Simply Visual Basic® 2005
Second Edition

D1304325

Deitel® Series Page

Simply Series

Simply C++: An Application-Driven Tutorial Approach

Simply C#: An Application-Driven Tutorial Approach

Simply Java™ Programming: An Application-Driven Tutorial Approach

Simply Visual Basic® .NET: An Application Driven Tutorial Approach (Visual Studio .NET 2003 Edition)

Simply Visual Basic® 2005, 2/E: An Application Driven Tutorial Approach

How to Program Series

Advanced Java™ 2 Platform How to Program

C How to Program, 5/E

C++ How to Program, 5/E - Including Cyber Classroom

e-Business and e-Commerce How to Program

Internet and World Wide Web How to Program, 3/E

Java™ How to Program, 6/E - Including Cyber Classroom

Perl How to Program

Python How to Program

Small C++ How to Program, 5/E - Including Cyber Classroom

Small Java™ How to Program, 6/E - Including Cyber Classroom

Visual Basic® 2005 How to Program, 3/E

Visual C++® .NET How to Program

Visual C#® 2005 How to Program, 2/E

XML How to Program

Also Available

SafariX Web Books

www.SafariX.com

To follow the Deitel publishing program, please register for the free *DEITEL® BUZZ ONLINE* e-mail newsletter at:

www.deitel.com/newsletter/subscribe.html

To communicate with the authors, send e-mail to:

deitel@deitel.com

For information on corporate on-site seminars offered by Deitel & Associates, Inc. worldwide, visit:

www.deitel.com

or write to:

deitel@deitel.com

For continuing updates on Prentice Hall/Deitel publications visit:

www.deitel.com,

www.prenhall.com/deitel

www.InformIT.com/deitel

Simply Visual Basic® 2005
Second Edition

P. J. Deitel
Deitel & Associates, Inc.

H. M. Deitel
Deitel & Associates, Inc.

PEARSON
Prentice
Hall

Upper Saddle River, NJ 07458

Library of Congress Cataloging-in-Publication Data

On file

Vice President and Editorial Director, ECS: *Marcia J. Horton*
Associate Editor: *Jennifer Cappello*
Assistant Editor: *Carole Snyder*
Executive Managing Editor: *Vince O'Brien*
Managing Editor: *Bob Engelhardt*
Production Editors: *Donna M. Crilly, Marta Samsel*
Director of Creative Services: *Paul Belfanti*
A/V Production Editor: *Xiaohong Zhu*
Art Studio: *Artworks, York, PA*
Creative Director: *Juan López*
Art Director: *Kristine Carney*
Cover Design: *Abbey S. Deitel, Harvey M. Deitel, Francesco Santalucia, Kristine Carney*
Interior Design: *Harvey M. Deitel, Kristine Carney*
Manufacturing Manager: *Alexis Heydt-Long*
Manufacturing Buyer: *Lisa McDowell*
Executive Marketing Manager: *Robin O'Brien*

© 2007 by Pearson Education, Inc.
Upper Saddle River, New Jersey 07458

The authors and publisher of this book have used their best efforts in preparing this book. These efforts include the development, research, and testing of the theories and programs to determine their effectiveness. The authors and publisher make no warranty of any kind, expressed or implied, with regard to these programs or to the documentation contained in this book. The authors and publisher shall not be liable in any event for incidental or consequential damages in connection with, or arising out of, the furnishing, performance, or use of these programs.

Many of the designations used by manufacturers and sellers to distinguish their products are claimed as trademarks and registered trademarks. Where those designations appear in this book, and Pearson Education, Inc. and the authors were aware of a trademark claim, the designations have been printed in initial caps or all caps. All product names mentioned remain trademarks or registered trademarks of their respective owners.

Printed in the United States of America

10 9 8 7 6 5 4 3 2 1

ISBN 0-13-243862-3

Pearson Education Ltd., *London*

Pearson Education Australia Pty. Ltd., *Sydney*

Pearson Education Singapore, Pte. Ltd.

Pearson Education North Asia Ltd., *Hong Kong*

Pearson Education Canada, Inc., *Toronto*

Pearson Educación de Mexico, S.A. de C.V.

Pearson Education–Japan, *Tokyo*

Pearson Education Malaysia, Pte. Ltd.

Pearson Education, Inc., *Upper Saddle River, New Jersey*

In memory of Anne Cashman:

To a gracious, kind, warm, woman, who always put
others before herself and who always saw the best in people.
Family and friends meant everything to her.

With love from her husband Marvin, her children Judy and Robert,
and her brother Paul Newman.

Trademarks:

Brief Table of Contents

Welcome to Visual Basic 2005 and the world of Microsoft Windows, Internet and World-Wide-Web programming with the .NET 2.0 platform! This book, which is part of our *Simply* series, has been updated based on Visual Studio 2005. Our goal was to write a book that focuses on core concepts and features of Visual Basic 2005 while keeping the discussion of this highly technical subject as simple as possible.

To achieve these goals, we implemented an innovative teaching methodology. We present the core concepts of leading-edge computing technologies using the tutorial-based, APPLICATION-DRIVEN approach, combined with the DEITEL® signature LIVE-CODE approach of teaching programming using complete, working, real-world applications. We merged the notion of a lab manual with that of a conventional textbook, creating a book that works well in a traditional classroom setting or with students sitting at computers and building each example application as they read the tutorials.

As students work through the tutorials, they learn about Visual Basic 2005 and its fundamental features, such as visual programming concepts, graphical-user-interface (GUI) components, multimedia (audio, images, animation and video), file processing, database processing and Internet and World-Wide-Web-based applications development. At the end of most sections, we provide self-review questions with answers so that students receive immediate feedback on their understanding of the material. Hundreds of additional self-review questions with answers are available on this book's Companion Web Site.

Features in Simply
Visual Basic 2005,
Second Edition

This book is loaded with pedagogic features, including:

- **APPLICATION-DRIVEN *Tutorial Approach.*** Each tutorial uses a contemporary, real-world application to teach programming concepts. The examples and exercises are up-to-the-minute with Internet/Web-related examples and with popular applications, such as an address book, game playing, graphics, multimedia and even a 3-tier Web-based bookstore. Most examples have a business, home or personal focus. At the beginning of each tutorial, students "test-drive" the completed application so they can see how it works. Then they build the application by following our step-by-step instructions. The book concentrates on the principles of good software engineering and stresses program clarity.

- ***LIVE-CODE Approach.*** This book contains several LIVE-CODE examples. Each tutorial ends with the complete, working program code and the students can run the application that they just created. We call this method of teaching and writing the ***LIVE-CODE Approach***. We feel that this approach is more effective than presenting only snippets of code out of the context of a complete application.

- ***Real-World Technologies.*** This text incorporates today's technologies to develop useful applications. For example, we use the Unified Modeling Language™ (UML) to replace flowcharts—an older standard. The UML has become the preferred graphical modeling language for designing object-oriented applications. In *Simply Visual Basic 2005, 2/e*, we use UML to show the flow of control for several control statements, so students gain practice reading the type of diagrams that are used in industry.

■ *Visual Programming and Graphical User Interface (GUI).* From the first tutorial, we immerse students in visual programming techniques and modifying Visual Basic 2005 GUIs. Students who learn these techniques can create graphical programs quickly and easily. The early tutorials provide students with a foundation for designing GUIs—concepts that they will apply throughout the book as we teach core programming concepts. Many tutorials contain GUI Design Tips that are summarized at the end of the tutorial for easy reference. Appendix C compiles all the GUI Design Tips to help students as they prepare for exams.

■ *Full-Color Presentation.* This book is in full color so that students can see sample outputs as they would appear on a monitor. Also, we syntax color the Visual Basic code, similar to the way Visual Studio 2005 colors the code in its editor window, so students can match what they see in the book with what they see on their screens. Our syntax-coloring conventions are as follows:

```
comments appear in green
keywords appear in dark blue
literal values appear in light blue
text, class, method, variable and property names appear in black
errors appear in red
```

■ *Graphics and Multimedia.* Graphics make applications fun to create and use. In our introduction to graphics, Tutorial 26, we discuss Graphical Device Interface (GDI+)—the Windows service that provides the graphical features used by Visual Studio 2005—to teach students to personalize a bank check. In Tutorial 27, we use a fun technology called Microsoft Agent to add interactive, animated characters to a phone book application. With Microsoft Agent's animated characters, your applications can speak to users and even respond to their voice commands!

■ *Databases.* Databases are crucial to businesses today, and we use real-world applications to teach the fundamentals of database programming. Tutorials 25 and 30 familiarize students with databases, presented in the context of two applications—an address book and a Web-based bookstore.

■ *Case Study.* This book includes a sequence of four tutorials in which the student builds a Web-based bookstore application. Tutorial 28 familiarizes readers with the ASP.NET Development Server (which enables testing of your Web applications), multi-tier architecture and simple Web transactions. Tutorials 29–31 use ASP.NET 2.0 and ADO.NET 2.0 to build an application that retrieves information from a database and displays the information in a Web page.

■ *Object-Oriented Programming.* Object-oriented programming is the most widely employed technique for developing robust, reusable software, and Visual Basic 2005 offers advanced object-oriented programming features. This book introduces students to defining classes and using objects, laying a solid foundation for future programming courses.

■ *Visual Studio 2005 Debugger.* Debuggers help programmers find and correct logic errors in program code. Visual Studio 2005 contains a powerful debugging tool that allows programmers to analyze their programs line-by-line as they execute. Throughout the book, we teach the Visual Studio 2005 Debugger; we explain how to use its key features and offer many debugging exercises.

To the Instructor   ***Focus of the Book***

Our goal was clear: Produce a Visual Basic 2005 textbook for introductory-level courses in computer programming aimed at students with little or no programming experience. This book teaches computer programming principles and the Visual Basic 2005 language, including data types, control statements, object-oriented programming, Visual Basic 2005 classes, GUI concepts, event-driven programming and more. After mastering the material in this book, students will be able to program in Visual Basic 2005 and to employ many key capabilities of the .NET 2.0 platform.

We also wanted a textbook that was up-to-date with Microsoft's latest release of Visual Studio—Visual Studio 2005, which includes Visual Basic 2005. We have rebuilt every application in the book using the 2005 software. All applications and solutions have been fully tested and run on this new platform.

A Note Regarding Software for the Book

On November 7, 2005 Microsoft released its Visual Studio 2005 development tools, including the Visual Basic® 2005 Express Edition. Per Microsoft's web site, Microsoft Express Editions are "lightweight, easy-to-use and easy-to-learn tools for the hobbyist, novice and student developer." According to the Microsoft Express Editions FAQ page (`msdn.microsoft.com/vstudio/express/support/faq/`), "Effective April 19th, 2006, all Visual Studio 2005 Express Editions are free permanently. SQL Server 2005 Express Edition has always been and will continue to be a free download."

You may use this software to compile and execute the example programs in the book. The Visual Basic 2005 Express Edition Software is available on the CD-ROM included with this book. You can also download Visual Basic 2005 Express Edition at:

> `msdn.microsoft.com/vstudio/express/vb/default.aspx`

When you install this software, you should install the help documentation and SQL Server 2005 Express. Microsoft provides a dedicated forum for help using the Express Edition:

> `forums.microsoft.com/msdn/ShowForum.aspx?ForumID=24`

Other Software Requirements

In Tutorial 27, we use Microsoft Agent, which can be downloaded from

> `www.microsoft.com/msagent/downloads/default.asp`

For Tutorial 25 and for the case study in Tutorials 28–31, you will need SQL Server 2005 Express Edition, which is available at

> `msdn.microsoft.com/vstudio/express/sql/`

Note that you *do not* need to download SQL Server 2005 Express separately if you select the option to install it during the Visual Basic 2005 Express installation.

Tutorials 28–31 require Visual Web Developer 2005 Express (or a complete version of Visual Studio 2005). Visual Web Developer 2005 Express is available at

> `msdn.microsoft.com/vstudio/express/vwd/`

For updates on the software used in this book visit **www.deitel.com/books/ SimplyVB2005** or subscribe to our free e-mail newsletter at `www.deitel.com/ newsletter/subscribe.html`. Also, be sure to check out our Visual Basic resource center (`www.deitel.com/VisualBasic`) frequently for new Visual Basic resources.

Lab Setup

To install some of the required software for this book, students and instructors will need Administrator-level access to the computer. For university computer labs where students do not have Administrator-level access, instructors and system administrators must ensure that the proper software is installed on the lab computers. In Tutorial 27 certain Microsoft Agent software components must be installed to execute and develop the **Phone Book** application. If students are not allowed to install software on lab computers, the Microsoft Agent components discussed in Tutorial 27 must be installed in advance.

A Note Regarding Terminology Used in the Book

In Tutorial 13, we discuss methods as Sub procedures (sometimes called subroutines) and Function procedures (sometimes called functions). We use this terminology for two reasons. First, the keywords Sub and Function are used in procedure definitions, so this naming is logical for students. Second, Visual Basic professionals have used this terminology for years and will continue to do so in the future. We also use the term "function" at certain points in this text to refer to Visual Basic 6 Function procedures that remain in Visual Basic 2005 (such as Val and Pmt). When we introduce object-oriented programming concepts in Tutorial 19, we discuss the difference between procedures and methods and indicate that the procedures defined throughout the text are, in fact, methods. We hope our use of terminology helps you present the material in a simple and understandable manner.

Exception Handling: Bonus Tutorial (Tutorial 32)

Exception handling is one of the most important topics in Visual Basic 2005 for building mission-critical and business-critical applications. Programmers need to know how to recognize the exceptions (errors) that could occur in software components and handle those exceptions effectively, allowing programs to deal with problems and continue executing instead of "crashing." Tutorial 32 overviews the proper use of exception handling, including the termination model of exception handling, throwing exceptions and catching exceptions.

Objectives

Each tutorial begins with objectives that inform students of what to expect and give them an opportunity, after reading the tutorial, to determine whether they have met the intended goals.

Outline

The tutorial outline enables students to approach the material in top-down fashion. Along with the tutorial objectives, the outline helps students anticipate future topics and set a comfortable and effective learning pace.

Example Applications (with Outputs)

We present Visual Basic 2005 features in the context of complete, working Visual Basic 2005 programs. We call this our LIVE-CODE approach. All examples are available as downloads from our web site:

    www.deitel.com/books/SimplyVB2005

Illustrations/Figures

An abundance of charts, line drawings and application outputs are included. The discussion of control statements, for example, features carefully drawn UML activity diagrams. [*Note:* We do not teach UML diagramming as an application-development tool, but we do use UML diagrams to explain the precise operation of many of Visual Basic 2005's control statements.]

Programming Tips

Hundreds of programming tips help students focus on important aspects of application development. These tips and practices represent the best the authors have gleaned from a combined seven decades of programming and teaching experience.

Good Programming Practice

Good Programming Practices highlight techniques that help students write programs that are clearer, more understandable and more maintainable.

 Common Programming Error

Students learning a language—especially in their first programming course—frequently make errors. Pointing out these *Common Programming Errors* in the text reduces the likelihood that students will make the same mistakes.

 Error-Prevention Tip

These tips describe aspects of Visual Basic 2005 that prevent errors from getting into programs in the first place, which simplifies the testing and debugging process.

 Performance Tip

Teaching students to write clear and understandable programs is the most important goal for a first programming course. But students want to write programs that run the fastest, use the least memory, require the smallest number of keystrokes, etc. *Performance Tips* highlight opportunities for improving program performance.

 Portability Tip

The *Portability Tips* provide insights on how Visual Basic 2005 achieves its high degree of portability among .NET 2.0 platforms.

 Software Design Tip

The *Software Design Tips* highlight architectural and design issues that affect the construction of software systems.

 GUI Design Tip

The GUI Design Tips highlight graphical-user-interface conventions to help students design attractive, user-friendly GUIs and use GUI features. Appendix C compiles all the GUI Design Tips to help students as they prepare for exams.

Skills Summary

Each tutorial includes a bullet-list-style summary of the new programming concepts presented. This reinforces key actions taken to build the application in each tutorial.

Key Terms

Each tutorial includes a list of important terms defined in the tutorial. These terms also appear in the index and in a book-wide glossary, so the student can locate terms and their definitions quickly.

Self-Review Questions and Answers

Self-review multiple-choice questions and answers are included after most sections to build students' confidence with the material and prepare them for the regular exercises. Students should be encouraged to attempt all the self-review exercises and check their answers.

Exercises (Solutions in Instructor's Manual)

Each tutorial concludes with exercises. Typical exercises include 10 multiple-choice questions, a "What does this code do?" exercise, a "What's wrong with this code?"

exercise, three programming exercises and a programming challenge. [*Note:* In the "What does this code do?" and "What's wrong with this code?" exercises, we show only portions of the code in the text.]

The questions involve simple recall of important terminology and concepts, writing individual Visual Basic 2005 statements, writing small portions of Visual Basic 2005 applications and writing complete Visual Basic 2005 methods, classes and applications. Every programming exercise uses a step-by-step methodology to suggest how to solve the problems. The solutions for the exercises are *available only to instructors* through their Prentice-Hall representatives. [*NOTE:* **Please do not write to us requesting the instructor's manual. Distribution of this publication is strictly limited to instructors teaching from the book. Instructors may obtain the solutions manual only from their regular Prentice Hall representatives. We regret that we cannot provide the solutions to professionals.**]

GUI Design Guidelines

Consistent and proper graphical user interface design is crucial to visual programming. In each tutorial, we summarize the GUI design guidelines that were introduced. Appendix C presents a cumulative list of these GUI design guidelines for easy reference.

Controls, Events, Properties & Methods Summaries

Each tutorial includes a summary of the controls, events, properties and methods covered in the tutorial. The summary includes a picture of each control, shows the control "in action" and lists the control's properties, events and methods that were discussed up to and including that tutorial.

"Double Indexing" of Visual Basic 2005 Code Examples

The extensive index includes important terms both under main headings and as separate entries so that students can search for any term or concept by keyword. The code examples and the exercises also are included in the index. Every Visual Basic 2005 source-code program in the book is indexed under the appropriate application. We also double-indexed various features, such as controls and properties. This makes it easier to find examples using particular features.

Teaching Resources for Simply Visual Basic 2005, Second Edition

Simply Visual Basic 2005, 2/e, has extensive instructor resources. The Prentice Hall *Instructor's Resource Center* contains the *Solutions Manual* with solutions to the vast majority of the end-of-chapter exercises, a *Test Item File* of multiple-choice questions (approximately two per book section) and PowerPoint® slides containing all the code and figures in the text, plus bulleted items that summarize the key points in the text. Instructors can customize the slides. If you are not already a registered faculty member, contact your Prentice Hall representative or visit

```
vig.prenhall.com/replocator/
```

DEITEL BUZZ® Online Free E-mail Newsletter

Our free e-mail newsletter, the *Deitel® Buzz Online*, includes commentary on industry trends and developments, links to free articles and resources from our published books and upcoming publications, product-release schedules, errata, challenges, anecdotes, information on our corporate instructor-led training courses and more. It's also a good way for you to keep posted about issues related to *Simply Visual Basic 2005, 2/e*. To subscribe, visit

```
www.deitel.com/newsletter/subscribe.html
```

What's New at Deitel

Free Content Initiative. We are pleased to bring you guest articles and free tutorials selected from our current and forthcoming publications as part of our Free Content Initiative. In each issue of our *Deitel® Buzz Online* newsletter, we announce the latest additions to our free content library. Let us know what topics you'd like to see and let us know if you'd like to submit guest articles!

www.deitel.com/articles/

Resource Centers and the Deitel Internet Business Initiative. We have created many online Resource Centers (at www.deitel.com) on such topics as Visual Basic, .NET, C#, C++, C, Java, Java EE 5, Java SE 6, AJAX, Ruby, PHP, Perl, Python, MySQL, RSS, XML, Web Services, Windows Vista, Linux, OpenGL, Google Analytics, Google Base, Google Video, Search Engines, Search Engine Optimization, Alert Services, IE7, the Internet Business Initiative, Mash-Ups, Podcasting, Computer Games, Game Programming, Virtual Worlds, Attention Economy, Affiliate Programs, Sudoku, WinFX and Web 2.0, with many more coming.

www.deitel.com/resourcecenters.html

These Resource Centers enhance students' learning experience, providing lots of alternate readings and project ideas, and connecting students to the professional community. The Resource Centers include links to tutorials, sample code, podcasts, articles, newsgroups, forums, blogs, RSS feeds, software downloads, open source projects, books, eBooks, sample chapters and more. We announce new resource centers in each issue of the *Deitel*® *Buzz Online* as well.

Acknowledgments

It is a great pleasure to acknowledge the efforts of many people whose names may not appear on the cover, but whose hard work, cooperation, friendship and understanding were crucial to the production of the book. Many people at Deitel & Associates, Inc. devoted long hours to this project—thanks especially to Abbey Deitel, Christi Kelsey and Barbara Deitel.

We would also like to thank the participants in the Deitel & Associates, Inc., Honors Internship Program: William Chen and Matt Gist.[1]

We are fortunate to have worked on this project with the talented and dedicated team of publishing professionals at Prentice Hall. We appreciate the extraordinary efforts of Marcia Horton, Editorial Director of Prentice Hall's Engineering and Computer Science Division. Jennifer Cappello and Dolores Mars did an extraordinary job recruiting the book's review team and managing the review process. Francesco Santalucia (an independent artist) and Kristine Carney did a wonderful job designing the book's cover. Vince O'Brien, Bob Engelhardt, Donna Crilly and Marta Samsel did a marvelous job managing the book's production.

We wish to acknowledge the efforts of our reviewers. Adhering to a tight time schedule, they scrutinized the text and the programs, providing countless suggestions for improving the accuracy and completeness of the presentation.

Simply Visual Basic 2005, Second Edition reviewers:

Karen Arlien (Bismarck State College)
Harlan Brewer (Select Engineering Services, Inc.)
Carol Buser (Owens Community College)

---

1. The Deitel & Associates, Inc. Honors Internship Program offers a limited number of salaried positions to college students majoring in Computer Science, Information Technology, Marketing and English. Students work at our corporate headquarters in Maynard, Massachusetts full-time in the summers and (for those attending college in the Boston area) part-time during the academic year. We also offer full-time co-op positions for students interested in taking a semester off from school to gain industry experience. Regular full-time positions are available to college graduates. For more information, please contact Abbey Deitel at deitel@deitel.com, visit our Web site, www.deitel.com, and subscribe to our free e-mail newsletter at www.deitel.com/newsletter/subscribe.html.

Nelson Capaz (Pasco Hernando Community College)
John Chen (Microsoft)
Bunny Howard (St. John's River Community College)
Sachin Korgaonkar (Cyquator Technologies Ltd.)
Chuck Litecky (Southern Illinois University)
José Antonio González Seco (Andalusia's Parliament)

Simply Visual Basic 2003 Reviewers

Cameron McColl (Microsoft)
Colin Merry (Microsoft)
Jeffrey Welton (Microsoft)
Judith Ashworth (Orillion USA, Inc.)
James Ball (Indiana State University)
Robert Benavides (Collin County Community College)
Chadi Boudiab (Georgia Perimeter College)
Charles Cadenhead (Brookhaven College)
Kunal Cheda (DotNetExtreme.com)
Mave Coxon (Lansing Community College)
Chris Crane (Independent Consultant)
Sergio Davalos (University of Washington-Tacoma)
David Fullerton (Yeshiva University)
George Gintowt (William Rainey Harper College)
James Gips (Boston College)
Manu Gupta (Patni Computer Systems)
Richard Hewer (Ferris State University)
James Huddleston (Independent Consultant)
Terrell Hull (Sun Certified Java Architect, Rational Qualified Practitioner)
Jeff Jones (A.D.A.M. Inc.)
Faisal Kaleem (Florida International University)
Yashavant Kanetkar (KICIT Pvt. Ltd.)
Dhananjay Katre (Patni Computer Systems, Ltd.)
Kurt Kominek (Northeast State Technical CC)
Stan Kurkovsky (Columbus State University)
Brian Larson (Modesto Junior College)
Sukan Makmuri (DeVry-Fremont)
Ken McLean (Northern Virginia CC)
Gordon McNorton (Collin County Community College)
Manish Mehta (Independent Consultant)
Marilyn Meyer (Fresno City College)
John Mueller (DataCon Services)
Narayana Rao Surapaneni (Patni Computer Systems)
Michael Rudisill (Northern Michigan University)
Sara Rushinek (University of Miami)
Praveen Sadhu (Infodat Solutions, Inc.)
Kenneth Schoonover (Chubb Technical Institute)
Andrea Shelly (Florida International University)
Robert Taylor (Lansing Community College)
Yateen Thakkar (Syntel India Ltd.)
Catherine Wyman (DeVry-Phoenix)
David Zeng (DeVry-Calgary)

Well, there you have it! Visual Basic is a powerful programming language that will help you write programs quickly and effectively. Visual Basic scales nicely into the realm of enterprise systems development to help organizations build their business-critical and mission-critical information systems. As you read the book, we would sincerely appreciate your comments, criticisms, corrections and suggestions for improvement. Please address all correspondence to:

deitel@deitel.com

We will respond promptly, and we will post corrections and clarifications on our Web site:

www.deitel.com

We hope you enjoy reading *Simply Visual Basic 2005, Second Edition* as much as we enjoyed writing it!

Paul J. Deitel
Dr. Harvey M. Deitel

About the Authors

Paul J. Deitel, CEO and Chief Technical Officer of Deitel & Associates, Inc., is a graduate of the MIT's Sloan School of Management, where he studied Information Technology. Through Deitel & Associates, Inc., he has delivered C#, Java, C and C++ courses to industry clients, including IBM, Sun Microsystems, Dell, Lucent Technologies, Fidelity, NASA at the Kennedy Space Center, the National Severe Storm Laboratory, White Sands Missile Range, Rogue Wave Software, Boeing, Stratus, Cambridge Technology Partners, Open Environment Corporation, One Wave, Hyperion Software, Adra Systems, Entergy, CableData Systems, Nortel Networks, Puma, Invensys and many more. He has also lectured on C++ and Java for the Boston Chapter of the Association for Computing Machinery. He and his father, Dr. Harvey M. Deitel, are the world's best-selling programming language textbook authors.

Dr. Harvey M. Deitel, Chairman and Chief Strategy Officer of Deitel & Associates, Inc., has 45 years of academic and industry experience in the computer field. Dr. Deitel earned B.S. and M.S. degrees from the Massachusetts Institute of Technology and a Ph.D. from Boston University. He has 20 years of college teaching experience, including earning tenure and serving as the Chairman of the Computer Science Department at Boston College before founding Deitel & Associates, Inc., with his son, Paul J. Deitel. He and Paul are the co-authors of several dozen books and multimedia packages and they are writing many more. With translations published in Japanese, German, Russian, Spanish, Traditional Chinese, Simplified Chinese, Korean, French, Polish, Italian, Portuguese, Greek, Urdu and Turkish, the Deitels' texts have earned international recognition. Dr. Deitel has delivered hundreds of professional seminars to major corporations, academic institutions, government organizations and the military.

About Deitel & Associates, Inc.

Deitel & Associates, Inc., is an internationally recognized corporate training and content-creation organization specializing in computer programming languages, Internet and World Wide Web software technology, object technology education and Internet business development. The company provides instructor-led courses on major programming languages and platforms, such as Java, Advanced Java, C, C++, C#, Visual C++, Visual Basic, XML, Perl, Python, object technology and Internet and World Wide Web programming. The founders of Deitel & Associates, Inc., are Dr. Harvey M. Deitel and Paul J. Deitel. The company's clients include many of the world's largest computer companies, government agencies, branches of the military and business organizations. Through its 30-year publishing partnership with Prentice Hall, Deitel & Associates, Inc. publishes leading-edge programming textbooks, professional books, interactive multimedia Cyber Classrooms, Complete Training Courses, Web-based training courses and e-content for popular course management systems such as WebCT, Blackboard and Pearson's CourseCompass. Deitel & Associates, Inc., and the authors can be reached via e-mail at:

deitel@deitel.com

To learn more about Deitel & Associates, Inc., its publications and its worldwide *DIVE INTO*® Series Corporate Training curriculum, see the last few pages of this book or visit:

www.deitel.com

and subscribe to the free *Deitel*® *Buzz Online* e-mail newsletter at:

www.deitel.com/newsletter/subscribe.html

Individuals wishing to purchase Deitel books, Cyber Classrooms, Complete Training Courses and Web-based training courses can do so through:

www.deitel.com/books/index.html

Bulk orders by corporations, the government, the military and academic institutions should be placed directly with Prentice Hall.

P lease follow the instructions in this section to ensure that your computer is set up properly before you begin using this book.

Font and Naming Conventions

We use fonts to distinguish between IDE features (such as menu names and menu items) and other elements that appear in the IDE. Our convention is to emphasize IDE features in a sans-serif bold **Helvetica** font (for example, **Properties** window) and to emphasize program text in a sans-serif Lucida font (for example, Private Boolean x = True).

A Note Regarding Software for the Book

This textbook includes a CD which contains Microsoft® Visual Basic® 2005 Express Edition version integrated development environment. The express edition is fully functional and there is no time limit for using the software. Tutorials 28–31 require Microsoft Visual Web Developer 2005 Express Edition which you can download from Microsoft at msdn.microsoft.com/vstudio/express/vwd. This textbook assumes that you are using Windows 2000 or Windows XP.

Hardware and Software Requirements for Visual Basic 2005 Express

To install and run Visual Basic 2005 Express Edition, Microsoft recommends that PCs have these minimum requirements:

- **Operating System:** Windows 2000 Service Pack 4, Windows XP Service Pack 2, Windows Server 2003 Service Pack 1, Windows x64 editions or Windows Vista.

- **Processor:** Computer with a 600 mhz or faster processor (1 GHz or higher recommended).

- **RAM minimum:** 192 MB but Microsoft recommends 256 MB (512 MB or more with SQL Express).

- **Hard Drive:** 500 MB (minimum)

- Mouse or other Microsoft-compatible pointing device

- To test and build the examples in Tutorial 25 and Tutorials 28-31, **you must install Microsoft's SQL Server 2005 Express**, which is an option during the Visual Basic 2005 Express Edition installation.

Monitor Display Settings

Simply Visual Basic 2005, 2/e includes hundreds of screenshots of applications. Your monitor-display settings may need to be adjusted so that the screenshots in the book will match what you see on your computer screen as you develop each application. [*Note:* We refer to single clicking with the left mouse button as **selecting** or **clicking**. We refer to double clicking with the left mouse button simply as **double clicking**.] Follow these steps to set your monitor display correctly:

1. Open the **Control Panel** and double click **Display**.
2. Click the **Settings** tab.
3. Click the **Advanced...** button.
4. In the **General** tab, make sure **Small Fonts** is selected; this should indicate that **96 dpi** is now the setting. [*Note:* If you already have this setting, you do not need to do anything else.]
5. Click **Apply**.

If you choose to use different settings, the Size and Location values we provide for different GUI elements (such as Buttons and Labels) in each application might not appear correctly on your screen. If so, simply adjust Size and Location values so the GUI elements in your application appear similar to those in the screenshots in the book.

Theme Settings for Windows XP Users

If you are using Windows XP, we assume that your theme is set to Windows XP Style. Follow these steps to set Windows XP as your desktop theme:

1. Open the **Control Panel**, then double click **Display**.
2. Click the **Themes** tab. Select **Windows XP** from the **Theme:** drop-down list.
3. Click **OK** to save the settings.

Viewing File Extensions

Several screenshots in *Simply Visual Basic 2005, 2/e* display file names on a user's system, including the file extension of each file. Your settings may need to be adjusted to display file extensions. Follow these steps to set your machine to display file extensions:

1. In the **Start** menu, select **All Programs**, then **Accessories**, then **Windows Explorer**.
2. Select **Folder Options...** from **Windows Explorer**'s **Tools** menu.
3. In the dialog that appears, select the **View** tab.
4. In the **Advanced settings:** pane, uncheck the box to the left of the text **Hide extensions for known file types**. [*Note*: If this item is already unchecked then no action needs to be taken.]

Copying and Organizing Files

The examples for *Simply Visual Basic 2005, 2/e* are available for download at

www.deitel.com/books/SimplyVB2005

Follow the steps in the next box to create the Examples directory on your hard drive. Screen shots in this box might differ slightly from what you see on your computer, depending on your version of Windows. We used Windows XP to prepare the screenshots for this book.

Downloading the Book Examples from the Deitel Website

1. ***Downloading the book's code examples.*** Open a Web browser and go to www.deitel.com/books/SimplyVB2005. Click the Examples link to download the SimplyVB2005_Examples.zip file to your computer.

2. ***Extracting the Examples directory.*** Use an extraction tool to unzip the file that you have downloaded in the previous step to your C: drive. If you do not already have extraction software installed on your computer, a popular extractor called WinZip is available at www.winzip.com and will help you to accomplish this task. Once you have successfully completed this step, your C: drive will include the ***Examples*** directory (Fig. 1).

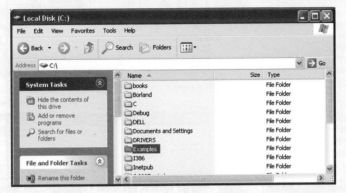

Figure 1 Successfully extracted Examples directory.

As you work through this book, you will be developing your own applications. In the following box, you create a directory on your C: drive in which you will save all of these personally developed applications.

Creating a Working Directory

1. ***Selecting the drive.*** Double click the **My Computer** icon on your desktop to access a list of your computer drives (Fig. 2). Double click the C: drive. The contents of the C: drive are displayed.

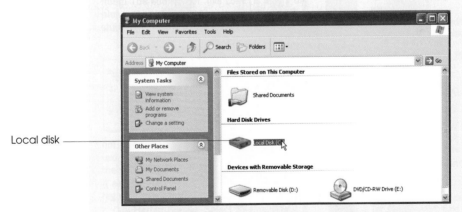

Local disk

Figure 2 Computer drives listed under **My Computer**.

2. ***Creating a new directory.*** Select the **File** menu. Under the **New** submenu, select **Folder** (Fig. 3). A new, empty directory appears on your C: drive (Fig. 4). [*Note:* From now on, we use the > character to indicate the selection of a menu command. For example, we use the notation **File > Open** to indicate the selection of the **Open** command from the **File** menu.]

(cont.)

New folder option
(selected)

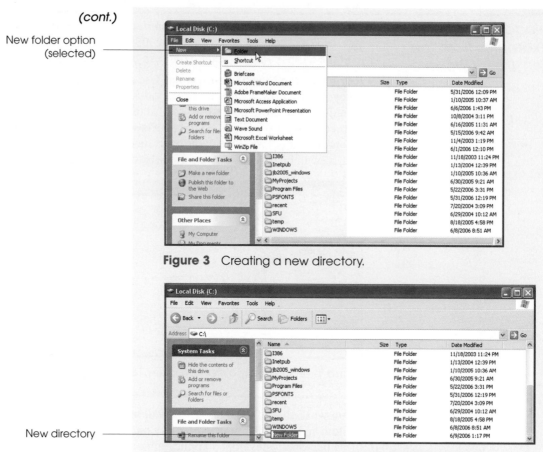

Figure 3 Creating a new directory.

New directory

Figure 4 New directory appears on the C: drive.

3. ***Naming the directory.*** Enter a name for the directory. We suggest that you choose a name that you recognize and remember. We chose `SimplyVB` (Fig. 5). You can use this directory to save the examples from this book, your own applications and your exercise solutions.

Newly created
working directory

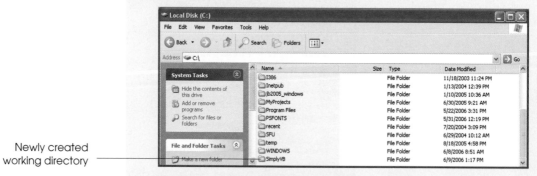

Figure 5 New working directory on the C: drive.

Before you can run the applications in *Simply Visual Basic 2005, 2/e* or build your own applications, you must install a Visual Basic development tool. We use Microsoft's Visual Basic 2005 Express Edition in the examples throughout this book. You too may use this software to compile and execute the example programs in the book. Visual Basic 2005 Express Edition is included on a CD bundled with this textbook and is also available for download at:

msdn.microsoft.com/vstudio/express/vb

Installing Visual Basic Express 2005 Express Edition

1. ***Beginning the installation.*** Load the Visual Basic 2005 Express Edition CD which accompanies this book to launch the software installer.

2. ***Accepting the license agreement.*** Carefully read the license agreement. Click the **I agree** button to agree to the terms. [*Note:* If you do not choose to accept the license agreement, the software will not install and you will not be able to execute or create Visual Basic applications.

3. ***Selecting the installation options.*** Select both the **Microsoft MSDN 2005 Express Edition** and **Microsoft SQL Server 2005 Express Edition x86** options to install (Fig. 6). For the examples in Tutorials 25 and 28–31, you must have Microsoft SQL Server 2005 installed on your machine. Installing the MSDN documentation is not required but is highly recommended.

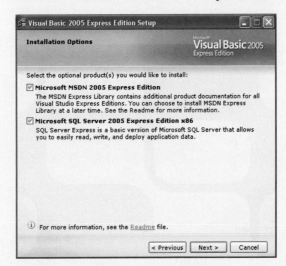

Figure 6   Installation options dialog.

4. ***Continuing and finishing the installation.*** Select **Next >** to continue with the installation. The installer will now begin copying the files required by Visual Basic 2005 and SQL Server 2005. Depending on your system, this process could take up to an hour.

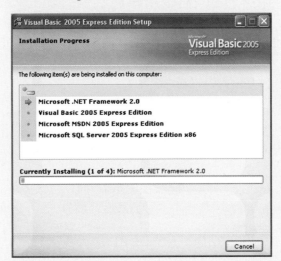

Figure 7   Installation (in progress) of Visual Basic 2005 Express Edition.

You are now ready to begin your Visual Basic studies with *Simply Visual Basic 2005, 2/e.* We hope you enjoy the book!

Drawing Application

Introducing Computers, the Internet and Visual Basic

Welcome to Visual Basic 2005! This book uses a straightforward, step-by-step tutorial approach to teach the fundamentals of Visual Basic programming. We hope that you will be informed and entertained as you learn Visual Basic.

The core of the book teaches Visual Basic using our **application-driven approach**, which provides step-by-step instructions for creating and interacting with useful, real-world computer applications. With this approach and our signature **live-code approach**, which shows dozens of complete, working Visual Basic applications and depicts their outputs, you learn the basic skills that underlie good programming. You will study bonus tutorials on graphics, multimedia and Web programming. All of the book's program examples are available on our Web site, www.deitel.com/books/simplyVB2005.

Computer use is increasing in almost every field. In an era of rising costs, computing costs are actually decreasing dramatically because of rapid developments in both hardware and software technology. Silicon-chip technology has made computing so economical that hundreds of millions of general-purpose computers are in use worldwide, helping people in business, industry, government and their personal lives.

Reading this text will start you on a challenging and rewarding educational path. If you'd like to communicate with us, send an e-mail to deitel@deitel.com, and we will respond promptly. For more information, visit www.deitel.com.

1.1 What Is a Computer?

A **computer** is a device capable of performing computations and making logical decisions at speeds millions, billions and even trillions of times faster than humans can. For example, many of today's personal computers can perform billions of additions per second. A person operating a desk calculator might require a lifetime to complete the same number of calculations that a powerful personal computer can perform in one second. Today's fastest supercomputers are already performing trillions of additions per second!

Computers process data, using sets of instructions called **computer programs**. These programs guide computers through orderly sets of actions that are specified by people known as **computer programmers**. In this book, we generally use

1

the term "application" instead of the term "program." An application is a program that does something particularly useful. Each tutorial in this book, on average, presents five applications—one in the main example and four in the exercises—for a total of more than 100 applications in the book.

A computer is composed of various devices (such as the keyboard, screen, mouse, hard drive, memory, DVD drive and processing units) known as **hardware**. The programs that run on a computer are referred to as **software**. Object-oriented programming (which models real-world objects with software counterparts), available in Visual Basic and other programming languages, is a significant breakthrough that can greatly enhance programmers' productivity.

SELF-REVIEW   1. Computers process data, using sets of instructions called _____.

    a) hardware   b) computer programs

    c) processing units   d) programmers

2. The devices that make up a computer are called _____.

    a) hardware   b) software

    c) programs   d) programmers

Answers: 1) b. 2) a.

1.2 Computer Organization

Computers can be thought of as being divided into six units:

1. **Input unit**. This "receiving" section of the computer obtains information (data and computer programs) from various **input devices**, such as the keyboard and the mouse. Other input devices include microphones (for recording speech to the computer), scanners (for scanning images) and digital cameras (for taking photographs and making videos).

2. **Output unit.** This "shipping" section of the computer takes information that the computer has processed and places it on various **output devices**, making the information available for use outside the computer. Output can be displayed on screens, played on audio/video devices, printed on paper, transmitted over the Internet, etc. Output also can be used to control other devices, such as robots used in manufacturing.

3. **Memory unit.** This rapid-access, relatively low-capacity "warehouse" section of the computer stores data temporarily while an application is running. The memory unit retains information that has been entered through input devices, so that information is immediately available for processing. To be executed, computer programs must be in memory. The memory unit also retains processed information until that information can be sent to output devices on which it is made available to users. Often, the memory unit is called either **memory** or **primary memory**. **Random-access memory (RAM)** is an example of primary memory. Primary memory is usually **volatile**, which means that it is erased when the machine is powered off.

4. **Arithmetic and logic unit (ALU).** The ALU is the "manufacturing" section of the computer. It performs calculations such as addition, subtraction, multiplication and division. It also makes decisions, allowing the computer to perform such tasks as determining whether two items stored in memory are equal.

5. **Central processing unit (CPU).** The CPU serves as the "administrative" section of the computer, supervising the operation of the other sections. The CPU alerts the input unit when information should be read into the

memory unit, instructs the ALU when to use information from the memory unit in calculations and tells the output unit when to send information from the memory unit to certain output devices.

6. **Secondary storage unit.** This unit is the long-term, high-capacity "warehousing" section of the computer. Secondary storage devices, such as hard drives, CD-ROM and DVD drives, zip drives and floppy disk drives, normally hold programs or data that other units are not actively using. The computer can retrieve this information when it is needed—hours, days, months or even years later. Information in secondary storage takes much longer to access than information in primary memory. However, secondary storage is much less expensive than primary memory. Secondary storage is nonvolatile, retaining information even when the computer is powered off.

SELF-REVIEW

1. The _____ is responsible for performing calculations, and contains decision-making mechanisms.
   a) central processing unit
   b) memory unit
   c) arithmetic and logic unit
   d) output unit

2. Information stored in _____ is normally erased when the computer is turned off.
   a) primary memory
   b) secondary storage
   c) CD-ROM drives
   d) hard drives

Answers: 1) c. 2) a.

1.3 Machine Languages, Assembly Languages and High-Level Languages

Programmers write instructions in various programming languages. Some of these are directly understandable by computers, and others require intermediate translation steps. Although hundreds of computer languages are in use today, they can be divided into three general types:

1. Machine languages

2. Assembly languages

3. High-level languages

A computer can directly understand only its own **machine language**. As the "natural language" of a particular computer, machine language is defined by the computer's hardware design. Machine languages generally consist of streams of numbers (ultimately reduced to 1s and 0s) that instruct computers how to perform their most elementary operations. Machine languages are machine dependent, which means that a particular machine language can be used on only one type of computer. The following section of a machine-language program, which adds *over-time pay* to *base pay* and stores the result in *gross pay*, demonstrates the incomprehensibility of machine language to humans:

```
+1300042774
+1400593419
+1200274027
```

As the popularity of computers increased, machine-language programming proved to be slow and error prone. Instead of using the strings of numbers that computers could directly understand, programmers began using English-like abbreviations to represent the basic operations of the computer. These abbreviations formed the basis of **assembly languages**. **Translator programs** called **assemblers** convert assembly-language programs to machine language at computer speeds. The following section of an assembly-language program also adds *overtime pay* to *base pay* and stores the result in *gross pay*, but presents the steps somewhat more clearly to human readers than the machine-language example:

```
LOAD    BASEPAY
ADD     OVERPAY
STORE   GROSSPAY
```

This assembly-language code is clearer to humans, but computers cannot understand it until it is translated into machine language by an assembler program.

Although the speed at which programmers could write programs increased rapidly with the creation of assembly languages, these languages still require many instructions to accomplish even the simplest tasks. To speed up the programming process, **high-level languages**, in which single program statements accomplish more substantial tasks, were developed. Translator programs called **compilers** convert high-level-language programs into machine language. High-level languages enable programmers to write instructions that look almost like everyday English and contain common mathematical notations. For example, a payroll application written in a high-level language might contain a statement such as

```
grossPay = basePay + overTimePay
```

From these examples, it is clear why programmers prefer high-level languages to either machine languages or assembly languages. Visual Basic is one of the world's most popular high-level programming languages. In the next section, you will learn about Microsoft's latest version of this language, called Visual Basic 2005.

SELF-REVIEW

1. The only programming language that a computer can directly understand is its own _____.

   a) high-level language   b) assembly language
   c) machine language   d) English

2. Programs that translate high-level language programs into machine language are called _____.

   a) assemblers   b) compilers
   c) programmers   d) converters

Answers: 1) c. 2) b.

1.4 Visual Basic

Visual Basic evolved from **BASIC** (Beginner's All-Purpose Symbolic Instruction Code), developed in the mid-1960s by Professors John Kemeny and Thomas Kurtz of Dartmouth College as a language for writing simple programs quickly and easily. BASIC's primary purpose was to teach novices fundamental programming techniques.

When Bill Gates founded Microsoft Corporation in the 1970s, he implemented BASIC on several early personal computers. In the late 1980s and the early 1990s, Microsoft developed the Microsoft Windows **graphical user interface (GUI)**—the visual part of the application with which users interact. With the creation of the Windows GUI, the natural evolution of BASIC was to Visual Basic, introduced by Microsoft in 1991 to make programming Windows applications easier.

Until Visual Basic appeared, developing Microsoft Windows-based applications was a difficult process. Visual Basic is a so-called object-oriented, event-driven (OOED) visual programming language in which programs are created with the use of a software tool called an **Integrated Development Environment (IDE)**. With Microsoft's Visual Studio IDE, a programmer can write, run, test and debug Visual Basic programs quickly and conveniently.

The latest versions of Visual Basic are fully object oriented—you'll learn some basics of object technology shortly and will study a rich treatment in the remainder of the book. Visual Basic is event driven—you'll write programs that respond to user-initiated events such as mouse clicks and keystrokes. It is a visual programming language—instead of writing detailed program statements to build your applications, you will use Visual Studio's graphical user interface, in which you conveniently drag and drop predefined objects into place and label and resize them. Visual Studio will write much of the program for you. We discuss .NET in more detail in Section 1.9.

Microsoft introduced its **.NET** (pronounced "dot-net") strategy in 2000. The **.NET platform**—the set of software components that enables .NET programs to run—allows applications to be distributed to a variety of devices (such as cell phones) as well as to desktop computers. The .NET platform offers a new programming model that allows programs created in different programming languages to communicate with each other, whether they reside on the same computer or on different computers connected to a network such as the Internet.

SELF-REVIEW   1. Microsoft created _____ in 1991 to make it easier to program Windows applications.

    a) Windows   b) BASIC

    c) Visual Basic   d) C#

2. Visual Basic evolved from _____, which was created as a language for writing simple programs quickly and easily.

    a) .NET   b) Windows

    c) Java   d) BASIC

Answers: 1) c. 2) d.

1.5 Other High-Level Languages

Although hundreds of high-level languages have been developed, only a few have achieved broad acceptance. IBM Corporation developed **Fortran** in the mid-1950s to create scientific and engineering applications that require complex mathematical computations. Fortran is still widely used.

COBOL was developed in the late 1950s by a group of computer manufacturers in conjunction with government and industrial computer users. COBOL is used primarily for business applications that require the manipulation of large amounts of data. A considerable portion of today's business software is still programmed in COBOL.

The C language, which Dennis Ritchie developed at Bell Laboratories in the early 1970s, gained widespread recognition as a development language of the UNIX operating system. C++, an extension of C, was developed by Bjarne Stroustrup in the early 1980s at Bell Laboratories. C++ provides capabilities for object-oriented programming (OOP). Many of today's major operating systems are written in C or C++.

Objects are reusable software components that model items in the real world. Object-oriented programs are often easier to understand, correct and modify than programs developed with previous techniques. Visual Basic .NET provides full object-oriented programming capabilities.

In the early 1990s, many organizations, including Sun Microsystems, predicted that intelligent consumer-electronic devices would be the next major market in which **microprocessors**—the chips that make computers work—would have a profound impact. But the marketplace for intelligent consumer-electronic devices did not develop as quickly as Sun had anticipated. By sheer good fortune, the World Wide Web exploded in popularity in 1993, and Sun saw an immediate potential for using its new Java programming language to create **dynamic content** (animated and interactive content) for Web pages. Sun announced Java to the public in 1995, grabbing the immediate attention of the business community because of the widespread interest in the Web. Developers now use Java to create Web pages with dynamic content, to build large-scale enterprise applications, to enhance the functionality of Web servers (the computers that provide the content distributed to your Web browser when you browse Web sites), to provide applications for consumer devices (for example, cell phones, pagers and PDAs) and for many other purposes.

In 2000, Microsoft announced C# (pronounced "C-Sharp") at the same time that it announced its .NET strategy. The C# programming language was designed specifically for the .NET platform. It has roots in C, C++ and Java, adapting the best features of each. Like Visual Basic, C# is object oriented and has access to .NET's powerful library of prebuilt components, enabling programmers to develop applications quickly. C#, Java and Visual Basic have comparable capabilities, so learning Visual Basic may create many career opportunities for you.

SELF-REVIEW

1. _____ is an extension of C and offers object-oriented capabilities.
   a) Visual Basic   b) C++
   c) assembly language   d) Windows

2. _____ is a programming language originally developed for Microsoft's .NET platform.
   a) C#   b) Java
   c) C++   d) Visual Basic

3. _____, developed in the late 1950s, is still used to produce a considerable portion of today's business software.
   a) COBOL   b) Fortran
   c) Java   d) C

4. _____, developed in the 1950s, is still used to create scientific and engineering applications that require complex mathematical computations.
   a) Visual Basic   b) Fortran
   c) COBOL   d) C#

Answers: 1) b. 2) a. 3) a. 4) b.

1.6 Structured Programming

During the 1960s, software-development efforts often ran behind schedule, costs greatly exceeded budgets and the finished products were unreliable. People began to realize that software development was a far more complex activity than they had imagined. Research activity intended to address these issues resulted in the evolution of **structured programming**—a disciplined approach to creating programs that are clear, correct and easy to modify.

One of the results of this research was the development of the **Pascal** programming language in 1971. Pascal, named after the 17th-century mathematician and philosopher Blaise Pascal, was designed for teaching structured programming and rapidly became the preferred introductory programming language in most colleges. Unfortunately, the language lacked many features needed to make it useful in commercial, industrial and government applications. By contrast, C, which also arose from research on structured programming, did not have the limitations of Pascal, and professional programmers quickly adopted it.

The **Ada** programming language, based on Pascal, was developed under the sponsorship of the U.S. Department of Defense (DOD) during the 1970s and early 1980s. The language was named after **Ada Byron**, **Lady Lovelace**, daughter of the poet Lord Byron. Lady Lovelace is generally credited as the world's first computer programmer because of an application she wrote in the early 1800s for the Analytical Engine mechanical computing device designed by Charles Babbage.

SELF-REVIEW

1. During the 1960s and 1970s, research to address such software-development problems as running behind schedule, exceeding budgets and creating unreliable products led to the evolution of _____.

    a) multithreading   b) object-oriented programming

    c) Ada   d) structured programming

2. _____ was designed to teach structured programming in academic environments.

    a) C++   b) C

    c) Java   d) Pascal

Answers: 1) d. 2) d.

1.7 Key Software Trend: Object Technology

As the benefits of structured programming were realized in the 1970s, improved software technology began to appear. However, it was not until object-oriented programming became widely used in the 1980s and 1990s that software developers finally felt they had the necessary tools to improve the software-development process dramatically.

What are objects, and why are they special? **Object technology** is a packaging scheme for creating meaningful software units. There are date objects, time objects, paycheck objects, invoice objects, automobile objects, people objects, audio objects, video objects, file objects, record objects and so on. In fact, almost any noun can be reasonably represented as a software object. Objects have **properties** (also called **attributes**), such as color, size and weight; and perform **actions** (also called **behaviors** or **methods**), such as moving, sleeping or drawing. **Classes** are types of related objects. For example, all cars belong to the "car" class, even though individual cars vary in make, model, color and options packages. A class specifies the general format of its objects, and the properties and actions available to an object depend on its class. An object is related to its class in much the same way as a building is related to its blueprint.

Before object-oriented languages appeared, **procedural programming languages** (such as Fortran, Pascal, BASIC and C) focused on actions (verbs) rather than things or objects (nouns). This made programming a bit awkward. However, using today's popular object-oriented languages, such as Visual Basic, C++, Java and C#, programmers can program in an object-oriented manner that more naturally reflects the way in which they perceive the world. This has resulted in significant productivity gains.

With object technology, properly designed classes can be reused on future projects. Using libraries of classes can greatly reduce the amount of effort required to implement new systems. Some organizations report that software reusability is not, in fact, the key benefit that they get from object-oriented programming. They indicate that object-oriented programming tends to produce software that is more understandable because it is better organized and has fewer maintenance requirements.

Object orientation allows the programmer to focus on the "big picture." Instead of worrying about the minute details of how reusable objects are implemented, the programmer can focus on the behaviors and interactions of objects. A road map that showed every tree, house and driveway would be difficult, if not impossible, to read. When such details are removed and only the essential information (roads) remains, the map becomes easier to understand. In the same way, an application that is divided into objects is easy to understand, modify and update because it hides much of the detail. It is clear that object-oriented programming will be the key programming methodology for the next several decades. Visual Basic is one of the world's most widely used fully object-oriented languages.

1. _____ focuses on actions (verbs) rather than things (nouns).

    a) C#   b) Object-oriented programming

    c) Visual Basic   d) Procedural programming

2. In object-oriented programming, _____, which are in a sense like blueprints, are types of related objects.

    a) classes   b) attributes

    c) behaviors   d) properties

Answers: 1) d. 2) a.

1.8 The Internet and the World Wide Web

In the late 1960s, ARPA—the Advanced Research Projects Agency of the Department of Defense—rolled out the blueprints for networking the main computer systems of approximately a dozen ARPA-funded universities and research institutions. The computers were to be connected with communications lines operating at a then-stunning 56 Kbps (1 Kbps is equal to 1,024 bits per second), at a time when most people (of the few who even had networking access) were connecting over telephone lines to computers at a rate of 110 bits per second. Academic research was about to take a giant leap forward. ARPA proceeded to implement what quickly became known as the ARPAnet, the grandparent of today's **Internet**.

Things worked out differently from the original plan. Although the ARPAnet enabled researchers to network their computers, its main benefit proved to be the capability for quick and easy communication via what came to be known as electronic mail (e-mail). This is true even on today's Internet, with e-mail, instant messaging and file transfer allowing hundreds of millions of people worldwide to communicate with each other.

The protocol (in other words, the set of rules) for communicating over the ARPAnet became known as the **Transmission Control Protocol (TCP)**. TCP ensured that messages, consisting of pieces called "packets," were properly routed from sender to receiver and arrived intact.

In parallel with the early evolution of the Internet, organizations worldwide were implementing their own networks for both intraorganization (that is, within an organization) and interorganization (that is, between organizations) communication. A huge variety of networking hardware and software appeared. One challenge was to enable these different networks to communicate with each other. ARPA accomplished this by developing the **Internet Protocol (IP)**, which created a true "network of networks," the current architecture of the Internet. The combined set of protocols is now commonly called **TCP/IP**.

Businesses rapidly realized that by using the Internet, they could improve their operations and offer new and better services to their clients. Companies started spending large amounts of money to develop and enhance their Internet presence. This generated fierce competition among communications carriers and hardware and software suppliers to meet the increased infrastructure demand. As a result, **bandwidth**—the information-carrying capacity of communications lines—on the Internet has increased tremendously, while hardware costs have plummeted.

The **World Wide Web** is a collection of hardware and software associated with the Internet that allows computer users to locate and view multimedia-based documents (documents with various combinations of text, graphics, animations, audios and videos) on almost any subject. Even though the Internet was developed more than three decades ago, the introduction of the World Wide Web (WWW) was a relatively recent event. In 1989, Tim Berners-Lee of CERN (the European Organization for Nuclear Research) began to develop a technology for sharing information via "hyperlinked" text documents. Berners-Lee called his invention the **HyperText Markup Language (HTML)**. He also wrote communication protocols such as

HyperText Transfer Protocol (HTTP) to form the backbone of his new hypertext information system, which he referred to as the World Wide Web.

In October 1994, Berners-Lee founded an organization, called the **World Wide Web Consortium** (**W3C**, `www.w3.org`), that is devoted to developing technologies for the World Wide Web. One of the W3C's primary goals is to make the Web universally accessible to everyone regardless disabilities, language or culture.

The Internet and the World Wide Web will surely be listed among the most important creations of humankind. In the past, most computer applications ran on "stand-alone" computers (computers that were not connected to one another). Today's applications can be written with the aim of communicating among the world's hundreds of millions of computers. In fact, as you will see, this is the focus of Microsoft's .NET strategy. The Internet and the World Wide Web make information instantly and conveniently accessible to large numbers of people, enabling even individuals and small businesses to achieve worldwide exposure. They are profoundly changing the way we do business and conduct our personal lives. To highlight the importance of Internet and Web programming, we include four tutorials at the end of the book in which you'll actually build and run a Web-based bookstore application.

SELF-REVIEW

1. Today's Internet evolved from the _____, which was a Department of Defense project.
   a) ARPAnet   b) HTML
   c) CERN   d) WWW

2. The combined set of protocols for communicating over the Internet is now commonly called _____.
   a) HTML   b) TCP/IP
   c) ARPA   d) TCP

Answers: 1) a. 2) b.

1.9 Introduction to Microsoft .NET

In June 2000, Microsoft announced its .NET initiative (`www.microsoft.com/net`), a broad new vision for using the Internet and the Web in the development, engineering, distribution and use of software. Rather than forcing developers to use a single programming language, the .NET initiative permits developers to create .NET applications in any .NET-compatible language (such as Visual Basic, Visual C++, C# and others). Part of the initiative includes Microsoft's **ASP.NET** technology, which allows programmers to create applications for the Web. You'll be introduced to ASP.NET as you build the Web-based bookstore application later in the book.

The .NET strategy extends the idea of **software reuse** to the Internet by allowing programmers to concentrate on their specialties without having to implement every component of every application. Instead, companies can buy Web services, which are Web-based programs that organizations can incorporate into their systems to speed the Web application development process. Visual programming (which you will learn throughout this book) has become popular because it enables programmers to create Windows applications easily, using such prepackaged graphical components as buttons, textboxes and scrollbars.

The Microsoft **.NET Framework** is at the heart of the .NET strategy. This framework executes applications and Web services, contains a class library (called the **Framework Class Library** or **FCL**) and provides many other programming capabilities that you'll use to build Visual Basic applications. In this book, you'll develop .NET software with Visual Basic. Steve Ballmer, Microsoft's CEO, stated in May 2001 that Microsoft was "betting the company" on .NET. Such a dramatic commitment surely indicates a bright future for Visual Basic programmers.

1. _____ is a technology specifically designed for the .NET platform and intended for programmers to create Web-based applications.

    a) Visual Basic   b) C++

    c) HTML   d) ASP.NET

2. _____ are existing Web-based programs that can be incorporated into other applications.

    a) Web services   b) Wire services

    c) Attributes   d) Properties

3. Programmers use the _____, a part of the .NET Framework, to build Visual Basic .NET applications.

    a) Visual Basic Library (VBL)   b) Framework Class Library (FCL)

    c) Microsoft Class Library (MCL)   d) Visual Basic Framework (VBF)

Answers: 1) d. 2) a. 3) b.

1.10 Test-Driving the Visual Basic Drawing Application

In each tutorial, you are given a chance to "test-drive" that tutorial's featured application. You'll actually run and interact with the completed application. Then, you'll learn the Visual Basic features you need to build the application. Finally, you'll "put it all together," creating your own working version of the application. You begin here in Tutorial 1 by running an application that allows the user to draw with "brushes" of four different colors and three different sizes. You'll actually build a similar application in the exercises of Tutorial 21.

The following box, *Test-Driving the **Drawing** Application*, will show you how the application allows the user to draw with different brush styles. The elements and functionality you see in this application are typical of what you will learn to program in this text. [*Note*: We use fonts to distinguish between IDE features (such as menu names and menu items) and other elements that appear in the IDE. Our convention is to emphasize IDE features (such as the **File** menu) in a semibold **sans-serif Helvetica** font and to emphasize other elements, such as file names (for example, `Form1.cs`), in a `sans-serif Lucida` font. Each term that is being defined is set in **heavy bold**.]

Test-Driving the Drawing Application

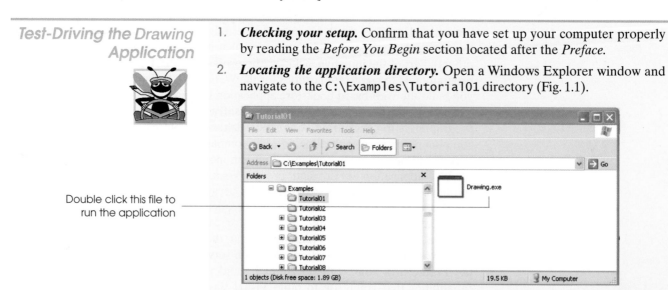

1. ***Checking your setup.*** Confirm that you have set up your computer properly by reading the *Before You Begin* section located after the *Preface*.

2. ***Locating the application directory.*** Open a Windows Explorer window and navigate to the `C:\Examples\Tutorial01` directory (Fig. 1.1).

Double click this file to run the application

Figure 1.1 Contents of `C:\Examples\Tutorial01`.

(cont.)   3. ***Running the Drawing application.*** Now that you are in the proper directory, double click the file name `Drawing.exe` (Fig. 1.1) to run the application (Fig. 1.2).

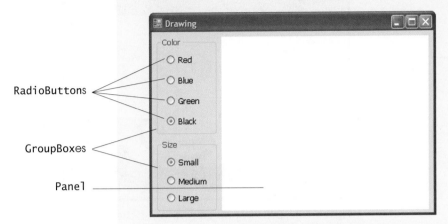

Figure 1.2 Visual Basic **Drawing** application.

In Fig. 1.2, several graphical elements—called **controls**—are labeled. The controls include `GroupBoxes`, `RadioButtons` and a `Panel` (these controls will be discussed in depth later in the text). The application allows you to draw with a black, blue, green or red brush of small, medium or large size. You will explore these options in this test-drive.

The use of existing controls—which are objects—enables you to get powerful applications running in Visual Basic much faster than if you had to write all the code yourself. In this text, you'll learn how to use many preexisting controls, as well as how to write your own program code to customize your applications.

The brush's properties, selected in the `RadioButtons` labeled **Black** and **Small**, are default settings—the initial settings you see when you first run the application. Programmers include default settings to provide visual cues for users to choose their own settings. Now you'll choose your own settings.

4. ***Changing the brush color.*** Click the `RadioButton` labeled **Red** to change the color of the brush. Click the `Panel`, and hold down the mouse to draw with the brush. Draw flower petals as shown in Fig. 1.3. Then click the `RadioButton` labeled **Green** to change the color of the brush once again.

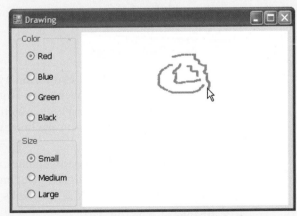

Figure 1.3 Drawing with a new brush color.

(cont.)

5. ***Changing the brush size.*** Click the RadioButton labeled **Large** to change the size of the brush. Draw grass and a flower stem, as shown in Fig. 1.4.

Figure 1.4   Drawing with a new brush size.

6. ***Finishing the drawing.*** Click the RadioButton labeled **Blue**. Then click the RadioButton labeled **Medium**. Draw raindrops, as shown in Fig. 1.5, to complete the drawing.

              Close box

Figure 1.5   Finishing the drawing.

7. ***Closing the application.*** Close your running application by clicking its **close box**, ☒ (Fig. 1.5).

1.11 Web Resources

The Internet and the Web are extraordinary resources. This section includes links to interesting and informative Web sites. Hot links to all these sites are included at www.deitel.com/books/simplyVB2005 to save you time. Reference sections like this one are included throughout the book where appropriate.

www.deitel.com
Visit this site for code downloads, updates, corrections and additional resources for Deitel & Associates publications, including *Simply Visual Basic 2005* errata, Frequently Asked Questions (FAQs), hot links and code downloads.

www.prenhall.com/deitel
The Deitel & Associates page on the Prentice Hall Web site contains information about our publications and code downloads for this book.

msdn.microsoft.com/vbasic
This is Microsoft's Visual Basic Web site.

www.deitel.com/visualbasic
Our Visual Basic Resource Center focuses on the enormous amount of Visual Basic content available online. Search for resources, downloads, tutorials, documentation, books, e-books, journals, articles, blogs and more that will help you develop Visual Basic applications.

www.GotDotNet.com
A site with abundant .NET resources.

www.softlord.com/comp
Visit this site to learn more about the history of computers.

www.elsop.com/wrc/h_comput.htm
This site presents the history of computing. It includes content about famous people in the computer field, the evolution of programming languages and the development of operating systems.

www.w3.org/History.html
Visit this site for the history of the World Wide Web.

www.netvalley.com/intval/07262/main.htm?sdf=1
This site presents the history of the Internet.

1.12 Wrap-Up

In this tutorial, you learned how computers are organized. You studied the levels of programming languages and which kinds of languages, including Visual Basic, require translators. You became familiar with some of the most popular programming languages. You learned the importance of structured programming and object-oriented programming. You studied a brief history of the Internet and the World Wide Web, were introduced to Microsoft's .NET initiative and learned some key aspects of .NET.

You took a working Visual Basic application out for a "test-drive." In the process of doing this, you learned that Visual Basic provides lots of prebuilt controls that perform useful functions, and that by familiarizing yourself with the capabilities of these controls, you can develop powerful applications much faster than if you tried to build them completely yourself. You were encouraged to explore several Web sites with additional information on this book, computers, the Internet, the Web, .NET and Visual Basic.

In the next tutorial, you'll learn about the Visual Basic 2005 Integrated Development Environment (IDE). This will help you prepare to create your own Visual Basic applications. You'll continue to learn with our application-driven approach, in which you'll see Visual Basic features in useful applications and will

1. study the user requirements for an application,

2. test-drive a working version of the application,

3. learn the technologies you'll need to build the application yourself, and

4. build your own version of the application.

As you work through the book, if you have any questions about Visual Basic 2005, just send an e-mail to deitel@deitel.com, and we'll respond promptly. We sincerely hope you enjoy learning the latest version of Microsoft's powerful Visual Basic language—one of the most widely used programming languages in the world—with *Simply Visual Basic 2005, 2/e*. Good luck!

KEY TERMS   **Ada**—A programming language, named after Lady Ada Lovelace, that was developed under the sponsorship of the U.S. Department of Defense (DOD) in the 1970s and early 1980s.

arithmetic and logic unit (ALU)—The "manufacturing" section of the computer. The ALU performs calculations and makes decisions.

ASP.NET—.NET software that helps programmers create applications for the Web.

assembler—A translator program that converts assembly-language programs to machine language at computer speeds.

assembly language—A type of programming language that uses English-like abbreviations to represent the fundamental operations on the computer.

attribute—Another name for a property of an object.

bandwidth—The information-carrying capacity of communications lines.

BASIC (Beginner's All-Purpose Symbolic Instruction Code)—A programming language that was developed in the mid-1960s by Professors John Kemeny and Thomas Kurtz of Dartmouth College as a language for writing simple programs. Its primary purpose was to familiarize novices with programming techniques.

Central Processing Unit (CPU)—The part of the computer's hardware that is responsible for supervising the operation of the other sections of the computer.

class—The type of a group of related objects. A class specifies the general format of its objects; the properties and actions available to an object depend on its class. An object is to its class much as a house is to its blueprint.

COBOL (COmmon Business Oriented Language)—A programming language that was developed in the late 1950s by a group of computer manufacturers in conjunction with government and industrial computer users. This language is used primarily for business applications that manipulate large amounts of data.

compiler—A translator program that converts high-level-language programs into machine language.

computer—A device capable of performing computations and making logical decisions at speeds millions and even billions of times faster than the speeds at which human beings carry out the same tasks.

computer program—A set of instructions that guides a computer through an orderly series of actions.

computer programmer—A person who writes computer programs.

control—A reusable GUI component, such as a `GroupBox`, `RadioButton`, `Button` or `Label`.

dynamic content—A type of content that is animated or interactive.

event-driven program—A program that responds to user-initiated events, such as mouse clicks and keystrokes.

Fortran (Formula Translator)—A programming language developed by IBM Corporation in the mid-1950s to create scientific and engineering applications that require complex mathematical computations.

Framework Class Library (FCL)—.NET's collection of "prepackaged" classes and methods for performing mathematical calculations, string manipulations, character manipulations, input/output operations, error checking and many other useful operations.

Graphical User Interface (GUI)—The visual part of an application with which users interact.

hardware—The various devices that make up a computer, including the keyboard, screen, mouse, hard drive, memory, CD-ROM, DVD and processing units.

high-level language—A type of programming language in which a single program statement accomplishes a substantial task. High-level languages use instructions that look almost like everyday English and contain common mathematical notations.

HyperText Markup Language (HTML)—A language for marking up information to share over the World Wide Web via hyperlinked text documents.

HyperText Transfer Protocol (HTTP)—The protocol that enables HTML files to be transmitted over the World Wide Web.

input device—Devices such as the keyboard and the mouse that are used to interact with a computer.

input unit—The "receiving" section of the computer that obtains information (data and computer programs) from various input devices, such as the keyboard and the mouse.

Integrated Development Environment (IDE)—A software tool that enables programmers to write, run, test and debug programs quickly and conveniently.

Internet—A worldwide computer network. Most people today access the Internet through the World Wide Web.

machine language—A computer's natural language, generally consisting of streams of numbers that instruct the computer how to perform its most elementary operations.

memory unit—The rapid-access, relatively low-capacity "warehouse" section of the computer, which stores data temporarily while an application is running.

memory—Another name for the memory unit.

method—A portion of a class that performs a task and possibly returns information when it completes the task.

microprocessor—The chip that makes a computer work (that is, the "brain" of the computer).

Microsoft .NET—Microsoft's vision for using the Internet and the Web in the development, engineering and use of software. .NET includes tools such as Visual Studio and programming languages such as Visual Basic.

.NET Framework—Microsoft-provided software that executes applications, provides the Framework Class Library (FCL) and supplies many other programming capabilities.

objects—Reusable software components that model items in the real world.

object technology—A packaging scheme for creating meaningful software units. The units are large and are focused on particular application areas. There are date objects, time objects, paycheck objects, file objects and the like.

output device—A device to which information that is processed by the computer can be sent.

output unit—The section of the computer that takes information the computer has processed and places it on various output devices, making the information available for use outside the computer.

Pascal—A programming language designed for teaching structured programming, named after the 17th-century mathematician and philosopher Blaise Pascal.

primary memory—Another name for the memory unit.

procedural programming language—A programming language (such as Fortran, Pascal, BASIC and C) that focuses on actions (verbs) rather than things or objects (nouns).

properties—Object attributes, such as size, color and weight.

Random-access memory—An example of primary memory.

secondary storage unit—The long-term, high-capacity "warehouse" section of the computer.

software—The set of applications that run on computers.

software reuse—The reuse of existing pieces of software, an approach that enables programmers to avoid "reinventing the wheel," helping them develop applications faster.

structured programming—A disciplined approach to creating programs that are clear, correct and easy to modify.

Transmission Control Protocol/Internet Protocol (TCP/IP)—The combined set of communications protocols for the Internet.

volatile memory—Memory that is erased when the machine is powered off.

visual programming with Visual Basic—Instead of writing detailed program statements, the programmer uses Visual Studio's graphical user interface to conveniently drag and drop predefined controls into place, and to label and resize them. Visual Studio writes much of the Visual Basic program, saving the programmer considerable effort.

World Wide Web (WWW)—A communications system that allows computer users to locate and view multimedia documents (such as documents with text, graphics, animations, audios and videos).

World Wide Web Consortium (W3C)—A forum through which qualified individuals and companies cooperate to develop and standardize technologies for the World Wide Web.

MULTIPLE-CHOICE QUESTIONS

1.1 The World Wide Web was developed _____.

a) by ARPA   b) at CERN by Tim Berners-Lee

c) before the Internet   d) as a replacement for the Internet

1.2 Microsoft's _____ initiative integrates the Internet and the Web into software development.

a) .NET

b) BASIC

c) Windows

d) W3C

1.3 TextBoxes, Buttons and RadioButtons are examples of _____.

a) platforms

b) high-level languages

c) IDEs

d) controls

1.4 _____ is an example of primary memory.

a) TCP

b) RAM

c) ALU

d) CD-ROM

1.5 Visual Basic is an example of a(n) _____ language, in which single program statements accomplish more substantial tasks.

a) machine

b) intermediate-level

c) high-level

d) assembly

1.6 Which protocol is primarily intended to create a "network of networks?"

a) TCP

b) IP

c) OOP

d) FCL

1.7 A major benefit of _____ programming is that it produces software that is more understandable and better organized than software produced with previously used techniques.

a) object-oriented

b) centralized

c) procedural

d) HTML

1.8 .NET's collection of prepackaged classes and methods is called the _____.

a) NCL

b) WCL

c) FCL

d) PPCM

1.9 The information-carrying capacity of communications lines is called _____.

a) networking

b) secondary storage

c) traffic

d) bandwidth

1.10 Which of these programming languages was specifically created for .NET?

a) C#

b) C++

c) BASIC

d) Visual Basic

EXERCISES

1.11 Categorize each of the following items as either hardware or software:

a) CPU

b) Compiler

c) Input unit

d) A word-processor program

e) A Visual Basic program

1.12 Translator programs, such as assemblers and compilers, convert programs from one language (referred to as the source language) to another language (referred to as the target language). Determine which of the following statements are _true_ and which are _false_:

a) A compiler translates high-level-language programs into target-language programs.

b) An assembler translates source-language programs into machine-language programs.

c) A compiler translates source-language programs into target-language programs.

d) High-level languages are generally machine dependent.

e) A machine-language program requires translation before it can run on a computer.

1.13 Computers can be thought of as being divided into six units.

    a) Which unit can be thought of as the "boss" of the other units?

    b) Which unit is the high-capacity "warehouse" and retains information even when the computer is powered off?

    c) Which unit might determine whether two items stored in memory are identical?

    d) Which unit obtains information from devices like the keyboard and the mouse?

1.14 Expand each of the following acronyms:

    a) W3C   b) TCP/IP

    c) OOP   d) FCL

    e) HTML

1.15 What are the advantages to using object-oriented programming techniques?

T U T O R I A L

Welcome Application

Introducing the Visual Basic 2005 Express Edition IDE

Visual Studio® **2005** is Microsoft's **Integrated Development Environment (IDE)** for creating, running and debugging applications written in a variety of .NET programming languages. The IDE allows you to create applications by dragging and dropping existing building blocks into place—a technique called visual programming—greatly simplifying application development. In this tutorial, you will learn the Visual Studio 2005 IDE features that you will need to create Visual Basic applications.

2.1 Test-Driving the Welcome Application

In this section, you continue learning with our application-driven approach as you prepare to build an application that displays a welcome message and a picture. This application must meet the following requirements:

> **Application Requirements**
>
> *A software company (Deitel & Associates) has asked you to develop a Visual Basic application that will display the message "Welcome to Visual Basic 2005!" and a picture of the company's bug mascot. To build this application, you must first familiarize yourself with the Visual Basic 2005 Express Edition IDE.*

In this tutorial, you will begin to develop the **Welcome** application. Then, in Tutorial 3, you will "put it all together" and create the **Welcome** application by following our step-by-step boxes. [*Note*: Our convention is to display application names in the **Helvetica** font.] You begin by test-driving the completed application. Then you will learn the additional Visual Basic technologies that you will need to create your own version of this application.

Test-Driving the
Welcome Application

1. ***Checking your setup.*** Confirm that you have set up your computer properly by reading the *Before You Begin* tutorial located at the beginning of this book just after the *Preface.*

2. ***Locating the application directory.*** Open Windows Explorer and navigate to the C:\Examples\Tutorial02 directory (Fig. 2.1).

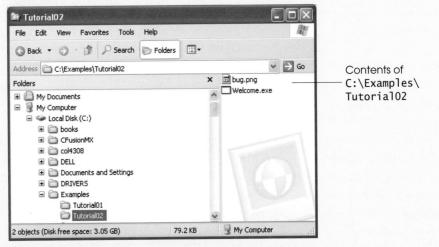

Contents of
C:\Examples\
Tutorial02

Figure 2.1   Contents of C:\Examples\Tutorial02.

3. ***Running the Welcome application.*** Double click Welcome.exe (Fig. 2.1) to run the application (Fig. 2.2).

Close
box

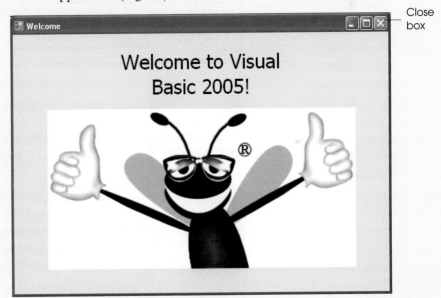

Figure 2.2   **Welcome** application executing.

4. ***Closing the application.*** Close your running application by clicking its close box, ⊠.

2.2 Overview of the Visual Basic 2005 Express Edition IDE

There are many versions of Visual Studio available. The book's examples are based on the *Microsoft Visual Basic 2005 Express Edition*, which supports only the Visual Basic programming language. You also can purchase a full version of Visual Studio 2005, which includes support for other languages in addition to Visual Basic, such as

Visual C# and Visual C++. Our screen captures and discussions focus on the IDE of the Visual Basic 2005 Express Edition. We assume that you have some familiarity with Microsoft Windows.

This section introduces you to the Visual Basic 2005 Express Edition IDE. To start Microsoft Visual Basic 2005 Express Edition in Windows XP, select **Start > All Programs > Microsoft Visual Basic 2005 Express Edition**. For Windows 2000 users, select **Start > Programs > Microsoft Visual Basic 2005 Express Edition**. We use the **>** character to indicate the selection of a menu command from a menu. For example, we use the notation **File > Open File** to indicate that you should select the **Open File** command from the **File** menu. Once the Express Edition begins execution, the **Start Page** displays (Fig. 2.3).

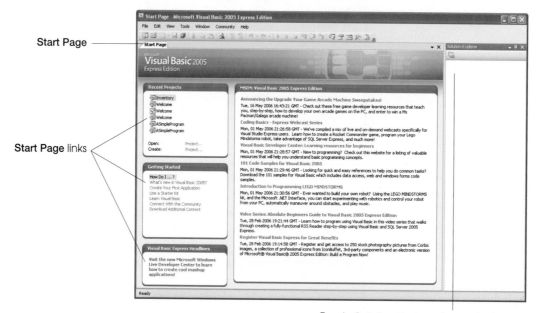

Figure 2.3 **Start Page** in Visual Basic 2005 Express Edition with an empty project list.

Depending on your version of Visual Studio, the **Start Page** may look different from the image in Fig. 2.3. For new programmers unfamiliar with Visual Basic, the **Start Page** contains a list of links to resources in the Visual Basic 2005 Express Edition IDE and on the Internet. For experienced developers, this page provides links to the latest developments in Visual Basic (such as updates and bug fixes) and to information on advanced programming topics. From this point forward we will refer to the Visual Basic 2005 Express Edition IDE simply as "Visual Basic" or "the IDE." Once you start exploring the IDE, you can return to the **Start Page** by selecting **View > Other Windows > Start Page**.

Links on the Start Page

The **Start Page** links are organized into sections—**Recent Projects**, **Getting Started**, **Visual Basic Express Headlines** and **MSDN: Visual Basic 2005 Express Edition**—that contain links to helpful programming resources. Clicking any link on the **Start Page** displays relevant information associated with the specific link. We refer to single clicking with the left mouse button as selecting, or clicking; we refer to double clicking with the left mouse button simply as double clicking.

The **Recent Projects** section contains information on projects you have recently created or modified. You can also open existing projects or create new ones by clicking the links in the section. The **Getting Started** section focuses on using the IDE for creating programs, learning Visual Basic, connecting to the Visual Basic developer community (i.e., other software developers with whom you can communicate through newsgroups and Web sites) and providing various development tools such as starter kits. For example, clicking the link **Use a Starter Kit** provides you with resources and links for building a simple screen saver application or a movie collection application. The screen saver application builds a screen saver that displays current news articles. The movie collection starter kit builds an application that lets you maintain a catalog of your DVDs and VHS movies, or the application can be changed to track anything else you might collect (e.g., CDs and video games).

The **Visual Basic Express Headlines** and **MSDN: Visual Basic 2005 Express Edition** sections provide links to information about programming in Visual Basic, including a tour of the language, new Visual Basic 2005 features and online courses. To access more extensive information on Visual Studio, you can browse the **MSDN (Microsoft Developer Network)** online library at msdn2.microsoft.com. The MSDN site contains articles, downloads and tutorials on technologies of interest to Visual Basic developers. You can also browse the Web from the IDE using Internet Explorer (also called the **internal Web browser** in the IDE). To request a Web page, type its URL into the **location bar** (Fig. 2.4) and press the *Enter* key—your computer, of course, must be connected to the Internet. (If the location bar is not already displayed, select **View > Other Windows > Web Browser** or press <*Ctrl*> <*Alt*> *R*.) The Web page that you wish to view will appear as another **tab**, which you can select, inside the Visual Basic IDE (Fig. 2.4). Other windows appear in the IDE in addition to the **Start Page** and the internal Web browser; we discuss several of them later in this tutorial.

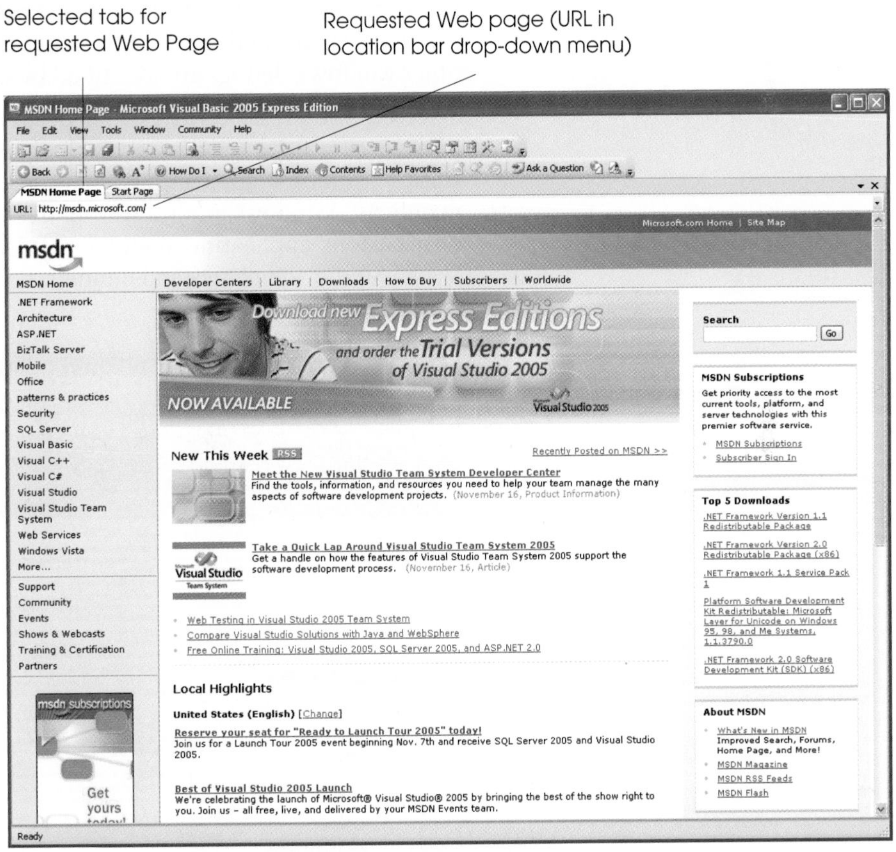

Selected tab for requested Web Page

Requested Web page (URL in location bar drop-down menu)

Figure 2.4   Displaying a Web page in the Visual Basic 2005 Express Edition IDE.

SELF-REVIEW   1. When you first open the Visual Basic 2005 Express Edition, the _____ displays.

    a) **What's New Page**   b) **Start Page**

    c) **Welcome Page**   d) None of the above.

2. The _____ section in the **Start Page** contains a listing of projects opened or created in Visual Basic.

    a) **MSDN**   b) **Getting Started**

    c) **Recent Projects**   d) **Visual Basic Express Headlines**

Answers: 1) b. 2) c.

2.3 Creating a Project for the Welcome Application

In this section, you will create a simple Visual Basic **Windows application**. Visual Basic organizes applications into **projects** and **solutions**. A project is a group of related files, such as the Visual Basic code and any images that might make up a program. Solutions contain one or more projects. Every application always contains exactly one solution. Large-scale applications can contain many projects, in which each project performs a single well-defined task. In this book, each application you build will contain only one project.

Creating a Project for the Welcome Application

1. *Creating a new project.* If you have not already done so, start Visual Basic. There are two ways to create a new project or open an existing project: 1) Select either **File > New Project…**, which creates a new project, or **File > Open Project…**, which opens an existing project. 2) From the **Start Page**, under the **Recent Projects** section, click the links **Create: Project…** or **Open: Project…**. Click the **New Project** Button (Fig. 2.5), causing the **New Project** dialog to display (Fig. 2.6). **Dialogs** are windows that can display information for, and gather information from, the application's user. Like other windows, dialogs are identified by the text in their **title bar**.

2. *Selecting the project type.* Visual Basic provides templates for a variety of projects (Fig. 2.7). Templates are the project types you can create in Visual Basic—Windows applications, console applications and others (you will mainly use Windows applications in this textbook). You can also create your own custom application templates. [*Note:* Depending on your version of Visual Studio, the names and number of items shown in the **Templates:** pane could differ.]

New Project button ——

Recent Projects listing ——

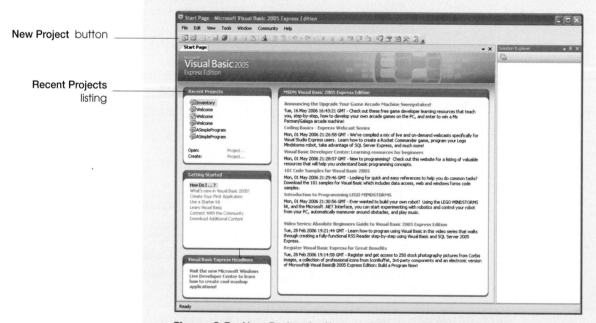

Figure 2.5 **New Project** button and **Recent Projects** listing.

(cont.)

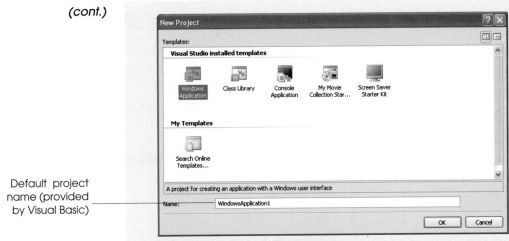

Default project
name (provided
by Visual Basic)

Figure 2.6   **New Project** dialog.

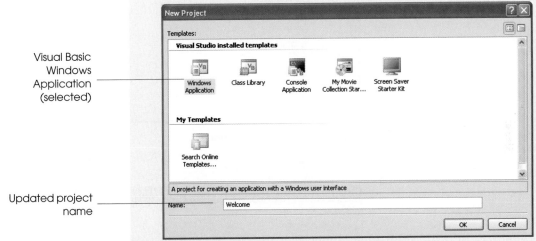

Visual Basic
Windows
Application
(selected)

Updated project
name

Figure 2.7   **New Project** dialog with updated project information.

3. *Selecting the template.* Select **Windows Application**, which is an application that executes within a Windows operating system (e.g., Windows 2000 or XP) and typically has a **graphical user interface (GUI)**—the visual part of the application with which the user interacts. Windows applications include Microsoft software products like Microsoft Word, Internet Explorer and Visual Studio; software products created by other vendors; and customized software that you and other programmers create.

4. *Changing the name of the project.* By default, Visual Basic assigns the name **WindowsApplication1** to the project (Fig. 2.6) and places these files in a directory named `WindowsApplication1`. To rename the project, type `Welcome` in the **Name:** TextBox (Fig. 2.7). Then click **OK**.

5. *Changing the location of the project.* Save this project in your `SimplyVB` directory. To change the project's location, select **File > Save All**, which causes the **Save Project** dialog to appear (Fig. 2.8). In this dialog, use the **Browse...** Button to locate your `SimplyVB` directory, and click **Open** (Fig. 2.9). After providing the project's name and location in the **Save Project** dialog, click **Save**. This displays the IDE in **design view** (Fig. 2.10), which contains the features you need to begin creating a Windows application. Note that your screen may look slightly different—some windows, such as the **Solution Explorer**, may not immediately appear. We will demonstrate how to open these windows shortly.

(cont.)

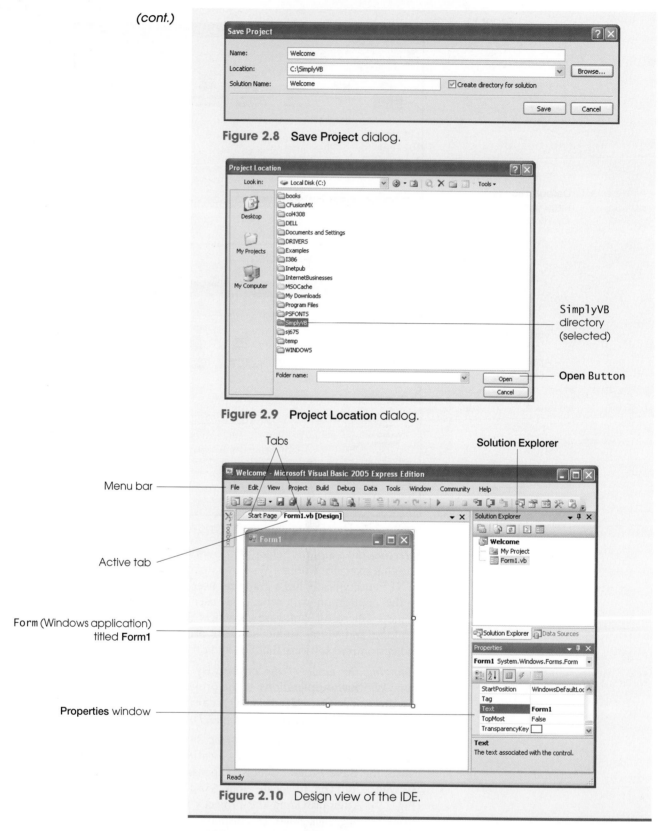

Figure 2.8 **Save Project** dialog.

Figure 2.9 **Project Location** dialog.

Figure 2.10 Design view of the IDE.

The name of each open file is listed on a tab (**Start Page** and **Form1.vb [Design]** in Fig. 2.10). To view a file, click its tab. Tabs provide easy access to multiple files. The **active tab** is displayed in bold text (**Form1.vb [Design]** in Fig. 2.10).

The content of the **Form1.vb [Design]** tab, which includes the gray rectangle (called a **Form**), is the Windows Form Designer. The Form (titled **Form1**) represents the main window of the Windows application that you are creating. Forms can be enhanced by adding controls (i.e., reusable components), such as Buttons. Collectively, the Form and controls make up the application's GUI. Users enter data (inputs) into the application by typing at the keyboard, by clicking the mouse buttons and in a variety of other ways. Applications display instructions and other information (outputs) for users to read in the GUI. For example, the **New Project** dialog in Fig. 2.6 is a GUI in which users click with the mouse to select project types and input project names and locations from the keyboard.

GUI controls (such as Buttons) aid both in data entry by users and in formatting and presenting data outputs to users. For example, Internet Explorer (Fig. 2.11) displays Web pages requested by users. Internet Explorer's GUI has a menu bar that contains six menus: **File**, **Edit**, **View**, **Favorites**, **Tools** and **Help**. These menus allow users to print files, save files and more. Below the menu bar is a **toolbar** that contains Buttons. Each Button contains an image (called an **icon)** that identifies the Button. When clicked, toolbar Buttons execute tasks (such as printing and searching). Beneath the toolbar is a ComboBox in which users can type the locations of Web sites to visit. Users also can click the ComboBox's drop-down arrow to select Web sites that they have visited previously. To the left of the ComboBox is a Label (**Address**) that identifies the purpose of the ComboBox. The menus, Buttons and Label are part of Internet Explorer's GUI; they allow users to interact with the Internet Explorer application. Using Visual Basic you can create your own applications that have all the GUI controls shown in Fig. 2.11 and many more.

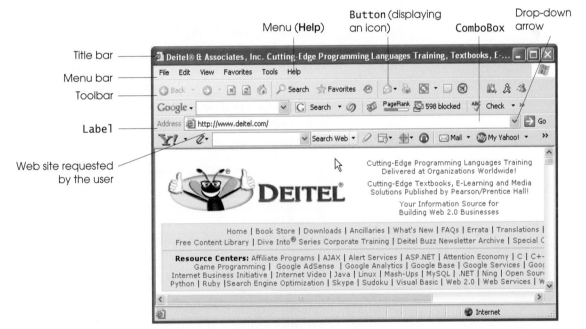

Figure 2.11   Internet Explorer window with GUI controls labeled. (Web site content courtesy of Deitel & Associates, Inc.)

SELF-REVIEW

1. The visual part of the application with which users interact is the application's _____.

    a) graphical user interface   b) project

    c) solution   d) title bar

2. A _____ contains one or more projects that collectively form a Visual Basic application.

    a) dialog   b) Form

    c) solution   d) GUI

Answers: 1) a. 2) c.

2.4 Menu Bar and Toolbar

Visual Basic programmers use **menus** (located on the Visual Basic IDE menu bar shown in Fig. 2.12) that contain commands for managing the IDE and for developing and executing applications. The set of menus displayed depends on what you are currently doing in the IDE.

Each menu has a group of related **menu items** that, when selected, cause the IDE to perform specific actions, such as opening windows, saving files, printing files and executing applications. For example, to display the **Toolbox** window, select **View > Toolbox**. The menus in Fig. 2.12 are summarized in Fig. 2.13—you will learn to use many of these menus throughout the book. In Tutorial 22, **Typing** Application (Introducing Keyboard Events, Menus and Dialogs), you learn how to create and add your own menus and menu items to your applications.

| File | Edit | View | Project | Build | Debug | Data | Format | Tools | Window | Community | Help |

Figure 2.12 Visual Basic 2005 IDE menu bar.

Menu	Description
File	Contains commands for opening, closing, adding and saving projects, as well as printing project data and exiting Visual Studio.
Edit	Contains commands for editing applications, such as **Cut**, **Paste**, and **Undo**.
View	Contains commands for displaying IDE windows (e.g., **Solution Explorer**, **Toolbox**, **Properties** window) and toolbars.
Project	Contains commands for managing projects and their files.
Build	Contains commands for compiling Visual Basic applications.
Debug	Contains commands for debugging (i.e., identifying and correcting problems in applications) and running applications.
Data	Contains commands for interacting with databases, which store the data an application processes. [*Note*: You will learn database concepts in Tutorial 25, **Address Book** Application.]
Format	Contains commands for aligning and modifying a Form's controls. Note that the **Format** menu appears only when a GUI component is selected in **Design** view.
Tools	Contains commands for accessing additional IDE tools and options that enable customization of the IDE.
Window	Contains commands for hiding, opening, closing and displaying IDE windows.
Community	Contains commands for sending questions directly to Microsoft, checking question status, sending feedback on Visual Basic and searching the Code-Zone developer center and the Microsoft developers community site.
Help	Contains commands for accessing the IDE's help features.

Figure 2.13 Visual Basic IDE menu summary.

Rather than navigate the menus from the menu bar, you can access many of the more common commands from the IDE toolbar (Fig. 2.14), which contains icons that graphically represent commands. To execute a command via the IDE toolbar, simply click its icon. Some icons have associated down arrows that, when clicked, display additional commands.

Toolbar icon indicates a
command to open a project

Down arrow indicates
additional commands
are available

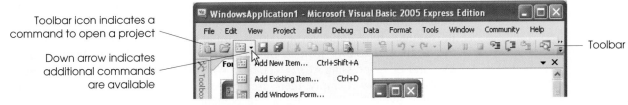

Figure 2.14   IDE toolbar.

It is difficult to remember what each of the icons on the toolbar represents. Positioning the mouse pointer over an icon highlights it and, after a brief pause, displays a description of the icon called a **tool tip** (Fig. 2.15). Tool tips help you become familiar with the IDE's features.

Tool tip displayed
when the mouse
pointer has rested
on the icon for a
few seconds

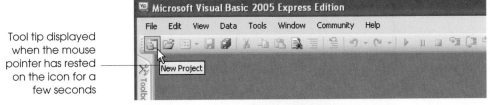

Figure 2.15   Tool tip demonstration.

SELF-REVIEW   1. _____ contain groups of related commands.

a) Menu items   b) Menus

c) Tool tips   d) None of the above

2. When the mouse pointer is positioned over an IDE toolbar icon for a few seconds, a _____ is displayed.

a) toolbox   b) toolbar

c) menu   d) tool tip

Answers: 1) b. 2) d.

2.5 Visual Basic 2005 Express Edition IDE Windows

The IDE provides windows for accessing project files and for customizing forms and controls by changing their attributes (names, colors, etc.). These windows provide visual aids for common programming tasks, such as managing files in a project. In this section, you will become familiar with several windows—**Solution Explorer**, **Properties** and **Toolbox**—that are essential for creating Visual Basic applications. You can access these windows by using the IDE toolbar icons (Fig. 2.16) or by selecting the window name, using the **View** menu. [*Note*: These icons may not appear if the IDE window has been minimized. If you cannot view the icons shown in Fig. 2.16, maximize the IDE window.]

Properties icon

Solution Explorer icon

Toolbox icon

Figure 2.16   Toolbar icons for three Visual Basic IDE windows.

Solution Explorer

The **Solution Explorer** window (located on the right side of the IDE, as shown in Fig. 2.10) provides access to solution files. This window allows you to manage files visually. The **Solution Explorer** window displays a list of all the files in a project and all the projects in a solution. (In this book you will create only single-project applications, but remember that a Visual Basic solution can contain more than one or more projects.) If the **Solution Explorer** window is not shown in the IDE, you can display it by clicking the **Solution Explorer** icon in the IDE (Fig. 2.16), by selecting **View > Solution Explorer** or by pressing *<Ctrl> <Alt> L*. When the IDE is first loaded, the **Solution Explorer** window is empty; there are no files to display. Once a project is open, the **Solution Explorer** window displays its contents. Figure 2.17 displays the contents for the **Welcome** application. By default, the IDE displays only files that you may need to edit—other files generated by the IDE are hidden. Click the **Show All Files** icon (Fig. 2.18) to display all the files in the solution, including those generated by the IDE.

Toolbar —

Show All Files icon —

Form file —

Properties window icon

— Project name

Figure 2.17 **Solution Explorer** with an open project.

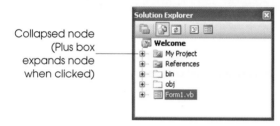

Collapsed node (Plus box expands node when clicked)

Figure 2.18 Using the **Show All Files** icon to display all the files in a solution.

For your single-project solution, **Welcome** is the only project. The file, which corresponds to the Form shown in Fig. 2.10, is named Form1.vb. (Visual Basic Form files use the .vb file name extension, which is short for "Visual Basic.")

The **plus** and **minus** boxes to the left of the **My Project, References, bin** and **obj** and **Form1.vb** items are called **nodes**. The plus and minus boxes expand and collapse information, respectively.

Navigating a Project with the Solution Explorer

1. ***Expanding a node.*** After clicking the **Show All Files** icon (Fig. 2.18), click the plus box to the left of the **My Project** folder to expand the node. The **Solution Explorer** window should look like Fig. 2.19.

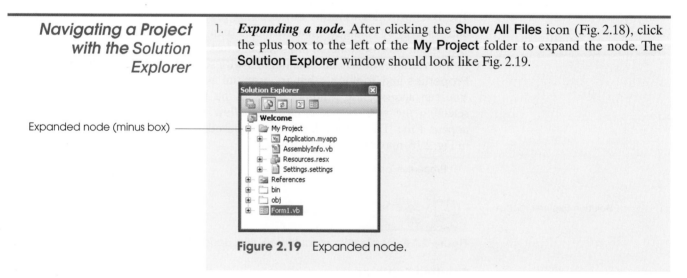

Expanded node (minus box) —

Figure 2.19 Expanded node.

(cont.)   2. ***Collapsing a node.*** Click the minus box to the left of the **My Project** folder
(Fig. 2.19) to collapse the node. The minus box now becomes a plus box as in
(Fig. 2.20).

Collapsed node (plus box) ——

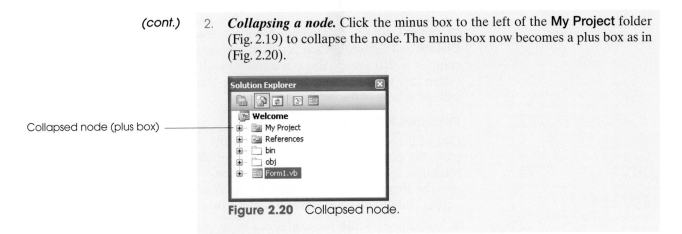

Figure 2.20   Collapsed node.

Toolbox

Using visual programming, you can "drag and drop" controls onto the Form quickly
and easily instead of building them from scratch, which is a slow and complex process. Just as you do not need to know how to build an engine to drive a car, you do
not need to know how to build controls to create effective GUIs. The **Toolbox**
(Fig. 2.21) contains a wide variety of controls for building GUIs. You will use the
Toolbox as you finish creating the **Welcome** application in Tutorial 3. If the **Toolbox** is not visible, select **View > Toolbox**.

Group names ——

Controls ——

Additional group
names ——

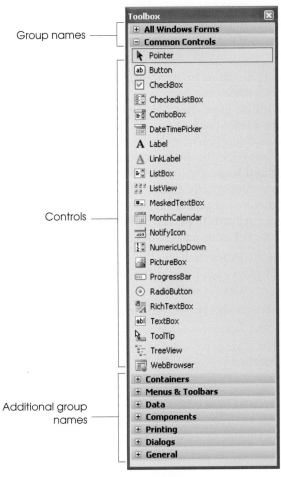

Figure 2.21   **Toolbox** displaying the contents of the **Common Controls** tab.

The **Toolbox** groups prebuilt controls into categories—**All Windows Forms, Common Controls, Containers, Menus & Toolbars, Data, Components, Printing, Dialogs** and **General.** When you click a group name, the **Toolbox** displays all of the controls in that group. You can scroll through the controls using the **scroll arrows** (when they are present) to the right of the **Toolbox.** In the remaining tutorials, you will use dozens of the **Toolbox**'s controls.

Properties **Window**

One of the windows you will use frequently is the **Properties window**, which displays the **properties** for Form and control objects. Properties specify an object's attributes, such as its size, color and position.

The **Properties** window allows you to set object properties visually without writing code. Setting properties visually provides a number of benefits:

- You can see which properties can be modified and, in many cases, you can learn the acceptable values for a given property.

- You do not have to remember or search the Visual Basic documentation (see Section 2.7) for a property's settings.

- You can see a brief description of the selected property that helps you understand the property's purpose.

- You can set a property quickly.

These features are designed to help ensure that settings are correct and consistent throughout the project. If the **Properties** window is not visible, select **View > Properties Window** (or press *F4*). Figure 2.22 shows a Form's **Properties** window:

- Each Form or control object has its own set of properties. At the top of the **Properties** window is the **component object box**, which allows you to select the object whose properties you wish to display in the **Properties** window.

- You can confirm that you're manipulating the correct object's properties because the object's name and class type are displayed in the component object box. Form objects have class type System.Windows.Forms.Form and are assigned generic names (such as Form1). You'll learn about the class types for controls in the next tutorial. Icons on the toolbar sort the properties either alphabetically (if you click the **Alphabetical icon**) or categorically (if you click the **Categorized icon**). Figure 2.22 shows the **Properties** window with its properties sorted categorically. Each gray horizontal bar to the left of the scrollbar is a category that groups related properties. For example, the **Design** category groups four related properties. The categories visible in Fig. 2.22 are **Behavior, Data, Design, Focus** and **Layout.** Note that each category is a node.

- The left column of the **Properties** window lists the object's property names; the right column displays each property's value. In the next tutorial, you will learn how to set properties for objects.

- You can scroll through the list of properties by dragging the scrollbar's scrollbox up or down.

- Whenever you select a property, a description of the property displays at the bottom of the **Properties** window.

SELF-REVIEW

1. The _____ allows you to add controls to the Form in a visual manner.
     a) **Solution Explorer**   b) **Properties** window
     c) **Toolbox**   d) **Dynamic Help** window

2. The _____ window allows you to view a solution's files.
     a) **Properties**   b) **Solution Explorer**
     c) **Toolbox**   d) None of the above.

Answers: 1) c. 2) b.

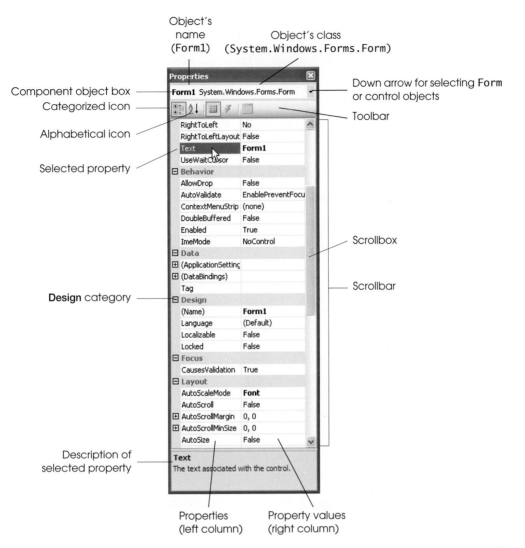

Figure 2.22 **Properties** window displaying a Form's properties.

2.6 Auto-Hide

Visual Basic provides a space-saving feature called **auto-hide** that allows you to hide or show certain windows of the Visual Basic IDE, such as the **Toolbox**, **Solution Explorer** and **Properties** window. When auto-hide is enabled for these windows, tabs representing the hidden windows appear along one of the edges of the IDE window.

Using Auto-Hide   1. ***Enabling auto-hide and displaying a hidden window.*** Auto-hide is enabled by clicking the window's vertical pin icon to change it to a horizontal pin icon. The toolbar along one of the edges of the IDE contains one or more tabs, each of which identifies a hidden window (Fig. 2.23). Place the mouse pointer over the **Toolbox** tab to display the **Toolbox** (Fig. 2.24).

(cont.)

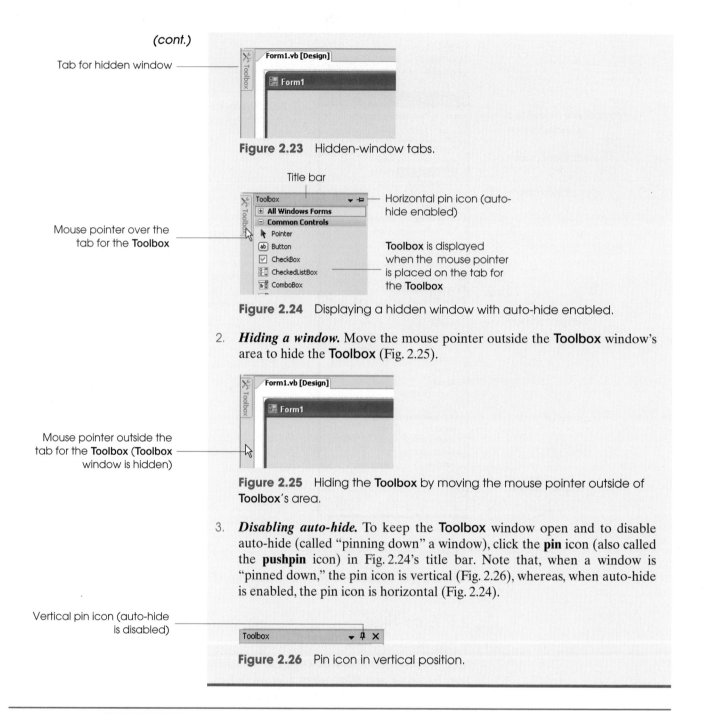

Tab for hidden window

Figure 2.23   Hidden-window tabs.

Title bar

Horizontal pin icon (auto-hide enabled)

Mouse pointer over the tab for the **Toolbox**

Toolbox is displayed when the mouse pointer is placed on the tab for the **Toolbox**

Figure 2.24   Displaying a hidden window with auto-hide enabled.

2. *Hiding a window.* Move the mouse pointer outside the **Toolbox** window's area to hide the **Toolbox** (Fig. 2.25).

Mouse pointer outside the tab for the **Toolbox** (**Toolbox** window is hidden)

Figure 2.25   Hiding the **Toolbox** by moving the mouse pointer outside of **Toolbox**'s area.

3. *Disabling auto-hide.* To keep the **Toolbox** window open and to disable auto-hide (called "pinning down" a window), click the **pin** icon (also called the **pushpin** icon) in Fig. 2.24's title bar. Note that, when a window is "pinned down," the pin icon is vertical (Fig. 2.26), whereas, when auto-hide is enabled, the pin icon is horizontal (Fig. 2.24).

Vertical pin icon (auto-hide is disabled)

Figure 2.26   Pin icon in vertical position.

SELF-REVIEW   1. Visual Basic provides a space-saving feature called _____.

    a) auto-close   b) hide

    c) collapse   d) auto-hide

2. When auto-hide is enabled, its pin icon is _____.

    a) horizontal   b) vertical

    c) down   d) diagonal

Answers: 1) d. 2) a.

2.7 Using Help

Visual Basic provides extensive help features. The **Help** menu commands are summarized in Fig. 2.27. Using **Help** is an excellent way to get information quickly about the IDE and its features. It provides a list of articles pertaining to the "current content" (i.e., the items around the location of the mouse cursor). Visual Basic also provides **context-sensitive help**, which displays relevant help articles rather than a generalized list of articles (Fig. 2.28). To use context-sensitive help, click an item, such as the form, then press the *F1* key. The help window provides help topics, code samples and Getting Started information. There is also a toolbar that provides access to the **How Do I**, **Search**, **Index** and **Contents** help features. To return to the IDE, either close the help window or select the icon for the IDE in your Windows task bar.

Command	Description
How Do I?	Contains links to relevant topics, including how to upgrade applications and learn more about Web services, architecture and design, files, data and more.
Search	Finds help articles based on search keywords.
Index	Displays an alphabetized list of topics which you can browse.
Contents	Displays a categorized table of contents in which help articles are organized by topic.

Figure 2.27   **Help** menu commands.

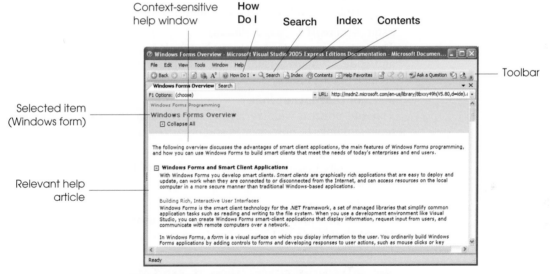

Figure 2.28   Context-sensitive help window.

SELF-REVIEW
1. _____ displays relevant help articles, based on the selected object.
   a) Internal help
   b) Context-sensitive help
   c) External help
   d) Context-driven help

2. **Help** command _____ displays an alphabetized list of topics through which you can browse.
   a) **Search**
   b) **Browse**
   c) **Contents**
   d) **Index**

Answers: 1) b. 2) d.

2.8 Saving and Closing Projects in Visual Basic

Once you are finished with a project, you will want to save the project's files and close it.

Closing the Project for the Welcome Application

1. *Saving the project's files.* Before closing the project for the **Welcome** application, you will want to save its files, ensuring that any changes made to the project are not lost. Although you did not make any changes to the project's files for this particular tutorial, you will be making such changes in most of the tutorials, so for practice, save your project files by selecting **File > Save All**.

2. *Closing the project.* Select **File > Close Project**.

2.9 Web Resources

Please take a moment to visit each of these sites briefly. To save typing time, use the hot links at www.deitel.com.

msdn.microsoft.com/vstudio
This site is the home page for Microsoft Visual Studio. This site includes news, documentation, downloads and other resources.

msdn.microsoft.com/vbasic/default.aspx
This site provides information on the newest release of Visual Basic, including downloads, community information and resources.

forums.microsoft.com/MSDN/default.aspx?ForumGroupID=10&SiteID=1
This site provides access to the Microsoft Visual Basic forums. You can use this site to get your Visual Basic language and IDE questions answered.

msdn.microsoft.com/msdnmag/
This is the Microsoft Developer Network Magazine site. This site provides articles and code on many Visual Basic and .NET programming topics. There is also an archive of past issues.

www.worldofdotnet.net
This site offers a wide variety of information on Visual Studio, including articles, news and links to newsgroups and other resources.

www.vbi.org
This site has Visual Basic articles, reviews of books and software, documentation, downloads, links and more.

www.vbcity.com
This site provides Visual Basic articles, tutorials, FAQs and more. Submit your Visual Basic code to be reviewed and rated by other developers. Includes polls on Visual Basic topics.

www.only4gurus.com/v3/showcat.asp?Cat=VB.Net
This site is an excellent resource for both beginners and advanced Visual Basic programmers. The site also provides information on many other programming languages and technologies.

2.10 Wrap-Up

This tutorial introduced the Visual Basic 2005 Express Edition integrated development environment (IDE). You learned key features, including tabs, menus, menu bars, toolbars, icons, auto-hide and more.

You created a Visual Basic Windows application that contained a Form object named Form1.vb. Controls placed on a Form represent the application's graphical user interface (GUI).

You worked with the **Solution Explorer**, **Toolbox** and **Properties** windows, all of which are essential to developing Visual Basic applications. The **Solution Explorer** window allows you to manage your solution's files visually. The **Toolbox** window contains a rich collection of controls (organized in groups) that allow you to create GUIs. The **Properties** window allows you to set the attributes of the Form and its controls.

You explored Visual Basic's help features, including the **Help** window, the **Help** menu and context-sensitive help. The **Help** window displays links related to the item you select with the mouse pointer. You learned about Web sites that provide additional Visual Basic information.

In the next tutorial, you will begin creating Visual Basic applications. You will follow step-by-step instructions for completing the **Welcome** application by using visual programming and the IDE features you learned in this tutorial.

SKILLS SUMMARY

Creating a New Project

- Select **File > New Project...** or **File > Open Project...**
- Click the links **Create: Project...** or **Open: Project...** (from the **Start Page**, under the **Recent Projects** section).
- Select **Windows Application** in the **Templates:** pane.
- Provide the project's name in the **Name:** TextBox.
- Click the **OK** Button.

Saving a Project

- Select **File > Save All**.
- Provide the project's name in the **Name:** TextBox.
- Provide the project's directory information in the **Location:** TextBox.

Viewing a Tool Tip for a Visual Basic Icon

- Place the mouse pointer on the icon, and keep it there until the tool tip appears.

Collapsing a Node in the Solution Explorer

- Click the node's minus box.

Expanding a Node in the Solution Explorer

- Click the node's plus box.

Scrolling Through the List of Controls in the Toolbox

- Click the scroll arrows.

Viewing the Properties Window

- Select **View > Properties Window** or press *F4*.

Displaying a Hidden Window

- Place the mouse pointer over the hidden window's tab.

Disabling Auto-Hide and "Pinning Down" a Window

- Click the window's horizontal pin icon to change it to a vertical pin icon.

Enabling Auto-Hide

- Click the window's vertical pin icon to change it to a horizontal pin icon.

Opening the Help Window

- Select **Help > How Do I**, **Help > Search**, **Help > Contents** or **Help > Index**.
- Select an item on which you want help and press the *F1* key.

KEY TERMS

active tab—The tab of the document displayed in the IDE.

Alphabetical icon—The icon in the **Properties** window that, when clicked, sorts properties alphabetically.

auto-hide—A space-saving IDE feature used for windows such as **Toolbox**, **Properties** and **Dynamic Help** that hides a window until the mouse pointer is placed on the hidden window's tab.

Categorized icon—The icon in the **Properties** window that, when clicked, sorts properties categorically.

component object box—The ComboBox at the top of the **Properties** window that allows you to select the Form or control object whose properties you want set.

context-sensitive help—A help option (launched by pressing *F1*) that provides links to articles that apply to the current content (that is, the item selected with the mouse pointer).

Community menu—The menu of the IDE that contains commands for sending questions directly to Microsoft, checking question status, sending feedback on Visual Basic and searching the CodeZone developer center and the Microsoft developers community site.

Contents command—The command that displays a categorized table of contents in which help articles are organized by topic.

Data menu—The menu of the IDE that contains commands for interacting with databases.

Debug menu—The menu of the IDE that contains commands for debugging and running an application.

design view—The IDE view that contains the features necessary to begin creating Windows applications.

dialog—A window that can display and gather information.

Form—The object that represents the Windows application's graphical user interface (GUI).

graphical user interface (GUI)—The visual part of the application with which the user interacts.

icon—The graphical representation of commands in the Visual Studio .NET IDE.

Integrated Development Environment (IDE)—The software used to create, document, run and debug applications.

internal Web browser—The Web browser (Internet Explorer) included in Visual Basic 2005 Express, with which you can browse the Web.

location bar—The ComboBox in Visual Basic's internal Web browser where you can enter the name of a Web site to visit.

menu—A group of related commands.

menu item—A command located in a menu that, when selected, causes an application to perform a specific action.

Microsoft Developer Network (MSDN)—An online library that contains articles, downloads and tutorials on technologies of interest to Visual Basic developers.

minus box—The icon that, when clicked, collapses a node.

New Project dialog—A dialog that allows you to choose what type of application you wish to create.

pin icon—An icon that enables or disables the auto-hide feature.

plus box—An icon that, when clicked, expands a node.

project—A group of related files that compose an application.

Properties window—The window that displays the properties for a Form or control object.

property—Specifies a control or Form object's attributes, such as size, color and position.

solution—Contains one or more projects.

Solution Explorer—A window that provides access to all the files in a solution.

Start Page—The initial page displayed when Visual Studio .NET is opened.

tool tip—The description of an icon that appears when the mouse pointer is held over that icon for a few seconds.

toolbar—A bar that contains Buttons that, when clicked, execute commands.

toolbar icon—A picture on a toolbar Button.

Toolbox—A window that contains controls used to customize Forms.

Tools menu—A menu of the IDE that contains commands for accessing additional IDE tools and options that enable customization of the IDE.

Visual Studio—Microsoft's integrated development environment (IDE), which allows developers to create applications in a variety of .NET programming languages.

Windows application—An application that executes on a Windows operating system.

2.1 The _____ integrated development environment is used for creating applications written in programming languages such as Visual Basic.

a) **Solution Explorer** b) Gates

c) Visual Studio d) Microsoft

2.2 The .vb file name extension indicates a _____.

a) Visual Basic file b) dynamic help file

c) help file d) very big file

2.3 The pictures on toolbar Buttons are called _____.

a) prototypes b) icons

c) tool tips d) tabs

2.4 The _____ allows programmers to modify controls visually, without writing code.

a) **Properties** window b) **Solution Explorer**

c) menu bar d) **Toolbox**

2.5 The _____ hides the **Toolbox** when the mouse pointer is moved outside the **Toolbox**'s area.

a) component-selection feature b) auto-hide feature

c) pinned command d) minimize command

2.6 A _____ appears when the mouse pointer is positioned over an IDE toolbar icon for a few seconds.

a) drop-down list b) menu

c) tool tip d) down arrow

2.7 The Visual Basic IDE provides _____.

a) help documentation b) a toolbar

c) windows for accessing project files d) All of the above.

2.8 The _____ contains a list of helpful links, such as **Getting Started** and **Visual Basic Express Headlines**.

a) **Solution Explorer** window b) **Properties** window

c) **Start Page** d) **Toolbox** link

2.9 The **Properties** window contains _____.

a) the component object box b) a **Solution Explorer**

c) menus d) a menu bar

2.10 A _____ can be enhanced by adding reusable components such as Buttons.

a) control b) Form

c) tab d) property

2.11 For Web browsing, Visual Basic includes _____.

a) Web View b) Excel

c) a **Web** tab d) Internet Explorer

2.12 An application's GUI can include _____.

a) toolbars b) icons

c) menus d) All of the above.

2.13 The _____ does not contain a pin icon.

a) Context-sensitive help window b) **Solution Explorer** window

c) **Toolbox** window d) active tab

2.14 When clicked, _____ in the **Solution Explorer** window will expand nodes and _____ will collapse nodes.

a) minus boxes; plus boxes
b) plus boxes; minus boxes
c) up arrows; down arrows
d) left arrows; right arrows

2.15 Form _____ specify attributes such as size and position.

a) nodes
b) inputs
c) properties
d) title bars

EXERCISES

2.16 (*Closing and Opening the Start Page*) In this exercise, you will learn how to close and reopen the **Start Page**. To accomplish this task, perform the following steps:

a) Close Visual Basic if it is open by selecting **File > Exit** or by clicking its close box.

b) Start Visual Basic 2005 Express Edition.

c) Close the **Start Page** by clicking its close box (Fig. 2.29).

d) Select **View > Other Windows > Start Page** to display the **Start Page**.

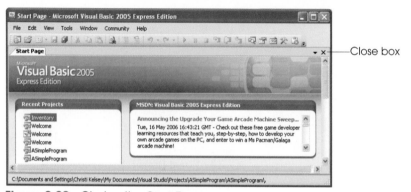

Close box

Figure 2.29 Closing the **Start Page**.

2.17 (*Enabling Auto-Hide for the Solution Explorer Window*) In this exercise, you will learn how to use the **Solution Explorer** window's auto-hide feature by performing the following steps:

a) Open the **Start Page**.

b) In the **Start Page**, click the **Open Project** Button to display the **Open Project** dialog. You can skip to *Step e*) if the **Welcome** application is already open.

c) In the **Open Project** dialog, navigate to `C:\SimplyVB\Welcome`, and click **Open**.

d) In the **Open Project** dialog, select `Welcome` (this might display as `Welcome.sln`), and click **Open**.

e) Position the mouse pointer on the vertical pin icon in the **Solution Explorer** window's title bar (Fig. 2.30).

Vertical pin icon

Figure 2.30 Enabling auto-hide.

f) Click the vertical pin icon. This action causes a **Solution Explorer** tab to appear on the right side of the IDE and changes the vertical pin icon to a horizontal pin icon (Fig. 2.31). Auto-hide has now been enabled for the **Solution Explorer** window.

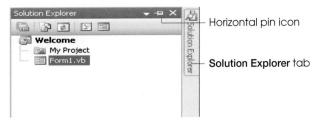

Figure 2.31 **Solution Explorer** window with auto-hide enabled.

g) Position the mouse pointer outside the **Solution Explorer** window to hide the window.

h) Position the mouse pointer on the **Solution Explorer** tab to view the **Solution Explorer** window.

2.18 (*Sorting Properties Alphabetically in the Properties Window*) In this exercise, you will learn how to sort the **Properties** window's properties alphabetically by performing the following steps:

a) Open the **Welcome** application by performing *Steps a–d* of Exercise 2.17. If the **Welcome** application is already open, you can skip this step.

b) Locate the **Properties** window. If it is not visible, display it by selecting **View > Properties Window.**

c) Click the Form.

d) To sort properties alphabetically, click the **Properties** window's **Alphabetical** icon (Fig. 2.32). The properties will display in alphabetic order.

Alphabetical icon ———

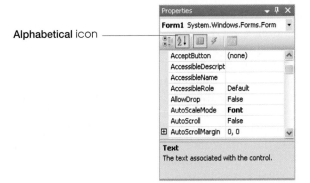

Figure 2.32 Sorting properties alphabetically.

TUTORIAL

Welcome Application

Introduction to Visual Programming

Today, users prefer software with interactive graphical user interfaces (GUIs) that respond to actions such as Button clicks, data input and much more. As a result, the vast majority of Windows applications, such as Microsoft Word and Internet Explorer, are GUI based. With Visual Basic, you can create Windows applications that input and output information in a variety of ways, which you will learn throughout the book.

In this tutorial, you use visual programming to complete the **Welcome** application you began creating in Tutorial 2. You will build the application's GUI by placing two controls—a Label and a PictureBox—on the Form. You will use the Label control to display text and the PictureBox control to display an image. You will customize the appearance of the Form, Label and PictureBox objects by setting their values in the **Properties** window. You will set many property values, including the Form's background color, the PictureBox's image and the Label's text. You also will learn how to execute your application from within the Visual Basic 2005 IDE.

3.1 Test-Driving the Welcome Application

The last tutorial introduced you to the Visual Basic 2005 IDE. In this tutorial, you will use Visual Basic to build the **Welcome** application mentioned in Tutorial 2. This application must meet the following requirements:

> **Application Requirements**
>
> *Recall that a software company (Deitel & Associates) has asked you to develop a simple **Welcome** application that includes the greeting "Welcome to Visual Basic 2005!" and a picture of the company's bug mascot. Now that you are familiar with the Visual Basic IDE, your task is to develop this application to satisfy the company's request.*

You begin by test-driving the completed application. Then you will learn the additional Visual Basic technologies that you will need to create your own version of this application.

1. ***Opening the completed application.*** Start Visual Basic and select **File >**
   Open Project... (Fig. 3.1) to display the **Open Project** dialog (Fig. 3.2).
   Select the C:\Examples\Tutorial03\CompletedApplication\Welcome
   directory from the **Look in:** ComboBox. Select the **Welcome** solution file
   (Welcome.sln) and click the **Open** Button.

Open Project... command
(selected) opens an existing
project

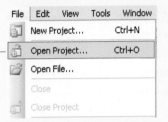

Figure 3.1 Opening an existing project with the **File** menu's **Open Project...**
command.

Open Project dialog ⎯

Look in: ComboBox ⎯

Welcome solution file ⎯

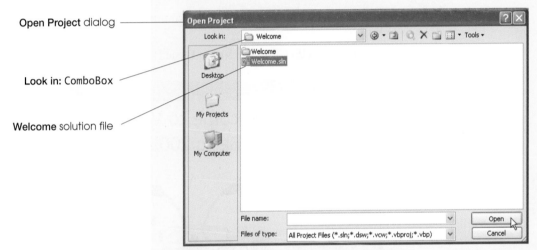

Figure 3.2 **Open Project** dialog displaying the contents of the **Welcome**
solution.

2. ***Opening the Form in design view.*** Double click on Welcome.vb in the **Solution**
   Explorer to open the **Welcome** application's Form in design view (Fig. 3.3).

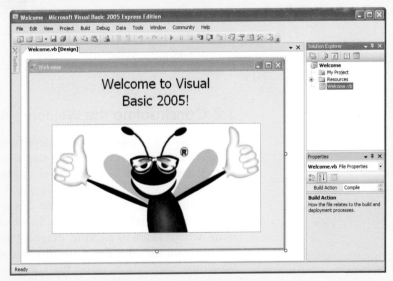

Figure 3.3 **Welcome** application's Form in design view.

(cont.)

3. ***Running the Welcome application.*** Select **Debug > Start Debugging** (Fig. 3.4). The **Start Debugging** command runs the application. The **Welcome** Form shown in Fig. 3.5 will appear.

Start Debugging command (selected) runs the application

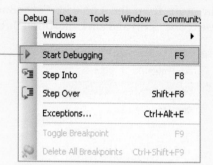

Figure 3.4 Running the **Welcome** application using the **Debug** menu's **Start Debugging** command.

4. ***Closing the application.*** Close the running application by clicking its close box, ☒.

5. ***Closing the IDE.*** Close the Visual Basic IDE by clicking its close box.

Close box

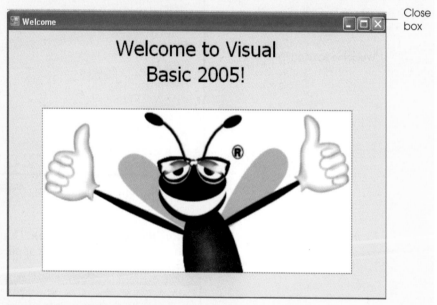

Figure 3.5 **Welcome** application running.

3.2 Constructing the Welcome Application

In this section, you perform the steps necessary to develop the **Welcome** application. The application consists of a single Form that uses a Label control and a PictureBox control. A **Label** control displays text that the user cannot change. A **PictureBox** control displays an image that the user cannot change. You will not write a single line of code to create this application. Instead, you will use the technique called **visual programming**, in which Visual Basic processes your programming actions (such as clicking, dragging and dropping controls) and actually writes the program for you! The following box shows you how to begin constructing the **Welcome** application, using the solution you created in Tutorial 2 as a starting point.

Changing the Form's File Name and Title Bar Text

1. *Opening the Welcome application's project.* Double click the `C:\Sim-plyVB\Welcome\Welcome.sln` file that you created in Tutorial 2 to open your application. Double click `Form1.vb` in the **Solution Explorer** window to display the blank **Form**. Figure 3.6 shows the **Welcome** application open in the IDE.

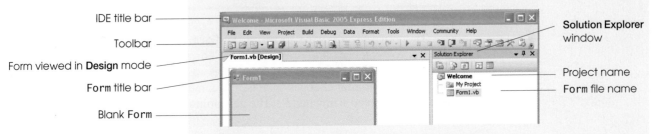

IDE title bar
Toolbar
Form viewed in **Design** mode
Form title bar
Blank **Form**

Solution Explorer window
Project name
Form file name

Figure 3.6 Blank **Form**.

Good Programming Practice

Change your application's **Form** file name (`Form1.vb`) to a name that describes the application's purpose.

2. *Changing the Form's file name.* When a Windows application is created, Visual Basic names the **Form** file `Form1.vb`. Select `Form1.vb` in the **Solution Explorer** window (Fig. 3.6) to display the file's properties in the **Properties** window (the window on the left in Fig. 3.7). If either window is not visible, you can select **View > Properties Window** or **View > Solution Explorer** to display the appropriate window. Double click the field to the right of the **File Name** property's box to select the current file name, and type `Welcome.vb` (Fig. 3.7). Press the *Enter* key to update the **Form**'s file name. Note that the file name changes in the **Solution Explorer** window (the window on the right in Fig. 3.7) and in the **Properties** window.

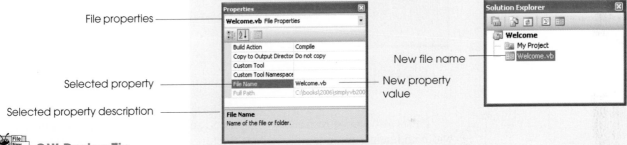

File properties
Selected property
Selected property description

New file name
New property value

Figure 3.7 Changing the **Form**'s file name.

GUI Design Tip

Choose short, descriptive **Form** titles. Capitalize words that are not articles, prepositions or conjunctions. Do not use punctuation.

3. *Setting the text in the Form's title bar.* The title bar is the top portion of the window that contains the window's title. To change the text in the **Form**'s title bar from **Form1** to **Welcome**, use the **Properties** window (Fig. 3.8). Click the gray area in the **Form**. Double click the field to the right of the **Text** property in the **Properties** window to select the current text, and type `Wel-come`. Press the *Enter* key to update the **Form**'s title bar (Fig. 3.9).

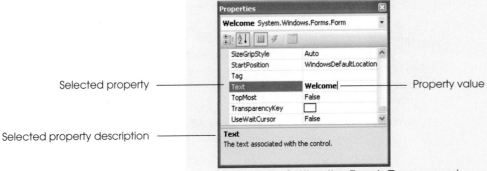

Selected property
Selected property description

Property value

Figure 3.8 Setting the **Form**'s **Text** property.

(cont.)

Updated title bar ——————

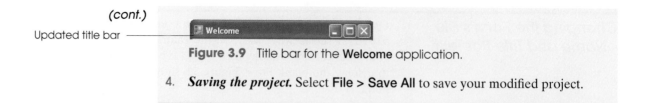

Figure 3.9 Title bar for the **Welcome** application.

4. ***Saving the project.*** Select **File > Save All** to save your modified project.

There are several ways to resize the Form. If the resizing does not have to be precise, you can click and drag one of the Form's enabled **sizing handles** (the small white squares that appear around the Form, as shown in Fig. 3.10). The appearance of the mouse pointer changes (that is, it becomes a pointer with two arrows) when it is over an enabled sizing handle. The new pointer indicates the direction(s) in which resizing is allowed.

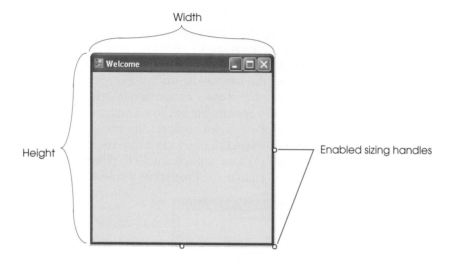

Figure 3.10 Form with sizing handles.

Forms also can be resized by using the **Size** property, which specifies the Form's width and height in units called **pixels** (*pic*ture *el*ements). A pixel is a tiny point on your computer screen that displays a color. The Size property has two members—the **Width** and **Height** properties. The Width property indicates the width of the Form in pixels, and the Height property specifies the height in pixels. Next, you learn how to set the Form's width and height.

Setting the Form's Size Property

1. ***Setting the Form's width and height.*** For your **Welcome** application GUI to look exactly like Fig. 3.5, you will need to resize the Form and its controls. Click the Form. Locate the Form's Size property in the **Properties** window (Fig. 3.11). Click the plus box, ⊞, next to this property to expand the node. Type 616 for the Width property value, and press *Enter*. Type 440 for the Height property value and press *Enter*. Note that the Size property value (616, 440) updates when either the Width or the Height is changed. You also can enter the width and height (separated by a comma) in the Size property's value field.

2. ***Saving the project.*** Select **File > Save All** to save your modified project.

(cont.)

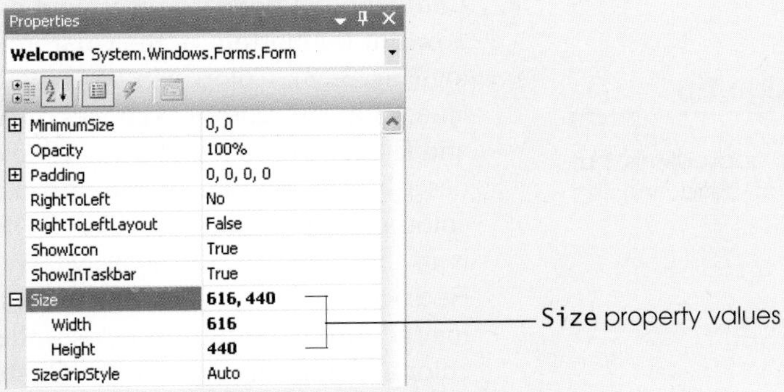

Figure 3.11 **Size** property values for the **Form**.

Now that you have set the Form's size, you will customize the Form further by changing its background color from gray to yellow.

Setting the Form's Background Color

1. **Exploring the available colors.** Click the Form to display its properties in the **Properties** window. The **BackColor** property specifies an object's background color. When you click the **BackColor** property's value in the **Properties** window, a down-arrow (▼) Button appears (Fig. 3.12). When clicked, the down-arrow Button displays three tabs: **System** (the default), **Web** and **Custom**. Each tab offers a series of colors called a **palette**. The **System** tab displays a palette containing the colors used in the Microsoft Windows GUI. This palette includes the colors for Windows controls and the Windows desktop. The **System** tab's colors are based on the Windows 2000/XP settings in the **Display Properties** dialog. To access this dialog in Windows XP or 2000, right click the desktop and select **Properties**. Click the **Appearance** tab to view the colors used by Windows. The **Web** tab displays a palette of **Web-safe colors**—colors that display the same on different computers. The **Custom** tab palette allows you to choose from a series of predefined colors or to create your own color. Click the **Custom** tab to display its palette as shown in Fig. 3.12.

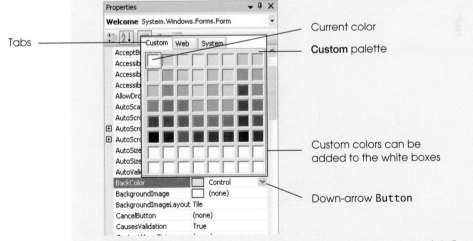

Figure 3.12 Viewing the **Custom** palette in the **Form**'s **BackColor** property value field.

(cont.)

GUI Design Tip

Use colors in your applications, but not to the point of distracting the user.

2. ***Changing the Form's background color.*** Right click any one of the 16 white boxes at the bottom of the **Custom** palette to display the **Define Color** dialog (Fig. 3.13). Colors can be created either by entering three values in the **Hue:**, **Sat:** and **Lum:** TextBoxes or by providing values for the **Red:**, **Green:** and **Blue:** TextBoxes. The values for the **Red:**, **Green:** and **Blue:** TextBoxes describe the amount of red, green and blue needed to create the custom color and are commonly called **RGB values**. Each red, green and blue value is in the range 0–255, inclusive. We use RGB values in this book. Set the **Red:** value to 255, the **Green:** value to 237 and the **Blue:** value to 169. Clicking the **Add Color** Button closes the dialog, changes the Form's background color and adds the color to the **Custom** palette (Fig. 3.14).

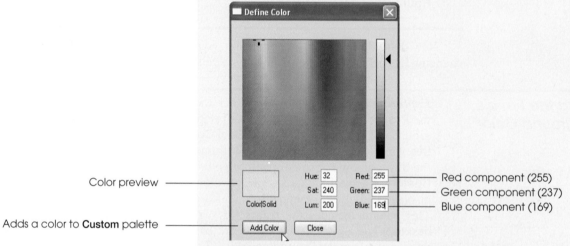

Color preview

Adds a color to **Custom** palette

Red component (255)
Green component (237)
Blue component (169)

Figure 3.13 Adding a color to the **Custom** palette.

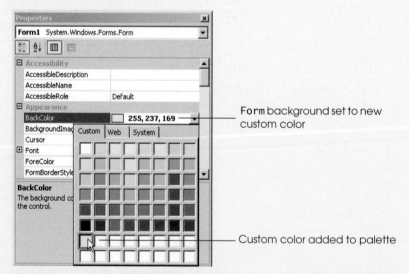

Form background set to new custom color

Custom color added to palette

Figure 3.14 **Properties** window after the new custom color has been added.

3. ***Saving the project.*** Select **File > Save All** to save your modified project.

Now that you have finished customizing the Form, you can add a control to the Form—a customized Label that displays a greeting.

GUI Design Tip

Use Labels to display text that users cannot change.

1. ***Adding a Label control to the Form.*** Click the **All Windows Forms** group in the **Toolbox** (Fig. 3.15). If the **Toolbox** is not visible, select **View > Toolbox**. Double click the Label control in the **Toolbox**. A Label will appear in the upper-left corner of the Form (Fig. 3.16). You also can drag the Label from the **Toolbox** and drop it on the Form. You will use this Label control to display the welcome message. The Label displays the text **Label1** by default.

   Note that the Label's background color is the same as the Form's background color. When a control is added to the Form, the IDE initially sets the control's BackColor property value to the Form's BackColor property value.

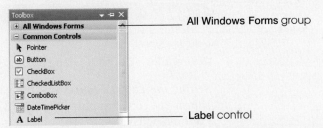

Figure 3.15   Clicking the **Windows Forms** tab in the **Toolbox**.

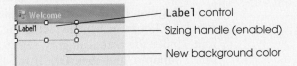

Figure 3.16   Adding a Label to the Form.

2. ***Setting the Label's AutoSize property.*** Click the Label to select it. You will notice that the Label's properties now appear in the **Properties** window. Visual Basic by default does not provide sizing handles (Fig. 3.16) for you to resize a Label. To enable resizing, you must set the Label's **AutoSize** property to False (Fig. 3.17). You can do this by double clicking this property's value or by selecting False from the drop-down list.

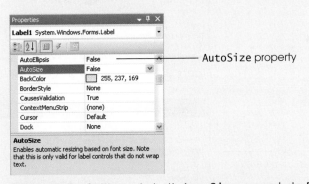

Figure 3.17   Setting a Label's AutoSize property to False.

3. ***Customizing the Label's appearance.*** The Label's Text property specifies the text (**Label1**) that the Label displays. Type Welcome to Visual Basic 2005! for the Label's Text property value and press *Enter*. Note that this text does not fit in the Label (Fig. 3.18). Use the sizing handles to enlarge the Label so all the text is displayed (Fig. 3.19)

GUI Design Tip

Ensure that all Label controls are large enough to display their text.

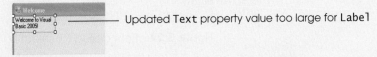

Figure 3.18   Label after updating its Text property.

(cont.)

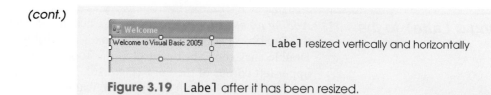

Label resized vertically and horizontally

Figure 3.19 Label after it has been resized.

4. *Aligning the Label.* Drag the Label to the top center of the Form. You also can center the Label by selecting **Format > Center In Form > Horizontally** (Fig. 3.20).

Centered Label

Figure 3.20 Centered Label.

GUI Design Tip

Use **Tahoma** font to improve readability for controls that display text.

5. *Setting the Label's font.* Click the value of the **Font** property to cause an ellipsis Button to appear (Fig. 3.21). Click the ellipsis Button to display the **Font** dialog (Fig. 3.22). The ellipsis is a convention used for each property that displays a dialog to help you set the property's value. In this dialog, you can select the font name (**Tahoma, Times New Roman,** etc.), font style (**Regular, Italic,** etc.) and font size (**16, 18,** etc.) in points (one point equals 1/72 of an inch). The text in the **Sample** Label displays the selected font. Under the **Size:** category, select **24** points. Under the **Font** category, select **Tahoma,** and click **OK**. If the Label's text does not fit on a single line, it wraps to the next line. Use the sizing handles to enlarge the Label vertically so that the text appears on two lines.

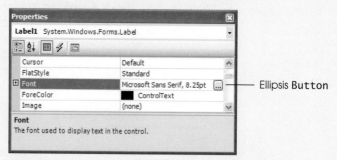

Ellipsis Button

Figure 3.21 Properties window displaying the Label's properties.

Font dialog

Current font

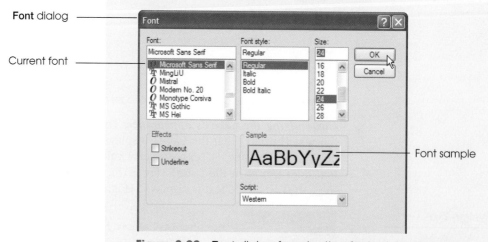

Font sample

Figure 3.22 Font dialog for selecting fonts, styles and sizes.

(cont.)   6. ***Aligning the Label's text.*** To align text inside a `Label`, use the `Label`'s
`TextAlign` property. Clicking the `TextAlign` property displays a down-
arrow `Button`. Click the down-arrow `Button` to display a three-by-three grid
of `Button`s (Fig. 3.23). The position of each `Button` shows where the text
will appear in the `Label`. Click the middle-center `Button` in the three-by-
three grid to align the text at the middle-center position in the `Label`. The
value `MiddleCenter` is assigned to property `TextAlign`. You may also set
this property's value by repeatedly clicking the property value to the right of
the property's name. This enables you to cycle through all the allowed `Text-
Align` property values. This technique works for any property that provides
a set of options to you via a down-arrow `Button` to the right of the property
value in the **Properties** window.

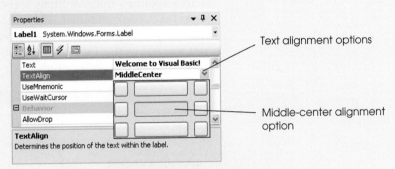

Text alignment options

Middle-center alignment
option

Figure 3.23   Centering the `Label`'s text.

7. ***Saving the project.*** Select **File > Save All** to save your modified project.

To finish this first Visual Basic Windows application, you need to insert an
image and execute the application. We use a `PictureBox` control to add an image
to the `Form` before running the application. The following box guides you step-by-
step through the process of adding an image to your `Form`.

***Inserting an Image and
Running the Welcome
Application***

1. ***Adding a PictureBox control to the Form.*** The `PictureBox` allows you to
display an image. To add a `PictureBox` control to the `Form`, double click the
`PictureBox` control icon

 PictureBox

in the `ToolBox`. When the `PictureBox` appears, click and drag it to a position centered below the `Label` (Fig. 3.24).

Updated `Label`

PictureBox

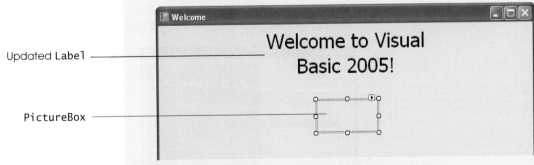

Figure 3.24   Inserting and aligning the `PictureBox`.

(cont.)

GUI Design Tip

Use PictureBoxes to enhance GUIs with graphics that users cannot change.

2. **Setting the Image property.** Click the PictureBox to display its properties in the **Properties** window. Locate the **Image** property, which displays a preview of the image (if one exists). No picture has yet been assigned to the Image property, so its value is (none) (Fig. 3.25). You can use any of several popular image formats, including

- *PNG (Portable Network Graphics)*
- *GIF (Graphic Interchange Format)*
- *JPEG (Joint Photographic Experts Group)*
- *BMP (Windows Bitmap)*

For this application, you will use a PNG-format image. Creating new images requires image-editing software, such as Jasc® Paint Shop Pro™ (www.jasc.com), Adobe® Photoshop™ (www.adobe.com), Macromedia® Fireworks® (www.adobe.com) or Microsoft Paint (provided with Windows). You will not create images in this book; instead, you will be provided with the images used in the tutorials.

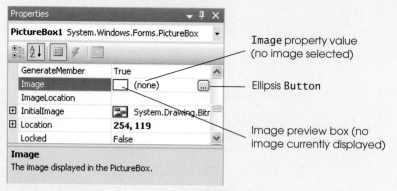

Figure 3.25 Image property of the PictureBox.

3. **Displaying an image.** In the **Properties** window, click the value of the PictureBox's Image property to display an ellipsis Button (Fig. 3.25). Click the ellipsis button to display the **Select Resource dialog** (Fig. 3.26). This dialog is used to import files, such as images, to any application. Click the **Import...** button to browse for an image to insert. In our case, the picture is bug.png. In the **Open** dialog that appears, navigate to the C:\Examples\ Tutorial03\CompletedApplication directory. Select bug.png and click the **Open** Button. (Fig. 3.27). The image is previewed in the **Select Resource** dialog (Fig. 3.28). Click **OK** to place the image in your application. Note that the PictureBox does not display the entire image (Fig. 3.29). You will solve this problem in the next step. Also, note that the Image property now shows a preview image in the **Properties** window (Fig. 3.30).

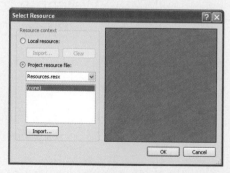

Figure 3.26 **Select Resource** dialog to select an image for the PictureBox.

(cont.)

bug.png file (may display
bug depending on whether
your computer is set to
display file name extensions)

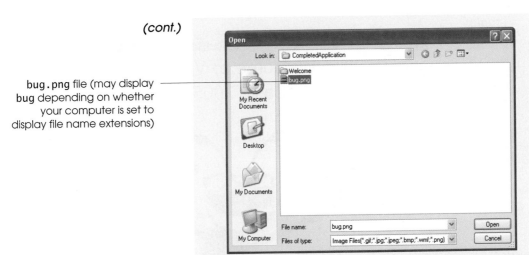

Figure 3.27   **Open** dialog used to browse for a `PictureBox` image.

Figure 3.28   **Select Resource** dialog displaying preview of selected image.

Welcome to Visual Basic 2005!

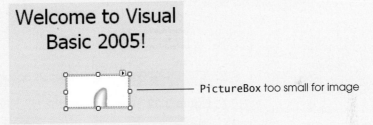

PictureBox too small for image

Figure 3.29   Newly inserted image.

Previewed image

Figure 3.30   Image previewed in the `Image` property value field.

GUI Design Tip

Images should fit inside their PictureBoxes. This can be achieved by setting `PictureBox` property SizeMode to `StretchImage`.

4. **Sizing the image to fit the PictureBox.** We want the image to fit in the PictureBox. PictureBox property **SizeMode** specifies how an image is displayed in a PictureBox. To size the image to fit in the PictureBox, change the SizeMode property to **StretchImage**, which **scales** the image (changes its width and height) to the size of the PictureBox. To resize the PictureBox, double click the Size property and enter 500, 250. Center the image horizontally on the Form by clicking the PictureBox and selecting **Format > Center in Form > Horizontally**. The Form should now look like Fig. 3.31. [*Note*: You may need to move the PictureBox up or down at this point to make your Form appear as it does in Fig. 3.31. To do this, you can simply click on the PictureBox, then use the up and down arrow keys.]

(cont.)

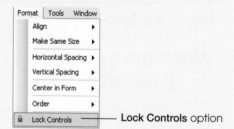

Newly inserted image —

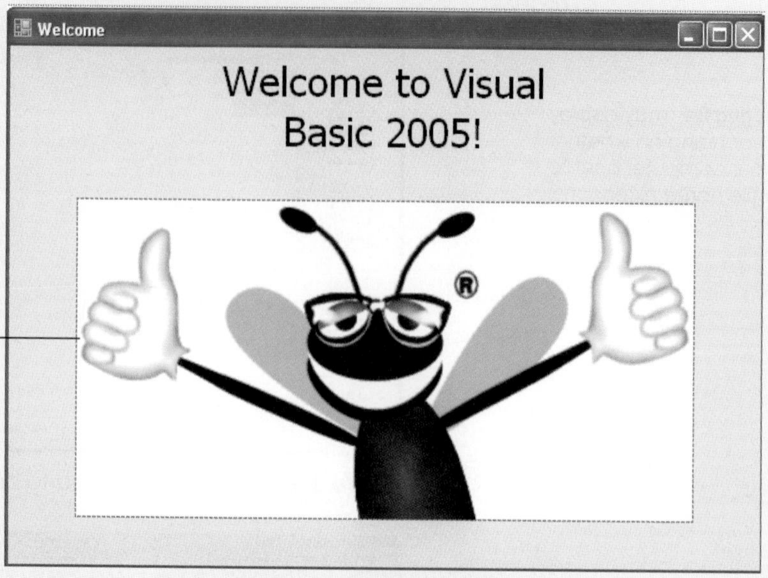

Figure 3.31 `PictureBox` displaying an image.

5. ***Locking the Form controls.*** Often, programmers accidentally alter the size and location of controls on the `Form`. To ensure that the controls remain in position, use the **Lock Controls** feature. First, select all the controls by using the **Edit > Select All** command. Next, select **Format > Lock Controls** (Fig. 3.32). A locked control appears in **Design** mode with a padlock icon in its upper-left corner.

Figure 3.32 Locking controls by using the **Format** menu.

6. ***Saving the project.*** Select **File > Save All** to save your modified project. You should save your files to your `C:\SimplyVB` directory frequently. Note, however, that it is not necessary to save project files if you are about to run the application. When a Visual Basic application is run in the IDE, the project files are automatically saved for you.

7. ***Running the application.*** The text **Welcome.vb [Design]** in the IDE's project tab (Fig. 3.6) indicates that we have been working in the IDE **design mode**. (That is, the application being created is not executing.) While in design mode, programmers have access to all the IDE windows (for example, **Toolbox**, **Properties**), menus and toolbars. In **run mode**, the application is running, and programmers can interact with fewer IDE features. Features that are not available are disabled ("grayed out"). Select **Debug > Start Debugging** to run the application. Figure 3.33 shows the IDE in run mode. Note that many toolbar icons and menus are disabled.

(cont.)

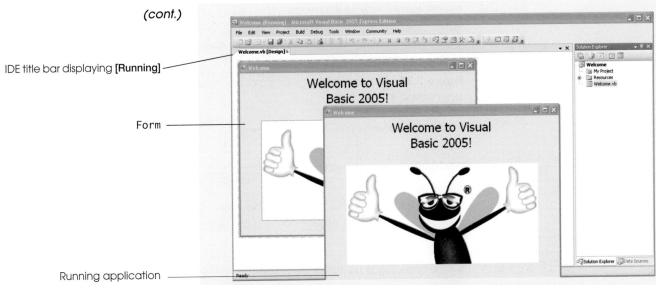

IDE title bar displaying **[Running]**

Form

Running application

Figure 3.33   IDE in run mode with the application running in the foreground.

8. ***Closing the application.*** Close the running application by clicking its close box, ☒. This action returns the IDE to design mode.

9. ***Closing the IDE.*** Close the IDE by clicking its close box.

SELF-REVIEW   1. The Form's _____ property specifies the text that is displayed in the Form's title bar.
   a) `Title`   b) `Text`
   c) `(Name)`   d) `Name`

2. Property _____ specifies how text is aligned within a `Label`'s boundaries.
   a) `Alignment`   b) `AlignText`
   c) `Align`   d) `TextAlign`

Answers: 1) b. 2) d.

3.3 Objects Used in the Welcome Application

In Tutorials 1 and 2, you learned that controls are reusable software components called objects. The **Welcome** application used a `Form` object, a `Label` object and a `PictureBox` object to create a GUI that displayed text and an image. Each of these objects is an instance of a class defined in the .NET Framework Class Library (FCL). The `Form` object was created by the Visual Basic IDE when you created the project. The `Label` and `PictureBox` objects were created by the IDE when you double clicked their respective icons in the **Toolbox**.

We used the **Properties** window to set the properties (attributes) for each object. Recall that the `ComboBox`—also called the component object box—at the top of the **Properties** window displays the names and class types of `Form` and control objects (Fig. 3.34). In Fig. 3.35, the component object box displays the name (`Welcome`) and class type (`Form`) of the `Form` object. In the FCL, classes are organized by functionality into directory-like entities called **namespaces**. The class types used in this application have namespace `System.Windows.Forms`. This namespace contains control classes and the `Form` class. You will be introduced to additional namespaces in later tutorials.

Figure 3.34 Component object box expanded to show the **Welcome** application's objects.

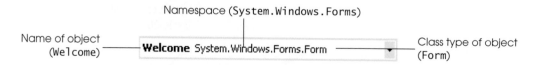

Figure 3.35 The name and class type of an object are displayed in the **Properties** window's component object box.

SELF-REVIEW

1. The ComboBox at the top of the **Properties** window is the _____.
   a) component object box
   b) control box
   c) control object box
   d) component box

2. The Framework Class Library (FCL) organizes classes into _____.
   a) collections
   b) name boxes
   c) namespaces
   d) class spaces

Answers: 1) a. 2) c.

3.4 Wrap-Up

This tutorial introduced you to visual programming in Visual Basic. You learned that visual programming helps you to design and create the graphical user interface portions of applications quickly and easily, by dragging and dropping controls onto Forms.

In creating your **Welcome** application, you used the **Properties** window to set the Form's title-bar text, size (width and height) and background color using properties Text, Size and BackColor, respectively. You learned that Labels are controls that display text and that PictureBoxes are controls that display images. You displayed text in a Label by setting its Text and TextAlign properties, and you displayed an image by setting a PictureBox control's Image and SizeMode properties.

You also examined the relationship between controls and classes. You learned that FCL classes are grouped into directory-like entities called namespaces and that controls are instances (objects) of FCL classes. The FCL classes used in this tutorial (Form, Label and PictureBox) belong to namespace System.Windows.Forms. You used the **Properties** window's component object box to view an object's name, namespace and class type.

In the next tutorial, you continue learning visual programming. In particular, you will create an application with controls that are designed to accept user input.

SKILLS SUMMARY

Creating GUIs Quickly and Efficiently

■ Use visual programming techniques.

Placing a Control on the Form

■ Double click the control in the **Toolbox** to place the control in the upper-left corner of the Form, or drag the control from the **Toolbox** onto the Form.

Aligning Controls

■ Use the **Format** menu's commands.

Resizing the Form or Control with Sizing Handles

■ Click and drag one of the object's enabled sizing handles.

Setting the Dimensions of the Form or Control by Using Property Size

■ Enter the height and width of the Form or control in the Size field.

Setting the Width and Height of the Form or Control

■ Enter values in the Width and Height property fields (or use the Size property field).

Setting the Form's Background Color

■ Set the Form's BackColor property.

Adding a Label Control to the Form

■ Double click the Label control in the **Toolbox** to place the control in the upper-left corner of the Form.

Setting a Label's Text Property

■ Set the Label's Text property.

Setting a Label's Font Property

■ Click the value of the Font property, which causes an ellipsis Button to appear next to the value. When the ellipsis Button is clicked, the **Font** dialog is displayed; it allows programmers to change the font name, style and size of the Label's text.

Aligning Text in a Label

■ Use the Label's TextAlign property.

Resizing a Label

■ Set the AutoSize property to False. Then use the sizing handles.

Adding an Image to the Form

■ Use a PictureBox control to display the image. Click the ellipsis Button next to the PictureBox Image property's value to browse for an image to insert using the **Select Resource** dialog.

■ Scale the image to the size of the PictureBox by setting property SizeMode to value StretchImage.

Displaying a Form or Control's Properties in the Properties Window

■ Click the Form or a control on the Form.

KEY TERMS

AutoSize property of a Label—Specifies whether a Label is automatically resized to accomodate the text in the Label.

BackColor property—Specifies the background color of the Form or a control.

design mode—IDE mode that allows you to create applications using Visual Studio .NET's windows, toolbars and menu bar.

Font property—Specifies the font name, style and size of any displayed text in the Form or one of its controls.

Height property—This property, a member of property Size, indicates the height of the Form or one of its controls in pixels.

Image property—Indicates the file name of the image displayed in a PictureBox.

Label—Control that displays text the user cannot modify.

namespace—Classes in the FCL are organized by functionality into these directory-like entities.

palette—A set of colors.

PictureBox—Control that displays an image.

pixel—A tiny point on your computer screen that displays a color.

RGB value—The amount of red, green and blue needed to create a color.

run mode—IDE mode indicating that the application is executing.

scale an image—The process of changing an image's width and height to fit a specified area.

Select Resource dialog—Used to import files, such as images, to any application.

Size property—Property that specifies the height and width, in pixels, of the `Form` or one of its controls.

SizeMode property—Property that specifies how an image is displayed in a `PictureBox`.

sizing handle—Square that, when enabled, can be used to resize the `Form` or one of its controls.

StretchImage—Value of `PictureBox` property `SizeMode` that scales an image to fill the `PictureBox`.

Text property—Specifies the text displayed by the `Form` or a `Label`.

TextAlign property—Specifies how text is aligned within a `Label`.

visual programming—Technique in which Visual Basic processes your programming actions (such as clicking, dragging and dropping controls) and writes code for you.

Web-safe colors—Colors that display the same on different computers.

Width property—This setting, a member of property `Size`, indicates the width of the `Form` or one of its controls, in pixels.

GUI DESIGN GUIDELINES

Overall Design

■ Use colors in your applications, but not to the point of distracting the user.

Forms

■ Choose short, descriptive `Form` titles. Capitalize words that are not articles, prepositions or conjunctions. Do not use punctuation.

■ Use **Tahoma** font to improve readability for controls that display text.

Labels

■ Use `Label`s to display text that users cannot change.

■ Ensure that all `Label` controls are large enough to display their text.

PictureBoxes

■ Use `PictureBox`es to enhance GUIs with graphics that users cannot change.

■ Images should fit inside their `PictureBox`es. This can be achieved by setting `PictureBox` property `SizeMode` to `StretchImage`.

CONTROLS, EVENTS, PROPERTIES & METHODS

Label `A Label`   This control displays on the `Form` text that the user cannot modify.

■ *In action*

> # Welcome to Visual Basic 2005!

■ *Properties*

`Text`—Specifies the text displayed on the `Label`.

`Font`—Specifies the font name, style and size of the text displayed in the `Label`.

`TextAlign`—Determines how the text is aligned within the `Label`.

`AutoSize`—Allows for automatic resizing of the `Label`.

PictureBox `PictureBox`   This control displays an image on the `Form`.

■ *In action*

■ *Properties*

`Image`—Specifies the file path of the image.

`SizeMode`—Specifies the how to size the image that is displayed in the `PictureBox`.

`Size`—Specifies the height and width (in pixels) of the `PictureBox`.

MULTIPLE-CHOICE QUESTIONS

3.1 Property _____ determines the Form's background color.

a) `BackColor`   b) `BackgroundColor`

c) `RGB`   d) `Color`

3.2 To save all the project's files, select _____.

a) **Save > Solution > Save Files**   b) **File > Save**

c) **File > Save All**   d) **File > Save As...**

3.3 When the ellipsis `Button` to the right of the **Font** property value is clicked, the _____ is displayed.

a) **Font Property** dialog   b) **New Font** dialog

c) **Font Settings** dialog   d) **Font** dialog

3.4 `PictureBox` property _____ contains a preview of the image displayed in the `PictureBox`.

a) `Picture`   b) `ImageName`

c) `Image`   d) `PictureName`

3.5 The _____ tab allows you to create your own color.

a) **Custom**   b) **Web**

c) **System**   d) **User**

3.6 The `PictureBox` class has namespace _____.

a) `System.Windows.Forms`   b) `System.Form.Form`

c) `System.Form.Font`   d) `System.Form.Control`

3.7 A `Label` control displays the text specified by property _____.

a) `Caption`   b) `Data`

c) `Text`   d) `Name`

3.8 In _____ mode, the application is executing.

a) start   b) run

c) break   d) design

3.9 The _____ command prevents programmers from accidentally altering the size and location of the Form's controls.

a) **Lock Controls**   b) **Anchor Controls**

c) **Lock**   d) **Bind Controls**

3.10 Pixels are _____.

a) picture elements   b) controls in the **Toolbox**

c) a set of fonts   d) a set of colors on the **Web** tab

EXERCISES

For Exercises 3.11–3.16, you are asked to create the GUI shown in each exercise. You will use the visual programming techniques presented in this tutorial to create a variety of GUIs. You are creating only GUIs, therefore your applications will not be fully operational. For example, the **Calculator** GUI in Exercise 3.11 will not behave like a calculator when its `Buttons` are clicked. You will learn how to make your applications fully operational in later tutorials. Create each application as a separate project. If you accidentally double click a control in **Design** view, the IDE will display the Form's source code. To return to **Design** view, select **View > Designer**.

3.11 _(Calculator GUI)_ Create the GUI for the calculator shown in Fig. 3.36.

a) _Creating a new project._ Create a new **Windows Application** named `Calculator`.

b) _Renaming the Form file._ Name the Form file `Calculator.vb`.

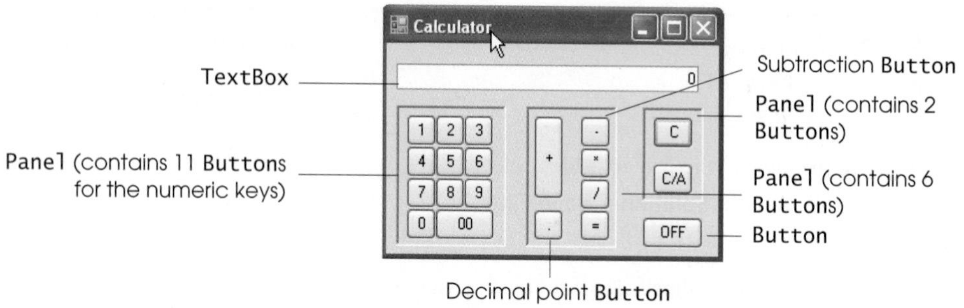

Figure 3.36 Calculator GUI.

TextBox

Panel (contains 11 Buttons for the numeric keys)

Subtraction Button

Panel (contains 2 Buttons)

Panel (contains 6 Buttons)

Button

Decimal point Button

c) *Manipulating the Form's properties.* Change the Size property of the Form to 272, 204. Change the Text property of the Form to Calculator. Change the Font property to Tahoma.

d) *Adding a TextBox to the Form.* Add a TextBox control by double clicking it in the **Toolbox**. A TextBox control is used to enter input into applications. Set the Text-Box's Text property in the **Properties** window to 0. Change the Size property to 240, 21. Set the TextAlign property to Right; this right aligns text displayed in the TextBox. Finally, set the TextBox's Location property to 8, 16—this property specifies where the upper-left corner of the control will be placed on the form.

e) *Adding the first Panel to the Form.* Panel controls are used to group other controls. Double click the Panel icon (☐ Panel) in the **Toolbox** to add a Panel to the Form. Change the Panel's BorderStyle property to Fixed3D to make the inside of the Panel appear recessed. Change the Size property to 88, 112. Finally, set the Location property to 8, 48. This Panel contains the calculator's numeric keys.

f) *Adding the second Panel to the Form.* Click the Form outside the first Panel to ensure that the second Panel is placed directly on the Form, rather than inside the first Panel. Double click the Panel icon in the **Toolbox** to add another Panel to the Form. Change the Panel's BorderStyle property to Fixed3D. Change the Size property to 72, 112. Finally, set the Location property to 112, 48. This Panel contains the calculator's operator keys.

g) *Adding the third (and last) Panel to the Form.* Click the Form outside the first and second Panels to ensure that the third Panel is placed directly on the Form. Double click the Panel icon in the **Toolbox** to add another Panel to the Form. Change the Panel's BorderStyle property to Fixed3D. Change the Size property to 48, 72. Finally, set the Location property to 200, 48. This Panel contains the calculator's **C** (clear) and **C/A** (clear all) keys.

h) *Adding Buttons to the Form.* There are 20 Buttons on the calculator. To add a Button to a Panel, double click the Button control (ab| Button) in the **Toolbox**. Then add the Button to the Panel by dragging and dropping it on the Panel. Change the Text property of each Button to the calculator key it represents. The value you enter in the Text property will appear on the face of the Button. Finally, resize the Buttons, using their Size properties. Each Button labeled 0–9, x, /, -, = and . should have a size of 24, 24. The **00** and **OFF** Buttons have size 48, 24. The **+** Button is sized 24, 64. The **C** (clear) and **C/A** (clear all) Buttons are sized 38, 24.

i) *Saving and closing the project.* Select **File > Save All** to save your changes. Then select **File > Close Project** to close the project for this application.

3.12 *(Alarm Clock GUI)* Create the GUI for the alarm clock in Fig. 3.37.

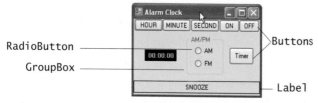

RadioButton

GroupBox

Buttons

Label

Figure 3.37 Alarm Clock GUI.

a) *Creating a new project.* Create a new **Windows Application** named `AlarmClock`.

b) *Renaming the Form file.* Name the Form file `AlarmClock.vb`.

c) *Manipulating the Form's properties.* Change the `Size` property of the Form to 256, 176. Change the `Text` property of the Form to `Alarm Clock`.

d) *Adding Buttons to the Form.* Add six Buttons to the Form. Change the `Text` property of each `Button` to the appropriate text. Change the `Size` properties of the **Hour**, **Minute** and **Second** Buttons to 60, 23. The **ON** and **OFF** Buttons get size 40, 23. The **Timer** Button gets size 48, 32. Align the Buttons as shown in Fig. 3.37.

e) *Adding a Label to the Form.* Add a Label to the Form. Change the `Text` property to **Snooze**. Set its `AutoSize` to `False` and its `Size` to 248, 23. Set the Label's `Text-Align` property to `MiddleCenter`. Finally, to draw a border around the edge of the **Snooze** Label, change the `BorderStyle` property of the **Snooze** Label to `FixedSingle`.

f) *Adding a GroupBox to the Form. GroupBoxes* are like `Panel`s, except that GroupBoxes can display a title. To add a GroupBox to the Form, click the Form, then double click the GroupBox control (<kbd>xy GroupBox</kbd>) in the **Toolbox**. Change the `Text` property to **AM/PM**, and set the `Size` property to 72, 72. To place the GroupBox in the correct location on the Form, set the `Location` property to 104, 38.

g) *Adding AM/PM RadioButtons to the GroupBox.* Add two RadioButtons to the Form by dragging the RadioButton control (<kbd>⊙ RadioButton</kbd>) in the **Toolbox** and dropping it onto the GroupBox twice. Change the `Text` property of one RadioButton to AM and the other to PM. Then place the RadioButtons as shown in Fig. 3.37 by setting the `Location` of the **AM** RadioButton to 16, 16 and that of the **PM** RadioButton to 16, 40. Set their `AutoSize` properties to `False`, then set their `Size` properties to 48, 24.

h) *Adding the time Label to the Form.* Add a Label to the Form and change its `Text` property to `00:00:00`. Change the `BorderStyle` property to `Fixed3D` and the `Back-Color` to `Black`. Set `AutoSize` to `False` and the `Size` property to 100, 23. Use the `Font` property to make the time bold. Change the `ForeColor` to `Silver` (located in the **Web** tab) to make the time stand out against the black background. Set `Text-Align` to `MiddleCenter` to center the text in the Label. Position the Label as shown in Fig. 3.37.

i) *Saving and closing the project.* Select **File > Save All** to save your changes. Then select **File > Close Project** to close the project for this application.

3.13 *(Microwave Oven GUI)* Create the GUI for the microwave oven shown in Fig. 3.38.

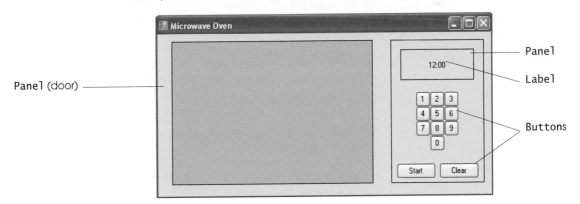

Figure 3.38 Microwave Oven GUI.

a) *Creating a new project.* Create a new **Windows Application** named `Microwave`.

b) *Renaming the Form file.* Name the Form file `Microwave.vb`.

c) *Manipulating the Form's properties.* Change the `Size` property of the Form to 552, 288. Change the `Text` property of the Form to `Microwave Oven`.

d) *Adding the microwave oven door.* Add a Panel to the Form by double clicking the Panel (<kbd>□ Panel</kbd>) in the **Toolbox**. Select the Panel and change the `BackColor` property to `Silver` (located in the **Web** tab) in the **Properties** window. Then change the Size to 328, 224. Next, change the BorderStyle property to FixedSingle. Position the Panel as shown in Fig. 3.38.

e) *Adding another Panel.* Add another Panel and change its Size to 152, 224 and its BorderStyle to FixedSingle. Place the Panel to the right of the door Panel, as shown in Fig. 3.38.

f) *Adding the microwave oven clock.* Add a Label to the right Panel by clicking the Label in the **Toolbox** once, then clicking once inside the right Panel. Change the Label's Text to 12:00, BorderStyle to FixedSingle, AutoSize to False and Size to 120, 48. Change TextAlign to MiddleCenter. Place the clock as shown in Fig. 3.38.

g) *Adding a keypad to the microwave oven.* Place a Button in the right Panel by clicking the Button control in the Toolbox once, then clicking inside the Panel. Change the Text to 1 and the Size to 24, 24. Repeat this process for nine more Buttons, changing the Text property in each to the next number in the keypad. Then add the **Start** and **Clear** Buttons, each of Size 64, 24. Do not forget to set the Text properties for each of these Buttons. Finally, arrange the Buttons as shown in Fig. 3.38. The 1 Button is located at 40, 80 and the **Start** Button is located at 8, 192.

h) *Saving and closing the project.* Select **File > Save All** to save your changes. Then select **File > Close Project** to close the project for this application.

3.14 *(Cell Phone GUI)* Create the GUI for the cell phone shown in Fig. 3.39.

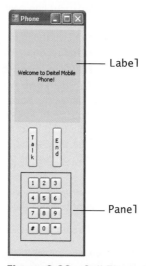

Figure 3.39 **Cell Phone** GUI.

a) *Creating a new project.* Create a new **Windows Application** named Phone.

b) *Renaming the Form file.* Name the Form file Phone.vb.

c) *Manipulating the Form's properties.* Change the Form's Text property to Phone and the Size to 160, 488. Change the Font property to Tahoma.

d) *Adding the display Label.* Add a Label to the Form. Change its BackColor to Aqua (in the **Web** tab palette), the Text to Welcome to Deitel Mobile Phone!, AutoSize to False and the Size to 136, 184. Change the TextAlign property to Middle-Center. Then place the Label as shown in Fig. 3.39.

e) *Adding the keypad Panel.* Add a Panel to the Form. Change its BorderStyle property to FixedSingle and its Size to 104, 136.

f) *Adding the keypad Buttons.* Add the keypad Buttons to the Form (12 Buttons in all). Each Button on the number pad should be of Size 24, 24 and should be placed in the Panel. Change the Text property of each Button such that numbers 0–9, the pound (#) and the star (*) keys are represented. Then add the final two Buttons such that the Text property for one is Talk and the other is End. Change the Size of each Button to 20, 80, and notice how the small Size causes the Text to align vertically.

g) *Placing the controls.* Arrange all the controls so that your GUI looks like Fig. 3.39.

h) *Saving and closing the project.* Select **File > Save All** to save your changes. Then select **File > Close Project** to close the project for this application.

3.15 *(Vending Machine GUI)* Create the GUI for the vending machine in Fig. 3.40.

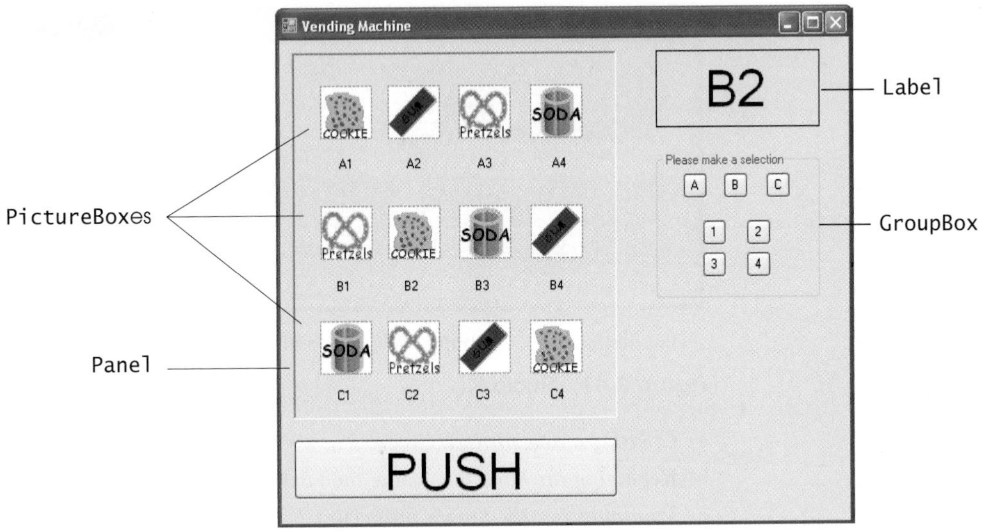

Figure 3.40 Vending Machine GUI.

a) *Creating a new project.* Create a new **Windows Application** named Vending-Machine.

b) *Renaming the Form file.* Name the Form file VendingMachine.vb.

c) *Manipulating the Form's properties.* Set the Text property of the Form to Vending Machine and the Size to 560, 488.

d) *Adding the food-selection Panel.* Add a Panel to the Form, and change its Size to 312, 344 and BorderStyle to Fixed3D. Add a PictureBox to the Panel, and change its Size to 50, 50. Then set the Image property by clicking the ellipsis Button and choosing a file from the C:\Examples\Tutorial03\ExerciseImages\VendingMachine directory. Repeat this process for 11 more PictureBoxes.

e) *Adding Labels for each vending item.* Add a Label under each PictureBox. Change the Text property of the Label to A1, the TextAlign property to MiddleCenter, AutoSize to False and the Size to 56, 16. Place the Label so that it is located as in Fig. 3.40. Repeat this process for A2 through C4 (11 Labels).

f) *Creating the vending machine door (as a Button).* Add a Button to the Form by dragging the Button control in the **Toolbox** and dropping it below the Panel. Change the Button's Text property to PUSH, its Font Size to 36 and its Size to 312, 56. Then place the Button on the Form as shown in Fig. 3.40.

g) *Adding the selection-display Label.* Add a Label to the Form, and change the Text property to B2, BorderStyle to FixedSingle, Font Size to 36, TextAlign to MiddleCenter, AutoSize to False and Size to 160, 72.

h) *Grouping the input Buttons.* Add a GroupBox below the Label, and change the Text property to Please make selection and the Size to 160, 136.

i) *Adding the input Buttons.* Finally, add Buttons to the GroupBox. For the seven Buttons, change the Size property to 24, 24. Then change the Text property of the Buttons such that each Button has one of the values A, B, C, 1, 2, 3 or 4, as shown in Fig. 3.40. When you are done, move the controls on the Form so that they are aligned as shown in the figure.

j) *Saving and closing the project.* Select **File > Save All** to save your changes. Then select **File > Close Project** to close the project for this application.

Programming Challenge ▶ **3.16** *(Radio GUI)* Create the GUI for the radio in Fig. 3.41. [*Note:* All colors used in this exercise are from the **Web** palette.] In this exercise, you will create this GUI on your own. Feel free to experiment with different control properties. For the image in the PictureBox, use the file (MusicNote.gif) found in the C:\Examples\Tutorial03\ExerciseImages\ Radio directory.

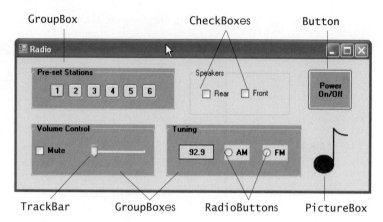

Figure 3.41 Radio GUI.

a) *Creating a new project.* Create a new **Windows Application** named Radio.

b) *Renaming the Form file.* Name the Form file Radio.vb.

c) *Manipulating the Form's properties.* Change the Form's Text property to Radio and the Size to 576, 240. Change the Font property to Tahoma. Set BackColor to Peach-Puff.

d) *Adding the Pre-set Stations GroupBox and Buttons.* Add a GroupBox to the Form. Set its Size to 232, 64, its Text to Pre-set Stations, its ForeColor to Control-Text and its BackColor to RosyBrown. Change its Font to bold. Finally, set its Location to 24, 16. Add six Buttons to the GroupBox. Set each BackColor to PeachPuff and each Size to 24, 23. Change the Buttons' Text properties to 1, 2, 3, 4, 5, 6, respectively.

e) *Adding the Speakers GroupBox and CheckBoxes.* Add a GroupBox to the Form. Set its Size to 160, 72, its Text to Speakers and its ForeColor to Black. Set its Location to 280, 16. Add two CheckBoxes to the Form. Set each CheckBox's AutoSize to False and its Size to 56, 24. Set the Text properties for the CheckBoxes to Rear and Front.

f) *Adding the Power On/Off Button.* Add a Button to the Form. Set its Text to Power On/Off, its BackColor to RosyBrown, its ForeColor to Black and its Size to 72, 64. Change its Font style to Bold.

g) *Adding the Volume Control GroupBox, the Mute CheckBox and the Volume Track-Bar.* Add a GroupBox to the Form. Set its Text to Volume Control, its BackColor to RosyBrown, its ForeColor to Black and its Size to 200, 80. Set its Font style to Bold. Add a CheckBox to the GroupBox. Set its Text to Mute, its AutoSize to False and its Size to 56, 24. Add a TrackBar to the GroupBox.

h) *Adding the Tuning GroupBox, the radio station Label and the AM/FM RadioButtons.* Add a GroupBox to the Form. Set its Text to Tuning, its ForeColor to Black and its BackColor to RosyBrown. Set its Font style to Bold and its Size to 216, 80. Add a Label to the Form. Set its BackColor to PeachPuff, its ForeColor to Black, its BorderStyle to FixedSingle, its Font style to Bold, its TextAlign to Middle-Center, its AutoSize to False and its Size to 56, 23. Set its Text to 92.9. Place the Label as shown in the figure. Add two RadioButtons to the GroupBox. Change the BackColor to PeachPuff, change AutoSize to False and change the Size to 46, 24. Set one's Text to AM and the other's Text to FM.

i) *Adding the image.* Add a PictureBox to the Form. Set its BackColor to Transparent, its SizeMode to StretchImage and its Size to 56, 72. Set its Image property to C:\Examples\Tutorial03\ExerciseImages\Radio\MusicNote.gif.

j) *Saving and closing the project.* Select **File > Save All** to save your changes. Then select **File > Close Project** to close the project for this application.

Objectives

In this tutorial, you will learn to:
- Visually program, using GUI design guidelines.
- Rename the Form.
- Add Labels, TextBoxes and a Button to the Form.
- Use the TextAlign and BorderStyle properties for Labels.

Outline

Designing the Inventory Application

Introducing TextBoxes and Buttons

This tutorial introduces you to the fundamentals of visual programming. You will design the graphical user interface for a simple inventory application. Through each set of steps, you will enhance the application's user interface by adding controls. You will design a Form on which you place Labels, TextBoxes and a Button. You will learn new properties for Labels and TextBoxes. At the end of the tutorial, you will find a list of new GUI design guidelines to help you create appealing and easy-to-use graphical user interfaces.

4.1 Test-Driving the Inventory Application

In this tutorial, you will create an inventory application that calculates the number of textbooks received by a college bookstore. This application must meet the following requirements:

Application Requirements

A college bookstore receives cartons of textbooks. In each shipment, cartons contain the same number of textbooks. The inventory manager wants to use a computer to calculate the total number of textbooks arriving at the bookstore for each shipment from the number of cartons and the number of textbooks in each carton. The inventory manager will enter the number of cartons received and the fixed number of textbooks in each carton for each shipment; then the application will calculate the total number of textbooks in the shipment.

This application performs a simple calculation. The user (the inventory manager) inputs into TextBoxes the number of cartons and the number of items in each carton. The user then clicks a Button, which causes the application to multiply the two numbers and display the result—the total number of textbooks received. You will begin by test-driving the completed application. Then you will learn the additional Visual Basic technologies that you will need to create your own version of this application.

Test-Driving the Inventory Application

1. ***Opening the completed application.*** Open the directory C:\Examples\ Tutorial04\CompletedApplication\Inventory to locate the **Inventory** application. Double click Inventory.sln to open the application in the Visual Basic IDE. Depending on your system configuration, you may not see the .sln file name extension. In this case, double click the file named Inventory that contains a solution file icon, .

2. ***Running the Inventory application.*** Select **Debug > Start Debugging** to run the application. The **Inventory** Form shown in Fig. 4.1 will appear.

Label

TextBoxes

Label

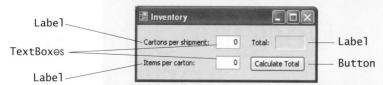

Label

Button

Figure 4.1 **Inventory** application Form with default data displayed by the application.

Note that there are two controls that you did not use in the **Welcome** application—the TextBox and Button controls. A **TextBox** is a control that the user can enter data into from the keyboard and that can display data to the user. A **Button** is a control that causes the application to perform an action when clicked.

3. ***Entering quantities in the application.*** Some controls (such as TextBoxes) are not used to display descriptive text for other controls; therefore, we refer to these controls by using the Labels that identify them. For example, we will refer to the TextBox to the right of the **Cartons per shipment:** Label as the **Cartons per shipment:** TextBox. Enter 3 in the **Cartons per shipment:** TextBox. Enter 15 in the **Items per carton:** TextBox. Figure 4.2 shows the Form after these values have been entered.

Figure 4.2 **Inventory** application with new quantities entered.

4. ***Calculating the total number of items received.*** Click the **Calculate Total** Button. This causes the application to multiply the two numbers you entered and to display the result (45) in the Label to the right of **Total:** (Fig. 4.3).

Result of calculation

Figure 4.3 Result of clicking the **Calculate Total** Button in the **Inventory** application.

5. ***Closing the application.*** Close your running application by clicking its close box.

6. ***Closing the project.*** Select **File > Close Project**.

4.2 Constructing the Inventory Application

Now that you have test-driven the completed application, you will begin creating your own version of the application. You will create a new project that contains the Form on which you will place the controls required for the **Inventory** application. Then you will save the solution containing the Form to your work directory, C:\SimplyVB (ensuring that you will know which directory contains your solution if you take a break from building the application). Finally, the initial steps conclude with instructions for renaming the Form.

Creating a New Application

1. ***Creating the new project.*** To create a Windows application, select **File > New Project...,** to display the **New Project** dialog (Fig. 4.4). From the list of templates, select **Windows Application**. Type Inventory in the **Name:** Textbox, and click the **OK** Button.

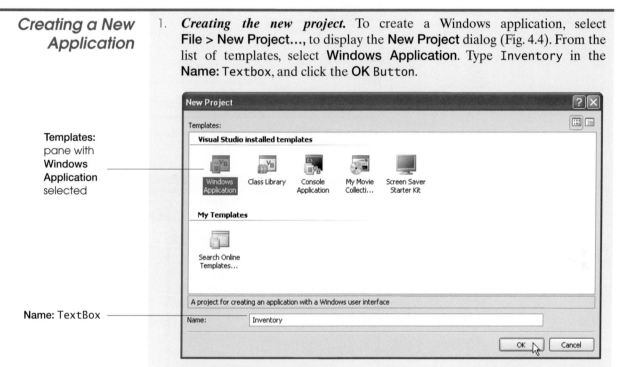

Templates: pane with **Windows Application** selected

Name: TextBox

Figure 4.4 **New Project** dialog for creating new applications.

2. ***Saving the project to your working directory.*** Now that a blank workspace has loaded, select **File > Save All,** to display the **Save Project** dialog (Fig. 4.5). Click the **Browse...** Button and the **Project Location** dialog appears (Fig. 4.6). Because you already created the SimplyVB directory, navigate to C:\SimplyVB. Click **Open** to select the directory and dismiss the dialog. The selected directory will then appear in the **Location:** TextBox.

Figure 4.5 **Save Project** dialog for saving the newly created application

3. ***Viewing the Form.*** Click the **Save** Button (Fig. 4.5) to close the **Save Project** dialog. The IDE will then reveal the application, containing a Form named **Form1** (Fig. 4.7). If the Form does not appear as in Fig. 4.7, select **View > Designer**. Then click the Form in the IDE to select it.

(cont.)

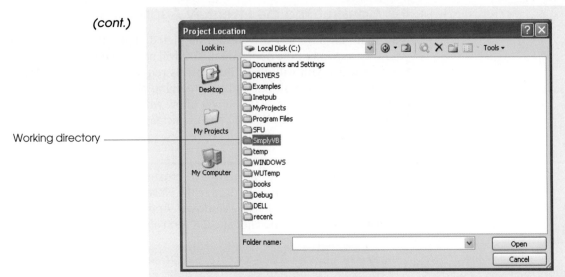

Figure 4.6 **Project Location** dialog used to specify the directory in which the project files reside.

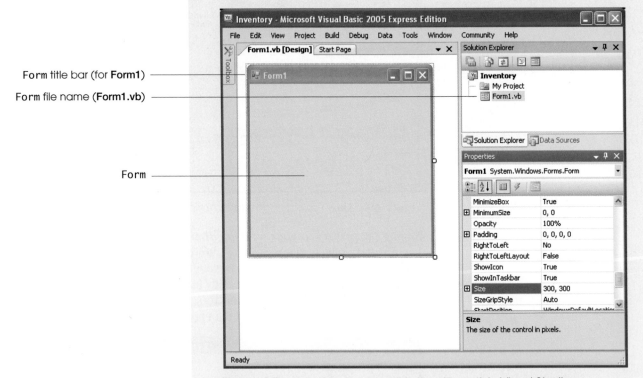

Figure 4.7 New Windows application (**Form1**) in Visual Studio.

4. **Renaming the Form file.** It is a good practice to change the Form's file name to a name more meaningful for your application. To change the Form's file name, click its name (**Form1.vb**) in the **Solution Explorer**. Then select **File Name** in the **Properties** window, and type **Inventory.vb** in the field to the right. Press *Enter* to update the file name. Unless otherwise noted, you need to press *Enter* for changes made in the properties window to take effect.

(cont.)

Good Programming Practice

Change the **Form** name to a unique and meaningful name for easy identification.

Good Programming Practice

Use standard suffixes for names of objects (controls and **Forms**) so that you can easily tell them apart. Append **Form** names with the suffix Form. Capitalize the first letter of the **Form** name because **Form** is a class. Objects (such as controls) should begin with lowercase letters.

Name property ──────────

GUI Design Tip

Change the **Form**'s font to Tahoma to be consistent with Microsoft's recommended font for Windows.

5. ***Renaming the Form object.*** Each Form object needs a unique and meaning-ful name for easy identification. In the Visual Basic IDE, you set the Form's name by using the **Name** property. By default, the Visual Basic IDE names the Form Form1. When you change the Form's file name, the Visual Basic IDE updates the form's Name property automatically to the name of the file without the .vb extension—in this case, Inventory. Click the Form in the Windows Form Designer. In the **Properties** window (Fig. 4.8), double click the field to the right of the Name property, listed as (Name). Type the name InventoryForm, then press *Enter* to update the name.

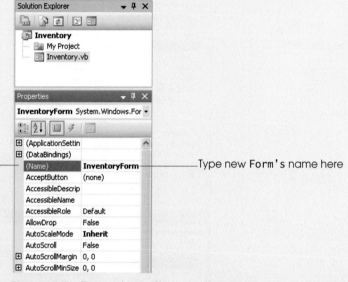

Name property ──────────(Name)────────── Type new **Form**'s name here

Figure 4.8 Renaming a file in the **Solution Explorer** and **Properties** windows.

6. ***Saving the project.*** Select **File > Save All** to save your changes. Saving your work often will prevent losing changes to the application.

Next, you will learn how to modify your Form by setting its font. As in all our examples, you should set the Form's font to **Tahoma**, the Microsoft-recommended font for GUIs. Changing the Form's font to Tahoma ensures that controls added to the Form use the Tahoma font. You will also learn how to change the Form's title and size. Although you have already changed the file name to Inventory.vb, you still need to change the title bar text to help users identify the Form's purpose. Changing the Form's size to be more appropriate for its content improves its appearance.

Customizing the Form

1. ***Setting the Form's font.*** In the preceding tutorial, you used the **Font** dialog to change the font. You will now use the **Properties** window to change the Form's font. Select the Form in the Windows Form Designer. If the **Proper-ties** window is not already open, click the properties icon in the IDE toolbar or select **View > Properties Window**. To change the Form's font to Tahoma, click the plus box ⊞ to the left of the **Font** property in the **Properties** win-dow (Fig. 4.9). This causes other properties related to the Form's Font to be displayed. In the list that appears, select the font's Name property, then click the down arrow to the right of the property value. In the list that appears, select Tahoma. [*Note*: This list may appear slightly different, depending on the fonts that are installed on your system.]

(cont.)

Click plus box to display
Font properties

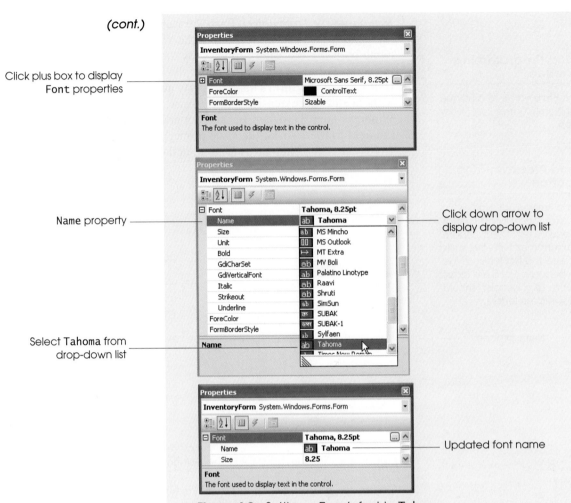

Name property

Click down arrow to
display drop-down list

Select Tahoma from
drop-down list

Updated font name

Figure 4.9 Setting a Form's font to Tahoma.

You will notice that several properties, such as Font, have a plus box ⊞ next to the property name to indicate that there are additional properties available for this node. For example, the Font Name, Size and Bold properties of a Font each have their own listings in the **Properties** window when you click the plus box.

2. ***Setting the text in the Form's title bar.*** The text in the Form's title bar is determined by the Form's **Text** property. To display the Form's properties in the **Properties** window, click the Form in the Windows Form Designer. Double click the field to the right of the Text property in the **Properties** window, type Inventory and press *Enter*. Form titles should use book-title capitalization. **Book-title capitalization** is a style that capitalizes the first letter of each significant word in the text and does not end with any punctuation (for example, *Capitalization in a Book Title*). The updated title bar is shown in Fig. 4.10.

GUI Design Tip

Form titles should use book-title capitalization.

3. ***Resizing the Form.*** Double click the field to the right of the Size property in the **Properties** window, then enter 296, 112 and press *Enter* (Fig. 4.10). Note that the Form is now the same size as the completed application you test-drove at the beginning of the tutorial.

4. ***Saving the project.*** Select **File > Save All** to save your changes.

(cont.)

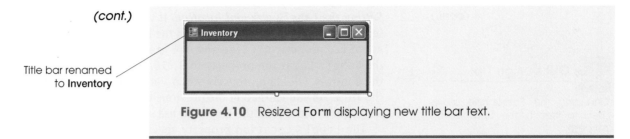

Figure 4.10   Resized **Form** displaying new title bar text.

Title bar renamed
to **Inventory**

Now that you have created and modified the Form, you will add controls to the GUI. Labels describe the purpose of controls on the Form and can be used to display results of calculations. In the next section, you will learn how to add Label controls and set each Label's name, text and position on the Form.

---

1. _____ is the Microsoft-recommended font for GUIs.

    a) Arial   b) Microsoft Sans Serif

    c) Tahoma   d) Times New Roman

2. Form titles should use _____ capitalization.

    a) book-title   b) complete

    c) no   d) sentence-style

Answers: 1) c. 2) a.

4.3 Adding **Label**s to the **Inventory** Application

Although you might not have noticed it, there are four Labels in this application. You can easily recognize three of the Labels from the application you designed in Tutorial 3. The fourth Label, however, has a border and contains no text until the user clicks the **Calculate Total** Button (Fig. 4.11). As the control's name indicates, Labels are often used to identify other controls on the Form. **Descriptive Labels** help the user understand each control's purpose and **output Labels** are used to display program output.

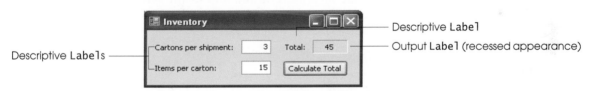

Descriptive Labels ——

——— Descriptive **Label**

——— Output **Label** (recessed appearance)

Figure 4.11   **Label**s used in the **Inventory** application.

---

1. ***Adding a Label control to the Form.*** Click the **All Windows Forms** group in the **Toolbox**. Then, double click the **Label** control in the **Toolbox** to place a Label on the Form (Fig. 4.12).

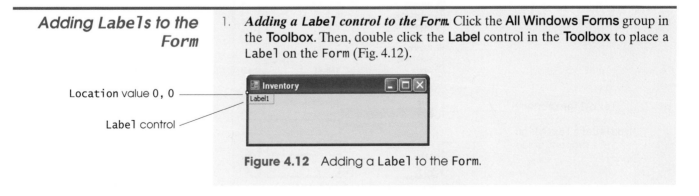

Location value 0, 0 ———

Label control ———

Figure 4.12   Adding a **Label** to the **Form**.

(cont.)

GUI Design Tip

Changing the Form's title allows users to identify the application's purpose.

GUI Design Tip

Although you can drag a Label control to a location on the Form, the Location property can be used to specify a precise position.

Good Programming Practice

Append the Label suffix to all Label control names.

GUI Design Tip

A Label used to describe the purpose of a control should use sentence-style capitalization and end with a colon. These types of Labels are called descriptive Labels.

GUI Design Tip

The TextAlign property of a descriptive Label should be set to MiddleLeft. This ensures that text within groups of Labels align.

2. **Setting the Label's size and location.** If the **Properties** window is not open, select **View > Properties Window**. In the **Properties** window, set the Label's AutoSize property to False and its Size property to 120, 21. Similarly, set the Label's Location property to 8, 16. Using these numbers ensures that the controls will align properly when you have added all of the controls to the Form. As you learned in the previous tutorial, you also can click and drag a control to place it on the Form and use sizing handles to resize it.

The Label's **Location** property specifies the position of the upper-left corner of the control on the Form. The IDE assigns the value 0, 0 to the top-left corner of the Form, not including the title bar (Fig. 4.12). A control's Location property is set according to its distance from that point on the Form. As the first number of the Location property increases, the control moves to the right. As the second number of the Location property increases, the control moves toward the bottom of the Form. In this case, the value of 8, 16 indicates that the Label is placed 8 pixels to the right of the top-left corner of the Form and 16 pixels down from the top-left corner of the Form (Fig. 4.14). A Location value of 16, 48 would indicate that the Label is placed 16 pixels to the right of the top-left corner of the Form and 48 pixels down from the top-left corner of the Form.

3. **Setting the Label's Name and Text properties.** In the **Properties** window, double click the field to the right of the Text property, then type Cartons per shipment:. Set the Name property to cartonsLabel.

When entering values for a Label's Text property, you should use sentence-style capitalization. **Sentence-style capitalization** means that you capitalize the first letter of the first word in the text. Every other letter in the text is lowercase unless it is the first letter of a proper noun (for example, *Deitel*).

4. **Modifying the Label's text alignment.** Select the TextAlign property in the **Properties** window; then, in the field to the right, click the down arrow (Fig. 4.13). Property TextAlign sets the alignment of text within a control such as a Label. Clicking the down arrow opens a window in which you can select the alignment of the text in the Label (Fig. 4.13). In this window, select the middle-left rectangle, which indicates that the Label's text aligns to the middle, vertically, and to the left, horizontally, in the control. The value of the property changes to MiddleLeft. Figure 4.14 displays the Label after you set its properties.

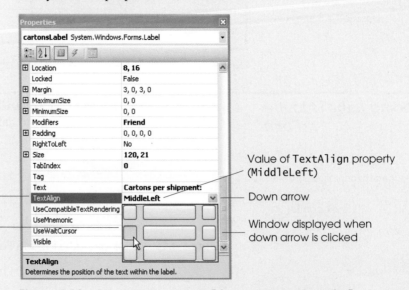

TextAlign property

MiddleLeft TextAlign property value

Value of TextAlign property (MiddleLeft)

Down arrow

Window displayed when down arrow is clicked

Figure 4.13 Changing the TextAlign property of a Label.

(cont.)

Location 8, 16 ——

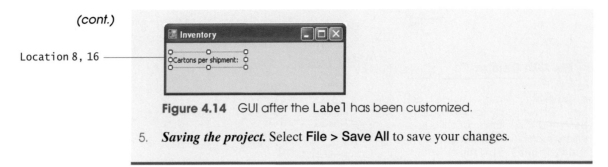

Figure 4.14 GUI after the Label has been customized.

5. *Saving the project.* Select **File > Save All** to save your changes.

Now you will add the remaining Labels to the Form. They will help the user understand what inputs to provide and interpret the application's output. These Labels will identify the controls that you will add to the Form later.

Placing Additional Labels on the Form

GUI Design Tip

Align the left sides of a group of descriptive Labels if the Labels are arranged vertically.

GUI Design Tip

As you drag controls around a Form in **Design** view, the IDE displays blue lines called snaplines that help you align and space your controls on the Form.

GUI Design Tip

Use a descriptive Label to identify an output Label.

GUI Design Tip

Place an application's output below and/or to the right of the Form's input controls.

GUI Design Tip

Output Labels should be distinguishable from descriptive Labels. This can be done by setting the BorderStyle property of an output Label to Fixed3D.

1. *Adding a second descriptive Label.* Double click the Label control on the **Toolbox** to add a second Label. Set the Label's AutoSize property to False. Then, set the Label's Size property to 104, 21 and the Label's Location property to 8, 48. Set the Label's Text property to Items per carton:, and change the Name property of this Label to itemsLabel. Then set the Label's TextAlign property to MiddleLeft.

2. *Adding a third descriptive Label.* Double click the Label control on the **Toolbox** to add a third Label. Set the Label's AutoSize property to False. Then, set the Label's Size property to 40, 21 and the Label's Location property to 184, 16. Set the Label's Text property to Total: and change the Name property of this Label to totalLabel. Then set the Label's TextAlign property to MiddleLeft.

3. *Adding an output Label.* To add the fourth Label, double click the Label control on the **Toolbox**. Set the Label's AutoSize property to False. Then, set the Label's Size property to 48, 21 and the Label's Location property to 224, 16. Then name this Label totalResultLabel. Set the Label's TextAlign property to MiddleCenter. For the previous Labels, you set this property to MiddleLeft. To select value MiddleCenter, follow the same actions as in *Step 2*, but select the center rectangle shown in Fig. 4.15. You should use MiddleCenter text alignment to display results of calculations because it distinguishes the value in the output Label from the values in the descriptive Labels (whose TextAlign property is set to MiddleLeft).

4. *Changing a Label's BorderStyle property.* The totalResultLabel displays the result of the application's calculation; therefore, you should make this Label appear different from the other Labels. To do this, you'll change the appearance of the Label's border by changing the value of the **BorderStyle** property. Assign the value Fixed3D (Fig. 4.16) to totalResultLabel's BorderStyle property to make the Label seem three-dimensional (Fig. 4.17). [*Note*: If selected, FixedSingle displays a single dark line as a border.]

5. *Clearing a Label's Text property.* When a Label is added to a Form, the Text property is assigned the default name of the Label. In this case, you should clear the text of the Label because you will not be adding meaningful text to totalResultLabel until later. To do this, delete the text to the right of the Text property in the **Properties** window and press *Enter*. Figure 4.17 displays the GUI with all Labels added.

6. *Saving the project.* Select **File > Save All** to save your changes.

(cont.)

GUI Design Tip

If several output Labels are arranged vertically to display numbers used in a mathematical calculation (such as in an invoice), use the MiddleRight TextAlign property.

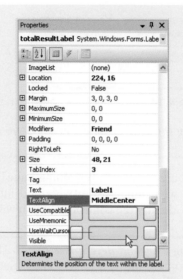

MiddleCenter TextAlign property value

Figure 4.15 Setting the TextAlign property to MiddleCenter.

Good Programming Practice

Clear the value of output Labels initially. When the application performs the calculation for that value, the Label's Text property should be updated to the new value. You will learn how to do this in the next tutorial.

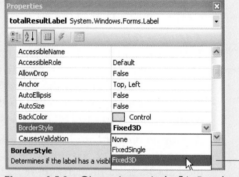

Fixed3D BorderStyle property highlighted

Figure 4.16 Changing a Label's BorderStyle property to Fixed3D.

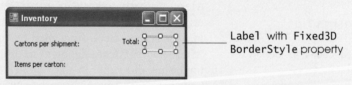

Label with Fixed3D BorderStyle property

Figure 4.17 GUI with all Labels added.

SELF-REVIEW

1. The value _____ for the Location property indicates the top-left corner (not including the title bar) of the Form.

   a) 1, 1   b) 0, 0

   c) 1, 0   d) 0, 1

2. An output Label should _____.

   a) be distinguishable from other Labels   b) initially have an empty Text property

   c) use Fixed3D for the BorderStyle property

   d) All of the above.

Answers: 1) b. 2) d.

4.4 Adding TextBoxes and a Button to the Form

The **Inventory** application requires user input to calculate the total number of textbooks that have arrived per shipment. Specifically, the user types in the number of cartons and the fixed number of books per carton. Because this type of data is entered from the keyboard, you use a TextBox control. Next, you will learn how to add TextBoxes to your Form and set their properties. Then, you will add a Button control to complete your GUI.

Adding TextBoxes to the Form

Good Programming Practice

Append the TextBox suffix to the name of every TextBox control.

GUI Design Tip

Use TextBoxes to input data from the keyboard.

1. ***Adding a TextBox to the Form.*** Double click the TextBox control,

     `abl TextBox`

    in the **Toolbox** to add a TextBox to the Form. Setting properties for a Text-Box is similar to setting the properties for a Label. To name a TextBox, select the Name property in the **Properties** window, and enter cartonsText-Box in the field to the right of the property (Fig. 4.18). Set the TextBox's Size property to 40, 21 and Location property to 128, 16. These size and location properties will cause the top of the TextBox to align with the top of the Label that describes it. Set the TextBox's Text property to 0 (Fig. 4.19). This will cause the value for your TextBox to be initially 0 when the application runs.

Name property set to cartonsTextBox

Location property set to 128, 16

Size property set to 40, 21

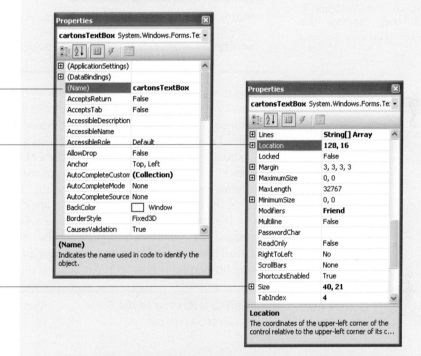

Figure 4.18 Properties window for the cartonsTextBox TextBox.

GUI Design Tip

Each TextBox should have a descriptive Label indicating the input expected from the user.

GUI Design Tip

Place each descriptive Label either above or to the left of the control (for instance, a TextBox) that it identifies.

2. ***Changing the TextAlign property of a TextBox.*** Change cartonsText-Box's TextAlign property to Right. Note that, when you click the down arrow to the right of this property, the window in Fig. 4.13 does not appear. This is because TextBoxes have fewer TextAlign options, which are displayed simply as a list. Select Right from this list (Fig. 4.19).

3. ***Adding a second TextBox to the Form.*** Double click the TextBox control in the **Toolbox**. Name the TextBox itemsTextBox. Set the Size property to 40, 21 and the Location property to 128, 48. These settings ensure that the left sides of the two TextBoxes align. The settings also align the top of the TextBox and the top of the Label that describes it. Set the Text property to 0 and the TextAlign property to Right. Figure 4.20 shows the Form after the TextBoxes have been added and their properties have been set.

(cont.)

GUI Design Tip

Make TextBoxes wide enough for their expected inputs.

GUI Design Tip

A descriptive Label and the control it identifies should be aligned on the left if they are arranged vertically.

GUI Design Tip

A descriptive Label should have the same height as the TextBox it describes if the controls are arranged horizontally.

GUI Design Tip

A descriptive Label and the control it identifies should be aligned on the top if they are arranged horizontally.

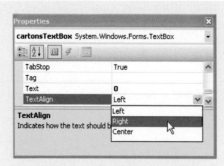

Figure 4.19　Selecting value `Right` of the `TextAlign` property of a Text-Box control.

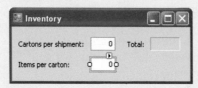

Figure 4.20　GUI after TextBoxes have been added and modified.

4. ***Saving the project.*** Select **File > Save All** to save your changes.

Note that your controls are aligning horizontally and vertically. In general, you should place each descriptive Label above or to the left of the control it describes (for instance, a TextBox). If you are arranging your controls on the same line, the descriptive Label and the control it describes should be the same height. However, if you arrange your controls vertically, the Label should be placed above the control it describes and the left sides of the controls should align. Following these simple guidelines will make your applications more appealing visually and easier to use by making the controls on the application less crowded.

Now that the user can enter data using a TextBox, you need a way for the user to command the application to perform the multiplication calculation and display the result. The most common way for a user to do this is by clicking a Button. The following box explains how to add a Button to the **Inventory** application.

Adding a Button to the Form

GUI Design Tip

Buttons should be stacked downward from the top right of a Form or arranged on the same line starting from the bottom right of a Form.

Good Programming Practice

Append the Button suffix to Button control names.

1. ***Adding a Button to the Form.*** Add a Button to the Form by double clicking the Button control,

```
ab  Button
```

in the **Toolbox**. Setting the properties for a Button is similar to setting the properties for a Label or a TextBox. Enter `calculateButton` in the Button's Name property.

Set the Button's Size to 88, 24 and Location to 184, 48. Note that these settings cause the left and right sides of the Button to align with the Labels above it (Fig. 4.21). Enter `Calculate Total` in the Button's Text property. A Button's Text property displays its value on the face of the Button. You should use book-title capitalization in a Button's Text property. When labeling Buttons, keep the Text as short as possible while still clearly indicating the Button's function.

(cont.)

2. ***Running the application.*** Select **Debug > Start Debugging** to run the application (Fig. 4.21). Note that no action occurs if you click the **Calculate Total** Button. This is because you have not written code that tells the application how to respond to your click. In Tutorial 5, you will write code to display (in totalResultLabel) the total number of books in the shipment when you click the Button.

GUI Design Tip

Buttons are labeled using their Text property. These labels should use book-title capitalization and be as short as possible while still being meaningful to the user.

Figure 4.21   Running the application after completing its design.

3. ***Closing the application.*** Close your running application by clicking its close box.

4. ***Closing the IDE.*** Close the Visual Basic IDE by clicking its close box.

SELF-REVIEW

1. A Button's _____ property sets the text on the face of the Button.
   a) Name
   b) Text
   c) Title
   d) Face

2. Buttons should be _____ of the Form.
   a) on the same line, from the bottom right
   b) stacked from the top left
   c) aligned with the title bar text
   d) Either a or c.

Answers: 1) b. 2) a.

4.5 Wrap-Up

In this tutorial, you began constructing your **Inventory** application by designing its graphical user interface. You learned how to use Labels to describe controls and how to set a Label's TextAlign and BorderStyle properties. You used these properties to distinguish between descriptive and output Labels.

After labeling your Form, you added TextBoxes to allow users to input data from the keyboard. Finally, you added a Button to the **Inventory** application, allowing a user to signal the application to perform an action (in this case, to multiply two numbers and display the result). While adding controls to the Form, you also learned some GUI design tips to help you create appealing and intuitive graphical user interfaces.

The next tutorial teaches you to program code in Visual Basic that will run when the user clicks the **Calculate Total** Button. When the Button is clicked, the application receives a signal called an event. You will learn how to program your application to respond to that event by performing the multiplication calculation and displaying the result.

SKILLS SUMMARY   **Creating a New Project**

■ Select **File > New Project...** to create a project

■ Select **File > Save All** to save a project to your working directory (C:\SimplyVB) by selecting it from the **Project Location** dialog.

Setting the Application's Font to Tahoma

■ Select Tahoma from the Font Name property ComboBox in the Form's **Properties** window.

Creating a Descriptive Label

- Add a Label to your Form, then change the TextAlign property to MiddleLeft.

Creating an Output Label

- Add a Label to your Form, and change the BorderStyle property to Fixed3D and the TextAlign property to MiddleCenter.

Enabling User Input from the Keyboard

- Add a TextBox control to your Form.

Signaling That the Application Should Perform an Action

- Add a Button to the Form, and write program code to perform that action. (You will learn how to add program code in Tutorial 5.)

KEY TERMS

book-title capitalization—A style that capitalizes the first letter of the each word in the text (for example, **Calculate Total**).

BorderStyle property—Specifies the appearance of a Label's border, which allows you to distinguish one control from another visually. The BorderStyle property can be set to None (no border), FixedSingle (a single dark line as a border), or Fixed3D (giving the Label a "sunken" appearance).

Button control—Commands the application to perform an action.

descriptive Label—A Label used to describe another control on the Form. This helps users understand a control's purpose.

Location property—Specifies the location of the upper-left corner of a control. This property is used to place a control on the Form precisely.

Name property—Assigns a unique and meaningful name to a control for easy identification.

output Label—A Label used to display calculation results.

sentence-style capitalization—A style that capitalizes the first letter of the first word in the text. Every other letter in the text is lowercase, unless it is the first letter of a proper noun (for example, **Cartons per shipment**).

Tahoma font—The Microsoft-recommended font for use in Windows applications.

Text property—Sets the text displayed on a control.

TextBox control—Retrieves user input from the keyboard.

GUI DESIGN GUIDELINES

Overall Design

- Although you can drag a Label control to a location on the Form, the Location property can be used to specify a precise position.
- Place an application's output below and/or to the right of the Form's input controls.

Buttons

- Buttons are labeled using their Text property. These labels should use book-title capitalization and be as short as possible while still meaningful to the user.
- Buttons should be stacked downward from the top right of a Form or arranged on the same line starting from the bottom right of a Form.

Forms

- Changing the Form's title allows users to identify the application's purpose.
- Form titles should use book-title capitalization.
- Change the Form font to Tahoma to be consistent with Microsoft's recommended font for Windows.

Labels

- The TextAlign property of a descriptive Label should be set to MiddleLeft. This ensures that text within groups of Labels aligns.
- A Label used to describe the purpose of a control should use sentence-style capitalization and end with a colon. These types of Labels are called descriptive Labels.

- Place each descriptive `Label` above or to the left of the control that it identifies.
- A descriptive `Label` should have the same height as the `TextBox` it describes if the controls are arranged horizontally.
- A descriptive `Label` and the control it identifies should be aligned on the left if they are arranged vertically.
- Align the left sides of a group of descriptive `Label`s if the `Label`s are arranged vertically.
- Use a descriptive `Label` to identify an output `Label`.
- Output `Label`s should be distinguishable from descriptive `Label`s. This can be done by setting the `BorderStyle` property of an output `Label` to `Fixed3D`.
- If several output `Label`s are arranged vertically to display numbers used in a mathematical calculation, use the `MiddleRight` value for the `TextAlign` property.
- A descriptive `Label` and the control it identifies should be aligned on the top if they are arranged horizontally.

TextBoxes

- Use `TextBox`es to input data from the keyboard.
- Each `TextBox` should have a descriptive `Label` indicating the input expected from the user.
- Make `TextBox`es wide enough for their expected inputs.

CONTROLS, EVENTS, PROPERTIES & METHODS

Button 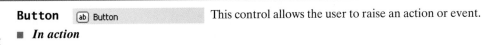   This control allows the user to raise an action or event.

- ***In action***

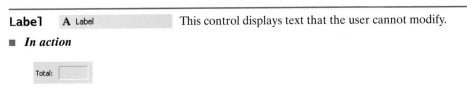

- ***Properties***

  `Name`—Specifies the name used to identify the `Button`. The name should include the `Button` suffix.

  `Size`—Specifies the height and width (in pixels) of the `Button`.

  `Text`—Specifies the text displayed on the `Button`.

Label A Label   This control displays text that the user cannot modify.

- ***In action***

  Total: [   ]

- ***Properties***

  `BorderStyle`—Specifies the appearance of the `Label`'s border.

  `Font`—Specifies the font name, style and size of the text displayed in the `Label`.

  `Location`—Specifies the location of the `Label` on the `Form` relative to the `Form`'s top-left corner.

  `Name`—Specifies the name used to identify the `Label`. The name should include the `Label` suffix.

  `Size`—Specifies the height and width (in pixels) of the `Label`.

  `Text`—Specifies the text displayed in the `Label`.

  `TextAlign`—Determines how the text is aligned within the `Label`.

TextBox 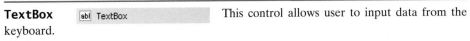   This control allows user to input data from the keyboard.

- ***In action***

■ *Properties*

Name—Specifies the name used to identify the TextBox. The name should include the TextBox suffix.

Size—Specifies the height and width (in pixels) of the TextBox.

Text—Specifies the text displayed in the TextBox.

TextAlign—Specifies how the text is aligned within the TextBox.

MULTIPLE-CHOICE QUESTIONS

4.1 A new Windows application is created by selecting _____ from the **File** menu.
a) **New Program**
b) **New File...**
c) **New Project...**
d) **New Application**

4.2 A Label's BorderStyle property can be set to _____.
a) Fixed3D
b) Single
c) 3D
d) All of the above.

4.3 When creating a Label, you can specify the _____ of that Label.
a) alignment of the text
b) border style
c) size
d) All of the above.

4.4 Changing the value stored in the _____ property will change the name of the Form file.
a) Name
b) File
c) File Name
d) Full Path

4.5 _____ should be appended as a suffix to all TextBox names.
a) Text Box
b) Text
c) Box
d) TextBox

4.6 A(n) _____ helps the user understand a control's purpose.
a) Button
b) descriptive Label
c) output Label
d) title bar

4.7 A _____ is a control in which the user can enter data from a keyboard.
a) Button
b) TextBox
c) Label
d) PictureBox

4.8 A descriptive Label uses _____.
a) sentence-style capitalization
b) book-title capitalization
c) a colon at the end of its text
d) Both a and c.

4.9 You should use the _____ font in your Windows applications.
a) Tahoma
b) MS Sans Serif
c) Times
d) Palatino

4.10 _____ should be appended as a suffix to all Button names.
a) Press
b) Label
c) Click
d) Button

EXERCISES

At the end of each tutorial, you will find a summary of new GUI design tips listed in the GUI Design Guidelines section. A cumulative list of GUI design guidelines, organized by control, appears in Appendix C. In these exercises, you will find Visual Basic Forms that do not follow the GUI design guidelines presented in this tutorial. For each exercise, you must modify control properties so that your end result is consistent with the guidelines presented in the tutorial. Note that these applications do not provide any functionality.

4.11 *(Address Book GUI)* In this exercise, you apply the GUI design guidelines you have learned to a graphical user interface for an address book (Fig. 4.22).

Figure 4.22   **Address Book** application without GUI design guidelines applied.

a) *Copying the template to your working directory.* Copy the directory C:\Examples\ Tutorial04\Exercises\AddressBook to your C:\SimplyVB directory.

b) *Opening the application's template file.* Double click AddressBook.sln in the AddressBook directory to open the application.

c) *Applying GUI design guidelines.* Rearrange the controls and modify properties so that the GUI conforms to the design guidelines you have learned.

d) *Saving the project.* Select **File > Save All** to save your changes.

4.12 *(Mortgage Calculator GUI)* In this exercise, you apply the GUI design guidelines you have learned to a graphical user interface for a mortgage calculator (Fig. 4.23).

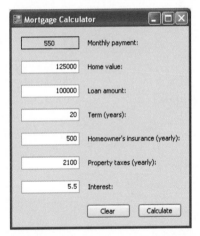

Figure 4.23   **Mortgage Calculator** application without GUI design guidelines applied.

a) *Copying the template to your working directory.* Copy the directory C:\Examples\ Tutorial04\Exercises\MortgageCalculator to your C:\SimplyVB directory.

b) *Opening the application's template file.* Double click MortgageCalculator.sln in the MortgageCalculator directory to open the application.

c) *Applying GUI design guidelines.* Rearrange the controls and modify properties so that the GUI conforms to the design guidelines you have learned.

d) *Saving the project.* Select **File > Save All** to save your changes.

4.13 *(Password GUI)* In this exercise, you apply the GUI design guidelines you have learned to a graphical user interface for a password-protected message application (Fig. 4.24).

a) *Copying the template to your working directory.* Copy the directory C:\Examples\ Tutorial04\Exercises\Password to your C:\SimplyVB directory.

b) *Opening the application's template file.* Double click Password.sln in the Password directory to open the application.

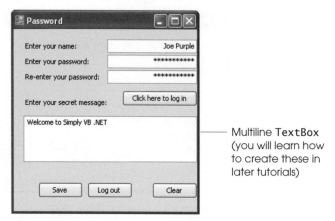

Figure 4.24   **Password** application without GUI design guidelines applied.

c) *Applying GUI design guidelines.* Rearrange the controls and modify properties so that the GUI conforms to the design guidelines you have learned.

d) *Saving the project.* Select **File > Save All** to save your changes.

Programming Challenge ▶

4.14 *(Monitor Invoice GUI)* In this exercise, you apply the GUI design guidelines you have learned to a graphical user interface for an invoice application (Fig. 4.25).

Figure 4.25   **Invoice** application without GUI design guidelines applied.

a) *Copying the template to your working directory.* Copy the directory C:\Examples\Tutorial04\Exercises\MonitorInvoice to your C:\SimplyVB directory.

b) *Opening the application's template file.* Double click the MonitorInvoice.sln file to open the application.

c) *Applying GUI design guidelines.* Rearrange the controls and modify properties so that the GUI conforms to the design guidelines you have learned.

d) *Saving the project.* Select **File > Save All** to save your changes.

Objectives

In this tutorial, you will learn to:
- Add an event handler for a **Button** control.
- Insert code into an event handler.
- Access a property's value by using Visual Basic code.
- Use the assignment and multiplication operators.

Outline

5.1 Test-Driving the Inventory Application

5.2 Introduction to Visual Basic Code

5.3 Inserting an Event Handler

5.4 Performing a Calculation and Displaying the Result

5.5 Using the Debugger: Syntax Errors

5.6 Wrap-Up

Completing the Inventory Application

Introducing Programming

This tutorial introduces fundamentals of nonvisual programming to create an application with which users can interact. You will learn these concepts as you add functionality (with Visual Basic code) to the **Inventory** application you designed in Tutorial 4. The term **functionality** describes the actions an application can execute. In this tutorial, you will examine **events**, which represent user actions, such as clicking a **Button** or altering a value in a **TextBox**, and **event handlers**, which are pieces of code that are executed (called) when such events occur (that is, when the events are raised). You will learn why events and event handlers are crucial to programming Windows applications.

5.1 Test-Driving the Inventory Application

In this tutorial, you will complete the **Inventory** application you designed in Tutorial 4. Recall that the application must meet the following requirements:

Application Requirements

A college bookstore receives cartons of textbooks. In each shipment, each carton contains the same number of textbooks. The inventory manager wants to use a computer to calculate the total number of textbooks arriving at the bookstore for each shipment from the number of cartons and the number of textbooks in each carton. The inventory manager will enter the number of cartons received and the fixed number of textbooks in each carton for each shipment; then the application will calculate the total number of textbooks in a shipment.

The inventory manager has reviewed and approved your design. Now you must add code that, when the user clicks a **Button**, will make the application multiply the number of cartons by the number of textbooks per carton and display the result—the total number of textbooks received. You will begin by test-driving the completed application. Then you will learn the additional Visual Basic technologies you will need to create your own version of this application.

Test-Driving the Inventory Application

1. ***Opening the completed application.*** Open the directory `C:\Examples\Tutorial05\CompletedApplication\Inventory2` to locate the **Inventory** application. Double click `Inventory2.sln` to open the application in the Visual Basic IDE.

2. ***Running the Inventory application.*** Select **Debug > Start Debugging** to run the application (Fig. 5.1). Enter 3 in the **Cartons per shipment:** Text-Box. Enter 15 in the **Items per carton:** TextBox. Figure 5.1 shows the Form after these values have been entered.

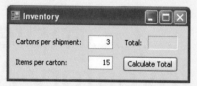

Figure 5.1 **Inventory** application with quantities entered.

3. ***Calculating the total number of items received.*** Click the **Calculate Total** Button. The application multiplies the two numbers you entered and displays the result (45) in the **Label** to the right of **Total:** (Fig. 5.2).

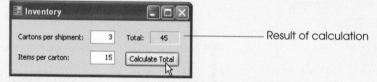

Result of calculation

Figure 5.2 Result of clicking the **Calculate Total** Button in the **Inventory** application.

4. ***Closing the application.*** Close your running application by clicking its close box.

5. ***Closing the IDE.*** Close the Visual Basic IDE by clicking its close box.

5.2 Introduction to Visual Basic Code

In Tutorial 3 and Tutorial 4, you were introduced to a concept called visual programming, which allows you to create GUIs without writing any program code. In this section, you will combine visual programming with conventional programming techniques to enhance the **Inventory** application.

Before you begin to view and edit code, you should customize the way the IDE displays and formats your code. In the following box, you open the template application and change the display and format settings to make it easy for you to work with code and follow our discussions. Adding line numbers, adjusting tab sizes and setting fonts and colors help you to navigate your code more easily.

Customizing the IDE

1. ***Copying the template to your working directory.*** Copy the `C:\Examples\Tutorial05\TemplateApplication\Inventory2` directory to your `C:\SimplyVB` directory. This directory contains the application created by following the steps in Tutorial 4.

2. ***Opening the Inventory application's template file.*** Double click `Inventory2.sln` in the `Inventory2` directory to open the application in the Visual Basic IDE. If an error occurs when you try to copy or modify the template, please consult your system administrator to ensure that you have proper privileges to edit these applications.

(cont.)

3. ***Displaying line numbers.*** In all of our programming discussions, we refer to specific code elements by line number. To help you locate where you will insert code in the examples, you need to enable the IDE's capability to show line numbers in your code.

   Select **Tools > Options…**, and, in the **Options** dialog that appears (Fig. 5.3), click the node beside the **Text Editor Basic** category to expand the collapsed options. Select the **Editor** category that subsequently appears (Fig. 5.4) and locate the **Interaction** group of Checkboxes within this category. If the Checkbox next to **Line numbers** is not checked, click inside the box to add a checkmark. If the box is already checked, you need not do anything; however, do not close the dialog.

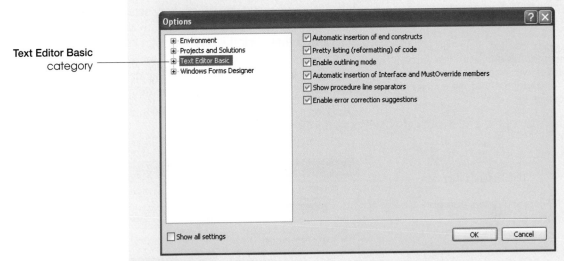

Text Editor Basic category

Figure 5.3   **Options** dialog.

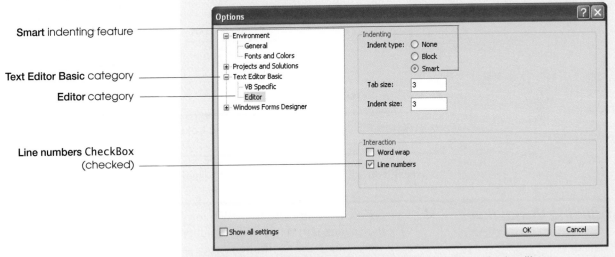

Smart indenting feature

Text Editor Basic category

Editor category

Line numbers CheckBox (checked)

Figure 5.4   **General** settings page for Visual Basic text editor.

4. ***Setting the tab size.*** Just as you indent the first line of each paragraph when writing a letter, it is important to use proper spacing when writing code. Indenting code improves program readability. You can control indents with tabs. In the options dialog that you opened in the preceding step, enter 3 for both the tab size and indent size fields.

(cont.)

The tab size setting indicates the number of spaces each tab character (inserted when you press the *Tab* key) represents. The **Indent size:** setting determines the number of spaces each indent inserted by the Visual Basic IDE represents. The IDE will now insert three spaces for you if you are using the **Smart** indenting feature (Fig. 5.4); however, you can insert them yourself with one keystroke by pressing the *Tab* key.

5. *Exploring fonts and colors.* Click the node beside the **Environment** category; then click the **Fonts and Colors** category that appears. The subsequent screen allows you to customize fonts and colors used to display code. The Visual Basic IDE can apply colors and fonts to make it easier for you to read and edit code. Note that, if your settings are not consistent with the default settings, what you see on your screen will appear different from what is presented in this book. If you need to reset your settings to the default for fonts and colors, click the **Use Defaults** Button (Fig. 5.5).

In the book's examples, you will see code with the **Selected Text** background set to yellow for emphasis. The default setting for **Selected Text** is a blue background. You should use the default settings on your machine.

6. *Applying your changes.* Click the **OK** Button to apply your changes and dismiss the **Options** dialog.

Good Programming Practice

You can change the font and color settings if you prefer a different appearance for your code. To remain consistent with this book, however, we recommend that you not change the default font and color settings.

Use Defaults `Button`

Fonts and Colors category

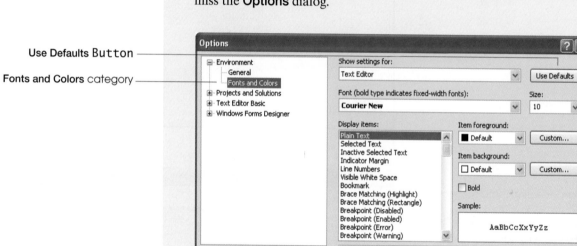

Figure 5.5 Examining the **Fonts and Colors** page.

Next, you will take your first peek at Visual Basic code.

Introducing Visual Basic Code

1. *Viewing application code.* If the Windows Form Designer is not open, double click the `Inventory.vb` file in the **Solutions Explorer** window. Then switch to **code view** (where the application's code is displayed in an editor window) by selecting **View > Code**. The tabbed window (`Inventory.vb`) in Fig. 5.6, also called a **code editor**, appears. Note that when you are asked to select **View > Code**, the `Inventory.vb` file must be selected in the **Solutions Explorer**.

You will notice that the IDE through which we present code to you may appear different than your IDE. To improve readability, we have hidden the **Toolbox** and closed any extra windows, such as the **Solutions Explorer**, **Properties** and **Error List** windows.

(cont.)

Inventory.vb tabbed window ────

Class definition ────

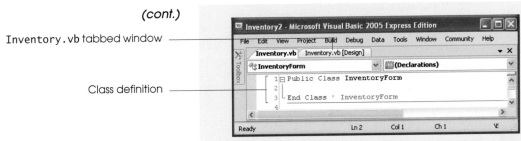

Figure 5.6 IDE showing code for the **Inventory** application.

Most Visual Basic programs consist of pieces called classes, which simplify application organization. Recall from Tutorial 1 that classes contain groups of code statements that perform tasks and return information when the tasks are completed. The code in this application defines your **Inventory** application class. (These lines collectively are called a **class definition**.) Most Visual Basic applications consist of a combination of code written by programmers (like you) and preexisting classes written and provided by Microsoft in the Framework Class Library (FCL). Again, the key to successful Visual Basic application development is achieving the right mix of the two. You will learn how to use both techniques in your programs.

2. *Examining class definitions.* Line 1 (Fig. 5.6) begins the class definition. The **Class keyword** introduces a class definition in Visual Basic and is immediately followed by the **class name** (InventoryForm in this application, the value you entered in the Form's Name property).

The name of the class is an **identifier**, which is a series of characters consisting of letters, digits and underscores (_). Identifiers cannot begin with a digit and cannot contain spaces. Examples of valid identifiers are value1, label_Value and exitButton. The name 7welcome is not a valid identifier, because it begins with a digit, and the name input field is not a valid identifier, because it contains a space. The class definition ends at line 3 with the keywords **End Class**. **Keywords** (or reserved words) are reserved for use by Visual Basic (you will learn the various keywords throughout the text). Note that keywords appear in blue by default in the IDE. A complete list of Visual Basic keywords can be found in Appendix E, Keyword Chart.

The Class keyword is preceded by the Public keyword. The code for every Form you design in the Visual Basic IDE begins with the Public keyword. You will learn about this keyword in Tutorial 19.

Visual Basic keywords and identifiers are not **case sensitive**. This means that uppercase and lowercase letters are considered to be identical; this practice causes InventoryForm and inventoryform to be understood by Visual Basic as the same identifier. Although the first letter of every keyword is capitalized, keywords are nevertheless not case sensitive. The IDE applies the correct case to each letter of a keyword and identifier, so when you type clasS, it is changed to Class when the *Enter* key is pressed.

Good Programming Practice

Capitalize the first letter of each class identifier, such as the Form name.

Good Programming Practice

Always type a keyword with the correct capitalization, even though the Visual Basic IDE will correct any capitalization errors.

SELF-REVIEW   1. Identifiers _____.

a) can begin with any character, but cannot contain spaces

b) must begin with a digit, but cannot contain spaces

c) cannot begin with a digit or contain spaces

d) cannot begin with a digit, but can contain spaces

2. Visual Basic keywords are _____ .

    a) case sensitive   b) comments

    c) not identifiers   d) not case sensitive

Answers: 1) c. 2) d.

5.3 Inserting an Event Handler

Now that you have finalized the GUI, you are ready to modify your application so that it will respond to user input. You will do this by inserting code manually. Most of the Visual Basic applications in this book provide functionality in the form of event handlers. Recall that an event handler is executed when an event occurs, such as the clicking of a `Button`. The next box shows you how to add an event handler to your application.

Adding a Button's Click Event Handler	1. ***Adding an event handler for the Button.*** In this step, you use the Windows Form Designer to create an event handler and enter code view. Begin by clicking the `Inventory.vb [Design]` tab to enter the Windows Form Designer. Then double click the Form's **Calculate Total** `Button` to enter code view. Note that the code for the application, which now includes the new event handler in lines 3–5 of Fig. 5.7, is displayed. Note too that we have added a blank line after the event handler by placing the cursor at the end of line 5, then pressing *Enter*.

Asterisks indicate unsaved changes to application

Empty event handler

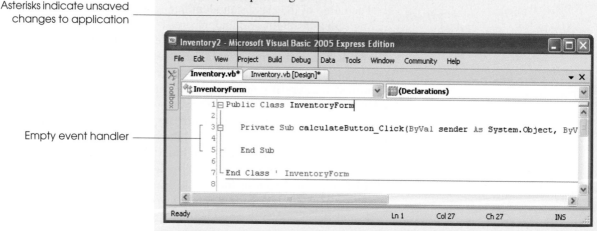

Figure 5.7 Event handler `calculateButton_Click` before you add your program code.

Double clicking the **Calculate Total** `Button` in design view caused the Visual Basic IDE to generate the `Button`'s `Click` event handler—the code that will execute when the user clicks the **Calculate Total** `Button`. When any control is double clicked in design view, the IDE inserts an event handler for that control. The event that the handler is associated with may differ based on the control that is double clicked. For instance, double clicking `Button` controls causes `Click` event handlers to be created. Double clicking other types of controls will cause other types of event handlers to be generated. Each control has a default type of event handler that is generated when that control is double clicked in design view.

(cont.)

In Visual Basic, event handlers by convention follow the naming scheme *controlName_eventName*. The word *controlName* refers to the name of the control provided in its Name property (in this case, calculateButton). The word *eventName* represents the name of the event (in this case, Click) raised by the control. When event *eventName* occurs, event handler *controlName_eventName* executes. In this application, calculate-Button_Click handles the **Calculate Total** Button's Click events—in other words, the code in calculateButton_Click executes when the user clicks the **Calculate Total** Button.

2. ***Running the application.*** Select **Debug > Start Debugging** to run the application (Fig. 5.8). The IDE automatically saves your work before running the application. Click the **Calculate Total** Button.

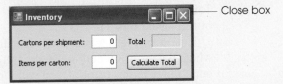

Figure 5.8 Running application without functionality.

Although you have added an event handler for the Button's Click event, no action occurs when you click the Button because you have not yet added any code to the event handler. In the next box, you add code to the event handler so that, when a user clicks the Button, text displays in the output Label (totalResultLabel).

3. ***Closing the application.*** Close the running application by clicking its close box.

Now that you have created an event handler for the **Calculate Total** Button, you need to insert code to perform an action. Specifically, you need to make the application multiply the number of cartons in a shipment by the fixed number of items per carton when a user clicks the **Calculate Total** Button. You write your first Visual Basic statement in the following box.

Adding Code to an Empty Event Handler

1. ***Changing to code view.*** If you are not already in code view, select **View > Code** to view the application's code.

2. ***Adding code to the event handler.*** In the event handler, insert lines 5–6 of Fig. 5.9 by typing the text on the screen then press *Enter*. Add the comment in line 8 following the keywords End Sub.

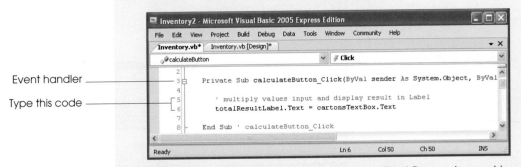

Figure 5.9 Code added to the **Calculate Total** Button's event handler.

(cont.)

Good Programming Practice

Comments written at the end of a line should be preceded by one or more spaces, to enhance program readability.

Line 5 of Fig. 5.9 begins with a **single-quote character** ('), which indicates that the remainder of the line is a **comment**. Programmers insert comments in programs to improve the readability of their code. These comments explain the code so that other programmers who need to work with the application can understand it more easily.

Comments also help you read your own code, especially when you have not looked at it for a while. Comments can be placed either on their own lines (these are called "full-line comments") or at the end of a line of Visual Basic code (these are called "end-of-line comments").

The Visual Basic compiler ignores comments, which means that comments do not cause the computer to perform any actions when your applications run. The comment used in line 5 simply indicates that the next line displays the value entered into the **Cartons per shipment:** TextBox in the **Total:** Label. Comments appear in green when displayed in the code editor of the Visual Basic IDE.

Line 6 of Fig. 5.9 presents your first executable Visual Basic **statement**, which performs an action. By default, statements end when the current line ends. Later in this tutorial, you will see how to continue a statement past one line. This statement (line 6) accesses the Text properties of cartonsText-Box and totalResultLabel. In Visual Basic, properties are accessed in code by placing a period between the control name (for example, totalRe-sultLabel) and property name (for example, Text). This period, which is placed to the right of the control name, is called the **member access operator** (.), or the **dot operator**. When the control name and member access operator are typed, a window appears listing that object's members (Fig. 5.10). This feature, known as the Visual Basic IDE's *IntelliSense*, displays all the members in a class for your convenience. You scroll to the member you are interested in and select it. Click the member name once to display a description of that member; double click it to add the name of the member to your application. You can also press *Enter* or *Tab* to insert the member. *IntelliSense* can be useful in discovering a class's members and their purpose. Note that the *IntelliSense* window in Fig. 5.10 shows two tabs—**Common** and **All**. The **Common** tab shows the most commonly used features that can appear to the right of the dot operator. The **All** tab shows every feature that can appear to the right of the dot operator.

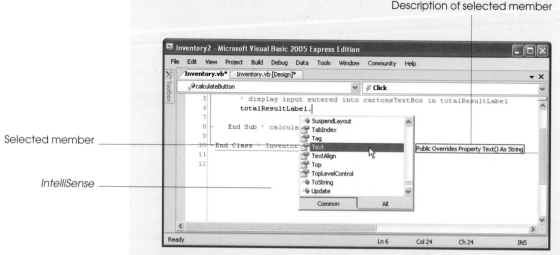

Figure 5.10 *IntelliSense* activating while entering code.

(cont.)

Let's examine line 6 of Fig. 5.9 more closely. Reading the line from left to right, we see totalResultLabel's Text property, followed by an "equals" sign (=), followed by cartonsTextBox's Text property value. The "=" symbol, as used here, is known as the **assignment operator**. The expressions on either side of the assignment operator are referred to as its **operands**. This assignment operator assigns the value on the right of the operator (the **right operand**) to the variable on the left of the operator (the **left operand**). The assignment operator is known as a **binary operator** because it has two operands—totalResultLabel.Text and cartonsTextBox.Text.

The entire statement is called an **assignment statement** because it assigns a value to the left operand. In this example, you are assigning the value of cartonsTextBox's Text property to totalResultLabel's Text property. The statement is read as, "The Text property of totalResultLabel *gets* the value of cartonTextBox's Text property." Note that the right operand is unchanged by the assignment statement.

When the user clicks the **Calculate Total** Button, the event handler will execute, displaying the value the user entered in the **Cartons per shipment:** TextBox in the output Label totalResultLabel. Clearly, this is not the correct result—the correct result is the number of items per carton times the number of cartons per shipment. In the box *Completing the Inventory Application*, you correct this error. Note that we have added a comment in line 8 of Fig. 5.9, indicating the end of our event handler.

Good Programming Practice

Add comments following the **End Sub** keywords to indicate the end of an event handler.

3. ***Running the application.*** Select **Debug > Start Debugging** to run the application (Fig. 5.11). Type 5 into the **Cartons per shipment:** TextBox and 10 into the **Items per carton:** TextBox, then click the **Calculate Total** Button. As you will see, the text of totalResultLabel now incorrectly displays the data, 5, that was entered into the **Cartons per shipment:** TextBox, rather than the correct result, 50.

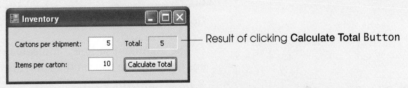
— Result of clicking **Calculate Total** Button

Figure 5.11   Running the application with event handler.

4. ***Closing the application.*** Close the running application by clicking its close box.

SELF-REVIEW

1. Event handlers generated by the Visual Basic IDE follow the naming convention _____.

    a) *controlName_eventName*   b) *eventName_controlName*

    c) *eventNameControlName*   d) *controlNameEventName*

2. The expressions on either side of the assignment operator are referred to as its _____.

    a) operator values   b) results

    c) operands   d) arguments

Answers: 1) a. 2) c.

5.4 Performing a Calculation and Displaying the Result

Now that you are familiar with displaying output in a Label, you will complete the **Inventory** application by displaying the product of the number of cartons per shipment and the number of items per carton. In the following box, you will learn how to perform mathematical operations in Visual Basic.

Completing the Inventory Application

Common Programming Error

Placing anything, including comments, to the right of a line-continuation character is a syntax error. Syntax errors are introduced in the box, *Using the Debugger: Syntax Errors*.

Modified **Inventory** application code

1. *Changing the event handler.* If you are not already in code view, select **View > Code** or click the Inventory.vb tab. Insert underscore (_) characters as shown at the right of lines 3–4. Indent lines 4–5 as shown in Fig. 5.12 by placing the cursor at the beginning of each line's text and pressing the *Tab* key. Then replace the body of calculateButton_Click with the code in lines 7–9 of Fig. 5.12.

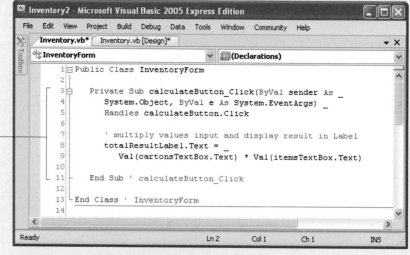

Figure 5.12 Using multiplication in the **Inventory** application.

The comment in line 7 indicates that you will be multiplying the two values input by the user and displaying the result in a Label.

2. *Adding multiline code.* Lines 7–9 perform the multiplication and assignment. You again use the assignment operator to assign a value to totalResultLabel.Text in line 8. To the right of the assignment operator is a space followed by an underscore (_), known as the **line-continuation character**. This character indicates that the next line is a continuation of the previous line. A single statement can contain as many line-continuation characters as necessary. However, at least one whitespace character must precede each line-continuation character. A **whitespace character** is a space, tab or newline (the character inserted by pressing the *Enter* key). This statement has been continued past the current line, so look to the next line for the assignment operator's right operand. We have also used the line-continuation character in lines 3–4 to split the first line of the event handler into three lines; this enables all the program code to fit in the window. The line-continuation character has no effect when placed at the end of a comment.

The assignment operator in line 8 assigns the result of multiplying the numbers input by the user to totalResultLabel.Text. In line 9, Val(cartonsTextBox.Text) is followed by an asterisk (*) and then Val(itemsTextBox.Text). The asterisk is known as the **multiplication operator**—the operator's left and right operands are multiplied together.

Good Programming Practice

A lengthy statement may be spread over several lines. If a single statement must be split across lines, choose breaking points that make sense, such as after an operator. If a statement is split across two or more lines, indent all subsequent lines with one "level" of indentation.

Common Programming Error

Splitting a statement over several lines without including the line-continuation character is a syntax error.

(cont.)

Your **Inventory** application cannot prevent users from accidentally entering nonnumeric input, such as letters and special characters like $ and @. Line 9 uses the **Val function** to prevent inputs like this from terminating the application. A function is a portion of code that performs a task when called (executed) and sends, or returns, a value to the location from which it was called. In this case, the values returned by Val become the values used to perform multiplication (line 9). We call functions (as in line 9) by typing their name followed by parentheses. Any values inside the parentheses (for example, cartonsTextBox.Text) are known as function **arguments**. Arguments are inputs to the function that provide information the function needs to perform its task. In this case, the argument specifies which value you want to send to function Val. You will learn how to create your own functions in Tutorial 13.

Function Val can be used to obtain a value from a string of characters (keyboard input) that is guaranteed to be a number. We use Val because this application is not intended to perform arithmetic calculations with characters that are not numbers. Val reads its argument one character at a time until it encounters a character that is not a number. Once a nonnumeric character is read, Val returns the number it has read up to that point. Val ignores whitespace characters (for example, "33 5" will be converted to 335). Figure 5.13 presents samples of Val calls and their results. Val recognizes the decimal point as a numeric character, and the plus and minus signs when they appear at the beginning of the string (to indicate that a number is positive or negative). Val does not recognize such symbols as commas and dollar signs. If function Val receives an argument that cannot be converted to a number (for example, "b35", which begins with a nonnumeric character), it returns 0. The result of the calculation is assigned to totalResult-Label.Text (line 8), to display the result to the user.

Be careful when using Val, however. Although the value returned is a number, it is not always the value the user intended (see Fig. 5.13). If incorrect data is entered from the user, Val makes no indication of the error. The function returns a value (usually not the value intended by the user) and the application continues, possibly using the incorrect input in calculations. For example, someone entering a monetary amount may enter the text $10.23, which Val will evaluate to 0. Note how a common mistake causes an application to execute incorrectly. Visual Basic provides two ways to handle invalid input. One way is to use Visual Basic's string-processing capabilities to examine input. You will learn about such capabilities as you read this book. The other form of handling invalid input is called exception handling, where you write code to handle errors that may be raised as the application executes. You will learn about exception handling in Tutorial 32.

3. ***Running the application.*** Select **Debug > Start Debugging** to run your application. Now the user can enter data in both TextBoxes. When the **Calculate Total** Button is clicked, the application will multiply the two numbers entered and display the result in totalResultLabel.

4. ***Closing the application.*** Close the running application by clicking its close box.

5. ***Saving the project.*** Select **File > Save All** to save your modified code.

Val Function Call Samples	Results
Val("16")	16
Val("-3")	-3
Val("1.5")	1.5
Val("67a4")	67
Val("8+5")	8
Val("14 Main St.")	14
Val("+1 2 3 4 5")	12345
Val("hello")	0

Figure 5.13 Val function call examples.

Figure 5.14 presents the **Inventory** application's code. The lines of code that contain new programming concepts that you learned in this tutorial are highlighted.

```
1   Public Class InventoryForm
2
3       Private Sub calculateButton_Click(ByVal sender As _
4           System.Object, ByVal e As System.EventArgs) _
5           Handles calculateButton.Click
6
7           ' multiply values input and display result in Label
8           totalResultLabel.Text = _
9               Val(cartonsTextBox.Text) * Val(itemsTextBox.Text)
10
11      End Sub ' calculateButton_Click
12
13  End Class ' InventoryForm
```

Figure 5.14 **Inventory** application code.

SELF-REVIEW

1. _____ provide information that functions need to perform their tasks.
   a) Inputs
   b) Arguments
   c) Outputs
   d) Both a and b.

2. What is the result of Val("%5")?
   a) 5
   b) 0
   c) 500
   d) 0.05

Answers: 1) d. 2) b.

5.5 Using the Debugger: Syntax Errors

So far in this book, you have executed applications by selecting **Debug > Start Debugging**. This compiles and runs the application. If you do not write your code correctly, errors appear in a window known as the **Error List** when the application is compiled. **Debugging** is the process of fixing errors in an application. There are two types of errors: syntax errors and logic errors.

Syntax errors (or compilation errors) occur when code statements violate the grammatical rules of the programming language. Examples of syntax errors include misspellings of keywords or identifiers and failure to use the line-continuation character when splitting a statement across multiple lines. An application cannot be executed until all of its syntax errors are corrected.

Logic errors do not prevent the application from compiling successfully, but do cause the application to produce erroneous results. The Visual Basic IDE contains software called a **debugger** that allows you to analyze the behavior of your application to determine whether it is executing correctly.

You can compile an application without executing it by selecting **Build > Build** *[Project Name]*, where project name appears as the name of your current project. Programmers frequently do this when they wish to determine whether there are any syntax errors in their code. Using either **Debug > Start Debugging** or **Build > Build** *[Project Name]* will display any syntax errors in the **Error List** window. The **Output** window will display the result of the compilation. If this window is not visible, select **Debug > Windows > Output** to view it while debugging. Figure 5.15 displays the output window for an application with no errors.

Figure 5.15 Results of successful build in the **Output** window.

In the Visual Basic IDE, syntax errors appear in the **Error List** window along with a description of each error. Figure 5.16 displays the error that appears when the line-continuation character is left out of a multiple-line statement. For additional information on a syntax error, right click the error statement in the **Error List** window, and select **Show Error Help**. This displays a help page explaining the error message and suggests corrections. Next, you will create syntax errors, view the results and fix the errors.

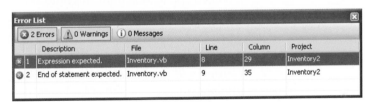

Figure 5.16 **Error List** lists syntax errors.

Using the Debugger: Syntax Errors

1. *Opening the completed application.* If the **Inventory** application is not currently open, locate the `Inventory2.sln` file, then double click it to load your application in the IDE.

2. *Creating your own syntax errors.* You will now create your own syntax errors, for demonstration purposes. If you are not in code view, select **View > Code**. Open the Error List window by selecting **View > Error List**. Add an additional character (`s`) to Label `totalResultLabel` on line 8 and delete the right parenthesis at the end of the assignment statement in line 9. Note the changes to the IDE (Fig. 5.17).

   The Visual Basic IDE provides **real-time error checking**. While manipulating the code in the code editor, you may have noticed that violations of Visual Basic syntax are immediately reported in the **Error List**. The precise location of the syntax error in your code is also emphasized by a blue jagged line. Unrecognized identifier `totalResultsLabel` and the missing parenthesis are reported in the **Error List** (Fig. 5.18).

(cont.)

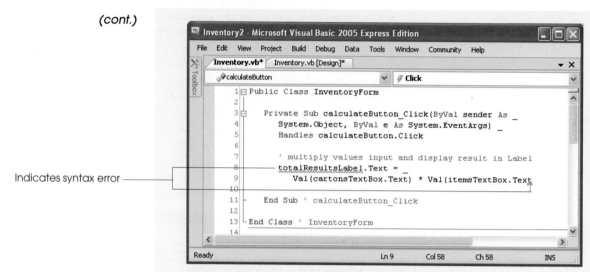

Figure 5.17 IDE with syntax errors.

Indicates syntax error ——

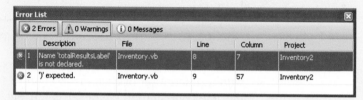

Figure 5.18 **Error List** displaying the syntax errors.

These features notify you of possible errors and give you a chance to fix the error before compiling the application. The IDE will refuse to run your modified application until *all* syntax errors have been corrected.

3. *Locating the syntax errors.* Double clicking an error in the **Error List** window selects the code containing that error. Double click the first error to highlight the error in line 8 (Fig. 5.19).

4. *Getting additional help.* Additional help regarding the syntax error is also available through the **Error List** item's context menu, which you can access by right clicking an item. Right click the **Name 'totalResultsLabel' is not declared** error message from the **Error List**, and select **Show Error Help** (Fig. 5.20). This displays a reference page with information regarding the general form of the syntax error, possible solutions and links to other documentation (Fig. 5.21). After viewing this information, close the help page by clicking its close box.

5. *Fixing the syntax error.* Now that you know how to locate and fix the syntax error, go back to code view and correct the two errors you created in *Step 2.* Notice that the error will be removed from the **Error List** window. When you correct the errors, that the jagged lines do not disappear immediately. However, when you move the cursor to another line, the debugger rechecks the code for errors and removes the jagged underline for each corrected syntax error.

6. *Saving the project.* Select **File > Save All** to save your modified code. The application is now ready to be compiled and executed.

7. *Closing the IDE.* Close the Visual Basic IDE by clicking its close box.

(cont.)

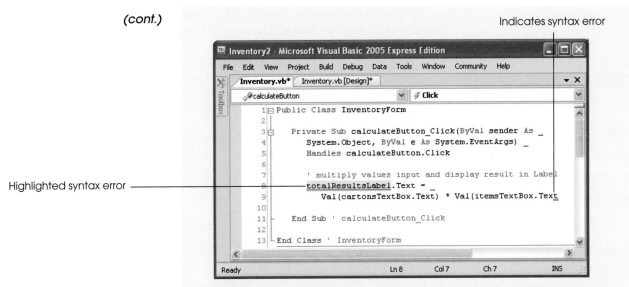

Figure 5.19   Highlighting the portion of code where a syntax error occurs.

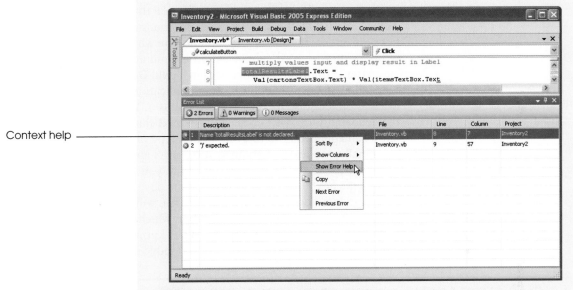

Figure 5.20   Getting additional help.

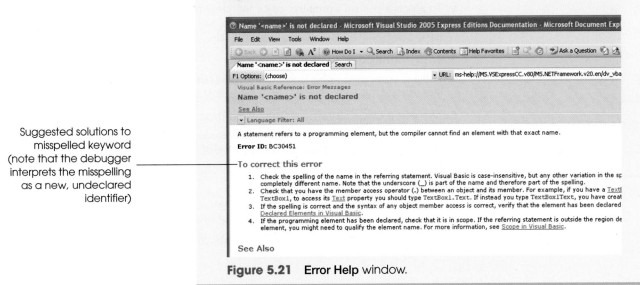

Figure 5.21   **Error Help** window.

In this section, you learned about syntax errors and how to find and correct them. In later tutorials, you will learn to detect and remove logic errors by using the Visual Basic IDE run-time debugger.

---

1. If there are syntax errors in an application, they will appear in a window known as the _____ when the application is compiled.

   a) **Task List**

   b) **Output**

   c) **Properties**

   d) **Error List**

2. A syntax error occurs when _____.

   a) the application terminates unexpectedly

   b) a statement breaks over several lines

   c) a parenthesis is omitted

   d) All of the above.

   Answers: 1) d. 2) d.

5.6 Wrap-Up

In this tutorial, you were introduced to Visual Basic programming. You learned how to use a `TextBox` control to allow users to input data and how to use a `Button` control to signal to your running application that it is to perform a particular action. You learned that the key to good programming is to achieve the right balance between employing visual programming (in which the IDE writes code for you) and writing your own code (nonvisual programming).

After learning about operators in Visual Basic, you wrote a few lines of code as you added an event handler to your application to perform a simple multiplication calculation and display the result to the user. You also used comments to improve the readability of your code. You learned that placing code in an event handler allows an application to respond to that type of event, such as a click of a `Button`.

Finally, you learned about syntax errors and how to use the Visual Basic IDE's debugger to reduce the number of errors you see when you try to run an application. In the next tutorial, you continue the developing of your **Inventory** application by using identifiers to create variables. You will also enhance your **Inventory** application by using the `TextChanged` event, which is raised when the user changes the value in a `TextBox`. After applying your knowledge of variables, you will use the debugger while an application runs to remove a logic error from that application.

SKILLS SUMMARY

Accessing a Property's Value by Using Visual Basic Code

- To access a control's property, place the property name after the control name and the member access operator (`.`). For example, to access the `Text` property of a `TextBox` named `cartonsTextBox`, use `cartonsTextBox.Text`.

Inserting Visual Basic Comments in Code

- Begin the comment with a single-quote character (`'`). A comment can be placed either on its own line (full-line comment) or at the end of a line of code (end-of-line comment).

Continuing a Code Statement Over More Than One Line

- Insert a line-continuation character (`_`), preceded by one or more whitespace characters, to indicate that the next line is a continuation of the preceding line. Only whitespace characters may follow a line-continuation character.

Naming an Event Handler

- Use the format for an event handler, *controlName_eventName*, where *controlName* is the name of the control that the event is related to and *eventName* is the name of the event. When event *eventName* is raised on control *controlName*, event handler *controlName_eventName* executes.

Inserting an Event Handler for a Button Control's Click Event

■ Double click the Button in design view to create an empty event handler; then insert the code that will execute when the event occurs.

Using an Assignment Statement

■ Use the = ("equals" sign) to assign the value of its right operand to its left operand. The entire statement is called an assignment statement because it assigns a value to the left operand (for example, a property).

Using the Multiplication Operator

■ Use an asterisk (*) between the two expressions to be multiplied. The multiplication operator multiplies the right and left operands if both operands contain numeric values. It is a syntax error to use the multiplication operator on values of nonnumeric data types.

Obtaining a Numeric Value from a TextBox

■ Pass the value of the TextBox's Text property to function Val.

Finding a Syntax Error

■ Double click the error message in the **Error List** window, or locate the jagged blue underlined text in your code.

Obtaining Help for a Syntax Error

■ Right click the error message in the **Error List** window, and select **Show Error Help** from the context menu.

KEY TERMS

argument—Inputs to a function that provide information the function needs to perform its task.

assignment operator—The "=" symbol used to assign values in an assignment statement.

assignment statement—A statement that copies one value to another. An assignment statement contains an "equals"-sign (=) operator that causes the value of its right operand to be copied to its left operand.

binary operator—Requires two operands.

case sensitive—The instance where two words that are spelled identically are treated differently if the capitalization of the two words differs.

class definition—The code that belongs to a class, beginning with keywords Public Class and ending with keywords End Class.

class name—The identifier used to identify the name of a class in code.

Class keyword—Begins a class definition.

Click event—An event raised when a user clicks a control.

code editor—A window where a user can create, view or edit an application's code.

code view—A mode of the Visual Basic IDE where the application's code is displayed in an editor window.

comment—A line of code that follows a single-quote character (') and is inserted to improve an application's readability.

debugger—A tool that allows you to analyze the behavior of your application to determine whether it is executing correctly.

debugging—The process of fixing errors in an application.

default property—The value of a property that provides the initial characteristics of an object when it is first created.

dot operator—See member access operator.

End Class keywords—Marks the end of a class definition.

event—A user action that can trigger an event handler.

event handler—A section of code that is executed (called) when a certain event is raised (occurs).

functionality—The actions an application can execute.

identifier—A series of characters consisting of letters, digits and underscores used to name program units such as classes, controls and variables.

***IntelliSense* feature**—Visual Basic IDE feature that aids the programmer during development by providing windows listing available class members and pop-up descriptions for those members.

keyword—A word in code reserved for a specific purpose. By default, these words appear in blue in the IDE and cannot be used as identifiers.

left operand—The expression on the left side of a binary operator.

line-continuation character—An underscore character (_) preceded by one or more spaces, used to continue a statement to the next line of code.

logic error—An error that does not prevent the application from compiling successfully, but does cause the application to produce erroneous results.

member access operator—Also known as the dot operator (.). Allows programmers to access a control's properties using code.

multiplication operator—The asterisk (*) used to multiply two operands, producing their product as a result.

operand—An expression on which an operator performs its task.

real-time error checking—Feature of the Visual Basic IDE that provides immediate notification of possible errors in your code. For example, syntax errors are indicated by blue, jagged underlines in code.

right operand—The expression on the right side of a binary operator.

single-quote character(')—Indicates the beginning of a code comment.

statement—A unit of code that, when compiled and executed, performs an action.

syntax error—An error that occurs when program statements violate the grammatical rules of a programming language.

Val function—Filters a number from its argument if possible. This avoids errors introduced by the entering of nonnumeric data when only numbers are expected. However, the result of the `Val` function is not always what the programmer intended.

whitespace character—A space, tab or newline character.

CONTROLS, EVENTS, PROPERTIES & METHODS

Button   ⓐⓑ Button   This control allows user to raise an action or event.

■ ***In action***

     Calculate Total

■ ***Event***

`Click`—Raised when the user clicks the `Button`.

■ ***Properties***

`Location`—Specifies the location of the `Button` on the `Form` relative to the top-left corner.

`Name`—Specifies the name used to identify the `Button`. The name should be appended with the Button suffix.

`Size`—Specifies the height and width (in pixels) of the `Button`.

`Text`—Specifies the text displayed on the `Button`.

MULTIPLE-CHOICE QUESTIONS

5.1 A(n) _____ represents a user action, such as clicking a `Button`.

     a) statement   b) event

     c) application   d) function

5.2 To switch to code view, select _____.

     a) **Code > View**   b) **Design > Code**

     c) **View > Code**   d) **View > File Code**

5.3 Code that performs the functionality of an application _____.

a) normally is provided by the programmer

b) can never be in the form of an event handler

c) always creates a graphical user interface

d) is always generated by the IDE

5.4 Comments _____.

a) help improve program readability

b) are preceded by the single-quote character

c) are ignored by the compiler　　　d) All of the above.

5.5 The _____ allows a statement to continue past one line (when that character is preceded by one or more whitespace characters).

a) single-quote (') character　　　b) hyphen (-) character

c) underscore (_) character　　　d) plus (+) character

5.6 A(n) _____ causes an application to produce erroneous results.

a) logic error　　　　　　　　b) event

c) assignment statement　　　　d) syntax error

5.7 A portion of code that performs a specific task and returns a value is known as a(n) _____.

a) variable　　　　　　　　b) function

c) operand　　　　　　　　d) identifier

5.8 Visual Basic keywords are _____.

a) identifiers　　　　　　　b) reserved words

c) case sensitive　　　　　　d) properties

5.9 The Visual Basic IDE will refuse to run your application until all _____ errors are corrected.

a) logical　　　　　　　　b) serious

c) syntax　　　　　　　　d) run-time

5.10 An example of a whitespace character is a _____ character.

a) space　　　　　　　　b) tab

c) newline　　　　　　　d) All of the above.

EXERCISES

5.11 *(Inventory Enhancement)* Extend the **Inventory** application to include a TextBox in which the user can enter the number of shipments received in a week. Assume that every shipment has the same number of cartons (each of which has the same number of items). Then modify the code so that the **Inventory** application uses that value in its calculation.

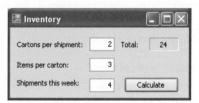

Figure 5.22　Enhanced **Inventory** application GUI.

a) *Copying the template application to your working directory.* Copy the directory C:\Examples\Tutorial05\Exercises\InventoryEnhancement to your C:\SimplyVB directory.

b) *Opening the application's template file.* Double click InventoryEnhancment.sln in the InventoryEnhancement directory to open the application.

c) ***Resizing the Form.*** Resize the Form you used in this tutorial by setting the Size property to 296, 144. Move the Button toward the bottom of the Form, as shown in Fig. 5.22. Its new location should be 184, 78.

d) ***Adding a Label.*** Add a Label to the Form and change the Text property to Shipments this week:. Set the Location property to 8, 80. Set the AutoSize property to False. Then, resize the Label so that the entire text displays. Set the Label's Name property to shipmentsLabel.

e) ***Adding a TextBox.*** Add a TextBox to the right of the Label. Set its Text property to 0 and the Location property to 128, 80. Set the TextAlign and Size properties to the same values as for the other TextBoxes in this tutorial's example. Set the TextBox's Name property to shipmentsTextBox.

f) ***Modifying the code.*** Modify the **Calculate Total** Click event handler so that it multiplies the number of shipments per week with the product of the number of cartons in a shipment and the number of items in a carton.

g) ***Running the application.*** Select **Debug > Start Debugging** to run your application. Enter values for the number of cartons per shipment, items per carton and shipments in the current week. Click the **Calculate** Button and verify that the total displayed is equal to the result when the three values entered are multiplied together. Enter a few sets of input and verify the total each time.

h) ***Closing the application.*** Close your running application by clicking its close box.

i) ***Closing the IDE.*** Close the Visual Basic IDE by clicking its close box.

5.12 *(Counter Application)* Create a counter application. Your counter application will consist of a Label and Button on the Form. The Label initially displays 0, but, each time a user clicks the Button, the value in the Label is increased by 1. When incrementing the Label, you will need to write a statement such as totalLabel.Text = Val(totalLabel.Text) + 1.

Figure 5.23 Counter GUI.

a) ***Creating the application.*** Create a new project named Counter.

b) ***Changing the name of the Form file.*** Change the name of Form1.vb to Counter.vb.

c) ***Modifying a new Form.*** Change your Form's Size property to 168, 144. Modify the Form so that the title reads **Counter**. Change the name of the Form to CounterForm.

d) ***Adding a Label.*** Add a Label to the Form, and place it as shown in Fig. 5.23. Make sure that the Label's Text property is set to 0 and that TextAlign property is set so that any text will appear in the middle (both horizontally and vertically) of the Label. This can be done by using the TextAlign property's MiddleCenter value. Set the BorderStyle property to Fixed3D. Set the Label's Name property to countTotalLabel.

e) ***Adding a Button.*** Add a Button to the Form so that it appears as shown in Fig. 5.23. Set the Button's Text property to contain the text **Count**. Set the Button's Name property to countButton.

f) ***Creating an event handler.*** Add an event handler to the **Count** Button such that the value in the Label increases by 1 each time the user clicks the **Count** Button.

g) ***Running the application.*** Select **Debug > Start Debugging** to run your application. Click the **Count** Button several times and verify that the output value is incremented each time.

h) ***Closing the application.*** Close your running application by clicking its close box.

i) ***Closing the IDE.*** Close the Visual Basic IDE by clicking its close box.

5.13 *(Account Information Application)* Create an application that allows a user to input a name, account number and deposit amount. The user then clicks the **Enter** Button, which causes the name and account number to be copied and displayed in two output Labels. The deposit amount entered will be added to the deposit amount displayed in another output Label. The result is displayed in the same output Label. Every time the **Enter** Button is clicked, the deposit amount entered is added to the deposit amount displayed in the output Label, keeping a cumulative total. When updating the Label, you will need to write a statement such as depositsLabel.Text = Val(depositsLabel.Text) + Val(depositAmount-TextBox).

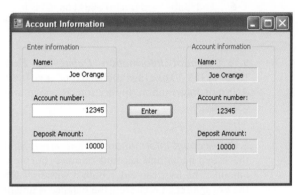

Figure 5.24   **Account Information** GUI.

a) *Copying the template application to your working directory.* Copy the directory C:\Examples\Tutorial05\Exercises\AccountInformation to your C:\SimplyVB directory.

b) *Opening the application's template file.* Double click AccountInformation.sln in the AccountInformation directory to open the application.

c) *Creating an event handler.* Add an event handler for the **Enter** Button's Click event.

d) *Coding the event handler.* Code the event handler to copy information from the **Name:** and **Account number:** TextBoxes to their corresponding output Labels. Then add the value in the **Deposit amount:** TextBox to the **Deposit amount:** output Label, and display the result in the **Deposit amount:** output Label.

e) *Running the application.* Select **Debug > Start Debugging** to run your application. Enter the values in Fig. 5.24 and click the **Enter** Button. Verify that the account information is displayed in the Labels on the right. Enter varying deposit amounts and click the **Enter** Button after each. Verify that the deposit amount on the right has the new values added.

f) *Closing the application.* Close your running application by clicking its close box.

g) *Closing the IDE.* Close the Visual Basic IDE by clicking its close box.

What does this code do? ▶ **5.14** After entering 10 in priceTextBox and 1.05 in taxTextBox, a user clicks the Button named enterButton. What is the result of the click, given the following code?

```
1   Private Sub enterButton_Click(ByVal sender As _
2       System.Object, ByVal e As System.EventArgs) _
3       Handles enterButton.Click
4
5       outputLabel.Text = Val(priceTextBox.Text) * Val(taxTextBox.Text)
6
7   End Sub ' enterButton_Click
```

What's wrong with this code? ▷ **5.15** The following event handler should execute when the user clicks a **Calculate** Button. Identify the error(s) in its code.

```
1  Private Sub calculateButton_Click(ByVal sender As
2     System.Object, ByVal e As System.EventArgs) _ ' second line
3     Handles calculateButton.Click
4
5     resultLabel.Text = priceTextBox.Text * taxTextBox.Text
6  End Sub ' calculateButton_Click
```

Using the Debugger ▷ **5.16** *(Account Information Debugging Exercise)* Copy the directory `C:\Examples\Tutorial05\Exercises\DebuggingExercise` to your `C:\SimplyVB` directory, then run the **Account Information** application. Remove any syntax errors, so that the application runs correctly.

Programming Challenge ▷ **5.17** *(Account Information Enhancement)* Modify Exercise 5.13 so that it no longer asks for the user's name and account number, but now asks the user for a withdrawal or deposit amount. The user can enter both a withdrawal and deposit amount at the same time. When the **Enter** Button is clicked, the balance is updated appropriately.

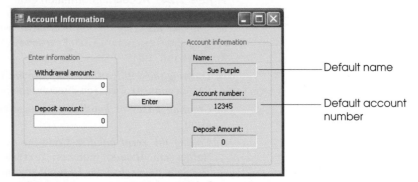

Figure 5.25 Enhanced **Account Information** GUI.

a) *Copying the template application to your working directory.* If you have not already done so, copy the `C:\Examples\Tutorial05\Exercises\AccountInformation` directory to your `C:\SimplyVB` directory.

b) *Opening the application's template file.* Double click `AccountInformation.sln` in the `AccountInformation` directory to open the application.

c) *Modifying the GUI.* Modify the GUI so that it appears as in Fig. 5.25.

d) *Setting the default values.* Set the default name and account number to the values shown in Fig. 5.25 using the **Properties** window.

e) *Writing code to add functionality.* Update the account balance for every withdrawal (which decreases the balance) and every deposit (which increases the balance). When the balance is updated, reset the TextBoxes to "0".

f) *Running the application.* Select **Debug > Start Debugging** to run your application. Enter various withdrawal and deposit amounts, click the **Enter** Button after each. Verify that the balance on the right of the application is updated appropriately after each time the **Enter** Button is clicked.

g) *Closing the application.* Close your running application by clicking its close box.

h) *Closing the IDE.* Close the Visual Basic IDE by clicking its close box.

Objectives

In this tutorial, you will learn to:
- Create variables.
- Handle the **TextChanged** event.
- Apply basic memory concepts using variables.
- Use the precedence rules of arithmetic operators.
- Set breakpoints to debug applications.

Outline

Enhancing the Inventory Application

Introducing Variables, Memory Concepts and Arithmetic

In the previous tutorial, you developed an **Inventory** application that used multiplication to calculate the number of items received into inventory. You learned how to create TextBoxes to read user input from the keyboard. You also added a Button to a Form and programmed that Button to respond to a user's click. In this tutorial, you will enhance your **Inventory** application using additional programming concepts, including variables, events and arithmetic.

6.1 Test-Driving the Enhanced Inventory Application

In this tutorial, you will enhance the previous tutorial's **Inventory** application by inserting code rather than dragging and dropping Visual Basic controls. You will use variables to perform arithmetic in Visual Basic, and you will study memory concepts to help you understand how applications run on computers. Recall that your **Inventory** application from Tutorial 5 calculated the number of items received from information supplied by the user—the number of cartons and the number of textbooks per carton. The enhanced application must meet the following requirements:

> ### Application Requirements
>
> *The inventory manager notices a flaw in your **Inventory** application. Although the application calculates the correct result, that result continues to display even after new data is entered. The only time the output changes is when the inventory manager clicks the **Calculate Button** again. You need to alter the **Inventory** application to clear the result as soon as the user enters new information into either of the TextBoxes, to avoid any confusion over the accuracy of your calculated result.*

You will begin by test-driving the completed application. Then you will learn the additional Visual Basic technologies that you will need to create your own version of this application. At first glance, the application does not seem to operate any differently from the application in the previous tutorial. However, you should notice that the **Total:** Label clears when you enter new data into either of the TextBoxes.

Test-Driving the Enhanced Inventory Application

1. *Opening the completed application.* Open the C:\Examples\Tutorial06\ CompletedApplication\Inventory3 directory to locate the enhanced **Inventory** application. Double click Inventory3.sln to open the application in the Visual Basic IDE. If the Form does not appear in design view, double click Inventory.vb in the **Solutions Explorer** window. In general, if the IDE does not open the Form in design view, you will need to double click the Form's file name in the **Solution Explorer** window.

2. *Running the Inventory application.* Select **Debug > Start Debugging** to run the application (Fig. 6.1).

Figure 6.1 **Inventory** application GUI displayed when the application runs.

3. *Calculating the number of items in the shipment.* Enter 5 in the **Cartons per shipment:** TextBox and 6 in the **Items per carton:** TextBox. Click the **Calculate Total** Button. The result will be displayed in the **Total:** output Label (Fig. 6.2).

Figure 6.2 Running the **Inventory** application.

4. *Entering new quantities.* After you modify the application, the result displayed in the **Total:** Label will be removed when the user enters a new quantity in either TextBox. Enter 13 as the new number of cartons—the last calculation's result is cleared (Fig. 6.3). This is explained later in this tutorial.

— Cleared output Label

Figure 6.3 Enhanced **Inventory** application clears output Label after new input.

5. *Closing the application.* Close your running application by clicking its close box.

6. *Closing the IDE.* Close the Visual Basic IDE by clicking its close box.

Good Programming Practice

Typically, variable-name identifiers begin with a lowercase letter. Every word in the name after the first word should begin with a capital letter, for example, firstNumber.

6.2 Variables

A **variable** holds data for your application, much as the Text property of a Label holds the text to be displayed to the user. Unlike the Text property of a Label, however, variable values are not shown to the user by default. Using variables in an application allows you to store and manipulate data without necessarily showing the data to the user and to store data without adding or using controls. Variables store such data as numbers, the date, the time and so on. However, each variable used in Visual Basic corresponds to exactly one type of information. For example, a variable that stores a number cannot be used to store text.

In Visual Basic, all variables must be **declared**, or reported, to the compiler by using program code. All **declarations** that you will make within event handlers begin with the keyword **Dim**. Recall that keywords are reserved for use by Visual Basic. (A complete list of Visual Basic keywords is presented in Appendix E.)

The following box introduces programming with variables. A variable name can be any valid identifier, which, as you learned in Tutorial 5, is a name that the compiler will recognize (and is not a keyword). As you also learned in the last tutorial, there are many valid characters for identifiers.

Good Programming Practice

Use only letters and digits as characters for your variable names.

Using Variables in the Inventory Application

1. *Copying the template to your working directory.* Copy the `C:\Examples\ Tutorial06\TemplateApplication\Inventory3` directory to your `C:\SimplyVB` directory.

2. *Opening the Inventory application's template file.* Double click `Inventory3.sln` in the `Inventory3` directory to open the application in the Visual Basic IDE.

3. *Adding variable declarations to event handler* `calculateButton_Click`. If you are in design view, enter code view by selecting **View > Code**. Add lines 7–10 of Fig. 6.4 to event handler `calculateButton_Click`. Lines 8–10 are declarations, which begin with keyword `Dim`. Note that, when you type the word `Dim`, as with all keywords, the IDE colors it blue by default. The words `cartons`, `items` and `result` are the names of variables. Lines 8–10 declare that variables `cartons`, `items` and `result` store data of type **Integer**, using the **As** keyword. The `As` keyword indicates that the following word (in this case `Integer`) is the variable type. `Integer` variables store **integer** values (whole numbers such as 919, 0 and –11). Data types already defined in Visual Basic, such as `Integer`, are known as **built-in data types** or **primitive data types**. Primitive data type names are also keywords. The 15 primitive data types are listed in Fig. 6.6. You will use some of these data types throughout the book. Notice that the IDE initially underlines the variables to indicate that they have not been used in the application. This is to safeguard against including any unnecessary variables in your application.

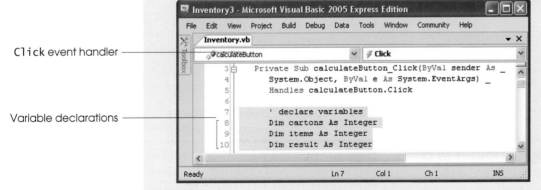

Click event handler

Variable declarations

Figure 6.4   Declaring variables in event handler `calculateButton_Click`.

(cont.)

4. **Retrieving input from TextBoxes.** Skip one line after the variable declarations, and add lines 12–14 of Fig. 6.5 in event handler calculateButton_Click. Once the user enters numbers and clicks **Calculate Total**, the values found in the Text property of the TextBox controls are converted to numerical values by the Val function. Then the numbers are assigned to variables cartons (line 13) and items (line 14) with the assignment operator, =. Line 13 is read as "cartons *gets* the result of the Val function applied to cartonsTextBox.Text."

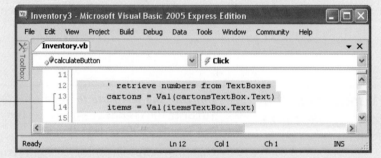

Assigning user input to variables

Figure 6.5 Retrieving numerical input from TextBoxes.

5. **Saving the project.** Select **File > Save All** to save your modified code.

The Val function returns a numerical value as data type **Double** when converting a value retrieved from a TextBox's Text property. Data type Double is used to store both whole and fractional numbers. Normally, Doubles store floating-point numbers, which are numbers with decimal points such as 2.3456 and –845.4680. Variables of data type Double can hold much larger values than variables of data type Integer.

After Val converts the two values typed by the user to Doubles, lines 13–14 implicitly convert the Doubles to Integer values. The integer value obtained by converting the Double in line 13 is assigned to variable cartons. Likewise, the integer value obtained by converting the Double in line 14 is assigned to variable items. Because Doubles and Integers are different types of variables, Visual Basic performs a conversion from one type to the other. This process is called **implicit conversion** because the conversion takes place without any additional code. Now that you have assigned values to your new variables, you use the variables to calculate the number of textbooks received.

Built-in (primitive) data types

Boolean	Date	Integer	Long	Short
Byte	Decimal	Single	Char	Double
SByte	String	UInteger	ULong	UShort

Figure 6.6 Visual Basic built-in data types.

Using Variables in a Calculation

1. **Performing the multiplication operation.** Skip one line from the end of the last statement you inserted and insert lines 16–17 in event handler calculateButton_Click (Fig. 6.7). The statement in line 17 will multiply the Integer variable cartons by items and assign the result to variable result, using the assignment operator =. The statement is read as, "result *gets* the value of cartons * items." (Most calculations are performed in assignment statements.)

(cont.)

2. ***Displaying the result.*** Add lines 19–20 of Fig. 6.7 to event handler `calculateButton_Click`. After the calculation is completed, line 20 will display the result of the multiplication operation. The number sets the value of Label `totalResultLabel`'s Text property. Once the property is updated, the Label will display the result of the multiplication operation (Fig. 6.8).

3. ***Running the application.*** Select **Debug > Start Debugging** to run your application. Enter 5 in the **Cartons per shipment:** TextBox and 6 in the **Items per carton:** TextBox. Then click the **Calculate Total** Button to test your application.

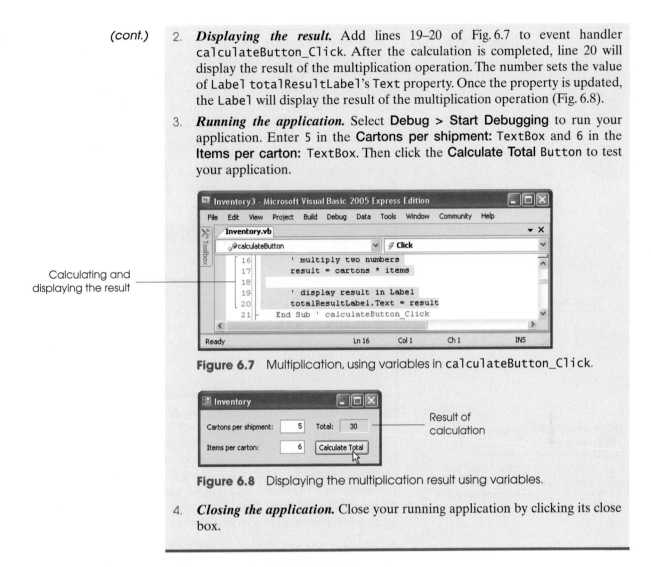

Calculating and displaying the result

Figure 6.7   Multiplication, using variables in `calculateButton_Click`.

Result of calculation

Figure 6.8   Displaying the multiplication result using variables.

4. ***Closing the application.*** Close your running application by clicking its close box.

SELF-REVIEW   1. When Visual Basic converts a `Double` to an `Integer` without requiring any code, this is referred to as a(n) _____.

   a) explicit conversion   b) implicit conversion
   c) data-type change   d) transformation

2. Data types already defined in Visual Basic, such as `Integer`, are known as _____ data types.

   a) provided   b) existing
   c) defined   d) built-in

Answers: 1) b. 2) d.

6.3 Handling the TextChanged Event

You may have noticed that the flaw, or **bug**, mentioned in the application requirements at the beginning of this tutorial remains in your application. Although `totalResultLabel` displays the current result, once you enter a new number into a TextBox, that result is no longer valid. However, the result displayed does not change again until you click the **Calculate Total** Button, potentially confusing anyone using the application. Visual Basic provides a convenient way to deal with this problem. In the next box, you will add event handlers to clear the output whenever new data is entered.

Handling the TextChanged Event

1. ***Adding an event handler for cartonsTextBox's TextChanged event.*** Switch to the IDE's Design View and double click the **Cartons per shipment:** TextBox to generate an event handler for the **TextChanged** event, which is raised when the TextBox's text changes. This is the default event for Text-Boxes. The IDE will then generate an event handler with an empty body (no additional code) and place the cursor in the body. Insert line 28 of Fig. 6.9 into your code. Note that we have added line-continuation characters (_) at the ends of lines 24 and 25 of this code, as well as a comment in line 23, before the event handler. Recall from Tutorial 5 that using line-continuation characters increases code readability by avoiding long lines that don't fit in the window.

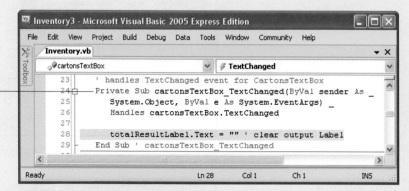

TextChanged event handler

Figure 6.9   TextChanged event handler for **Cartons per shipment:** TextBox.

According to the application requirements for this tutorial, the application should clear the value in `totalResultLabel` every time users change the text in either TextBox. Line 28 clears the value in `totalResultLabel`. The notation "" (side-by-side double quotes) in line 28 is called an **empty string**, which is a value that does not contain any characters. This empty string replaces whatever is stored in `totalResultLabel.Text`.

2. ***Adding an event handler for itemsTextBox's TextChanged event.*** We want the result cleared regardless of which TextBox changes value first. Return to design view by clicking the **Inventory.vb [Design]** tab. Then double click the **Items per carton:** TextBox, and insert line 36 from Fig. 6.10 into the new event handler. Note that these lines perform the same task as line 28—we want the same action to occur, namely, the clearing of a TextBox.

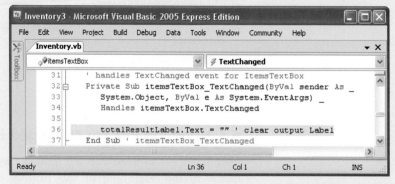

Figure 6.10   TextChanged event handler for **Items per carton:** TextBox.

Good Programming Practice

If a statement is wider than the code editor window, use the line-continuation character within the statement to continue it on the next line.

(cont.)   3. ***Running the application.*** Select **Debug > Start Debugging** to run your
application. To test the application, enter 8 in the **Cartons per shipment:**
TextBox and 7 in the **Items per carton:** TextBox. When you click the **Cal-
culate Total** Button, the number 56 should appear in the output Label.
Then enter 9 in the **Items per carton:** TextBox to ensure that the Text-
Changed event handler clears the output Label.

4. ***Closing the application.*** Close your running application by clicking its close
box.

Figure 6.11 presents the source code for the enhanced **Inventory** application.
The lines of code that contain new programming concepts that you learned in this
tutorial are highlighted.

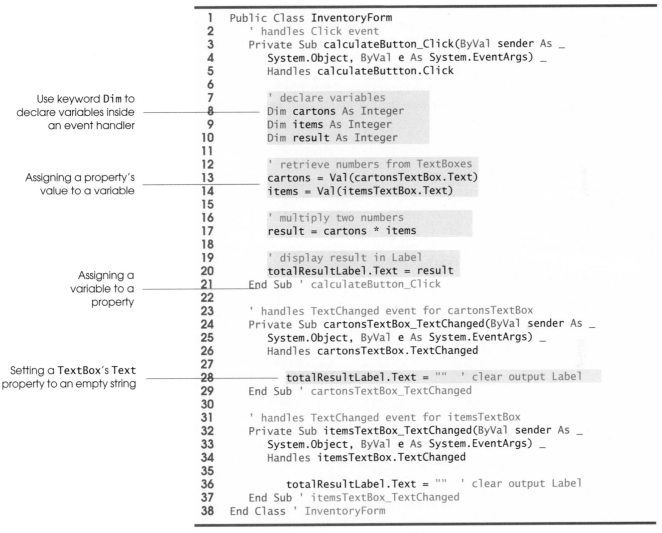

Use keyword **Dim** to
declare variables inside
an event handler

Assigning a property's
value to a variable

Assigning a
variable to a
property

Setting a **TextBox**'s **Text**
property to an empty string

```
 1  Public Class InventoryForm
 2      ' handles Click event
 3      Private Sub calculateButton_Click(ByVal sender As _
 4          System.Object, ByVal e As System.EventArgs) _
 5          Handles calculateButtton.Click
 6
 7          ' declare variables
 8          Dim cartons As Integer
 9          Dim items As Integer
10          Dim result As Integer
11
12          ' retrieve numbers from TextBoxes
13          cartons = Val(cartonsTextBox.Text)
14          items = Val(itemsTextBox.Text)
15
16          ' multiply two numbers
17          result = cartons * items
18
19          ' display result in Label
20          totalResultLabel.Text = result
21      End Sub ' calculateButton_Click
22
23      ' handles TextChanged event for cartonsTextBox
24      Private Sub cartonsTextBox_TextChanged(ByVal sender As _
25          System.Object, ByVal e As System.EventArgs) _
26          Handles cartonsTextBox.TextChanged
27
28          totalResultLabel.Text = ""  ' clear output Label
29      End Sub ' cartonsTextBox_TextChanged
30
31      ' handles TextChanged event for itemsTextBox
32      Private Sub itemsTextBox_TextChanged(ByVal sender As _
33          System.Object, ByVal e As System.EventArgs) _
34          Handles itemsTextBox.TextChanged
35
36          totalResultLabel.Text = ""  ' clear output Label
37      End Sub ' itemsTextBox_TextChanged
38  End Class ' InventoryForm
```

Figure 6.11   **Inventory** application code.

SELF-REVIEW   1. The _____ is represented by "" in Visual Basic.

a) empty character   b) empty string

c) empty value   d) None of the above.

2. Use property _____ to remove any text displayed in a TextBox.
   a) `ClearText`
   b) `Remove`
   c) `Display`
   d) `Text`

Answers: 1) b. 2) d.

6.4 Memory Concepts

Variable names—such as `cartons`, `items` and `result`—correspond to actual locations in the computer's memory. Every variable has a **name**, **type**, **size** and **value**. In the **Inventory** application code listing in Fig. 6.11, when the assignment statement (line 13)

```
cartons = Val(cartonsTextBox.Text)
```

executes, the user input stored in `cartonsTextBox.Text` is converted to an Integer. This Integer is placed in the memory location to which the name `cartons` has been assigned by the compiler. Suppose that the user enters the characters 12 in the **Cartons per shipment:** TextBox. This input is stored in `cartonsTextBox.Text`. When the user clicks **Calculate Total**, line 13 converts the user input to an Integer and places the Integer value 12 in location `cartons`, as shown in Fig. 6.12.

Figure 6.12 Memory location showing name and value of variable `cartons`.

Whenever a value is placed in a memory location, this value replaces the value previously stored in that location. The previous value is overwritten (lost).

Suppose that the user then enters the characters 10 in the **Items per carton:** TextBox and clicks **Calculate Total**. Line 14 of Fig. 6.11

```
items = Val(itemsTextBox.Text)
```

converts `itemsTextBox.Text` to an Integer, placing the Integer value 10 in location `items`, and memory appears as shown in Fig. 6.13.

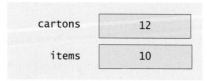

Figure 6.13 Memory locations after values for variables `cartons` and `items` have been input.

Once the **Calculate Total** Button is clicked, line 17 multiplies these values and places their total into variable `result`. The statement

```
result = cartons * items
```

performs the multiplication and replaces (that is, overwrites) `result`'s previous value. After `result` is calculated, the memory appears as shown in Fig. 6.14. Note that the values of `cartons` and `items` appear exactly as they did before they were used in the calculation of `result`. Although these values were used when the computer performed the calculation, they were not destroyed. This illustrates that when a value is read from a memory location, the process is **nondestructive** (meaning that the value is not overwritten).

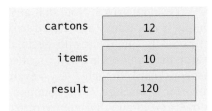

Figure 6.14 Memory locations after a multiplication operation.

SELF-REVIEW
1. When a value is placed into a memory location, the value _____ the previous value into that location.

   a) copies
   b) replaces
   c) adds itself to
   d) moves

2. When a value is read from memory, that value is _____.

   a) overwritten
   b) replaced with a new value
   c) moved to a new location in memory
   d) not overwritten

Answers: 1) b. 2) d.

6.5 Arithmetic

Most programs perform arithmetic calculations. In the last tutorial, you performed the arithmetic operation multiplication by using the multiplication operator (*). The **arithmetic operators** are summarized in Fig. 6.15. Note the use of various special symbols not used in algebra. For example, the **asterisk** (*) indicates multiplication, the keyword **Mod** represents the **modulus operator**, the **backslash** (\) represents integer division and the **caret** (^) represents exponentiation. Most of the arithmetic operators in Fig. 6.15 are binary operators, each requiring two operands.

Visual Basic .NET operation	Arithmetic operator	Algebraic expression	Visual Basic .NET expression
Addition	+	$f + 7$	f + 7
Subtraction	–	$p - c$	p - c
Multiplication	*	bm	b * m
Division (float)	/	x / y or $\frac{x}{y}$ or $x \div y$	x / y
Division (integer)	\	none	v \ u
Modulus	Mod	r mod s	r Mod s
Exponentiation	^	q^p	q ^ p
Unary Negative	–	$-e$	-e
Unary Positive	+	$+g$	+g

Figure 6.15 Arithmetic operators.

For example, the expression sum + value contains the binary operator + and the two operands sum and value. Visual Basic also provides **unary operators**, which are operators that take only one operand. For example, unary versions of plus (+) and minus (–) are provided so that programmers can write expressions such as +9 (a positive number) and –19 (a negative number).

Visual Basic has separate operators for **integer division** (the backslash, \) and **floating-point division** (the forward slash, /). Floating-point division divides two numbers (whole or fractional) and returns a floating-point number (a number with a decimal point). The operator for integer division treats its operands as integers and returns an integer result. Integer division takes two Integer operands and yields an Integer result; for example, the expression 7 \ 4 evaluates to 1, and the expression 17 \ 5 evaluates to 3. Note that any fractional part in the Integer division result simply is discarded (also called truncated)—no rounding occurs. When floating-point numbers (numbers with decimal points) are used with the integer-division operator, the numbers are first rounded to the nearest whole number, then divided. This means that, although 7.1 \ 4 evaluates to 1 as expected, the statement 7.7 \ 4 evaluates to 2, because 7.7 is rounded to 8 before the division occurs. Neither division operator allows division by zero. If your code divides by zero, a run-time error occurs. By default, this error will terminate the application.

The modulus operator, Mod, yields the remainder after division. The expression x Mod y yields the remainder after x is divided by y. Thus, 7 Mod 4 yields 3, and 17 Mod 5 yields 2. This operator is used most commonly with Integer operands, but also can be used with other types. The modulus operator can be applied to several interesting problems, such as discovering whether one number is a multiple of another. If a and b are numbers, a Mod b yields 0 if a is a multiple of b. 8 Mod 3 yields 2, so 8 is not a multiple of 3. But 8 Mod 2 and 8 Mod 4 each yield 0, because 8 is a multiple both of 2 and of 4.

Arithmetic expressions in Visual Basic must be written in **straight-line form** so that you can type them into a computer. For example, the division of 7.1 by 4.3 cannot be written

$$\frac{7.1}{4.3}$$

but is written in straight-line form as 7.1 / 4.3. Raising 3 to the 2nd power cannot be written as 3^2, but is written in straight line form as 3 ^ 2.

Parentheses are used in Visual Basic expressions to group operations in the same manner as in algebraic expressions. To multiply *a* times the quantity *b* + *c*, you write

a * (b + c)

Visual Basic applies the operators in arithmetic expressions in a precise sequence, determined by the **rules of operator precedence,** which are generally the same as those followed in algebra. These rules enable Visual Basic to apply operators in the correct order.

Common Programming Error

Attempting to divide by zero is a **runtime error** (that is, an error that has its effect while the application executes). Dividing by zero terminates an application.

Rules of Operator Precedence

1. *Operators in expressions contained within a pair of parentheses are evaluated first*. Thus, *parentheses can be used to force the order of evaluation to occur in any sequence desired by the programmer*. Parentheses are at the highest level of precedence. With **nested** (or **embedded**) parentheses, the operators contained in the innermost pair of parentheses are applied first.

2. *Exponentiation is applied next*. If an expression contains several exponentiation operations, operators are applied from left to right.

3. *Unary positive and negative, + and -, are applied next*. If an expression contains several sign operations, operators are applied from left to right.

4. *Multiplication and floating-point division operations are applied next*. If an expression contains several multiplication and floating-point division operations, operators are applied from left to right.

5. *Integer division is applied next*. If an expression contains several Integer division operations, operators are applied from left to right.

6. *Modulus operations are applied next*. If an expression contains several modulus operations, operators are applied from left to right.

7. *Addition and subtraction operations are applied last*. If an expression contains several addition and subtraction operations, operators are applied from left to right.

Note that we mention nested parentheses. Not all expressions with several pairs of parentheses contain nested parentheses. For example, although the expression

    a * (b + c) + c * (d + e)

contains multiple pairs of parentheses, none of the parentheses are nested. These sets of parentheses are referred to as being "on the same level" and are evaluated from left to right.

Let's consider several expressions in light of the rules of operator precedence. Each example lists an algebraic expression and its Visual Basic equivalent.

The following calculates the average of three numbers:

Algebra: $m = \dfrac{(a + b + c)}{3}$

Visual Basic: m = (a + b + c) / 3

The parentheses are required because floating-point division has higher precedence than addition. The entire quantity (a + b + c) is to be divided by 3. If the parentheses are omitted, erroneously, we obtain a + b + c / 3, which evaluates as

$a + b + \dfrac{c}{3}$

The following is the equation of a straight line:

Algebra: $y = mx + b$

Visual Basic: y = m * x + b

No parentheses are required. The multiplication is applied first, because multiplication has a higher precedence than addition. The assignment occurs last because it has a lower precedence than multiplication and addition.

To develop a better understanding of the rules of operator precedence, consider how the expression $y = ax^2 + bx + c$ is evaluated:

    y = a * x ^ 2 + b * x + c
          ⑥   ②   ①   ④   ③   ⑤

The circled numbers under the statement indicate the order in which Visual Basic applies the operators. Remember that in Visual Basic x^2 is represented as x ^ 2. Also, note that the assignment operator is applied last because it has a lower precedence than any of the arithmetic operators.

As in algebra, it is acceptable to place unnecessary parentheses in an expression to make the expression easier to read—these parentheses are called **redundant parentheses**. For example, the preceding assignment statement might use redundant parentheses to emphasize terms:

    y = (a * x ^ 2) + (b * x) + c

Good Programming Practice

Using redundant parentheses in complex arithmetic expressions can make the expressions easier to read.

SELF-REVIEW

1. Arithmetic expressions in Visual Basic must be written _____ to facilitate entering applications into the computer.

    a) using parentheses   b) on multiple lines

    c) in straight-line form   d) None of the above.

2. The expression to the right of the assignment operator (=) is always evaluated _____ the assignment occurs.

    a) before   b) after

    c) at the same time   d) None of the above.

Answers: 1) c. 2) a.

6.6 Using the Debugger: Breakpoints

The debugger will be one of your most important tools in developing applications, once you become familiar with its features. You were introduced to the debugger in Tutorial 5, where you used it to locate and eliminate syntax errors. In this tutorial, you continue your study of the debugger, learning about breakpoints, which allow you to examine what your application is doing while it is running. A **breakpoint** is a marker that can be set at any executable line of code. When application execution reaches a breakpoint, execution pauses, allowing you to peek inside your application and ensure that there are no logic errors, such as an incorrect calculation. In the next box, *Using the Debugger: Breakpoints*, you learn how to use breakpoints in the Visual Basic IDE debugger.

Using the Debugger:
Breakpoints

1. ***Inserting breakpoints in the Visual Basic IDE.*** Ensure that the Inventory3 project is open in the IDE's Code view. To insert a breakpoint in the IDE, either click inside the **margin indicator bar** (the gray margin indicator at the left of the code window, Fig. 6.16) next to the line of code at which you wish to break, or right click that line of code and select **Breakpoint > Insert Breakpoint**. You can set as many breakpoints as necessary. Set breakpoints at lines 17 and 20 of your code. A solid maroon circle appears where you clicked, indicating that a breakpoint has been set (Fig. 6.16). When the application runs, it suspends execution at any line that contains a breakpoint. The application is said to be in **break mode** when the debugger pauses the application's execution. Breakpoints can be set during design mode, break mode and run mode.

Margin indicator bar ——

Breakpoints ——

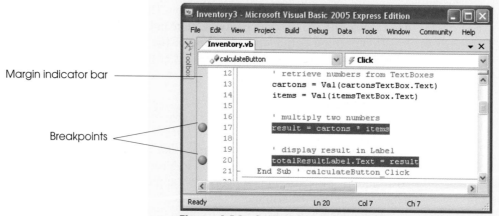

Figure 6.16 Setting two breakpoints.

2. ***Beginning the debugging process.*** After setting breakpoints in the code editor, select **Debug > Start Debugging** to begin the debugging process. During debugging of a Windows application, the application window appears (Fig. 6.17), allowing application interaction (input and output). Enter 10 and 7 into the Textboxes and click **Calculate Total** to continue. The title bar of the IDE will now display **(Debugging)** (Fig. 6.18), indicating that the IDE is in break mode.

3. ***Examining application execution.*** Application execution suspends at the first breakpoint, and the IDE becomes the **active window** (Fig. 6.19). The yellow arrow to the left of line 17 indicates that this line contains the next statement to execute.

(cont.)

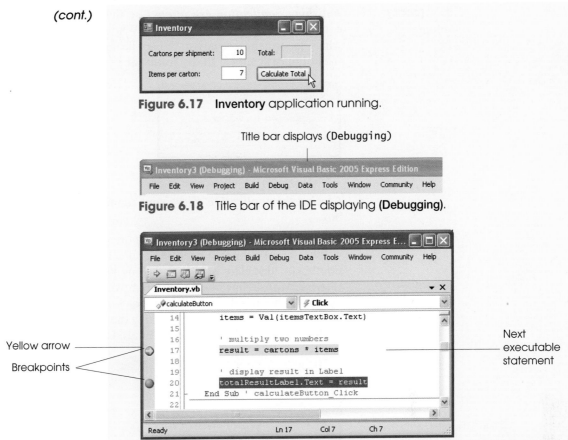

Figure 6.17　**Inventory** application running.

Title bar displays **(Debugging)**

Figure 6.18　Title bar of the IDE displaying **(Debugging)**.

Yellow arrow

Breakpoints

Next executable statement

Figure 6.19　Application execution suspended at the first breakpoint.

4. ***Using the Continue command to resume execution.*** To resume execution, select **Debug > Continue**. The application executes until it stops at the next breakpoint, in line 20. Note that when you place your mouse pointer over the variable name `result`, the value that the variable stores is displayed in a *Quick Info* box (Fig. 6.20). In a sense, you are peeking inside the computer at the value of one of your variables. As you'll see, this can help you spot logic errors in your applications.

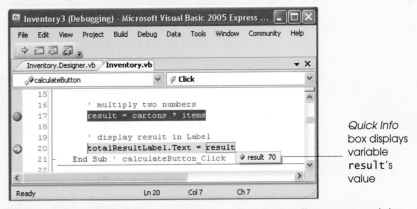

Quick Info box displays variable `result`'s value

Figure 6.20　Displaying a variable value by placing the mouse pointer over a variable name.

(cont.)

5. ***Finishing application execution.*** Use the **Debug > Continue** command to complete the application execution. When there are no more breakpoints at which to suspend execution, the application will execute to completion and the output will appear in the **Total:** Label (Fig. 6.21).

Figure 6.21 Application output.

6. ***Closing the application.*** Close your running application by clicking its close box.

7. ***Disabling a breakpoint.*** To disable a breakpoint, right click a line of code in which a breakpoint has been set, and select **Breakpoint > Disable Breakpoint**. The disabled breakpoint is indicated by a hollow maroon circle (Fig. 6.22). Disabling rather than removing a breakpoint allows you to re-enable the breakpoint (by clicking inside the hollow circle) in an application. This also can be done by right clicking the line marked by the hollow maroon circle and selecting **Breakpoint > Enable Breakpoint**.

Disabled breakpoint ——

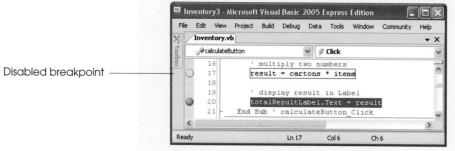

Figure 6.22 Disabled breakpoint.

8. ***Removing a breakpoint.*** To remove a breakpoint that you no longer need, right click a line of code in which a breakpoint has been set and select **Breakpoint > Delete Breakpoint**. You also can remove a breakpoint by clicking the maroon circle in the margin indicator bar.

9. ***Saving the project.*** Select **File > Save All** to save your modified code.

10. ***Closing the IDE.*** Close the Visual Basic IDE by clicking its close box.

In this section, you learned how to enable the debugger and set breakpoints so that you can examine the results of code while an application is running. You also learned how to continue execution after an application suspends execution at a breakpoint and how to disable and remove breakpoints.

SELF-REVIEW

1. A breakpoint cannot be set at a(n) _____.
   a) comment
   b) executable line of code
   c) assignment statement
   d) arithmetic statement

2. When application execution suspends at a breakpoint, the next statement to be executed is the statement _____ the breakpoint.
   a) before
   b) after
   c) at
   d) None of the above.

Answers: 1) a. 2) c.

6.7 Internet and Web Resources

Please take a moment to visit each of these sites briefly. To save typing time, use the hot links on the enclosed CD or at www.deitel.com.

www.devx.com/dotnet
This Web site contains information about the .NET platform, which includes Visual Basic. The site includes links to articles, books and news.

www.vbcity.com
This site lists numerous links to articles, books and tutorials on Visual Basic. The site allows programmers to submit code and have it rated by other developers. The site also polls visitors on a variety of Visual Basic topics and provides access to archives that include code listings and news.

www.cyber-matrix.com/vb.htm
This site links to Visual Basic tutorials, books, tips and tricks, controls, programming tools, magazines, newsgroups and more.

searchvb.techtarget.com
This site offers a search engine designed specifically to discover Visual Basic Web sites.

6.8 Wrap-Up

You have now added variables to your **Inventory** application. You began by using variables to produce the same results as your previous **Inventory** application. Then you enhanced the **Inventory** application, using the TextChanged event, which allowed you to execute code that cleared the value in the output Label when the user changed a value in either TextBox.

You learned about memory concepts, including how variables are read and written. You will apply these concepts to the applications that you will build in later tutorials, which rely heavily on the use of variables. You learned how to perform arithmetic in Visual Basic, and you studied the rules of operator precedence to evaluate mathematical expressions correctly. Finally, you learned how to insert breakpoints in the debugger. Breakpoints allow you to pause application execution and examine variable values. This capability will prove useful to you in finding and fixing logic errors.

In the next tutorial, you will design a graphical user interface and write code to create a wage calculator. You will use pseudocode, an informal language that will help you design the application. You will learn to use the debugger's **Watch** window, another useful tool that will help you remove logic errors.

SKILLS SUMMARY

Declaring a Variable
- Use the keyword Dim.
- Use a valid identifier as a variable name.
- Use the keyword As to indicate that the following word specifies the variable's data type.
- Specify a type such as Integer or Double.

Handling a TextBox's TextChanged Event
- Double click a TextBox on a Form to generate an empty TextChanged event handler.
- Insert code into the event handler that executes when the text in a TextBox changes.

Reading a Value from a Memory Location
- Use the variable's name (as declared in the variable's Dim statement) on the right side of an assignment statement.

Replacing a Value in a Memory Location
- Use the variable name, followed by the assignment operator (=), followed by an expression giving the new value.

Representing Positive and Negative Numbers

■ Use the unary versions of plus (+) and minus (−).

Performing Arithmetic Operations

■ Write arithmetic expressions in Visual Basic in straight-line form.

■ Use the operator precedence rules to determine the order in which operators are applied.

■ Use operator + to perform addition.

■ Use operator − to perform subtraction.

■ Use operator * to perform multiplication.

■ Use operator / to perform floating-point division.

■ Use operator \ (backslash) to perform Integer division, which treats the operands as Integers and returns an Integer result.

■ Use operator ^ to perform exponentiation.

■ Use the modulus operator, Mod, to report the remainder after division.

■ Use parenthesis to manage the order of operations or to clarify expressions.

Setting a Breakpoint

■ Click the margin indicator bar (the gray margin indicator at the left of the code window) next to the line at which you wish to break, or right click a line of code and select **Breakpoint > Insert Breakpoint**.

Resuming Application Execution after Entering Break Mode

■ Select **Debug > Continue**.

Disabling a Breakpoint

■ Right click a line of code containing a breakpoint, and select **Breakpoint > Disable Breakpoint**.

Removing a Breakpoint

■ Right click a line of code containing a breakpoint, and select **Breakpoint > Delete Breakpoint**.

■ You also can remove a breakpoint by clicking the maroon circle in the margin indicator bar.

Enabling a Breakpoint

■ Enable a disabled breakpoint by clicking inside the hollow circle in the margin indicator bar.

■ You also can enable a disabled breakpoint by right clicking the line marked by the hollow maroon circle and selecting **Breakpoint > Enable Breakpoint**.

KEY TERMS

active window—The front-most window on your screen.

arithmetic operators—The operators +, −, *, /, \, ^ and Mod.

As keyword—Used in variable declarations. Indicates that the following word (such as Integer) is the variable type.

asterisk (*)—Multiplication operator. The operator's left and right operands are multiplied together.

backslash (\)—Integer division operator. The operator divides its left operand by its right and returns an integer result.

break mode—The IDE mode when application execution is suspended. This mode is entered through the debugger.

breakpoint—A location where execution is to suspend, indicated by a solid maroon circle.

bug—A flaw in a program that prevents it from executing correctly.

built-in data type—A data type already defined in Visual Basic, such as an Integer (also known as a primitive data type).

caret (^)—Exponentiation operator. This operator raises its left operand to a power specified by the right operand.

declaration—The reporting of a new variable to the compiler. The variable can then be used in the Visual Basic code.

declare a variable—Report the name and type of a variable to the compiler.

Dim keyword—Indicates the declaration of a variable.

Double data type—Stores both whole and fractional numbers. Normally, `Doubles` store floating-point numbers.

embedded parentheses—Another term for nested parentheses.

empty string—A string that does not contain any characters.

floating-point division—Divides two numbers (whole or fractional) and returns a floating-point number.

implicit conversion—A conversion from one data type to another performed by Visual Basic.

integer—A whole number, such as 919, –11, 0 and 138624.

Integer data type—Stores integer values.

integer division—Integer division takes two `Integer` operands and yields an `Integer` result. The fractional portion of the result is discarded.

margin indicator bar—A margin in the IDE where breakpoints are displayed.

Mod (modulus operator)—The modulus operator yields the remainder after division.

name of a variable—The identifier used in an application to access or modify a variable's value.

nested parentheses—When an expression in parentheses is found within another expression surrounded by parentheses. With nested parentheses, the operators contained in the innermost pair of parentheses are applied first.

nondestructive memory operation —A process that does not overwrite a value in memory.

primitive data type—A data type already defined in Visual Basic, such as `Integer` (also known as a built-in data type).

redundant parentheses—Unnecessary parentheses in an expression to make the expression easier to read.

rules of operator precedence—Rules that determine the precise order in which operators are applied in an expression.

runtime error—An error that has its effect at execution time.

size of a variable—The number of bytes required to store a value of the variable's type.

straight-line form—The manner in which arithmetic expressions must be written left to right to be represented in Visual Basic code.

TextChanged event—Occurs when the text in a `TextBox` changes.

type of a variable—Specifies the kind of data that can be stored in a variable and the range of values that can be stored.

unary operators—An operator that takes only one operand.

value of a variable—The piece of data that is stored in a variable's location in memory.

variable—A location in the computer's memory where a value can be stored.

CONTROLS, EVENTS, PROPERTIES & METHODS

TextBox   `abl TextBox`   This control allows the user to input data from the keyboard.

■ *In action*

`| 0 |`

■ *Event*

`TextChanged`—Raised when the text in the `TextBox` is changed.

■ *Properties*

`Location`—Specifies the location of the `Label` on the `Form` relative to the top-left corner.

`Name`—Specifies the name used to access the `TextBox` programmatically. The name should be appended with the `TextBox` suffix.

`Size`—Specifies the height and width (in pixels) of the `TextBox`.

`Text`—Specifies the text displayed in the `TextBox`.

`TextAlign`—Specifies how the text is aligned within the `TextBox`.

MULTIPLE-CHOICE QUESTIONS

6.1 Parentheses that are added to an expression simply to make it easier to read are known as _____ parentheses.

a) necessary   b) redundant

c) embedded   d) nested

6.2 The _____ operator performs `Integer` division.

a) `\`   b) `+`

c) `Mod`   d) `^`

6.3 Every variable has a _____.

a) name   b) value

c) type   d) All of the above.

6.4 In Visual Basic, arithmetic expressions must be written in _____ form.

a) straight-line   b) top-bottom

c) left-right   d) right-left

6.5 Arithmetic expressions are evaluated _____.

a) from right to left   b) from left to right

c) according to the rules of operator precedence

d) from the lowest level of precedence to the highest level of precedence

6.6 Variable declarations in event handlers begin with the keyword _____.

a) `Declare`   b) `Dim`

c) `Sub`   d) `Integer`

6.7 Entering a value in a `TextBox` raises the _____ event.

a) `TextAltered`   b) `ValueChanged`

c) `ValueEntered`   d) `TextChanged`

6.8 The _____ function converts user input from a `TextBox` to a variable of type `Double`.

a) `Convert`   b) `MakeDouble`

c) `Val`   d) `WriteDouble`

6.9 Variables to store integer values should be declared with keyword _____.

a) `Integer`   b) `Int`

c) `IntVariable`   d) None of the above.

6.10 Keyword _____ in a variable declaration indicates that the data type is the next word.

a) `IsA`   b) `Type`

c) `Dim`   d) `As`

EXERCISES

6.11 *(Simple Encryption Application)* This application uses a simple technique to encrypt a number. Encryption is the process of modifying data so that only those intended to receive the data can undo the changes and view the original data. The user enters the data to be encrypted via a `TextBox`. The application then multiplies the number by 7 and adds 5. The application displays the encrypted number in a `Label` as shown in Fig. 6.23.

Figure 6.23   Result of completed **Simple Encryption** application.

a) *Copying the template to your working directory.* Copy the directory `C:\Examples\Tutorial06\Exercises\SimpleEncryption` to your `C:\SimplyVB` directory.

b) *Opening the application's template file.* Double click `SimpleEncryption.sln` in the `SimpleEncryption` directory to open the application.

c) *Coding the `Click` event handler.* Encrypt the number in the `Click` event handler for the Encrypt **Button** by using the preceding technique. The user input should be stored in an `Integer` variable (number) before it is encrypted. The event handler then should display the encrypted number.

d) *Clearing the result.* Add an event handler for the **Enter number to encrypt:** Text-Box's `TextChanged` event. This event handler should clear the **Encrypted number:** TextBox whenever the user enters new input.

e) *Running the application.* Select **Debug > Start Debugging** to run your application. Enter the value 25 into the **Enter number to encrypt:** TextBox and click the Encrypt `Button`. Verify that the value 180 is displayed in the **Encrypted number:** output `Label`. Enter other values and click the Encrypt `Button` after each. Verify that the appropriate encrypted value is displayed each time.

f) *Closing the application.* Close your running application by clicking its close box.

g) *Closing the IDE.* Close the Visual Basic IDE by clicking its close box.

6.12 *(Temperature Converter Application)* Write an application that converts a Celsius temperature, *C*, to its equivalent Fahrenheit temperature, *F*. Figure 6.24 displays the completed application. Use the following formula:

$$F = \frac{9}{5}C + 32$$

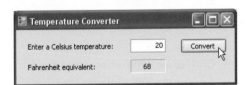

Figure 6.24 Completed **Temperature Converter.**

a) *Copying the template to your working directory.* Copy the directory `C:\Examples\Tutorial06\Exercises\TemperatureConversion` to your `C:\SimplyVB` directory.

b) *Opening the application's template file.* Double click `TemperatureConversion.sln` in the `TemperatureConversion` directory to open the application.

c) *Coding the `Click` event handler.* Perform the conversion in the **Convert** `Button`'s `Click` event handler. Define `Integer` variables to store the user-input Celsius temperature and the result of the conversion. Display the Fahrenheit equivalent of the temperature conversion.

d) *Clearing user input.* Clear the result in the **Enter a Celsius temperature:** TextBox's `TextChanged` event.

e) *Running the application.* Select **Debug > Start Debugging** to run your application. Enter the value 20 into the **Enter a Celsius temperature:** TextBox and click the **Convert** `Button`. Verify that the value 68 is displayed in the output `Label`. Enter other Celsius temperatures, click the **Convert** `Button` after each. Use the formula provided above to verify that the proper Fahrenheit equivalent is displayed each time.

f) *Closing the application.* Close your running application by clicking its close box.

g) *Closing the IDE.* Close the Visual Basic IDE by clicking its close box.

6.13 *(Simple Calculator Application)* In this exercise, you will add functionality to a simple calculator application. The calculator will allow a user to enter two numbers in the Text-Boxes. There will be four `Buttons` labeled +, -, / and *. When the user clicks the `Button` labeled as addition, subtraction, multiplication or division, the application will perform that operation on the numbers in the TextBoxes and displays the result. The calculator also should clear the calculation result when the user enters new input. Figure 6.25 displays the completed calculator.

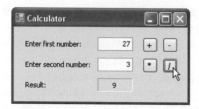

Figure 6.25 Result of **Calculator** application.

a) *Copying the template to your working directory.* Copy the directory `C:\Examples\Tutorial06\Exercises\SimpleCalculator` to your `C:\SimplyVB` directory.

b) *Opening the application's template file.* Double click `SimpleCalculator.sln` in the `SimpleCalculator` directory to open the application.

c) *Coding the addition `Click` event handler.* This event handler should add the two numbers and display the result.

d) *Coding the subtraction `Click` event handler.* This event handler should subtract the second number from the first number and display the result.

e) *Coding the multiplication `Click` event handler.* This event handler should multiply the two numbers and display the result.

f) *Coding the division `Click` event handler.* This event handler should divide the first number by the second number and display the result.

g) *Clearing the result.* Write event handlers for the TextBoxes' TextChanged events. Write code to clear `resultLabel` after the user enters new input into either TextBox.

h) *Running the application.* Select **Debug > Start Debugging** to run your application. Enter a first number and a second number, then verify that each of the Buttons works by clicking each, and viewing the output. Repeat this process with two new values and again verify that the proper output is displayed based on which Button is clicked.

i) *Closing the application.* Close your running application by clicking its close box.

j) *Closing the IDE.* Close the Visual Basic IDE by clicking its close box.

What does this code do? ▶ **6.14** This code modifies variables `number1`, `number2` and `result`. What are the final values of these variables?

```
1   Dim number1 As Integer
2   Dim number2 As Integer
3   Dim result As Integer
4
5   number1 = 5 * (4 + 6)
6   number2 = 2 ^ 2
7   result = number1 \ number2
```

What's wrong with this code? ▶ **6.15** Find the error(s) in the following code, which uses variables to perform a calculation.

```
1   Dim number1 As Integer
2   Dim number2 As Integer
3   Dim result As Integer
4
5   number1 = (4 * 6 ^ 4) / (10 Mod 4 - 2)
6   number2 = (16 \ 3) ^ 2 * 6 + 1
7   result = number1 - number2
```

Using the Debugger ▶ **6.16** *(Average Three Numbers)* You have just written an application that takes three numbers as input in TextBoxes, stores the three numbers in variables, then finds the average of the numbers (note that the average is rounded to the nearest integer value). The output is displayed in a Label (Fig. 6.26, which displays the incorrect output). You soon realize, however, that the number displayed in the Label is not the average, but rather a number that does not make sense given the input. Use the debugger to help locate and remove this error.

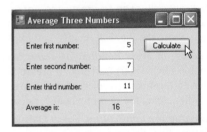

Figure 6.26   **Average Three Numbers** application.

a) *Copying the template to your working directory.* Copy the directory C:\Examples\ Tutorial06\Exercises\AverageDebugging to your C:\SimplyVB directory.

b) *Opening the application's template file.* Double click AverageDebugging.sln in the AverageDebugging directory to open the application.

c) *Running the application.* Select **Debug > Start Debugging** to run your application. View the output to observe that the output is incorrect.

d) *Closing the application.* Close the application, and view the Average.vb file in code view.

e) *Setting breakpoints.* Set a breakpoint in the calculateButton_Click event handler. Run the application again, and use the debugger to help find the error(s).

f) *Finding and correcting the error(s).* Once you have found the error(s), modify the application so that it correctly calculates the average of three numbers.

g) *Running the application.* Select **Debug > Start Debugging** to run your application. Enter the three values from Fig. 6.26 into the input TextBoxes provided and click the **Calculate** Button. Verify that the output now accurately reflects the average of these values, which is 8.

h) *Closing the application.* Close your running application by clicking its close box.

i) *Closing the IDE.* Close the Visual Basic IDE by clicking its close box.

Programming Challenge ▶

6.17 *(Digit Extraction)* Write an application that allows the user to enter a five-digit number into a TextBox. The application then separates the number into its individual digits and displays each digit in a Label. The application should look and behave similarly to Fig. 6.27. [*Hint:* You can use the Mod operator to extract the ones digit from a number. For instance, 12345 Mod 10 is 5. You can use integer division (\) to "peel off" digits from a number. For instance, 12345 \ 100 is 123. This allows you to treat the 3 in 12345 as a ones digit. Now you can isolate the 3 by using the Mod operator. Apply this technique to the rest of the digits.]

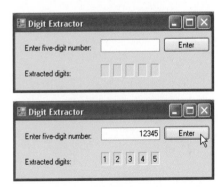

Figure 6.27   **Digit Extractor** application GUI.

a) *Creating the application.* Create a new project named DigitExtractor. Rename the Form1.vb file DigitExtractor.vb. Change the name of the Form to DigitExtractorForm. Add Labels, a TextBox and a Button to the application's Form.

Name the TextBox `inputTextBox` and name the Button `enterButton`. Name the other controls logically based on the tips provided in earlier tutorials.

b) *Adding an event handler for enterButton's `Click` event.* In design view, double click `enterButton` to create the `enterButton_Click` event handler. In this event handler, create five variables of type `Integer`. Use the `Mod` operator to extract each digit. Store the digits in the five variables created.

c) *Adding an event handler for inputTextBox's `TextChanged` event.* In design view, double click `inputTextBox` to create the `inputTextBox_TextChanged` event handler. In this event handler, clear the five `Label`s used to display each digit. This event handler clears the output whenever new input is entered.

d) *Running the application.* Select **Debug > Start Debugging** to run your application. Enter a five-digit number and click the **Enter** Button. Enter a new five-digit number and verify that the previous output is cleared.

e) *Closing the application.* Close your running application by clicking its close box.

f) *Closing the IDE.* Close the Visual Basic IDE by clicking its close box.

Wage Calculator Application

Introducing Algorithms, Pseudocode and Program Control

B efore writing an application, it is essential to have a thorough understanding of the problem you need to solve. This will allow you to design a carefully planned approach to solving the problem. When writing an application, it is equally important to recognize the types of building blocks that are available and to use proven application-construction principles. In this tutorial, you will learn the theory and principles of **structured programming**. Structured programming is a technique for organizing program control that will help you develop applications that are clear and easier to debug and modify. The techniques presented are applicable to most high-level languages, including Visual Basic.

7.1 Test-Driving the Wage Calculator Application

In this section, we preview this tutorial's **Wage Calculator** application. This application must meet the following requirements:

> **Application Requirements**
>
> *A payroll company calculates the gross earnings per week of employees. Employees' weekly salaries are based on the number of hours they worked and their hourly wages. Create an application that accepts this information and calculates each employee's total (gross) earnings. The application assumes a standard work week of 40 hours. The wages for 40 or fewer hours are calculated by multiplying the employee's hourly salary by the number of hours worked. Any time worked over 40 hours in a week is considered "over-time" and earns time and a half. Salary for time and a half is calculated by multiplying the employee's hourly wage by 1.5 and multiplying the result of that calculation by the number of overtime hours worked. The total overtime earned is added to the user's gross earnings for the regular 40 hours of work to calculate the total earnings for that week.*

This application calculates wages from hourly salary and hours worked per week. Normally, an employee who has worked 40 or fewer hours is paid regular wages. The calculation differs if the employee has worked more than the standard 40-hour work week. In this tutorial, we introduce a programming tool known as a **control structure** that allows us to make this distinction and perform different calculations based on different user inputs. You begin by test-driving the completed application. Then you will learn the additional Visual Basic technologies that you will need to create your own version of this application.

Test-Driving the Wage Calculator Application

1. ***Opening the completed application.*** Open the directory C:\Examples\ Tutorial07\CompletedApplication\WageCalculator to locate the **Wage Calculator** application. Double click WageCalculator.sln to open the application in the Visual Basic IDE.

2. ***Running the application.*** Select **Debug > Start Debugging** to run the application (Fig. 7.1). Note that we have placed the TextBoxes vertically, rather than horizontally, in this application. To make our GUI well organized, we have aligned the right sides of each TextBox and made the TextBoxes the same size. We have also left aligned the TextBoxes' descriptive Labels.

Figure 7.1 **Wage Calculator** application.

3. ***Enter the employee's hourly wage.*** Enter **10** in the **Hourly wage:** TextBox.

4. ***Enter the number of hours the employee worked.*** Enter **45** in the **Weekly hours:** TextBox.

5. ***Calculate the employee's gross earnings.*** Click the **Calculate** Button. The result (**$475.00**) is displayed in the **Gross earnings:** TextBox (Fig. 7.2). Note that the employee's salary is the sum of the wages for the standard 40-hour work week (40 * 10) and the overtime pay (5 * 10 * 1.5).

Figure 7.2 Calculating wages by clicking the **Calculate** Button.

6. ***Closing the application.*** Close your running application by clicking its close box.

7. ***Closing the IDE.*** Close the Visual Basic IDE by clicking its close box.

 **GUI Design Tip**

When using multiple TextBoxes vertically, align the TextBoxes on their right sides, and where possible make the TextBoxes the same size. Left align the descriptive Labels for such TextBoxes.

7.2 Algorithms

Computing problems can be solved by executing a series of actions in a specific order. A procedure for solving a problem, in terms of:

1. the actions to be executed and

2. the order in which these actions are to be executed

is called an **algorithm**. The following example demonstrates the importance of correctly specifying the order in which the actions are to be executed. Consider the "rise-and-shine algorithm" followed by one junior executive for getting out of bed and going to work: (1) get out of bed, (2) take off pajamas, (3) take a shower, (4) get dressed, (5) eat breakfast and (6) carpool to work. This routine prepares the executive for a productive day at the office.

However, suppose that the same steps are performed in a slightly different order: (1) get out of bed, (2) take off pajamas, (3) get dressed, (4) take a shower, (5) eat breakfast, (6) carpool to work. In this case, our junior executive shows up for work soaking wet.

Indicating the appropriate sequence in which to execute actions is equally crucial in computer programs. **Program control** refers to the task of ordering an application's statements correctly. In this tutorial, you will begin to investigate the program-control capabilities of Visual Basic.

SELF-REVIEW

1. _____ refer(s) to the task of ordering an application's statements correctly.

    a) Actions   b) Program control

    c) Control structures   d) Visual programming

2. A(n) _____ is a plan for solving a problem in terms of the actions to be executed and the order in which these actions are to be executed.

    a) chart   b) control structure

    c) algorithm   d) ordered list

Answers: 1) b. 2) c.

7.3 Pseudocode

Pseudocode is an informal language that helps programmers develop algorithms. The pseudocode we present is particularly useful in the development of algorithms that will be converted to structured portions of Visual Basic applications. Pseudocode resembles everyday English; it is convenient and user-friendly, but it is not an actual computer-programming language.

Pseudocode statements are not executed on computers. Rather, pseudocode helps you think out an application before attempting to write it in a programming language, such as Visual Basic. In this tutorial, we provide several examples of pseudocode.

The pseudocode that we present consists solely of characters, so that you can create and modify the pseudocode by using editor programs, such as the Visual Basic code editor or Notepad. A carefully prepared pseudocode program can be converted easily to a corresponding Visual Basic application. Much of this conversion is as simple as replacing pseudocode statements with their Visual Basic equivalents. Let us look at an example of a pseudocode statement:

    Assign 0 to the counter

This pseudocode statement provides an easy-to-understand task. You can put several such statements together to form an algorithm that can be used to meet application requirements. When the pseudocode algorithm has been completed, the programmer can then convert pseudocode statements to their equivalent Visual Basic statements. The pseudocode statement above, for instance, can be converted to the following Visual Basic statement:

```
counter = 0
```

Pseudocode normally describes only **executable statements**—the actions performed when the corresponding Visual Basic application is run. An example of a programming statement that is not executed is a declaration. The declaration

Software Design Tip

Pseudocode helps the programmer conceptualize an application during the application-design process. Pseudocode statements can be converted to Visual Basic at a later point.

```
Dim number As Integer
```

informs the compiler of `number`'s type and instructs the compiler to reserve space in memory for this variable. The declaration does not cause any action, such as input, output or a calculation, to occur when the application executes, so we would not include this information in the pseudocode.

SELF-REVIEW

1. _____ is an artificial and informal language that helps programmers develop algorithms.
   a) Pseudocode
   b) VB-Speak
   c) Notation
   d) None of the above.

2. Pseudocode _____.
   a) usually describes only declarations
   b) is executed on computers
   c) usually describes only executable lines of code
   d) usually describes declarations and executable lines of code

Answers: 1) a. 2) c.

7.4 Control Structures

Normally, statements in an application are executed one after another in the order in which they are written. This is called **sequential execution**. However, Visual Basic allows you to specify that the next statement to be executed may not be the next one in sequence. A **transfer of control** occurs when an executed statement does not directly follow the previously executed statement in the written application. This is common in computer programs.

All programs can be written in terms of only three control structures: the **sequence structure**, the **selection structure** and the **repetition structure**. The sequence structure is built into Visual Basic—unless directed to act otherwise, the computer executes Visual Basic statements sequentially—that is, one after the other in the order in which they appear in the application. The **activity diagram** in Fig. 7.3 illustrates a typical sequence structure, in which two calculations are performed in order. We discuss activity diagrams in detail following Fig. 7.3.

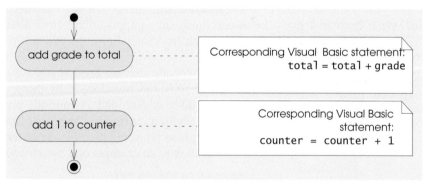

Figure 7.3 Sequence structure activity diagram.

Activity diagrams are part of the **Unified Modeling Language (UML)**—an industry standard for modeling software systems. An activity diagram models the activity (also called the **workflow**) of a portion of a software system. Such activities may include a portion of an algorithm, such as the sequence structure in Fig. 7.3. Activity diagrams are composed of special-purpose symbols, such as the **action-state symbol** (a rectangle with its left and right sides replaced with arcs curving outward), the **diamond symbol** and the **small circle symbol**; these symbols are connected by **transition arrows**, which represent the flow of the activity. Figure 7.3 does not include any diamond symbols—these will be used in later activity diagrams, beginning with Fig. 7.6.

Like pseudocode, activity diagrams help programmers develop and represent algorithms, although many programmers prefer pseudocode. Activity diagrams clearly show how control structures operate.

Consider the activity diagram for the sequence structure in Fig. 7.3. The activity diagram contains two **action states** that represent actions to perform. Each action state contains an **action expression**—for example, "add grade to total" or "add 1 to counter"—that specifies a particular action to perform. Other actions might include calculations or input/output operations. The arrows in the activity diagram are called transition arrows. These arrows represent **transitions** indicating the order in which the actions represented by the action states occur—the application that implements the activities illustrated by the activity diagram in Fig. 7.3 first adds grade to total, then adds 1 to counter.

The **solid circle** located at the top of the activity diagram represents the activity's **initial state**—the beginning of the workflow before the application performs the modeled activities. The solid circle surrounded by a hollow circle that appears at the bottom of the activity diagram represents the **final state**—the end of the workflow after the application performs its activities.

Notice, in Fig. 7.3, the rectangles with the upper-right corners folded over. They look like sheets of paper and are called **notes** in the UML. Notes are like comments in Visual Basic applications—they are explanatory remarks that describe the purpose of symbols in the diagram. Figure 7.3 uses UML notes to show the Visual Basic code that the programmer might associate with each action state in the activity diagram. A **dotted line** connects each note with the element that the note describes. Activity diagrams normally do not show the Visual Basic code that implements the activity, but we use notes here to show you how the diagram relates to Visual Basic code.

Visual Basic provides three types of **selection structures**, which we discuss in this tutorial and in Tutorial 11. The **If...Then** selection structure performs (selects) an action (or sequence of actions) based on a condition. A **condition** is an expression with a **true** or **false** value that is used to make a decision. Conditions are **evaluated** (that is, tested) to determine whether their value is true or false. These values are of data type **Boolean** and are specified in Visual Basic code by using the keywords **True** and **False**. Sometimes we refer to a condition as a Boolean expression.

If the condition evaluates to true, the actions specified by the If...Then structure will execute. If the condition evaluates to false, the actions specified by the If...Then structure will be skipped. The **If...Then...Else** selection structure performs an action (or sequence of actions) if a condition is true and performs a different action (or sequence of actions) if the condition is false. The Select Case structure, discussed in Tutorial 12, performs one of many actions (or sequences of actions), depending on the value of an expression.

The If...Then structure is called a **single-selection structure** because it selects or ignores a single action (or a sequence of actions). The If...Then...Else structure is called a **double-selection structure** because it selects between two different actions (or sequences of actions). The Select Case structure is called a **multiple-selection structure** because it selects among many different actions or sequences of actions.

Visual Basic provides seven types of **repetition structures**—While...End While, Do While...Loop, Do...Loop While, Do Until...Loop, Do...Loop Until, For...Next and For Each...Next. Repetition structures Do While...Loop and Do Until...Loop are covered in Tutorial 9; Do...Loop While and Do...Loop Until are covered in Tutorial 10; For...Next is covered in Tutorial 11; and For Each...Next is covered in Tutorial 20.[1] The words If, Then, Else, End, Select, Case, While, Do, Until, Loop, For, Next and Each are all Visual Basic keywords—Appendix E includes a com-

---

1. We do not discuss the While...End While loop in this book. This repetition structure behaves identically to the Do While...Loop and is provided for programmers familiar with previous versions of Visual Basic.

plete list of Visual Basic keywords. We discuss many of Visual Basic's keywords and their respective purposes throughout this book. Visual Basic has a much larger set of keywords than most other popular programming languages.

Visual Basic has 11 control structures—the sequence structure, three types of selection structures and seven types of repetition structures. All Visual Basic applications are formed by combining as many of each type of control structure as is necessary. As with the sequence structure in Fig. 7.3, each control structure is drawn with two small circle symbols—a solid black one to represent the entry point to the control structure, and a solid black one surrounded by a hollow circle to represent the exit point.

All Visual Basic control structures are **single-entry/single-exit control structures**—each has exactly one entry point and one exit point. Such control structures make it easy to build applications—the control structures are attached to one another by connecting the exit point of one control structure to the entry point of the next. This is similar to stacking building blocks, so we call it **control-structure stacking**. The only other way to connect control structures is through **control-structure nesting**, whereby one control structure can be placed inside another. Thus, algorithms in Visual Basic applications are constructed from only 11 different types of control structures combined in only two ways—this is a model of simplicity. Control structures in Visual Basic are implemented as statements, so from this point forward (after the following exercises), we use the term "statement" in preference to the term "structure."

---

1. All Visual Basic applications can be written in terms of _____ types of control structures.

    a) one   b) two

    c) three   d) four

2. The process of application statements executing one after another in the order in which they are written is called _____.

    a) transfer of control   b) sequential execution

    c) workflow   d) None of the above.

Answers: 1) c. 2) b.

7.5 If...Then Selection Statement

A selection statement chooses among alternative courses of action in an application. For example, suppose that the passing grade on a test is 60 (out of 100). The pseudocode statement

If student's grade is greater than or equal to 60
    Display "Passed"

Common Programming Error

Omitting the **Then** keyword in an **If...Then** statement is a syntax error. The IDE helps prevent this error by inserting the **Then** keyword after you write the condition.

determines whether the condition "student's grade is greater than or equal to 60" is true or false. If the condition is true, then "Passed" is displayed, and the next pseudocode statement in order is "performed." (Remember that pseudocode is not a real programming language.) If the condition is false, the display statement is ignored, and the next pseudocode statement in order is performed.

The preceding pseudocode *If* statement may be written in Visual Basic as

```
If studentGrade >= 60 Then
    displayLabel.Text = "Passed"
End If
```

The Visual Basic code corresponds closely to the pseudocode, demonstrating the usefulness of pseudocode as an application-development tool. The body (sometimes called a **block**) of the If...Then statement displays the string "Passed" in a Label. The keywords End If close an If...Then statement.

Note the indentation in the If...Then statement. Such indentation enhances application readability. The Visual Basic compiler ignores whitespace characters, such as spaces, tabs and newlines used for indentation and vertical spacing, unless the whitespace characters are contained in strings.

The condition between keywords If and Then determines whether the statement(s) within the If...Then statement will execute. If the condition is true, the body of the If...Then statement executes. If the condition is false, the body is not executed. Conditions in If...Then statements can be formed by using the **equality operators** and **relational operators** (also called **comparison operators**), which are summarized in Fig. 7.4. The relational and equality operators all have the same level of precedence.

Algebraic equality or relational operators	Visual Basic equality or relational operators	Example of Visual Basic condition	Meaning of Visual Basic condition
Relational operators			
>	>	x > y	x is greater than y
<	<	x < y	x is less than y
≥	>=	x >= y	x is greater than or equal to y
£	<=	x <= y	x is less than or equal to y
Equality operators			
=	=	x = y	x is equal to y
≠	<>	x <> y	x is not equal to y

Figure 7.4 Equality and relational operators.

Figure 7.5 shows the **syntax** of the If...Then statement. A statement's syntax specifies how the statement must be formed to compile without syntax errors. Let's look closely at the syntax of an If...Then statement. The first line of Fig. 7.5 specifies that the statement must begin with the keyword If and be followed by a condition and the keyword Then. Note that we have italicized *condition*. This indicates that, when creating your own If...Then statement, you should replace the text *condition* with the actual condition that you would like evaluated. The second line indicates that you should replace *statements* with the actual statements that you want to be included in the body of the If...Then statement. These statements make up the body of the If...Then statement. Note that the text *statements* is placed within square brackets. These brackets do not appear in the actual If...Then statement. Instead, the square brackets indicate that certain portions of the statement are optional. In this example, the square brackets indicate that all statements in the If...Then statement's body are optional. Of course, if there are no statements in the body of the If...Then statement, then no actions will occur as part of that statement, regardless of the condition's value. The final line indicates that the statement ends with the End If keywords.

Syntax

```
If condition Then
    [ statements ]
End If
```

Figure 7.5 If...Then statement syntax.

Figure 7.6 illustrates the single-selection If...Then statement. This activity diagram contains what is perhaps the most important symbol in an activity diagram—the diamond, or **decision symbol**, which indicates that a decision is to be made. Note the two sets of square brackets above or next to the arrows leading from the decision symbol; these are called **guard conditions**. A decision symbol indicates that the workflow will continue along a path determined by the symbol's associated guard conditions, which can be true or false. Each transition arrow emerging from a decision symbol has a guard condition (specified in square brackets above or next to the transition arrow). If a particular guard condition is true, the workflow enters the action state to which that transition arrow points. For example, in Fig. 7.6, if the grade is greater than or equal to 60, the application displays "Passed," then transitions to the final state of this activity. If the grade is less than 60, the application immediately transitions to the final state without displaying a message. Only one guard condition associated with a particular decision symbol can be true at once.

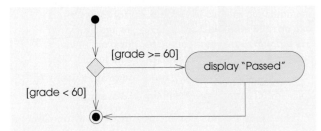

Figure 7.6 If...Then single-selection statement activity diagram.

Note that the If...Then statement (Fig. 7.6), is a single-entry/single-exit statement. The activity diagrams for the remaining control structures also contain (aside from small circle symbols and flowlines called transitions) only action-state symbols, indicating actions to be performed, and diamond symbols, indicating decisions to be made. Representing control structures in this way emphasizes the **action/decision model of programming**. To understand the process of structured programming better, we can envision 11 bins, each containing a different type of the 11 possible control structures. The control structures in each bin are empty, meaning that nothing is written in the action-state symbols and no guard conditions are written next to the decision symbols. The programmer's task is to assemble an application, using as many control structures as the algorithm demands, combining those control statements in only two possible ways (stacking or nesting) and filling in the actions and decisions (with the decisions' guard conditions) in a manner appropriate to the algorithm. Again, each of these control structures is implemented in Visual Basic as a statement.

SELF-REVIEW 1. Which of the following If...Then statements correctly displays that a student received an A on an exam if the score was 90 or above?

a) If studentGrade <> 90 Then
       displayLabel.Text = "Student received an A"
   End If

b) If studentGrade > 90 Then
       displayLabel.Text = "Student received an A"
   End If

c) If studentGrade = 90 Then
       displayLabel.Text = "Student received an A"
   End If

d) If studentGrade >= 90 Then
       displayLabel.Text = "Student received an A"
   End If

2. The symbol _____ is not a Visual Basic operator.

    a) *   b) ∧

    c) %   d) <>

Answers: 1) d. 2) c.

7.6 If...Then...Else Selection Statement

As you have learned, the If...Then selection statement performs an indicated action (or sequence of actions) only when the condition evaluates to true; otherwise, the action (or sequence of actions) is skipped. The If...Then...Else selection statement allows the programmer to specify that a different action (or sequence of actions) is to be performed when the condition is true than when the condition is false. For example, the pseudocode statement

> If student's grade is greater than or equal to 60
>   Display "Passed"
>
> Else
>   Display "Failed"

displays "Passed" if the student's grade is greater than or equal to 60, but displays "Failed" if the student's grade is less than 60. In either case, after output occurs, the next pseudocode statement in sequence is "performed."

The preceding pseudocode *If...Else* statement may be written in Visual Basic as

```
If studentGrade >= 60 Then
    displayLabel.Text = "Passed"
Else
    displayLabel.Text = "Failed"
End If
```

Good Programming Practice

Apply a standard indentation convention consistently throughout your applications to enhance readability.

Note that the body of the **Else** clause is indented so that it lines up with the indented body of the If clause. A standard indentation convention should be applied consistently throughout your applications. It is difficult to read programs that do not use uniform spacing conventions. The IDE helps you maintain consistent indentation with its "smart indenting" feature, which is enabled by default for Visual Basic. The If...Then...Else selection statement follows the same general syntax as the If...Then statement. The Else keyword and any related statements are placed between the If...Then and closing End If statements, as in Fig. 7.7.

Syntax

```
If condition Then
    [ statements ]
Else
    [ statements ]
End If
```

Figure 7.7   If...Then...Else statement syntax.

Figure 7.8 illustrates the flow of control in the If...Then...Else double-selection statement. Once again, aside from the initial state, transition arrows and final state, the only symbols in the activity diagram represent action states and decisions. In this example, the grade is either less than 60 or greater than or equal to 60. If the grade is less than 60, the application displays "Failed". If the grade is equal to or greater than 60, the application displays "Passed". We continue to emphasize this action/decision model of computing. Imagine again a deep bin containing as many empty double-selection statements as might be needed to build any Visual

Basic application. Your job as a programmer is to assemble these selection statements (by stacking and nesting) with any other control statements required by the algorithm. You fill in the action states and decision symbols with action expressions and guard conditions appropriate to the algorithm.

Good Programming Practice

Indent both body statements of an If...Then...Else statement to improve readability.

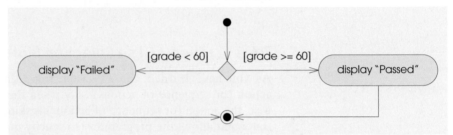

Figure 7.8 If...Then...Else double-selection statement activity diagram.

Nested If...Then...Else statements test for multiple conditions by placing If...Then...Else statements inside other If...Then...Else statements. For example, the following pseudocode (Fig. 7.9) will display "A" for exam grades greater than or equal to 90, "B" for grades in the range 80–89, "C" for grades in the range 70–79, "D" for grades in the range 60–69 and "F" for all other grades:

```
If student's grade is greater than or equal to 90
    Display "A"
Else
    If student's grade is greater than or equal to 80
        Display "B"
    Else
        If student's grade is greater than or equal to 70
            Display "C"
        Else
            If student's grade is greater than or equal to 60
                Display "D"
            Else
                Display "F"
```

Figure 7.9 Pseudocode for an application that displays a student's grades.

Good Programming Practice

If there are several levels of indentation, each level should be indented farther to the right by the same amount of space.

The pseudocode in Fig. 7.9 may be written in Visual Basic as shown in Fig. 7.10.

```
1   If studentGrade >= 90 Then
2       displayLabel.Text = "A"
3   Else
4       If studentGrade >= 80 Then
5           displayLabel.Text = "B"
6       Else
7           If studentGrade >= 70 Then
8               displayLabel.Text = "C"
9           Else
10              If studentGrade >= 60 Then
11                  displayLabel.Text = "D"
12              Else
13                  displayLabel.Text = "F"
14              End If
15          End If
16      End If
17  End If
```

Figure 7.10 Visual Basic code converted from the pseudocode in Fig. 7.9.

If `studentGrade` is greater than or equal to 90, the first condition evaluates to `True` and the statement `displayLabel.Text = "A"` is executed. With a value for `studentGrade` greater than or equal to 90, the remaining three conditions will evaluate to `True`. These conditions, however, are never evaluated, because they are placed within the `Else` portion of the outer `If...Then...Else` statement. The first condition is `True`, so all statements within the `Else` clause are skipped. Let's now assume that `studentGrade` contains the value 75. The first condition is `False`, so the application will execute the statements within the `Else` clause of this statement. This `Else` clause also contains an `If...Then...Else` statement, with the condition `studentGrade >= 80`. This condition evaluates to `False`, causing the statements in this `If...Then...Else` statement's `Else` clause to execute. This `Else` clause contains yet another `If...Then...Else` statement, with the condition `studentGrade >= 70`. This condition is `True`, causing the statement `displayLabel.Text = "C"` to execute. The `Else` clause of this `If...Then...Else` statement is then skipped.

Most Visual Basic programmers prefer to use the **ElseIf keyword** to write the preceding `If...Then...Else` statement, as shown in Fig. 7.11.

```
 1   If studentGrade >= 90 Then
 2       displayLabel.Text = "A"
 3   ElseIf studentGrade >= 80 Then
 4       displayLabel.Text = "B"
 5   ElseIf studentGrade >= 70 Then
 6       displayLabel.Text = "C"
 7   ElseIf studentGrade >= 60 Then
 8       displayLabel.Text = "D"
 9   Else
10       displayLabel.Text = "F"
11   End If
```

Figure 7.11 `If...Then...Else` statement using the `ElseIf` keyword.

The two statements are equivalent, but the latter statement is popular because it avoids deep indentation of the code. Such deep indentation often leaves little room on a line, forcing lines to be split and decreasing code readability. Note that the final portion of the `If...Then...Else` statement uses the `Else` keyword to handle all the remaining possibilities. The `Else` clause must always be last in an `If...Then...Else` statement—following an `Else` clause with another `Else` or `ElseIf` clause is a syntax error. You should also note that the latter statement requires only one `End If`.

SELF-REVIEW

1. `If...Then...Else` is a _____-selection statement.

   a) single   b) double

   c) triple   d) nested

2. Placing an `If...Then...Else` statement inside another `If...Then...Else` statement is an example of _____.

   a) nesting `If...Then...Else` statements   b) stacking `If...Then...Else` statements

   c) creating sequential `If...Then...Else`   d) None of the above.
      statements

Answers: 1) b. 2) a.

7.7 Constructing the Wage Calculator Application

The following section teaches you how to build the **Wage Calculator** by using the `If...Then...Else` statement. The `If...Then...Else` statement allows you to select between calculating regular wages and including overtime pay based on the number of hours worked. The following pseudocode describes the basic operation of the **Wage Calculator** application, which runs when the user clicks **Calculate:**

> When the user clicks the Calculate Button
> > Retrieve the number of hours worked and hourly wage from the TextBoxes
> >
> > If the number of hours worked is less than or equal to 40 hours
> > > Gross earnings equals hours worked times hourly wage
> >
> > Else
> > > Gross earnings equals 40 times hourly wage plus hours
> > > above 40 times wage and a half
> >
> > Display gross earnings

Visual Studio provides many programming tools to aid you in creating powerful and effective applications. With so many tools available, it is often helpful to create a table to organize and choose the best GUI elements. Like pseudocode, these tables simplify the task of creating the application by outlining the application's actions. In addition to listing the application's actions, the table assigns controls and events to the actions described in the pseudocode.

Now that you have test-driven the **Wage Calculator** application and studied its pseudocode representation, you will use an Action/Control/Event (ACE) table to help you convert the pseudocode to Visual Basic. Figure 7.12 lists the actions, controls and events that will help you complete your own version of this application.

The `Label`s in the first row display information about the application to the user. These `Label`s guide the user through the application. The `Button` control, `calculateButton`, is used to calculate the employee's wages. Note that the third column of the table specifies that we will be using this control's `Click` event to perform any calculations. The `TextBox`es will contain input from the user. The final control, `earningsResultLabel`, is a `Label` that displays the application's output.

Action/Control/Event (ACE) Table for the Wage Calculator Application

Action	Control	Event

Label the application's controls	`wageLabel,`
	`hoursLabel,`
	`earningsLabel`
		Application is run

	`calculateButton`	`Click`
Retrieve the number of hours worked and hourly wage from the TextBoxes	`wageTextBox,` `hoursTextBox`	
If the number of hours worked is less than or equal to 40 hours Gross earnings equals hours worked times hourly wage		
Else Gross earnings equals 40 times hourly wage plus hours above 40 times wage and a half		
Display gross earnings	`earningsResultLabel`	

Figure 7.12   Action/Control/Event table for the **Wage Calculator** application.

We now apply our pseudocode and the ACE table to complete the **Wage Calculator** application. The following box will guide you through the process of adding a `Click` event to the **Calculate** `Button` and declaring the variables you will need to calculate the employee's wages. If you forget to add code to this `Click` event, the application will not respond when the user clicks the **Calculate** `Button`.

*Declaring Variables in
the Calculate Button's
Click Event Handler*

1. ***Copying the template to your working directory.*** Copy the `C:\Examples\Tutorial07\TemplateApplication\WageCalculator` directory to your `C:\SimplyVB` directory.

2. ***Opening the Wage Calculator application's template file.*** Double click `WageCalculator.sln` in the `WageCalculator` directory to open the application in the Visual Basic IDE. If the application does not open in design view, double click the **WageCalculator.vb** file in the **Solution Explorer**. If the **Solution Explorer** is not open, select **View > Solution Explorer**.

3. ***Adding the Calculate Button Click event handler.*** In this example, the event handler calculates the gross wages when the **Calculate** Button's `Click` event occurs. Double click the **Calculate** Button. An event handler will be generated, and you will be switched to code view. Lines 3–6 of Fig. 7.13 display the generated event handler. Be sure to add the comments and line-continuation characters as shown in Fig. 7.13 so that the line numbers in your code match those presented in this tutorial.

Generated event handler ————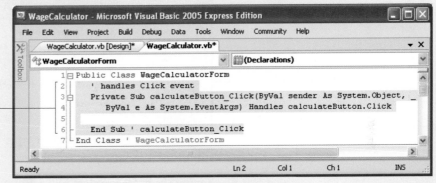

Figure 7.13 Calculate Button event handler.

In line 6, the End Sub keywords indicate the end of event handler calculateButton_Click. In line 7, the End Class keywords indicate the end of class WageCalculatorForm. We often add such comments so that the reader can easily determine which event handler or class is being closed without having to search for the beginning of that event handler or class in the file.

4. ***Declaring variables.*** This application uses the primitive data types Double and **Decimal**. A Double holds numbers with decimal points. Because hours and wages are often fractional numbers, Integers are not appropriate for this application. Add lines 6–9 of Fig. 7.14 into the body of event handler calculateButton_Click. Line 7 contains a variable declaration for Double hours, which holds the number of hours input by the user.

Type Decimal is used to store monetary amounts because this data type ensures rounding accuracy in arithmetic calculations involving monetary amounts. Lines 8–9 declare wage, which stores the hourly wage input by the user, and earnings, which stores the total amount of earnings for the week.

5. ***Declaring a constant.*** Add line 11 of Fig. 7.15 to the end of event handler calculateButton_Click. Line 11 contains a **constant**, a variable whose value cannot be changed after its initial declaration. Constants are declared with keyword **Const**. In this case, we assign to the constant HOUR_LIMIT the maximum number of hours worked before mandatory overtime pay (40). Note that we capitalize the constant's name to emphasize that it is a constant.

**Good Programming
Practice**

Constant variables (sometimes called named constants) help make programs more readable by providing names for constant values.

**Good Programming
Practice**

Capitalize the name of a constant. Separate each word in the name of a constant with an underscore.

(cont.)

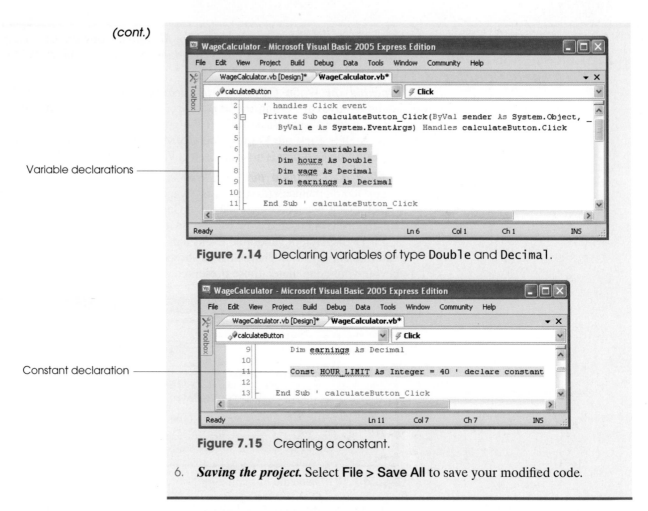

Figure 7.14 Declaring variables of type `Double` and `Decimal`.

Variable declarations

Constant declaration

Figure 7.15 Creating a constant.

6. ***Saving the project.*** Select **File > Save All** to save your modified code.

Now that you have declared variables, you can use them to receive input from the user, then use that input to compute and display the user's wages. The following box walks you through using the `If...Then...Else` statement to determine the user's wages.

Determining the User's Wages

1. ***Obtaining inputs from the TextBoxes.*** Add lines 13–15 of Fig. 7.16 to the end of event handler `calculateButton_Click`. Lines 14–15 assign values to `hours` and `wage` from the TextBoxes into which the user enters data. The `Val` function returns the user input as `Doubles` (lines 14–15). Visual Basic implicitly converts the `Double` result of `Val` to data type `Decimal` to assign the result to `wage` (line 15).

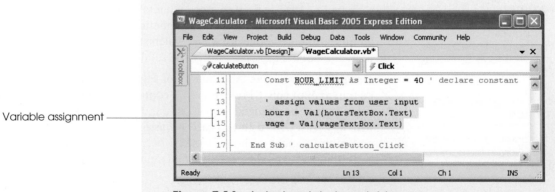

Variable assignment

Figure 7.16 Assigning data to variables.

(cont.)

Error-Prevention Tip

To reduce errors, the IDE sometimes adds keywords for you. One example is the adding of the keywords End If when an If...Then or an If...Then...Else statement is created. This eliminates the possibility that such keywords will be forgotten or misspelled.

2. ***Determining wages based on hours worked.*** Begin to add the If...Then...Else statement shown in lines 17–28 of Fig. 7.17 to the end of event handler calculateButton_Click. First type lines 17–18, then press *Enter*. Note that the keywords End If are added for you by the IDE. Continue by adding lines 19–28 to the If...Then...Else statement. You might need to indent as you go. This If...Then...Else statement determines whether employees earn overtime in addition to their usual wages. Line 18 determines whether the value stored in hours is less than or equal to HOUR_LIMIT. If it is, then line 20 assigns the value of the product of hours and wage to earnings. When you multiply a variable of data type Double by a variable of data type Decimal, Visual Basic implicitly converts the Decimal variable to a Double. The Double result is implicitly converted to a Decimal when it is assigned to earnings.

Added
If...Then...Else ——
statement

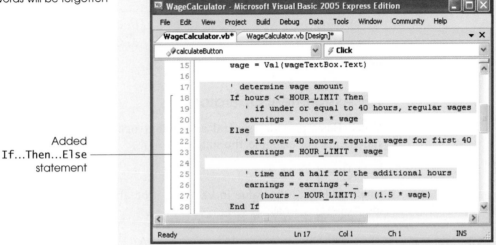

Figure 7.17 If...Then...Else statement to determine wages.

If, on the other hand, hours is not less than or equal to HOUR_LIMIT, then the application proceeds to the Else keyword in line 21. Line 23 computes the wage for the hours worked up to the limit set by HOUR_LIMIT and assigns it to earnings. Lines 26–27 determine how many hours over HOUR_LIMIT there are (by using the expression hours – HOUR_LIMIT) and then multiplies that by 1.5 and the user's hourly wages. This calculation results in the user's time-and-a-half pay for overtime hours. The value of this statement is then added to the value of earnings, and the result is assigned to earnings.

3. ***Displaying the result.*** Add lines 30–31 of Fig. 7.18 to the end of event handler calculateButton_Click. Line 31 assigns the value in earnings to the Text property of the Label earningsResultLabel, implicitly converting earnings from a Decimal to a string.

Displaying output ——

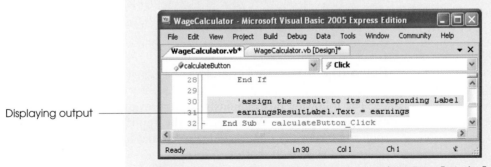

Figure 7.18 Assigning the result to earningsResultLabel.

(cont.)

4. ***Running the application.*** Select **Debug > Start Debugging** to run your application. Note that the output is not yet formatted as it should be in the completed application. Your will learn how to add this functionality in Section 7.9.

5. ***Closing the application.*** Close your running application by clicking its close box.

SELF-REVIEW

1. The Decimal data type is used to store _____.

    a) letters and digits   b) integers

    c) strings   d) monetary amounts

2. Constants are declared with keyword _____.

    a) Fixed   b) Constant

    c) Final   d) Const

Answers: 1) d. 2) d.

7.8 Assignment Operators

Visual Basic provides several assignment operators for abbreviating assignment statements. For example, the statement

```
value = value + 3
```

which adds 3 to the value in value, can be abbreviated with the addition assignment operator += as

```
value += 3
```

The += operator adds the value of the right operand to the value of the left operand and stores the result in the left operand. Visual Basic provides assignment operators for several binary operators, including +, -, *, ^, / and \. When an assignment statement is evaluated, the expression to the right of the operator is always evaluated first, then assigned to the variable on the left. Figure 7.19 includes the assignment operators, sample expressions using these operators and explanations.

Assignment operators	Sample expression	Explanation	Assigns
Assume: c = 4			
+=	c += 7	c = c + 7	11 to c
-=	c -= 3	c = c - 3	1 to c
*=	c *= 4	c = c * 4	16 to c
/=	c /= 2	c = c / 2	2 to c
\=	c \= 3	c = c \ 3	1 to c
^=	c ^= 2	c = c ^ 2	16 to c

Figure 7.19 Assignment operators.

The following box demonstrates abbreviating our time-and-a-half calculation with the += operator. When you run the application again, you will notice that the application runs the same as before—all that has changed is that one of the longer statements was made shorter.

Using the Addition Assignment Operator

1. ***Adding the addition assignment operator.*** Replace lines 26–27 of Fig. 7.17 with line 26 of Fig. 7.20.

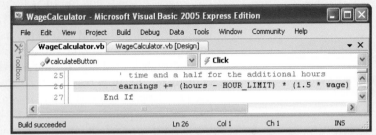

Addition assignment operator shortens statement

Figure 7.20   Using the addition assignment operator in a calculation.

In this step, we have used the addition assignment operator to make our statement shorter. Note that the statement still performs the same action—the time-and-a-half pay for the user is calculated and added to the regular wages earned.

2. ***Running the application.*** Select **Debug > Start Debugging** to run your application. Note that the application still does not format the output properly. The functionality of the application is the same as it was in the last box—we are now only using the += operator to abbreviate a statement.

3. ***Closing the application.*** Close your running application by clicking its close box.

SELF-REVIEW 1. The *= operator _____.

a) squares the value of the right operand and stores the result in the left operand

b) adds the value of the right operand to the value of the left operand and stores the result in the left operand

c) creates a new variable and assigns the value of the right operand to that variable

d) multiplies the value of the left operand by the value of the right operand and stores the result in the left operand

2. If intX is initialized with the value 5, what value will intX contain after the expression intX -= 3 is executed?

a) 3   b) 5
c) 7   d) 2

Answers: 1) d. 2) d.

7.9 Formatting Text

There are several ways to format output in Visual Basic. In this section, we introduce method **String.Format** to control how text displays. Modifying the appearance of text for display purposes is known as text **formatting**. This method takes as an argument a **format control string**, followed by arguments that indicate the values to be formatted. The format control string argument specifies how the remaining arguments are to be formatted.

Recall that your **Wage Calculator** does not display the result of its calculation with the appropriate decimal and dollar sign that you saw when test-driving the application. Next, you learn how to apply currency formatting to the value in the **Gross earnings:** TextBox.

Formatting the Gross Earnings

GUI Design Tip

Format all monetary amounts using the C (currency) format specifier.

1. **Modifying the Calculate Button's *Click* event.** If the IDE is not already in code view, select **View > Code**. Replace line 30 of Fig. 7.18 with line 30 of Fig. 7.21. Line 30 sends the format control string, "{0:C}", and the value to be formatted, earnings, to the String.Format method. The number zero indicates that argument 0 (earnings—the first argument after the format control string) should take the format specified by the letter after the colon; this letter is called the **format specifier**. In this case, we use the format defined by the uppercase letter C, which represents the **currency format**, used to display values as monetary amounts. The effect of the C format specifier varies, depending on the locale setting of your computer. In our case, the result is preceded with a dollar sign ($) and displayed with two decimal places (representing cents) because we are in the United States.

Formatting output as currency ————

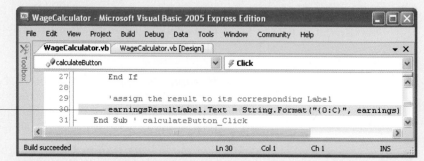

Figure 7.21 Using the Format method to display the result as currency.

2. **Running the application.** Select **Debug > Start Debugging** to run your application. The application should now output gross earnings as currency.

3. **Closing the application.** Close your running application by clicking its close box.

4. **Saving the project.** Select **File > Save All** to save your modified code.

Figure 7.22 shows several format specifiers. All format specifiers are case insensitive, so the uppercase letters may be used interchangeably with their lowercase equivalents. Note that format code D must be used only with Integers.

Format Specifier	Description
C	Currency. Formats the currency based on the computer's locale setting. For U.S. currency, precedes the number with $, separates every three digits with commas and sets the number of decimal places to two.
E	Scientific notation. Displays one digit to the left of the decimal point and six digits to the right of the decimal point, followed by the character E and a three-digit integer representing the exponent of a power of 10. For example, 956.2 is formatted as 9.562000E+002.
F	Fixed point. Sets the number of decimal places to two.
G	General. Visual Basic chooses either E or F for you, depending on which representation generates a shorter string.
D	Decimal integer. Displays an integer as a whole number in standard base-10 format.
N	Number. Separates every three digits with a comma and sets the number of decimal places to two.

Figure 7.22 Format specifiers for strings.

Figure 7.23 presents the source code for the **Wage Calculator** application. The lines of code that contain new programming concepts that you learned in this tutorial are highlighted.

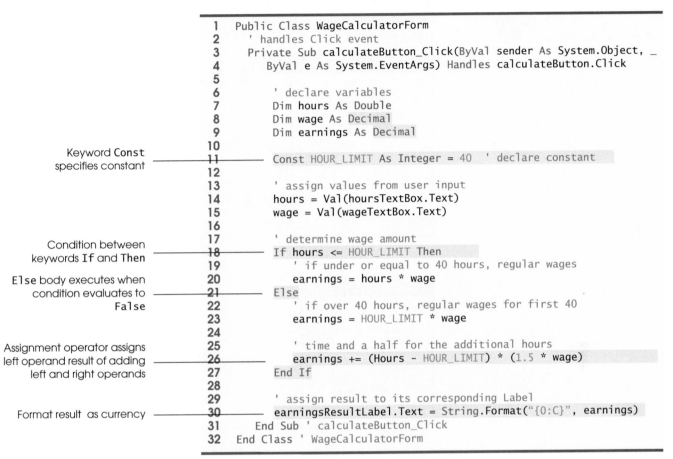

```
 1  Public Class WageCalculatorForm
 2      ' handles Click event
 3      Private Sub calculateButton_Click(ByVal sender As System.Object, _
 4          ByVal e As System.EventArgs) Handles calculateButton.Click
 5
 6          ' declare variables
 7          Dim hours As Double
 8          Dim wage As Decimal
 9          Dim earnings As Decimal
10
11          Const HOUR_LIMIT As Integer = 40   ' declare constant
12
13          ' assign values from user input
14          hours = Val(hoursTextBox.Text)
15          wage = Val(wageTextBox.Text)
16
17          ' determine wage amount
18          If hours <= HOUR_LIMIT Then
19              ' if under or equal to 40 hours, regular wages
20              earnings = hours * wage
21          Else
22              ' if over 40 hours, regular wages for first 40
23              earnings = HOUR_LIMIT * wage
24
25              ' time and a half for the additional hours
26              earnings += (Hours - HOUR_LIMIT) * (1.5 * wage)
27          End If
28
29          ' assign result to its corresponding Label
30          earningsResultLabel.Text = String.Format("{0:C}", earnings)
31      End Sub ' calculateButton_Click
32  End Class ' WageCalculatorForm
```

Keyword **Const** specifies constant

Condition between keywords **If** and **Then**

Else body executes when condition evaluates to **False**

Assignment operator assigns left operand result of adding left and right operands

Format result as currency

Figure 7.23   **Wage Calculator** application code.

SELF-REVIEW

1. Method `String.Format` is used to _____.
   a) create constant variables   b) control how text is formatted
   c) format Visual Basic statements   d) All of the above.

2. The _____ format displays values as monetary amounts.
   a) monetary   b) cash
   c) currency   d) dollar

Answers: 1) b. 2) c.

7.10 Using the Debugger: The Watch Window

Visual Studio includes several debugging windows that are accessible from the **Debug > Windows** submenu. The **Watch window**, which is available only in break mode, allows the programmer to examine the value of a variable or expression. You can use the **Watch** window to view changes in a variable's value as the application executes, or you can change a variable's value yourself by entering the new value directly into the **Watch** window. Each expression or variable that is added to the **Watch** window is called a watch. In the following box, we demonstrate how to add, remove and manipulate watches by using the **Watch** window.

1. ***Starting debugging.*** If the IDE is not in code view, switch to code view now. Set breakpoints in lines 15 and 20 (Fig. 7.24). Select **Debug > Start Debugging** to run the application. The **Wage Calculator** Form appears. Enter 12 into the **Hourly wage:** TextBox and 40 into the **Weekly hours:** TextBox (Fig. 7.25). Click the **Calculate** Button.

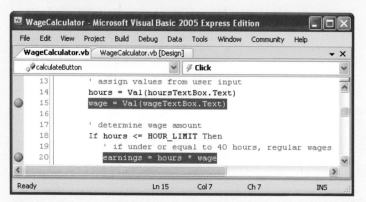

Figure 7.24 Breakpoints added to **Wage Calculator** application.

Figure 7.25 **Wage Calculator** application.

2. ***Suspending application execution.*** Clicking the **Calculate** Button will cause event handler calculateButton_Click to execute until the breakpoint is reached. When the breakpoint is reached, application execution is paused, and the IDE switches into break mode. Note that the **active window** has been changed from the running application to the IDE. The active window is the window that is currently being used and is sometimes referred to as the window that has the **focus**. The **Wage Calculator** application is still running, but it is hidden behind the IDE.

3. ***Examining data.*** Once the application has entered break mode, you are free to explore the values of various variables, using the debugger's **Watch** window. To display the **Watch** window, select **Debug > Windows > Watch**. The **Watch** window (Fig. 7.26) is initially empty. To add a watch, you can type an expression into the **Name** column. Single click in the first field of the **Name** column. Type hours, then press *Enter*. The value and type will be added by the IDE (Fig. 7.26). Note that this value is 40.0—the value assigned to hours in line 14. Type wage in the next row, then press *Enter*. The value displayed for wage is 0D. The D indicates that the number stored in wage is of type Decimal. You can also highlight a variable name in the code and drag-and-drop that variable into the **Watch** window or right click the variable in the code and select **Add Watch**.

(cont.)

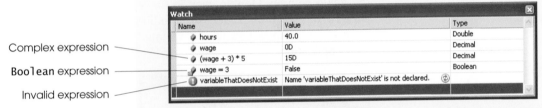

Figure 7.26 **Watch** window.

4. ***Examining different expressions.*** Add the expression (wage + 3) * 5 into the **Watch** window. Note that the **Watch** window can evaluate arithmetic expressions, returning the value **15D**. Add the expression wage = 3 into the **Watch** window. Expressions containing the = symbol are treated as Boolean expressions instead of assignment statements. The value returned is **False**, because wage does not currently contain the value 3. Add the expression variableThatDoesNotExist into the **Watch** window. This identifier does not exist in the current application, and therefore cannot be evaluated. An appropriate message is displayed in the **Value** field. Your **Watch** window should look similar to Fig. 7.27.

	Name	Value	Type
	hours	40.0	Double
	wage	0D	Decimal
Complex expression ———	(wage + 3) * 5	15D	Decimal
Boolean expression ———	wage = 3	False	Boolean
Invalid expression ———	variableThatDoesNotExist	Name 'variableThatDoesNotExist' is not declared.	

Figure 7.27 Examining expressions.

5. ***Removing an expression from the Watch window.*** At this point, we would like to clear the final expressions from the **Watch** window. To remove an expression, simply right click the expression in the **Watch** window and select **Delete Watch** (Fig. 7.28). Alternatively, you can click a variable in the **Watch** window and press *Delete* to remove the expression. Remove all the expressions that you added in *Step 4*.

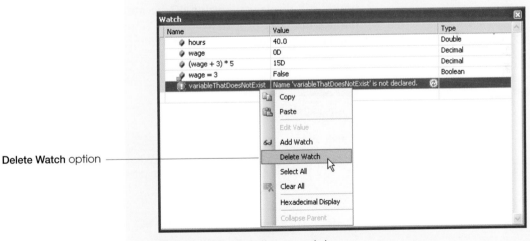

Figure 7.28 Deleting a watch.

(cont.)

6. ***Viewing modified values in a Watch window.*** Continue debugging by selecting **Debug > Continue**. The application will continue to execute until the next breakpoint, in line 20. Line 15 executes, assigning the wage value entered (12) to wage. The If...Then continuation condition evaluates to True in line 18, and the application is once again suspended in line 20. Note that the value of wage has changed not only in the application, but also in the **Watch** window. Because the value has changed since the last time the application was suspended, the modified value is displayed in red (Fig. 7.29).

Modified value appears in red —

Figure 7.29 Modified values in **Watch** window.

7. ***Modifying values directly in a Watch window.*** The **Watch** window can be used to change the value of a variable by simply entering the new value in the **Value** column. Double click in the **Value** field for hours, replace 40.0 with 10.0, then press *Enter*. The modified value appears in red (Fig. 7.30). This option enables you to test various values to confirm the behavior of your application.

Value modified directly —

Figure 7.30 Modifying values in a **Watch** window.

8. ***Viewing the application result.*** Select **Debug > Continue** to continue application execution. Event handler calculateButton_Click finishes execution and displays the result in a Label. The result is $120.00, because we changed hours to 10.0 in the last step. The TextBox to the right of **Weekly hours:** still displays the value **40**, because we changed the value of hours, but not the Text property of either TextBox. Once the application has finished running, the focus is returned to the **Wage Calculator** window, and the final results are displayed (Fig. 7.31).

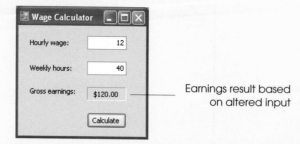

Earnings result based on altered input

Figure 7.31 Output displayed after the debugging process.

9. ***Closing the application.*** To close your application, either click the running application's close box or select **Debug > Stop Debugging**.

10. ***Saving the project.*** Select **File > Save All** to save your modified code.

11. ***Closing the IDE.*** Close the Visual Basic IDE by clicking its close box.

SELF-REVIEW   1. An application enters break mode when _____.

       a) **Debug > Start** is selected   b) a breakpoint is reached

       c) the **Watch** window is used   d) there is a syntax error

    2. The **Watch** window allows you to _____.

       a) change variable values   b) view variable type information

       c) evaluate expressions   d) All of the above.

Answers: 1) b. 2) d.

7.11 Wrap-Up

In this tutorial, we discussed techniques of solving programming problems. We introduced algorithms, pseudocode, the UML and control structures. We discussed different types of control structures and when each might be used.

You began by test-driving an application that used the `If...Then...Else` statement to determine an employee's weekly pay. You studied different control statements and used the UML to diagram the decision-making processes of the `If...Then` and the `If...Then...Else` statements.

You learned how to format text by using the method `String.Format` and how to abbreviate mathematical statements by using the assignment operators.

In the *Using the Debugger* section, you learned how to use the **Watch** window to view an application's data. You learned how to add watches, remove watches and change variable values.

In the next tutorial you will learn how to display message dialogs based on user input. You will study the logical operators, which give you more expressive power for forming the conditions in your control statements. You will use the `CheckBox` control to allow the user to select from various options in an application.

SKILLS SUMMARY

Choosing Among Alternate Courses of Action

■ Use the `If...Then` or `If...Then...Else` control statements.

Conceptualizing the Application Before Using Visual Studio .NET

■ Use pseudocode.

■ Create an Action/Control/Event (ACE) table.

Understanding Control Statements

■ View the control statement's corresponding UML diagram.

Performing Comparisons

■ Use the equality and relational operators.

Creating a Constant

■ Use the `Const` keyword.

■ Assign a value to the constant in the declaration.

Abbreviating Assignment Expressions

■ Use the assignment operators.

Formatting a Value as a Monetary Amount

■ Use the format code `C` in method `String.Format`.

Examining Data During Application Execution

■ Use the debugger to set a breakpoint, and examine the **Watch** window.

KEY TERMS

action/decision model of programming—Representing control statements as UML activity diagrams with rounded rectangles indicating *actions* to be performed and diamond symbols indicating *decisions* to be made.

action expression (in the UML)—Used in an action state within a UML activity diagram to specify a particular action to perform.

action state—An action to perform in a UML activity diagram that is represented by an action-state symbol.

action-state symbol—A rectangle with its left and right sides replaced with arcs curving outward that represents an action to perform in a UML activity diagram.

active window—The window that is currently being used—sometimes referred to as the window that has the focus.

activity diagram—A UML diagram that models the activity (also called the workflow) of a portion of a software system.

algorithm—A procedure for solving a problem, specifying the actions to be executed and the order in which they are to be executed.

block—A group of code statements.

Boolean data type—A data type that has the value True or False.

condition—An expression with a true or false value that is used to make a decision.

control structure (control statement)—An application component that specifies the order in which statements execute (also known as the flow of control).

control structure (statement) nesting—Placing one control statement in the body of another control statement.

control structure (statement) stacking—A set of control statements in sequence. The exit point of one control statement is connected to the entry point of the next control statement in sequence.

constant—A variable whose value cannot be changed after its initial declaration.

currency format—Used to display values as monetary amounts.

Decimal data type—Used to store monetary amounts.

decision symbol—The diamond-shaped symbol in a UML activity diagram that indicates that a decision is to be made.

diamond symbol—A symbol (also known as the decision symbol) in a UML activity diagram; this symbol indicates that a decision is to be made.

dotted line—A UML activity diagram symbol that connects each UML-style note with the element that the note describes.

double-selection statement—A statement, such as If…Then…Else, that selects between two different actions or sequences of actions.

ElseIf keyword—Keyword used for the nested conditions in nested If…Then…Else statements.

equality operators—Operators = (is equal to) and <> (is not equal to) that compare two values.

executable statement—Actions that are performed when the corresponding Visual Basic application is run.

final state—Represented by a solid circle surrounded by a hollow circle in a UML activity diagram; the end of the workflow after an application performs its activities

focus—Designates the window currently in use.

format control string—A string that specifies how data should be formatted.

format specifier—Code that specifies the type of format that should be applied to a string for output.

formatting—Modifying the appearance of text for display purposes.

guard condition—An expression contained in square brackets above or next to the arrows leading from a decision symbol in a UML activity diagram that determines whether workflow continues along a path.

If…Then—Selection statement that performs an action (or sequence of actions) based on a condition. This is also called the single-selection statement.

If...Then...Else—Selection statement that performs an action (or sequence of actions) if a condition is `true` and performs a different action (or sequence of actions) if the condition is `false`. This is also called the double-selection statement.

initial state—Represented by a solid circle in a UML activity diagram; the beginning of the workflow before the application performs the modeled activities.

multiple-selection statement—A statement that selects from among many different actions or sequences of actions.

nested statement—A statement that is placed inside another control statement.

note—An explanatory remark (represented by a rectangle with a folded upper-right corner) describing the purpose of a symbol in a UML activity diagram.

program control—The task of ordering an application's statements in the correct order.

pseudocode—An informal language that helps programmers develop algorithms.

relational operators—Operators < (less than), > (greater than), <= (less than or equal to) and >= (greater than or equal to) that compare two values (also known as comparison operators)

repetition structure (or repetition statement)—Allows the programmer to specify that an action or actions should be repeated, depending on the value of a condition.

selection structure (or selection statement)—Selects among alternative courses of action.

sequence structure (or sequence statement)—Built into Visual Basic—unless directed to act otherwise, the computer executes Visual Basic statements sequentially.

sequential execution—Statements in an application are executed one after another in the order in which they are written.

single-entry/single-exit control structure (or statement)—A control statement that has one entry point and one exit point. All Visual Basic control statements are single-entry/single-exit control statements.

single-selection statement—The `If...Then` statement, which selects or ignores a single action or sequence of actions.

small circles (in the UML)—The solid circle in an activity diagram represents the activity's initial state, and the solid circle surrounded by a hollow circle represents the activity's final state.

solid circle (in the UML)—A UML activity diagram symbol that represents the activity's initial state.

String.Format method—Formats a string.

structured programming—A technique for organizing program control to help you develop applications that are easy to understand, debug and modify.

syntax—Specifies how a statement must be formed to compile without syntax errors.

transfer of control—Occurs when an executed statement does not directly follow the previously executed statement in the written application.

transition—A change from one action state to another that is represented by transition arrows in a UML activity diagram.

UML (Unified Modeling Language)—An industry standard for modeling software systems graphically.

Watch window—A Visual Basic IDE window that allows you to view variable values as an application is being debugged.

workflow—The activity of a portion of a software system.

GUI DESIGN GUIDELINES

Overall Design

■ Format all monetary amounts using the C (currency) format specifier.

TextBox

■ When using multiple TextBoxes vertically, align the TextBoxes on their right sides, and where possible make the TextBoxes the same size. Left-align the descriptive Labels for such TextBoxes.

CONTROLS, EVENTS, PROPERTIES & METHODS

String This class represents a series of characters treated as a single unit.
- *Method*

Format—Arranges the String in a specified format.

MULTIPLE-CHOICE QUESTIONS

7.1 The _____ operator returns False if the left operand is larger than the right operand.

a) =

b) <

c) <=

d) All of the above.

7.2 A _____ occurs when an executed statement does not directly follow the previously executed statement in the written application.

a) transition

b) flow

c) logical error

d) transfer of control

7.3 A variable or an expression that is added to the **Watch** window is known as a _____.

a) watched variable

b) watched expression

c) watch

d) watched value

7.4 The If...Then statement is called a _____ statement because it selects or ignores one action.

a) single-selection

b) multiple-selection

c) double-selection

d) repetition

7.5 The three types of control statements are the sequence statement, the selection statement and the _____ statement.

a) repeat

b) looping

c) redo

d) repetition

7.6 In an activity diagram, a rectangle with curved sides represents _____.

a) a complete algorithm

b) a comment

c) an action

d) the termination of the application

7.7 The If...Then...Else selection statement ends with the keywords _____.

a) End If Then Else

b) End If Else

c) End Else

d) End If

7.8 A variable of data type Boolean can be assigned keyword _____ or keyword _____.

a) True, False

b) Off, On

c) True, NotTrue

d) Yes, No

7.9 A variable whose value cannot be changed after its initial declaration is called a _____.

a) Double

b) constant

c) standard

d) Boolean

7.10 The _____ operator assigns the result of adding the left and right operands to the left operand.

a) +

b) =+

c) +=

d) none of the above

EXERCISES

7.11 *(Currency Converter Application)* Develop an application that functions as a currency converter, as shown in Fig. 7.32. Users must provide a number in the **Dollars:** TextBox and a currency name (as text) in the **Convert from Dollars to:** TextBox. Clicking the **Convert** Button will convert the specified amount into the indicated currency and display it in a

Label. Limit yourself to the following currencies as user input: Dollars, Euros, Yen and Pesos. Use the following exchange rates: **1 Dollar = .79 Euros, 115 Yen** and **11 Pesos.**

Figure 7.32 **Currency Converter** GUI.

a) ***Copying the template to your working directory.*** Copy the directory `C:\Examples\Tutorial07\Exercises\CurrencyConverter` to your `C:\SimplyVB` directory.

b) ***Opening the application's template file.*** Double click `CurrencyConverter.sln` in the `CurrencyConverter` directory to open the application.

c) ***Add an event handler for the Convert Button's Click event.*** Double click the **Convert** Button to generate an empty event handler for the Button's Click event. The code for *Steps d–f* belongs in this event handler.

d) ***Obtaining the user input.*** Use the Val function to convert the user input from the **Dollars:** TextBox to a Double. Assign the result to a Decimal variable amount. Visual Basic implicitly performs this conversion from Double to Decimal.

e) ***Performing the conversion.*** Use an If...ElseIf...ElseIf statement to determine which currency the user entered. Assign the result of the conversion to amount.

f) ***Displaying the result.*** Display the result using method String.Format with format specifier F.

g) ***Running the application.*** Select **Debug > Start Debugging** to run your application. Enter a value in dollars to be converted and the name of the currency you wish to convert to. Click the **Convert** Button and, using the exchange rates above, verify that the correct output is displays.

h) ***Closing the application.*** Close your running application by clicking its close box.

i) ***Closing the IDE.*** Close the Visual Basic IDE by clicking its close box.

7.12 *(Wage Calculator That Performs Tax Calculations)* Develop an application that calculates an employee's wages, as shown in Fig. 7.33. The user should provide the hourly wage and number of hours worked per week. When the **Calculate** Button is clicked, the gross earnings of the user should display in the **Gross earnings:** TextBox. The **Less FWT:** TextBox should display the amount deducted for federal taxes and the **Net earnings:** TextBox displays the difference between the gross earnings and the federal tax amount. Assume that overtime wages are 1.5 times the hourly wage and federal taxes are 15% of gross earnings. The **Clear** Button should clear all fields.

Figure 7.33 **Wage Calculator** GUI.

a) *Copying the template to your working directory.* Copy the directory `C:\Examples\Tutorial07\Exercises\ExpandedWageCalculator` to your `C:\SimplyVB` directory.

b) *Opening the application's template file.* Double click `WageCalculator.sln` in the `ExpandedWageCalculator` directory to open the application.

c) *Modifying the* Calculate *Button's* Click *event handler.* Add the code for *Steps d–f* to `calculateButton_Click`.

d) *Adding a new variable.* Declare `federalTaxes` to store the amount deducted for federal taxes.

e) *Calculating and displaying the federal taxes deducted.* Multiply the total earnings (`earnings`) by 0.15 (that is, 15%) to determine the amount to be removed for taxes. Assign the result to `federalTaxes`. Display this value using method `String.Format` with format specifier C.

f) *Calculating and displaying the employee's net pay.* Subtract `federalTaxes` from `earnings` to calculate the employee's net earnings. Display this value using method `String.Format` with format specifier C.

g) *Creating an event handler for the* Clear *Button.* Double click the **Clear** `Button` to generate an empty event handler for the `Click` event. This event handler should clear user input from the two `TextBox`es and the results from the three `Label`s.

h) *Running the application.* Select **Debug > Start Debugging** to run your application. Enter an hourly wage and the number of hours worked. Click the **Calculate** `Button` and verify that the appropriate output is displayed for gross earnings, amount taken out for federal taxes and net earnings. Click the **Clear** `Button` and check that all fields are cleared.

i) *Closing the application.* Close your running application by clicking its close box.

j) *Closing the IDE.* Close the Visual Basic IDE by clicking its close box.

7.13 *(Customer Charge Account Analyzer Application)* Develop an application (as shown in Fig. 7.34) that determines whether a department-store customer has exceeded the credit limit on a charge account. Each customer enters an account number (an `Integer`), a balance at the beginning of the month (a `Decimal`), the total of all items charged this month (a `Decimal`), the total of all credits applied to the customer's account this month (a `Decimal`), and the customer's allowed credit limit (a `Decimal`). The application should input each of these facts, calculate the new balance (= *beginning balance – credits + charges*), display the new balance and determine whether the new balance exceeds the customer's credit limit. If the customer's credit limit is exceeded, the application should display a message (in a `Label` at the bottom of the `Form`) informing the customer of this fact.

Figure 7.34 Credit Checker GUI.

a) *Copying the template application to your working directory.* Copy the directory `C:\Examples\Tutorial07\Exercises\CreditChecker` to `C:\SimplyVB`.

b) *Opening the application's template file.* Double click `CreditChecker.sln` in the `CreditChecker` directory to open the application.

c) *Adding the Calculate Button's Click event handler.* Double click the **Calculate Balance** Button to generate the empty event handler for the Click event. The code for *Steps d–g* is added to this event handler.

d) *Declaring variables.* Declare an Integer variable to store the account number. Declare four Decimal variables to store the starting balance, charges, credits and credit limit. Declare a fifth Decimal variable to store the new balance in the account after the credits and charges have been applied.

e) *Obtaining user input.* Obtain the user input from the TextBoxes' Text properties.

f) *Calculating and displaying the new balance.* Calculate the new balance by adding the total credits to the starting balance and subtracting the charges. Assign the result to a variable. Display the result formatted as currency.

g) *Determining if the credit limit has been exceeded.* If the new balance exceeds the specified credit limit, a message should be displayed in errorLabel.

h) *Handling the Account number: TextBox's TextChanged event.* Double click the **Account number:** TextBox to generate its TextChanged event handler. This event handler should clear the other TextBoxes, the error message Label and the result Label.

i) *Running the application.* Select **Debug > Start Debugging** to run your application. Enter an account number, your starting balance, the amount charged to your account, the amount credited to your account and your credit limit. Click the **Calculate Balance** Button and verify that the new balance displayed is correct. Enter an amount charged that exceeds your credit limit. Click the **Calculate Balance** Button and ensure that a message is displayed in the lower Label.

j) *Closing the application.* Close your running application by clicking its close box.

k) *Closing the IDE.* Close the Visual Basic IDE by clicking its close box.

What does this code do? ▶ **7.14** Assume that ageTextBox is a TextBox control and that the user has entered the value 27 into this TextBox. Determine the action performed by the following code:

```
1   Dim age As Integer
2
3   age = Val(ageTextBox.Text)
4
5   If age < 0 Then
6      ageLabel.Text = "Enter a value greater than or equal to zero."
7   ElseIf age < 13 Then
8      ageLabel.Text = "Child"
9   ElseIf age < 20 Then
10     ageLabel.Text = "Teenager"
11  ElseIf age < 30 Then
12     ageLabel.Text = "Young Adult"
13  ElseIf age < 65 Then
14     ageLabel.Text = "Adult"
15  Else
16     ageLabel.Text = "Senior Citizen"
17  End If
```

What's wrong with this code? ▶ **7.15** Assume that ampmLabel is a Label control. Find the error(s) in the following code:

```
1   Dim hour As Integer
2
3   hour = 14
4
5   If hour < 11 Then
6      If hour > 0 Then
7          ampmLabel.Text = "AM"
8      End If
```

```
9   Else
10      ampmLabel.Text = "PM"
11   ElseIf hour > 23 Then
12      ampmLabel.Text = "Time Error."
13   End If
```

Using the Debugger ▶

7.16 *(Grade Calculator Application)* Copy the `C:\Examples\Tutorial07\Debugger` directory to your working directory. This directory contains the `Grades` application, which takes a number from the user and displays the corresponding letter grade. For values 90–100 it should display **A**; for 80–89, **B**, for 70–79, **C**, for 60–69, **D** and for anything lower, an **F**. Run the application. Enter the value 85 in the TextBox and click **Calculate**. Note that the application displays **D** when it ought to display **B**. Select **View > Code** to enter the code editor and set as many breakpoints as you feel necessary. Select **Debug > Start Debugging** to use the debugger to help you find the error(s). Figure 7.35 shows the incorrect output when the value 85 is input.

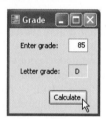

Figure 7.35 Incorrect output for **Grade** application.

Programming Challenge ▶

7.17 *(Encryption Application)* A company transmits data over the telephone, but it is concerned that its phones could be tapped. All its data is transmitted as four-digit `Integers`. The company has asked you to write an application that encrypts its data so that it may be transmitted more securely. Encryption is the process of transforming data for security reasons. Create a `Form` similar to Fig. 7.36. Your application should read four-digits entered by the user and encrypt the information. Assume that the user inputs a single digit in each TextBox. Use the following technique to encrypt the number:

a) Replace each digit by *(the sum of that digit plus 7)* Mod *10*.

b) Swap the first digit with the third, and swap the second digit with the fourth.

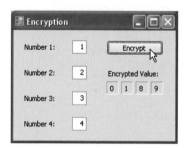

Figure 7.36 **Encryption** application.

Objectives

In this tutorial, you will learn to:
- Use **CheckBoxes** to allow users to select options.
- Use dialogs to display messages.
- Use logical operators to form more powerful conditions.

Outline

Dental Payment Application

Introducing CheckBoxes and Message Dialogs

Many Visual Basic applications use **dialogs** (also called **message dialogs**). These are windows that display messages to users. You encounter many dialogs while using a computer, from those that instruct you to select files or enter passwords to others that notify you of problems while using an application. In this tutorial, you will learn how to use message dialogs to inform users of input problems.

You may have noticed that TextBoxes allow users to enter nearly any value as input. In some cases, you may want to use controls that provide users with predefined options. One way to do this is by providing CheckBoxes in your application. You also will learn about logical operators, which you can use in your applications to make more involved decisions based on user input.

8.1 Test-Driving the Dental Payment Application

When you visit the dentist, there are many procedures that the dentist can perform. The office assistant may present you with a bill generated by a computer. In this tutorial, you will program an application that prepares a bill for some basic dental procedures. This application must meet the following requirements:

> **Application Requirements**
>
> *A dentist's office administrator wishes to create an application that employees can use to bill patients. The application must allow users to enter the patient's name and specify which services were performed during the visit. The application will then calculate the total charges. If a user attempts to calculate a bill before any services are specified, or before the patient's name is entered, an error message informing the user that necessary input is missing will be displayed.*

In the **Dental Payment** application, you will use CheckBox controls and a message dialog to assist the user in entering data. You begin by test-driving the completed application. Then you will learn the additional Visual Basic technologies that you will need to create your own version of this application.

155

1. *Opening the completed application.* Open the directory `C:\Examples\Tutorial08\CompletedApplication\DentalPayment` to locate the **Dental Payment** application. Double click `DentalPayment.sln` to open the application in the Visual Basic IDE.

2. *Running the Dental Payment application.* Select **Debug > Start Debugging** to run the application (Fig. 8.1).

   Note that there are three square-shaped controls in the left column of the Form. These are known as **CheckBox** controls. A CheckBox is a small square that either is blank or contains a check mark. When a CheckBox is selected, a check mark appears in the box (☑). A CheckBox can be selected by simply clicking within the CheckBox's small square or by clicking on the text of the CheckBox. A selected CheckBox can be unchecked in the same way. You will learn how to add CheckBox controls to a Form shortly.

CheckBox controls (unchecked)

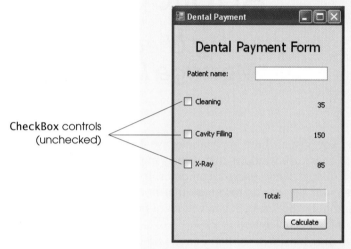

Figure 8.1 Running the completed **Dental Payment** application.

3. *Attempting to calculate a total without entering input.* Leave the **Patient name** field blank, and deselect any CheckBoxes that you have selected. Click the **Calculate** Button. Note that a message dialog appears indicating that you must enter data (Fig. 8.2). Close this dialog by clicking its **OK** Button.

Figure 8.2 Message dialog appears when no name is entered and/or no CheckBoxes are selected.

4. *Entering quantities in the application.* The **Dental Payment** Form is still displayed. Type Bob Jones in the **Patient name** field. Check all three CheckBoxes by clicking each one. As you will see, a check mark appears in each CheckBox (Fig. 8.3).

5. *Unchecking the Cavity Filling CheckBox.* Click the **Cavity Filling** CheckBox to remove its check mark. Only the **Cleaning** and **X-Ray** CheckBoxes should now be selected (Fig. 8.4).

6. *Determining the bill.* Click the **Calculate** Button. This causes the application to total the price of the services performed during the dentist visit. The result is displayed in the **Total:** field (Fig. 8.5).

(cont.)

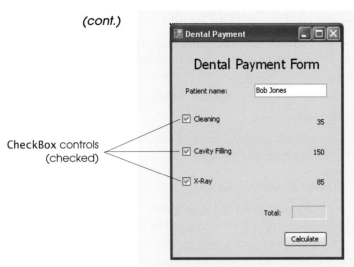

CheckBox controls
(checked)

Figure 8.3 Dental Payment application with input entered.

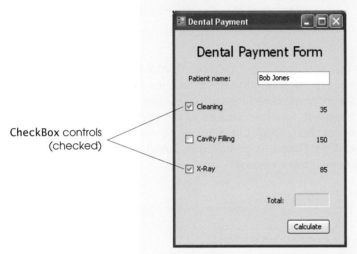

CheckBox controls
(checked)

Figure 8.4 Dental Payment application with input entered.

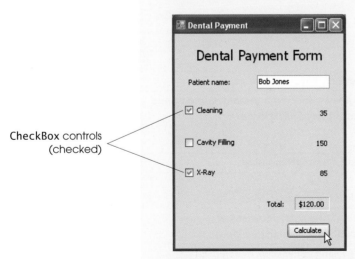

CheckBox controls
(checked)

Figure 8.5 Dental Payment application with input entered.

7. ***Closing the application.*** Close your running application by clicking its close box.

8. ***Closing the IDE.*** Close the Visual Basic IDE by clicking its close box.

8.2 Designing the Dental Payment Application

Recall that pseudocode is an informal language that helps programmers develop algorithms. The following pseudocode describes the basic operation of the **Dental Payment** application, which runs when the user clicks **Calculate**:

When the user clicks the Calculate Button

    Clear previous total

    If user has not entered a patient name or has not selected any CheckBoxes
        Display message in dialog
    Else
        Initialize the total to zero

        If "Cleaning" CheckBox is selected
            Add cost of a cleaning to the total

        If "Cavity Filling" CheckBox is selected
            Add cost of receiving a cavity filling to the total

        If "X-Ray" CheckBox is selected
            Add cost of receiving an x-ray to the total

        Format total to be displayed as currency
        Display total

Now that you have test-driven the **Dental Payment** application and studied its pseudocode representation, you will use an ACE table to help you convert the pseudocode to Visual Basic. Figure 8.6 lists the actions, controls and events that will help you complete your own version of this application. Data is input using a Text-Box (`nameTextBox`) and CheckBoxes (`cleanCheckBox`, `cavityCheckBox` and `xrayCheckBox`). Output is displayed in Label `totalResultLabel` when a Button (`calculateButton`) is clicked.

<table>
<tr><td rowspan="11">Action/Control/Event (ACE) Table for the Dental Payment Application
</td><td>**Action**</td><td>**Control/Class/Object**</td><td>**Event**</td></tr>
<tr><td>Label all the application's controls</td><td>`titleLabel`,
`nameLabel`,
`totalLabel`,
`cleanCostLabel`,
`fillingCostLabel`,
`xrayCostLabel`</td><td>Application is run</td></tr>
<tr><td></td><td>`calculateButton`</td><td>Click</td></tr>
<tr><td>Clear previous total</td><td>`totalResultLabel`</td><td></td></tr>
<tr><td>If user has not entered a patient name or has not selected any CheckBoxes</td><td>`nameTextBox`,
`cleanCheckBox`,
`cavityCheckBox`,
`xrayCheckBox`</td><td></td></tr>
<tr><td>   Display message in dialog</td><td>`MessageBox`</td><td></td></tr>
<tr><td>Else
   Initialize the total to zero</td><td></td><td></td></tr>
<tr><td>If "Cleaning" CheckBox is selected
   Add cost of a cleaning to the total</td><td>`cleanCheckBox`</td><td></td></tr>
<tr><td>If "Cavity Filling" CheckBox is selected
   Add cost of receiving a cavity filling to the total</td><td>`cavityCheckBox`</td><td></td></tr>
</table>

Figure 8.6 Action/Control/Event table for **Dental Payment** application. (Part 1 of 2.)

Action	Control/Class/Object	Event
If "X-Ray" CheckBox is selected Add cost of receiving an x-ray to the total	xrayCheckBox	
Format total to be displayed as currency	String	
Display total	totalResultLabel	

Figure 8.6   Action/Control/Event table for **Dental Payment** application. (Part 2 of 2.)

8.3 Using CheckBoxes

As mentioned earlier, a CheckBox is a small square that either is blank or contains a check mark. (A CheckBox is known as a **state button** because it can be in the on/off [true/false] state.) When a CheckBox is selected, a check mark appears in the box. Any number of CheckBoxes can be selected at a time, including none at all. The text that appears alongside a CheckBox is called the **CheckBox label**.

GUI Design Tip

A CheckBox's label should be descriptive and as short as possible. When a CheckBox's label contains more than one word, use book-title capitalization.

You can determine whether a CheckBox is on (that is, checked) by using the **Checked property**. If the CheckBox is checked, the Checked property returns the Boolean value True when accessed. If the CheckBox is not checked, the Checked property returns False when accessed.

You will now create the **Dental Payment** application from the template provided. The following box demonstrates how to add the CheckBoxes to your application. The application you will build in the next two boxes will not display a dialog if the TextBox is empty and/or all the CheckBoxes are unchecked when the **Calculate Button** is clicked. You will learn how to display that dialog in Section 8.4.

Adding CheckBoxes to the Form

1. ***Copying the template application to your working directory.*** Copy the C:\Examples\Tutorial08\TemplateApplication\DentalPayment directory to your C:\SimplyVB directory.

2. ***Opening the Dental Payment application's template file.*** Double click DentalPayment.sln in the DentalPayment directory to open the application in the Visual Basic IDE. Be sure to double click Inventory.vb in the **Solution Explorer** if the form does not appear.

3. ***Adding CheckBox controls to the Form.*** Add a CheckBox to the Form by double clicking the

icon in the **Toolbox**. Repeat this process until three CheckBoxes have been added to the Form.

GUI Design Tip

Align groups of CheckBoxes either horizontally or vertically.

4. ***Customizing the CheckBoxes.*** For this application, you will be modifying the AutoSize, Location, Text, Size and Name properties of each CheckBox. First, set the AutoSize property of all three checkboxes to false. This property is similar to the one that you modified for labels in Tutorial 2. Next, change the Size property of all three CheckBoxes to 122, 24. Change the Name property of the first CheckBox to cleanCheckBox and set its Location property to 16, 112 and its Text property to Cleaning. Change the Name property of the second CheckBox to cavityCheckBox, its Location property to 16, 159 and its Text property to Cavity Filling. Change the Name property of the final CheckBox to xrayCheckBox, its Location property to 16, 206 and its Text property to X-Ray.

5. ***Saving the project.*** Select **File > Save All** to save your changes.

After placing the CheckBoxes on the Form and setting their properties, you need to code an event handler to enhance the application's functionality when users select CheckBoxes and click **Calculate**.

Adding the Calculate Button's Event Handler	1. ***Adding an event handler for calculateButton's Click event.*** Double click the **Calculate** Button on the Form to create an event handler for that control's Click event.

2. ***Adding If...Then statements to calculate the patient's bill.*** Add lines 6–28 of Fig. 8.7 to your application. Be sure to include all blank lines and line-continuation characters shown in Fig. 8.7 to improve code readability and to ensure that your line numbers correspond to the figure's.

Line 7 clears any text in the output Label that may be present from a previous calculation. Line 10 declares variable total, which stores the total charges for the patient as an Integer. This variable is initialized to 0. Lines 12–25 define three If...Then statements that determine whether the user has checked any of the Form's CheckBoxes. Each If...Then statement's condition compares a CheckBox's Checked property to True. For each If...Then statement, the dollar value of the service is added to total if the current CheckBox is checked. The first If...Then statement, for example, adds 35 to total in line 14 if CheckBox cleanCheckBox is selected (line 13). Note that the numeric values added to total correspond to the monetary values indicated on the GUI, to the right of each service. Line 28 displays the total (formatted as a currency amount) in totalResultLabel.

Add this highlighted code ———

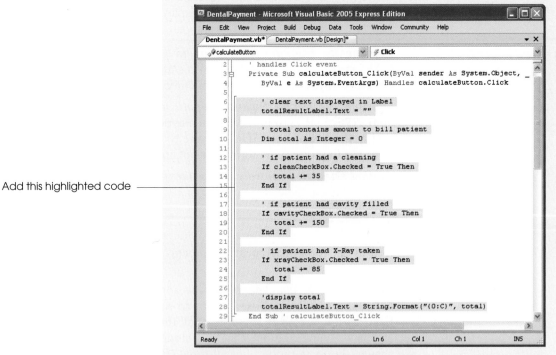

Figure 8.7   Using the Checked property.

3. ***Running the application.*** Select **Debug > Start Debugging** to run your application. Note that the user is not required to enter a name or select any CheckBoxes before clicking the **Calculate** Button. If no CheckBoxes are selected, the bill displays the value **$0.00** (Fig. 8.8).

(cont.)

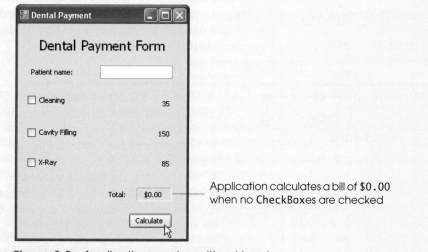

Figure 8.8   Application running without input.

4. *Selecting a CheckBox.* Select the **Cleaning** CheckBox, and click the **Calcu-late** Button. The **Total:** field now displays **$35.00**.

5. *Closing the application.* Close your running application by clicking its close box.

SELF-REVIEW
1. The _____ property sets a CheckBox's label.

    a) `Text`   b) `Value`

    c) `Label`   d) `Checked`

2. Which property determines whether a CheckBox is selected?

    a) `Selected`   b) `Checked`

    c) `Clicked`   d) `Check`

Answers: 1.) a. 2.) b.

8.4 Using a Dialog to Display a Message

In the completed application, a message is displayed in a dialog if the user attempts to calculate the total charges without specifying which services were performed and/or without entering a name. In this section, you will learn how to display a dialog when a patient name is not input. When the dialog is closed, control is returned to the application's Form. The message dialog used in your application is displayed in Fig. 8.9.

Title bar ————
Icon indicates the tone of the message ————
OK Button allows the user to close the dialog ————

———— Close box

———— Dialog sized to accommodate contents

Figure 8.9   Dialog displayed by the application.

The message dialog contains a title bar and a close box. This dialog also contains a message (`Please enter a name and check at least one item`), an **OK** Button that allows the user to **dismiss** (close) the dialog (which the user must do to proceed) and an icon that indicates the tone of the message. (In this case, ⚠ indicates that a problem has occurred.)

GUI Design Tip

Text displayed in a dialog should be descriptive and as short as possible.

Message dialogs are defined by class **MessageBox** and can be displayed by using method **MessageBox.Show**. The message dialog is customized by the arguments passed to method MessageBox.Show. The following box demonstrates displaying a message dialog based on a condition.

Displaying a Message Dialog Using **MessageBox.Show**

1. ***Adding an If...Then statement to the event handler for calculateButton's Click event.*** The message should display only if the user does not enter the patient's name. Later, you will add the code to determine if no CheckBox has been marked. Place the cursor in line 8 and press *Enter*. Then insert lines 9–12 of Fig. 8.10 into your event handler. Be sure to include a blank line after the End If statement.

   Line 10 tests whether data was entered in the **Patient name:** TextBox. If no data has been entered, the expression nameTextBox.Text = "" evaluates to True. You will add the body of this If...Then statement in *Step 2*.

Add this highlighted code ⎯⎯⎯⎯⎯

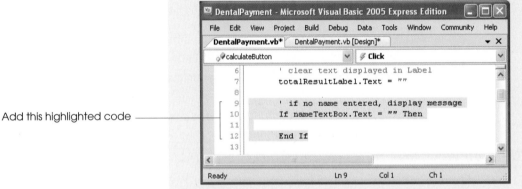

Figure 8.10 Adding an If...Then statement to the calculateButton Click event handler to display a message dialog.

2. ***Adding code to display a message dialog.*** Insert lines 12–16 from Fig. 8.11 into the body of the If...Then statement you created in the preceding step. Change the End If (line 12 of Fig. 8.10) to Else (line 17 of Fig. 8.11). Note that the code you added to the Click event earlier (Fig. 8.7) now composes the body of the Else portion of your If...Then...Else statement. The Else is marked as a syntax error because the If...Then...Else statement is now missing an End If statement. You will add this statement in *Step 3*.

Add this highlighted code ⎯⎯⎯⎯⎯

Change End If to Else ⎯⎯⎯⎯⎯

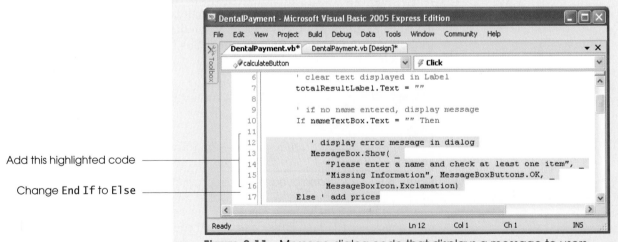

Figure 8.11 Message dialog code that displays a message to users.

Lines 13–16 call method `MessageBox.Show` using four arguments separated by commas. The first argument specifies the text that displays in the dialog, the second argument specifies the text that appears in its title bar, the third argument indicates which `Button`(s) to display at the bottom of the dialog and the fourth argument indicates which icon appears to the left of the dialog's text. We discuss the final two arguments in more detail shortly.

3. ***Closing the If...Then...Else statement.*** Scroll to the end of your event handler code. Notice that the IDE automatically inserted the keywords `End If` (line 39 of Fig. 8.12) to terminate the `If...Else` statement. Figure 8.13 displays the entire method `calculateButton_Click` after the new code has been added. Compare this code to your own to ensure that you have added the new code correctly.

Add this highlighted code ⟶

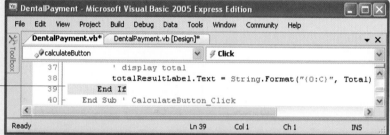

Figure 8.12 Ending the `If...Else` statement.

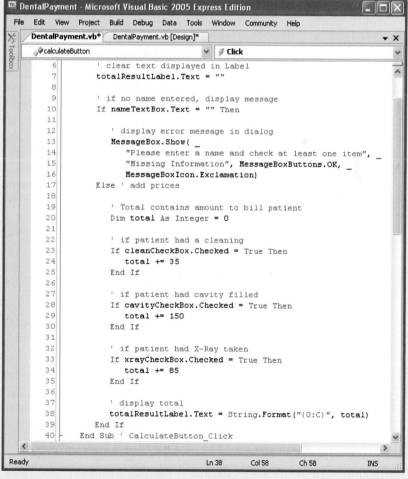

Figure 8.13 Completed `calculateButton_Click` event handler.

(cont.)

4. ***Running the application.*** Select **Debug > Start Debugging** to run your application. Note that the user does not have to select any CheckBoxes before clicking the **Calculate** Button but must enter a name in the **Patient name:** TextBox. If none of the CheckBoxes is selected, the bill will contain the value **$0.00** (Fig. 8.14). In the next section, you will modify the code to test whether the user has selected any CheckBoxes.

5. ***Closing the application.*** Close your running application by clicking its close box.

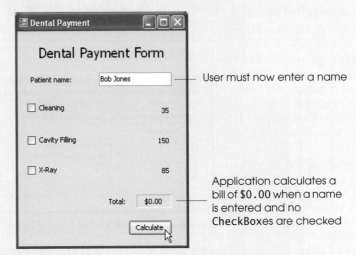

Figure 8.14 Application running without any CheckBoxes selected.

In this example, you passed four arguments to method `MessageBox.Show`. The first two arguments indicate the text of the dialog's message and the text of the dialog's title bar, respectively. The third argument specifies the Button that displays in the dialog. To accomplish this task, you passed one of the FCL's **MessageBoxButtons** constants to method `MessageBox.Show`. You will use only the `MessageBoxButtons.OK` constant in this book. Figure 8.15 lists the available Button constants. Note that several Buttons can be displayed at once. The fourth argument specifies the icon that displays in the dialog. To set the icon to display, you passed one of Visual Basic's **MessageBoxIcon** constants to method `MessageBox.Show`. The available icon constants are shown in Fig. 8.16.

MessageBoxButtons Constants	Description
`MessageBoxButtons.OK`	**OK** Button. Allows the user to acknowledge a message.
`MessageBoxButtons.OKCancel`	**OK** and **Cancel** Buttons. Allow the user to either continue or cancel an operation.
`MessageBoxButtons.YesNo`	**Yes** and **No** Buttons. Allow the user to respond to a question.
`MessageBoxButtons.YesNoCancel`	**Yes**, **No** and **Cancel** Buttons. Allow the user to respond to a question or cancel an operation.
`MessageBoxButtons.RetryCancel`	**Retry** and **Cancel** Buttons. Allow the user either to retry or to cancel an operation that has failed.
`MessageBoxButtons.AbortRetryIgnore`	**Abort**, **Retry** and **Ignore** Buttons. When one of a series of operations has failed, these Buttons allow the user to abort the entire sequence, retry the failed operation or ignore the failed operation and continue.

Figure 8.15 Message dialog Button constants.

MessageBoxIcon Constants	Icon	Description
MessageBox- Icon.Exclamation	⚠	Icon containing an exclamation point. Typically used to caution the user against potential problems.
MessageBox- Icon.Information	ⓘ	Icon containing the letter "i." Typically used to display information about the state of the application.
MessageBox- Icon.Question	❔	Icon containing a question mark. Typically used to ask the user a question.
MessageBox- Icon.Error	✖	Icon containing an ∞ in a red circle. Typically used to alert the user to errors or critical situations.

Figure 8.16   Message dialog icon constants.

SELF-REVIEW

1. Which constant, when passed to method `MessageBox.Show`, indicates that a question is being asked?

   a) `MessageBox.Question`   b) `MessageBoxIcon.QuestionMark`

   c) `MessageBox.QuestionMark`   d) `MessageBoxIcon.Question`

2. What is the message dialog icon containing the letter "i" typically used for?

   a) To display information about the state of the application

   b) To caution the user against potential problems

   c) To ask the user a question   d) To alert the user to critical situations

Answers: 1.) d. 2.) a.

8.5 Logical Operators

So far, you have studied only **simple conditions**, such as `count <= 10`, `total > 1000`, and `number <> value`. Each selection statement that you used evaluated only one condition with one of the operators >, <, >=, <=, = or <>.

To handle multiple conditions more efficiently, Visual Basic provides **logical operators** that can be used to form complex conditions by combining simple ones. The logical operators are **AndAlso**, **OrElse**, **Xor** and **Not**. We will consider examples that use each of these operators. After you learn about logical operators, you will use them to create a complex condition in your **Dental Payment** application to confirm `CheckBox` entries.

Using AndAlso

Suppose that you wish to ensure that two conditions are *both* true in an application before choosing a certain path of execution. In that case, you can use the logical `AndAlso` operator as follows:

```
If genderTextBox.Text = "Female" AndAlso age >= 65 Then
    seniorFemales += 1
End If
```

This `If...Then` statement contains two simple conditions. The condition `gender-TextBox.Text = "Female"` determines whether a person is female, and the condition `age >= 65` determines whether a person is a senior citizen. The = and >= operators have a higher precedence than operator `AndAlso`. In this case, the two simple conditions are evaluated first, then the `AndAlso` operator is evaluated using their result. The `If...Then` statement then considers the combined condition

```
genderTextBox.Text = "Female" AndAlso age >= 65
```

This condition evaluates to true *if and only if* both of the simple conditions are true, meaning that `genderTextBox.Text` contains the value `"Female"` and `age` contains

Error-Prevention Tip

Always write the simplest condition possible by limiting the number of logical operators used. Conditions with many logical operators can be hard to read and can introduce subtle bugs into your applications.

a value greater than or equal to 65. When this combined condition is true, the count of `seniorFemales` is incremented by 1. However, if either or both of the simple conditions are false, the application skips the increment and proceeds to the statement following the `If...Then` statement. The readability of the preceding combined condition can be improved by adding redundant (that is, unnecessary) parentheses:

```
(genderTextBox.Text = "Female") AndAlso (age >= 65)
```

Figure 8.17 illustrates the outcome of using the `AndAlso` operator with two expressions. The table lists all four possible combinations of `True` and `False` values for *expression1* and *expression2*, which represent the left operand and the right operand, respectively. Such tables are called **truth tables**. Visual Basic evaluates to `True` or `False` expressions that include relational operators, equality operators and logical operators.

expression1	expression2	expression1 AndAlso expression2
False	False	False
False	True	False
True	False	False
True	True	True

Figure 8.17 Truth table for the `AndAlso` operator.

Using `OrElse`

Now let's consider the `OrElse` operator. Suppose that you wish to ensure that either *or* both of two conditions are true before you choose a certain path of execution. You would use the `OrElse` operator, as in the following application segment:

```
If (semesterAverage >= 90 OrElse finalExam >= 90) Then
    MessageBox.Show("Student grade is A", "Student Grade", _
        MessageBoxButtons.OK, MessageBoxIcon.Information)
End If
```

This statement also contains two simple conditions. The condition `semesterAverage >= 90` is evaluated to determine whether the student deserves an "A" in the course because of an outstanding performance throughout the semester. The condition `finalExam >= 90` is evaluated to determine whether the student deserves an "A" in the course because of an outstanding performance on the final exam. The `If...Then` statement then considers the combined condition

```
(semesterAverage >= 90 OrElse finalExam >= 90)
```

Error-Prevention Tip

When writing conditions that contain combinations of `AndAlso` and `OrElse` operators, use parentheses to ensure that the conditions evaluate properly. Otherwise, logic errors could occur because `AndAlso` has higher precedence than `OrElse`.

and awards the student an "A" if either or both of the conditions are true, meaning that the student performed well during the semester, performed well on the final exam or both. Note that the text `"Student grade is A"` is displayed unless both of the conditions are false. Figure 8.18 provides a truth table for the `OrElse` operator. Note that the `AndAlso` operator has a higher precedence than the `OrElse` operator. See Appendix A for a complete listing of operator precedence in Visual Basic.

expression1	expression2	expression1 OrElse expression2
False	False	False
False	True	True
True	False	True
True	True	True

Figure 8.18 Truth table for the `OrElse` operator.

Short-Circuit Evaluation

An expression containing operator `AndAlso` is evaluated only until truth or falsity is known. For example, evaluation of the expression

```
(genderTextBox.Text = "Female" AndAlso age >= 65)
```

stops immediately if `genderTextBox.Text` is not equal to `"Female"` (which would mean that the entire expression is false). In this case, the evaluation of the second expression is irrelevant; once the first expression is known to be false, the whole expression must be false. Evaluation of the second expression occurs if and only if `genderTextBox.Text` is equal to `"Female"` (which would mean that the entire expression could still be true if the condition `age >= 65` is true).

Similarly, an expression containing `OrElse` is evaluated only until its truth or falsity is known. For example, evaluation of the expression

```
If (semesterAverage >= 90 OrElse finalExam >= 90) Then
```

stops immediately if `semesterAverage` is greater than or equal to 90 (which would mean that the entire expression is `True`). In this case, the evaluation of the second expression is irrelevant; once the first expression is known to be true, the whole expression must be true.

This way of evaluating logical expressions requires fewer operations, and therefore takes less time. This performance feature for the evaluation of `AndAlso` and `OrElse` expressions is called **short-circuit evaluation**.[1]

Using Xor

A condition containing the **logical exclusive OR (Xor)** operator is `True` *if and only if one of its operands results in a `True` value and the other results in a `False` value.* If both operands are `True` or both are `False`, the entire condition is `False`. Figure 8.19 presents a truth table for the logical exclusive OR operator (`Xor`). This operator always evaluates both of its operands (that is, there is no short-circuit evaluation).

expression1	expression2	expression1 Xor expression2
False	False	False
False	True	True
True	False	True
True	True	False

Figure 8.19   Truth table for the logical exclusive OR (`Xor`) operator.

Using Not

Visual Basic's **Not** (logical negation) operator enables a programmer to "reverse" the meaning of a condition. Unlike the logical operators `AndAlso`, `OrElse` and `Xor`, each of which combines two expressions (that is, these are all binary operators), the logical negation operator is a unary operator, requiring only one operand. The logical negation operator is placed before a condition to choose a path of execution if

---

1. Visual Basic also provides the `And` and `Or` operators, which do not short-circuit. (They always evaluate their right operand regardless of whether or not the condition's truth or falsity is already known.) In Visual Basic applications, the performance benefit of using `AndAlso` and `OrElse` is negligible. One potential problem of using `AndAlso`/`OrElse` instead of `And`/`Or` is when the right operand contains a side effect, such as a function call that modifies a variable. Because such side effects might not occur when using short-circuit evaluation, subtle logic errors could occur. As a good programming practice, most Visual Basic programmers who use operators `AndAlso` and `OrElse` try to avoid writing conditions that contain side effects.

the original condition (without the logical negation operator) is False. The logical negation operator is demonstrated by the following application segment:

```
If Not (grade = value) Then
    displayLabel.Text = "They are not equal!"
End If
```

The parentheses around the condition grade = value are necessary because the logical negation operator (Not) has a higher precedence than the equality operator. Most programmers prefer to write

```
Not (grade = value)
```

as

```
(grade <> value)
```

Figure 8.20 provides a truth table for the logical negation operator. The following box provides an example of using complex expressions. You will modify your **Dental Payment** application to use a complex expression.

expression	Not expression
False	True
True	False

Figure 8.20 Truth table for the **Not** operator (logical NOT).

Using Logical Operators in Complex Expressions

1. **Inserting a complex expression into the Click event handler.** Double click the **Calculate** Button on the Form. Replace lines 9–10 of Fig. 8.10 with lines 9–13 of Fig. 8.21.

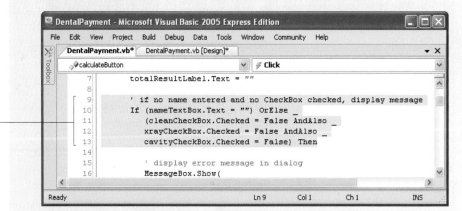

Add the highlighted code

Figure 8.21 Using the AndAlso and OrElse logical operators.

Lines 10–13 define a more sophisticated logical expression than others we have used in this book. Note the use of OrElse and AndAlso. If the name is blank or if no CheckBox is checked, a dialog should appear. After the original expression (nameTextBox.Text = ""), you use OrElse to indicate that either the expression on the left (nameTextBox.Text = "") or the expression "on the right" (which ensures that no CheckBoxes have been checked) needs to be True for the entire expression to evaluate to True to execute the body of the If...Then statement. The complex expression "on the right" uses AndAlso twice to determine whether all of the CheckBoxes are unchecked. Note that because AndAlso has a higher precedence than OrElse, the parentheses in lines 10, 11 and 13 are redundant (unnecessary).

(cont.)

2. ***Running the application.*** Select **Debug > Start Debugging** to run your application. Note that users must enter a name and select at least one CheckBox before they click the **Calculate** Button. The application appears the same as in Figs. 8.1 and 8.4. (You have finally corrected the weakness from your earlier implementation of the **Dental Payment** application.)

3. ***Closing the application.*** Close your running application by clicking its close box.

4. ***Closing the IDE.*** Close the Visual Basic IDE by clicking its close box.

Figure 8.22 presents the source code for the **Dental Payment** application. The lines of code that contain new programming concepts that you learned in this tutorial are highlighted.

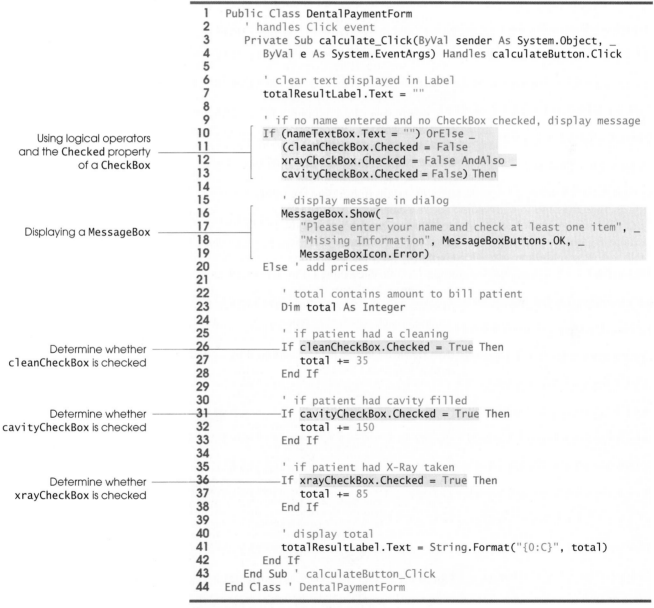

```vb
1   Public Class DentalPaymentForm
2       ' handles Click event
3       Private Sub calculate_Click(ByVal sender As System.Object, _
4           ByVal e As System.EventArgs) Handles calculateButton.Click
5
6           ' clear text displayed in Label
7           totalResultLabel.Text = ""
8
9           ' if no name entered and no CheckBox checked, display message
10          If (nameTextBox.Text = "") OrElse _
11              (cleanCheckBox.Checked = False
12              xrayCheckBox.Checked = False AndAlso _
13              cavityCheckBox.Checked = False) Then
14
15              ' display message in dialog
16              MessageBox.Show( _
17                  "Please enter your name and check at least one item", _
18                  "Missing Information", MessageBoxButtons.OK, _
19                  MessageBoxIcon.Error)
20          Else ' add prices
21
22              ' total contains amount to bill patient
23              Dim total As Integer
24
25              ' if patient had a cleaning
26              If cleanCheckBox.Checked = True Then
27                  total += 35
28              End If
29
30              ' if patient had cavity filled
31              If cavityCheckBox.Checked = True Then
32                  total += 150
33              End If
34
35              ' if patient had X-Ray taken
36              If xrayCheckBox.Checked = True Then
37                  total += 85
38              End If
39
40              ' display total
41              totalResultLabel.Text = String.Format("{0:C}", total)
42          End If
43      End Sub ' calculateButton_Click
44  End Class ' DentalPaymentForm
```

Figure 8.22 Code for the **Dental Payment** application.

Labels pointing to code:

- Using logical operators and the **Checked** property of a **CheckBox** (lines 10–13)
- Displaying a **MessageBox** (lines 16–19)
- Determine whether `cleanCheckBox` is checked (line 26)
- Determine whether `cavityCheckBox` is checked (line 31)
- Determine whether `xrayCheckBox` is checked (line 36)

1. A unary operator _____.

   a) requires exactly one operand   b) requires two operands

   c) must use the AndAlso keyword   d) can have no operands

2. The _____ operator is used to ensure that two conditions are both true.

   a) Xor   b) AndAlso

   c) Also   d) OrElse

Answers: 1.) a. 2.) b.

8.6 Designer-Generated Code

In Tutorial 6, you learned that every variable must be declared with a name and a type before you can use it in an application. Like the variables you've declared, GUI controls also must be declared before they are used. You might be wondering where these declarations are, since you have not seen them in any of the examples so far. A nice aspect of Visual Basic 2005 is that when you work **Design** view to build and configure your application's GUI, Visual Basic automatically declares the controls for you. It also generates code that creates each control and configures its properties—including any changes that you make to the properties through the **Properties** window or by dragging and resizing controls on the Form.

To improve the readability of your application code, Visual Basic "hides" the GUI declarations and other GUI code it generates in a separate file that starts with the same name as the Form's .vb file, but ends with **Designer.vb**—in this tutorial, the file is named DentalPaymentForm.Designer.vb. By placing this code in a separate file, Visual Basic allows you to focus on you application's logic rather than the tedious details of building the GUI.

You can view these separate files and even edit them—though editing them is not recommended. To view the Designer.vb file for the **Dental Payment** application, click the **Show All Files** button (discussed in Section 2.5) in the **Solution Explorer**, then click the plus (+) sign next to DentalPayment.vb to expand its node. Double click DentalPaymentForm.Designer.vb to view the code.

Figure 8.23 shows the declarations that the IDE generated for all of the controls used in the **Dental Payment** application (lines 166–177). Note that the IDE declares each control's type with its fully qualified type name—that is, the namespace System.Windows.Forms followed by the type of the control. The controls declared in Fig. 8.23 are created by lines 22–33 in the completed application's DentalPaymentForm.Designer.vb file.

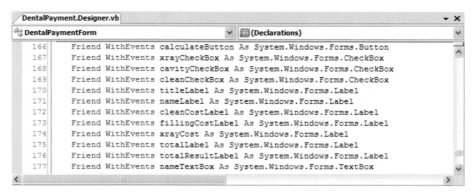

Figure 8.23 GUI declarations for the controls in the **Dental Payment** application.

In *Step 4* of the box *Adding CheckBoxes to the Form* earlier in this tutorial, you placed three CheckBoxes on the Form and configured several of their properties. Figure 8.24 shows some of the statements that the IDE created based on your actions. For example, you set the Size property of each CheckBox to 122,24. Lines

49, 58 and 67 are the generated statements that change the size of the CheckBoxes to these values. Similarly, you changed the locations of the CheckBoxes. The statements that change their locations appear in lines 47, 56 and 65, respectively.

```
DentalPayment.Designer.vb                                                    ▼ ✕
DentalPaymentForm                              ▼   InitializeComponent                    ▼
 44        '
 45        'xrayCheckBox
 46        '
 47        Me.xrayCheckBox.Location = New System.Drawing.Point(16, 206)
 48        Me.xrayCheckBox.Name = "xrayCheckBox"
 49        Me.xrayCheckBox.Size = New System.Drawing.Size(122, 24)
 50        Me.xrayCheckBox.TabIndex = 9
 51        Me.xrayCheckBox.Text = "X-Ray"
 52        Me.xrayCheckBox.UseVisualStyleBackColor = True
 53        '
 54        'cavityCheckBox
 55        '
 56        Me.cavityCheckBox.Location = New System.Drawing.Point(16, 159)
 57        Me.cavityCheckBox.Name = "cavityCheckBox"
 58        Me.cavityCheckBox.Size = New System.Drawing.Size(122, 24)
 59        Me.cavityCheckBox.TabIndex = 10
 60        Me.cavityCheckBox.Text = "Cavity Filling"
 61        Me.cavityCheckBox.UseVisualStyleBackColor = True
 62        '
 63        'cleanCheckBox
 64        '
 65        Me.cleanCheckBox.Location = New System.Drawing.Point(16, 112)
 66        Me.cleanCheckBox.Name = "cleanCheckBox"
 67        Me.cleanCheckBox.Size = New System.Drawing.Size(122, 24)
 68        Me.cleanCheckBox.TabIndex = 3
 69        Me.cleanCheckBox.Text = "Cleaning"
 70        Me.cleanCheckBox.UseVisualStyleBackColor = True
```

Figure 8.24 Statements that configure the CheckBox properties.

Everything you do with visual programming in **Design** view has consequences in the Designer.vb file, but the IDE handles the GUI code for you. This greatly simplifies the programming process and makes you more productive. This also eliminates many common programming errors and typos, since the IDE does not make mistakes when it generates this code.

GUIs are tremendous tools for interfacing with computers. However, they require lots of code. Visual programming in **Design** view enables the IDE to generate most of this code for you, and the hidden Designer.vb file gets the GUI "out of the way" so you can concentrate on the logic of your application.

8.7 Wrap-Up

In this tutorial, you used CheckBox controls to provide a series of choices to users in the **Dental Payment** application. CheckBoxes provide options that can be selected by clicking them. When a CheckBox is selected, its square contains a check mark. You can determine whether a CheckBox is selected in your code by accessing its Checked property.

Your **Dental Payment** application also used message dialogs to display messages to the user when information was not entered appropriately. To implement dialogs in your application, you used the MessageBox class, which provides methods and constants necessary to display a dialog containing Buttons and an icon. You used an If...Then...Else statement to calculate the cost of the dental visit or display a message dialog if the user was missing input. Later in this book you will learn to avoid checking for invalid user input by disabling a control (such as a Button) when its events should not cause any action to occur.

You learned to use the logical AndAlso operator when both conditions must be true for the overall condition to be true—if either condition is false, the overall condition is false. You also learned that the logical OrElse operator requires at least one of its conditions to be true for the overall condition to be true—if both conditions are false, the overall condition is false. The logical Xor operator requires that exactly one of its conditions be true for the overall condition to be true—if both conditions are false or if both conditions are true, the overall condition is false. The logical Not operator reverses the Boolean result of a condition—True becomes False, and False becomes True. You then used the AndAlso and OrElse operators to form a complex expression.

Finally, you learned about the Designer.vb file that the IDE generates to store the code that builds the controls in your GUI. This file also contains the statements that configure the controls based on your actions in **Design** mode.

In the next tutorial, you will learn more about Visual Basic's control structures. Specifically, you will use **repetition statements**, which allow the programmer to specify that an action or a group of actions should be performed many times.

SKILLS SUMMARY

Adding a CheckBox to a Form

■ Double click the CheckBox in the **ToolBox**.

Selecting a CheckBox

■ Click the CheckBox, and a check mark will appear in the box.

Deselecting a CheckBox

■ Click a checked CheckBox to remove its check mark.

Determining Whether a CheckBox Is Selected

■ Access the CheckBox's Checked property.

Displaying a Dialog

■ Use method MessageBox.Show.

Combining Multiple Conditions

■ Use the logical operators to form complex conditions by combining simple ones.

KEY TERMS

AndAlso operator—A logical operator used to ensure that two conditions are *both* true before choosing a certain path of execution. Performs short-circuit evaluation.

CheckBox control—A small square GUI element that either is blank or contains a check mark.

CheckBox label—The text that appears alongside a CheckBox.

Checked property of the CheckBox control—Specifies whether the CheckBox is checked (True) or unchecked (False).

Designer.vb file—The file containing the declarations and statements that build an application's GUI.

dialog (message dialog)—A window that displays messages to users or gathers input from users.

dismiss—Synonym for close.

logical exclusive OR (Xor) operator—A logical operator that is True if and only if one of its operands results in True and the other results in False.

logical operators—The operators (for example, AndAlso, OrElse, Xor and Not) that can be used to form complex conditions by combining simple ones.

MessageBox class—Provides a method for displaying message dialogs.

MessageBoxButtons constants—The identifiers that specify Buttons that can be displayed in a MessageBox dialog.

MessageBoxIcon constants—Identifiers that specify icons that can be displayed in a MessageBox dialog.

MessageBox.Show method—Displays a message dialog.

Not (logical negation) operator—A logical operator that enables a programmer to reverse the meaning of a condition: A True condition, when logically negated, becomes False, and a False condition, when logically negated, becomes True.

OrElse operator—A logical operator used to ensure that either *or* both of two conditions are

True in an application before a certain path of execution is chosen.

repetition statements—Statements that allow the programmer to specify that an action or a group of actions should be performed many times.

short-circuit evaluation—The evaluation of the right operand in AndAlso and OrElse expressions occurs only if the first condition meets the criteria for the condition.

simple condition—Contains one expression.

state button—A button that can be in the on/off (true/false) state.

truth table—A table that displays the Boolean result of a logical operator for all possible combinations of True and False values for its operands.

GUI DESIGN GUIDELINES

CheckBoxes

■ A CheckBox's label should be descriptive and as short as possible. When a CheckBox label contains more than one word, use book-title capitalization.

■ Align groups of CheckBoxes either horizontally or vertically.

Message Dialogs

■ Text displayed in a dialog should be descriptive and as short as possible.

CONTROLS, EVENTS, PROPERTIES & METHODS

CheckBox ☑ CheckBox   This control allows user to select an option.

■ *In action*

☑ Cleaning

☐ Cavity Filling

■ *Properties*

Checked—Specifies whether the CheckBox is checked (True) or unchecked (False).

Location—Specifies the location of the CheckBox on the Form.

Name—Specifies the name used to access the CheckBox control programmatically. The name should be appended with the CheckBox suffix.

Text—Specifies the text displayed next to the CheckBox.

MULTIPLE-CHOICE QUESTIONS

8.1 How many CheckBoxes in a GUI can be selected at once?

a) 0   b) 1
c) 4   d) any number

8.2 The text that appears alongside a CheckBox is referred to as the _____.

a) CheckBox label   b) CheckBox name
c) CheckBox value   d) CheckBox data

8.3 The first argument passed to method MessageBox.Show is _____.

a) the text displayed in the dialog's title bar
b) a constant representing the Buttons displayed in the dialog
c) the text displayed inside the dialog
d) a constant representing the icon that appears in the dialog

8.4 You can specify the Button(s) and icon to be displayed in a message dialog by using the MessageBoxButtons and _____ constants.

a) MessageIcon   b) MessageBoxImages
c) MessageBoxPicture   d) MessageBoxIcon

8.5 _____ are used to create complex conditions.

a) Assignment operators   b) Activity diagrams
c) Logical operators   d) Formatting codes

8.6 Operator AndAlso _____.
a) performs short-circuit evaluation
b) is not a keyword
c) is a comparison operator
d) evaluates to false if both operands are true

8.7 A CheckBox is selected when its Checked property is set to _____.
a) On
b) True
c) Selected
d) Checked

8.8 The condition *expression1* AndAlso *expression2* evaluates to True when _____.
a) *expression1* is True and *expression2* is False
b) *expression1* is False and *expression2* is True
c) both *expression1* and *expression2* are True
d) both *expression1* and *expression2* are False

8.9 The condition *expression1* OrElse *expression2* evaluates to False when _____.
a) *expression1* is True and *expression2* is False
b) *expression1* is False and *expression2* is True
c) both *expression1* and *expression2* are True
d) both *expression1* and *expression2* are False

8.10 The condition *expression1* Xor *expression2* evaluates to True when _____.
a) *expression1* is True and *expression2* is False
b) *expression1* is False and *expression2* is True
c) both *expression1* and *expression2* are True
d) Both a and b.

EXERCISES

8.11 (***Enhanced Dental Payment Application***) Modify the **Dental Payment** application from this tutorial to include additional services, as shown in Fig. 8.25. Add the proper functionality (using If...Then statements) to determine whether any of the new CheckBoxes are selected, and, if so, add the price of the service to the total bill.

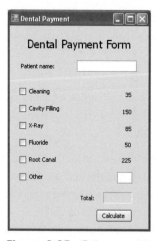

Figure 8.25 Enhanced **Dental Payment** application.

a) ***Copying the template to your working directory.*** Copy the directory C:\Examples\ Tutorial08\Exercises\DentalPaymentEnhanced to your C:\SimplyVB directory.

b) ***Opening the application's template file.*** Double click DentalPaymentEnhanced.sln in the DentalPaymentEnhanced directory to open the application.

c) ***Adding CheckBoxes and Labels and a TextBox.*** Add two CheckBoxes and two Labels to the Form. The new CheckBoxes should be labeled **Fluoride** and **Root Canal**, respectively. Add these CheckBoxes and Labels beneath the X-Ray CheckBox and its price Label. The price for a fluoride treatment is $50; the price for a root canal is $225. Add a CheckBox labeled **Other** and a Label containing a dollar sign (**$**) to the Form, as shown in Fig. 8.25. Then add a TextBox to the right of the **$** Label in which the user can enter the cost of the service performed.

d) *Modifying the C1ick event handler code.* Add code to the calculateButton_Click event handler that determines whether the new CheckBoxes have been selected. This can be done my modifying the compound condition in the first If...Then statement in the event handler. Also, use If...Then statements to update the bill amount.

e) *Running the application.* Select **Debug > Start Debugging** to run your application. Test your application by checking one or more of the new services. Click the **Calculate** Button and verify that the proper total is displayed. Test the application again by checking some of the services, then checking the Other CheckBox and entering a dollar value for this service. Click the **Calculate** Button and verify that the proper total is displayed, and that it includes the price for the "other" service.

f) *Closing the application.* Close your running application by clicking its close box.

g) *Closing the IDE.* Close the Visual Basic IDE by clicking its close box.

8.12 (*Fuzzy Dice Order Form Application*) Write an application that allows users to process orders for fuzzy dice, as shown in Fig. 8.26. The application should calculate the total price of the order, including tax and shipping. TextBoxes for inputting the order number, the customer name and the shipping address are provided. Initially, these fields contain text that describes their purpose. Provide CheckBoxes for selecting the fuzzy-dice color and TextBoxes for inputting the quantities of fuzzy dice to order. The application should also contain a Button that, when clicked, calculates the subtotals for each type of fuzzy dice ordered and the total of the entire order (including tax and shipping). Use 5% for the tax rate. Shipping charges are $1.50 for up to 20 pairs of dice. If more than 20 pairs of dice are ordered, shipping is free.

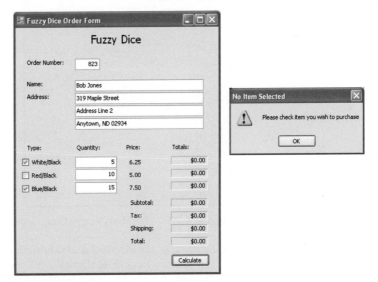

Figure 8.26 **Fuzzy Dice Order Form** application.

a) *Copying the template to your working directory.* Copy the directory C:\Examples\ Tutorial08\Exercises\FuzzyDiceOrderForm to your C:\SimplyVB directory.

b) *Opening the application's template file.* Double click FuzzyDiceOrderForm.sln in the FuzzyDiceOrderForm directory to open the application.

c) *Adding CheckBoxes to the Form.* Add three CheckBoxes to the Form. Label the first CheckBox **White/Black**, the second one **Red/Black** and the third **Blue/Black**.

d) *Adding a C1ick event handler and its code.* Create the C1ick event handler for the **Calculate** Button. For this application, users should not be allowed to specify an item's quantity unless the item's corresponding CheckBox is checked. For the total to be calculated, the user must enter an order number, a name and a shipping address. Use logical operators to ensure that these terms are met. If they are not, display a message in a dialog.

e) *Calculating the total cost.* Calculate the subtotal, tax, shipping and total, and display the results in their corresponding `Label`s.

f) *Running the application.* Select **Debug > Start Debugging** to run your application. Test the application by providing quantities for checked items. For instance, ensure that your application is calculating 5% sales tax. If more than 20 pairs of dice are ordered, verify that shipping is free. Also, determine whether your code containing the logical operators works correctly by specifying a quantity for an item that is not checked. For instance, in Fig. 8.26, a quantity is specified for **Red/Black** dice, but the corresponding `CheckBox` is not selected. This should cause the message dialog in Fig. 8.26 to appear.

g) *Closing the application.* Close your running application by clicking its close box.

h) *Closing the IDE.* Close the Visual Basic IDE by clicking its close box.

8.13 (*Modified Fuzzy Dice Order Form Application*) Modify the **Fuzzy Dice Order Form** application from Exercise 8.12 to determine whether customers should receive a 7% discount on their purchase. Customers ordering more than $500 (before tax and shipping) in fuzzy dice are eligible for this discount.

a) *Opening the application.* Open the application you created in Exercise 8.12.

b) *Determining whether the total cost is over $500.* Use an `If...Then` statement to determine whether the amount ordered is greater than $500.

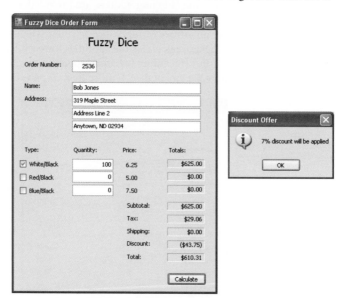

Figure 8.27   Modified **Fuzzy Dice Order Form** application.

c) *Displaying the discount and subtracting the discount from the total.* If a customer orders more than $500, display a message dialog, as shown in Fig. 8.27, that informs the user that the customer is entitled to a 7% discount. The message dialog should contain an `Information` icon and an **OK** `Button`. Calculate 7% of the total amount, and display the discount amount in the **Discount:** field. Subtract this amount from the total, and update the **Total:** field.

d) *Running the application.* Select **Debug > Start Debugging** to run your application. Confirm that your application calculates and displays the discount properly.

e) *Closing the application.* Close your running application by clicking its close box.

f) *Closing the IDE.* Close the Visual Basic IDE by clicking its close box.

What does this code do? ▶   **8.14** Assume that `nameTextBox` is a `TextBox` and that `otherCheckBox` is a `CheckBox` next to which is another `TextBox` called `otherTextBox`, in which the user should specify a value. What does this code segment do?

```
1   If (nameTextBox.Text = "" OrElse _
2       (otherCheckBox.Checked = True AndAlso _
3       otherTextBox.Text = "")) Then
4
5       MessageBox.Show("Please enter a name or value", _
6           "Input Error", MessageBoxButtons.OK, _
7           MessageBoxIcon.Exclamation)
8
9   End If
```

What's wrong with this code? ▶ **8.15** Assume that nameTextBox is a TextBox. Find the error(s) in the following code:

```
1   If nameTextBox.Text = "John Doe" Then
2
3       MessageBox.Show("Welcome, John!", _
4           MessageBoxIcon.Exclamation)
5
6   End If
```

Using the Debugger ▶ **8.16** (*Sibling Survey Application*) The **Sibling Survey** application displays the siblings selected by the user in a dialog. If the user checks either the **Brother(s)** or **Sister(s)** CheckBox and the **No Siblings** CheckBox, the user is asked to verify the selection. Otherwise, the user's selection is displayed in a MessageBox. While testing this application, you noticed that it does not execute properly. Use the debugger to find and correct the logic error(s) in the code. This exercise is located in the C:\Examples\Tutorial08\Debugger\SiblingSurvey directory. Figure 8.28 shows the correct output for the application.

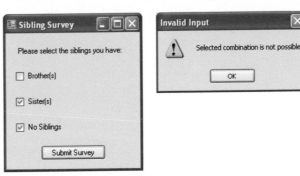

Figure 8.28   Correct output for the **Sibling Survey** application.

Programming Challenge ▶ **8.17** (*Enhanced Fuzzy Dice Order Form Application*) Enhance the **Fuzzy Dice Order Form** application from Exercise 8.12 by replacing the **Calculate** Button with a **Clear** Button. The application should update the total cost, tax and shipping when the user changes any one of the three **Quantity** field's values (Fig. 8.29). The **Clear** Button should return all fields to their original values. [*Hint*: You will need to use the CheckBox **CheckedChanged** event for each CheckBox. This event is raised when the state of a CheckBox changes. Double click a CheckBox in design view to create an event handler for that CheckBox's Checked-Changed event. You also will need to assign Boolean values to the CheckBoxes' Checked properties to control their states.]

Figure 8.29 Enhanced **Fuzzy Dice Order Form** application.

Objectives

In this tutorial, you will learn to:
- Use the **Do While...Loop** and **Do Until...Loop** repetition statements to execute statements in an application repeatedly.
- Use counter-controlled repetition.
- Display information in **ListBoxes**.
- Concatenate strings.

Outline

9.1 Test-Driving the Car Payment Calculator Application

9.2 **Do While...Loop** Repetition Statement

9.3 **Do Until...Loop** Repetition Statement

9.4 Constructing the Car Payment Calculator Application

9.5 Wrap-Up

Car Payment Calculator Application

Introducing the Do While...Loop and Do Until...Loop Repetition Statements

This tutorial continues the discussion of structured programming that we began in Tutorial 7. We introduce repetition statements, which are control statements that can repeat actions on the basis of a condition's value. You perform many repetitive tasks based on conditions. For example, each time you turn a page in this book (while there are more pages to read), you are repeating a simple task, namely turning a page, based on a condition, namely that there are more pages to read.

The ability to perform tasks repeatedly is an important part of structured programming. Repetition statements are used in many types of applications. In this tutorial, you will learn to use the Do While...Loop and the Do Until...Loop repetition statements. You will include a repetition statement in the **Car Payment Calculator** application that you build. Later tutorials will introduce additional repetition statements.

9.1 Test-Driving the Car Payment Calculator Application

The following problem statement requires an application that repeats a calculation four times—you will use a repetition statement to solve this problem. The application must meet the following requirements:

Application Requirements

Typically, banks offer car loans for periods ranging from two to five years (24 to 60 months). Borrowers repay the loans in monthly installments. The amount of each monthly payment is based on the length of the loan, the amount borrowed and the interest rate. Create an application that allows the customer to enter the price of a car, the down-payment amount and the annual interest rate of the loan. The application should display the loan's duration in months and the monthly payments for two-, three-, four- and five-year loans. The variety of options allows the user to easily compare repayment plans and choose the one that is most convenient.

You begin by test-driving the completed application. Then you will learn the additional Visual Basic technologies that you will need to create your own version of this application.

Test-Driving the Car Payment Calculator Application

1. **Opening the completed application.** Open the directory C:\Examples\ Tutorial09\CompletedApplication\CarPaymentCalculator to locate the **Car Payment Calculator** application. Double click CarPayment-Calculator.sln to open the application in the Visual Basic IDE.

2. **Running the application.** Select **Debug > Start Debugging** to run the application (Fig. 9.1). Note the new GUI control—the **ListBox** control, which allows users to view and select from multiple items in a list. Users cannot add items to, or remove items from, a ListBox by interacting directly with it. The ListBox does not accept keyboard input; users cannot add or delete selected items. You need to add code to your application to add or remove items from a ListBox.

ListBox control ———

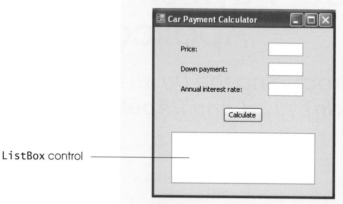

Figure 9.1 **Car Payment Calculator** application before data has been entered.

3. **Entering quantities in the application.** Enter 16900 in the **Price:** TextBox. Enter 6000 in the **Down payment:** TextBox. Enter 7.5 in the **Annual interest rate:** TextBox. The Form appears as in Fig. 9.2.

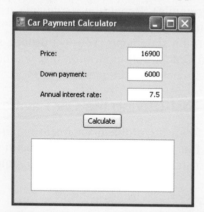

Figure 9.2 **Car Payment Calculator** application after data has been entered.

4. **Calculating the monthly payment amounts.** Click the **Calculate** Button. The application displays the monthly payment amounts in the ListBox (Fig. 9.3). The information is organized in tabular format.

5. **Closing the application.** Close your running application by clicking its close box.

6. **Closing the IDE.** Close the Visual Basic IDE by clicking its close box.

(cont.)

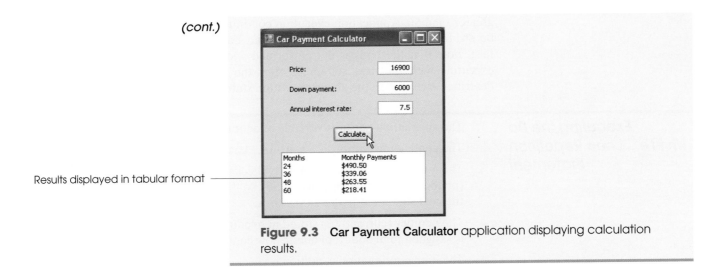

Results displayed in tabular format ——————

Figure 9.3   Car Payment Calculator application displaying calculation results.

9.2 Do While...Loop Repetition Statement

A **repetition statement** can repeat actions, depending on the value of a condition (which can be either true or false). For example, if you go to the grocery store with a list of items to purchase, you go through the list until you have each item. This process is described by the following pseudocode statements:

> *Do while there are more items on my shopping list*
>> *Purchase next item*
>> *Cross it off my list*

These statements describe the repetitive actions that occur during a shopping trip. The condition "there are more items on my shopping list" can be true or false. If it is true, then the actions "Purchase next item" and "Cross it off my list" are performed in sequence. In an application, these actions execute repeatedly while the condition remains true. The statement(s) indented in this repetition statement constitute its **body**. When the last item on the shopping list has been purchased and crossed off the list, the condition becomes false. At this point, the repetition terminates, and the first statement after the repetition statement executes. In the shopping example, you would proceed to the checkout station.

As an example of a Do While...Loop statement, let's look at an application segment designed to find the first power of 3 greater than 50.

Common Programming Error

Provide in the body of every **Do While...Loop** statement an action that eventually causes the condition to become false. If you do not, the repetition statement never terminates, causing an error called an **infinite loop**. Such an error causes the application to "hang up." When an infinite loop occurs in an application, right click the application in the task bar and select **Close**. In the dialog box that pops up, click **End Now**.

```
Dim product As Integer = 3

Do While product <= 50
    product *= 3
Loop
```

The application segment initializes variable product to 3, taking advantage of a Visual Basic feature that allows variable initialization to be incorporated into a declaration. The condition in the Do While...Loop statement, product <= 50, is referred to as the **loop-continuation condition**. While the loop-continuation condition remains true, the Do While...Loop statement executes its body repeatedly. When the loop-continuation condition becomes false, the Do While...Loop statement finishes executing, and product contains the first power of 3 larger than 50. Let's examine the execution of the preceding code in detail.

When the Do While...Loop statement is entered, the value of product is 3. Each time the loop executes, the variable product is multiplied by 3, taking on the values 3, 9, 27 and 81, successively. When product becomes 81, the condition in the Do While...Loop statement, product <= 50, is evaluated to false. When the repetition ends, the final value of product is 81, which is, indeed, the first power of 3 greater than 50. Application execution continues with the next statement after the Do While...Loop statement. If a Do While...Loop statement's condition is initially false, note that the body is not performed and your application simply continues executing with the next statement after the keyword Loop. The following box describes each step as the above repetition statement executes.

Executing the Do While...Loop Repetition Statement

1. The application declares variable product and sets its value to 3.

2. The application enters the Do While...Loop repetition statement.

3. The loop-continuation condition is checked. The condition evaluates to True (product is less than or equal to 50), so the application resumes execution at the next statement in the loop's body.

4. The number (currently 3) stored in product is multiplied by 3 and the result is assigned to product; product now contains the number 9.

5. The loop-continuation condition is checked. The condition evaluates to True (product is less than or equal to 50), so the application resumes execution at the next statement in the loop's body.

6. The number (currently 9) stored in product is multiplied by 3 and the result is assigned to product; product now contains the number 27.

7. The loop-continuation condition is checked. The condition evaluates to True (product is less than or equal to 50), so the application resumes execution at the next statement in the loop's body.

8. The number (currently 27) stored in product is multiplied by 3 and the result is assigned to product; product now contains the number 81.

9. The loop-continuation condition is checked. The condition evaluates to False (product is not less than or equal to 50), so the application exits the Do While...Loop repetition statement and the application resumes execution at the first statement after the Loop statement.

Let's use a UML activity diagram to illustrate the flow of control in the preceding Do While...Loop repetition statement. The UML activity diagram in Fig. 9.4 contains an initial state, transition arrows, a merge, a decision, two guard conditions, three notes and a final state. The oval represents the action state in which the value of product is multiplied by 3.

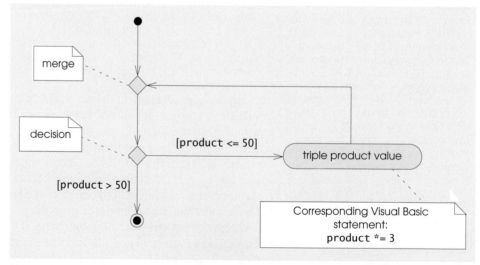

Figure 9.4 Do While...Loop repetition statement UML activity diagram.

The activity diagram clearly shows the repetition. The transition arrow emerging from the action state wraps back to the merge, creating a **loop**. The guard conditions are tested each time the loop iterates until the guard condition product > 50 eventually becomes true. At this point, the Do While...Loop statement is exited, and control passes to the next statement in the application following the loop.

Figure 9.4 introduces the UML's **merge symbol**. The UML represents both the merge symbol and the decision symbol as diamonds. The merge symbol joins two flows of activity into one flow of activity. In this diagram, the merge symbol joins the transitions from the initial state and from the action state, so they both flow into the loop-continuation guard decision, which is the decision that determines whether the loop body statement should begin executing (or continue executing). In this case, the UML diagram enters its action state when the loop-continuation guard condition product <= 50 is true.

Although the UML represents both the decision and the merge symbols with the diamond shape, the symbols can be distinguished by the number of "incoming" and "outgoing" transition arrows. A decision symbol has one transition arrow pointing to the diamond and two (or more) transition arrows pointing out from the diamond to indicate possible transitions from that point. In addition, each transition arrow pointing out of a decision symbol has a guard condition next to it. A merge symbol has two (or more) transition arrows pointing to the diamond and only one transition arrow pointing from the diamond, to indicate multiple activity flows merging to continue the activity.

SELF-REVIEW

1. The body of a Do While...Loop statement executes _____.
   a) at least once   b) never
   c) if its condition is true   d) if its condition is false

2. The UML represents both the merge symbol and the decision symbol as _____.
   a) rectangles with rounded sides   b) diamonds
   c) small black circles   d) ovals

   Answers: 1) c. 2) b.

9.3 Do Until...Loop Repetition Statement

Common Programming Error

Failure to provide the body of a Do Until...Loop statement with an action that eventually causes the condition in the Do Until...Loop to become true creates an infinite loop.

Unlike the Do While...Loop repetition statement, the **Do Until...Loop** repetition statement determines whether its condition is false before repetition can continue, and the loop terminates when its condition becomes true. This is known as a **loop-termination condition**. For example, you can think of grocery shopping as looping through the list of items until there are none left on the list. Note that the condition "there are no more items on my shopping list" must be false for the loop to continue. This process is described by the following pseudocode statements:

```
Do until there are no more items on my shopping list
    Purchase next item
    Cross it off my list
```

These statements describe the repetitive actions that occur during a shopping trip. Statements in the body of a Do Until...Loop are executed repeatedly for as long as the loop-termination condition remains False. As an example of a Do Until...Loop repetition statement, let's look again at an application segment designed to find the first power of 3 larger than 50:

```
Dim product As Integer = 3

Do Until product > 50
    product *= 3
Loop
```

The following box describes each step as the repetition statement executes.

Executing the Do Until...Loop Repetition Statement

1. The application declares variable product and sets its value to 3.

2. The application enters the Do Until...Loop repetition statement.

3. The loop-termination condition is checked. The condition evaluates to False (product is not greater than 50), so the application resumes execution at the next statement in the loop's body.

4. The number (currently 3) stored in product is multiplied by 3 and the result is assigned to product; product now contains the number 9.

5. The loop-termination condition is checked. The condition evaluates to False (product is not greater than 50), so the application resumes execution at the next statement in the loop's body.

6. The number (currently 9) stored in product is multiplied by 3 and the result is assigned to product; product now contains the number 27.

7. The loop-termination condition is checked. The condition evaluates to False (product is not greater than 50), so the application resumes execution at the next statement in the loop's body.

8. The number (currently 27) stored in product is multiplied by 3 and the result is assigned to product; product now contains the number 81.

9. The loop-termination condition is checked. The condition now evaluates to True (product is greater than 50), so the application exits the Do Until...Loop repetition statement and the application resumes execution at the first statement after the Loop statement.

The UML activity diagram in Fig. 9.5 illustrates the flow of control for the Do Until...Loop repetition statement. Once again, note that (besides the initial state, transition arrows, a final state and three notes) the only other symbols in the diagram represent an action state, a decision and a merge.

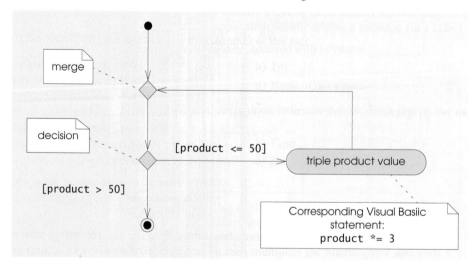

merge

decision

[product <= 50]

triple product value

[product > 50]

Corresponding Visual Basiic statement:
product *= 3

Figure 9.5 Do Until...Loop repetition statement UML activity diagram.

SELF-REVIEW

1. A Do Until...Loop repetition statement differs from a Do While...Loop repetition statement in _____.

   a) that a Do While...Loop repetition statement loops as long as the loop-continuation condition remains False, whereas a Do Until...Loop repetition statement loops as long as the loop-continuation condition remains True

b) that a `Do Until...Loop` repetition statement loops as long as the loop-termination condition remains `False`, whereas a `Do While...Loop` repetition statement loops as long as the loop-continuation condition remains `True`

c) that a `Do Until...Loop` repetition statement always executes at least once

d) no way. There is no difference between the `Do Until...Loop` and `Do While...Loop` repetition statements

2. Statements in the body of a `Do Until...Loop` are executed repeatedly for as long as the _____ remains `False`.

a) loop-continuation condition   b) do-loop condition

c) loop-termination condition   d) until-loop condition

Answer: 1) b. 2) c.

9.4 Constructing the Car Payment Calculator Application

Now that you have learned the `Do While...Loop` and `Do Until...Loop` repetition statements, you are ready to construct the **Car Payment Calculator** application.

The following pseudocode describes the basic operation of the **Car Payment Calculator** application that occurs when a user enters information and clicks the **Calculate** Button:

```
When the user clicks the Calculate Button
        Initialize loan length to two years
        Clear the ListBox of any previous calculation results
        Add a header to the ListBox

        Get down payment from a TextBox
        Get sticker price from a TextBox
        Get interest rate from a TextBox

        Calculate loan amount (sticker price – down payment)
        Calculate monthly interest rate (interest rate / 12)

        Do while loan length is less than or equal to five years
            Convert the loan length in years to number of months

            Calculate monthly payment based on loan amount, monthly interest rate
            and loan length in months

            Insert result into ListBox
            Increment loan length in years by one year
```

You have test-driven the **Car Payment Calculator** application and studied its pseudocode representation. Now you will use an Action/Control/Event (ACE) table to help you convert the pseudocode to Visual Basic. Figure 9.6 lists the actions, controls and events that will help you complete your own version of this application.

Note in the pseudocode that the retrieval of the user input and the of the loan amount and the monthly interest rate occur before the repetition statement because they need to be performed only once. Statements that have different results in each iteration are included in the repetition statement. The repetition statement's body includes: converting loan length in years to loan length in months, calculating the monthly payment amount, displaying the calculation's result and incrementing the loan length in years.

Action/Control/Event (ACE) Table for the Car Payment Calculator

Action	Control	Event
Label all the application's controls	stickerPriceLabel, downPaymentLabel, interestLabel	Application is run
	calculateButton	Click
Initialize loan length to two years		
Clear the ListBox of any previous calculation results	paymentsListBox	
Add a header to the ListBox	paymentsListBox	
Get down payment from a TextBox	downPaymentTextBox	
Get sticker price from a TextBox	stickerPriceTextBox	
Get interest rate from a TextBox	interestTextBox	
Calculate loan amount		
Calculate monthly interest rate		
Do while loan length is less than or equal to five years Convert the loan length in years to number of months		
Calculate monthly payment based on loan amount, monthly interest rate and loan length in months		
Insert result into ListBox	paymentsListBox	
Increment loan length in years by one year		

Figure 9.6   **Car Payment Calculator** application ACE table.

The application displays the calculation results in a ListBox. Next, you will add and customize the ListBox that displays the results.

Adding a ListBox to the Car Payment Calculator Application

Good Programming Practice

Append the ListBox suffix to all ListBox control names.

GUI Design Tip

A ListBox should be large enough to display all of its contents or large enough that scrollbars can be used easily.

1. *Copying the template to your working directory.* Copy the C:\Examples\Tutorial09\TemplateApplication\CarPaymentCalculator directory to your C:\SimplyVB directory.

2. *Opening the Car Payment Calculator application's template file.* Double click CarPaymentCalculator.sln in the CarPaymentCalculator directory to open the application in the Visual Basic IDE (Fig. 9.7). The TextBoxes for user input and the **Calculate** Button are provided for you.

3. *Adding a ListBox control to the Form.* Double click the ListBox control,

> 🔳 ListBox

in the **Toolbox**. Change the Name property of the ListBox to paymentsListBox. Set the Location property to 28, 168 and the Size property to 232, 82. Figure 9.8 shows the Form with the ListBox control.

4. *Saving the project.* Select **File > Save All** to save your changes.

(cont.)

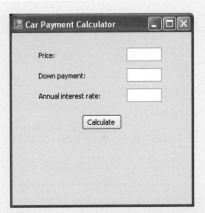

Figure 9.7   **Car Payment Calculator** application's Form in design mode.

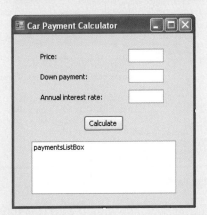

Figure 9.8   ListBox added to **Car Payment Calculator** application's Form.

After adding the ListBox, you must add an event handler to the application so that the application can respond to the user's clicking the **Calculate** Button. Event handler calculateButton_Click updates the ListBox's contents. The following box describes how to add items to a ListBox and how to clear a ListBox.

Using Code to Change a ListBox's Contents	1. ***Adding the Calculate Button's event handler.*** Double click the **Calculate** Button to generate the empty event handler calculateButton_Click.
	2. ***Clearing the ListBox control.*** Add lines 6–7 of Fig. 9.9 to calculateButton_Click. Each time users click the **Calculate** Button, any content previously displayed in the ListBox is removed. To remove all content from the ListBox, call method **Clear** on property **Items** (line 7). Content can be added and deleted from the ListBox by using its Items property. The Items property returns an object that contains a list of items displayed in the ListBox. Note that we have added comments in lines 2 and 8, and broken the first line of calculateButton_Click into two lines for readability.
 **GUI Design Tip**	3. ***Adding content to the ListBox control.*** Add lines 9–11 of Fig. 9.10 to calculateButton_Click. The ListBox displays the number of monthly payments and the amount per payment. To clarify what information is being displayed, a line of text—called a **header**—needs to be added to the List-Box. Method **Add** (lines 10–11 of Fig. 9.10) adds the header—the column headings "Months" and "Monthly Payment" separated by two tab characters—to the ListBox's Items property.
Use headers in a ListBox when you are displaying tabular data. Adding headers improves readability by indicating the information that will be displayed in the ListBox.	

(cont.)

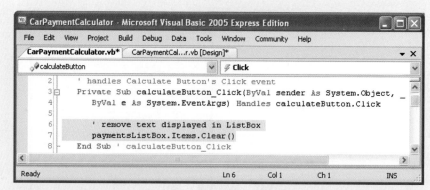

Figure 9.9 Clearing the contents of a ListBox.

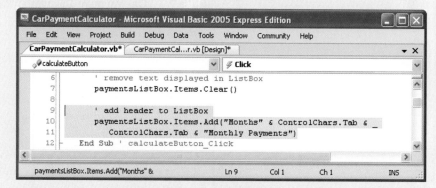

Figure 9.10 Adding a header to a ListBox.

The ampersand symbol (&) is called the **string-concatenation operator**. This operator combines (or concatenates) its two operands into one value. In lines 10–11, the header is created by joining the values "Months" and "Monthly Payments" with two ControlChars.Tab constants. The constant ControlChars.Tab inserts a tab character into the string. The application uses two tab characters of separation between the columns (Fig. 9.3).

4. **Saving the project.** Select **File > Save All** to save your modified code.

Now that you have learned how to change a ListBox's contents, you need to declare variables and obtain user input for the calculation. The following box shows you how to initialize the **Car Payment Calculator** application's variables. The box also guides you through converting the annual interest to the monthly interest rate and shows you how to calculate the amount of the loan.

Declaring Variables and Receiving User Input

1. **Declaring variables.** Place the cursor in the blank line immediately preceding the code you added in the box *Using Code to Change a ListBox's Contents*. Add lines 6–13 of Fig. 9.11 to the application above the code you added in the preceding box. Variables years and months store the length of the loan in years and months. The calculation requires the length in months, but the loop-continuation condition will use the number of years. Variables price, downPayment and interest store the user input from the Text-Boxes. Normally price and downPayment would be represented as type Decimal, because they represent monetary values. For simplicity in this application, we have used Integers. Variable monthlyPayment stores the result of the monthly payment calculation. Variables loanAmount and monthlyInterest store calculation results.

(cont.)

Variables to store the length of the loan

Variables to store user input

Variables to store calculation results

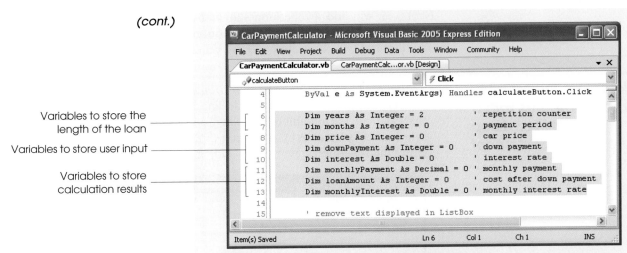

Figure 9.11 Variables for the **Car Payment Calculator** application.

2. *Retrieving user input needed for the calculation.* Add lines 22–26 of Fig. 9.12 below the code you added in the preceding box. Lines 24–26 receive the down payment (downPayment), the price (price) and the annual interest rate (interest) provided by the user. Note that line 26 divides the interest rate by 100 to obtain the decimal equivalent (for example, 5% becomes .05).

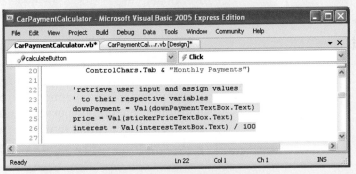

Figure 9.12 Retrieving input in the **Car Payment Calculator** application.

3. *Calculating values used in the calculation.* The application computes the amount of the loan by subtracting the down payment from the price. Add lines 28–30 of Fig. 9.13 to calculate the amount borrowed (line 29) and the monthly interest rate (line 30). These calculations need to occur only once, so they are placed before the Do While...Loop. Variables loanAmount and monthlyInterest will be used in the calculation of monthly payments, which will be added to your application shortly.

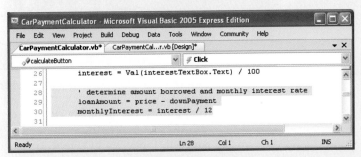

Figure 9.13 Determining amount borrowed and monthly interest rate.

4. *Saving the project.* Select **File > Save All** to save your modified code.

Next, you will add a repetition statement to the application to calculate the monthly payment for four loans. The repetition statement performs this calculation for loans that last two, three, four and five years.

Calculating the Monthly Payment Amounts with a Do While...Loop Repetition Statement

1. *Setting the loop-continuation condition.* Place the cursor after the code you entered in the preceding box. Add lines 32–33 of Fig. 9.14 below the lines that calculate the amount of the loan (`loanAmount`) and the monthly interest rate (`monthlyInterest`). After you type line 33 and press *Enter*, the IDE closes the repetition statement by adding the keyword `Loop` in line 35.

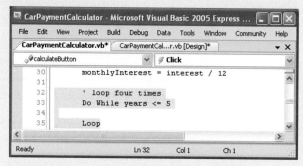

Figure 9.14 Loop-continuation condition.

Recall that the shortest loan in this application lasts two years, so you initialized `years` to 2 in line 6 (Fig. 9.11). The loop-continuation condition (`years <= 5`) in Fig. 9.14 specifies that the `Do While...Loop` statement executes while `years` remains less than or equal to 5. This loop is an example of **counter-controlled repetition**. This technique uses a variable called a **counter** (`years`) to control the number of times that a set of statements will execute. Counter-controlled repetition also is called **definite repetition**, because the number of repetitions is usually known before the loop begins executing. In this example, repetition terminates when the counter (`years`) exceeds 5.

2. *Calculating the payment period.* Add lines 34–35 of Fig. 9.15 to the Do While...Loop repetition statement to calculate the number of payments (that is, the length of the loan in months). The number of months changes with each iteration of the loop, and the calculation result changes as the length of the payment period changes. Variable `months` will have the values 24, 36, 48 and 60, on successive iterations of the loop.

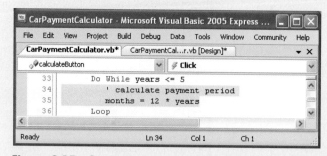

Figure 9.15 Converting the loan duration from years to months.

3. *Computing the monthly payment.* Add lines 37–39 of Fig. 9.16 to the Do While...Loop repetition statement immediately after the code you just entered. Lines 38–39 (Fig. 9.16) use the `Pmt` function to calculate the user's monthly payment. The **Pmt** function returns a `Double` value that specifies the monthly payment amount on a loan for a constant interest rate (`monthlyInterest`) and a given time period (`months`).

(cont.)

Line 39 passes to Pmt the interest rate, the total number of payments (equal to the number of months in the payment period) and the amount borrowed. Borrowed amounts are represented by negative values, because they represent a removal of cash from the person or organization that is lending money. Monetary amounts are stored in variables of type Decimal. Method **Convert.ToDecimal** converts the Double return value of Pmt to type Decimal and assigns this value to monthlyPayment.

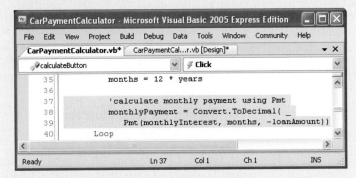

Figure 9.16 Pmt function returns monthly payment.

4. ***Displaying the monthly payment amount.*** Add lines 41–44 of Fig. 9.17 to the application. The number of monthly payments and the monthly payment amounts are displayed beneath the header. To add this content to the List-Box, call method Add (lines 42–44 of Fig. 9.17). Lines 43–44 use method String.Format to display monthlyPayment in currency format. Note that the two tab characters ensure that the monthly payment amount is placed in the second column. The space provided by the extra tab character makes the application's output more readable.

5. ***Incrementing the counter variable.*** Add line 46 of Fig. 9.18 before the closing keyword of the repetition statement. Line 46 increments the counter variable (years). Variable years will be incremented until it equals 6. Then the loop-continuation condition (years <= 5) will evaluate to False and the repetition will end.

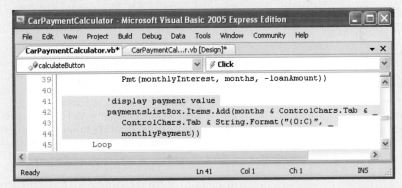

Figure 9.17 Displaying the number of months and the amount of each monthly payment.

6. ***Running the application.*** Select **Debug > Start Debugging** to run your application. The application should calculate and display monthly payments. Enter values for a car's price, down payment and annual interest rate and click the **Calculate** Button to verify that the application is working correctly.

(cont.)

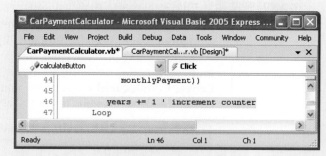

Figure 9.18 Incrementing the counter.

7. ***Closing the application.*** Close your running application by clicking its close box.

8. ***Closing the IDE.*** Close the Visual Basic IDE by clicking its close box.

Figure 9.19 presents the source code for the **Car Payment Calculator** application. The lines of code that contain new programming concepts that you learned in this tutorial are highlighted.

```
1   Public Class CarPaymentForm
2      ' handles Calculate Button's Click event
3      Private Sub calculateButton_Click(ByVal sender As System.Object, _
4         ByVal e As System.EventArgs) Handles calculateButton.Click
5
6         Dim years As Integer = 2          ' repetition counter
7         Dim months As Integer = 0         ' payment period
8         Dim price As Integer = 0          ' car price
9         Dim downPayment As Integer = 0    ' down payment
10        Dim interest As Double = 0        ' interest rate
11        Dim monthlyPayment As Decimal = 0 ' monthly payment
12        Dim loanAmount As Integer = 0     ' cost after down payment
13        Dim monthlyInterest As Double = 0 ' monthly interest rate
14
15        ' remove text displayed in ListBox
16        paymentsListBox.Items.Clear()
17
18        ' add header to ListBox
19        paymentsListBox.Items.Add("Months" & ControlChars.Tab & _
20           ControlChars.Tab & "Monthly Payments")
21
22        ' retrieve user input and assign values
23        ' to their respective variables
24        downPayment = Val(downPaymentTextBox.Text)
25        price = Val(stickerPriceTextBox.Text)
26        interest = Val(interestTextBox.Text) / 100
27
28        ' determine amount borrowed and monthly interest rate
29        loanAmount = price - downPayment
30        monthlyInterest = interest / 12
31
32        ' loop four times
33        Do While years <= 5
34           ' calculate payment period
35           months = 12 * years
36
37           ' calculate monthly payment using Pmt
38           monthlyPayment = Convert.ToDecimal( _
39              Pmt(monthlyInterest, months, -loanAmount))
```

Figure 9.19 **Car Payment Calculator** application code. (Part 1 of 2.)

```
40
41                       ' display payment value
42               paymentsListBox.Items.Add(months & ControlChars.Tab & _
43                  ControlChars.Tab & String.Format("{0:C}", _
44                  monthlyPayment))
45
46               years += 1 ' increment counter
47           Loop
48       End Sub ' calculateButton_Click
49   End Class ' CarPaymentForm
```

Figure 9.19   **Car Payment Calculator** application code. (Part 2 of 2.)

---

1. Counter-controlled repetition is also called _____ because the number of repetitions is usually known before the loop begins executing.

   a) definite repetition   b) known repetition

   c) sequential repetition   d) counter repetition

2. The line of text added to a ListBox to clarify the information that will be displayed is called a _____.

   a) title   b) starter

   c) header   d) clarifier

Answers: 1) a. 2) c.

9.5 Wrap-Up

In this tutorial, you began using repetition statements. You used the Do While...Loop and the Do Until...Loop statements to repeat actions in an application, depending on a loop-continuation condition or a loop-termination condition, respectively.

The Do While...Loop repetition statement executes as long as its loop-continuation condition is True. When the loop-continuation condition becomes False, the repetition terminates. An infinite loop occurs if this condition never becomes False.

The Do Until...Loop repetition statement executes as long as its loop-termination condition is False. The repetition terminates when the loop-termination condition becomes True. An infinite loop occurs if this condition never becomes True.

You learned about counter-controlled repetition, in which a repetition statement "knows" the number of times it will iterate because a variable known as a counter precisely counts the number of iterations. You used a repetition statement to develop a **Car Payment Calculator** application in which you calculated the monthly payments for a given loan amount and a given interest rate for loan durations of two, three, four and five years.

In the **Car Payment Calculator** application, you used the ListBox control to display several payment options on a car loan. You learned about the ListBox control, which is used to maintain a list of items. Items can be added to and removed from the ListBox programmatically. Values are added to a ListBox control by invoking method Add on the ListBox control's Items property. The Items property returns an object that contains all the values displayed in the ListBox.

In the next tutorial, you will learn two other Do repetition statements, and you will continue exploring counter-controlled repetition. The **Car Payment Calculator** application demonstrated one common use of repetition statements—performing a calculation for several different values. The next application introduces another common application of repetition statements—summing a series of numbers.

SKILLS SUMMARY

Displaying Values in a ListBox

- Property Items of the ListBox control returns an object that contains the values to be displayed in a ListBox.
- Invoke method Add to add values to the Items property.

Clearing a ListBox's Contents

- Method Clear of the Items's property deletes (clears) all the values in the ListBox.

Repeating Actions in an Application

- Use a repetition statement that depends on the true or false value of a loop-continuation condition or a loop-termination condition.

Executing a Repetition Statement for a Known Number of Repetitions

- Use counter-controlled repetition with a counter variable to determine the number of times that a set of statements will execute.

Using the Do While...Loop Repetition Statement

- This repetition statement executes while the loop-continuation condition is True.
- An infinite loop occurs if the condition never becomes False.

Using the Do Until...Loop Repetition Statement

- This repetition statement executes while the loop-termination condition is False.
- An infinite loop occurs if the condition never becomes True.

Concatenating Strings

- Use the & operator to build a new String from two existing Strings. The contents of the right operand are appended to the contents of the left operand to create the new String.

KEY TERMS

Add method of Items—Adds an item to a ListBox control.

body of a control statement—The set of statements that are enclosed in a control statement.

Clear method of Items—Deletes all the values in a ListBox's control.

ControlChars.Tab constant—Represents a tab character.

Convert.ToDecimal method—Converts a value to type Decimal, which is appropriate for monetary calculations.

counter—A variable often used to determine the number of times a block of statements in a loop will execute.

counter-controlled repetition—A technique that uses a counter variable to determine the number of times that a block of statements will execute. Also called definite repetition.

definite repetition—See counter-controlled repetition.

Do Until...Loop repetition statement—A control statement that executes a set of body statements until its loop-termination condition becomes True.

Do While...Loop repetition statement—A control statement that executes a set of body statements while its loop-continuation condition is True.

header—A line of text at the top of a ListBox that clarifies the information being displayed.

infinite loop—An error in which a repetition statement never terminates.

Items property of the ListBox control—Returns an object containing all the values in the ListBox.

ListBox control—Allows the user to view items in a list. Items can be added to or removed from the list programmatically.

loop—Another name for a repetition statement.

loop-continuation condition—The condition used in a repetition statement (such as a Do While...Loop) that enables repetition to continue while the condition is True and that causes repetition to terminate when the condition becomes False.

loop-termination condition—The condition used in a repetition statement (such as a Do Until...Loop) that enables repetition to continue while the condition is False and that causes repetition to terminate when the condition becomes True.

merge symbol (in the UML)—A diamond symbol in the UML that joins two flows of activity into one flow of activity.

Pmt function—A function that, given an interest rate, a time period and a monetary loan amount, returns a Double value specifying the payment amount per specified time period.

repetition statement—Allows the programmer to specify that an action or actions should be repeated, depending on the value of a condition.

string-concatenation operator (&)—This operator combines its two operands into one value.

GUI DESIGN GUIDELINES

ListBox

■ A ListBox should be large enough to display all of its content or large enough that scroll-bars may be used easily.

■ Use headers in a ListBox when you are displaying tabular data. Adding headers improves readability by indicating the information that will be displayed in the ListBox.

CONTROLS, EVENTS, PROPERTIES & METHODS

Convert The Convert class converts the value of a data type to another data type.

■ *Methods*

ToDecimal—Converts its argument to a Decimal value.

ListBox   ⯐ ListBox   This control allows the user to view and select from items in a list.

■ *In action*

Months	Monthly Payments
24	$490.50
36	$339.06
48	$263.55
60	$218.41

■ *Properties*

Items—Returns an object that contains the items displayed in the ListBox.

Location—Specifies the location of the ListBox on the Form.

Name—Specifies the name used to access the properties of the ListBox programatically. The name should be appended with the ListBox suffix.

Size—Specifies the height and width (in pixels) of the ListBox.

■ *Methods*

Items.Add—Adds an item to the Items property.

Items.Clear—Deletes all the values in the ListBox's Items property.

MULTIPLE-CHOICE QUESTIONS

9.1 The _____ statement executes until its loop-termination condition becomes True.

a) Do While...Loop   b) Do Until...Loop

c) Do   d) Loop

9.2 The _____ statement executes until its loop-continuation condition becomes False.

a) Do While...Loop   b) Do Until...Loop

c) Do   d) Do While

9.3 A(n) _____ loop occurs when a condition in a Do While...Loop never becomes False.

a) infinite   b) undefined

c) nested   d) indefinite

9.4 A _____ is a variable that helps control the number of times that a set of statements will execute.

a) repeater b) counter

c) loop d) repetition control statement

9.5 The _____ control allows users to add and view items in a list.

a) `ListItems` b) `SelectBox`

c) `ListBox` d) `ViewBox`

9.6 In a UML activity diagram, a(n) _____ symbol joins two flows of activity into one flow of activity.

a) merge b) combine

c) action state d) decision

9.7 Property _____ returns an object containing all the values in a `ListBox`.

a) `All` b) `List`

c) `ListItemValues` d) `Items`

9.8 Method _____ deletes all the values in a `ListBox`.

a) `Remove` b) `Delete`

c) `Clear` d) `Del`

9.9 Items's method _____ adds an item to a `ListBox`.

a) `Include` b) `Append`

c) `Add` d) `Insert`

9.10 Function _____ calculates monthly payments on a loan based on a fixed interest rate.

a) `MonPmt` b) `Payment`

c) `MonthlyPayment` d) `Pmt`

EXERCISES

9.11 *(Table of Powers Application)* Write an application that displays a table of numbers from 1 to an upper limit, along with each number's squared value (for example, the number *n* to the power 2, or *n* ^ 2) and cubed value (the number *n* to the power 3, or *n* ^ 3). The user specifies the upper limit, and the results are displayed in a `ListBox`, as in Fig. 9.20.

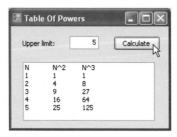

Figure 9.20 **Table of Powers** application's Form.

a) *Copying the template to your working directory.* Copy the directory `C:\Examples\Tutorial09\Exercises\TableOfPowers` to your `C:\SimplyVB` directory.

b) *Opening the application's template file.* Double click `TableOfPowers.sln` in the `TableOfPowers` directory to open the application.

c) *Adding a ListBox.* Add a `ListBox` to the application, as shown in Fig. 9.20. Name the `ListBox` `resultsListBox`.

d) *Adding the Upper limit: TextBox event handler.* Double click the **Upper limit:** Text-Box to generate an event handler for this `TextBox`'s `TextChanged` event. In this event handler, clear the `ListBox`.

e) *Adding the Calculate Button event handler.* Double click the **Calculate** Button to generate the empty event handler `calculateButton_Click`. Add the code specified by the remaining steps to this event handler.

f) **Clearing the ListBox.** Use method Clear on the Items property to clear the List-Box from any previous data.

g) **Obtaining the upper limit supplied by the user.** Assign the value entered by the user in the **Upper limit:** TextBox to a variable. Note that the TextBox's Name property is set to inputTextBox.

h) **Adding a header.** Use method Add on the Items property to insert a header in the ListBox. The header should label three columns—N, N^2 and N^3. Column headings should be separated by tab characters.

i) **Calculating the powers from 1 to the specified upper limit.** Use a Do Until...Loop to calculate the squared value and the cubed value of each number from 1 to the upper limit, inclusive. Add an item to the ListBox containing the current number being analyzed, its squared value and its cubed value.

j) **Incrementing the counter.** Remember to increment the counter appropriately each time through the loop.

k) **Running the application.** Select **Debug > Start Debugging** to run your application. Enter an upper limit and click the **Calculate** Button. Verify that the table of powers displayed contains the correct values.

l) **Closing the application.** Close your running application by clicking its close box.

m) **Closing the IDE.** Close the Visual Basic IDE by clicking its close box.

9.12 (Mortgage Calculator Application) A bank offers mortgages that can be repaid in 5, 10, 15, 20, 25 or 30 years. Write an application that allows a user to enter the price of a house (the amount of the mortgage) and the annual interest rate. When the user clicks a Button, the application displays a table of the mortgage length in years together with the monthly payment, as shown in Fig. 9.21.

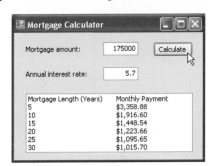

Figure 9.21 **Mortgage Calculator** application's Form.

a) **Copying the template to your working directory.** Copy the directory C:\Examples\ Tutorial09\Exercises\MortgageCalculator to your C:\SimplyVB directory.

b) **Opening the application's template file.** Double click MortgageCalculator.sln in the MortgageCalculator directory to open the application.

c) **Adding a ListBox to display the results.** Add a ListBox as shown in Fig. 9.21. Name the ListBox resultsListBox.

d) **Adding a Calculate Button event handler.** Double click the **Calculate** Button to generate the empty event handler calculateButton_Click. Add the code specified in the remaining steps to your event handler.

e) **Converting the annual interest rate to the monthly interest rate.** To convert the annual interest rate from a percent value into its Double equivalent, divide the annual rate by 100. Then divide the Double annual rate by 12 to obtain the monthly rate.

f) **Clearing the ListBox.** Use method Clear on the Items property to clear the List-Box from any previous data.

g) **Displaying a header.** Use method Add to display a header in the ListBox. The header should be the column headers "Mortgage Length (Years)" and "Monthly Payment", separated by a tab character.

h) *Using a repetition statement.* Add a Do While...Loop repetition statement to calculate six monthly payment options for the user's mortgage. Each option has a different number of years that the mortgage can last. For this exercise, use the following numbers of years: 5, 10, 15, 20, 25 and 30.

i) *Converting the length of the mortgage from years to months.* Convert the number of years to months.

j) *Calculating the monthly payments for six different mortgages.* Use the Pmt function to compute the monthly payments. Pass to the function the monthly interest rate, the number of months in the mortgage and the mortgage amount. Remember that the mortgage amount must be negative, because it represents an amount of money being paid out by the lender.

k) *Displaying the results.* Use method Add on the Items property to display the length of the mortgage in years and the monthly payment in the ListBox. You will need to use three tab characters to ensure that the monthly payment appears in the second column.

l) *Running the application.* Select **Debug > Start Debugging** to run your application. Enter a mortgage amount and annual interest rate, then click the **Calculate** Button. Verify that the monthly payments displayed contain the correct values.

m) *Closing the application.* Close your running application by clicking its close box.

n) *Closing the IDE.* Close the Visual Basic IDE by clicking its close box.

9.13 *(Office Supplies Application)* Create an application that allows a user to make a list of office supplies to buy, as shown in Fig. 9.22. The user should enter the supply item in a TextBox and click the **Buy** Button to add it to the ListBox. The **Clear** Button removes all the items from the ListBox.

Figure 9.22 **Office Supplies** application's Form.

a) *Copying the template to your working directory.* Copy the directory C:\Examples\Tutorial09\Exercises\OfficeSupplies directory to your C:\SimplyVB directory.

b) *Opening the application's template file.* Double click OfficeSupplies.sln in OfficeSupplies directory to open the application.

c) *Adding a ListBox.* Add a ListBox to the Form. Name the ListBox suppliesListBox. Place and size it as shown in Fig. 9.22.

d) *Adding an event handler for the Buy Button.* Double click the **Buy** Button to generate the event handler buyButton_Click. The event handler should obtain the user input from the TextBox. The user input is then added as an item into the ListBox. After the input is added to the ListBox, clear the **Supply:** TextBox.

e) *Adding an event handler for the Clear Button.* Double click the **Clear** Button to generate the event handler clearButton_Click. The event handler should use the Clear method on the Items property to clear the ListBox.

f) *Running the application.* Select **Debug > Start Debugging** to run your application. Enter several items into the **Supply:** TextBox and click the **Buy** Button after entering each item. Verify that each item is added to the ListBox. Click the **Clear** Button and verify that all items are removed from the ListBox.

g) *Closing the application.* Close your running application by clicking its close box.

h) *Closing the IDE.* Close the Visual Basic by clicking its close box.

What does this code do? ▷ **9.14** What is the result of the following code?

```
1   Dim x As Integer = 1
2   Dim mysteryValue As Integer = 1
3
4   Do While x < 6
5
6      mysteryValue *= x
7      x += 1
8   Loop
9
10  displayLabel.Text = mysteryValue
```

What's wrong with this code? ▷ **9.15** Find the error(s) in the following code:

a) Assume that the variable x is declared and initialized to 1. The loop should total the numbers from 1 to 10.

```
1   Dim total As Integer = 0
2
3   Do Until x <= 10
4
5      total += x
6      x += 1
7   Loop
```

b) Assume that the variable counter is declared and initialized to 1. The loop should sum the numbers from 1 to 100.

```
1   Do While counter <= 100
2
3      total += counter
4   Loop
5
6   counter += 1
```

c) Assume that the variable counter is declared and initialized to 1000. The loop should iterate from 1000 to 1.

```
1   Do While counter > 0
2
3      displayLabel.Text = counter
4      counter += 1
5   Loop
```

d) Assume that the variable counter is declared and initialized to 1. The loop should execute five times, adding the numbers 1–5 to a ListBox.

```
1   Do While counter < 5
2
3      numbersListBox.Items.Add(counter)
4      counter += 1
5   Loop
```

Using the Debugger ▷ **9.16** (*Odd Numbers Application*) The **Odd Numbers** application should display all of the odd integers between one and the number input by the user. Copy the **Odd Numbers** application from C:/Examples/Tutorial09/Exercises/Debugger to your working directory. Run the application. Note that an infinite loop occurs after you enter a value into the **Upper**

limit: TextBox and click the **View** Button. Use the debugger to find and fix the error(s) in the application. Figure 9.23 displays the correct output for the application.

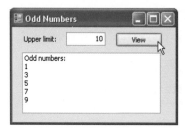

Figure 9.23 Correct output for the **Odd Numbers** application.

Programming Challenge ▶ **9.17** *(To-Do List Application)* Use a ListBox as a to-do list. Enter each item in a TextBox, and add it to the ListBox by clicking a Button. The item should be displayed in a numbered list, as in Fig. 9.24. To do this, we introduce property Count, which returns the number of items in a ListBox's Items property. The following is a sample call to assign the number of items displayed in sampleListBox to an Integer variable:

```
count = sampleListBox.Items.Count
```

Figure 9.24 **To-Do List** application's Form.

10

Class Average Application

Introducing the Do...Loop While and Do...Loop Until Repetition Statements

This tutorial continues the discussion of repetition statements that we began in Tutorial 9. In the preceding tutorial, we examined Do While...Loop and Do Until...Loop repetition statements, which test their loop-continuation and loop-termination conditions before an iteration. This tutorial introduces two additional repetition statements, Do...Loop While and Do...Loop Until, which perform their tests after each iteration. As a result, the body statements contained in these repetition statements are performed at least once.

You will also learn how to disable and enable controls on a Form. When a control, such as a Button, is disabled, it will no longer respond to the user. You will use this feature to prevent the user from causing errors in your applications. This tutorial also introduces the concept of transferring the focus of the application to a control. Proper use of the focus makes an application easier to use.

10.1 Test-Driving the Class Average Application

This application must meet the following requirements:

> **Application Requirements**
>
> *A teacher regularly gives quizzes to a class of 10 students. The grades on these quizzes are integers in the range from 0 to 100 (0 and 100 are both valid grades). The teacher would like you to develop an application that computes the class average for a quiz.*

The class average is equal to the sum of the grades divided by the number of students who took the quiz. The algorithm for solving this problem must input each of the grades, total the grades, perform the averaging calculation and display the result. You begin by test-driving the completed application. Then you will learn the additional Visual Basic technologies that you will need to create your own version of this application.

1. *Opening the completed application.* Open the directory C:\Examples\ Tutorial10\CompletedApplication\ClassAverage to locate the **Class Average** application. Double click ClassAverage.sln to open the application in the Visual Basic IDE.

2. *Running the Class Average application.* Select **Debug > Start Debugging** to run the application (Fig. 10.1).

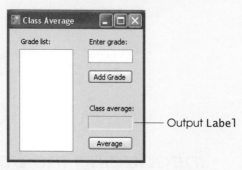

Figure 10.1   **Class Average** application's Form in run mode.

3. *Entering quiz grades.* Enter 85 as the first quiz grade in the **Enter grade:** TextBox, and click the **Add Grade** Button. The grade entered will display in the ListBox, as in Fig. 10.2. After you click the **Add Grade** Button, the cursor appears in the **Enter grade:** TextBox. When a control is selected (for example, the **Enter grade:** TextBox), it is said to have the **focus** of the application. You will learn to set the focus to a control as you build this tutorial's application. As a result of the application's focus being transferred to the **Enter grade:** TextBox, you can type another grade without navigating to the TextBox with the mouse or the *Tab* key. Transferring the focus to a particular control tells the user what information the application expects next. [*Note:* If you click the **Average** Button before 10 grades have been input, an error occurs. In the dialog that displays, click the close button and stop debugging to return to design mode. Repeat *Step 2.* You will fix this problem in the exercises.]

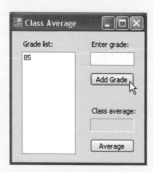

Figure 10.2   Entering grades in the **Class Average** application.

4. *Repeat* **Step 3** *nine times.* Enter nine other grades between 0 and 100, and click the **Add Grade** Button after each entry. After 10 grades are displayed in the **Grade list:** ListBox, the Form will look similar to Fig. 10.3. Note that the **Add Grade** Button is disabled once you have entered 10 grades. That is, its color is gray, and clicking the Button does not invoke its event handler.

5. *Calculating the class average.* Click the **Average** Button to calculate the average of the 10 quizzes. The class average will be displayed in an output Label above the **Average** Button (Fig. 10.4). Note that the **Add Grade** Button is now enabled.

(cont.)

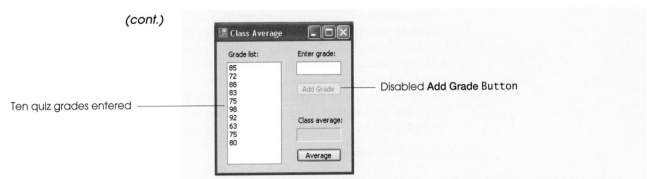

Figure 10.3   **Class Average** application after 10 grades have been input.

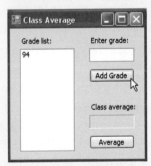

Figure 10.4   Displaying the class average.

6. ***Entering another set of grades.*** You can calculate the class average for another set of 10 grades without restarting the application. Enter a grade in the TextBox, and click the **Add Grade** Button. Note that the **Grade list:** ListBox and the **Class average:** field are cleared when you start entering another set of grades (Fig. 10.5).

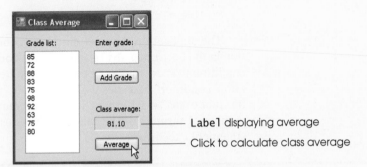

Figure 10.5   Entering a new set of grades.

7. ***Closing the application.*** Close your running application by clicking its close box.

8. ***Closing the IDE.*** Close the Visual Basic IDE by clicking its close box.

10.2 Do...Loop While Repetition Statement

The **Do...Loop While** repetition statement is similar to the Do While...Loop statement; both statements iterate while their loop-continuation conditions are True. In the Do While...Loop statement, the loop-continuation condition is tested at the beginning of the loop, before the body of the loop is performed. The Do...Loop While statement performs the loop-continuation condition *after* the loop body is performed. Therefore, in a Do...Loop While statement, the loop body always executes at least once. Recall that a Do While...Loop executes only if its loop-continua-

Common Programming Error

An infinite loop occurs when the loop-continuation condition in a Do...Loop While statement never becomes False.

tion condition evaluates to true. When a Do...Loop While statement terminates, execution continues with the statement after the Loop While clause.

To illustrate the Do...Loop While repetition style, consider the example of packing a suitcase: Before you begin packing, the suitcase is empty. You place an item in the suitcase, then determine whether the suitcase is full. As long as the suitcase is not full, you continue to put items in the suitcase. As an example of a Do...Loop While statement, let's look at the following application segment designed to display the numbers 1 through 3 in a ListBox:

```
Dim counter As Integer = 1

Do
    displayListBox.Items.Add(counter)
    counter += 1
Loop While counter <= 3
```

The application segment initializes counter to 1. The loop-continuation condition in the Do...Loop While statement is counter <= 3. While the loop-continuation condition is True, the Do...Loop While statement executes. When the loop-continuation condition becomes False (that is, when counter is greater than 3), the Do...Loop While statement finishes executing and displayListBox contains the numbers 1 through 3. The following box describes each step as the above repetition statement executes.

Executing the Do...Loop While Repetition Statement	1. The application declares variable counter and sets its value to 1.
	2. The application enters the Do...Loop While repetition statement.
	3. The number (currently 1) stored in counter is added to displayListBox's Items property.
	4. The value of counter is increased by 1; counter now contains 2.
	5. The loop-continuation condition is checked. The condition evaluates to True (counter is less than or equal to 3), so the application resumes execution at the first statement after the Do statement.
	6. The number (currently 2) stored in counter is added to displayListBox's Items property.
	7. The value of counter is increased by 1; counter now contains 3.
	8. The loop-continuation condition is checked. The condition evaluates to True (counter is less than or equal to 3), so the application resumes execution at the first statement after the Do statement.
	9. The number (currently 3) stored in counter is added to the displayListBox's Items property.
	10. The value of counter is increased by 1; counter now contains 4.
	11. The loop-continuation condition is checked. The condition evaluates to False (counter is not less than or equal to 3), so the application exits the Do...Loop While repetition statement.

Error-Prevention Tip

Including a final value in the condition of a repetition statement (and choosing the appropriate relational operator) can reduce the occurrence of off-by-one errors. For example, in a Do While...Loop statement used to print the values 1–10, the loop-continuation condition should be counter <= 10, rather than counter < 10 (which is an off-by-one error) or counter < 11 (which is correct, but less clear).

If you mistyped the loop-continuation condition as counter < 3 or counter <= 2, the ListBox would display only 1 and 2. Including an incorrect relational operator (such as the less than sign in counter < 3) or an incorrect final value for a loop counter (such as the 2 in counter <= 2) in the condition of any repetition statement can cause **off-by-one errors**, which occur when a loop executes for one more or one fewer iteration than is necessary.

Figure 10.6 illustrates the UML activity diagram for the general Do...Loop While statement. This diagram makes it clear that the loop-continuation guard condition ([counter <= 3]) does not evaluate until after the loop performs the action state at least once. Recall that action states can include one or more Visual Basic statements executed one after the other (sequentially) as in the preceding example. When you use a Do...Loop While repetition statement in building an application, you would provide the appropriate action state and the guard conditions for your application.

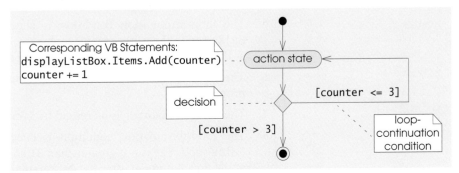

Figure 10.6 Do...Loop While repetition statement UML activity diagram.

1. The Do...Loop While statement tests the loop-continuation condition _____.
   a) for False after the loop body executes   b) for False before the loop body executes
   c) for True after the loop body executes   d) for True before the loop body executes

2. An infinite loop occurs when the loop-continuation condition in a Do While...Loop or Do...Loop While statement _____.
   a) never becomes True   b) never becomes False
   c) is False   d) is tested repeatedly

Answers: 1) c. 2) b.

10.3 Do...Loop Until Repetition Statement

Error-Prevention Tip

An infinite loop occurs when the loop-termination condition in a Do...Loop Until statement never becomes True.

The **Do...Loop Until** statement is similar to the Do Until...Loop statement, except that in the Do...Loop Until statement the loop-termination condition is tested after the loop body is performed. Therefore, the loop body executes at least once. When a Do...Loop Until terminates, execution continues with the statement after the Loop Until clause.

Again, consider the suitcase-packing example. Before you begin packing, the suitcase is empty. You place an item in the suitcase, then determine whether the suitcase is still empty. As long as the condition "the suitcase is full" is False, you continue to put items into the suitcase.

As an example of a Do...Loop Until statement, let's look at another application segment designed to display the numbers 1 through 3 in a ListBox:

```
Dim counter As Integer = 1

Do
    displayListBox.Items.Add(counter)
    counter += 1
Loop Until counter > 3
```

The application segment initializes the counter counter to 1, and the loop-termination condition in the Do...Loop Until statement is counter > 3. While the loop-termination condition is False, the Do...Loop Until statement executes. When the loop-termination condition becomes True, the Do...Loop Until statement finishes executing and displayListBox contains the numbers 1 through 3. The following box describes each step as the repetition statement executes.

Executing the Do...Loop Until Repetition Statement

1. The application declares variable counter and sets its value to 1.

2. The application enters the Do...Loop Until repetition statement.

3. The number (1) stored in counter is Added to the displayListBox's Items property.

4. The value of counter is increased by 1; counter now contains 2.

5. The loop-termination condition is checked. The condition evaluates to False (counter is not greater than 3), so the application resumes execution at the first statement after the Do statement.

6. The number (2) stored in counter is Added to the displayListBox's Items property.

7. The value of counter is increased by 1; counter now contains 3.

8. The loop-termination condition is checked. The condition evaluates to False (counter is not greater than 3), so the application resumes execution at the first statement after the Do statement.

9. The number (3) stored in counter is Added to the displayListBox's Items property.

10. The value of counter is increased by 1; counter now contains 4.

11. The loop-termination condition is checked. The condition now evaluates to True (counter is greater than 3), so the application exits the Do...Loop Until repetition statement.

The Do...Loop Until UML activity diagram (Fig. 10.7) makes it clear that the loop-termination guard condition is not evaluated until after the body is executed at least once. This UML diagram indicates the exact same guard conditions as detailed in Fig. 10.6. The only difference for a Do...Loop Until repetition statement is that it continues to execute when the loop-termination guard condition is False. When the guard condition evaluates to True, the repetition ends and program control moves to the next statement following the Loop Until clause.

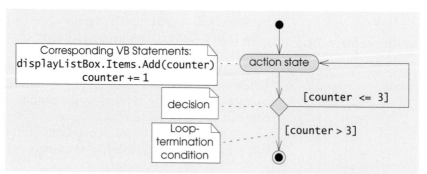

Figure 10.7 Do...Loop Until repetition statement activity diagram.

SELF-REVIEW

1. The Do...Loop Until statement checks the loop-termination condition _____.

   a) for False after the loop body executes   b) for False before the loop body executes

   c) for True after the loop body executes   d) for True before the loop body executes

2. When a Do...Loop Until terminates, execution continues with the _____.

   a) Loop Until clause   b) statement after the Loop Until clause

   c) statements inside Do and Loop Until   d) Do clause

Answers: 1) c. 2) b.

10.4 Creating the Class Average Application

Now that you have learned the Do...Loop While and Do...Loop Until repetition statements, you can begin to develop the **Class Average** application. First, you will use pseudocode to list the actions to be executed and to specify the order of execution. You will use counter-controlled repetition to input the grades one at a time. Recall that this technique uses a variable called a counter to determine the number of times that a set of statements executes. In this example, repetition terminates when the counter exceeds 10 because we are assuming, for simplicity, that the user will only enter 10 grades. The following pseudocode describes the basic operation of the **Class Average** application when the **Add Grade** Button is clicked and when the **Average** Button is clicked:

When the user clicks the Add Grade Button

    If an average has already been calculated for a set of grades
        Clear the output Label and the ListBox

    Retrieve grade entered by user in the Enter grade: TextBox
    Display the grade in the ListBox
    Clear the Enter grade: TextBox
    Transfer focus to the Enter grade: TextBox

    If the user has entered more than 10 grades
        Disable the Add Grade Button
        Transfer focus to the Average Button

When the user clicks the Average Button
    Set total to zero
    Set grade counter to zero

    Do
        Read the next grade in the ListBox
        Add the grade to the total
        Add one to the grade counter
    Loop While the grade counter is less than 10

    Calculate the class average by dividing the total by 10
    Display the class average
    Enable the Add Grade Button
    Transfer focus to the Enter grade: TextBox

Now that you have test-driven the **Class Average** application and studied its pseudocode representation, you will use an ACE table to help you convert the pseudocode to Visual Basic. Figure 10.8 lists the actions, controls and events that will help you complete your own version of this application.

We label the application's GUI, using Labels promptLabel, describeOutputLabel and gradeListLabel. The user enters grades in inputTextBox and clicks addButton. The Click event then Adds the value that the user entered in inputTextBox to the ListBox, using method gradesListBox.Items.Add(). When the user has entered 10 grades and clicked averageButton, the application will retrieve each value from the ListBox, add it to the total and compute the class average by dividing by 10. The class average then will be displayed in outputLabel.

Action/Control/Event Table for the Class Average Application

Action	Control	Event
Label all the application's controls	promptLabel, gradeListLabel, describeOutputLabel	
	addButton	Click
If an average has already been calculated for a set of grades	outputLabel	
Clear the output Label and the ListBox	outputLabel, gradesListBox	
Retrieve grade entered by user in the Enter grade: TextBox	inputTextBox	
Display the grade in the ListBox	gradesListBox	
Clear the Enter grade: TextBox	inputTextBox	
Transfer focus to the Enter grade: TextBox	inputTextBox	
If the user has entered more than 10 grades	gradesListBox	
Disable the Add Grade Button	addButton	
Transfer focus to the Average Button	averageButton	
	averageButton	Click
Set total to zero		
Set grade counter to zero		
Do		
Read the next grade in the ListBox	gradesListBox	
Add the grade to the total		
Add one to the grade counter		
Loop While the grade counter is less than 10		
Calculate the class average by dividing the total by 10		
Display the class average	outputLabel	
Enable the Add Grade Button	addButton	
Transfer focus to the Enter grade: TextBox	inputTextBox	

Figure 10.8 ACE table for the **Class Average** application.

Now that we have formulated an algorithm for solving the **Class Average** problem, we can begin adding functionality to the template application. To display in the **Grade list:** ListBox a grade entered in the **Enter grade:** TextBox, the user clicks the **Add Grade** Button. If the application is already displaying grades in the **Grade list:** ListBox and the class average in the **Class average:** Label, the values are first cleared. The following box guides you through adding this functionality to the **Add Grade** Button's event handler.

Entering Grades in the Class Average Application

1. ***Copying the template to your working directory.*** Copy the C:\Examples\ Tutorial10\TemplateApplication\ClassAverage directory to your C:\SimplyVB directory.

2. ***Opening the Class Average application's template file.*** Double click ClassAverage.sln in the ClassAverage directory to open the application in the Visual Basic IDE. Double click ClassAverage.vb in the **Solution Explorer** to display the Form (Fig. 10.9).

(cont.)

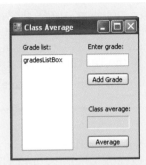

Figure 10.9   **Class Average** application's **Form** in design view.

3. *Adding an event handler for the **Add Grade Button**.* Each time users enter grades in the **Class Average** application, they must click the **Add Grade** Button. Double click the Button labeled **Add Grade** to create event handler addButton_Click.

4. *Clearing the ListBox and the **Class average:** Label of any output from a previous calculation.* Add lines 6–10 (Fig. 10.10) to event handler addButton_Click. Remember to place a comment before each event handler (line 2), and recall that we use the line-continuation character to split long lines (lines 3–4). To determine whether there was a previous calculation, test whether outputLabel displays any text by comparing the Text property's value to the empty string (line 7). If outputLabel displays the result of a previous calculation, set its Text property to the empty string (line 8). Line 9 clears the grades from the ListBox.

Clearing the grade list and class average

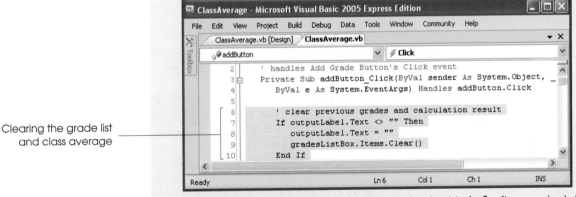

Figure 10.10   Clearing the ListBox and output Label after a calculation.

5. *Displaying each grade in the ListBox control.* Add lines 12–14 of Fig. 10.11 to event handler addButton_Click below the If...Then statement. Line 13 Adds the grade entered in inputTextBox to gradesList-Box's Items property. The grade is displayed in the ListBox.

Adding a numeric grade to the ListBox and clearing the user input from the TextBox

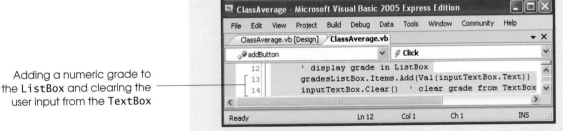

Figure 10.11   Adding the grade input to the ListBox and clearing the **Enter grade:** TextBox.

(cont.)

6. ***Preparing for the next grade to be entered.*** Method Clear (line 14 of Fig. 10.11) deletes the grade from the TextBox to prepare the application for the next grade to be entered. Using this method functions the same as assigning "" to the TextBox's Text property.

7. ***Saving the project.*** Select **File > Save All** to save your modified code.

You have added the code to display the grade entered in the **Enter grade:** TextBox in the ListBox when the user clicks the **Add Grade** Button. Next, you learn how to transfer the focus to the TextBox for the next grade entry after the user clicks the **Add Grade** Button. The following box also shows you how to disable the **Add Grade** Button after 10 grades have been entered and its functionality is no longer needed.

Transferring the Focus to a Control and Disabling a Button

1. ***Transferring the focus to a control.*** Add line 15 (Fig. 10.12) to event handler addButton_Click. Line 15 calls inputTextBox's **Focus** method to place the cursor in the TextBox for the next grade input. This process is called **transferring the focus.** Here the focus is transferred from the Button to the TextBox.

Transferring the focus of the application to the TextBox

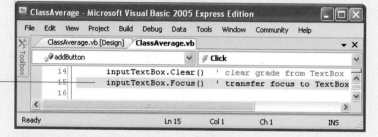

Figure 10.12 Transferring the focus to the TextBox control.

2. ***Disabling the Add Grade Button to prohibit users from entering more than 10 grades.*** Your application should accept exactly 10 grades. If the number of grades already entered by the user is equal to 10, then the application should prevent the user from entering more grades. Add lines 17–21 of Fig. 10.13 to event handler addButton_Click. Line 18 determines whether 10 or more grades have been entered, using the >= comparison operator. Items's **Count** property returns the number of items displayed in the **Grade list:** ListBox. If 10 grades have been entered, line 19 disables addButton by setting its **Enabled** property to False. Clicking the disabled **Add Grade** Button will not cause the addButton_Click event handler to execute.

GUI Design Tip

Disable Buttons when their function should not be available to users.

Disabling the **Add grade** Button and transferring the focus to the **Average** Button

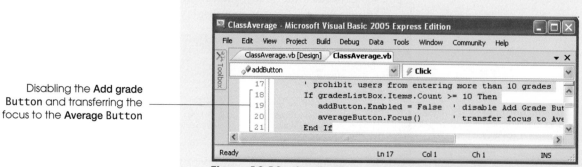

Figure 10.13 Application accepts only 10 grades.

(cont.)

3. ***Transferring the focus to the Average Button after 10 grades have been entered.*** After 10 grades have been entered, it does not make sense for the application to transfer the focus to the TextBox. Instead, line 20 invokes method Focus to transfer the focus to the **Average** Button. This way, you can press *Enter* to invoke **Average** Button's event handler, without navigating to the Button or using the mouse pointer.

4. ***Saving the project.*** Select **File > Save All** to save your modified code.

After 10 grades have been entered and displayed in the ListBox, the **Add Grade** Button's event handler transfers the focus to the **Average** Button. When the user clicks the **Average** Button, the application calculates and displays the average of the 10 grades. The following box shows you how to sum the grades with a Do…Loop Until repetition statement before the average calculation. The box also covers displaying the result in the **Class average:** Label.

Calculating the Class Average

1. ***Adding an event handler for the Average Button.*** Double click the Button labeled **Average** to generate event handler averageButton_Click.

2. ***Initializing variables used in the class-average calculation.*** Add lines 28–32 of Fig. 10.14 to event handler averageButton_Click. Line 29 declares Integer total. You will use total to calculate the sum of 10 grades (you will need this sum later when you calculate the average grade). Line 30 declares the counter (gradeCounter). It is important that variables used as totals and counters have appropriate initial values before they are used. If a numerical variable is not initialized before its first use, Visual Basic initializes it to a default value of 0. However, notice in Figure 10.14 that all of the variables are manually initialized to 0. This has been done simply to make the program clearer. Variable grade (line 31) temporarily stores each grade read from the ListBox. Although the grades entered are Integers, the result of the averaging calculation can be a floating-point value (such as the 81.10 result in Fig. 10.4); therefore, you declare Double variable average (line 32) to store the class average.

3. ***Summing the grades displayed in the ListBox.*** Add lines 34–40 of Fig. 10.15 to event handler averageButton_Click. The Do…Loop Until statement (lines 35–40) sums the grades that it reads from the ListBox. Line 40 indicates that the statement should iterate until the value of gradeCounter is greater than or equal to 10. Line 37 reads the current value from the ListBox, using property **Item** from the ListBox's Items collection, and stores that value in grade. The items in a ListBox are accessed by their position number, starting from position number 0. Line 38 adds grade to the previous value of total and assigns the result to total, using the += assignment operator. Variable gradeCounter is incremented (line 39) to indicate that another grade has been processed. (Incrementing the counter ensures that the condition at line 40 eventually becomes True, terminating the loop.)

4. ***Calculating and displaying the average.*** Add lines 42–45 of Fig. 10.16 to event handler averageButton_Click. Line 42 assigns the result of the average calculation to variable average. Line 43 displays the value of variable average. Note the use of the F format specifier to display average in floating point format. After the average is displayed, another set of 10 grades can be entered. To allow this, you need to enable the **Add Grade** Button by setting property Enabled to True (line 44). Line 45 transfers the focus to the **Enter grade:** TextBox.

 **GUI Design Tip**

Enable a disabled **Button** when its function should be available to the user once again.

(cont.)

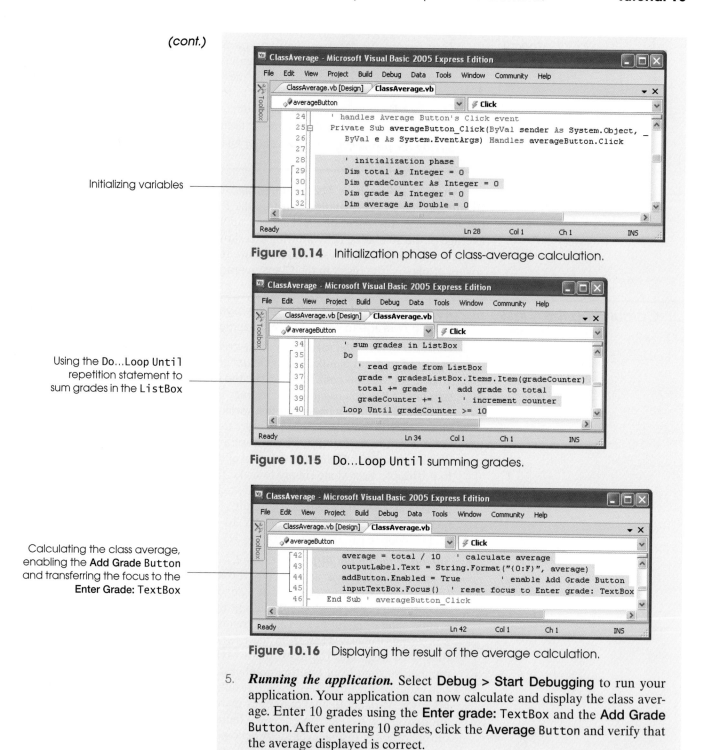

Initializing variables

Figure 10.14 Initialization phase of class-average calculation.

Using the Do...Loop Until repetition statement to sum grades in the ListBox

Figure 10.15 Do...Loop Until summing grades.

Calculating the class average, enabling the **Add Grade** Button and transferring the focus to the **Enter Grade:** TextBox

Figure 10.16 Displaying the result of the average calculation.

5. ***Running the application.*** Select **Debug > Start Debugging** to run your application. Your application can now calculate and display the class average. Enter 10 grades using the **Enter grade:** TextBox and the **Add Grade** Button. After entering 10 grades, click the **Average** Button and verify that the average displayed is correct.

6. ***Closing the application.*** Close your running application by clicking its close box.

7. ***Closing the IDE.*** Close the Visual Basic IDE by clicking its close box.

Figure 10.17 presents the source code for the **Class Average** application. The lines of code that contain new programming concepts that you learned in this tutorial are highlighted.

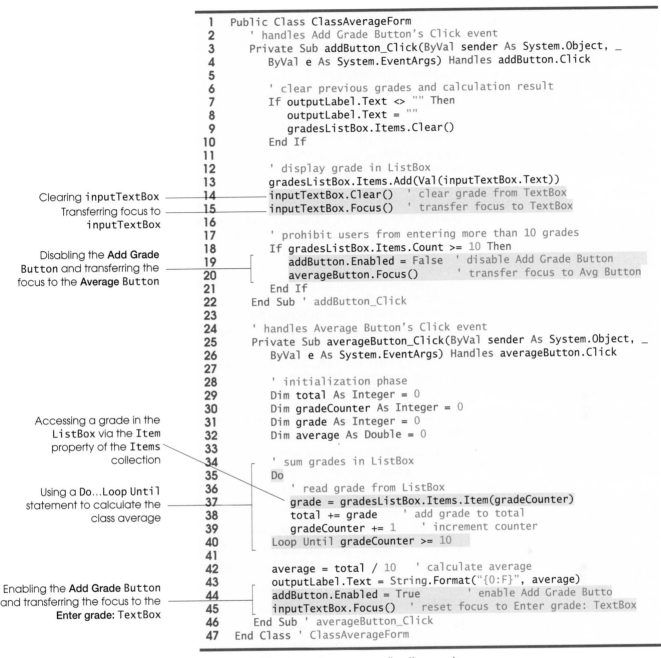

```
 1  Public Class ClassAverageForm
 2     ' handles Add Grade Button's Click event
 3     Private Sub addButton_Click(ByVal sender As System.Object, _
 4        ByVal e As System.EventArgs) Handles addButton.Click
 5
 6        ' clear previous grades and calculation result
 7        If outputLabel.Text <> "" Then
 8           outputLabel.Text = ""
 9           gradesListBox.Items.Clear()
10        End If
11
12        ' display grade in ListBox
13        gradesListBox.Items.Add(Val(inputTextBox.Text))
14        inputTextBox.Clear()  ' clear grade from TextBox
15        inputTextBox.Focus()  ' transfer focus to TextBox
16
17        ' prohibit users from entering more than 10 grades
18        If gradesListBox.Items.Count >= 10 Then
19           addButton.Enabled = False  ' disable Add Grade Button
20           averageButton.Focus()      ' transfer focus to Avg Button
21        End If
22     End Sub ' addButton_Click
23
24     ' handles Average Button's Click event
25     Private Sub averageButton_Click(ByVal sender As System.Object, _
26        ByVal e As System.EventArgs) Handles averageButton.Click
27
28        ' initialization phase
29        Dim total As Integer = 0
30        Dim gradeCounter As Integer = 0
31        Dim grade As Integer = 0
32        Dim average As Double = 0
33
34        ' sum grades in ListBox
35        Do
36           ' read grade from ListBox
37           grade = gradesListBox.Items.Item(gradeCounter)
38           total += grade     ' add grade to total
39           gradeCounter += 1    ' increment counter
40        Loop Until gradeCounter >= 10
41
42        average = total / 10   ' calculate average
43        outputLabel.Text = String.Format("{0:F}", average)
44        addButton.Enabled = True      ' enable Add Grade Butto
45        inputTextBox.Focus()  ' reset focus to Enter grade: TextBox
46     End Sub ' averageButton_Click
47  End Class ' ClassAverageForm
```

Clearing inputTextBox — line 14
Transferring focus to — line 15
inputTextBox

Disabling the **Add Grade** — lines 19–20
Button and transferring the
focus to the **Average** Button

Accessing a grade in the — line 37
ListBox via the Item
property of the Items
collection

Using a Do...Loop Until — lines 35–40
statement to calculate the
class average

Enabling the **Add Grade** Button — lines 44–45
and transferring the focus to the
Enter grade: TextBox

Figure 10.17   **Class Average** application code.

SELF-REVIEW   1. If you do not want a Button to call its event handler method when the Button is clicked,
set property _____ to _____

    a) Enabled, False   b) Enabled, True

    c) Disabled, True   d) Disabled, False

2. _____ a TextBox selects that TextBox to receive user input.

    a) Enabling   b) Clearing

    c) Transferring the focus to   d) Disabling

Answers: 1) a. 2) c.

10.5 Wrap-Up

In this tutorial, you learned how to use the Do...Loop While and the Do...Loop Until repetition statements. We provided the syntax and included UML activity diagrams that explained how each statement executes. You used the Do...Loop Until statement in the **Class Average** application that you developed.

The Do...Loop While repetition statement executes as long as its loop-continuation condition is True. This repetition statement always executes at least once. When the loop-continuation condition becomes False, the repetition terminates. This repetition statement enters an infinite loop if the loop-continuation condition never becomes False.

The Do...Loop Until repetition statement also executes at least once. It executes as long as its loop-termination condition is False. When the loop-termination condition becomes True, the repetition terminates. The Do...Loop Until statement enters an infinite loop if the loop-termination condition never becomes True.

You also learned more sophisticated techniques for creating polished graphical user interfaces for your applications. You now know how to invoke method Focus to transfer the focus in an application, indicating that the next action the user takes should involve this control. You also learned how to disable Buttons that should not be available to a user at certain times during an application's execution, and you learned how to enable those Buttons again.

In the next tutorial, you will continue studying repetition statements. You will learn how to use the For...Next repetition statement, which is particularly useful for counter-controlled repetition.

SKILLS SUMMARY

Do...Loop While Repetition Statement

- Iterates while its loop-continuation condition is True.
- Tests the loop-continuation condition after the loop body is performed.
- Always executes the loop at least once.
- Becomes an infinite loop if the loop-continuation condition can never become False.

Do...Loop Until Repetition Statement

- Iterates until its loop-termination condition becomes True.
- Tests the loop-termination condition after the loop body is performed.
- Always executes the loop at least once.
- Becomes an infinite loop if the loop-termination condition can never become True.

Disabling a Button

- Set Button property Enabled to False.

Enabling a Button

- Set Button property Enabled to True.

Transferring the Focus to a Control

- Call method Focus.

KEY TERMS

Count property of Items—Returns the number of ListBox items.

Do...Loop Until repetition statement—A control statement that executes a set of statements until the loop-termination condition becomes True after the loop executes.

Do...Loop While repetition statement—A control statement that executes a set of statements while the loop-continuation condition is True; the condition is tested after the loop executes.

Enabled property—Specifies whether a control such as a Button appears enabled (True) or disabled (False).

Focus method—Transfers the focus of the application to the control on which the method is called.

Item property of Items—Returns the value stored in the ListBox at the specified index.

off-by-one error—The kind of logic error that occurs when a loop executes for one more or one fewer iteration than is intended.

transferring the focus—Selecting a control in an application.

GUI DESIGN GUIDELINES

Button

- Disable a Button when its function should not be available to users.
- Enable a disabled Button when its function should once again be available to users.

CONTROLS, EVENTS, PROPERTIES & METHODS

Button      This control allows the user to raise an action or event.

- *In action*

    Calculate Total

- *Event*

    Click—Raised when the user clicks the Button.

- *Properties*

    Enabled—Determines whether the Buttons event handler executes when the Button is clicked.

    Location—Specifies the location of the Button on the Form relative to the top-left corner.

    Name—Specifies the name used to access the Button programmatically. The name should be appended with the Button suffix.

    Size—Specifies the height and width (in pixels) of the Button.

    Text—Specifies the text displayed on the Button.

- *Method*

    Focus—Transfers the focus of the application to the Button that calls it.

ListBox   ≣↕ ListBox   This control allows the user to view and select from items in a list.

- *In action*

Months	Monthly Payments
24	$490.50
36	$339.06
48	$263.55
60	$218.41

- *Properties*

    Items—Returns an object that contains the items displayed in the ListBox.

    Items.Count—Returns the number of items in the ListBox.

    Items.Item—Returns the values at the specified index in the ListBox.

    Location—Specifies the location of the ListBox on the Form relative to the top-left corner.

    Name—Specifies the name used to access the ListBox programmatically. The name should be appended with the ListBox suffix.

    Size—Specifies the height and width (in pixels) of the ListBox.

- *Methods*

    Items.Add—Adds an item to the Items property.

    Items.Clear—Deletes all the values in the ListBox's Items property.

TextBox `abl TextBox` This control allows the user to input data from the keyboard.

- ■ *In action*

  ```
  0
  ```

- ■ *Event*

  TextChanged—Raised when the text in the TextBox is changed.
- ■ *Properties*

  Location—Specifies the location of the TextBox on the Form relative to the top-left corner.

  Name—Specifies the name used to access the TextBox programmatically. The name should be appended with the TextBox suffix.

  Size—Specifies the height and width (in pixels) of the TextBox.

  Text—Specifies the text displayed in the TextBox.

  TextAlign—Specifies how the text is aligned within the TextBox.
- ■ *Methods*

  Clear—Removes the text from the TextBox that calls it.

  Focus—Transfers the focus of the application to the TextBox that calls it.

MULTIPLE-CHOICE QUESTIONS

10.1 A(n) _____ occurs when a loop-continuation condition in a Do...Loop While never becomes False.

    a) infinite loop   b) counter-controlled loop

    c) control statement   d) nested control statement

10.2 Set property _____ to True to enable a Button.

    a) Disabled   b) Focus

    c) Enabled   d) ButtonEnabled

10.3 The _____ statement executes at least once and continues executing until its loop-termination condition becomes True.

    a) Do While...Loop   b) Do...Loop Until

    c) Do...Loop While   d) Do Until...Loop

10.4 The _____ statement executes at least once and continues executing until its loop-continuation condition becomes False.

    a) Do...Loop Until   b) Do Until...Loop

    c) Do While...Loop   d) Do...Loop While

10.5 Method _____ transfers the focus to a control.

    a) GetFocus   b) Focus

    c) Transfer   d) Activate

10.6 A _____ contains the sum of a series of values.

    a) total   b) counter

    c) condition   d) loop

10.7 Property _____ of _____ contains the number of items in a ListBox.

    a) Count, ListBox   b) ListCount, Items

    c) ListCount, ListBox   d) Count, Items

10.8 A(n) _____ occurs when a loop executes for one more or one less iteration than is necessary.

    a) infinite loop   b) counter-controlled loop

    c) off-by-one error   d) nested control statement

10.9 A Do...Loop Until repetition statement's loop-termination condition is evaluated _____.

a) only the first time the body executes   b) before the body executes

c) after the body executes   d) None of the above.

10.10 If its continuation condition is initially False, a Do...Loop While repetition statement _____.

a) never executes   b) executes while the condition is False

c) executes until the condition becomes   d) executes only once
True

EXERCISES

10.11 *(Modified Class Average Application)* Modify the **Class Average** application, as in Fig. 10.18, so that **Average** Button is disabled until 10 grades have been entered.

 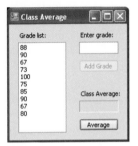

Figure 10.18 Modified **Class Average** application.

a) *Copying the template to your working directory.* Copy the directory C:\Examples\ Tutorial10\Exercises\ModifiedClassAverage to your C:\SimplyVB directory.

b) *Opening the application's template file.* Double click ClassAverage.sln in the ModifiedClassAverage directory to open the application.

c) *Initially disabling the Average Button.* Use the **Properties** window to modify the **Average** Button in the Form so that it is disabled when the application first executes by initially setting its Enabled property to False.

d) *Enabling the Average Button after 10 grades have been entered.* Add code to the addButton_Click event handler so that the **Average** Button becomes enabled when 10 grades have been entered.

e) *Disabling the Average Button after the calculation has been performed.* Add code to the averageButton_Click event handler so that the **Average** Button is disabled once the calculation result has been displayed.

f) *Running the application.* Select **Debug > Start Debugging** to run your application. Enter 10 grades and ensure that the **Average** Button is disabled until all 10 grades are entered. Verify that the **Add Grade** Button is disabled after 10 grades are entered. Once the **Average** Button is enabled, click it and verify that the average displayed is correct. The **Average** Button should then become disabled again, and the **Add Grade** Button should be enabled.

g) *Closing the application.* Close your running application by clicking its close box.

h) *Closing the IDE.* Close the Visual Basic IDE by clicking its close box.

10.12 *(Class Average Application That Handles Any Number of Grades)* Rewrite the **Class Average** application to handle any number of grades, as in Fig. 10.19. Note that the application does not know how many grades the user will enter, so the Buttons must be enabled at all times.

a) *Copying the template to your working directory.* Copy the directory C:\Examples\ Tutorial10\Exercises\UndeterminedClassAverage to C:\SimplyVB.

b) *Opening the application's template file.* Double click ClassAverage.sln in the UndeterminedClassAverage directory to open the application.

c) *Never disabling the Add Grade Button.* Remove code from the addButton_Click event handler so that the **Add Grade** Button is not disabled after entering 10 grades.

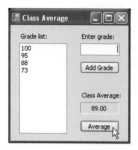

Figure 10.19 Modified **Class Average** application handling an unspecified number of grades.

d) *Summing the grades in the ListBox.* Modify code in the averageButton_Click event handler so that gradeCounter is incremented until it is equal to the number of grades entered. Use gradesListBox.Items.Count to determine the number of items in the ListBox. The number returned by the Count property will be zero if there are no grades entered. Use an If...Then selection statement to avoid division by zero and display a message dialog to the user if there are no grades entered when the user clicks the **Average** Button.

e) *Calculating the class average.* Modify the code in the averageButton_Click event handler so that average is computed by using gradesListBox.Items.Count rather than the value 10.

f) *Running the application.* Select **Debug > Start Debugging** to run your application. Enter 10 grades and click the **Average** Button. Verify that the average displayed is correct. Follow the same actions but this time for 15 grades, then for 5 grades. Each time, verify that the appropriate average is displayed.

g) *Closing the application.* Close your running application by clicking its close box.

h) *Closing the IDE.* Close the Visual Basic IDE by clicking its close box.

10.13 *(Arithmetic Calculator Application)* Write an application that allows users to enter a series of numbers and manipulate them. The application should provide users with the option of adding or multiplying the numbers. Users should enter each number in a TextBox. After entering each number, users click a Button and the number is inserted in a ListBox. The GUI should behave as in Fig. 10.20.

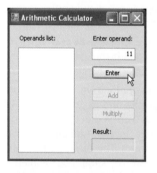
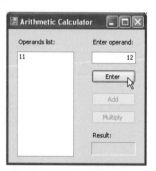

Figure 10.20 **Arithmetic Calculator** application.

a) *Copying the template to your working directory.* Copy the directory C:\Examples\ Tutorial10\Exercises\ArithmeticCalculator to your C:\SimplyVB directory.

b) *Opening the application's template file.* Double click ArithmeticCalculator.sln in the ArithmeticCalculator directory to open the application.

c) *Add a ListBox to display the entered numbers.* Add a ListBox. Place and size it as in Fig. 10.20.

d) *Creating an event handler for the Enter Button.* Create the Click event handler for the **Enter** Button. If the result of a previous calculation is displayed, this event handler should clear the result, clear the ListBox and disable the addition and multiplication Buttons. It should then insert the current number in the **Operands list:** ListBox. When the ListBox contains at least two numbers, the event handler should then enable the addition and multiplication Buttons.

e) *Summing the grades in the ListBox.* Define the Click event handler for the **Add** Button. This event handler should compute the sum of all the values in the **Operands list:** ListBox and display the result in resultLabel.

f) *Define the Click event handler for the Multiply Button.* This event handler should compute the product of all the values in the **Operands list:** ListBox and display the result in resultLabel.

g) *Running the application.* Select **Debug > Start Debugging** to run your application. Enter two values, then click the **Add** and **Multiply** Buttons. Verify that the results displayed are correct. Also, make sure that the **Add** and **Multiply** Buttons are not enabled until two values have been entered.

h) *Closing the application.* Close your running application by clicking its close box.

i) *Closing the IDE.* Close the Visual Basic IDE by clicking its close box.

What does this code do? ▶ **10.14** What is the result of the following code?

```
1   Dim y As Integer
2   Dim x As Integer
3   Dim mysteryValue As Integer
4
5   x = 1
6   mysteryValue = 0
7
8   Do
9       y = x ^ 2
10      displayListBox.Items.Add(y)
11      mysteryValue += 1
12      x += 1
13  Loop While x <= 10
14
15  resultLabel.Text = mysteryValue
```

What's wrong with this code? ▶ **10.15** Find the error(s) in the following code. This code should add 10 to the value in y and store it in z. It then should reduce the value of y by one and repeat until y is less than 10. Lastly, resultLabel should display the final value of z.

```
1   Dim y As Integer = 10
2   Dim z As Integer = 2
3
4   Do
5       z = y + 10
6   Loop Until y < 10
7
8   y -= 1
9
10  resultLabel.Text = z
```

Using the Debugger ▷ **10.16** (*Factorial Application*) The **Factorial** application calculates the factorial of an integer input by the user. The factorial of an integer is the product of the integers from one to that number. For example, the factorial of 3 is 6 (1 × 2 × 3). While testing the application you noticed that it does not execute correctly. Use the debugger to find and correct the logic error(s) in the application. Figure 10.8 displays the correct output for the **Factorial** application.

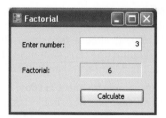

Figure 10.21 Correct output for the **Factorial** application.

Programming Challenge ▷ **10.17** (*Restaurant Bill Application*) Develop an application that calculates a restaurant bill. The user should be able to enter the item ordered, the quantity of the item ordered and the price per item. When the user clicks the **Add Item** Button, your application should display the number ordered, the item ordered and the price per unit in three ListBoxes, as shown in Fig. 10.22. When the user clicks the **Total Bill** Button, the application should calculate the total cost. For each entry in the ListBox, multiply the cost of each item by the number of items ordered.

Figure 10.22 Restaurant Bill application's Form.

Objectives

In this tutorial, you will learn to:
- Execute statements repeatedly with the For...Next repetition statement.
- Obtain user input with the NumericUpDown control.
- Display information, using a multiline TextBox.
- Use type String.

Outline

11.1 Test-Driving the Interest Calculator Application

11.2 Essentials of Counter-Controlled Repetition

11.3 Introducing the For...Next Repetition Statement

11.4 Examples Using the For...Next Statement

11.5 Constructing the Interest Calculator Application

11.6 Wrap-Up

Interest Calculator Application

Introducing the For...Next Repetition Statement

As you learned in Tutorials 9 and 10, applications are often required to repeat actions. Using a Do repetition statement allowed you to specify a condition and test it either before entering the loop or after execution of the body of the loop. In the **Car Payment Calculator** application and the **Class Average** application, a counter was used to determine the number of times the loop should iterate. In fact, the use of counters in repetition statement is so common in applications that Visual Basic provides an additional control statement specially designed for such cases: the For...Next repetition statement. In this tutorial, you will use the For...Next repetition statement to create an **Interest Calculator** application.

11.1 Test-Driving the Interest Calculator Application

The **Interest Calculator** application calculates the amount of money in your savings account after you begin with a certain amount of money and are paid a certain interest rate for a certain amount of time. Users specify the principal amount (the initial amount of money in the account), the interest rate and the number of years for which interest will be calculated. The application then displays the results. This application must meet the following requirements:

Application Requirements

You are considering investing $1,000.00 in a savings account that yields 5% interest, and you want to forecast how your investment will grow. Assuming that you will leave all interest on deposit, calculate and print the amount of money in the account at the end of each year over a period of n years. To compute these amounts, use the following formula:

$$a = p(1 + r)^n$$

where

p is the original amount of money invested (the principal)

r is the annual interest rate (for example, .05 is equivalent to 5%)

n is the number of years

a is the amount on deposit at the end of the nth year.

You begin by test-driving the completed application. Then, you will learn the additional Visual Basic technologies that you will need to create your own version of this application.

Test-Driving the Interest Calculator Application

1. *Opening the completed application.* Open the directory C:\Examples\ Tutorial11\CompletedApplication\InterestCalculator to locate the **Interest Calculator** application. Double click InterestCalculator.sln to open the application in the Visual Basic IDE.

2. *Running the Interest Calculator application.* Select **Debug > Start Debugging** to run the application (Fig. 11.1).

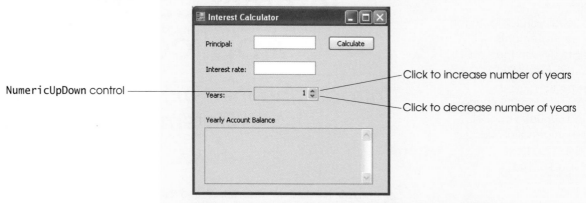

NumericUpDown control

Click to increase number of years

Click to decrease number of years

Figure 11.1 Completed **Interest Calculator** application.

3. *Providing a principal value.* Once the application is running, provide a value in the **Principal:** TextBox. Input 1000, as specified in the problem statement.

4. *Providing an interest-rate value.* Next, type a value in the **Interest Rate:** TextBox. We specified the interest rate 5% in the problem statement, so enter 5 in the **Interest Rate:** TextBox.

5. *Providing the duration of the investment.* Now, choose the number of years for which you want to calculate the amount in the savings account. In this case, select 10 by clicking the up arrow in the **Years:** NumericUpDown control repeatedly until the value reads 10.

6. *Calculating the amount.* After you input the necessary information, click the **Calculate** Button. The amount of money in your account at the end of each year during a period of 10 years displays in the multiline TextBox. The application should look similar to Fig. 11.2.

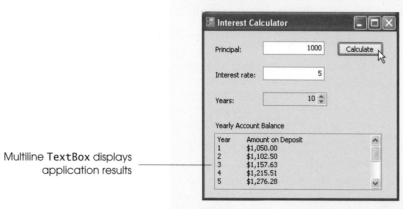

Multiline **TextBox** displays application results

Figure 11.2 Output of completed **Interest Calculator** application.

(cont.)   7. ***Closing the application.*** Close your running application by clicking its close box.

   8. ***Closing the IDE.*** Close the Visual Basic IDE by clicking its close box.

11.2 Essentials of Counter-Controlled Repetition

In Tutorial 10, you learned how to use counter-controlled repetition. The four essential elements of counter-controlled repetition are:

1. the *name* of a *control variable* (or loop counter) that is used to determine whether the loop continues to iterate

2. the *initial value* of the control variable

3. the *increment* (or *decrement*) by which the control variable is modified during each iteration of the loop (that is, each time the loop is performed)

4. the condition that tests for the *final value* of the control variable (to determine whether looping should continue).

The example of Fig. 11.3 uses the four elements of counter-controlled repetition. This Do While...Loop is similar to the **Car Payment Calculator** application's loop in Tutorial 9.

```
1    Dim counter As Integer = 2 ' repetition counter
2
3    Do While counter <= 5
4       months = 12 * counter ' calculate payment period
5
6       ' calculate payment value
7       value = Convert.ToDecimal( _
8          Pmt(monthlyInterest, months, -loanAmount))
9
10      ' display payment value
11      paymentsListBox.Items.Add(months & ControlChars.Tab & _
12         ControlChars.Tab & String.Format("{0:C}", value))
13
14      counter += 1 ' increment counter
15   Loop
```

Figure 11.3   Counter-controlled repetition example.

Recall that the **Car Payment Calculator** application calculates and displays monthly car payments over periods of two to five years. The declaration in line 1 *names* the control variable (counter), indicating that it is of data type Integer. This declaration includes an initialization, which sets the variable to an *initial value* of 2.

Consider the Do While...Loop statement (lines 3–15). Line 4 uses the counter variable to calculate the number of months over which car payments are to be made. Lines 7–8 use the Pmt function to determine the monthly payment for the car. This value depends on the interest rate, the duration of the loan in months, the car's price, and the down-payment amount. Lines 11–12 display the amount in a ListBox. Line 14 increments the control variable counter by 1 for each iteration of the loop. The condition in the Do While...Loop statement (line 3) tests for whether the value of the control variable is less than or equal to 5, meaning that 5 is the *final value* for which the condition is true. The body of this Do While...Loop is performed even when the control variable is 5. The loop terminates when the control variable exceeds 5 (that is, when counter has a value of 6).

1. The control variable's _____ is not one of the four essential elements of counter-controlled repetition.

   a) name

   b) initial value

   c) type

   d) final value

2. What aspect of the control variable determines whether looping should continue?

   a) name

   b) initial value

   c) type

   d) final value

Answers: 1) c. 2) d.

11.3 Introducing the For...Next Repetition Statement

The **For...Next** repetition statement makes it easier for you to write code to perform counter-controlled repetition. This statement specifies all four elements essential to counter-controlled repetition. The For...Next statement takes less time to code and is easier to read than an equivalent Do repetition statement.

Let's examine the first line of the For...Next repetition statement (Fig. 11.4), which we call the **For...Next header**. The For...Next header specifies all four essential elements for counter-controlled repetition. The line should be read "*for each value of counter starting at 2 and ending at 10, do the following statements, then add (step) two to counter.*"

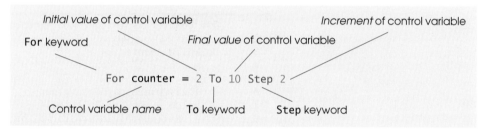

Figure 11.4 For...Next header components.

Each For...Next statement begins with the keyword **For**. Then the statement names and initializes a control variable (in this case, counter is set to 2). [*Note:* We suggest that you declare (using the Dim keyword) the counter variable before the For statement.] Following the initial value of the control variable is the keyword **To**, followed by the final value of the control variable to be used in the loop. You can then use the **Step** keyword to specify the amount by which to increase (or decrease) the control variable each time the loop body completes execution. If you wish to decrease the value of the control variable each time through the loop, simply use a negative number after the Step keyword. The following box describes each step as the above repetition statement executes.

Executing the
For...Next Repetition
Statement

1. The application sets variable counter's value to 2.

2. The loop-continuation condition is checked. The condition evaluates to True (counter is 2, which is less than or equal to 10), so the application executes the body of the For...Next repetition statement.

3. The value of counter is increased by 2; counter now contains 4.

4. The loop-continuation condition is checked. The condition evaluates to True (counter is 4, which is less than or equal to 10), so the application executes the body of the For...Next repetition statement.

(cont.)

5. The value of `counter` is increased by 2; `counter` now contains 6.

6. The loop-continuation condition is checked. The condition evaluates to `True` (`counter` is 6, which is less than or equal to 10), so the application executes the body of the `For…Next` repetition statement.

7. The value of `counter` is increased by 2; `counter` now contains 8.

8. The loop-continuation condition is checked. The condition evaluates to `True` (`counter` is 8, which is less than or equal to 10), so the application executes the body of the `For…Next` repetition statement.

9. The value of `counter` is increased by 2; `counter` now contains 10.

10. The loop-continuation condition is checked. The condition evaluates to `True` (`counter` is 10, which is less than or equal to 10), so the application executes the body of the `For…Next` repetition statement.

11. The value of `counter` is increased by 2; `counter` now contains 12.

12. The loop-continuation condition is checked. The condition evaluates to `False` (`counter` is 12, which is not less than or equal to 10), so the application exits the `For…Next` repetition statement.

Good Programming Practice

Place a blank line before and after each control statement to make it stand out in the code.

Using the keyword `Step` is optional. If you omit the `Step` keyword, the control variable is incremented by one after each repetition, by default.

The `For…Next` statement can be represented by repetition statements. For example, an equivalent `Do While…Loop` statement for Fig. 11.4 is

```
counter = 2

Do While counter <= 10
    body statement(s)
    counter += 2
Loop
```

Note that the `For…Next` statement's header (Fig. 11.4) implies the loop-continuation condition (`counter <= 10`), which is shown explicitly in the preceding `Do While…Loop` statement. The starting value, ending value and increment portions of a `For…Next` statement can contain arithmetic expressions. The expressions are evaluated once (when the `For…Next` statement begins executing) and then used as the starting value, ending value and increment of the `For…Next` header. For example, assume that a = 2 and b = 10. The header

```
For i = a To (4 * a * b) Step (b \ a)
```

is equivalent to the header

```
For i = 2 To 80 Step 5
```

Error-Prevention Tip

Although the value of the control variable can be changed in the body of a `For…Next` loop, avoid doing so, because this practice can lead to subtle errors.

If the implied loop-continuation condition is initially `False` (for example, if the starting value is greater than the ending value and the increment value is positive), the `For…Next`'s body is not performed. Instead, execution proceeds with the statement after the `For…Next` statement.

The control variable frequently is displayed or used in calculations in the `For…Next` body, but it does not have to be. It is common to use the control variable only to control repetition and not use it in the `For…Next` body.

The UML activity diagram for the `For…Next` statement is similar to that of the `Do While…Loop` statement. For example, the UML activity diagram of the `For…Next` statement

```
For counter = 1 To 10
    displayListBox.Items.Add(counter * 10)
Next
```

is shown in Fig. 11.5. This activity diagram shows that the initialization occurs only once and that incrementing occurs *after* each execution of the body statement. Note that, besides small circles and flowlines, the activity diagram contains only rounded rectangle symbols and small diamond symbols. The rounded rectangle symbols are filled with the actions, and the flowlines coming out of the small diamond symbols are labeled with the appropriate guard conditions for this algorithm.

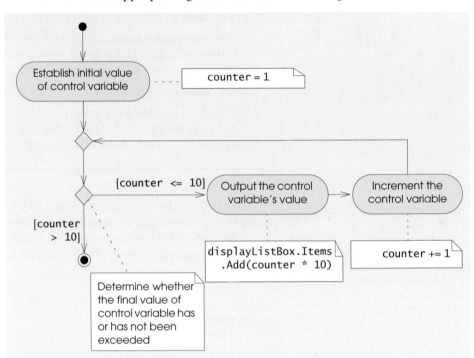

Figure 11.5   For...Next repetition statement UML activity diagram.

The For...Next header indicates each item needed to conduct counter-controlled repetition with a control variable. To help solidify your understanding of this new repetition statement, you will now learn how the Do While...Loop statement of Fig. 11.3 can be replaced by a For...Next statement.

The converted code is shown in Fig. 11.6. When the For...Next statement begins execution, line 3 of Fig. 11.6 initializes control variable counter to 1.

The implied loop-continuation condition counter <= 5 (which depends on the counter's final value) is tested in line 3. Keyword To is required in the For...Next statement. The value before this keyword specifies the initial value of counter; the value that follows it specifies the value tested for loop continuation (in this case, 5). Keyword Step is optional and is not used here. Step specifies the increment (the amount that is added to counter each time the For...Next body is executed.) If Step is not included, then the increment is 1, by default.

The initial value of counter is 1, so the implied loop-continuation condition is satisfied and the payment calculations within the For...Next body are executed.

After executing the For...Next body, the Next keyword is reached (line 13). This keyword marks the end of the For...Next repetition statement. When Next is reached, counter is incremented by 1 (the default increment amount), and the loop begins again with the implied loop-continuation condition test.

This process repeats until the implied loop-continuation condition becomes False as counter becomes greater than 5, then repetition terminates.

```
1   Dim counter As Integer
2
3   For counter = 2 To 5
4      months = 12 * counter ' calculate payment period
5
6      ' calculate payment value
7      value = Convert.ToDecimal( _
8         Pmt(monthlyRate, months, -loanAmount))
9
10     ' display payment value
11     paymentsListBox.Items.Add(months & ControlChars.Tab & _
12        ControlChars.Tab & String.Format("{0:C}", value))
13  Next
```

Figure 11.6   Code segment for the **Car Payment Calculator** application that demonstrates the **For...Next** statement.

Common Programming Error

Counter-controlled loops should not be controlled with floating-point variables. These are represented only approximately in the computer's memory, possibly resulting in imprecise counter values and inaccurate tests for termination that could lead to logic errors.

SELF-REVIEW

1. If the Step clause is omitted, the increment of a For...Next statement defaults to _____.

 a) 2   b) 1

 c) 0   d) –1

2. The value before the To keyword in a For...Next statement specifies the _____.

 a) initial value of the counter variable b) final value of the counter variable

 c) increment   d) number of times the statement iterates

Answers: 1) b. 2) a.

11.4 Examples Using the For...Next Statement

The following examples demonstrate different ways of varying the control variable in a For...Next statement. In each case, we write the appropriate For...Next header:

a) Vary the control variable from 1 to 100 in increments of 1.

```
For i = 1 To 100
or
For i = 1 To 100 Step 1
```

b) Vary the control variable from 100 to 1 in increments of –1 (decrements of 1).

```
For i = 100 To 1 Step -1
```

c) Vary the control variable from 7 to 77 in increments of 7.

```
For i = 7 To 77 Step 7
```

d) Vary the control variable from 20 to 2 in increments of –2 (decrements of 2).

```
For i = 20 To 2 Step -2
```

e) Vary the control variable over the sequence of the following values: 2, 5, 8, 11, 14, 17, 20.

```
For i = 2 To 20 Step 3
```

f) Vary the control variable over the sequence of the following values: 99, 88, 77, 66, 55, 44, 33, 22, 11, 0.

```
For i = 99 To 0 Step -11
```

SELF-REVIEW

1. Which of the following is the appropriate For...Next header for varying the control variable over the following sequence of values: 25, 20, 15, 10, 5?

 a) For i = 5 To 25 Step 5   b) For i = 25 To 5 Step -5

 c) For i = 5 To 25 Step -5   d) For i = 25 To 5 Step 5

2. Which of the following statements describes the For...Next header

   `For i = 81 To 102`?

   a) Vary the control variable from 81 to 102 in increments of 1.
   b) Vary the control variable from 81 to 102 in increments of 0.
   c) Vary the control variable from 102 to 81 in increments of -1.
   d) Vary the control variable from 81 to 102 in increments of 2.

Answers: 1) b. 2) a.

11.5 Constructing the Interest Calculator Application

Our solution to this tutorial's problem statement computes interest over a given number of years by using the For...Next statement. This repetition statement will perform the calculation for every year that the money remains on deposit.

The following pseudocode describes the basic operation of the **Interest Calculator** application when the **Calculate** Button is clicked:

```
When the user clicks the Calculate Button
    Get the values for the principal, interest rate and years entered by the user
    Store a header to be added to the output TextBox

    For each year (starting at 1 and ending with the number of years entered)
        Calculate the current value of the investment
        Display the year and the current value of the investment
```

The template application we provide for this tutorial contains the **Calculate** Button plus two Labels and their corresponding TextBoxes: for **Principal:** and for **Interest Rate:**. The Form has a **Years:** Label, but you will insert the NumericUpDown control for this input. The **NumericUpDown** control limits a user's choices for the number of years to a specific range. You will then create a multiline TextBox with a scrollbar and add it to the application's GUI. Finally, you will add functionality with a For...Next statement. Now that you have test-driven the **Interest Calculator** application and studied its pseudocode representation, you will use an ACE table to help you convert the pseudocode to Visual Basic. Figure 11.7 lists the actions, controls and events that will help you complete your own version of this application.

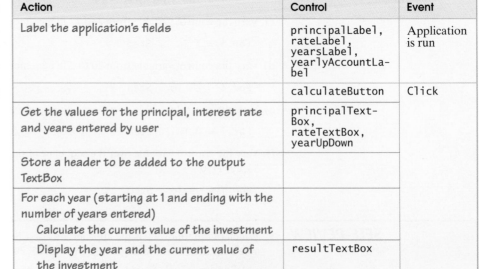

Action/Control/Event (ACE) Table for the Interest Calculator Application

Action	Control	Event
Label the application's fields	principalLabel, rateLabel, yearsLabel, yearlyAccountLabel	Application is run
	calculateButton	Click
Get the values for the principal, interest rate and years entered by user	principalTextBox, rateTextBox, yearUpDown	
Store a header to be added to the output TextBox		
For each year (starting at 1 and ending with the number of years entered) Calculate the current value of the investment		
Display the year and the current value of the investment	resultTextBox	

Figure 11.7 ACE table for **Interest Calculator** application.

In the following box, you will begin building the **Interest Calculator** application. First, you will add a NumericUpDown control to allow the user to specify the number of years. This control provides up and down arrows that allow the user to scroll through the control's range of values. The following box shows you how to set the limits of the range (maximum and minimum values). We will use 10 as the maximum value and 1 as the minimum value for this control. The **Increment** property specifies by how much the current number in the NumericUpDown control changes when the user clicks the control's up (for incrementing) or down (for decrementing) arrow. This application uses the Increment property's default value, 1.

Adding and Customizing a NumericUpDown Control	1. ***Copying the template to your working directory.*** Copy the C:\Examples\ Tutorial11\TemplateApplication\InterestCalculator directory to your C:\SimplyVB directory.

2. ***Opening the Interest Calculator application's template file.*** Double click InterestCalculator.sln in the InterestCalculator directory to open the application in the Visual Basic IDE (Fig. 11.8). Double click the InterestCalculator.vb file in the **Solution Explorer** if the form is not already visible.

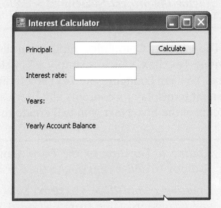

Figure 11.8   Template **Interest Calculator** application **Form** in design view.

3. ***Adding a NumericUpDown control.*** Double click NumericUpDown

in the **Toolbox** to add it to the Form (Fig. 11.9). Change the control's Name property to yearUpDown. To improve code readability, append the UpDown suffix to NumericUpDown control names.

GUI Design Tip

A NumericUpDown control should follow the same GUI Design Guidelines as a TextBox. (See Appendix C.)

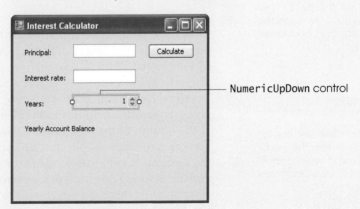

NumericUpDown control

Figure 11.9   NumericUpDown control added to **Interest Calculator** application.

(cont.)

4. *Setting the NumericUpDown control's location and size.* Set yearUpDown's `Location` property to 96, 96 and its `Size` property to 104, 21, so that it aligns horizontally and vertically with the `TextBoxes` above it.

5. *Setting property TextAlign.* Set property `TextAlign` to `Right`. The number now appears right aligned in the control.

6. *Setting property ReadOnly.* To ensure that the user cannot enter invalid values in the **Years:** `NumericUpDown` control, set the **ReadOnly** property to `True`. The `ReadOnly` property changes the background color of the control to gray, indicating that the user can change its value only by using the up and down arrows.

7. *Setting range limits for the NumericUpDown control.* By default, this control sets 0 as the minimum and 100 as the maximum. You will change these values. Set the **Maximum** property of the **Years:** `NumericUpDown` control to 10. Then set its **Minimum** property to 1. This (combined with setting its `ReadOnly` property to `True`) limits users to selecting values between 1 and 10 for the number of years. Note that the `NumericUpDown` control displays 1, the value of its `Minimum` property. Your `Form` should now look like Fig. 11.9.

8. *Saving the project.* Select **File > Save All** to save your modified code.

Good Programming Practice

Append the UpDown suffix to `NumericUpDown` control names.

GUI Design Tip

Use a `NumericUpDown` control to limit the range of user input.

The **Interest Calculator** application displays the results of its calculations in a multiline `TextBox`, which is simply a `TextBox` that can display more than one line of text. You can configure the `TextBox` to have a scrollbar, so that, if the `TextBox` is too small to display its contents, the user can scroll up and down to view the entire contents of the box. Next, you will create this `TextBox`.

Adding and Customizing a Multiline TextBox with a Scrollbar

1. *Adding a TextBox to the Form.* Double click the `TextBox` control in the **Toolbox** to add a `TextBox` to the Form. Name the `TextBox` resultTextBox.

2. *Creating a multiline TextBox.* Select the `TextBox`'s **Multiline** property, and change its value from `False` to `True`. Doing so allows the `TextBox` to contain multiple lines.

3. *Setting the size and location of the TextBox.* Set the `TextBox`'s `Location` property to 16, 160 and the `Size` property to 272, 88, so that it aligns horizontally with the controls above it.

4. *Setting property ReadOnly.* To ensure that the user cannot change the output in the **Yearly account balance:** `TextBox`, set the `ReadOnly` property to `True`.

5. *Inserting a vertical scrollbar.* Using scrollbars allows you to keep the size of a `TextBox` small while still allowing the user to view all the information in that `TextBox`. The length of the text could exceed the height of the `TextBox`, so enable the vertical scrollbar by setting resultTextBox's **ScrollBars** property to **Vertical**. A vertical scrollbar appears on the right side of the `TextBox`. By default, property `ScrollBars` is set to **None**. You can also set property `ScrollBars` to **Horizontal** or **Both**. A horizontal scrollbar appears at the bottom of the `TextBox`. The value `Both` indicates that horizontal and vertical scrollbars should be displayed. Note that, even without scrollbars, the user can scroll through the text by using the arrow keys. The scrollbar is initially disabled on your `Form`. A scrollbar is enabled only when it is needed (that is, when there is enough text in the `TextBox`). Your `Form` should look like Fig. 11.10.

GUI Design Tip

If a `TextBox` will display multiple lines of output, set the `Multiline` property to `True` and left align the output by setting the `TextAlign` property to `Left`.

GUI Design Tip

If a multiline `TextBox` will display many lines of output, limit the `TextBox` height and use a vertical scrollbar to allow users to view additional lines of output.

(cont.)

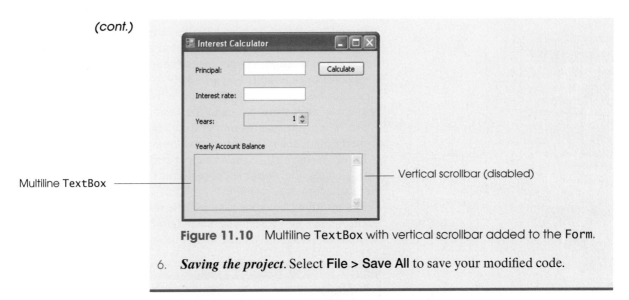

Figure 11.10   Multiline **TextBox** with vertical scrollbar added to the **Form**.

6. ***Saving the project.*** Select **File > Save All** to save your modified code.

Now that you have finished designing the GUI, you will add functionality to your application. When the user clicks the **Calculate** Button, you want the application to retrieve the input and then output a table containing the amount on deposit at the end of each year. You will do this by adding code to the Button's Click event handler.

Adding a Click Event Handler

1. ***Creating the event handler.*** Double click the **Calculate** Button. The **Calculate** Button Click event handler appears in the application's code.

2. ***Adding code to event handler calculateButton_Click.*** Add lines 6–17 of Fig. 11.11 to the calculateButton_Click event handler. Lines 6–12 declare the variables needed to store user inputs, calculation results and the output. Variable principal stores the amount of the principal as entered by the user, rate stores the interest rate and year stores the number of years the user selected in the NumericUpDown control. Variable amount stores the result of the interest calculation.

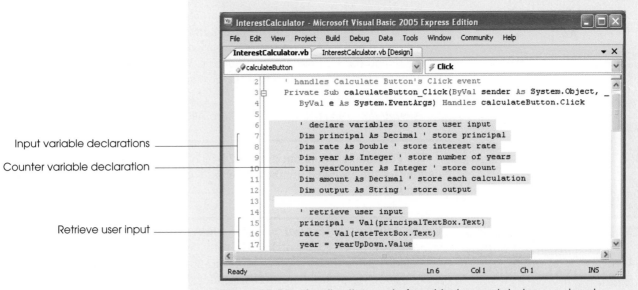

Figure 11.11   Application code for retrieving and storing user input.

(cont.)

Line 12 declares a `String` variable `output`. **String variables** store a series of characters. The most commonly used characters are letters and numbers, although there are also many special characters, such as $, *, ^, tabs and newlines. A list of characters you are likely to use is found in Appendix B, ASCII Character Set. You actually have been using `String`s all along—`Label`s and `TextBox`es both store values in the `Text` property as values of type `String`. In fact, when you assign a numeric data type, such as an `Integer`, to the `Text` property of a `Label`, the `Integer` value is implicitly converted to a `String`.

Lines 15–16 retrieve the principal and the interest rate from `TextBox`es. Line 17 uses the `NumericUpDown` control's `Value` property to obtain the user's selection.

The multiline `TextBox` displays the results in two columns. Add lines 19–21 of Fig. 11.12 to assign the header to `output`. The header labels the two columns as `Year` and `Amount on Deposit`, respectively.

Appending header text to the output `String`

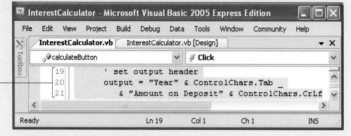

Figure 11.12 Application code for displaying a header in a multiline `TextBox`.

Recall that you cleared values in a `Label` in Tutorial 6 by setting the `Text` property to the empty string (`""`), which represents a `String` value with no characters. When assigning new text to a `String` variable, you must begin and end the text with a double quotation mark (`"`). For example, if you want to store the word `Year` in the `String` variable `year`, you would use the following statement:

```
year = "Year"
```

You can append a `String` or a character to the end of another `String` by using the concatenation operator (`&`). In lines 20–21 of Fig. 11.12, we use the `ControlChars.Tab` constant to insert a tab character between the word `Year` and the text `Amount on Deposit`. We then insert a newline character (`ControlChars.CrLf`), so that the next series of text will appear in the next line of output.

3. ***Saving the project.*** Select **File > Save All** to save your modified code.

The `For...Next` statement in lines 24–29 of Fig. 11.13 performs the interest calculations for the specified number of years. You create the `For...Next` statement in the next box.

Calculating Cumulative Interest with a For...Next Statement

1. ***Initializing the control variable and establishing the loop-continuation test.*** Add lines 23–24 of Fig. 11.13 to the `calculateButton_Click` event handler. Note that the keyword `Next` appears.

Line 24 is the `For...Next` header which initializes control variable `yearCounter` to 1. The value after the keyword `To` sets the implied loop-continuation condition. This loop continues while the control variable is less than or equal to the number of years specified by the user.

(cont.)

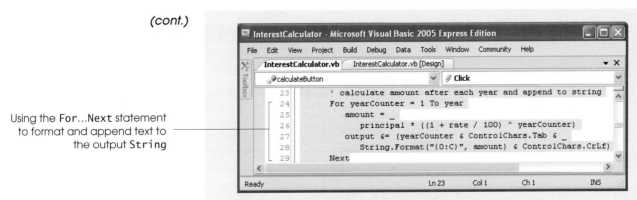

Using the **For…Next** statement to format and append text to the output **String**

Figure 11.13 Application code for **For…Next** statement.

2. *Performing the interest calculation.* The For…Next statement executes its body once for each year up to the value of year, varying control variable yearCounter from 1 to year in increments of 1. Add lines 25–26 of Fig. 11.13 to perform the calculation from the formula

$$a = p \ (1 + r)^{\,n}$$

where *a* is amount, *p* is principal, *r* is rate and *n* is yearCounter.

Note that the calculation in line 26 also divides rate 100. This implies that the user must enter an interest rate value in percentage format (for example, the user should enter the number 5.5 to represent 5.5%).

3. *Appending the calculation to the output string.* Add lines 27–28 of Fig. 11.13. These lines append additional text to the end of output, using the **&=** operator. The **&=** operator (which behaves much like the **+=** operator) appends the right operand to the text in the left operand. This new value is then assigned to the variable in the left operand. The text includes the current yearCounter value, a tab character (ControlChars.Tab) to position to the second column, the result of the call String.Format("{0:C}", amount) and, finally, a newline character (ControlChars.CrLf) to start the next output on the next line. Recall that the C (for "currency") formatting code indicates that its corresponding argument (amount) should be displayed in monetary format.

4. *Reaching the Next keyword.* After the body of the loop is performed, application execution reaches keyword Next, which is now in line 29. The counter (yearCounter) is incremented by 1, and the loop begins again with the implied loop-continuation test.

5. *Terminating the For…Next statement.* The For…Next statement executes until the control variable exceeds the number of years specified by the user.

6. *Displaying the result of the calculations.* After exiting the For…Next statement, output is ready to be displayed to the user in resultTextBox. Add line 30 of Fig. 11.14 to display the header and the results in the multiline TextBox.

7. *Running the application.* Select **Debug > Start Debugging** to run your application. Your application can now calculate and display the amount on deposit for each year. Enter 1000 in the **Principal:** TextBox, 5 in the **Interest Rate:** TextBox and 10 in the **Years:** NumericUpDown control. Click the **Calculate** Button and verify that the results are the same as those displayed in Fig. 11.2.

(cont.)

Displaying in the multiline TextBox the result of the calculations performed in the For...Next statement

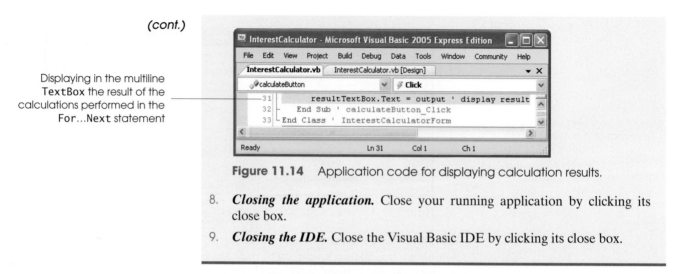

Figure 11.14 Application code for displaying calculation results.

8. ***Closing the application.*** Close your running application by clicking its close box.

9. ***Closing the IDE.*** Close the Visual Basic IDE by clicking its close box.

Figure 11.15 presents the source code for the **Interest Calculator** application. The lines of code that contain new programming concepts that you learned in this tutorial are highlighted.

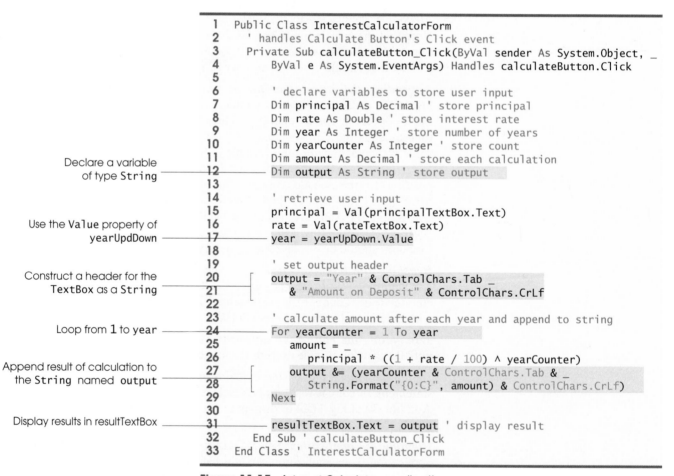

Declare a variable of type `String`

Use the `Value` property of `yearUpdDown`

Construct a header for the TextBox as a `String`

Loop from `1` to `year`

Append result of calculation to the `String` named `output`

Display results in `resultTextBox`

```
1   Public Class InterestCalculatorForm
2       ' handles Calculate Button's Click event
3       Private Sub calculateButton_Click(ByVal sender As System.Object, _
4           ByVal e As System.EventArgs) Handles calculateButton.Click
5
6           ' declare variables to store user input
7           Dim principal As Decimal ' store principal
8           Dim rate As Double ' store interest rate
9           Dim year As Integer ' store number of years
10          Dim yearCounter As Integer ' store count
11          Dim amount As Decimal ' store each calculation
12          Dim output As String ' store output
13
14          ' retrieve user input
15          principal = Val(principalTextBox.Text)
16          rate = Val(rateTextBox.Text)
17          year = yearUpDown.Value
18
19          ' set output header
20          output = "Year" & ControlChars.Tab _
21              & "Amount on Deposit" & ControlChars.CrLf
22
23          ' calculate amount after each year and append to string
24          For yearCounter = 1 To year
25              amount = _
26                  principal * ((1 + rate / 100) ^ yearCounter)
27              output &= (yearCounter & ControlChars.Tab & _
28                  String.Format("{0:C}", amount) & ControlChars.CrLf)
29          Next
30
31          resultTextBox.Text = output ' display result
32      End Sub ' calculateButton_Click
33  End Class ' InterestCalculatorForm
```

Figure 11.15 **Interest Calculator** application.

SELF-REVIEW

1. The _____ property determines by how much the current number in a NumericUp-Down control changes when the user clicks the up arrow or the down arrow.

   a) Amount   b) Step

   c) Increment   d) Next

2. Which For...Next header alters the control variable from 1 to 50 in increments of 5?

   a) `For i = 1 To 50 Step 50`   b) `For 1 To 50 Step 5`

   c) `For i = 1 To 50 Step = 5`   d) `For i = 1 To 50 Step 5`

Answers: 1) c. 2) d.

11.6 Wrap-Up

In this tutorial, you learned that the essential elements of counter-controlled repetition are the name of a control variable, the initial value of the control variable, the increment (or decrement) by which the control variable is modified each time through the loop and the condition that tests the final value of the control variable. We then explored the For...Next repetition statement, which combines these essentials of counter-controlled repetition in its header.

After becoming familiar with the For...Next repetition statement, you changed the **Car Payment Calculator** application's Do While...Loop statement into a For...Next statement. You then built an **Interest Calculator** after analyzing the pseudocode and the ACE table for this application. In the **Interest Calculator**'s GUI, you added new design elements, including a NumericUpDown control and a multiline TextBox that contained a scrollbar.

In the next tutorial, you will learn to use the Select Case multiple-selection statement. You have learned that the If...Then...Else selection statement can be used in code to select between multiple courses of action on the value of a condition. You will see that a Select Case multiple-selection statement can save development time and improve code readability if the number of conditions is large. You will then use a Select Case multiple-selection statement to build a **Security Panel** application.

SKILLS SUMMARY

Using the For...Next Repetition Statement
- Specify the initial value of the control variable before keyword To.
- Specify the value tested for loop continuation after keyword To.
- Use optional keyword Step to specify the increment (or decrement).
- Use keyword Next to mark the end of the repetition statement.
- Using the For...Next statement helps eliminate off-by-one errors.

Creating a Multiline TextBox with a Vertical Scrollbar
- Insert a TextBox onto the Form.
- Set TextBox property Multiline to True.
- Set TextBox property ScrollBar to Vertical.

Specifying a NumericUpDown Control's Maximum Value
- Use NumericUpDown property Maximum.

Specifying a NumericUpDown Control's Minimum Value
- Use NumericUpDown property Minimum.

Changing the Current Number in a NumericUpDown Control
- Click the NumericUpDown control's up or down arrow.

Specifying by How Much the Current Number in a NumericUpDown Control Changes When the User Clicks an Arrow
- Use NumericUpDown property Increment.

Obtaining the Value of a NumericUpDown Control
- Use NumericUpDown property Value.

KEY TERMS

Both value of ScrollBars property—Used to display both horizontal and vertical scrollbars on the bottom and right side of a TextBox.

For...Next header—The first line of a For...Next repetition statement. The For...Next header specifies all four essential elements for the counter-controlled repetition of a For...Next repetition statement.

For...Next repetition statement—Repetition statement that handles the details of counter-controlled repetition. The For...Next statement uses all four elements essential to counter-controlled repetition in one line of code (the name of a control variable, the initial value, the increment or decrement value and the final value).

For keyword—Begins the For...Next statement.

Horizontal value of ScrollBars property—Used to display a horizontal scrollbar on the bottom of a TextBox.

Increment property of a NumericUpDown control—Specifies by how much the current number in the NumericUpDown control changes when the user clicks the control's up (for incrementing) or down (for decrementing) arrow.

Maximum property of a NumericUpDown control—Determines the maximum input value in a particular NumericUpDown control.

Minimum property of a NumericUpDown control—Determines the minimum input value in a particular NumericUpDown control.

Multiline property of a TextBox control—Specifies whether the TextBox is capable of displaying multiple lines of text. If the property value is True, the TextBox may contain multiple lines of text; if the value of the property is False, the TextBox can contain only one line of text.

None value of ScrollBars property—Used to display no scrollbars on a TextBox.

NumericUpDown control—Allows you to specify maximum and minimum numeric input values. Also allows you to specify an increment (or decrement) when the user clicks the up (or down) arrow.

ReadOnly property of a NumericUpDown control—Determines whether the input value can be typed by the user.

ScrollBars property of a TextBox control—Specifies whether a TextBox has a scrollbar and, if so, of what type. By default, property ScrollBars is set to None. Setting the value to Vertical places a scrollbar along the right side of the TextBox.

Step keyword—Optional component of the For...Next header that specifies the increment (that is, the amount added to the control variable each time the loop is executed).

String variable—A variable that stores a series of characters.

To keyword—Used to specify a range of values. Commonly used in For...Next headers to specify the initial and final values of the statement's control variable.

Vertical value of ScrollBars property—Used to display a vertical scrollbar on the right side of a TextBox.

GUI DESIGN GUIDELINES

TextBox

- If a TextBox will display multiple lines of output, set the Multiline property to True and left align the output by setting the TextAlign property to Left.
- If a multiline TextBox will display many lines of output, limit the TextBox height and use a vertical scrollbar to allow users to view additional lines of output.

NumericUpDown

- A NumericUpDown control should follow the same GUI Design Guidelines as a TextBox.
- Use a NumericUpDown control to limit the range of user input.

CONTROLS, EVENTS, PROPERTIES & METHODS

NumericUpDown   NumericUpDown   This control allows you to specify maximum and minimum numeric input values.

■ *In action*

6 ⬍

■ *Properties*

Increment—Specifies by how much the current number in the NumericUpDown control changes when the user clicks the control's up (for incrementing) or down (for decrementing) arrow.

Location—Specifies the location of the NumericUpDown control on the Form relative to the top-left corner.

Maximum—Determines the maximum input value in a particular NumericUpDown control.

Minimum—Determines the minimum input value in a particular NumericUpDown control.

Name—Specifies the name used to access the NumericUpDown control programmatically. The name should be appended with the UpDown suffix.

ReadOnly—Determines whether the input value can be typed by the user.

Size—Specifies the height and width (in pixels) of the NumericUpDown control.

TextAlign—Specifies how the text is aligned within the NumericUpDown control.

Value—Specifies the value in the NumericUpDown control.

TextBox   abl TextBox   This control allows the user to input data from the keyboard.

■ *In action*

0

■ *Event*

TextChanged—Raised when the text in the TextBox is changed.

■ *Properties*

Location—Specifies the location of the TextBox on the Form relative to the top-left corner.

Multiline—Specifies whether the TextBox is capable of displaying multiple lines of text.

Name—Specifies the name used to access the TextBox programmatically. The name should be appended with the TextBox suffix.

ReadOnly—Determines whether the value of a TextBox can be changed.

ScrollBars—Specifies whether the TextBox contains a scrollbar.

Size—Specifies the height and width (in pixels) of the TextBox.

Text—Specifies the text displayed in the TextBox.

TextAlign—Specifies how the text is aligned within the TextBox.

■ *Method*

Focus—Transfers the focus of the application to the TextBox that calls it.

MULTIPLE-CHOICE QUESTIONS

11.1 "Hello" has data type _____.

   a) String

   b) StringLiteral

   c) Character

   d) StringText

11.2 A _____ provides the ability to enter or display multiple lines of text in the same control.

   a) TextBox

   b) NumericUpDown

   c) MultilineTextBox

   d) multiline NumericUpDown

11.3 The NumericUpDown control allows you to specify _____.

   a) a maximum value the user can select   b) a minimum value the user can select

   c) an increment for the values presented   d) All of the above.
      to the user

11.4 _____ is optional in a For...Next header when the control variable's increment is 1.

   a) Keyword To   b) The initial value of the control variable

   c) Keyword Step   d) The final value of the control variable

11.5 Setting TextBox property ScrollBars to _____ creates a vertical scrollbar.

   a) True   b) Vertical

   c) Up   d) Both

11.6 _____ is used to determine whether a For...Next loop continues to iterate.

   a) The initial value of the control variable   b) Keyword For

   c) Keyword Step   d) The control variable

11.7 In a For...Next loop, the control variable is incremented (or decremented) _____.

   a) after the body of the loop executes   b) when keyword To is reached

   c) while the loop-continuation condition   d) while the body of the loop executes
      is False

11.8 Setting a NumericUpDown control's _____ property to True ensures that the user cannot enter invalid values in the control.

   a) Increment   b) ScrollBars

   c) ReadOnly   d) InValid

11.9 The _____ and _____ properties limit the values users can select in the NumericUpDown control.

   a) Maximum, Minimum   b) Top, Bottom

   c) High, Low   d) Max, Min

11.10 The For...Next header _____ can be used to vary the control variable over the odd numbers between 1 and 10.

   a) For i = 1 To 10 Step 1   b) For i = 1 To 10 Step 2

   c) For i = 1 To 10 Step -1   d) For i = 1 To 10 Step -2

EXERCISES

11.11 (*Present Value Calculator Application*) A bank wants to show its customers how much they would need to invest to achieve a specified financial goal (future value) in 5, 10, 15, 20, 25 or 30 years. Users must provide their financial goal (the amount of money desired after the specified number of years has elapsed), an interest rate and the length of the investment in years. Create an application that calculates and displays the principal (initial amount to invest) needed to achieve the user's financial goal. Your application should allow the user to invest money for 5, 10, 15, 20, 25 or 30 years. For example, a customer who wants to reach the financial goal of $15,000 over a period of 5 years when the interest rate is 6.6% would need to invest $10,896.96, as shown in Fig. 11.16. Use the &= operator and a For...Next loop to accomplish this.

   a) *Copying the template to your working directory.* Copy the directory C:\Examples\ Tutorial11\Exercises\PresentValue to your C:\SimplyVB directory.

   b) *Opening the application's template file.* Double click PresentValue.sln in the PresentValue directory to open the application.

   c) *Adding the NumericUpDown control.* Place and size the NumericUpDown so that it follows the GUI Design Guidelines. Set the NumericUpDown control's Name property to yearUpDown. Set the NumericUpDown control to allow only multiples of five for the number of years. Allow the user to select only a duration that is in the specified range of values.

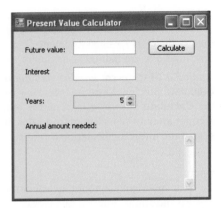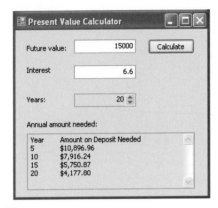

Figure 11.16   Present Value Calculator GUI.

d) *Adding a multiline TextBox.* Add a TextBox to the Form below the NumericUpDown control. Change the size to 272, 88, and position the TextBox on the Form so that it follows the GUI Design Guidelines. Then set the TextBox to display multiple lines and a vertical scrollbar. Ensure that the user cannot modify the text in the TextBox.

e) *Adding a Click event handler and adding code.* Add a Click event handler for the **Calculate** Button. Once in code view, add code to the application such that, when the **Calculate** Button is clicked, the multiline TextBox displays the necessary principal for each five-year interval. Use the following version of the present-value calculation formula:

$$p = a / (1 + r)^n$$

where

   p is the amount needed to achieve the future value
   r is the annual interest rate (for example, .05 is equivalent to 5%)
   n is the number of years
   a is the future-value amount.

f) *Running the application.* Select **Debug > Start Debugging** to run your application. Enter amounts for the future value, interest rate and number of years. Click the **Calculate** Button and verify that the year intervals and the amount on deposit needed for each are correct. Test the application again, this time entering 30 for the number of years. Verify that the vertical scrollbar appears to display all of the output.

g) *Closing the application.* Close your running application by clicking its close box.

h) *Closing the IDE.* Close the Visual Basic IDE by clicking its close box.

11.12 *(Compound Interest: Comparing Rates Application)* Write an application that calculates the amount of money in an account after 10 years for interest rate amounts of 5–10%. For this application, users must provide the initial principal.

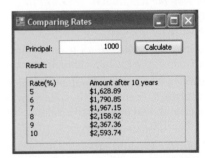

Figure 11.17   Comparing Rates GUI.

a) *Copying the template to your working directory.* Copy the directory C:\Examples\ Tutorial11\Exercises\ComparingRates to your C:\SimplyVB directory.

b) *Opening the application's template file.* Double click ComparingRates.sln in the ComparingRates directory to open the application.

c) *Adding a multiline TextBox.* Add a TextBox to the Form below the **Result:** Label control. Change the size to 256, 104, and position the TextBox on the Form so that it follows the GUI Design Guidelines (Fig. 11.17). Then set the TextBox to display multiple lines. Ensure that the user cannot modify the text in the TextBox.

d) *Adding a Click event handler and adding code.* Add a Click event handler for the **Calculate** Button. Once in code view, add code to the application such that, when the **Calculate** Button is clicked, the multiline TextBox displays the amount in the account after 10 years for interest rates of 5, 6, 7, 8, 9 and 10%. Use the following version of the interest-calculation formula:

$$a = p\,(1 + r)^{\,n}$$

where

p is the original amount invested (the principal)
r is the annual interest rate (for example, .05 is equivalent to 5%)
n is the number of years
a is the investment's value at the end of the nth year.

e) *Running the application.* Select **Debug > Start Debugging** to run your application. Enter the principal amount for an account and click the **Calculate** Button. Verify that the correct amounts after 10 years are then displayed, based on interest rate amounts of 5–10%.

f) *Closing the application.* Close your running application by clicking its close box.

g) *Closing the IDE.* Close the Visual Basic IDE by clicking its close box.

11.13 *(Validating Input to the Interest Calculator Application)* Enhance the **Interest Calculator** application with error checking. Test for whether the user has entered valid values for the principal and interest rate. If the user enters an invalid value, display a message in the multiline TextBox. Figure 11.18 demonstrates the application handling an invalid input.

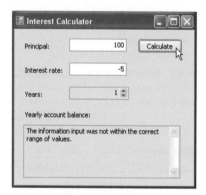

Figure 11.18 **Interest Calculator** application with error checking.

a) *Copying the template to your working directory.* Copy the directory C:\Examples\Tutorial11\Exercises\InterestCalculatorEnhancement to your C:\SimplyVB directory.

b) *Opening the application's template file.* Double click InterestCalculator.sln in the InterestCalculatorEnhancement directory to open the application.

c) *Adding a Click event handler and adding code.* Add a Click event handler for the **Calculate** Button. Once in code view, modify the code to validate the input. The principal should be a positive amount. The interest rate should be greater than 0, but less than 100.

d) *Displaying the error message.* Display the text "The information was not within the correct range of values." in resultTextBox if the values are not valid.

e) *Running the application.* Select **Debug > Start Debugging** to run your application. Enter invalid data for the principal and interest rate. The invalid data can include negative numbers and letters. Verify that entering invalid data and clicking the **Calculate** Button results in the error message displayed in Fig. 11.18.

f) *Closing the application.* Close your running application by clicking its close box.

g) *Closing the IDE.* Close the Visual Basic IDE by clicking its close box.

What does this code do? ▶ **11.14** What is the value of `result` after the following code executes? Assume that `power`, `i`, `result` and `number` are all declared as `Integers`.

```
1   power = 5
2   number = 10
3   result = number
4
5   For i = 1 To (power - 1)
6       result *= number
7   Next
```

What's wrong with this code? ▶ **11.15** Assume that the variable `counter` is declared as an `Integer` for both a and b. Identify and correct the error(s) in each of the following:

a) This statement should display in a `ListBox` all numbers from 100 to 1 in decreasing order.

```
1   For counter = 100 To 1
2       displayListBox.Items.Add(counter)
3   Next
```

b) The following code should display in a `ListBox` the odd `Integers` from 19 to 1 in decreasing order.

```
1   For counter = 19 To 1 By -1
2       displayListBox.Add(counter)
3   Next
```

Using the Debugger ▶ **11.16** (*Savings Calculator Application*) The **Savings Calculator** application calculates the amount that the user will have on deposit after one year. The application gets the initial amount on deposit from the user, and assumes that the user will add $100 to the account every month for the entire year. No interest is added to the account. While testing the application, you noticed that the amount calculated by the application was incorrect. Use the debugger to locate and correct any logic error(s). Figure 11.19 displays the correct output for this application.

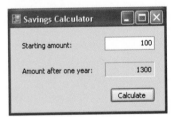

Figure 11.19   Correct output for the **Savings Calculator** application.

Programming Challenge ▶ **11.17** (*Pay Raise Calculator Application*) Develop an application that computes the amount of money an employee makes each year over a user-specified number of years. The employee receives an hourly wage and a pay raise once every year. The user specifies the hourly wage and the amount of the raise (in percentages per year) in the application.

a) *Copying the template to your working directory.* Copy the directory `C:\Examples\Tutorial11\Exercises\PayRaise` to your `C:\SimplyVB` directory.

b) *Opening the application's template file.* Double click `PayRaise.sln` in the `PayRaise` directory to open the application.

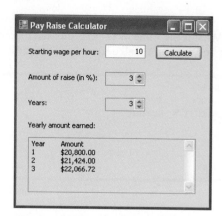

Figure 11.20 Pay Raise GUI.

c) *Adding controls to the Form.* Add two NumericUpDown controls to the Form. The first NumericUpDown control should allow the user to specify the pay raise percentage. The user should only be able to specify percentages in the range of 3–8%. Create the second NumericUpDown control for users to select the number of years in the range 1–50. Then add a multiline TextBox control to the application. Ensure that the user cannot modify the text in the NumericUpDown and TextBox controls. Resize and move the controls you created so that they follow the GUI Design Guidelines as in Fig. 11.20.

d) *Adding a Click event handler and adding code.* Add a Click event handler for the **Calculate** Button. Once in code view, add code to use the For...Next statement to compute the yearly salary amounts, based on the yearly pay raise.

e) *Running the application.* Select **Debug > Start Debugging** to run your application. Enter a starting wage per hour, the size of the yearly raise and the number of years worked. Click the **Calculate** Button and verify that the correct amount after each year is displayed in the **Yearly amount earned:** TextBox.

f) *Closing the application.* Close your running application by clicking its close box.

g) *Closing the IDE.* Close the Visual Basic IDE by clicking its close box.

Security Panel Application

Introducing the Select Case Multiple-Selection Statement

Objectives

In this tutorial, you will learn to:
- Use the Select Case multiple-selection statement.
- Use Case statements.
- Use the Is keyword.
- Obtain the current date and time.
- Display the date and time.
- Use TextBox property PasswordChar.

Outline

In the last tutorial, you learned to use the For...Next statement, which is the most concise statement for performing counter-controlled repetition. In this tutorial, you will learn about the Select Case multiple-selection statement. The Select Case statement is used to simplify code that uses several ElseIf statements sequentially when an application must choose among many possible actions to perform.

12.1 Test-Driving the Security Panel Application

In this tutorial, you will use the Select Case multiple-selection statement to construct a **Security Panel** application. This application must meet the following requirements:

Application Requirements

A lab wants to install a security panel outside a laboratory room. Only authorized personnel may enter the lab, using their security codes. The following are valid security codes (also called access codes) and the groups of employees they represent:

Values	Group
1645–1689	Technicians
8345	Custodians
9998, 1006–1008	Scientists

Once a security code is entered, access is either granted or denied. All access attempts are written to a window below the keypad. If access is granted, the date, time and group (scientists, custodians, etc.) are written to the window. If access is denied, the date, the time and the message "Access Denied" are written to the window. Furthermore, the user can enter any one-digit access code to summon a security guard for assistance. The date, the time and the message "Restricted Access" are then written to the window to indicate that the request has been received.

You begin by test-driving the completed application. Then you will learn the additional Visual Basic technologies that you will need to create your own version of this application.

Test-Driving the Security Panel Application

1. **Opening the completed application.** Open the directory `C:\Examples\Tutorial12\CompletedApplication\SecurityPanel` to locate the **Security Panel** application. Double click `SecurityPanel.sln` to open the application in the Visual Basic IDE.

2. **Running the Security Panel application.** Select **Debug > Start Debugging** to run the application (Fig. 12.1). At the top of the `Form`, you are provided with a `TextBox` that displays an asterisk for each digit in the security code entered using the GUI keypad. Note that the GUI keypad looks much like a real-world keypad. (We will mimic real-world conditions when possible.) The **C** `Button` clears your current input, and the **#** `Button` causes the application to process the security code entered. Results are displayed in the `ListBox` at the bottom of the `Form`.

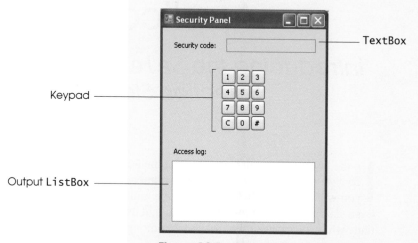

Figure 12.1 **Security Panel** application executing.

3. **Entering an invalid security code.** Use the keypad to enter the invalid security code 1212. Note that an asterisk (*) is displayed in the `TextBox` (Fig. 12.2) for each numeric key pressed (by clicking its `Button` on the `Form`). These characters do not allow other people to see the code entered. When finished, click the **#** `Button`. A message indicating that access is denied will appear in the `ListBox`, as in Fig. 12.3. Note that the `TextBox` is cleared when the **#** `Button` is pressed.

GUI Design Tip

If your GUI is modeling a real-world object, your GUI design should mimic the physical appearance of the object.

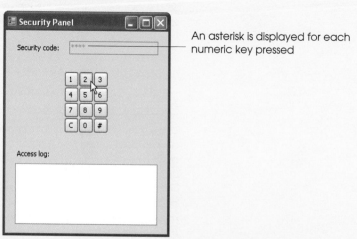

Figure 12.2 Asterisks displayed in **Security code:** field.

(cont.)

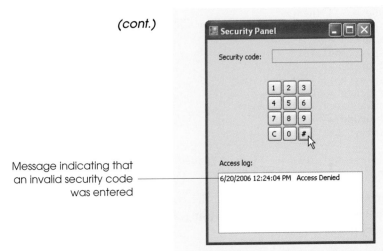

Figure 12.3   **Security Panel** displaying **Access Denied** message.

Message indicating that
an invalid security code
was entered

4. *Using the C Button*. Press a few numeric keys, then click the **C** Button. Note that all the asterisks displayed in the TextBox disappear. Users often make mistakes when keystroking or when clicking Buttons, so the **C** Button allows users to make a "fresh start."

5. *Entering a valid security code*. Use the keypad to enter 1006, then click the # Button. Note that a second message appears in the ListBox, as in Fig. 12.4.

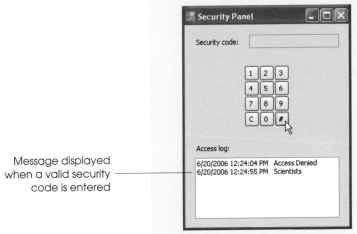

Message displayed
when a valid security
code is entered

Figure 12.4   **Security Panel** application confirming a valid security-code entry.

6. *Closing the application*. Close your running application by clicking its close box.

7. *Closing the IDE*. Close the Visual Basic IDE by clicking its close box.

12.2 Introducing the Select Case Multiple-Selection Statement

In this section, you will learn how to use the **Select Case multiple-selection statement**. For comparison purposes, we will first provide an If...Then...Else multiple-selection statement that displays a text message based on a student's grade:

```
If grade = "A" Then
   displayLabel.Text = "Excellent!"
ElseIf grade = "B" Then
   displayLabel.Text = "Very good!"
ElseIf grade = "C" Then
   displayLabel.Text = "Good."
ElseIf grade = "D" Then
   displayLabel.Text = "Poor."
ElseIf grade = "F" Then
   displayLabel.Text = "Failure."
Else
   displayLabel.Text = "Invalid grade."
End If
```

This statement can be used to produce the correct output when selecting among multiple values of grade. However, by using the `Select Case` statement, you can simplify every instance like

```
If grade = "A" Then
```

to one like

```
Case "A"
```

and eliminate the `If` and `ElseIf` keywords.

The following `Select Case` multiple-selection statement performs the same functionality as the preceding `If...Then...Else` statement:

```
Select Case grade

   Case "A"
      displayLabel.Text = "Excellent!"

   Case "B"
      displayLabel.Text = "Very good!"

   Case "C"
      displayLabel.Text = "Good."

   Case "D"
      displayLabel.Text = "Poor."

   Case "F"
      displayLabel.Text = "Failure."

   Case Else
      displayLabel.Text = "Invalid grade."

End Select
```

Good Programming Practice

Placing a blank line before and after each `Case` in a `Select Case` statement improves readability.

Good Programming Practice

Indenting the statements in the body of a `Case` improves readability.

Common Programming Error

When using the optional `Case Else` statement in a `Select Case` statement, failing to place the `Case Else` as the last `Case` is a syntax error.

Common Programming Error

Case statements whose controlling expressions result in the same value are logic errors. At run time, only the body of the first matching `Case` is executed.

The `Select Case` statement begins with the keywords `Select Case` followed by a **test expression** (also called a **controlling expression**) and terminates with keywords **End Select**. The preceding `Select Case` statement contains five **Case statement**s and the optional **Case Else statement**. Each Case uses grade as the test expression. It also contains the keyword Case followed by an **expression list**. The expression list can contain strings such as "A" and numeric values such as 707 and 9.9. Although a `Select Case` statement can have any number of Cases, it must have at most one Case Else.

Figure 12.5 shows the UML activity diagram for this `Select Case` multiple-selection statement. The first condition to be evaluated is grade = "A". If this condition is True, the text "Excellent!" is displayed, and control proceeds to the first statement after the `Select Case` statement. If the condition is False (that is, grade <> "A"), the statement continues by testing the next condition, grade = "B". If this condition is True, the text "Very good!" is displayed, and control proceeds to the first statement after the `Select Case` statement. If the condition is False (that is, grade <> "B"), the statement continues to test the next condition. This process continues until a matching Case is found or until the final condition evaluates to False (grade <> "F"). If the latter occurs, the Case Else's body is executed, and the text "Invalid grade." is displayed. The application then continues with the first statement after the Select Case statement.

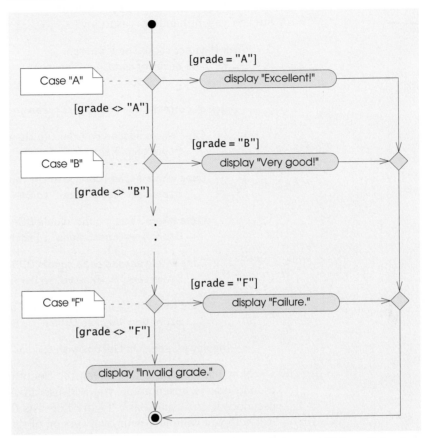

Figure 12.5   Select Case multiple-selection statement UML activity diagram.

SELF-REVIEW

1. Select Case is a _____-selection statement.
   a) multiple   b) double
   c) single   d) None of the above.

2. When does the Case Else body execute?
   a) Every time a Select Case statement executes
   b) When more than one Case is matched
   c) When all Cases are matching Case statements in a Select Case statement
   d) None of the above.

Answers: 1) a. 2) d.

12.3 Constructing the Security Panel Application

The **Security Panel** application contains 10 Buttons that display digits. (We call these numeric Buttons.) You will create an event handler for each Button's Click event. These Buttons make up the GUI keypad. The following pseudocode describes the Click event handler for each of these numeric Buttons:

    If a numeric Button is clicked
        Concatenate Button's digit to the TextBox's Text property value

Later in this tutorial, you will convert this pseudocode into the Visual Basic code and create the Click event handlers for each numeric Button. The user then will be able to use the numeric Buttons to enter digits and have them concatenated to the text in a TextBox.

In addition to the numeric Buttons, this application also contains a **C** Button and a **#** Button. The **C** Button clears the Form's TextBox. The pseudocode for the **#** Button's event handler is as follows:

```
When the user clicks the # Button:
    Retrieve security code input by user
    Clear input TextBox

    Select correct Case based on access code

        Case where access code is less than 10
            Store text "Restricted Access" to String variable

        Case where access code is in the range 1645 to 1689
            Store text "Technicians" to String variable

        Case where access code equals 8345
            Store text "Custodians" to String variable

        Case where access code equals 9998 or is in the range 1006 to 1008
            Store text "Scientists" to String variable

        Case where none of the preceding Cases match
            Store text "Access Denied" to String variable

    Display message in ListBox with current time and String variable's contents
```

Now that you have test-driven the **Security Panel** application and studied its pseudocode representation, you will use an ACE table to help you convert the pseudocode to Visual Basic. Figure 12.6 lists the actions, controls and events that will help you complete your own version of this application. The first row specifies that you will be using Labels to identify the TextBox and ListBox controls. The second row introduces the Buttons for the numeric keypad. When these Buttons are clicked, their values are concatenated to the text in the TextBox's Text property. The next row indicates that securityCodeTextBox will store the security code that is input by the user. The next two rows specify Buttons that the user can click to clear the TextBox (clearButton) and enter the security code (enterButton). The last row indicates that the ListBox will be used to display a message to the user.

Action/Control/Event (ACE) Table for the Interest Calculator Application

Action	Control	Event
Label the application's fields	securityCodeLabel, accessLogLabel	
	enterButton	Click
Retrieve security code input by user	securityCodeTextBox	
Clear input TextBox	securityCodeTextBox	
Select correct Case based on access code		
Case where access code is less than 10 Store text "Restricted Access"		

Figure 12.6 ACE table for **Security Panel** application. (Part 1 of 2.)

Action	Control	Event
Case where access code is in the range 1645 to 1689 Store text "Technicians"		
Case where access code equals 8345 Store text "Custodians"		
Case where access code equals 9998 or is in the range 1006 to 1008 Store text "Scientists"		
Case where none of preceding Cases match Store text "Access Denied"		
Display message in ListBox with current time and String variable's contents	logEntryListBox	

Figure 12.6   ACE table for **Security Panel** application. (Part 2 of 2.)

Now that you are familiar with the Select Case multiple-selection statement, you will use it to build the **Security Panel** application.

Using the PasswordChar Property

GUI Design Tip

Mask passwords or other sensitive pieces of information in TextBoxes.

1. ***Copying the template to your working directory.*** Copy the C:\Examples\Tutorial12\TemplateApplication\SecurityPanel directory to your C:\SimplyVB directory.

2. ***Opening the Security Panel application's template file.*** Double click SecurityPanel.sln in the SecurityPanel directory.

3. ***Displaying the * character in the TextBox.*** Select the **Security code:** TextBox at the top of the Form, and set this TextBox's PasswordChar property to * in the **Properties** window. Text displayed in a TextBox can be hidden or **masked** with the character specified in property **PasswordChar**. **Masking characters** are displayed rather than the actual TextBox text that the user types. However, the TextBox's Text property does contain the text the user typed. For example, if a user enters 5469, the TextBox displays ****, yet stores "5469" in its Text property. Now any character displayed in your interface's TextBox displays as the * character.

4. ***Disabling the TextBox.*** The primary reason for using a TextBox instead of a Label to display the access code is to use the PasswordChar property. To prevent users from modifying the text in the TextBox, set its **Enabled** property to False.

5. ***Create the enterButton_Click event handler.*** Double click the # Button to create the enterButton_Click event handler.

6. ***Declaring and initializing variables.*** Add lines 6–10 of Fig. 12.7 to the enterButton_Click event handler. Lines 6–7 declare variables accessCode and message. Variable accessCode will be used to store the user's security code (access code), and variable message will store the message that will be displayed to the user, based on the access code entered. Line 9 sets the accessCode variable to the security code input by the user. Line 10 clears the **Security code:** TextBox.

7. ***Saving the project.*** Select **File > Save All** to save your modified code.

(cont.)

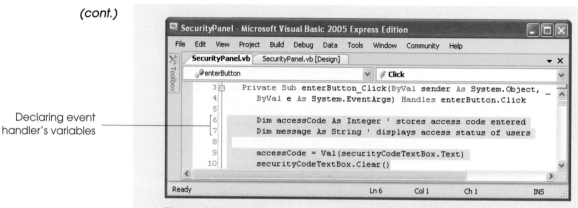

Figure 12.7 Variable declarations for enterButton_Click.

Now that you have designed the GUI for your application, declared the variables for your event handler and obtained a value for variable accessCode, let's continue by creating your Select Case statement, as shown in the following box. This statement will determine the user's access level based on the code input.

Adding a Select Case Statement to the Application

1. **Adding a Select Case statement to enterButton_Click.** Press *Enter* twice, add line 12 from Fig. 12.8 to the enterButton_Click event handler and press *Enter*. Keywords End Select (line 14) immediately appear below the Select Case line that you just added. Line 12 begins the Select Case statement, which contains the controlling expression accessCode—the access code entered by the user. Remember that this expression (the value accessCode) is compared sequentially with each Case until either a match occurs or the End Select statement is reached. If a matching Case is found, the body of the Case executes and program control proceeds to the first statement after the End Select statement.

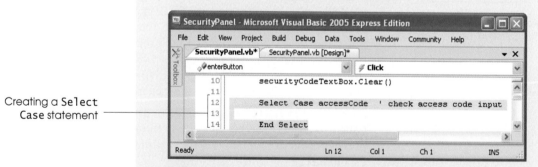

Figure 12.8 Select Case statement.

2. **Adding a Case to the Select Case statement.** Add lines 13–15 from Fig. 12.9 to the Select Case statement. [*Note:* The indentation on your machine may not appear exactly as shown in Fig. 12.9. This is because we turned off **Smart** indenting to display code in our own style. Indentation does not affect program execution, so you do not need to turn off **Smart** indenting.] The first Case statement tests whether accessCode is less than 10. Keyword **Is** along with the comparison operator < specify a range of values to test. You can use the Is keyword followed by a comparison operator to compare the controlling expression and the value to the right of the operator. In this case, if the value in accessCode is less than 10, the code in the body of the Case statement executes and message is assigned the string "Restricted Access", which is displayed after the body of the Select Case statement completes.

(cont.)

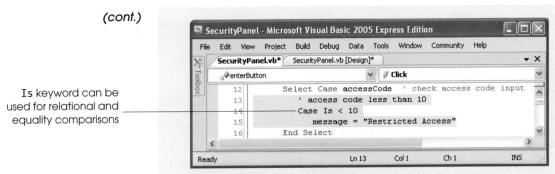

Figure 12.9 First `Case` added to `Select Case` statement.

Is keyword can be used for relational and equality comparisons

3. *Specifying Cases for the remaining access codes.* Press *Enter* twice and add lines 17–28 from Fig. 12.10 to the `Select Case` statement.

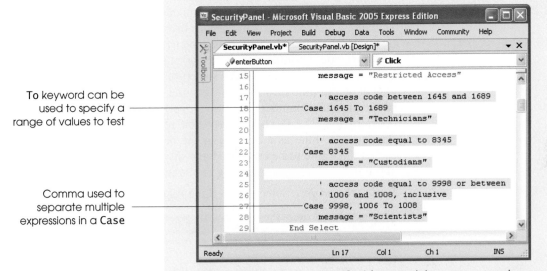

To keyword can be used to specify a range of values to test

Comma used to separate multiple expressions in a `Case`

Figure 12.10 `Cases` specified for remaining access codes.

The `Case` statement in lines 18–19 determines whether the value of `accessCode` is in the range 1645 to 1689, inclusive. Keyword `To` is used to specify the range. If the user enters an access code in this range, the body of the `Case` statement sets `message` to `"Technicians"`.

The next `Case` statement (lines 22–23) checks for a specific number. If `accessCode` matches the value 8345, then the statement in that `Case` is executed. Specifying a single value in a `Case` statement is common.

The next `Case` statement (lines 27–28) determines whether `accessCode` is 9998 or a number in the range 1006 to 1008, inclusive. Note that when multiple values are provided in a `Case` statement, they are separated by commas.

4. *Adding a Case Else to the Select Case statement.* Add lines 30–32 from Fig. 12.11 to the `Select Case` statement. These lines contain the optional **Case Else**, which is executed when the controlling expression does not match any of the previous `Cases`. If used, the `Case Else` must follow all other `Case` statements. In your application, the body of the `Case Else` statement sets variable `message` to `"Access Denied"`. The required keywords `End Select` (line 33 of Fig. 12.11) terminate the `Select Case` statement.

Common Programming Error

If the value on the left side of the `To` keyword in a `Case` statement is larger than the value on the right side, the `Case` is ignored during application execution, potentially causing a logic error.

(cont.)

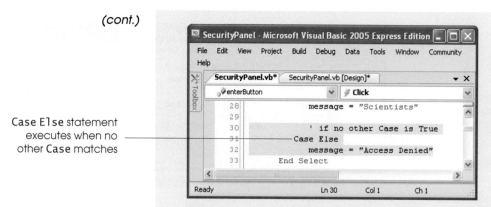

Case Else statement executes when no other Case matches

Figure 12.11 Case Else of the Select Case statement.

5. *Displaying results in the ListBox.* Insert lines 34–35 of Fig. 12.12 after the `Select Case` statement. The statement at line 35 displays a `String` in `logEntryListBox` consisting of the current system date and time, followed by three spaces and the value assigned to `message`. The first part of method `Add`'s argument contains the expression **Date.Now**. The Framework Class Library (FCL) provides a **Date** structure that can be used to store and display date and time information. Like the objects that you have used in this book, structure members such as properties are accessed by using the dot operator (`.`). The `Date` property `Now` returns the system time and date. Passing this value as a `String` in the argument to method `Add` (line 35) causes this value to be converted and displayed as a `String`. You will learn about how a date is stored using the `Date` structure in Tutorial 14.

6. *Saving the project.* Select **File > Save All** to save your modified code.

Figure 12.12 Updating the **Security Panel** application's ListBox.

Now that you have defined the `enterButton_Click` event handler, you will focus on the numeric Buttons. You will create event handlers for each numbered Button and for the **C** Button.

Programming the Remaining Event Handlers

1. *Create the `zeroButton_Click` event handler.* In design view, double click the **0** Button (zeroButton) to create the zeroButton_Click event handler.

2. *Coding the `zeroButton_Click` event handler.* Insert line 41 of Fig. 12.13 to the event handler. Line 41 appends the `String` "0" to the end of security-CodeTextBox's `Text` property value. You do this to append the numeric Button's value to the access code in the TextBox.

(cont.)

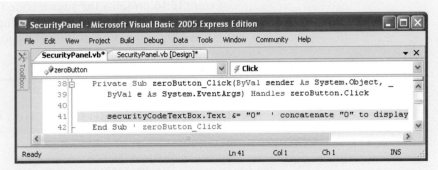

Figure 12.13   Event handler `zeroButton_Click`.

3. ***Define the other numeric Buttons' event handlers.*** Repeat *Steps 1–2* for the remaining numeric Buttons (**1** through **9**). Be sure to substitute the Button's number for the value between the quotes (for example, `oneButton_Click` sets `securityCodeTextBox`'s number as `&= "1"`). Figure 12.14 shows the event handlers for Buttons `oneButton` and `twoButton`.

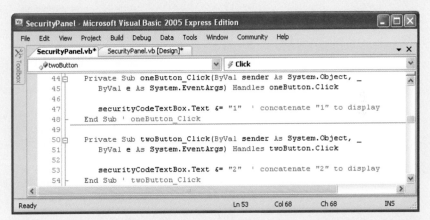

Figure 12.14   Event handlers `oneButton_Click` and `twoButton_Click`.

4. ***Define the `clearButton_Click` event handler.*** Double click the **C** Button, and add line 101 as shown in Fig. 12.15. Line 101 clears the **Security code:** TextBox.

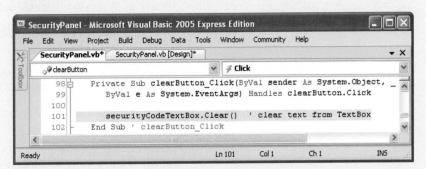

Figure 12.15   Event handler `clearButton_Click` defined.

5. ***Running the application.*** Select **Debug > Start Debugging** to run your application.

6. ***Closing the application.*** Close your running application by clicking its close box.

7. ***Closing the IDE.*** Close the Visual Basic IDE by clicking its close box.

Figure 12.16 presents the source code for the **Security Panel** application. The lines of code that contain new programming concepts that you have learned in this tutorial are highlighted. Look over the code carefully to make sure that you have added all of the event handlers correctly.

```
1   Public Class SecurityPanelForm
2
3       Private Sub enterButton_Click(ByVal sender As System.Object, _
4           ByVal e As System.EventArgs) Handles enterButton.Click
5
6           Dim accessCode As Integer ' stores access code entered
7           Dim message As String ' displays access status of users
8
9           accessCode = Val(securityCodeTextBox.Text)
10          securityCodeTextBox.Clear()
11
12          Select Case accessCode   ' check access code input
13              ' access code less than 10
14              Case Is < 10
15                  message = "Restricted Access"
16
17              ' access code between 1645 and 1689
18              Case 1645 To 1689
19                  message = "Technicians"
20
21              ' access code equal to 8345
22              Case 8345
23                  message = "Custodians"
24
25              ' access code equal to 9998 or between
26              ' 1006 and 1008, inclusive
27              Case 9998, 1006 To 1008
28                  message = "Scientists"
29
30              ' if no other Case is True
31              Case Else
32                  message = "Access Denied"
33          End Select
34          ' display time and message in ListBox
35          logEntryListBox.Items.Add(Date.Now & "    " & message)
36      End Sub ' enterButton_Click
37
38      Private Sub zeroButton_Click(ByVal sender As System.Object, _
39          ByVal e As System.EventArgs) Handles zeroButton.Click
40
41          securityCodeTextBox.Text &= "0"   ' concatenate "0" to display
42      End Sub ' zeroButton_Click
43
44      Private Sub oneButton_Click(ByVal sender As System.Object, _
45          ByVal e As System.EventArgs) Handles oneButton.Click
46
47          securityCodeTextBox.Text &= "1"   ' concatenate "1" to display
48      End Sub ' oneButton_Click
49
50      Private Sub twoButton_Click(ByVal sender As System.Object, _
51          ByVal e As System.EventArgs) Handles twoButton.Click
52
53          securityCodeTextBox.Text &= "2"   ' concatenate "2" to display
54      End Sub ' twoButton_Click
55
56      Private Sub threeButton_Click(ByVal sender As System.Object, _
57          ByVal e As System.EventArgs) Handles threeButton.Click
58
```

Labels pointing to the code:
- Declaring variables → lines 6–7
- Retrieving access code and clearing TextBox → lines 9–10
- Using a `Select Case` statement to determine user access level → line 12
- Obtain the current date and time using `Date.Now` → line 35
- Appending the numeric **Button** value to the text stored in the TextBox → lines 38–41

Figure 12.16 **Security Panel** application. (Part 1 of 2.)

```
59              securityCodeTextBox.Text &= "3"  ' concatenate "3" to display
60        End Sub ' threeButton_Click
61
62        Private Sub fourButton_Click(ByVal sender As System.Object, _
63           ByVal e As System.EventArgs) Handles fourButton.Click
64
65              securityCodeTextBox.Text &= "4"  ' concatenate "4" to display
66        End Sub ' fourButton_Click
67
68        Private Sub fiveButton_Click(ByVal sender As System.Object, _
69           ByVal e As System.EventArgs) Handles fiveButton.Click
70
71              securityCodeTextBox.Text &= "5"  ' concatenate "5" to display
72        End Sub ' fiveButton_Click
73
74        Private Sub sixButton_Click(ByVal sender As System.Object, _
75           ByVal e As System.EventArgs) Handles sixButton.Click
76
77              securityCodeTextBox.Text &= "6"  ' concatenate "6" to display
78        End Sub ' sixButton_Click
79
80        Private Sub sevenButton_Click(ByVal sender As System.Object, _
81           ByVal e As System.EventArgs) Handles sevenButton.Click
82
83              securityCodeTextBox.Text &= "7"  ' concatenate "7" to display
84        End Sub ' sevenButton_Click
85
86        Private Sub eightButton_Click(ByVal sender As System.Object, _
87           ByVal e As System.EventArgs) Handles eightButton.Click
88
89              securityCodeTextBox.Text &= "8"  ' concatenate "8" to display
90        End Sub ' eightButton_Click
91
92        Private Sub nineButton_Click(ByVal sender As System.Object, _
93           ByVal e As System.EventArgs) Handles nineButton.Click
94
95              securityCodeTextBox.Text &= "9"  ' concatenate "9" to display
96        End Sub ' nineButton_Click
97
98        Private Sub clearButton_Click(ByVal sender As System.Object, _
99           ByVal e As System.EventArgs) Handles clearButton.Click
100
101             securityCodeTextBox.Clear()  ' clear text from TextBox
102       End Sub ' clearButton_Click
103 End Class ' SecurityPanelForm
```

Figure 12.16　Security Panel application. (Part 2 of 2.)

SELF-REVIEW

1. A Case that handles all values larger than a specified value must precede the > operator with keyword _____.

   a) `Select`　　　　　　　　　　　b) `Is`

   c) `Case`　　　　　　　　　　　　d) `All`

2. Use a(n) _____ to separate multiple conditions in a Case statement.

   a) period　　　　　　　　　　　b) asterisk

   c) comma　　　　　　　　　　　d) colon

Answers: 1) b. 2) c.

12.4 Wrap-Up

In this tutorial, you learned how to use the `Select Case` multiple-selection statement and discovered its similarities to the `If...Then...Else` statement. You studied a UML activity diagram that illustrates the flow of control in `Select Case` statements.

You then applied what you learned to create your **Security Panel** application. You set a TextBox's PasswordChar property to * in the **Properties** window to mask the text within the TextBox. You used a `Select Case` statement to determine whether the user inputted a correct security code. You also defined several Cases and included a `Case Else` statement, which executes if a valid security code is not provided. Finally, you used `Date.Now` to obtain the system time and date.

In the next tutorial, you will learn how to construct applications from small, manageable pieces of reusable code called procedures. You will use this capability to enhance an example you created earlier in the book.

SKILLS SUMMARY

Creating a `Select Case` Statement

- Use the keywords `Select Case` followed by a controlling expression.

- Use the keyword Case followed by an expression to compare with the controlling expression.

- Define the statements that execute if the Case's expression matches the controlling expression.

- Use the keywords `Case Else` followed by statements to execute if the controlling expression does not match any of the provided Cases. `Case Else`, if used, must be the last Case statement.

Masking User Input in a TextBox

- Set the TextBox's PasswordChar property to the desired character, typically the asterisk (*), to mask the user input.

- Retrieve the value typed by the user in the Text property.

Retrieving the Current Date and Time

- Use property Now of structure Date, which, when converted to a String, displays the current date in the format 12/31/2002 11:59:59 P.M.

KEY TERMS

`Case Else` statement—Optional statement whose body executes if the `Select Case`'s test expression does not match an expression of any Case.

Case statement—Statement whose body executes if the `Select Case`'s test expression matches an expression of any Case.

controlling expression—Value compared sequentially with each Case until either a match occurs or the `End Select` statement is reached. Also known as a test expression.

`Date.Now`—Returns the current system time and date.

Date structure—A structure whose properties can be used to store and display date and time information.

`Enabled` property of a TextBox—Determines whether the TextBox will respond to user input.

`End Select` keywords—Terminates the `Select Case` statement.

expression list—Multiple expressions separated by commas. Used for Cases in `Select Case` statements, when certain statements should execute based on more than one condition.

`Is` keyword—A keyword that when followed by a comparison operator, can be used to compare the controlling expression of a `Select Case` statement and a value.

masking—Hiding text such as passwords or other sensitive pieces of information that should not be observed by other people as they are typed. Masking is achieved by using the PasswordChar property of the TextBox for which you would like to hide data. The actual data entered is retained in the TextBox's Text property.

masking character—Used to replace each character displayed in a TextBox when the TextBox's data is masked for privacy.

multiple-selection statement—Performs one of many actions (or sequences of actions) depending on the value of the controlling expression.

`PasswordChar` property of a TextBox—Specifies the masking character for a TextBox.

`Select Case` statement—The multiple-selection statement used to make a decision by comparing an expression to a series of conditions. The algorithm then takes different actions based on those values.

GUI DESIGN GUIDELINES

Overall Design

- If your GUI is modeling a real-world object, its design should mimic the physical appearance of the object.

TextBox

- Mask passwords or other sensitive pieces of information in TextBoxes.

CONTROLS, EVENTS, PROPERTIES & METHODS

TextBox | abl TextBox | This control allows the user to input data from the keyboard.

- *In action*

| 0 |

- *Event*

  TextChanged—Raised when the text in the TextBox is changed.

- *Properties*

  Enabled—Determines whether the user can enter data (True) in the TextBox or not (False).

  Location—Specifies the location of the TextBox on the Form relative to the top-left corner.

  Multiline—Specifies whether the TextBox is capable of displaying multiple lines of text.

  Name—Specifies the name used to access the TextBox programmatically. The name should be appended with the TextBox suffix.

  PasswordChar—Specifies the masking character to be used when displaying data in the TextBox.

  ReadOnly—Determines whether the value of a TextBox can be changed.

  ScrollBars—Specifies whether the TextBox contains scrollbars.

  Size—Specifies the height and width (in pixels) of the TextBox.

  Text—Specifies the text displayed in the TextBox.

  TextAlign—Specifies how the text is aligned within the TextBox.

- *Methods*

  Clear—Removes text from the TextBox that calls it.

  Focus—Transfers the focus of the application to the TextBox that calls it.

MULTIPLE-CHOICE QUESTIONS

12.1 The _____ keywords signify the end of a Select Case statement.

    a) End Case
    b) End Select
    c) End Select Case
    d) Case End

12.2 The expression _____ returns the current system time and date.

    a) Date.DateTime
    b) Date.SystemDateTime
    c) Date.Now
    d) Date.SystemTimeDate

12.3 You can hide information entered into a TextBox by setting the TextBox's _____ property to a character that will be displayed for every character the user enters.

    a) PrivateChar
    b) Mask
    c) MaskingChar
    d) PasswordChar

12.4 Which of the following is a syntax error?

    a) Having duplicate Case statements in the same Select Case statement
    b) Having a Case statement in which the value to the left of a To keyword is larger than the value to the right
    c) Preceding a Case statement with the Case Else statement in a Select Case statement
    d) Using keyword Is in a Select Case statement

12.5 Keyword _____ is used to specify a range in a Case statement.

a) Also   b) Between

c) To   d) From

12.6 _____ separates multiple values tested in a Case statement.

a) A comma   b) An underscore

c) Keyword Also   d) A semicolon

12.7 The _____ method inserts a value in a ListBox.

a) Append   b) Items.Insert

c) Insert   d) Items.Add

12.8 If the value on the left of the To keyword in a Case statement is larger than the value on the right, _____.

a) a syntax error occurs   b) the body of the Case statement executes

c) the body of the Case statement never executes

d) the statement causes a runtime error

12.9 The expression following the keywords Select Case is called a _____.

a) guard condition   b) controlling expression

c) selection expression   d) case expression

12.10 To prevent a user from modifying text in a TextBox, set its _____ property to False.

a) Enabled   b) Text

c) TextChange   d) Editable

EXERCISES

12.11 *(Sales Commission Calculator Application)* Develop an application that calculates a salesperson's commission from the number of items sold (Fig. 12.17). Assume that all items have a fixed price of $10 per unit. Use a Select Case statement to implement the following sales commission schedule:

> Fewer than 10 items sold = 1% commission
> Between 10 and 40 items sold = 2% commission
> Between 41 and 100 items sold = 4% commission
> More than 100 items sold = 8% commission

Figure 12.17   Sales Commission Calculator GUI.

a) *Copying the template to your working directory.* Copy the directory C:\Examples\ Tutorial12\Exercises\SalesCommissionCalculator to your C:\SimplyVB directory.

b) *Opening the application's template file.* Double click SalesCommissionCalculator.sln in the SalesCommissionCalculator directory to open the application.

c) *Defining an event handler for the Button's Click event.* Create an event handler for the **Calculate** Button's Click event.

d) *Display the salesperson's gross sales.* In your new event handler, multiply the number of items that the salesperson has sold by 10, and display the resulting gross sales as a monetary amount.

e) *Calculate the salesperson's commission percentage.* Use a Select Case statement to compute the salesperson's commission percentage from the number of items sold. The rate that is selected is applied to all the items the salesperson sold.

f) *Display the salesperson's earnings.* Multiply the salesperson's gross sales by the commission percentage determined in the preceding step to calculate the salesperson's earnings. Remember to divide by 100 to obtain the percentage.

g) *Running the application.* Select **Debug > Start Debugging** to run your application. Enter a value for the number of items sold and click the **Calculate** Button. Verify that the gross sales displayed is correct, that the percentage of commission is correct and that the earnings displayed is correct based on the commission assigned.

h) *Closing the application.* Close your running application by clicking its close box.

i) *Closing the IDE.* Close the Visual Basic IDE by clicking its close box.

12.12 *(Cash Register Application)* Use the numeric keypad from the **Security Panel** application to build a **Cash Register** application (Fig. 12.18). In addition to numbers, the cash register should include a decimal point Button. Apart from this numeric operation, there should be **Enter, Delete, Clear** and **Total** Buttons. Sales tax should be calculated on the amount purchased. Use a Select Case statement to compute sales tax. Add the tax amount to the subtotal to calculate the total. Display the subtotal, tax and total for the user. Use the following sales-tax percentages, which are based on the amount of money spent:

Amounts under \$100 = 5% (.05) sales tax
Amounts between \$100 and \$500 = 7.5% (.075) sales tax
Amounts above \$500 = 10% (.10) sales tax

Figure 12.18   Cash Register GUI.

a) *Copying the template to your working directory.* Copy the directory `C:\Examples\Tutorial12\Exercises\CashRegister` to your `C:\SimplyVB` directory.

b) *Opening the application's template file.* Double click `CashRegister.sln` in the `CashRegister` directory to open the application.

c) *Define event handlers for the numeric Buttons and decimal point in the keypad.* Create event handlers for each of these Button's Click events. Have each event handler concatenate the proper value to the TextBox at the top of the Form.

d) *Define an event handler for the Enter Button's Click event.* Create an event handler for this Button's Click event. Have this event handler add the current amount to the subtotal and display the new subtotal.

e) *Define an event handler for the Total Button's Click event.* Create an event handler for this Button's Click event. Have this event handler use the subtotal to compute the tax amount.

f) *Define an event handler for the Clear Button's Click event.* Create an event handler for this Button's Click event. Have this event handler clear the user input and display the value \$0.00 for the subtotal, sales tax and total.

g) *Define an event handler for the Delete Button's Click event.* Create an event handler for this Button's Click event. Have this event handler clear only the data in the TextBox.

h) *Running the application.* Select **Debug > Start Debugging** to run your application. Use the keypad to enter various dollar amounts, clicking the **Enter** Button after each. After several amounts have been entered, click the **Total** Button and verify that the appropriate sales tax and total are displayed. Enter several values again and click the **Delete** Button to clear the current input. Click the **Clear** Button to clear all the output values.

i) *Closing the application.* Close your running application by clicking its close box.

j) *Closing the IDE.* Close the Visual Basic IDE by clicking its close box.

12.13 *(Income Tax Calculator Application)* Create an application that computes the amount of income tax that a person must pay, depending upon salary. Your application should perform as shown in Fig. 12.19. Use the following income ranges and corresponding tax rates:

Under $20,000 = 2% income tax
$20,000 – 50, 000 = 5% income tax
$50,001 – 75,000 = 10% income tax
$75,001 – 100,000= 15% income tax
Over $100,000 = 20% income tax

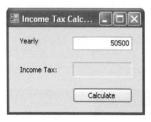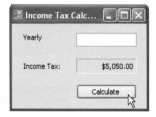

Figure 12.19 Income Tax Calculator GUI.

a) *Copying the template to your working directory.* Copy the directory C:\Examples\ Tutorial12\Exercises\IncomeTaxCalculator to your C:\SimplyVB directory.

b) *Opening the application's template file.* Double click IncomeTaxCalculator.sln in the IncomeTaxCalculator directory to open the application.

c) *Define an event handler for the Calculate Button's Click event.* Use the designer to create an event handler for this Button's Click event. Have this event handler use a Select Case statement to determine the user's income-tax percentage. For simplicity, this value should then be multiplied by the user's salary and displayed in the output Label.

d) *Running the application.* Select **Debug > Start Debugging** to run your application. Enter a yearly salary and click the **Calculate** Button. Verify that the appropriate income tax is displayed, based on the ranges listed in the exercise description.

e) *Closing the application.* Close your running application by clicking its close box.

f) *Closing the IDE.* Close the Visual Basic IDE by clicking its close box.

What does this code do? ▶ **12.14** What is output by the following code? Assume that donationButton is a Button, donationTextBox is a TextBox and messageLabel is an output Label.

```
1   Private Sub donationButton_Click(ByVal sender As _
2      System.Object, ByVal e As System.EventArgs) _
3      Handles donationButton.Click
4
5      Select Case Val(donationTextBox.Text)
6
7         Case 0
8            messageLabel.Text = "Please consider donating to our cause."
9
```

```
10          Case 1 To 100
11              messageLabel.Text = "Thank you for your donation."
12
13          Case Is > 100
14              messageLabel.Text = "Thank you very much for your donation!"
15
16          Case Else
17              messageLabel.Text = "Please enter a valid amount."
18
19      End Select
20
21  End Sub
```

What's wrong with this code? ▶ **12.15** This `Select Case` statement should determine whether an `Integer` is even or odd. Find the error(s) in the following code:

```
1  Select Case value Mod 2
2
3      Case 0
4          outputLabel.Text = "Odd Integer"
5
6      Case 1
7          outputLabel.Text = "Even Integer"
8
9  End Select
```

Using the Debugger ▶ **12.16** (*Discount Calculator Application*) The **Discount Calculator** application determines the discount the user will receive, based on how much money the user spends. A 15% discount is received for purchases over $200, a 10% discount is received for purchases between $150 and $199, a 5% discount is received for purchases between $100 and $149 and a 2% discount is received for purchases between $50 and $99. While testing your application, you notice that the application is not calculating the discount properly for some values. Use the debugger to find and fix the logic error(s) in the application. Figure 12.20 displays the correct output for the application.

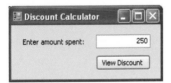

Figure 12.20   Correct output for the **Discount Calculator** application.

Programming Challenge ▶ **12.17** (*Enhanced Cash Register Application*) Modify the **Cash Register** application (Exercise 12.12) to include the operations addition, subtraction and multiplication. Remove the **Enter** Button, and replace it with the addition (**+**), subtraction (**–**) and multiplication (*****) Buttons. These Buttons should take the value displayed in the **Subtotal:** field and the value displayed in the upper Label and perform the operation of the clicked Button. The result should be displayed in the **Subtotal:** field. Fig. 12.21 displays the enhanced **Cash Register** application GUI.

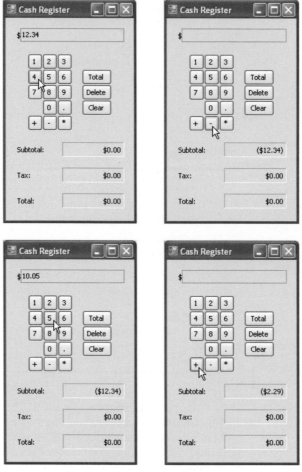

Figure 12.21 Enhanced Cash Register GUI.

Objectives

In this tutorial, you will learn to:
- Construct applications modularly from pieces called procedures.
- Work with "built-in" procedures.
- Distinguish between Function procedures and Sub procedures, and determine when each should be used.
- Create your own Function procedures and Sub procedures.
- Use the Debug Toolbar

Outline

13.1 Test-Driving the Enhanced Wage Calculator Application

13.2 Classes and Procedures

13.3 Function Procedures

13.4 Using Sub Procedures in the Wage Calculator Application

13.5 Using the Debugger: Debug Toolbar

13.6 Wrap-Up

Enhancing the Wage Calculator Application

Introducing *Function* Procedures and *Sub* Procedures

Most software applications that solve real-world problems are much larger than the applications presented in the first few tutorials of this text. Experience has shown that the best way to develop and maintain a large application is to construct it from smaller, more manageable pieces. This technique is known as **divide and conquer**. These manageable pieces include program components, known as **procedures**, that simplify the design, implementation and maintenance of large applications. In this tutorial, you will learn how to create two kinds of procedures—namely, Function procedures and Sub procedures.

13.1 Test-Driving the Enhanced Wage Calculator Application

Next, you will use procedures to enhance the **Wage Calculator** application that you created in Tutorial 7. This application must meet the following requirements:

Application Requirements

Recall the problem statement from Tutorial 7: A payroll company calculates the gross earnings per week of employees. Employees' weekly salaries are based on the number of hours they worked and their hourly wages. Create an application that accepts this information and calculates the employee's total (gross) earnings. The application assumes a standard work week of 40 hours. The wages for 40 or fewer hours are calculated by multiplying the employee's hourly salary by the number of hours worked. Any time worked over 40 hours in a week is considered "overtime" and earns time and a half. Salary for time and a half is calculated by multiplying the employee's hourly wage by 1.5 and multiplying the result of that calculation by the number of overtime hours worked. The total overtime earned is added to the user's gross earnings for the regular 40 hours of work to calculate the total earnings for that week.

The completed application has the same functionality as the application in Tutorial 7, but uses procedures to better organize the code. This application calculates wages that are based on an employee's hourly salary and the number of hours worked per week. Normally, an employee who works 40 or fewer hours earns the hourly wage multiplied by the number of hours worked. The calcula-

263

tion differs if the employee has worked more than the standard 40-hour work week. In this tutorial, you learn about procedures that perform calculations based on input values that may differ with each execution of the application. You begin by test-driving the completed application. Then you will learn the additional Visual Basic technologies that you will need to create your own version of this application.

Test-Driving the Wage Calculator Application

1. ***Opening the completed application.*** Open the directory `C:\Examples\Tutorial13\CompletedApplication\WageCalculator2` to locate the **Wage Calculator** application. Double click `WageCalculator2.sln` to open the application in the Visual Basic IDE.

2. ***Running the Wage Calculator application.*** Select **Debug > Start Debugging** to run the application.

3. ***Entering the employee's hourly wage.*** Enter 10 in the **Hourly wage:** Text-Box (Fig. 13.1).

Figure 13.1 **Wage Calculator** running.

4. ***Entering the number of hours the employee worked.*** Enter 45 in the **Weekly hours:** TextBox.

5. ***Calculating wages earned.*** Click the **Calculate** Button. The result (`$475.00`) is displayed in the **Gross earnings:** Label.

6. ***Closing the application.*** Close the running application by clicking its close box.

7. ***Closing the IDE.*** Close the Visual Basic IDE by clicking its close box.

13.2 Classes and Procedures

The key to creating large applications is to break the applications into smaller pieces. In object-oriented programming, these pieces consist primarily of classes, which can be further broken down into **methods**. In Visual Basic programming, methods are implemented (created) by writing procedures.

Programmers typically combine **programmer-defined** classes and methods with preexisting (also predefined) code available in the FCL. Using preexisting code saves time, effort and money. The concept of **reusing code** increases efficiency for application developers. Figure 13.2 explains and demonstrates several preexisting Visual Basic procedures.

You have already used several preexisting classes and methods in the FCL. For example, all of the GUI controls you have used in your applications are defined in the FCL as classes. You have also used FCL class methods, such as method `Format` of class `String`, to display output properly in your applications. Without method `String.Format`, you would have needed to code this functionality yourself—a task that would have included many lines of code and programming techniques that have not been introduced yet. You will learn many more FCL classes and methods in this book.

Procedure	Description	Example
`Math.Max(x, y)`	Returns the larger value of x and y	`Math.Max(2.3, 12.7)` is `12.7` `Math.Max(-2.3, -12.7)` is `-2.3`
`Math.Min(x, y)`	Returns the smaller value of x and y	`Math.Min(2.3, 12.7)` is `2.3` `Math.Min(-2.3, -12.7)` is `-12.7`

`Math.Sqrt(x)`	Returns the square root of x	`Math.Sqrt(9)` is `3.0`
		`Math.Sqrt(2)`
		  is `1.4142135623731`

`Pmt(x, y, z)`	Calculates loan payments where x specifies the interest rate, y specifies the number of payment periods and z specifies the principal value of the loan	`Pmt(0.05, 12, -4000)` is `451.301640083261`

`Val(x)`	Returns a numeric value for x	`Val("5")` is `5`
		`Val("5a8")` is `5`
		`Val("a5")` is `0`

`String.Format(x, y)`	Returns String values where x is a format string, and y is a value to be formatted as a `String`	`String.Format("{0:C}", 1.23)` is `"$1.23"`

Figure 13.2 Some predefined Visual Basic procedures.

However, the FCL cannot provide every conceivable feature that you might want, so Visual Basic allows you to create your own programmer-defined procedures to meet the unique requirements of your particular applications. Two types of procedures exist: **Function procedures** and **Sub procedures**. In the next section, you will learn about `Function` procedures; in Section 13.4, you will learn about Sub procedures. Throughout this tutorial, the term "procedure" refers to both `Function` procedures and Sub procedures, unless otherwise noted.

SELF-REVIEW

1. _____ provides the programmer with preexisting classes that perform common tasks.
   a) The Framework Class Library
   b) The `PreExisting` keyword
   c) The Framework Code Library
   d) The `Library` keyword

2. Programmers normally use _____.
   a) programmer-defined procedures
   b) preexisting procedures
   c) both programmer-defined and preexisting procedures
   d) neither programmer-defined nor preexisting procedures

Answers: 1) a. 2) c.

13.3 Function Procedures

The applications presented earlier in this book call FCL methods (such as `String.Format`) to help accomplish the applications' tasks. You will now learn how to write your own programmer-defined procedures. You will first learn how to create procedures in the context of two small applications, before you create the enhanced **Wage Calculator** application. The first application uses the Pythagorean Theorem to calculate the length of the hypotenuse of a right triangle, and the second application determines the maximum of three numbers. Let us begin by reviewing the Pythagorean Theorem. A right triangle (a triangle with a 90-degree angle) always satisfies the following relationship—the sum of the squares of the two smaller sides of the triangle equals the square of the largest side of the triangle, which is known as the hypotenuse. In this application, the two smaller sides are called sides A and B, and their lengths are used to calculate the length of the hypotenuse. Follow the steps in the next box to create the application.

Creating the Hypotenuse Calculator Application	1. ***Copying the template to your working directory.*** Copy the `C:\Examples\Tutorial13\TemplateApplication\HypotenuseCalculator` directory to your `C:\SimplyVB` directory.

2. ***Opening the Hypotenuse Calculator application's template file.*** Double click `HypotenuseCalculator.sln` in the `HypotenuseCalculator` directory to open the application in the Visual Basic IDE. You will see the GUI shown in Fig. 13.3. When this application is running, the user enters the lengths of a triangle's two shorter sides into the **Length of side A:** and **Length of side B:** TextBoxes, then clicks the **Calculate Hypotenuse** Button. The completed application will calculate the length of the hypotenuse at this time and display the result in the **Length of hypotenuse:** output Label.

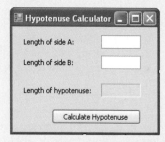

Figure 13.3   Hypotenuse Calculator GUI.

3. ***Viewing the template application code.*** Switch to code view, and examine the code provided in the template, shown in Fig. 13.4. We have provided an incomplete event handler for the **Calculate Hypotenuse** Button. This event handler contains six declarations (lines 6–11). Variables `sideA` and `sideB` will contain the lengths of sides A and B, entered by the user. Variable `hypotenuse` will contain the length of the hypotenuse, which will be calculated shortly. Variable `squareSideA` will be used to store the length of side A, squared. Similarly, variables `squareSideB` and `squareHypotenuse` will be used to store the squares of the lengths of sides B and the hypotenuse, respectively. Lines 13–14 store the user input for the lengths of sides A and B. Lines 17–23 contain an `If...Then...Else` statement. The `If` statement's body displays a message dialog if a negative value (or zero) is input as the length of side A or side B, or both. The `Else`'s body, which will execute if values greater than zero are entered, will be used to calculate the length of the hypotenuse.

4. ***Creating an empty Function procedure.*** Add lines 26–28 of Fig. 13.5 after event handler `calculateButton_Click`. The keywords `End Function` will appear (line 30). You will learn about these keywords shortly. Note that we have added a comment in line 30 to identify the procedure being terminated.

5. ***Understanding the Function procedure.*** The procedure begins in line 28 (Fig. 13.5) with keyword **Function**, followed by a **procedure name** (in this case, `Square`). The procedure name can be any valid identifier. The procedure name is followed by a set of parentheses containing a variable declaration.

(cont.)

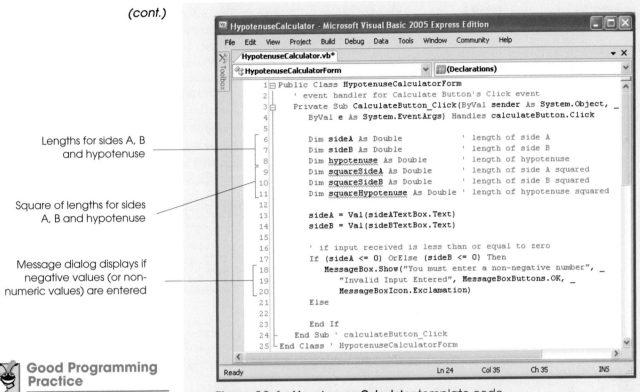

Figure 13.4   **Hypotenuse Calculator** template code.

Lengths for sides A, B and hypotenuse

Square of lengths for sides A, B and hypotenuse

Message dialog displays if negative values (or non-numeric values) are entered

Good Programming Practice

Add comments at the end of your procedures, indicating which procedure is being terminated. Such comments remind the reader of the procedure that is being terminated.

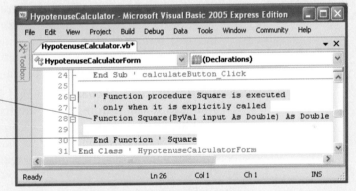

Figure 13.5   `Function` procedure `Square`.

`Function` procedure header

`End Function` keywords mark the end of a `Function` procedure

Software Design Tip

To promote reusability, each procedure should perform a single well-defined task, and the procedure name should express that task effectively.

The declaration within the parentheses is known as the **parameter list**, where variables (called **parameters**) are declared. Although this parameter list contains only one declaration, the parameter list can contain multiple declarations separated by commas. The parameter list declares each parameter's name and type. Note that the declarations of parameter variables here use the keyword `ByVal` instead of keyword `Dim`. We will discuss keyword `ByVal` shortly. Parameter variables are used in the `Function` procedure body.

The parameter list is followed by the keyword `As`, which is in turn followed by the data type `Double`. The type that follows `As`, known as the **return type**, indicates the type of the result returned from the `Function` (in this case, `Double`). The first line of a procedure (including the keyword `Function`, the procedure name, the parameter list and the return type) is often called the **procedure header**. The procedure header for `Square` declares one parameter variable, `input`, to be of type `Double` and sets the return type of `Square` to be `Double`.

(cont.)

The Function procedure of Fig. 13.5 ends on line 30 with the keywords **End Function**. The declarations and statements that appear after the procedure header but before the keywords End Function form the **procedure body**. The procedure body contains Visual Basic code that performs actions, generally by manipulating or interacting with the parameters from the parameter list. In the next step, you will add statements to the body of procedure Square. The procedure header, the body and the keywords End Function collectively make up the **procedure definition**.

6. *Adding code to the body of a Function procedure.* You want your Function procedure to perform the squaring functionality needed in this application. Add lines 30–31 of Fig. 13.6 to Square's body.

Calculating squares by using the ∧ operator

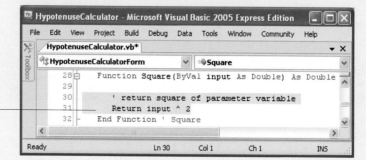

Figure 13.6 Square procedure definition.

Line 31 uses the ∧ operator to calculate the square of input—the parameter of this procedure. Line 31 uses a **Return statement** to return this value. This statement begins with the keyword **Return**, followed by an expression. The Return statement returns the result of the expression following keyword Return, in this case input ∧ 2, and terminates execution of the procedure. This value is returned to the point at which the procedure was called. You will write the code to call the procedure in the next step.

7. *Calling procedure Square.* Now that you have created your procedure, you will need to call it from your event handler. Add lines 22–24 of Fig. 13.7 to your application, in the Else block of the If...Then...Else statement. These lines call Square by using the procedure name followed by a set of parentheses that contain the procedure's argument. In this case, the arguments are the result of Val(sideATextBox.Text) and Val(sideBTextBox.Text).

Calling procedure Square

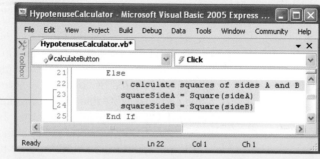

Figure 13.7 Invoking procedure Square.

Note that typing the opening parenthesis after a procedure name causes the Visual Basic IDE to display a window containing the procedure's argument names and types (Fig. 13.8). This is the *Parameter Info* feature of the IDE, which provides you with information about procedures and their arguments. The *Parameter Info* feature displays information for programmer-defined procedures as well as for FCL methods.

(cont.)

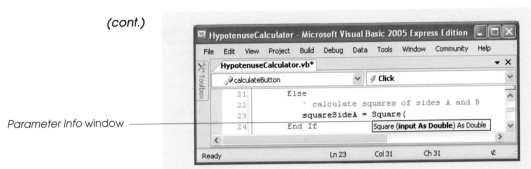

Figure 13.8   *Parameter Info* window.

Parameter Info window

A procedure is **invoked** (that is, made to perform its designated task) by a **procedure call**. The procedure call specifies the procedure name and provides information (**arguments**) that the **callee** (the procedure being called) requires to do its job. When the called procedure completes its task, it returns control to the **caller** (the **calling procedure**). For example, we have typically called function `Val` as follows:

```
result = Val(inputTextBox.Text)
```

where `Val` is the name of the function, and `inputTextBox.Text`'s value is the argument passed to this function. The procedure uses this value to perform its defined task (returning the value of `inputTextBox.Text` as a number).

When program control reaches line 23 of Fig. 13.7, the application calls `Function` procedure `Square`. At this point, the application makes a copy of the value entered into the **Length of side A:** TextBox (after this value has been passed to function `Val`), and program control transfers to the first line of `Square`.

Keyword **ByVal**, specified in the header of procedure `Square`, indicates that a copy of the argument's value (the length of side A) should be passed to `Square`. `Square` receives the copy of the value input by the user and stores it in the parameter `input`. When the `Return` statement in `Square` is reached, the value to the right of keyword `Return` is returned to the point in line 23 where `Square` was called, and the procedure's execution completes (any remaining statements of the procedure's body will not be executed).

Program control will also be transferred to this point, and the application will continue by assigning the return value of `Square` to variable `squareSideA`. These same actions will occur again when program control reaches the second call to `Square` in line 24. With this call, the value passed to `Square` is the value entered into the **Length of side B:** TextBox (after this value has been passed to function `Val`), and the value returned is assigned to variable `squareSideB`.

8. ***Calling a preexisting method of the FCL.*** Add lines 26–34 of Fig. 13.9 to the `Else`'s body of the `If...Then...Else` statement in your application. Line 28 adds the square of side A and the square of side B, resulting in the square of the hypotenuse, which is assigned to variable `squareHypotenuse`. Line 32 then calls FCL method **Sqrt** of class `Math` (by using the dot operator). This method will calculate the square root of the square of the hypotenuse to find the length of the hypotenuse.

9. ***Running the application.*** Select **Debug > Start Debugging** to run your application. Enter 3 into the **Length of side A:** TextBox and 4 into the **Length of side B:** TextBox. Click the **Calculate Hypotenuse** Button. The output is shown in Fig. 13.10.

Error-Prevention Tip

Small procedures are easier to test, debug and understand than large ones.

(cont.)

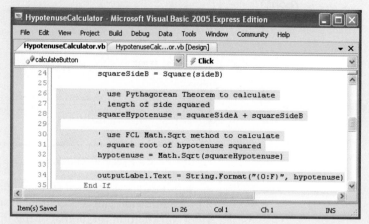

Figure 13.9 Completing the `calculateButton_Click` event handler.

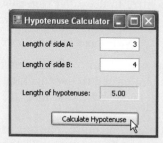

Figure 13.10 **Hypotenuse Calculator** application running.

10. ***Closing the application***. Close your running application by clicking its close box.

11. ***Closing the IDE***. Close the Visual Basic IDE by clicking its close box.

You have now successfully created a Function procedure. You have also tested this Function procedure (by running the application) to confirm that it works correctly. This Function procedure can now be used in any Visual Basic application where you wish to calculate the square of a Double. All you need to do is include the procedure definition in your application. This is an example of code reuse, which helps programmers create applications faster.

As demonstrated in the **Hypotenuse Calculator** application, the procedure call used to call a Function procedure follows the format

> *name*(*argument list*)

There must be one argument in the argument list of the procedure call for each parameter in the parameter list of the procedure header. The arguments also must be compatible with the parameters' types (that is, Visual Basic must be able to assign the value of the argument to its corresponding parameter variable). For example, a parameter of type Double could receive the value of 53547.350009, 22 or -.03546, but not "hello", because a Double variable cannot contain a String. If a procedure does not receive any values, the parameter list is empty (that is, the procedure name is followed by an empty set of parentheses). You will study procedure parameters in detail in Tutorial 15.

As you saw in the preceding example, the statement

> `Return` *expression*

can occur anywhere in a Function procedure body and returns the value of *expression* to the caller. If necessary, Visual Basic attempts to convert the value of *expres-*

sion to the `Function` procedure's return type. Functions `Return` exactly one value. When a `Return` statement is executed, control returns immediately to the point at which that `Function` procedure was called.

You will now create another `Function` procedure. This procedure, which is part of the **Maximum** application, returns the largest of three numbers input by the user. In the following box, you will create the **Maximum** application.

Creating a *Function* Procedure That Returns the Largest of Three Numbers

1. **Copying the template to your working directory.** Copy the `C:\Examples\Tutorial13\TemplateApplication\Maximum` directory to your `C:\SimplyVB` directory.

2. **Opening the Maximum application's template file.** Double click `Maximum.sln` in the `Maximum` directory to open the application in the Visual Basic IDE. Switch to design view (Fig. 13.11).

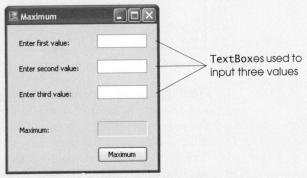

Figure 13.11   **Maximum** application in design view.

3. **Creating an event handler for the Maximum Button.** Double click the **Maximum** Button to create an event handler for this Button's `Click` event. Add a comment in line 2 of Fig. 13.12 and split the header over two lines, as shown in lines 3–4. Add lines 6–7 to the event handler. Lines 6–7 call `Function` procedure `Maximum` and pass it the three values the user has input into the application's `TextBoxes`. Note that `Maximum` has been underlined in blue, indicating a syntax error. This occurs because `Function` procedure `Maximum` has not yet been defined. You will define `Maximum` in the next step. This syntax error will occur whenever you call a procedure that is not recognized by the Visual Basic IDE. Misspelling the name of a procedure in a procedure call will likewise cause a syntax error. Finally, add the comment after keywords **End Sub** in line 8.

Common Programming Error

Calling a procedure that does not yet exist or misspelling the procedure name in a procedure call results in a syntax error.

Calling a procedure that has not yet been defined is an error

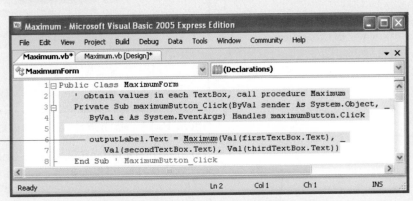

Figure 13.12   Invoking `Function` procedure `Maximum`.

(cont.)

4. ***Creating Function procedure Maximum.*** Add lines 10–12 of Fig. 13.13 after event handler maximumButton_Click, then press *Enter*. Note that the keywords End Function will be added for you by the IDE. The parameter list specifies that the values of the three arguments passed to Maximum will be stored in parameters one, two and three. The parameter list is followed by the keyword As and the return type Double.

Empty Function
procedure Maximum

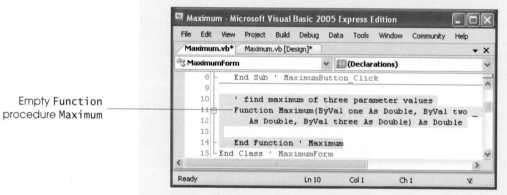

Figure 13.13   Maximum Function procedure.

5. ***Adding functionality to Function procedure Maximum.*** Add lines 14–20 of Fig. 13.14 to the body of Maximum. Line 14 creates a variable that will contain the maximum of the first two numbers passed to this procedure. This maximum is determined in line 17 by using the **Max** method of FCL class Math. This method takes two Doubles and returns the maximum of these two values. The value returned is assigned to variable temporaryMaximum in line 17. You then compare that value to Function procedure Maximum's third parameter, three, in line 18. The maximum determined in this line, finalMaximum, is the maximum of the three values. Line 20 uses a Return statement to return this value. The Return statement terminates execution of the procedure and returns the result of finalMaximum to the calling procedure. The result is returned to the point (line 6 of Fig. 13.12) where Maximum was called and is assigned to outputLabel's Text property.

Calling Math.Max to determine
the maximum of two values

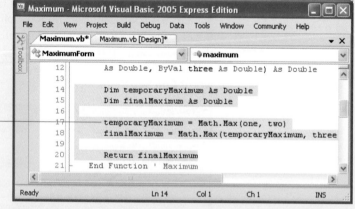

Figure 13.14   Math.Max returns the larger of its two arguments.

6. ***Running the application.*** Select **Debug > Start Debugging** to run your application (Fig. 13.15). Enter a numeric value into each TextBox, and click the **Maximum** Button. Note that the largest of the three values is displayed in the output Label.

(cont.)

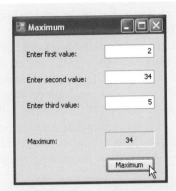

Figure 13.15 **Maximum** application running.

7. ***Closing the application.*** Close your running application by clicking its close box.

8. ***Closing the IDE.*** Close the Visual Basic IDE by clicking its close box.

13.4 Using Sub Procedures in the Wage Calculator Application

The **Calculate** `Button`'s `Click` event handler in the original version of the **Wage Calculator** application (Tutorial 7) calculated wages and displayed the result in a `Label`. In the following box, you'll write `Sub` procedure `DisplayPay` to perform these tasks. **Sub procedures** are similar to `Function` procedures, with one important difference: Sub procedures do not return a value to the caller. When the user clicks the **Calculate** Button, event handler `calculateButton_Click` calls Sub procedure `DisplayPay`.

Creating a Sub Procedure within the Wage Calculator Application

1. ***Copying the template to your working directory.*** Copy the `C:\Examples\Tutorial13\TemplateApplication\WageCalculator2` directory to your `C:\SimplyVB` directory.

2. ***Opening the Wage Calculator application's template file.*** Double click `WageCalculator2.sln` in the `WageCalculator2` directory to open the application in the Visual Basic IDE.

3. ***Creating the `calculateButton_Click` event handler.*** View the application's Form in design view. Double click the **Calculate** Button to generate the `Click` event handler.

(cont.)

4. **Entering functionality to *calculateButton_Click*.** Add lines 6–15 of Fig. 13.16 to the empty event handler. This code calls procedure DisplayPay to calculate and display the wages. Lines 11–12 retrieve the user input from the TextBoxes and assign the values to variables declared in lines 7–8. Line 15 calls procedure DisplayPay, which you will define shortly. This procedure call takes two arguments: the hours worked (userHours) and the hourly wage (wage). Note that the call to DisplayPay is underlined in blue because the procedure has not yet been defined; for the moment, this is a syntax error. Also note that the procedure's arguments in this example are variables. Arguments also can be constants or expressions.

Software Design Tip

The procedure header and procedure calls all must agree with regard to the number, types and order of parameters.

Call to DisplayPay

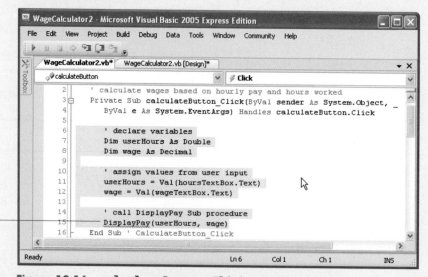

Figure 13.16 calculateButton_Click calls DisplayPay.

5. **Creating a Sub procedure.** After event handler calculateButton_Click, add Sub procedure DisplayPay to your application (lines 18–40 of Fig. 13.17).

Procedure DisplayPay receives the argument values and stores them in the parameters hours and rate. Note that the syntax of a Sub procedure is the same as the syntax of a Function procedure, with a few small changes. One change is that the Function keywords are replaced with **Sub** keywords (lines 19 and 40 of Fig. 13.17). Another difference is that there is no return type, because Sub procedures do not return a value.

Common Programming Error

Declaring a variable in a procedure's body with the same name as a parameter variable in the procedure header is a syntax error.

Note that the variable earnings and the constant HOUR_LIMIT have been moved to the DisplayPay procedure. (In Fig. 7.15 of Tutorial 7, they were located within the calculateButton_Click event handler.) They are no longer needed in calculateButton_Click, so they have been removed from that event handler.

Lines 27–37 define the If...Then...Else statement that determines whether overtime must be calculated. The condition for this statement determines whether hours is less than or equal to constant HOUR_LIMIT. If it is, then the employee's earnings without overtime are calculated. Otherwise, the employee's earnings including overtime are calculated. Line 39 displays the result (formatted as currency) in a Label.

When the End Sub statement in line 40 is encountered, control is returned to the calling procedure, calculateButton_Click (line 15 of Fig. 13.16).

6. **Saving the project.** Select **File > Save All** to save your modified code.

(cont.)

DisplayPay calculates and displays the user's gross earnings

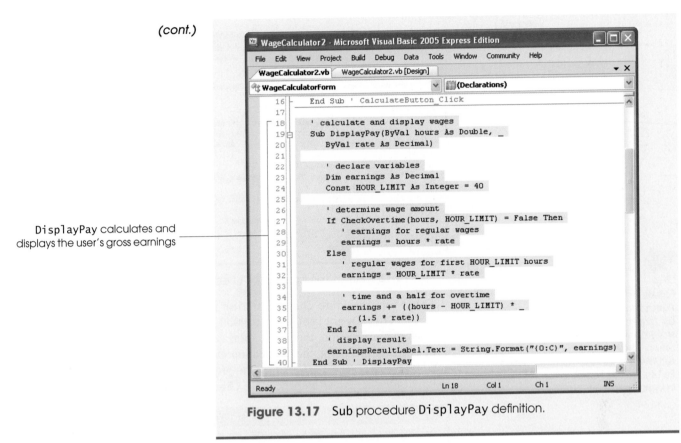

Figure 13.17 Sub procedure DisplayPay definition.

The following box shows you how to add Function procedure CheckOvertime to the **Wage Calculator** application. CheckOvertime will be used to determine whether an employee has worked overtime.

Creating a Function Procedure within the Wage Calculator Application

1. ***Creating a Function procedure header.*** Add Function procedure Check-Overtime (lines 42–51 of Fig. 13.18) to your application, after the Display-Pay procedure definition. Note that the return type of the procedure is Boolean. This indicates that the value returned by the procedure must be a Boolean (that is, a constant, variable or expression that evaluates to True or False).

   When CheckOvertime is called, program control is transferred to the beginning of this procedure in line 43. The arguments passed to this procedure (passed in the procedure call, which you will write in the next step) are stored in the parameter variables total and limit. Line 47 returns the Boolean value True, to indicate that the employee has worked overtime; line 49 returns the Boolean value False, to indicate that the employee has not worked any overtime. Program control and the value (either True or False) are returned to the line where CheckOvertime was initially called.

2. ***Modifying Sub procedure DisplayPay.*** In Sub procedure DisplayPay, replace the statement (line 27 of Fig. 13.17)

   ```
   If hours <= HOUR_LIMIT Then
   ```

   with line 27 of Fig. 13.19. We modify DisplayPay so that it now calls Function procedure CheckOvertime to determine whether the employee qualifies for overtime pay.

(cont.)

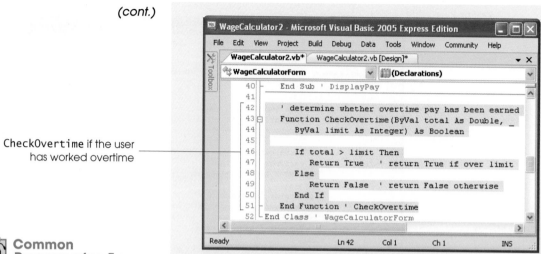

CheckOvertime if the user has worked overtime

Figure 13.18 Function procedure CheckOverTime definition.

Common Programming Error

Failure to return a value from a Function procedure (for example, by forgetting to provide a Return statement) causes the procedure to return the default value for the *return-type* (0 for numeric types, False for Booleans), often resulting in logic errors.

Function procedure CheckOvertime is called (line 27) with the procedure call CheckOvertime(hours, HOUR_LIMIT). When program control reaches this expression, the application calls Function procedure CheckOvertime. At this point, the application makes a copy of the value of hours and HOUR_LIMIT (the arguments in the procedure call), and control transfers to the header of Function procedure CheckOvertime.

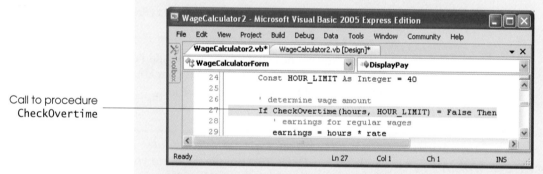

Call to procedure CheckOvertime

Figure 13.19 DisplayPay calls Function procedure CheckOvertime.

The parameter variables in CheckOvertime's header are initialized to copies of hours's value and HOUR_LIMIT's value. The value returned from CheckOvertime is compared to the value False in line 27. Note that this line can also be written as

```
If Not CheckOvertime(hours, HOUR_LIMIT) Then
```

Now when the **Calculate** Button is clicked, DisplayPay is called and executed. Recall that Function procedure CheckOvertime is called by the DisplayPay Sub procedure. This sequence of calls is repeated every time the user clicks the **Calculate** Button.

3. ***Running the application***. Select **Debug > Start Debugging** to run your application. Enter an hourly wage and number of hours worked (under 40), then click the **Calculate** Button. Verify that the appropriate earnings are displayed. Change the number of hours worked to a value over 40 and click the **Calculate** Button again. Verify that the appropriate output is displayed.

4. ***Closing the application***. Close your running application by clicking its close box.

Figure 13.20 presents the source code for the **Wage Calculator** application. The lines of code that contain new programming concepts that you learned in this tutorial are highlighted.

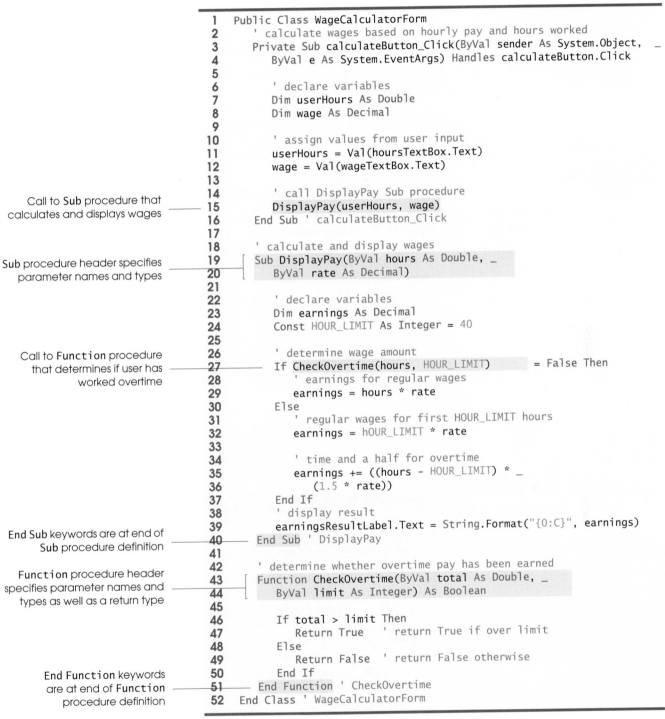

Call to **Sub** procedure that calculates and displays wages

Sub procedure header specifies parameter names and types

Call to **Function** procedure that determines if user has worked overtime

End **Sub** keywords are at end of **Sub** procedure definition

Function procedure header specifies parameter names and types as well as a return type

End **Function** keywords are at end of **Function** procedure definition

```
1   Public Class WageCalculatorForm
2       ' calculate wages based on hourly pay and hours worked
3       Private Sub calculateButton_Click(ByVal sender As System.Object, _
4           ByVal e As System.EventArgs) Handles calculateButton.Click
5
6           ' declare variables
7           Dim userHours As Double
8           Dim wage As Decimal
9
10          ' assign values from user input
11          userHours = Val(hoursTextBox.Text)
12          wage = Val(wageTextBox.Text)
13
14          ' call DisplayPay Sub procedure
15          DisplayPay(userHours, wage)
16      End Sub ' calculateButton_Click
17
18      ' calculate and display wages
19      Sub DisplayPay(ByVal hours As Double, _
20          ByVal rate As Decimal)
21
22          ' declare variables
23          Dim earnings As Decimal
24          Const HOUR_LIMIT As Integer = 40
25
26          ' determine wage amount
27          If CheckOvertime(hours, HOUR_LIMIT) = False Then
28              ' earnings for regular wages
29              earnings = hours * rate
30          Else
31              ' regular wages for first HOUR_LIMIT hours
32              earnings = hOUR_LIMIT * rate
33
34              ' time and a half for overtime
35              earnings += ((hours - HOUR_LIMIT) * _
36                  (1.5 * rate))
37          End If
38          ' display result
39          earningsResultLabel.Text = String.Format("{0:C}", earnings)
40      End Sub ' DisplayPay
41
42      ' determine whether overtime pay has been earned
43      Function CheckOvertime(ByVal total As Double, _
44          ByVal limit As Integer) As Boolean
45
46          If total > limit Then
47              Return True     ' return True if over limit
48          Else
49              Return False    ' return False otherwise
50          End If
51      End Function ' CheckOvertime
52  End Class ' WageCalculatorForm
```

Figure 13.20   Code for **Wage Calculator** application.

SELF-REVIEW   1. Arguments to a procedure can be _____.

     a) constants   b) expressions

     c) variables   d) All of the above.

2. The _____ is a comma-separated list of declarations in a procedure header.
   a) argument list
   b) parameter list
   c) value list
   d) variable list

Answers: 1) d. 2) b.

13.5 Using the Debugger: Debug Toolbar

You will now continue your study of the debugger by learning about the debug toolbar, which contains Buttons for controlling the debugging process. These Buttons provide convenient access to actions in the **Debug** menu. In this section, you will learn how to use the debug toolbar's Buttons to verify that a procedure's code is executing correctly. In the following box, we use the debug toolbar Buttons to examine the **Wage Calculator** application.

Using the Debugger: Debug Toolbar

1. ***Opening the completed application.*** Open the **Wage Calculator2** application.

2. ***Opening the debug toolbar.*** The debug toolbar contains Buttons for controlling the debugging process. These Buttons provide easy access to the **Debug** menu commands. To display the debug toolbar (Fig. 13.21), select **View > Toolbars > Standard**. The debug toolbar appears below the IDE menu bar (Fig. 13.22).

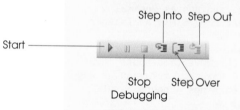

Figure 13.21 Debug toolbar.

3. ***Setting a breakpoint.*** Set a breakpoint in line 15 by clicking in the margin indicator bar (Fig. 13.22).

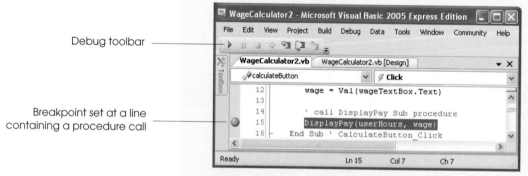

Figure 13.22 Setting a breakpoint.

4. ***Starting the debugger.*** To start the debugger, select **Debug > Start Debugging**. The WageCalculator2 application executes. Enter the value 7.50 in the **Hourly wage:** TextBox, and enter 35 in the **Weekly hours:** TextBox. Click the **Calculate** Button.

(cont.)   5. ***Using the Step Into Button.*** The Step Into Button (Fig. 13.21) executes the next statement (the yellow highlighted line) in the application. If the next statement to execute is a procedure call (Fig. 13.23) and the Step Into Button is clicked, control is transferred to the called procedure. The Step Into Button allows you to enter a procedure and confirm its execution. Click the Step Into Button to enter procedure `DisplayPay` (Fig. 13.24).

Next statement to execute is a procedure call

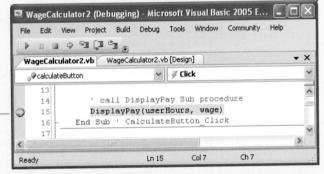

Figure 13.23   Statement calls procedure `DisplayPay`.

Control is transferred to the procedure definition

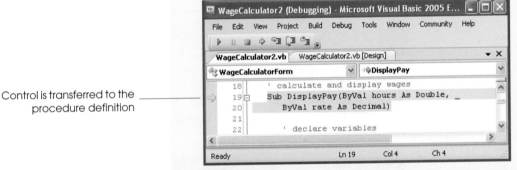

Figure 13.24   Using the debug toolbar's Step Into Button.

6. ***Clicking the Step Over Button.*** Click the Step Over Button to execute the current statement (lines 19–20 in Fig. 13.24) and transfer control to line 27 (Fig. 13.25).

Procedure `CheckOverTime` will be executed without stepping into it when the Step Over Button is clicked

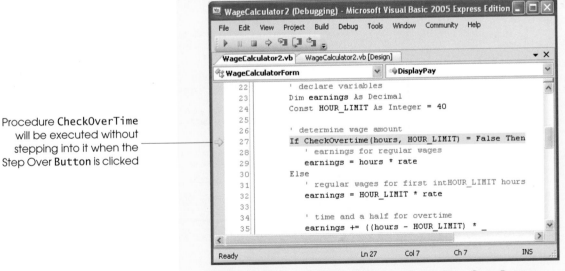

Figure 13.25   Using the debug toolbar's Step Over Button.

(cont.)

7. ***Clicking the Step Over Button again***. Click the Step Over Button. This Button behaves like the Step Into Button when the next statement to execute does not contain a procedure call. If the next statement to execute contains a procedure call, the called procedure executes in its entirety (without transferring control and entering the procedure), and the yellow arrow advances to the next executable line in the current procedure (Fig. 13.26).

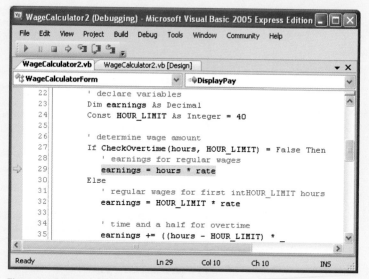

Figure 13.26 Using the debug toolbar's Step Over Button again.

8. ***Setting a breakpoint***. Set a breakpoint at the end of procedure `DisplayPay` in line 40 (End Sub) of Fig. 13.27. You will make use of this breakpoint in the next step.

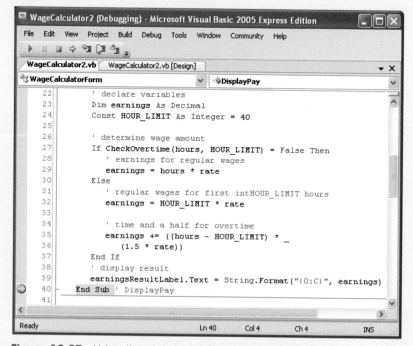

Figure 13.27 Using the debug toolbar's Continue Button.

(cont.)   9. ***Using the Continue Button.*** Clicking the Continue `Button` will execute any statements between the next executable statement and the next breakpoint or the end of the current event handler, whichever comes first. Note that there is one executable statement (line 39) before the breakpoint that was set in *Step 8*. Click the Continue `Button`. The next executable statement is now line 40 (Fig. 13.27). This feature is particularly useful when you have many lines of code before the next breakpoint that you do not want to step through line by line.

10. ***Using the Stop Debugging Button.*** Click the **Stop Debugging** `Button` to end the debugging session and return the IDE to design mode.

11. ***Starting the debugger.*** We have one last feature we wish to present that will require you to start the debugger again. Start the debugger, as you did in *Step 4*, entering the same values as input.

12. ***Using the Step Into Button.*** Keep the breakpoint in line 15 (Fig. 13.22) and remove the breakpoint from line 40. Repeat *Step 5*.

13. ***Clicking the Step Out Button***. After you have stepped into the `DisplayPay` procedure, click the Step Out `Button` to execute the statements in the procedure and return control to line 15, which contains the procedure call. Often, in lengthy procedures, you will want to look at a few key lines of code and then continue debugging the caller's code. This feature is useful for such situations, where you do not want to continue stepping through the entire procedure line by line.

14. ***Clicking the Stop Debugging Button***. Click the Stop Debugging `Button` to end the debugging session.

15. ***Close the IDE.*** Close the Visual Basic IDE by clicking its close box.

SELF-REVIEW

1. During debugging, the _____ `Button` executes the remaining statements in the current procedure call and returns program control to the place where the procedure was called.

   a) Step Into   b) Step Out
   c) Step Over   d) Steps

2. The _____ `Button` behaves like the Step Into `Button` when the next statement to execute does not contain a procedure call.

   a) Step Into   b) Step Out
   c) Step Over   d) Steps

Answers: 1) b. 2) c.

13.6 Wrap-Up

In this tutorial, you learned about the difference between `Function` and `Sub` procedures, and you learned how procedures can be used to better organize an application. This tutorial introduced you to the concept called code reuse, showing how time and effort can be saved by using preexisting code. You used preexisting code provided by the FCL and learned to create your own code that can be used in other applications.

You were introduced to the syntax for creating and invoking the two types of procedures. You learned the components of a procedure, including the procedure header, parameter list, and (in the case of `Function` procedures) the return type and `Return` statement. After learning how to develop and write procedures, you learned about the order of execution that occurs from the line where a procedure is called (invoked) to the procedure definition, and returning control back to the point of invocation. In this tutorial's applications, you created three Function procedures—Square, Maximum and CheckOvertime—and a Sub procedure (DisplayPay).

After creating the procedures in this tutorial, you learned how to debug the procedures in the application by using the Buttons in the debug toolbar. These Buttons (including the Step Into, Step Out and Step Over Buttons) can be used to determine whether a procedure is executing correctly.

In the next tutorial, you learn about such controls as GroupBoxes and DateTime-Pickers and use them to build a **Shipping Time** application. This application controls information about a package being shipped from one location to another.

SKILLS SUMMARY

Invoking a Procedure

- Specify the procedure name and any arguments in parentheses.
- Ensure that the arguments passed match the procedure definition's parameters in number, type and order.

Using a Function Procedure

- Use a Function procedure when a value needs to be returned to the caller.

Creating a Function Procedure

- Use keyword Function to begin the procedure.
- Specify a parameter list declaring each parameter's name and type. In the parameter list, use keyword ByVal in place of keyword Dim.
- Place the keyword As and the return type after the parenthesis that terminates the parameter list.
- Press *Enter* to generate the terminating End Function statement.
- Add code to the procedure's body to perform a specific task.
- Return a value with the Return statement.

Returning a Value from a Function Procedure

- Use the Return keyword followed by the value to be returned.

Creating a Sub Procedure

- Start the procedure header with keyword Sub.
- Specify a parameter list declaring each parameter's name and type. In the parameter list, use keyword ByVal in place of keyword Dim.
- Press *Enter* to generate the terminating End Sub statement.
- Add code to the procedure's body to perform a specific task.

Using the Debug Toolbar

- To execute a procedure while stepping through your code in the debugger, click the **Step Into** Button if you'd like to view the execution of that procedure's body statements.
- To step out of a procedure in the debugger, click the **Step Out** Button to return to the caller.
- When you wish to execute a procedure in your code without stepping through it in the debugger, click the **Step Over** Button.

KEY TERMS

argument—Information provided to a procedure call.

ByVal—The keyword specifying that the calling procedure should pass a copy of its argument's value in the procedure call to the called procedure.

callee—The procedure being called.

caller—The procedure that calls another procedure. Also known as the calling procedure.

divide-and-conquer technique—Constructing large applications from small, manageable pieces to make development and maintenance of large applications easier.

End Function Keywords—Indicates the end of a Function procedure.

End Sub Keywords—Indicates the end of a Sub procedure.

Function keyword—Begins the definition of a Function procedure.

Function procedure—A procedure similar to a Sub procedure, with one important difference: Function procedures return a value to the caller, whereas Sub procedures do not.

invoking a procedure—Causing a procedure to perform its designated task.

Max method of class Math—A Shared method of class Math which returns the greater of its two arguments.

method—A procedure contained in a class.

Parameter Info **feature of the Visual Basic IDE**—Provides the programmer with information about procedures and their arguments.

parameter list—A comma-separated list in which the procedure declares each parameter variable's name and type.

parameter variable—A variable declared in a procedure's parameter list that can be used in the body of the procedure.

procedure—A set of instructions for performing a particular task.

procedure body—The declarations and statements that appear after the procedure header but before the keywords End Sub or End Function. The procedure body contains Visual Basic code that performs actions, generally by manipulating or interacting with the parameters from the parameter list.

procedure call—Invokes a procedure, specifies the procedure name and provides arguments that the callee (the procedure being called) requires to perform its task.

procedure definition—The procedure header, body and ending statement.

procedure header—The first line of a procedure (including the keyword Sub or Function, the procedure name, the parameter list and the Function procedure return type).

procedure name—Follows the keyword Sub or Function and distinguishes one procedure from another. A procedure name can be any valid identifier.

programmer-defined procedure—A procedure created by a programmer to meet the unique needs of a particular application.

Return keyword—Signifies the return statement that sends a value back to the procedure's caller.

Return statement—Used to return a value from a procedure.

return type—Data type of the result returned from a Function procedure.

reusing code—The practice of using existing code to build new code. Reusing code saves time, effort and money.

Sqrt method of class Math—A Shared method of class Math which returns the square root of its argument.

Sub keyword—Begins the definition of a Sub procedure.

Sub procedure—A procedure similar to a Function procedure, with one important difference: Sub procedures do not return a value to the caller, whereas Function procedures do.

CONTROLS, EVENTS, PROPERTIES & METHODS

Math This class provides methods used to perform common arithmetic calculations.

■ *Methods*

Min—Returns the smaller of two numeric values.

Max—Returns the larger of two numeric values.

Sqrt—Returns the square root of a numeric value.

MULTIPLE-CHOICE QUESTIONS

13.1 A procedure defined with keyword Sub _____.

a) must specify a return type   b) does not accept arguments

c) returns a value   d) does not return a value

13.2 The technique of developing large applications from small, manageable pieces is known as _____.

a) divide and conquer   b) returning a value

c) click and mortar   d) a building-block algorithm

13.3 What is the difference between Sub and Function procedures?

    a) Sub procedures return values, Function procedures do not.

    b) Function procedures return values, Sub procedures do not.

    c) Sub procedures accept parameters, Function procedures do not.

    d) Function procedures accept parameters, Sub procedures do not.

13.4 What occurs after a procedure call is made?

    a) Control is given to the called procedure. After the procedure is run, the application continues execution at the point where the procedure call was made.

    b) Control is given to the called procedure. After the procedure is run, the application continues execution with the statement after the called procedure's definition.

    c) The statement before the procedure call is executed.

    d) The application terminates.

13.5 Functions can return _____ value(s).

    a) zero   b) exactly one

    c) one or more   d) any number of

13.6 Which of the following must be true when making a procedure call?

    a) The number of arguments in the procedure call must match the number of parameters in the procedure header.

    b) The argument types must be compatible with their corresponding parameter types.

    c) Both a and b.   d) None of the above.

13.7 Which of the following statements correctly returns the variable value from a Function procedure?

    a) `Return Dim value`   b) `Return value As Integer`

    c) `value Return`   d) `Return value`

13.8 The _____ Button executes the next statement in the application. If the next statement to execute contains a procedure call, the called procedure executes in its entirety.

    a) Step Into   b) Step Out

    c) Step Over   d) Steps

13.9 The first line of a procedure (including the keyword Sub or Function, the procedure name, the parameter list and the Function procedure return type) is known as the procedure _____.

    a) body   b) title

    c) caller   d) header

13.10 Method _____ of class Math calculates the square root of the value passed as an argument.

    a) `SquareRoot`   b) `Root`

    c) `Sqrt`   d) `Square`

EXERCISES

13.11 (*Temperature Converter Application*) Write an application that performs temperature conversions (Fig. 13.28). The application should be capable of performing two types of conversions: degrees Fahrenheit to degrees Celsius, and degrees Celsius to degrees Fahrenheit.

    a) *Copying the template to your working directory.* Copy the directory `C:\Examples\Tutorial13\Exercises\TemperatureConversion` to your `C:\SimplyVB` directory.

    b) *Opening the application's template file.* Double click `TemperatureConversion.sln` in the `TemperatureConversion` directory to open the application.

    c) *Convert Fahrenheit to Celsius.* To convert degrees Fahrenheit to degrees Celsius, use this formula:

```
celsius = (5 / 9) * (fahrenheit - 32)
```

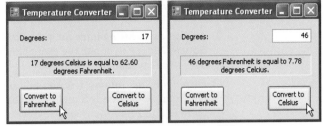

Figure 13.28   **Temperature Converter** GUI.

d) *Convert Celsius to Fahrenheit.* To convert degrees Celsius to degrees Fahrenheit, use this formula:

```
fahrenheit = (9 / 5) * celsius + 32
```

e) *Adding event handlers to your application.* Double click each Button to add the proper event handlers to your application. These event handlers will call procedures (that you will define in the next step) to convert the degrees entered to either Fahrenheit or Celsius. Each event handler will display the result in the application's output Label.

f) *Adding* Function *procedures to your application.* Create Function procedures to perform each conversion, using the formulas above. The user should provide the temperature to convert.

g) *Formatting the temperature output.* To format the temperature information, use the String.Format method. Use F as the formatting code to limit the temperature to two decimal places.

h) *Running the application.* Select **Debug > Start Debugging** to run your application. Enter a temperature value. Click the **Convert to Fahrenheit** Button and verify that the correct output is displayed based on the formula given. Click the **Convert to Celsius** Button and again verify that the output is correct.

i) *Closing the application.* Close your running application by clicking its close box.

j) *Closing the IDE.* Close the Visual Basic IDE by clicking its close box.

13.12 *(Display Square Application)* Write an application that displays a solid square composed of a character input by the user (Fig. 13.29). The user also should input the size.

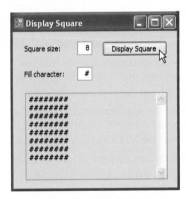

Figure 13.29   **Display Square** application.

a) *Copying the template to your working directory.* Copy the directory C:\Examples\ Tutorial13\Exercises\DisplaySquare to your C:\SimplyVB directory.

b) *Opening the application's template file.* Double click DisplaySquare.sln in the DisplaySquare directory to open the application.

c) *Adding a Sub procedure.* Write a Sub procedure DisplaySquare to display the solid square. The size (the length of each side) should be specified by the Integer parameter size. The character that fills the square should be specified by the String parameter fillCharacter. Use a For...Next statement nested within another For...Next statement to create the square. The outer For...Next specifies what row is currently being displayed. The inner For...Next appends all the characters that form the row to a display String.

d) *Adding an event handler for your Button's Click event.* Double click the **Display Square** Button to create the event handler. Program the event handler to call procedure DisplaySquare.

e) *Displaying the output.* Use the multiline TextBox provided to display the square. For example, if size is 8 and fillCharacter is #, the application should look similar to Fig. 13.29.

f) *Running the application.* Select **Debug > Start Debugging** to run your application. Enter a size for the square (that is, the length of each side) and a fill character. Click the **Display Square** Button. A square should be displayed of the size you specified, using the character you specified.

g) *Closing the application.* Close your running application by clicking its close box.

h) *Closing the IDE.* Close the Visual Basic IDE by clicking its close box.

13.13 (*Miles Per Gallon Application*) Drivers often want to know the miles per gallon their cars get so they can estimate gasoline costs. Develop an application that allows the user to input the number of miles driven and the number of gallons used for a tank of gas.

Figure 13.30 **Miles Per Gallon** application.

a) *Copying the template to your working directory.* Copy the directory C:\Examples\Tutorial13\Exercises\MilesPerGallon to your C:\SimplyVB directory.

b) *Opening the application's template file.* Double click MilesPerGallon.sln in the MilesPerGallon directory to open the application.

c) *Calculating the miles per gallon.* Write a Function procedure MilesPerGallon that takes the number of miles driven and gallons used (entered by the user), calculates the amount of miles per gallon and returns the miles per gallon for a tankful of gas.

d) *Displaying the result.* Create a Click event handler for the **Calculate MPG** Button that invokes the Function procedure MilesPerGallon and displays the result returned from the procedure as in Fig. 13.30.

e) *Running the application.* Select **Debug > Start Debugging** to run your application. Enter a value for the number of miles driven and the amount of gallons used. Click the **Calculate MPG** Button and verify that the correct output is displayed.

f) *Closing the application.* Close your running application by clicking its close box.

g) *Closing the IDE.* Close the Visual Basic IDE by clicking its close box.

What does this code do? ▶ **13.14** What does the following code do? Assume that this procedure is invoked by using Mystery(70, 80).

```
1   Sub Mystery(ByVal number1 As Integer, ByVal _
2       number2 As Integer)
3
4       Dim x As Integer
5       Dim y As Double
6
7       x = number1 + number2
8       y = x / 2
9
```

```
10        If y <= 60 Then
11            resultLabel.Text = "<= 60 "
12        Else
13            resultLabel.Text = "Result is " & y
14        End If
15
16    End Sub ' Mystery
```

What's wrong with this code? ▶ **13.15** Find the error(s) in the following code, which should take an `Integer` value as an argument and return the value of the argument multiplied by two.

```
1    Function TimesTwo(ByVal number As Integer) As Integer
2
3        Dim result As Integer
4
5        result = number * 2
6    End Function ' CheckValue
```

Using the Debugger ▶ **13.16** (*Gas Pump Application*) The **Gas Pump** application (Fig. 13.31) calculates the cost of gas at a local gas station. This gas station charges $1.41 per gallon for **Regular** grade gas, $1.47 per gallon for **Special** grade gas and $1.57 per gallon for **Super+** grade gas. The user enters the number of gallons to purchase and clicks the desired grade. The application calls a Sub procedure to compute the total cost from the number of gallons entered and the selected grade. While testing your application, you noticed that one of your totals was incorrect, given the input.

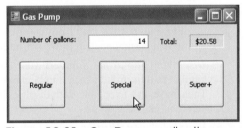

Figure 13.31   **Gas Pump** application executing correctly.

a) *Copying the template to your working directory.* Copy the directory C:\Examples\ Tutorial13\Debugger\GasPumpIncorrect to your C:\SimplyVB directory.

b) *Opening the application's template file.* Double click GasPump.sln in the GasPump-Incorrect directory to open the application.

c) *Running the application.* Select **Debug > Start Debugging** to run your application. Determine which total is incorrect.

d) *Setting a breakpoint.* Set a breakpoint at the beginning of the event handler that is providing incorrect output. For instance, if the **Regular** Button is providing incorrect output when clicked, add a breakpoint at the beginning of that Button's Click event handler. Use the debugger to help find any logic error(s) in the application.

e) *Modifying the application.* Once you have located the error(s), modify the application so that it behaves correctly.

f) *Running the application.* Select **Debug > Start Debugging** to run your application. Enter a number of gallons and click the **Regular**, **Special** and **Super+** Buttons. After each Button is clicked, verify that the total displayed is correct based on the prices given in this exercise's description.

g) *Closing the application.* Close your running application by clicking its close box.

h) *Closing the IDE.* Close the Visual Basic IDE by clicking its close box.

Programming Challenge ▷ **13.17** (*Prime Numbers Application*) An Integer greater than 1 is said to be prime if it is divisible by only 1 and itself. For example, 2, 3, 5 and 7 are prime numbers, but 4, 6, 8 and 9 are not. Write an application that takes two numbers (representing a lower bound and an upper bound) and determines all of the prime numbers within the specified bounds, inclusive.

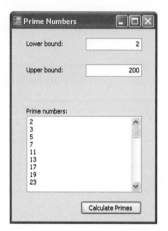 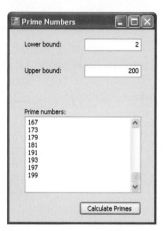

Figure 13.32 Prime Numbers application.

a) *Creating the application.* Create an application named PrimeNumbers and have its GUI appear as shown in Fig. 13.32. Add an event handler for the **Calculate Primes** Button's Click event.

b) *Checking for prime numbers.* Write a Function procedure Prime that returns True if a number is prime, False otherwise.

c) *Limiting user input.* Allow users to enter a lower bound (lower) and an upper bound (upper). Prevent the user from entering bounds less than or equal to 1, or an upper bound that is smaller than the lower bound.

d) *Displaying the prime numbers.* Call Function procedure Prime from your event handler to determine which numbers between the lower and upper bounds are prime. Then have the event handler display the prime numbers in a multiline, scrollable TextBox, as in Fig. 13.32.

e) *Running the application.* Select **Debug > Start Debugging** to run your application. Enter a lower bound and an upper bound that is smaller than the lower bound. Click the **Calculate Primes** Button. You should receive an error message. Enter negative bounds and click the **Calculate Primes** Button. Again, you should receive an error message. Enter valid bounds and click the **Calculate Primes** Button. This time, the primes within that range should be displayed.

f) *Closing the application.* Close your running application by clicking its close box.

g) *Closing the IDE.* Close the Visual Basic IDE by clicking its close box.

Objectives

In this tutorial, you will learn to:
- Create and manipulate **Date** variables.
- Execute code at regular intervals using a **Timer** control.
- Retrieve **Date** input with a **DateTimePicker** control.
- Group controls using a **GroupBox** control.

Outline

Shipping Time Application

Using Dates and Timers

Many companies, from airlines to shipping companies, rely on date and time information in their daily operations. These companies often require applications that reliably perform date and time calculations. In this tutorial, you will create an application that performs calculations using the **Date** structure, which allows you to store and manipulate date and time information. You will also learn how to use a **DateTimePicker** control to retrieve date and time information from the user. Finally, you will learn how to use a **Timer**— a Visual Basic control that allows you to execute code at specified time intervals.

14.1 Test-Driving the Shipping Time Application

In this tutorial, you will build the **Shipping Time** application. This application must meet the following requirements:

> **Application Requirements**
>
> *A seafood distributor has asked you to create an application that will calculate the delivery time for fresh seafood shipped from Portland, Maine, to its distribution center in Las Vegas, Nevada, where only the freshest seafood is accepted. The distributor has arrangements with local airlines to guarantee that seafood will ship on flights that leave either at noon or at midnight. However, for security reasons, the airport requires the distributor to drop off the seafood at the airport at least one hour before each flight. When the distributor specifies the drop-off time, the application should display the delivery time in Las Vegas. This application should take into account the three-hour time difference (it's three hours earlier in Las Vegas) and the six-hour flight time between the two cities. The application should allow the user to select drop-off times within the current day (seafood must be shipped within a day to guarantee freshness). The application should also include a running clock that displays the current time.*

This application calculates the shipment's delivery time from the user's drop-off time, taking into account such factors as transit time and time zones. You will use the **DateTimePicker** control to enable the user to enter the drop-off time.

You will use the Date structure properties and methods to calculate the delivery time. You begin by test-driving the completed application. Then you will learn the additional Visual Basic technologies that you will need to create your own version of this application.

1. ***Opening the completed application.*** Open the directory `C:\Examples\Tutorial14\CompletedApplication\ShippingTime` to locate the **Shipping Time** application. Double click `ShippingTime.sln` to open the application in the Visual Basic IDE.

2. ***Running the Shipping Time application.*** Select **Debug > Start Debugging** to run the application (Fig. 14.1).

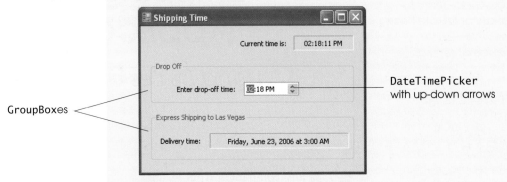

GroupBoxes

DateTimePicker with up-down arrows

Figure 14.1 **Shipping Time** application.

3. ***Entering a drop-off time.*** The default drop-off time is set to your computer's current time when the application is loaded (opened). When you change the drop-off time, the `Label` displaying the delivery time will display the delivery time based on the new time. Note that if you select a time before 11:00 A.M., the shipment will arrive in Las Vegas at 3:00 P.M. If you specify a time between 11:00 A.M. and 11:00 P.M., the shipment will arrive in Las Vegas at 3:00 A.M. the following day. Finally, if you specify a time after 11:00 P.M., the shipment will not arrive until 3:00 P.M. the following day.

    The time displayed in the **Current time is:** `Label` will update to the current time once each second. However, the drop-off time displayed in the `DateTimePicker` will change only if you select different values by using the up and down arrows or by typing in a new value.

4. ***Closing the application.*** Close your running application by clicking its close box.

5. ***Closing the IDE.*** Close the Visual Basic IDE by clicking its close box.

14.2 Date Variables

Choosing the correct data type in which to store information can decrease development time by simplifying code. For example, if you are counting whole numbers, variables of type `Integer` are your best choice; if you need to store monetary values, you should use variables of type `Decimal`. If you want to store date information (such as the day, month, year and time), you could use separate variables to keep track of the month, day of the week, year and other date-related information. This would be a complicated task and could slow the development of applications that require date and time information.

Declaring a Date Variable

The primitive type Date simplifies manipulation, storage and display of date (and time) information. Date is the Visual Basic keyword that corresponds to the DateTime Structure in the FCL. A **Date** variable stores information about a point in time (for example, 12:00:00 A.M. on January 1, 2003). Using code, you can access a Date's properties, including the day, the hour and the minute. Your **Shipping Time** application requires calculations involving time, so you will use Date variables to store and manipulate this information.

The Date type is a structure, so you must use the New keyword when creating a Date value. In the code,

Date constructor ———————————————————————

```
Dim delivery As Date = New Date(2003, 1, 1, 0, 0, 0)
```

Date variable ———————

a new Date variable named delivery is declared. The **New** keyword calls the Date structure's constructor. A **constructor** is a procedure that initializes a class object or structure value when it is created. You will use FCL class constructors in Tutorial 16. You will also learn how to write your own constructors in Tutorial 19. Note that this particular constructor takes six arguments: year, month, day, hour, minute and second. These values are described in Fig. 14.2.

Argument	Range	Description
Initializing a Date variable using New Date(*year*, *month*, *day*, *hour*, *minute*, *second*)		
year	Integer values 1–9999	Specifies the year.
month	Integer values 1–12	Specifies the month of the year.
day	Integer values 1–*number of days in month*	Specifies the day of the month. Each month has 28 to 31 days depending on the month and year.
hour	Integer values 0–23	Specifies the hour of the day. The value 0 represents 12:00 A.M.
minute	Integer values 0–59	Specifies the minute of the hour.
second	Integer values 0–59	Specifies the number of elapsed seconds in the current minute.

Figure 14.2 Date constructor arguments.

Using Date Members

After assigning a value to a Date variable, you can access its properties using the member-access (dot) operator, as follows:

```
year = delivery.Year      ' retrieves Date delivery's year
month = delivery.Month    ' retrieves Date delivery's month
day = delivery.Day        ' retrieves Date delivery's day
hour = delivery.Hour      ' retrieves Date delivery's hour
minute = delivery.Minute  ' retrieves Date delivery's minute
second = delivery.Second  ' retrieves Date delivery's second
```

In this tutorial, you will use several Date properties and methods that can be accessed through the member-access operator.

Values in Date variables cannot be added like numeric-primitive-data types such as Integers and Decimals. Instead of using arithmetic operators to add or subtract values in Date variables, you must call the correct method, using the member-access operator. Figure 14.3 demonstrates how to perform various calculations with Date variables.

Visual Basic .NET statement	Result
Assume delivery *has been initialized with a* Date *value.*	
delivery = delivery.AddHours(3)	Add 3 hours.
delivery = delivery.AddMinutes(-5)	Subtract 5 minutes.
delivery = delivery.AddDays(1)	Add 1 day.
delivery = delivery.AddMinutes(30)	Add 30 minutes.
delivery = delivery.AddHours(-12)	Subtract 12 hours.

Figure 14.3 Date methods that perform various calculations.

Note that an "add" method does not actually change the value of the Date variable on which it is called. Instead, each "add" method returns a Date value containing the result of the calculation. To change the value of Date variable delivery, you must assign to delivery the value returned by the "add" method.

Visual Basic provides a simple way to assign the current date and time to a Date variable. You can use the **Now** property to assign your computer's current date and time to a Date variable:

```
Dim currentTime As Date = Date.Now
```

Much like methods MessageBox.Show and String.Format, you can access the Now property of the Date structure by following the name of the structure with the member-access operator and the name of the property. Note that this assignment does not require keyword New. This is because the Date.Now property returns a Date value.

Now that you are familiar with Date variables, you will design the **Shipping Time** application by using two new controls—the GroupBox control and the DateTimePicker control. A **GroupBox** control groups related controls visually by drawing a labeled box around them. The **DateTimePicker** control allows users to enter date and time information.

SELF-REVIEW

1. The _____ property of the Date structure retrieves your computer's current date and time.

   a) Time

   b) Now

   c) CurrentTime

   d) DateTime

2. The fourth argument to the Date constructor specifies the variable's _____.

   a) day

   b) year

   c) hour

   d) minute

Answers: 1) b. 2) c.

14.3 Building the Shipping Time Application: Design Elements

You are now ready to begin analyzing the problem statement and developing pseudocode. The following pseudocode describes the basic operation of the **Shipping Time** application:

When the Form loads:
    Set range of possible drop-off times to any time in the current day
    Determine the shipment's delivery time
    Display the shipment's delivery time

When the user changes the drop-off time:
    Determine the shipment's delivery time
    Display the shipment's delivery time

After one second has elapsed:
    Update the current time displayed

When the DisplayDeliveryTime procedure gets called:
    Determine the time the shipment's flight will depart
    Add three hours to determine the delivery time (takes into account 6 hours
        for time of flight minus 3 hours for the time difference)
    Display the delivery time

When the DepartureTime procedure gets called:

    Select correct Case based on the hour the shipment was dropped off

      Case where the drop-off hour is between the values 0 and 10
        Delivery set to depart on noon flight of current day

      Case where the drop off hour is 23
        Delivery set to depart on noon flight of next day

      Case where none of the preceding Cases match
        Delivery set to depart on midnight flight of current day

Now that you have test-driven the **Shipping Time** application and studied its pseudocode representation, you will use an ACE table to help you convert the pseudocode to Visual Basic. Figure 14.4 lists the actions, controls and events that will help you complete your own version of this application.

Action/Control/Event (ACE) Table for the Shipping Time Application

Action	Control	Event/Method
Label the application's controls	currentTime-IsLabel, dropOffLabel, deliveryTime-Label	Application is run
	ShippingTime-Form	Load
Set range of possible drop-off times to any time in the current day	dropOff-DateTimePicker	
Determine the shipment's delivery time	dropOff-DateTimePicker	
Display the shipment's delivery time	lasVegasTime-Label	
	dropOff-DateTimePicker	ValueChanged
Determine the shipment's delivery time	dropOff-DateTimePicker	
Display the shipment's delivery time	lasVegasTime-Label	
	clockTimer	Tick
Update and display the current time	currentTime-Label	
		Display-DeliveryTime
Determine the time the shipment's flight will depart	dropOff-DateTimePicker	
Add three hours to determine the delivery time		
Display the delivery time	lasVegasTime-Label	

Figure 14.4   ACE table for the **Shipping Time** application. (Part 1 of 2.)

(cont.)	Action	Control	Event/Method
			DepartureTime
	Select correct Case based on the hour the shipment was dropped off	dropOff- DateTimePicker	
	Case where drop-off hour is 0–10		
	Delivery set to depart on noon flight		
	Case where drop-off hour is 23		
	Delivery set to depart on noon flight of next day		
	Case were none of the preceding Cases match		
	Delivery set to depart on midnight flight		

Figure 14.4 ACE table for the **Shipping Time** application. (Part 2 of 2.)

The following box demonstrates how to insert a GroupBox control into your application.

Placing Controls in a GroupBox

1. *Copying the template to your working directory.* Copy the C:\Examples\ Tutorial14\TemplateApplication\ShippingTime to your C:\SimplyVB directory.

2. *Opening the Shipping Time application's template file.* Double click Ship-pingTime.sln in the ShippingTime directory to open the application in the Visual Basic IDE.

3. *Displaying the template Form.* Double click ShippingTime.vb in the **Solution Explorer** window to display the Form in the IDE.

4. *Inserting a GroupBox control in the Form.* The template includes a Group-Box that displays the seafood-shipment delivery time. Add a second Group-Box to contain the drop-off time by double clicking the **GroupBox** control,

in the **Toolbox**. Change the Text property to Drop Off and the Name property to dropOffGroupBox. Change the Location property to 16, 56 and the Size property to 328, 64. After these modifications, your Form should look like Fig. 14.5.

> **Good Programming Practice**
>
> Append the GroupBox suffix to GroupBox control names.

Newly created GroupBox displaying the text **Drop Off**

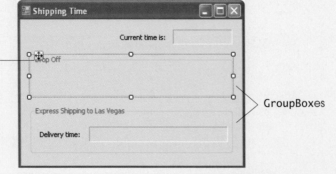

Figure 14.5 GroupBox controls on the **Shipping Time** Form.

 **GUI Design Tip**

GroupBox titles should be concise and should use book-title capitalization.

(cont.)

5. ***Creating Labels inside the GroupBox.*** To place a Label inside the GroupBox, click the **Label** tab in the **Toolbox**, then click inside the GroupBox (Fig. 14.6). Change the Text property of the Label to Enter drop-off time: and the Name property to dropOffLabel. Then change the position and size of the Label by setting its Location property to 40, 32, the AutoSize property to false, and the Size property to 104, 21. Change the Label's TextAlign property to MiddleLeft.

Before clicking inside the GroupBox

Figure 14.6 Adding a Label to a GroupBox.

Note that the Location values you entered are measured from the top-left corner of the GroupBox and not from the top-left corner of the Form. Objects, that contain controls, such as Forms, GroupBoxes and Panels (which you will use in Tutorial 19), are called **containers**. Location values for controls in an application are measured from the top-left corner of the object that contains them.

If a GroupBox is placed over a control that is already on the Form, the control will be behind the GroupBox (that is, the GroupBox hides the control by covering it). To avoid this problem, remove all controls from the area in which you wish to place the GroupBox control before inserting it. You can then either drag and drop existing controls into the GroupBox or add new controls as needed by using the method described earlier.

6. ***Saving the project.*** Select **File > Save All** to save your changes.

GUI Design Tip

Use GroupBoxes to group related controls on the Form visually.

You have now added a GroupBox and a Label to the **Shipping Time** application to display the drop-off time. In the following box, you will add a DateTimePicker control to retrieve the drop-off time from the user.

Recall that the DateTimePicker retrieves date and time information from the user. The DateTimePicker allows you to select from a variety of predefined date and time formats to present to the user (for example, date formats like 12/31/02 and December 31, 2002; and time formats like 2:00 PM and 14:00) or you can create your own format. The date and time information is then stored in a variable of type Date, which you can manipulate using Date methods. Note that the format limits the date and/or time information the user can specify. However, the format used to present the date and/or time does not alter the Date value stored in the DateTimePicker.

Creating and Customizing the DateTimePicker

1. ***Adding the DateTimePicker.*** To add a DateTimePicker to your application, click the **DateTimePicker** control,

(cont.)

in the **Toolbox**, then click to the right of dropOffLabel to place the DateTimePicker. Your Form should look similar to Fig. 14.7. (Your control will contain your computer's current date.)

2. *Modifying the DateTimePicker.* With the DateTimePicker selected, change the Name property of the DateTimePicker to dropOffDateTime-Picker.

GUI Design Tip

Use a DateTimePicker to retrieve date and time information from a user.

GUI Design Tip

Each DateTimePicker should have a corresponding descriptive Label.

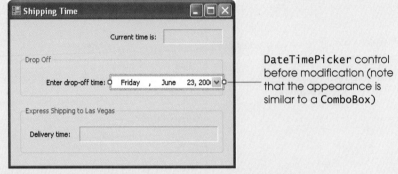

Figure 14.7 DateTimePicker control on the Form.

Align the DateTimePicker with its Label by setting its Size property to 88, 21 and its Location property to 152, 32. Next, change its **Format** property to Custom. This indicates that you will specify how the date will appear in the DateTimePicker.

3. *Specifying a custom display format.* When the DateTimePicker's Format property is set to Custom, it uses the custom format that you specify in the **CustomFormat** property. Note that the DateTimePicker now displays the date in the format 1/1/2003, the default format when the CustomFormat property has not been set.

Set the value of the CustomFormat property to hh:mm tt. The "hh" displays the hour as a number from 01 to 12, the ":" inserts a colon and the "mm" indicates that the number of minutes from 00 to 59 should follow the colon. The "tt" indicates that AM or PM should appear, depending on the time of day. Note that this property eliminates the problem of a user entering a letter or symbol when the application expects a number—the DateTimePicker will not allow values in any format other than what you specify in the CustomFormat property.

Good Programming Practice

Append the DateTimePicker suffix to DateTimePicker control names.

4. *Using up-down arrows in the DateTimePicker.* Set the DateTimePicker's **ShowUpDown** property to True. This setting allows the user to select the date or time by clicking the up or down arrows that appear on the right side of the control, much like a NumericUpDown control. When the property is set to False (which is the default), a down arrow will appear on the right side of the control (Fig. 14.7), much like a ComboBox. Clicking the down arrow will cause a month calendar to appear, allowing the user to select a date (but not a time). A demonstration of the month calendar is shown in the Controls, Events, Properties & Methods section at the end of this tutorial. The user only needs to enter the time of day, so you will use up-down arrows to display the time (Fig. 14.8).

GUI Design Tip

If the user is to specify a time of day or a date and time, set the Date-TimePicker's ShowUpDown property to True. If the user is to specify only a date, set the DateTimePicker's ShowUpDown property to False to allow the user to select a day from the month calendar.

5. *Saving the project.* Select **File > Save All** to save your modified code.

(cont.)

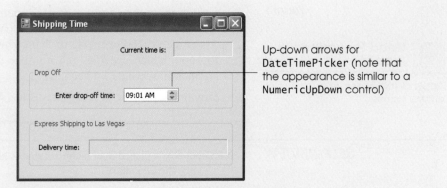

Up-down arrows for
`DateTimePicker` (note that
the appearance is similar to a
`NumericUpDown` control)

Error-Prevention Tip

If the user is to specify a date and/or time, use a `DateTimePicker` control to prevent the user from entering invalid date or time values.

Figure 14.8   Customized `DateTimePicker` control on the `Form`.

The final control you will add to the `Form` is a `Timer`. You will use the `Timer` to place a clock on the `Form` so that users can see the current time of day while using the application.

Creating a Timer Control

1. *Adding a Timer control.* A **Timer** control is an object that can "wake up" every millisecond (1/1000 of a second) by generating a **Tick** event. By default, the `Timer` "wakes up" every 100 milliseconds (1/10 of a second). Each time the `Tick` event is generated, its event handler is executed. You can customize the "wake period" (the amount of time between `Timer` `Tick` events) and the code it executes (the event handler for the `Tick` event) so that a certain task is performed once every "wake up" period.

   Add a `Timer` to the `Form` by clicking the **Timer** control,

    Timer

   in the **Toolbox** and dragging and dropping it anywhere on the `Form`. Note that the `Timer` does not actually appear on the `Form`; it appears below the Windows Form Designer in an area called the **component tray** (Fig. 14.9). The `Timer` control is placed in the component tray because it is not part of the graphical user interface—users never see the `Timer` control.

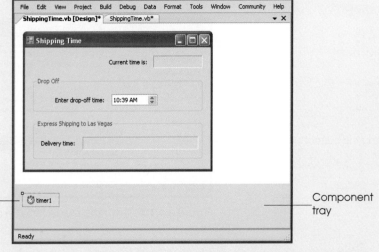

Timer control ———

Component tray

Figure 14.9   `Timer` control is displayed in the component tray.

(cont.)

Good Programming Practice

Append the Timer suffix to Timer control names.

2. **Customizing the Timer control.** Rename the Timer by setting its Name property to clockTimer. To allow the Timer's Tick event to be raised, set the Timer's Enabled property to True. Then set the Timer's **Interval** property to 1000, which specifies the number of milliseconds between Tick events (1,000 milliseconds = 1 second).

3. **Saving the project.** Select **File > Save All** to save your modified code.

SELF-REVIEW

1. If a GroupBox is placed over a control that is already on the Form, the control will be _____ the GroupBox.

   a) replaced by   b) inside

   c) behind   d) in front of

2. Setting the Format property of the DateTimePicker control to _____ indicates that you will specify how the date will appear in the DateTimePicker.

   a) Custom   b) Unique

   c) User   d) Other

Answers: 1) c. 2) a.

14.4 Creating the Shipping Time Application: Inserting Code

Now that you have completed the visual design of the **Shipping Time** application, you will complete the application by inserting code. You will begin coding the application's functionality by creating a clock on the application that updates the current time every second. You will then write code that displays the delivery time from Portland to Las Vegas. You will implement this feature by inserting code that is run when the Form loads or whenever the user specifies a new drop-off time. In the following box, you will write the code to create the clock.

Coding the Shipping Time Application's Clock

1. **Inserting code to handle the Timer's Tick event.** Double click the Timer control in the component tray to generate the empty event handler for the Tick event. (A Tick event is raised once per Interval, as set in the Timer's Interval property.) Add lines 6–8 of Fig. 14.10 to the body of the event handler. Be sure to format the event handler as shown in Fig. 14.10 to ensure that your line numbers match those in the text.

Printing the current time —

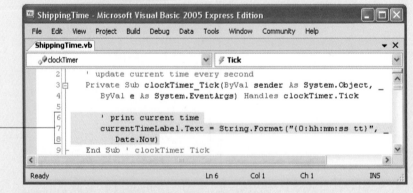

Figure 14.10 Inserting code for a Tick event.

(cont.)

Lines 3–9 display the event handler for the `Tick` event, which executes every second. `Date` property `Now` retrieves your computer's time when it is accessed. The event handler takes this information and formats it to match the format you specify, `"hh:mm:ss tt"`. The `Text` property of `currentTimeLabel` is then set to the formatted `String` for display to the user. Recall that the 0 corresponds to `Date.Now` and the text following the first colon contains your format information. You are already familiar with the purpose of `hh:mm` and `tt`. The `:ss` following `mm` indicates that a colon followed by the number of seconds (00–59) should be displayed.

2. ***Saving the project.*** Select **File > Save All** to save your modified code.

Now that you have coded your application's clock, using the `Timer`'s `Tick` event handler, you will insert code to display a delivery time when the application opens. You will begin by creating a `Load` event handler for your application.

Using Code to Display a Delivery Time	1. ***Adding the ShippingTimeForm_Load event handler.*** When an application runs, the `Form` is displayed. However, sometimes you also want a specific action to occur when the application opens but before the `Form` displays. To run code when the application first opens, create an event handler for the **Load** event. To create a `Load` event handler, return to the Windows Form Designer by clicking the **ShippingTime.vb [Design]** tab. Double click an empty area of the `Form` to generate the `Load` event handler and enter code view.
	2. ***Storing the current date.*** Add line 16 from Fig. 14.11 into the `Load` event handler. Line 16 stores the current date in variable `currentTime`. (You will store the date as a variable so that you can preserve information about the current date for use later in the event handler.) Be sure to add the comments and line-continuation characters as shown in Fig. 14.11 so that the line numbers in your code match those presented in this tutorial.

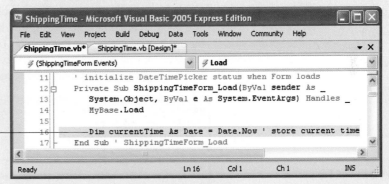

Storing the current time in `currentTime`

Figure 14.11   Storing the current time.

3. ***Setting the drop-off hours.*** Add lines 18–23 of Fig. 14.12 to the `ShippingTimeForm_Load` event handler. These lines set the `MinDate` and `MaxDate` properties for `dropOffDateTimePicker`. The **MinDate** property specifies the earliest value that the `DateTimePicker` will allow the user to enter. The **MaxDate** property specifies the latest value that the `DateTimePicker` will allow the user to enter. Together, these two properties set the range of drop-off times from which the user can select.

(cont.)

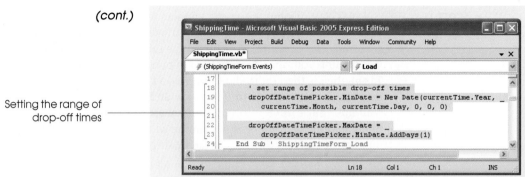

Setting the range of drop-off times

Figure 14.12 Setting the `MinDate` and `MaxDate` properties.

To guarantee freshness, the seafood shipment should be dropped off at the airline within the current day; therefore, the earliest drop-off time (`MinDate`) is set to 12:00 A.M. of the current day (lines 19–20), and the latest drop-off time (`MaxDate`) is set to 12:00 A.M. the following day (lines 22–23). Note that the `MaxDate` value is calculated by adding one day to the `MinDate` value using the `AddDays` method. Recall that the `AddDays` method does not change the `Date` value on which it operates—it returns a new `Date` value. This value is assigned to the `MaxDate` property in line 22.

The `Date` constructor (called in line 19) creates a value that stores a time. Recall that the first parameter is the year, the second is the month and the third is the day. The last three parameters specify the hour, minute and number of seconds. A `Date` variable's `Year` property returns the value of its year as an `Integer` (for example, 2003). Its `Month` property returns the value of the `Date` variable's month as an `Integer` (for example, 6 for June). Finally, the `Date` variable's `Day` property returns the day of the month (an `Integer` between 1 and 31, depending on the month and year). You assigned to the `currentTime` variable the value of the current time (using `Date.Now`); therefore, the first three arguments combine to specify the current date.

4. ***Calling the DisplayDeliveryTime procedure.*** Add lines 25–26 of Fig. 14.13 to call the `DisplayDeliveryTime` procedure. Note that `DisplayDelivery-Time` is underlined in blue. This is due to the syntax error you introduce when you call a procedure that has not yet been written. You will write this procedure later in this tutorial. The `DisplayDeliveryTime` calculates the delivery time in Las Vegas and displays the result in the **Delivery time:** `Label`.

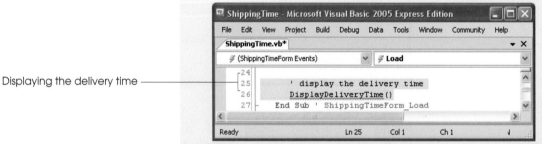

Displaying the delivery time

Figure 14.13 Calling the `DisplayDeliveryTime` procedure.

5. ***Saving the project.*** Select **File > Save All** to save your modified code.

So far, you have added functionality that calculates the delivery time and calls `DisplayDeliveryTime` when the application runs initially. However, you should allow a user to select any drop-off time and instantly see when the seafood shipment will be delivered. In the following box, you will learn how to handle the `DateTime-`

Picker's **ValueChanged** event, which is raised when the user changes the time in the DateTimePicker.

Coding the ValueChanged Event Handler	1. ***Creating the ValueChanged event handler.*** Click the **ShippingTime.vb [Design]** tab. Double click the DateTimePicker control dropOffDateTime-Picker to generate the ValueChanged event handler.
	2. ***Inserting code in the event handler.*** Insert lines 34–35 of Fig. 14.14 into the event handler. This code will run when the user changes the time in the DateTimePicker. Be sure to add the comments and line-continuation characters as shown in Fig. 14.14 so that the line numbers in your code match those presented in this tutorial.

Calculating and displaying the delivery time

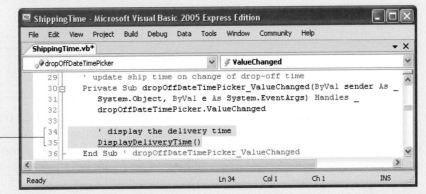

Figure 14.14   Inserting code in the **ValueChanged** event handler.

The ValueChanged event handler also uses the DisplayDeliveryTime procedure to calculate and display the delivery time in Las Vegas. In the next box, you will write the DisplayDeliveryTime procedure, after which the syntax error will no longer appear.

3. ***Saving the solution.*** Select **File > Save All** to save your modified code.

Though you have called the DisplayDeliveryTime procedure in two event handlers, you still need to write the procedure. Next, you will use Date methods to display the delivery time in an output Label.

Coding the DisplayDeliveryTime Procedure	1. ***Creating the DisplayDeliveryTime procedure.*** Add lines 38–48 of Fig. 14.15 below the ValueChanged event handler. Line 42 calls the DepartureTime procedure. Note that DepartureTime is underlined in blue. This is due to the syntax error you introduce when you call a procedure that has not yet been written. You will write this procedure in the following box. The DepartureTime procedure determines which flight (midnight or noon) the seafood shipment will use. It returns a Date value representing the flight's departure time. Line 42 stores this value in the Date variable delivery.
	2. ***Calculating and displaying the delivery time.*** Line 45 calculates the delivery time by adding three hours to the departure time (see the discussion following this box). Lines 46–47 display the Las Vegas delivery time by calling the Date structure's ToLongDateString and ToShortTimeString methods. A Date variable's **ToLongDateString** method returns the date as a String in the format "Wednesday, October 30, 2002." A Date variable's **ToShortTimeString** returns the time as a String in the format "4:00 PM."
	3. ***Saving the project.*** Select **File > Save All** to save your modified code.

(cont.)

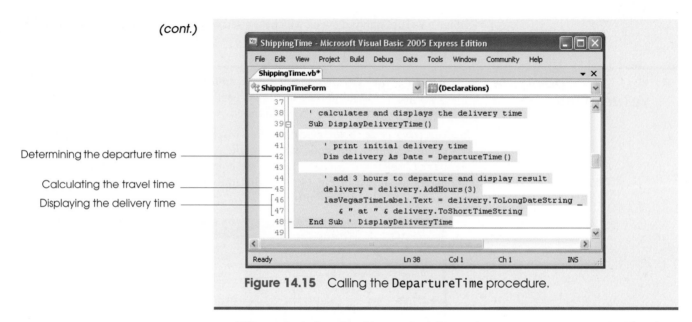

Determining the departure time

Calculating the travel time

Displaying the delivery time

Figure 14.15   Calling the DepartureTime procedure.

When calculating the shipment's delivery time, you must account for the time-zone difference and the flight time. For instance, if you send a shipment from Portland to Las Vegas, it will travel west three time zones (the time in Las Vegas is three hours earlier) and spend six hours in transit. If you drop off the shipment at 5:00 P.M. in Portland, the shipment will leave on the midnight flight and arrive in Las Vegas at

12:00 A.M. + *(time zone change + flight time)* = 12:00 A.M. + *(-3 + 6) hours,*

which is 3:00 A.M. Las Vegas time. Similarly, if the shipment takes the noon flight to Las Vegas, it will arrive at 3:00 P.M. in Las Vegas.

To complete the application, you need to code the DepartureTime procedure. You will use a Select Case statement and Date methods to return a Date containing the departure time (noon or midnight) for the seafood shipment's flight.

Coding the
DepartureTime
Procedure

1. ***Writing the DepartureTime procedure and declaring variables.*** Insert lines 50–55 of Fig. 14.16 into your code below the DisplayDeliveryTime procedure. Line 53 stores the current date in the Date variable currentDate. Line 54 declares the Date variable departTime, the variable you will use to store the DepartureTime Function procedure's return value.

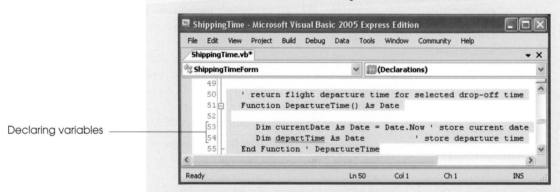

Declaring variables

Figure 14.16   Inserting procedure DepartureTime into the application.

(cont.)

2. ***Determining which flight the shipment uses.*** Insert lines 56–72 of Fig. 14.17 after the variable declarations and before the End Function statement. The Select Case statement that begins at line 57 uses the hour specified by the user in the DateTimePicker as the controlling expression. The value selected by the user in the DateTimePicker is located in its **Value** property. The Date structure's Hour property returns the hour of the Date stored in the DateTimePicker's Value property.

The body of the first Case statement (line 59) executes if the value in the DateTimePicker is between midnight (Hour = 0) and 10:59 A.M. (Hour = 10). If the drop-off time occurs between midnight and 10:59:59 A.M., the seafood shipment takes the noon flight to Las Vegas (recall that the shipment leaves for the airport one hour before the flight leaves). The body of the first Case (lines 60–61) then stores the departure time of noon on the current day in the return variable departTime.

The body of the next Case statement (line 63) executes if the value in the DateTimePicker is between 11:00 P.M. and 11:59 P.M. (Hour = 23). If the drop-off time occurs between 11:00 P.M. and 11:59 P.M, the seafood shipment takes the noon flight to Las Vegas the next day. The body of this Case (lines 64–66) then stores the departure time of noon on the next day in the return variable departTime.

The body of the Case Else statement (line 68) executes if the controlling expression of neither of the other two Case statements evaluates to True (the value in the DateTimePicker is between 11:00 A.M. and 10:59 P.M.). In this case, the seafood shipment takes the midnight flight to Las Vegas. The body of this Case (lines 69–71) then stores the departure time of midnight in the return variable departTime. Note that because midnight occurs on the following day, the Date variable representing midnight should contain a Day property value corresponding to the next day. Line 69 ensures that this occurs.

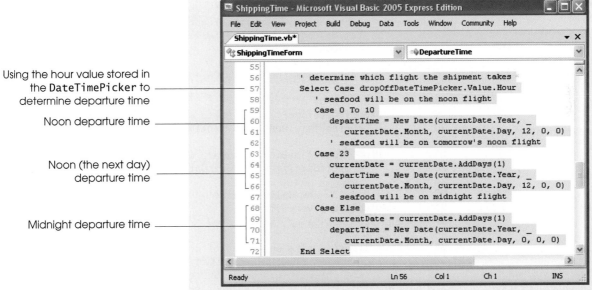

Using the hour value stored in the DateTimePicker to determine departure time

Noon departure time

Noon (the next day) departure time

Midnight departure time

Figure 14.17 Determining the seafood shipment's flight departure time.

3. ***Returning the delivery time.*** Insert line 73 of Fig. 14.18 into the DepartureTime procedure following the End Select statement. Line 73 returns the Date value containing the flight departure time.

4. ***Running the application.*** Select **Debug > Start Debugging** to run your application.

(cont.)

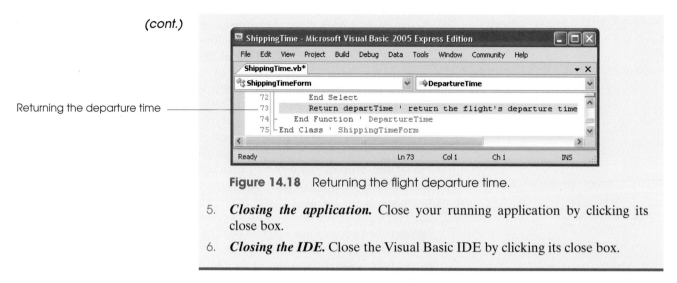

Returning the departure time

Figure 14.18 Returning the flight departure time.

5. ***Closing the application.*** Close your running application by clicking its close box.

6. ***Closing the IDE.*** Close the Visual Basic IDE by clicking its close box.

Figure 14.19 presents the source code for the **Shipping Time** application. The lines of code that contain new programming concepts that you learned in this tutorial are highlighted.

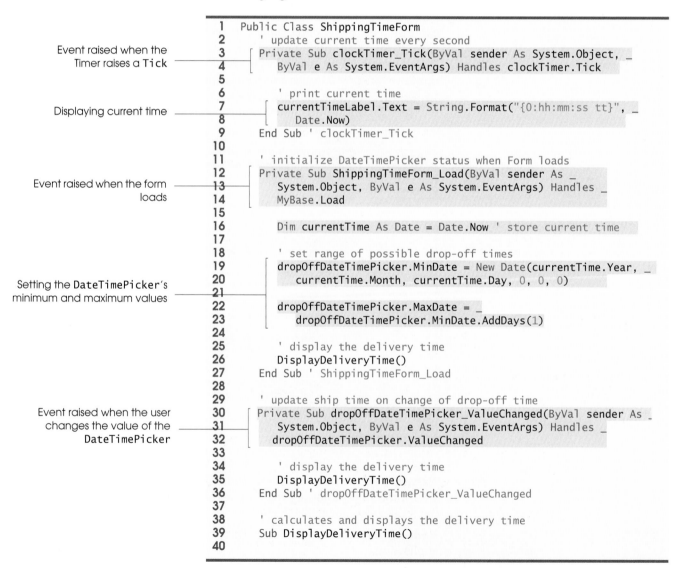

Event raised when the Timer raises a Tick

Displaying current time

Event raised when the form loads

Setting the DateTimePicker's minimum and maximum values

Event raised when the user changes the value of the DateTimePicker

```
1  Public Class ShippingTimeForm
2     ' update current time every second
3     Private Sub clockTimer_Tick(ByVal sender As System.Object, _
4        ByVal e As System.EventArgs) Handles clockTimer.Tick
5
6        ' print current time
7        currentTimeLabel.Text = String.Format("{0:hh:mm:ss tt}", _
8           Date.Now)
9     End Sub ' clockTimer_Tick
10
11    ' initialize DateTimePicker status when Form loads
12    Private Sub ShippingTimeForm_Load(ByVal sender As _
13       System.Object, ByVal e As System.EventArgs) Handles _
14       MyBase.Load
15
16       Dim currentTime As Date = Date.Now ' store current time
17
18       ' set range of possible drop-off times
19       dropOffDateTimePicker.MinDate = New Date(currentTime.Year, _
20          currentTime.Month, currentTime.Day, 0, 0, 0)
21
22       dropOffDateTimePicker.MaxDate = _
23          dropOffDateTimePicker.MinDate.AddDays(1)
24
25       ' display the delivery time
26       DisplayDeliveryTime()
27    End Sub ' ShippingTimeForm_Load
28
29    ' update ship time on change of drop-off time
30    Private Sub dropOffDateTimePicker_ValueChanged(ByVal sender As _
31       System.Object, ByVal e As System.EventArgs) Handles _
32       dropOffDateTimePicker.ValueChanged
33
34       ' display the delivery time
35       DisplayDeliveryTime()
36    End Sub ' dropOffDateTimePicker_ValueChanged
37
38    ' calculates and displays the delivery time
39    Sub DisplayDeliveryTime()
40
```

Figure 14.19 **Shipping Time** application code. (Part 1 of 2.)

Calculating and displaying the
delivery time in Las Vegas

Using a **Select Case** statement
to determine departure time

```
41          ' print initial delivery time
42          Dim delivery As Date = DepartureTime()
43
44          ' add 3 hours to departure and display result
45          delivery = delivery.AddHours(3)
46          lasVegasTimeLabel.Text = delivery.ToLongDateString _
47             & " at " & delivery.ToShortTimeString
48       End Sub ' DisplayDeliveryTime
49
50       ' returns flight departure time for selected drop-off time
51       Function DepartureTime() As Date
52
53          Dim currentDate As Date = Date.Now ' store current date
54          Dim departTime As Date              ' store departure time
55
56          ' determine which flight the shipment takes
57          Select Case dropOffDateTimePicker.Value.Hour
58             ' seafood will be on the noon flight
59             Case 0 To 10
60                departTime = New Date(currentDate.Year, _
61                   currentDate.Month, currentDate.Day, 12, 0, 0)
62             ' seafood will be on tomorrow's noon flight
63             Case 23
64                currentDate = currentDate.AddDays(1)
65                departTime = New Date(currentDate.Year, _
66                   currentDate.Month, currentDate.Day, 12, 0, 0)
67             ' seafood will be on midnight flight
68             Case Else
69                currentDate = currentDate.AddDays(1)
70                departTime = New Date(currentDate.Year, _
71                   currentDate.Month, currentDate.Day, 0, 0, 0)
72          End Select
73          Return departureTime ' return the flight's departure time
74       End Function ' DepartureTime
75    End Class ' ShippingTimeForm
```

Figure 14.19   Shipping Time application code. (Part 2 of 2.)

SELF-REVIEW   1. DateTimePicker properties _____ and _____ specify the earliest and latest
dates that can be selected, respectively.

a) MinDate, MaxDate   b) Now, Later

c) Minimum, Maximum   d) Early, Late

Answers: 1) d. 2) a.

14.5 Wrap-Up

In this tutorial, you learned how to use the Date type, a structure for manipulating time and date information. You used variables of this type to calculate and display delivery times in your **Shipping Time** application. To help users enter date and time information, you used a DateTimePicker control. You observed how a DateTime-Picker control can display custom date and time formats and limit user input. To help you group controls on the Form visually, you used the GroupBox control. You also learned how to use the Timer control on the Form, which allowed your application to execute code every specified number of milliseconds.

You then learned how to use three new event handlers to help you complete the **Shipping Time** application. You learned that the Form's Load event handler allows your application to execute code when the application is opened initially. You used this event to set initial values in your application. You then learned how to use the DateTimePicker control's ValueChanged event handler, which allows you to execute code when the control's value changes. You used this event handler to update the delivery time each time the user entered a new time. Finally, you learned about the Timer's Tick event handler, which you used to update and display the current time in a Label that serves as a clock.

In the next tutorial, you will use the **Fund Raiser** to introduce two programming concepts: arguments and scope rules. Learning these concepts will help you build more powerful and dependable applications because you will understand how Visual Basic keeps track of variables throughout your application.

SKILLS SUMMARY

Storing and Manipulating Date and Time Information

- Use a Date variable to store and manipulate date and time information. A Date variable stores information about a point in time (for example, 12:00:00 A.M. on January 1, 2003). This information can be formatted for display in predefined long or short formats or in custom (programmer-defined) formats.

Using Date variables

- Use keyword New to declare a new Date value.
- Use property Date.Now to obtain your computer's current date and time.
- Use the member-access operator to access properties of a Date variable, such as Years, Hours, etc.
- Use Date methods, such as AddHours and AddDays, to add or subtract time from values in Date variables. Then assign the value returned by the method to a Date variable.

Using a GroupBox Control

- Use a GroupBox control to group related controls visually. To add a GroupBox to the Form, double click the **GroupBox** control in the **Toolbox**.
- Use property Text to configure the title of a GroupBox.

Placing Controls Inside a GroupBox

- Place a control inside the GroupBox by clicking the control's name in the **Toolbox** and clicking inside the GroupBox.

Using the DateTimePicker Control

- Use a DateTimePicker control to get date and time information from the user.
- Set property Format to Custom to indicate that you will specify how the date will appear in the DateTimePicker. The format is specified in property CustomFormat.
- Set property ShowUpDown to True to allow the user to select the date or time by clicking an up or down arrow. If this property's value is False, a monthly calendar will drop down, allowing the user to pick a date.

Using the Timer Control

- Use a Timer control to execute code (the Tick event handler) at specified intervals. To add a Timer control to the Form, click **Timer** in the **Windows Forms** tab of the **Toolbox**, and click anywhere on the Form. The Timer control will appear in the component tray.
- Customize the time between Tick events by using the Interval property, which specifies the number of milliseconds between Tick events.
- Set the Enabled property to True so that the Tick event is raised once per Interval.

KEY TERMS

component tray—The area below the Windows Form Designer that contains controls, such as Timers, that are not part of the graphical user interface.

constructor—A procedure that initializes a class object or structure value when it is created.

container—An object that contains controls such as a GroupBox.

CustomFormat property of a DateTimePicker control—The DateTimePicker property that contains the programmer-specified format string with which to display the date and/or time when DateTimePicker Format property is set to Custom.

Date variable—A variable of type Date, capable of storing date and time data.

DateTimePicker control—Retrieves date and time information from the user.

Format property of a DateTimePicker control—The DateTimePicker property that allows the programmer to specify a predefined or custom format with which to display the date and/or time.

GroupBox control—Groups related controls visually.

Interval property of a Timer control—The Timer property that specifies the number of milliseconds between Tick events.

Load event of a Form—Raised when an application initially executes.

MaxDate property of a DateTimePicker control—The DateTimePicker property that specifies the latest value that the DateTimePicker will allow the user to enter.

MinDate property of a DateTimePicker control—The DateTimePicker property that specifies the earliest value that the DateTimePicker will allow the user to enter.

New keyword—Used to call a constructor when creating an object.

Now property—The property of structure Date that retrieves your computer's current time.

ShowUpDown property of a DateTimePicker control—The DateTimePicker property that, when true, allows the user to specify the time using up and down arrows, and, when false, allows the user to specify the date using a calendar.

Tick event of a Timer control—Raised after the number of milliseconds specified in the Timer control's Interval property has elapsed (if Enabled is True).

Timer control—Wakes up at specified intervals to execute code in its Tick event handler.

ToLongDateString method of type Date—Returns a String containing the date in the format "Wednesday, October 30, 2002."

ToShortTimeString method of type Date—Returns a String containing the time in the format "4:00 PM."

Value property of a DateTimePicker control—Stores the value (such as a time) in a DateTimePicker control.

ValueChanged event of a DateTimePicker control—Raised when a user selects a new day or time in the DateTimePicker control.

GUI DESIGN GUIDELINES

DateTimePicker

- Use a DateTimePicker to retrieve date and time information from the user.
- Each DateTimePicker should have a corresponding descriptive Label.
- If the user is to specify a time of day or a date and time, set the DateTimePicker's ShowUpDown property to True. If the user is to specify a date, set the DateTimePicker's ShowUpDown property to False to allow the user to select a day from the month calendar.

GroupBox

- GroupBox titles should be concise and should use book-title capitalization.
- Use GroupBoxes to group related controls on the Form visually.

CONTROLS, EVENTS, PROPERTIES & METHODS

Date This structure provides properties and methods to store and manipulate date and time information.

- *Properties*

  Day—Returns the day stored in a Date variable.

  Hour—Returns the hour stored in a Date variable.

  Month—Returns the month stored in a Date variable.

  Now—Returns the system's current date and time.

  Year—Returns the year stored in a Date variable.

- *Methods*

  AddDays—Creates a new Date value that is the specified number of days later (or earlier) in time.

  AddHours—Creates a new Date value that is the specified number of hours later (or earlier) in time.

  AddMinutes—Creates a new Date value that is the specified number of minutes later (or earlier) in time.

ToLongDateString—Returns a String containing the date in the format "Wednesday, October 30, 2002."

ToShortTimeString—Returns a String containing the time in the format "4:00 PM."

DateTimePicker [≣ DateTimePicker] This control is used to retrieve date and time information from the user.

■ *In action*

DateTimePicker using default format

■ *Event*
ValueChanged—Raised when the Value property is changed.

■ *Properties*
CustomFormat—Sets which format string to use when displaying the date and/or time.

Format—Specifies the format in which the date and time are displayed on the control. Long specifies that the date is to be displayed in the format "Monday, December 09, 2002." Short specifies that the date is to be displayed in the format "12/9/2002." Time specifies that the time is to be displayed in the format "8:39:53 PM." Custom allows the programmer to specify a custom format in which to display the date and/or time.

Hour—Stores the hour in the DateTimePicker control.

Location—Specifies the location of the DateTimePicker control on its container relative to the container's top-left corner.

MinDate—Specifies the minimum date and/or time that can be selected when using this control.

MaxDate—Specifies the maximum date and/or time that can be selected when using this control.

Name—Specifies the name used to access the DateTimePicker control programmatically. The name should be appended with the DateTimePicker suffix.

ShowUpDown—Specifies whether the up-down arrows (True) are displayed on the control for time values. If False, a down arrow is displayed for accessing a drop-down calendar.

Value—Stores the date and/or time in the DateTimePicker control.

GroupBox [⬚ GroupBox] This control groups related controls visually.

■ *In action*

Drop Off

Enter drop-off time: 09:29 AM

■ *Properties*
Name—Specifies the name used to access the GroupBox control programmatically. The name should be appended with the GroupBox suffix.

Location—Specifies the location of the GroupBox control on the Form.

Size—Specifies the height and width (in pixels) of the GroupBox control.

Text—Specifies the text displayed on the GroupBox.

Timer [🕑 Timer] This control wakes up at specified intervals of time to execute code in its Tick event handler.

■ *Event*

Tick—Raised after the number of milliseconds specified in the Interval property has elapsed.

■ *Properties*

Enabled—Determines whether the Timer is running (True). The default is False.

Interval—Determines the time interval between Tick events.

Name—Specifies the name used to access the Timer control programmatically. The name should be appended with the Timer suffix.

MULTIPLE-CHOICE QUESTIONS

14.1 The _____ allows you to store and manipulate date information easily.

  a) Date structure   b) DatePicker control

  c) GroupBox control   d) Now property

14.2 You can _____ to a Date variable.

  a) add hours   b) add days

  c) subtract hours   d) All of the above.

14.3 To subtract one day from Date variable day's value, assign the value returned by _____ to day.

  a) day.AddHours(-24)   b) day.SubtractDays(1)

  c) day.AddDays(-1)   d) Both a and c.

14.4 The time 3:45 and 35 seconds in the afternoon would be formatted as 03:45:35 PM according to the format string _____.

  a) "hh:mm:ss"   b) "hh:mm:ss tt"

  c) "hh:mm:ss am:pm"   d) "h:m:s tt"

14.5 A(n) _____ event occurs before the Form is displayed.

  a) LoadForm   b) InitializeForm

  c) Load   d) FormLoad

14.6 Timer property Interval sets the rate at which Tick events occur in _____.

  a) nanoseconds   b) microseconds

  c) milliseconds   d) seconds

14.7 To set Date now's time five hours earlier, use _____.

  a) now = now.SubtractHours(5)   b) now = now.AddHours(-5)

  c) now = now.AddHours(5)   d) now.AddHours(-5)

14.8 A _____ is a container.

  a) GroupBox   b) Form

  c) Timer   d) Both a and b.

14.9 A Date variable stores hour values in the range _____.

  a) 1 to 12   b) 0 to 12

  c) 0 to 24   d) 0 to 23

14.10 A DateTimePicker's _____ property specifies the format string with which to display the date.

  a) CustomFormat   b) FormatString

  c) Format   d) Text

EXERCISES

14.11 (*World Clock Application*) Create an application that displays the current time in Los Angeles, Atlanta, London and Tokyo. Use a Timer to update the clock every second. Assume that your local time is the time in Atlanta. Atlanta is three hours later than Los Angeles. London is five hours later than Atlanta. Tokyo is eight hours later than London. The application should look similar to Fig. 14.20.

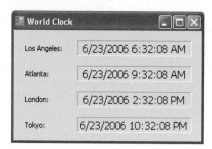

Figure 14.20   World Clock GUI.

a) *Copying the template to your working directory.* Copy the directory C:\Examples\ Tutorial14\Exercises\WorldClock to your C:\SimplyVB directory.

b) *Opening the application's template file.* Double click WorldClock.sln in the WorldClock directory to open the application.

c) *Adding a Timer to the Form.* Add a Timer control to the **World Clock** application. Set the Timer control's name property to clockTimer.

d) *Adding a Tick event handler for clockTimer.* Add a Tick event handler for Timer clockTimer. The event handler should calculate and display the current times for Los Angeles, Atlanta, London and Tokyo. Use the Date variable's ToShortDate-String and ToLongTimeString methods to create the display text.

e) *Running the application.* Select **Debug > Start Debugging** to run your application. Look at the clock on your machine to verify that the time for Los Angeles is three hours earlier, the time in Atlanta is the same as what your clock says, the time in London is five hours later, and the time in Tokyo is 13 hours later (eight hours later than London).

f) *Closing the application.* Close your running application by clicking its close box.

g) *Closing the IDE.* Close the Visual Basic IDE by clicking its close box.

14.12 (*Shipping Time Application Enhancement*) During the winter, a distribution center in Denver, Colorado, needs to receive seafood shipments to supply the local ski resorts. Enhance the **Shipping Time** application by adding Denver, Colorado, as another shipping destination. Denver is two time zones west of Portland, meaning that the time is two hours earlier than Portland, Maine. Because there are no direct flights to Denver, shipments from Portland will take eight hours.

a) *Copying the template to your working directory.* Copy the directory C:\Examples\ Tutorial14\Exercises\ShippingTimeEnhanced to your C:\SimplyVB directory.

b) *Opening the application's template file.* Double click ShippingTime.sln in the ShippingTimeEnhanced directory to open the application.

c) *Inserting a GroupBox.* Resize the Form to fit the **Express Shipping to Denver** GroupBox as shown in Fig. 14.21. Add a GroupBox to the Form. Change the Text property of the GroupBox to indicate that it will contain the delivery time in Denver. Resize and move the GroupBox so that it resembles the GUI shown in Fig. 14.21.

d) *Inserting Labels.* In the GroupBox you just created, add an output Label to display the delivery time for a seafood shipment to Denver and a corresponding descriptive Label.

e) *Inserting code to the DisplayDeliveryTime procedure.* Add code to Display-DeliveryTime procedure to compute and display the delivery time in Denver.

f) *Running the application.* Select **Debug > Start Debugging** to run your application. Select various drop-off times, and ensure that the delivery times are correct for both Las Vegas and Denver.

g) *Closing the application.* Close your running application by clicking its close box.

h) *Closing the IDE.* Close the Visual Basic IDE by clicking its close box.

Figure 14.21   Enhanced Shipping Time GUI.

14.13 (*Alarm Application*) Create an application that allows the user to set an alarm clock. The application should allow the user to set the exact time of the alarm by using a DateTime-Picker. While the alarm is set, the user should not be able to modify the DateTimePicker. If the alarm is set and the current time matches or exceeds the time in the DateTimePicker, play the computer's "beep" sound. (Your computer must have the necessary hardware for sound.) The user should be able to cancel an alarm by using a **Reset** Button. This Button is disabled when the application starts.

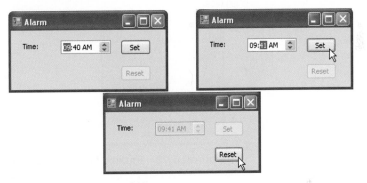

Figure 14.22   Alarm GUI.

a) *Copying the template to your working directory.* Copy the directory C:\Examples\ Tutorial14\Exercises\AlarmClock to your C:\SimplyVB directory.

b) *Opening the application's template file.* Double click AlarmClock.sln in the AlarmClock directory to open the application.

c) *Inserting a DateTimePicker.* Add a DateTimePicker control to the Form. Set the DateTimePicker to display only the time, as shown in Fig. 14.22. Set the DateTime-Picker control's Size property to 80, 21, and move the control so that it appears as it does in Fig. 14.22.

d) *Coding the Set Button's Click event handler.* Add a Click event handler for the **Set** Button. This event handler should disable the **Set** Button and the DateTimePicker and enable the **Reset** Button.

e) *Coding the Timer's Tick event handler.* Define the Tick event handler for the Timer. A Tick event should occur every 1,000 milliseconds (one second). If the alarm is set and the current time matches or exceeds the time in the DateTimePicker, play the computer's "beep" sound by calling the Beep function. To call the Beep function, type Beep() on its own line in your code.

f) *Coding the Reset Button's Click event handler.* Define the Click event handler for the **Reset** Button. When the **Reset** Button is clicked, the GUI should be set back to its original state.

g) *Running the application.* Select **Debug > Start Debugging** to run your application. Use the DateTimePicker and the **Set** Button to set a time for the alarm to go off.

Wait for that time to verify that the alarm will make beeping sounds. Click the **Reset Button** to set a new time for the alarm to go off.

h) *Closing the application.* Close your running application by clicking its close box.

i) *Closing the IDE.* Close the Visual Basic IDE by clicking its close box.

What does this code do? ▶ **14.14** This code creates a `Date` variable. What date does this variable contain?

```
Dim day As Date = New Date(2003, 1, 2, 3, 4, 5)
```

What's wrong with this code? ▶ **14.15** The following lines of code are supposed to create a `Date` variable and increment its hour value by two. Find the error(s) in the code.

```
Dim currentDay As Date = Date.Now
currentDay.AddHours(2)
```

Programming Challenge ▶ **14.16** (*Parking Garage Fee Calculator*) Create an application that computes the fee for parking a car in a parking garage (Fig. 14.23). The user should provide the **Time In:** and **Time Out:** values by using `DateTimePicker`s. The application should calculate the cost of parking in the garage for the specified amount of time. Assume that parking costs $3 an hour. When calculating the total time spent in the garage, you can ignore the seconds value, but treat the minutes value as a fraction of an hour (1 minute is 1/60 of an hour). For simplicity, assume that no overnight parking is allowed, so each car leaves the garage on the same day in which it arrives.

Figure 14.23   Parking Garage Fee Calculator GUI.

a) *Copying the template to your working directory.* Copy the directory `C:\Examples\Tutorial14\Exercises\ParkingGarageFeeCalculator` to your `C:\SimplyVB` directory.

b) *Opening the application's template file.* Double click `ParkingGarageFeeCalculator.sln` in the `ParkingGarageFeeCalculator` directory to open the application.

c) *Inserting the DateTimePicker controls.* Add two `DateTimePicker` controls to the Form. Set the `DateTimePicker`s so that they show the time only. Set the `Size` property of each `DateTimePicker` control to 80, 21, and move the `DateTimePicker`s so that they are positioned as in Fig. 14.23.

d) *Writing the Function procedure Fee.* Define a `Function` procedure Fee that accepts four `Integer`s as parameters—the hour value of the **Time In:**, the hour value of the **Time Out:**, the minute value of the **Time In:** and the minute value of the **Time Out:**. Using this information, procedure Fee should calculate the fee for parking in the garage. The `Function` procedure should then return this value as a `Decimal`.

e) *Coding the Calculate Button's Click event handler.* Add the `Click` event handler for the **Calculate Button**. This event handler should call Fee to obtain the amount due. It should then display the amount (formatted as currency) in a `Label`.

f) *Running the application.* Select **Debug > Start Debugging** to run your application. Use the `DateTimePicker`s' up and down arrows to select a time the car was placed in the garage and the time the car was taken out of the garage. Click the **Calculate** Button and verify that the correct fee is displayed.

g) *Closing the application.* Close your running application by clicking its close box.

h) *Closing the IDE.* Close the Visual Basic IDE by clicking its close box.

Objectives

In this tutorial, you will learn to:
- Create variables that can be used in all the Form's procedures.
- Pass arguments by reference, using ByRef, so that the called procedure can modify the caller's variables.
- Eliminate subtle data-type errors by enabling Option Strict.
- Change a value from one data type to another, using methods of class Convert.

Outline

Fund Raiser Application

Introducing Scope, Pass-by-Reference and Option Strict

In this tutorial, you will learn several important Visual Basic concepts. First, you will learn how to declare variables that can be referenced from any procedure within your Form's code. Next, you will learn another technique for passing arguments to procedures. In the procedures that you have created so far, the application has made a copy of the argument's value, and any changes the called procedure made to the copy did not affect the original variable's value. You will learn how to pass an argument to a procedure—using a technique called pass-by-reference—so that changes made to the parameter's value in the procedure are also made to the original variable in the caller. You will learn how the Visual Basic compiler handles conversions between different data types and how to enable a feature called Option Strict to avoid subtle errors that can occur when a value of one type is assigned to a variable of another type. In addition, you will be introduced to methods from class Convert that allow you to convert data from one type to another.

15.1 Test-Driving the Fund Raiser Application

In this tutorial, you will create a fund raiser application that determines how much donated money is available after operating costs. This application must meet the following requirements:

> ### Application Requirements
>
> *An organization is hosting a fund raiser to collect donations. A portion of each donation is used to cover the operating expenses of the organization; the rest of the donation goes to the charity. Create an application that allows the organization to keep track of the total amount of money raised. The application should deduct 17% of each donation for operating costs; the remaining 83% is given to the charity. The application should display the amount of each donation after the 17% operating expenses are deducted; it also should display the total amount raised for the charity (that is, the total amount donated less all operating costs) for all donations up to that point.*

The user inputs the amount of a donation into a TextBox and clicks a Button to calculate the net amount of the donation that the charity receives after operating expenses have been deducted. In addition, the total amount of money raised for the charity is updated and displayed. You begin by test-driving the completed application. Then you will learn the additional Visual Basic technologies that you will need to create your own version of this application.

Test-Driving the Fund Raiser Application

1. ***Opening the completed application.*** Open the directory `C:\Examples\Tutorial15\CompletedApplication\FundRaiser` to locate the **Fund Raiser** application. Double click `FundRaiser.sln` to open the application in the Visual Basic IDE.

2. ***Running the* Fund Raiser *application.*** Select **Debug > Start Debugging** to run the application (Fig. 15.1).

Figure 15.1 **Fund Raiser** application's Form.

3. ***Entering a donation in the application.*** Enter 1500 in the **Donation:** Text-Box. Click the **Make Donation** Button. The application calculates the amount of the donation after the operating expenses have been deducted and displays the result ($1245.00) in the **After expenses:** field. Because this is the first donation entered, this amount is repeated in the **Total raised:** field (Fig. 15.2).

Figure 15.2 **Fund Raiser** application's Form with first donation entered.

4. ***Entering additional donations.*** Enter more donations, and click the **Make Donation** Button. Note that the total raised increases with each additional donation (Fig. 15.3).

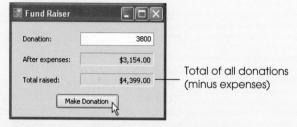

Total of all donations (minus expenses)

Figure 15.3 Making further donations.

5. ***Closing the application.*** Close your running application by clicking its close box.

6. ***Closing the IDE.*** Close the Visual Basic IDE by clicking its close box.

15.2 Constructing the Fund Raiser Application

The following pseudocode statements describe the basic operation of the **Fund Raiser** application:

> When the user changes the current donation amount in the TextBox:
>   Clear Label that displays amount of current donation that goes toward charity
>
> When the user clicks the Make Donation Button:
>   Obtain amount of current donation from TextBox
>   Call CalculateDonation to calculate amount of current donation that goes toward charity (amount after operating costs)
>   Display amount of current donation that goes toward charity
>   Update total amount raised for charity (from all donations received)
>   Display total amount raised for charity
>
> When the CalculateDonation procedure gets called:
>   Calculate operating costs (multiply the donated amount by the operating cost percentage)
>   Calculate amount of donation that goes to charity (Subtract operating costs
>   from donated amount)

Now that you have test-driven the **Fund Raiser** application and studied its pseudocode representation, you will use an ACE table to help you convert the pseudocode to Visual Basic. Figure 15.4 lists the actions, controls and events that will help you complete your own version of this application.

Action/Control/Event Table for the Fund Raiser Application

Action	Control	Event/Method
Label all the application's controls	donationsLabel, donatedLabel, totalLabel	Application is run
	donationTextBox	TextChanged
Clear Label that displays amount of current donation that goes toward charity	donatedValueLabel	
	donateButton	Click
Obtain user donation from TextBox	donationTextBox	
Calculate amount of current donation that goes toward charity		
Display amount of current donation that goes toward charity	donatedValueLabel	
Update total amount raised for charity		
Display total amount raised for charity	totalValueLabel	
		Calculate-Donation
Calculate operating costs		
Calculate amount of donation that goes to charity		

Figure 15.4 Fund Raiser application's ACE table.

You're now ready to begin programming the **Fund Raiser** application. First, you will declare the variables needed in the application. In this discussion, you will learn a new concept—scope. The **scope** of a variable identifier is the portion of an application in which the variable's identifier can be referenced. Some identifiers can be referenced throughout an application; others can be referenced only from limited portions of an application (such as within a single procedure). You will now add code to your application to illustrate these various scopes.

Examining Scope with the *Fund Raiser* Application

1. ***Copying the template to your working directory.*** Copy the `C:\Examples\Tutorial15\TemplateApplication\FundRaiser` directory to your `C:\SimplyVB` directory.

2. ***Opening the Fund Raiser application's template file.*** Double click `FundRaiser.sln` in the `FundRaiser` directory to open the application in the Visual Basic IDE (Fig. 15.5).

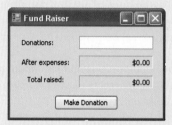

Figure 15.5 **Fund Raiser** template application's Form.

3. ***Placing declarations in the code file.*** Select **View > Code**, and add lines 2–3 of Fig. 15.6 to `FundRaiser.vb`. In this application, you need a variable that stores the total amount of money raised for charity.

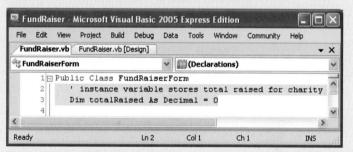

Figure 15.6 Declaring an instance variable in the application.

This variable is initialized when the application first runs and must retain its value while the application executes (that is, it cannot be created each time a procedure is invoked). Variable `totalRaised` stores the total amount of money raised. This variable is an **instance variable**—a variable declared inside a class, but outside any procedure definitions of that class. All procedures in class `FundRaiserForm` will have access to this variable and will be able to modify its value.

Instance variables have **module scope**. Module scope begins at the identifier after keyword `Class` and terminates at the `End Class` statement. This scope enables any procedure in a class to access all instance variables defined in the same class. Form instance variables with module scope are created when the application begins executing.

4. ***Creating the Click event handler for the Make Donation Button.*** Select **View > Designer** to return to design view. Double click the **Make Donation** Button to generate its Click event handler `donateButton_Click`. Split the procedure header over two lines, as in lines 28–29 of Fig. 15.7, and place the comments in lines 27 and 31 around the event handler.

(cont.)

5. ***Declaring local variables in event handler donateButton_Click.*** Add lines 31–32 of Fig. 15.8 to event handler donateButton_Click. Variable donation (line 31) stores the donation amount. Variable afterCosts (line 32) stores the donation amount after the operating expenses have been deducted.

In Visual Basic, identifiers, such as donation and afterCosts, that are declared inside a procedure (but outside of a control statement, such as a Do While...Loop) have **procedure scope**. Identifiers with procedure scope cannot be referenced outside of the procedure in which they are declared. Parameters to procedures are also considered to have procedure scope.

Identifiers declared inside control statements, such as inside an If...Then statement, have **block scope**. Block scope begins at the identifier's declaration and ends at the block's final statement (for example, End If).

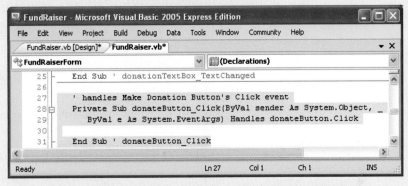

Figure 15.7 Adding a Click event handler to the application.

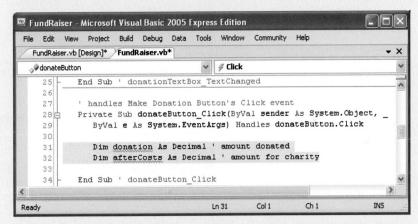

Figure 15.8 Declaring local variables in the **Fund Raiser** application.

Variables with either procedure scope or block scope are called **local variables**, because they cannot be referenced outside the procedure or block in which they are declared. If a local variable (that is, a variable with either block scope or procedure scope) has the same name as an instance variable (that is, a variable with module scope), the instance variable is hidden in the procedure or block. Any expression containing the variable name will use the local variable's value and not the instance variable's value. The instance variable's value is not destroyed, though—it is still available for access outside the procedure or block.

Error-Prevention Tip

Hidden variable names can sometimes lead to subtle logic errors. Use unique names for all variables, regardless of scope, to prevent an instance variable from becoming hidden.

(cont.)

6. ***Examining the CalculateDonation procedure.*** The template application provides the CalculateDonation Function procedure (lines 5–17 of Fig. 15.9). Line 9 declares constant COSTS, which stores the operating-cost percentage. This constant also is "local" to the procedure and cannot be used elsewhere. The Function procedure accepts one parameter value—the total donation amount (donatedAmount). The amount of the donation that goes toward operating costs is 17% of the initial donation. The net donation (the amount that goes toward charity) is calculated by multiplying local constant COSTS, whose value is 0.17, by the initial donation amount and subtracting this result from the donation amount.

Procedure CalculateDonation subtracts the operating cost from the initial donation amount (donatedAmount) and assigns the result to netDonation (lines 13–14). The Function procedure then returns the Decimal result (line 16).

Parameter donatedAmount has procedure scope because it is declared in the procedure header

Local variable netDonation has procedure scope because it is declared in the procedure body

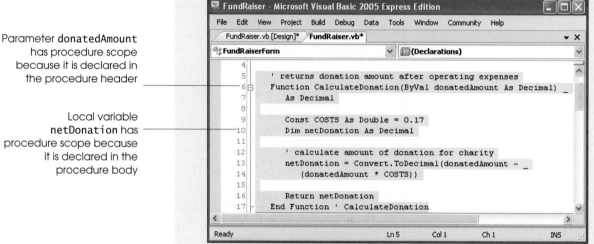

Figure 15.9 Function procedure CalculateDonation provided by the template application.

7. ***Demonstrating the difference between module scope and procedure scope.*** Now you are going to demonstrate the limits of procedure scope. Temporarily replace constant COSTS with donation, donateButton_Click's local variable (line 14 in Fig. 15.10). Note the jagged line under donation to indicate an error. Variables with procedure scope can be accessed and modified only in the procedure in which they are defined. The error message displayed when the mouse pointer rests on donation indicates that donation is not declared. This variable is "local" to donateButton_Click, so Function CalculateDonation cannot "see" the declaration of donation. Replace donation with COSTS.

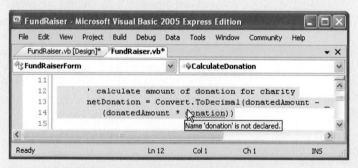

Figure 15.10 Demonstrating procedure scope.

(cont.)   8. ***Obtaining the donation amount.*** Add lines 34–35 of Fig. 15.11 to event handler `donateButton_Click`. You obtain the total donation amount from TextBox `donationTextBox` (line 35).

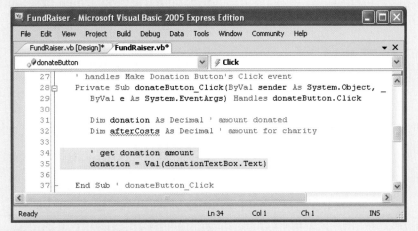

Figure 15.11   Obtaining the donation amount.

9. ***Calculating and displaying the donation amount after the operating expenses.*** Add lines 37–41 of Fig. 15.12 to the event handler. Line 38 invokes procedure `CalculateDonation` with the amount of the donation (`donation`). The result of this procedure—the net amount that goes to charity after the deduction for operating costs—is assigned to variable `afterCosts`. The donation amount after operating costs is formatted as a currency string and displayed in the **After expenses:** field (line 41).

10. ***Updating and displaying the fund raiser total.*** Add lines 43–47 of Fig. 15.13 to the event handler. Line 44 updates instance variable `totalRaised`, which stores the total amount given to the charity after the operating costs have been deducted. Line 47 displays the total amount raised for charity.

Note that `totalRaised` is not declared as a local variable in this event handler and does not have a jagged line beneath it. Recall that `totalRaised` is an instance variable, declared in line 3 of Fig. 15.6. Instance variables may be used in any of the class's procedures.

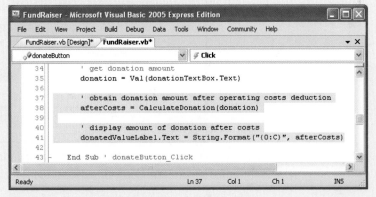

Figure 15.12   Calculating and displaying the donation amount after operating expenses.

(cont.)

Instance variable `totalRaised` has module scope, and therefore maintains its value between procedure calls. Variables with procedure scope, such as `donation`, do not retain their values between procedure calls and are reinitialized each time their procedure is invoked.

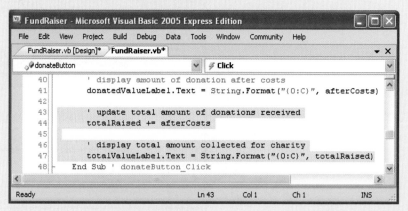

Figure 15.13 Updating and displaying the total amount raised for charity.

11. ***Clearing the After expenses: field to display the next result.*** The template application includes event handler `donationTextBox_TextChanged` (lines 19–25 of Fig. 15.14) for the **Donation:** TextBox's TextChanged event. When the user enters data into the TextBox, the TextChanged event occurs and line 24 clears the donation for charity from the **After expenses:** field.

12. ***Running the application.*** Select **Debug > Start Debugging** to run your application. Enter several donation values to see that they are added to the total donation amount each time the **Make Donation** Button is clicked. The application will now run and display the correct output. We can also solve this problem using a sophisticated technique known as pass-by-reference. You will modify your application to use pass-by-reference in the next section.

13. ***Closing the application.*** Close your running application by clicking its close box.

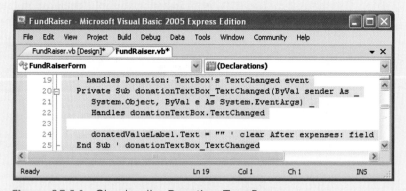

Figure 15.14 Clearing the **Donation:** TextBox.

SELF-REVIEW

1. Instance variables have _____ scope.

   a) block

   b) procedure

   c) module

   d) None of the above.

2. Variables with either procedure scope or block scope are called _____.
   a) instance variables   b) local variables
   c) class variables   d) hidden variables

Answers: 1) c. 2) b.

15.3 Passing Arguments: Pass-by-Value vs. Pass-by-Reference

Arguments are passed to procedures in one of two ways: **pass-by-value** and **pass-by-reference** (also called **call-by-value** and **call-by-reference**). The keyword ByVal (which we have used in all our procedures until now, including event handlers generated by Visual Basic) indicates that a variable has been passed by value. When an argument is passed by value, the application makes a copy of the argument's value and passes the copy to the called procedure. Changes made to the copy in the called procedure do not affect the original variable's value in the calling procedure.

In contrast, when an argument is passed by reference (using keyword **ByRef**), the original data can be accessed and modified directly by the called procedure. This is useful in some situations, such as when a procedure needs to produce more than one result. However, it can cause subtle errors and is used largely only by experienced programmers. In the following box, you will learn to use keyword ByRef to pass an argument by reference to the procedure that calculates the donation amount after operating costs.

Passing Arguments with ByRef in the Fund Raiser Application

1. ***Passing variable afterCosts by reference.*** Replace line 38 in event handler donateButton_Click with line 38 of Fig. 15.15. The procedure call in line 38 of Fig. 15.15 passes two variables to procedure CalculateDonation. Note that because procedure CalculateDonation currently only accepts one argument, the second argument (afterCosts) is flagged as a syntax error. In the following steps, we will rewrite procedure CalculateDonation so that it accepts two arguments, resolving the syntax error. The first argument (in this case, donation) will be passed by value; the second argument (in this case, afterCosts) will be passed by reference. When the CalculateDonation procedure returns, variable afterCosts will contain the portion of the donation that the charity receives. Therefore, no assignment statement is necessary.

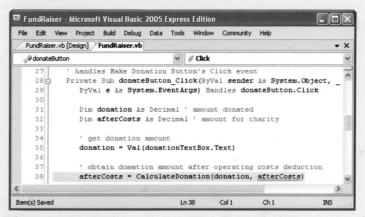

Figure 15.15 Passing variable afterCosts by reference.

2. ***Removing the old CalculateDonation Function procedure.*** Delete the CalculateDonation Function procedure (lines 6–17 of Fig. 15.16) from FundRaiser.vb.

(cont.)

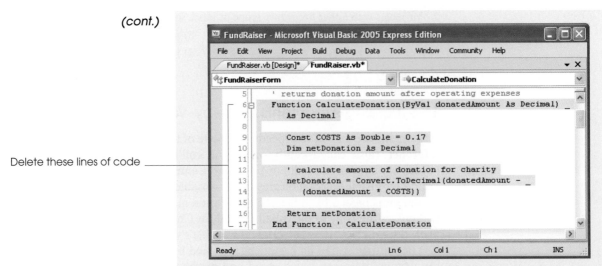

Delete these lines of code

Figure 15.16 `Function` procedure `CalculateDonation` to be removed.

3. *Coding the new CalculateDonation Sub procedure.* Add lines 6–9 of Fig. 15.17 in your code. Lines 6–7 specify procedure `CalculateDonation`'s header. Keyword `ByRef` (line 7) indicates that variable `netDonation` is passed by reference. This means that any changes made to variable `netDonation` in `CalculateDonation` affect `donateButton_Click`'s local variable `afterCosts`. Since it is no longer necessary for `CalculateDonation` to return a value, `CalculateDonation` is now created as a `Sub` procedure rather than a `Function` procedure.

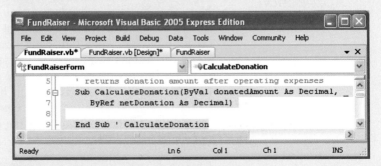

Figure 15.17 `CalculateDonation` `Sub` procedure.

4. *Calculating the donation amount for charity after operating costs.* Add lines 9–13 of Fig. 15.18 to `Sub` procedure `CalculateDonation`. Lines 12–13 calculate the amount of the donation that goes toward charity after operating costs have been deducted. Note that this is the same calculation that was performed in lines 13–14 of the `Function` procedure `CalculateDonation` in Fig. 15.16. The only difference is that assigning the calculation result to variable `netDonation` actually assigns the value to `donateButton_Click`'s local variable `afterCosts`. You do not need to return the calculation result.

5. *Running the application.* Select **Debug > Start Debugging** to run your application. Again, the application will display the correct results, adding to the total donation amount for each input. This solution, however, uses pass-by-reference rather than pass-by-value. In the next section you will improve upon this application again by using `Option Strict`, which will help you write cleaner code.

(cont.)

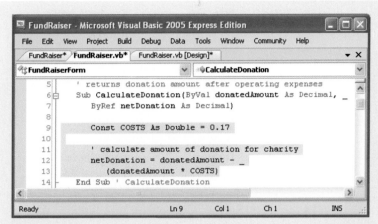

Figure 15.18   Calculating the donation that goes toward charity after operating costs have been deducted.

6. ***Closing the application.*** Close your running application by clicking its close box.

---

1. Keyword _____ indicates pass-by-reference.

   a) `Reference`   b) `ByRef`

   c) `ByReference`   d) `PassByRef`

2. When an argument is passed by reference, the called procedure can access and modify _____.

   a) the caller's original data directly   b) a copy of the caller's data

   c) other procedures' local variables   d) None of the above.

Answers: 1) b. 2) a.

15.4 Option Strict

When a computer accesses data, it needs to know what type that data is for the data to make sense. Imagine you are purchasing a book from an online store that ships internationally. You notice that the price for the book is 20, but no currency is associated with the price; it could be dollars, euros, pesos, yen or some other currency. Therefore, it is important to know what type of currency is being used. If the currency is different from the one that you normally use, you will need to perform a conversion to get the price.

Similar conversions occur many times in an application. The computer determines a data type, and, with that knowledge, it can add two `Integers` or combine two `Strings` of text. Visual Basic can convert one data type to another, as long as the conversion makes sense. For example, you are allowed to assign an `Integer` value to a `Decimal` variable without writing code that tells the application how to do the conversion. These types of assignments perform conversions called **implicit conversions.** When an attempted conversion does not make sense, such as assigning `"hello"` to an `Integer` variable, an error occurs. Figure 15.19 lists Visual Basic's data types and their allowed implicit conversions. [*Note:* We do not discuss every data type in this book. Consult the Visual Basic documentation to learn more about Visual Basic data types.]

The types listed in the right column are "larger" types in that they can store more data than the types in the left column. For example, `Integer` types (left column) can be converted to `Long` types (right column, which includes four other data types). An `Integer` variable can store values in the approximate range ±2.1 billion;

Data Type	Can be implicitly converted to these (larger) types
Boolean	Object
Byte	Short, Integer, Long, Decimal, Single, Double or Object
Char	String or Object
Date	Object
Decimal	Single, Double or Object
Double	Object
Integer	Long, Decimal, Single, Double or Object
Long	Decimal, Single, Double or Object
Object	none
Short	Integer, Long, Decimal, Single, Double or Object
Single	Double or Object
String	Object

Figure 15.19   Data types and their allowed conversions.

a Long variable can store numbers in the approximate range $\pm 9 \times 10^{18}$ (9 followed by 18 zeros). This means that any Integer value can be assigned to a Long variable without losing any data. These kinds of conversions are called implicit **widening conversions**, because the value of a "smaller" type (Integer) is being assigned to a variable of a "larger" type (Long).

When a "larger" type, such as Double, is assigned to a "smaller" type, such as Integer, either a run-time error will occur because the value being assigned is too large to be stored in the smaller type or the assignment will be permitted. Consider the following code:

```
Dim value1 As Double = 4.6
Dim value2 As Integer = value1
```

![Common Programming Error icon] **Common Programming Error**

Narrowing conversions can result in loss of data, which can cause subtle logic errors.

Variable value2 will be assigned 5—the result of implicitly converting the Double value 4.6 to an Integer. These types of conversions are called implicit **narrowing conversions**. They can introduce subtle errors in applications, because the actual value being assigned could have been altered without you being aware of it—a dangerous practice. For example, if the programmer was expecting variable value2 to be assigned a value other than 5 (such as 4.6 or 4), a logic error would occur.

Visual Basic provides a feature called **Option Strict** that, when set to On, disallows implicit narrowing conversions. If you attempt an implicit narrowing conversion, the compiler issues a syntax error. Later, we will show you how programmers can override this by performing narrowing conversions explicitly. First, however, you will learn how to enable Option Strict, which is set to Off by default. The following box demonstrates how to set Option Strict to On through the Visual Basic IDE.

Enabling Option Strict

1. *Activating Option Strict.* In the **Solution Explorer** window, right click the project name (FundRaiser) to display a context menu. Select **Properties** to open the **FundRaiser Property Pages** tab (Fig. 15.20).

2. *Selecting the Compile option.* On the left side of the **FundRaiser Property Pages** tab, select the **Compile** category (Fig. 15.21). In the middle of the dialog is a ComboBox labeled **Option Strict:**. By default, the option is set to Off.

(cont.)

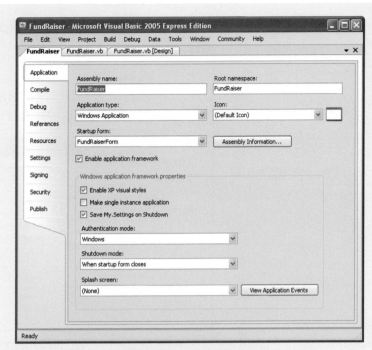

Figure 15.20 FundRaiser **Property Pages** tab.

Compile category ⎯⎯⎯⎯

ComboBox containing value
for Option Strict, which is ⎯⎯⎯⎯
set to Off by default

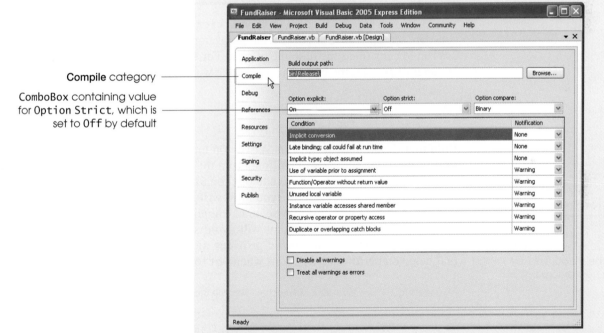

Figure 15.21 Selecting **Build** in the **FundRaiser Property Pages** tab.

3. ***Setting Option Strict to On.*** Select On in the ComboBox labeled **Option Strict:** (Fig. 15.22). Option Strict is now set to On for this application. You will need to set Option Strict to On for each application you create.

4. ***Saving the project.*** Select **File > Save All** to save your modified code.

5. ***Closing the Property Pages window.*** Close the **Property Pages** window by clicking its close box.

(cont.)

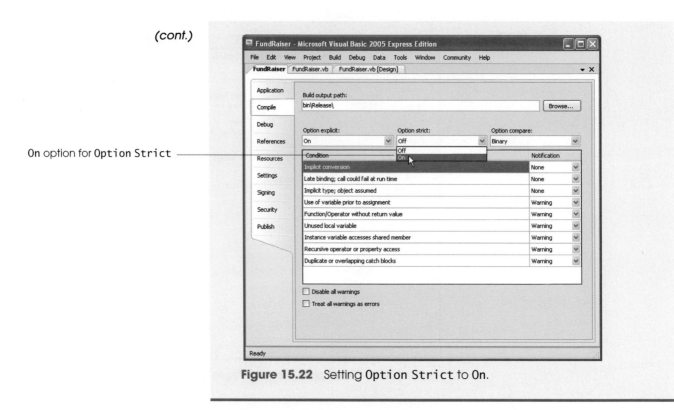

On option for `Option Strict` —————

Figure 15.22 Setting `Option Strict` to On.

As an alternative to setting `Option Strict` to On through the Visual Basic IDE, you can set `Option Strict` to On programmatically by writing the statement `Option Strict On` as the first line of code. For example, to set `Option Strict` to On in `FundRaiser.vb`, the beginning of the file would appear as

```
Option Strict On

Public Class FundRaiserForm
```

Note that the statement `Option Strict On` must appear before any other code in the file, including the class definition. From this point forward, all code examples in the remainder of this book have had `Option Strict` set to On through the IDE.

Error-Prevention Tip

Set `Option Strict` to On in every application to avoid subtle errors that can be introduced by implicit narrowing conversions.

When `Option Strict` is On, you must write code to perform narrowing conversions explicitly. At first, this may seem like a nuisance. However, it will help you create more robust applications that will avoid subtle errors that could result from implicit conversions. Visual Basic provides methods in class **Convert** (Fig. 15.23) that help you perform conversions when `Option Strict` is On.

Convert To	Use Convert Method	Sample Statement
`Integer`	`ToInt32`	`value = Convert.ToInt32( _` `   Val(inputTextBox.Text))`

`Decimal`	`ToDecimal`	`value = Convert.ToDecimal( _`
		`   Pmt(monthlyInterest, _`
		`   months,-loanAmount))`

`Double`	`ToDouble`	`rate = Convert.ToDouble( _` `   Val(rateTextBox.Text)) / 100`
`String`	`ToString`	`result = Convert.ToString(total)`

Figure 15.23 Four of class **Convert**'s methods.

The name of each conversion method is the word To, followed by the name of the data type to which the method converts its argument. For example, to convert a `String` input by the user in `inputTextBox` to an `Integer` use the statement

```
number = Convert.ToInt32(Val(inputTextBox.Text))
```

Int32 is the FCL type that Visual Basic's `Integer` keyword represents.

Conversions in statements that call `Convert` methods are called **explicit conversions**. In the following box, you will learn to use explicit conversions.

Using Class Convert in the Fund Raiser Application	1. ***Converting a Double donation amount to a Decimal value.*** Note that lines 12–13 in Fig. 15.24 are underlined. Place the mouse pointer over the jagged lines. An error message now displays, indicating that `Option Strict` prohibits an implicit conversion from `Double` to `Decimal`. This is because converting from `Double` to `Decimal` could result in data loss.

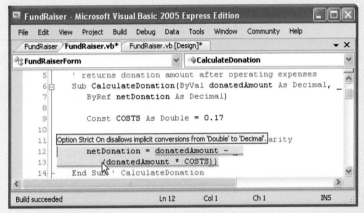

Figure 15.24 `Option Strict` prohibits implicit narrowing conversions.

Replace the underlined expression with lines 12–13 of Fig. 15.25. Method `Convert.ToDecimal` converts the `Double` value to a `Decimal` value. When the conversion is performed explicitly with a call to method `Convert.ToDecimal`, the jagged lines disappear.

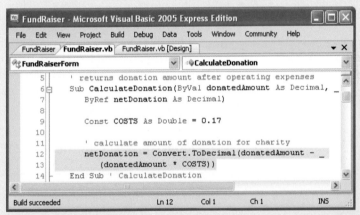

Figure 15.25 Explicitly performing a narrowing conversion with `Convert.ToDecimal`.

2. ***Converting the user input from a String to a Decimal.*** Line 32 of Fig. 15.26 is underlined. The error message that appears when the mouse pointer rests on this line indicates that `Option Strict` prohibits an implicit conversion from `Double` to `Decimal`.

Replace the underlined expression with line 32 of Fig. 15.27. Method `Convert.ToDecimal` explicitly converts the `Double` to a `Decimal`. After this change is made, the jagged line disappears.

(cont.)

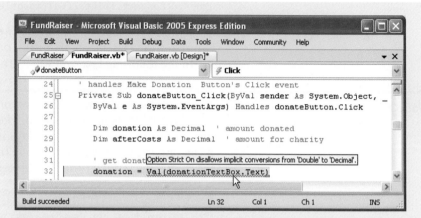

Figure 15.26 `Option Strict` prohibits a narrowing conversion from type `Double` to type `Decimal`.

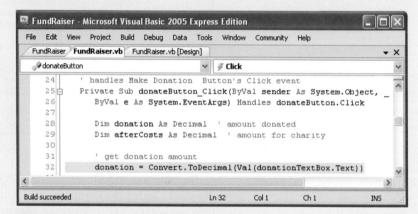

Figure 15.27 Explicitly converting a `Double` to type `Decimal` with `Convert.ToDecimal`.

3. ***Running the application.*** Select **Debug > Start Debugging** to run your application. Enter a donation amount and click the **Make Donation** Button. Verify that the total raised and the amount after expenses are correct. Enter more donations, each time verifying the output. Note that the total amount raised should also reflect previous donation amounts.

4. ***Closing the application.*** Close your running application by clicking its close box.

5. ***Closing the IDE.*** Close the Visual Basic IDE by clicking its close box.

Figure 15.28 presents the source code for the **Fund Raiser** application. The lines of code that contain new programming concepts that you learned in this tutorial are highlighted.

Instance variable declaration

Procedure `CalculateDonation` determines the amount of donation after operating costs; parameter `netDonation` is modified directly (using `ByRef`)

```
1   Public Class FundRaiserForm
2       ' instance variable stores total raised for charity
3       Dim totalRaised As Decimal = 0
4
5       ' returns donation amount after operating expenses
6       Sub CalculateDonation(ByVal donatedAmount As Decimal, _
7           ByRef netDonation As Decimal)
8
```

Figure 15.28 **Fund Raiser** application's code. (Part 1 of 2.)

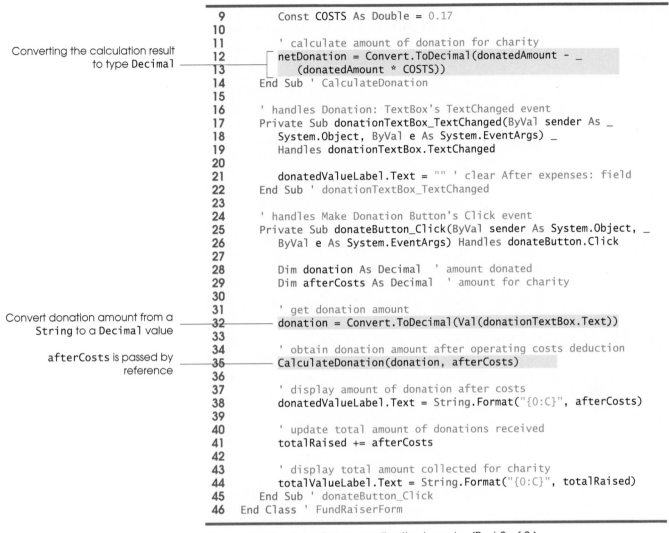

Converting the calculation result to type `Decimal`

Convert donation amount from a `String` to a `Decimal` value

`afterCosts` is passed by reference

```
 9            Const COSTS As Double = 0.17
10
11            ' calculate amount of donation for charity
12            netDonation = Convert.ToDecimal(donatedAmount - _
13               (donatedAmount * COSTS))
14         End Sub ' CalculateDonation
15
16         ' handles Donation: TextBox's TextChanged event
17         Private Sub donationTextBox_TextChanged(ByVal sender As _
18            System.Object, ByVal e As System.EventArgs) _
19            Handles donationTextBox.TextChanged
20
21            donatedValueLabel.Text = "" ' clear After expenses: field
22         End Sub ' donationTextBox_TextChanged
23
24         ' handles Make Donation Button's Click event
25         Private Sub donateButton_Click(ByVal sender As System.Object, _
26            ByVal e As System.EventArgs) Handles donateButton.Click
27
28            Dim donation As Decimal   ' amount donated
29            Dim afterCosts As Decimal   ' amount for charity
30
31            ' get donation amount
32            donation = Convert.ToDecimal(Val(donationTextBox.Text))
33
34            ' obtain donation amount after operating costs deduction
35            CalculateDonation(donation, afterCosts)
36
37            ' display amount of donation after costs
38            donatedValueLabel.Text = String.Format("{0:C}", afterCosts)
39
40            ' update total amount of donations received
41            totalRaised += afterCosts
42
43            ' display total amount collected for charity
44            totalValueLabel.Text = String.Format("{0:C}", totalRaised)
45         End Sub ' donateButton_Click
46      End Class ' FundRaiserForm
```

Figure 15.28   Fund Raiser application's code. (Part 2 of 2.)

SELF-REVIEW

1. When `Option Strict` is set to `On`, the programmer must explicitly perform _____.

   a) narrowing conversions   b) widening conversions

   c) all type conversions   d) no conversions

2. The methods in _____ are used to change data types explicitly.

   a) class `Strict`   b) class `Change`

   c) class `Convert`   d) class `Conversion`

Answers: 1) a. 2) c.

15.5 Wrap-Up

In this tutorial, you learned concepts about data types and variables, and you built the **Fund Raiser** application to demonstrate these concepts.

You learned how to create instance variables, which are declared inside a class, but outside any procedure definitions. Instance variables have module scope, which means that they are accessible to all procedures in the class in which they are declared. In this tutorial, you declared your instance variable in the `Form` class. In Tutorial 19, you will learn how to create your own classes and how to declare instance variables in them. Until now, all the variables you have declared have been local variables—that is, variables with either procedure scope or block scope. Variables with procedure scope are modifiable only within the procedure in which they are declared. Variables with block scope are modifiable only within the block (such as the body of an `If...Then` statement) in which they are declared.

You learned the difference between passing arguments by reference and passing arguments by value. When using pass-by-value, the calling procedure makes a copy of the argument's value and passes the copy to the called procedure. Changes to the called procedure's copy do not affect the original variable value in the calling procedure. When using pass-by-reference, the original data can be accessed and modified directly by the called procedure. You now know how to use keyword `ByVal` to pass arguments by value and keyword `ByRef` to pass arguments by reference.

You also learned about data-type conversions. You learned that narrowing conversions (such as converting a `Double` to a `Decimal`) can result in data loss and that widening conversions (such as a conversion from `Integer` to `Double`) don't have this problem. You learned that setting `Option Strict` to On causes Visual Basic to flag implicit narrowing conversions as syntax errors and forces the programmer to perform such conversions explicitly.

In the next tutorial, you will learn about random-number generation, and you will create an application that simulates the dice game called craps.

SKILLS SUMMARY

Setting `Option Strict` to On

- Right click the project name in the **Solution Explorer**, and select **Properties**.
- Select **Compile** from the categories in the **Property Pages** dialog.
- Set the **Option Strict:** ComboBox to **On**.

Passing Arguments

- Arguments can be passed in two ways: pass-by-value (`ByVal`) and pass-by-reference (`ByRef`).

Passing Arguments by Value

- In the procedure header, place keyword `ByVal` before the name of each argument that is to be passed by value.
- The application makes a copy of the argument's value and passes the copy to the called procedure.
- Changes to the called procedure's copy do not affect the original argument value.

Passing Arguments by Reference

- In the procedure header, place keyword `ByRef` before the name of each argument that is to be passed by reference.
- Called procedures can access and modify original arguments directly.

Understanding Scope

- You learned the differences between module scope, procedure scope and block scope.
- Instance variables have module scope and can be accessed by all procedures in the same class.
- Local variables have either procedure scope or block scope.
- Variables with procedure scope cannot be referenced outside the procedure in which they are declared.
- Variables with block scope cannot be referenced outside the block (such as the body of an `If...Then` statement) in which they are declared.
- Block scope begins at the identifier's declaration and ends at the block's end statement.

KEY TERMS

block scope—Variables declared inside control statements, such as an `If...Then` statement, have block scope. Block scope begins at the identifier's declaration and ends at the block's final statement (for example, `End If`).

ByRef keyword—Used to pass an argument by reference.

call-by-reference—See *pass-by-reference*.

call-by-value—See *pass-by-value*.

Convert class—Provides methods for converting data types.

explicit conversion—An operation that converts a value of one type to another type using code to (explicitly) tell the application to do the conversion. An example of an explicit conversion is to convert a value of one type to another type using a `Convert` method.

implicit conversion—An operation that converts a value of one type to another type without writing code to (explicitly) tell the application to do the conversion.

instance variable—Declared inside a class but outside any procedure of that class. Instance variables have module scope.

local variable—Declared inside a procedure or block, such as the body of an `If...Then` statement. Local variables have either procedure scope or block scope.

module scope—Begins at the identifier after keyword `Class` and terminates at the `End Class` statement, enables all procedures in the same class to access all instance variables defined in that class.

narrowing conversion—A conversion where the value of a "larger" type is being assigned to a variable of a "smaller" type, where the larger type can store more data than the smaller type. Narrowing conversions can result in loss of data, which can cause subtle logic errors.

`Option Strict`—When set to `On`, `Option Strict` causes the compiler to check all conversions and requires the programmer to perform an explicit conversion for all narrowing conversions (for example, conversion from `Double` to `Decimal`).

pass-by-reference—When an argument is passed by reference, the called procedure can access and modify the caller's original data directly. Keyword `ByRef` indicates pass-by-reference (also called call-by-reference).

pass-by-value—When an argument is passed by value, the application makes a copy of the argument's value and passes the copy to the called procedure. With pass-by-value, changes to the called procedure's copy do not affect the original variable's value. Keyword `ByVal` indicates pass-by-value (also called call-by-value).

procedure scope—Variables declared inside a procedure but outside a control structure have procedure scope. Variables with procedure scope cannot be referenced outside the procedure in which they are declared.

scope—The portion of an application in which an identifier (such as a variable name) can be referenced. Some identifiers can be referenced throughout an application; others can be referenced only from limited portions of an application (such as within a single procedure or block).

widening conversion—A conversion in which the value of a "smaller" type is assigned to a variable of a "larger" type—that is, a type that can store more data than the smaller type.

MULTIPLE-CHOICE QUESTIONS

15.1 In the **Property Pages** dialog, _____ must be selected to access `Option Strict`.

a) **Compile**
b) **Designer Defaults**
c) **General**
d) **Imports**

15.2 When `Option Strict` is set to `On`, variables _____.

a) are passed by value
b) are passed by reference
c) might need to be converted explicitly to a different type to avoid errors
d) are used only within the block in which they are declared

15.3 A variable declared inside a class, but outside a procedure, is called a(n) _____.

a) local variable
b) hidden variable
c) instance variable
d) constant variable

15.4 Visual Basic provides methods in class _____ to convert from one data type to another.

a) `ChangeTo`
b) `Convert`
c) `ConvertTo`
d) `ChangeType`

15.5 When `Option Strict` is _____, the conversion from a `Decimal` to an `Integer` results in an error.

a) `On`   b) `True`

c) `Off`   d) `False`

15.6 Keyword _____ indicates pass-by-reference.

a) `ByReference`   b) `ByRef`

c) `Ref`   d) `Reference`

15.7 With _____, changes made to a parameter variable's value do not affect the value of the variable in the calling procedure.

a) `Option Strict`   b) pass-by-value

c) pass-by-reference   d) None of the above.

15.8 Instance variables _____.

a) can be accessed by a procedure in the   b) have module scope
   same class

c) Neither of the above.   d) Both of the above.

15.9 Assigning a "smaller" type to a "larger" type is a _____ conversion.

a) narrowing   b) shortening

c) widening   d) lengthening

15.10 A value of type `Single` can be implicitly converted to _____.

a) `Integer`   b) `Double`

c) Neither of the above.   d) Both of the above.

EXERCISES

15.11 (*Task List Application*) Create an application that allows users to add items to a daily task list. The application should also display the number of tasks to be performed. Use method `Convert.ToString` to display the number of tasks in a `Label`. The application should look like the GUI in Fig. 15.29.

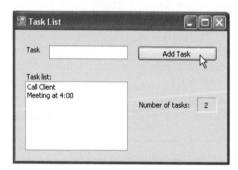

Figure 15.29   **Task List** application's GUI.

a) *Copying the template to your working directory.* Copy the directory `C:\Examples\Tutorial15\Exercises\TaskList` to your `C:\SimplyVB` directory.

b) *Opening the application's template file.* Double click `TaskList.sln` in the `TaskList` directory to open the application.

c) *Setting `Option Strict` to `On`.* Use the directions provided in the box, *Enabling Option Strict*, to set `Option Strict` to `On`.

d) *Creating an instance variable.* Declare `numberOfTaks` as an instance variable of class `TaskListForm`. This variable will be used to keep track of how many tasks have been entered.

e) *Adding the Add Task Button's `Click` event handler.* Double click the **Add Task** Button to generate the empty event handler `addButton_Click`. This event handler should display the user input in the `ListBox` and clear the user input from the Text-Box. The event handler should also update the `Label` that displays the number of tasks. Use method `Convert.ToString` to display the number of tasks in the `Label`. Finally, the event handler should transfer the focus to the `TextBox`.

f) ***Running the application.*** Select **Debug > Start Debugging** to run your application. Enter several tasks, and click the **Add Task** `Button` after each. Verify that each task is added to the **Task list:** `ListBox`, and that the number of tasks is incremented with each new task.

g) ***Closing the application.*** Close your running application by clicking its close box.

h) ***Closing the IDE.*** Close the Visual Basic IDE by clicking its close box.

15.12 (*Quiz Average Application*) Develop an application that computes a student's average quiz score for all of the quiz scores entered. The application should look like the GUI in Fig. 15.30. Use method `Convert.ToInt32` to convert the user input to an `Integer`. Use instance variables with module scope to keep track of the sum of all the quiz scores entered and the number of quiz scores entered.

Figure 15.30 **Quiz Average** application's GUI.

a) ***Copying the template to your working directory.*** Copy the directory `C:\Examples\Tutorial15\Exercises\QuizAverage` to your `C:\SimplyVB` directory.

b) ***Opening the application's template file.*** Double click `QuizAverage.sln` in the `QuizAverage` directory to open the application.

c) ***Setting `Option Strict` to `On`.*** Use the directions provided in the box, *Enabling Option Strict*, to set `Option Strict` to `On`.

d) ***Adding instance variables.*** Add two instance variables—`totalScore`, which keeps track of the sum of all the quiz scores entered, and `taken`, which keeps track of the number of quiz scores entered.

e) ***Adding the Submit Score Button's event handler.*** Double click the **Submit Score** `Button` to generate the empty event handler `calculateButton_Click`. The code required in *Steps f–k* should be placed in this event handler.

f) ***Obtaining user input.*** Use method `Convert.ToInt32` to convert the user input from the `TextBox` to an `Integer`.

g) ***Updating the number of quiz scores entered.*** Increment the number of quiz scores entered.

h) ***Updating the sum of all the quiz scores entered.*** Add the current quiz score to the current total to update the sum of all the quiz scores entered.

i) ***Calculating the average score.*** Divide the sum of all the quiz scores entered by the number of quiz scores entered to calculate the average score.

j) ***Displaying the average score.*** Use method `Convert.ToString` to display the average quiz grade in the **Average:** field.

k) ***Displaying the number of quizzes taken.*** Use method `Convert.ToString` to display the number of quiz scores entered in the **Number taken:** field.

l) ***Running the application.*** Select **Debug > Start Debugging** to run your application. Enter several quiz scores, clicking the **Submit Score** `Button` after each. With each new score, verify that the **Number taken:** field is incremented and that the average is updated correctly.

m) ***Closing the application.*** Close your running application by clicking its close box.

n) ***Closing the IDE.*** Close the Visual Basic IDE by clicking its close box.

15.13 (*Maximum Application*) Modify the **Maximum** application from Tutorial 13 (Fig. 15.31) to use keyword `ByRef` to pass a fourth argument to procedure `Maximum` by reference. Use methods from class `Convert` to perform any necessary type conversions.

Figure 15.31 **Maximum** application's GUI.

a) *Copying the template to your working directory.* Copy the directory `C:\Examples\Tutorial15\Exercises\Maximum` to your `C:\SimplyVB` directory.

b) *Opening the application's template file.* Double click `Maximum.sln` in the `Maximum` directory to open the application.

c) *Setting `Option Strict` to `On`.* Use the directions provided in the box *Enabling Option Strict* to set `Option Strict` to `On`.

d) *Adding a local variable.* Add local variable `max` of type `Double` to event handler `maximumButton_Click`. The code required in *Steps d–f* should be placed in this event handler. Variable `max` will store the result of procedure `Maximum`.

e) *Passing four arguments to procedure `Maximum`.* Use method `Convert.ToDouble` to convert the user input from the `TextBox`es to `Double`s. Pass these three values as the first three arguments to procedure `Maximum`. Pass local variable `max` as the fourth argument to procedure `Maximum`.

f) *Displaying the maximum value.* Use method `Convert.ToString` to display local variable `max` in the **Maximum:** field.

g) *Changing procedure `Maximum` to a Sub procedure.* Change procedure `Maximum` to a Sub procedure. Make sure that Sub procedure `Maximum` no longer returns a value and does not specify a return type. The modifications required in *Steps g–h* should be performed on this Sub procedure.

h) *Adding a fourth parameter to procedure `Maximum`.* Add a fourth parameter `finalMaximum` of type `Double` to `Maximum`'s procedure header. Use keyword `ByRef` to specify that this argument will be passed by reference. Remove the declaration of variable `finalMaximum` from the body of procedure `Maximum`.

i) *Running the application.* Select **Debug > Start Debugging** to run your application. Enter three different values into the input fields and click the **Maximum** Button. Verify that the largest value is displayed in the **Maximum:** field.

j) *Closing the application.* Close your running application by clicking its close box.

k) *Closing the IDE.* Close the Visual Basic IDE by clicking its close box.

What does this code do? ▶ **15.14** What is displayed in `displayLabel` when the following code is executed?

```
1   Public Class ScopeTestForm
2
3      Dim value2 As Integer = 5
4
5      Private Sub enterButton_Click(ByVal sender As System.Object, _
6         ByVal e As System.EventArgs) Handles enterButton.Click
7
8         Dim value1 As Integer = 10
9         Dim value2 As Integer = 3
10
11        Test(value1)
12        displayLabel.Text = Convert.ToString(value1)
13     End Sub ' enterButton_Click
```

```
14
15      Sub Test(ByRef value1 As Integer)
16        value1 *= value2
17      End Sub ' Test
18
19   End Class ' ScopeTestForm
```

What's wrong with this code? ▶ **15.15** Find the error(s) in the following code (the procedure should assign the value 14 to variable `result`).

```
1    Sub Sum()
2       Dim numberWords As String = "4"
3       Dim number As Integer = 10
4       Dim result As Integer
5
6       result = numberWords + number
7    End Sub ' Sum
```

Programming Challenge ▶ **15.16** (*Schedule Book Application*) Develop an application that allows a user to enter a schedule of appointments and their respective times. Create the Form in Fig. 15.32 and name the application **Schedule Book**. Add a `Function` procedure called `TimeTaken` that returns a `Boolean` value. Each time a user enters a new appointment, `Function` procedure `TimeTaken` determines whether the user has scheduled more than one appointment at the same time. If `TimeTaken` returns `True`, the user will be notified via a message dialog. Otherwise, the appointment will be added to the `ListBox`es. Set `Option Strict` to `On`, and use methods from class `Convert` as necessary.

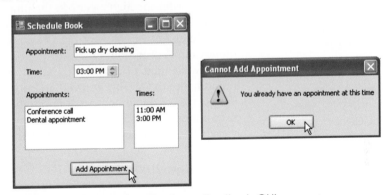

Figure 15.32   **Schedule Book** application's GUI.

Craps Game Application

Introducing Random-Number Generation

Objectives

In this tutorial, you will learn to:
- Code simulation techniques that employ random-number generation.
- Use class **Random** methods to generate random numbers.
- Use enumerations to enhance code readability.
- Read images from files.
- Use classes from other namespaces.

Outline

16.1 Test-Driving the **Craps Game** Application

16.2 Random-Number Generation

16.3 Using Enumerations in the **Craps Game** Application

16.4 Using Random Numbers in the **Craps Game** Application

16.5 Wrap-Up

You will now be introduced to a popular type of application—simulation and game playing. In this tutorial, you will develop a **Craps Game** application. There is something in the air of a gambling casino that invigorates many people—from the high rollers at the plush mahogany-and-felt craps tables to the quarter-poppers at the one-armed bandits. Many of these individuals are drawn by the element of chance—the possibility that luck will convert a pocketful of money into a mountain of wealth.

The element of chance can be introduced into computer applications using random numbers. This tutorial's **Craps Game** application introduces several new concepts, including random-number generation and enumerations. It also uses important concepts that you learned earlier in this book, including instance variables, procedures and the `Select Case` multiple-selection control structure.

16.1 Test-Driving the Craps Game Application

One of the most popular games of chance is a dice game known as "craps," played in casinos throughout the world. This application must meet the following requirements:

Application Requirements

Create an application that simulates playing the game of craps. In this game, a player rolls two dice. Each die has six faces. Each face contains one, two, three, four, five or six spots. After the dice have come to rest, the sum of the spots on the two top faces is calculated. If the sum is 7 or 11 on the first throw, the player wins. If the sum is 2, 3 or 12 on the first throw (called "craps"), the player loses (the "house" wins). If the sum is 4, 5, 6, 8, 9 or 10 on the first throw, that sum becomes the player's "point." To win, a player must continue rolling the dice until the point value is rolled. The player loses by rolling a 7 before rolling the point.

Creating this application will teach you two important concepts: random-number generation and enumerations. You begin by test-driving the completed application. Then you will learn the additional Visual Basic technologies that you will need to create your own version of this application.

*Test-Driving the Craps
Game Application*

1. ***Opening the completed application.*** Open the directory C:\Examples\ Tutorial16\CompletedApplication\CrapsGame to locate the **Craps Game** application. Double click CrapsGame.sln to open the application in the Visual Basic IDE.

2. ***Running the Craps Game application.*** Select **Debug > Start Debugging** to run the application (Fig. 16.1).

Figure 16.1   **Craps Game** application's initial appearance.

3. ***Starting the game.*** Click the **Play** Button. There are three possible outcomes at this point: The player wins by rolling a 7 or an 11 (Fig. 16.2). The player loses by rolling 2, 3 or 12 (Fig. 16.3). Otherwise, the roll becomes the player's point (4, 5, 6, 8, 9 or 10), which is then displayed for the remainder of the game (Fig. 16.4). Note that unlike the real game of craps, the value of the roll is computed using the forward-facing die faces instead of the top faces in this application.

Figure 16.2   Player wins on first roll by rolling 7 or 11.

Figure 16.3   Player loses on first roll by rolling 2, 3 or 12.

(cont.)

Figure 16.4 First roll sets the point that the player must match to win.

4. ***Continuing the game.*** If the application displays **Roll again!**, as in Fig. 16.4, click the **Roll** Button repeatedly until either you win by matching your point value (Fig. 16.5) or you lose by rolling a 7 (Fig. 16.6). When the game ends, you can click **Play** to start over.

Figure 16.5 Winning the game by matching your point before rolling a 7.

Figure 16.6 Losing by rolling a 7 before matching your point.

5. ***Closing the application.*** Close your running application by clicking its close box.

6. ***Closing the IDE.*** Close the Visual Basic IDE by clicking its close box.

16.2 Random-Number Generation

Now you will learn how to use an object of class **Random** to introduce the element of chance into your computer applications. You will learn more about working with objects of existing classes over the next few tutorials, then you will learn to create your own classes and create objects of those classes in Tutorial 19. Consider the following statements:

```
Dim randomObject As Random = New Random
Dim randomNumber As Integer = randomObject.Next()
```

The first statement declares `randomObject` as a reference of type `Random` and assigns it a Random object. A **reference** is a variable to which you assign an object. Recall that keyword `New` creates a new object in memory.

The second statement declares `Integer` variable `randomNumber`. It then assigns it the value returned by calling Random's Next method on `randomObject` using the dot operator. The **Next** method generates a positive `Integer` value between zero and the largest possible `Integer`, which is the constant **Int32.Max-Value** (the value 2,147,483,647). You can use the Next method to generate random values of type `Integer` or use **NextDouble** method to generate random values of type `Double`. The `NextDouble` method returns a positive `Double` value between 0.0 and 1.0 (not including 1.0). Class `Random` does not contain a Next method for any other data type.

If the `Next` method were to produce truly random values, then every value in this range would have an equal chance (or probability) of being chosen when `Next` is called. However, the values returned by `Next` are actually **pseudorandom numbers**, a sequence of values produced by a complex mathematical calculation. This mathematical calculation comes close, but is not exactly random in choosing numbers.

The range of values produced by `Next` (that is, values between 0 and 2,147,483,647) often is different from the range needed in a particular application. For example, an application that simulates coin tossing might require only 0 for heads and 1 for tails. An application that simulates the rolling of a six-sided die would require random `Integers` from 1 to 6. Similarly, an application that randomly predicts the next type of spaceship (out of four possibilities) that flies across the horizon in a video game might require random `Integers` from 1 to 4.

By passing an argument to the `Next` method as follows

```
value = 1 + randomObject.Next(6)
```

you can produce integers in the range from 1 to 6. When a single argument is passed to `Next`, the values returned by `Next` will be in the range from 0 to (but not including) the value of that argument (that is, 5 in the preceding statement). You can change the range of numbers produced by adding 1 to the previous result, so that the return values are between 1 and 6, rather than 0 and 5. This new range, 1 to 6, corresponds nicely with the roll of a six-sided die, for example.

Visual Basic simplifies the process of setting the range of numbers by allowing the programmer to pass two arguments to `Next`. For example, the preceding statement also could be written as

```
value = randomObject.Next(1, 7)
```

Note that you must use 7 as the second argument to the `Next` method to produce integers in the range from 1 to 6. The first argument indicates the minimum value in the desired range; the second is equal to *one more than the maximum value desired*.

As with method `Next`, the range of values produced by method `NextDouble` (that is, values greater than or equal to 0.0 and less than 1.0) is also usually different from the range needed in a particular application. By multiplying the value returned from method `NextDouble` as follows

```
value = 6 * randomObject.NextDouble()
```

you can produce `Double` values in the range from 0.0 to 6.0 (not including 6.0). Figure 16.7 shows examples of the ranges returned by calls to methods `Next` and `NextDouble`.

Method call	Resulting range
`randomObject.Next()`	0 to one less than `Int32.MaxValue`
`randomObject.Next(30)`	0 to 29
`10 + randomObject.Next(10)`	10 to 19
`randomObject.Next(10, 20)`	10 to 19
`randomObject.Next(5, 100)`	5 to 99
`randomObject.NextDouble()`	0.0 to less than 1.0
`8 * randomObject.NextDouble()`	0.0 to less than 8.0

Figure 16.7 `Next` and `NextDouble` method calls with corresponding ranges.

SELF-REVIEW

1. The statement _____ returns a number in the range from 8 to 300.
   a) `randomObject.Next(8, 300)` b) `randomObject.Next(8, 301)`
   c) `1 + randomObject.Next(8, 300)` d) None of the above.

2. The statement _____ returns a number in the range 15 to 35.
   a) `randomObject.Next(15, 36)` b) `randomObject.Next(15, 35)`
   c) `10 + randomObject.Next(5, 26)` d) Both a and c.

Answers: 1) b. 2) d.

16.3 Using Enumerations in the Craps Game Application

The following pseudocode describes the basic operation of the **Craps Game** application:

```
When the player clicks the Play Button:
     Roll the dice using random numbers
     Display images corresponding to the numbers on the rolled dice
     Calculate the sum of both dice

     Select correct case based on the sum of the two dice:

     Case where first roll is 7 or 11
          Disable the Roll Button
          Display the winning message

     Case where first roll is 2, 3 or 12
          Disable the Roll Button
          Display the losing message

     Case where none of the preceding Cases are true
          Set the value of the point to the sum of the dice
          Display point value
          Display message to roll again
          Display images for user's point
          Disable the Play Button
          Enable the Roll Button

When the player clicks the Roll Button:
     Roll the dice using random numbers
     Display images corresponding to the numbers on the rolled dice
     Calculate the sum of both dice

     If the player rolls the same value as the point
          Display the winning message
          Disable the Roll Button
          Enable the Play Button
```

> Else If the player rolls a 7
>   Display the losing message
>   Disable the Roll Button
>   Enable the Play Button

Now that you have test-driven the **Craps Game** application and studied its pseudocode representation, you will use an ACE table to help you convert the pseudocode to Visual Basic. Figure 16.8 lists the actions, controls and events that will help you complete your own version of this application.

Action/Control/Event (ACE) Table for the Craps Game Application

Action	Control/Object	Event
Label the application's controls	resultLabel, pointDiceGroup-Frame	
	playButton	Click
Roll the dice using random numbers	randomObject	
Display images corresponding to the numbers on the rolled dice	die1Picture, die2Picture	
Calculate the sum of both dice		
Select correct case based on sum:		
Case where first roll is 7 or 11 Disable the Roll Button	rollButton	
Display the winning message	statusLabel	
Case where first roll is 2, 3 or 1 Disable the Roll Button	rollButton	
Display the losing message	statusLabel	

Case where none of the preceding Cases are true
    Set the value of the point to
    the sum of the dice		

Display the point value	pointDiceGroup-Frame	
Display message to roll again	statusLabel	
Display images for user's point	pointDie1Picture, pointDie2Picture	
Disable the Play Button	playButton	
Enable the Roll Button	rollButton	
	rollButton	Click
Roll the dice using random numbers	randomObject	
Display images corresponding to the numbers on the rolled dice	die1Picture, die2Picture	
Calculate the sum of both dice		
If the player rolls the same value as the point Display the winning message	statusLabel	
Disable the Roll Button	rollButton	
Enable the Play Button	playButton	
If the player rolls a 7 Display the losing message	statusLabel	
Disable the Roll Button	rollButton	
Enable the Play Button	playButton	

Figure 16.8   ACE table for the **Craps Game** application.

In the following boxes, you will create an application to simulate playing the game of craps. The steps that follow show you how to add code to import the System.IO namespace. As you have already learned, Visual Basic has access to the Framework Class Library (FCL), which is a rich collection of classes that can be used to enhance applications. The FCL includes classes that provide methods for using files, graphics, multimedia and more. These FCL classes are grouped (by functionality) in units called **namespaces**. The **System.IO namespace** provides classes and methods for accessing files (such as images and text) and directories (such as C:\SimplyVB). You will need to use code to access image files for the **Craps Game** application; therefore, you import the System.IO namespace. Importing a namespace (using the **Imports** statement) allows you to access its members.

Viewing the Craps Game Template Application and Importing its Required Namespaces	1. ***Copying the template to your working directory.*** Copy the C:\Examples\ Tutorial16\TemplateApplication\CrapsGame directory to your C:\SimplyVB directory.

2. ***Opening the application's template file.*** Double click CrapsGame.sln in the CrapsGame directory to open the application in the Visual Basic IDE. Figure 16.9 displays the Form in design view. Remember to turn **Option Strict** On before going any further.

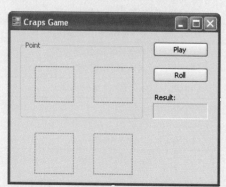

Figure 16.9 Template **Craps Game** Form in design view.

3. ***Allowing image-file access.*** The application will display images; therefore, you need to import the System.IO namespace to allow access to methods to help you read image files. Select **View > Code**. Add Imports System.IO (line 1) into your code before the class definition (Fig. 16.10).

Importing the System.IO namespace

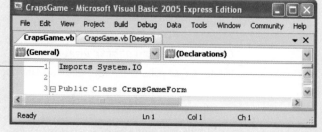

Figure 16.10 Imports statement added in the **Craps Game** application.

4. ***Saving the project.*** Select **File > Save All** to save your modified code.

Note that the numbers 2, 3, 7, 11 and 12 have special meanings during a game of craps. Throughout the course of a craps game, you will use these numbers (as constants) quite often. In this case, it would be helpful to create a group of related constants and assign them meaningful names for use in your application. Visual Basic allows you to accomplish this by using an **enumeration**. You will learn how to create constant identifiers that describe various significant dice combinations in craps (such as SNAKE_EYES, TREY, CRAPS, LUCKY_SEVEN, YO_LEVEN and BOX_CARS). By providing descriptive identifiers for a group of related constants, enumerations enhance program readability and ensure that numbers are consistent throughout the application. Next, you will learn how to use enumerations.

Introducing Enumerations and Declaring Instance Variables

1. **Declaring an enumeration.** Add lines 4–5 of Fig. 16.11 to your application, then press *Enter*. Note that keywords End Enum appear. Enumerations begin with the keyword **Enum** (line 5), and end with the keywords **End Enum** (line 12). The name of the enumeration (DiceNames) follows the keyword Enum (line 5). Now add lines 6–11 of Fig. 16.11 into your application between the lines containing keywords Enum and End Enum.

Defining an enumeration ——

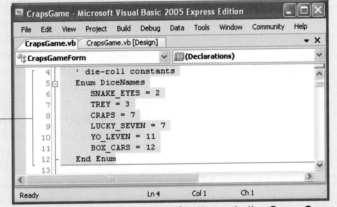

Figure 16.11 Enumeration DiceNames in the **Craps Game** application.

Enumerations are used in this application to make the code easier to read, especially for someone who is unfamiliar with the application. You can refer to the numbers using the enumeration constants and the member-access operator. For instance, use DiceNames.SNAKE_EYES for the number 2, DiceNames.TREY for the number 3, DiceNames.CRAPS and DiceNames.LUCKY_SEVEN for the number 7, DiceNames.YO_LEVEN for the number 11 and Dice-Names.BOX_CARS for the number 12. Note that you can assign the same value to multiple enumeration constants, as you did in lines 8 and 9.

2. **Declaring constants and instance variables.** Several methods will require the use of the same variables throughout the lifetime of the application. You will declare instance variables for this purpose. Add lines 14–20 of Fig. 16.12 below the enumeration definition.

Good Programming Practice

Use enumerations to group related constants and enhance code readability.

Common Programming Error

An enumeration type can be specified after the enumeration name by using the keyword As followed by Byte, Integer, Long or Short. Enumerations use type Integer if no type is specified. Attempting to create enumeration values of type String, Decimal and Double results in a syntax error.

(cont.)

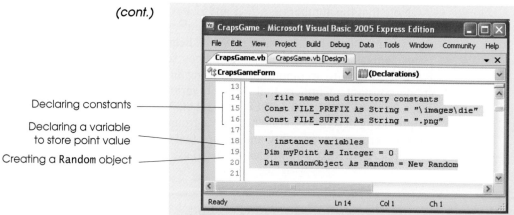

Declaring constants

Declaring a variable
to store point value

Creating a **Random** object

Figure 16.12   Instance variables added to the **Craps Game** application.

In this application, you will need to access images that display the six faces of a die. For convenience, each image file has a name that differs only by one number. For example, the image for the die face displaying 1 is named `die1.png`, and the image for the die face displaying 6 is named `die6.png`. Recall that `png` is an image-file name extension that is short for Portable Network Graphic. These images are stored in the folder named `images` in your project's `bin\Debug` directory. As such, the `String` `images\die1.png` would correctly indicate the location of the die face displaying 1 relative to the `bin\Debug` directory. [*Note:* You also can indicate the location of the die face by using the `String images\die1.png`.] To help create a `String` representing the path to the image, `Strings` `FILE_PREFIX` (`images\die`) and `FILE_SUFFIX` (`.png`) are used (as constants) to store the prefix and suffix of the file name (lines 15–16).

The game of craps requires that you store the user's point, once established on the first roll, for the duration of the game. Therefore, variable `myPoint` (line 19 of Fig. 16.12) is declared as an `Integer` to store the value of the dice on the first roll. You will use the `Random` object referenced by `randomObject` (line 20) to "roll" the dice and generate those values.

3. *Saving the project.* Select **File > Save All** to save your modified code.

SELF-REVIEW

1. Use keyword _____ to define groups of related constants.
   a) `ReadOnly`
   b) `Enum`
   c) `Constants`
   d) `Enumeration`

2. Namespace _____ is used to access files and directories.
   a) `System.File`
   b) `System.FileDirectory`
   c) `System.FileAccess`
   d) `System.IO`

Answers: 1) b. 2) d.

16.4 Using Random Numbers in the Craps Game Application

Now that you have declared an enumeration and instance variables, you will add code to execute when the user clicks the **Craps Game** application's `Buttons`. The following box explains how to add the code that executes when the user clicks the **Play** `Button`.

Coding the Play Button's Click Event Handler

1. **Creating the Play Button's Click event handler.** Return to the **Design View** to display the Form. Double click the **Play** Button to generate the **Play** Button's Click event handler and view the code file. (The **Play** Button is used to begin a new game of craps.)

2. **Removing Images from a PictureBox and rolling dice.** Begin coding the Click event handler by adding lines 26–35 from Fig. 16.13 into the playButton_Click event handler. Be sure to add the comments and line-continuation characters, as shown in Fig. 16.13, so that the line numbers in your code match those presented in this tutorial. [*Note:* RollDice() will be underlined in blue because the procedure is not yet defined.]

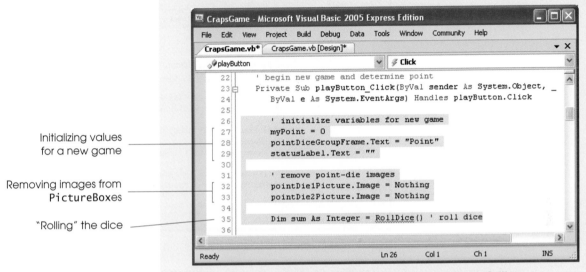

Initializing values for a new game

Removing images from PictureBoxes

"Rolling" the dice

Figure 16.13 playButton_Click event handler definition.

Lines 27–29 initialize variables for a new game. Line 27 sets variable myPoint, the craps game point value, to 0. Line 28 changes the text displayed on the GroupBox to Point, using the GroupBox's Text property. As you saw in the test-drive, the GroupBox's Text property will be used to display the point value. Finally, line 29 clears the value of the output Label because the user is starting a new game.

Lines 32–33 remove any images from the PictureBoxes used to display the point die. Though there are no images when the application is first run, if the user chooses to continue playing after completing a game, the images from the previous game must be cleared. Setting the Image property to keyword Nothing indicates that there is no image to display. Keyword **Nothing** is used to clear a reference's value, much as the empty string ("") is used to clear a String's value.

Line 35 declares the variable sum and assigns it the value returned by rolling the dice. This is accomplished by calling the RollDice procedure, which you will define later in this tutorial. [*Note:* RollDice() will be underlined in blue because the procedure is not yet defined.] The RollDice procedure will not only roll dice and return the sum of their values, but also will display the die images in the lower two PictureBoxes.

(cont.)

3. ***Using a Select Case statement to determine the result of rolling the dice.***
Recall that if the player rolls 7 or 11 on the first roll, the player wins. However,
if the player rolls 2, 3 or 12 on the first roll, the player loses. Add lines 37–38 of
Fig. 16.14 to the playButton_Click event handler beneath the code you
added in the previous step. Press *Enter*. Note that the keywords End Select
are auto-generated. Now add lines 39–50 of Fig. 16.14 into the
playButton_Click event handler between the Select and End Select keywords.

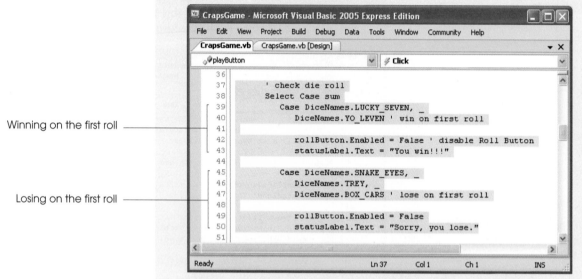

Figure 16.14 Select Case statement in playButton_Click.

The first Case statement (lines 39–43) selects values 7 and 11, using the
enumeration values DiceNames.LUCKY_SEVEN and DiceNames.YO_LEVEN.
Recall that several expressions can be specified in the same Case statement
when they are separated by commas. If the sum of the dice is 7 or 11, the
code in lines 42–43 disables the **Roll** Button and displays "You win!!!" in
the output statusLabel. If the dice add up to 2 (DiceNames.SNAKE_EYES),
3 (DiceNames.TREY) or 12 (DiceNames.BOX_CARS), the code in the second
Case statement executes (lines 45–50). This code disables the **Roll** Button
and displays a message in statusLabel indicating that the player has lost.

4. ***Using the Case Else statement to continue the game.*** If the player did not
roll a 2, 3, 7, 11 or 12, then the value of the dice becomes the point and the
player must roll again. Add lines 52–60 of Fig. 16.15 within the Select Case
statement to implement this rule.

The first line of the Case Else statement's body (line 53) sets the instance
variable myPoint to the sum of the die values. Next, line 54 changes the text
in the GroupBox, using its Text property to display the value of the current
point. The statusLabel is changed to notify the user to roll again (line 55).

If the user must match the point, you display the die images corresponding to the result of the dice roll. In Tutorial 3, you learned how to insert an
image into a PictureBox in the Windows Form Designer. To set the image
for a PictureBox, you used its Image property. You can also use code to set
this property. To display the die faces for the point in the GroupBox, set the
Image property of each PictureBox in the GroupBox to the same Image
property value as its corresponding PictureBox below the GroupBox (lines
56–57). Finally, the **Play** Button is disabled (line 58) and the **Roll** Button is
enabled (line 59), limiting users to clicking the **Roll** Button for the rest of the
game. Line 60 ends the Select Case statement.

(cont.)

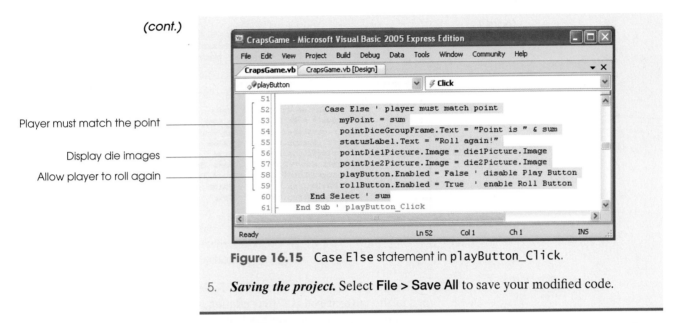

Player must match the point

Display die images

Allow player to roll again

Figure 16.15 `Case Else` statement in `playButton_Click`.

5. **Saving the project.** Select **File > Save All** to save your modified code.

The **Roll** Button is enabled after the user clicks **Play**, so you must code an event handler for it. You define the event handler in the following box.

Coding the Roll Button's `Click` Event Handler

1. **Generating the Roll Button's `Click` event handler.** Return to design view, and double click the **Roll** Button. This generates the **Roll** Button's `Click` event handler and opens the code window.

2. **Rolling the dice.** The user clicks the **Roll** Button to try to match the point, which requires rolling dice. Add line 67 of Fig. 16.16, which will roll the dice, display the die images and store the sum of the dice in variable `sum`. [*Note:* `RollDice()` is underlined in blue because the procedure is not yet defined. You will define it to roll the dice and display the die images shortly.]

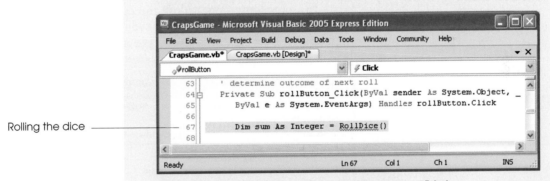

Rolling the dice

Figure 16.16 Rolling the dice in `rollButton_Click`.

3. **Determining the output of the roll.** If the roll matches the point, the user wins and the game ends. However, if the user rolls a 7 (`DiceNames.CRAPS`), the user loses and the game ends. Add lines 69–78 of Fig. 16.17 into the `rollButton_Click` event handler to incorporate this processing into your **Craps Game** application.

The `If...Then` statement (lines 70–73) determines whether the sum of the dice in the current roll matches the point. If the sum and point match, the program displays a winning message in `statusLabel`. It then allows the user to start a new game, by disabling the **Roll** Button and enabling the **Play** Button.

(cont.)

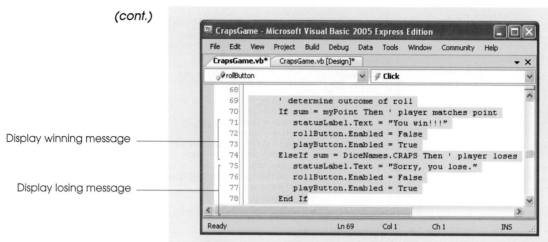

Display winning message

Display losing message

Figure 16.17 Determining the outcome of a roll.

The ElseIf statement (lines 74–77) determines whether the sum of the dice in the current roll is 7 (DiceNames.CRAPS). If so, the application displays a message that the user has lost (in statusLabel) and ends the game by disabling the **Roll** Button and enabling the **Play** Button. If the player neither matches the point nor rolls a 7, then the player is allowed to roll again. The player rolls the dice again by clicking the **Roll** Button.

4. ***Saving the project.*** Select **File > Save All** to save your modified code.

In the following box, you add code into the application to simulate rolling dice and use code to display the dice in the appropriate PictureBoxes.

Using Random Numbers to Simulate Rolling Dice

1. ***Creating a Random object and simulating die rolling.*** This application will roll and display dice many times as it executes. Therefore, it is a good idea to create two procedures: one to roll the dice (RollDice) and one to display the dice (DisplayDie). Define Function procedure RollDice first, by adding lines 81–93 of Fig. 16.18. [*Note:* The calls to DisplayDie will be underlined in blue because the procedure is not yet defined.]

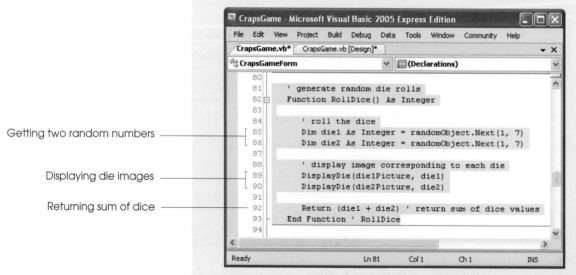

Getting two random numbers

Displaying die images

Returning sum of dice

Figure 16.18 RollDice procedure definition.

(cont.)

This code sets the values of `die1` and `die2` to the values returned by `randomObject.Next(1, 7)`, which is an `Integer` random number between 1 and 6 (lines 85 and 86). Remember that the number returned is always less than the second argument.

The procedure then makes two calls to `DisplayDie` (lines 89 and 90), a procedure that displays the image of the die face corresponding to each number. The first parameter in `DisplayDie` is the `PictureBox` that will display the image, and the second parameter is the number that appears on the face of the die. The calls to `DisplayDie` are underlined in blue as syntax errors because the procedure has not yet been defined. You will define the `DisplayDie` procedure in *Step 2*. Finally, the procedure returns the sum of the values of the dice (line 92), which the application uses to determine the outcome of the craps game.

2. ***Displaying the dice images.*** You will now define procedure `DisplayDie` to display the die images corresponding to the random numbers generated in procedure `RollDice`. Add lines 95–103 of Fig. 16.19 (after the `RollDice` procedure) to create the `DisplayDie` procedure.

Displaying a die image ————

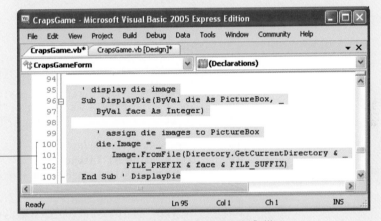

Figure 16.19   `DisplayDie` procedure definition.

Line 100 begins the statement that sets the `Image` property for the specified `PictureBox`. Because the `Image` property must be set using an object of type `Image`, you must create an `Image` object.

The `Image` class contains a `FromFile` method to help create `Image` objects. **`Image.FromFile`** returns an `Image` object containing the image located at the path you specify. To specify the location, use the path (as a `String`) as the parameter to the `FromFile` method. In this case, you can begin by using the `Directory.GetCurrentDirectory` method (line 101). The **`Directory.Get-CurrentDirectory`** method (contained in the `System.IO` namespace) returns the location of the folder from which your application was loaded (the `bin` directory). In this case, `Directory.GetCurrentDirectory` will return the string `C:\SimplyVB\CrapsGame\bin\debug`.

Now append `FILE_PREFIX & face & FILE_SUFFIX` to create the rest of the location of the file (line 102). If the value of `face` is 1, the expression would represent the string `images\die1.png`. This is the location of the image of a die face showing 1. If you combine the value of `Directory.Get-CurrentDirectory` with the expression mentioned earlier, the result is `C:\SimplyVB\CrapsGame\bin\debug\images\die1.png`, the location of the image on your computer. You can use Windows Explorer to verify that this is the correct location. This image is then displayed in the `PictureBox` by using its `Image` property.

Good Programming Practice

Using `Directory` method `GetCurrentDirectory` makes an application more portable, because the application does not require knowledge of the user's directory structure to locate files related to the application.

(cont.)

3. ***Running the application.*** Select **Debug > Start Debugging** to run your completed application and enjoy the game!

4. ***Closing the application.*** Close your running application by clicking its close box.

5. ***Closing the IDE.*** Close the Visual Basic IDE by clicking its close box.

Figure 16.20 presents the source code for the **Craps Game** application. The lines of code that contain new programming concepts that you learned in this tutorial are highlighted. As part of the project settings, Option Strict is set to On (to ensure explicit narrowing conversions).

Importing the System.IO namespace

Defining an enumeration

Creating a Random object

Removing the images from both point PictureBoxes

```vb
1   Imports System.IO
2
3   Public Class CrapsGameForm
4      ' die-roll constants
5      Enum DiceNames
6         SNAKE_EYES = 2
7         TREY = 3
8         CRAPS = 7
9         LUCKY_SEVEN = 7
10        YO_LEVEN = 11
11        BOX_CARS = 12
12     End Enum
13
14     ' file-name and directory constants
15     Const FILE_PREFIX As String = "\images\die"
16     Const FILE_SUFFIX As String = ".png"
17
18     ' instance variables
19     Dim myPoint As Integer = 0
20     Dim randomObject As Random = New Random
21
22     ' begin new game and determine point
23     Private Sub playButton_Click(ByVal sender As System.Object, _
24        ByVal e As System.EventArgs) Handles playButton.Click
25
26        ' initialize variables for new game
27        myPoint = 0
28        pointDiceGroupBox.Text = "Point"
29        statusLabel.Text = ""
30
31        ' remove point-die images
32        pointDie1Picture.Image = Nothing
33        pointDie2Picture.Image = Nothing
34
35        Dim sum As Integer = RollDice() ' roll dice
36
37        ' check die roll
38        Select Case sum
39           Case DiceNames.LUCKY_SEVEN, _
40              DiceNames.YO_LEVEN ' win on first roll
41
42              rollButton.Enabled = False ' disable Roll Button
43              statusLabel.Text = "You win!!!"
44
45           Case DiceNames.SNAKE_EYES, _
46              DiceNames.TREY, _
47              DiceNames.BOX_CARS ' lose on first roll
48
49              rollButton.Enabled = False
50              statusLabel.Text = "Sorry, you lose."
```

Figure 16.20 **Craps Game** application code listing. (Part 1 of 2.)

```
51
52                    Case Else ' player must match point
53                        myPoint = sum
54                        pointDiceGroupBox.Text = "Point Is " & sum
55                        statusLabel.Text = "Roll again!"
56                        pointDie1Picture.Image = die1Picture.Image
57                        pointDie2Picture.Image = die2Picture.Image
58                        playButton.Enabled = False ' disable Play Button
59                        rollButton.Enabled = True   ' enable Roll Button
60                End Select ' sum
61        End Sub ' playButton_Click
62
63        ' determine outcome of next roll
64        Private Sub rollButton_Click(ByVal sender As System.Object, _
65            ByVal e As System.EventArgs) Handles rollButton.Click
66
67            Dim sum As Integer = RollDice()
68
69            ' determine outcome of roll
70            If sum = myPoint Then ' player matches point
71                statusLabel.Text = "You win!!!"
72                rollButton.Enabled = False
73                playButton.Enabled = True
74            ElseIf sum = DiceNames.CRAPS Then ' player loses
75                statusLabel.Text = "Sorry, you lose."
76                rollButton.Enabled = False
77                playButton.Enabled = True
78            End If
79        End Sub ' rollButton_Click
80
81        ' generate random die rolls
82        Function RollDice() As Integer
83
84            ' roll the dice
85            Dim die1 As Integer = randomObject.Next(1, 7)
86            Dim die2 As Integer = randomObject.Next(1, 7)
87
88            ' display image corresponding to each die
89            DisplayDie(die1Picture, die1)
90            DisplayDie(die2Picture, die2)
91
92            Return (die1 + die2) ' return sum of dice values
93        End Function ' RollDice
94
95        ' display die image
96        Sub DisplayDie(ByVal die As PictureBox, _
97            ByVal face As Integer)
98
99            ' assign die images to PictureBox
100           die.Image = _
101               Image.FromFile(Directory.GetCurrentDirectory & _
102                   FILE_PREFIX & face & FILE_SUFFIX)
103       End Sub ' DisplayDie
104   End Class ' CrapsGameForm
```

Generating random numbers — (lines 85–86)

Using code to display an image — (lines 100–102)

Figure 16.20 Craps Game application code listing. (Part 2 of 2.)

SELF-REVIEW

1. _____ returns a string that, by default, represents the location from which the application was loaded.

   a) `Directory.GetWorkingDirectory`   b) `Directory.GetDirectory`

   c) `Directory.GetCurrentDirectory`   d) `Directory.ActiveDirectory`

2. To clear the image in a `PictureBox`, set its `Image` property to _____.

    a) `""` (double quotes)   b) `Nothing`

    c) `None`   d) `Empty`

Answers: 1) c. 2) b.

16.5 Wrap-Up

In this tutorial, you created the **Craps Game** application to simulate playing the popular dice game called craps. You learned about the `Random` class and how it can be used to generate random numbers by creating a `Random` object and calling method `Next` on it. You then learned how to specify the range of values within which random numbers should be generated by passing various arguments to method `Next`. You were also introduced to enumerations, which enhance program readability by using descriptive identifiers to represent constants in an application.

Using your knowledge of random-number generation and event handlers, you wrote code that added functionality to your **Craps Game** application. You used random-number generation to simulate the element of chance. In addition to "rolling dice" in code, you learned how to use a `PictureBox` to display an image by using code. You used the `System.IO` namespace to help access images located in a file.

In the next tutorial, you will learn how to use arrays, which allow you to use one name to store many values. You will apply your knowledge of random numbers and arrays to create a **Flag Tutor** application that tests your knowledge of various nations' flags.

SKILLS SUMMARY

Generating Random Numbers

- Create an object of class `Random`, and call this object's `Next` method.

Generating Random Numbers within a Specified Range

- Call the `Random` class's `Next` method with one argument. This argument represents one more than the maximum possible desired value for the random numbers.

- Call the `Random` class's `Next` method with two arguments. The first argument represents the minimum possible value; the second argument represents one more than the maximum possible desired value.

Declaring Enumerations

- Begin an enumeration with keyword `Enum`; then use a list of descriptive names, and set each one to the value it represents. End the enumeration with keywords `End Enum`.

KEY TERMS

`Directory.GetCurrentDirectory`—A method of class `Directory` in the `System.IO` namespace that returns a `String` containing the path to the directory that contains the application.

End Enum keywords—End an enumeration.

Enum keyword—Begins an enumeration.

enumeration—A group of related, named constants.

`Image.FromFile`—A method of class `Image` that returns an `Image` object containing the image located at the path you specify.

Imports keyword—Used to import namespaces.

`Int32.MaxValue` **constant**—The largest possible `Integer`—more specifically, 2,147,483,647.

namespace—A group of related classes in the Framework Class Library.

Next method of class Random—A method of class `Random` that, when called with no arguments, generates a positive `Integer` value between zero and the constant `Int32.MaxValue`, and, when called with arguments, generates an `Integer` value in a range constrained by those arguments.

NextDouble method of class Random—A method of class `Random` that generates a positive `Double` value that is greater than or equal to 0.0 and less than 1.0.

Nothing keyword—Used to clear a reference's value.

pseudorandom numbers—A sequence of values produced by a complex mathematical calculation that simulates random-number generation.

Random class—Contains methods to generate pseudorandom numbers.

reference—A variable to which you assign an object.

System.IO namespace—Contains methods to access files and directories.

CONTROLS, EVENTS, PROPERTIES & METHODS

Directory This class provides functionality to manipulate directories, such as creating, moving, and navigating through them.

■ *Method*

GetCurrentDirectory—Returns a string that, by default, represents the location from which the application was loaded.

Image This class provides functionality to manipulate images.

■ *Method*

FromFile—Used to specify the image to load and where it is located.

Random This class is used to generate random numbers.

■ *Methods*

Next—When called with no arguments, generates a positive Integer value between zero and the largest possible Integer, which is the constant Int32.MaxValue (2,147,483,647). When called with one argument, generates a positive Integer value between zero and one less than the argument passed to it. When called with two arguments, generates a positive Integer value between those two arguments, inclusive of the first and exclusive of the second.

NextDouble—Generates a positive Double value that is greater than or equal to 0.0 and less than 1.0.

MULTIPLE-CHOICE QUESTIONS

16.1 A Random object can generate pseudorandom numbers of type _____.

a) Integer
b) Single
c) Double
d) Both a and c.

16.2 A _____ is a group of related classes in the Framework Class Library.

a) class space
b) directory
c) namespace
d) library

16.3 Constant identifiers within enumerations (e.g. SNAKE_EYES, TREY, CRAPS, etc.) _____ be assigned the same numeric value.

a) cannot
b) can
c) must
d) should

16.4 The Next method of class Random can be called using _____.

a) one argument
b) no arguments
c) two arguments
d) All of the above.

16.5 The statement _____ assigns value a random number in the range from 5 to 20.

a) value = randomObject.Next(5, 21)
b) value = randomObject.Next(4, 20)
c) value = randomObject.Next(5, 20)
d) value = randomObject.Next(4, 21)

16.6 The _____ method specifies the file from which an image is loaded.

a) Next in class Random
b) FromFile in class Image
c) GetCurrentDirectory in class Directory
d) None of the above.

16.7 The System.IO namespace contains classes and methods to _____.

a) access files and directories

b) display graphics in an application

c) insert multimedia into an application

d) All of the above.

16.8 The values returned by the _____ method of class Random are actually pseudorandom numbers.

a) NextRandom

b) Pseudorandom

c) Next

d) Pseudo

16.9 When creating random numbers, the second argument passed to the Next method is _____.

a) equal to the maximum value you wish to be generated

b) equal to one more than the maximum value you wish to be generated

c) equal to one less than the maximum value you wish to be generated

d) equal to the minimum value you wish to be generated

16.10 A(n) _____ is a group of related, named constants.

a) namespace

b) variable

c) enumeration

d) None of the above.

EXERCISES

16.11 (*Guess the Number Application*) Develop an application that generates a random number and prompts the user to guess the number (Fig. 16.21). When the user clicks the **New Game** Button, the application chooses a number in the range 1 to 100 at random. The user enters guesses into the **Guess:** TextBox and clicks the **Enter** Button. If the guess is correct, the game ends, and the user can start a new game. If the guess is not correct, the application should indicate whether the guess is higher or lower than the correct number.

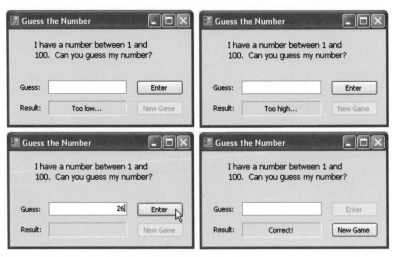

Figure 16.21 Guess the Number application.

a) *Copying the template to your working directory.* Copy the directory C:\Examples\ Tutorial16\Exercises\GuessNumber to your C:\SimplyVB directory.

b) *Opening the application's template file.* Double click GuessNumber.sln in the GuessNumber directory to open the application. Remember to turn **Option Strict** On before going any further.

c) *Creating a Random object.* Create two instance variables. The first variable should reference a Random object, and the second variable should store a random-generated number.

d) *Adding a Click event handler for the Enter Button.* Add a Click event handler for the **Enter** Button that retrieves the value entered by the user and compares it to the random number. If the guess is correct, display **Correct!** in the output Label. Then disable the **Enter** Button and enable the **New Game** Button. If the user's guess is higher than the correct answer, display **Too high...** in the output Label. If the user's guess is lower than the correct answer, display **Too low...** in the output Label.

e) *Adding a Click event handler for the New Game Button.* Add a Click event handler for the **New Game** Button that generates a new random number for the instance variable. The event handler should then disable the **New Game** Button, enable the **Enter** Button and clear the **Result:** TextBox.

f) *Running the application.* Select **Debug > Start Debugging** to run your application. Enter guesses (clicking the **Enter** Button after each) until you have successfully determined the answer. Click the **New Game** Button and test the application again.

g) *Closing the application.* Close your running application by clicking its close box.

h) *Closing the IDE.* Close the Visual Basic IDE by clicking its close box.

16.12 (*Dice Simulator Application*) Develop an application that simulates rolling two six-sided dice. Your application should have a **Roll Button** that, when clicked, displays two dice images corresponding to random numbers. It should also display the number of times each face has appeared. Your application should look like Fig. 16.22.

Figure 16.22 Dice Simulator application.

a) *Copying the template to your working directory.* Copy the directory C:\Examples\ Tutorial16\Exercises\DiceSimulator to your C:\SimplyVB directory.

b) *Opening the application's template file.* Double click DiceSimulator.sln in the DiceSimulator directory to open the application. Remember to turn **Option Strict** On before going any further.

c) *Adding a Click event handler for the Roll Button.* Add a Click event handler for the **Roll** Button. Call method DisplayDie in this event handler to display the images for both dice

d) *Displaying the die image.* Create a Sub procedure named DisplayDie that takes a PictureBox control as an argument. This method should generate a random number to simulate a die roll, then display the die image in the corresponding PictureBox control on the Form. The die image should correspond to the random number that was generated. To set the image, refer to the code presented in Fig. 16.20.

e) *Displaying the frequency.* Add a Sub procedure called DisplayFrequency to be called from DisplayDie that uses a Select Case statement to update the number of times each face has appeared. Create an enumeration for the dice faces which will be used in the Select Case statement.

f) *Running the application.* Select **Debug > Start Debugging** to run your application. Click the **Roll** Button several times. Each time, two die faces are displayed. Verify after each roll that the appropriate face values on the left are incremented.

g) *Closing the application.* Close your running application by clicking its close box.

h) *Closing the IDE.* Close the Visual Basic IDE by clicking its close box.

16.13 (*Lottery Picker Application*) A lottery commission offers four different lottery games to play: Three-number, Four-number, Five-number and Five-number + one lotteries. Each game has independent numbers. Develop an application that randomly picks numbers for all four games and displays the generated numbers in a GUI (Fig. 16.23). You should use two digits to display all numbers by using the D2 format specifier in a call to String.Format. The games are played as follows:

- Three-number lotteries require players to choose three numbers in the range 0–9.
- Four-number lotteries require players to choose four numbers in the range 0–9.
- Five-number lotteries require players to choose five numbers in the range 1–39.
- Five-number + 1 lotteries require players to choose five numbers in the range 1–49 and an additional number in the range of 1–42.

Figure 16.23 **Lottery Picker** application.

a) *Copying the template to your working directory.* Copy the directory `C:\Examples\Tutorial16\Exercises\LotteryPicker` to your `C:\SimplyVB` directory.

b) *Opening the application's template file.* Double click `LotteryPicker.sln` in the `LotteryPicker` directory to open the application. Remember to turn **Option Strict** On before going any further.

c) *Generating random numbers.* Create a `Function` procedure that will generate the random numbers for all four games.

d) *Drawing numbers for the games.* Add code into your application to call the previously created procedure in order to generate numbers for all four games. To make the applications simple, allow repetition of numbers.

e) *Running the application.* Select **Debug > Start Debugging** to run your application. Click the **Generate** Button multiple times. Make sure the values displayed are within the ranges described in the exercise description.

f) *Closing the application.* Close your running application by clicking its close box.

g) *Closing the IDE.* Close the Visual Basic IDE by clicking its close box.

What does this code do? ▶ **16.14** What does the following code do?

```
1   Sub PickRandomNumbers()
2
3       Dim number1 As Integer
4       Dim number As Double
5       Dim number2 As Integer
6       Dim randomObject As Random = New Random
7
8       number1 = randomObject.Next()
9       number = 5 * randomObject.NextDouble()
10      number2 = randomObject.Next(1, 10)
11      integer1Label.Text = Convert.ToString(number1)
12      double1Label.Text = Convert.ToString(number)
13      integer2Label.Text = Convert.ToString(number2)
14  End Sub ' PickRandomNumbers
```

What's wrong with this code? ▶ **16.15** This Sub procedure should assign a random Decimal number (in the range 0 to `Int32.MaxValue`) to Decimal `decNumber`. (Assume that `Option Strict` is On.) Find the error(s) in the following code.

```
1   Sub RandomDecimal()
2
3       Dim number As Decimal
4       Dim randomObject As Random = New Random
5
6       number = randomObject.Next()
7       displayLabel.Text = Convert.ToString(number)
8
9   End Sub ' RandomDecimal
```

Programming Challenge ▶ **16.16** (*Multiplication Teacher Application*) Develop an application that helps children learn multiplication. Use random-number generation to produce two positive one-digit integers that display in a question, such as "How much is 6 times 7?" The student should type the answer into a TextBox. If the answer is correct, then the application randomly displays one of three messages in a Label, **Very Good!**, **Excellent!** or **Great Job!** and displays the next question. If the student is wrong, the Label displays the message **No. Please try again**. The GUI and sample user interactions are shown in Fig. 16.24.

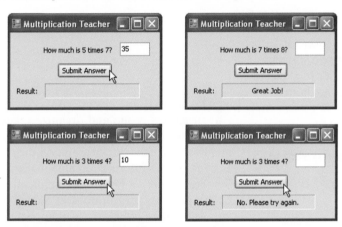

Figure 16.24 **Multiplication Teacher** application.

a) *Copying the template to your working directory.* Copy the directory C:\Examples\ Tutorial16\Exercises\MultiplicationTeacher to your C:\SimplyVB directory.

b) *Opening the application's template file.* Double click Multiplication-Teacher.sln in the MultiplicationTeacher directory to open the application. Remember to turn **Option Strict** On before going any further.

c) *Generating the questions.* Add a procedure into your application to generate each new question.

d) *Determining whether the right answer was entered.* Add code into your application to call the procedure created in the preceding step. After this procedure has been called, determine whether the student answered the question correctly, and display the appropriate message.

e) *Displaying a random message.* Add a procedure GenerateOutput that displays a random message congratulating the student for answering correctly. This method should be called if the student answered the question correctly.

f) *Running the application.* Select **Debug > Start Debugging** to run your application. Enter several correct answers and at least one incorrect answer. Verify that **No. Please try again** is displayed when you are incorrect, and one of the other responses is displayed at random when you are correct.

g) *Closing the application.* Close your running application by clicking its close box.

h) *Closing the IDE.* Close the Visual Basic IDE by clicking its close box.

17

TUTORIAL

Objectives

In this tutorial, you will learn to:
- Create and initialize arrays.
- Store information in an array.
- Refer to individual elements of an array.
- Sort arrays.
- Use **ComboBox**es to display options in a drop-down list.
- Determine whether a specific character is in a `String`.
- Remove a character from a `String`.
- Convert a `String` to lowercase characters.
- Insert characters in a `String`.

Outline

Flag Quiz Application

Introducing One-Dimensional Arrays and ComboBoxes

This tutorial introduces basic concepts and features of **data structures**. Data structures group and organize related data. **Arrays** are data structures that consist of data items of the same type. You will learn how to create arrays and how to access the information they contain. You will also learn how to sort a `String` array's information alphabetically.

This tutorial's **Flag Quiz** application includes a ComboBox control. A ComboBox presents user options in a drop-down list. This will be the first time that you will add a ComboBox to an application, but you have used them many times before in the Visual Studio environment. For example, when you activated `Option Strict` in Tutorial 15, you selected `On` from a ComboBox.

17.1 Test-Driving the Flag Quiz Application

You will now create an application that tests a student's knowledge of the flags of various countries. The application will use arrays to store information, such as the country names and `Boolean` values that determine whether a country name has been previously selected by the application as a correct answer. This application must meet the following requirements:

Application Requirements

A geography teacher would like to quiz students on their knowledge of the flags of various countries. The teacher has asked you to write an application that displays a flag and allows the student to select the corresponding country from a list. The application should inform the user of whether the answer is correct and display the next flag. The application should display five flags randomly chosen from the flags of Australia, Brazil, China, Italy, Russia, South Africa, Spain and the United States. When the application is run, a given flag should be displayed only once.

You begin by test-driving the completed application. Then you will learn the additional Visual Basic technologies that you will need to create your own version of this application.

358

Test-Driving the Flag Quiz Application

1. ***Opening the completed application.*** Open the directory `C:\Examples\Tutorial17\CompletedApplication\FlagQuiz` to locate the **Flag Quiz** application. Double click `FlagQuiz.sln` to open the application in the Visual Basic IDE.

2. ***Running the Flag Quiz application.*** Select **Debug > Start Debugging** to run the application (Fig. 17.1). Note that you might see a different flag when you run the application, because the application randomly selects which flag to display.

PictureBox displays flag ⎯⎯⎯⎯⎯

ComboBox contains answers (country names)

Figure 17.1   **Flag Quiz** application's `Form`.

3. ***Selecting an answer.*** The ComboBox contains eight country names. One country name corresponds to the displayed flag and is the correct answer. The scrollbar allows you to browse through the ComboBox's drop-down list. Select an answer from the ComboBox, as shown in Fig. 17.2.

Answer being selected ⎯⎯⎯⎯⎯

Scrollbar in **ComboBox**'s drop-down list

Figure 17.2   Selecting an answer from the ComboBox.

4. ***Submitting a correct answer.*** Click the **Submit** Button to check your answer. If it is correct, the message `"Correct!"` is displayed in an output `Label` (Fig. 17.3). Note that the **Submit** Button is now disabled and the **Next Flag** Button is enabled.

Figure 17.3   Submitting the correct answer.

5. ***Displaying the next flag.*** Click the **Next Flag** Button to display a different flag (Fig. 17.4). Note that the **Submit** Button is now enabled, the **Next Flag** Button is disabled, the ComboBox displays **Australia** (the first country listed in the ComboBox) and the output `Label` is cleared.

Figure 17.4   Displaying the next flag.

(cont.)   6.   ***Submitting an incorrect answer.*** To demonstrate the application's response, select an incorrect answer and click **Submit**, as in Fig. 17.5. The application displays "Sorry, incorrect." in the output Label.

Figure 17.5   Submitting an incorrect answer.

7.   ***Finishing the quiz.*** After the application displays five flags and the user has submitted five answers, the quiz ends (Fig. 17.6). Note that the two Buttons and the ComboBox are disabled.

ComboBox is disabled when the quiz ends

Figure 17.6   Finishing the quiz.

8.   ***Closing the application.*** Close your running application by clicking its close box.

9.   ***Closing the IDE.*** Close the Visual Basic IDE by clicking its close box.

17.2 Introducing Arrays

An array is a group of memory locations that all contain data items of the same name and type. Array names follow the same conventions that apply to other identifiers. To refer to a particular location in an array, you specify the name of the array and the **position number** of the location, which is a value that indicates a specific location within an array. Position numbers begin at 0 (zero).

Figure 17.7 depicts an Integer array named netUnitsSold. This array contains 13 items, also called **elements**. Each array element represents the net number of "units sold" of a particular book in one month at a bookstore. For example, netUnitsSold(1) is the net sales of that book for January (month 1), netUnitsSold(2) is the net sales for February, and so on. In this example, you simply ignore the first element of the array, because there is no month zero.

Each array element is referred to by providing the name of the array followed by the position number of the element in parentheses (). The position numbers for the elements in an array begin with 0. Thus, the **zeroth element** of array netUnitsSold is referred to as netUnitsSold(0), element 1 of array netUnitsSold is referred to as netUnitsSold(1), element 6 of array netUnitsSold is referred to as netUnitsSold(6) and so on. Element *i* of array netUnitsSold is referred to as netUnitsSold(i). The position number in parentheses is called an **index** or a **subscript**. An index must be either zero, a positive integer or an integer expression that yields a positive result. If an application uses an expression as an index, the expression is evaluated first to determine the index. For example, if variable value1 is equal to 5, and variable value2 is equal to 6, then the statement

```
netUnitsSold(value1 + value2) += 2
```

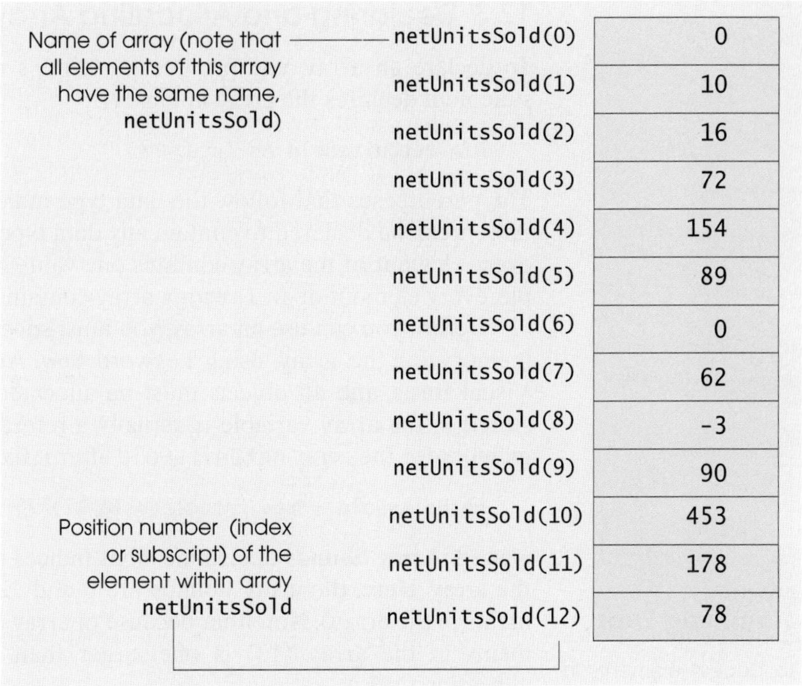

Name of array (note that all elements of this array have the same name, netUnitsSold)	netUnitsSold(0) 0
	netUnitsSold(1) 10
	netUnitsSold(2) 16
	netUnitsSold(3) 72
	netUnitsSold(4) 154
	netUnitsSold(5) 89
	netUnitsSold(6) 0
	netUnitsSold(7) 62
	netUnitsSold(8) -3
	netUnitsSold(9) 90
Position number (index or subscript) of the element within array netUnitsSold	netUnitsSold(10) 453
	netUnitsSold(11) 178
	netUnitsSold(12) 78

Figure 17.7 Array consisting of 13 elements.

adds 2 to array element `netUnitsSold(11)`. Note that an **indexed array name** (the array name followed by an index enclosed in parentheses)—like any other variable name—can be used on the left side of an assignment statement to place a new value into an array element.

Let's examine array `netUnitsSold` in Fig. 17.7 more closely. The name of the array is `netUnitsSold`. The 13 elements of the array are referred to as `netUnitsSold(0)` through `netUnitsSold(12)`. The value of `netUnitsSold(1)` is 10, the value of `netUnitsSold(2)` is 16, the value of `netUnitsSold(3)` is 72, the value of `netUnitsSold(7)` is 62 and the value of `netUnitsSold(11)` is 178. A positive value for an element in this array indicates that more books were sold than were returned. A negative value for an element in this array indicates that more books were returned than were sold. A value of zero indicates that the number of books sold was equal to the number of books returned.

Values stored in arrays can be used in various calculations and applications. For example, to determine the net units sold in the first three months of the year, then store the result in variable `firstQuarterUnits`, we would write

```
firstQuarterUnits = netUnitsSold(1) + netUnitsSold(2) + _
   netUnitsSold(3)
```

You will deal exclusively with **one-dimensional** arrays, such as `netUnitsSold`, in this tutorial. The indexed array names of one-dimensional arrays use only one index. In the next tutorial, you will study two-dimensional arrays; their indexed array names use two indices.

SELF-REVIEW

1. The number that refers to a particular element of an array is called its _____.

   a) value
   b) size
   c) indexed array name
   d) index (or subscript)

2. The indexed array name of one-dimensional array `units`'s element 2 is _____.

   a) `units{2}`
   b) `units(2)`
   c) `units[0,2]`
   d) `units[2]`

Answers: 1) d. 2) b.

17.3 Declaring and Allocating Arrays

To declare an array, you provide the array's name and data type. The following statement declares the array in Fig. 17.7:

```
Dim netUnitsSold As Integer()
```

The parentheses that follow the data type indicate that `netUnitsSold` is an array. Arrays can be declared to contain any data type. In an array of primitive data types, every element of the array contains one value of the declared data type. For example, every element of an `Integer` array contains an `Integer` value.

Before you can use an array, you must specify the size of the array and allocate memory for the array, using keyword `New`. Arrays are represented as objects in Visual Basic, and all objects must be allocated by using keyword `New`. The value stored in the array variable is actually a reference to the array object. To allocate memory for the array `netUnitsSold` after it has been declared, the statement

```
netUnitsSold = New Integer(0 To 12) {}
```

Common Programming Error

Attempting to access elements in the array by using an index outside the array bounds is a run-time error.

is used. **Array bounds** determine what indices can be used to access an element in the array. Here, the array bounds are 0 and 12 (one less than the number of elements in the array). Note that because of array element 0, the actual number of elements in the array (13) is one larger than the upper bound specified in the allocation (12).

The required braces ({ and }) are called an **initializer list** and specify the initial values of the elements in the array. When the initializer list is empty, as it is here, the elements in the array are initialized to the default value for the array's data type. Again, these default values are 0 for numeric primitive-data-type variables (such as `Integer`), `False` for `Boolean` variables and `Nothing` for references. Recall that keyword `Nothing` denotes an empty reference (that is, a value indicating that a reference variable has not been assigned an object). The initializer list also can contain a comma-separated list specifying the initial values of the elements in the array. For example,

```
Dim salesPerDay As Integer()
salesPerDay = New Integer() {0, 2, 3, 6, 1, 4, 5, 6}
```

Common Programming Error

If you specify an upper bound when initializing an array, it is a syntax error if you provide too many or too few values in the initializer list.

declares and allocates an array containing eight `Integer` values. Visual Basic can determine the array bounds from the number of elements in the initializer list. Thus, it is not necessary to specify the size of the array when a nonempty initializer list is present.

You can specify both the array bounds and an initializer list, as in the following statement:

```
Dim temperatures As Double() = _
    New Double(0 To 3) {23.45, 34.98, 78.98, 53.23}
```

Note that the upper bound is one less than the number of items in the array.

In older versions of Visual Basic, arrays were initialized using implicit array bounds. Thus the preceding statement would have been written as follows:

```
Dim temperatures As Double() = _
    New Double(3) {23.45, 34.98, 78.98, 53.23}
```

Software Design Tip

Programming languages evolve. Students tend to learn the newest language features. When you go into industry, you will no doubt also work on "legacy" software (that is, pre-existing software that uses older language features).

Note that the value 0 and the keyword `To` are not included in the parentheses.

Often, the elements of an array are used in a calculation. The following box demonstrates declaring and initializing an array and accessing its elements.

Computing the Sum of an Array's Elements

1. ***Copying the template to your working directory.*** Copy the C:\Examples\Tutorial17\TemplateApplication\SumArray directory to your C:\SimplyVB directory.

2. ***Opening the Sum Array application's template file.*** Double click SumArray.sln in the SumArray directory to open the application in the Visual Basic IDE.

3. ***Adding the Button's Click event handler.*** Double click the **Sum Array** Button in design view (Fig. 17.8) to generate the empty event handler sumButton_Click.

Figure 17.8 **Sum Array** application's Form in design view.

4. ***Combining the declaration and allocation of an array.*** Add lines 6–11 of Fig. 17.9 to the event handler. Lines 7–8 combine the declaration and allocation of an array into one statement.

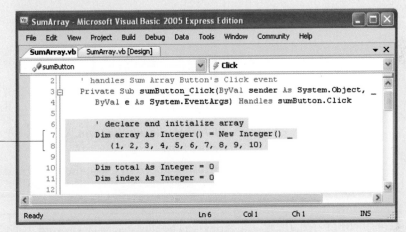

Creating an array of Integers

Figure 17.9 Declaring an array in the event handler.

 Error-Prevention Tip

Use method GetUpperBound when you need to find the largest index in an array. Using an actual numerical value for the upper bound instead could lead to errors if you change the number of array elements.

 Error-Prevention Tip

It is important to note the difference between the "seventh element of the array" and "array element seven." Array indices begin at 0, which means that the former has the index 6, whereas the latter has the index 7. This confusion is a common source of "off-by-one" errors.

5. ***Calculating the sum.*** Add lines 13–20 (Fig. 17.10) to the event handler. The For…Next loop (lines 14–18) retrieves each element's value (one at a time), which is added to total. Method **GetUpperBound** returns the index of the last element in the array. Method GetUpperBound takes one argument, indicating a dimension of the array. We discuss arrays with two dimensions in Tutorial 18. For one-dimensional arrays, such as array, the argument passed to GetUpperBound is always 0, to indicate the first (and only) dimension (or row) of the array. In this case, array.GetUpperBound(0) returns 9.

Every array in Visual Basic "knows" its own length. The **length** (or the number of elements) of the array (10 in this case) is returned by the expression array.Length.

We could have set the upper bound in the For…Next loop as

```
array.Length - 1
```

which returns 9. The value returned by method GetUpperBound is one less than the value of the array's **Length** property.

(cont.)

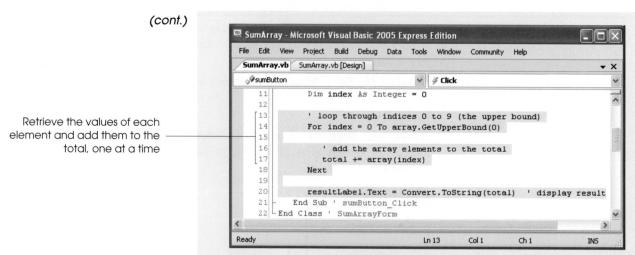

Retrieve the values of each element and add them to the total, one at a time

Figure 17.10 Calculating the sum of the values of an array's elements.

6. ***Displaying the result.*** Line 20 displays the sum of the array element values.

7. ***Running the application.*** Select **Debug > Start Debugging** to run your application. The result of adding the integers from 1 to 10, inclusive, is displayed when you click the **Sum Array** Button (Fig. 17.11).

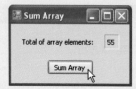

Figure 17.11 Displaying the sum of the values of an array's elements.

8. ***Closing the application.*** Close your running application by clicking its close box.

9. ***Closing the IDE.*** Close the Visual Basic IDE by clicking its close box.

SELF-REVIEW

1. Arrays can be allocated using keyword _____.
   a) `Declare`   b) `Create`
   c) `New`   d) `Allocate`

2. An array's length is _____.
   a) one more than the array's last index   b) one less than the array's last index
   c) the same as the array's last index   d) returned by method `GetUpperBound`

Answers: 1) c. 2) a.

17.4 Constructing the Flag Quiz Application

Before you can begin building the **Flag Quiz** application, you will need to develop the application using pseudocode and an ACE table. The following pseudocode describes the basic operation of the **Flag Quiz** application:

> When the Form loads:
>   Sort the country names alphabetically
>   Place country names in the ComboBox
>   Randomly select a flag
>   Display the flag

When the user clicks the Submit Button:
    Retrieve the selected country name from the ComboBox

    If the selected value matches the correct answer
        Display "Correct!" in the Label
    Else
        Display "Sorry, incorrect." in the Label

    If five images have been displayed
        Append "Done!" to the Label's text
        Disable the Buttons and ComboBox
    Else
        Disable Submit Button
        Enable Next Flag Button

When the user clicks the Next Flag Button:
    Randomly select a flag that has not been chosen previously
    Display the new flag
    Clear the Label's text
    Set ComboBox to display its first item
    Update the number of flags shown
    Enable Submit Button
    Disable Next Flag Button

Now that you have test-driven the **Flag Quiz** application and studied its pseudocode representation, you will use an ACE table to help you convert the pseudocode to Visual Basic. Figure 17.12 lists the actions, controls and events that will help you complete your own version of this application.

Action/Control/Event (ACE) Table for the Flag Quiz Application

Action	Control/Class/Object	Event
Label the application's controls	flagGroupBox, chooseLabel	
	flagQuizForm	Load
Sort the countries alphabetically	Array	
Place countries in the ComboBox	optionsComboBox	
Randomly select a flag	randomObject	
Display the flag	flagPicture	
	submitButton	Click
Retrieve the selected country	optionsComboBox	
If selected value matches the correct answer Display "Correct!" in the Label	feedbackLabel	
Else Display "Sorry, incorrect." in Label	feedbackLabel	
If five images have been displayed Append "Done!" to Label's text	feedbackLabel	
Disable the Buttons and ComboBox	nextButton, submitButton, optionsComboBox	
Else Disable Submit Button	submitButton	
Enable Next Flag Button	nextButton	

Figure 17.12 Flag Quiz application's ACE table. (Part 1 of 2.)

Action	Control/Class/Object	Event
	nextButton	Click
Randomly select a flag that has not been chosen previously	randomObject	
Display the new flag	flagPicture	
Clear the Label's text	feedbackLabel	
Set ComboBox to display first item	optionsComboBox	
Update the number of flags shown		
Enable Submit Button	submitButton	
Disable Next Flag Button	nextButton	

Figure 17.12 **Flag Quiz** application's ACE table. (Part 2 of 2.)

The following box shows you how to initialize the variables used in the application. In particular, the application requires two one-dimensional arrays.

Initializing Important Variables

1. *Copying the template to your working directory.* Copy the C:\Examples\Tutorial17\TemplateApplication\FlagQuiz directory to your C:\SimplyVB directory.

2. *Opening the Flag Quiz application's template file.* Double click FlagQuiz.sln in the FlagQuiz directory to open the application in the Visual Basic IDE.

3. *Declaring the array of country names.* Add lines 3–6 of Fig. 17.13 to the application. Lines 4–6 declare and initialize array options as an instance variable of class FlagQuizForm. Each element is a String containing the name of a country. These lines assign the initializer list to the array, combining the declaration and initialization into one statement. The compiler allocates the size of the array (in this case, eight elements) to suit the number of items in the initializer list.

Creating an array of Strings to store country names

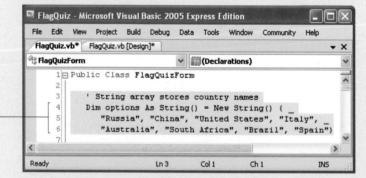

Figure 17.13 String array that stores country names.

4. *Creating a Boolean array.* The application should not display any flag more than once. Since the application uses random-number generation to pick a flag, the same flag could be selected more than once—just as, when you roll a six-sided die many times, a die face could be repeated. You will use a Boolean array to keep track of which flags have been displayed. Add lines 8–10 of Fig. 17.14 to FlagQuiz.vb. Lines 9–10 declare and create Boolean array used.

(cont.)

Creating an array of `Boolean` values with the same number of elements as the array of country names

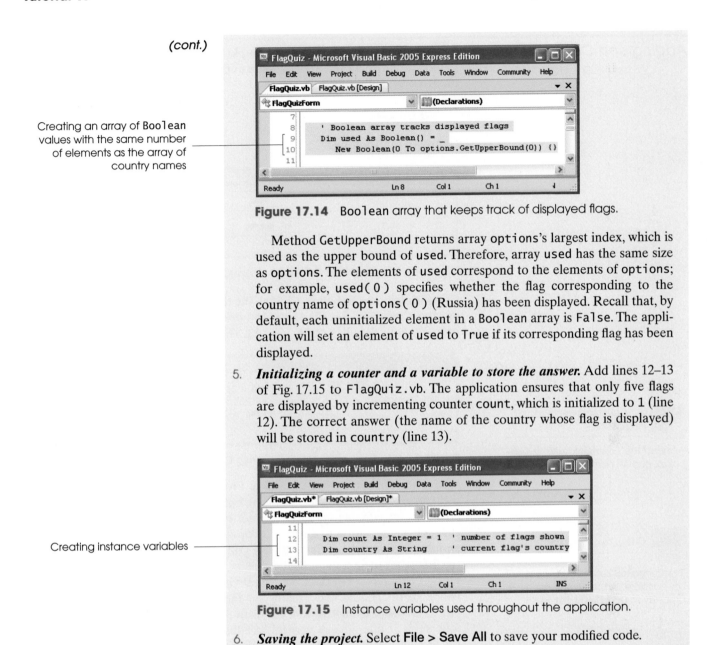

Figure 17.14 `Boolean` array that keeps track of displayed flags.

Method `GetUpperBound` returns array `options`'s largest index, which is used as the upper bound of `used`. Therefore, array `used` has the same size as `options`. The elements of `used` correspond to the elements of `options`; for example, `used( 0 )` specifies whether the flag corresponding to the country name of `options( 0 )` (Russia) has been displayed. Recall that, by default, each uninitialized element in a `Boolean` array is `False`. The application will set an element of `used` to `True` if its corresponding flag has been displayed.

5. ***Initializing a counter and a variable to store the answer.*** Add lines 12–13 of Fig. 17.15 to `FlagQuiz.vb`. The application ensures that only five flags are displayed by incrementing counter `count`, which is initialized to 1 (line 12). The correct answer (the name of the country whose flag is displayed) will be stored in `country` (line 13).

Creating instance variables

Figure 17.15 Instance variables used throughout the application.

6. ***Saving the project.*** Select **File > Save All** to save your modified code.

GUI Design Tip

Each `ComboBox` should have a descriptive `Label` that describes the `ComboBox`'s contents.

Now you will add another control to the **Flag Quiz** application template. The **Flag Quiz** application allows students to select answers from a ComboBox. The **ComboBox** control combines a `TextBox` and a `ListBox`. A ComboBox usually appears as a `TextBox` with a down arrow to its right. The user can click the down arrow to display a list of predefined items. If a user chooses an item from this list, that item is displayed in the ComboBox. If the list contains more items than the drop-down list can display at one time, a vertical scrollbar appears. The following box shows you how to assign an array's elements to a ComboBox before the Form is displayed to users.

Adding and Customizing a ComboBox

1. **Adding a ComboBox to the Form.** Double click FlagQuiz.vb in the **Solution Explorer** to display the application's Form (Fig. 17.16). Add a ComboBox to the Form by double clicking the

control in the **Toolbox**.

Figure 17.16   Flag Quiz template application's Form.

2. **Customizing the ComboBox.** Change the Name property of the ComboBox to optionsComboBox. Set the Location property to 136, 32. Leave the Size property at its default setting, 121, 21. The Form should look like Fig. 17.17.

Figure 17.17   ComboBox added to **Flag Quiz** application's Form.

3. **Setting the appearance of ComboBox.** Property **DropDownStyle** determines the ComboBox's appearance. Value **DropDownList** specifies that the ComboBox is not editable (the user cannot type text in its TextBox). You can click the arrow button to display a drop-down list from which you can select an item. In this style of ComboBox, if you press the key that corresponds to the first letter of an item in the ComboBox, that item is selected and displayed in the ComboBox's TextBox. Set the DropDownStyle property of the ComboBox to DropDownList. Finally, set the **MaxDropDownItems** property of optionsComboBox to 4, so that the drop-down list can display a maximum of four items at one time. A vertical scrollbar will be added to the drop-down list, to allow users to select the remaining items.

4. **Generating an event handler to add items to the ComboBox during the Load event.** The ComboBox should contain a list of country names when the Form is displayed. The Form's Load event occurs before the Form is displayed; as a result, you should add the items to the ComboBox in the Form's Load event handler. Double click the Form to generate the empty event handler FlagQuizForm_Load.

5. **Displaying items in the ComboBox.** Add lines 19–20 of Fig. 17.18 to the FlagQuizForm_Load. ComboBox property **DataSource** specifies the source of the items displayed in the ComboBox. In this case, the source is array options (discussed shortly).

6. **Saving the project.** Select **File > Save All** to save your modified code.

Good Programming Practice

Append the **ComboBox** suffix to ComboBox control names.

GUI Design Tip

If a **ComboBox**'s content should not be editable, set its **DropDownStyle** property to **DropDownList**.

(cont.)

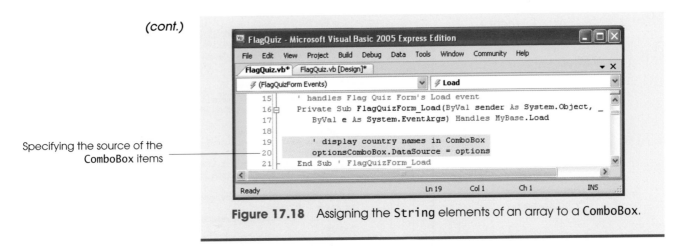

Specifying the source of the ComboBox items

Figure 17.18 Assigning the `String` elements of an array to a `ComboBox`.

Recall that to specify the image displayed in a `PictureBox`, you need to set its `Image` property to the image's file name. The flag images are stored in `C:\SimplyVB\FlagQuiz\bin\Debug\images`. The name of each flag-image file is of the form *countryname*`.png`, where *countryname* has no whitespace. The following box shows how the application constructs the full path name needed to locate and display each flag.

Building a Flag-Image File's Path Name

1. *Creating a procedure to build the flag-image file's path name.* Add lines 23–27 of Fig. 17.19 to the **Flag Quiz** application after event handler `FlagQuizForm_Load`. Function `BuildPathName` constructs a full path name for a flag-image file, beginning with the country name. The country name is retrieved from instance variable `country` (the correct answer) and stored in local variable `output`.

2. *Removing whitespace from the country name.* Some countries—for example, South Africa and the United States—have a space character in their names, but the flag-image file names do not contain whitespace characters. Add lines 29–35 of Fig. 17.19 to procedure `BuildPathName`. Line 30 uses `String` method **IndexOf** to assign to `space` the index where the space character (`" "`) in the country name occurs. For instance, if `output` were `"South Africa"`, `space` would be 5, because the space appears at index 5 of the name, counting from position zero. If the country does not have a space character, method `IndexOf` returns –1. Line 33 tests for whether `space` is a positive number. In this application, method `IndexOf` returns a number greater than 0 if the country name is "South Africa" or "United States."

   If a space is found, the **Remove** method is called to eliminate the space character (line 34). Method `Remove` receives an index as its first argument and the number of characters to remove as its second argument. For example, the words "South Africa" would become the word "SouthAfrica." Method `Remove` returns a copy of the `String` without the space character. The copy is assigned to variable `output`. [*Note:* `String` methods, such as `Remove`, do not modify the `String` object for which they are called. The `String` object returned by these methods contains a copy of the modified `String`.]

3. *Ensuring that all characters are lowercase.* Add line 37 of Fig. 17.20 to procedure `BuildPathName`. Now that `output` contains a country name without whitespace, line 37 invokes method **ToLower**, which returns a copy of the `String` with any uppercase letters in the name converted to lowercase. All the flag-image file names are in lowercase for consistency. Note that there is also a **ToUpper** method for converting a `String` to uppercase.

(cont.)

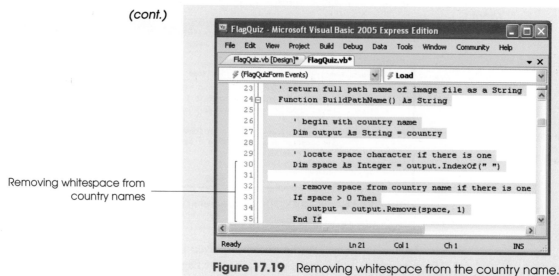

Removing whitespace from country names

Figure 17.19 Removing whitespace from the country name.

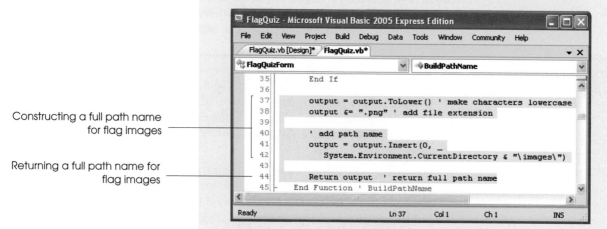

Constructing a full path name for flag images

Returning a full path name for flag images

Figure 17.20 Building the flag-image file path name.

4. *Adding the file extension.* Add line 38 of Fig. 17.20 to procedure Build-PathName. The flag-image files are in PNG format. Line 38 appends the file extension ".png" to output.

5. *Adding the fully qualified path name.* Add lines 40–42 of Fig. 17.20 to procedure BuildPathName. The flag-image files are stored in an images directory in the directory containing the application's executable file. Property **CurrentDirectory** of class System.Environment (line 42) returns the directory from which the application is executing as a fully qualified path name (for example, C:\SimplyVB\FlagQuiz\bin\Debug). Method **Insert** combines this path name and "\images\" and *countryname*.png. The first argument to Insert specifies at what index the String will be added, and the second argument is the String to insert. Method Insert returns a copy of the string with the inserted characters. This copy is assigned to output.

6. *Returning the full path name.* Add line 44 of Fig. 17.20 to procedure BuildPathName. Line 44 returns the fully qualified path name of the specified country's flag image file.

7. *Saving the project.* Select **File > Save All** to save your modified code.

To ensure that the user is not asked the same question twice, a flag must be displayed no more than once when running the application. The application uses `Boolean` array `used` to track which flags have been displayed. The following box shows you how to ensure that the application displays a flag no more than once.

Selecting a Unique Flag to Display	1. ***Creating the GetUniqueRandomNumber procedure.*** Add lines 47–48 of Fig. 17.21 to the **Flag Quiz** application after procedure `BuildPathName`. Line 48 is the header for the `GetUniqueRandomNumber` procedure. `GetUniqueRandomNumber` returns the index of a country name whose flag has not been displayed.

2. ***Generating a random index.*** Add line 50 of Fig. 17.21 to the procedure `GetUniqueRandomNumber`. To select the next flag to display, you create a reference, `randomObject` (line 50), to a `Random` object.

Determining whether a
country's flag has been
displayed previously

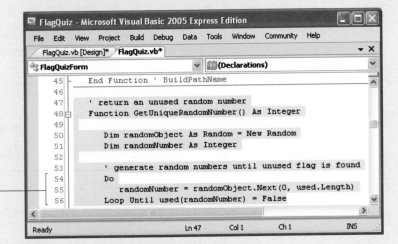

Figure 17.21   Generating a unique index.

3. ***Ensuring that each flag displays only once.*** Add lines 51–56 of Fig. 17.21 to `GetUniqueRandomNumber`. Method `Next` (line 55) of class `Random` generates a random index between 0 and `used.Length` (the number of country names). If the index has been selected previously, the element of `used` at the generated index is `True`. The `Do...Loop Until` statement (lines 54–56) iterates until it finds a unique index (that is, until `used(random)` is `False`).

4. ***Indicating that the index has been used.*** Add lines 58–59 of Fig. 17.22 to the `GetUniqueRandomNumber` procedure. Line 59 sets the element at the selected index of `used` to `True`. This indicates that the flag has been used. Checking the values in this array ensures that the index will not be used again in the application.

Indicating that the unused flag
will be displayed and return the
flag's index for use

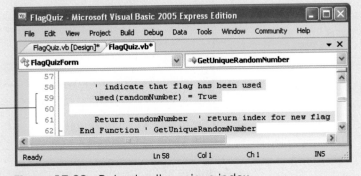

Figure 17.22   Returning the unique index.

(cont.)

5. **Returning the unique random number.** Add line 61 of Fig. 17.22 to the Get-UniqueRandomNumber procedure. Line 61 returns the unique random index.

6. **Saving the project.** Select **File > Save All** to save your modified code.

With the full path name and a unique flag selected, the application can display that flag. The following box shows how to display the selected flag.

Displaying a Flag

1. **Creating the DisplayFlag procedure.** Add lines 64–65 of Fig. 17.23 to the **Flag Quiz** application after procedure GetUniqueRandomNumber. Procedure DisplayFlag selects a random country name and displays that country's flag.

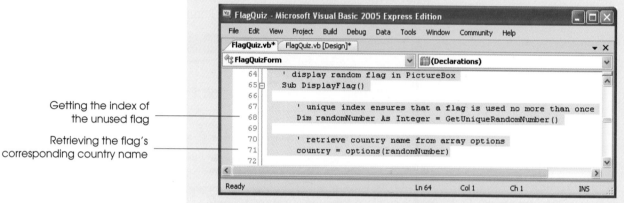

Getting the index of the unused flag

Retrieving the flag's corresponding country name

Figure 17.23 Choosing a random country name.

2. **Obtaining a unique index.** Add lines 67–68 of Fig. 17.23 to the DisplayFlag procedure. Line 68 invokes GetUniqueRandomNumber to find an index of a flag that has not been displayed during the application's execution and assigns it to randomNumber.

3. **Retrieving a country name.** Add lines 70–71 of Fig. 17.23 to the Display-Flag procedure. Line 71 assigns to country the flag's corresponding country name at index randomNumber of String array options.

4. **Building the flag image's path name.** Add lines 73–74 of Fig. 17.24 to the DisplayFlag procedure. Line 74 invokes procedure BuildPathName. The procedure returns the flag image's path name, which is assigned to path.

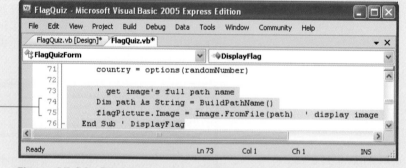

Getting the path name of the flag and displaying the flag image

Figure 17.24 Displaying a flag image.

5. **Displaying the flag image.** Add line 75 of Fig. 17.24 to the DisplayFlag procedure. Line 75 sets flagPicture's Image property to the Image object returned by method Image.FromFile. Recall that method Image.FromFile returns an Image object from the specified file.

(cont.)   6. ***Displaying a flag when the application is run.*** When the Form loads, the
first flag image in the quiz is displayed. The Form Load event handler should
invoke procedure `DisplayFlag`. Add line 22 of Fig. 17.25 to event handler
`FlagQuizForm_Load`.

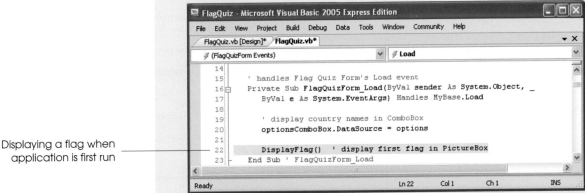

Displaying a flag when
application is first run

Figure 17.25   Displaying a flag when the **Form** is loaded.

7. ***Saving the project.*** Select **File > Save All** to save your modified code.

The user submits an answer by selecting a country name from the ComboBox
and clicking the **Submit** Button. The application displays whether the user's
answer is correct. If the application is finished (that is, five flags have been displayed), the application informs the user that the quiz is done; otherwise, the application enables the user to view the next flag. The following box implements this
functionality.

Processing a User's Answer

1. ***Adding the Submit Button's Click event handler.*** Return to design view
(**View > Designer**). Double click the **Submit** Button to generate the Click
event handler `submitButton_Click`.

2. ***Retrieving the selected ComboBox item.*** Add lines 84–86 of Fig. 17.26 to the
empty event handler. Lines 85–86 retrieve the user's answer, convert it to a
`String` and assign it to `response`. Property **SelectedValue** returns the
value of the ComboBox's selected item. Visual Basic method `Con-
vert.ToString` converts the selected item to a `String`. Recall that we now
use `Option Strict`, which requires explicit conversions. Variable `response`
contains the selected country's name.

3. ***Verifying the user's answer.*** Add lines 88–93 of Fig. 17.26 to
`submitButton_Click`. The If...Then...Else statement (lines 89–93) determines whether the user's response matches the correct answer. Line 90 displays `"Correct!"` in the Label if the user's response matches the correct
answer. Otherwise, line 92 displays `"Sorry, incorrect."`.

4. ***Informing the user that the quiz is over when five flags have been displayed.***
Add lines 95–104 of Fig. 17.27 to the `submitButton_Click` event handler. If
five flags have been displayed (lines 96–100), the Label displays text informing the user that the quiz is over, and both Buttons are disabled. The ComboBox is also disabled, by setting its **Enabled** property to `False`.

(cont.)

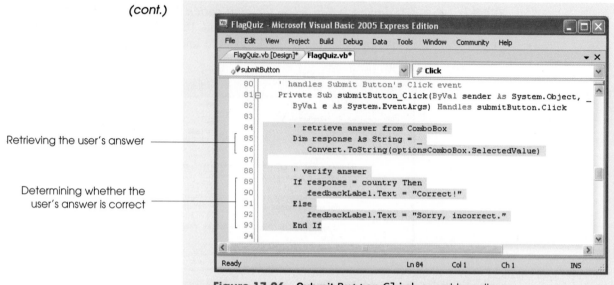

Figure 17.26 Submit `Button` `Click` event handler.

Retrieving the user's answer ⟶

Determining whether the user's answer is correct ⟶

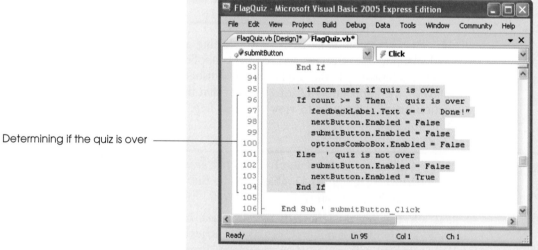

Determining if the quiz is over ⟶

Figure 17.27 Testing whether the quiz is finished.

5. ***Continuing the quiz when fewer than five flags have been shown.*** If the quiz is not finished (that is, `count` is less than 5), the application disables the **Submit** `Button` and enables the **Next Flag** `Button` (lines 102–103). The functionality of the **Next Flag** `Button` will be discussed shortly.

6. ***Saving the project.*** Select **File > Save All** to save your modified code.

The user requests the next flag in the quiz by clicking the **Next Flag** `Button`. The application then displays the next flag and increments the number of flags shown. In the following box, you will implement this functionality.

Displaying the Next Flag

1. ***Adding the Next Flag Button's `Click` event handler to the application.*** Return to design view (**View > Designer**). Double click the **Next Flag** `Button` to generate the `Click` event handler `nextButton_Click`.

2. ***Displaying the next flag.*** Add line 112 of Fig. 17.28 to the empty event handler. This line calls procedure `DisplayFlag` to place the next flag in the `PictureBox`.

(cont.)

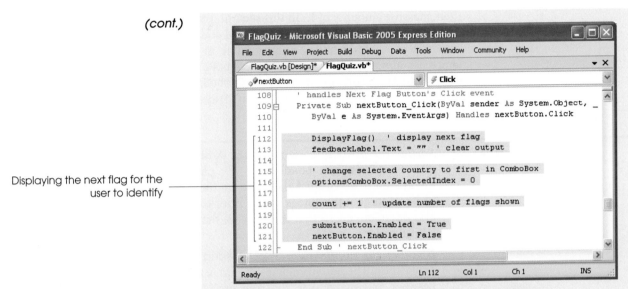

Displaying the next flag for the
user to identify

Figure 17.28 Next Flag Button Click event handler.

3. *Clearing the previous results.* Add line 113 of Fig. 17.28 to nextButton_Click to clear the output Label, deleting the results of the previous question.

4. *Resetting the ComboBox.* Add lines 115–116 of Fig. 17.28 to nextButton_Click. Line 116 sets property **SelectedIndex** of ComboBox options to 0, the first item in the ComboBox's drop-down list.

5. *Updating the number of flags shown.* Add line 118 of Fig. 17.28 to nextButton_Click to update instance variable count to indicate that one more flag has been shown.

6. *Enabling the Submit Button and disabling the Next Flag Button.* Add lines 120–121 of Fig. 17.28 to nextButton_Click. Line 120 enables the **Submit Button**; line 121 disables the **Next Flag Button**. This is a visual reminder to the user that an answer must be submitted before another flag can be displayed.

7. *Saving the project.* Select **File > Save All** to save your modified code.

---

1. Property _____ specifies the source of the data displayed in the ComboBox.

    a) ComboData   b) Source

    c) DataList   d) DataSource

2. ComboBox property _____ is 0 when the first ComboBox item is selected.

    a) SelectedIndex   b) SelectedValue

    c) Index   d) SelectedNumber

Answers: 1) d. 2) a.

17.5 Sorting Arrays

Sorting data refers to arranging the data into some particular order, such as ascending or descending order. Sorting is one of the most popular computing capabilities. For example, a bank sorts checks by account number so that it can prepare individual bank statements at the end of each month. Telephone companies sort account information by last name and, within last-name listings, by first name, to make it easy to find phone numbers. Virtually every organization must sort some data, and often, massive amounts of it. In this section, you learn how to sort the values in an array so that you can alphabetize the list of countries in the **Flag Quiz** application.

Users are able to find a country name in the ComboBox faster if the country names are alphabetized. [*Note:* Class ComboBox contains property **Sorted**, which, when set to True, sorts the items in the ComboBox alphabetically. We do not use this property because this tutorial focuses on arrays.] The following box shows you how to sort an array.

Sorting an Array	1. ***Sorting the array of country names.*** Add line 19 of Fig. 17.29 to event handler FlagQuizForm_Load. Line 19 passes array options to method **Array.Sort**, which sorts the values in the array into ascending alphabetical order. Note that this line is placed prior to the assigning of options to property DataSource, so that the items in the ComboBox are displayed in alphabetical order.
	2. ***Running the application.*** Select **Debug > Start Debugging** to run your application. The country names should now be alphabetized. Enter different answers and make sure that the proper message is displayed based on whether the answer is correct. Make sure that after five answers have been entered, the text **Done!** is appended to the current message displayed.
	3. ***Closing the application.*** Close your running application by clicking its close box.
	4. ***Closing the IDE.*** Close the Visual Basic IDE by clicking its close box.

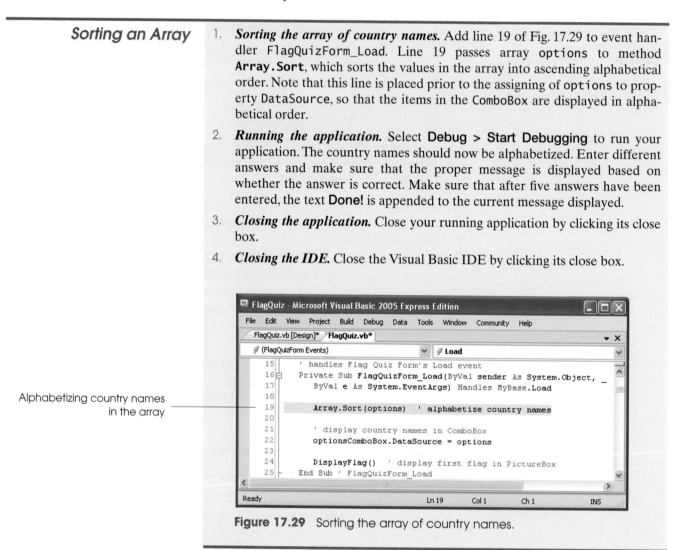

Alphabetizing country names in the array

Figure 17.29 Sorting the array of country names.

Figure 17.30 presents the source code for the **Flag Quiz** application. The lines of code that contain new programming concepts that you learned in this tutorial are highlighted.

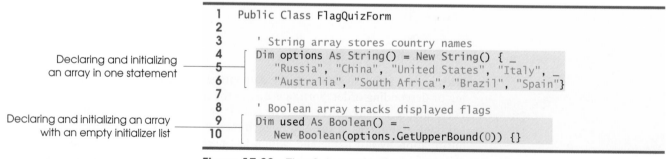

Declaring and initializing an array in one statement

Declaring and initializing an array with an empty initializer list

```
1   Public Class FlagQuizForm
2
3      ' String array stores country names
4      Dim options As String() = New String() { _
5         "Russia", "China", "United States", "Italy", _
6         "Australia", "South Africa", "Brazil", "Spain"}
7
8      ' Boolean array tracks displayed flags
9      Dim used As Boolean() = _
10        New Boolean(options.GetUpperBound(0)) {}
```

Figure 17.30 **Flag Quiz** application's code. (Part 1 of 3.)

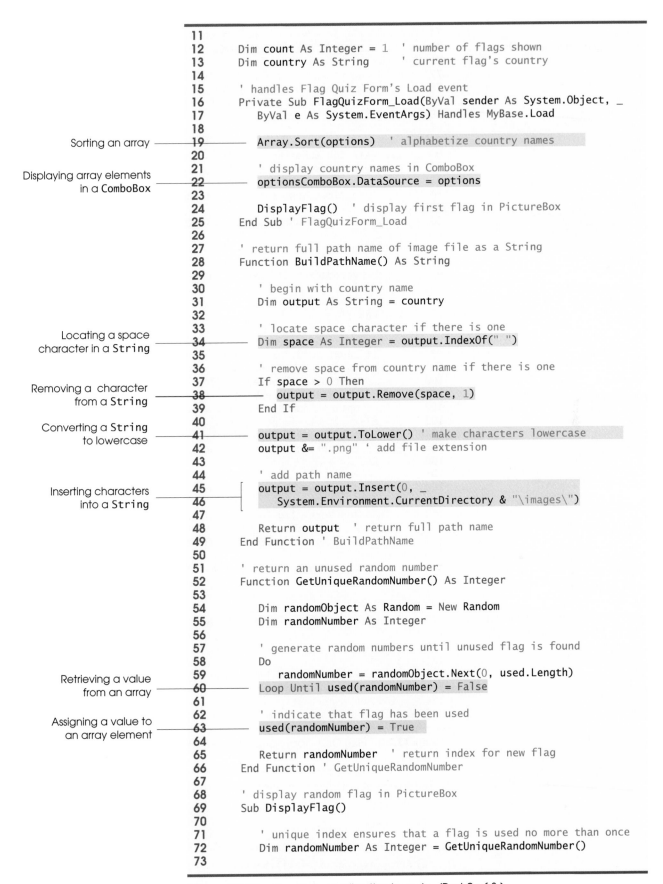

```
 11
 12      Dim count As Integer = 1  ' number of flags shown
 13      Dim country As String      ' current flag's country
 14
 15      ' handles Flag Quiz Form's Load event
 16      Private Sub FlagQuizForm_Load(ByVal sender As System.Object, _
 17         ByVal e As System.EventArgs) Handles MyBase.Load
 18
 19         Array.Sort(options)  ' alphabetize country names
 20
 21         ' display country names in ComboBox
 22         optionsComboBox.DataSource = options
 23
 24         DisplayFlag()  ' display first flag in PictureBox
 25      End Sub ' FlagQuizForm_Load
 26
 27      ' return full path name of image file as a String
 28      Function BuildPathName() As String
 29
 30         ' begin with country name
 31         Dim output As String = country
 32
 33         ' locate space character if there is one
 34         Dim space As Integer = output.IndexOf(" ")
 35
 36         ' remove space from country name if there is one
 37         If space > 0 Then
 38            output = output.Remove(space, 1)
 39         End If
 40
 41         output = output.ToLower() ' make characters lowercase
 42         output &= ".png" ' add file extension
 43
 44         ' add path name
 45         output = output.Insert(0, _
 46            System.Environment.CurrentDirectory & "\images\")
 47
 48         Return output  ' return full path name
 49      End Function ' BuildPathName
 50
 51      ' return an unused random number
 52      Function GetUniqueRandomNumber() As Integer
 53
 54         Dim randomObject As Random = New Random
 55         Dim randomNumber As Integer
 56
 57         ' generate random numbers until unused flag is found
 58         Do
 59            randomNumber = randomObject.Next(0, used.Length)
 60         Loop Until used(randomNumber) = False
 61
 62         ' indicate that flag has been used
 63         used(randomNumber) = True
 64
 65         Return randomNumber  ' return index for new flag
 66      End Function ' GetUniqueRandomNumber
 67
 68      ' display random flag in PictureBox
 69      Sub DisplayFlag()
 70
 71         ' unique index ensures that a flag is used no more than once
 72         Dim randomNumber As Integer = GetUniqueRandomNumber()
 73
```

Annotations (left margin):
- Sorting an array → line 19
- Displaying array elements in a ComboBox → line 22
- Locating a space character in a String → line 34
- Removing a character from a String → line 38
- Converting a String to lowercase → line 41
- Inserting characters into a String → lines 45–46
- Retrieving a value from an array → line 60
- Assigning a value to an array element → line 63

Figure 17.30   **Flag Quiz** application's code. (Part 2 of 3.)

Retrieving a value from an array ——

```
74          ' retrieve country name from array options
75          country = options(randomNumber)
76
77          ' get image's full path name
78          Dim path As String = BuildPathName()
79          flagPicture.Image = Image.FromFile(path) ' display image
80       End Sub ' DisplayFlag
81
82       ' handles Submit Button's Click event
83       Private Sub submitButton_Click(ByVal sender As System.Object, _
84          ByVal e As System.EventArgs) Handles submitButton.Click
85
86          ' retrieve answer from ComboBox
87          Dim response As String = _
88             Convert.ToString(optionsComboBox.SelectedValue)
89
90          ' verify answer
91          If response = country Then
92             feedbackLabel.Text = "Correct!"
93          Else
94             feedbackLabel.Text = "Sorry, incorrect."
95          End If
96
97          ' inform user if quiz is over
98          If count >= 5 Then   ' quiz is over
99             feedbackLabel.Text &= "   Done!"
100            nextButton.Enabled = False
101            submitButton.Enabled = False
102            optionsComboBox.Enabled = False
103         Else   ' quiz is not over
104            submitButton.Enabled = False
105            nextButton.Enabled = True
106         End If
107
108      End Sub ' submitButton_Click
109
110      ' handles Next Flag Button's Click event
111      Private Sub nextButton_Click(ByVal sender As System.Object, _
112         ByVal e As System.EventArgs) Handles nextButton.Click
113
114         DisplayFlag()   ' display next flag
115         feedbackLabel.Text = ""   ' clear output
116
117         ' change selected country to first in ComboBox
118         optionsComboBox.SelectedIndex = 0
119
120         count += 1   ' update number of flags shown
121
122         submitButton.Enabled = True
123         nextButton.Enabled = False
124      End Sub ' nextButton_Click
125   End Class ' FlagQuizForm
```

Converting the selected value from the **ComboBox** into a **String** —— (lines 87–88)

Setting the selected **ComboBox** item —— (line 118)

Figure 17.30   Flag Quiz application's code. (Part 3 of 3.)

SELF-REVIEW

1. The process of ordering the elements of an array is called _____ the array.

    a) allocating   b) sorting

    c) declaring   d) initializing

2. Which of the following sorts array `averageRainfall`?

    a) `Array(averageRainfall).Sort()`   b) `Sort.Array(averageRainfall)`

    c) `Sort(averageRainfall)`   d) `Array.Sort(averageRainfall)`

Answers: 1) b. 2) d.

17.6 Wrap-Up

In this tutorial, you learned about data structures called arrays, which contain elements of the same type. You then learned how to create, initialize and access one-dimensional arrays. You created a simple application called **SumArray**, which calculated the sum of the Integer values stored in an array. You studied pseudocode and an ACE table to help you begin creating the **Flag Quiz** application.

In building the **Flag Quiz** application, you were introduced to the ComboBox control. You learned how to add a ComboBox to the Form and modify the ComboBox's appearance. You then populated the ComboBox with data from an array. You reviewed how to display images in a PictureBox and how to generate random numbers by using an object of class Random.

You were introduced to several new String methods, including method Insert (for inserting characters), method Remove (for removing characters), method ToLower (for converting uppercase letters to lowercase letters) and method IndexOf (for returning the index of a character in a String). You learned how to sort an array alphabetically by using method Array.Sort.

In the next tutorial, you will learn how to create more sophisticated arrays with two dimensions, and you will use them to implement a student grades application. You will see that two-dimensional arrays are like tables organized in rows and columns.

SKILLS SUMMARY

Creating an Array

■ Declare the array using the format:

> Dim *arrayName* As *arrayType*()

where *arrayName* is the reference name of the array, and *arrayType* is the type of data that will be stored in the array.

Assigning an Object to an Array Reference

■ Use keyword New as in the statement:

> *arrayName* = New *arrayType*() {*arrayInitializerList*}

where *arrayInitializerList* is a comma-separated list of the items that will initialize the elements of the array.

Referring to Element *n* of an Array

■ Use index *n*.
■ Enclose the index in parentheses after the array name.

Obtaining the Length of an Array

■ Use property Length.

Obtaining the Index of the Last Element in a One-Dimensional Array

■ Invoke method GetUpperBound with 0 as its argument.

Combining TextBox Features With ListBox Features

■ Use a ComboBox control.

Setting the Maximum Number of Drop-Down Items a ComboBox's List Displays

■ Use property MaxDropDownItems.

Specifying the Source of Data Displayed in a ComboBox

■ Use property DataSource.

Obtaining a User's Selection in a ComboBox

■ Use property SelectedValue.

Changing the Style of a ComboBox

■ Use property DropDownStyle.

Sorting an Array

■ Invoke method `Array.Sort`.

Determining Whether a `String` Contains a Specified Character

■ Method `IndexOf` returns the index of a specified character in a `String`.

■ If the character is not in the `String`, method `IndexOf` returns `-1`.

Converting a `String` to Lowercase

■ Method `ToLower` returns a copy of a `String` with all uppercase characters converted to lowercase.

Inserting Characters into a `String`

■ Method `Insert` returns a copy of a `String` with specified characters added at a specified index.

Removing Characters from a `String`

■ Method `Remove` returns a copy of the `String` with a specified number of characters removed.

KEY TERMS

array—A data structure containing data items of the same type.

array bounds—Integers that determine what indices can be used to access an element in an array. The lower bound is 0; the upper bound is the length of the array minus one.

`Array.Sort` method—Sorts the values of an array into ascending order.

`ComboBox` control—Combines a `TextBox` with a `ListBox`.

`CurrentDirectory` property of `System.Environment`—Returns the directory from which the application is executing as a fully qualified path name.

`DataSource` property of class `ComboBox`—Specifies the source of items listed in a `ComboBox`.

data structure—Groups and organizes related data.

`DropDownList` value of `DropDownStyle` property—Specifies that a `ComboBox` is not editable.

`DropDownStyle` property of class `ComboBox`—Property of the `ComboBox` control that specifies the appearance of the `ComboBox`.

element—An item in an array.

`Enabled` property of class `ComboBox`—Specifies whether a user can select an item from a `ComboBox`.

`GetUpperBound` method of class `Array`—Returns the largest index of an array.

index—An array element's position number, also called a subscript. An index must be zero, a positive integer or an integer expression. If an application uses an expression as an index, the expression is evaluated first, to determine the index.

indexed array name—The array name followed by an index enclosed in parentheses. The indexed array name can be used on the left side of an assignment statement to place a new value into an array element. The indexed array name can be used in the right side of an assignment to retrieve the value of that array element.

`IndexOf` method of class `String`—`String` method that accepts as an argument a substring to search for in a `String`. The method returns the index of the specified substring in a `String`. If the `String` does not contain the substring, the method returns `-1`.

initializer list—The required braces ({ and }) surrounding the initial values of the elements in an array. When the initializer list is empty, the elements in the array are initialized to the default value for the array's data type.

`Insert` method of class `String`—`String` method that inserts its second argument (a `String`) at the position specified by the first argument.

length of an array—The number of elements in an array.

`Length` property of class `Array`—Contains the length (or number of elements in) an array.

`MaxDropDownItems` property of class `ComboBox`—Property of the `ComboBox` class that specifies how many items can be displayed in the drop-down list. If the `ComboBox` has more elements than this, it will provide a scrollbar to access all of them.

one-dimensional array—An array that uses only one index.

position number—A value that indicates a specific location within an array. Position numbers begin at 0 (zero).

Remove method of class String—String method that deletes a specified number of characters (the second argument) starting at the index specified by the first argument.

SelectedIndex property of class ComboBox—Specifies the index of the selected item. Returns –1 if no item is selected.

SelectedValue property of class ComboBox—Specifies the value of the selected item.

Sorted property of class ComboBox—When set to True, sorts the items in a ComboBox alphabetically.

subscript—See *index*.

ToLower method of class String—Returns a copy of the String for which it is called with any uppercase letters converted to lowercase letters.

ToUpper method of class String—Returns a copy of the String for which it is called with any lowercase letters converted to uppercase letters.

zeroth element—The first element in an array.

GUI DESIGN GUIDELINES	**ComboBoxes** ■ Each ComboBox should have a descriptive Label that describes the ComboBox's contents. ■ If a ComboBox's content should not be editable, set its DropDownStyle property to DropDownList.

CONTROLS, EVENTS, PROPERTIES & METHODS

ComboBox This control allows users to select from a drop-down list of options.

■ *In action*

■ *Properties*

DataSource–Specifies the source of the items listed in a ComboBox.

DropDownStyle–Specifies a ComboBox's appearance.

Enabled–Specifies whether a user can select an item from the ComboBox.

Location—Specifies the location of the ComboBox control on the container control relative to the top-left corner.

MaxDropDownItems—Specifies the maximum number of items the ComboBox can display in its drop-down list. If the ComboBox has more elements than this, it will provide a scrollbar to access all of them.

Name—Specifies the name used to access the ComboBox control programmatically. The name should be appended with the ComboBox suffix.

SelectedIndex—Specifies the index of the selected item. Returns –1 if no item is selected.

SelectedValue—Specifies the selected item.

Size—Specifies the height and width (in pixels) of the ComboBox control.

Sorted—When set to True, displays the ComboBox options in alphabetical order or ascending order.

Array This data structure stores a fixed number of elements of the same type.

■ *Property*

Length—Specifies the number of elements in the array.

■ *Methods*

GetUpperBound—Method returns the largest index of the array.

Sort—Orders an array's elements. An array of numerical values would be organized in ascending order, and an array of Strings would be organized in alphabetical order.

String The String class represents a series of characters treated as a single unit.

■ *Methods*

Format—Arranges the String in a specified format.

IndexOf—Returns the index of the specified character(s) in a String.

Insert—Returns a copy of the String for which it is called with the specified character(s) inserted.

Remove—Returns a copy of the String for which it is called with the specified character(s) removed.

ToLower—Returns a copy of the String for which it is called with any uppercase letters converted to lowercase letters.

MULTIPLE-CHOICE QUESTIONS

17.1 Arrays can be declared to hold values of _____.

a) type Double

b) type Integer

c) type String

d) any data type

17.2 The elements of an array are related by the fact that they have the same name and _____.

a) constant value

b) subscript

c) type

d) value

17.3 Method _____ returns the largest index in the array.

a) GetUpperBound

b) GetUpperLimit

c) GetLargestIndex

d) GetUpperSubscript

17.4 The first element in every array is the _____.

a) subscript

b) zeroth element

c) length of the array

d) smallest value in the array

17.5 Arrays _____.

a) are controls

b) always have one dimension

c) keep data in sorted order at all times

d) are objects

17.6 The initializer list can _____.

a) be used to determine the size of the array

b) contain a comma-separated list of initial values for the array elements

c) be empty

d) All of the above.

17.7 Which method call sorts array words in ascending order?

a) Array.Sort(words)

b) words.SortArray()

c) Array.Sort(words, 1)

d) Sort(words)

17.8 The ComboBox control combines a TextBox with a _____ control.

a) DateTimePicker

b) ListBox

c) NumericUpDown

d) Label

17.9 To search for a period (.) in a String called test, call method _____.

a) String.Search(test, ".")

b) String.IndexOf(test, ".")

c) test.IndexOf(".")

d) test.Search(".")

17.10 Property _____ contains the size of an array.

a) Elements

b) ArraySize

c) Length

d) Size

EXERCISES

17.11 (*Enhanced Flag Quiz Application*) Enhance the **Flag Quiz** application by counting the number of questions that were answered correctly (Fig. 17.31). After all the questions have been answered, display a message in a Label that describes how well the user performed. The following table shows which messages to display:

Number of correct answers	Message
5	Excellent!
4	Very good
3	Good
2	Poor
1 or 0	Fail

Figure 17.31 Enhanced **Flag Quiz** application's GUI.

a) *Copying the template to your working directory.* Copy the directory C:\Examples\ Tutorial17\Exercises\FlagQuiz2 to your C:\SimplyVB directory.

b) *Opening the application's template file.* Double click FlagQuiz.sln in the FlagQuiz2 directory to open the application.

c) *Adding a variable to count the number of correct answers.* Add an instance variable numberCorrect, and initialize it to 0. You will use this variable to count the number of correct answers submitted by the user.

d) *Counting the correct answers.* Increment numberCorrect in the **Submit** Button's event handler whenever the submitted answer is correct.

e) *Displaying the message.* Write a procedure DisplayMessage that displays a message in scoreLabel depending on the value of numberCorrect. Call this procedure from the **Submit** Button's event handler when the quiz is completed.

f) *Running the application.* Select **Debug > Start Debugging** to run your application. The finished application should behave as in Fig. 17.31. Run the application a few times and enter a different number of correct answers each time to verify that the correct feedback is displayed.

g) *Closing the application.* Close your running application by clicking its close box.

h) *Closing the IDE.* Close the Visual Basic IDE by clicking its close box.

17.12 (*Salary Survey Application*) Use a one-dimensional array to solve the following problem: A company pays its salespeople on a commission basis. The salespeople receive $200 per week, plus 9% of their gross sales for that week. For example, a salesperson who grosses $5,000 in sales in a week receives $200 plus 9% of $5,000, a total of $650. Write an application (using an array of counters) that determines how many of the salespeople earned salaries in each of the following ranges (assuming that each salesperson's salary is truncated to an integer amount): $200–299, $300–399, $400–499, $500–599, $600–699, $700–799, $800–899, $900–999 and over $999.

Allow the user to enter the sales for each employee in a TextBox. The user clicks the **Calculate** Button to calculate the salesperson's salary. When the user is done entering this information, clicking the **Show Totals** Button displays how many of the salespeople earned salaries in each of the above ranges. The finished application should behave like Fig. 17.32.

a) *Copying the template to your working directory.* Copy the directory C:\Examples\ Tutorial17\Exercises\SalarySurvey to your C:\SimplyVB directory.

b) *Opening the application's template file.* Double click SalarySurvey.sln in the SalarySurvey directory to open the application.

c) *Creating an array of salary ranges.* Create a String array, and initialize it to contain the salary ranges (the Strings displayed in the ListBox's first column).

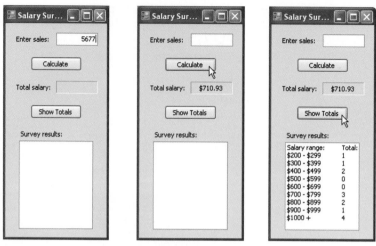

Figure 17.32 **Salary Survey** application's GUI.

d) *Create an array that represents the number of salaries in each range.* Create an empty `Decimal` array to store the number of employees who earn salaries in each range.

e) *Creating an event handler for the Calculate Button.* Write event handler `calculateButton_Click`. Obtain the user input from the **Enter sales:** TextBox. Calculate the commission due to the employee and add that amount to the base salary. Increment the element in array `salaries` that corresponds to the employee's salary range. This event handler should also display the employee's salary in the **Total salary:** Label.

f) *Writing an event handler for the Show Totals Button.* Create event handler `showTotalsButton_Click` to display the salary distribution in the ListBox. Use a For...Next statement to display the range (an element in array `salaryRanges`) and the number of employees whose salary falls in that range (an element in array `salaries`).

g) *Running the application.* Select **Debug > Start Debugging** to run your application. Enter several sales amounts using the **Calculate** Button. Click the **Show Totals** Button and verify that the proper amounts are displayed for each salary range, based on the salaries calculated from your input.

h) *Closing the application.* Close your running application by clicking its close box.

i) *Closing the IDE.* Close the Visual Basic IDE by clicking its close box.

17.13 (*Cafeteria Survey Application*) Twenty students were asked to rate, on a scale from 1 to 10, the quality of the food in the student cafeteria, with 1 being "awful" and 10 being "excellent." Allow the user input to be entered using a ComboBox. Place the 20 responses in an `Integer` array, and determine the frequency of each rating. Display the frequencies as a histogram in a multiline, scrollable TextBox. Figure 17.33 demonstrates the completed application.

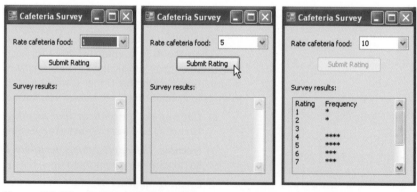

Figure 17.33 **Cafeteria Survey** GUI.

a) *Copying the template to your working directory.* Copy the directory C:\Examples\ Tutorial17\Exercises\CafeteriaSurvey to your C:\SimplyVB directory.

b) *Opening the application's template file.* Double click CafeteriaSurvey.sln in the CafeteriaSurvey directory.

c) *Creating an array of the possible ratings.* Create an array of 10 consecutive integers, called choices to contain the integers in the range 1–10, inclusive.

d) *Adding a ComboBox.* Add a ComboBox to the GUI as in Fig. 17.33. The ComboBox will display the possible ratings. Set property DropDownStyle to DropDownList.

e) *Displaying the possible ratings when the application starts.* Write the event handler for the Load event so that the DataSource of the ComboBox is set to choices when the application starts.

f) *Creating an array to store the responses.* Create an Integer array of length 11 named responses. This will be used to store the number of responses in each of the 10 categories (element 0 will not be used).

g) *Counting the number of responses.* Create an Integer variable named response Counter to keep track of how many responses have been input.

h) *Storing the responses.* Write the event handler submitButton_Click to increment responseCounter. Store the response in array responses. Call procedure Display-Histogram to display the results.

i) *Creating procedure DisplayHistogram.* Note that the procedure template is already provided for you in the application template. Add a header to the TextBox. Use nested For...Next loops to display the ratings in the first column. The second column uses asterisks to indicate how many students surveyed submitted the corresponding rating.

j) *Running the application.* Select **Debug > Start Debugging** to run your application. Enter 20 responses using the **Submit Rating** Button. Verify that the resulting histogram displays the responses entered.

k) *Closing the application.* Close your running application by clicking its close box.

l) *Closing the IDE.* Close the Visual Basic IDE by clicking its close box.

What does this code do? ▶ **17.14** This function declares numbers as its parameter. What does it return?

```
1   Function Mystery(ByVal numbers As Integer()) As Integer()
2
3      Dim i As Integer
4      Dim length As Integer = numbers.Length - 1
5      Dim tempArray As Integer() = _
6         New Integer(0 To length) {}
7
8      For i = length To 0 Step -1
9         tempArray(length - i) = numbers(i)
10     Next
11
12     Return tempArray
13  End Function ' Mystery
```

What's wrong with this code? ▶ **17.15** The code that follows uses a For...Next loop to sum the elements in an array. Find the error(s) in the following code:

```
1   Sub SumArray()
2      Dim sum As Integer
3      Dim counter As Integer
4      Dim numbers As Integer() = _
5         New Integer() {1, 2, 3, 4, 5, 6, 7, 8}
6
```

```
7        For counter = 0 To numbers.Length
8            sum += numbers(counter)
9        Next
10
11   End Sub ' SumArray
```

Programming Challenge ▶

17.16 (*Road Sign Test Application*) Write an application that will test the user's knowledge of road signs. Your application should display a random sign image and ask the user to select the sign name from a ComboBox. This application should look like Fig. 17.34. [*Hint:* The application is similar to the **Flag Quiz** application.] You can find the images in `C:\Examples\Tutorial17\Exercises\images`. Remember to set `Option Strict` to `On`.

Figure 17.34 **Road Sign Test** GUI.

T U T O R I A L

18

Objectives

In this tutorial, you will learn to:

- Understand the differences between one-dimensional and two-dimensional arrays.
- Declare and manipulate two-dimensional arrays.
- Understand the usefulness of two-dimensional arrays.
- Use RadioButtons to enable users to select exactly one option out of several.

Outline

Student Grades Application

Introducing Two-Dimensional Arrays and RadioButtons

In this tutorial, you will learn about two-dimensional arrays, which, like one-dimensional arrays, store multiple values. However, two-dimensional arrays allow you to store multiple rows of values. You will also learn about the RadioButton control, which you will employ to enable users to choose only one option out of many.

18.1 Test-Driving the Student Grades Application

You will implement the **Student Grades** application by using a two-dimensional array. This application must meet the following requirements:

Application Requirements

A teacher issues three tests to a class of 10 students. The grades on these tests are integers in the range from 0 to 100. The teacher has asked you to develop an application to keep track of each student's average and the average of the class as a whole. The teacher has also asked that there be a choice to view the grades as either numbers or letters. Letter grades should be calculated according to the grading system:

90–100	*A*
80–89	*B*
70–79	*C*
60–69	*D*
Below 60	*F*

The application should allow a user to input the student's name and three test grades, then compute each student's average and the class average. The application should display number grades by default.

The student's average is equal to the sum of the student's three grades divided by three. The class average is equal to the sum of all of the students' averages divided by the number of students in the class (10 in this case). You begin by test-driving the completed application. Then you will learn the additional Visual Basic technologies you will need to create your own version of this application.

Test-Driving the Student Grades Application

1. **Opening the completed application.** Open the C:\Examples\ Tutorial18\CompletedApplication\StudentGrades directory to locate the **Student Grades** application. Double click StudentGrades.sln to open the application in the Visual Basic IDE.

2. **Running the Student Grades application.** Select **Debug > Start Debugging** to run the application (Fig. 18.1).

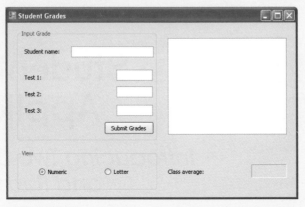

Figure 18.1 Running the completed **Student Grades** application.

3. **Entering data.** Type Gretta Green in the **Student Name:** TextBox. Type 87, 94 and 93 in the **Test 1:**, **Test 2:** and **Test 3:** TextBoxes, respectively (Fig. 18.2). Click the **Submit Grades** Button to display the data in the List-Box (Fig. 18.3).

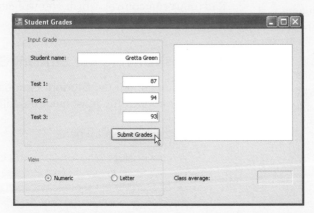

Figure 18.2 Inputting data to the **Student Grades** application.

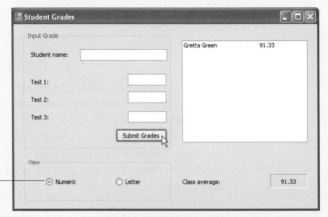

Numeric RadioButton selected as the default

Figure 18.3 Displaying the student's numerical grade.

(cont.)   4. ***Changing the ListBox's appearance.*** Change the ListBox's appearance by clicking the white circle of the **Letter** RadioButton (Fig. 18.4). The ListBox will display the data using the letter grading system. Click the **Numeric** RadioButton to once again display the data in numeric form. (Fig. 18.3).

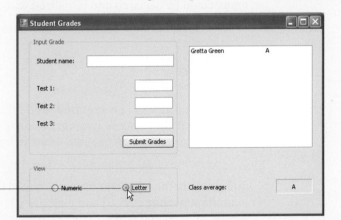

Select the **Letter** RadioButton

Figure 18.4   Displaying the student's resulting letter grade.

5. ***Closing the application.*** Close your running application by clicking its close box.

6. ***Closing the IDE.*** Close the Visual Basic IDE by clicking its close box.

18.2 Two-Dimensional Rectangular Arrays

So far, you have studied one-dimensional arrays, which contain one sequence (or row) of values. In this section, we introduce **two-dimensional arrays** (often called **double-subscripted arrays**), which require two indices to identify particular elements. **Rectangular arrays** are two-dimensional arrays that are often used to represent **tables** of values consisting of information arranged in **rows** and **columns**. Each row is the same size and therefore has the same number of columns (hence, the term "rectangular"). To identify a particular table element, you must specify the two indices—by convention, the first identifies the element's row, and the second identifies the element's column. Figure 18.5 illustrates a two-dimensional rectangular array, named array, which contains three rows and four columns. A rectangular two-dimensional array with *m* rows and *n* columns is called an ***m-by-n* array**; therefore, the array in Fig. 18.5 is a 3-by-4 array.

	Column 0	Column 1	Column 2	Column 3
Row 0	array(0, 0)	array(0, 1)	array(0, 2)	array(0, 3)
Row 1	array(1, 0)	array(1, 1)	array(1, 2)	array(1, 3)
Row 2	array(2, 0)	array(2, 1)	array(2, 2)	array(2, 3)

Column index (or subscript)

Row index (or subscript)

Array name

Figure 18.5   Two-dimensional rectangular array with three rows and four columns.

Every element in array is identified in Fig. 18.5 by an element name of the form array(i, j), where array is the name of the array and i and j are the indices that uniquely identify the row and column of each element in array. All row numbers and column numbers in two-dimensional arrays begin with zero, so the elements in the first row each have a first index of 0; the elements in the last column each have a second index of 3 (Fig. 18.5).

Two-dimensional arrays are initialized much like one-dimensional arrays. For example, a two-dimensional rectangular array, numbers, with two rows and two columns, could be declared and initialized with

```
Dim numbers As Integer(,) = New Integer(0 To 1, 0 To 1) {}
numbers(0, 0) = 1
numbers(0, 1) = 2
numbers(1, 0) = 3
numbers(1, 1) = 4
```

Note that a comma (,) is required inside the parenthesis following the data type to indicate that the array is two-dimensional. Alternatively, the preceding initialization could be written on one line using an initializer list:

```
Dim numbers As Integer(,) = New Integer(,) {{1, 2}, {3, 4}}
```

The values in the initializer list are grouped by row using nested braces, with 1 and 2 initializing numbers(0, 0) and numbers(0, 1), respectively, and 3 and 4 initializing numbers(1, 0) and numbers(1, 1), respectively.

Recall from Tutorial 17 that you can specify the bounds of an array implicitly or explicitly. The same is true for two-dimensional arrays. Accordingly, the array numbers also can be allocated as follows:

```
Dim numbers As Integer(,) = New Integer(1, 1) {}
```

SELF-REVIEW

1. Arrays that use two indices are referred to as _____ arrays.

   a) single-subscripted
   b) two-dimensional
   c) double
   d) one-dimensional

2. The expression _____ creates an integer array of two rows and five columns.

   a) New Integer(0 To 2, 0 To 5) {}
   b) New Integer(0 To 1, 0 To 5) {}
   c) New Integer(0 To 1, 0 To 4) {}
   d) New Integer(0 To 2, 0 To 4) {}

Answers: 1) b. 2) c.

18.3 Using RadioButtons

A **RadioButton** is a small white circle that either is blank or contains a smaller dot. When a RadioButton is selected, a dot appears in the circle. A RadioButton is known as a state button because it can only be in the "on" state or the "off" state. (The other state button you have learned is the CheckBox, which was introduced in Tutorial 8.)

RadioButtons are similar to CheckBoxes in that they are state buttons, but RadioButtons normally appear as a group; only one RadioButton in the group can be selected at a time. Like car-radio preset buttons, which can select only one station at a time, RadioButtons are used to represent a set of mutually exclusive options. **Mutually exclusive options** are a set of options of which only one can be selected at a time. By default, all RadioButtons added directly to the Form become part of the same group. To separate RadioButtons into several groups, each RadioButton group must be in a different container (such as a GroupBox).

The RadioButton control's **Checked** property indicates whether the RadioButton is checked (contains a small black dot) or unchecked (blank). If the RadioButton is checked, the Checked property returns the Boolean value True. If the RadioButton is not checked, the Checked property returns False.

A RadioButton also generates an event when its checked state changes. Event **CheckedChanged** occurs when a RadioButton is either selected or deselected.

The following pseudocode describes the basic operation of the **Student Grades** application:

GUI Design Tip

Use RadioButtons when the user is to choose only one option from a group.

GUI Design Tip

Always place each group of RadioButtons in a separate container (such as a GroupBox).

When the user clicks the Submit Grades Button:
    Retrieve the grades from the TextBoxes
    Add the student's name and test average to the arrays
    Display each student's name and test average in the ListBox
    Display the class's average in the Class average: TextBox
    Clear the student's name and test average from the TextBoxes

    If 10 students have been entered
        Disable the Submit Grades Button

When the user selects the Numeric RadioButton:
    Display each student's name and numeric average in the ListBox
    Display the class's numeric average in the Class average: TextBox

When the user selects the Letter RadioButton:
    Display each student's name and letter average in the ListBox
    Display the class's letter average in the Class average: TextBox

Your **Student Grades** application uses the RadioButton control's Checked-Changed event handler to update the ListBox when the user selects either letter or numeric grades for display. Now that you have test-driven the **Student Grades** application and studied its pseudocode representation, you will use an ACE table to help you convert the pseudocode to Visual Basic. Figure 18.6 lists the actions, controls and events that will help you complete your own version of this application.

Action/Control/Event (ACE) Table for the Student Grades Application

Action	Control	Event
Label the application's components	inputGroupBox, viewGroupBox, nameLabel, test1Label, test2Label, test3Label, classAverageLabel, averageLabel	Application is run
	submitButton	Click
Retrieve grades from the TextBoxes	nameTextBox, test1TextBox, test2TextBox, test3TextBox	
Add the student's name and test average to the arrays	nameTextBox, grades	
Display each student's name and test average in the ListBox	gradesListBox	
Display the class's average in the Class average: TextBox	averageLabel	
Clear the student's name and test average from the TextBoxes	nameTextBox, test1TextBox, test2TextBox, test3TextBox	
If 10 students have been entered		
Disable the Submit Grades Button	submitButton	
	numericRadio-Button	Checked-Changed
	letterRadioButton	
Display each student's name and numeric average in the ListBox	gradesListBox	

Figure 18.6 ACE table for the **Student Grades** application.

Now you will build your **Student Grades** application, using two-dimensional arrays and RadioButtons. The RadioButtons will allow the user to view the students' grades as letters or numbers.

Adding RadioButtons to the View GroupBox

1. ***Copying the template to your working directory.*** Copy the C:\Examples\ Tutorial18\TemplateApplication\StudentGrades directory to your C:\SimplyVB directory.

2. ***Opening the Student Grades application's template file.*** Double click StudentGrades.sln in the StudentGrades directory to open the application in the Visual Basic IDE.

3. ***Adding RadioButtons to the View GroupBox.*** Click the **View** GroupBox on the Form. Add a RadioButton to the GroupBox by double clicking the **RadioButton** control,

in the **Toolbox**. Repeat this process so that two RadioButtons are added to the GroupBox. Note that, as with CheckBoxes, each RadioButton control contains a label.

GUI Design Tip

Align groups of RadioButtons either horizontally or vertically.

Good Programming Practice

Append the RadioButton suffix to RadioButton control names.

4. ***Customizing the RadioButtons.*** To align the RadioButtons horizontally, set the Location property of one RadioButton to 42, 33, and set the other RadioButton's Location property to 174, 33. Set the AutoSize property of each RadioButton to False. Then, resize the RadioButton labels by setting each RadioButton's Size property to 95, 19. Rename the left RadioButton by changing its Name property to numericRadioButton, and set its Text property to Numeric. Then set the right RadioButton control's Name property to letterRadioButton, and set its Text property to Letter. Set the Checked property of numericRadioButton to True. Your Form should now look similar to Fig. 18.7.

Error-Prevention Tip

To avoid subtle logic errors, one RadioButton in a group should be selected by default, by setting its Checked property to True. This can be done using code or by setting the value using the **Properties** window.

Figure 18.7 RadioButtons placed in the GroupBox.

5. ***Saving the project.*** Select **File > Save All** to save your modified code.

SELF-REVIEW

1. The _____ property determines whether a RadioButton is selected.

   a) Selected
   b) Clicked
   c) Checked
   d) Enabled

2. The _____ event is raised when a RadioButton is either selected or deselected.
   a) CheckedChanged   b) Changed
   c) SelectedChanged   d) None of the above.

Answers: 1) c. 2) a.

18.4 Inserting Code into the Student Grades Application

Now that you have placed the controls on the Form, you are ready to write code to interact with the data given by the user. First you will declare a two-dimensional array to contain the student information.

Declaring a Two-Dimensional Array	1. ***Declaring a two-dimensional array.*** Add lines 3–4 of Fig. 18.8 to your code. Line 3 declares a 10-by-2 array of strings to contain the student information. The first column of grades will contain each student's name. The second column will contain each student's test average. Note the studentCount instance variable (line 4), which contains the number of students entered by the user.

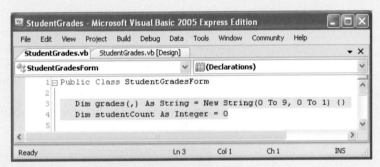

Figure 18.8   Declaring a two-dimensional array.

2. ***Saving the project.*** Select **File > Save All** to save your modified code.

The template code provides an incomplete version of the **Submit Grades** Button's Click event handler. You will now use the two-dimensional array that you declared in the previous box to finish this event handler.

*Finishing the Submit Grades **Button's Click** Event Handler*	1. ***Completing the submitButton_Click event handler.*** Add lines 13–19 of Fig. 18.9 to your code. Line 14 adds the student's name to the first column of the two-dimensional grades array. Lines 15–17 add the student's test average to the second column of the array. Note that the TestAverage method (line 16) is underlined in blue, indicating a syntax error. This occurs because the TestAverage method has not been defined yet; you will soon create this method to calculate the average of three test scores. By using the format control string "{0:F}", the String.Format method converts the test average to a string with exactly two digits following the decimal point. This string is then stored in the array. Line 19 increments the number of students in the class.

(cont.)

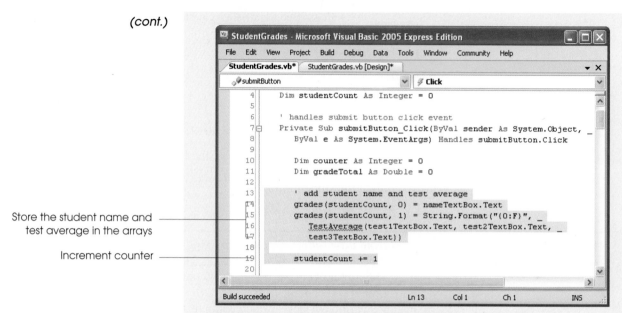

Store the student name and test average in the arrays

Increment counter

Figure 18.9 Storing the student information.

2. *Displaying the output.* Insert lines 21–41 of Fig. 18.10 into your code. The loop in lines 21–24 calculates the sum of all the student averages. Line 26 uses the Checked method of letterRadioButton control to determine how the user would like the students' grades to be displayed. Line 29 calls the LetterGrade method to determine the letter grade corresponding to a given numeric grade. This method has already been provided for you in the template. The Else branch of the decision (lines 35–40) represents displaying the information in gradesListBox in numeric form.

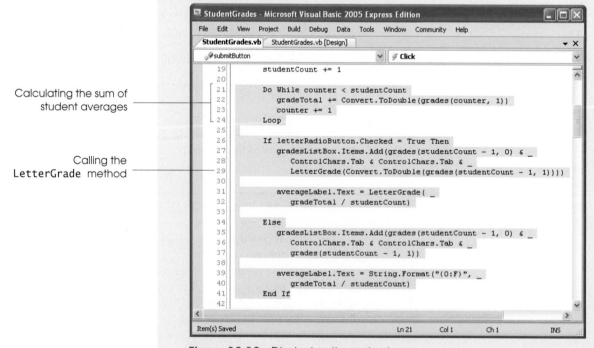

Calculating the sum of student averages

Calling the LetterGrade method

Figure 18.10 Displaying the output.

(cont.)   3. ***Disabling the Submit Grades* `Button` *and* `clearing` *input.*** Insert lines 43–52 of Fig. 18.11 into your code. Lines 44–47 remove the user's input from each `TextBox` in `inputFrame`. If 10 students have already been entered into the array, line 51 will disable the **Submit Grades** `Button` so that no more grades can be entered.

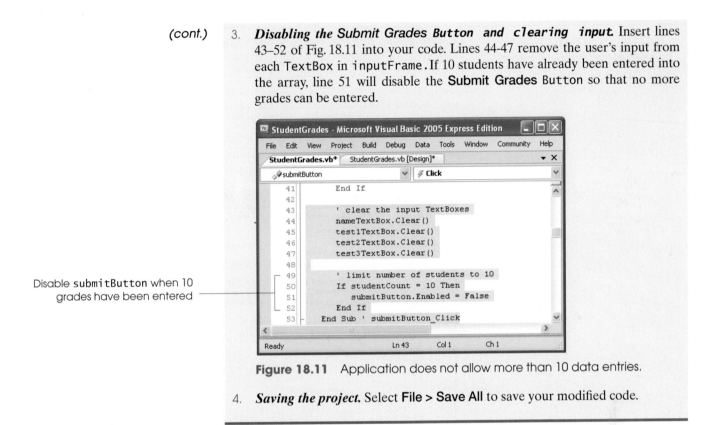

Disable `submitButton` when 10 grades have been entered

Figure 18.11   Application does not allow more than 10 data entries.

4. ***Saving the project.*** Select **File > Save All** to save your modified code.

In one of the previous boxes, you called the `TestAverage` method, which is not yet defined, to display the appropriate data. Next you will code the `TestAverage` method.

Coding a Method to Average Test Grades

1. ***Coding the* `TestAverage` *method.*** Add lines 55–60 of Fig. 18.12 below your `submitButton_Click` event handler. Line 59 returns the sum of three test scores passed to the method as string arguments. Passing the test scores as string arguments allows for easy input from the three test `TextBoxes` but requires the use of the `Val` method to ensure proper numeric interpretation.

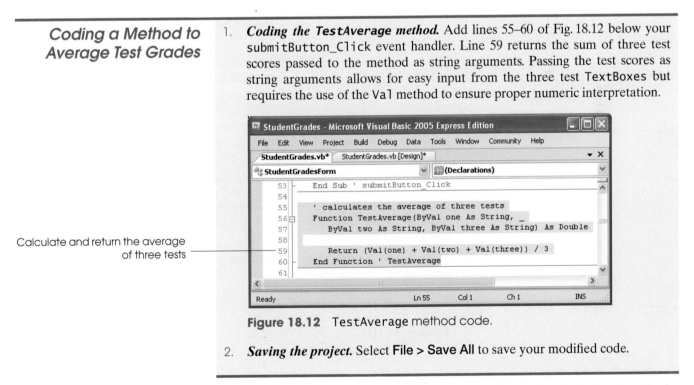

Calculate and return the average of three tests

Figure 18.12   `TestAverage` method code.

2. ***Saving the project.*** Select **File > Save All** to save your modified code.

You will now code event handlers to enhance the application's functionality by allowing the user to select whether the results will be presented as letter grades or numeric grades.

Coding Event Handlers for the RadioButtons

1. *Creating the numericRadioButton_CheckedChanged event handler.* In design view, double click the **Numeric** RadioButton to generate its CheckedChanged event handler. Add lines 66–84 of Fig. 18.13 to the event handler. Lines 73–79 present a loop to populate the ListBox with the student names and grades stored in the two-dimensional array. Simultaneously, the loop sums the students' grades (line 77) in order to later calculate the class average in a subsequent line. Using String.Format, lines 82–83 divide the summed scores by the number of students and assign the result to averageLabel.

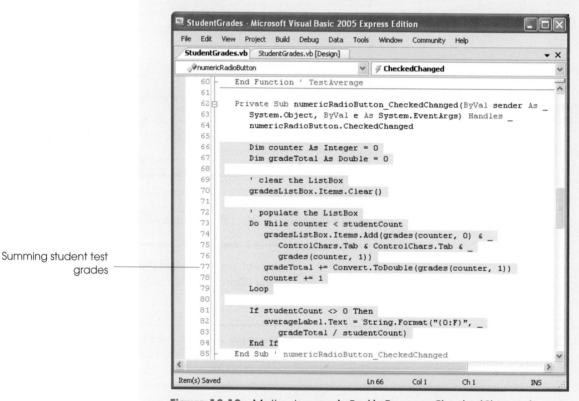

Summing student test grades

Figure 18.13   Method numericRadioButton_CheckedChanged.

2. *Creating the letterRadioButton_CheckedChanged event handler.* In design view, double click the **Letter** RadioButton to generate its CheckedChanged event handler. Add lines 91–104 of Fig. 18.14 to the event handler. Lines 97–102 present another loop to populate the ListBox with the student names and grades stored in the two-dimensional array. However, this time the grades are to be displayed in letter form, so the LetterGrade method is called in lines 100 and 104. Be sure to add the comments in line 105 and format the event handler as in Fig. 18.14.

3. *Running the application.* Select **Debug > Start Debugging** to run your application. You can now select to view the grades as letters or numbers.

4. *Closing the application.* Close your running application by clicking its close box.

5. *Closing the IDE.* Close the Visual Basic IDE by clicking its close box.

(cont.)

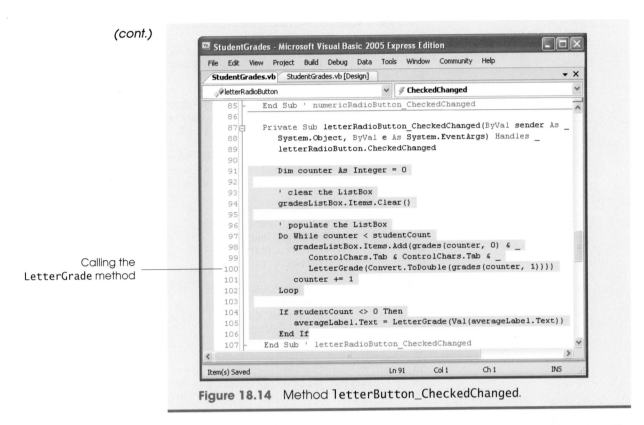

Calling the
LetterGrade method

Figure 18.14 Method `letterButton_CheckedChanged`.

Figure 18.15 presents the source code for the **Student Grades** application. The lines of code that contain new programming concepts that you learned in this tutorial are highlighted.

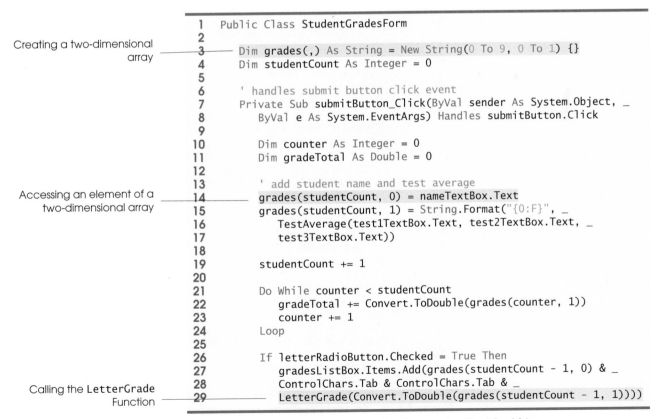

Creating a two-dimensional array

Accessing an element of a two-dimensional array

Calling the LetterGrade Function

```
1   Public Class StudentGradesForm
2
3       Dim grades(,) As String = New String(0 To 9, 0 To 1) {}
4       Dim studentCount As Integer = 0
5
6       ' handles submit button click event
7       Private Sub submitButton_Click(ByVal sender As System.Object, _
8           ByVal e As System.EventArgs) Handles submitButton.Click
9
10          Dim counter As Integer = 0
11          Dim gradeTotal As Double = 0
12
13          ' add student name and test average
14          grades(studentCount, 0) = nameTextBox.Text
15          grades(studentCount, 1) = String.Format("{0:F}", _
16              TestAverage(test1TextBox.Text, test2TextBox.Text, _
17              test3TextBox.Text))
18
19          studentCount += 1
20
21          Do While counter < studentCount
22              gradeTotal += Convert.ToDouble(grades(counter, 1))
23              counter += 1
24          Loop
25
26          If letterRadioButton.Checked = True Then
27              gradesListBox.Items.Add(grades(studentCount - 1, 0) & _
28                  ControlChars.Tab & ControlChars.Tab & _
29                  LetterGrade(Convert.ToDouble(grades(studentCount - 1, 1))))
```

Figure 18.15   Student Grades application code. (Part 1 of 3.)

```vbnet
30
31        averageLabel.Text = LetterGrade( _
32           gradeTotal / studentCount)
33
34     Else
35        gradesListBox.Items.Add(grades(studentCount - 1, 0) & _
36           ControlChars.Tab & ControlChars.Tab & _
37           grades(studentCount - 1, 1))
38
39        averageLabel.Text = String.Format("{0:F}", _
40           gradeTotal / studentCount)
41     End If
42
43     ' clear the input TextBoxes
44     nameTextBox.Clear()
45     test1TextBox.Clear()
46     test2TextBox.Clear()
47     test3TextBox.Clear()
48
49     ' limit number of students to 10
50     If studentCount = 10 Then
51        submitButton.Enabled = False
52     End If
53  End Sub ' submitButton_Click
54
55  ' calculates the average of three tests
56  Function TestAverage(ByVal one As String, _
57     ByVal two As String, ByVal three As String) As Double
58
59     Return (Val(one) + Val(two) + Val(three)) / 3
60  End Function ' TestAverage
61
62  Private Sub numericRadioButton_CheckedChanged(ByVal sender As _
63     System.Object, ByVal e As System.EventArgs) Handles _
64     numericRadioButton.CheckedChanged
65
66     Dim counter As Integer = 0
67     Dim gradeTotal As Double = 0
68
69     ' clear the ListBox
70     gradesListBox.Items.Clear()
71
72     ' populate the ListBox
73     Do While counter < studentCount
74        gradesListBox.Items.Add(grades(counter, 0) & _
75           ControlChars.Tab & ControlChars.Tab & _
76           grades(counter, 1))
77        gradeTotal += Convert.ToDouble(grades(counter, 1))
78        counter += 1
79     Loop
80
81     If studentCount <> 0 Then
82        averageLabel.Text = String.Format("{0:F}", _
83           gradeTotal / studentCount)
84     End If
85  End Sub ' numericRadioButton_CheckedChanged
86
87  Private Sub letterRadioButton_CheckedChanged(ByVal sender As _
88     System.Object, ByVal e As System.EventArgs) Handles _
89     letterRadioButton.CheckedChanged
90
91     Dim counter As Integer = 0
92
```

Figure 18.15   **Student Grades** application code. (Part 2 of 3.)

```
93           ' clear the ListBox
94           gradesListBox.Items.Clear()
95
96           ' populate the ListBox
97           Do While counter < studentCount
98              gradesListBox.Items.Add(grades(counter, 0) & _
99                 ControlChars.Tab & ControlChars.Tab & _
100                LetterGrade(Convert.ToDouble(grades(counter, 1))))
101             counter += 1
102          Loop
103
104          If studentCount <> 0 Then
105             averageLabel.Text = LetterGrade(Val(averageLabel.Text))
106          End If
107       End Sub ' letterRadioButton_CheckedChanged
108
109       ' determines a letter grade corresponding to a numeric grade
110       Function LetterGrade(ByVal grade As Double) As String
111
112          If grade >= 90 Then
113             Return "A"
114          ElseIf grade >= 80 Then
115             Return "B"
116          ElseIf grade >= 70 Then
117             Return "C"
118          ElseIf grade >= 60 Then
119             Return "D"
120          Else
121             Return "F"
122          End If
123       End Function ' LetterGrade
124 End Class ' StudentGradesForm
```

Figure 18.15   Student Grades application code. (Part 3 of 3.)

SELF-REVIEW   1. A container can contain _____ RadioButton(s).

a) exactly two   b) no more than one

c) no more than three   d) any number of

2. When one RadioButton in a container is selected, _____.

a) others can be selected at the same time   b) a logic error will occur

c) all others will be deselected   d) Both a and c.

Answers: 1.) d. 2.) c.

18.5 Wrap-Up

In this tutorial, you learned how to declare and assign values to a two-dimensional array. You used code to store user input in a two-dimensional array.

To help you complete the **Student Grades** application, you used RadioButtons. You learned that you must group related RadioButtons in separate containers. Initially, zero or one RadioButton in a container will be selected. Once a RadioButton has been selected, only one RadioButton can be selected at a time. You also learned that selecting or deselecting a RadioButton calls its CheckedChanged event handler.

In the next tutorial, you will learn about classes. (Recall that you have been using classes all along, from the Form class that represents the application's GUI to the Random class that you use to generate random numbers.) You will learn how to create your own classes for use in your applications.

SKILLS SUMMARY

Using Two-Dimensional Arrays

- Declare a rectangular array to create a table of values (each row will contain the same number of columns).

Using a `RadioButton`

- Use a `RadioButton` in an application to present the user with mutually exclusive options.

Selecting a `RadioButton` at Runtime

- Click the white circle of the `RadioButton`. (A small dot will appear inside the white circle.)

Determining Whether a `RadioButton` Is Selected

- Access the `RadioButton`'s `Checked` property.

Executing Code When a `RadioButton`'s State Has Changed

- Use the `CheckedChanged` event handler, which executes when a `RadioButton` is selected or deselected.

KEY TERMS

Checked property of `RadioButton` control—When `True`, displays a small dot in the control. When `False`, the control displays an empty white circle.

CheckedChanged event—Raised when a `RadioButton`'s state changes.

column—The second dimension of a two-dimensional array.

double-subscripted array—*See two-dimensional array.*

m-by-n array—A two-dimensional array with m rows and n columns.

mutually exclusive options—A set of options of which only one can be selected at a time.

`RadioButton` control—Appears as a small circle that is either blank (unchecked) or contains a smaller dot (checked). Usually these controls appear in groups of two or more. Exactly one `RadioButton` in a group is selected at one time.

rectangular array—A type of two-dimensional array that can represent tables of values consisting of information arranged in rows and columns. Each row contains the same number of columns.

row—The first dimension of a two-dimensional array.

table—A two-dimensional array used to contain information arranged in rows and columns.

two-dimensional array—A double-subscripted array that contains multiple rows of values.

GUI DESIGN GUIDELINES

RadioButton

- Use `RadioButton`s when the user is to choose only one option from a group.
- Always place each group of `RadioButton`s in a separate container (such as a `GroupBox`).
- Align groups of `RadioButton`s either horizontally or vertically.

CONTROLS, EVENTS, PROPERTIES & METHODS

RadioButton   This component is used to enable users to select only one of several options.

- *In action*

- *Event*

    `CheckedChanged`—Raised when the control is either selected or deselected.

- *Properties*

    `Checked`—Set to `True` if the control is selected and `False` if it is not selected.

    `Location`—Specifies the location of the `RadioButton` control on the container control relative to the top-left corner.

Name—Specifies the name used to access the RadioButton control programmatically. The name should be appended with the RadioButton suffix.

Size—Specifies the height and width (in pixels) of the RadioButton control.

Text—Specifies the text displayed in the label to the right of the RadioButton.

MULTIPLE-CHOICE QUESTIONS

18.1 A(n) _____ is required inside parentheses in order to indicate that an array is two-dimensional.

a) comma   b) asterisk

c) period   d) apostrophe

18.2 A two-dimensional array in which each row contains the same number of columns is called a _____ array.

a) data   b) rectangular

c) tabular   d) All of the above.

18.3 In an *m*-by-*n* array, the *m* stands for _____.

a) the number of columns in the array   b) the total number of array elements

c) the number of rows in the array   d) the number of elements in each row

18.4 The _____ statement assigns an array of three columns and five rows to a two-dimensional `integer` array named `array`.

a) `array = _`
   `New Integer(0 To 5, 0 To 3) {}`

b) `array = _`
   `New Integer(0 To 4, 0 To 2){}`

c) `array = _`
   `New Integer(0 To 4, 0 To 3) {}`

d) `array = _`
   `New Integer(0 To 5, 0 To 2) {}`

18.5 A RadioButton is a type of _____ button.

a) check   b) change

c) state   d) action

18.6 Use a _____ to group RadioButtons on the Form.

a) GroupBox control   b) ComboBox control

c) ListBox control   d) None of the above.

18.7 The _____ event handler is invoked when selecting a RadioButton control.

a) Selected   b) CheckedChanged

c) ButtonChanged   d) CheckSelected

18.8 The _____ property is set to True when a RadioButton is selected.

a) Selected   b) Chosen

c) On   d) Checked

18.9 Two-dimensional arrays are often used to represent _____.

a) a pie chart   b) distances

c) lines   d) tables

18.10 The statement _____ assigns an array of three columns and three rows to a two-dimensional array of integers `array`.

a) `Dim array As Integer()() = _`
   `New Integer()() {{1, 2, 3}, {4, 5, 6}, {7, 8, 9}}`

b) `Dim array As Integer(,) = _`
   `{{1, 2, 3}, {4, 5, 6}, {7, 8, 9}}`

c) `Dim array As Integer(,) = _`
   `New Integer(,) {{1, 2, 3}, {4, 5, 6}, {7, 8, 9}}`

d) `Dim array As Integer() = _`
   `{{1, 2, 3}, {4, 5, 6}, {7, 8, 9}}`

EXERCISES

18.11 *(Food Survey Application)* A school cafeteria is giving an electronic survey to its students to improve their lunch menu. Create an application that will use a two-dimensional array to hold counters for the survey (Fig. 18.16). You will also provide RadioButtons for the students to indicate whether they like or dislike a particular food.

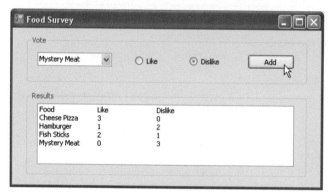

Figure 18.16 **Food Survey** application.

a) *Copying the template to your working directory.* Copy the directory C:\Examples\ Tutorial18\Exercises\FoodSurvey to your C:\SimplyVB directory.

b) *Opening the application's template file.* Double click FoodSurvey.sln in the Food-Survey directory to open the application.

c) *Adding RadioButtons to the Vote GroupBox.* Add two RadioButtons to the **Vote** GroupBox. Name one likeRadioButton and the other dislikeRadioButton. Change their Text properties to Like and Dislike, respectively. Set the Checked property of likeRadioButton to True. Rearrange and comment the control declarations appropriately.

d) *Declaring a two-dimensional integer array.* Declare a two-dimensional integer array named display, with four rows and two columns.

e) *Creating event handler addButton_Click.* Generate the Click event handler for the **Add** Button. In the event handler, clear the ListBox, then add the header "Food" & ControlChars.Tab & ControlChars.Tab & "Like" & ControlChars.Tab & ControlChars.Tab & "Dislike" to the ListBox. Create a local integer variable index. This variable should contain the index of the selected item in foodsComboBox.

f) *Using a For loop to display the data.* Insert a For statement into the event handler to loop through each row in the display array (rows 0–3). In the body of the loop, insert an if statement that checks whether likeRadioButton is selected and whether the variable index is equal to the counter of your For statement. If both conditions are True, increment the counter in column 0 in the display array. Insert an else if statement that determines whether dislikeRadioButton is selected and whether the variable index is equal to the counter of your For statement. If both conditions are True, increment the counter in column 1 of the display array.

g) *Adding the current row to the ListBox.* Inside the For statement, add the current row to the ListBox. The counter variable of the For statement will be used as the index of the display array. Use the ControlChars.Tab character to align the results.

h) *Running the application.* Select **Debug > Start Debugging** to run your application. Choose either the **Like** or **Dislike** RadioButton. Click the **Add** Button and check to make sure all strings and numbers in the **Results** GroupBox are correct. Add several other selections to the **Food Survey** and make sure that the numbers are correct.

i) *Closing the application.* Close your running application by clicking its close box.

j) *Closing the IDE.* Close the Visual Basic IDE by clicking its close box.

18.12 *(Sales Report Application)* A clothing manufacturer has asked you to create an application that will calculate its total sales for a week. Sales values should be input separately for each clothing item, but the amount of sales for all five weekdays should be input at once. The application should calculate the total amount of sales for each item in the week and also the total sales for the manufacturer for all the items in the week. Because the manufacturer is a small company, it will produce at most 10 items in any week. The application is shown in Fig. 18.17.

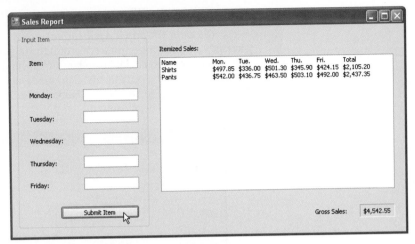

Figure 18.17 **Sales Report** application.

a) *Copying the template to your working directory.* Copy the directory C:\Examples\ Tutorial18\Exercises\SalesReport to your C:\SimplyVB directory.

b) *Opening the application's template file.* Double click SalesReport.sln in the SalesReport directory to open the application.

c) *Declaring a two-dimensional decimal array.* Declare a two-dimensional decimal array named itemSales, with 10 rows and five columns.

d) *Inputting data from the user.* Add code to the beginning of the submitButton_Click event handler to input the data from the user. Assign the item name to the one-dimensional itemNames array, indexed with itemCount (which stores the number of items added). Assign the daily sales data to the two-dimensional itemSales array. The first index to this array should be itemCount, and the second will range from 0 to 4 depending on the day of the week. Finally, increment variable itemCount to record that another item's sales data has been added.

e) *Iterating over all the items added.* Inside the DisplaySales method, after the output variable has been declared, add code to begin a For statement. This For statement should iterate from 0 to itemCount - 1. Declare the counterItem variable as the For statement's counter. Insert code in the For statement to set output to the item's name. Remember that the items' names are stored in string array itemNames. Append two tab characters to format the output properly.

f) *Iterating over the days in the week.* Add code to initialize the weekTotal variable to 0. This variable keeps track of the total sales for each item over the course of the week. Add code to start a For statement. This For statement will iterate from 0 to 4, which is one less than the number of days in the work week. This is an example of a nested For statement, which is comparable to a nested if statement.

g) *Appending the daily sales and summing sales for the week.* Add code in this For statement to append the daily sales to output. These sales are stored in the itemSales array. This array must be accessed with the current item and the day of the week. The output is money, so use the String.Format method to format the value. Append a tab character to format the output properly.

h) *Calculating the weekly sales.* Insert code to add the amount of the daily sales to the weekTotal variable. This variable stores the weekly sales for each item.

i) *Calculating the total sales and outputting an item's sales.* Insert code to add the weekly sales to the salesTotal variable. This variable keeps track of the total sales for all the items and is formatted and displayed in grossSalesLabel. Add code to append the weekly sales to output. The weekly sales are also stored as money, so use the String.Format method again. Then add output to the ListBox using the Add method of ListBox property Items.

j) *Running the application.* Select **Debug > Start Debugging** to run your application. Test your application to ensure that it runs correctly, as in Fig. 18.17.

k) *Closing the application.* Close your running application by clicking its close box.

l) *Closing the IDE.* Close the Visual Basic IDE by clicking its close box.

18.13 *(Student Grades 2 Application)* A teacher needs an application that computes each student's grade average (on a scale of 0 to 100 points) and the class average for ten students. The application should add a student's name and test average (separated by a tab character) to a `ListBox` and calculate the class grade average each time the user clicks the **Submit Grades** Button (Fig. 18.18). The **Submit Grades** Button should be disabled after ten students' grades have been entered.

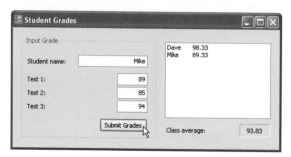

Figure 18.18 **Student Grades 2** application.

a) *Copying the template to your working directory.* Copy the directory `C:\Examples\Tutorial18\Exercises\StudentGrades2` to your `C:\SimplyVB` directory.

b) *Opening the application's template file.* Double click `StudentGrades.sln` in the `StudentGrades2` directory to open the application.

c) *Declare instance variables.* Declare an `Integer` counter and a 10-by-2 `String` array as instance variables.

d) *Coding the Submit Grades Button's `Click` event handler.* Double click the **Submit Grades** Button to generate its `Click` event handler. Write code in the event handler to retrieve input from the `TextBoxes`. Then store the student's name in the first column of the two-dimensional `String` array and the student's test average in the second column of the array. Use a `Function` procedure to calculate the student's test average.

e) *Computing the class average.* Add the student's name and the student's test average (separated by a tab character) to the `ListBox`. Then calculate and display the class average, using a Function procedure. [*Hint:* Use the two-dimensional `String` array and the `Integer` counter to calculate the class average.]

f) *Completing the event handler.* Increment the counter by one after calculating the class average. If 10 students' grades have been entered, disable the **Submit Grades** Button.

g) *Running the application.* Select **Debug > Start Debugging** to run your application. Test your application to ensure that it runs correctly, as in Fig. 18.18.

h) *Closing the application.* Close your running application by clicking its close box.

i) *Closing the IDE.* Close the Visual Basic IDE by clicking its close box.

What does this code do? ▶

18.14 What is returned by the following code? Assume that `GetStockPrices` is a `Function` procedure that returns a 2-by-31 array, with the first row containing the stock price at the beginning of the day and the last row containing the stock price at the end of the day, for each day of the month.

```
1   Function Mystery() As Integer()
2       Dim prices As Integer(,) = New Integer(0 To 1, 0 To 30) {}
3
4       prices = GetStockPrices()
5
6       Dim result As Integer() = New Integer(30) {}
7       Dim i As Integer
```

```
 8
 9        For i = 0 To 30
10            result(i) = prices(0, i) - prices(1, i)
11        Next
12
13        Return result
14    End Function ' Mystery
```

What's wrong with this code? ▶ **18.15** Find the error(s) in the following code. The `TwoDArrays` procedure should create a two-dimensional array and initialize all its values to one.

```
 1    Sub TwoDArrays()
 2        Dim array As Integer(,)
 3
 4        array = New Integer(0 To 3, 0 To 3) {}
 5
 6        Dim i As Integer
 7
 8        ' assign 1 to all cell values
 9        For i = 0 To 3
10            array(i, i) = 1
11        Next
12
13    End Sub ' TwoDArrays
```

Programming Challenge ▶ **18.16** (*Enhanced Lottery Picker Application*) A lottery commission offers four different lottery games to play: three-number, four-number, five-number and five-number + 1. In Tutorial 16, your **Lottery Picker** application selected duplicate numbers for each lottery. In this exercise, you enhance the **Lottery Picker** to prevent duplicate numbers for the five-number and five-number + 1 lotteries (Fig. 18.19). According to this new requirement, the games are now played as follows:

- Three-number lotteries require players to choose three numbers in the range 0–9.
- Four-number lotteries require players to choose four numbers in the range 0–9.
- Five-number lotteries require players to choose five unique numbers in the range 1–39.
- Five-number + 1 lotteries require players to choose five unique numbers in the range 1–49 and an additional unique number in the range 1–42.

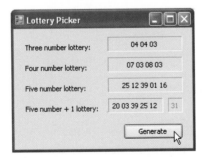

Figure 18.19 Enhanced **Lottery Picker** application.

a) *Copying the template to your working directory.* Copy the directory `C:\Examples\Tutorial18\Exercises\EnhancedLotteryPicker` to your `C:\SimplyVB` directory.

b) *Opening the application's template file.* Double click `EnhancedLotteryPicker.sln` in the `EnhancedLotteryPicker` directory to open the application.

c) *Declaring a two-dimensional array to maintain unique random numbers.* Declare the variable numbers instance that stores a 2-by-50 bool array. You will use this array later in this exercise to test whether a lottery number has already been chosen.

d) *Initializing the array.* Each time the user clicks the **Generate** Button, the application initializes the array by declaring its rows and setting the initial values. Write a ClearArray method that uses a For statement to assign each value in the numbers array to False. Call the ClearArray method at the beginning of the **Generate** Button's Click event handler.

e) *Modifying the Generate method.* You will modify the Generate method to use the bool array to pick unique random numbers. Begin by writing a statement that generates a random number and assigns its value to an Integer variable number.

f) *Determining whether the random number has already been selected.* Use an if statement to determine whether the maximum lottery number is equal to 40. (This happens when the upper limit on the random number equals 40.) In this case, you will examine the first row of the array. To maintain unique numbers, you will set the value of the element in that row whose index equals the random number to True (indicating that it has been picked). For example, if the random number 34 has been picked, numbers[0, 34] would contain the value True. To test whether a number has been picked, use a While statement inside the If statement to access that element of the array. If the array element's value is True, use the body of the loop to assign a new random number to number. If the value in the array is False, use the condition in the while header to ignore the body of the loop. Just outside the While statement, include a statement that modifies the array to indicate that the number has now been picked.

g) *Completing the application.* Use a second if statement to determine whether the maximum lottery number is greater than 40. In this case, you will examine the second row of the array. Repeat the process in the preceding step. Remember to return the value stored in number at the end of the Generate method.

h) *Running the application.* Select **Debug > Start Debugging** to run your application. Click the **Generate** Button and check to make sure all the numbers in both five-number lotteries are unique. Do this several more times to make sure.

i) *Closing the application.* Close your running application by clicking its close box.

j) *Closing the IDE.* Close the Visual Basic IDE by clicking its close box.

Objectives

In this tutorial, you will learn to:
- Create your own classes.
- Create and use objects of your own classes.
- Control access to object instance variables.
- Use keyword Private.
- Create your own properties.
- Use the Panel control.
- Use String methods PadLeft and Substring.

Outline

Microwave Oven Application

Building Your Own Classes and Objects

In earlier tutorials, you used the following application-development methodology: You analyzed many typical problems that required an application to be built and determined what classes from the FCL were needed to implement each application. You then selected appropriate methods from these classes and created any necessary procedures to complete each application.

You have now seen several FCL classes. Each GUI control is defined as a class. When you add a control to your application from the **Toolbox**, an object (also known as an instance) of that class is created and added to your application. You have also seen FCL classes that are not GUI controls. Classes String and Random, for example, have been used to create String objects (for textual data) and Random objects (for generating random numbers), respectively. When you create and use an object of a class in an application, your application is known as a **client** of that class.

In this tutorial, you'll learn to create and use your own classes (sometimes known as **programmer-defined classes** or **programmer-defined types**). Creating your own classes is a key part of object-oriented programming (OOP). As with procedures, classes can be reused. Visual Basic applications typically are created by using a combination of FCL classes and methods and programmer-defined classes and procedures. You have already created several procedures in this book. Note that all of these procedures were created within classes, because all of your applications have been defined as classes (each Form you've created is a class). In this tutorial (and for the remainder of the book), you will refer to a class's procedures as methods, which is the industry-preferred term for procedures located within a class.

You will create a microwave oven simulator where the user will enter an amount of time for the microwave to cook food. To handle the time data, you will create a class called Time. This class will store a number of minutes and seconds (which your **Microwave Oven** application will use to keep track of the remaining cook time) and provide properties whereby clients of this class can change the number of minutes and seconds.

19.1 Test-Driving the Microwave Oven Application

In this tutorial you will build your own class as you construct your **Microwave Oven** application. This application must meet the following requirements:

Application Requirements

*An electronics company is considering building microwave ovens. The company has asked you to develop an application that simulates a microwave oven. The oven will contain a keypad that allows the user to specify the microwave cook time, which is displayed for the user. Once a time is entered, the user clicks the **Start Button** to begin the cooking process. The microwave's glass window changes color (from gray to yellow) to simulate the oven's light that remains on while the food is cooking, and a timer counts down one second at a time. Once the time expires, the color of the microwave's glass window returns to gray (indicating that the microwave's light is now off) and the microwave displays the text "Done!" The user can click the **Clear Button** at any time to stop the microwave and enter a new time. The user should be able to enter a number of minutes no larger than 59 and a number of seconds no larger than 59; otherwise, the invalid cook time will be set to zero. A beep will be sounded whenever a **Button** is clicked and when the microwave oven has finished a countdown.*

You begin by test-driving the completed application. Then you will learn the additional Visual Basic technologies that you will need to create your own version of this application.

Test-Driving the Microwave Oven Application

1. ***Opening the completed application.*** Open the directory C:\Examples\ Tutorial19\CompletedApplication\MicrowaveOven to locate the **Microwave Oven** application. Double click MicrowaveOven.sln to open the application in the Visual Basic IDE.

2. ***Running the Microwave Oven application.*** Select **Debug > Start Debugging** to run the application (Fig. 19.1). The application contains a large rectangle on the left (representing the microwave oven's glass window) and a keypad on the right, including a Label with the text **Microwave Oven**. The numeric Buttons are used to enter the cook time, which will be displayed in the Label on the top right. Note that the keypad Buttons appear flat, to give the application a more "real-world" appearance. To create this appearance, the Buttons' **FlatStyle** property has been set to **Flat**. Similarly, the Label's BorderStyle property has been set to **FixedSingle**.

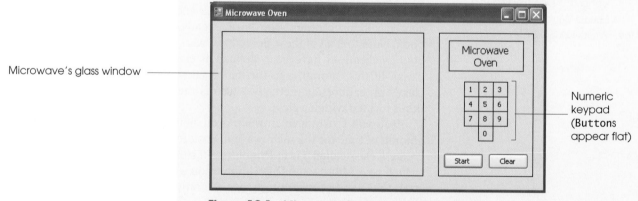

Microwave's glass window ⎯⎯⎯⎯⎯⎯

Numeric keypad (Buttons appear flat)

Figure 19.1 **Microwave Oven** application's Form.

(cont.)   3.   ***Entering a time.*** Click the following numeric Buttons in order: **1**, **2**, **3**, **4** and
                  5. Each time you click a keypad Button, you will hear a beeping sound. (If you
                  do not hear a beeping sound, please check your computer's settings to ensure
                  that the volume of your machine's speaker has not been lowered or muted.)

                  Note that you can enter no more than four digits (the first two for the
                  minutes and the second two for the seconds)—any extra digits will not
                  appear (Fig. 19.2). The number of minutes and the number of seconds must
                  each be 59 or less. If the user enters an invalid number of minutes or seconds
                  (such as 89), the invalid amount will be set to zero.

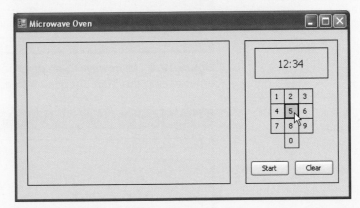

Figure 19.2   **Microwave Oven** application accepts only four digits.

         4.   ***Entering invalid data.*** Click the **Clear** Button to clear your input. Click the
              following numeric Buttons in order: **7**, **2**, **3** and **5** (Fig. 19.3). This input is
              invalid because the number of minutes, 72, is larger than the maximum
              allowed value, 59, so the number of minutes is reset to zero when the **Start**
              Button is clicked. Click the **Start** Button now. Note that the number of min-
              utes has been reset to **00** (Fig. 19.4). Also note that the microwave oven's
              window has changed to yellow, to simulate the light that goes on inside the
              oven so that the user can watch the food cooking.

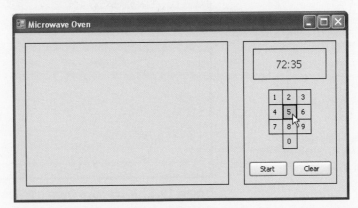

Figure 19.3   **Microwave Oven** application with invalid input.

         5.   ***Entering valid data.*** Click the **Clear** Button to enter a new cook time. Click
              Button **5** (to indicate five seconds); then, click **Start** (Fig. 19.5).

         6.   ***Viewing the application after the cooking time has expired.*** Wait five sec-
              onds. Note that the display Label shows the time counting down by 1 each
              second. When the time has reached zero, the oven beeps, the display Label
              changes to contain the text **Done!** and the microwave oven's window
              changes back to the same color as the Form (Fig. 19.6).

(cont.)

Color yellow simulates
microwave light

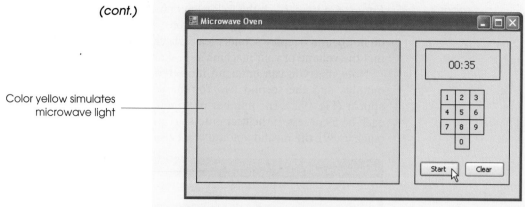

Figure 19.4 Microwave Oven application after invalid input has been entered and the **Start Button** clicked.

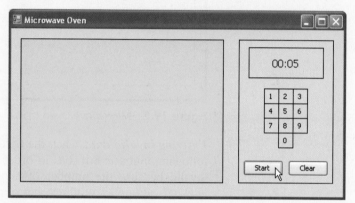

Figure 19.5 Microwave Oven application with valid time entered and inside light turned on (it is now cooking).

Label displays **Done!**
when cooking is finished

Color returns to default
color to simulate that
cooking has finished

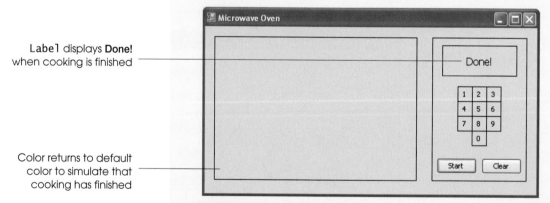

Figure 19.6 Microwave Oven application after the cooking time has elapsed.

7. ***Closing the application.*** Close your running application by clicking its close box.

8. ***Closing the IDE.*** Close the Visual Basic IDE by clicking its close box.

19.2 Designing the Microwave Oven Application

In Tutorial 14, you learned to use GroupBoxes to group various controls. The **Microwave Oven** application also groups controls, using a **Panel control**. The main difference between Panels and GroupBoxes is that GroupBoxes can display a caption,

GUI Design Tip

Use Panels to organize groups of related controls where the purpose of the controls is obvious. If the purpose of the controls is not obvious, use a GroupBox in place of a Panel, because GroupBoxes can contain captions.

and Panels cannot. The **Microwave Oven** application requires two Panels—one to contain the controls of the application, and the other to represent the microwave oven's glass window. The template application provided for you contains one of these Panels.

The **Microwave Oven** application contains a class (called Time) whose objects store the cook time in minutes and seconds. All the controls you have used (including the Form itself) are defined as classes. You will create the Time class before you create the class for the **Microwave Oven**. The following pseudocode describes the basic operation of class Time:

> When the time object is created:
>> Assign input to variables for number of minutes and number of seconds
>
> When setting the number of minutes:
>
>> If the number of minutes is less than 60
>>> Set the number of minutes to specified value
>> Else
>>> Set the number of minutes to 0
>
> When setting the number of seconds:
>
>> If the number of seconds is less than 60
>>> Set the number of seconds to specified value
>> Else
>>> Set the number of seconds to 0

When an object of class Time is created, the number of minutes and number of seconds will be initialized. Invalid data will cause both the number of minutes and the number of seconds to be set to 0. The following pseudocode describes the basic operation of your **Microwave Oven** class:

> When the user clicks a numeric Button:
>> Sound beep
>> Display the formatted time
>
> When the user clicks the Start Button:
>> Store the minutes and seconds
>> Display the formatted time
>> Begin countdown—Start timer
>> Turn the microwave light on
>
> When the timer ticks (once per second):
>> Decrease time by one second
>
>> If new time is zero
>>> Stop the countdown
>>> Sound beep
>>> Display text "Done!"
>>> Turn the microwave light off
>> Else
>>> Display new time
>
> When the user clicks the Clear Button:
>> Display the text "Microwave Oven"
>> Clear input and time data
>> Stop the countdown
>> Turn the microwave light off

The user enters input by clicking the numeric Buttons. Each time a numeric Button is clicked, the number on that Button is appended to the end of the cook time displayed in the GUI's Label. At most, four digits can be displayed. After entering the cook time, the user can click the **Start** Button to begin the cooking process or click the **Clear** Button and enter a new time. Each Button makes a beeping sound when clicked. If the **Start** Button is clicked, a countdown using a Timer control begins, and the microwave oven's window changes to yellow, indicating that the microwave oven's light is on (so that the user can watch the food cook). Each second, the display is updated to show the remaining cooking time. When the countdown finishes, another beep is sounded, the display Label displays the text **Done!** and the microwave oven's light is turned off by changing the window's color back to its default gray.

Now that you have test-driven the **Microwave Oven** application and studied its pseudocode representation, you will use an ACE table to help you convert the pseudocode to Visual Basic. Figure 19.7 lists the actions, controls and events that will help you complete your own version of this application.

Action/Control/Event (ACE) Table for the Microwave Oven Application

Action	Control/Object	Event
	oneButton, twoButton, threeButton, fourButton, fiveButton, sixButton, sevenButton, eightButton, nineButton, zeroButton	Click
Sound beep		
Display the formatted time	displayLabel	
	startButton	Click
Store the minutes and seconds	timeObject	
Display the formatted time	displayLabel	
Begin countdown—Start timer	clockTimer	
Turn microwave light on	windowPanel	
	clockTimer	Tick
Decrease time by one second	timeObject	
If new time is zero	timeObject	
Stop the countdown	clockTimer	
Sound beep		
Display text "Done!"	displayLabel	
Turn the microwave light off	windowPanel	
Else Display new time	displayLabel	
	clearButton	Click
Display the text "Microwave Oven"	displayLabel	
Clear input and time data	timeIs, timeObject	
Stop the countdown	clockTimer	
Turn microwave light off	windowPanel	

Figure 19.7 ACE table for the **Microwave Oven** application.

Input is sent to the application when the user clicks one of the numeric Buttons. Values are displayed in displayLabel as they are entered. Once all input has been entered, the user clicks the **Start** Button to begin the countdown. The form's windowPanel background color is set to yellow to simulate the microwave oven's light being turned on, and clockTimer will update displayLabel each second during the countdown. To clear the input and start over, the user can click the **Clear** Button. In the following box, you begin creating your **Microwave Oven** application by adding the second Panel to the Form and viewing the template code.

Adding a Panel Control to the Microwave Oven Application

1. *Copying the template to your working directory.* Copy the C:\Examples\ Tutorial19\TemplateApplication\MicrowaveOven directory to your C:\SimplyVB directory.

2. *Opening the Microwave Oven application's template file.* Double click MicrowaveOven.sln in the MicrowaveOven directory to open the application in the Visual Basic IDE.

3. *Adding a Panel to the Form.* Add a Panel control to the Form by double clicking the **Panel** control (☐ Panel) in the **Toolbox**. Name the control windowPanel because this Panel will represent your microwave oven's window. Set the Panel's Size property to 328, 224 and its Location property to 16, 16. Set the BorderStyle property to FixedSingle, to display a thin black rectangle surrounding your Panel.

4. *Viewing the template code.* Before you add code to this application, switch to code view, and examine the code provided. Line 4 of Fig. 19.8 declares instance variable timeIs, a String that will store user input.

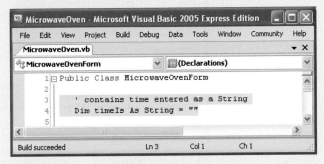

Figure 19.8 Variable timeIs contains the user's input.

The template code also contains event handlers for the numeric Buttons' Click events. Each Button is clicked when the user wants to append the current Button's digit to the amount of cooking time. Let's look at one of these event handlers closely (Fig. 19.9). Line 10 calls function **Beep**, which causes your computer to make a beeping sound. Each event handler for the numeric keypad Buttons begins with a call to Beep, appends the current Button's number to timeIs (line 11) and calls method DisplayTime (line 12), which displays the current cooking time in the application's Label. There are 10 of these event handlers—one for each digit from 0 to 9.

MicrowaveOven.vb contains four more methods that you will define in this tutorial. The first is the startButton_Click event handler in lines 96–100 of Fig. 19.10. This event handler will be used to start the microwave oven's cooking process, which in this simulation consists of a time countdown and a change in the window's color to yellow, simulating the oven's light being on.

Event handler clearButton_Click (lines 102–106) will be used to clear the time entered. The **Clear** Button is used to change the time entered or terminate cooking early. The event handler resets the time to all zeros and displays the text **Microwave Oven**. Method DisplayTime (lines 108–111) will be used to display the cooking time as it is being entered. Event handler clockTimer_Tick (lines 113–117) will be used to change the application's Label during the countdown.

5. *Saving the project.* Select **File > Save All** to save your modified code.

(cont.)

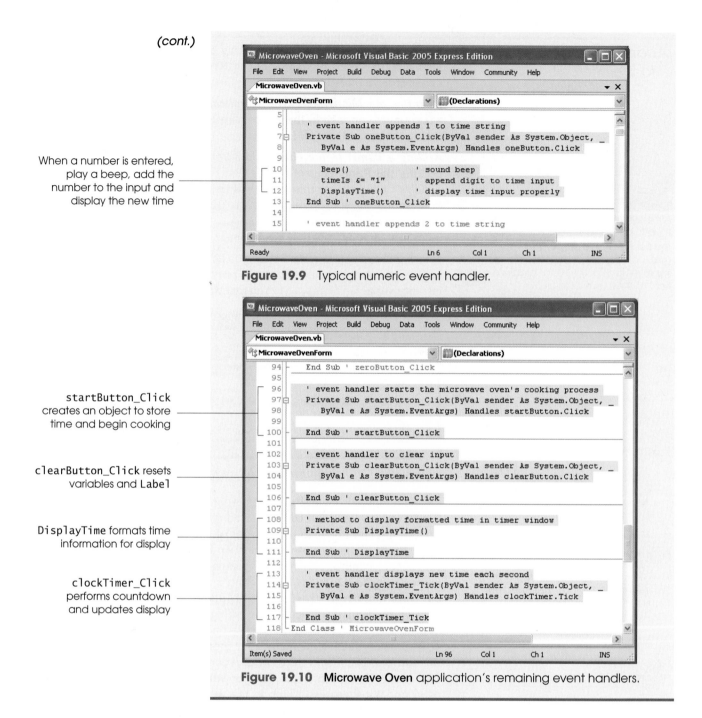

When a number is entered, play a beep, add the number to the input and display the new time

Figure 19.9 Typical numeric event handler.

`startButton_Click` creates an object to store time and begin cooking

`clearButton_Click` resets variables and `Label`

`DisplayTime` formats time information for display

`clockTimer_Click` performs countdown and updates display

Figure 19.10 **Microwave Oven** application's remaining event handlers.

SELF-REVIEW

1. A `Panel` is different from a `GroupBox` in that a _____.

   a) `GroupBox` can be used to organize controls, whereas a `Panel` cannot
   b) `Panel` contains a caption, whereas a `GroupBox` does not
   c) `GroupBox` contains a caption, whereas a `Panel` does not
   d) `Panel` can be used to organize controls, whereas a `GroupBox` cannot

2. Function `Beep` causes the computer to _____.

   a) make three beeping sounds in sequence
   b) make a beeping sound
   c) display a message dialog and make a beeping sound
   d) set off the system alarm and pause the application

Answers: 1) c. 2) b.

19.3 Adding a New Class to the Project

Next, you will learn how to add a class to your application. This class will be used to create objects that contain the time in minutes and seconds.

Adding a Class to the Microwave Oven Application

1. ***Adding a new class to the project.*** Select **Project > Add Class**. In the dialog that appears (Fig. 19.11), enter the class name (`Time`) in the **Name:** field and click **Add**. Note that the class name (ending with the `.vb` file extension) appears in the **Solution Explorer** below the project name (Fig. 19.12).

Select **Class** as new item ⎯⎯⎯

Name of new class ⎯⎯⎯

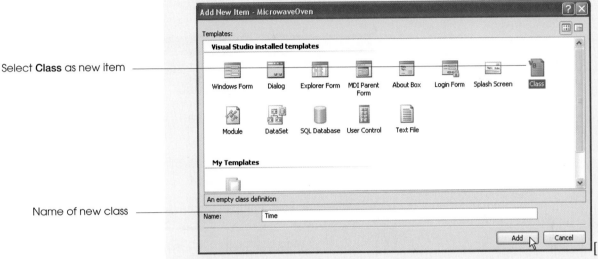

Figure 19.11 **Add New Item** dialog allows you to create a new class.

New file displayed in **Solution Explorer** ⎯⎯⎯

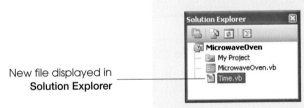

Figure 19.12 **Solution Explorer** displaying new class file.

2. ***Viewing the code that has been added to this class.*** If `Time.vb` does not open for you when it is created, double click the file in the **Solution Explorer**. Note that a few lines of code have been added for you (Fig. 19.13). Line 1, which begins the `Time` class definition, contains the keywords `Public` and `Class`, followed by the name of the class (in this case, `Time`). Keyword **`Class`** indicates that what follows is a class definition. You will learn about keyword `Public` in Section 19.7. The keywords **End Class** (line 3) indicate the end of the class definition. Any code placed between these two lines forms the class definition's body. Any methods or variables defined in the body of a class are considered to be **members** of that class.

3. ***Adding instance variables to your application.*** Add lines 1–2 of Fig. 19.14 to `Time.vb`, above the class definition. Add comments indicating the name and purpose of your class files. Add lines 6–8 to the `Time` class definition.

   Lines 7 and 8 declare each of the two `Integer` instance variables—`minuteValue` and `secondValue`. The `Time` class will store a time value containing minutes and seconds—the value for minutes is stored in `minuteValue`, and the value for seconds is stored in `secondValue`. Finally, be sure to add a comment in line 10 where the class definition is terminated.

Good Programming Practice

Add comments at the beginning of programmer-defined classes to increase readability. The comments should indicate the name of the file that contains the class and the purpose of the class being defined.

(cont.)

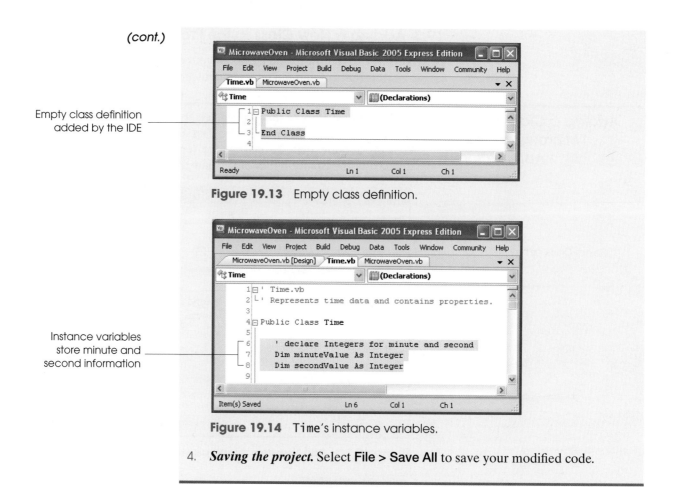

Empty class definition added by the IDE

Figure 19.13   Empty class definition.

Instance variables store minute and second information

Figure 19.14   `Time`'s instance variables.

4. *Saving the project.* Select **File > Save All** to save your modified code.

SELF-REVIEW

1. To add a class to a project in the Visual Basic IDE, select _____.

   a) **File > Add Class**   b) **File > Add File > Add Class**

   c) **Project > Add Class**   d) **Project > Add File > Add Class**

2. A class definition ends with the keyword(s) _____.

   a) `Class End`   b) `End Class`

   c) `EndClass`   d) `End`

Answers: 1) c. 2) b.

19.4 Initializing Class Objects: Constructors

A class can contain methods as well as instance variables. You have already used method `Format` from class `String` and method `Next` from class `Random`. A **constructor** is a special method within a class definition that is used to initialize a class's instance variables. In Tutorial 16, you learned how to use constructors to create objects (e.g., `New Random`). In the following box, you will create a constructor for your `Time` class that allows clients to create `Time` objects and initialize their data.

Defining a Constructor

1. *Adding a constructor to a class.* Add lines 10–12 of Fig. 19.15 to the body of class `Time`, then press *Enter*. The keywords `End Sub` will be added for you, just as with the other `Sub` procedures you have created in this text.

(cont.)

New is the constructor method. You write code for the constructor that is invoked whenever an object of that class is **instantiated** (created). This constructor method then performs the actions in its body, which you will add in the next few steps. A constructor's actions consist mainly of statements that initialize the class's instance variables.

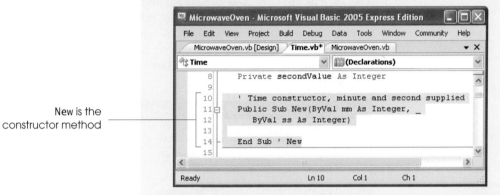

New is the
constructor method

Figure 19.15 Empty constructor.

Constructors can take arguments (you'll see how to provide arguments to constructors momentarily) but cannot return values. An important difference between constructors and other methods is that constructors cannot specify a return data type—for this reason, Visual Basic constructors are implemented as Sub procedures rather than Function procedures, because Sub procedures cannot return values. A class's instance variables can be initialized in the constructor or when they are defined in the class definition. Variable secondValue, for instance, can be initialized where it is declared (line 8) or it can be initialized in Time's constructor.

2. *Initializing variables in a constructor.* Add lines 14 and 15 of Fig. 19.16 to the constructor. These lines initialize Time's instance variables to the values of the constructor's parameter variables (lines 11–12 of Fig. 19.15). When an object is created in a client of a class, values are often specified for that object. A Time object can now be created with the statement

```
timeObject = New Time(5, 3)
```

This Time object will be created and the constructor will execute. The values 5 and 3 are assigned to the constructor's parameters, which will be used to initialize secondValue and minuteValue.

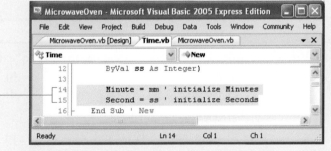

Initialize instance variables

Figure 19.16 Constructor initializing instance variables.

Common Programming Error

Attempting to declare a constructor as a Function procedure instead of as a Sub procedure and attempting to Return a value from a constructor are both syntax errors.

Error-Prevention Tip

Providing a constructor to ensure that every object is initialized with meaningful values can help eliminate logic errors.

(cont.)

3. **Creating a Time object.** After defining the class, you can use it as a type (just as you would use `Integer` or `Double`) in declarations. View `Microwave-Oven.vb` by selecting the **MicrowaveOven.vb** tab above the code editor. Add lines 6–7 of Fig. 19.17 to your application. Note the use of the class name, `Time`, as a type. Just as you can create many variables from a data type, such as `Integer`, you can create many objects from class types. You can create your own class types as needed; this is one reason why Visual Basic is known as an **extensible language**—the language can be "extended" with new data types. Note that, after you type As in line 8, *IntelliSense* displays a window of available types. New class `Time` will be displayed in the *IntelliSense* window (Fig. 19.18).

Declare `timeObject` of programmer-defined type `Time`

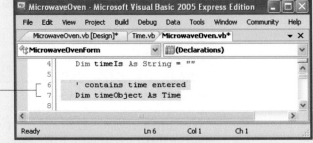

Figure 19.17 Declaring an object of type `Time`.

`Time` appears as a type in the IDE

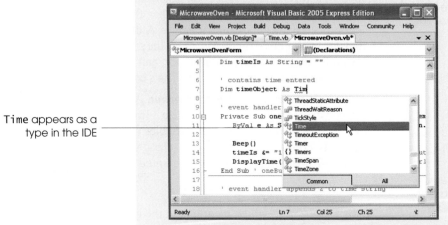

Figure 19.18 `Time` appearing as a type in an *IntelliSense* window.

4. **Saving the project.** Select **File > Save All** to save your modified code.

SELF-REVIEW
1. A(n) _____ language is one that can be "extended" with new data types.
   a) data   b) extensible
   c) typeable   d) extended

2. Variables can be initialized _____.
   a) when they are declared   b) to their default values
   c) in a constructor   d) All of the above.

Answers: 1) b. 2) d.

19.5 Properties

Clients of a class usually want to manipulate that class's instance variables. For example, assume a class (`Person`) that stores information about a person, including age information (stored in `Integer` instance variable `age`). Clients who create an object of class `Person` might want to modify `age`—perhaps incorrectly, by assigning a negative value to `age`, for example. Classes often provide **properties** to allow clients to access and modify instance variables safely. The syntax used to access properties is the same as the syntax used to access instance variables. You have already seen and used several properties in previous tutorials. For instance, many GUI controls contain a `Text` property, used to retrieve or modify the text displayed by a control. When a value is to be assigned to a property, the code in the property definition is executed. The code in the property typically checks the value to be assigned and rejects invalid data. In this tutorial, you learn how to create your own properties to help clients of a class read and modify the class's instance variables. You will create two properties, `Minute` and `Second`, for your `Time` class. `Minute` allows clients to access variable `minuteValue` safely, and `Second` allows clients to access variable `secondValue` safely.

A **property definition** may consist of two **accessors**—method-like code units that handle the details of modifying and returning data. The **Set accessor** allows clients to set (that is, assign values to) properties. For example, when the code

```
timeObject.Minute = 35
```

executes, the `Set` accessor of the `Minute` property executes. `Set` accessors typically provide data-validation capabilities (such as range checking) to ensure that the value of each instance variable is set properly. In your **Microwave Oven** application, users can specify an amount of minutes only in the range 0 to 59. Values not in this range will be discarded by the `Set` accessor, and `minuteValue` will be assigned the value 0. The **Get accessor** allows clients to get (that is, obtain the value of) a property. When the code

```
minuteValue = timeObject.Minute
```

executes, the `Get` accessor of the `Minute` property executes (and returns the value of the `minuteValue` instance variable).

Each property is typically defined to perform validity checking—to ensure that the data assigned to the property is valid. Keeping an object's data valid is also known as keeping that data in a **consistent state**. Property `Minute` keeps instance variable `minuteValue` in a consistent state. In the following box, you will create properties `Minute` and `Second` for your `Time` class, defining `Get` and `Set` accessors for each.

Defining Properties	1. ***Adding property Minute to class Time.*** View `Time.vb` by selecting the **Time.vb** tab above the code editor. Add lines 18–19 of Fig. 19.19, then press *Enter* to add property `Minute` to class `Time`. Lines 21–23 and lines 26–28 will be added for you automatically by the IDE. Note the syntax used in a property definition. You begin in line 19 with the keyword `Public` (which will be discussed in Section 19.7), followed by the keyword **Property**, which indicates that you are defining a property. The keyword `Property` is followed by the name of the property (in this case, `Minute`) and a set of parentheses, which is similar to the way you define methods. The first line of the property then concludes with the keyword `As` followed by a data type (in this case, `Integer`), indicating the data type of any value assigned to, or read from, this property.

Good Programming Practice

Name each property with a capital first letter.

(cont.)

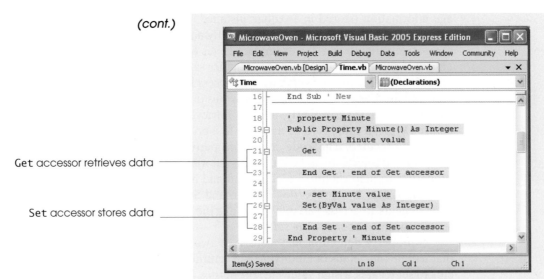

Figure 19.19 Empty `Minute` property.

Get accessor retrieves data

Set accessor stores data

Error-Prevention Tip

A property that sets the value of an instance variable should verify that the intended new value is correct. If it is not, the `Set` accessor should place the instance variable into an appropriate consistent state.

The keyword **Get** in line 21 indicates the beginning of this property's Get accessor. The keywords **End Get** in line 23 indicate the end of the Get accessor. Any code that you insert between these two lines will make up the Get accessor's body and will be executed when a client of this class attempts to read a value from the Minute property, as with the code `minutes = timeObject.Minute`.

The keyword **Set** in line 26 indicates the beginning of this property's Set accessor. The keywords **End Set** in line 28 indicate the end of the Set accessor. Any code that you insert between these two lines will make up the Set accessor's body and will be executed automatically (that's the beauty of properties) when a client of this class attempts to assign a value to the Minute property, as with the code `timeObject.Minute = 35`. The value assigned is stored in the parameter specified in line 26, which by default uses the identifier `value`. This identifier is used to access the value assigned to property Minute. The property ends in line 29 with the keywords **End Property**. Note that we have added a comment to this line, indicating the name of the property being terminated.

2. ***Defining the Get accessor.*** Add line 22 of Fig. 19.20 to your Get accessor. Also add a comment (line 20) above the Get accessor, to increase readability. When property Minute is referenced, you want your Get accessor to return the value of `minuteValue` just as a method (function) would return a value, so you use the keyword Return in line 22, followed by the identifier `minuteValue`. Finally, add a comment in line 23 to indicate the end of the Get accessor.

3. ***Defining the Set accessor.*** Add lines 28–33 of Fig. 19.21 to your Set accessor. Also add a comment (line 25) above the Set accessor, to increase readability. When property Minute is assigned a value, you want to test whether the value to be assigned is valid. You do not want to accept a minutes value greater than 59, a condition that is tested in line 29. If the number of minutes is valid, it will be assigned to `minuteValue` in line 30. Otherwise, the value 0 will be assigned to `minuteValue` in line 32. Finally, add a comment at line 34 to indicate the end of the Set accessor.

(cont.)

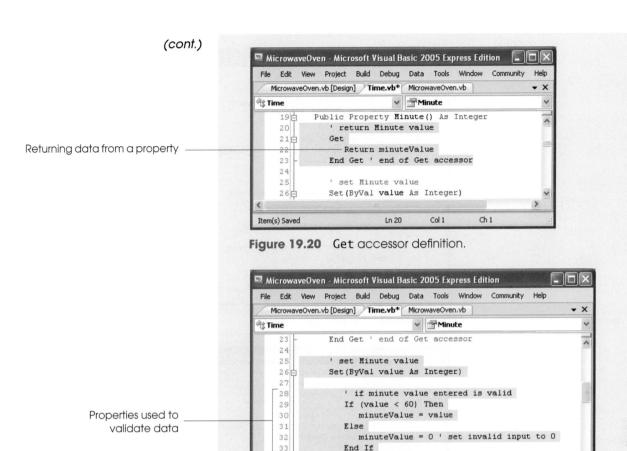

Returning data from a property

Figure 19.20   **Get** accessor definition.

Properties used to validate data

Figure 19.21   **Set** accessor definition.

4. *Adding property **Second** to class **Time***. Add lines 37–38 of Fig. 19.22 to your application, then press *Enter*. Lines 40–42 and 45–47 are added for you automatically by the IDE. You should add the comments at lines 37 and 48 manually.

5. *Defining the **Second** property's accessors.* Add comments above each accessor (lines 39 and 44 of Fig. 19.23). Add line 41 to property Second's Get accessor and lines 47–52 to property Second's Set accessor. Note that this property is similar to Minute, except that variable secondValue is being modified and read, as opposed to variable minuteValue. Finally, you should add comments at the end of each accessor (lines 42 and 53) to increase readability.

6. *Assigning values to properties.* Change lines 14–15 of Fig. 19.16 to lines 14–15 of Fig. 19.24. Now that you have defined properties to ensure that only valid data will be assigned to minuteValue and secondValue, you can use these properties to safely initialize instance variables in the class's constructor. So when client calls New and passes mm and ss values, the constructor will call the property method to validate the values.

7. *Saving the project.* Select **File > Save All** to save your modified code.

(cont.)

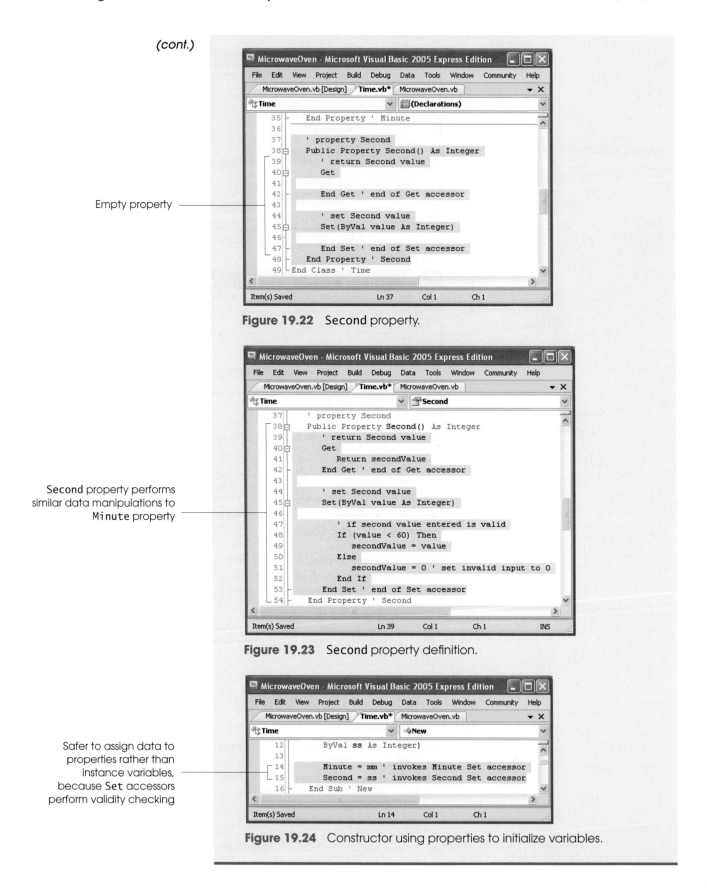

Empty property

Figure 19.22 Second property.

Second property performs similar data manipulations to **Minute** property

Figure 19.23 Second property definition.

Safer to assign data to properties rather than instance variables, because **Set** accessors perform validity checking

Figure 19.24 Constructor using properties to initialize variables.

1. A(n) _____ can ensure that a value is appropriate for a data member before the data member is assigned that value.

     a) `Get` accessor   b) `Access` accessor

     c) `Modify` accessor   d) `Set` accessor

2. Properties can contain both _____ accessors.

     a) `Return` and `Value`   b) `Get` and `Value`

     c) `Get` and `Set`   d) `Return` and `Set`

Answers: 1) d. 2) c.

19.6 Completing the Microwave Oven Application

Now that you have completed your `Time` class, you will use an object of this class to maintain the cooking time in your application. Follow the steps in the next box to add this functionality to your application.

Completing the Microwave Oven Application	1. *Formatting user input.* View `MicrowaveOven.vb` by selecting the **MicrowaveOven.vb** tab above the code editor. Add lines 103–108 of Fig. 19.25 to event handler `startButton_Click`. Variables `second` and `minute` (lines 103–104) will be used to store the second and minute values entered by the user. Lines 107–108 use `String` method **PadLeft**, which appends characters to the beginning of a `String` based on the `String`'s length. This method can be used to guarantee the length of a `String`—if the `String` has fewer characters than desired, method `PadLeft` will add characters to the beginning of the `String` until it has the proper number of characters. You want `timeIs` to contain four characters (for example, `"0325"` rather than `"325"` for a time of `"3:25"`, representing 3 minutes and 25 seconds). Having four digits makes the conversion to minutes and seconds easier. You can now simply convert the first two digits (03) to a minute value and the last two digits (25) to a second value. The first argument in the `PadLeft` call, 4, specifies the length that `timeIs` will have after characters have been appended. If `timeIs` already contains four or more characters, `PadLeft` will not have any effect. The second argument (the character 0) specifies the character that will be appended to the beginning of the `String`. Note that specifying only `"0"` as the second argument will cause an error, because `"0"` is of type `String`. Method `PadLeft` expects the second argument to be a single character of data type **Char**. You obtain the character 0 by calling method **Convert.ToChar**, which converts your `String` zero to a character zero. You can also use the literal value `"0"c`.

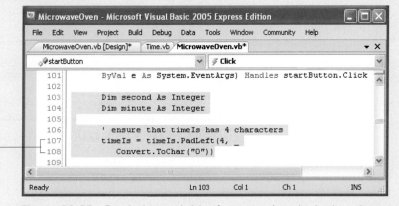

Ensure `timeIs` has four characters for conversion purposes

Figure 19.25   Declaring variables for second and minute values.

(cont.)

2. ***Converting user input to Integers.*** Add lines 110–112 of Fig. 19.26 to event handler startButton_Click. Line 111 calls method Convert.ToInt32 to convert the last two characters of timeIs to an Integer and assign this value to second. The last two characters are selected from timeIs by using method **Substring**. This is another String method, used to return only a portion of a String from timeIs. The argument passed to Substring, 2, indicates that the subset of characters returned from this method should begin with the character at position 2, and continue until the end of the string. Remember that the character at position 2 is actually the third character in the String, because the position values of a String begin at 0. In the example "0325", calling Substring with the argument 2 returns "25". Line 112 selects the first two characters of timeIs, converts the value to an Integer, and assigns this value to minute. The call to Substring in line 112 takes two arguments. The first argument, 0, indicates that the characters returned from this method start with the first character (at position 0) of timeIs. The second argument, 2, indicates that only two characters from the starting position are to be returned. In the example "0325", calling Substring with the arguments 0 and 2 returns "03".

Convert input to seconds and minutes

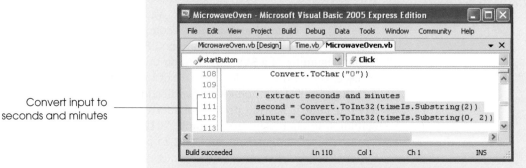

Figure 19.26 Form minute and second values from input.

3. ***Creating a Time object.*** Add lines 114–115 of Fig. 19.27 to startButton_Click. Line 115 creates an object of type Time. When the object is instantiated, keyword New allocates the memory in which the Time object will be stored; then the Time constructor is called (with the values of minute and second) to initialize the instance variables of the Time object. The constructor then returns a reference to the newly created object; this reference is assigned to timeObject.

Use keyword New to create a new object

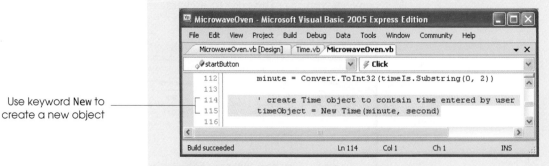

Figure 19.27 Creating a Time object.

(cont.)   4. ***Accessing a Time object's properties.*** Add lines 117–118 of Fig. 19.28 to
`startButton_Click`. These lines use the newly created `Time` object and
method `String.Format` to display the cooking time properly. You want the
resulting `String` to contain two digits (for the minute), a colon (:) and
finally another two digits (for the second). For example, if the time entered
was 3 minutes and 20 seconds, the `String` that will display for the user is
`"03:20"`. To achieve this result, you pass to the method the format control
string `"{0:D2}:{1:D2}"`, which indicates that arguments 0 and 1 (the first
and second arguments after the format `String` argument) take the format
D2 (base 10 decimal number format using two digits) for display purposes—
thus, 8 would be converted to 08. The colon between the curly braces } and {
will be included in the output, separating the minutes from the seconds. The
arguments after the format-control string access `timeObject`'s minute and
second values, using the `Minute` and `Second` properties. Note that `Time`'s
properties appear in the *IntelliSense* window (Fig. 19.29) when you try to
access the object's members (using the dot operator).

Display cooking time ——————

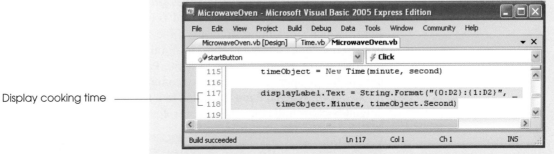

Figure 19.28   Displaying time information with separating colon.

Time's properties
appear in *IntelliSense* —————

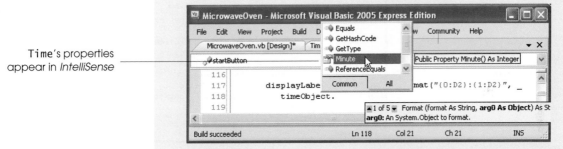

Figure 19.29   Properties of a programmer-defined type also appear in
IntelliSense.

5. ***Starting the cooking process.*** Add lines 120–124 of Fig. 19.30 to your application. Line 120 clears the user's input, so that the user can enter new input
at any time. Line 122 starts the `Timer` by setting its `Enabled` property to
`True`. The `Timer`'s `Tick` event will now be raised each second. You will
implement the event handler for this event shortly. Line 124 sets the `Panel`'s
`BackColor` property to yellow to simulate the light inside the microwave
oven. The color yellow is assigned to property `BackColor` using property
`Yellow` of structure `Color`. The **Color** structure contains several predefined
colors as properties.

(cont.)

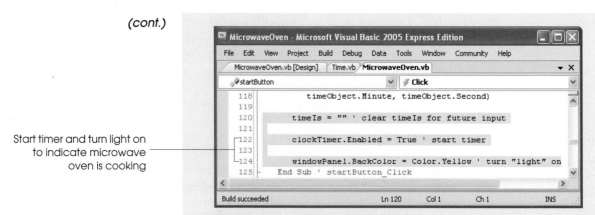

Start timer and turn light on to indicate microwave oven is cooking

Figure 19.30 Starting the microwave oven countdown.

6. ***Clearing the cook time.*** Add lines 131–136 of Fig. 19.31 to event handler `clearButton_Click`. Line 132 sets the application's `Label` to **Microwave Oven**. Line 133 clears the input values stored in `timeIs`, and line 134 resets the `Time` object to zero minutes and zero seconds. Line 135 disables the `Timer`, which stops the countdown. Line 136 sets the `Panel`'s background back to the `Panel`'s original color to simulate turning off the light inside the microwave oven. Note that we set the `Panel`'s color using the **DefaultBackColor** property. This property contains the default background color for a control. When a `Panel` is added to a `Form`, its background takes on the default background color of the control.

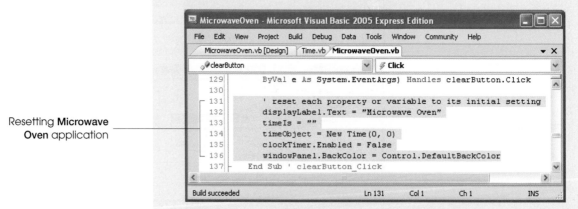

Resetting **Microwave Oven** application

Figure 19.31 Clearing the **Microwave Oven** input.

7. ***Displaying data as it is being input.*** Add lines 142–150 of Fig. 19.32 to method `DisplayTime`. This method will be called each time the user enters another digit for the cooking time. Lines 142–143 declare variables `second` and `minute`, which will store the current number of seconds and minutes. Line 145 declares `display`, which will store the user's current input in the proper display format. Lines 148–150 remove any extra digits entered by the user. (Recall that the user may enter a maximum of four digits.) Line 148 uses `String` property **Length**, which returns the number of characters in a `String`, to determine whether `timeIs` has more than four digits.

If it does, line 149 uses `String` method `Substring` to remove the extra digits. The arguments (0 followed by 4) indicate that the substring returned should begin with the first character in `timeIs` and continue for four characters. The result is assigned back to `timeIs`, ensuring that any characters appended past the first four will be removed.

(cont.)

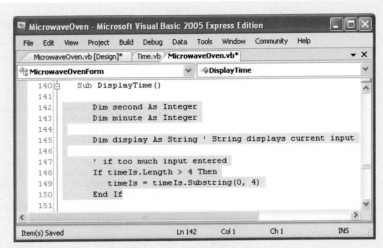

Figure 19.32 Modifying invalid user input.

8. *Completing the DisplayTime method.* Add lines 152–160 of Fig. 19.33 to method `DisplayTime`. These lines are similar to those of event handler `startButton_Click`. Line 152 appends zeros to the front of `timeIs` if fewer than four digits were entered. Lines 155–156 use method `Substring` to isolate the number of seconds and minutes currently entered. Lines 159–160 then use method `Format` to display the input correctly.

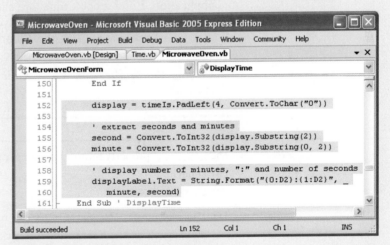

Figure 19.33 Display current input.

9. *Performing the countdown.* Add lines 167–182 of Fig. 19.34 to event handler `clockTimer_Tick`. Remember that this event handler executes every second for as long as the `Timer` is enabled. Lines 168–179 modify the display `Label` once per second so that the time remaining is shown to the user.

If the value of seconds is greater than zero (line 168), the number of seconds is decremented by one (line 169). If the value of seconds is zero but the value of minutes is greater than zero (line 170), the number of minutes is decremented by one (line 171) and the number of seconds is reset to 59 for the new minute (line 172). If the number of seconds is zero and the number of minutes is zero, the cooking process is stopped—the `Timer` is disabled (line 174), a beep is sounded (line 175), the display `Label` is set to **Done!** (line 176) and the window `Panel`'s background color is set back to its default background color (line 177).

(cont.)

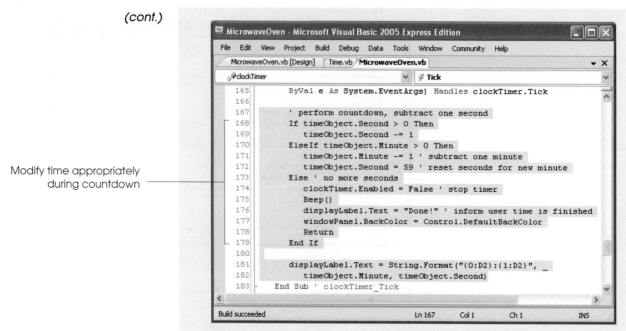

Modify time appropriately during countdown

```
      165          ByVal e As System.EventArgs) Handles clockTimer.Tick
      166
      167          ' perform countdown, subtract one second
      168          If timeObject.Second > 0 Then
      169             timeObject.Second -= 1
      170          ElseIf timeObject.Minute > 0 Then
      171             timeObject.Minute -= 1 ' subtract one minute
      172             timeObject.Second = 59 ' reset seconds for new minute
      173          Else ' no more seconds
      174             clockTimer.Enabled = False ' stop timer
      175             Beep()
      176             displayLabel.Text = "Done!" ' inform user time is finished
      177             windowPanel.BackColor = Control.DefaultBackColor
      178             Return
      179          End If
      180
      181          displayLabel.Text = String.Format("{0:D2}:{1:D2}", _
      182             timeObject.Minute, timeObject.Second)
      183       End Sub ' clockTimer_Tick
```

Figure 19.34 Modifying the display during countdown.

10. ***Running the application.*** Select **Debug > Start Debugging** to run your application. Enter a cook time and click the **Start** Button. The application should now countdown correctly, as you have defined the Tick event handler for clockTimer. Click the **Clear** Button and verify that the input is cleared and the countdown is stopped.

11. ***Closing the application.*** Close your running application by clicking its close box.

SELF-REVIEW

1. The _____ property returns the number of characters in a String.

   a) Length   b) Size

   c) Char   d) Width

2. The expression example.Substring(0, 7) returns the character(s) _____.

   a) that begin at position seven and run backward to position zero

   b) that begin at position zero and continue for seven characters

   c) at position zero and position seven   d) at position zero, repeated seven times

Answers: 1) a. 2) b.

19.7 Controlling Access to Members

Common Programming Error

Attempting to access a Private class member from outside its class is a syntax error.

Keywords **Public** and **Private** are called **member-access modifiers**. You defined properties with member-access modifier Public earlier in this tutorial. Class members that are declared with access modifier Public are available to any Time object. Declaring instance variables, properties or methods with member-access modifier Private makes them available only to methods and properties of the class. Attempting to access a class's Private data from outside the class definition is a compilation error. Normally, instance variables are declared Private, whereas methods and properties are declared Public. In the following box, you will declare this application's instance variables as Private.

Controlling Access to Members

1. ***Declaring Time's instance variables as Private.*** View Time.vb by selecting the **Time.vb** tab above the code editor. Replace keyword Dim in lines 7 and 8 with keyword Private (as in Fig. 19.35), indicating that these instance variables are accessible only to members of class Time. A class's Private instance variables may be accessed only by methods and properties of the class.

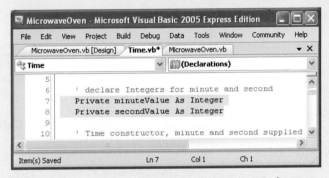

Figure 19.35 Time's instance variables are `Private`.

2. ***Declaring MicrowaveOvenForm's instance variables as Private.*** View MicrowaveOven.vb by selecting the **MicrowaveOven.vb** tab above the code editor. Replace keyword Dim in lines 4 and 7 with keyword Private (as in Fig. 19.36), indicating that these instance variables are accessible only to members of class MicrowaveOvenForm. When an object of the class contains such instance variables, only methods, properties and events of the object's class can access the variables.

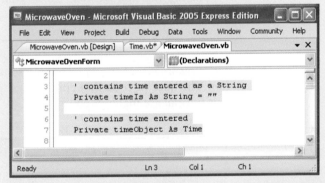

Figure 19.36 Microwave Oven's instance variables are `Private`.

3. ***Setting method DisplayTime as Private.*** Add keyword Private to the beginning of method DisplayTime (line 140 of Fig. 19.37). As with variables, methods are declared Private to make them accessible only to other members of the current class. In this example only the class that defines your **Microwave Oven** uses method DisplayTime, so you should make this method Private.

Note that the event handlers you have created throughout this book have the keyword Private automatically added to their headers. You now know that this occurs because event handlers are specific to the Form's class, and not the entire application, which includes class Time.

(cont.)

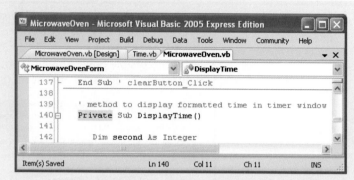

Figure 19.37 **Microwave Oven**'s methods are `Private`.

4. ***Running the application.*** Select **Debug > Start Debugging** to run your application. Note that the application performs exactly as it did at the end of the last box. This occurs because when instance variables are declared by using keyword `Dim`, they are by default `Private` variables. For example, recall that the instance variables of `Time` did not appear in the *IntelliSense* window of Fig. 19.29. These variables were `Private` by default, and therefore not accessible outside of class `Time`. Inaccessible variables do not appear in the *IntelliSense* window. It is a good practice always to precede instance variables with a member-access modifier (usually `Private`). Changing `DisplayTime` to be `Private` did not affect the application either, because your code does not attempt to access this method from outside the class in which it is defined.

5. ***Closing the application.*** Close your running application by clicking its close box.

Software Design Tip

Declare all instance variables of a class as `Private`. When necessary, provide `Public` properties to set and get the values of `Private` instance variables.

Figures 19.38 and 19.39 present the source code for the **Microwave Oven** application. The lines of code that contain new programming concepts that you learned in this tutorial are highlighted.

```
1   Public Class MicrowaveOvenForm
2
3      ' contains time entered as a String
4      Private timeIs As String = ""
5
6      ' contains time entered
7      Private timeObject As Time
8
9      ' event handler appends 1 to time string
10     Private Sub oneButton_Click(ByVal sender As System.Object, _
11        ByVal e As System.EventArgs) Handles oneButton.Click
12
13        Beep()                ' sound beep
14        timeIs &= "1"         ' append digit to time input
15        DisplayTime()         ' display time input properly
16     End Sub ' oneButton_Click
17
18     ' event handler appends 2 to time string
19     Private Sub twoButton_Click(ByVal sender As System.Object, _
20        ByVal e As System.EventArgs) Handles twoButton.Click
21
22        Beep()                ' sound beep
```

Figure 19.38 **Microwave Oven** application code. (Part 1 of 4.)

```
23          timeIs &= "2"          ' append digit to time input
24          DisplayTime()          ' display time input properly
25       End Sub ' twoButton_Click
26
27       ' event handler appends 3 to time string
28       Private Sub threeButton_Click(ByVal sender As System.Object, _
29          ByVal e As System.EventArgs) Handles threeButton.Click
30
31          Beep()                 ' sound beep
32          timeIs &= "3"          ' append digit to time input
33          DisplayTime()          ' display time input properly
34       End Sub ' threeButton_Click
35
36       ' event handler appends 4 to time string
37       Private Sub fourButton_Click(ByVal sender As System.Object, _
38          ByVal e As System.EventArgs) Handles fourButton.Click
39
40          Beep()                 ' sound beep
41          timeIs &= "4"          ' append digit to time input
42          DisplayTime()          ' display time input properly
43       End Sub ' fourButton_Click
44
45       ' event handler appends 5 to time string
46       Private Sub fiveButton_Click(ByVal sender As System.Object, _
47          ByVal e As System.EventArgs) Handles fiveButton.Click
48
49          Beep()                 ' sound beep
50          timeIs &= "5"          ' append digit to time input
51          DisplayTime()          ' display time input properly
52       End Sub ' fiveButton_Click
53
54       ' event handler appends 6 to time string
55       Private Sub sixButton_Click(ByVal sender As System.Object, _
56          ByVal e As System.EventArgs) Handles sixButton.Click
57
58          Beep()                 ' sound beep
59          timeIs &= "6"          ' append digit to time input
60          DisplayTime()          ' display time input properly
61       End Sub ' sixButton_Click
62
63       ' event handler appends 7 to time string
64       Private Sub sevenButton_Click(ByVal sender As System.Object, _
65          ByVal e As System.EventArgs) Handles sevenButton.Click
66
67          Beep()                 ' sound beep
68          timeIs &= "7"          ' append digit to time input
69          DisplayTime()          ' display time input properly
70       End Sub ' sevenButton_Click
71
72       ' event handler appends 8 to time string
73       Private Sub eightButton_Click(ByVal sender As System.Object, _
74          ByVal e As System.EventArgs) Handles eightButton.Click
75
76          Beep()                 ' sound beep
77          timeIs &= "8"          ' append digit to time input
78          DisplayTime()          ' display time input properly
79       End Sub ' eightButton_Click
80
81       ' event handler appends 9 to time string
82       Private Sub nineButton_Click(ByVal sender As System.Object, _
83          ByVal e As System.EventArgs) Handles nineButton.Click
84
85          Beep()                 ' sound beep
86          timeIs &= "9"          ' append digit to time input
```

Figure 19.38   Microwave Oven application code. (Part 2 of 4.)

```
87          DisplayTime()        ' display time input properly
88     End Sub ' nineButton_Click
89
90     ' event handler appends 0 to time string
91     Private Sub zeroButton_Click(ByVal sender As System.Object, _
92        ByVal e As System.EventArgs) Handles zeroButton.Click
93
94        Beep()               ' sound beep
95        timeIs &= "0"        ' append digit to time input
96        DisplayTime()        ' display time input properly
97     End Sub ' zeroButton_Click
98
99     ' event handler starts the microwave oven's cooking process
100    Private Sub startButton_Click(ByVal sender As System.Object, _
101       ByVal e As System.EventArgs) Handles startButton.Click
102
103       Dim second As Integer
104       Dim minute As Integer
105
106       ' ensure that timeIs has 4 characters
107       timeIs = timeIs.PadLeft(4, _
108          Convert.ToChar("0"))
109
110       ' extract seconds and minutes
111       second = Convert.ToInt32(timeIs.Substring(2))
112       minute = Convert.ToInt32(timeIs.Substring(0, 2))
113
114       ' create Time object to contain time entered by user
115       timeObject = New Time(minute, second)
116
117       displayLabel.Text = String.Format("{0:D2}:{1:D2}", _
118          timeObject.Minute, timeObject.Second)
119
120       timeIs = "" ' clear timeIs for future input
121
122       clockTimer.Enabled = True ' start timer
123
124       windowPanel.BackColor = Color.Yellow ' turn "light" on
125    End Sub ' startButton_Click
126
127    ' event handler to clear input
128    Private Sub clearButton_Click(ByVal sender As System.Object, _
129       ByVal e As System.EventArgs) Handles clearButton.Click
130
131       ' reset each property or variable to its initial setting
132       displayLabel.Text = "Microwave Oven"
133       timeIs = ""
134       timeObject = New Time(0, 0)
135       clockTimer.Enabled = False
136       windowPanel.BackColor = Control.DefaultBackColor
137    End Sub ' clearButton_Click
138
139    ' method to display formatted time in timer window
140    Private Sub DisplayTime()
141
142       Dim second As Integer
143       Dim minute As Integer
144
145       Dim display As String ' String displays current input
146
147       ' if too much input entered
148       If timeIs.Length > 4 Then
149          timeIs = timeIs.Substring(0, 4)
150       End If
```

Annotations (left margin):

- Creating a new object of a programmer-defined type → (line 115)
- Accessing variables of a programmer-defined type → (lines 117–118)
- Start timer to begin countdown → (line 122)
- Use property **BackColor** to change the **Panel**'s color → (line 124)
- Method **Substring** returns a subset of characters in a **String** → (lines 148–149)

Figure 19.38 Microwave Oven application code. (Part 3 of 4.)

```
151
152    display = timeIs.PadLeft(4, Convert.ToChar("0"))
153
154        ' extract seconds and minutes
155        second = Convert.ToInt32(display.Substring(2))
156        minute = Convert.ToInt32(display.Substring(0, 2))
157
158        ' display number of minutes, ":" and number of seconds
159        displayLabel.Text = String.Format("{0:D2}:{1:D2}", _
160            minute, second)
161     End Sub ' DisplayTime
162
163     ' event handler displays new time each second
164     Private Sub clockTimer_Tick(ByVal sender As System.Object, _
165        ByVal e As System.EventArgs) Handles clockTimer.Tick
166
167        ' perform countdown, subtract one second
168        If timeObject.Second > 0 Then
169            timeObject.Second -= 1
170        ElseIf timeObject.Minute > 0 Then
171            timeObject.Minute -= 1 ' subtract one minute
172            timeObject.Second = 59 ' reset seconds for new minute
173        Else ' no more seconds
174            clockTimer.Enabled = False ' stop timer
175            Beep()
176            displayLabel.Text = "Done!" ' inform user time is finished
177            windowPanel.BackColor = Control.DefaultBackColor
178            Return
179        End If
180
181        displayLabel.Text = String.Format("{0:D2}:{1:D2}", _
182            timeObject.Minute, timeObject.Second)
183     End Sub ' clockTimer_Tick
184 End Class ' MicrowaveOvenForm
```

Method **PadLeft** called — (points to line 152)

Figure 19.38   Microwave Oven application code. (Part 4 of 4.)

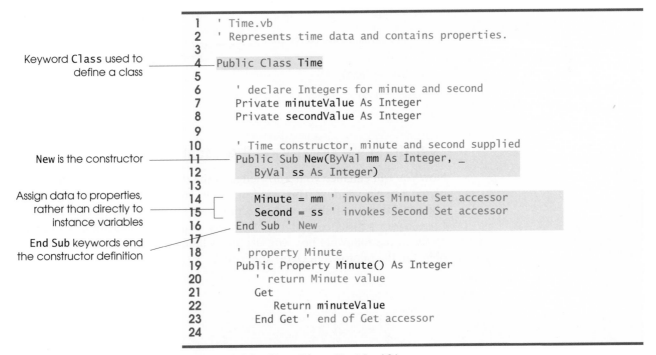

```
1   ' Time.vb
2   ' Represents time data and contains properties.
3
4   Public Class Time
5
6       ' declare Integers for minute and second
7       Private minuteValue As Integer
8       Private secondValue As Integer
9
10      ' Time constructor, minute and second supplied
11      Public Sub New(ByVal mm As Integer, _
12         ByVal ss As Integer)
13
14          Minute = mm ' invokes Minute Set accessor
15          Second = ss ' invokes Second Set accessor
16      End Sub ' New
17
18      ' property Minute
19      Public Property Minute() As Integer
20          ' return Minute value
21          Get
22              Return minuteValue
23          End Get ' end of Get accessor
24
```

Keyword **Class** used to define a class — (points to line 4)

New is the constructor — (points to line 11)

Assign data to properties, rather than directly to instance variables — (points to lines 14–15)

End Sub keywords end the constructor definition — (points to line 16)

Figure 19.39   Class Time. (Part 1 of 2.)

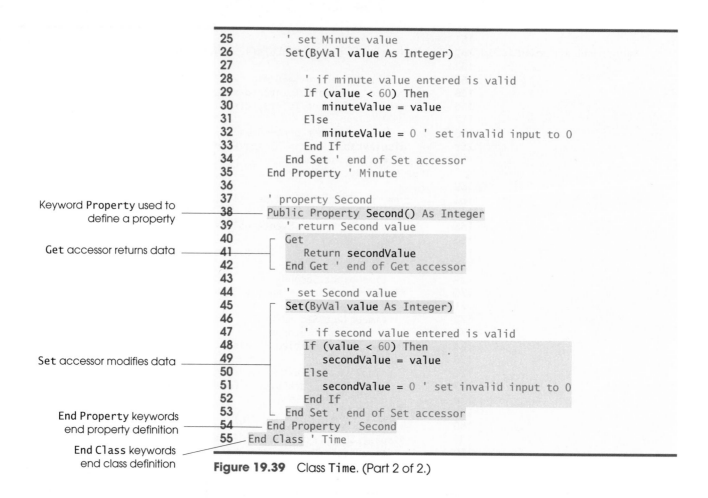

```
25       ' set Minute value
26       Set(ByVal value As Integer)
27
28          ' if minute value entered is valid
29          If (value < 60) Then
30             minuteValue = value
31          Else
32             minuteValue = 0 ' set invalid input to 0
33          End If
34       End Set ' end of Set accessor
35    End Property ' Minute
36
37    ' property Second
38    Public Property Second() As Integer
39       ' return Second value
40       Get
41          Return secondValue
42       End Get ' end of Get accessor
43
44       ' set Second value
45       Set(ByVal value As Integer)
46
47          ' if second value entered is valid
48          If (value < 60) Then
49             secondValue = value
50          Else
51             secondValue = 0 ' set invalid input to 0
52          End If
53       End Set ' end of Set accessor
54    End Property ' Second
55 End Class ' Time
```

Keyword **Property** used to define a property

Get accessor returns data

Set accessor modifies data

End Property keywords end property definition

End Class keywords end class definition

Figure 19.39 Class **Time**. (Part 2 of 2.)

SELF-REVIEW

1. Instance variable declarations must be preceded by which of the following keywords?

   a) `Dim`

   b) `Private`

   c) `Public`

   d) Any of the above.

2. Instance variables are considered _____ by default.

   a) `Private`

   b) `Public`

   c) `Dimensional`

   d) None of the above.

Answers: 1) d. 2) a.

19.8 Using the Debugger: The Locals Window

Now you will enhance your knowledge of the debugger by studying the capabilities of the **Locals** window. This window allow you to view the values stored in an object's instance variables. In this section, you will learn how to view the contents of `timeObject`'s instance variables to verify that your application is executing correctly. In the following box, you use this window to examine the state of the `Time` object in the **Microwave Oven** application.

*Using the Debugger:
Using the Locals Window*

1. **Viewing the application code.** View MicrowaveOven.vb by selecting the **MicrowaveOven.vb** tab above the code editor.

2. **Setting breakpoints.** Set breakpoints in lines 168 and 177 by clicking in the margin indicator bar (Fig. 19.40). You can set breakpoints in your application to examine an object's instance variables at certain places during execution. In the **Microwave Oven** application, the clockTimer's Tick event handler modifies the properties of timeObject. Setting breakpoints in lines 168 and 177 allows you to suspend execution before and after certain properties have been modified, ensuring that data is being modified properly.

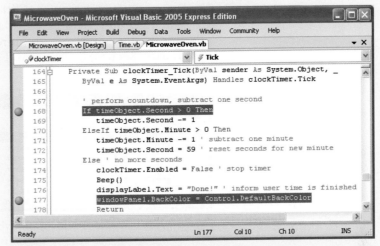

Figure 19.40 **Microwave Oven** application with breakpoints added.

3. **Starting the debugger.** Start the debugger by selecting **Debug > Start Debugging**.

4. **Opening the Locals window.** Open the **Locals** window (Fig. 19.41) by selecting **Debug > Windows > Locals** while the debugger is running. The **Locals** window allows you to view the state of the variables in the current scope. Recall that the scope of a variable's identifier is the portion of an application in which the identifier can be referenced. The Timer's Tick event is a method of the Form class, so all the instance variables and controls of the Form are viewable in the **Locals** window. This means that you will be able to view the values of the properties of timeObject, because timeObject is an instance variable of the Form class.

Figure 19.41 Empty **Locals** window.

5. **Setting the time.** Set the microwave oven's time to 1:01, and click the **Start** Button.

6. **Using the Locals window.** While execution is still halted, look at the **Locals** window. If the **Locals** window is now hidden, reselect **Debug > Windows > Locals**. The **Locals** window lists all the variables that are in the scope of the Timer's Tick event handler. To view the contents of timeObject, click the plus box next to the word **Me**. Scroll down until you reach timeObject, and click the plus box next to it. This will show all the members of timeObject, their current values and their types (Fig. 19.42).

(cont.)

Instance variables
of `timeObject`

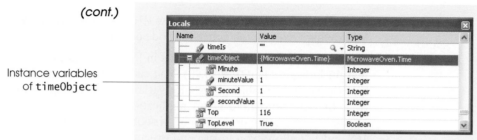

Figure 19.42 **Locals** window displaying the state of `timeObject`.

7. *Continuing program execution.* Click the debug toolbar's **Continue** Button, and view the values of the `timeObject`'s members. Note that the value for the amount of seconds (as represented by variable `secondValue` and property `Second`) has changed (Fig. 19.43). Click the **Continue** Button again.

Changed values

Figure 19.43 **Locals** window displaying changed variables.

8. *Changing the value of a variable.* In the **Locals** window, double click the value for property `Second`. Type 0 and press *Enter* to set the microwave oven's time to zero (Fig. 19.44). Note that the changed value appears in red after you have pressed *Enter*. The **Locals** window allow you to change the values of variables to verify that program execution is correct at certain points without having to run the program again for each value.

Value changed by user

Figure 19.44 Changing the value of a variable in the **Locals** window.

9. *Continuing execution.* Click the **Continue** Button. Execution continues until the breakpoint in line 177 is reached.

10. *Stopping the debugger.* Click the **Stop Debugging** Button to end the debugging session.

11. *Closing the application.* Close your running application by clicking its close box.

12. *Closing the IDE.* Close the Visual Basic IDE by clicking its close box.

In this section, you learned how to use the **Locals** window to view the state of an object and verify that your application is executing correctly.

1. The **Locals** window allows you to _____.

    a) change the value stored in an instance variable of an object

    b) view all of the variables in the current scope

    c) view the values stored in all of the variables in the current scope

    d) All of the above.

2. When a variable's value is changed by the user, it becomes _____ in the **Locals** window.

    a) red   b) italic

    c) blue   d) bold

Answers: 1) d. 2) a.

19.9 Wrap-Up

In previous tutorials, you used FCL classes and methods to add functionality to your applications. In this tutorial, you learned how to create your own classes, also known as programmer-defined classes, to provide functionality not available in the FCL. Visual Basic applications typically are created by using a combination of FCL classes and methods and programmer-defined classes and methods.

    You created a microwave-oven simulator using a programmer-defined class called `Time`. You added a file to your application to create the `Time` class; then you added a constructor, instance variables and properties to that class. You defined your constructor to initialize the class's instance variables. For each property, you defined `Get` and `Set` accessors that allow the class's instance variables to be safely accessed and modified. You then applied what you have already learned about using classes and properties to create a `Time` object. You used the properties of class `Time` to access and display the number of minutes and number of seconds that the user has specified as the microwave oven's cook time. You also learned how to control access to the members of class `Time` through the use of `Public` and `Private` designations. You also learned how `Panel`s can organize controls (much like `GroupBox`es), and used a `Panel` to simulate the microwave oven's door. You even learned some new ways to manipulate strings using the `Substring` and `PadLeft` methods. You concluded the tutorial by learning how to view an application's values using the debugger's **Locals** window.

    In the next tutorial, you will learn about collections. The FCL provides several collection classes that enable you to store collections of data in an organized way. A collection can be thought of as a group of items. You will use collections to create a **Shipping Hub** application that stores information about several packages that are being shipped to various states. Each package will be defined by using a `Package` programmer-defined class. Several `Package` objects will be maintained by using collections.

SKILLS SUMMARY

Defining a `Public` Property

- Use keyword `Public` and `Property` followed by the name of the property and a set of parentheses.
- After the parentheses, specify the property's type with the `As` keyword.
- Press *Enter*. Empty `Get` and `Set` accessors will be added for you by the IDE, followed by the keywords `End Property`. The `Get` accessor begins with keyword `Get` and ends with keywords `End Get`. The `Set` accessor begins with keyword `Set` and ends with keywords `End Set`.
- In the `Get` accessor, provide code to return the requested data.
- In the `Set` accessor, provide code to modify the relevant data. Be sure to do validity checking.

Adding a Class File to Your Project

■ Select **Project > Add Class.**

■ Enter a name for the class.

Creating a Constructor

■ Use keywords `Public Sub New`, followed by a set of parentheses enclosing any parameter variables for the constructor.

■ Press *Enter.* The keywords End Sub will be provided by the IDE.

■ Add code to initialize the object's data.

Adding a Panel to Your Application

■ Double click the `Panel` control in the **Toolbox,** or drag the `Panel` control from the **Toolbox** to the Form. We recommend appending `Panel` to `Panel` control names.

KEY TERMS

accessor—Method-like code units that handle the details of modifying and returning data.

Beep function—Causes your computer to make a beep sound.

Class Keyword—Reserved word required to begin a class defintion.

client—When an application creates and uses an object of a class, the application is known as a client of the class.

Color structure—Contains several predefined colors as properties.

consistent state—A way to maintain the values of an object's instance variables such that the values are always valid.

constructor—A special class method that initializes a class's variables.

DefaultBackColor property—Contains the default background color for a `Panel` control.

End Class Keywords—Reserved words required to end a class defintion.

extensible language—A language that can be "extended" with new data types. Visual Basic is an extensible language.

FixedSingle value of the BorderStyle property of a Label—Specifies that the `Label` will display a thin, black border.

Flat value of the FlatStyle property of a Button—Specifies that a `Button` will appear flat.

FlatStyle property of a Button—Determines whether the `Button` will appear flat or three-dimensional.

Get accessor—Used to retrieve a value of a property.

instantiate an object—Create an object of a class.

Length property of class String—Returns the number of characters in a `String`.

Locals window—Allows you to view the state of the variables in the current scope during debugging.

members of a class—Methods, variables, and properties declared within the body of a class.

member-access modifier—Keywords used to specify what members of a class a client may access. Includes keywords `Public` and `Private`.

PadLeft method of class String—Adds characters to the beginning of a string until the length of the string equals the specified length.

Panel control—Used to group controls. Unlike GroupBoxes, `Panel`s do not have captions.

Private keyword—Member-access modifier that makes members accessible only to that class.

programmer-defined class (programmer-defined type)—A class defined by a programmer, as opposed to classes predefined in the Framework Class Library.

property—Contains accessors: portions of code that handle the details of modifying and returning data.

Property keyword—Reserved word indicating the definition of a class property.

Public keyword—Member-access modifier that makes instance variables or methods accessible wherever the application has a reference to that object.

Set accessor—Provides data-validation capabilities to ensure that the value is set properly.

Substring method of class `String`—Returns characters from a string, corresponding to the arguments passed by the user, that indicate the start and the end positions within a `String`.

ToChar method of class `Convert`—Converts a single character `String` to type `Char`.

GUI DESIGN GUIDELINES	**Panel**

- Use `Panel`s to organize groups of related controls where the purpose of the controls is obvious. If the purpose of the controls is not obvious, use a `GroupBox` in place of a `Panel`, because `GroupBox`es can contain captions.

- A `Panel` can display scrollbars for use when the `Panel` is not large enough to display all of its controls at once. For usability, we suggest avoiding scrollbars on a `Panel`. If the `Panel` is not large enough to display all of its contents, increase the size of the `Panel`.

- Although it is possible to have a `Panel` without a border (by setting the `BorderStyle` property to `None`), use borders on your `Panel`s to improve readability and organization.

CONTROLS, EVENTS, PROPERTIES & METHODS	

Button      This control allows the user to raise an action or event.

- *In action*

- *Event*

  `Click`—Raised when the user clicks the `Button`.

- *Properties*

  `Enabled`—Determines whether the `Button`'s event handler is executed when the `Button` is clicked.

  `FlatStyle`—Determines whether the `Button` will appear flat or three-dimensional.

  `Location`—Specifies the location of the `Button` on the `Form` relative to the top-left corner.

  `Name`—Specifies the name used to access the `Button` programmatically. The name should be appended with the `Button` suffix.

  `Size`—Specifies the height and width (in pixels) of the `Button`.

  `Text`—Specifies the text displayed on the `Button`.

- *Method*

  `Focus`—Transfers the focus of the application to the `Button` that calls it.

Convert   The `Convert` class converts the value of a data type to another data type.

- *Methods*

  `ToChar`—Converts a value into a character (of data type `Char`).

  `ToDecimal`—Converts the value from another data type to type `Decimal`.

  `ToDouble`—Converts the value from another data type to type `Double`.

Label   This control displays text on the `Form` that the user cannot modify.

- *In action*

- *Properties*

  `BorderStyle`—Specifies the appearance of the `Label`'s border.

  `Font`—Specifies the font name, style and size of the text displayed in the `Label`.

  `Location`—Specifies the location of the `Label` on the `Form` relative to the top-left corner.

  `Name`—Specifies the name used to access the `Label` programmatically. The name should be appended with the `Label` suffix.

Size—Specifies the height and width (in pixels) of the Label.

Text—Specifies the text displayed on the Label.

TextAlign—Specifies how the text is aligned within the Label.

Panel ☐ Panel   This control is used to organize various controls. Unlike a GroupBox control, the Panel control does not display a caption.

■ *In action*

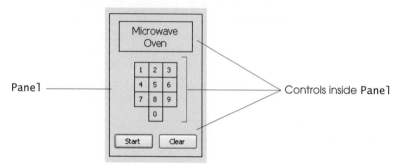

Panel ——————— Controls inside Panel

■ *Properties*

DefaultBackColor—Returns the default background color of a Panel control.

Name—Specifies the name of the Panel.

Size—Specifies the size of the Panel.

Location—Specifies the Panel's location on the Form relative to the top-left corner.

BorderStyle—Specifies the Panel's border style. Options include None (displaying no border), FixedSingle (a single-line border) and Fixed3D (a three-dimensional border).

   None—Specifies that the Panel's will not display a border.

   FixedSingle—Specifies that the Panel will display a thin, black border.

   Fixed3D—Specifies that the Panel will display a three-dimensional border.

BackColor—Specifies the background color of the Panel.

String The String class represents a series of characters treated as a single unit.

■ *Property*

Length—Returns the number of characters in the String.

■ *Methods*

Format—Arranges the string in a specified format.

IndexOf—Returns the index of the specified character(s) in a String.

Insert—Returns a copy of the String for which it is called with the specified character(s) inserted.

PadLeft—Inserts characters at the beginning of a String.

Remove—Returns a copy of the String for which it is called with the specified character(s) removed.

Substring—Returns a substring from a String.

ToLower—Returns a copy of the String for which it is called with any uppercase letters converted to lowercase letters.

MULTIPLE-CHOICE QUESTIONS

19.1 A Button appears flat if its _____ property is set to Flat.

a) BorderStyle   b) FlatStyle

c) Style   d) BackStyle

19.2 Keyword _____ introduces a class definition.

a) NewClass   b) ClassDef

c) VBClass   d) Class

19.3 Keyword _____ is used to create an object.

   a) `CreateObject`

   b) `Instantiate`

   c) `Create`

   d) `New`

19.4 String characters are of data type _____.

   a) `Char`

   b) `StringCharacter`

   c) `Character`

   d) `strCharacter`

19.5 The _____ is used to retrieve the value of an instance variable.

   a) `Get` accessor of a property

   b) `Retrieve` method of a class

   c) `Client` method of a class

   d) `Set` accessor of a property

19.6 When you enter the header for a constructor in the Visual Basic IDE and then press *Enter*, the keywords _____ are created for you.

   a) `End Public Class`

   b) `End Procedure`

   c) `End Sub`

   d) `End`

19.7 An important difference between constructors and other methods is that _____.

   a) constructors cannot specify a return data type

   b) constructors cannot specify any parameters

   c) other methods are implemented as Sub procedures

   d) constructors can assign values to instance variables

19.8 A class can yield many _____, just as a primitive data type can yield many variables.

   a) names

   b) objects

   c) values

   d) types

19.9 The Set accessor enables you to _____.

   a) provide range checking

   b) modify data

   c) provide data validation

   d) All of the above.

19.10 Instance variables declared `Private` are not accessible _____.

   a) outside the class

   b) by other methods of the same class

   c) by other members of the same class

   d) inside the same class

EXERCISES

19.11 (*Triangle Creator Application*) Create an application that allows the user to enter the lengths for the three sides of a triangle as `Integers`. The application should then determine whether the triangle is a right triangle (two sides of the triangle form a 90-degree angle), an equilateral triangle (all sides of equal length) or neither. The application's GUI is completed for you (Fig. 19.45). You must create a class to represent a triangle object and define the event handler for the **Create** Button.

   a) *Copying the template to your working directory.* Copy the directory `C:\Examples\Tutorial19\Exercises\Triangle` to your `C:\SimplyVB` directory.

   b) *Opening the application's template file.* Double click `Triangle.sln` in the `Triangle` directory to open the application.

   c) *Creating the Triangle class.* Add a class to the project, and name it `Triangle`. This is where you will define the properties of the `Triangle` class.

   d) *Defining the necessary constructor and properties.* Define a constructor that will take the lengths of the three sides of the triangle as arguments. Create three properties that enable clients to access and modify the lengths of the three sides. If the user enters a negative value, that side should be assigned the value zero.

   e) *Adding additional features.* Create two more properties in the `Triangle` class: One determines whether the sides form a right triangle, the other an equilateral triangle. These properties are considered **read-only**, because you would naturally define only the `Get` accessor. There is no simple `Set` accessor that can make a triangle a right triangle or an equilateral triangle without first modifying the lengths of the triangle's sides. To create a read-only property (where the `Set` accessor is omitted), precede keyword **Property** with the keyword **ReadOnly**.

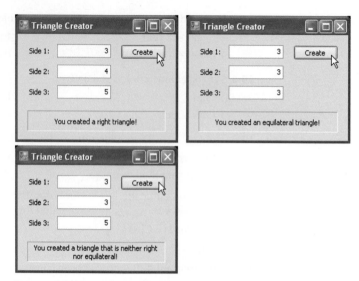

Figure 19.45 **Triangle Creator** application with all possible outputs.

f) ***Adding code to event handler.*** Now that you have created your `Triangle` class, you can use it to create objects in your application. Double click the **Create** Button in **Design View** to generate the event handler. Create new variables to store the three lengths from the `TextBoxes`; then use those values to create a new `Triangle` object.

g) ***Displaying the result.*** Use an `If...ElseIf` statement to determine whether the triangle is a right triangle, an equilateral triangle or neither. Display the result in a `Label`.

h) ***Running the application.*** Select **Debug > Start Debugging** to run your application. Add various inputs until you have created an equilateral triangle, a right triangle and a triangle that is neither right nor equilateral. Verify that the proper output is displayed for each.

i) ***Closing the application.*** Close your running application by clicking its close box.

j) ***Closing the IDE.*** Close the Visual Basic IDE by clicking its close box.

19.12 (*Modified Microwave Oven Application*) Modify the tutorial's **Microwave Oven** application to include an additional digit to would represent the hour. Allow the user to enter up to 9 hours, 59 minutes, and 59 seconds (Fig. 19.46).

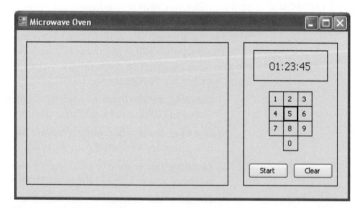

Figure 19.46 Modified **Microwave Oven** application's GUI.

a) ***Copying the template to your working directory.*** Copy the directory `C:\Examples\Tutorial19\Exercises\MicrowaveOven2` to your `C:\SimplyVB` directory.

b) ***Opening the application's template file.*** Double click `MicrowaveOven2.sln` in the `MicrowaveOven2` directory to open the application.

c) ***Adding the hour variable.*** To allow cooking time that includes the hour digit, you will need to modify the `Time` class. Define a new `Private` instance variable to represent the hour. Change the `Time` constructor to take in the hour amount as its first argument (now `Time` should have three arguments). You will also have to modify the **Start** Button event handler, **Clear** Button event handler and the DisplayTime method to include an hour variable.

d) ***Adding the Hour property.*** Use the Minute and Second properties as your template to create the property for the hour. Remember, we are allowing an additional digit to represent the hour (hour < 10).

e) ***Changing the padding amount.*** Change the calls to the PadLeft method to be consistent with the new time format.

f) ***Extracting the hour.*** Add a call to the Substring method so that hour gets the first digit in the timeIs String. Also, change the calls to the Substring method for minute and second so that they extract the proper digits from the timeIs String.

g) ***Accessing the first five digits.*** Change the If...Then statement from the DisplayTime method to take and display the first five digits entered by the user.

h) ***Edit the Timer object.*** Edit the clockTimer_Tick event handler to provide changes to hours and its corresponding minutes and seconds.

i) ***Displaying the time.*** Edit the Format String so that the display Label includes the hour.

j) ***Running the application.*** Select **Debug > Start Debugging** to run your application. Enter various times and verify that the application counts down properly. Enter an amount of time that is 10 hours or longer, and verify that the application handles invalid input correctly.

k) ***Closing the application.*** Close your running application by clicking its close box.

l) ***Closing the IDE.*** Close the Visual Basic IDE by clicking its close box.

19.13 (***Account Information Application***) The local bank wants you to create an application that will allow it to view clients' information. The interface is created for you; you need to implement the Client class (Fig. 19.47). Once the application is completed, the bank manager should be able to click the **Next** or **Previous** Button to run through each client's information. The information is stored in four arrays containing first names, last names, account numbers and account balances.

Figure 19.47   **Account Information** application GUI.

a) ***Copying the template to your working directory.*** Copy the directory C:\Examples\ Tutorial19\Exercises\AccountInformation to your C:\SimplyVB directory.

b) ***Opening the application's template file.*** Double click AccountInformation.sln in the AccountInformation directory to open the application.

c) ***Determining variables for the class.*** Examine the code from AccountInformation.vb, including all the properties that the Client object uses to retrieve the information.

d) ***Creating the Client class.*** Create a new class, and call it Client. Add this class to the project. Define four Private instance variables to represent each property value, to ensure that each Client object contains all the required information about each client. Use these variables to define a constructor.

e) ***Defining each property.*** Each Private variable should have a corresponding property allowing the user to set or get the Private variable's value.

f) ***Adding more information***. In the AccountInformationForm_Load event handler, add one more account. Include name, account number, and balance for each corresponding array.

g) ***Running the application.*** Select **Debug > Start Debugging** to run your application. Click the **Previous** and **Next** Buttons to ensure that each account's information is displayed properly.

h) ***Closing the application.*** Close your running application by clicking its close box.

i) ***Closing the IDE.*** Close the Visual Basic IDE by clicking its close box.

What does this code do? ▶ **19.14** What does the following code do? The first code listing contains the definition of class Shape. Each Shape object represents a closed shape with a number of sides. The second code listing contains a method (Mystery) created by a client of class Shape. What does this method do?

```
1   Public Class Shape
2
3       Private sides As Integer
4
5       ' constructor with number of sides
6       Public Sub New(ByVal value As Integer)
7          Side = value
8       End Sub ' New
9
10      ' set and get side value
11      Public Property Side() As Integer
12
13         ' return sides
14         Get
15            Return sides
16         End Get ' end of Get accessor
17
18         ' set sides
19         Set(ByVal value As Integer)
20
21            If value > 0 Then
22               sides = value
23            Else
24               sides = 0
25            End If
26
27         End Set ' end of Set accessor
28
29      End Property ' Side
30
31   End Class ' Shape
```

```
1   Public Function Mystery(ByVal shapeObject As Shape) As String
2      Dim shape As String
3
4      ' determine case with shapeObject.Side
5      Select Case shapeObject.Side
6
7         Case Is < 3
8            shape = "Not a Shape"
9
10        Case 3
11           shape = "Triangle"
12
13        Case 4
14           shape = "Square"
15
```

(cont.)

```
16          Case Else
17             shape = "Polygon"
18
19       End Select
20
21       Return shape
22  End Function ' Mystery
```

What's wrong with this code? ▶ **19.15** Find the error(s) in the following code. The following method should create a new Shape object with numberSides sides. Assume the Shape class from Exercise 19.14.

```
1  Private Sub ManipulateShape(ByVal numberSides As Integer)
2     Dim shapeObject As Shape = New Shape(3)
3
4     shape.sides = numberSides
5  End Sub ' ManipulateShape
```

Using the Debugger ▶ **19.16** (*View Name Application*) The **View Name** application allows the user to enter the user's first and last names. When the user clicks the **View Name** Button, a MessageBox that displays the user's first and last names appears. The application creates an instance of Class Name. This class uses its property definitions to set the first-name and last-name instance variables. Copy the Names folder from C:\Examples\Tutorial19\Exercises\Debugger to your C:\SimplyVB folder. Open and run the application. While testing your application, you noticed that the MessageBox did not display the correct output. Use the debugger to find the logic error(s) in the application. The application with the correct output is displayed in Fig. 19.48.

Figure 19.48   **View Name** application with correct output.

Programming Challenge ▶ **19.17** (*DVD Burner Application*) Create an application that simulates a DVD burner. Users create a DVD with their choice of title and bonus materials. The GUI is provided for you (Fig. 19.49). You will create a class (DVD) to represent the DVD object and another class (Bonus) to represent bonus materials for a DVD object.

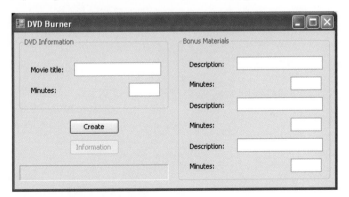

Figure 19.49   **DVD Burner** application's GUI.

a) *Copying the template to your working directory.* Copy the directory `C:\Examples\Tutorial19\Exercises\DVDBurner` to your `C:\SimplyVB` directory.

b) *Opening the application's template file.* Double click `DVDBurner.sln` in the DVD-Burner directory to open the application.

c) *Creating the bonus material object.* Create a class, and name it `Bonus`. The class's objects will each represent one bonus-material item on the DVD. Each `Bonus` object should have a name (description) and a length (in minutes). Use this tutorial's `Time` class as your guide in creating the properties for the name and length of each bonus material.

d) *Creating the DVD class.* Create a class, and name it `DVDObject`. This class contains the movie title and the length of the movie. The class should also include an array of three `Bonus` items.

e) *Creating the necessary variables.* Before you define the **Create** `Button`'s event handler, create a `DVDObject` class instance variable. Inside the **Create** `Button`'s event handler, create the necessary variables to store the information from the `TextBox`es on the GUI. This is also where you need to create the array of `Bonus` objects to store the bonus materials.

f) *Adding bonus-material information.* Add the description and length of each bonus item to the `Bonus` array you created from the preceding step.

g) *Creating a DVD object.* Use information about the movie, its title, length and the array of bonus materials to make your DVD object.

h) *Displaying the output.* The **Information** `Button`'s `Click` event is already defined for you. Locate the event handler, add a `String` containing the complete information on the DVD object that you created earlier and display this `String` to a `MessageBox`.

i) *Running the application.* Select **Debug > Start Debugging** to run your application. Enter information for several DVDs. After information is entered for each, click the **Create** `Button`. Then click the **Information** `Button` and verify that the information being displayed is correct for your newly created DVD.

j) *Closing the application.* Close your running application by clicking its close box.

k) *Closing the IDE.* Close the Visual Basic IDE by clicking its close box.

Objectives

In this tutorial, you will learn to:
- Create and manipulate an `ArrayList` object.
- Set the `MaxLength` property of a **TextBox.**
- Set the `TabStop` and `TabIndex` properties of a control.
- Create an access key for a control.
- Use a `For Each...Next` loop to iterate through an `ArrayList`.
- Obtain a `String` representation of an object.

Outline

Shipping Hub Application

Introducing Collections, the For Each...Next Statement and Access Keys

Though most business can be conducted over phone lines and using e-mail messages, often it is necessary to send documents by a shipping company. As the pace of business increases, it is essential that shipping companies develop an efficient means to transfer packages from one location to another. To accomplish this task, many shipping companies send packages to a central location (a hub) before the packages reach their final destination. In this tutorial, you'll develop a **Shipping Hub** application to simulate package processing at a shipping warehouse. You'll use collections, which provide a quick and easy way to organize and manipulate the data used by your application. This tutorial focuses on the `ArrayList` collection, which provides data-storage capabilities similar to an array, but with much greater flexibility. You'll also learn to use the `For Each...Next` repetition statement to iterate through the objects in a collection.

20.1 Test-Driving the Shipping Hub Application

In this section, you will test-drive the **Shipping Hub** application. This application must meet the following requirements:

Application Requirements

*A shipping company receives packages at its headquarters, which functions as its shipping hub. After receiving the packages, the company ships them to a distribution center in one of the following states: Alabama, Florida, Georgia, Kentucky, Mississippi, North Carolina, South Carolina, Tennessee, West Virginia or Virginia. The company needs an application to track the packages that pass through its shipping hub. The application generates a package ID number for each package that arrives at the shipping hub when the user clicks the application's **Scan New** Button. Once a package has been scanned, the user should be able to enter the shipping address for the package. The user should be able to navigate through the list of scanned packages by using **< BACK** or **NEXT >** Buttons and by viewing a list of all packages destined for a particular state.*

This application stores a list of packages in an ArrayList. You will use the For Each...Next repetition statement to access the objects stored in the ArrayList. You begin by test-driving the completed application. Then you will learn the additional Visual Basic technologies that you will need to create your own version of this application.

Test-Driving the Shipping Hub Application

1. ***Opening the completed application***. Open the directory C:\Examples\Tutorial20\CompletedApplication\ShippingHub to locate the **Shipping Hub** application. Double click ShippingHub.sln to open the application in the Visual Basic IDE.

2. ***Running the Shipping Hub application***. Select **Debug > Start Debugging** to run the application (Fig. 20.1).

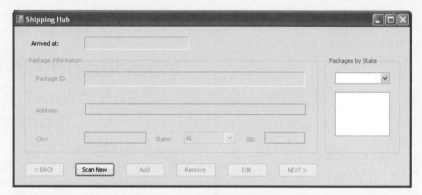

Figure 20.1 **Shipping Hub** application when first run.

3. ***Scanning a new package***. Click the **Scan New** Button. The application displays a package ID number, enables the TextBoxes and allows the user to enter the package information (Fig. 20.2). The package ID number for your first package will most likely be different than the one above because it is randomly generated each time the application executes.

Figure 20.2 Scanning a new package.

4. ***Using the Tab key***. Type 318 Some Street in the **Address:** TextBox, then press the *Tab* key. Note that the cursor moves to the **City:** TextBox (Fig. 20.3).

5. ***Adding a package to the list of packages***. Type Point Pleasant in the **City:** field, then press the *Tab* key. Select **WV** from the **State:** ComboBox, then press the *Tab* key. Type 25550 in the **Zip:** field, and click the **Add** Button to add the package to the application's ArrayList.

(cont.)

Figure 20.3   Pressing the *Tab* key moves the cursor to the next **TextBox**.

Note that you cannot enter more than five numbers in the **Zip:** field because the **Zip:** TextBox's MaxLength property is set to 5. The value in the **MaxLength** property determines the maximum number of characters that the user can enter into a TextBox. The values in the **State:** ComboBox were added using its **Items** property in the Windows Form Designer. When you open the template application, examine the values stored in the Items property to see how this is accomplished.

6. ***Removing, editing and browsing packages.*** The application's **NEXT >** and **< BACK** Buttons allow the user to navigate the list of packages. The **Remove** Button allows the user to delete packages, and the **Edit** Button allows the user to update a particular package's information. Experiment with the various Buttons by adding, removing and editing packages. We suggest using the following sample data:

   - 9 Some Road, Goose Creek, SC, 29445
   - 234 Some Place, Tamassee, SC, 29686
   - 46 Some Avenue, Mammoth Cave, KY, 42259
   - 3 Some Street, Yazoo City, MS, 39194

7. ***Viewing all packages going to a state.*** The ComboBox on the right side of the application allows the user to select a state. When a state is selected, all of the package ID numbers of packages destined for that state are displayed in the ListBox (Fig. 20.4). If the ListBox contains more package numbers than it can display, a vertical scrollbar will be added to the ListBox.

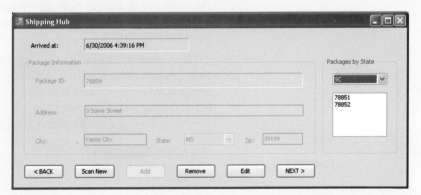

Figure 20.4   Viewing all packages going to South Carolina.

8. ***Closing the application.*** Close your running application by clicking its close box.

9. ***Closing the IDE.*** Close the Visual Basic IDE by clicking its close box.

20.2 Package Class

Your application must store data retrieved from the packages' shipping information. Each package ships to one location with an address, city, state and zip code. However, since multiple packages can be shipped to the same location, each package will need a unique identification number to distinguish it from other packages. As you learned in Tutorial 20, a convenient way to group related information is by creating instances of a class. The `Package` class included with the template application (but not yet added to the project) provides the necessary properties to keep track of package information. It also provides properties that ensure that only methods of class `Package` can access the instance variables of the class. The table in Fig. 20.5 describes the properties for class `Package`.

Property	Description
Address	Provides access to instance variable `addressValue`. Represents the package's address as a `String`.
City	Provides access to instance variable `cityValue`, which represents the package's city as a `String`.
State	Provides access to instance variable `stateValue`, which stores the package's state as a `String`. It uses the standard two-letter state abbreviations. For example, NC is used for North Carolina.
Zip	Provides access to instance variable `zipValue`. Represents the zip code as a five-digit `Integer`.
PackageNumber	Provides access to instance variable `packageNumberValue`, which stores the package's identification number as an `Integer`.
ArrivalTime	Provides access to instance variable `timeValue`, which stores the package's arrival time as a `Date`.

Figure 20.5   Properties listing for class `Package`.

The `Package` class must be added to the **Shipping Hub** application before objects of this class can be created. You will learn how to add the `Package` class to the **Shipping Hub** application in the following box.

Adding a Class to an Application

1. ***Copying the template to your working directory.*** Copy the `C:\Examples\Tutorial20\TemplateApplication\ShippingHub` directory to your `C:\SimplyVB` directory.

2. ***Opening the Shipping Hub application's template file.*** Double click `ShippingHub.sln` in the `ShippingHub` directory to open the application in the Visual Basic IDE.

3. ***Adding class Package.*** In the **Solution Explorer**, right click the **ShippingHub** project. Select **Add > Existing Item...** from the context menu that appears. When the **Add Existing Item** dialog appears, select the `Package.vb` file and click **Add**. The `Package` class is now included in the application and shown in the **Solution Explorer** (Fig. 20.6).

Package class added to the ShippingHub project ——

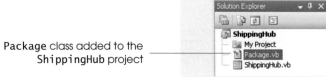

Figure 20.6   **Solution Explorer** with `Package.vb` added.

20.3 Using Properties TabIndex and TabStop

Many applications require users to enter information into multiple TextBoxes. It is awkward for users to have to select each TextBox using the mouse. It is often easier to allow the user to use the *Tab* key to navigate the controls on the Form. To ensure ease of use, the focus must be transferred to the proper control when the *Tab* key is pressed. The **TabIndex** property allows you to specify the order in which focus is transferred to controls when *Tab* is pressed. However, some controls, such as a read-only TextBox, should not be selected using the *Tab* key. The **TabStop** property specifies whether the user can select the control using the *Tab* key. Setting this property to False prevents the control from being selected. You set both of these properties in the following box.

Setting Properties TabIndex and TabStop	1. **Opening ShippingHub.vb.** Double click ShippingHub.vb in the **Solution Explorer** to open the file in design view. The **Shipping Hub** application requires that the user enter the package information into its TextBoxes. To make it easy for the user to enter the data, allow the user to press the *Tab* key to access the proper control.

2. **Setting property TabStop.** The TabStop property defaults to True for controls that receive user input. Make sure that the TabStop property is set to True for the **Address:**, **City:**, and **Zip:** TextBoxes, the **State:** and **Packages by State** ComboBox and the **Scan New** Button.

3. **Disabling property TabStop.** Be sure to set the TabStop property to False for the other controls on the Form. The user should only be given access to certain controls, so you must prevent the *Tab* key from transferring the focus to an improper control, such as a disabled TextBox.

4. **Using the Tab Order view in the Windows Form Designer.** The IDE provides a view called **Tab Order** to help visualize the tab order. To use the **Tab Order** view, select the Form by clicking it, then select **View > Tab Order**. White numbers indicating the TabIndex appear in blue boxes in the upper-left corner of the control (Fig. 20.7). The first time you click a control in this view, its TabIndex value will be set to zero, as displayed in the TabIndex box (Fig. 20.7). Subsequent clicks will increment the value by one. |

GUI Design Tip

Set a control's TabStop property to True only if the control is used to receive user input.

GUI Design Tip

Use the TabIndex property to define the logical order in which the user should enter data. Usually the order transfers the focus of the application from top to bottom and left to right.

TabIndex box set to zero ————

TabIndex boxes (not modified) ◄——

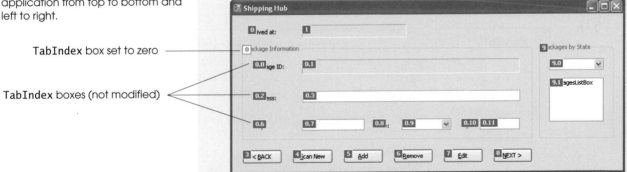

Figure 20.7 Setting the TabIndex properties using the **Tab Order** view of the **Shipping Hub** application.

Begin by clicking the **Package Information** GroupBox. Note that its value becomes 0 and the background of the surrounding box changes to white (Fig. 20.7). Then click the **Address:** TextBox. Now the value changes to 0.0. The first zero refers to the TabIndex of the container (in this case, the GroupBox), and the second zero refers to the TabIndex for that control within the container.

(cont.)   Continue setting the tab indices by clicking the **City:** TextBox, then the **State:** ComboBox and finally the **Zip:** TextBox. Finish setting the tab indices for the GroupBox by clicking each control that has not been changed. Controls that have not been changed display a box with a blue background.

5. ***Setting the TabIndex properties for the rest of the application***. Continue setting the TabIndex properties by clicking the **Scan New** Button. Then click the remaining unchanged controls in the order indicated in Fig. 20.8. When all the application's controls have been ordered, the TabIndex boxes will once again display a blue background. Exit the **Tab Order** view by selecting **View > Tab Order** or by pressing the *Escape* key.

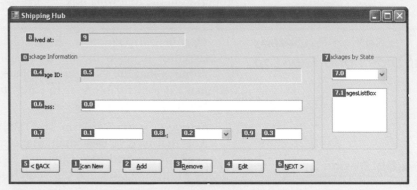

Figure 20.8   **Tab Order** view of the **Shipping Hub** application.

6. ***Saving the project***. Select **File > Save All** to save your modified code.

Using the TabIndex and TabStop properties properly enables users to enter data into an application more efficiently. Most controls have TabIndex and TabStop properties. TabIndex values on a Form or within a GroupBox must be unique—two controls cannot receive the focus at the same time. By default, the first control added to the Form has a value of 0 for its TabIndex property. The second control added has a value of 1 for its TabIndex property. The third control has a value of 2 (one more than the last control's value) for its TabIndex property, and so on.

SELF-REVIEW

1. Property _____ specifies the order in which controls receive the focus when *Tab* is pressed.

    a) `Text`   b) `TabStop`

    c) `Index`   d) `TabIndex`

2. To prevent the focus from being transferred to a control using the *Tab* key, set property _____ to _____.

    a) `TabIndex, 0`   b) `TabStop, False`

    c) `TabControl, True`   d) `TabIndex, Nothing`

Answers: 1) d. 2) b.

20.4 Using Access Keys

Applications that require the user to enter a great deal of text data should enable the ability to enter data by using only the keyboard. Setting the TabIndex and TabStop properties, for instance, helps the user enter data in a logical order by using the *Tab* key. **Access keys** (or keyboard shortcuts) allow the user to perform an action on a control using the keyboard.

To specify an access key for a control, insert an & (ampersand) symbol in the Text property before the letter you wish to use as an access key. If you wish to use "s" as the access key on the **Scan New** Button, set its Text property to &Scan New. You can specify many access keys in an application, but each letter used as an access key in a container must be unique. To use the access key, you must press and hold the *Alt* key, then press the access key character on the keyboard (release both keys after pressing the access key character). In this case of the **Scan New** Button, you would press and hold the *Alt* key, then press the *S* key (also written as *Alt+S*) You would then release both keys. The effect of using the access key is the same as clicking the button.

Access keys are often used on Button controls and on the MainMenu control, which will be introduced in Tutorial 22. If you wish to display an ampersand character on a control, you must type && in its Text property. Follow the steps in the next box to use access keys in your **Shipping Hub** application.

Creating Access Keys

1. ***Creating an access key for the Scan New Button.*** Insert an & symbol before the letter S in the Text property of the **Scan New** Button (Fig. 20.9). Press *Enter* or click outside the field to update the property. Note that the letter S is now underlined on the Button (Fig. 20.9). If the user presses *Alt* then *S* during execution, this will have the same effect as "clicking" the **Scan New** Button. (The Click event will be raised.) Depending on your system configuration, you may need to press the *Alt* key to display the underline under the access key character.

GUI Design Tip

Use access keys to allow users to "click" a control using the keyboard.

Using the & symbol to create an access key (there is no space between & and S)

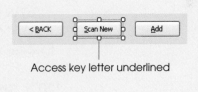

Access key letter underlined

Figure 20.9 Creating an access key.

2. ***Inserting access keys for the remaining Buttons.*** Use the Text properties of the remaining Buttons to create access keys. Precede the B on the **< BACK** Button with an ampersand. Repeat this process for the A on the **Add** Button, the R on the **Remove** Button, the E on the **Edit** Button and the N on the **NEXT >** Button.

3. ***Saving the project.*** Select **File > Save All** to save your modified code.

SELF-REVIEW

1. When creating an access key, the _____ the ampersand is underlined.
   a) character preceding
   b) character following
   c) characters following
   d) characters preceding

2. Press the _____ key then the underlined character on a Button to use the access key.
   a) *Control*
   b) *Shift*
   c) *Alt*
   d) *Tab*

Answers: 1) b. 2) c.

20.5 Collections

The .NET Framework provides several classes, called **collections**, which you can use to store groups of related objects. These classes provide methods that facilitate the storage and organization of your data without requiring any knowledge of the details of how the objects are being stored. This capability improves your application-development time because you do not have to write code to organize your data efficiently—the methods in the collection classes are proven to be reliable and efficient.

In Tutorials 17 and 18, you learned how to declare and use arrays in your applications. You may have noticed a limitation to arrays—once an array is declared, its size will not change to match its data set. This poses a problem if the number of items in an array will change over time.

Class `ArrayList` (a member of the `System.Collections` namespace) provides a convenient solution to this problem. The **ArrayList** collection provides all of the capabilities of an array, but also provides dynamic resizing capabilities. **Dynamic resizing** enables the `ArrayList` object to increase its size to accommodate new elements and to decrease its size when elements are removed.

> **Software Design Tip**
>
> Use an `ArrayList` to store a group of values when the number of elements in the group varies during the running of an application.

SELF-REVIEW

1. Collections _____.
   a) force you to focus on how your data is stored
   b) speed up application development
   c) allow you to focus on the details of your application
   d) Both b and c.

2. One limitation of arrays is that _____.
   a) their size cannot change dynamically   b) they can only store primitive data types
   c) `Strings` cannot be placed in them   d) All of the above.

Answers: 1) d. 2) a.

20.6 Shipping Hub Application: Using Class `ArrayList`

By now, you are familiar with designing GUIs and writing methods and event handlers. This tutorial's template file provides much of the application's functionality so that you can concentrate on using an `ArrayList`. You are encouraged to study the full source code at the end of the tutorial to understand how the application is implemented. The following pseudocode statements describe the basic operation of your **Shipping Hub** application:

```
When the Form loads:
    Generate an initial package ID number
    Create an empty ArrayList

When the user clicks the Scan New Button:
    Generate a unique package ID number
    Enable TextBoxes, the ComboBox and the Add Button

When the user clicks the Add Button:
    Retrieve address, city, state and zip code values; and disable input controls
    Add the package to the ArrayList
    Add the package number to the ListBox
    Change the ComboBox value to the package's destination state

When the user clicks the < BACK Button:
    Display the previous package in the list

When the user clicks the NEXT > Button:
    Display the next package in the list
```

When the user clicks the Remove Button:
    Remove the package from the list

When the user clicks the Edit Button:
    Change the Button to read Update
    Allow the user to modify package address information

When the user clicks the Update Button:
    Update the package's information in the list
    Disable controls that allow user input, and change the
        Update Button to read Edit

When the user chooses a different state in the ComboBox:
    Display the package number for each package destined for that
        state in the ListBox

The **Shipping Hub** application must store a list of packages through which the user can navigate using the **NEXT >** and **< BACK** Buttons. Each time the application runs, it must allow for any number of packages to be added. Using arrays, you would be limited by the number of values that you could store in the array. The ArrayList collection solves this problem by combining the functionality of an array with dynamic resizing capabilities.

Now that you have test-driven the **Shipping Hub** application and studied its pseudocode representation, you will use an ACE table to help you convert the pseudocode to Visual Basic. Figure 20.10 lists the actions, controls and events that will help you complete your own version of this application.

*Action/Control/Event
(ACE) Table for the
Shipping Hub
Application*

Action	Control/Object	Event
Label the application's controls	addressFrame, listByStateFrame, arrivedLabel, packageIDLabel, addressLabel, cityLabel, stateLabel, zipLabel	Application is run
	ShippingHubForm	Load
Generate an initial package ID number	randomObject	
Create an empty ArrayList	list	
	newButton	Click
Generate a random package ID number for the first package	randomObject	
Enable TextBoxes, the ComboBox and the Add Button	addButton, addressTextBox, cityTextBox, stateComboBox, zipTextBox	
	addButton	Click
Retrieve address, city, state and zip code values; and disable input controls	addressTextBox, cityTextBox, stateComboBox, zipTextBox	
Add the package to the ArrayList	list	
Add the package number to the ListBox	packagesListBox	
Change the ComboBox value to the package's destination state	stateComboBox	

Figure 20.10   ACE table for the **Shipping Hub** application. (Part 1 of 2.)

(cont.)

Action	Control/Object	Event
	backButton	Click
Display the previous package in the list	list, address-TextBox, cityText-Box, stateComboBox, zipTextBox	
	nextButton	Click
Display the next package in the list	list, address-TextBox, cityText-Box, stateComboBox, zipTextBox	
	removeButton	Click
Remove the package from the list	list	
	editUpdateButton	Click
Change the Button to read Update	editUpdateButton	
Allow the user to modify package address information	addressTextBox, cityTextBox, stateComboBox, zipTextBox	
	editUpdateButton	Click
Update the package's information in the list	list	
Disable controls that allow user input, and change the Update Button to read Edit	addressTextBox, cityTextBox, stateComboBox, zipTextBox, editUpdateButton	
	viewPackagesCom-boBox	Selected-Index-Changed
Display the package number for each package destined for that state in the ListBox	packagesListBox	

Figure 20.10 ACE table for the **Shipping Hub** application. (Part 2 of 2.)

In this tutorial, you focus on using an ArrayList in the **Shipping Hub** application. You begin by creating an ArrayList object.

Creating a List of Packages

1. ***Declaring an ArrayList***. Insert line 3 of Fig. 20.11 in the Shipping Hub class to declare ArrayList list. Note the use of the member-access operator (.) to gain access to the ArrayList class, which is located in namespace System.Collections. Alternatively, you could place the following Imports statement at the beginning of your file to import the **Collections** namespace:

   Imports System.Collections

   In this case, you would not need to use the member-access operator because the namespace has been imported. In the following discussion, we will refer to the Collections.ArrayList object as an ArrayList.

(cont.)

Declaring an `ArrayList` reference

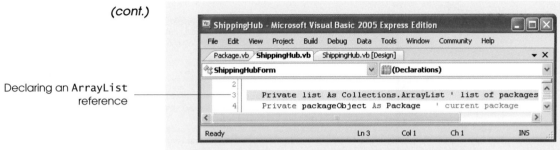

Figure 20.11　Declaring the `ArrayList` reference.

2. ***Initializing the ArrayList.*** To use the `ArrayList` instance variable declared in *Step 1*, you must create a new `ArrayList` object. You will then assign a reference to the `ArrayList` object to the instance variable. Insert line 21 (Fig. 20.12) to the Form's `Load` event handler. This line uses the `New` keyword to create an empty `ArrayList` object when the application loads. Note that line 20 uses the `ComboBox`'s `Items.Item` property to show the first state in the list. The **`Items.Item`** property retrieves the value stored in the `ComboBox` at the specified index.

Initializing the `ArrayList` reference

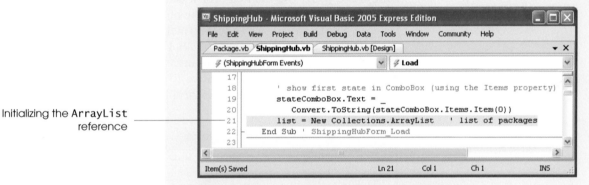

Figure 20.12　Creating an `ArrayList` object.

3. ***Saving the project.*** Select **File > Save All** to save your modified code.

Now that you have created an `ArrayList` object, you will need to insert code that allows the user to add packages to the `ArrayList`. To accomplish this, you will create a reference to an object of class `Package` and use the `ArrayList`'s `Add` method to store the reference in the `ArrayList`. Recall that you have already added the `Package` class to your application. You will now create packages and add them to your list.

Adding and Removing Packages	1. ***Creating a package.*** The user clicks the **Scan New** Button when a new package arrives at the shipping hub. When this occurs, the application creates a package number and allows the user to enter the shipping address. Insert lines 28–29 from Fig. 20.13 into the **Scan New** Button's `Click` event handler. Line 28 increments `packageID` to ensure that all packages have a unique identification number. Line 29 passes the package number as an argument to the constructor for class `Package`. The value that you pass to the `Package` constructor can then be accessed using its `PackageNumber` property. Note that line 29 uses the same reference, `packageObject`, many times to reference a new `Package` object. However, the previous `Package` object will not be destroyed each time the reference is changed. This is because each package reference will be stored in the `ArrayList`.

(cont.)

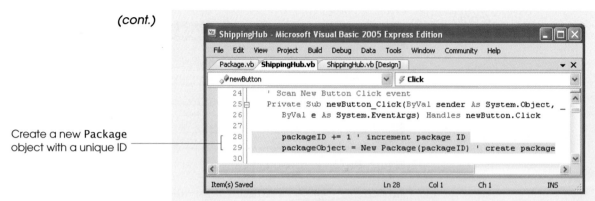

Figure 20.13 Creating a Package object.

Create a new **Package** object with a unique ID

2. ***Displaying the package number and arrival time.*** After the package has been "scanned," the application should display the new package's arrival time and package number to the user. Insert lines 32–35 of Fig. 20.14 into the newButton_Click event handler. Lines 32–33 use the Package's PackageNumber property to display the package identification number in a Label. The **ToString** method, which is defined for most objects and data types, returns a value representing the object as text (of type String). For instance, a Date structure's ToString method returns the date as a String, in the format 11/11/2002 9:34:00 AM. However, be aware that for many FCL classes, ToString merely returns the class name. The ToString method can be used as an alternative to the Convert.ToString method. Lines 34–35 use the Package's ArrivalTime property to display the arrival time (the current time) in a Label.

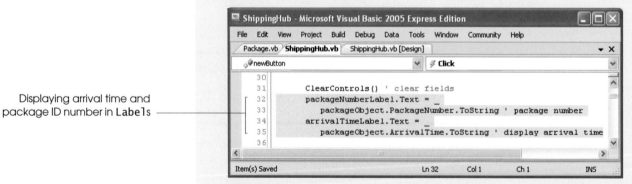

Displaying arrival time and package ID number in Labels

Figure 20.14 Displaying the package's number and arrival time.

3. ***Adding a package to the ArrayList.*** To add the package to the ArrayList after entering the package's information, the user clicks the **Add** Button. Add line 50 of Fig. 20.15 to the **Add** Button's Click event handler. This line stores the package information by adding the Package object to list using the ArrayList's **Add** method.

Each time you add an object to the ArrayList by calling the Add method, the object is placed at the end of the ArrayList. With arrays, you refer to a value's location by its index. Similarly, in an ArrayList, you refer to an object's location in the ArrayList as the object's **index**. Like an array, the index of an object at the beginning of the ArrayList is zero, and the index of an object at the end of the ArrayList is one less than the number of objects in the ArrayList.

(cont.)

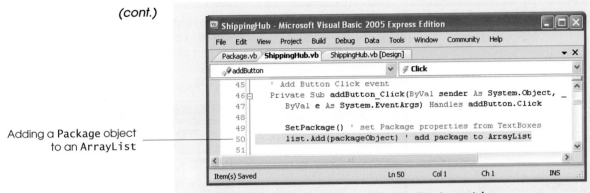

Adding a **Package** object to an **ArrayList**

Figure 20.15 Adding a package to the **ArrayList**.

4. *Removing a package from the **ArrayList**.* When the user selects a package and clicks the **Remove** Button, the application should remove the package from the **ArrayList**. The **ArrayList** class provides a simple way to remove objects from the **ArrayList**. Insert line 105 (Fig. 20.16) into the **Remove** Button's **Click** event handler. This line uses the **RemoveAt** method to remove a package from the **ArrayList**. The argument passed to the RemoveAt method is the index (stored in variable position) of the package in the **ArrayList**. Variable position keeps track of the index and is incremented or decremented each time the user clicks the **NEXT >** or **< BACK** Buttons.

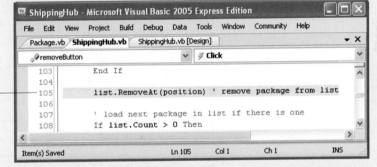

Removing the current package from the **ArrayList**

Figure 20.16 Removing a package from the **ArrayList**.

If a package at index 3 is removed from the **ArrayList**, the package that was previously at index 4 will then be located at index 3. Whenever an object is removed from an **ArrayList**, the indices update accordingly. Note that line 108 of Fig. 20.16 uses the Count property of class **ArrayList**. Like the Length property of an array, the **Count** property returns the number of objects contained in the **ArrayList**.

5. *Saving the project.* Select **File > Save All** to save your modified code.

Once a package has been added to the **ArrayList**, the **Shipping Hub** application disables the TextBoxes so that the user does not accidentally modify the package information. An **Edit** Button is provided to allow users to modify any of the package information except for the arrival time and the package identification number. When the user clicks the **Edit** Button, its event handler should enable the controls that allow the user to modify the package data. You will add functionality to accomplish this in the following box.

Updating Package Information

1. ***Changing the Edit Button's Text property.*** Add lines 132–133 of Fig. 20.17 to your application. When the **Edit** Button is clicked, line 133 changes the text on the **Edit** Button to &Update (using U as the access key). This indicates that the user should click the same Button, which now is labeled **Update**, to submit changes to the package information.

Using code to change the text displayed on a Button

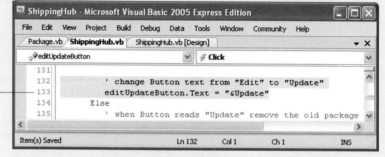

Figure 20.17 Changing the **Edit** Button to display **Update**.

2. ***Updating the package data.*** Insert lines 138–139 of Fig. 20.18 into the editUpdateButton_Click event handler. When the user chooses to alter the package information, the package is removed from the ArrayList and a new one with the updated address information is added.

Updating the ArrayList with new package information

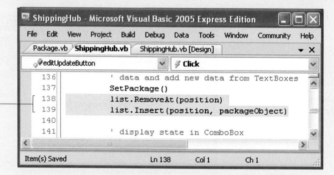

Figure 20.18 Removing and inserting a package to update data.

Line 138 removes the old package object from the ArrayList. Line 139 uses class ArrayList's Insert method to add the package to the Array-List. The **Insert** method is like the Add method, but Insert allows you to specify the index in the ArrayList at which to insert the package. The first argument to the Insert method is the index at which to insert the package (in this case, position), and the second argument contains the package to insert into the ArrayList (package). Using the Insert method allows you to place the updated package object at the same index in the ArrayList as the package object you just removed.

3. ***Changing the Button's Text property to Edit.*** After the user clicks the **Update** Button, the TextBoxes are once again disabled. Since the user's changes have been applied you should reset the text on the **Update** Button to read **Edit**. Insert line 149 of Fig. 20.19 into the event handler to reset the text on the Button to **Edit**. Note once again the use of the & to enable the Button's access key.

4. ***Saving the project.*** Select **File > Save All** to save your modified code.

(cont.)

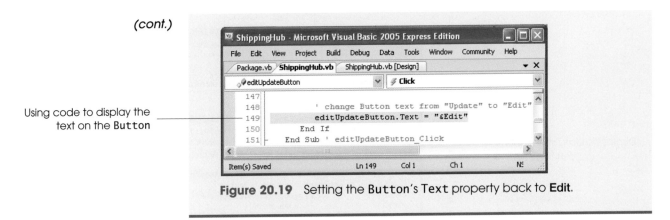

Figure 20.19 Setting the **Button**'s **Text** property back to **Edit**.

Using code to display the text on the **Button**

The user navigates the **ArrayList** by clicking the **NEXT >** and **< BACK** Buttons. Each time the user chooses to view a different package in the **ArrayList**, the package information displayed in the **Form**'s controls must be updated. To display a package's information, you must retrieve the information from the **ArrayList** that you created. You will learn how to do this in the following box.

Displaying a Package

1. ***Retrieving package data.*** Insert lines 165–167 from Fig. 20.20 into your application's **LoadPackage** method. To display the information, you must retrieve the data from the **ArrayList** using the **Item** method, which returns the object stored at the index specified by the method's argument. Lines 166–167 assign to **packageObject** the package stored at index **position**. Function **CType** converts its first argument to the type of object specified by the second argument. In this case, the item returned is being converted to a **Package**.

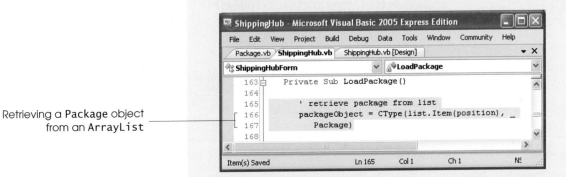

Retrieving a **Package** object from an **ArrayList**

Figure 20.20 Retrieving a package from the **ArrayList**.

Note that the code you inserted explicitly converts the object returned by the **ArrayList** to an object of type **Package**. An **ArrayList** stores references to objects of type **Object**—which means that it can store *any* object you choose, from predefined objects (like a **Random** object) to programmer-defined objects (like a **Package** object). To use and access the properties and methods of a package returned from an **ArrayList**, you must explicitly convert it to a **Package** object.

2. ***Displaying the package information.*** Insert lines 169–177 of Fig. 20.21 into your application. These lines retrieve the package information from **packageObject** and display the data in the corresponding controls on the **Form**, using the **ToString** method.

3. ***Saving the project.*** Select **File > Save All** to save your modified code.

(cont.)

Displaying data stored in the **Package** object

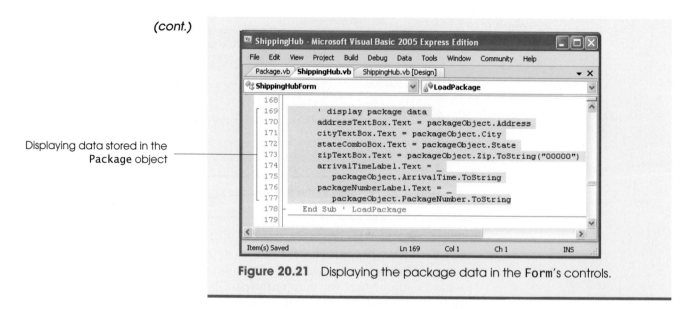

Figure 20.21 Displaying the package data in the **Form**'s controls.

In the preceding box, you learned that an `ArrayList` stores references to `Objects`, and this allows objects of any type to be referenced from an `ArrayList`. Visual Basic 2005 introduced a capability called generics that enables a collection to store references to objects of specific types rather than references to `Objects`. Generics are beyond the scope of this book. If you plan to continue your Visual Basic studies, we provide a thorough treatment of generics and generic collections in *Visual Basic 2005 How to Program, Third Edition*. We also provide tutorials and resource centers with additional Visual Basic 2005 information at www.deitel.com. You can find tutorials on Visual Basic generics and many other topics at

www.deitel.com/articles/index.html

Our Visual Basic Resource Center

www.deitel.com/visualbasic

includes articles on many Visual Basic 2005 features, including generics. Go to our resource centers for lots of additional information on the subjects in this book and new developments in VB.

SELF-REVIEW

1. Method _____ of class `ArrayList` can be used to add an object at a specific location in the `ArrayList`.

   a) AddAt
   b) Insert
   c) AddObjectAt
   d) Add

2. The **Shipping Hub** application uses an `ArrayList` because class `ArrayList` _____.

   a) can store a variable number of objects
   b) allows the addition and removal of packages
   c) allows the insertion of items into any index in the `ArrayList`
   d) All of the above.

Answers: 1) b. 2) d.

Good Programming Practice

Use a For Each...Next repetition statement to iterate through values in an array or collection without using a counter variable.

20.7 For Each...Next Repetition Statement

Visual Basic provides the **For Each...Next** repetition statement for iterating through the values in an array or a collection. Instead of setting initial and final values for a counter variable, the For Each...Next statement uses a control variable (a reference) that can reference each object in the collection. Assuming that you have created an `ArrayList` called `list` that contains only `Package` objects, the code

```
Dim packageObject As Package

For Each packageObject In list
    packagesListBox.Items.Add(packageObject.PackageNumber)
Next
```

adds each package's ID number to a ListBox. The For Each...Next statement requires both a collection type and an element. The **collection type** specifies the array or collection (in this case, list) through which you wish to iterate. The **element** (in this case, packageObject) is used to store a reference to a value in the collection type. If the For Each...Next statement contains an element of the same type as the collection type (or one that can be converted to the same type), the statement assigns the collection type's object to the element (in this case, packageObject). The body of the For Each...Next statement is then executed. Note that the For Each...Next statement does not require you to specify initial and final counter values, and thus it simplifies access to groups of values.

Figure 20.22 shows the UML activity diagram for the preceding For Each...Next statement. It is similar to the UML diagram for the For...Next statement in Tutorial 11. The only difference is that the For Each...Next continues to execute the body until all elements in the array (or collection) have been accessed.

Common Programming Error

If the element in a For Each...Next statement cannot be converted to the same type as the collection type's objects, a runtime error occurs. For example, if an Array-List contained only Date values, declaring a reference to a Package object as the element would cause a runtime error.

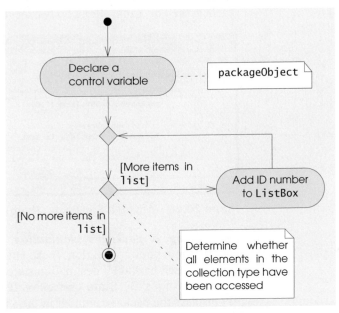

Figure 20.22   UML activity diagram for For Each...Next repetition statement.

When the user selects a state from the ComboBox, the application displays the package number for each package destined for that state. You will use the For Each...Next statement in the **Shipping Hub** application to add this functionality.

Inserting a For Each...Next Statement

1. *Declaring a control variable (reference)*. Add line 215 of Fig. 20.23 to your application. This line declares reference viewPackage of type Package. The reference viewPackage will be used to reference each Package object in your ArrayList (one at a time) as you iterate through the ArrayList of Package objects. Note that you have added code to a ComboBox's SelectedIndexChanged event handler. The **SelectedIndexChanged** event is raised when the value selected in the ComboBox changes.

(cont.)

Declaring the control variable for the For Each...Next repetition statement

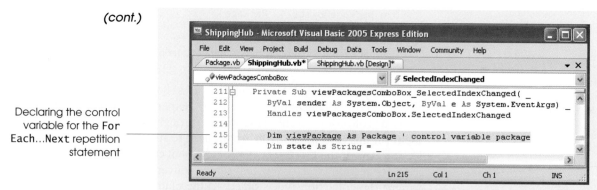

Figure 20.23 Declaring a reference for use in For Each...Next loop.

2. *Inserting a For Each...Next statement.* Add lines 221–222 of Fig. 20.24 to your application, then press *Enter*. Note that the Next statement has been added for you in line 224. Line 222 is the header for the repetition statement. This loop will iterate through list, assigning the next element in the ArrayList (beginning with the first package object) to reference viewPackage before executing the body of the loop. When a new package is reached, the For Each...Next body executes.

For Each...Next header

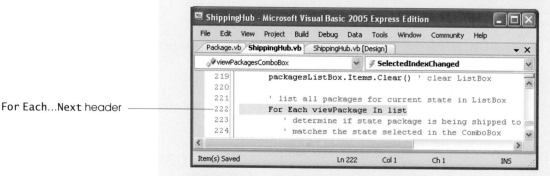

Figure 20.24 Writing a For Each...Next statement.

3. *Determining a package's destination state.* Insert lines 223–228 of Fig. 20.25 into your application. These lines contain an If...Then statement that tests each package's destination state against the state name displayed in the **Packages By State** ComboBox. If the two state names match, line 227 displays the package number in the ListBox.

Displaying package ID numbers only for packages destined for the specified state

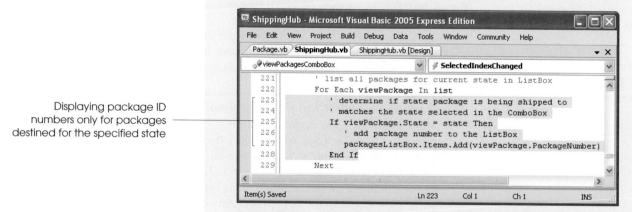

Figure 20.25 Displaying all packages going to selected state.

(cont.)

4. ***Running the application.*** Select **Debug > Start Debugging** to run your application. Enter information for several packages going to the same state. Select that state in the **Packages by State** GroupBox and verify that the correct packages are listed. Click the application's Buttons and make sure that you can remove, cycle through or modify the packages.

5. ***Closing the application.*** Close your running application by clicking its close box.

6. ***Closing the IDE.*** Close the Visual Basic IDE by clicking its close box.

Figure 20.26 presents the source code for the **Shipping Hub** application. The lines of code that contain new programming concepts that you learned in this tutorial are highlighted.

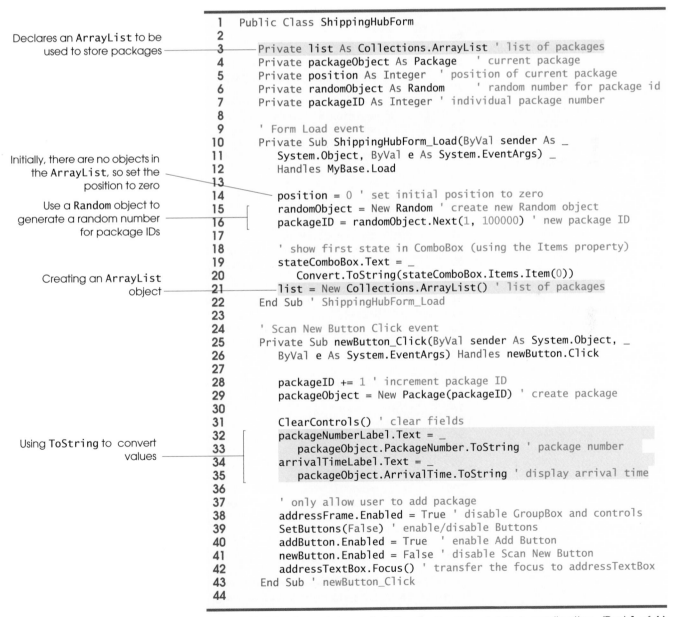

Declares an `ArrayList` to be used to store packages

Initially, there are no objects in the `ArrayList`, so set the position to zero

Use a `Random` object to generate a random number for package IDs

Creating an `ArrayList` object

Using `ToString` to convert values

```
1   Public Class ShippingHubForm
2
3       Private list As Collections.ArrayList ' list of packages
4       Private packageObject As Package   ' current package
5       Private position As Integer  ' position of current package
6       Private randomObject As Random     ' random number for package id
7       Private packageID As Integer ' individual package number
8
9       ' Form Load event
10      Private Sub ShippingHubForm_Load(ByVal sender As _
11          System.Object, ByVal e As System.EventArgs) _
12          Handles MyBase.Load
13
14          position = 0 ' set initial position to zero
15          randomObject = New Random ' create new Random object
16          packageID = randomObject.Next(1, 100000) ' new package ID
17
18          ' show first state in ComboBox (using the Items property)
19          stateComboBox.Text = _
20              Convert.ToString(stateComboBox.Items.Item(0))
21          list = New Collections.ArrayList() ' list of packages
22      End Sub ' ShippingHubForm_Load
23
24      ' Scan New Button Click event
25      Private Sub newButton_Click(ByVal sender As System.Object, _
26          ByVal e As System.EventArgs) Handles newButton.Click
27
28          packageID += 1 ' increment package ID
29          packageObject = New Package(packageID) ' create package
30
31          ClearControls() ' clear fields
32          packageNumberLabel.Text = _
33              packageObject.PackageNumber.ToString ' package number
34          arrivalTimeLabel.Text = _
35              packageObject.ArrivalTime.ToString ' display arrival time
36
37          ' only allow user to add package
38          addressFrame.Enabled = True ' disable GroupBox and controls
39          SetButtons(False) ' enable/disable Buttons
40          addButton.Enabled = True   ' enable Add Button
41          newButton.Enabled = False ' disable Scan New Button
42          addressTextBox.Focus() ' transfer the focus to addressTextBox
43      End Sub ' newButton_Click
44
```

Figure 20.26 Complete code listing for the **Shipping Hub** application. (Part 1 of 4.)

```
45        ' Add Button Click event
46        Private Sub addButton_Click(ByVal sender As System.Object, _
47           ByVal e As System.EventArgs) Handles addButton.Click
48
49           SetPackage() ' set Package properties from TextBoxes
50           list.Add(packageObject) ' add package to ArrayList
51
52           addressFrame.Enabled = False ' disable GroupBox and controls
53           SetButtons(True) ' enable appropriate Buttons
54
55           ' package cannot be added until Scan New is clicked
56           addButton.Enabled = False ' disable Add Button
57
58           ' if package's state displayed, add ID to ListBox
59           If stateComboBox.Text = viewPackagesComboBox.Text Then
60              packagesListBox.Items.Add(packageObject.PackageNumber)
61           End If
62
63           viewPackagesComboBox.Text = packageObject.State ' list package
64           newButton.Enabled = True ' enable Scan New Button
65        End Sub ' addButton_Click
66
67        ' Back Button Click event
68        Private Sub backButton_Click(ByVal sender As System.Object, _
69           ByVal e As System.EventArgs) Handles backButton.Click
70
71           ' move backward one package in the list
72           If position > 0 Then
73              position -= 1
74           Else ' wrap to end of list
75              position = list.Count - 1
76           End If
77
78           LoadPackage() ' load package data from item in list
79        End Sub ' backButton_Click
80
81        ' Next Button Click event
82        Private Sub nextButton_Click(ByVal sender As System.Object, _
83           ByVal e As System.EventArgs) Handles nextButton.Click
84
85           ' move forward one package in the list
86           If position < list.Count - 1 Then
87              position += 1
88           Else
89              position = 0 ' wrap to beginning of list
90           End If
91
92           LoadPackage() ' load package data from item in list
93        End Sub ' nextButton_Click
94
95        ' Remove Button click event
96        Private Sub removeButton_Click(ByVal sender As _
97           System.Object, ByVal e As System.EventArgs) _
98           Handles removeButton.Click
99
100          ' remove ID from ListBox if state displayed
101          If stateComboBox.Text = viewPackagesComboBox.Text Then
102             packagesListBox.Items.Remove(packageObject.PackageNumber)
103          End If
104
105          list.RemoveAt(position) ' remove package from list
106
```

When the user clicks the **< BACK** Button, decrement the position. If the position was zero, set the position to the last object in the **ArrayList**

When the user clicks the **NEXT >** Button, increment the position. If the position was the last object in the array, set the position to zero

Figure 20.26   Complete code listing for the **Shipping Hub** application. (Part 2 of 4.)

```
107        ' load next package in list if there is one
108        If list.Count > 0 Then
109           ' if not at first position, go to previous one
110           If position > 0 Then
111              position -= 1
112           End If
113           LoadPackage() ' load package data from item in list
114        Else
115           ClearControls() ' clear fields
116        End If
117        SetButtons(True) ' enable appropriate Buttons
118     End Sub ' removeButton_Click
119
120     ' Edit/Update Button Click event
121     Private Sub editUpdateButton_Click(ByVal sender As _
122        System.Object, ByVal e As System.EventArgs) _
123        Handles editUpdateButton.Click
124
125        ' when Button reads "Edit", allow user to
126        ' edit package information only
127        If editUpdateButton.Text = "&Edit" Then
128           addressFrame.Enabled = True
129           SetButtons(False)
130           editUpdateButton.Enabled = True
131
132           ' change Button text from "Edit" to "Update"
133           editUpdateButton.Text = "&Update"
134        Else
135           ' when Button reads "Update" remove the old package
136           ' data and add new data from TextBoxes
137           SetPackage()
138           list.RemoveAt(position)
139           list.Insert(position, packageObject)
140
141           ' display state in ComboBox
142           viewPackagesComboBox.Text = packageObject.State
143
144           ' when done, return to normal operating state
145           addressFrame.Enabled = False  ' disable GroupBox
146           SetButtons(True) ' enable appropriate Buttons
147
148           ' change Button text from "Update" to "Edit"
149           editUpdateButton.Text = "&Edit"
150        End If
151     End Sub ' btnEditUpdate_Click
152
153     ' set package properties
154     Private Sub SetPackage()
155        packageObject.Address = addressTextBox.Text
156        packageObject.City = cityTextBox.Text
157        packageObject.State = _
158           Convert.ToString(stateComboBox.SelectedItem)
159        packageObject.Zip = Convert.ToInt32(Val(zipTextBox.Text))
160     End Sub ' SetPackage
161
162     ' load package information into Form
163     Private Sub LoadPackage()
164
165        ' retrieve package from list
166        packageObject = CType(list.Item(position), _
167           Package)
168
169        ' display package data
170        addressTextBox.Text = packageObject.Address
```

Set the position to the next package in the **ArrayList** — *lines 108–112*

Using **&** in the **Text** property of a **Button** to create an access key — *line 133*

Removing and inserting items from/into an **ArrayList** — *lines 138–139*

Using **&** in the **Text** property of a **Button** to create an access key — *line 149*

Retrieve data from user, and store it in the **Package** object — *lines 154–160*

Figure 20.26 Complete code listing for the **Shipping Hub** application. (Part 3 of 4.)

```
171         cityTextBox.Text = packageObject.City
172         stateComboBox.Text = packageObject.State
173         zipTextBox.Text = packageObject.Zip.ToString("00000")
174         arrivalTimeLabel.Text = _
175            packageObject.ArrivalTime.ToString
176         packageNumberLabel.Text = _
177            packageObject.PackageNumber.ToString
178      End Sub ' LoadPackage
179
180      ' clear all the input controls on the Form
181      Private Sub ClearControls()
182         addressTextBox.Clear()
183         cityTextBox.Clear()
184         zipTextBox.Clear()
185         stateComboBox.SelectedText = ""
186         arrivalTimeLabel.Text = ""
187         packageNumberLabel.Text = ""
188      End Sub ' ClearControls
189
190      ' enable/disable Buttons
191      Private Sub SetButtons(ByVal state As Boolean)
192         removeButton.Enabled = state
193         editUpdateButton.Enabled = state
194         nextButton.Enabled = state
195         backButton.Enabled = state
196
197         ' disable navigation if not multiple packages
198         If list.Count < 2 Then
199            nextButton.Enabled = False
200            backButton.Enabled = False
201         End If
202
203         ' if no items, disable Remove and Edit/Update Buttons
204         If list.Count = 0 Then
205            editUpdateButton.Enabled = False
206            removeButton.Enabled = False
207         End If
208      End Sub ' SetButtons
209
210      ' event raised when user selects a new state in ComboBox
211      Private Sub viewPackagesComboBox_SelectedIndexChanged( _
212         ByVal sender As System.Object, ByVal e As System.EventArgs) _
213         Handles viewPackagesComboBox.SelectedIndexChanged
214
215         Dim viewPackage As Package ' control variable package
216         Dim state As String = _
217            Convert.ToString(viewPackagesComboBox.SelectedItem)
218
219         packagesListBox.Items.Clear() ' clear ListBox
220
221         ' list all packages for current state in ListBox
222         For Each viewPackage In list
223            ' determine if state package is being shipped to
224            ' matches the state selected in the ComboBox
225            If viewPackage.State = state Then
226               ' add package number to the ListBox
227               packagesListBox.Items.Add(viewPackage.PackageNumber)
228            End If
229         Next
230      End Sub ' viewPackagesComboBox_SelectedIndexChanged
231   End Class ' ShippingHubForm
```

Using ToString to convert values — (lines 173–177)

Enable or disable Buttons depending on value of state — (lines 192–195)

Figure 20.26   Complete code listing for the **Shipping Hub** application. (Part 4 of 4.)

1. The collection type in a For Each...Next repetition statement represents _____.
    a) the counter used for iteration
    b) the reference used for iteration
    c) an array or collection
    d) the guard condition

2. The _____ statement provides a convenient way to iterate through values in an array or collection.
    a) Do While...Loop
    b) For...Next
    c) For Each...Next
    d) None of the above.

Answers: 1) c. 2) c.

20.8 Wrap-Up

In this tutorial, you learned how to use the TabStop and TabIndex properties to enhance the **Shipping Hub** application's usability. You learned how to determine which controls receive the application's focus when the *Tab* key is pressed using the TabStop property. You then set the TabIndex property, to specify the order in which controls receive the focus of the application when the *Tab* key is pressed. To further enhance the user interface, you created access keys to allow the user to "click" Buttons in the **Shipping Hub** application by pressing the *Alt* key and then the access key for the particular Button.

You learned about using the ArrayList collection. You used ArrayList methods to add a package object to an ArrayList and delete the package from a specific index in an ArrayList. You then wrote code to insert a Package object into the ArrayList at a specific index. These methods helped you store, edit and navigate an ArrayList of packages in the **Shipping Hub** application.

Finally, you learned about the For Each...Next repetition statement. You declared a control variable for use in the loop and used that reference in the For Each...Next statement to iterate through each element in a collection type (which can be an array or a collection). Then you used the For Each...Next statement to iterate through package objects in the ArrayList in your **Shipping Hub** application.

In the next tutorial, you will learn about mouse events, which are events raised when the user moves or clicks the mouse. You will use mouse events to allow the user to draw art on a Form.

SKILLS SUMMARY

Using the TabIndex and TabStop Properties

■ Set the TabIndex properties of controls on your Form using numbers to specify the order in which to transfer the focus of the application when the user presses the *Tab* key. Using **View > Tab Order** helps in configuring the order of this process.

■ Set the TabStop property of a control to False if a control is not used by the user to input data. Set the TabStop property of a control to True if focus should be transferred to the control using the *Tab* key.

Creating Access Keys

■ Insert the & symbol in a control's Text property before the character you wish you use as an access key (keyboard shortcut).

Creating an ArrayList

■ Assign a reference to an ArrayList to an object of type Collections.ArrayList using keyword New.

Using an ArrayList

■ Call ArrayList method Add on an ArrayList object to add the method's argument to the ArrayList.

■ Call ArrayList method RemoveAt on an ArrayList object to remove the object from the ArrayList at the index specified by the method's argument.

- Call `ArrayList` method `Insert` on an `ArrayList` object to add the object specified by the second argument to the `ArrayList` at the index specified by the first argument.

- Call `ArrayList` method `Count` on an `ArrayList` object to obtain the number of its elements.

- Call `ArrayList` method `Item` on an `ArrayList` object to access an `ArrayList` element by index.

Using a For Each...Next Repetition Statement

- Declare a reference of the same type as the elements you wish to access in a collection type (array or collection).

- Specify the reference as the control variable in the For Each...Next repetition statement and the array or collection through which you wish to iterate. The loop repeats and the body of the For Each...Next repetition statement executes for each element in the collection type. The value accessed at the beginning of each iteration is stored in the element reference for the body of the loop.

KEY TERMS

access key—Keyboard shortcut that allows the user to perform an action on a control using the keyboard.

Add method of class `ArrayList`—Adds a specified object to the end of an `ArrayList`.

`ArrayList` class—Performs the same functionality as an array, but has resizing capabilities.

collection—A class used to store groups of related objects.

collection type of a For Each...Next statement—Specifies the array or collection through which you wish to iterate.

`Collections` namespace—Contains collection classes such as `ArrayList`.

`Count` property of `ArrayList`—Returns the number of objects contained in the `ArrayList`.

`CType` function—Function that converts the type of its first argument to the type specified by the second argument.

dynamic resizing—A capability that allows certain objects (such as `ArrayLists`) to increase or decrease in size based on the addition or removal of elements from that object. Enables the `ArrayList` object to increase its size to accommodate new elements and to decrease its size when elements are removed.

element of a For Each...Next statement—Used to store a reference to the current value of the collection being iterated.

For Each...Next repetition statement—Iterates through elements in an array or collection.

index of an `ArrayList`—The value with which you can refer to a specific element in an `ArrayList`, based on the element's location in the `ArrayList`.

`Insert` method of class `ArrayList`—Inserts a specified object into the specified location of an `ArrayList`.

`Items` property of `ComboBox`—Specifies the values the user can select from the `ComboBox`.

`Items.Item` property of `ComboBox`—Retrieves the value at the specified index of a `ComboBox`.

`MaxLength` property of `TextBox`—Specifies the maximum number of characters that can be input into a `TextBox`.

`RemoveAt` method of class `ArrayList`—Removes the object located at a specified location of an `ArrayList`.

`SelectedIndexChanged` event of `ComboBox`—Raised when a new value is selected in a `ComboBox`.

`TabIndex` property—A control property that specifies the order in which focus is transferred to controls on the Form when the *Tab* key is pressed.

`TabStop` property—A control property that specifies whether a control can receive the focus when the *Tab* key is pressed.

`ToString` method—Returns a `String` representation of the object or data type on which the method is called.

GUI DESIGN GUIDELINES	**Overall Design** ■ Set a control's TabStop property to True only if the control is used to receive user input. ■ Use the TabIndex property to define the logical order in which the user is to enter data. Usually the tab order transfers the focus of the application from top to bottom and left to right. ■ Use access keys to allow users to click a control using the keyboard.

CONTROLS, EVENTS, PROPERTIES & METHODS	**ArrayList** This class is used to store a variable number of objects. ■ *Properties* Count—Returns the number of objects contained in the ArrayList. Item—Accesses elements of the ArrayList by index. ■ *Methods* Add—Adds an object to the ArrayList object. Insert—Adds an object to the ArrayList object at a specific index. RemoveAt—Removes an object from the ArrayList object at the specified index.

ComboBox   ▣ ComboBox   This control allows users to select options from a drop-down list.

■ *In action*

■ *Event*

SelectedIndexChanged—Raised when a new value is selected in the ComboBox.

■ *Properties*

DataSource—Allows you to add items to the ComboBox.

DropDownStyle—Determines the ComboBox's style.

Enabled—Determines whether the user can enter data (True) in the ComboBox or not (False).

Items.Item—Retrieves the value at the specified index.

Items—Specifies the values the user can select from the ComboBox.

Location—Specifies the location of the ComboBox control on its container control relative to the top-left corner.

MaxDropDownItems—Determines the maximum number of items to be displayed when the user clicks the drop-down arrow.

Name—Specifies the name used to access the ComboBox control programmatically. The name should be appended with the ComboBox suffix.

SelectedValue—Contains the item selected by the user.

TabIndex—Specifies the order in which focus is transferred to controls when *Tab* is pressed.

TabStop—Specifies whether the user can select the control using the *Tab* key.

Text—Specifies the text displayed in the ComboBox.

TextBox   abl TextBox   This control allows the user to input data from the keyboard.

■ *In action*

■ *Event*

TextChanged—Raised when the text in the TextBox is changed.

- ■ *Properties*

  Enabled—Determines whether the user can enter data in the TextBox or not.

  Location—Specifies the location of the TextBox on its container control relative to the top-left corner.

  MaxLength—Specifies the maximum number of characters that can be input into the TextBox.

  Multiline—Specifies whether the TextBox is capable of displaying multiple lines of text.

  Name—Specifies the name used to access the TextBox programmatically. The name should be appended with the TextBox suffix.

  PasswordChar—Specifies the masking character to be used when displaying data in the TextBox.

  ReadOnly—Determines whether the value of a TextBox can be changed.

  ScrollBars—Specifies whether a multiline TextBox contains a scrollbar.

  Size—Specifies the height and width (in pixels) of the TextBox.

  TabIndex—Specifies the order in which focus is transferred to controls when *Tab* is pressed.

  TabStop—Specifies whether the user can select the control using the *Tab* key.

  Text—Specifies the text displayed in the TextBox.

  TextAlign—Specifies how the text is aligned within the TextBox.

- ■ *Method*

  Focus—Transfers the focus of the application to the TextBox that calls it.

MULTIPLE-CHOICE QUESTIONS

20.1 _____ are specifically designed to store groups of values.

    a) Collections   b) Properties

    c) Accessors   d) None of the above.

20.2 The _____ key provides a quick and convenient way to navigate through controls on a Form.

    a) *Tab*   b) *Enter*

    c) *Caps Lock*   d) *Alt*

20.3 An ArrayList differs from an array of type Object in that an ArrayList can _____.

    a) store objects of any type   b) resize dynamically

    c) be accessed programmatically   d) All of the above.

20.4 The element in a For Each...Next statement _____.

    a) must be of type Integer

    b) must be of (or convertible to) the same type as the collection or array type

    c) must be of type ArrayList   d) None of the above.

20.5 The control that receives the focus the first time *Tab* is pressed has a TabIndex property set to _____.

    a) First   b) 0

    c) Next   d) 1

20.6 Users should be able to use the *Tab* key to transfer the focus to _____.

    a) only Buttons   b) only TextBoxes

    c) only controls that have an AcceptTab property

    d) only the controls that receive user input

20.7 To ensure that the proper controls obtain the focus when the *Tab* key is pressed, use the _____.

    a) TabIndex property   b) TabStop and TabIndex properties

    c) TabStop property   d) Focus property

20.8 To add a value to the end of an ArrayList, call the _____ method.

a) Add

b) AddToEnd

c) AddAt

d) InsertAt

20.9 To remove a value from a specific index in the ArrayList, use method _____.

a) Remove

b) RemoveAt

c) Delete

d) DeleteAt

20.10 To display an ampersand character on a control, type a _____ in its Text property.

a) &_

b) &

c) &&

d) _&

EXERCISES

20.11 (*Modified Salary Survey Application*) Modify the **Salary Survey** application you created in Exercise 17.12 by using a For Each...Next loop to replace the For...Next loop that is used in Tutorial 17 (Fig. 20.27).

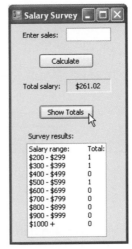

Figure 20.27   Modified **Salary Survey** GUI.

a) *Copying the template to your working directory.* Copy the directory C:\Examples\ Tutorial20\Exercises\SalarySurveyModified to your C:\SimplyVB directory.

b) *Opening the application's template file.* Double click SalarySurveyModified.sln in the SalarySurvey directory to open the application.

c) *Locating the event handler.* In **Design View**, double click the **Show Totals** Button to bring up the event handler. The code to handle the Click event should include two statements, one to clear the items in the ListBox and the other to add a header.

d) *Creating a counter variable.* The For Each...Next loop allows you to loop through each element in a specified collection. The For...Next loop from Exercise 17.12 handles the String (salaryRanges) and Integer (salaries) arrays. This presents a problem. You cannot loop through both of these arrays using the same element reference. (One is an Integer and the other is a String.) To handle this you need to create a common counter variable, one that you will use to loop through the indices of both arrays. This is possible because the lengths of both arrays are the same.

e) *Adding an element reference.* It does not matter which array you decide to use in this exercise, because these arrays are of the same length. Declare an element reference with the correct data type.

f) *Create the For Each...Next loop.* Use the new element reference that you have created along with the array of your choice to create the For Each...Next loop statement.

g) *Adding text to the ListBox.* Adding the statement to output to the ListBox is exactly the same as in Exercise 17.12. The only difference will be the name of the counter variable that you decide to use.

h) *Increment the counter variable.* To successfully loop through both arrays and output the data, you need to increment the counter variable. This ensures that the proper data is added to the ListBox through each iteration.

i) *Running the application.* Select **Debug > Start Debugging** to run your application. Enter several sales amounts using the **Calculate** Button. Click the **Show Totals** Button and verify that the proper amounts are displayed for each salary range, based on the salaries calculated from your input.

j) *Closing the application.* Close your running application by clicking its close box.

k) *Closing the IDE.* Close the Visual Basic IDE by clicking its close box.

20.12 (*Modified Shipping Hub Application*) Modify the **Shipping Hub** application created in this tutorial, so that the user can double click a package in the packagesListBox. When a package number is double clicked, the package's information should be displayed in a MessageBox (Fig. 20.28).

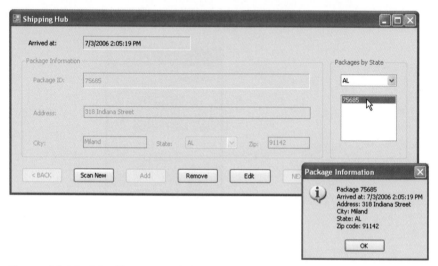

Figure 20.28 Modified **Shipping Hub** application GUI.

a) *Copying the template to your working directory.* Copy the directory C:\Examples\Tutorial20\Exercises\ShippingHubModified to your C:\SimplyVB directory.

b) *Opening the application's template file.* Double click ShippingHubModified.sln in the ShippingHubModified directory to open the application.

c) *Viewing the event handler.* Click **ShippingHub.vb** in the **Solution Explorer** and select **View > Code**. Scroll to the end of the code listing to locate the ListBox's DoubleClick event handler. A ListBox's DoubleClick event is raised when the control is double clicked.

d) *Initializing necessary variables.* To loop through the packages in the ArrayList of Packages, you need to create a reference of type Package. It is also helpful to create a String variable to store the information about the given package. Write code in the DoubleClick event handler to declare the Package tempPackage and the String packageInfo.

e) *Check whether the user has selected a valid item.* To determine whether the user has selected a valid item (and not an empty element in the ListBox), write an If...Then statement to make sure that the ListBox was not empty when the user selected an item. [*Hint:* A SelectedIndex value of -1 means that no item is currently selected.]

f) *Writing a For Each...Next loop.* Use the Package reference you declared in *Step d* to create a For Each...Next loop with the list collection.

g) *Determining whether the current selected package is correct.* Insert an If...Then statement to determine whether the current object that is selected from the list collection matches the selected item from the ListBox. The packages are listed in the ListBox by their package numbers, so use that information in your If...Then statement. Once the correct package is matched, store its information in the packageInfo String.

h) *Inserting the Else statement.* Make sure to notify the user if an invalid item has been selected from the ListBox. If this occurs, add a message to the packageInfo String that will be displayed in the MessageBox.

i) *Displaying the MessageBox.* Call the MessageBox's Show method to display the text you have added to the packageInfo String. This displays either the information for the package selected or a message stating that an invalid package has been selected.

j) *Running the application.* Select **Debug > Start Debugging** to run your application. Add several packages. In the **Packages by State** GroupBox, select a state for which there are packages being sent. Double click one of the packages listed in the **Packages by State** ListBox, and verify that the correct information is displayed in a MessageBox.

k) *Closing the application.* Close your running application by clicking its close box.

l) *Closing the IDE.* Close the Visual Basic IDE by clicking its close box.

20.13 (*Controls Collection Application*) Visual Basic provides many different types of collections. One such collection is the Controls collection, which is used to provide access to all of the controls on a Form. Create an application that uses the Controls collection and a For Each...Next loop to iterate through each control on the Form. As each control is encountered, add its name to a ListBox, and change the control's background color (in Fig. 20.29, Color.Wheat, is used).

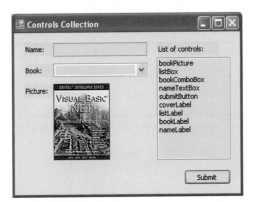

Figure 20.29   Controls Collection GUI.

a) *Copying the template to your working directory.* Copy the directory C:\Examples\ Tutorial20\Exercises\ControlsCollection to your C:\SimplyVB directory.

b) *Opening the application's template file.* Double click ControlsCollection.sln in the ControlsCollection directory to open the application.

c) *Generating an event handler.* Switch to Design view. Double click the **Submit** Button in design view to create an event handler for the click event.

d) *Declaring a control variable.* Declare a reference of type Control. This reference represents each element in the For Each...Next statement as it iterates through each Control on the Form.

e) *Clearing the ListBox.* To ensure that the information in the ListBox is updated each time the **Submit** Button is clicked, clear the ListBox of all items.

f) *Writing a For Each...Next loop.* To create the For Each...Next loop, use the control variable that you created to iterate through the Form's Controls collection.

g) *Adding each control's name to the ListBox.* Use the ListBox's Add method to insert the name of each control on the Form. Recall that a control's Name property contains the name of the control.

h) *Changing the control's background color.* Use the Control's BackColor property to change the control's background color. Set the property to a new color using a member of the Color structure. [*Hint:* Type the word Color followed by the member-access operator to display a list of predefined colors using the *IntelliSense* feature.] Note that the color of the PictureBox does not appear to change because its image displays in the control's foreground.

i) *Running the application.* Select **Debug > Start Debugging** to run your application. Click the **Submit** Button. Verify that the controls' background colors change, and that all the controls are listed in the **List of controls:** ListBox.

j) *Closing the application.* Close your running application by clicking its close box.

k) *Closing the IDE.* Close the Visual Basic IDE by clicking its close box.

What does this code do? ▶   **20.14** What is the result of the following code?

```
1   Dim list As Collections.ArrayList
2   Dim listItems As Integer
3   Dim output As String
4
5   list = New ArrayList
6   list.Add(1)
7   list.Add(3)
8   list.Add(5)
9
10  For Each listItems In list
11      output &= (" " & listItems.ToString)
12  Next
13
14  MessageBox.Show(output, "Mystery", _
15      MessageBoxButtons.OK, MessageBoxIcon.Information)
```

What's wrong with this code? ▶   **20.15** This code should iterate through an array of Packages in list and print each package's number in displayLabel. Find the error(s) in the following code.

```
1   Dim value As Collections.ArrayList
2
3   For Each value In list
4     displayLabel.Text &= (" " & value.PackageNumber)
5   Next
```

Programming Challenge ▶   **20.16** (*Enhanced Shipping Hub Application*) Enhance the **Shipping Hub** application created in Exercise 20.12 to allow the user to move a maximum of five packages from the warehouse to a truck for shipping (Fig. 20.30). If you have not completed Exercise 20.12, follow the steps in Exercise 20.12 before proceeding to the next step. If you have completed Exercise 20.12, copy the code you added to the packagesListBox DoubleClick event handler to the same event handler in this application before beginning the exercise.

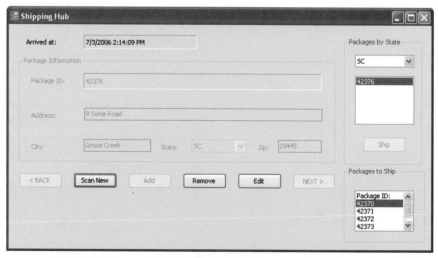

Figure 20.30   Enhanced **Shipping Hub** GUI.

a) *Copying the template to your working directory.* Copy the directory C:\Examples\ Tutorial20\Exercises\ShippingHubEnhanced to your C:\SimplyVB directory.

b) *Opening the application's template file.* Double click ShippingHubEnhanced.sln in the ShippingHubEnhanced directory to open the application.

c) *Enabling the Ship Button.* The **Ship** Button should not be enabled until a package is selected in packageListBox. Double click packageListBox from design view to define the event handler. Use the Button's Enabled property to enable the Button if the SelectedIndex of the ListBox is not -1. This means that when the user selects a package from the ListBox, the user can send it to the truck by clicking the **Ship** Button. Also, insert a line of code after the For Each...Next statement in the viewPackagesCombBox_SelectedIndexChanged event handler to disable the **Ship** Button when a user chooses a different state.

d) *Defining the Ship Button's Click Event.* Double click the **Ship** Button in **Design View** to define the Click event.

e) *Creating temporary variables.* Create two temporary Package references to store the correct package's information. Use tempPackage as the reference to the element in the collection type of a For Each...Next statement, and the truckPackage as a reference to the package added to the truck.

f) *Incrementing the counter.* You are only allowing five packages to be shipped, so declare an instance variable that will track how many packages have been placed onto the truck. Increment the variable each time the **Ship** Button is clicked.

g) *Using the If...Then...Else statement.* Use an If...Then...Else statement to allow packages to be placed onto the truck if the number of packages on the truck is less than five.

h) *Using the For Each...Next loop.* Use a For Each...Next loop to iterate through the values in list. Each iteration should determine whether the current package is the one selected from the ListBox.

i) *Adding the package to the truck.* When the For Each...Next loop has located the correct package, add it to the truck by adding the reference to tempPackage to the truck's ArrayList, truckList. Then assign the value in tempPackage (the package sent to the truck) to truckPackage.

j) *Removing the package.* When the For Each...Next loop completes, remove the package meant for the truck from list and packagesListBox.

k) *Displaying the package in the ListBox.* Use a For Each...Next loop that iterates through each package in the truckList ArrayList and displays each package in truckListBox.

l) *Refreshing the GUI.* Call the ClearControls and SetButtons methods to clear the TextBoxes and enable the appropriate Buttons. Set the **Ship** Button's Enabled property to False.

m) *Coding the Else statement.* Display a MessageBox that notifies the user if the number of packages on the truck is already five. Then disable the **Ship** Button.

n) *Running the application.* Select **Debug > Start Debugging** to run your application. Add several packages. In the **Packages by State** GroupBox, select several packages and add them to the **Packages to Ship** ListBox. Verify that you can add only five packages to this ListBox.

o) *Closing the application.* Close your running application by clicking its close box.

p) *Closing the IDE.* Close the Visual Basic IDE by clicking its close box.

21

TUTORIAL

"Cat and Mouse" Painter Application

Introducing the Graphics Object and Mouse Events

The computer mouse is one of the most important input devices and is essential to the GUIs of Windows applications. With the mouse, the user can point to, click and drag items in applications. Clicking and releasing a mouse button are associated with events, as is moving the mouse. Every time you move the mouse, Windows interprets that event and redraws the mouse pointer as it moves across the screen.

In this tutorial, you create a **Painter** application that handles mouse events. The user clicks the left mouse button over the Form to enable drawing. By moving the mouse pointer over the Form with the left mouse button pressed, the user can create line drawings composed of small circles. You'll learn how to set the shape's color. You'll also learn how to stop drawing when the user releases the mouse button and how to enable the user to erase a drawing by holding down the right mouse button.

21.1 Test-Driving the Painter Application

In this tutorial, you will create a **Painter** application. This application must meet the following requirements:

Application Requirements

The principal of an elementary school wants to introduce computers to children by appealing to their creative side. Many elementary-level applications test skills in mathematics, but the principal wishes to use an application that allows children to express their artistic skills. Develop an application that allows the student to "paint" on a Form, using the mouse. The application should draw when the user moves the mouse with the left mouse button held down and stop drawing when the left mouse button is released. The application draws many small blue-violet circles side by side to trace out lines, curves and shapes. An important part of any drawing application is the ability to erase mistakes or to clear the Form for more drawing room. The user can erase portions of the drawing by moving the mouse with the right mouse button held down.

You begin by test-driving the completed application. Then you will learn the additional Visual Basic technologies that you will need to create your own version of this application.

1. *Opening the completed application.* Open the directory `C:\Examples\Tutorial21\CompletedApplication\Painter` to locate the **Painter** application. Double click `Painter.sln` to open the application in the Visual Basic IDE.

2. *Running the Painter application.* Select **Debug > Start Debugging** to run the application (Fig. 21.1).

Figure 21.1   **Painter** application before drawing.

3. *Drawing with the mouse.* To draw on the Form using the **Painter** application, press and hold down the left mouse button while the mouse pointer is anywhere over the Form (Fig. 21.2). To stop drawing, release the mouse button. Note that the application draws little blue-violet circles as you move the mouse while pressing the left mouse button. The size of these circles will vary depending on your display settings.

Drawing lines composed of small, colored circles

Figure 21.2   Drawing on the **Painter** application's Form.

4. *Being creative.* Draw a cat and a computer mouse, as shown in Fig. 21.3. Be creative and have fun—your drawing need not look like the image shown.

5. *Using the eraser.* Hold down the right mouse button and move the mouse pointer over part of your drawing. This "erases" the drawing wherever the mouse pointer comes into contact with the colored line (Fig. 21.4). When you add code to the application to erase, you will see, that you are actually drawing circles in the Form's background color.

(cont.)

Figure 21.3 Drawing a cat and a computer mouse on the Form.

Erasing by drawing circles that are the same color as the Form's background

Figure 21.4 Erasing part of the drawing.

6. ***Closing the application.*** Close your running application by clicking its close box.

7. ***Closing the IDE.*** Close the Visual Basic IDE by clicking its close box.

21.2 Constructing the Painter Application

Before you begin building the **Painter** application, you should review the application's functionality. The following pseudocode describes the basic operation of the **Painter** application and what happens when the user moves the mouse pointer over the application's Form:

When a mouse button is pressed:

    If the left mouse button is pressed
        Enable user to draw
    Else if the right mouse button is pressed
        Enable the user to erase

When a mouse button is released:
    Disable the user from drawing
    Disable the user from erasing

When the mouse is moved:

    If the user is allowed to paint
        Draw a blue-violet circle at the position of the mouse pointer
    Else If the user is allowed to erase
        "Erase" by drawing a circle at the position of the mouse pointer in the
        Form's background color

Now that you have test-driven the **Painter** application and studied its pseudocode representation, you will use an ACE table to help you convert the pseudocode to Visual Basic. Figure 21.5 lists the actions, controls and events that will help you complete your own version of this application.

Action/Control/Event (ACE) Table for the Painter Application

Action	Control/Object/Class	Event
	PainterForm	MouseDown
If the left mouse button is pressed	MouseEventArgs	
Enable user to draw		
Else if the right mouse button is pressed	MouseEventArgs	
Enable the user to erase		
	PainterForm	MouseUp
Disable the user from drawing		
Disable the user from erasing		
	PainterForm	MouseMove

If the user is allowed to paint
  Draw blue-violet circle at position
  of mouse pointer
	graphicsObject	

Else If the user is allowed to erase
  "Erase" by drawing a circle at the
  position of the mouse in the Form's
  background color
	graphicsObject	

Figure 21.5 **Painter** application's ACE table.

This tutorial starts by showing you how to use two mouse events—the event that occurs when you press a mouse button and the event that occurs when you release that mouse button. At first, your **Painter** application will draw a circle when the user presses or releases any mouse button. Next, you will modify the application so that it draws when the user moves the mouse with a button pressed. If the user moves the mouse without pressing a mouse button, nothing will be drawn.

To complete the **Painter** application, you'll add the eraser capability, which requires you to determine which mouse button the user presses. The last section of the tutorial will show you how to assign the drawing capability to the left mouse button and the eraser capability to the right mouse button.

21.3 Using a Graphics Object

Now that you have seen the pseudocode and the ACE table, you are ready to begin building the **Painter** application. You will use a **Graphics** object to enable the user to draw on the Form. Class Graphics contains methods used for drawing text, lines, rectangles and other shapes. The following box shows you how to create the **Painter** application's Graphics object.

Creating a Graphics Object

1. ***Copying the template to your working directory.*** Copy the C:\Examples\ Tutorial21\TemplateApplication\Painter directory to your C:\SimplyVB directory.

2. ***Opening the Painter application's template file.*** Double click Painter.sln in the Painter directory to open the application in the Visual Basic IDE. Open Painter.vb in code view.

(cont.)

3. ***Creating a Graphics object.*** Add lines 6–7 of Fig. 21.6 into the **Painter** application. Line 7 declares **Graphics** variable **graphicsObject**. The **CreateGraphics** method (which is a member of class **Form**) creates a **Graphics** object with which you will draw shapes on the **Form**. You are writing code in the **Form's** class (**PainterForm**), so you do not need to use the member-access operator (**.**) to access the **Form's** **CreateGraphics** method. Note that the template already contains a declaration of constant DIAMETER (line 4). We will discuss this constant shortly.

Creating a **Graphics** object ———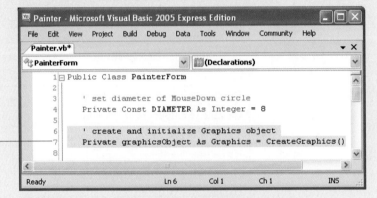

Figure 21.6 Declaring a **Graphics** reference.

4. ***Saving the project.*** Select **File > Save All** to save your modified code.

SELF-REVIEW

1. To draw on a Form, use an object of class _____.

    a) Graphics

    b) Drawing

    c) Paint

    d) Sketch

2. The _____ method of class **Form** creates a **Graphics** object.

    a) GetGraphics

    b) MakeGraphics

    c) CreateGraphics

    d) InitializeGraphics

Answers: 1) a. 2) c.

21.4 Handling the MouseDown Event

This section begins our discussion of handling **mouse events**, which occur when the user interacts with the **Form** or controls on the **Form** using the mouse. In the **Painter** application, the user interacts exclusively with the **Form**. (There are no controls on the **Form**.)

A Form's **MouseDown** event occurs when a mouse button is pressed while the mouse pointer is over the **Form**. You will learn how to add a MouseDown event handler to your application in the following box. When you run your application after following the steps in this box, you'll be able to press any mouse button to draw a circle on the **Form**. When you add the eraser capability to the **Painter** application in Section 21.7, you'll learn how to determine which mouse button was pressed.

Handling the MouseDown Event

1. ***Generating the MouseDown event handler.*** To generate the MouseDown event handler, select **(PainterForm Events)** from the **Class Name** ComboBox (Fig. 21.7) in the code view. Then select MouseDown from the **Method Name** ComboBox.

(cont.)

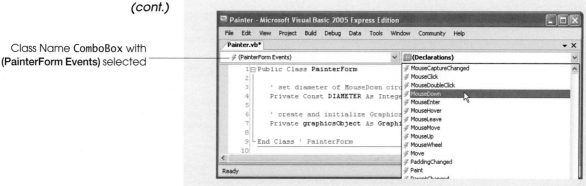

Class Name **ComboBox** with
(PainterForm Events) selected

Figure 21.7 Creating a **MouseDown** event handler.

This generates the event handler **PainterForm_MouseDown** (Fig. 21.8). As always, you should add a comment and format your code to improve readability (lines 9–14). The application invokes **PainterForm_MouseDown** when the user generates the Form's **MouseDown** event by pressing a mouse button when the mouse pointer is over **PainterForm**.

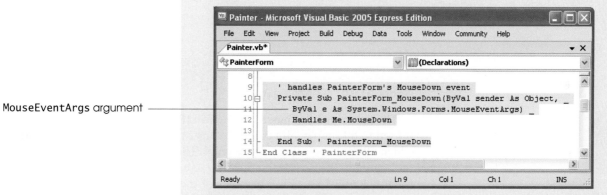

MouseEventArgs argument

Figure 21.8 **MouseDown** event handler generated for **PainterForm**.

The second argument passed to event handler **Painter-Form_MouseDown** is a variable of type **MouseEventArgs** (line 11). This **MouseEventArgs** object (referenced by **e**) contains information about the **MouseDown** event, including the coordinates of the mouse pointer when the mouse button is pressed on the Form.

Note that the *x*- and *y*-coordinates of the **MouseEventArgs** object are relative to the top-left corner of the Form or control that raises the event. Point *(0,0)* represents the upper-left corner of the Form. If you wish to access the *x*-coordinate of the mouse, use property **X** of reference **e**. To access the *y*-coordinate of the mouse, use property **Y** of reference **e**.

2. ***Drawing on the Form whenever a mouse button is clicked.*** Add lines 14–16 of Fig. 21.9 to the **MouseDown** event handler and remove the blank line at line 17. The **FillEllipse** method of class **Graphics** draws an ellipse on the Form. Recall that you declared **graphicsObject** and assigned it a **Graphics** object earlier in this tutorial. Figure 21.10 shows a diagram of a general ellipse. The dotted rectangle—known as the ellipse's **bounding box**—specifies an ellipse's height, width and location on the Form.

(cont.)

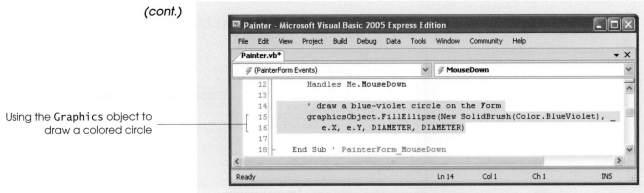

Figure 21.9 Adding code to the **MouseDown** event handler.

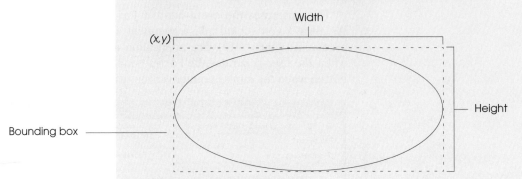

Figure 21.10 General ellipse.

The first argument passed to the **FillEllipse** method is a **brush**, which is used to fill shapes with colors. In this case, we specify a new **SolidBrush**, which fills a shape using a single color. The color of the brush is specified as the argument passed to the **SolidBrush** constructor. The color you select (**Color.BlueViolet**) is a member of the **Color** structure. For a complete list of predefined colors in Visual Basic, simply type the word **Color** followed by a dot, and the *IntelliSense* feature will provide a drop-down list of over 100 predefined colors (Fig. 21.11).

The second and third arguments to the **FillEllipse** method specify the *x*- and *y*-coordinates of the upper-left corner of the bounding box, relative to the upper-left corner of the **Form**. In this application, you use the *x*- and *y*- coordinates of the mouse (returned by properties X and Y of **Mouse-EventArgs** reference e). The fourth and fifth arguments passed to the **FillEllipse** method (constant DIAMETER) specify the height and width of the bounding box. An ellipse with equal width and height is a circle—this method call draws a blue-violet circle.

The **Graphics** object provides methods for drawing shapes other than ellipses. You will learn about these methods in Tutorial 26. Note that the *x*- and *y*-coordinates the **Graphics** object uses to draw a shape are relative to the control or **Form** that created it. In this case, the **Graphics** object draws shapes at positions relative to the **Form**.

3. ***Running the application.*** Select **Debug > Start Debugging** to run your application. Notice that a small blue-violet circle is drawn when a mouse button is pressed while the mouse pointer is over the **Form** (Fig. 21.12).

4. ***Closing the application.*** Close your running application by clicking its close box.

(cont.)

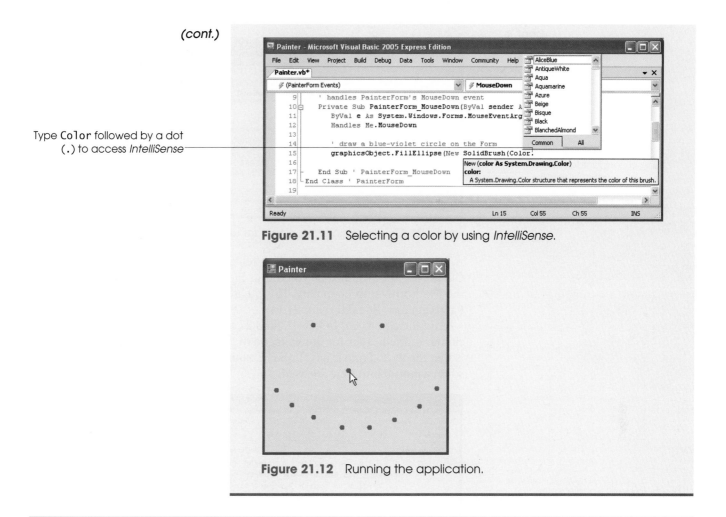

Figure 21.11　Selecting a color by using *IntelliSense*.

Type **Color** followed by a dot (.) to access *IntelliSense*

Figure 21.12　Running the application.

---

1. To draw a solid shape, the `FillEllipse` method uses a _____.

    a) `Pencil` object　　　　　　　　　b) `Marker` object
    c) `PaintBrush` object　　　　　　　d) `SolidBrush` object

2. `BlueViolet` is a member of the _____ structure.

    a) `SolidColor`　　　　　　　　　　b) `FillColor`
    c) `Color`　　　　　　　　　　　　d) `SystemColor`

Answers: 1) d. 2) c.

21.5 Handling the MouseUp Event

Using the application, you can click anywhere on the Form and place a blue-violet circle. To enhance the application further, you will place a green circle on the Form when the user releases the mouse button. A Form's **MouseUp** event occurs when the user releases a mouse button after previously pressing it while the mouse pointer was over the Form. You will add this functionality in the following box.

Handling the MouseUp Event

1. ***Adding a second diameter.*** Add lines 6–7 of Fig. 21.13 to your application (above the initialization of the `Graphics` reference and below the initialization of constant `DIAMETER`). These lines declare a second constant that stores the diameter of a smaller circle. A circle with this diameter (in pixels) will be drawn whenever the user releases a mouse button.

(cont.)

Using a constant to store a circle's diameter

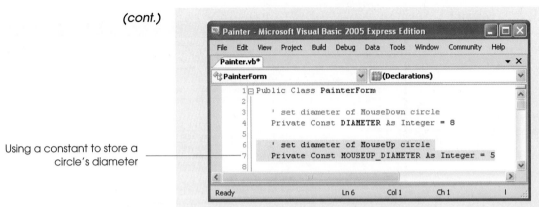

Figure 21.13 Declaring a constant for use in the `MouseUp` event handler.

2. *Adding the MouseUp event handler.* Select **(PainterForm Events)** from the **Class Name** ComboBox, as you did in Fig. 21.7. Then select `MouseUp` from the **Method Name** ComboBox. This creates an empty event handler called `PainterForm_MouseUp` (Fig. 21.14).

Add the comments in lines 22 and 27 to your application. This header is similar to the header for the `MouseDown` event handler (the only difference is that the word `Down` is now `Up`). The `MouseUp` event handler executes only when a mouse button is released.

`MouseUp` event handler after commenting and formatting

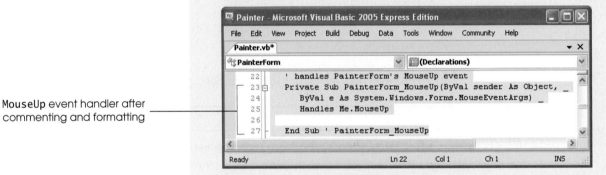

Figure 21.14 `MouseUp` empty event handler.

3. *Drawing a circle when the user releases a mouse button.* Add lines 27–28 of Fig. 21.15 to the `MouseUp` event handler to draw a circle at the position of the mouse pointer on the `Form` whenever the user releases the mouse button. The diameter of each "mouse up" circle is smaller than the diameter of the `BlueViolet` circles drawn by the `MouseDown` event handler that is called when a mouse button is pressed.

Drawing a green circle with half the diameter of the blue-violet circle

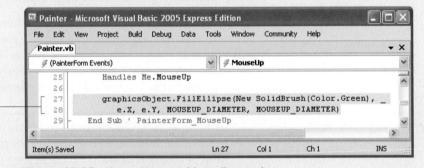

Figure 21.15 `MouseUp` event handler code.

(cont.)   4. ***Running the application.*** Select **Debug > Start Debugging** to run your application (Fig. 21.16). Press and hold a mouse button, move the mouse pointer to a new location and release the button. Note that a BlueViolet circle is drawn when you press any mouse button and that a Green circle is drawn when you release the mouse button.

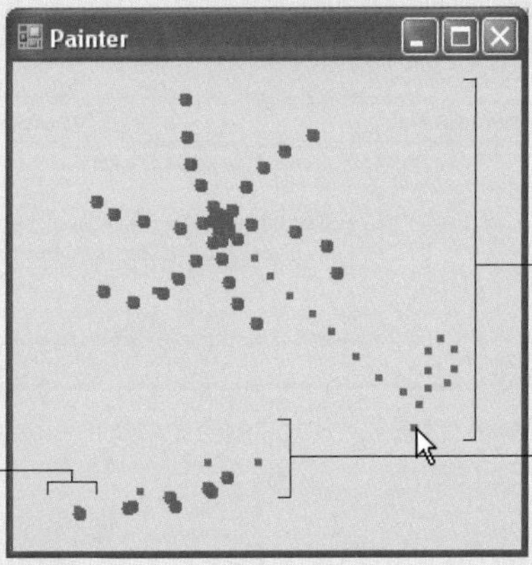

Pressing the mouse button and releasing it without moving the mouse pointer

Drawing a flower using only MouseUp and MouseDown event handlers

Pressing mouse button, then releasing it after moving pointer

Figure 21.16 Running the application.

5. ***Closing the application.*** Close your running application by clicking its close box.

SELF-REVIEW 1. Releasing a mouse button generates a _____ event.

a) MouseRelease   b) MouseUp

c) MouseOff   d) MouseClick

2. The second and third arguments of the FillEllipse method specify the *x*- and *y*-coordinates of the _____.

a) ellipse's center   b) bounding box's lower-left corner

c) bounding box's upper-right corner d) bounding box's upper-left corner

Answers: 1) b. 2) d.

21.6 Handling the MouseMove Event

Currently, the application allows you to draw only isolated circles when a mouse button is pressed or released. It does not yet allow you to draw more sophisticated shapes and designs. Next, you will enhance your application to provide more drawing capabilities. The application will be able to continuously draw BlueViolet circles as long as the mouse is being dragged (that is, moved with a button pressed). If the mouse button is not pressed, moving the mouse across the Form will not draw anything. To add this functionality, you will begin by modifying your two event handlers.

Modifying the *Painter*
Application

1. ***Adding a Boolean variable to specify whether a mouse button is pressed.*** Delete the constant MOUSEUP_DIAMETER (lines 6–7 of Fig. 21.13) and add lines 3–4 of Fig. 21.17 to your application (above the initialization of DIAMETER). Line 4 declares and initializes the Boolean variable shouldPaint. The application must be able to determine whether a mouse button is pressed, because the application is to draw on the Form only when a mouse button is held down.

(cont.)

You will alter the `MouseDown` and `MouseUp` event handlers so that `shouldPaint` is `True` when any mouse button is held down and `False` when the mouse button is released. When the application is first loaded, it should not "paint" anything, so this instance variable is initialized to `False`.

Declaring and setting an instance variable to control painting

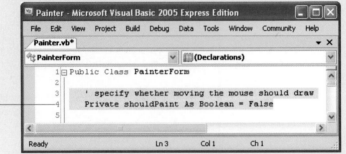

Figure 21.17   `Boolean` instance variable `shouldPaint` is declared and set to `False`.

2. *Altering the MouseDown event handler.* Remove the code inside the Mouse-Down event handler, leaving just the procedure header and the `End Sub` statement. Add line 20 of Fig. 21.18 to the `MouseDown` event handler to set `shouldPaint` to `True`. This indicates that a mouse button has been pressed.

Allow drawing when mouse button is pressed

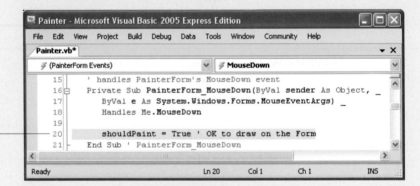

Figure 21.18   Setting `shouldPaint` to `True`.

3. *Altering the MouseUp event handler.* Remove the code inside the `MouseUp` event handler, leaving just the procedure header and the `End Sub` statement. Add line 30 of Fig. 21.19 to set `shouldPaint` to `False`. This indicates that a mouse button has been released.

Disable drawing when mouse button is released

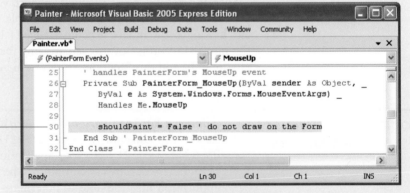

Figure 21.19   Setting `shouldPaint` to `False`.

4. *Saving the project.* Select **File > Save All** to save your modified code.

You have altered the event handlers to set the value of the shouldPaint variable to indicate whether a mouse button is pressed. Next, you will handle the **MouseMove** event, which is raised whenever the mouse moves. Whenever you move the mouse over the **Painter** application's Form, the application invokes the Mouse-Move event handler. You define the MouseMove event handler in the following box.

Adding the MouseMove Event Handler

1. *Adding the MouseMove event handler.* Select **(PainterForm Events)** from the **Class Name** ComboBox as in Fig. 21.7. Then select MouseMove from the **Method Name** ComboBox to generate the empty MouseMove event handler PainterForm_MouseMove (Fig. 21.20). Add comments to lines 23 and 28.

MouseMove event handler after commenting and formatting

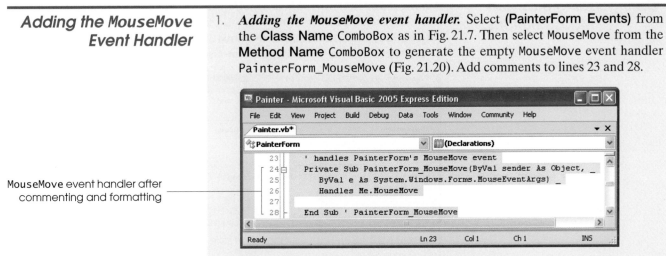

Figure 21.20 MouseMove empty event handler.

2. *Adding code to the MouseMove event handler.* Add lines 28–32 of Fig. 21.21 to the MouseMove event handler, which executes each time the user moves the mouse. The If...Then statement tests the value of shouldPaint. If it's True (a mouse button is pressed), the FillEllipse method draws a Blue-Violet circle on the Form. If it's False (no mouse button is pressed), then nothing is drawn.

Drawing a circle when the mouse moves and a mouse button is pressed

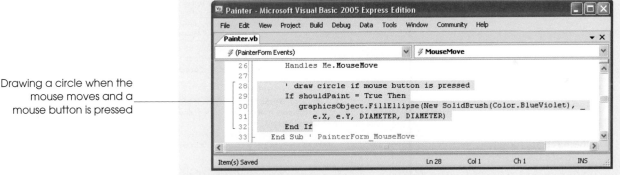

Figure 21.21 MouseMove event handler draws circles on the Form if a mouse button is held down.

3. *Running the application.* Select **Debug > Start Debugging** to run your application. Try drawing various shapes and designs on the Form. Note that you can draw using any mouse button.

4. *Closing the application.* Close your running application by clicking its close box.

21.7 Distinguishing Between Mouse Buttons

Now that your application allows the user to draw using the mouse, you are going to add the code that allows the user to "erase" by moving the mouse over the drawing with the right mouse button pressed. You also will alter the application so that the user can draw by moving the mouse with only the left mouse button pressed. To do this, you'll need to determine which mouse button has been pressed. You learn how to do this in the following box.

Distinguishing Between Mouse Buttons

1. ***Adding a Boolean variable to specify whether the application should erase while the mouse pointer is moving.*** Add lines 3–4 of Fig. 21.22 to your application (above the initialization of shouldPaint). Instance variable should-Erase specifies whether moving the mouse pointer should act like an eraser.

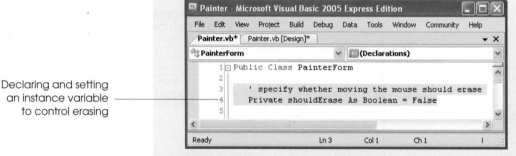

Declaring and setting an instance variable to control erasing

Figure 21.22 Boolean instance variable shouldErase is declared and set to False.

2. ***Determining which mouse button was pressed.*** Replace the code in event handler PainterForm_MouseDown with lines 20–26 of Fig. 21.23. The **Button** property of the MouseEventArgs object (referenced by e) specifies which mouse button has been pressed. The **MouseButtons enumeration** defines constants that represent the mouse buttons.

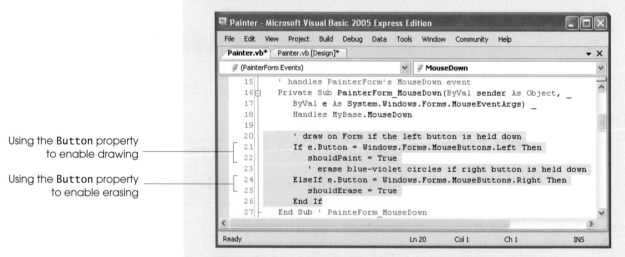

Using the **Button** property to enable drawing

Using the **Button** property to enable erasing

Figure 21.23 Determining which mouse button was pressed.

The two most common mouse buttons—**Right** and **Left**—are included in MouseButtons. If the left mouse button is pressed (line 21), line 22 sets shouldPaint to True to indicate that dragging the mouse will draw. If the right mouse button is pressed (line 24), line 25 sets shouldErase to True to indicate that dragging the mouse will erase any blue-violet circles touched by the mouse pointer. Note that only one of the variables can be True at a time. For example, if shouldPaint is True, then shouldErase is False. To ensure this, both variables are set to False when the mouse button is released. (See *Step 3*.)

(cont.)

3. **Changing the MouseUp event handler.** Add line 35 of Fig. 21.24 to the PainterForm_MouseUp event handler. The application should not erase or draw when no mouse buttons are pressed. Line 35 sets shouldErase to False to indicate that the mouse pointer will not act as an eraser. Note that shouldPaint is also set to False (line 34).

Disabling erasing when a mouse button is released

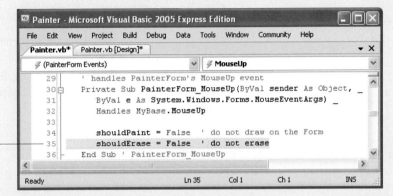

```
29      ' handles PainterForm's MouseUp event
30      Private Sub PainterForm_MouseUp(ByVal sender As Object, _
31          ByVal e As System.Windows.Forms.MouseEventArgs) _
32          Handles MyBase.MouseUp
33
34          shouldPaint = False   ' do not draw on the Form
35          shouldErase = False   ' do not erase
36      End Sub ' PainterForm_MouseUp
```

Figure 21.24   Setting shouldErase to False when a mouse button is released.

4. **Drawing when the left mouse button is pressed.** Replace the code in event handler PainterForm_MouseMove with lines 43–51 of Fig. 21.25. If should-Paint is True (line 44), lines 45–46 draw a BlueViolet circle. Your changes to the MouseDown event handler make shouldPaint True when the left mouse button is pressed. As a result, the application draws BlueViolet circles only when the user drags the mouse while pressing the left mouse button.

Drawing circles if left mouse button is pressed while the mouse moves

Erasing by drawing circles with the Form's background color

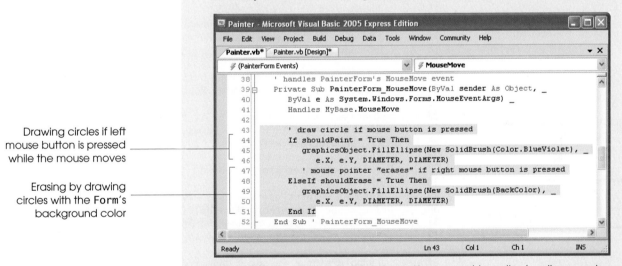

```
38      ' handles PainterForm's MouseMove event
39      Private Sub PainterForm_MouseMove(ByVal sender As Object, _
40          ByVal e As System.Windows.Forms.MouseEventArgs) _
41          Handles MyBase.MouseMove
42
43          ' draw circle if mouse button is pressed
44          If shouldPaint = True Then
45              graphicsObject.FillEllipse(New SolidBrush(Color.BlueViolet), _
46                  e.X, e.Y, DIAMETER, DIAMETER)
47          ' mouse pointer "erases" if right mouse button is pressed
48          ElseIf shouldErase = True Then
49              graphicsObject.FillEllipse(New SolidBrush(BackColor), _
50                  e.X, e.Y, DIAMETER, DIAMETER)
51          End If
52      End Sub ' PainterForm_MouseMove
```

Figure 21.25   Changing the MouseMove event handler to allow erasing.

5. **Erasing when the right mouse button is pressed.** The MouseMove event handler does not actually erase anything. Instead, when shouldErase is True (line 48 of Fig. 21.25), the FillEllipse method (lines 49–50) draws a circle that is the same size as the BlueViolet circle and has the same color as the Form's background. This allows the mouse pointer to act like an eraser. Note that the first argument to FillEllipse is BackColor. Much like the Create-Graphics method, the BackColor property of the Form can be accessed without the member-access operator because it's a property of the same class that is using the property. The **BackColor** property returns the Form's background color as a Color value.

(cont.)

6. *Running the application*. Select **Debug > Start Debugging** to run your application. Try drawing various shapes and designs on the Form, then try to erase them.

7. *Closing the application*. Close your running application by clicking its close box.

8. *Closing the IDE*. Close the Visual Basic IDE by clicking its close box.

Figure 21.26 presents the source code for the **Painter** application. The lines of code that contain new programming concepts that you learned in this tutorial are highlighted.

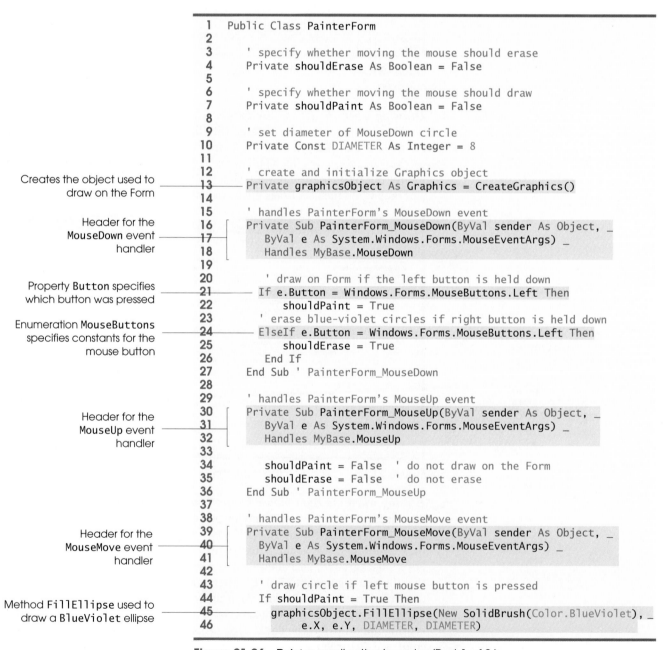

```
 1   Public Class PainterForm
 2
 3       ' specify whether moving the mouse should erase
 4       Private shouldErase As Boolean = False
 5
 6       ' specify whether moving the mouse should draw
 7       Private shouldPaint As Boolean = False
 8
 9       ' set diameter of MouseDown circle
10       Private Const DIAMETER As Integer = 8
11
12       ' create and initialize Graphics object
13       Private graphicsObject As Graphics = CreateGraphics()
14
15       ' handles PainterForm's MouseDown event
16       Private Sub PainterForm_MouseDown(ByVal sender As Object, _
17          ByVal e As System.Windows.Forms.MouseEventArgs) _
18          Handles MyBase.MouseDown
19
20          ' draw on Form if the left button is held down
21          If e.Button = Windows.Forms.MouseButtons.Left Then
22             shouldPaint = True
23          ' erase blue-violet circles if right button is held down
24          ElseIf e.Button = Windows.Forms.MouseButtons.Left Then
25             shouldErase = True
26          End If
27       End Sub ' PainterForm_MouseDown
28
29       ' handles PainterForm's MouseUp event
30       Private Sub PainterForm_MouseUp(ByVal sender As Object, _
31          ByVal e As System.Windows.Forms.MouseEventArgs) _
32          Handles MyBase.MouseUp
33
34          shouldPaint = False   ' do not draw on the Form
35          shouldErase = False   ' do not erase
36       End Sub ' PainterForm_MouseUp
37
38       ' handles PainterForm's MouseMove event
39       Private Sub PainterForm_MouseMove(ByVal sender As Object, _
40          ByVal e As System.Windows.Forms.MouseEventArgs) _
41          Handles MyBase.MouseMove
42
43          ' draw circle if left mouse button is pressed
44          If shouldPaint = True Then
45             graphicsObject.FillEllipse(New SolidBrush(Color.BlueViolet), _
46                e.X, e.Y, DIAMETER, DIAMETER)
```

Creates the object used to draw on the Form — line 13

Header for the MouseDown event handler — lines 16–18

Property **Button** specifies which button was pressed — line 21

Enumeration **MouseButtons** specifies constants for the mouse button — line 24

Header for the MouseUp event handler — lines 30–32

Header for the MouseMove event handler — lines 39–41

Method **FillEllipse** used to draw a **BlueViolet** ellipse — lines 45

Figure 21.26 **Painter** application's code. (Part 1 of 2.)

Create a **Brush** with the
Form's background color

```
47            ' mouse pointer "erases" if right mouse button is pressed
48            ElseIf shouldErase = True Then
49               graphicsObject.FillEllipse(New SolidBrush(BackColor),
50                  e.X, e.Y, DIAMETER, DIAMETER)
51            End If
52         End Sub ' PainterForm_MouseMove
53      End Class ' PainterForm
```

Figure 21.26   Painter application's code. (Part 2 of 2.)

SELF-REVIEW   1. Moving the mouse pointer generates a _____ event.

    a) `MouseMove`   b) `MousePositionChanged`

    c) `MouseMoved`   d) `MouseChanged`

2. The _____ enumeration specifies constants for the mouse buttons.

    a) `MouseButtons`   b) `Buttons`

    c) `MouseOptions`   d) `ButtonOptions`

Answers: 1) a. 2) a.

21.8 Wrap-Up

In this tutorial, you learned the essentials of mouse-event handling. You handled three common mouse events—`MouseMove`, `MouseUp` and `MouseDown`—and how to create mouse event handlers associated with a `Form`. You generated these event handlers by selecting the appropriate mouse event from the **Method Name** ComboBox after selecting **(PainterForm Events)** from the **Class Name** ComboBox.

You used a `Graphics` object in the **Painter** application. You invoked the Form's `CreateGraphics` method to create a `Graphics` object. You used the `Graphics` method `FillEllipse` to draw a solid circle on the `Form`. You learned how to use a `SolidBrush` object to draw a shape in a solid color specified by one of the predefined colors in the `Color` structure.

The **Painter** application uses mouse events to determine what the user wants to do. The user moves the mouse with the left mouse button held down to draw on the `Form`. Moving the mouse across the `Form` without pressing a button does not draw anything on the `Form`. You learned to distinguish which mouse button was pressed. You used this to provide the **Painter** application with an eraser. When users move the mouse with the right mouse button pressed, the **Painter** application draws circles with the Form's background color.

To build the **Painter** application, you used `MouseEventArgs` objects, which are passed to mouse event handlers and provide information about mouse events. Properties `X` and `Y` of the `MouseEventArgs` object specify the *x*- and *y*-coordinates where the mouse event occurred. The `Button` property specifies which (if any) mouse button was pressed. You used constants defined by the `MouseButtons` enumeration to determine which button the `Button` property specified.

In the next tutorial, you'll learn how to use event handlers that respond to user interactions with the keyboard, then build an application that uses keyboard events. The application will also teach you how to create menus and dialogs.

SKILLS SUMMARY   Raising Events with a Mouse

■ Pressing a mouse's buttons and moving the mouse raise events.

Handling Mouse Events

■ The `MouseEventArgs` class contains information about mouse events, such as the *x*- and *y*-coordinates where the mouse event occurred. Each mouse-event handler receives an object of class `MouseEventArgs` as an argument.

- Moving the mouse raises event MouseMove.
- Pressing a mouse button raises event MouseDown.
- Releasing a mouse button raises event MouseUp.

Distinguishing Between Mouse Buttons

- The Button property of MouseEventArgs specifies which mouse button was pressed.
- The MouseButtons enumeration specifies the constants Left and Right for mouse buttons. These are used to determine which button was pressed.

Creating an Event Handler for a Mouse Event Associated with a Form

- Select (*FormName* Events) from the Class Name ComboBox, where *FormName* is the name of the application's Form. Then select the appropriate event from the Method Name ComboBox.

Drawing on a Form

- Graphics methods are used to draw shapes on a Form or a control.
- Create a Graphics object (by invoking the Form's CreateGraphics method) to access methods for drawing shapes on the Form.

Drawing a Solid Ellipse

- Use the Graphics method FillEllipse to draw a solid ellipse.
- Pass a SolidBrush object to the FillEllipse method to specify the shape's color.
- Specify the color, the coordinates of the bounding box's upper-left corner and the width and height of the bounding box. When the width and height of the bounding box are equal, a circle is drawn.

KEY TERMS

BackColor property of class Form—Returns the Color value used as the background color of the Form.

bounding box of an ellipse—Specifies an ellipse's location, width and height.

brush—Used to fill shapes with colors.

Button property of class MouseEventArgs—Specifies which (if any) mouse button is pressed.

CreateGraphics method—Creates a Graphics object on a Form or control.

FillEllipse method of class Graphics—The method of the Graphics class that draws an ellipse. This method takes as arguments a brush, a Color, the coordinates of the upper-left corner of the ellipse's bounding box and the width and height of the bounding box. If the width and height are the same, a circle is drawn.

Graphics class—Provides methods for drawing shapes.

Left value of MouseButtons enumeration—Used to represent the left mouse button.

mouse event—Generated when a user interacts with an application using the computer's mouse.

MouseButtons enumeration—Defines constants, such as Left and Right, to specify mouse buttons.

MouseDown event—Generated when a mouse button is pressed.

MouseEventArgs class—Specifies information about a mouse event.

MouseMove event—Generated when a mouse pointer is moved.

MouseUp event—Generated when the mouse button is released.

Right value of MouseButtons enumeration—Used to represent the right mouse button.

SolidBrush class—Defines a brush that draws with a single color.

X property of class MouseEventArgs—The property of class MouseEventArgs that specifies the *x*-coordinate of the mouse event.

Y property of class MouseEventArgs—The property of class MouseEventArgs that specifies the *y*-coordinate of the mouse event.

CONTROLS, EVENTS, PROPERTIES & METHODS

Form The class that represents an application's GUI.

- *Events*

  Load—Raised when an application initially executes.

  MouseDown—Raised when a mouse button is clicked.

  MouseMove—Raised when the mouse pointer is moved.

  MouseUp—Raised when a mouse button is released.

- *Property*

  BackColor—Specifies the background color of the Form.

- *Method*

  CreateGraphics—Creates a Graphics object.

Graphics The class that contains methods used to draw text, lines and shapes.

- *Method*

  FillEllipse—Draws a solid ellipse of a specified size and color at the specified location. If the width and height specified are the same, a circle will be drawn.

MouseEventArgs The class that contains information about mouse events.

- *Properties*

  Buttons—Specifies which (if any) mouse button was pressed.

  X—Specifies the *x*-coordinate of the mouse event.

  Y—Specifies the *y*-coordinate of the mouse event.

MULTIPLE-CHOICE QUESTIONS

21.1 The *x*- and *y*-coordinates of the MouseEventArgs object are relative to _____.

a) the screen

b) the application

c) the Form or control that contains the control that raised the event

d) None of the above.

21.2 The _____ method of the Graphics class draws a solid ellipse.

a) FillEllipse

b) Ellipse

c) SolidEllipse

d) FilledEllipse

21.3 The _____ object passed to a mouse event handler contains information about the mouse event that was raised.

a) EventHandler

b) MouseEventHandler

c) MouseEventArgs

d) EventArgs

21.4 The _____ event is raised when a mouse button is pressed.

a) MousePress

b) MouseClick

c) MouseDown

d) MouseButtonDown

21.5 A _____ is used to fill a shape with color using a Graphics object.

a) painter

b) brush

c) paint bucket

d) marker

21.6 A _____ event is raised every time the mouse interacts with a control.

a) control

b) mouse pointer

c) mouse

d) user

21.7 The _____ property of MouseEventArgs specifies which mouse button was pressed.

a) Source

b) Button

c) WhichButton

d) ButtonPressed

21.8 The _____ class contains methods for drawing text, lines, rectangles and other shapes.

a) `Pictures`
b) `Drawings`
c) `Graphics`
d) `Illustrations`

21.9 An ellipse with its _____ is a circle.

a) height twice the length of its width
b) width set to zero
c) height half the length of its width
d) height equal to its width

21.10 The _____ method creates a `Graphics` object.

a) `NewGraphics`
b) `CreateGraphics`
c) `PaintGraphics`
d) `InitializeGraphics`

EXERCISES

21.11 _(Line Length Application)_ The **Line Length** application will draw a straight black line on the Form and calculate the length of the line (Fig. 21.27). The line begins at the coordinates where the mouse button is pressed and stops at the point where the mouse button is released. The application displays the line's length (that is, the distance between the two endpoints) in the Label **Length =**. Use the following formula to calculate the line's length, where (x_1, y_1) is the first endpoint (the coordinates where the mouse button is pressed) and (x_2, y_2) is the second endpoint (the coordinates where the mouse button is released). To calculate the distance (or length) between the two points, use the following equation:

$$d = \sqrt{(x_1 - x_2)^2 + (y_1 - y_2)^2}$$

To draw a straight line, you need to use the **DrawLine** method on a `Graphics` object. When drawing lines, use a **Pen** object, which is an object used to specify characteristics of lines and curves. Use the following method call to draw a black line between the two points using a `Graphics` object reference `graphicsObject`:

```
graphicsObject.DrawLine(New Pen(Color.Black), x₁, y₁, x₂, y₂)
```

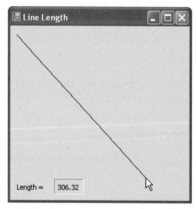

Figure 21.27 **Line Length** application's GUI.

a) _Copying the template to your working directory._ Copy the directory `C:\Examples\Tutorial21\Exercises\LineLength` to your `C:\SimplyVB` directory.

b) _Opening the application's template file._ Double click `LineLength.sln` in the Line-Length directory to open the application.

c) _Declaring instance variables._ Declare and initialize a reference to a `Graphics` object that you will use to draw a line. Then declare four `Integer`s in which you will store the _x-_ and _y-_coordinates of the two points.

d) _Adding a MouseDown event handler._ Create a `MouseDown` event handler. Add code to the `MouseDown` event handler to store the coordinates of the first endpoint of the line.

e) _Creating the Distance method._ Define a `Function` procedure named `Length` that returns the distance between two endpoints as a `Double`. The `Function` procedure should use the following statement to perform the line length calculation, where xDistance is the difference between the *x*-coordinates of the two points and yDistance is the difference between the *y*-coordinates of the two points:

```
Math.Sqrt((xDistance ^ 2) + (yDistance ^ 2))
```

f) *Adding a MouseUp event handler.* Create a MouseUp event handler. First store the coordinates of the line's second endpoint. Then call the Length method to obtain the distance between the two endpoints (the line's length). Finally, display the line on the Form and the line's length in the **Length =** Label, as in Fig. 21.27.

g) *Running the application.* Select **Debug > Start Debugging** to run your application. Draw several lines and view their lengths. Verify that the length values are accurate.

h) *Closing the application.* Close your running application by clicking its close box.

i) *Closing the IDE.* Close the Visual Basic IDE by clicking its close box.

21.12 *(Circle Painter Application)* The **Circle Painter** application will draw a blue circle of a randomly chosen size when the user presses a mouse button anywhere over the Form (Fig. 21.28). The application will randomly select a circle diameter in the range from 5 to 199, inclusive. To draw a blue circle with a given diameter (diameter), use the following statement:

```
graphicsObject.DrawEllipse(New Pen(Color.Blue), e.X, e.Y, _
    diameter, diameter)
```

The **DrawEllipse** method, when passed a Pen (instead of a brush) as an argument, draws the outline of an ellipse. Recall that an ellipse is a circle if the height and width arguments are the same (in this case, the randomly selected diameter). Use the *x*- and *y*-coordinates of the MouseDown event as the *x*- and *y*-coordinates of the circle's bounding box (that is, the second and third arguments to the DrawEllipse method). Note that the first argument to the DrawEllipse method is a Pen object. See Exercise 21.11 for a description of Pen.

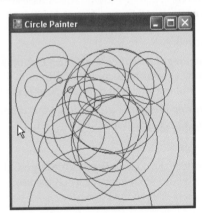

Figure 21.28 **Circle Painter** application's GUI.

a) *Copying the template to your working directory.* Copy the directory C:\Examples\Tutorial21\Exercises\CirclePainter to your C:\SimplyVB directory.

b) *Opening the application's template file.* Double click CirclePainter.sln in the CirclePainter directory to open the application.

c) *Adding a MouseDown event handler.* Create a MouseDown event handler. In the event handler, retrieve the *x*- and *y*-coordinates of the location of the mouse pointer when a mouse button was pressed. Then generate a random number to use as the circle's diameter, using a Random object, and store it in a variable. Finally, call the DrawEllipse method on a reference to a Graphics object to draw a blue circle on the Form with the diameter generated by the Random object.

d) *Running the application.* Select **Debug > Start Debugging** to run your application. Draw several blue circles and make sure that they are of different sizes.

e) *Closing the application.* Close your running application by clicking its close box.

f) *Closing the IDE.* Close the Visual Basic IDE by clicking its close box.

21.13 *(Advanced Circle Painter Application)* In this exercise, you will enhance the application you created in Exercise 21.12. The advanced **Circle Painter** application will draw blue circles with randomly generated diameters when the user presses the left mouse button. When the user presses the right mouse button, the application will draw a red circle with a randomly generated diameter (Fig. 21.29).

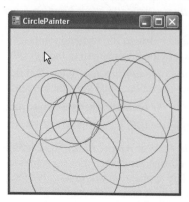

Figure 21.29   Advanced **Circle Painter** application's GUI.

a) *Copying the template to your working directory.* Make a copy of the `CirclePainter` directory from Exercise 21.12 in your `C:\SimplyVB` directory. Rename the copied directory `AdvancedCirclePainter`. If you have not completed Exercise 21.12, follow the steps in Exercise 21.12 to complete the application.

b) *Opening the application's template file.* Double click `CirclePainter.sln` file in the `AdvancedCirclePainter` directory to open the application.

c) *Drawing the appropriate circle.* Use the `Button` property of the `MouseEventArgs` reference, e, to determine which mouse button was pressed. Finally, call the `DrawEllipse` method on a reference to a `Graphics` object to draw a blue circle on the `Form` if the left mouse button was clicked, or a red circle if the right mouse button was clicked.

d) *Running the application.* Select **Debug > Start Debugging** to run your application. Draw several blue circles of different sizes using the left mouse button, then draw several red circles of different sizes using the right mouse button.

e) *Closing the application.* Close your running application by clicking its close box.

f) *Closing the IDE.* Close the Visual Basic IDE by clicking its close box.

What does this code do? ▶   **21.14** Consider the code in Fig. 21.26. Suppose that we change the `MouseMove` event handler to the code below. What happens when the user moves the mouse? Assume that `displayLabel` has been placed on the `Form`.

```
1   Private Sub PainterForm_MouseMove(ByVal sender As Object, _
2      ByVal e As System.Windows.Forms.MouseEventArgs)
3      Handles MyBase.MouseMove
4
5      displayLabel.Text = "I'm at " & e.X & ", " & e.Y & "."
6   End Sub ' PainterForm_MouseMove
```

What's wrong with this code? ▶   **21.15** The following code should draw a `BlueViolet` circle of diameter 4 that corresponds to the movement of the mouse. Find the error(s) in the following code:

```
1   Private Sub PainterForm_MouseMove(ByVal sender As Object, _
2      ByVal e As System.Windows.Forms.MouseEventArgs) _
3      Handles MyBase.MouseMove
4
5      If shouldPaint = True Then
6         Dim graphicsObject As Graphics = Graphics()
```

(cont.)

```
 7
 8              graphicsObject.FillEllipse = ( _
 9                  New SolidBrush(Color.BlueViolet), e.Y, e.X, 5, 4)
10      End If
11  End Sub ' PainterForm_MouseMove
```

Programming Challenge ▶ **21.16** *(Advanced Painter Application)* Extend the `Painter` application to enable a user to change the size and color of the circles drawn (Fig. 21.30).

Figure 21.30 **Advanced Painter** application's GUI.

a) *Copying the template to your working directory.* Copy the directory `C:\Examples\Tutorial21\Exercises\AdvancedPainter` to your `C:\SimplyVB` directory.

b) *Opening the application's template file.* Double click `AdvancedPainter.sln` in the `AdvancedPainter` directory to open the application.

c) *Understanding the provided instance variables.* The template already provides you with four instance variables. Variable `brushColor` is a `Color` value that specifies the color of the brush used in the **Advanced Painter** application. The `shouldPaint` and `shouldErase` variables perform the same functions as in this tutorial's **Painter** application. The `diameter` variable stores the diameter of the circle to be drawn.

d) *Declaring an enumeration to store the circle diameter sizes.* Declare an enumeration `Sizes` to store the possible values of `diameter`. Set constant `SMALL` to 4, `MEDIUM` to 8 and `LARGE` to 10.

e) *Adding event handlers for the Color RadioButtons.* The **Color** `RadioButton`'s event handlers should set `brushColor` to their specified colors (`Color.Red`, `Color.Blue`, `Color.Green` or `Color.Black`).

f) *Adding event handlers for the Size RadioButtons.* The **Size** `RadioButton`'s event handlers should set `diameter` to `Sizes.SMALL` (for the **Small** `RadioButton`), `Sizes.MEDIUM` (for the **Medium** `RadioButton`) or `Sizes.LARGE` (for the **Large** `RadioButton`).

g) *Adding a mouse event handler to a Panel.* To associate mouse events with the `Panel`, select `painterPanel` from the Class Name ComboBox. Then select the appropriate mouse event from the Method Name ComboBox.

h) *Coding the MouseDown and MouseUp event handlers.* The `MouseUp` and `MouseDown` event handlers behave exactly as they do in the **Painter** application.

i) *Coding the MouseMove event handler.* The `MouseMove` event handler behaves the same way as the one in the **Painter** application. The color of the brush that draws the circle when `shouldPaint` is `True` is specified by `brushColor`. The eraser color is specified by the `Panel`'s `BackColor` property and its size is specified by `diameter`.

j) *Running the application.* Select **Debug > Start Debugging** to run your application. Start drawing on the `Panel` using different brush sizes and colors. Use the right mouse button to erase part of your drawing.

k) *Closing the application.* Close your running application by clicking its close box.

l) *Closing the IDE.* Close the Visual Basic IDE by clicking its close box.

22

Objectives

In this tutorial, you will learn to:
- Handle keyboard events.
- Create menus for your Windows applications.
- Use dialogs to display messages.
- Use the ShowDialog method of the **Font** and **Color** dialogs.
- Display the **Font** dialog to enable users to choose fonts.
- Display the **Color** dialog to enable users to choose colors.
- Use operator IsNot to compare references

Outline

Typing Application

Introducing Keyboard Events, Menus and Dialogs

Text editor applications enable you to perform many tasks, from writing e-mails to creating business proposals. These applications often use menus and dialogs to help you customize the appearance of your document. They also respond to keys pressed on the keyboard either by displaying characters or by performing actions (such as accessing menus or dialogs). In this tutorial, you'll learn how to handle **keyboard events**, which occur when keys on the keyboard are pressed and released. Handling keyboard events allows you to specify the action that the application is to take when a key is pressed. You will then learn how to add menus to your application. By now, you are familiar with using various menus and dialogs provided by Windows applications. You will learn to create menus that group related commands and allow the user to select various actions the application can take. Finally, you will learn about the **Font** and **Color** dialogs, which allow the user to change the appearance of text in the application.

22.1 Test-Driving the Typing Application

In this tutorial, you will create a **Typing** Application to help students learn how to type. This application must meet the following requirements:

> **Application Requirements**
>
> *A high-school course teaches students how to type. The instructor would like to use a Windows application that allows students to watch what they are typing on the screen without looking at the keyboard. You have been asked to create an application that displays what the student types. The application has to display a virtual keyboard that highlights any key the student presses on the real keyboard. This application must also contain menu commands for selecting the font style and color of the text displayed, clearing the text displayed and inverting the background and foreground colors of the display.*

This application allows the user to type text. As the user presses each key, the application highlights the corresponding key on the GUI and adds the character to a TextBox. The user can select the color and style of the characters typed, invert the background and foreground colors and clear the TextBox. You will begin by test-driving the completed application. Then you will learn the additional Visual Basic technologies that you will need to create your own version of this application.

Test-Driving the Typing Application

1. ***Opening the completed application.*** Open the directory C:\Examples\ Tutorial22\CompletedApplication\Typing to locate the **Typing** Application. Double click Typing.sln to open the application in the Visual Basic IDE.

2. ***Running the Typing application.*** Select **Debug > Start Debugging** to run the application. Once the application has loaded, type the sentence "Programming in Visual Basic is simple." As you type, the corresponding keys light up on the Form's virtual keyboard and the text is displayed in the TextBox (Fig. 22.1).

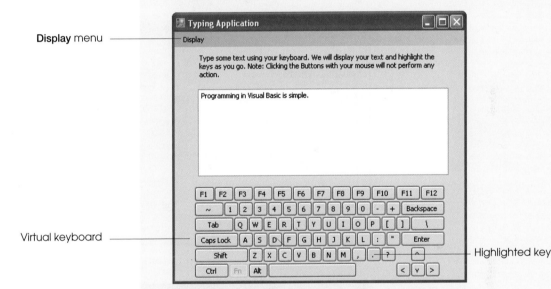

Display menu ——

Virtual keyboard ——

—— Highlighted key

Figure 22.1 **Typing** Application with key pressed.

3. ***Changing the font.*** Select **Display > Text > Font…** (Fig. 22.2) to open the **Font** dialog shown in Fig. 22.3. The **Font** dialog allows you to choose the font style that will display the application's output. Select Tahoma from the **Font:** ComboBox, select Bold from the **Font style:** ComboBox and select 11 from the **Size:** ComboBox. Click the **OK** Button. Note that the text you typed in *Step 2* is now bold and bigger.

4. ***Changing the color of the font.*** Select **Display > Text > Color…** to display the **Color** dialog (Fig. 22.4). This dialog is similar to the **Font** dialog, except that it allows you to choose the color of the text displayed. Select a color, and click **OK**.

(cont.)

Menu item ————
Submenu ————

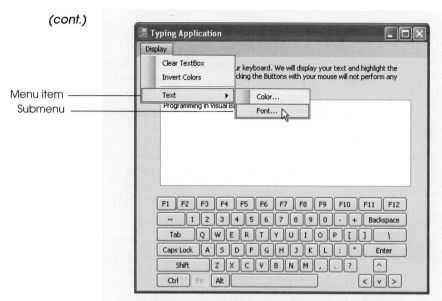

Figure 22.2 Selecting the **Font...** menu item.

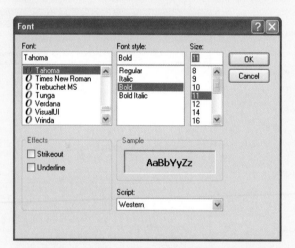

Figure 22.3 **Font** dialog displayed when **Display > Text > Font...** is selected.

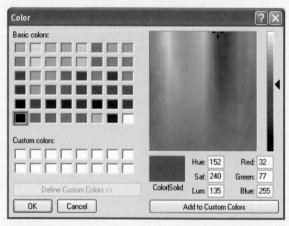

Figure 22.4 **Color** dialog displayed when **Display > Text > Color...** is selected.

(cont.)   5.   ***Inverting the background and foreground colors***. Select **Display > Invert Colors** (Fig. 22.5). This option allows you to swap the background and foreground colors. The result is shown in Fig. 22.6.

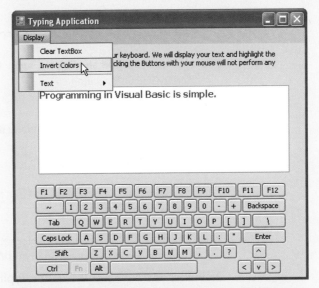

Figure 22.5   Selecting the **Invert Colors** menu item.

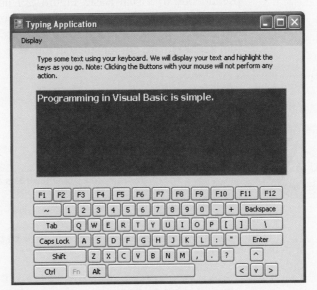

Figure 22.6   Output with colors inverted.

6.   ***Clearing the TextBox***. Select **Display > Clear TextBox** to remove all the text from the TextBox.

7.   ***Closing the application***. Close your running application by clicking its close box.

8.   ***Closing the IDE***. Close the Visual Basic IDE by clicking its close box.

22.2 Analyzing the Typing Application

Before you begin building the **Typing Application**, you should analyze the application's components. The following pseudocode describes the basic operation of the **Typing Application**:

> When the user presses a key:
>> Highlight the corresponding Button on the GUI
>> Display the key's value in the TextBox
>
> When the user releases a key:
>> Reset the corresponding Button's color to the Button's default color
>
> When the user selects the Color... menu item:
>> Display the Color dialog
>> Update the TextBox text's color
>
> When the user selects the Font... menu item:
>> Display the Font dialog
>> Update the TextBox text's font
>
> When the user selects the Clear TextBox menu item:
>> Clear the TextBox
>
> When the user selects the Invert Colors menu item:
>> Swap the TextBox's background and foreground colors

Now that you have test-driven the **Typing Application** application and studied its pseudocode representation, you will use an ACE table to help you convert the pseudocode to Visual Basic. Figure 22.7 lists the actions, controls and events that will help you complete your own version of this application. [*Note:* The number of Buttons is large and no Button events are used; therefore, the Buttons in the virtual keyboard are not included in the ACE table.]

Action/Control/Event (ACE) Table for the Typing Application

Action	Control	Event
Label the application's controls	promptLabel	Application is run
	outputTextBox	KeyPress, KeyDown
Highlight the corresponding Button on the GUI	keyboard Buttons	
Display the key's value in the TextBox	outputTextBox	
	outputTextBox	KeyUp
Reset the corresponding Button's color to the Button's default color	keyboard Buttons	
	colorMenuItem	Click
Display the Color dialog	dialog	
Update the TextBox text's color	outputTextBox	
	fontMenuItem	Click
Display the Font dialog	dialog	
Update the TextBox text's font	outputTextBox	
	clearMenuItem	Click
Clear the TextBox	outputTextBox	
	invertMenuItem	Click
Swap the TextBox's background and foreground colors	outputTextBox	

Figure 22.7 ACE table for the **Typing Application**.

22.3 Keyboard Events

We now show how to handle keyboard events, which are generated when keys on the keyboard are pressed and released. All keyboard events are raised by the control that currently has the focus. In the **Typing Application**, these events are raised by the TextBox control. You'll first learn about the **KeyDown** event, which occurs when a key is pressed. Since there are many keys on the keyboard, you will find that the template application provides much of the required code. In the following box, you'll insert the remaining code to handle the event when the user presses a key.

Coding the KeyDown Event Handler

1. **Copying the template to your working directory.** Copy the C:\Examples\ Tutorial22\TemplateApplication\Typing directory to your C:\SimplyVB directory.

2. **Opening the Typing application's template file.** Double click Typing.sln in the Typing directory to open the application in the Visual Basic IDE.

3. **Adding the Backspace key case.** Add lines 12–19 of Fig. 22.8 to your code. These lines remove a character from the TextBox and highlight the **Back-Space** Button when the *Backspace* key is pressed.

Testing whether key pressed was the *Backspace* key

Highlighting the *Backspace*

Removing the last character in the TextBox

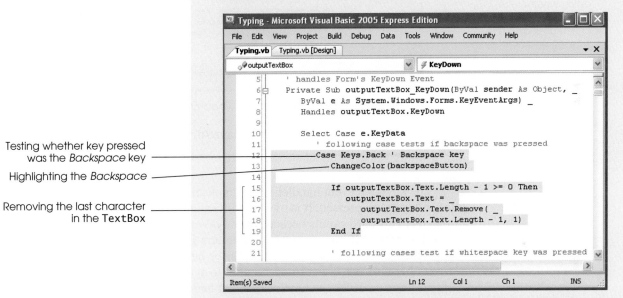

Figure 22.8 Removing a character when *Backspace* is pressed.

When a key is pressed, the KeyDown event is raised. As you have seen in previous tutorials, many event handlers specify two parameters—sender and e. The **sender** Object is the GUI component that raised the event (this is also known as the source of the event), and e contains data for the event. In this case, e (which is of type **KeyEventArgs**) contains a **KeyData** property (line 10) that specifies which key was pressed.

Visual Basic provides the **Keys enumeration** to represent keyboard keys using meaningful names. Recall that enumerations are used to assign meaningful names to constant values. In this case, each value in the Keys enumeration is an Integer that represents a key. Keys.Back (line 12) is the Keys enumeration's representation of the *Backspace* key. Line 13 calls method ChangeColor to highlight the **Backspace** Button. The ChangeColor method is provided for you in the template. The If...Then statement in lines 15–19 tests whether there is text in the TextBox. If the TextBox contains text, lines 16–18 remove the last character from the TextBox. If the TextBox is empty, no action is performed.

(cont.)

String method **Remove** deletes characters from a String. The first argument contains the index at which to begin removing characters, and the second argument specifies the number of characters to remove. The String property Length returns the number of characters in the String. The position of the first character in a String is zero; therefore, you must subtract 1 from the value returned by the Length property to indicate the position of the last character. Use 1 as the second argument to indicate that you want to remove only one character.

4. *Adding the* **Enter** *key case.* Add lines 22–24 of Fig. 22.9 to the Select Case statement in the KeyDown event handler. Keys.Enter (line 22) represents the *Enter* key. Line 23 changes the color of the **Enter** key on the GUI, and line 24 inserts a new line in the TextBox.

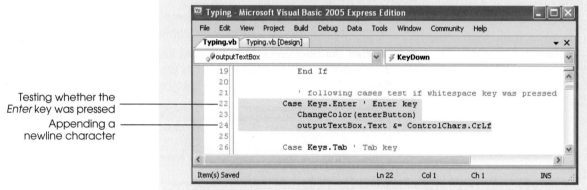

Testing whether the *Enter* key was pressed

Appending a newline character

Figure 22.9 Case that executes when *Enter* key is pressed.

5. *Saving the project.* Select **File > Save All** to save your modified code.

The KeyDown event handler in this application does not test whether any of the letter keys were pressed. It is often inconvenient to use the KeyDown event handler to detect keyboard events because the KeyEventArgs object's KeyData property is case insensitive. If you try to handle letters in the KeyDown event handler, only uppercase letters will be recognized. This is not appropriate for the **Typing Application** because the user should be able to type uppercase and lowercase letters. Visual Basic provides the **KeyPress** event handler, which can be used to recognize both uppercase and lowercase letters. You will learn how to use the KeyPress event handler in the following box.

Adding Code to the KeyPress Event Handler

1. *Writing the* **Select Case** *statement.* Add line 191 of Fig. 22.10 to the KeyPress event handler. Line 191 begins a Select Case statement that uses the uppercase equivalent of the pressed key for the controlling expression.

The key names in the Keys enumeration are in their uppercase form; therefore, the Case statement must use the uppercase representation of the key that was pressed. Structure **Char** provides methods for manipulating individual characters. Char method **ToUpper** returns the uppercase representation of its argument. Note that the value returned by the ToUpper method does not alter the data in its argument.

(cont.)

In this example, the argument that is passed to the ToUpper method uses the KeyChar property of e. (Type **KeyPressEventArgs**.) The **KeyChar** property is similar to KeyData property of the KeyEventArgs object, but contains only values representable as characters. Note that the e parameters for the KeyDown and KeyPress event handlers are of different types. The KeyChar property can represent both uppercase and lowercase character values.

Using the uppercase
representation of key pressed

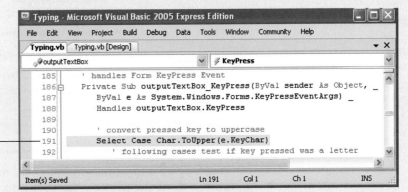

Figure 22.10   Converting the pressed key to an uppercase letter.

2. *Inserting the **A** key case.* Add lines 193–195 of Fig. 22.11 to the Select Case statement in the KeyPress event handler. These lines highlight the **A** Button in the application and display an **A** in the TextBox when the user presses the *A* key.

Converting to a character to
compare key values
Appending a key character

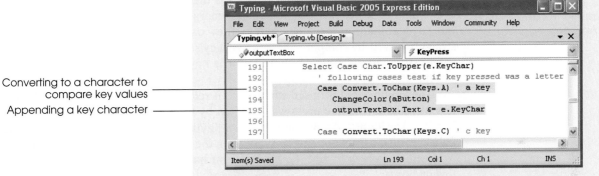

Figure 22.11   Performing actions when the *A* key is pressed.

Line 193 compares the key pressed to the value Keys.A, which represents the *A* key. The Keys enumeration stores numeric values, but the key pressed by the user is passed to the KeyPress event handler as a character; therefore, the Keys enumeration value needs to be converted to a character before the values can be compared. Line 193 uses method Convert.ToChar to convert that value into a character. Line 194 changes the color of the **A** Button on the GUI, and line 195 adds either the "a" or "A" character to the end of the text in the TextBox, depending on whether the user held the shift key while pressing the *A* key.

3. *Inserting the **B** key case.* Add lines 197–199 of Fig. 22.12 to the Select Case statement. These lines highlight the **B** Button and add a B to the TextBox when the user presses the *B* key. For each key pressed, its Button should be highlighted, and the correct output should be displayed in the TextBox.

4. *Saving the project.* Select **File > Save All** to save your modified code.

(cont.)

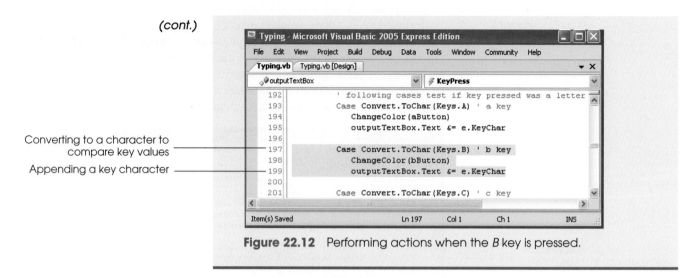

Converting to a character to compare key values ———————

Appending a key character ———————

Figure 22.12 Performing actions when the *B* key is pressed.

You may be wondering why you could not just use the KeyPress event handler to test for all of the keys on the keyboard. Like the KeyDown event handler, the KeyPress event handler has limitations. The KeyPress event handler cannot test for the modifier keys (*Ctrl*, *Shift* and *Alt*). **Modifier keys** do not display characters on the keyboard, but can be used to modify the way that applications respond to a keyboard event. For instance, pressing the *Shift* key while pressing a letter in a text editor displays the uppercase form of the letter. You used the KeyDown event handler to handle the event raised when a modifier key is pressed. Another reason not to use only the KeyPress event handler is that the KeyChar property used in this event handler stores the pressed key as a character, requiring explicit conversion of the Keys enumeration values before they can used in comparisons. It is more straightforward to compare the pressed key's numeric value against the numeric values stored in the Keys enumeration. The KeyData property used in the KeyDown event handler allows you to do this.

The **KeyUp** event is raised when a key is released by the user. It is raised regardless of whether the key press was handled by the KeyPress or the KeyDown event handler. The **Typing Application** uses the KeyUp event handler to remove the highlight color from Buttons on the GUI when the user releases the corresponding key. You will learn how to add the KeyUp event handler to your application in the following box.

Software Design Tip

Use the KeyPress event handler for letter key events. Use the KeyDown event handler for modifier, number and symbol key events.

Creating the KeyUp Event Handler

1. ***Creating the KeyUp event handler.*** An empty KeyUp event handler is provided, to maintain clarity in the template application. However, if you want to generate KeyUp, KeyDown or KeyPress event handlers for other controls, begin by selecting the control for which you wish to add the event handler. In the **Typing Application** select outputTextbox from the **Class Name** ComboBox. Then select the appropriate event handler from the **Method Name** ComboBox, as shown in Fig. 22.13. When you select an event name from the Method Name ComboBox, that event handler is generated in your code.

2. ***Writing code in the KeyUp event handler.*** Insert line 303 of Fig. 22.14 in your application. The KeyUp event handler executes whenever a key is released; therefore, you need to change the color of the released Button back to that Button's default color. Line 303 calls ResetColor, provided for you in the template, to perform this action.

3. ***Saving the project.*** Select **File > Save All** to save your modified code.

(cont.)

Class Name ComboBox

Method Name ComboBox
drop-down list

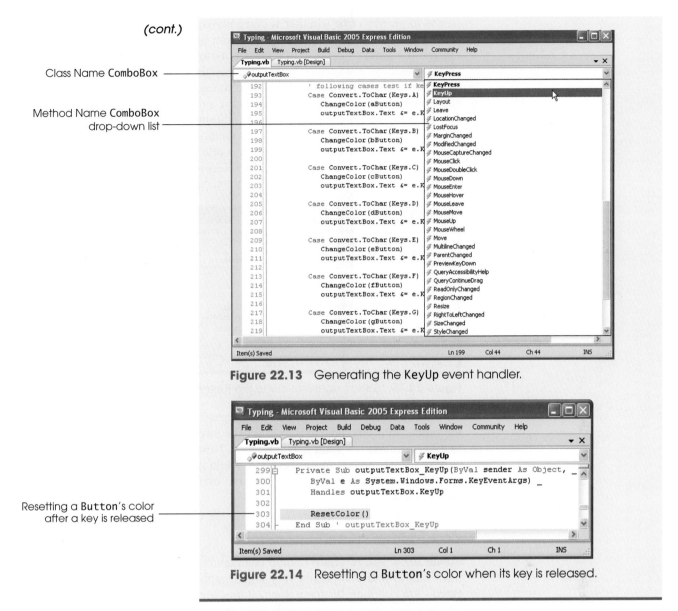

Figure 22.13   Generating the **KeyUp** event handler.

Resetting a **Button**'s color
after a key is released

Figure 22.14   Resetting a **Button**'s color when its key is released.

Next, you'll examine the `ResetColor` method that we provided for you in the template. This method uses the `IsNot` operator—a helpful tool for determining whether a variable refers to an object or contains the `Nothing` reference.

SELF-REVIEW

1. A _____ event is raised when a key on the keyboard is pressed or released.
    a) keyboard   b) `KeyDownEvent`
    c) `KeyChar`   d) `KeyUpEvent`

2. The _____ event is raised when a key is released.
    a) `KeyEventUp`   b) `KeyRelease`
    c) `KeyUp`   d) None of the above.

Answers: 1) a. 2) c.

22.4 IsNot Operator

In Tutorial 19, you learned how to create classes and objects of those classes. You also learned that you can use variables that store references to objects to interact with those objects. Sometimes it is useful to know whether a variable contains a reference to an object or whether it currently contains a `Nothing` reference, so that you can determine whether the variable can be used to manipulate an object. You can use the **IsNot** operator to compare a variable's value to the value `Nothing`. Such a condition evalutes to `True` if the variable refers to an object; otherwise, the condition evaluates to `False`. You can also use `IsNot` to compare two variables to determine whether or not they refer to the same object. If they do not, the condition evaluates to `True`; otherwise, the condition evaluates to `False`.

Figure 22.15 shows the `ResetColor` method that you called to restore the color of a button when the corresponding key is released. Line 317 uses the `IsNot` operator to ensure that `lastButton` actually refers to a `Button`. If `lastButton` does not refer to a `Button` object, line 318 will not execute.

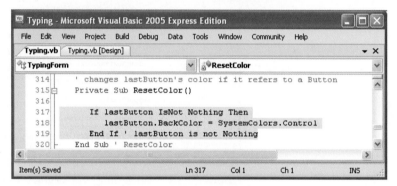

Figure 22.15 `IsNot` operator inside the `ResetColor` method

The code you have just added highlighs the corresponding `Buttons`, displays the output in a `TextBox`, and changes the `Buttons` back to their normal color, so that the user can see what is being typed. Now you will allow the user to alter the appearance of the text in the `TextBox`. To do this, you will use the **MenuStrip** control, which creates a menu that allows the user to select various options to format the `TextBox`.

22.5 Menus

Menus allow you to group related commands for Windows applications. Although most menus and commands vary among applications, some—such as **Open** and **Save**—are common to many applications. Menus are an important part of GUIs because they organize commands without cluttering the GUI. In this section, you will learn how to enhance the **Typing Application** by adding menus that allow the user to control how to display text in the `TextBox`.

Creating a Menu

1. ***Creating a MenuStrip control.*** Switch to **Design** view. Double click Menu-Strip in the **All Windows Forms** tab of the **Toolbox** to add a `MenuStrip` to your application (Fig. 22.16). When you do this, a `MenuStrip` control appears in the component tray. Also, a box that reads **Type Here** appears on the top of your Form. This represents a **menu item**—an item that the user can select in the `MenuStrip` control. When you type text in the **Type Here** field, Visual Studio creates a **ToolStripMenuItem** to represent the menu item. To edit menu items, click the **MenuStrip** icon in the component tray, the menu on the Form, or a menu item. This puts the IDE in **Menu Designer mode**, which allows you to create and edit menus and menu items. Change the `Name` property of the `MenuStrip` control to menuBar.

(cont.)

ToolStripMenuItem field ——————

MenuStrip control in
the component tray ——————

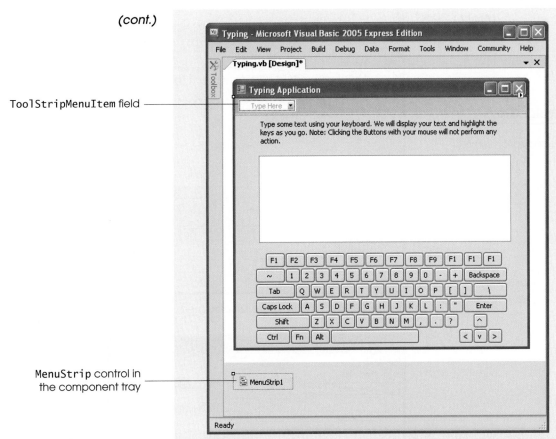

Figure 22.16   MenuStrip control added to the **Typing Application**.

2. *Creating the first menu item*. Click in the **Type Here** box, type &Display and press *Enter*. This sets the text to be displayed in that menu item and indicates that the letter D is the shortcut key. Then change the Name property of the ToolstripMenuItem to displayMenuItem. Note that when you clicked the **Type Here** field, two more fields appeared (Fig. 22.17). The one on the right represents a new menu item that can be created to the right of the **Display** menu item. The field below the **Display** menu item represents a menu item that will appear when the **Display** menu item is selected. You will use the **Display** menu item to display all of the options that allow the user to customize the output displayed in the TextBox.

3. *Creating additional menu items*. In the box below the **Display** menu, type &Clear TextBox. Set the Name property of this menu item to clearMenuItem. Once again, two more boxes appear. Every time you add an item to a menu, these two boxes will appear (Fig. 22.18). Entering text in the right box turns the menu item on the left into a submenu. The right box is now a menu item in that submenu. A **submenu** is a menu within another menu. The box that appears on the bottom of the menu allows you to add another item to that menu. Type &Invert Colors in this box to add another menu item. Set the Name property of this menu item to invertMenuItem.

4. *Inserting a separator bar*. Right click the box that appears below the **Invert Colors** menu item, and select **Insert Separator** from the context menu that appears. Note that a **separator bar**, which is a gray, recessed horizontal rule, appears below the **Invert Colors** menu item. Separator bars are used to group submenus and menu items. A separator bar also can be created by typing a hyphen (-) in the Text property of a menu item.

Good Programming Practice

We suggest appending the MenuItem suffix to ToolStripMenuItem controls.

GUI Design Tip

Use separator bars in a menu to group related menu items.

(cont.)

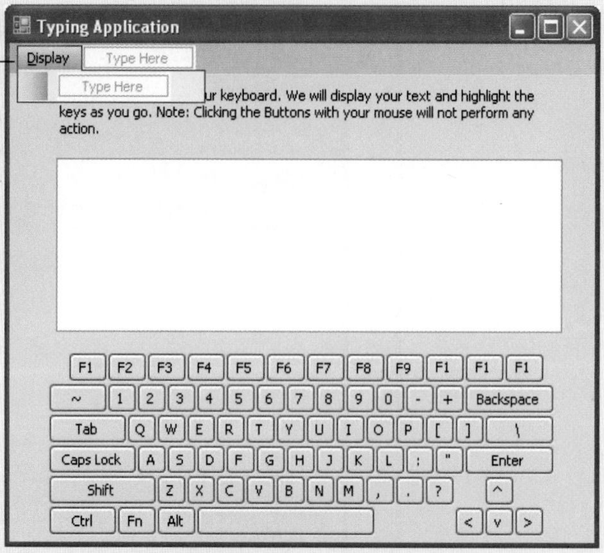

Menu item

Figure 22.17 Creating the **Display** menu.

Submenu item

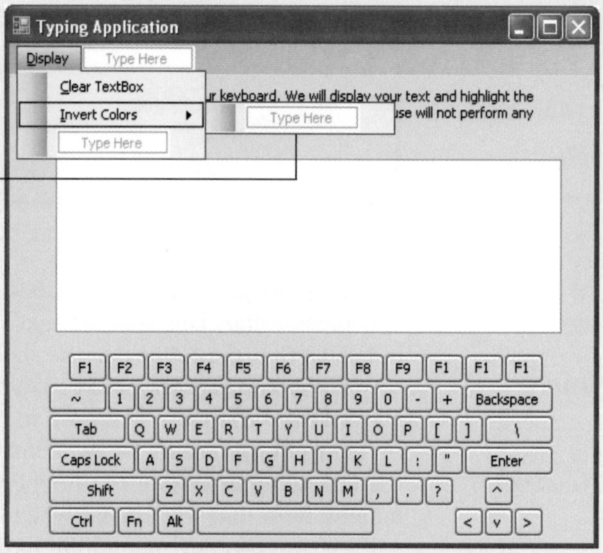

Figure 22.18 Adding items to the menu.

5. ***Creating a submenu.*** In the box under the separator bar, type **&Text**. This menu item will contain options to format the appearance of the text displayed in the **TextBox**. Set the **Name** property of this menu item to **textMenuItem**. All menu items can contain both menu items and submenus. Insert **&Color...** and **&Font...** as menu items in your submenu, naming them **colorMenuItem** and **fontMenuItem**, respectively. (Fig. 22.19)

6. ***Running the application.*** Select **Debug > Start Debugging** to run your application, and select a menu item. At this point, nothing happens because you have not created event handlers for the menu items.

7. ***Closing the application.*** Close the application by clicking its close box.

(cont.)

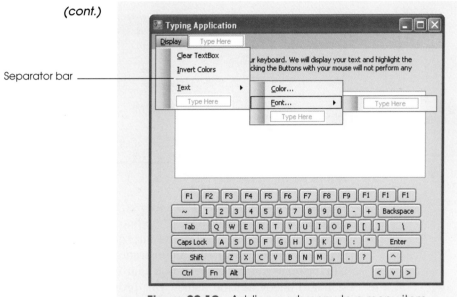

Separator bar

Figure 22.19   Adding a submenu to a menu item.

For a menu item to perform an action when it is selected, an event handler must be added for that item. The **Typing Application** introduces the **Font** dialog and the **Color** dialog to allow the user to customize the appearance of what is being typed. Dialogs allow you to receive input from and display messages to the user. You will learn how to use the **Font** dialog in the following box by displaying it from a menu item's event handler.

Coding the *Font... Menu Item's* Click *Event Handler*

1. ***Creating an event handler for the Font... menu item.*** In the Windows Form Designer, double click the **Font...** menu item that you have just created to generate its Click event handler.

2. ***Declaring the dialog variables.*** Add lines 327–328 of Fig. 22.20 to your code. Line 327 creates a new **FontDialog** object that will allow the user to select the font style to apply to the text. Line 328 declares a variable of type **DialogResult** that will store information indicating which **Button** the user clicked to exit the dialog.

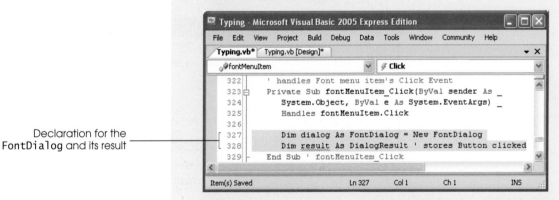

Declaration for the FontDialog and its result

Figure 22.20   Declarations for the **FontDialog** and its **DialogResult**.

3. ***Displaying the dialog.*** Add lines 330–331 of Fig. 22.21 to your event handler. These lines call the **ShowDialog** method to display the **Font** dialog to the user and assign the return value of ShowDialog to variable result.

(cont.)

Showing the dialog and assigning the result

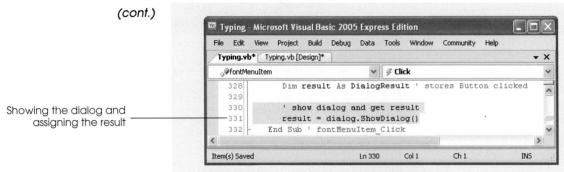

Figure 22.21 Opening the **Font** dialog.

4. *Exiting the event handler if the user clicks Cancel.* Add lines 333–336 of Fig. 22.22 to your application. These lines determine whether the user has clicked the **Font** dialog's **Cancel** Button. Line 334 compares the value stored in `result` with the enumeration value **DialogResult.Cancel**. **DialogResult** is an enumeration that contains values corresponding to standard dialog Button names. This provides a convenient way to determine which Button the user has clicked. If the user clicks the **Cancel** Button, no action takes place and the method exits using the Return statement (line 335).

Take no action if user cancels

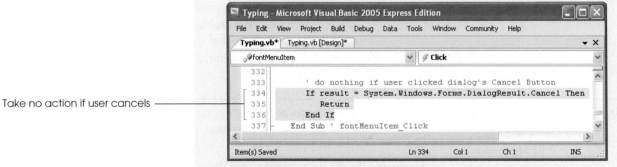

Figure 22.22 Exit the event handler if the user clicks **Cancel**.

5. *Setting the font.* Add lines 338–339 of Fig. 22.23 to give the text the style that the user has selected from the FontDialog. This statement immediately updates the font displayed in outputTextBox.

Assigning the new font value

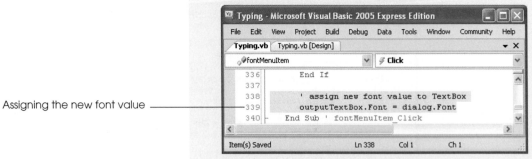

Figure 22.23 Changing the display font.

6. *Saving the project.* Select **File > Save All** to save your modified code.

The user of the **Typing Application** should also be able to select the color of the font displayed in the TextBox. You will learn how to display the **Color** dialog from an event handler in the following box.

*Coding the Color...
Menu Item's Click
Event Handler*

1. **Creating an event handler for the Color... menu item.** Double click the **Color...** menu item to generate its Click event handler.

2. **Declaring the dialog variables.** Add lines 347–348 of Fig. 22.24 to your application. Line 347 creates a new ColorDialog object that will allow the user to select the color of the text. Line 348 declares a DialogResult variable to store the value of the Button clicked by the user.

Declarations for the
ColorDialog and its result ───

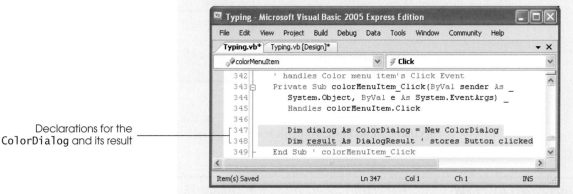

Figure 22.24 Declarations for the **Color** dialog and its DialogResult.

3. **Setting the ColorDialog's open mode.** Add lines 350–351 of Fig. 22.25 to your application. The **ColorDialog** object allows you to specify which color options the dialog presents to the user of your application. To display the **Color** dialog as shown in Fig. 22.4, the **FullOpen** option must be set to True (line 350). If this option is set to False, only the left half of the dialog will be displayed. Line 351 opens the **Color** dialog using the ShowDialog method.

Displaying the ColorDialog
with a complete color ───
selection

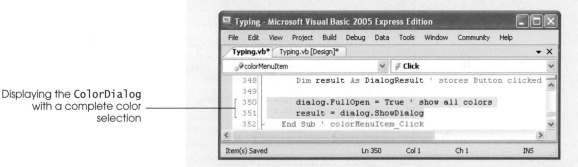

Figure 22.25 Displaying the **Color** dialog.

4. **Setting the font color.** Add lines 353–359 of Fig. 22.26 to your application. The If...Then statement on lines 354–356 prevents the color from being changed if the user clicks **Cancel**. Line 359 sets the text's color to the color the user selected in the **Color** dialog.

(cont.)

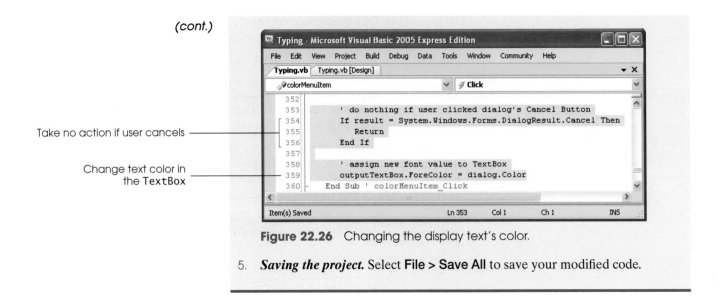

Take no action if user cancels

Change text color in the TextBox

Figure 22.26 Changing the display text's color.

5. *Saving the project.* Select **File > Save All** to save your modified code.

The user should be able to clear all of the text in the TextBox using the **Clear TextBox** menu item. You will learn how to do this in the following box.

Clearing the TextBox

1. *Generating an event handler.* Double click the **Clear TextBox** menu item to generate its Click event.

2. *Clearing the text.* Add line 367 of Fig. 22.27 to your application. This line calls the Clear method to erase the text in the TextBox. Calling the Clear method on a TextBox has the same effect as setting its Text property to the empty string.

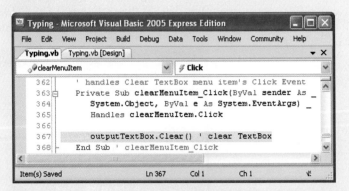

Figure 22.27 Calling the Clear method of class TextBox to erase the text.

3. *Saving the project.* Select **File > Save All** to save your modified code.

The user should be able to swap the foreground and background colors of the TextBox. You will learn how to accomplish this in the following box.

Inverting Colors

1. *Creating an event handler.* Double click the **Invert Colors** menu item in design view to create its Click event handler (Fig. 22.28).

(cont.)

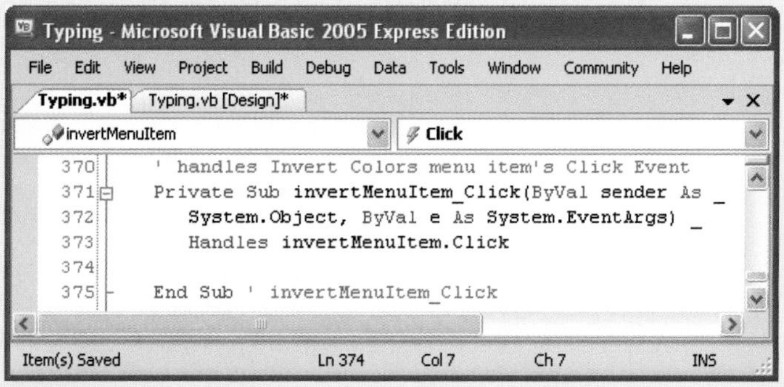

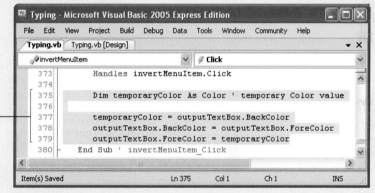

Figure 22.28   Empty event handler for **Invert Color** menu item.

2. ***Inverting the colors.*** Insert lines 375–379 of Fig. 22.29 to your application. Line 375 declares a Color variable to store a color value. To swap colors, you must use a temporary variable to hold one of the colors that you want to swap. A **temporary variable** is used to store data when swapping values. Such a variable is no longer needed after the swap occurs. Without a temporary variable, you would lose the value of one color property (by reassigning its value) before you could assign its color to the other property.

Line 377 assigns the temporary Color variable the background color of the TextBox. Line 378 then sets the background color to the foreground color. Finally, line 379 assigns the text color the value stored in the temporary Color variable, which contains the TextBox's background color from before the swap.

Using a temporary variable to swap color values

```
373           Handles invertMenuItem.Click
374
375           Dim temporaryColor As Color ' temporary Color value
376
377           temporaryColor = outputTextBox.BackColor
378           outputTextBox.BackColor = outputTextBox.ForeColor
379           outputTextBox.ForeColor = temporaryColor
380    End Sub ' invertMenuItem_Click
```

Figure 22.29   Swapping the background and foreground colors.

3. ***Running the application.*** Select **Debug > Start Debugging** to run your application. Enter text using your keyboard. The keys you press should be highlighted in the virtual keyboard on the Form. Use the menu to change the color of the text, then invert the colors of the text and the TextBox. Finally, use the menus to change the text's font, then clear the TextBox.

4. ***Closing the application.*** Close your running application by clicking its close box.

5. ***Closing the IDE.*** Close the Visual Basic IDE by clicking its close box.

Figure 22.30 presents the source code for the **Typing Application**. The lines of code that contain new programming concepts that you learned in this tutorial are highlighted.

Instance variable to store which **Button** the user pressed

Select Case determines which key was pressed

Handling the case when the *Backspace* key is pressed

Handling the case when the *Enter* key is pressed

```
1   Public Class TypingForm
2
3       Private lastButton As Button ' reference to last Button pressed
4
5       ' handles Form's KeyDown Event
6       Private Sub outputTextBox_KeyDown(ByVal sender As Object, _
7           ByVal e As System.Windows.Forms.KeyEventArgs) _
8           Handles outputTextBox.KeyDown
9
10          Select Case e.KeyData
11              ' following case tests if backspace was pressed
12              Case Keys.Back ' Backspace key
13                  ChangeColor(backspaceButton)
14
15                  If outputTextBox.Text.Length - 1 >= 0 Then
16                      outputTextBox.Text = _
17                          outputTextBox.Text.Remove( _
18                          outputTextBox.Text.Length - 1, 1)
19                  End If
20
21              ' following cases test if whitespace key was pressed
22              Case Keys.Enter ' Enter key
23                  ChangeColor(enterButton)
24                  outputTextBox.Text &= ControlChars.CrLf
25
26              Case Keys.Tab ' Tab key
27                  ChangeColor(tabButton)
28                  outputTextBox.Text &= ControlChars.Tab
29
30              Case Keys.Space ' space bar
31                  ChangeColor(spaceButton)
32                  outputTextBox.Text &= " "
33
34              ' following cases test if number key was pressed
35              Case Keys.D0 ' 0 key
36                  ChangeColor(zeroButton)
37                  outputTextBox.Text &= "0"
38
39              Case Keys.D1
40                  ChangeColor(oneButton)
41                  outputTextBox.Text &= "1"
42
43              Case Keys.D2
44                  ChangeColor(twoButton)
45                  outputTextBox.Text &= "2"
46
47              Case Keys.D3
48                  ChangeColor(threeButton)
49                  outputTextBox.Text &= "3"
50
51              Case Keys.D4
52                  ChangeColor(fourButton)
53                  outputTextBox.Text &= "4"
54
55              Case Keys.D5
56                  ChangeColor(fiveButton)
57                  outputTextBox.Text &= "5"
58
59              Case Keys.D6
60                  ChangeColor(sixButton)
61                  outputTextBox.Text &= "6"
62
63              Case Keys.D7
64                  ChangeColor(sevenButton)
65                  outputTextBox.Text &= "7"
```

Figure 22.30 Typing Application code listing. (Part 1 of 7.)

```
66
67          Case Keys.D8
68              ChangeColor(eightButton)
69              outputTextBox.Text &= "8"
70
71          Case Keys.D9
72              ChangeColor(nineButton)
73              outputTextBox.Text &= "9"
74
75          ' following cases test if one of the F keys was pressed
76          Case Keys.F1 ' F1 key
77              ChangeColor(f1Button)
78
79          Case Keys.F2 ' F2 key
80              ChangeColor(f2Button)
81
82          Case Keys.F3 ' F3 key
83              ChangeColor(f3Button)
84
85          Case Keys.F4 ' F4 key
86              ChangeColor(f4Button)
87
88          Case Keys.F5 ' F5 key
89              ChangeColor(f5Button)
90
91          Case Keys.F6 ' F6 key
92              ChangeColor(f6Button)
93
94          Case Keys.F7 ' F7 key
95              ChangeColor(f7Button)
96
97          Case Keys.F8 ' F8 key
98              ChangeColor(f8Button)
99
100         Case Keys.F9 ' F9 key
101             ChangeColor(f9Button)
102
103         Case Keys.F10 ' F10 key
104             ChangeColor(f10Button)
105
106         Case Keys.F11 ' F11 key
107             ChangeColor(f11Button)
108
109         Case Keys.F12 ' F12 key
110             ChangeColor(f12Button)
111
112         ' following cases test if a special character was pressed
113         Case Keys.OemOpenBrackets ' left square bracket
114             ChangeColor(leftBraceButton)
115             outputTextBox.Text &= "["
116
117         Case Keys.OemCloseBrackets ' right square bracket
118             ChangeColor(rightBraceButton)
119             outputTextBox.Text &= "]"
120
121         Case Keys.Oemplus ' plus sign
122             ChangeColor(plusButton)
123             outputTextBox.Text &= "+"
124
125         Case Keys.OemMinus ' minus sign
126             ChangeColor(hyphenButton)
127             outputTextBox.Text &= "-"
128
```

Figure 22.30   Typing Application code listing. (Part 2 of 7.)

```
129            Case Keys.Oemtilde ' tilde (~)
130                ChangeColor(tildeButton)
131                outputTextBox.Text &= "~"
132
133            Case Keys.OemPipe ' backslash
134                ChangeColor(slashButton)
135                outputTextBox.Text &= "\"
136
137            Case Keys.OemSemicolon ' colon
138                ChangeColor(colonButton)
139                outputTextBox.Text &= ":"
140
141            Case Keys.OemQuotes ' quotation marks
142                ChangeColor(quoteButton)
143                outputTextBox.Text &= ControlChars.Quote
144
145            Case Keys.OemPeriod ' period
146                ChangeColor(periodButton)
147                outputTextBox.Text &= "."
148
149            Case Keys.Oemcomma ' comma
150                ChangeColor(commaButton)
151                outputTextBox.Text &= ","
152
153            Case Keys.OemQuestion ' question mark
154                ChangeColor(questionButton)
155                outputTextBox.Text &= "?"
156
157            Case Keys.CapsLock ' Caps Lock key
158                ChangeColor(capsButton)
159
160            ' following cases test if an arrow key was pressed
161            Case Keys.Down ' down arrow
162                ChangeColor(downButton)
163
164            Case Keys.Up ' up arrow
165                ChangeColor(upButton)
166
167            Case Keys.Left ' left arrow
168                ChangeColor(leftButton)
169
170            Case Keys.Right ' right arrow
171                ChangeColor(rightButton)
172
173            ' following cases test if a modifier key was pressed
174            Case CType(e.Shift, Keys) ' Shift key
175                ChangeColor(shiftLeftButton)
176
177            Case CType(e.Control, Keys) ' Control key
178                ChangeColor(ctrlLeftButton)
179
180            Case CType(e.Alt, Keys) ' Alt key
181                ChangeColor(altLeftButton)
182        End Select
183    End Sub ' outputTextBox_KeyDown
184
185    ' handles Form KeyPress Event
186    Private Sub outputTextBox_KeyPress(ByVal sender As Object, _
187        ByVal e As System.Windows.Forms.KeyPressEventArgs) _
188        Handles outputTextBox.KeyPress
189
```

Figure 22.30 **Typing Application** code listing. (Part 3 of 7.)

Normalizing the character
using Char.ToUpper to
make it uppercase

Code executed when
the *a* key is pressed

Code executed when
the *b* key is pressed

Converting a number to a
Char using
Convert.ToChar

```
190      ' convert pressed key to uppercase
191      Select Case Char.ToUpper(e.KeyChar)
192         ' following cases test if key pressed was a letter
193         Case Convert.ToChar(Keys.A) ' a key
194            ChangeColor(aButton)
195            outputTextBox.Text &= e.KeyChar
196
197         Case Convert.ToChar(Keys.B) ' b key
198            ChangeColor(bButton)
199            outputTextBox.Text &= e.KeyChar
200
201         Case Convert.ToChar(Keys.C) ' c key
202            ChangeColor(cButton)
203            outputTextBox.Text &= e.KeyChar
204
205         Case Convert.ToChar(Keys.D) ' d key
206            ChangeColor(dButton)
207            outputTextBox.Text &= e.KeyChar
208
209         Case Convert.ToChar(Keys.E) ' e key
210            ChangeColor(eButton)
211            outputTextBox.Text &= e.KeyChar
212
213         Case Convert.ToChar(Keys.F) ' f key
214            ChangeColor(fButton)
215            outputTextBox.Text &= e.KeyChar
216
217         Case Convert.ToChar(Keys.G) ' g key
218            ChangeColor(gButton)
219            outputTextBox.Text &= e.KeyChar
220
221         Case Convert.ToChar(Keys.H) ' h key
222            ChangeColor(hButton)
223            outputTextBox.Text &= e.KeyChar
224
225         Case Convert.ToChar(Keys.I) ' i key
226            ChangeColor(iButton)
227            outputTextBox.Text &= e.KeyChar
228
229         Case Convert.ToChar(Keys.J) ' j key
230            ChangeColor(jButton)
231            outputTextBox.Text &= e.KeyChar
232
233         Case Convert.ToChar(Keys.K) ' k key
234            ChangeColor(kButton)
235            outputTextBox.Text &= e.KeyChar
236
237         Case Convert.ToChar(Keys.L) ' l key
238            ChangeColor(lButton)
239            outputTextBox.Text &= e.KeyChar
240
241         Case Convert.ToChar(Keys.M) ' m key
242            ChangeColor(mButton)
243            outputTextBox.Text &= e.KeyChar
244
245         Case Convert.ToChar(Keys.N) ' n key
246            ChangeColor(nButton)
247            outputTextBox.Text &= e.KeyChar
248
249         Case Convert.ToChar(Keys.O) ' o key
250            ChangeColor(oButton)
251            outputTextBox.Text &= e.KeyChar
252
```

Figure 22.30 **Typing Application** code listing. (Part 4 of 7.)

```
253              Case Convert.ToChar(Keys.P) ' p key
254                 ChangeColor(pButton)
255                 outputTextBox.Text &= e.KeyChar
256
257              Case Convert.ToChar(Keys.Q) ' q key
258                 ChangeColor(qButton)
259                 outputTextBox.Text &= e.KeyChar
260
261              Case Convert.ToChar(Keys.R) ' r key
262                 ChangeColor(rButton)
263                 outputTextBox.Text &= e.KeyChar
264
265              Case Convert.ToChar(Keys.S) ' s key
266                 ChangeColor(sButton)
267                 outputTextBox.Text &= e.KeyChar
268
269              Case Convert.ToChar(Keys.T) ' t key
270                 ChangeColor(tButton)
271                 outputTextBox.Text &= e.KeyChar
272
273              Case Convert.ToChar(Keys.U) ' u key
274                 ChangeColor(uButton)
275                 outputTextBox.Text &= e.KeyChar
276
277              Case Convert.ToChar(Keys.V) ' v key
278                 ChangeColor(vButton)
279                 outputTextBox.Text &= e.KeyChar
280
281              Case Convert.ToChar(Keys.W) ' w key
282                 ChangeColor(wButton)
283                 outputTextBox.Text &= e.KeyChar
284
285              Case Convert.ToChar(Keys.X) ' x key
286                 ChangeColor(xButton)
287                 outputTextBox.Text &= e.KeyChar
288
289              Case Convert.ToChar(Keys.Y) ' y key
290                 ChangeColor(yButton)
291                 outputTextBox.Text &= e.KeyChar
292
293              Case Convert.ToChar(Keys.Z) ' z key
294                 ChangeColor(zButton)
295                 outputTextBox.Text &= e.KeyChar
296           End Select ' ends test for letters
297        End Sub ' outputTextBox_KeyPress
298
299        Private Sub outputTextBox_KeyUp(ByVal sender As Object, _
300           ByVal e As System.Windows.Forms.KeyEventArgs) _
301           Handles outputTextBox.KeyUp
302
303           ResetColor()
304        End Sub ' outputTextBox_KeyUp
305
306        ' highlight Button passed as argument
307        Private Sub ChangeColor(ByVal buttonPassed As Button)
308
309           ResetColor()
310           buttonPassed.BackColor = Color.Yellow
311           lastButton = buttonPassed
312        End Sub ' ChangeColor
313
```

Figure 22.30   **Typing Application** code listing. (Part 5 of 7.)

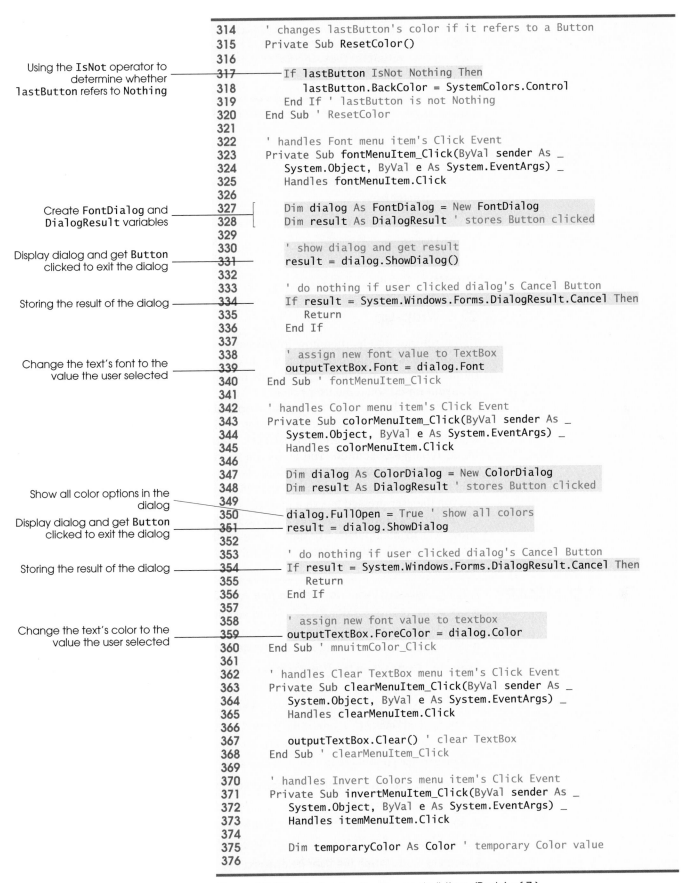

```
314        ' changes lastButton's color if it refers to a Button
315        Private Sub ResetColor()
316
317            If lastButton IsNot Nothing Then
318                lastButton.BackColor = SystemColors.Control
319            End If ' lastButton is not Nothing
320        End Sub ' ResetColor
321
322        ' handles Font menu item's Click Event
323        Private Sub fontMenuItem_Click(ByVal sender As _
324            System.Object, ByVal e As System.EventArgs) _
325            Handles fontMenuItem.Click
326
327            Dim dialog As FontDialog = New FontDialog
328            Dim result As DialogResult ' stores Button clicked
329
330            ' show dialog and get result
331            result = dialog.ShowDialog()
332
333            ' do nothing if user clicked dialog's Cancel Button
334            If result = System.Windows.Forms.DialogResult.Cancel Then
335                Return
336            End If
337
338            ' assign new font value to TextBox
339            outputTextBox.Font = dialog.Font
340        End Sub ' fontMenuItem_Click
341
342        ' handles Color menu item's Click Event
343        Private Sub colorMenuItem_Click(ByVal sender As _
344            System.Object, ByVal e As System.EventArgs) _
345            Handles colorMenuItem.Click
346
347            Dim dialog As ColorDialog = New ColorDialog
348            Dim result As DialogResult ' stores Button clicked
349
350            dialog.FullOpen = True ' show all colors
351            result = dialog.ShowDialog
352
353            ' do nothing if user clicked dialog's Cancel Button
354            If result = System.Windows.Forms.DialogResult.Cancel Then
355                Return
356            End If
357
358            ' assign new font value to textbox
359            outputTextBox.ForeColor = dialog.Color
360        End Sub ' mnuitmColor_Click
361
362        ' handles Clear TextBox menu item's Click Event
363        Private Sub clearMenuItem_Click(ByVal sender As _
364            System.Object, ByVal e As System.EventArgs) _
365            Handles clearMenuItem.Click
366
367            outputTextBox.Clear() ' clear TextBox
368        End Sub ' clearMenuItem_Click
369
370        ' handles Invert Colors menu item's Click Event
371        Private Sub invertMenuItem_Click(ByVal sender As _
372            System.Object, ByVal e As System.EventArgs) _
373            Handles itemMenuItem.Click
374
375            Dim temporaryColor As Color ' temporary Color value
376
```

Using the **IsNot** operator to determine whether **lastButton** refers to **Nothing**

Create **FontDialog** and **DialogResult** variables

Display dialog and get **Button** clicked to exit the dialog

Storing the result of the dialog

Change the text's font to the value the user selected

Show all color options in the dialog

Display dialog and get **Button** clicked to exit the dialog

Storing the result of the dialog

Change the text's color to the value the user selected

Figure 22.30   Typing Application code listing. (Part 6 of 7.)

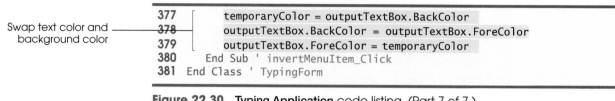

Swap text color and background color

```
377    temporaryColor = outputTextBox.BackColor
378    outputTextBox.BackColor = outputTextBox.ForeColor
379    outputTextBox.ForeColor = temporaryColor
380    End Sub ' invertMenuItem_Click
381  End Class ' TypingForm
```

Figure 22.30 **Typing Application** code listing. (Part 7 of 7.)

SELF-REVIEW

1. Menus can contain _____.

a) commands that the user can select   b) submenus

c) separator bars   d) All of the above.

2. _____ allow you to receive input from and display messages to users.

a) Dialogs   b) Menus

c) Separator bars   d) Enumerations

Answers: 1) d. 2) a.

22.6 Wrap-Up

In this tutorial, you learned how to process keyboard events by using the KeyDown and KeyPress event handlers that are invoked when the user presses various keys on the keyboard. You then learned how to use the KeyUp event handler to handle the event raised when the user releases a key.

You added menus to the **Typing Application.** You learned that menus allow you to add controls to your application without cluttering the GUI. You also learned how to code a menu item's Click event handler to alter the displayed text in the **Typing Application.** You learned how to display the **Color** and **Font** dialogs so that the user could specify the font style and color of the text in the TextBox. You also learned how to use the DialogResult enumeration to determine which Button the user pressed to exit a dialog.

In the next tutorial, you will learn about the methods in the String class that allow you to manipulate Strings. These methods will help you build a screen-scraper application that can search text for a particular value.

SKILLS SUMMARY

Adding Keyboard Event Handlers to Your Application

- Select the control for which you want to add the event handler from the **Class Name** ComboBox.
- Select the desired event handler from the **Method Name** ComboBox.

Executing Code When the User Presses a Letter Key on the Keyboard

- Use the KeyPress event handler.
- Use property KeyChar to determine which key was pressed.
- Use method ToUpper to convert the pressed key to an uppercase letter.
- Use a Select Case statement to perform an action depending on what key was pressed.
- Compare the pressed key to a Keys enumeration value in each Case.

Executing Code When the User Presses a Key That Is Not a Letter

- Use the KeyDown event handler.
- Use property KeyData to determine which key was pressed.
- Use CType(e.[*Key Name*], Keys) for the Alt, Ctrl, and Shift Keys

Executing Code When the User Releases a Key

- Use the KeyUp event handler.

Adding Menus to Your Application

■ Double click the MenuStrip control in the **Toolbox**.

■ Add menu items to the menu by typing the item's name in the **Type Here** boxes that appear in Menu Designer mode.

■ Add submenus by typing a menu item's name in the **Type Here** box that appears to the right of the submenu's name.

■ Use a menu item's Click event handler to perform an action when that menu item is selected by the user.

Adding a Font Dialog to Your Application

■ Use keyword New to create a new FontDialog object.

■ Use a DialogResult variable to store the Button the user clicked to exit the dialog.

■ Use method ShowDialog to display the dialog.

Adding a Color Dialog to Your Application

■ Use keyword New to create a new ColorDialog object.

■ Use a DialogResult variable to store the Button the user clicked to exit the dialog.

■ Set the FullOpen option to True to provide the user with the full range of colors.

■ Use method ShowDialog to display the dialog.

KEY TERMS

Cancel value of DialogResult enumeration—Used to determine whether the user clicked the **Cancel** Button of a dialog.

Char structure—Stores characters (such as letters and symbols).

ColorDialog class—Used to display a dialog from which the user can select colors.

DialogResult enumeration—An enumeration that contains values corresponding to standard dialog Button names.

FontDialog class—Used to display a dialog from which the user can choose a font and its style.

FullOpen property of class ColorDialog—Property that, when True, enables the Color-Dialog to provide a full range of color options when displayed.

IsNot operator—Determines whether two variables contain references to different objects or whether a variable refers to an object.

keyboard event—Raised when a key on the keyboard is pressed or released.

KeyChar property of class KeyPressEventArgs—Contains data about the key that raised the KeyPress event.

KeyData property of class KeyEventArgs—Contains data about the key that raised the KeyDown event.

KeyDown event—Generated when a key is initially pressed. Use to handle the event raised when a key that is not a letter key is pressed.

KeyEventArgs class—Stores information about special modifier keys.

KeyPress event—Generated when a key is pressed. Use to handle the event raised when a letter key is pressed.

KeyPressEventArgs class—Stores information about character keys.

Keys enumeration—Contains values representing keyboard keys.

KeyUp event—Generated when a key is released.

menu—Design element that groups related commands for Windows applications. Although these commands depend on the application, some—such as **Open** and **Save**—are common to many applications. Menus are an integral part of GUIs, because they organize commands without cluttering the GUI.

Menu Designer mode in the Visual Basic IDE—Design mode in the IDE that allows you to create and edit menus and menu items.

menu item—Command located in a menu that, when selected, causes the application to perform an action.

MenuStrip control—Allows you to add menus to your application.

modifier key—Key such as *Shift*, *Alt* or *Control* that modifies the way that an application responds to a keyboard event.

Remove method of class String—Deletes characters from a String. The first argument contains the index in the String at which to begin removing characters, and the second argument specifies the number of characters to remove.

sender event argument—Event argument that contains a reference to the GUI component that raised the event (also called the source of the event).

separator bar—Bar placed in a menu to separate related menu items.

ShowDialog method of class FontDialog or ColorDialog—The method that displays the dialog on which it is called.

submenu—Menu within another menu.

temporary variable—Used to store data when swapping values.

ToUpper method of structure Char—Returns the uppercase representation of the character passed as a parameter.

ToolStripMenuItem class—Class which allows you to add menu items to a MenuStrip control.

GUI DESIGN GUIDELINES

MenuStrip

- Use book-title capitalization in menu item text.
- Use separator bars in a menu to group related menu items.
- If clicking a menu item opens a dialog, an ellipsis (...) should follow the menu item's text.

CONTROLS, EVENTS, PROPERTIES & METHODS

Char This structure represents characters.

- *Method*

  ToUpper—Returns the uppercase equivalent of an alphabetic character.

ColorDialog ColorDialog   This control allows the user to select a color.

- *Properties*

  Color—Contains the color selected by the user. The default color is black.

  FullOpen—When True, displays an extended color palette. If this property is set to False, a dialog with fewer options is displayed.

- *Method*

  ShowDialog—Displays the **Color** dialog to the user.

FontDialog FontDialog   This control allows the user to select a font and customize its size and style.

- *Method*

  ShowDialog—Displays the **Font** dialog to the user.

- *Property*

  Font—Contains the font specified by the user.

KeyEventArgs This class represents arguments passed to the KeyDown event handler.

- *Property*

  KeyData—Contains data about the key that raised the KeyDown event.

KeyPressEventArgs This class represents arguments passed to the KeyPress event handler.

- *Property*

  KeyChar—Contains data about the key that raised the KeyPress event.

MenuStrip    This control allows you to group related commands for a Windows application.

■ *In action*

■ *Event*

Click—Raised when the user clicks a menu item or presses a shortcut key that represents an item.

TextBox ⎡abl⎤ TextBox   This control allows the user to input data from the keyboard.

■ *In action*

0

■ *Events*

KeyDown—Raised when a key is pressed. KeyDown is case insensitive. It cannot recognize lowercase letters.

KeyPress—Raised when a key is pressed. KeyPress cannot handle modifier keys.

KeyUp—Raised when a key is released by the user.

TextChanged—Raised when the text in the TextBox is changed.

■ *Properties*

Enabled—Determines whether the user can enter data (True) in the TextBox or not (False).

Location—Specifies the location of the TextBox on the container control relative to the top-left corner.

MaxLength—Specifies the maximum number of characters that can be input into the TextBox.

Multiline—Specifies whether the TextBox is capable of displaying multiple lines of text.

Name—Specifies the name used to access the TextBox programmatically. The name should be appended with the TextBox suffix.

PasswordChar—Specifies the masking character to be used when displaying data in the TextBox.

ReadOnly—Determines whether the value of a TextBox can be changed.

ScrollBars—Specifies whether the TextBox contains a scrollbar.

Size—Specifies the height and width (in pixels) of the TextBox.

Text—Specifies the text displayed in the TextBox.

TextAlign—Specifies how the text is aligned within the TextBox.

■ *Methods*

Clear—Removes the text from the TextBox that calls it.

Focus—Transfers the focus of the application to the TextBox that calls it.

MULTIPLE-CHOICE QUESTIONS

22.1 When creating a menu, typing a(n) _____ in front of a menu item name will create an access shortcut for that item.

    a) &
                  b) !
    c) $
                  d) #

22.2 *Alt*, *Shift* and *Control* are _____ keys.

    a) modifier
                  b) special
    c) function
                  d) None of the above.

22.3 KeyChar is a property of _____.

a) `KeyEventArgs`
b) `Key`
c) `KeyArgs`
d) `KeyPressEventArgs`

22.4 Typing a hyphen (–) as a menu item's `Text` property will create a(n) _____.

a) separator bar
b) access shortcut
c) new submenu
d) keyboard shortcut

22.5 A _____ provides a group of related commands for Windows applications.

a) separator bar
b) hot key
c) menu
d) margin indicator bar

22.6 The _____ enumeration specifies key codes and modifiers.

a) `Keyboard`
b) `Key`
c) `KeyboardTypes`
d) `Keys`

22.7 The _____ event is raised when a key is pressed by the user.

a) `KeyPress`
b) `KeyHeld`
c) `KeyDown`
d) Both a and c.

22.8 Which of the following is not a keyboard event?

a) `KeyPress`
b) `KeyDown`
c) `KeyUp`
d) `KeyClicked`

22.9 Which of the following is not a structure?

a) `Char`
b) `Color`
c) `String`
d) `Date`

22.10 The _____ type allows you to determine which `Button` the user clicked to exit a dialog.

a) `DialogButtons`
b) `DialogResult`
c) `Buttons`
d) `ButtonResult`

EXERCISES

22.11 (*Inventory Application with Keyboard Events*) Enhance the **Inventory** application that you developed in Tutorial 4 to prevent the user from entering input that is not a number. Use keyboard events to allow the user to press the number keys, the left and right arrows and the *Backspace* keys. If any other key is pressed, display a `MessageBox` instructing the user to enter a number (Fig. 22.31).

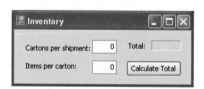 

Figure 22.31 Enhanced **Inventory** application.

a) *Copying the template to your working directory.* Copy the directory `C:\Examples\Tutorial22\Exercises\KeyEventInventory` to your `C:\SimplyVB` directory.

b) *Opening the application's template file.* Double click `KeyEventInventory.sln` in the `KeyEventInventory` directory to open the application.

c) *Adding the KeyDown event handler for the first TextBox.* Add an empty `KeyDown` event handler for the **Cartons per shipment:** `TextBox`.

d) *Adding a Select Case statement.* Add a `Select Case` statement to the `KeyDown` event handler that determines whether a number key, a left or right arrow or the *Backspace* key was pressed.

e) *Adding the Case Else statement.* Add a `Case Else` statement that will determine whether a key other than a valid one for this application was pressed. If an invalid key was pressed, display a `MessageBox` that instructs the user to enter a number.

f) **Adding the KeyDown event handler for the second TextBox.** Repeat *Steps c–e*, but this time create a KeyDown event handler for the **Items per carton:** TextBox. This event handler should have the same functionality as the one for the **Cartons per shipment:** TextBox.

g) **Running the application.** Select **Debug > Start Debugging** to run your application. Try entering letters or pressing the up- and down-arrow keys in the TextBoxes. A MessageBox should be displayed. Enter valid input and click the **Calculate Total** Button. Verify that the correct output is displayed.

h) **Closing the application.** Close your running application by clicking its close box.

i) **Closing the IDE.** Close the Visual Basic IDE by clicking its close box.

22.12 (**Bouncing Ball Game**) Write an application that allows the user to play a game, in which the goal is to prevent a bouncing ball from falling off the bottom of the Form. When the user presses the *S* key, a blue ball will bounce off the top, left and right sides (the "walls") of the Form. A horizontal bar on the bottom of the Form serves as a paddle to prevent the ball from hitting the bottom of the Form. (The ball can bounce off the paddle, but not the bottom of the Form.) The user can move the paddle using the left and right arrow keys. If the ball hits the paddle, it bounces up, and the game continues. If the ball hits the bottom of the Form, the game ends. The paddle's width decreases every 20 seconds to make the game more challenging. The GUI is provided for you (Fig. 22.32).

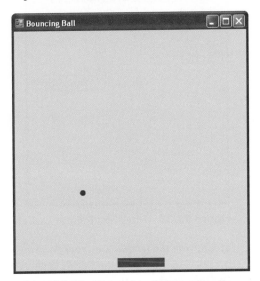

Figure 22.32 Bouncing Ball application.

a) **Copying the template to your working directory.** Copy the directory C:\Examples\Tutorial22\Exercises\BouncingBall to your C:\SimplyVB directory.

b) **Opening the application's template file.** Double click BouncingBall.sln in the BouncingBall directory to open the application.

c) **Creating the KeyDown event handler.** Insert a KeyDown event handler for the Form.

d) **Writing code to start the game.** Write an If...Then statement in the KeyDown event handler that tests whether the user presses the *S* key. You can use the KeyDown event handler for the *S* key in this case because you do not care whether the user presses an uppercase *S* or a lowercase *S*. If the user presses the *S* key, start the two Timers provided in the template (set their Enabled properties to True).

e) **Inserting code to move the paddle left.** Write an If...Then statement that tests whether the user pressed the left-arrow key and whether the paddle's horizontal position (rectangleX) is greater than zero. If the paddle's horizontal position equals zero, the left edge of the paddle is touching the left wall and the paddle should not be allowed to move farther to the left. If both the conditions in the If...Then are true, decrease the paddle's *x*-position by 10.

f) **Inserting code to move the paddle right.** Write an If...Then statement that tests whether the user pressed the right-arrow key and whether the paddle's *x*-coordinate is less than the width of the Form minus the width of the paddle (rectangleWidth). If the paddle's *x*-coordinate equals the Form's width minus the width of the paddle, the paddle's right edge is touching the right wall and the paddle should not be allowed to move farther to the right. If both the conditions in the If...Then statement are true, increase the paddle's *x*-coordinate by 10.

g) ***Running the application.*** Select **Debug > Start Debugging** to run your application. Press the *S* key to begin the game and use the paddle to keep the bouncing ball from dropping off the Form. Continue doing this until 20 seconds have passed, and verify that the paddle is decreased in size at that time.

h) ***Closing the application.*** Close your running application by clicking its close box.

i) ***Closing the IDE.*** Close the Visual Basic IDE by clicking its close box.

22.13 (***Modified Painter Application***) Modify the **Painter** application that you developed in Tutorial 21 to include menus that allow the user to select the size and color of the painted ellipses and the color of the Form (Fig. 22.33). (The menus replace the RadioButtons.) Add a multi-line TextBox that allows the user to type text to accompany the painting. The user should be able to use menus to select the font style and color of the text and the background color of the TextBox.

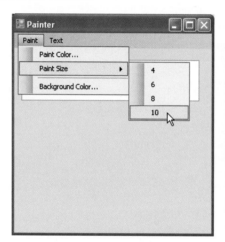

Figure 22.33 Modified **Painter** GUI.

a) ***Copying the template to your working directory.*** Copy the directory C:\Examples\Tutorial22\Exercises\ModifiedPainter to your C:\SimplyVB directory.

b) ***Opening the application's template file.*** Double click ModifiedPainter.sln in the ModifiedPainter directory to open the application.

c) ***Creating the menus.*** Create two menus. The first one should be titled **Paint** and should contain a **Paint Color...** menu item, a **Paint Size** submenu that contains menu items **4**, **6**, **8** and **10**, a separator bar and a **Background Color...** menu item. The second menu should be titled **Text** and have **Text Color...** and **Font...** menu items, and a **TextBox Color...** menu item.

d) ***Changing the paint color.*** Add an event handler for the **Paint Color...** menu item. This event handler should display a **Color** dialog that allows the user to change the value stored in paintColor.

e) ***Changing the paint size.*** Add an event handler for each of the **Size** submenu's menu items. Each event handler should change the value stored in diameter to the value displayed on the menu (that is, clicking the **4** menu item will change the value of diameter to 4).

f) ***Changing the background color.*** Add an event handler for the **Background Color...** menu item. This event handler should display a **Color** dialog that allows the user to change the value stored in backgroundColor and also change the BackColor property of the Form. To change the background color of the Form, assign the value specifying the background color to BackColor. For instance, the statement BackColor = Color.White changes the background color of the Form to white.

g) *Changing the text color.* Add an event handler for the **Text Color...** menu item. This event handler should display a **Color** dialog that allows the user to change the color of the text displayed in the TextBox.

h) *Changing the text style.* Add an event handler for the **Font...** menu item. This event handler should display a **Font** dialog that allows the user to change the style of the text displayed in the TextBox.

i) *Changing the TextBox's background color.* Add an event handler for the **TextBox Color...** menu item. This event handler should display a **Color** dialog that allows the user to change the background color of the TextBox.

j) *Running the application.* Select **Debug > Start Debugging** to run your application. Use the menus to draw shapes of various colors and brush sizes. Enter text to describe your drawing. Use the other menu options to change the color of the Form, the TextBox and the text in the TextBox.

k) *Closing the application.* Close your running application by clicking its close box.

l) *Closing the IDE.* Close the Visual Basic IDE by clicking its close box.

What does this code do? ▶ **22.14** What is the result of the following code?

```
1   Private Sub colorMenuItem_Click(ByVal sender As _
2      System.Object, ByVal e As System.EventArgs) _
3      Handles colorMenuItem.Click
4
5      Dim dialog As ColorDialog = New ColorDialog
6      Dim result As DialogResult
7
8      dialog.FullOpen = True
9
10     result = dialog.ShowDialog()
11
12     If result = System.Windows.Forms.DialogResult.Cancel Then
13        Return
14     End If
15
16     BackColor = dialog.Color
17  End Sub ' colorMenuItem_Click
```

What's wrong with this code? ▶ **22.15** This code should allow a user to pick a font from a **Font** dialog and set the text in displayTextBox to that font. Find the error(s) in the following code, assuming that a TextBox named displayTextBox exists on a Form.

```
1   Private Sub Fonts()
2      Dim dialog As FontDialog
3
4      dialog = New FontDialog
5      dialog.ShowDialog
6      displayTextBox.Font = dialog.Font
7   End Sub
```

Programming Challenge ▶ **22.16** (*Dvorak Keyboard Application*) Create an application that simulates the letters on the Dvorak keyboard. A Dvorak keyboard allows faster typing by placing the most commonly used keys in the most accessible locations. Use keyboard events to create an application similar to the **Typing Application** that simulates the Dvorak keyboard instead of the standard keyboard. The correct Dvorak key should be highlighted on the virtual keyboard, and the correct character should be displayed in the TextBox. The keys and characters map as follows:

- On the top row, the *P* key of the Dvorak keyboard maps to the *R* key on a standard keyboard, and the *L* key of the Dvorak keyboard maps to the *P* key on a standard keyboard.

- On the middle row, the *A* key remains in the same position, and the *S* key on the Dvorak keyboard maps to the semicolon key on the standard keyboard.
- On the bottom row, the *Q* key on the Dvorak keyboard maps to the *X* key on the standard keyboard, and the *Z* key maps to the question-mark key.
- All of the other keys on the Dvorak keyboard map to the locations shown in Fig. 22.34.

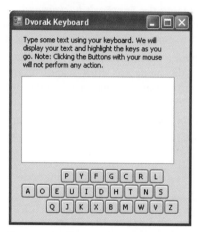

Figure 22.34 Dvorak Keyboard GUI.

a) *Copying the template to your working directory.* Copy the directory `C:\Examples\Tutorial22\Exercises\DvorakKeyboard` to your `C:\SimplyVB` directory.

b) *Opening the application's template file.* Double click `DvorakKeyboard.sln` in the DvorakKeyboard directory to open the application.

c) *Creating the KeyPress event handler.* Add a `KeyPress` event handler for the `TextBox`.

d) *Creating a Select Case statement.* Add a `Select Case` statement to the `KeyPress` event handler. The `Select Case` statement should test whether all of the letter keys on the Dvorak keyboard were pressed except for the *S*, *W*, *V* and *Z* keys. If a Dvorak key was pressed, highlight it on the GUI and display the character in the `TextBox`.

e) *Creating a KeyDown event handler.* Add a `KeyDown` event handler for the `TextBox`. The *S*, *W*, *V* and *Z* keys do not map to a letter key on the standard keyboard; therefore, a `KeyDown` event handler must be used to determine whether one of these keys was pressed.

f) *Adding a Select Case statement.* Add a `Select Case` statement to your `KeyDown` event handler that determines whether *S*, *W*, *V* or *Z* was pressed. If one of these keys was pressed, highlight the key, and add the character to the `TextBox`.

g) *Running the application.* Select **Debug > Start Debugging** to run your application. Use your keyboard to enter text. Verify that the text entered is correct based on the rules in the exercise description. Make sure that the correct `Buttons` on the `Form` are highlighted as you enter text.

h) *Closing the application.* Close your running application by clicking its close box.

i) *Closing the IDE.* Close the Visual Basic IDE by clicking its close box.

Screen Scraping Application

Introducing *String* Processing

Objectives

In this tutorial, you will learn to:
- Create and manipulate String objects.
- Use properties and methods of class String.
- Search for substrings within Strings.
- Extract substrings within Strings.
- Replace substrings within Strings.

Outline

This tutorial introduces Visual Basic's String-processing capabilities. The techniques presented in this tutorial can be used to create applications that process text. Earlier tutorials introduced class String from the System namespace and several of its methods. In this tutorial, you will learn how to search Strings, retrieve characters from String objects and replace characters in a String. You will create an application that uses these String-processing capabilities to manipulate a string containing **HTML (HyperText Markup Language)**. HTML is a technology for describing Web pages. Extracting desired information from the HTML that composes a Web page is called **screen scraping**. Applications that perform screen scraping can be used to extract specific information, such as weather conditions or stock prices, from Web pages so that the information can be formatted and manipulated more easily by computer applications. In this tutorial, you will create a simple **Screen Scraping** application.

23.1 Test-Driving the Screen Scraping Application

This application must meet the following requirements:

Application Requirements

An online European auction house wants to expand its business to include bidders from the United States. However, all of the auction house's Web pages currently display their prices in euros, not dollars. The auction house wants to generate separate Web pages for American bidders that will display the prices of auction items in dollars. These new Web pages will be generated by using screen-scraping techniques on the already existing Web pages. You have been asked to build a prototype application that will test the screen-scraping functionality. The application will have to search a sample string of HTML and extract information about the price of a specified auction item. For testing purposes, a ComboBox should be provided that contains auction items listed in the HTML. The selected item's amount must then be converted to dollars. For simplicity, assume that the exchange rate is one to one (that is, one euro is equivalent to one dollar). The price (in dollars) and sample HTML are displayed in Labels.

The **Screen Scraping** application searches for the name of a specified auction item in a string of HTML. Users select the item for which to search from a ComboBox. The application then extracts and displays the price in dollars of this item. You begin by test-driving the completed application. Then, you will learn the additional Visual Basic technologies that you will need to create your own version of the application.

Test-Driving the Screen Scraping Application

1. ***Opening the completed application.*** Open the directory `C:\Examples\Tutorial23\CompletedApplication\ScreenScraping` to locate the **Screen Scraping** application. Double click `ScreenScraping.sln` to open the application in the Visual Basic IDE.

2. ***Running the application.*** Select **Debug > Start Debugging** to run the application (Fig. 23.1). Note that the HTML string is displayed in a Label at the bottom of the Form.

Label containing HTML ⎯⎯⎯⎯

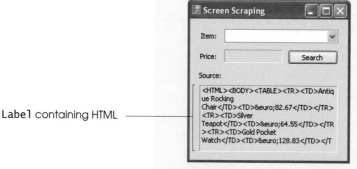

Figure 23.1 **Screen Scraping** application's Form.

3. ***Selecting an item name.*** The ComboBox contains three item names. Select an item name from the ComboBox, as shown in Fig. 23.2.

ComboBox's drop-down list ⎯⎯⎯⎯

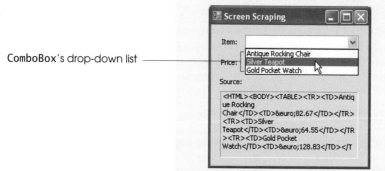

Figure 23.2 Selecting an item name from the ComboBox.

4. ***Searching for an item's price.*** Click the **Search** Button to display the price for the selected item. The extracted price is displayed in a Label (Fig. 23.3).

5. ***Closing the application.*** Close your running application by clicking its close box.

6. ***Closing the IDE.*** Close the Visual Basic IDE by clicking its close box.

(cont.)

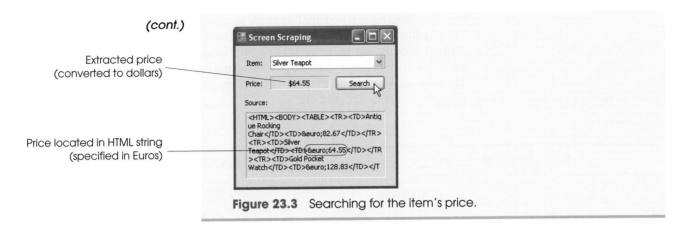

Extracted price
(converted to dollars)

Price located in HTML string
(specified in Euros)

Figure 23.3   Searching for the item's price.

23.2 Fundamentals of Strings

A string is a series of characters treated as a single unit. These characters can be uppercase letters, lowercase letters, digits and various **special characters**, such as +, -, *, /, $ and others. A string is an object of class String in the System namespace. We write **string literals**, or **string constants** (often called **literal String objects**), as sequences of characters in double quotation marks, as follows:

```
"This is a string!"
```

You've already created and used Strings in previous tutorials. You know that a declaration can assign a String literal to a String variable. For example, the declaration

```
Dim colorIs As String = "blue"
```

initializes colorIs to refer to the String literal object "blue".

Like arrays, Strings always know their own size. String property Length returns the length of the String (that is, the number of characters in the String). For example, the expression colorIs.Length evaluates to 4 for the String "blue".

Another useful property of class String is **Chars**, which returns the character located at a specific index in a String. Property Chars takes an Integer argument specifying the index and returns the character at that index. As in arrays, the first element of a String is at index 0. For example, the following code

```
If string1.Chars(0) = string2.Chars(0) Then
    messageLabel.Text = "The first characters are the same."
```

compares the character at index 0 (that is, the first character) of string1 with the character at index 0 of string2.

In earlier tutorials, you used several methods of class String to manipulate String objects. Figure 23.4 lists some of these methods. You will be introduced to new String methods later in this tutorial.

Method	Sample Expression Method Call (assume text = "My String")	Returns
Insert(*index*, *string*)	text.Insert(9,"!")	"My String!"
Remove(*index*, *count*)	text.Remove(2,1)	"MyString"
ToLower()	text.ToLower()	"my string"
ToUpper()	text.ToUpper()	"MY STRING"

Figure 23.4   String-class methods introduced in earlier tutorials.

Any String method that appears to modify a String actually returns a new String that contains the results. For example, String method ToUpper does not actually modify the original String, but instead returns a new String in which each lowercase letter has been converted to uppercase. This occurs because Strings are **immutable** objects—that is, characters in Strings cannot be changed after the Strings are created.

SELF-REVIEW

1. The _____ property of the class String returns the number of characters in the String.

   a) MaxChars   b) Length

   c) CharacterCount   d) TotalLength

2. A String can be composed of _____.

   a) digits   b) lowercase letters

   c) special characters   d) All of the above.

Answers: 1) b. 2) d.

23.3 Analyzing the Screen Scraping Application

Before building the **Screen Scraping** application, you must analyze its components. The following pseudocode describes the basic operation of the **Screen Scraping** application.

> When the Form loads:
>   Display the HTML that contains the items' prices in a Label
>
> When the user clicks the Search Button:
>   Search the HTML for the item the user selected from the ComboBox
>   Extract the item's price
>   Convert the item's price from euros to dollars
>   Display the item's price in a Label

Now that you have test-driven the **Screen Scraping** application and studied its pseudocode representation, you will use an ACE table to help you convert the pseudocode to Visual Basic. Figure 23.5 lists the actions, controls and events that will help you complete your own version of this application.

Action/Control/Event (ACE) Table for the Screen Scraping Application

Action	Control/Object	Event
Label the application's controls	itemLabel priceLabel sourceLabel	Application is run
	ScreenScraping-Form	Load
Display the HTML that contains the items' prices in a Label	htmlLabel	
	searchButton	Click
Search the HTML for the item the user selected from the ComboBox	html, itemsComboBox	
Extract the item's price	html	
Convert the item's price from euros to dollars	price	
Display the item's price in a Label	resultLabel	

Figure 23.5 ACE table for **Screen Scraping** application.

Now that you've analyzed the **Screen Scraping** application's components, you will learn about the `String` methods that you will use to construct the application.

23.4 Locating Substrings in `Strings`

In many applications, it is necessary to search for a character or set of characters in a `String`. For example, a programmer creating a word-processing application would want to provide capabilities that allow users to search their documents. Class `String` provides methods that make it possible to search for specified **substrings** (or sequences of characters) in a `String`. In the following box, you begin building the **Screen Scraping** application.

Locating the Selected Item's Price

1. *Copying the template to your working directory.* Copy the `C:\Examples\Tutorial23\TemplateApplication\ScreenScraping` directory to your `C:\SimplyVB` directory.

2. *Opening the Screen Scraping application's template file.* Double click `ScreenScraping.sln` in the `ScreenScraping` directory to open the application in the Visual Basic IDE. Double click `ScreenScraping.vb` in the **Solution Explorer** to display the application's Form in **Design** view.

3. *Creating a `Click` event handler for the Search Button.* Double click the **Search** Button on the application's Form to generate the event handler `searchButton_Click`. Add the comments in lines 13 and 17 of Fig. 23.6.

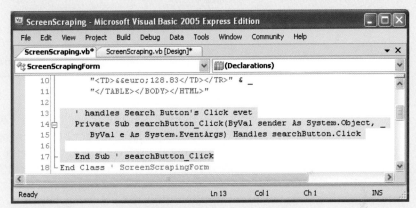

Figure 23.6 `searchButton_Click` event handler.

4. *Declaring three Integer variables and a String reference.* Add lines 17–20 of Fig. 23.7 to the `searchButton_Click` event handler. These lines declare `Integer` variables `itemLocation`, `priceBegin` and `priceEnd` and `String` variable `price`.

5. *Locating the specified item name.* Add lines 22–24 of Fig. 23.8 to event handler `searchButton_Click`. Lines 23–24 call `String` method **IndexOf** to locate the first occurrence of the specified item name in the HTML string (`html`). There are three versions of `IndexOf` that search for substrings in a `String`. Lines 23–24 use the version of `IndexOf` that takes a single argument—the substring for which to search. (The specified item name is the `SelectedItem` of `itemsComboBox`.)

(cont.)

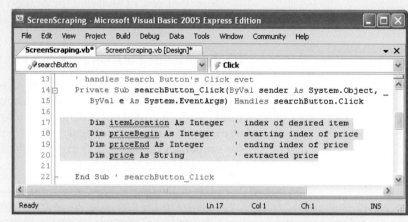

Figure 23.7   `searchButton_Click` event-handler declarations.

Search for the
`SelectedItem` in the
`String html`

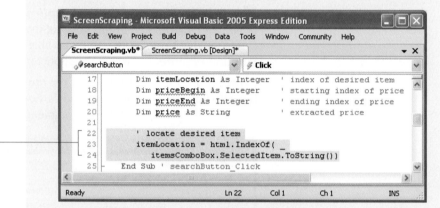

Figure 23.8   Locating the desired item name.

`Option Strict` is set to `On`, so we must first convert `SelectedItem` (which is of type `Object`) to a `String`, by using method `ToString`, before passing the selected item to method `IndexOf`. If `IndexOf` finds the specified substring (in this case, the item name), `IndexOf` returns the index at which the substring begins in the `String`. For example, the return value 0 means that the substring begins at the first element of the `String`. If `IndexOf` does not find the specified substring, it returns –1. The result is stored in variable `itemLocation`.

6. ***Locating the start of the price.*** Add lines 26–28 of Fig. 23.9 to event handler `searchButton_Click`. Lines 27–28 locate the index at which the item's price begins. Lines 27–28 use a version of method `IndexOf` that takes two arguments—the substring for which to search and the starting index in the `String` at which the search begins. The method does not examine any characters that occur prior to the starting index (specified by `itemLocation`). The third version of method `IndexOf` takes three arguments—the substring for which to search, the index at which to start searching and the number of characters to search. We do not use this version of `IndexOf` in the **Screen Scraping** application.

We know that the first price that follows the specified item name will be the desired price, therefore, we can begin our search at `itemLocation`. The substring we search for is `"&euro;"`. This is the HTML representation of the euro symbol, which appears before every price value in the HTML string in this application. The index returned from method `IndexOf` is stored in variable `priceBegin`.

(cont.)

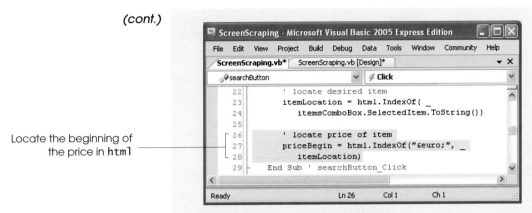

Figure 23.9   Locating the desired item price.

7. ***Locating the end of the price.*** Add line 29 of Fig. 23.10 to event handler `searchButton_Click`. Line 29 finds the index at which the desired price ends. Line 29 calls method `IndexOf` with the substring `"</TD>"` and the starting index `priceBegin`. A </TD> tag directly follows every price (excluding any spaces) in the HTML string, so the index of the first </TD> tag after `priceBegin` marks the end of the current price.

    The index returned from method `IndexOf` is stored in variable `priceEnd`. In the next box, we will use `priceBegin` and `priceEnd` to obtain the price substring from the string `html`.

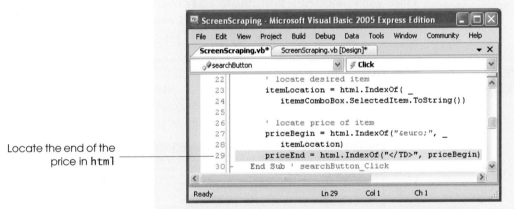

Figure 23.10   Locating the end of the item's price.

8. ***Saving the project.*** Select **File > Save All** to save your modified code.

The **LastIndexOf** method is similar to method `IndexOf`. Method `LastIndexOf` locates the last occurrence of a substring in a `String`; it performs the search starting from the end of the `String` and searches toward the beginning. If method `LastIndexOf` finds the substring, it returns the starting index of the specified substring in the `String`; otherwise, `LastIndexOf` returns –1.

There are three versions of `LastIndexOf` that search for substrings in a `String`. The first version takes a single argument—the substring for which to search. The second version takes two arguments—the substring for which to search and the highest index from which to begin searching backward for the substring. The third version of method `LastIndexOf` takes three arguments—the substring for which to search, the starting index from which to start searching backward and the number of characters to search. Figure 23.11 shows examples of the three versions of `LastIndexOf`. Note that the example expression (`String text`) begins with a blank space on purpose.

Method	Example Expression (assume text = " My String")	Returns
`LastIndexOf(string)`	`text.LastIndexOf("n")`	8
`LastIndexOf(string, integer)`	`text.LastIndexOf("n", 6)`	-1
`LastIndexOf(string, integer, integer)`	`text.LastIndexOf("m", 7, 3)`	-1

Figure 23.11   `LastIndexOf` examples.

SELF-REVIEW

1. Method _____ locates the first occurrence of a substring.

    a) `IndexOf`   b) `FirstIndexOf`

    c) `FindFirst`   d) `Locate`

2. The third argument passed to the `LastIndexOf` method is _____.

    a) the starting index from which to start searching backward

    b) the starting index from which to start searching forward

    c) the length of the substring to locate

    d) the number of characters to search

Answers: 1) a. 2) d.

23.5 Extracting Substrings from `Strings`

Once you've located a substring in a `String`, you might want to retrieve the substring from the `String`. The following box uses the `Substring` method to retrieve the price of the selected item from the HTML string.

Retrieving the Desired Item's Price

1. ***Extracting the price.*** Add lines 31–33 of Fig. 23.12 to the `search-Button_Click` event handler. Class `String` provides two versions of the **Substring** method, each of which returns a new `String` object that contains a copy of a part of an existing `String` object.

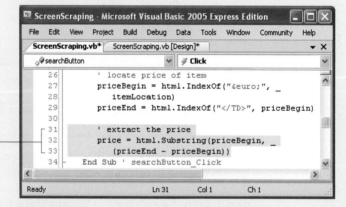

Extract price from `html`

Figure 23.12   Retrieving the desired price.

Lines 32–33 extract the price, using the version of the `Substring` method that takes two `Integer` arguments. The first argument (`priceBegin`) specifies the starting index from which the method copies characters from the original `String`.

The second argument (`priceEnd - priceBegin`) specifies the length of the substring to be copied. The substring returned (`price`) contains a copy of the specified characters from the original `String`. In this case, the substring returned is the item's price (in euros).

(cont.) The other version of method Substring takes one Integer argument. The argument specifies the starting index from which the method copies characters in the original String. The substring returned contains a copy of the characters from the starting index to the end of the String. We do not use this version of Substring in the **Screen Scraping** application.

2. *Saving the project.* Select **File > Save All** to save your modified code.

SELF-REVIEW

1. The Substring method _____.
   a) accepts either one or two arguments
   b) returns a new String object
   c) creates a String object by copying part of an existing String object
   d) All of the above.

2. The second argument passed to method Substring specifies _____.
   a) the last index of the String to copy
   b) the length of the substring to copy
   c) the index from which to begin copying backwards
   d) a character which, when reached, signifies that copying is to stop

Answers: 1) d. 2) b.

23.6 Replacing Substrings in Strings

Perhaps you want to replace certain characters in Strings. Class String provides the **Replace** method to replace occurrences of one substring with a different substring. The Replace method takes two arguments—a String to replace in the original String and a String with which to replace all occurrences of the first argument. Method Replace returns a new String with the specified replacements. The original String remains unchanged. If there are no occurrences of the first argument in the String, the method returns a copy of the original String. The following box uses method Replace to convert the extracted price from euros to dollars.

Converting the Price to Dollars

1. *Converting the price.* Add lines 35–36 of Fig. 23.13 to searchButton_Click. Line 36 converts the extracted price from euros to dollars. For simplicity, we assume that dollars are equal to euros.

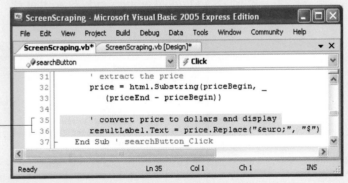

Replace "€" with "$"

Figure 23.13 Converting the price to dollars.

(cont.)

Therefore, to perform the conversion, we need to change only the currency's name. Line 36 uses `String` method `Replace` to return a new `String` object, replacing every occurrence (one in this example) in `price` of substring `"&euro;"` with substring `"$"`. Note that we assign the value returned from method `Replace` to `resultLabel.Text` to display the text in dollars.

2. *Saving the project.* Select **File > Save All** to save your modified code.

Method `Replace` also is used when the `Form` for the **Screen Scraping** application first loads. The following box uses method `Replace` to ensure that the HTML string displays correctly in a `Label`.

Displaying the HTML String

1. *Creating a Load event handler for the Form.* In **Design** view (**View > Designer**), double click the `Form` to generate an empty Load event handler. This event handler will execute when the application runs.

2. *Formatting the Load event handler.* Add the comments in lines 39 and 44 of Fig. 23.14 around event handler `ScreenScrapingForm_Load`. Also, split the procedure header over three lines using line-continuation characters (that is, underscores), as in lines 40–42 of Fig. 23.14, to improve its readability.

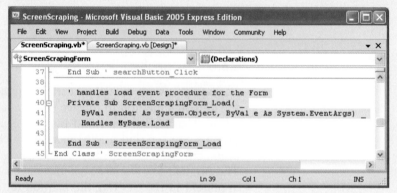

Figure 23.14 Load event for the Form.

3. *Displaying the HTML string in a Label.* Add lines 44–45 of Fig. 23.15 to `ScreenScrapingForm_Load`. Line 45 calls `String` method `Replace` to replace every occurrence of `"&euro;"` in the HTML string with `"&&euro;"`. As explained previously, the substring `"&euro;"` is the HTML for the euro symbol. For this text to display in a `Label` correctly, we must prefix it with an additional ampersand (&) so that the "e" in "euro" is not confused with an access shortcut. The value returned from `Replace` is displayed in `htmlLabel`.

Replace all occurrences of
"&euro" with "&&euro"

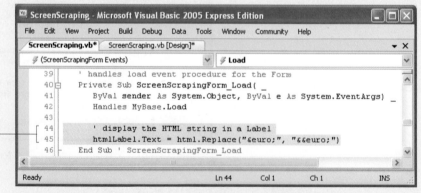

Figure 23.15 Displaying the HTML string in a `Label`.

(cont.)   4. ***Running the application.*** Select **Debug > Start Debugging** to run your application. Select the different items from the **Item** ComboBox, clicking the **Search** Button after each selection. Make sure that in each case, the proper price is extracted and displayed in dollar amounts.

5. ***Closing the application.*** Close your running application by clicking its close box.

6. ***Closing the IDE.*** Close the Visual Basic IDE by clicking its close box.

---

1. If there are no occurrences of the substring in the String, method Replace returns _____.

   a) 0   b) -1
   c) Nothing   d) a copy of the original String

Answer: 1) d.

23.7 Other String Methods

Class String provides several additional methods that allow you to manipulate Strings. Figure 23.16 lists some of these methods and provides a description of what each method does.

Method	Description	Sample Expression (assume text = " My String")
EndsWith(*string*)	Returns True if a String ends with the argument *string*; otherwise, returns False.	`text.EndsWith("ing")` Returns: True

Join(*separator, array*)	Concatenates the elements in a String array, separated by the first argument. A new String containing the concatenated elements is returned.	`Dim array As String() = New String() {"a", "b", "c"}`
		
		 `String.Join(";", array)`
		
		 Returns: "a;b;c"

Split()	Splits the words in a String whenever a space is reached.	`Dim array As String() = _`
		 `   text.Split()`
		
		 Returns: "My" and "String" in an array of Strings

StartsWith(*string*)	Returns True if a String starts with argument *string*; otherwise, returns False.	`text.StartsWith("Your")` Returns: False
Trim()	Removes any whitespace (that is, blank lines, spaces and tabs) from the beginning and end of a String.	`text.Trim()` Returns: "My String"

Figure 23.16   Description of other String methods.

Figure 23.17 presents the source code for the **Screen Scraping** application. The lines of code that contain new programming concepts that you learned in this tutorial are highlighted.

```
1   Public Class ScreenScrapingForm
2
3       ' String of HTML to extract prices from
4       Dim html As String = "<HTML><BODY><TABLE>" & _
5           "<TR><TD>Antique Rocking Chair</TD>" & _
6           "<TD>&&euro;82.67</TD></TR>" & _
7           "<TR><TD>Silver Teapot</TD>" & _
8           "<TD>&&euro;64.55</TD></TR>" & _
9           "<TR><TD>Gold Pocket Watch</TD>" & _
10          "<TD>&&euro;128.83</TD></TR>" & _
11          "</TABLE></BODY></HTML>"
12
13      ' handles Search Button's Click event
14      Private Sub searchButton_Click(ByVal sender As System.Object, _
15          ByVal e As System.EventArgs) Handles searchButton.Click
16
17          Dim itemLocation As Integer   ' index of desired item
18          Dim priceBegin As Integer     ' starting index of price
19          Dim priceEnd As Integer       ' ending index of price
20          Dim price As String           ' extracted price
21
22          ' locate desired item
23          itemLocation = html.IndexOf( _
24              itemsComboBox.SelectedItem.ToString())
25
26          ' locate price of item
27          priceBegin = html.IndexOf("&euro;", _
28              itemLocation)
29          priceEnd = html.IndexOf("</TD>", priceBegin)
30
31          ' extract the price
32          price = html.Substring(priceBegin, _
33              (priceEnd - priceBegin))
34
35          ' convert price to dollars and display
36          resultLabel.Text = price.Replace("&euro;", "$")
37      End Sub ' searchButton_Click
38
39      ' handles load event procedure for the Form
40      Private Sub ScreenScrapingForm_Load( _
41          ByVal sender As System.Object, ByVal e As System.EventArgs) _
42          Handles MyBase.Load
43
44          ' display the HTML string in a Label
45          htmlLabel.Text = html.Replace("&euro;", "&&euro;")
46      End Sub ' ScreenScrapingForm_Load
47  End Class ' ScreenScrapingForm
```

Annotations:
- Search for the SelectedItem in the String html (lines 23–24)
- Locate the beginning of the price in html (lines 27–28)
- Locate the end of the price in html (line 29)
- Extract the price from html (lines 32–33)
- Replace "€" with "$" (line 36)

Figure 23.17 Screen Scraping application.

SELF-REVIEW 1. The _____ method removes all whitespace characters that appear at the beginning and end of a String.

a) RemoveSpaces　　　　　b) NoSpaces
c) Trim　　　　　　　　　d) Truncate

2. The `StartsWith` method returns _____ if a `String` begins with the `String` text passed to `StartsWith` as an argument.

   a) `True`   b) `False`

   c) `1`   d) the index of the substring

Answers: 1) c. 2) a.

23.8 Wrap-Up

In this tutorial, we introduced you to class `String` from the `System` namespace. You learned how to create and manipulate `String` objects. You learned how to locate, retrieve and replace substrings in `Strings`. You reviewed several methods from class `String` that were used in earlier tutorials and learned several additional methods. You applied your knowledge of `Strings` in Visual Basic to create a simple **Screen Scraping** application that retrieved the price of an item from an HTML `String`.

    In the next tutorial, you will learn how data is represented in a computer. You will be introduced to the concepts of files and streams. You will learn how to store data in sequential-access files.

SKILLS SUMMARY

Determining the Size of a `String`

- Use `String` property `Length`.

Locating Substrings in `Strings`

- Use `String` method `IndexOf` to locate the first occurrence of a substring.
- Use `String` method `LastIndexOf` to locate the last occurrence of a substring.

Retrieving Substrings from `Strings`

- Use `String` method `Substring` with one argument to obtain a substring that begins at the specified starting index and contains the remainder of the original `String`.
- Use `String` method `Substring` with two arguments to specify the starting index and the length of the substring.

Replacing Substrings in `Strings`

- Use `String` method `Replace` to replace occurrences of one substring with another substring.
- Use method `Replace` to return a new `String` containing the replacements.

Comparing Substrings to the Beginning or End of a `String`

- Use `String` method `StartsWith` to determine whether a `String` starts with a particular substring.
- Use `String` method `EndsWith` to determine whether a `String` ends with a particular substring.

Removing Whitespace from a `String`

- Use `String` method `Trim` to remove all whitespace characters that appear at the beginning and end of a `String`.

KEY TERMS

Chars property of class `String`—Returns the character located at a specific index in a `String`.

EndsWith method of class `String`—Determines whether a `String` ends with a particular substring.

HTML (HyperText Markup Language)—A technology for describing Web content.

immutable—An object that cannot be changed after it is created. In Visual Basic, `Strings` are immutable.

IndexOf method of class `String`—Returns the index of the first occurrence of a substring in a `String`. Returns `-1` if the substring is not found.

Join method of class `String`—Concatenates the elements in a `String` array, separated by the first argument. A new `String` containing the concatenated elements is returned.

`LastIndexOf` method of class `String`—Returns the index of the last occurrence of a substring in a `String`. Returns -1 if the substring is not found.

literal `String` objects—A `String` constant written as a sequence of characters in double quotation marks (also called a string literal).

`Replace` method of class `String`—Returns a new `String` object in which every occurrence of a substring is replaced with a different substring.

screen scraping—The process of extracting desired information from the HTML that composes a Web page.

special characters—Characters that are neither digits nor letters.

`Split` method of class `String`—Splits the words in a `String` whenever a space is reached.

`StartsWith` method of class `String`—Determines whether a `String` starts with a particular substring.

string constant—A `String` constant written as a sequence of characters in double quotation marks (also called a string literal).

string literal—A `String` constant written as a sequence of characters in double quotation marks (also called a literal `String` object).

substring—A sequence of characters in a `String`.

`Substring` method of class `String`—Creates a new `String` object by copying part of an existing `String` object.

`ToLower` method of class `String`—Creates a new `String` object that replaces every uppercase letter in a `String` with its lowercase equivalent.

`ToUpper` method of class `String`—Creates a new `String` object that replaces every lowercase letter in a `String` with its uppercase equivalent.

`Trim` method of class `String`—Removes all whitespace characters from the beginning and end of a `String`.

CONTROLS, EVENTS, PROPERTIES & METHODS

`String` The `String` class represents a series of characters treated as a single unit.

■ *Property*

`Char`—Returns the character located at a specific index in the `String`.

`Length`—Returns the number of characters in the `String`.

■ *Methods*

`EndsWith`—Determines whether a `String` ends with a particular substring.

`Format`—Arranges the string in a specified format.

`IndexOf`—Returns the index of the specified character(s) in a `String`. It returns -1 if the substring is not found.

`Insert`—Returns a copy of the `String` for which it is called with the specified character(s) inserted.

`LastIndexOf`—Returns the index of the last occurrence of a substring in a `String`. It returns -1 if the substring is not found.

`PadLeft`—Inserts characters at the beginning of a `String`.

`Remove`—Returns a copy of the `String` for which it is called with the specified character(s) removed.

`Replace`—Returns a new `String` object in which every occurrence of a substring is replaced with a different substring.

`StartsWith`—Determines whether a `String` starts with a particular substring.

`Substring`—Returns a substring from a `String`.

`ToLower`—Returns a copy of the `String` for which it is called with any uppercase letters converted to lowercase letters.

`ToUpper`—Creates a new `String` object that replaces every lowercase letter in a `String` with its uppercase equivalent.

`Trim`—Removes all whitespace characters from the beginning and end of a `String`.

MULTIPLE-CHOICE QUESTIONS

23.1 Extracting desired information from Web pages is called _____.

a) Web crawling   b) screen scraping

c) querying   d) redirection

23.2 If `IndexOf` method does not find the specified substring, it returns _____.

a) `False`   b) `0`

c) `-1`   d) None of the above.

23.3 The `String` class allows you to _____ `String`s.

a) search   b) retrieve characters from

c) replace characters in   d) All of the above.

23.4 _____ is a technology for describing Web content.

a) Class `String`   b) A `String` literal

c) HTML   d) A screen scraper

23.5 The `String` class is located in the _____ namespace.

a) `String`   b) `System.Strings`

c) `System.IO`   d) `System`

23.6 The _____ method creates a new `String` object by copying part of an existing `String` object.

a) `StringCopy`   b) `Substring`

c) `CopyString`   d) `CopySubString`

23.7 All `String` objects are _____.

a) the same size   b) always equal to each other

c) preceded by at least one whitespace character

d) immutable

23.8 The `IndexOf` method does not examine any characters that occur prior to the _____.

a) starting index   b) first match

c) last character of the `String`   d) None of the above.

23.9 The _____ method determines whether a `String` ends with a particular substring.

a) `CheckEnd`   b) `StringEnd`

c) `EndsWith`   d) `EndIs`

23.10 The `Trim` method removes all whitespace characters that appear _____ a `String`.

a) in   b) at the beginning of

c) at the end of   d) at the beginning and end of

EXERCISES

23.11 (*Supply Cost Calculator Application*) Write an application that calculates the cost of all the supplies added to the user's shopping list (Fig. 23.18). The application should contain two `ListBox`es. The first `ListBox` contains all the supplies offered and their respective prices. Users should be able to select the desired supplies from the first `ListBox` and add them to the second `ListBox`. Provide a **Calculate** Button that displays the total price for the user's shopping list (the contents of the second `ListBox`).

     a) *Copying the template to your working directory.* Copy the directory `C:\Examples\Tutorial23\Exercises\SupplyCalculator` to your `C:\SimplyVB` directory.

     b) *Opening the application's template file.* Double click `SupplyCalculator.sln` in the `SupplyCalculator` directory to open the application.

     c) *Adding code to the Add >> Button.* Double click the **Add >>** Button to create an empty event handler. Insert code in the event handler that adds the selected item from the first `ListBox` to `stockListBox`. Be sure to check that at least one item is selected in the first `ListBox` before attempting to add an item to `stockListBox`.

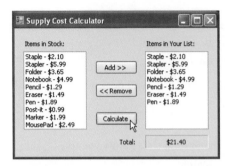

Figure 23.18 **Supply Cost Calculator** application's GUI.

d) *Enabling the Buttons.* Once the user adds something to the stockListBox, set the Enabled properties of the **<< Remove** and **Calculate** Buttons to True.

e) *Deselecting the items.* Once the items are added to the stockListBox, make sure that they are deselected in the supplyListBox. Also, clear the **Total:** Label to indicate to the user that a new total price must be calculated.

f) *Adding code to the << Remove Button.* Double click the **<< Remove** Button to create an empty event handler. Use a Do While loop to remove any selected items in the stockListBox. Be sure to check that at least one item is selected before attempting to remove an item. [*Hint:* Method stockListBox.Items.RemoveAt(index) will remove the item located at index from the stockListBox.]

g) *Adding code to the Calculate Button.* Double click the **Calculate** Button to create an empty event handler. Use a For...Next statement to loop through all the items in the stockListBox. Convert each item from the ListBox into a String. Then use the String method Substring to extract the price of each item.

h) *Displaying the total.* Convert the String representing each item's price to a Decimal, and add this to the overall total (of type Decimal). Remember to output the value in currency format.

i) *Running the application.* Select **Debug > Start Debugging** to run your application. Use the **Add >>** and **<< Remove** Buttons to add and remove items from the **Items in Your List:** ListBox. Click the **Calculate** Button and verify that the total price displayed is correct.

j) *Closing the application.* Close your running application by clicking its close box.

k) *Closing the IDE.* Close the Visual Basic IDE by clicking its close box.

23.12 (*Encryption Application*) Write an application that encrypts a message from the user (Fig. 23.19). The application should be able to encrypt the message in two different ways: substitution cipher and transposition cipher (both described below). The user should be able to enter the message in a TextBox and select the desired method of encryption. Display the encrypted message in a Label.

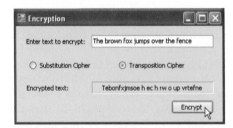

Figure 23.19 **Encryption** application's GUI.

In a substitution cipher, every character in the English alphabet is represented by a different character in the substitution alphabet. Every time a letter occurs in the English sentence, it is replaced by the letter in the corresponding index of the substitution string. In a transposition cipher, two Strings are created. The first new String contains all characters at the even indices of the input String. The second new String contains all of the characters at the odd indices. The new Strings separated by a white space are the encrypted text. For example a transposition cipher for the word "code" would be "cd oe."

a) *Copying the template to your working directory.* Copy the directory C:\Examples\ Tutorial23\Exercises\Encryption to your C:\SimplyVB directory.

b) *Opening the application's template file.* Double click Encryption.sln in the Encryption directory to open the application.

c) *Adding code to the Encrypt Button.* Double click the **Encrypt** Button to create an empty event handler.

d) *Determining the cipher method.* Use If...Then...Else statements to determine which method of encryption the user has selected and call the appropriate procedure.

e) *Locating the SubstitutionCipher method.* Locate the SubstitutionCipher procedure. The English and substitution alphabet Strings are defined for you in this procedure.

f) *Converting the text input to lowercase.* Add code to the SubstitutionCipher method that uses the ToLower method of class String to make all the characters in the input string (plainTextBox.Text) lowercase.

g) *Performing the substitution encryption.* Use nested For...Next loops to iterate through each character of the input String. When a character from the input String is found in the String holding the English alphabet, replace the character in the input String with the character located at the same index in the substitution String.

h) *Displaying the String.* Now that the String has been substituted with all the corresponding cipher characters, assign the cipher String to cipherTextLabel.

i) *Locating the TranspositionCipher method.* Locate the TranspositionCipher method. Define three variables—a counter variable and two Strings (each representing a word).

j) *Extracting the first word.* Use a Do While...Loop to retrieve all the "even" indices (starting from 0) from the input String. Increment the counter variable by 2 each time, and add the characters located at even indices to the first String created in *Step h*.

k) *Extracting the second word.* Use another Do While...Loop to retrieve all the "odd" indices (starting from 1) from the same input String. Increment the counter variable by 2, and add the characters at odd indices to the second String that you created in *Step h*.

l) *Outputting the result.* Add the two Strings together with a space in between, and output the result to cipherTextLabel.

m) *Running the application.* Select **Debug > Start Debugging** to run your application. Enter text into the **Enter text to encrypt:** TextBox. Select the **Substitution Cipher** RadioButton and click the **Encrypt** Button. Verify that the output is the properly encrypted text using the substitution cipher. Select the **Transposition Cipher** RadioButton and click the **Encrypt** Button. Verify that the output is the properly encrypted text using the transposition cipher.

n) *Closing the application.* Close your running application by clicking its close box.

o) *Closing the IDE.* Close the Visual Basic IDE by clicking its close box.

23.13 (*Anagram Game Application*) Write an **Anagram Game** that contains an array of 20 pre-set words (Fig. 23.20). The game randomly selects a word and scrambles its letters. A Label displays the scrambled word for the user to guess. If the user guesses correctly, display a message, then repeat the process with a different word. If the guess is incorrect, display a message, and let the user try again.

a) *Copying the template to your working directory.* Copy the directory C:\Examples\ Tutorial23\Exercises\Anagram to your C:\SimplyVB directory.

b) *Opening the application's template file.* Double click Anagram.sln in the Anagram directory to open the application.

c) *Locating the GenerateAnagram method.* Locate the GenerateAnagram method. It is the first method after the AnagramForm_Load event handler.

d) *Picking a random word.* Generate a random number to use as the index of the word in the anagram array. Retrieve word from the anagram array, using the first random number as an index. Store the word in another String variable. Generate a second random number to store the index of a character to be moved.

Figure 23.20 **Anagram Game** application's GUI.

e) *Generate the scrambled word*. Use a For...Next statement to iterate through the word 20 times. Each time the loop executes, pass the second random number created in *Step c* to the Chars property of class String. Append the character returned by Chars to the end of the String, and remove it from its original position. Next, generate a new random number to move a different character during the next iteration of the loop. Remember to output the final word to anagramLabel.

f) *Defining the Submit Button*. Double click the **Submit** Button to generate an empty event handler.

g) *Testing the user's input*. Use an If...Then...Else statement to determine whether the user's input matches the actual word. If the user is correct, clear and place the focus on the TextBox and generate a new word. Otherwise, select the user's text and place the focus on the TextBox.

h) *Running the application.* Select **Debug > Start Debugging** to run your application. Submit correct answers and incorrect answers, and verify that the appropriate message is displayed each time.

i) *Closing the application.* Close your running application by clicking its close box.

j) *Closing the IDE.* Close the Visual Basic IDE by clicking its close box.

What does this code do? ▶ **23.14** What is assigned to `result` when the following code executes?

```
1   Dim word1 As String = "CHORUS"
2   Dim word2 As String = "d i n o s a u r"
3   Dim word3 As String = "The theme is string."
4   Dim result As String
5
6   result = word1.ToLower()
7   result = result.Substring(4)
8   word2 = word2.Replace(" ", "")
9   word2 = word2.Substring(4, 4)
10  result = word2 & result
11
12  word3 = word3.Substring(word3.IndexOf(" ") + 1, 3)
13
14  result = word3.Insert(3, result)
```

What's wrong with this code? ▶ **23.15** This code should remove all commas from `test` and convert all lowercase letters to uppercase letters. Find the error(s) in the following code.

```
1   Dim test As String = "Bug,2,Bug"
2
3   test = test.ToUpper()
4   test = test.Replace("")
```

23.16 (*Pig Latin Application*) Write an application that encodes English-language phrases into pig Latin (Fig. 23.21). Pig Latin is a form of coded language often used for amusement. Many different methods are used to form pig Latin phrases. For simplicity, use the following method to form the pig Latin words:

> *To form a pig Latin word from an English-language phrase, the translation proceeds one word at a time. To translate an English word into a pig Latin word, place the first letter of the English word (if it is not a vowel) at the end of the English word and add the letters "ay." If the first letter of the English word is a vowel, place it at the end of the word and add "y." Using this method, the word "jump" becomes "umpjay," the word "the" becomes "hetay" and the word "ace" becomes "ceay." Blanks between words remain blanks.*

Assume the following: The English phrase consists of words separated by blanks, there are no punctuation marks and all words have two or more letters. Enable the user to input a sentence. The `TranslateToPigLatin` method will translate the sentence into pig Latin, word by word. [*Hint:* You will need to use the `Join` and `Split` methods of class `String` demonstrated in Fig. 23.16 to form the pig Latin phrases].

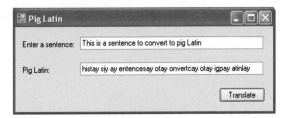

Figure 23.21   Pig Latin application.

a) *Copying the template to your working directory.* Copy the `C:\Examples\Tutorial23\Exercises\PigLatin` directory to your `C:\SimplyVB` directory.

b) *Opening the application's template file.* Double click `PigLatin.sln` in the `PigLatin` directory to open the application.

c) *Splitting the sentence.* Use method `Split` on the `String` passed to the `TranslateToPigLatin` method. Assign the result of this operation to `words`.

d) *Retrieving the word's first letter.* Declare a `For...Next` loop that iterates through your array of words. As you iterate through the array, store each word's first letter in `temporary`.

e) *Determining the suffix.* Use `If...Then...Else` statements to determine whether the first letter is a vowel, then determine the suffix for each word. Store this suffix in `suffix`.

f) *Generating new words.* Generate the new words by arranging each word's pieces in the proper order.

g) *Returning the new sentence.* When the `For...Next` loop finishes, use method `Join` to combine all of the elements in `words`, and `Return` the new pig Latin sentence.

h) *Running the application.* Select **Debug > Start Debugging** to run your application. Enter a sentence and click the **Translate** Button. Verify that the sentence is correctly converted into pig Latin.

i) *Closing the application.* Close your running application by clicking its close box.

j) *Closing the IDE.* Close the Visual Basic IDE by clicking its close box.

24

Objectives

In this tutorial, you will learn to:
- Create, read from, write to and update files.
- Understand a computer's data hierarchy.
- Become familiar with sequential-access file processing.
- Use `StreamReader` and `StreamWriter` classes to read from, and write to, sequential-access files.
- Use the `OpenFileDialog` control.
- Add and configure a `MonthCalendar` control.

Outline

Ticket Information Application

Introducing Sequential-Access Files

You have used variables and arrays to store data temporarily—the data is lost when a method or application terminates. When you want to store data for a longer period of time, you can use files. A **file** is a collection of data that is given a name such as `data.txt` or `Welcome.sln`. Data in files exists even after the application that created the data terminates. Such data often is called **persistent data**. Computers store files on **secondary storage media**, including magnetic disks (for example, the hard drive of your computer), optical disks (for instance, CD-ROMs or DVDs) and magnetic tapes.

File processing, which includes creating, reading from, writing to and updating files, is an important capability of Visual Basic. It enables Visual Basic to support commercial applications that typically process massive amounts of persistent data. In this tutorial, you will learn about **sequential-access files**, which contain information that is read from a file in the order that it was originally written to the file. You will learn how to create, open and write to a sequential-access file by building a **Write Event** application. This application allows the user to create or open a **text file** (a file containing human-readable characters) and to input the date, time and description of a community event (such as a concert or a sporting match).

You will then learn how to read data from a file by building the **Ticket Information** application. This application displays data from a text file named `calendar.txt` created by the **Write Event** application.

24.1 Test-Driving the Ticket Information Application

Many communities and businesses use computer applications to allow their members and customers to view information about upcoming events, such as movies, concerts, sports and other activities. The **Write Event** application that you build in Section 24.4 writes the community event information to a sequential-access file. The **Ticket Information** application that you build in this tutorial displays the data stored in the file generated by the **Write Event** application. This application must meet the following requirements:

Application Requirements

A local town has asked you to write an application that allows its residents to view community events for the current month. Events taking place in the town include concerts, sporting events, movies and other forms of entertainment. When the user selects a date, the application must indicate whether there are events scheduled for that day. The application must list the scheduled events and allow the user to select a listed event. When the user selects an event, the application must display the time and price of the event and a brief description of the event. The community event information is stored in a sequential-access file named `calendar.txt`.

Your application will allow a user to select a date from a **MonthCalendar** control. Then the application will open the `calendar.txt` file and read its contents to display information about events scheduled for the selected date. You begin by test-driving the completed application. Then you will learn the additional Visual Basic technologies that you will need to create your own version of this application.

Test-Driving the Ticket Information Application 	1. ***Opening the completed application.*** Open the directory C:\Examples\ Tutorial24\CompletedApplication\TicketInformation to locate the **Ticket Information** application. Double click TicketInformation.sln to open the application in the Visual Basic IDE. 2. ***Running the Ticket Information application.*** Select **Debug > Start Debugging** to run the application (Fig. 24.1). The calendar will look different, depending on the date that you test-drive the application. This is because the calendar reflects the day and month on which you actually run the application. The MonthCalendar control is similar to the DateTimePicker control (Tutorial 14), except that MonthCalendar allows you to select a range of dates, whereas the DateTimePicker allows you to select the time, but no more than one date. For simplicity, you should select only one date. In addition, the application deals only with the current month, but the Month-Calendar control allows the user to view calendars of previous or future months by using the arrow buttons.

Arrow buttons allow user to scroll through months

MonthCalendar control

ComboBox lists any events

TextBox displays event details

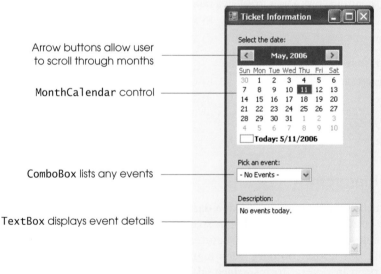

Figure 24.1   **Ticket Information** application's GUI.

(cont.)   3. ***Getting event information.*** Select the 18th day of the current month in the MonthCalendar. Note that the ComboBox displays the message "- No Events -" (Fig. 24.2). This is because there are no events scheduled for the 18th. Select the 19th day of the month. The ComboBox now displays "- Events -". Click the ComboBox to view the scheduled events and select **Comedy club**. The time, price and description of the event appear in the **Description:** TextBox (Fig. 24.2).

18th day of the month selected

No events displayed

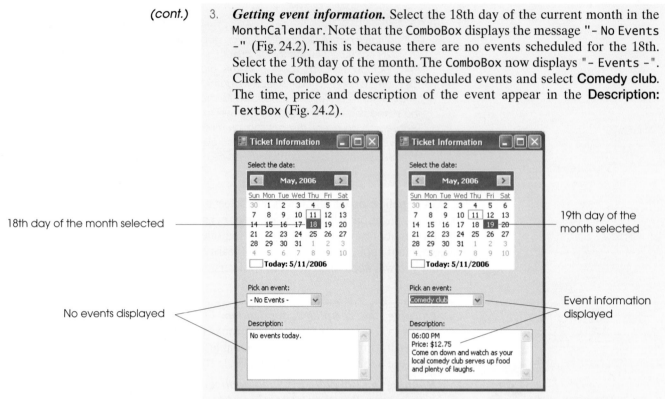

19th day of the month selected

Event information displayed

Figure 24.2   **Ticket Information** application displaying event information.

4. ***Testing the application.*** Select other dates (such as 1, 12 and 30) and view the results.

5. ***Closing the application.*** Close your running application by clicking its close box.

6. ***Closing the IDE.*** Close the IDE by clicking its close box.

SELF-REVIEW   1. The _____ control allows a user to select a range of dates.

a) DateTimePicker   b) MonthCalendar

c) ComboBox   d) TextBox

2. The MonthCalendar control is similar to the _____ control.

a) DateTimePicker   b) ComboBox

c) TextBox   d) Timer

Answers: 1) b. 2) a.

24.2 Data Hierarchy

Data items processed by computers form a **data hierarchy** (Fig. 24.3) in which data items become larger and more complex in structure as they progress from bits, to characters, to fields and to larger data structures.

Throughout this book, you have been manipulating data in your applications. The data has been in several forms—**decimal digits** (0, 1, 2, 3, 4, 5, 6, 7, 8 and 9), letters (A–Z and a–z) and **special symbols** ($, @, %, &, *, (,), -, +, ", :, ?, / and many others). Digits, letters and special symbols are referred to as characters. The set of all characters used to write applications and represent data items on a particular computer is called that computer's **character set**.

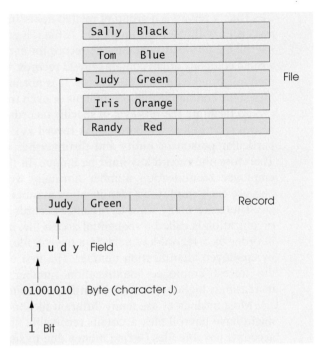

Figure 24.3 Data hierarchy.

The computer's character set is readable and understandable by humans. Ultimately, however, all data items processed by a computer are reduced to combinations of zeros and ones. The smallest data item that computers support is called a **bit**. "Bit" is short for "**binary digit**"—a digit that can hold only the value 0 or the value 1. Computer circuitry performs various simple bit manipulations, such as examining the value of a bit, setting the value of a bit and reversing the value of a bit (from 1 to 0 or from 0 to 1). This approach has been adopted because it is simple and economical to build electronic devices that can assume two stable states—0 representing one state and 1 representing the other. It is remarkable that the extensive functions performed by computers involve only the most fundamental manipulations of 0s and 1s.

Because computers can process only 0s and 1s, every character in a computer's character set is represented as a pattern of 0s and 1s. **Bytes** are composed of eight bits. Characters in Visual Basic are **Unicode** characters, which are composed of two bytes. Programming with data in the low-level form of bits is difficult, so programmers create applications and data items with characters, and computers manipulate and process these characters as patterns of bits.

Just as characters are composed of bits, **fields** are composed of characters. A field is a group of characters that conveys some meaning. For example, a field consisting of uppercase and lowercase letters can represent a person's name.

Typically, a **record** (which usually is represented as a Class in Visual Basic) is a collection of several related fields (called member variables in Visual Basic). In a payroll system, for example, a record for a particular employee might include the following fields:

1. Employee identification number

2. Name

3. Address

4. Hourly pay rate

5. Number of exemptions claimed

6. Year-to-date earnings

7. Amount of taxes withheld

Thus, a record is a group of related fields. In the preceding example, each field is associated with the same employee. A file is a group of related records. A company's payroll file normally contains one record for each employee. Hence, a payroll file for a small company might contain only 22 records, whereas a payroll file for a large company might contain 100,000 records. It is not unusual for a company to have many files, some containing millions, billions or even trillions of characters of information.

To facilitate the retrieval of specific records from a file, at least one field in each record is chosen as a record key. A **record key** identifies a record as belonging to a particular person or entity and distinguishes that record from all other records. Therefore, the record key must be unique. In the payroll record just described, the employee identification number normally would be chosen as the record key because each employee's identification number is different.

There are many ways to organize records in a file. The most common type of organization is called a sequential-access file, in which records typically are stored in order by a record-key field. In a payroll file, records usually are placed in order by employee identification number. The first employee record in the file contains the lowest employee identification number, and subsequent records contain increasingly higher employee identification numbers.

Most businesses use many different files to store data. For example, a company might have payroll files, accounts receivable files (listing money due from clients), accounts payable files (listing money due to suppliers), inventory files (listing facts about all the items handled by the business) and many other types of files. Sometimes, a group of related files is called a **database**. A collection of programs designed to create and manage databases is called a **database management system** (DBMS). You will learn about databases in Tutorial 25.

SELF-REVIEW

1. The smallest data item a computer can process is called a _____.

   a) database   b) byte

   c) file   d) bit

2. A _____ is a group of related records.

   a) file   b) field

   c) bit   d) byte

Answers: 1) d. 2) a.

24.3 Files and Streams

Visual Basic actually views each file as a sequential **stream** of bytes (Fig. 24.4). When a file is opened, Visual Basic creates an object and associates a stream with that object.

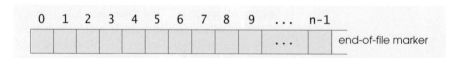

Figure 24.4   Visual Basic's conceptual view of an *n*-byte file.

To perform file processing in Visual Basic, namespace System.IO must be imported. This namespace includes definitions of stream classes, such as **StreamReader** (for text input from a file) and **StreamWriter** (for text output to a file).

24.4 Writing to a File: Creating the Write Event Application

An important aspect of the **Ticket Information** application is its ability to read data sequentially from a file. You will need to create the file from which the **Ticket Infor-**

mation application will read its data. Therefore, before you create the **Ticket Information** application, you must learn how to write to a file sequentially.

The **Write Event** application enables the user to create a new file or open an existing file. The user might want to create a new file for events or update an existing file by adding more event information. You will add this functionality in the following box.

Adding a Dialog to Open or Create a File

1. ***Copying the template to your working directory.*** Copy the C:\Examples\ Tutorial24\TemplateApplication\WriteEvent directory to your C:\SimplyVB directory.

2. ***Opening the Write Event application's template file.*** Double click WriteEvent.sln in the WriteEvent directory to open the application in the Visual Basic IDE.

3. ***Adding a dialog to the Form.*** The application uses the **OpenFileDialog** control to customize the **Open** dialog. To add an OpenFileDialog to the application, double click the OpenFileDialog control

   in the **All Windows Forms** category of the **Toolbox**. Change the control's Name property to openFileDialog. Change its **FileName** property to cal-endar.txt, which will be the default file name displayed in the **Open** dialog. [*Note:* This is the name of the file from which the **Ticket Information** application retrieves information.] The **Open** dialog normally allows the user to open only existing files, but you also want the user to be able to create a file. For this reason, set property **CheckFileExists** to False so that the **Open** dialog allows the user to specify a new file name. If the user specifies a file that does not exist, the file is created and opened. Figure 24.5 shows the application in design view after the OpenFileDialog control has been added and renamed.

OpenFileDialog control ——

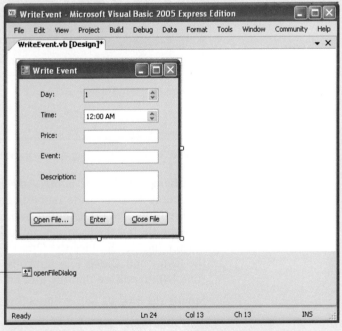

Figure 24.5 openFileDialog added and renamed.

4. ***Saving the project.*** Select **File > Save All** to save your modified code.

The **Write Event** application stores the user-input information in a text file. It expects the user to open or create a file with the extension .txt. If the user does not do so, the application displays an error message. The following box guides you through adding this functionality.

Determining Whether a File Name Is Valid

1. **Adding the header for method CheckValidity.** Add lines 3–7 of Fig. 24.6 to the application. Method CheckValidity receives a file name as a String and returns a Boolean value. If the file name is valid, the Function returns True. Otherwise, the Function returns False.

CheckValidity Function procedure header

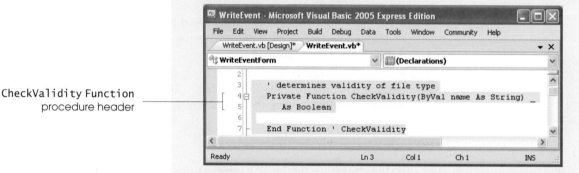

Figure 24.6   Method CheckValidity header.

2. **Displaying a MessageBox to indicate an invalid file name.** Add lines 7–14 of Fig. 24.7 to method CheckValidity. String method EndsWith (line 8) returns False if name does not end with .txt, the extension that indicates a text file. In this case, lines 9–11 display a MessageBox informing the user that the application expects a text file.

Displaying error message if incorrect file type is provided

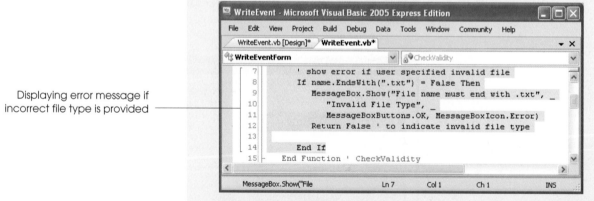

Figure 24.7   Displaying an error message indicating an invalid file name.

3. **Receiving a valid file name.** Add lines 13–18 of Fig. 24.8 to the If...Then statement. If a valid file name is entered, method CheckValidity should return True. The GUI should indicate that the user cannot create or open another file, but the user may enter data into the file or close the file. For this reason, line 15 disables the **Open File...** Button, while lines 16–17 enable the **Enter** and **Close File** Buttons, respectively. The method returns True (line 18) to indicate that the user entered a valid file name.

4. **Saving the project.** Select **File > Save All** to save your modified code.

(cont.)

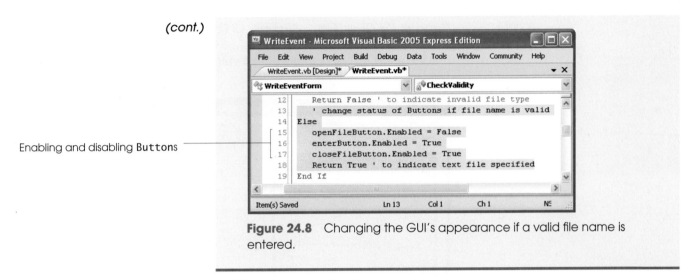

Enabling and disabling `Buttons`

Figure 24.8 Changing the GUI's appearance if a valid file name is entered.

You have added the `OpenFileDialog` control to allow users to open a file and a method that determines whether the user has entered a valid file name. Now you will add code that associates the specified file with a stream.

Creating a
StreamWriter Object

1. ***Importing namespace `System.IO` to enable file processing.*** To access the classes and methods that will enable you to perform file processing with sequential-access files, you must import namespace `System.IO`. Accordingly, add line 1 of Fig. 24.9.

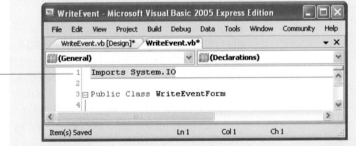

Importing namespace
`System.IO`

Figure 24.9 `System.IO` namespace imported into `WriteEventForm` class.

2. ***Declaring a `StreamWriter` variable.*** Namespace `System.IO` includes class `StreamWriter`, which is used to create objects for writing text to a file. You will use a `StreamWriter` to write data into the file created or opened by the user. Add line 5 of Fig. 24.10 to the `WriteEventForm` class definition to declare the variable that will be assigned a `StreamWriter` object.

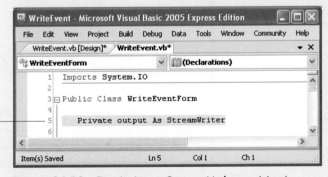

Declaring `StreamWriter` object

Figure 24.10 Declaring a `StreamWriter` object.

(cont.)

3. ***Creating the Open File... Button's* `Click` *event handler*.** Switch to **Design** view and double click the **Open File...** Button on the **Write Event** application's Form (Fig. 24.11) to create the empty `openFileButton_Click` event handler.

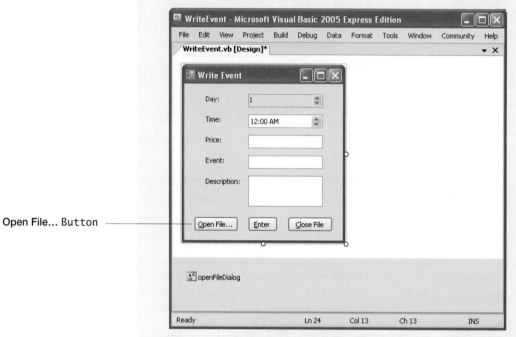

Open File... Button

Figure 24.11 **Write Event** application Form in design view.

4. ***Displaying the Open dialog*.** Add lines 30–39 of Fig. 24.12 to the event handler. When the user clicks the **Open File...** Button, the **ShowDialog** method of the `OpenFileDialog` control displays the **Open** dialog to allow the user to open a file (line 31). If the user specifies a file that does not exist, it will be created. Line 31 assigns the return value of method `ShowDialog` to a `DialogResult` variable named `result`. Be sure to add the comments and line-continuation characters, as shown in Fig. 24.12, so that the line numbers in your code match those presented in this tutorial.

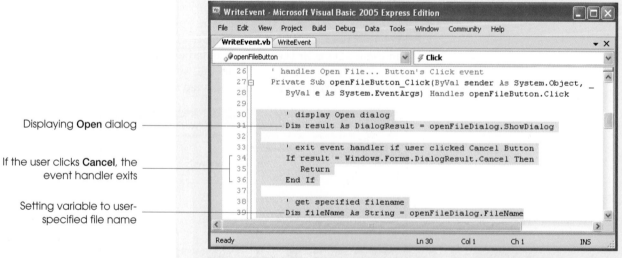

Displaying **Open** dialog

If the user clicks **Cancel**, the event handler exits

Setting variable to user-specified file name

Figure 24.12 Displaying the **Open** dialog and retrieving the result.

(cont.)

5. *Exiting event handler if the user clicks the Cancel Button.* Consider Fig. 24.12. The value of the DialogResult variable specifies whether the user clicked the **Cancel** Button in the **Open** dialog. If so, the event handler returns immediately (line 35). At this point, the user can still open or create a file by clicking the enabled **Open File...** Button again.

6. *Retrieving the file name.* Property FileName of OpenFileDialog specifies the file name that the user selected (line 39 of Fig. 24.12). The application stores the path and file name in fileName. The file name will be tested to determine whether it is valid and then used to initialize the StreamWriter object.

7. *Checking for a valid file type.* Add lines 41–45 of Fig. 24.13 to the event handler. Line 42 invokes method CheckValidity (which you defined earlier in this tutorial) to determine whether the specified file is a text file (that is, the file name ends with ".txt").

Check for valid filename ——————

Create StreamWriter object ——————

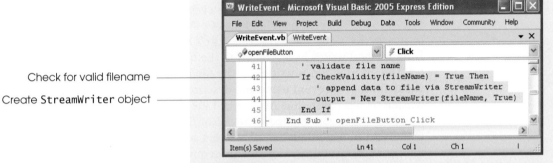

Figure 24.13   Validating the filename and initializing a StreamWriter object.

8. *Initializing a StreamWriter object.* The call to the StreamWriter constructor (line 44) initializes StreamWriter object output, which will be used to write to the new file specified by the user. Note that the StreamWriter constructor takes two arguments. The first indicates the name of the file (specified by variable fileName) to which you will write information. The second is a Boolean value that determines whether the StreamWriter will append information to the end of the file. You pass value True, so that any information written to the file will be appended to the end of the file if the file already exists.

9. *Saving the project.* Select **File > Save All** to save your modified code.

> **Common Programming Error**
>
> When you open an existing file by invoking the StreamWriter constructor with a False second argument, data previously contained in the file will be lost.

Now that the application can open a file, the user can input information that will be written to that file. In the following box, you will add code that makes the **Enter** Button's Click event handler write the data to the text file.

Writing Information to a Sequential-Access File

1. *Clearing user input from the TextBoxes and resetting the NumericUpDown control.* Add lines 48–54 of Fig. 24.14 to the application below the openFileButton_Click event handler. After the user's input is processed, the **Enter** Button's event handler will invoke method ClearUserInput to clear the TextBoxes and reset the NumericUpDown control's value to 1 (the first day of the month).

(cont.)

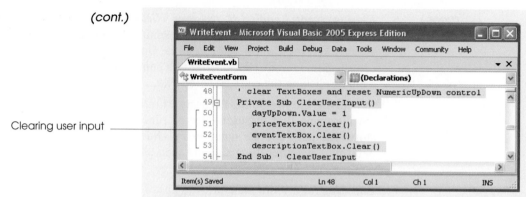

Figure 24.14 Clearing user input.

2. *Creating the enterButton_Click event handler*. In **Design** view, double click the **Enter** Button to add the enterButton_Click event handler.

3. *Defining the enterButton_Click event handler*. Add lines 60–66 of Fig. 24.15 to the event handler. Lines 61–65 write the user input line by line to the file by using the StreamWriter's **WriteLine** method. The Write-Line method writes its argument to the file, followed by a newline character. The information is written to the file in the following order: day of the event, time, price, event name and description. Each piece of information is written on a separate line of the file. Line 66 invokes the ClearUserInput procedure that you defined in *Step 1* of this box. Be sure to add the comments and line-continuation characters, as shown in Fig. 24.15, so that the line numbers in your code match those presented in this tutorial.

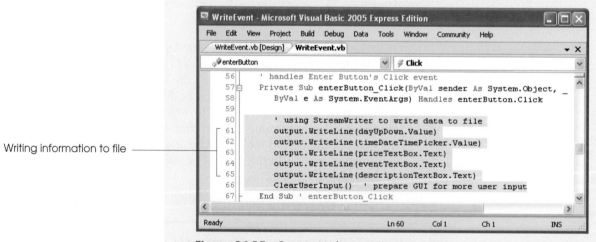

Figure 24.15 StreamWriter writing to a file.

4. *Saving the project*. Select **File > Save All** to save your modified code.

You should close the file after you have finished processing it. You will add this capability to the **Close File** Button's Click event handler in the following box.

Closing the StreamWriter

1. *Create the closeFileButton_Click event handler*. In **Design** view, double click the **Close File** Button of the **Write Event** application's Form. The closeFileButton_Click event handler appears in the WriteEvent.vb file.

(cont.)　　2. ***Defining the `closeFileButton_Click` event handler.*** Add lines 73–78 of Fig. 24.16 to the event handler. Line 73 uses the StreamWriter's **Close** method to close the stream. Line 76 reenables the **Open File...** Button in case the user would like to create or update another sequential-access file. Lines 77–78 disable the **Enter** and **Close File** Buttons because users should not be able to click these Buttons when a file is not open.

Closing `StreamWriter` object ——

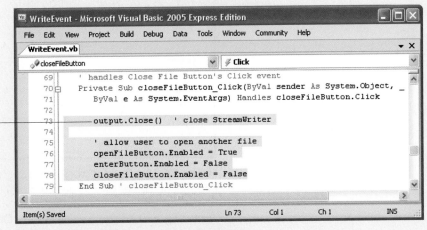

Figure 24.16 Closing the `StreamWriter`.

3. ***Saving the project.*** Select **File > Save All** to save your modified code.

You have now successfully created the **Write Event** application. You will test this application to see how it works and view the file contents in the following box.

**Writing Event
Information to a File**

1. ***Running the Write Event application.*** Select **Debug > Start Debugging** to run your application (Fig. 24.17).

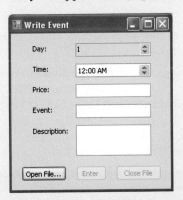

Figure 24.17 Write Event application running.

2. ***Creating a file.*** Click the **Open File...** Button to select a file. The **Open** dialog appears. Browse to C:\Examples\Tutorial24\TemplateApplication\TicketInformation\bin\Debug (Fig. 24.18). [*Note:* An existing calendar.txt file should appear in the **Open** dialog.] The file name calendar.txt should be displayed in the **File name:** field, as in Fig. 24.18. The **File name:** field may not display the extension (.txt), or calendar may be displayed with a capital "C" based on your computer's settings. Click the **Open** Button. This will open the existing calendar.txt file.

(cont.)

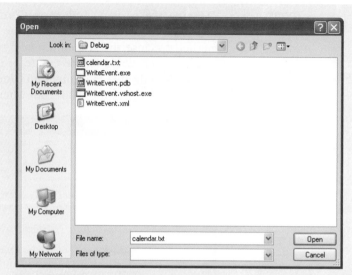

Figure 24.18   **Open** dialog displaying contents of the template **Ticket Information** application's **debug** folder.

3. *Inputting event information.* In the **Day:** NumericUpDown control, select 4 to indicate that the event is scheduled on the fourth day of the month. Enter 2:30 PM in the **Time:** DateTimePicker. Type 12.50 in the **Price:** TextBox. Enter Arts and Crafts Fair in the **Event:** TextBox. In the **Description:** TextBox, enter the information Take part in creating various types of arts and crafts at this fair. Click the **Enter** Button to add this event's information to the calendar.txt file.

4. *Inputting more event information.* Write more event information to the file by repeating *Step 3* with your own set of events.

5. *Closing the file.* When you have entered all the events you wish, click the **Close File** Button. This closes the calendar.txt file and prevents any more events from being written.

6. *Closing the application.* Close your running application by clicking its close box.

7. *Opening and closing the sequential-access file.* Use the IDE to open calendar.txt. Select **File > Open File...** to display the **Open** dialog. Navigate to C:\Examples\Tutorial24\TemplateApplication\TicketInformation\bin\Debug, select the calendar.txt file that you created and click **Open**. Scroll through the file. The information you entered in *Step 3* should appear in the file, similar to Fig. 24.19. Close the calendar.txt file.

Day and time of event, ticket price, event name and description

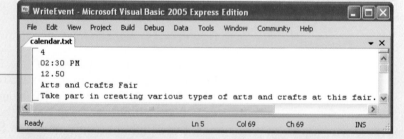

Figure 24.19   Sequential-access file generated by **Write Event** application.

8. *Closing the IDE.* Close the Visual Basic IDE by clicking its close box.

Figure 24.20 presents the source code for the **Write Event** application. The lines of code that contain new programming concepts that you have learned so far in this tutorial are highlighted.

Importing a namespace System.IO

StreamWriter that will write text to a file

Retrieve user input from **Open** dialog

Storing filename entered by user

Create StreamWriter object to associate a stream with the user-specified text file

```
1   Imports System.IO
2
3   Public Class WriteEventForm
4
5     Private output As StreamWriter
6
7     ' determine validity of file type
8     Private Function CheckValidity(ByVal name As String) _
9        As Boolean
10
11       ' show error if user specified invalid file
12       If name.EndsWith(".txt") = False Then
13         MessageBox.Show("File name must end with .txt", _
14            "Invalid File Type", _
15            MessageBoxButtons.OK, MessageBoxIcon.Error)
16         Return False   ' to indicate invalid file type
17       ' change status of Buttons if file name is valid
18       Else
19         openFileButton.Enabled = False
20         enterButton.Enabled = True
21         closeFileButton.Enabled = True
22         Return True   ' to indicate text file specified
23       End If
24     End Function ' CheckValidity
25
26     ' handles Open File... Button's Click event
27     Private Sub openFileButton_Click(ByVal sender As System.Object, _
28        ByVal e As System.EventArgs) Handles openFileButton.Click
29
30       ' display Open dialog
31       Dim result As DialogResult = openFileDialog.ShowDialog
32
33       ' exit event handler if user clicked Cancel Button
34       If result = Windows.Forms.DialogResult.Cancel Then
35         Return
36       End If
37
38       ' get specified filename
39       Dim fileName As String = openFileDialog.FileName
40
41       ' validate file name
42       If CheckValidity(fileName) = True Then
43         ' append data to file via StreamWriter
44         output = New StreamWriter(fileName, True)
45       End If
46     End Sub ' openFileButton_Click
47
48     ' clear TextBoxes and reset NumericUpDown control
49     Private Sub ClearUserInput()
50       dayUpDown.Value = 1
51       priceTextBox.Clear()
52       eventTextBox.Clear()
53       descriptionTextBox.Clear()
54     End Sub ' ClearUserInput
55
56     ' handles Enter Button's Click event
57     Private Sub enterButton_Click(ByVal sender As System.Object, _
58        ByVal e As System.EventArgs) Handles enterButton.Click
59
```

Figure 24.20 **Write Event** application's code. (Part 1 of 2.)

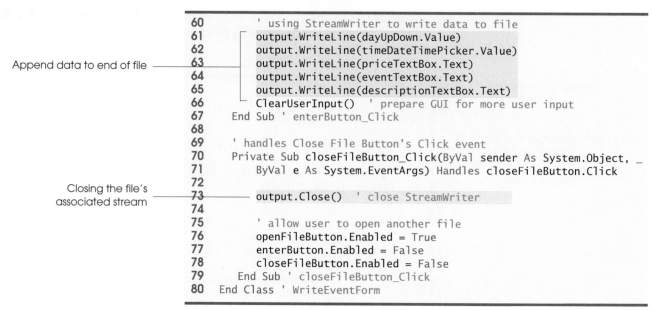

Append data to end of file

Closing the file's associated stream

```
60          ' using StreamWriter to write data to file
61          output.WriteLine(dayUpDown.Value)
62          output.WriteLine(timeDateTimePicker.Value)
63          output.WriteLine(priceTextBox.Text)
64          output.WriteLine(eventTextBox.Text)
65          output.WriteLine(descriptionTextBox.Text)
66          ClearUserInput()   ' prepare GUI for more user input
67       End Sub ' enterButton_Click
68
69       ' handles Close File Button's Click event
70       Private Sub closeFileButton_Click(ByVal sender As System.Object, _
71          ByVal e As System.EventArgs) Handles closeFileButton.Click
72
73          output.Close()   ' close StreamWriter
74
75          ' allow user to open another file
76          openFileButton.Enabled = True
77          enterButton.Enabled = False
78          closeFileButton.Enabled = False
79       End Sub ' closeFileButton_Click
80    End Class ' WriteEventForm
```

Figure 24.20   **Write Event** application's code. (Part 2 of 2.)

24.5 Building the Ticket Information Application

Now that you have created the **Write Event** application to enable a user to write community-event information to a sequential-access text file, you will create the **Ticket Information** application you test-drove at the beginning of the tutorial. First you need to analyze the application. The following pseudocode describes the basic operation of the **Ticket Information** application:

> When the Form loads:
>   Display the current day's events
>
> When the user selects a date on the calendar:
>   Display the selected day's events
>
> When the user selects an event from the Pick an event: ComboBox:
>   Retrieve index of selected item in the Pick an event: ComboBox
>   Display event information in the Description: TextBox
>
> When procedure CreateEventList is called:
>   Extract data for the current day from calendar.txt
>   Clear the Pick an event: ComboBox
>
>   If events are scheduled for that day
>   Add each event to the Pick an event: ComboBox
>   Display "- Events -" in the Pick an event: ComboBox
>   Display "Pick an event." in the Description: TextBox
>   Else
>   Display "- No Events -" in the Pick an event: ComboBox
>   Display "No events today." in the Description: TextBox
>
> When procedure ExtractData is called:
>   Retrieve the selected date from the calendar
>   Open calendar.txt file for reading
>   Read the first line of the file

While there are events left in the file and the number of events is less than 10

    If the current event is for the day selected by the user
        Store the event information
        Increment the number of events for the selected day
    Else
        Move to the beginning of the next record in the file

    Read the next line of the file

Now that you have test-driven the **Ticket Information** application and studied its pseudocode representation, you will use an ACE table to help you convert the pseudocode to Visual Basic. Figure 24.21 lists the actions, controls and events that will help you complete your own version of this application.

Action/Control/Event (ACE) Table for the Ticket Information Application

Action	Control	Event/Method
Label the application's controls	dateLabel, eventLabel, description-Label	Application is run
	EventsForm	Load
Display the current day's events	eventComboBox	
	dateMonthCal-endar	DateChanged
Display the selected day's events	description-TextBox	
	eventComboBox	Selected-IndexChanged
Retrieve index of selected item in the Pick an event: ComboBox	eventComboBox	
Display event information in the Description: TextBox	description-TextBox	
		Create-EventList
Extract data for the current day	dateMonthCal-endar	
Clear the Pick an event: ComboBox	eventComboBox	
If events are scheduled for that day Add each event to the Pick an event: ComboBox	eventComboBox, data	
Display "- Events -" in the Pick an event: ComboBox	eventComboBox	
Display "Pick an event." in the Description: TextBox	description-TextBox	
Else Display "- No Events -" in the Pick an event: ComboBox	eventComboBox	
Display "No events today." in the Description: TextBox	description-TextBox	

Figure 24.21   ACE table for the **Ticket Information** application. (Part 1 of 2.)

Action	Control	Event/Method
		ExtractData
Retrieve the selected date from the calendar	dateMonth-Calendar	
Open calendar.txt file for reading	input	
Read the first line of the file	input	
While there are events left in the file and the number of events is less than 10	input, numberOfEvents	
If the current event is for the day selected by the user Store the event information	data, line, input	
Increment the number of events for the selected day	numberOfEvents	
Else Move to the beginning of the next record in the file	input	
Read the next line of the file	input	

Figure 24.21 ACE table for the **Ticket Information** application. (Part 2 of 2.)

The **Ticket Information** application allows the user to view the information for a specific date by selecting the date from a MonthCalendar control. The following box guides you through configuring the MonthCalendar control.

Adding a MonthCalendar Control

1. ***Copying the template to your working directory.*** Copy the C:\Examples\Tutorial24\TemplateApplication\TicketInformation directory to your C:\SimplyVB directory.

2. ***Opening the Ticket Information template application.*** Double click TicketInformation.sln in the TicketInformation directory to open the application in the Visual Basic IDE and view the template's Form (Fig. 24.22). The template provides the empty methods CreateEventList and ExtractData. You will add code to these methods later.

Figure 24.22 Ticket Information template application's Form.

(cont.)

3. ***Adding a MonthCalendar control to the Form.*** Double click the MonthCalendar control

Good Programming Practice

Append the MonthCalendar suffix to MonthCalendar control names.

in the **All Windows Forms** group of the **Toolbox**. The **Properties** window should display the control's properties. Change the Name property to date-MonthCalendar. Set the Location of the MonthCalendar control to 16, 32.

4. ***Saving the project.*** Select **File > Save All** to save your modified code.

Now that you have added the MonthCalendar control, you can begin writing code for the **Ticket Information** application. For this application, you will define two Sub procedures named CreateEventList and ExtractData. Before adding any functionality to the application, you will import System.IO and create two instance variables in the next box.

Beginning to Build the
Ticket Information
Application

1. ***Importing namespace System.IO.*** Switch to **Code** view. You must import namespace System.IO to allow the application to use class StreamReader to read information from a sequential-access file. To do so, add line 1 of Fig. 24.23 before the class definition.

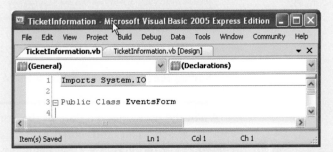

Figure 24.23   System.IO namespace imported to EventsForm.

2. ***Adding instance variables.*** Add lines 5–9 of Fig. 24.24 to the application. To keep track of information, you will store the event information read from the file in array data (line 6) and the number of events for a specified day in numberOfEvents (line 9). For simplicity, the array data is initialized with 10 rows of five items each (allowing up to 10 total events per day).

Creating an array of Strings ⎯⎯⎯⎯⎯⎯

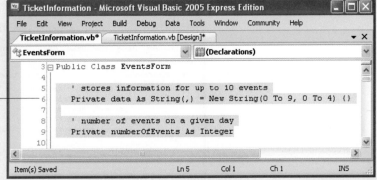

Figure 24.24   Instance variables declared in the **Ticket Information** application.

3. ***Saving the project.*** Select **File > Save All** to save your modified code.

When you run the **Ticket Information** application, by default, the current day is selected in the MonthCalendar control. The application shows the list of the day's events in the ComboBox. Recall that, if there are no events for the day, the ComboBox displays "- No Events -". In the following box, you will invoke a method from the Form's Load event handler to set the display in the ComboBox appropriately.

Handling the Form's Load Event

1. **Defining the Form's Load event.** Double click the Form in **Design** view to generate the event handler EventsForm_Load. Add lines 26–27 of Fig. 24.25 to the Load event handler. Line 26 selects today's date as the currently selected date in the MonthCalendar. Line 27 invokes method CreateEventList. You will soon add code to CreateEventList to populate the ComboBox with any events scheduled for the current day.

You will add code to CreateEventList procedure later

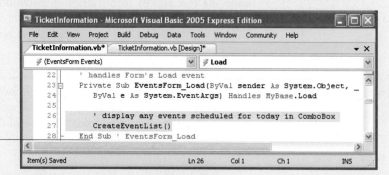

Figure 24.25 Load event handler calling method CreateEventList.

2. **Saving the project.** Select **File > Save All** to save your modified code.

When the user selects a date in the MonthCalendar control, the **DateChanged** event is raised. You add code to the event handler that invokes the CreateEventList method in the following box.

Handling the MonthCalendar's DateChanged Event

1. **Creating the MonthCalendar's DateChanged event handler.** In **Design** view, double click the MonthCalendar to generate the empty event handler dateMonthCalendar_DateChanged.

2. **Invoking the CreateEventList method.** Add lines 36–37 of Fig. 24.26 to the dateMonthCalendar_DateChanged event handler. Line 37 invokes method CreateEventList, which you will define in the next box.

Calling the CreateEventList method

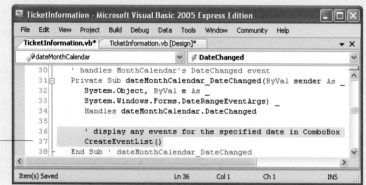

Figure 24.26 MonthCalendar's DateChanged event handler.

3. **Saving the project.** Select **File > Save All** to save your modified code.

The application invokes method CreateEventList from the Form's Load event and the MonthCalendar's DateChanged event. The CreateEventList method populates the ComboBox with event names if there are any events for the day the user chooses; otherwise, it indicates that the event list is empty. You define this functionality in the following box.

Defining the CreateEventList Method

1. **Setting variables and clearing the ComboBox in the CreateEventList method.** Add lines 14–21 of Fig. 24.27 to the CreateEventList method. The CreateEventList method first declares a counter, count (line 14), that will be used to iterate through the events. Line 18 invokes the ExtractData method (which you'll define in the next box), passing the Date that is currently selected in the MonthCalendar. The ExtractData method will store event information in array data and assign the number of events scheduled for the specified date to numberOfEvents. This date is specified by the MonthCalendar control's **SelectionStart** property. The Items.Clear method removes any events currently displayed in the ComboBox (line 21).

You will add code to the ExtractData procedure in the next box

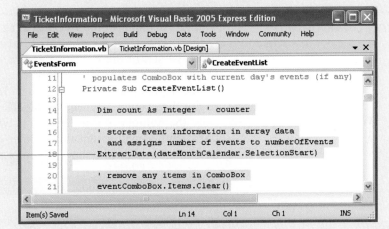

Figure 24.27 CreateEventList modified to call method ExtractData and clear the ComboBox.

2. **Setting events displayed in the ComboBox.** Add lines 23–36 of Fig. 24.28 to the CreateEventList method.

Extracting event name from array and displaying it in the ComboBox

Indicating that events are scheduled for the day

Indicating that no events are scheduled for the day

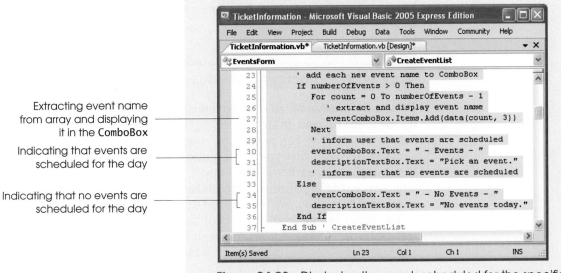

Figure 24.28 Displaying the events scheduled for the specified day.

(cont.)

If there are events scheduled for the chosen day (line 24), then lines 25–28 iterate through array `data` and add the name of each event to the `ComboBox`. The `CreateEventList` method informs the user that there are events scheduled for the specified day by using the `Text` properties of the `ComboBox` and `TextBox` (lines 30–31). If there are events for the chosen day, then the `ComboBox` displays `"- Events -"` and the `Textbox` displays `"Pick an event."`; otherwise, the `ComboBox` displays `"- No events -"` and the `Textbox` displays `"No events today."` (lines 34–35).

3. *Saving the project.* Select **File > Save All** to save your modified code.

As described in *Step 1* of the previous box, the `ExtractData` method uses a variable of type `Date` (`currentDate`) as its only parameter. The `ExtractData` method assigns the information about any events scheduled for that day to the `data` array and assigns the number of events for that day to the `numberOfEvents` variable. You define the `ExtractData` method in the following box.

Reading a Sequential-Access File

1. *Adding variables to the ExtractData method.* Add lines 43–48 of Fig. 24.29 to the `ExtractData` method. The `Date` selected in the `MonthCalendar` control is passed to the `ExtractData` method as the parameter `currentDate`. Line 44 assigns `chosenDay` the selected day returned by the `Day` property of the `currentDate` parameter. The `fileDay` variable (line 45) will store the day of the event read from the file. The `lineNumbers` variable (line 46) will store the number of lines to skip between events in the file. The `ExtractData` method will assign the number of events scheduled for the specified date to the variable `numberOfEvents`, which is initialized to 0 in line 48.

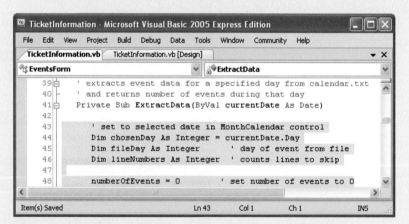

Figure 24.29 `ExtractData` method's variable declarations.

2. *Using a StreamReader to read from the file.* Add lines 50–54 of Fig. 24.30 to the method. To read from the file, `ExtractData` creates a new `Stream-Reader` object (line 51), passing the name of the file to be read (`"calendar.txt"`). Recall that you wrote information to this file using the **Write Event** application earlier in this tutorial. [*Note:* The data file is in the same directory as the application's executable (`C:\SimplyVB\TicketInformation\bin\Debug`), so you do not need to use the full path name.]

The **ReadLine** method (line 54) of the `StreamReader` reads one line of text from the specified stream (`input`) and returns the characters as a `String`. Line 54 assigns the first line of the file to `line`.

(cont.)

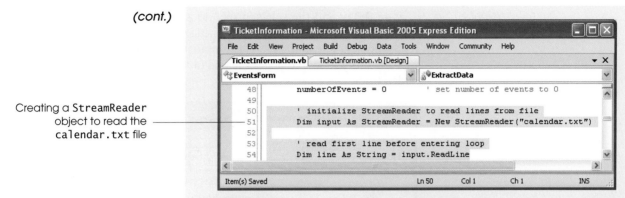

Figure 24.30　Using `StreamReader` to read data from a sequential-access file.

3. *Extracting the day from an event in the file.* Add lines 56–59 of Fig. 24.31 to the `ExtractData` method. The loop determines whether there is more information to read in the file. This condition ensures that the end of the file has not been reached. When this condition becomes `False`, looping should stop. The `StreamReader` object's **Peek** method returns the next character to be read or `-1` if there are no more characters to read in the file (that is, the end of the file has been reached). Line 57 also ensures that no more than 10 events for the specified day are read from the file. This constraint is necessary because of the fixed size of the array `data`. If these conditions are met, the body of the `Do While...Loop` executes. Line 58 converts the line read from the file (that is, the day of the event) to an `Integer` and assigns that value to `fileDay`. The first time the loop executes, `line` contains the first line in the file.

Creating a `StreamReader` object to read the `calendar.txt` file

Verify that the end of file has not been reached and fewer than 10 events are stored in the array

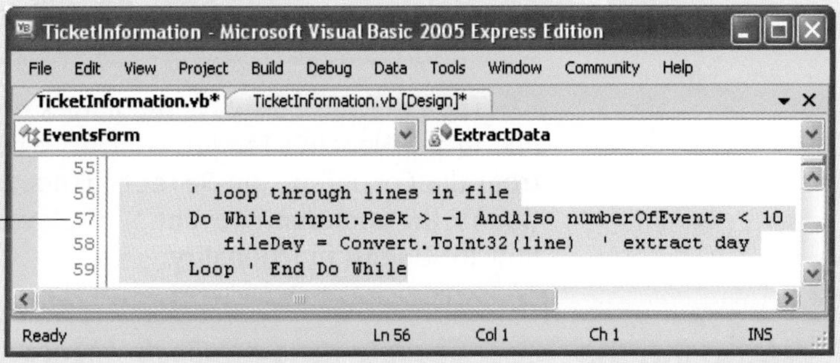

Figure 24.31　Extracting the day from an event entry in the file.

4. *Reading event information from the sequential-access file.* Add lines 60–76 of Fig. 24.32 to the `ExtractData` method's `Do While...Loop`. The loop reads each event sequentially from the file. If the day of the event read from the file (`fileDay`) and the specified day (`chosenDay`) are the same (line 61), then the event information (day, time, ticket price, name and description) is read from the file and is stored in array `data` (lines 62–66).

Recall that when you created the **Write Event** application, each piece of data (day, time, price, event and description) was written to `calendar.txt` on a separate line, so the event data is retrieved using the `ReadLine` method. Each event for the chosen day is placed in its own row of the array (indicated by `numberOfEvents`), and each piece of event information is placed in its own column of the array. Line 67 increments `numberOfEvents` to indicate that an event has been scheduled for that date.

(cont.)

If `fileDay` and the selected day do not match, then the `StreamReader` skips to the next event, using a `For...Next` loop (lines 70–72). Line 76 then reads the next line in the file that contains an event's date. The entire process repeats until the loop reaches the end of the file or until 10 events have been added to the `data` array.

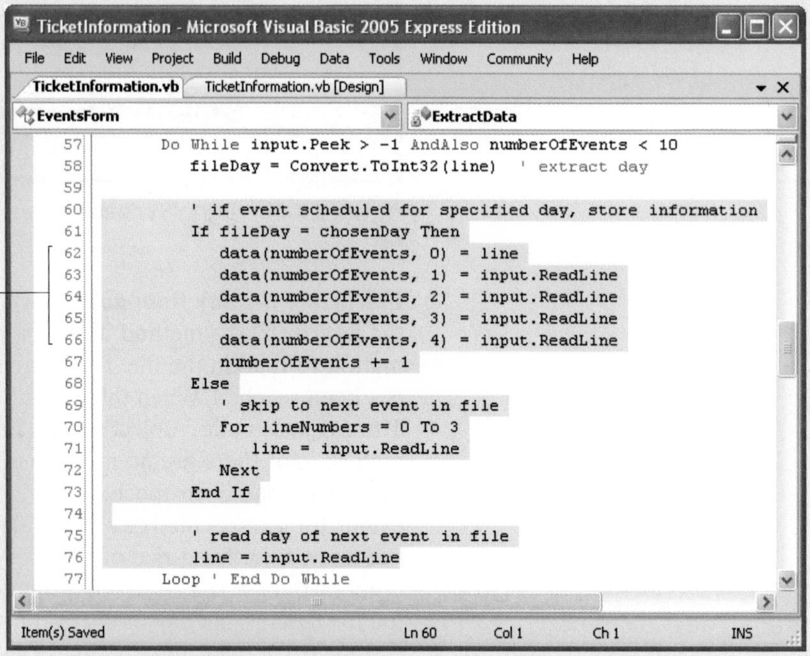

Store event information in a row of the array

```
57          Do While input.Peek > -1 AndAlso numberOfEvents < 10
58              fileDay = Convert.ToInt32(line)   ' extract day
59
60              ' if event scheduled for specified day, store information
61              If fileDay = chosenDay Then
62                  data(numberOfEvents, 0) = line
63                  data(numberOfEvents, 1) = input.ReadLine
64                  data(numberOfEvents, 2) = input.ReadLine
65                  data(numberOfEvents, 3) = input.ReadLine
66                  data(numberOfEvents, 4) = input.ReadLine
67                  numberOfEvents += 1
68              Else
69                  ' skip to next event in file
70                  For lineNumbers = 0 To 3
71                      line = input.ReadLine
72                  Next
73              End If
74
75              ' read day of next event in file
76              line = input.ReadLine
77          Loop ' End Do While
```

Figure 24.32 Sequentially reading event entries from the file.

5. **Saving the project.** Select **File > Save All** to save your modified code.

The `ComboBox` displays the names of any events scheduled for the date specified in the `MonthCalendar` control. When the user selects the community event from the `ComboBox`, the `SelectedIndexChanged` event is raised and the description of the community event is displayed in the `TextBox`. The next box explains how to add this functionality.

Handling the SelectedIndexChanged Event

1. **Creating the ComboBox's SelectedIndexChanged event handler.** Double click the **Pick an Event** ComboBox in **Design** view to generate the empty event handler `eventComboBox_SelectedIndexChanged`.

2. **Displaying event information.** Add lines 103–109 of Fig. 24.33 to the event handler. When the user selects an event in the ComboBox, the `eventComboBox_SelectedIndexChanged` event handler displays information about the event in the `descriptionTextBox`. The `SelectedIndex` property of the ComboBox returns the index number of the selected event, which is equivalent to the row number of the event in the `data` array. The event handler appends descriptive text, newline characters, the time that the event starts (line 104), the ticket price (lines 106–107) and the event's description (line 109) to the TextBox's `Text` property.

3. **Running the application.** Select **Debug > Start Debugging** to run your application. Select various dates and view the event information. Select the fourth day of the current month. You should be able to view the arts and crafts fair event added earlier in the tutorial.

(cont.)

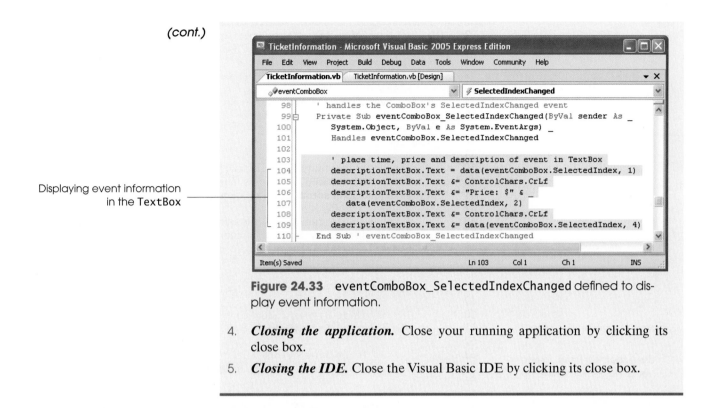

Displaying event information in the **TextBox**

Figure 24.33 eventComboBox_SelectedIndexChanged defined to display event information.

4. ***Closing the application.*** Close your running application by clicking its close box.

5. ***Closing the IDE.*** Close the Visual Basic IDE by clicking its close box.

Figure 24.34 presents the source code for the **Ticket Information** application. The lines of code that contain new programming concepts that you have learned so far in this tutorial are highlighted.

Importing namespace System.IO

```vb
1   Imports System.IO
2
3   Public Class EventsForm
4
5      ' stores information for up to 10 events
6      Private data As String(,) = New String(0 To 9, 0 To 4) {}
7
8      ' number of events on a given day
9      Private numberOfEvents As Integer
10
11     ' populates ComboBox with current day's events (if any)
12     Private Sub CreateEventList()
13
14        Dim count As Integer   ' counter
15
16        ' stores event information in array data
17        ' and assigns number of events to numberOfEvents
18        ExtractData(dateMonthCalendar.SelectionStart)
19
20        ' remove any items in ComboBox
21        eventComboBox.Items.Clear()
22
23        ' add each new event name to ComboBox
24        If numberOfEvents > 0 Then
25           For count = 0 To numberOfEvents - 1
26              ' extract and display event name
27              eventComboBox.Items.Add(data(count, 3))
28           Next
```

Figure 24.34 **Ticket Information** application's code. (Part 1 of 3.)

```
29              ' inform user that events are scheduled
30              eventComboBox.Text = " - Events - "
31              descriptionTextBox.Text = "Pick an event."
32          ' inform user that no events are scheduled
33          Else
34              eventComboBox.Text = " - No Events - "
35              descriptionTextBox.Text = "No events today."
36          End If
37      End Sub ' CreateEventList
38
39      ' extracts event data for a specified day from calendar.txt
40      ' and returns number of events during that day
41      Private Sub ExtractData(ByVal currentDate As Date)
42
43          ' set to selected date in MonthCalendar control
44          Dim chosenDay As Integer = currentDate.Day
45          Dim fileDay As Integer        ' day of event from file
46          Dim lineNumbers As Integer  ' counts lines to skip
47
48          numberOfEvents = 0           ' set number of events to 0
49
50          ' initialize StreamReader to read lines from file
51          Dim input As StreamReader = New StreamReader("calendar.txt")
52
53          ' read first line before entering loop
54          Dim line As String = input.ReadLine
55
56          ' loop through lines in file
57          Do While input.Peek > -1     AndAlso numberOfEvents < 10
58              fileDay = Convert.ToInt32(line)  ' extract day
59
60              ' if event scheduled for specified day, store information
61              If fileDay = chosenDay Then
62                  data(numberOfEvents, 0) = line
63                  data(numberOfEvents, 1) = input.ReadLine
64                  data(numberOfEvents, 2) = input.ReadLine
65                  data(numberOfEvents, 3) = input.ReadLine
66                  data(numberOfEvents, 4) = input.ReadLine
67                  numberOfEvents += 1
68              Else
69                  ' skip to next event in file
70                  For lineNumbers = 0 To 3
71                      line = input.ReadLine
72                  Next
73              End If
74
75              ' read day of next event in file
76              line = input.ReadLine
77          Loop ' End Do While
78      End Sub ' ExtractData
79
80      ' handles Form's Load event
81      Private Sub EventsForm_Load(ByVal sender As System.Object, _
82          ByVal e As System.EventArgs) Handles MyBase.Load
83
84          ' display any events scheduled for today in ComboBox
85          CreateEventList()
86      End Sub ' EventsForm_Load
87
88      ' handles MonthCalendar's DateChanged event
89      Private Sub dateMonthCalendar_DateChanged(ByVal sender As _
90          System.Object, ByVal e As _
91          System.Windows.Forms.DateRangeEventArgs) _
92          Handles dateMonthCalendar.DateChanged
```

Creating **StreamReader** object *(line 51)*

Using method **ReadLine** to read the first line of the file *(line 54)*

Ensuring that the end of the file has not been reached *(line 57)*

Reading information from a file and storing the data in an array *(lines 64)*

Using method **ReadLine** to skip to the next event in the file *(line 71)*

Using method **ReadLine** to read the day of the next event *(line 76)*

Figure 24.34   Ticket Information application's code. (Part 2 of 3.)

```
93
94            ' display any events for the specified date in ComboBox
95            CreateEventList()
96        End Sub ' dateMonthCalendar_DateChanged
97
98        ' handles ComboBox's SelectedIndexChanged event
99        Private Sub eventComboBox_SelectedIndexChanged(ByVal sender As _
100           System.Object, ByVal e As System.EventArgs) _
101           Handles eventComboBox.SelectedIndexChanged
102
103           ' place time, price and description of event in TextBox
104           descriptionTextBox.Text = data(eventComboBox.SelectedIndex, 1)
105           descriptionTextBox.Text &= ControlChars.CrLf
106           descriptionTextBox.Text &= "Price: $" & _
107              data(eventComboBox.SelectedIndex, 2)
108           descriptionTextBox.Text &= ControlChars.CrLf
109           descriptionTextBox.Text &= data(eventComboBox.SelectedIndex, 4)
110        End Sub ' eventComboBox_SelectedIndexChanged
111 End Class ' EventsForm
```

Figure 24.34   **Ticket Information** application's code. (Part 3 of 3.)

24.6 Wrap-Up

In this tutorial, you learned how to store data in sequential-access files. Data in files is called persistent data because it is maintained after the application that generated the data terminates. Computers store files on secondary storage devices.

Sequential-access files store data items in the order that they are written to the file. They are part of the data hierarchy in which computers process data items. These files are composed of records, which are collections of related fields. Fields contain characters composed of bytes. Bytes are composed of the smallest data items that computers can support—bits.

You learned how Visual Basic views each file as a sequential stream of bytes with an end-of-file marker. You learned how to create a sequential-access file in the **Write Event** application by associating a StreamWriter object with a specified file name. You used StreamWriter to add information to that file. After creating a file of community events with the **Write Event** application, you developed the **Ticket Information** application, which uses a StreamReader object to read information from that file sequentially. The user selects a date in the **Ticket Information** application's MonthCalendar control and extracts event information from a sequential-access file about any events scheduled for the specified date.

In the next tutorial, you will be introduced to databases, which were briefly mentioned earlier in this tutorial. Databases provide another common mechanism for maintaining persistent data.

SKILLS SUMMARY   **Displaying the Open Dialog**

■ Add an OpenFileDialog object to your application by double clicking OpenFileDialog in the **ToolBox**.

■ Invoke the OpenFileDialog's ShowDialog method.

Retrieving the Filename from the Open Dialog

■ Use the Filename property of the OpenFileDialog object.

Writing Lines of Text to a Sequential-Access File

■ Import namespace System.IO.

■ Create a StreamWriter object by passing two arguments to the constructor: the name of the file to open for writing and a Boolean value that determines whether information will be appended to the file.

■ Use the WriteLine method of StreamWriter to write information to the file.

Reading Lines of Text from a Sequential-Access File

■ Import namespace `System.IO`.

■ Create a `StreamReader` object by passing the name of the file to open for reading to the constructor.

■ Use the `ReadLine` method of `StreamReader` to read information from the file.

Adding a `MonthCalendar` Control

■ Double click the `MonthCalendar` control in the **ToolBox** to add a `MonthCalendar` to the application.

Handling a `MonthCalendar` Control's `DateChanged` Event

■ Double click the `MonthCalendar` control in **Design** view to generate the `DateChanged` event handler.

■ Property `SelectionStart` returns the first (or only) date selected.

Handling a `ComboBox` Control's `SelectedIndexChanged` Event

■ Double click the `ComboBox` control in **Design** view to generate the `SelectedIndex-Changed` event handler.

KEY TERMS

binary digit—A digit that can assume one of two values.

bit—Short for "binary digit." A digit that can assume one of two values.

byte—Eight bits.

character set—The set of all characters used to write applications and represent data items on a particular computer. Visual Basic uses the Unicode character set.

CheckFileExists property of class `OpenFileDialog`—Enables the user to display a warning if a specified file does not exist.

Close method of class `StreamWriter` or `StreamReader`—Used to close the stream.

database—Can be a group of related files.

database management system (DBMS)—Collection of programs designed to create and manage databases.

data hierarchy—Collection of data items processed by computers that become larger and more complex in structure as you progress from bits, to characters, to fields and up to larger data structures.

DateChanged event of `MonthCalendar` control—Raised when a new date (or a range of dates) is selected.

decimal digits—The digits 0, 1, 2, 3, 4, 5, 6, 7, 8 and 9.

field—Group of characters that conveys some meaning. For example, a field consisting of uppercase and lowercase letters can represent a person's name.

file—Collection of data that is assigned a name. Used for long-term persistence of large amounts of data, even after the application that created the data terminates.

FileName property of class `OpenFileDialog`—Specifies the file name displayed in the dialog.

MonthCalendar control—Displays a calendar from which a user can select a range of dates.

OpenFileDialog control—Enables an application to use the **Open** dialog, which allows users to specify a file to be opened

Peek method of class `StreamReader`—Returns the next character to be read or −1 if there are no more characters to read in the file (that is, the end of the file has been reached).

persistent data—Data maintained in files.

ReadLine method of class `StreamReader`—Method of class `StreamReader` that reads a line from a file and returns it as a `String`.

record—A collection of related fields. Usually a `Class` in Visual Basic composed of several fields (called member variables in Visual Basic).

record key—Identifies a record and distinguishes it from all other records.

secondary storage media—Devices such as magnetic disks, optical disks and magnetic tapes on which computers store files.

SelectionStart property of MonthCalendar control—Returns the first (or only) date selected.

sequential-access file—File which contains data that is read in the order that it was written to the file.

ShowDialog method of class OpenFileDialog—Displays the **Open** dialog and returns the result of the user interaction with the dialog.

special symbols—$, @, %, &, *, ( ), -, +, ", :, ?, / and the like.

stream—Object that has access to a sequence of characters.

StreamReader class—Provides methods for reading information from a file.

StreamWriter class—Provides methods for writing information to a file.

text file—A file containing human-readable characters.

Unicode—A character set containing characters that are composed of two bytes. Characters are represented in Visual Basic using the Unicode character set.

WriteLine method of class StreamWriter—Method of class StreamWriter that writes a String and a line terminator to a file.

CONTROLS, EVENTS, PROPERTIES & METHODS

ComboBox   ▤ ComboBox   This control allows users to select options from a drop-down list.

■ *In action*

■ *Event*

SelectedIndexChanged—Raised when a new value is selected in the ComobBox.

■ *Properties*

DropDownStyle—Determines the ComboBox's style.

Enabled—Determines whether the user can enter data (True) in the ComboBox or not (False).

Items—Specifies the values the user can select from the ComboBox.

Item—Retrieves the value at the specified index.

Location—Specifies the location of the ComboBox control on its container control relative to the top-left corner.

MaxDropDownItems—Determines the maximum number of items to be displayed when the user clicks the drop-down arrow.

Name—Specifies the name used to access the ComboBox control programmatically. The name should be appended with the ComboBox suffix.

SelectedIndex—Specifies the index of the item selected.

SelectedValue—Contains the item selected by the user.

Text—Specifies the text displayed in the ComboBox.

■ *Methods*

Items.Add—Adds an item to the ComboBox.

Items.Clear—Deletes all the values in the ComboBox.

MonthCalendar   ▦ MonthCalendar   This control displays a calendar from which the user can select a date or a range of dates.

■ *In action*

■ *Event*

DateChanged—Raised when a new date (or a range of dates) is selected.

■ *Properties*

Location—Specifies the location of the MonthCalendar control on the Form.

Name—Specifies the name used to access the properties of the MonthCalendar control in the application code. The name should be appended with the MonthCalendar suffix.

SelectionStart—Returns the first (or only) date selected.

OpenFileDialog   OpenFileDialog   This object enables an application to use the **Open** dialog.

■ *Properties*

CheckFileExists—Enables the user to display a warning if a specified file does not exist.

FileName—Sets the default file name displayed in the dialog. It can also be used to retrieve the name of the user-entered file.

Name—Specifies the identifier used to reference the control's properties and methods.

■ *Method*

ShowDialog—Displays the **Open** dialog and returns the result of the user interaction with the dialog.

StreamWriter This class is used to write data to a file.

■ *Methods*

Close—Used to close the stream.

WriteLine—Writes the data specified in its argument, followed by a newline character.

StreamReader This class is used to read data from a file.

■ *Methods*

Close—Closes the stream.

ReadLine—Reads a line of data from a particular file.

MULTIPLE-CHOICE QUESTIONS

24.1 Data maintained in a file is called _____.

a) persistent data
b) bits
c) secondary data
d) databases

24.2 Methods from the _____ class can be used to write data to a file.

a) StreamReader
b) FileWriter
c) StreamWriter
d) WriteFile

24.3 Namespace _____ provides the classes and methods that you need to use to perform file processing.

a) System.IO
b) System.Files
c) System.Stream
d) System.Windows.Forms

24.4 Sometimes a group of related files is called a _____.

a) field
b) database
c) collection
d) byte

24.5 A(n) _____ allows the user to select a file to open.

a) CreateFileDialog
b) OpenFileDialog
c) MessageBox
d) None of the above.

24.6 Digits, letters and special symbols are referred to as _____.

a) constants
b) Integers
c) Strings
d) characters

24.7 The _____ method reads a line from a file.

a) `ReadLine`   b) `Read`

c) `ReadAll`   d) `ReadToNewline`

24.8 A _____ contains information that is read in the order that it was written.

a) sequential-access file   b) `StreamWriter`

c) `StreamReader`   d) None of the above.

24.9 The smallest data item that a computer can support is called a _____.

a) character set   b) character

c) special symbol   d) bit

24.10 Methods from the _____ class can be used to read data from a file.

a) `StreamWriter`   b) `FileReader`

c) `StreamReader`   d) `ReadFile`

EXERCISES

24.11 (*Birthday Saver Application*) Create an application that stores people's names and birthdays in a file (Fig. 24.35). The user creates a file and inputs each person's first name, last name and birthday on the `Form`. The information is then written to the file.

Figure 24.35 **Birthday Saver** application's GUI.

a) *Copying the template to your working directory.* Copy the directory `C:\Examples\Tutorial24\Exercises\BirthdaySaver` to your `C:\SimplyVB` directory.

b) *Opening the application's template file.* Double click `BirthdaySaver.sln` in the `BirthdaySaver` directory to open the application (Fig. 24.35).

c) *Adding and customizing an* `OpenFileDialog` *component.* Add an `OpenFileDialog` component to the `Form`. Change its `Name` property to `openFileDialog`. Set the `CheckFileExists` property to `False`.

d) *Importing namespace* `System.IO`. Import `System.IO` to allow file processing.

e) *Declaring a* `StreamWriter` *object.* Declare a `StreamWriter` object that can be used throughout the entire class.

f) *Defining the Open File... Button's Click event handler.* Double click the **Open File...** `Button` to create the `openButton_Click` event handler. Write code to display the **Open** dialog. If the user clicks the **Cancel** `Button` in the dialog, the event handler will perform no further actions. Otherwise, determine whether the user provided a file name that has the `.txt` extension (indicating a text file). If the user did not, display a `MessageBox` asking the user to select an appropriate file. If the user specified a valid file name, perform *Step g*.

g) *Initializing the* `StreamWriter`. Initialize the `StreamWriter` in the event handler `openButton_Click`, passing the user-input file name as an argument. Allow the user to append information to the file by passing the `Boolean` value `True` as the second argument to the `StreamWriter`.

h) *Defining the Enter Button's Click event handler.* Double click the **Enter** `Button` to create the event handler `enterButton_Click`. This event handler writes the entire name of the person on one line in the file. Then the person's birthday is written on the next line in the file. Finally, the `TextBox`es on the `Form` are cleared, and the `DateTimePicker`'s value is set back to the current date.

i) *Defining the Close File Button's Click event handler.* Double click the **Close File** `Button` to create the `closeButton_Click` event handler. Close the `StreamWriter` connection in this event handler.

j) *Running the application.* Select **Debug > Start Debugging** to run your application. Open a file by clicking **Open File...** Button. After a file has been opened, use the input fields provided to enter birthday information. After each person's name and birthday are typed in, click the **Enter** Button. When you are finished, close the file by clicking the **Close File** Button. Browse to the file and ensure that its contents contain the birthday information that you entered.

k) *Closing the application.* Close your running application by clicking its close box.

l) *Closing the IDE.* Close the Visual Basic IDE by clicking its close box.

24.12 (*Photo Album Application*) Create an application that displays images for the user, as shown in Fig. 24.36. This application should display the current image in a large Picture-Box and display the previous and next images in smaller PictureBoxes. A description of the book represented by the large image should be displayed in a multiline TextBox. The application should use the Directory class's methods to facilitate the displaying of the images.

Figure 24.36 Photo Album application GUI.

a) *Copying the template to your working directory.* Copy the directory C:\Examples\ Tutorial24\Exercises\PhotoAlbum to your C:\SimplyVB directory.

b) *Opening the application's template file.* Double click PhotoAlbum.sln in the PhotoAlbum directory to open the application.

c) *Creating instance variables.* Create instance variable current to represent the current image that is displayed, and set it to 0. Create the largeImage array (to store the path names of five large images), the smallImage array (to store the path names of five small images) and the descriptions array (to store the descriptions of the five books represented by the images).

d) *Defining the RetrieveData procedure.* Create a Sub procedure named RetrieveData to store the path names of the larger images in largeImages and the path names of the smaller images in smallImage. Use the Directory class's GetCurrentDirectory method to determine the directory path for the images\large and images\small folders. Sequential-access file books.txt stores the file name of each image. The file is organized such that the file name of the small and large images are on the first line. These files have similar names. The small image's file name ends with _thumb.jpg (that is, *filename*_thumb.jpg) while the large image's file name ends with _large.jpg (that is, *filename*_large.jpg). The description of the book, which should be stored in array descriptions, follows the file name. Write code to read this data from the file and place it into arrays.

e) *Defining the DisplayPicture procedure.* Create a Sub procedure named DisplayPicture to display the current image in the large PictureBox, to display the previous and next images in the smaller PictureBoxes, and to place the description of the large image in the TextBox.

f) ***Using If...Then...Else in the DisplayPicture procedure.*** Use an If...Then...Else statement to display the images on the Form. If the Integer instance variable is 0, display the image of the first book. Also, display the next book's image in the next image PictureBox. However, since there is no previous image, nothing should be displayed in the previous image PictureBox, and the **Previous Image** Button should be disabled. If the last image is displayed in the large PictureBox, then disable the **Next Image** Button, and do not display anything in the next image PictureBox. Otherwise, all three PictureBoxes should display their corresponding images, and the **Previous Image** and **Next Image** Buttons should be enabled.

g) ***Defining the PhotoAlbumForm_Load event handler.*** Double click the Form to create the PhotoAlbumForm_Load event handler. Invoke methods RetrieveData and DisplayPicture in this event handler.

h) ***Defining the previousButton_Click event handler.*** Double click the **Previous Image** Button to create the previousButton_Click event handler. In this event handler, decrease the Integer instance variable by 1 and invoke procedure DisplayPicture.

i) ***Defining the nextButton_Click event handler.*** Double click the **Next Image** Button to create the nextButton_Click event handler. In this event handler, increment the Integer instance variable by 1 and invoke the DisplayPicture procedure.

j) ***Running the application.*** Select **Debug > Start Debugging** to run your application. Click the **Previous Image** and **Next Image** Buttons to ensure that the proper images and descriptions are displayed.

k) ***Closing the application.*** Close your running application by clicking its close box.

l) ***Closing the IDE.*** Close the Visual Basic IDE by clicking its close box.

24.13 (***Car Reservation Application***) Create an application that allows a user to reserve a car for the specified day (Fig. 24.37). A small car-reservation company can rent out only four cars per day. Let the application allow the user to specify a certain day. If four cars have already been reserved for that day, then indicate to the user that no vehicles are available.

Figure 24.37 **Car Reservation** application GUI.

a) ***Copying the template to your working directory.*** Copy the directory C:\Examples\Tutorial24\Exercises\CarReservation to your C:\SimplyVB directory.

b) ***Opening the application's template file.*** Double click CarReservation.sln in the CarReservation directory to open the application.

c) ***Adding a MonthCalendar control to the Form.*** Drag and drop a MonthCalendar control on the Form. Set the Location property of the control to 16, 40.

d) ***Importing System.IO namespace.*** Import namespace System.IO to allow file processing.

e) ***Defining a method.*** Create a method named NumberOfReservations that takes one argument of type Date. The procedure should create a StreamReader that reads from the reservations.txt file. Use a Do While Loop to allow the StreamReader to search through the entire reservations.txt file to see how many cars have been rented for the day selected by the user. The procedure should close the Stream-Reader connection and return the number of cars rented for the day selected.

f) *Defining a Sub procedure.* Create a Sub procedure named CheckReservations. This procedure should invoke the NumberOfReservations method, passing in the user-selected day as an argument. The CheckReservations method should then retrieve the number returned by NumberOfReservations and determine whether four cars have been rented for that day. If four cars have been rented, then display a message dialog to the user stating that no cars are available that day for rental. If fewer than four cars have been rented for that day, create a StreamWriter object, passing reservations.txt as the first argument and True as the second argument. Write the day and the user's name to the reservations.txt file and display a message dialog to the user stating that a car has been reserved.

g) *Defining the reserveButton_Click event handler.* Double click the **Reserve Car** Button to create the reserveButton_Click event handler. In this event handler, invoke the CheckReservations procedure and clear the **Name:** TextBox.

h) *Running the application.* Select **Debug > Start Debugging** to run your application. Enter several reservations, including four reservations for the same day. Enter a reservation for a day that already has four reservations to ensure that a message dialog will be displayed.

i) *Closing the application.* Close your running application by clicking its close box. Open reservations.txt to ensure that the proper data has been stored (based on the reservations entered in *Step h*).

j) *Closing the IDE.* Close the Visual Basic IDE by clicking its close box.

What does this code do? ▶ **24.14** What is the result of the following code?

```
1   Dim path1 As String = "oldfile.txt"
2   Dim path2 As String = "newfile.txt"
3   Dim line As String
4
5   Dim output As StreamWriter
6   output = New StreamWriter(path2)
7
8   Dim input As StreamReader
9   input = New StreamReader(path1)
10
11  line = input.ReadLine()
12
13  Do While line <> ""
14     output.WriteLine(line)
15     line = input.ReadLine()
16  Loop
17
18  output.Close()
19  input.Close()
```

What's wrong with this code? ▶ **24.15** Find the error(s) in the following code, which is supposed to read a line from some-file.txt, convert the line to uppercase and then append it to somefile.txt.

```
1   Dim path As String = "somefile.txt"
2   Dim contents As String
3
4   Dim output As StreamWriter
5   output = New StreamWriter(path, True)
6
7   Dim input As StreamReader
8   input = New StreamReader(path)
9
```

(cont.)

```
10   contents = input.ReadLine()
11
12   contents = contents.ToUpper()
13
14   output.Write(contents)
15
16   output.Close()
17   input.Close()
```

Programming Challenge ▶

24.16 (*File Scrape Application*) Create an application, similar to the screen-scraping application of Tutorial 23, that opens a user-specified file and searches the file for the price of a book, returning it to the user (Fig. 24.38). [*Hint:* You will need to use the ReadToEnd method of class StreamReader to retrieve the entire contents of the files. The book price appears, for example, in the sample booklist.htm file as Our Price: $59.99.]

Figure 24.38   **File Scrape** application GUI.

a) *Copying the template to your working directory.* Copy the directory C:\Examples\ Tutorial24\Exercises\FileScrape to your C:\SimplyVB directory. Note that two HTML files—booklist.htm and bookpool.htm—are provided for you.

b) *Opening the application's template file.* Double click FileScrape.sln in the File-Scrape directory to open the application.

c) *Creating an event handler.* Create an event handler for the **Open...** Button that allows the user to select a file to search for prices.

d) *Creating a second event handler.* Create an event handler for the **Search** Button. This event handler should search the specified HTML file for the book price. When the price is found, display it in the output Label.

e) *Running the application.* Select **Debug > Start Debugging** to run your application. Click the **Open...** Button and select one of the .htm files provided in the File-Scrape directory. Click the **Search** Button and view the price of the book. For booklist.htm, the price should be $59.99, and for bookpool.htm the price should be $39.50.

f) *Closing the application.* Close your running application by clicking its close box.

g) *Closing the IDE.* Close the Visual Basic IDE by clicking its close box.

25

Address Book Application

Introducing Database Programming

Objectives

In this tutorial, you will learn to:
- Connect to databases.
- View the contents of a SQL Server 2005 Express database.
- Add database controls to Windows Forms.
- Use the **Data Sources** window.
- Use the **Query Builder** dialog.
- Read information from and update information in databases.

Outline

25.1 Test-Driving the Address Book Application

25.2 Planning the Address Book Application

25.3 Creating Database Connections

25.4 Programming the Address Book Application

25.5 Wrap-Up

I n the last tutorial, you learned how to create sequential-access files and how to search through such files to locate information. Sequential-access files are inappropriate for so-called **instant-access applications**, in which information must be located immediately. An electronic address book can be constructed as an instant-access application for rapid access to specific contact information. A large company's address book may have hundreds of thousands of listings; however, when a specific person's contact information is requested, it is retrieved almost immediately. This type of instant access is made possible by databases. Individual database records can be accessed directly (and quickly) without sequentially searching through large numbers of other records, as is required with sequential-access files. In this tutorial, you will be introduced to databases and **ADO.NET**, the part of Microsoft.NET, for interacting with databases. You will learn about databases and ADO.NET as you create this tutorial's **Address Book** application.

25.1 Test-Driving the Address Book Application

An electronic address book provides quick and easy access to stored contact information. It also allows new contact information to be added and existing contact information to be updated or deleted. This application must meet the following requirements:

Application Requirements

You have been asked to create an address book application that stores the first name, last name, e-mail address and phone number of multiple people in a database table. Each entry should be stored as a different row in the table. The user should be able to navigate through the data, add rows, delete rows and save changes to the data. Specific entries should be retrievable by searching the data by last name.

You begin by test-driving the completed application. Then you will learn the additional Visual Basic 2005 technologies that you will need to create your own version of this application.

Test-Driving the Address Book Application

1. ***Opening the completed application.*** Open the directory `C:\Examples\Tutorial25\CompletedApplication\AddressBook` to locate the **Address Book** application. Double click `AddressBook.sln` to open the application in Visual Basic 2005.

2. ***Running the application.*** Select **Debug > Start Debugging** to run the application (Fig. 25.1). The database we provide with this example is initially empty, so the **Address ID:** TextBox (which is **ReadOnly**) is initially blank and the navigation Buttons in the **BindingNavigator** at the top of the Form are disabled. The BindingNavigator, discussed later in this chapter, is the strip of buttons below the window's title bar. It is an auto-generated control that allows you to manipulate the data displayed in the Form's other controls.

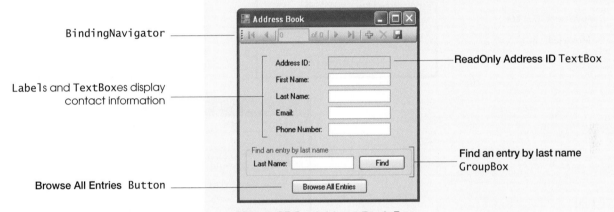

BindingNavigator

Labels and TextBoxes display contact information

Browse All Entries Button

ReadOnly Address ID TextBox

Find an entry by last name GroupBox

Figure 25.1   Address Book Form.

3. ***Adding a new entry.*** Click the **Add new** Button ⊕ in the BindingNavigator at the top of the Form. The **Address ID:** TextBox is automatically filled in with the value 0, and 1 of 1 is now displayed in the BindingNavigator to indicate that you are manipulating the first record and that the total number of records is one. Fill in the **First Name**, **Last Name**, **Email** and **Phone Number** TextBoxes as shown in Fig. 25.2 then click the **Save Data** Button 🖫 in the BindingNavigator.

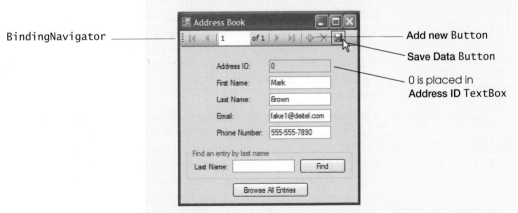

BindingNavigator

Add new Button

Save Data Button

0 is placed in Address ID TextBox

Figure 25.2   Adding an entry in the **Address Book** Form.

(cont.)

4. ***Adding more entries.*** As in *Step 3*, click the **Add new** Button to create another entry. Now the **Address ID:** TextBox contains 1, and 2 of 2 is displayed in the BindingNavigator. Also, the **Move first** and **Move previous** navigation Buttons in the BindingNavigator are now enabled since the first entry precedes the entry you just added. Fill in the fields as shown in Fig. 25.3, then click the **Add new** Button in the BindingNavigator. Repeat this process until you finish entering the other two contacts shown in Fig. 25.3, then click the **Save Data** Button.

Enabled
BindingNavigator
Buttons

Move first Button
Move previous Button

Move next Button
Move last Button

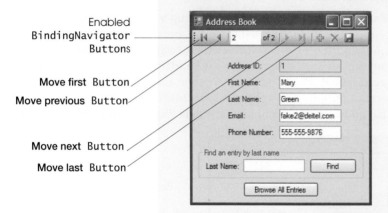

Figure 25.3   Adding additional entries in the **Address Book** Form.

5. ***Browsing all entries.*** After adding entries to the database table, you can view all of them by clicking the **Browse All Entries** Button at the bottom of the Form. Since the Form displays only one entry at a time, you need to use the **Move first**, **Move previous**, **Move next** and **Move last** Buttons in the BindingNavigator to navigate through the entries. You can also edit previous entries. [*Note:* If you edit entries, remember to click the **Save Data** Button after updating an entry.] Before proceeding with *Step 6*, click the **Move last** Button.

6. ***Searching all entries by last name.*** To search all the entries by **Last Name**, enter a last name in the **Last Name** TextBox of the **Find an entry by last name** GroupBox, then click the **Find** Button. Using this method, search for the last name Brown. Your first entry should now be displayed in the Form (Fig. 25.4). If you search for a last name that is not in your database table, then nothing is returned by the application and the Form's TextBoxes are cleared. Note that the BindingNavigator now shows 1 of 1, because there is only one entry with the last name Brown.

(cont.)

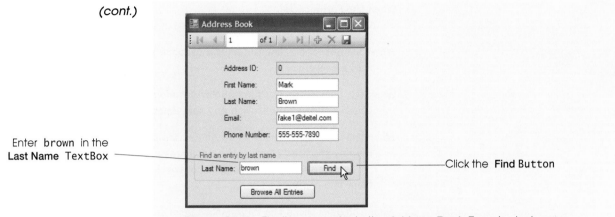

Figure 25.4 Finding an entry in the **Address Book** Form by last name.

Enter `brown` in the
Last Name `TextBox`

Click the **Find** `Button`

7. *Deleting an entry.* Click the **Browse All Entries** `Button` to return to view-ing all entries, then navigate to the second entry (the entry you will delete). When the second entry is displayed in the Form, click the **Delete** `Button` ✕ in the `BindingNavigator` (Fig. 25.5). Now click the **Save Data** But-ton. Browse the entries with the `BindingNavigator` to confirm that the Mary Green entry was deleted.

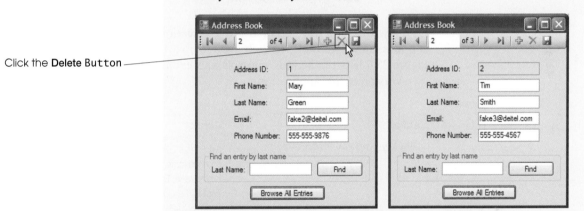

Click the **Delete** `Button`

Figure 25.5 Deleting an entry in the **Address Book** Form.

8. *Closing the application.* Close the application by clicking its close box. [*Note:* When you close the application, then run it again, you will notice that any changes you made to the database were not stored. Every time you start the application in **Debug** mode, the IDE recopies the original database in the project's `bin\Debug` folder. To allow your database changes to be stored permanently, select `AddressBook.mdf` in the **Solution Explorer**, then set its **Copy To Output Directory** property to `Copy if newer`.]

9. *Closing the IDE.* Close Visual Basic 2005 by clicking its close box.

25.2 Planning the Address Book Application

Now that you have test-driven the **Address Book** application, you will begin by analyzing the application. The following pseudocode describes the basic operation of the **Address Book** application. As you will see, the features described here are generated automatically for you.

When the Form loads
    Display the first entry (if one exists) in the AddressBook database

When the user clicks the BindingNavigator's auto-generated Add new Button
    Add a new entry

When the user clicks the BindingNavigator's auto-generated Save Data Button
    Update the database with any new, deleted and updated entries

When the user clicks the Browse All Entries Button
    Display the first entry in the database and allow the user to browse all
        entries with the BindingNavigator
    Clear the search text box

When the user clicks the BindingNavigator's auto-generated Delete Button
    Delete the current entry displayed in the Form

When the user clicks the Find Button
    If no entries have a last name that matches the input string,
        then display empty TextBoxes
    Otherwise, display the first entry with the specified last name and allow the
        user to browse through all matching entries with BindingNavigator's
        auto-generated buttons

Now that you have studied the application's pseudocode representation, you will use an ACE table to help you convert the pseudocode to Visual Basic. Figure 25.6 lists the actions, controls and events that will help you complete your own version of this application.

Action/Control/Event (ACE) Table for the Address Book Application

Action	Control	Event
Display contact information	AddressIDTextBox, FirstNameTextBox, LastNameTextBox, EmailTextBox, PhoneNumberTextBox	
	AddressBookForm	Load
Display the first entry (if one exists) in the AddressBook database	AddressesTableAdapter, AddressBookDataSet.Addresses	
Add a new entry	BindingNavigatorAddDataItem, AddressIDTextBox, FirstNameTextBox, LastNameTextBox, EmailTextBox, PhoneNumberTextBox	Click the **Add new** Button on the AddressesBindingNavigator
Update the database with any new, deleted and updated entries	AddressesBindingNavigatorSaveItem, AddressesTableAdapter, AddressesBindingSource, AddressBookDataSet.Addresses	Click the **Save Data** Button on the AddressesBindingNavigator

Figure 25.6 ACE table for the **Address Book** application. (Part 1 of 2.)

Action	Control	Event
	`browseAllButton`	`Click`
Display the first entry in the database and allow the user to browse all entries with the BindingNavigator	`AddressesTable-Adapter`, `AddressBookData-Set.Addresses`	
Clear the search text box	`findTextBox`	
Delete the current entry displayed in the Form	`AddressesBinding-Navigator`, `AddressBookData-Set.Addresses`	Click the **Delete** Button on the `AddressesBinding-Navigator`
	`findButton`	`Click`
If no entries have a last name that matches the input string Display blank fields	`findTextBox`, `AddressesTable-Adapter`, `AddressBookData-Set.Addresses`	
Otherwise, display the first entry with the specified last name and allow the user to browse through all matching entries with BindingNavigator's auto-generated buttons	`findTextBox`, `AddressesTable-Adapter`, `AddressBookData-Set.Addresses`	

Figure 25.6   ACE table for the **Address Book** application. (Part 2 of 2.)

25.3 Creating Database Connections

In this tutorial, you will use the IDE's **Data Sources** window to connect to a database. A **database** is an organized collection of data. Many different strategies exist for organizing data in databases to allow easy access to and manipulation of the data. A **database management system** (**DBMS**) enables you to access and store data without worrying about how it is organized. In this tutorial, you use a SQL Server 2005 Express database. You connect to the database in the following box.

Adding a Database Connection to the Address Book Application

1. *Creating the project.* Create a new Windows Application named Address-Book. Change the name of the Form to AddressBookForm, and change the source file name to AddressBookForm.vb. Then set the Form's Text property to Address Book.

2. *Adding a data source to the project.* To interact with a data source (e.g., a database), you must add it to the project using the **Data Sources** window, which lists the databases that your project can access. Open the **Data Sources** window (Fig. 25.7) by selecting **Data > Show Data Sources**. In the **Data Sources** window, click the link **Add New Data Source...** to open the **Data Source Configuration Wizard** (Fig. 25.8). This wizard guides you through connecting to a database and choosing the parts of the database to use in your application.

3. *Choosing the data source type.* The first screen of the **Data Source Configuration Wizard** asks you to choose the data source type you wish to include in the project. Select **Database** and click **Next >**.

(cont.)

Add New Data Source `Button` ————

Add New Data Source `Label` ————

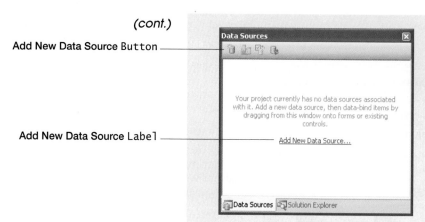

Figure 25.7 **Data Sources** window.

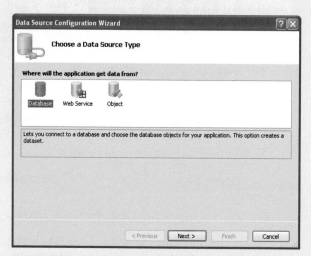

Figure 25.8 **Data Source Configuration Wizard** dialog.

4. *Adding a new database connection.* You must next choose the **connection** that will be used to connect to the database (i.e., the actual source of the data). Click the **New Connection...** `Button` to open the **Add Connection** dialog (Fig. 25.9). If the **Data Source** is not set to **Microsoft SQL Server Database File (SqlClient)**, click **Change...**, select **Microsoft SQL Server Database File** and click **OK**. Next, click **Browse...**, locate the `Address-Book.mdf` database file in the `C:\Examples\Tutorial25` directory, select it and click **Open**. You can click **Test Connection** to verify that the IDE can connect to the database through SQL Server 2005 Express. Click **OK** to create the connection.

5. *Choosing the `AddressBook.mdf` data connection.* Now that you have created a connection to the `AddressBook.mdf` database, you can select and use it to access the database. Click **Next >** to set the connection, then click the **Yes** `Button` when asked whether you want to copy the database file to your project.

6. *Saving the connection string.* The next screen (Fig. 25.10) asks you whether you want to save the connection string to the application configuration file. A **connection string** specifies the path to a database file on disk, as well as some additional settings that determine how to access the database. Saving the connection string in a configuration file makes it easy to change the connection settings at a later time. Leave the default selections and click **Next >** to proceed.

(cont.)

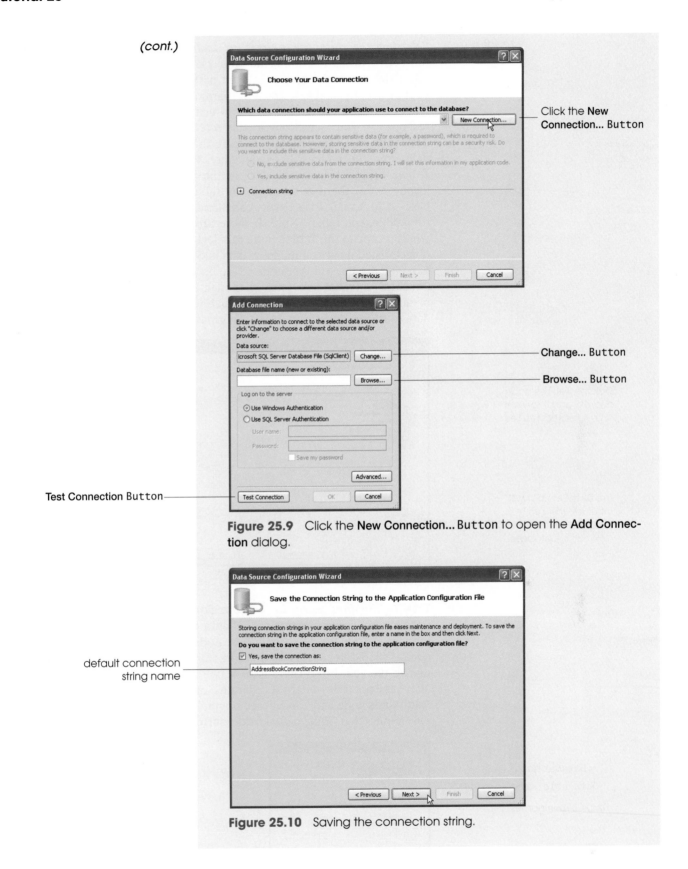

Figure 25.9   Click the **New Connection...** Button to open the **Add Connection** dialog.

Figure 25.10   Saving the connection string.

(cont.)

7. ***Selecting the database objects to include in your DataSet***. The IDE retrieves information about the database you selected and prompts you to select the database objects (i.e., the parts of the database) that you want your project to be able to access. Programs typically access a database's contents through a cache of the data, which is stored in a **DataSet** object. In response to your selections in this screen, the IDE will generate a class derived from System.Data.DataSet that is designed specifically to store data from the AddressBook database. Click the CheckBox to the left of **Tables** (Fig. 25.11) to indicate that the custom DataSet is to cache (i.e., locally store) the data from all the tables in the AddressBook.mdf database—AddressID, FirstName, LastName, PhoneNumber and Email fields in the Addresses table. [Note: If there are multiple tables in your database, you can expand the **Tables** node to select specific tables. The other database objects listed do not contain any data in our sample AddressBook.mdf database and are beyond the scope of the book.] By default, the IDE names the DataSet AddressBookDataSet, though it is possible to specify a different name in this screen. Finally, click **Finish** to complete the process of adding a data source to the project. [*Note:* This may take a few seconds.]

Click the **Tables** node and expand it to view selected **Tables**

The **DataSet** that will include the **Tables** extracted from the database

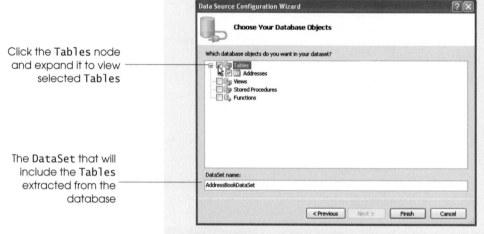

Figure 25.11 Select **Tables** node to add database tables to the dataset

8. ***Viewing the data source in the Data Sources window***. An AddressBook-DataSet node now appears in the **Data Sources** window with child nodes for each table in the database—these nodes represent the DataTables of the AddressBookDataSet. A **DataTable** stores data in memory (discussed further in the next box). There is only one node in this example because the AddressBook.mdf database contains only one DataTable. Expand the **Addresses** node and you will see the table's columns—the DataSet's structure mimics that of the actual **AddressBook** database (Fig. 25.12).

DataSet name

DataTable name

DataColumn names

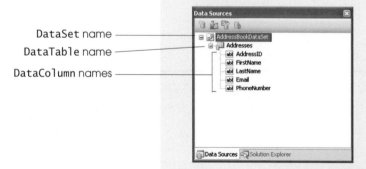

Figure 25.12 Updated **Data Sources** window.

(cont.)   9. ***Viewing the database in the Solution Explorer.*** AddressBook.mdf is now
               listed as a node in the **Solution Explorer** (Fig. 25.13), indicating that the
               database is part of this project. In addition, the **Solution Explorer** now lists a
               new node named AddressBookDataSet.xsd. The .xsd extension repre-
               sents an XML Schema document that specifies the structure of a set of XML
               documents. The IDE uses an XML Schema document to represent a
               DataSet's structure, including the tables that comprise the DataSet and the
               relationships among them. When you added the AddressBook database as a
               data source, the IDE created the AddressBookDataSet.xsd file based on
               the structure of the AddressBook database. The IDE then generated class
               AddressBookDataSet from the schema (i.e., structure) described by the
               .xsd file.

Database that was
added to this project

XML Schema document
generated by the IDE

Figure 25.13   Updated **Solution Explorer** window.

10. ***Saving the project.*** Select **File > Save All** to save your modified code. Save
    the project in the C:\SimplyVB directory.

Now that you have established a connection to the database by using the **Data
Sources** window, you will need to know how the AddressBook.mdf database organizes its data. You will use the **Database Explorer** window to view the database
information in the Visual Basic 2005 IDE. You will learn about the database in the
following box.

Understanding the   1. ***Opening the Database Explorer.*** Select **View > Database Explorer.**
AddressBook.mdf
Database Structure   2. ***Viewing the Addresses table of the AddressBook.mdf database in Data-***
                              base Explorer. Addresses is a table in the AddressBook.mdf database. A
                              Table, represented by keyword DataTable, stores related information in
                              rows and columns. Relational databases, such as SQL Server 2005 Express,
                              consist of one or more tables. To view the contents of the Addresses table,
                              first expand the AddressBook.mdf node, then the **Tables** node. Right click
                              Addresses, and select **Show Table Data** (Fig. 25.14). The contents of the
                              Addresses table display in Visual Basic 2005 (Fig. 25.15).

                          3. ***Understanding the database.*** Figure 25.15 displays the entire database
                              (because it consists of only one table) used in the **Address Book** application.
                              This table contains four **records** and five **fields**. A record is a table row, and a
                              field is a table column. For example, in this table, the **AddressID, FirstName,
                              LastName, Email** and **PhoneNumber** columns are fields that represent the
                              data in each record.

(cont.)

Click to display the **Tables** node ⎯⎯⎯⎯⎯

Right click the **Addresses** node ⎯⎯⎯⎯⎯

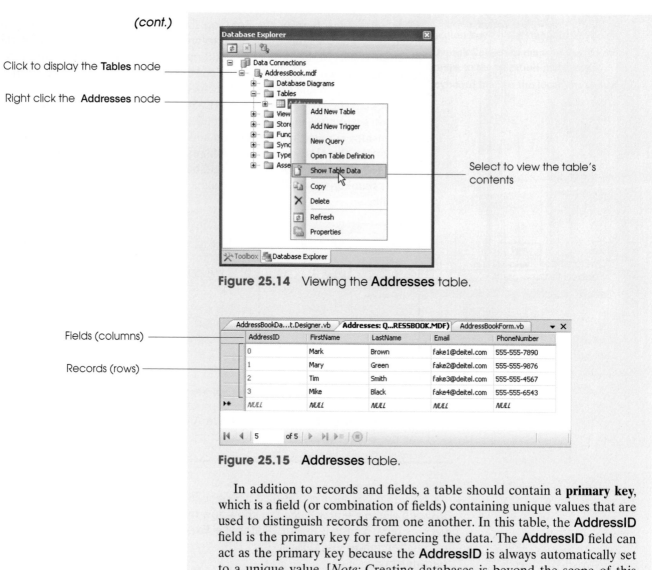

Select to view the table's contents

Figure 25.14 Viewing the **Addresses** table.

Fields (columns) ⎯⎯⎯⎯⎯

Records (rows) ⎯⎯⎯⎯⎯

Figure 25.15 **Addresses** table.

In addition to records and fields, a table should contain a **primary key**, which is a field (or combination of fields) containing unique values that are used to distinguish records from one another. In this table, the **AddressID** field is the primary key for referencing the data. The **AddressID** field can act as the primary key because the **AddressID** is always automatically set to a unique value. [*Note:* Creating databases is beyond the scope of this book, so we provide you with preconfigured databases for this tutorial's example and exercises.]

4. ***Closing the Addresses window.*** Right click the **Addresses** tab and select **Close**.

Now that you have added the AddressBook.mdf database as a data source, you can display the data from the database's **Addresses** table in your program. The IDE provides design tools that allow you to display data from a data source on a Form without writing *any* code. Simply drag and drop items from the **Data Sources** window onto a Form, and the IDE generates the GUI controls and code necessary to display the selected data source's content. In the following box, you will learn how to do this in the **Address Book** application.

Displaying the Address Book Fields on the Form

1. *Indicating that the IDE will create Labels and TextBoxes to display the fields in each row of data*. The IDE allows you to specify the type of control(s) that it creates when you drag and drop a data source member onto a Form in **Design** view. Make sure you viewing AddressBookForm in **Design** view, then click the **Addresses** node in the **Data Sources** window (Fig. 25.16). Note that this node becomes a drop-down list when you select it. [This does not occur if you are not in a Form's **Design** view.] Click the down arrow to view the items in the list. The icon to the left of DataGridView will initially be highlighted, because it is the default control to be used to display table data. Select the Details option in the drop-down list to indicate that the IDE is to create a set of Label–TextBox pairs for each name–column value pair when you drag and drop the **Addresses** table onto the Form. (You will see what this looks like in Fig. 25.17.) You can also choose the **Customize...** option to select other controls that are capable of being bound to a table's data.

Addresses node

Default control for displaying table data

Select Details to display data in a set of Labels and TextBoxes

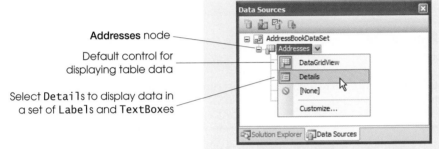

Figure 25.16   Selecting a display format for table data.

2. *Dragging the Addresses data source node onto the Form*. Drag the **Addresses** node from the **Data Sources** window to the Form. The IDE creates a series of Labels and TextBoxes (Fig. 25.17) because you selected Details in the preceding step. The IDE sets the text of each Label based on the corresponding column name in the database table, and uses regular expressions to insert spaces into multi-word column names to make the Labels more readable (e.g., FirstName becomes First Name).

   The IDE also creates a **BindingNavigator** and the other components in the component tray. A BindingNavigator's buttons resemble the controls on a CD or DVD player and allow you to move to the first row of data, the preceding row, the next row and the last row. The control also displays the currently selected row number in a text box. You can use this text box to enter the number of a row that you want to select. A BindingNavigator also has buttons that allow you to add a new row, delete a row and save changes to the underlying data source (that is, the Addresses table of the AddressBook.mdf database).

3. *Making the AddressID TextBox ReadOnly*. The AddressID column of the Addresses table is an auto-incremented column that is used to uniquely identify each record in the Addresses table, so users should not be allowed to edit the values of this column. Select the **Address ID** TextBox and set its ReadOnly property to True using the **Properties** window. Note that you may need to click in an empty part of the Form to deselect the other Labels and TextBoxes before selecting the **Address ID** TextBox.

4. *Executing the Address Book application*. At this point, execute the application by selecting **Debug > Start Debugging**, then test the BindingNavigator's capabilities. Note that you can already browse the database entries, add entries and delete entries even though you have not written *any* code!

(cont.)

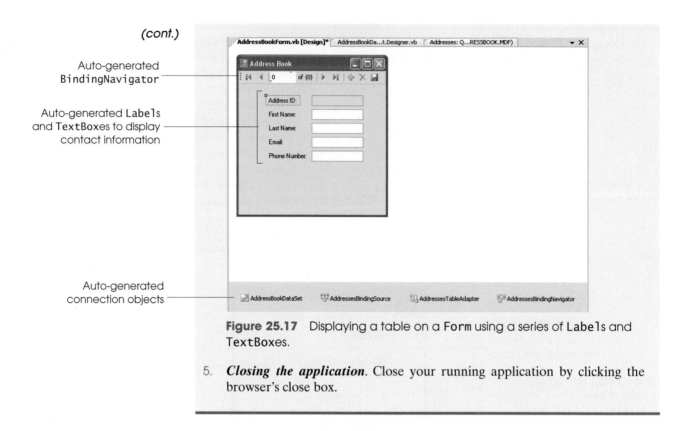

Auto-generated `BindingNavigator`

Auto-generated `Labels` and `TextBoxes` to display contact information

Auto-generated connection objects

Figure 25.17 Displaying a table on a `Form` using a series of `Labels` and `TextBoxes`.

5. *Closing the application.* Close your running application by clicking the browser's close box.

While the `BindingNavigator` allows you to browse the address book entries, it would be more convenient to be able to find a specific entry by last name. In the next box, you will use the **Query Builder** tool in the **TableAdapter Query Configuration Wizard** to create a SQL statement that searches the `AddressBook.mdf` database for entries with specific last names. Then you will add GUI controls to the `Form` that will allow the user to execute this search.

Searching the Last-Name Field in the AddressBook.mdf Database

1. *Using a query to select specific data from a database table.* To add this functionality to the application, you must add a new query to the AddressesTableAdapter using the **TableAdapter Query Configuration Wizard**. A **TableAdapter** object interacts with a database on disk (i.e., the AddressBook.mdf file). When other components need to retrieve data from the database or write data to the database, they invoke `TableAdapter` methods. AddressesTableAdapter is one of the objects that is auto-generated by the IDE when you drag a table from the **Data Sources** window onto the Form.

To create a `TableAdapter` method that returns all the records in the AddressBook.mdf database with a specific last name, first click the **Edit DataSet with Designer** icon (Fig. 25.18) in the **Data Sources** window. Select the AddressesTableAdapter. Right click the TableAdapter's name and select **Add Query...** In the **TableAdapter Query Configuration Wizard**, keep the default option **Use SQL Statements** and click **Next**. On the next screen, keep the default option **SELECT** which returns rows and click **Next**.

(cont.)

Click the **Edit DataSet** with Designer Button

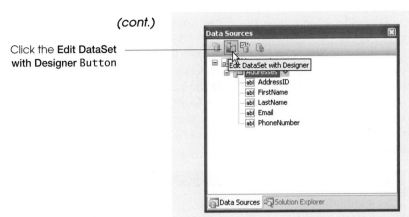

Figure 25.18   Click the **Edit DataSet with Designer** Button.

2. *Using Query Builder to create a query*. **Query Builder** is a tool which allows you to specify commands that retrieve information from and modify information in databases. In this dialog, click the **Query Builder...** Button (Fig. 25.19). Note that the lower portion of the **Query Builder** dialog contains some code (Fig. 25.20). This represents the **Structured Query Language (SQL)** statement that will be used to select information from the database. SQL is a language often used to perform database queries (requests for specified information) and to manipulate data. The FROM Addresses portion of the SQL statement indicates that the information you will select will be from the database's Addresses table.

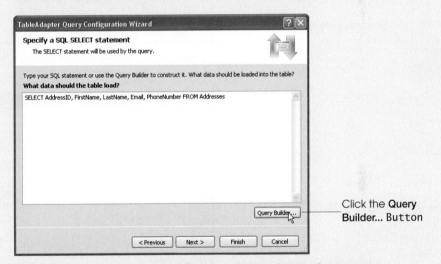

Click the **Query Builder...** Button

Figure 25.19   Click the **Query Builder...** Button to create a query.

By default, each column name is checked (Fig. 25.20), indicating that the query will return each column. The middle portion of the window contains a table in which each row corresponds to a column in the Addresses table. To the right of the column names are columns in which you can enter values or make selections that modify the query. We will use the **Filter** column to add a WHERE clause to the SELECT statement, returning only listings where the person's last name matches the last name for which the user is searching. WHERE clauses enable you to select subsets of the data in a database.

(cont.)   Type @lastName into the **Filter** column of the **LastName** field. This appends the clause WHERE LastName = @lastName to the end of the default query (Fig. 25.21). Note that @lastName is a parameter that will be replaced by a value when the query executes. Click the **Execute Query** Button to test the query, and display the results in the bottom portion of the **Query Builder** window. In the Value column of the **Query Parameters** window, type Brown and click **OK** to test the query. For more **Query Builder** information, see msdn2.microsoft.com/library/ms172013.aspx. Click **OK** to exit the **Query Builder**, then click **Next >**.

All columns are selected by default in the **Addresses** window

Filter Column

Corresponding SQL statement

Execute Query Button

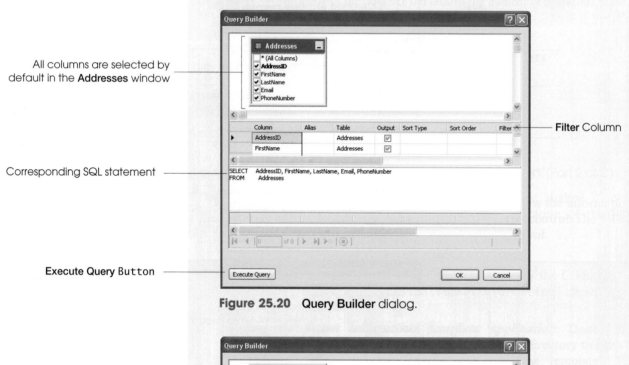

Figure 25.20   Query Builder dialog.

Enter @lastName into field LastName's **Filter** Column, then press *Enter*

Updated SQL statement

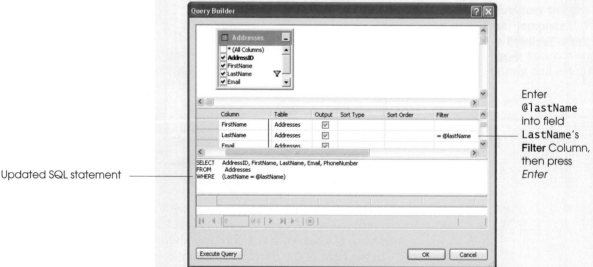

Figure 25.21   **Using the **Filter Column in the **Query Builder** dialog.

(cont.)   3. ***Naming data methods***. In the next screen, enter `FillByLastName` and `Get-DataByLastName` as the names for the two methods that the wizard will generate. The query contains a parameter, so each of these methods will take a parameter to set the value of `@lastName` in the query. You will see how to call the `FillByLastName` method and specify a value for `@lastName` shortly. Click **Finish** to complete the wizard and return to the **DataSet Designer** (Fig. 25.22). Note that the new `FillByLastName` and `GetDataByLastName` methods appear under the `AddressesTableAdapter` and that parameter `@lastName` is listed to the right of the method names.

New query created ———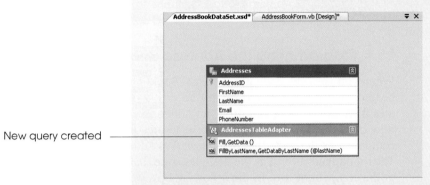

Figure 25.22   New query created in the **DataSet Designer**.

4. ***Adding controls to allow users to specify a last name to locate***. Now that you have created a query to locate rows with a specific last name, add controls to allow the user to enter a last name and execute this query. Open **Design** view and add to the Form a `Label` named `findLabel`, a `TextBox` named `findTextBox` and a `Button` named `findButton` (Fig. 25.23). Place these controls in a `GroupBox` named `findGroupBox`, then set the `GroupBox`'s `Text` property to `Find an entry by last name`. Set the `Text` properties of the `Label` and `Button` as shown in Fig. 25.23.

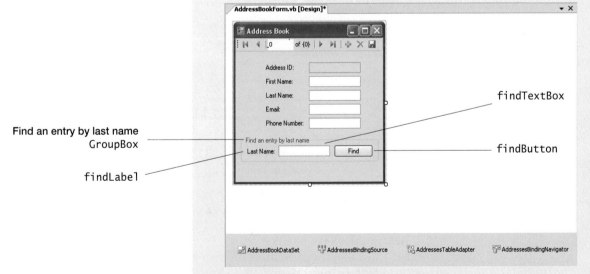

Figure 25.23   Add controls to search data by last name.

5. ***Saving the project***. Select **File > Save All** to save your modified code.

SELF-REVIEW

1. A database connection is added to an application in the _____ window.

   a) **Solution Explorer**   b) **Properties**
   c) **Data Sources**   d) None of the above.

2. After displaying the records in a database table on a Form, a _____ object allows you to navigate through theses records, add new records, delete records, and update the records.

   a) BindingNavigator   b) DataSet
   c) TableAdapter   d) None of the above.

Answers: 1) c. 2) a.

25.4 Programming the Address Book Application

When you view the code file (AddressBookForm.vb), you will notice that code has been provided for you. You do not need to write any of this code—the IDE generates it when you drag and drop the Addresses table from the **Data Sources** window onto the Form. The IDE also generates a considerable amount of additional code, such as the code that defines classes AddressBookDataSet and Addresses-TableAdapter, as well as the designer code that declares the auto-generated objects in the component tray. In the following box, we present only the code in Address-BookForm.vb, because it is the only file you'll need to modify.

Examining the Auto-Generated Code in AddressBookForm.vb

1. **The Click event handler for the Save Data Button.** Lines 6–14 in Fig. 25.24 contain the Click event handler for the **Save Data** Button in the Addresses-BindingNavigator. [*Note:* We've added comments and formatted the code in Fig. 25.24.] You click this button to save changes to the underlying data source (that is, the Addresses table of the AddressBook.mdf database). Saving the changes is a two-step process. First, the DataSet associated with the databound control (indicated by its BindingSource) must be updated to include any changes made by the user. Second, the database on disk must be updated to match the new contents of the DataSet.

Click event for the
Save Data Button

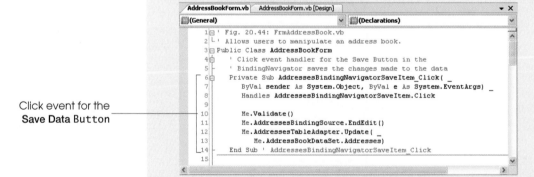

Figure 25.24 Click event handler for the **Save Data** Button.

Before the event handler saves any changes, line 10 invokes Me.Validate() to validate the controls on the Form. If you implement Validating or Validated events for any of the Form's controls, these events enable you to validate user input and indicate errors for invalid data. Line 11 invokes AddressesBindingSource's EndEdit method to ensure that the object's associated data source (AddressBookDataSet.Addresses) is updated with any changes made by the user to the currently selected row (for example, adding a row, changing a column value). Any changes to other rows were applied to the DataSet when you selected another row.

(cont.)

Line 12 invokes AddressesTableAdapter's Update method to write the modified version of the Addresses table (in memory) to the SQL Server database on disk. The Update method executes the SQL statements necessary to make the data in the database's Addresses table match the data in AddressBookDataSet.Addresses.

2. ***The Load event handler for AddressBookForm Form.*** Lines 16–22 in Fig. 25.25 contain the event handler for the Form's Load event. It fills the in-memory DataSet with data from the database on disk. Once the DataSet is filled, the GUI control bound to it can display its data. Line 21 calls AddressesTableAdapter's Fill method to retrieve information from the database, placing this information in the DataSet object provided as an argument. Recall that the IDE generated AddressesTableAdapter to execute SQL commands over the connection we created within the **Data Source Configuration Wizard**. Thus, the Fill method executes a SELECT statement to retrieve all the rows of the Addresses table of the Address-Book.mdf database, then places the result of this query in AddressBookDataSet.Addresses. The IDE bound the controls in the GUI to the Addresses table, so when the Form loads and method Fill is called, the first entry is displayed automatically.

Load event for
AddressBookForm

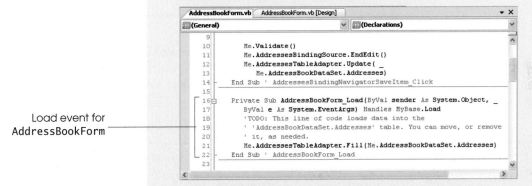

Figure 25.25   Click event handler for the **Save Data** Button.

3. ***Saving the project.*** Select **File > Save All** to save your modified code.

Now you will define the findButton_Click event handler to retrieve all listings with last names that match the user's search string (entered in findTextBox) and display them one at a time in the Form.

---

findButton_Click Event Handler

1. ***Creating the findButton_Click event handler.*** Double click the **Find** Button in **Design** View.

2. ***Retrieving and displaying listings with specific last names.*** Add lines 28–31 of Fig. 25.27 to the findButton_Click event handler. The FillByLastName method replaces the current data in AddressBookDataSet.Addresses with data for only those rows with last names that match the entered text in findTextBox. Note that when invoking FillByLastName, you must pass the DataTable to be filled, as well as an argument specifying the last name to find. This argument becomes the value of the @lastName parameter in the SELECT statement created in *Steps 1–3* of the box *Searching the Last Name Field in the AddressBook.mdf Database.*

(cont.)

When you search for a specific entry (i.e., enter a last name and click **Find**), the BindingNavigator allows the user to browse only the rows containing the specified last name. This is because the data source bound to the Form's controls (i.e., AddressBookDataSet.Addresses) has changed and now contains only rows containing the specified last name.

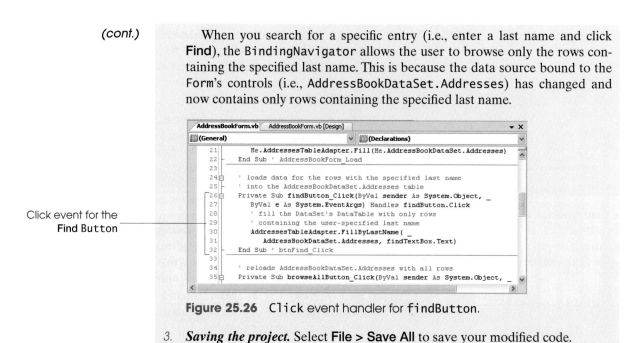

Click event for the
Find Button

Figure 25.26 Click event handler for findButton.

3. *Saving the project.* Select **File > Save All** to save your modified code.

Now you are ready to add the **Browse All Entries** Button and create the browseAllButton_Click event handler, which will allow users to return to browsing all the rows after searching for specific rows. You add this Button and create this method in the following box.

Adding the Browse All Entries Button and Its Click Event Handler

1. *Adding the browseAllButton to the Form.* Add a Button named browseAllButton and set its **Text** property to Browse All Entries. Set its **Location** property to 83, 238. Then set its **Size** property to 122px by 23px. The completed Form in **Design** View is shown in Fig. 25.28.

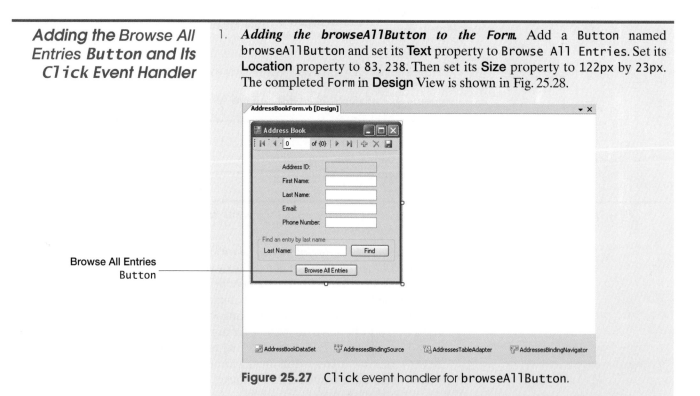

Browse All Entries
Button

Figure 25.27 Click event handler for browseAllButton.

2. *Creating the browseAllButton_Click event handler.* Double click the **Browse All Entries** Button in **Design** View.

(cont.)   3. ***Refilling Addresses DataTable with all the rows in the database table.***
Add lines 37–40 of Fig. 25.28 to the browseAllButton_Click event han-
dler. The Fill method replaces the current data in AddressBookData-
Set.Addresses with data for all the rows in the database table. Note that
this is the same method that is called in the AddressBookForm_Load event
handler when the DataTable is filled initially without being filtered by specific search conditions. Line 40 clears the findTextBox.

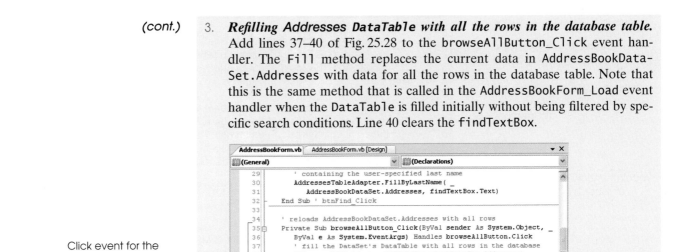

Click event for the
Browse All Entries Button

Figure 25.28 Click event handler for browseAllButton.

4. ***Saving the project.*** Select **File > Save All** to save your modified code.

Now that you have completed the **Address Book** application, you will test it in
the following box to ensure that it is functioning properly.

Testing Your Completed
Address Book
Application

1. ***Running the application.*** Select **Debug > Start Debugging** to run your
application. Enter a short list of contacts using the **Add new** Button of the
BindingNavigator, then click the **Save Data** Button. Next, search for the
last name of one of the contacts that you entered, using findTextBox and
findButton. Now refill the DataTable with all the data you previously
entered by clicking the **Browse All Entries** Button. Test the delete function
by deleting an entry and then clicking the **Save Data** Button. Click the
Browse All Entries Button again to see if the entry has been erased.

2. ***Closing the application.*** Close your running application by clicking the
browser's close box.

3. ***Closing the IDE.*** Close Visual Web Developer by clicking its close box.

Figure 25.29 presents the source code for the **Address Book** application. The
lines of code that contain new programming concepts that you learned in this tutorial are highlighted.

```
1   ' Fig. 25.29: AddressBookForm.vb
2   ' Allows users to manipulate an address book.
3   Public Class AddressBookForm
4       ' Click event handler for the Save Data Button in the
5       ' BindingNavigator saves the changes made to the data
6       Private Sub AddressesBindingNavigatorSaveItem_Click( _
7           ByVal sender As System.Object, ByVal e As System.EventArgs) _
8           Handles AddressesBindingNavigatorSaveItem.Click
9
```

Auto-generated Click
event handler for **Save
Data** Button

Figure 25.29 Address Book application code. (Part 1 of 2.)

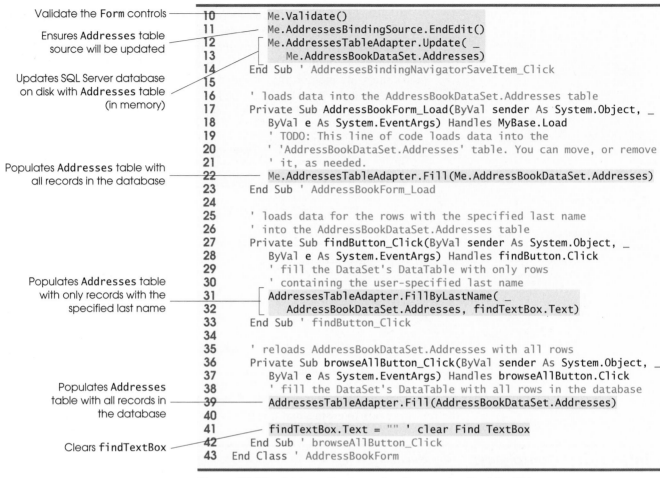

Validate the **Form** controls

Ensures **Addresses** table source will be updated

Updates SQL Server database on disk with **Addresses** table (in memory)

Populates **Addresses** table with all records in the database

Populates **Addresses** table with only records with the specified last name

Populates **Addresses** table with all records in the database

Clears **findTextBox**

```
10          Me.Validate()
11          Me.AddressesBindingSource.EndEdit()
12          Me.AddressesTableAdapter.Update( _
13             Me.AddressBookDataSet.Addresses)
14       End Sub ' AddressesBindingNavigatorSaveItem_Click
15
16       ' loads data into the AddressBookDataSet.Addresses table
17       Private Sub AddressBookForm_Load(ByVal sender As System.Object, _
18          ByVal e As System.EventArgs) Handles MyBase.Load
19          ' TODO: This line of code loads data into the
20          ' 'AddressBookDataSet.Addresses' table. You can move, or remove
21          ' it, as needed.
22          Me.AddressesTableAdapter.Fill(Me.AddressBookDataSet.Addresses)
23       End Sub ' AddressBookForm_Load
24
25       ' loads data for the rows with the specified last name
26       ' into the AddressBookDataSet.Addresses table
27       Private Sub findButton_Click(ByVal sender As System.Object, _
28          ByVal e As System.EventArgs) Handles findButton.Click
29          ' fill the DataSet's DataTable with only rows
30          ' containing the user-specified last name
31          AddressesTableAdapter.FillByLastName( _
32             AddressBookDataSet.Addresses, findTextBox.Text)
33       End Sub ' findButton_Click
34
35       ' reloads AddressBookDataSet.Addresses with all rows
36       Private Sub browseAllButton_Click(ByVal sender As System.Object, _
37          ByVal e As System.EventArgs) Handles browseAllButton.Click
38          ' fill the DataSet's DataTable with all rows in the database
39          AddressesTableAdapter.Fill(AddressBookDataSet.Addresses)
40
41          findTextBox.Text = "" ' clear Find TextBox
42       End Sub ' browseAllButton_Click
43    End Class ' AddressBookForm
```

Figure 25.29 Address Book application code. (Part 2 of 2.)

SELF-REVIEW

1. TableAdapter's _____ method writes the modified version of a table (in memory) to the database on disk.

   a) Update
   b) Fill
   c) GetData
   d) None of the above.

2. When calling a query method that executes a SQL statement with a WHERE condition, both the _____ and the parameter that will be checked in the WHERE condition need to be passed to the method.

   a) Database
   b) TableAdapter
   c) DataSet
   d) DataTable

Answers: 1) a. 2) d.

25.5 Wrap-Up

In this tutorial, you learned that a database is an organized collection of data and that database management systems provide mechanisms for storing and organizing data in a format consistent with that of a database. You then examined the contents of the Microsoft SQL Server 2005 Express database that was used in the **Address Book** application. While examining the AddressBook.mdf database, you learned that a field in a database table is a column and that a record is an entire table row. You also learned that each record must contain a primary key, which is used to distinguish one record from another.

After learning about the database, you used ADO.NET objects to communicate with the database. You learned how to obtain a `DataSet` by creating a connection to the database via the **Data Sources** window. Then you were introduced to the automatically-generated database objects that you used in the **Address Book** application. You learned how to generate GUI components that are bound to a database by dragging a database table from the **Data Sources** window onto a `Form`. You learned how to access and manipulate database data. To access the database data, you learned how to use Visual Basic 2005's **Query Builder** tool to build Structured Query Language (SQL) statements. These statements allowed you to retrieve and update information in the database. Using **Query Builder**, you created a customized SELECT statement.

In the next tutorial, you will learn about graphics. In particular, you will learn about coordinate systems and how to create colors and draw shapes. You will then use the concepts and techniques presented in the tutorial to create an application that can draw and print payroll checks.

SKILLS SUMMARY

Adding a Database Connection by Using the Data Sources Window

■ Open the **Data Sources** window by selecting **Data > Show Data Sources**.

■ In the **Data Sources** window, click **Add New Data Source...** to open the **Data Source Configuration Wizard**.

■ Select **Database** and click **Next >** in the first screen of the **Data Source Configuration Wizard**.

■ Choose the connection that will be used to connect to the database by clicking **New Connection...**, then selecting the database file in the **Add Connection** dialog.

■ Save the connection string in a configuration file to make it easy to change the connection settings at a later time.

■ Select the database objects to include in your `DataSet`.

Viewing Database Contents Using the Database Explorer Window

■ Open the **Database Explorer** window by selecting **View > Database Explorer**

■ Expand the database node in the **Database Explorer** window node, then expand the **Tables** node.

■ Right click desired table and select **Show Table Data**

Displaying Database Data on a Form Using Drag-and-Drop

■ While in **Design** view, open the **Data Sources** window by selecting **Data > Show Data Sources**.

■ Click the node of the table you want to display in the **Data Sources** window, thereby causing this node to become a drop-down list.

■ Select the format in which you want to display the data by clicking the table node.

■ Drag and drop the table node onto the `Form`.

Adding a query using the TableAdapter Query Configuration Wizard

■ Click the **Edit DataSet with Designer** icon in the **Data Sources** window.

■ Select the `TableAdapter`. Right click the `TableAdapter`'s name and select **Add Query...**.

■ In the **TableAdapter Query Configuration Wizard**, keep the default option **Use SQL Statements** and click **Next**.

■ On the next screen, keep the default option **SELECT which returns rows** and click **Next**.

■ In this dialog, create your SQL statement either manually or by clicking the **Query Builder...** `Button`.

■ In the next screen, enter names for the two methods that the wizard will generate.

■ Click **Finish** to complete the wizard and return to the **DataSet Designer**.

KEY TERMS

ADO.NET—Part of Microsoft.NET that is used to interact with databases.

BindingNavigator—A control that allows you to manipulate and navigate data on a databound Form.

criteria of WHERE clause—Indicates the specific records from which data will be retrieved or manipulated.

connection—Represents the connection between an application and its data source.

connection string—Specifies the path to a database file on disk, as well as some additional settings that determine how to access the database.

database—Organized collection of data.

Database Explorer window—Window used to view and manipulate database information in the Visual Basic 2005 IDE.

Data Sources window—Window used to connect application to a data source (e.g. a database) and create a series of databound controls.

database management system (DBMS)—Provides mechanisms for storing and organizing data in a manner that is consistent with the database's format.

DataSet—A class that is designed specifically to store data from databases that are connected to the application.

Data Source configuration Wizard—Wizard used to add a data source connection to the application.

DataTable—Allows you to store related information in memory in rows and columns.

field—Column in a table of a database.

FROM SQL keyword—Specifies table from which to get data.

instant-access application—Application that immediately locates a particular record of information.

.mdf file—A database file of SQL Server 2005 Express.

primary key—Field (or combination of fields) in a database table that contains unique values used to distinguish records from one another.

Query Builder—Visual Basic 2005 tool that allows you to specify the statements that retrieve information from and modify information in databases.

record—An entire table row in a database.

SELECT SQL keyword—Used to request specified information from a database.

SQL Server 2005 Express—A relational databases management system built by Microsoft.

Structured Query Language (SQL)—Language often used by relational databases to perform queries and manipulate data in relational databases.

table—Used to store related information in rows and columns. (Represented by key term DataTable.)

TableAdapter—Object that controls interactions between your application and a connected database.

TableAdapter Query Configuration Wizard—Wizard used to create queries that return specific data from a DataSet.

WHERE SQL keyword—Specifies criteria that determine which rows to retrieve.

CONTROLS, EVENTS, PROPERTIES & METHODS

BindingNavigator [BindingNavigator] This object allows the user to navigate through records in a DataSet. BindingNavigator also has buttons that allow you to add a new row, delete a row and save changes to the underlying data source.

MULTIPLE-CHOICE QUESTIONS

25.1 A _____ provides mechanisms for storing and organizing data in a manner that is consistent with a database's format.

a) relational database

b) connection object

c) data command

d) database management system

25.2 An entire row in a database table is known as a _____.

a) record

b) field

c) column

d) primary key

25.3 A primary key is used to _____.

a) create rows in a database

b) identify fields in a database

c) distinguish between records in a table

d) read information from a database

25.4 In a SELECT statement, what follows the SELECT keyword?

a) the name of the table

b) the names of fields

c) the name of the database

d) the criteria that the record must meet

25.5 What does the following SELECT statement do?

```
SELECT Age FROM People WHERE LastName = 'Purple'
```

a) It selects the age of the person (or people) with the last name `Purple` from the `People` table.

b) It selects the value `Purple` from the `Age` table of the `People` database.

c) It selects the age of the person with the last name `Purple` from the `People` database.

d) It selects the `People` field from the `Age` table with the `LastName` value `Purple`.

25.6 The SQL _____ modifies information in a database.

a) `SELECT` statement

b) `MODIFY` statement

c) `CHANGE` statement

d) `UPDATE` statement

25.7 A _____ is an organized collection of data.

a) record

b) database

c) data reader

d) primary key

EXERCISES

25.8 *(Stock Portfolio Application)* A stock broker wants an application that will display a client's stock portfolio (Fig. 25.30). All the companies that the user holds stock in should be displayed in a ComboBox when the application is loaded. When the user selects a company from the ComboBox, the stock information for that company will automatically displayed in Label—TextBox pairs.

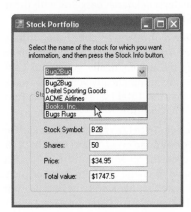

Figure 25.30   **Stock Portfolio** application.

a) *Creating a windows application.* Select **File > New Project...** and create a new **Windows Application** named StockPortfolio. In the **Solution Explorer**, rename the **Form1.vb** file to **StockPortfolioForm.vb**.

b) *Configuring the Form's properties.* Make sure the Form's **Name** property is set to StockPortfolioForm then change the **Text** property to Stock Portfolio. Change the Form's **Size** property to 295px by 322px.

c) *Adding a display Label to the Form.* Add a Label named displayLabel. Set its **Text** property to Select the name of the stock for which you want information, then press the Stock Info button. Set the Label's **Size** property to 241px by 32px. Set the **Location** property to 22, 19.

d) *Adding a data source to the Project.* Open the **Data Sources** window and click **Add New Data Source...** Add the Stocks table in the database C:\Examples\Tutorial25\Exercises\Databases\Stocks.mdf to the application by following the steps in the box *Adding a Database Connection to the Address Book Application* that guide you through the **Data Source Configuration Wizard**. StocksDataSet should now appear in the **Data Sources** window.

e) *Adding a display GroupBox to the Form.* Add a GroupBox named StockInfoGroup-Box. Set its **Size** property to 235px by 169px. Then set its **Location** property to 28, 97. The GroupBox should contain all the Label and TextBox controls.

f) *Adding controls that display stock portfolio data on the Form.* Just as in *Steps 1–2* in the box *Displaying the Address Book Fields on the Form*, choose Details from the **Stocks** drop-down list in the **Data Sources** window and drag-and-drop the **Stocks** node onto the Form. Move the automatically generated Labels and TextBoxes so that they are centered in StockInfoGroupBox.

g) *Deleting BindingNavigator control and StocksBindingNavigatorSave-Item_Click.* You will be navigating through the data with the StockNameComboBox, so you do not need the BindingNavigator control in this application. To delete it, just click the BindingNavigator in the Form and press *delete*. Since you deleted the BindingNavigator, you also do not need its automatically generated method StocksBindingNavigatorSaveItem_Click, which executes when the **Save Data Button** is pressed. To delete this method, right click the Form and select **View Code**, then delete this method from the file (StockPortfolioForm.vb).

h) *Adding a ComboBox that displays all the stock names onto the Form.* Add a ComboBox named stockNameComboBox. Then set the ComboBox's **Width** and **Height** to 178px and 21px, respectively, its **X** property to 51px and the **Y** property to 56px.

i) *Making the ComboBox databound to retrieve all the stock names.* Select StockName-ComboBox and click the black triangle in the upper-right corner of the control. This causes a **ComboBox Tasks** menu to appear. In this menu, check the **Use databound items** CheckBox, which causes four ComboBoxes to appear below the CheckBox. In the **Data Source** ComboBox select StocksBindingSource. Then, in the **Display Member** and **Value Member** ComboBoxes, select StockName. This will automatically populate StockNameComboBox with the names of all the stocks in the **Stocks** table of the Stocks.mdf database.

j) *Adding a Total value Label and Total value TextBox onto the Form.* Add a Label named TotalLabel and a TextBox named TotalTextBox. Place the Label directly under the automatically generated Labels from *Step e*, and the TextBox directly under the automatically generated TextBoxes. To make the application look neat, be sure that the **Total** Label and **Total** TextBox are the same size as the automatically generated controls.

k) *Updating TotalTextBox in StocksBindingSource's PositionChanged event and the Form's Load event.* Select the StocksBindingSource object in the component tray and click the **Events Button** in the **Properties** window. Double click Position-Changed to create an event handler for the this event. Now write an If statement to make sure that neither PriceTextBox nor SharesTextBox is equal to Nothing. Inside this If statement, add the line TotalTextBox.Text = "$" & SharesTextBox.Text * PriceTextBox.Text to calculate the total value of your stock holdings in the selected company and display this value with a dollar sign in front of it. Also add this line of code to the automatically-generated StockPortfolioForm_Load method.

l) *Running the application.* Select **Debug > Start Debugging** to run your application. Select different stocks from the ComboBoxes. Verify that the TextBoxes that display the stock information are modified appropriately when a new stock is chosen.

m) *Closing the application.* Close your running application by clicking its close box.

25.9 *(Airline Reservation Application)* An airline company wants you to develop an application that displays flight information (Fig. 25.31). The database contains two tables, one containing information about the flights, the other containing passenger information. The user should be able to choose a flight number from a ComboBox. When a flight number is chosen, the application should display the date of the flight, the flight's departure and arrival cities and the names of the passengers scheduled to take the flight.

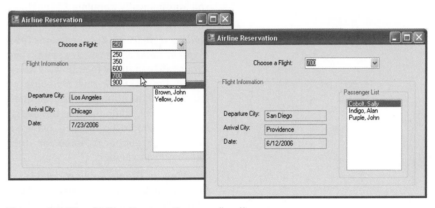

Figure 25.31   Airline Reservation application.

a) *Creating a windows application.* Select **File > New Project...** and create a new **Windows Application** named AirlineReservation. In the **Solution Explorer**, rename the **Form1.vb** file to **AirlineReservationForm.vb**.

b) *Configuring the Form's properties.* Make sure the Form's **Name** property is set to AirlineReservationForm then change the **Text** property to Airline Reservation. Then set the Form's **Size** property to 435px by 318px.

c) *Adding a data source to the Project.* Open the **Data Sources** window and click **Add New Data Source...** Add the Flights and Reservations tables in the database C:\Examples\Tutorial25\Exercises\Databases\Reservations.mdf to the application by following the steps in the box *Adding a Database Connection to the Address Book Application*, which guide you through the **Data Source Configuration Wizard**. ReservationsDataSet should now appear in the **Data Sources** window.

d) *Adding two GroupBoxes to the Form.* Add a GroupBox named flightGroupBox and one named passengerGroupBox. As seen in Fig. 25.31, set the **Text** property of passengerGroupBox to Passenger List, and place it around ReservationsListBox. Then set the **Text** property of flightGroupBox to Flight Information, and place it around all the controls except FlightNumberComboBox.

e) *Adding controls that display flight information on the Form.* Just as in *Steps 1–2* in the box *Displaying the Address Book Fields on the Form*, choose Details from the **Flights** table drop-down list in the **Data Sources** window and drag-and-drop the **Flights** node onto the Form. Delete the **Flights** Label and TextBox, because the selected flight number will be displayed in FlightNumberComboBox, which you will create in the next step. Move the automatically generated Labels and TextBoxes so that they are located in the left side of flightGroupBox as seen in Fig. 25.31.

f) *Deleting BindingNavigator control and FlightsBindingNavigatorSave- Item_Click.* You will be navigating through the data with the FlightNumberComboBox, so you do not need the BindingNavigator control. To delete it, just click the BindingNavigator in the Form and press delete. Since you have deleted the BindingNavigator, you do not need its automatically generated method FlightsBindingNavigatorSaveItem_Click, which executes when the **Save Data** Button is pressed. To delete this method, right click the Form and select **View Code**, then delete this method from the file (AirlineReservationForm.vb).

g) *Adding a ComboBox that displays all the flight numbers and a Label that describes the ComboBox onto the Form.* Add a ComboBox named FlightNumberComboBox. Then set the ComboBox's **Size** property to 145px by 21px and its **Location** property to 193, 24. Now create a label named flightLabel and set its **Text** property to Choose a flight:. Then set the **Position** of flightLabel equal to 83, 13.

h) *Making FlightNumberComboBox databound so that it displays all the flight numbers.* Select FlightNumberComboBox and click the black triangle in the upper-right corner of the control. This displays the **ComboBox Tasks** menu. In this menu, check the **Use databound items** CheckBox, which causes four ComboBoxes to appear below the CheckBox. In the **Data Source** ComboBox, select FlightsBindingSource. Then, in the **Display Member** and **Value Member** ComboBoxes, select FlightNumber. This will automatically populate FlightNumberComboBox with the names of all the stocks in the **Flights** table of the Reservations.mdf database.

i) *Adding a query to ReservationsTableAdapter table to retrieve passenger names by flight number.* In the ReservationsDataSet designer, add a query to ReservationsTableAdapter by following *Steps 1–3* in the box *Searching the Last Name Field in the AddressBook.mdf Database*, which guide you through the **TableAdapter Query Configuration Wizard**. The query should return the **Name** field of the Reservations table while filtering the query using the **FlightNumber** field. The final SQL statement should be SELECT Name FROM Reservations WHERE (FlightNumber=@flightNumber). Name the query methods FillByFlightNumber and GetDataByFlightNumber.

j) *Creating a FlightNumberComboBox event handler for SelectedIndexChanged.* Double click FlightNumberComboBox in design view to create the event handler FlightNumberComboBox_SelectedIndexChanged. In this method, place code that determines whether **FlightNumberComboBox.Text** is not equal to Nothing. If this condition is true, then use the ReservationsTableAdapter.FillByFlightNumber method you just created to populate the **ReservationsDataSet.Reservations** table, using **FlightNumberComboBox.Text** as the second query parameter. This causes the selected flight number in FlightNumberComboBox to be matched with the **FlightNumber** field in the **Reservations** table.

k) *Programming the AirlineReservationForm_Load event handler.* Code is automatically placed in this method to fill both the **Reservations** and **Flight** tables with every row of data. Only code for the **Flights** table is necessary, so delete the code that fills the **Reservations** table. However, you do need to fill the **Reservations** table with the rows where the **FlightNumber** field matches the flight number selected in FlightNumberComboBox. To achieve this, copy the line of code in the If statement of the FlightNumberComboBox_SelectedIndexChanged method that uses the ReservationsTableAdapter.FillByFlightNumber method. Then paste this code after the statement that fills the **Flight** table. Make sure that the FlightsTableAdapter.Fill method appears first, so that the FlightNumberComboBox is populated before you use it in a query.

l) *Adding a ListBox that displays the names of all the people on the selected flight onto the Form.* Add a ListBox named ReservationsListBox. Set the ListBox's **Size** property to 108px by 134px, and move it so its located in the center of passengerGroupBox as seen in Fig. 25.31.

m) *Making ReservationsListBox databound.* Follow the same procedure as in *Step g*, but in the **Data Source** ComboBox expand the **Other Data Sources** node, then the **Project Data Sources** node, and then the **ReservationsDataSet** node. Now click the **Reservations** table icon and ReservationsBindingSource will automatically be selected for you in the **Data Source** ComboBox. Then select Name and FlightNumber in the **Display Member** and **Value Member** ComboBoxes, respectively. This will automatically populate ReservationsListBox with the names of all the people on the selected flight and the corresponding flight number as the value associated with each item in the ComboBox.

n) *Running the application.* Select **Debug > Start Debugging** to run your application. Select a flight from the **Choose a Flight:** ComboBox. Verify that the flight information is correct. Repeat this process for the other flights.

o) *Closing the application.* Close your running application by clicking its close box.

CheckWriter Application

Introducing Graphics and Printing

In this tutorial, you will learn about Visual Basic's tools for drawing two-dimensional shapes and for controlling colors and fonts. Visual Basic supports graphics that allow you to visually enhance Windows applications. To build the **CheckWriter** application, you will take advantage of the GDI+ **Application Programming Interface (API)**. An API is the interface used by an application to access the operating system and various services on a computer. **GDI+ (Graphics Device Interface)** is a graphics API that provides classes for creating and manipulating two-dimensional vector graphics, fonts and images. A **vector graphic** is not represented as a grid of pixels, but is instead represented by a set of mathematical properties called vectors, which describe a graphic's dimensions, attributes and position. Using the GDI+ API, you can create robust graphics without worrying about the specific details of graphics hardware.

The Framework Class Library contains many sophisticated drawing capabilities as part of the `System.Drawing` namespace and the other namespaces that comprise GDI+. The `System.Drawing.Printing` namespace will be used in the **CheckWriter** application to specify how the check will be printed on the page.

As you will see, GDI+ graphics capabilities will help you preview and print a check using the **CheckWriter** application. To complete the application, you will learn some more powerful drawing capabilities, such as changing the styles of the lines used to draw shapes and controlling the colors of filled shapes. You will also learn how to specify a text style using fonts.

26.1 Test-Driving the CheckWriter Application

Before test-driving the completed **CheckWriter** application, you should understand the purpose of the application. This application must meet the following requirements:

> **Application Requirements**
>
> *A local business is responsible for distributing paychecks to its employees. The human-resources department needs a way to generate and print the paychecks. You have been asked to create an application that allows the human-resources department to input all the information necessary for a valid check, which includes the employee's name, the date, the amount that the employee should be paid and the company's address information. Your application should graphically draw the check so that it can be printed.*

This application prints a paycheck. The user inputs the check number, the date, the numeric amount of the check, the employee's name, the amount of the check written in words and the company's address information. The user can press the **Preview** Button, which displays the format of the check. The user can then press the **Print** Button if the format is acceptable, causing the check to print from the printer. You begin by test-driving the completed application. Then you will learn the additional Visual Basic technologies that you will need to create your own version of this application.

Test-Driving the CheckWriter Application

1. ***Opening the completed application.*** Open the directory `C:\Examples\Tutorial26\CompletedApplication\CheckWriter` to locate the **CheckWriter** application. Double click `CheckWriter.sln` to open the application in the Visual Basic IDE.

2. ***Running the CheckWriter application.*** Select **Debug > Start Debugging** to run the application (Fig. 26.1).

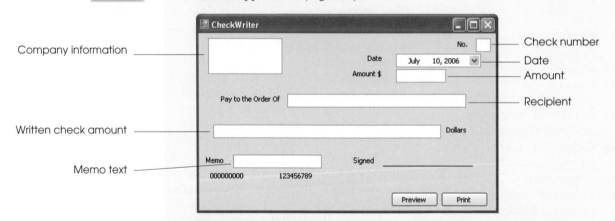

Figure 26.1 **CheckWriter** application displaying an empty check.

3. ***Providing inputs for the company information.*** In the company information TextBox, type The Company, then press *Enter* to proceed to the next line of the TextBox. Type 123 Fake Street. Press *Enter* to proceed to the third line of the TextBox. Type Any Town, MA 11111.

4. ***Providing values for the remaining information.*** For the **No.** field, input the check number 100. Leave the **Date** field (represented by a `DateTimePicker` control) as today's date, which is the default. Input 1,000.00 as the check amount. Enter John Smith as the recipient, and type One Thousand and 00/100 in the TextBox to the left of **Dollars**. In the **Memo** field, type Paycheck. The check should appear as shown in Fig. 26.2.

(cont.)

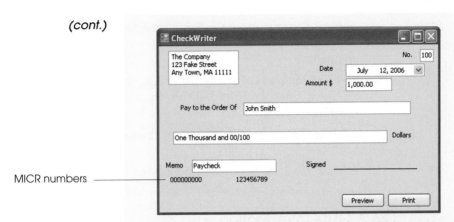

Figure 26.2   **CheckWriter** application displaying a completed check.

You may have noticed that at the bottom-left side of all bank checks is a string of numbers and symbols. These are called Magnetic Ink Character Recognition (MICR) numbers. MICR numbers are broken into three components. The first nine digits are the bank's routing number, followed by the account number and then the check number. Banks have special machines that read these numbers and route the check to the appropriate account. Using the MICR font, you can create MICR numbers in your check-writing application. (We did not use the MICR font in this application.) To download the MICR font, visit www.newfreeware.com/graphics/696/.

5. *Previewing the check.* Click the **Preview** Button. A **Print preview** dialog appears, displaying the completed check, as shown in Fig. 26.3. This dialog is actually a control of type `PrintPreviewDialog`, which is used to display how a document appears before it is printed.

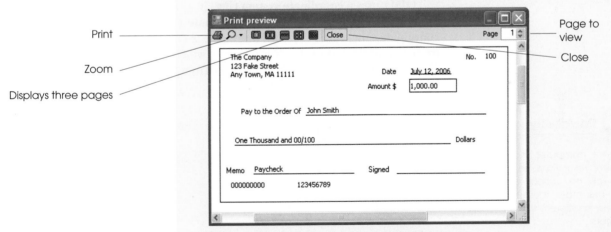

Figure 26.3   Preview of the completed check.

The **Print preview** dialog contains several toolbar `Button`s. The first `Button` is the print `Button` (🖨), which allows the user to print the document. The next `Button` (🔍) zooms in and out, allowing the user to view the document at different sizes. The next five `Button`s allow the user to specify the number of pages that can be displayed in the dialog at one time. The user can view one, two, three, four or six pages at a time in the dialog box. The **Close** `Button` closes the dialog box. Finally, the right-most control in the dialog box allows the user to specify which page of the document to view. The `PrintPreviewDialog` control is discussed in detail later in this tutorial. The document that displays in this dialog box is the `PrintDocument`, an object that you will create when coding the application.

(cont.)

Click **Close** to close the **Print preview** dialog. [*Note:* Printing or previewing the document is not possible when there is no printer installed on your computer.]

6. ***Printing the check.*** To print the check, your computer must be connected to a printer. Click the **Print** Button. The check prints from the default printer of your computer.

7. ***Closing the application.*** Close your running application by clicking its close box.

8. ***Closing the IDE.*** Close the Visual Basic IDE by clicking its close box.

26.2 GDI+ Introduction

This section introduces the graphics classes and structures used in this tutorial and discusses GDI+ graphics programming. Graphics typically consist of lines, shapes, colors and text drawn on the background of a control.

Objects of the Pen and Brush classes affect the appearance of the lines and shapes you draw. A **Pen** specifies the line style used to draw a shape (for example, line thickness, solid lines, dashed lines, etc.). A **Brush** specifies how to fill a shape (for example, solid color or pattern). As you learned in Tutorial 21, the Graphics class contains methods used for drawing. The drawing methods of the Graphics class usually require a Pen or Brush object to render a specified shape.

The Color structure contains pre-defined colors and methods that allow users to create new colors. Objects of the Font class affect the appearance of text. The **Font** class contains properties (such as Bold, Italic and Size) that describe font characteristics. The **FontFamily** class contains methods for obtaining font information (such as **GetName**).

GDI+ uses a **coordinate system** (Fig. 26.4) to identify every point on the screen. A coordinate pair has both an ***x*-coordinate** (the horizontal coordinate) and a ***y*-coordinate** (the vertical coordinate). The *x*-coordinate is the horizontal distance from zero at the left of the drawing area, which increases as you move to the right. The *y*-coordinate is the vertical distance from zero at the top of the drawing area, which increases as you move down.

Portability Tip

Different computer monitors have different resolutions, so the density of pixels on various monitors will vary. This may cause graphics to appear in different sizes on different monitors.

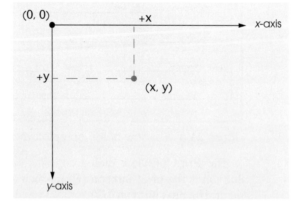

Figure 26.4 GDI+ coordinate system.

The ***x*-axis** defines every horizontal coordinate, and the ***y*-axis** defines every vertical coordinate. Programmers position text and shapes on the screen by specifying their (x, y) coordinates. The upper-left corner of a GUI component (such as a Panel or the Form) has the coordinates $(0, 0)$. In the diagram in Fig. 26.4, the red point at position (x, y) is x pixels from the left of position $(0, 0)$ along the *x*-axis and y pixels from the top of position $(0, 0)$ along the *y*-axis. Coordinate units are measured in pixels, which are the smallest units of resolution on a computer monitor.

　1. The _____ class contains properties that describe font characteristics.

　　　a) Font　　　　　　　　　　　　　　b) GDIFont

　　　c) SystemFont　　　　　　　　　　　d) FontStyle

2. The _____ corner of a GUI component has the coordinate $(0, 0)$.

　　　a) lower-left　　　　　　　　　　　b) upper-right

　　　c) upper-left　　　　　　　　　　　d) lower-right

Answers: 1) a.　2) c.

26.3 Constructing the CheckWriter Application

Now that you have learned about the features that you will use in your **Check-Writer** application, you need to analyze the application. The following pseudocode describes the basic operation of the **CheckWriter** application:

> When the user clicks the Preview Button
> 　　Retrieve input from the user
> 　　Display the check in a Print preview dialog
>
> When the user clicks the Print Button
> 　　Retrieve input from the user
> 　　Print the check on the printer

Now that you have test-driven the **CheckWriter** application and studied its pseudocode representation, you will use an ACE table to help you convert the pseudocode to Visual Basic. Figure 26.5 lists the actions, controls and events that will help you complete your own version of this application.

Action/Control/Event (ACE) Table for the CheckWriter Application

Action	Control/Object	Event
Label the application's controls	numberLabel, dateLabel, amountLabel, payeeLabel, dollarsLabel, memoLabel, signedLabel, underlineLabel, abaLabel, accountLabel	
	previewButton	Click
Retrieve input from the user	numberTextBox, dateTimePicker, amountTextBox, payeeTextBox, payment-TextBox, memoTextBox, payerTextBox	
Display the check in a Print preview dialog	previewObject	
	printButton	Click
Retrieve input from the user	numberTextBox, dateTimePicker, amountTextBox, payeeTextBox, paymentTextBox, memoTextBox, payerTextBox	
Print the check on the printer	document	

Figure 26.5　ACE table for the **CheckWriter** application.

Now that you have an understanding of the **CheckWriter** application, you can begin to create it. A template application is provided that contains many of the GUI's controls. You begin writing code for this application by creating a Print-PreviewDialog object in the following box.

Adding a *PrintPreviewDialog* *in the CheckWriter* *Application*	1. **Copying the template to your working directory.** Copy the C:\Examples\ Tutorial26\TemplateApplication\CheckWriter directory to your C:\SimplyVB directory.

2. **Opening the CheckWriter application's template file.** Double click Check-Writer.sln in the CheckWriter directory to open the application in the Visual Basic IDE.

3. **Adding the PrintPreviewDialog.** In the **Toolbox**, locate the **PrintPreview-Dialog** control

        PrintPreviewDialog

in the **All Windows Forms** group, and drag and drop it onto the Form. The control should appear in the component tray as shown in Fig. 26.6.

The **PrintPreviewDialog** control uses a dialog to allow users to view a document of different sizes, print a document and display multiple pages of a document before printing. Make sure the PrintPreviewDialog object that you just created is selected, and change its Name property to previewObject. This object has a Document property that specifies the document to preview. The document must be a PrintDocument object, as will be discussed later in the tutorial. For now, do not specify the document.

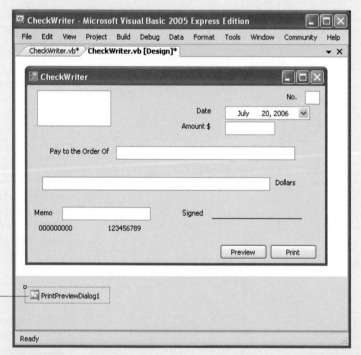

Added PrintPreviewDialog

Figure 26.6 **CheckWriter** application in **Design** view with PrintPreview-Dialog.

4. **Setting the UseAntiAlias property to True.** The PrintPreviewDialog also contains the **UseAntiAlias** property, which makes the text in the dialog appear smoother on the screen. To accomplish this, set the UseAntiAlias property to True.

(cont.)   5. ***Running the application.*** Select **Debug > Start Debugging** to run your
application (Fig. 26.7). Click the **Preview** Button, then click the **Print** Button. Currently, the application does nothing because you have not yet added
event handlers for the Buttons. You will add functionality to the application
in the next series of boxes.

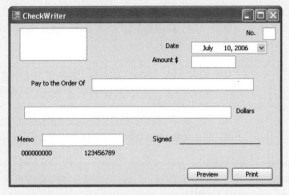

Figure 26.7   Running template application.

6. ***Closing the application.*** Close your application by clicking its close box.

---

1. Use a _____ control to preview a document before it is printed.

   a) PrintDialog   b) PrintPreviewDialog

   c) PrintPreviewControl   d) PrintDocument

2. A PrintPreviewDialog object has a _____ property that specifies the document to
   preview.

   a) Preview   b) PreviewDocument

   c) View   d) Document

Answers: 1) b. 2) d.

26.4 PrintPreviewDialogs and PrintDocuments

In the **CheckWriter** application, you use an object of the PrintPreviewDialog
class. As previously mentioned, this object displays a dialog that shows a document
as it will appear when it is printed. Recall that the dialog object contains the **Document** property, which allows you to specify the document to preview, and that the
object specified in the Document property must be of type PrintDocument. The
PrintPreviewDialog's ShowDialog method displays the preview dialog. You will
use this method later in the application.

The **PrintDocument** object allows you to specify how to print a specified document. The object can raise a **PrintPage** event. This occurs when the data required
to print the current page is needed (that is, when the Print method is called). You
can define this object's PrintPage event handler to specify what you want to print.
This object also contains a **Print** method that uses a Graphics object to print the
document. You will use method Print later in the application.

---

1. The object in the Document property must be of type _____.

   a) PrintPreviewDialog   b) PrintDocument

   c) PrintPreviewControl   d) PrintDialog

2. The _____ method of object `PrintDocument` uses a graphics object to print the document.

    a) `Graphics`   b) `Document`

    c) `Print`   d) None of the above.

Answers: 1) b. 2) c.

26.5 Creating an Event Handler for the `CheckWriter` Application

Now that you have created the `PrintPreviewDialog` object in the **CheckWriter** application, you can begin to add functionality to the application. Before you can use print features, you must import the `System.Drawing.Printing` namespace. You will also create an instance variable that will be used by several different methods. You will implement these features in the following box.

Importing a Namespace and Declaring an Instance Variable	1. *Switching to code view.* Select **View > Code** to view the `CheckWriter.vb` code.
	2. *Importing namespaces.* Add line 1 before the class `CheckWriterForm` definition, as shown in Fig. 26.8 to import the **System.Drawing.Printing** namespace. This statement allows your applications to access all services related to printing. After you import the namespace, the application can use `PrintDocument` objects. The namespace also enables access to the **PrintPageEventArgs.Graphics** property, which you will use to draw the graphics that will appear on the printed page.

Importing the
`System.Drawing.Printing`
namespace

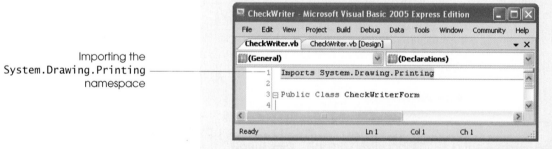

Figure 26.8   Import namespaces to class `CheckWriterForm`.

3. *Declaring the instance variable.* Add line 5 (Fig. 26.9) to the application to declare variable `fontObject`, which is used to specify the text font. This statement declares a `Font` variable named `fontObject` that you will use shortly to reference a `Font` object.

Declaring a `Font` object

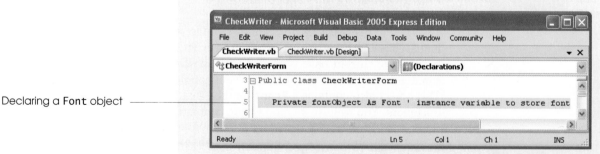

Figure 26.9   Instance variable `fontObject` created.

4. *Saving the project.* Select **File > Save All** to save your modified code.

Now that you have imported namespace `System.Drawing.Printing` and declared the `Font` variable, you can write code to enable printing and previewing. You will begin by defining the `document_PrintPage` method, which will specify what to print. When printing the check, you want the printed document to resemble the application's `Form`. This can be completed using a `For Each...Next` statement that draws the contents of each control in a `Graphics` object. You can then print the check using this `Graphics` object. You will begin writing code to perform these actions in the following box.

Defining an Event Handler to Print Pages	1. ***Creating the document_PrintPage method.*** Add lines 7–11 into the application code, as in Fig. 26.10. These lines create the event handler for the `PrintPage` event. You need to type these lines to create the event handler because the `PrintDocument` object has not yet been created. You will create this object later in the tutorial.

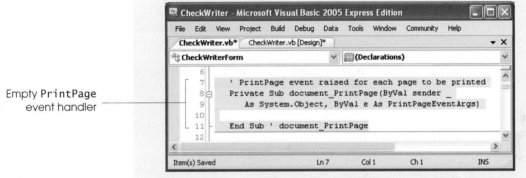

Empty `PrintPage` event handler

Figure 26.10 document_PrintPage event handler.

2. ***Declaring the variables.*** Add lines 11–20 of Fig. 26.11 to the event handler. Lines 11–12 declare `Single` variables that represent the *x*- and *y*-coordinates where controls appear on the `Form`. **Single** is a type that stores floating-point values. `Single` is similar to `Double`, but is less precise and requires less memory. Lines 15 and 18 declare `Single` variables, which specify the coordinates of the left and top margins of the page to be printed. These values are determined by using the **MarginBounds.Left** and **MarginBounds.Top** properties of the `PrintPageEventArgs` object (e from line 9) that is passed when the `PrintPage` event is raised.

   Line 19 declares the `String` variable `line`, which will be used to store text from the controls. Line 20 declares a **Control** variable (a variable that can reference any control on the `Form`), which you will use as the control variable in your `For Each...Next` statement.

3. ***Iterating through the controls on the Form.*** Add lines 22–25 of Fig. 26.12 to the method. This `For Each...Next` statement iterates through the controls on the `Form` to print the check. You'll define this statement's body in the next box.

4. ***Adding formatting lines and drawing the check's border.*** Add lines 27–45 of Fig. 26.13 into the event handler. Checks contain lines for payee, payment amount, and memo information. To draw these lines, call the **DrawLine** method on the `Graphics` object. This method takes five arguments, the first of which specifies the pen to use to draw the line. The next four arguments consist of the coordinates of the line's endpoints in the following order: x1, y1, x2, y2. Lines 28–31 draw the payee line, using the `Location` property of the `payeeTextBox` control as arguments in the method call. Lines 33–36 and lines 38–41 similarly use their respective control location properties to draw a line in the appropriate place on the check.

(cont.)

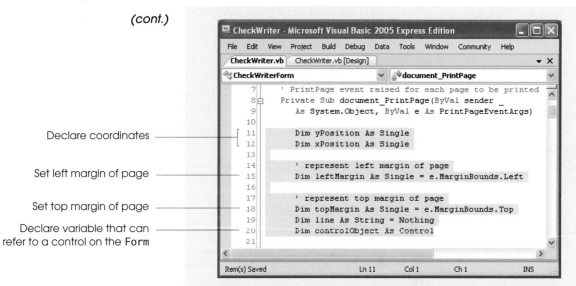

Declare coordinates

Set left margin of page

Set top margin of page

Declare variable that can refer to a control on the **Form**

Figure 26.11   Variables created for `document_PrintPage`.

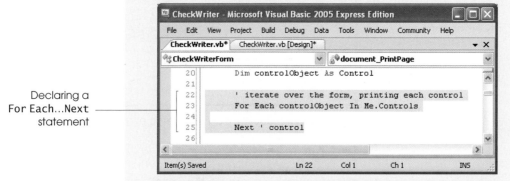

Declaring a For Each...Next statement

Figure 26.12   For Each...Next statement used for iteration.

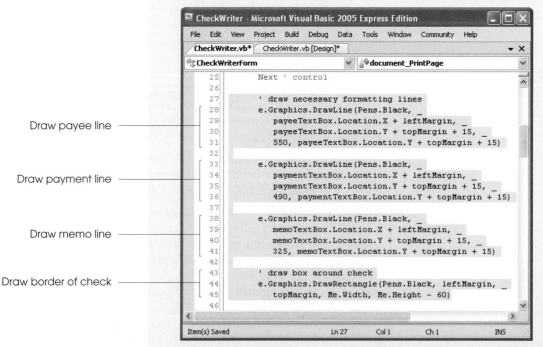

Draw payee line

Draw payment line

Draw memo line

Draw border of check

Figure 26.13   Event handler `document_PrintPage` modified to draw border of check.

(cont.) The Form's border is not contained in a control; therefore, you must use a Graphics object to draw a rectangle around the check to be printed.

To draw the rectangle around the check, use the PrintPageEventArgs object (e from line 9) that is passed when the PrintPage event is raised. The Graphics property of this object again allows you to specify what you want to print. By calling the **DrawRectangle** method on the Graphics object, you can specify the properties of the rectangle to draw.

The first argument you pass to the method is the Pens.Black object. This is a Pen object that uses a black color to draw the rectangle's border. The second argument specifies the *x*-coordinate that defines the left side of the rectangle you wish to draw. Use the leftMargin variable that you created in *Step 2* to represent the position of the left margin of the page on which the check will print. This value ensures that the rectangle will align with the left margin. The third argument in the method specifies the *y*-coordinate that defines the top of the rectangle. Use the topMargin variable that you created in *Step 2* to represent the position of the top margin of the page on which the check will print. Together, the *x*- and *y*-coordinates in the second and third arguments define the upper-left corner of the rectangle.

The fourth and fifth arguments specify the width and height of the rectangle. The width is set to Me.Width, which returns the width of the Form. Keyword **Me** references the current object—in this case, the Form. The height, on the other hand, is set to Me.Height - 60. This value is the height of the Form minus 60 pixels. You subtract 60 pixels because you do not want to print the Buttons on the bottom of the Form. These Buttons were created to allow users to print and preview the checks. (They were not intended to be printed on the checks.)

5. ***Indicating that there are no more pages to print.*** Add lines 47–48 of Fig. 26.14 to the method. Line 48 indicates that there are no more pages to print by setting the event argument's **HasMorePages** property to False.

Indicate no more pages to print ———

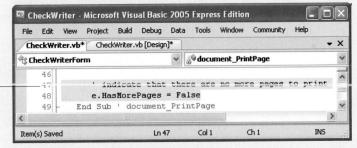

Figure 26.14 Event handler document_PrintPage modified to indicate that there are no more pages to print.

6. ***Saving the project.*** Select **File > Save All** to save your modified code.

SELF-REVIEW

1. Importing the System._____ namespace gives you access to print-related functions.

   a) Windows
   b) Printing
   c) Drawing.Printing
   d) Drawing

2. The _____ keyword references the current object.

   a) Me
   b) Current
   c) Form
   d) None of the above.

Answers: 1) c. 2) a.

26.6 Graphics Objects: Colors, Lines and Shapes

A `Graphics` object controls drawing in an application. In addition to providing methods for drawing various shapes, `Graphics` objects contain methods for font manipulation, color manipulation and other graphics-related actions. You can draw on many controls, such as `Labels` and `Buttons`, which have their own drawing areas. To draw on a control, first obtain a `Graphics` object for the control by invoking its `CreateGraphics` method, as in

```
Dim graphicsObject As Graphics = displayPanel.CreateGraphics()
```

Now you can use the methods provided in class `Graphics` to draw on the `display-Panel`. You will see many `Graphics` methods throughout this tutorial.

Colors

Colors can enhance an application's appearance and help convey meaning. For example, a red traffic light indicates stop, yellow indicates caution and green indicates go. The `Color` structure defines methods and constants used to manipulate colors.

Every color can be created from a combination of alpha, red, green and blue components. The alpha value determines the **opacity** (amount of transparency) of the color. For example, the alpha value 0 specifies a transparent color, and the value 255 specifies an opaque color. Alpha values between 0 and 255 (inclusive) result in a blending of the color's RGB value with that of any background color, causing a semi-transparent effect. All three RGB components are `Bytes` that represent integer values in the range 0–255. The first number in the RGB value defines the amount of red in the color, the second defines the amount of green and the third defines the amount of blue. The larger the value for a particular color, the greater the amount of that color. Visual Basic enables you to choose from almost 17 million colors. If a computer monitor cannot display all of these colors, it displays the color closest to the one specified, or it attempts to imitate the color using **dithering** (using small dots of existing colors to form a pattern that simulates the desired color). Figure 26.15 summarizes some predefined `Color` constants. You can also find a list of various RGB values and their corresponding colors at `http://www.pitt.edu/~nisg/cis/web/cgi/rgb.html`.

Good Programming Practice

When working with color, keep in mind that many people are color blind or have difficulty perceiving and distinguishing colors. So, use colors that can be distinguished easily.

Constant	RGB value	Constant	RGB value
Color.Orange	255, 200, 0	Color.White	255, 255, 255
Color.Pink	255, 175, 175	Color.Gray	128, 128, 128
Color.Cyan	0, 255, 255	Color.DarkGray	64, 64, 64
Color.Magenta	255, 0, 255	Color.Red	255, 0, 0
Color.Yellow	255, 255, 0	Color.Green	0, 255, 0
Color.Black	0, 0, 0	Color.Blue	0, 0, 255

Figure 26.15 `Color` structure constants and their RGB values.

You can use pre-existing colors, or you can create your own by using the **FromArgb** method. The statement

```
Dim colorSilver As Color = Color.FromArgb(192, 192, 192)
```

creates a silver color and assigns it to variable `colorSilver`. Now you can use `colorSilver` whenever you need a silver color. The `Color` method `FromArgb` is used to create this color and other colors by specifying the RGB values as arguments. The method sets the alpha value to 255 (that is, opaque) by default.

Drawing Lines, Rectangles and Ovals

This section presents several `Graphics` methods for drawing lines, rectangles and ovals. To draw shapes and `Strings`, you must specify the type of `Brushes` and `Pens` to use. A Pen, which functions much like an ordinary pen, is used to specify such characteristics as the color and width of the shape's lines. Most drawing methods require a Pen object. To fill the interior of objects, you must specify a Brush. All classes derived from the abstract class Brush define objects that fill the interiors of shapes with color patterns or images. For example, a SolidBrush specifies the Color that fills the interior of a shape. The following statement creates a Solid-Brush with the color orange:

```
Dim brush As SolidBrush = New SolidBrush(Color.Orange)
```

Many drawing methods have multiple versions. When employing methods that draw outlined hollow shapes, use versions that take a Pen argument. When employing methods that draw shapes filled with colors, patterns or images, use versions that take a Brush argument. Many of these methods require x, y, width and height arguments. The x and y arguments represent the shape's upper-left corner coordinate. The width and height arguments represent the width and height of the shape in pixels, respectively. Figure 26.16 summarizes several Graphics methods and their parameters.

Graphics Drawing Methods and Descriptions

Note: Many of these methods have multiple versions.

```
DrawLine(ByVal p As Pen, ByVal x1 As Single, ByVal y1 As Single,
    ByVal x2 As Single, ByVal y2 As Single)
```
Draws a line from the point (x1, y1) to the point (x2, y2). The Pen determines the color, style and width of the line.

```
DrawRectangle(ByVal p As Pen, ByVal x As Single, ByVal y As Single,
    ByVal width As Single, ByVal height As Single)
```
Draws a rectangle of the specified width and height. The top-left corner of the rectangle is at the point (x, y). The Pen determines the rectangle's color, style and border width.

```
FillRectangle(ByVal b As Brush, ByVal x As Single, ByVal y As Single,
    ByVal width As Single, ByVal height As Single)
```
Draws a solid rectangle of the specified width and height. The top-left corner of the rectangle is at the point (x, y). The Brush determines the fill pattern inside the rectangle.

```
DrawEllipse(ByVal p As Pen, ByVal x As Single, ByVal y As Single,
    ByVal width As Single, ByVal height As Single)
```
Draws an ellipse inside a rectangular area of the specified width and height. The top-left corner of the rectangular area is at the point (x, y). The Pen determines the color, style and border width of the ellipse.

```
FillEllipse(ByVal b As Brush, ByVal x As Single, ByVal y As Single,
    ByVal width As Single, ByVal height As Single)
```
Draws a filled ellipse inside a rectangular area of the specified width and height. The top-left corner of the rectangular area is at the point (x, y). The Brush determines the pattern inside the ellipse.

Figure 26.16 Graphics methods that draw lines, rectangles and ovals.

SELF-REVIEW   1. The RGB value of a Color represents _____.

   a) the index number of a color

   b) the amount of red, green and blue in a color

   c) the thickness of the drawing object

   d) the type of shape to draw

2. The _____ method is used to draw solid rectangles.
   - a) `DrawRectangle`
   - b) `FillRectangle`
   - c) `SolidRectangle`
   - d) `OpaqueRectangle`

Answers: 1) b. 2) b.

26.7 Printing Each Control of the CheckWriter Application

Recall earlier that you created the empty For Each...Next statement to iterate through all the controls on the Form. Now you will write code for the body of the For Each...Next statement to print all the controls on the Form except for the Buttons.

Iterating through All the Objects of the Form to Print Each Control

1. ***Checking for Buttons.*** In the body of the For Each...Next statement of document_PrintPage, add lines 24–27 of Fig. 26.17. Adding this If...Then statement determines whether the current control is a Button. If the control is not a Button, then the body of the If...Then statement executes. However, if the control is a Button, the For Each...Next statement continues to the next control on the Form.

Make sure current control is not a Button

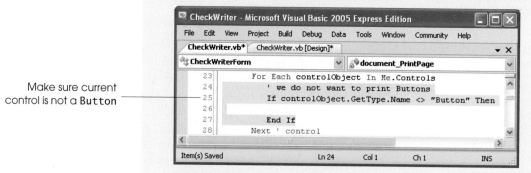

Figure 26.17 Code to determine whether the current control is a Button.

2. ***Defining the body of the If...Then statement.*** Now you must add code that properly prints the value that appears in each control on the check. Add lines 26–41 of Fig. 26.18 into the body of the If...Then statement.

Determine current control

Underline the text if displaying date from DateTimePicker

Draw box around dollar amount

Set the default font

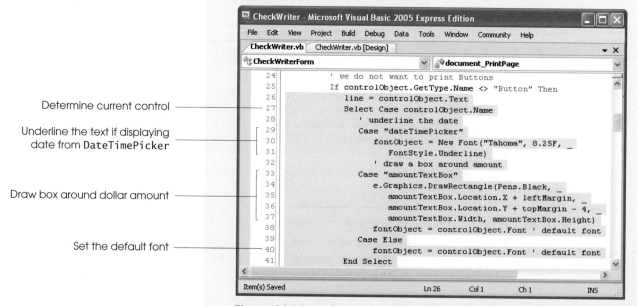

Figure 26.18 Select Case statement to print controls.

(cont.)

Line 26 sets the `line` variable that you created earlier to `controlObject.Text`. This property contains the value contained in the control's `Text` property (text displayed to the user or entered by the user). The `Select Case` statement (lines 27–41) specifies how each control prints. The controlling expression is set to the value `controlObject.Name`. This is the `Name` property of the control. You can use the `Name` property to select specific controls that need to be treated differently when printed.

The first `Case` (lines 29–31) determines what happens when the current control is `dateTimePicker`. This `Case` sets the `fontObject` reference to the font style of the date—an underlined Tahoma font, with a size of `8.25` (the same size as the text in the control). The date on the check will be underlined and will appear in `8.25` points in Tahoma font. Fonts are discussed in detail later in this tutorial.

The second `Case` (lines 33–38) executes if the control is `amountTextBox`. This `Case` draws the box that surrounds the decimal amount of the check. `DrawRectangle` (a `Graphics` method) is invoked by using the `e.Graphics` property. The outline of the rectangle prints in black, indicated by `Pens.Black`. The *x*- and *y*-coordinates are specified by adding the TextBox's *x-y* location on the `Form` to the `leftMargin` and `topMargin` variables, respectively. Recall that we begin printing the check at the corner of the top and left margins. Adding the margin values to the `Location` properties ensures that `amountTextBox` prints in the same position as it appears on the `Form`. (Line 36 subtracts four points of space to center the box on the text.) Line 38 sets the font of the text to draw to the same value as the font used to display text in the control.

The third `Case` (lines 39–40) executes for all the other controls. This `Case` sets the `fontObject` font style to the same value as the font used to display text in the control. Line 41 ends the `Select Case` statement.

3. ***Setting the positions of the text of each control.*** Add lines 43–52 of Fig. 26.19 to the body of the If...Then statement. Lines 44–45 set the `xPosition` variable to `leftMargin + controlObject.Location.X`. By adding the *x*-coordinate of the current control (represented by `controlObject.Location.X`) to the left margin, you ensure that the check will not draw outside the margins of the page.

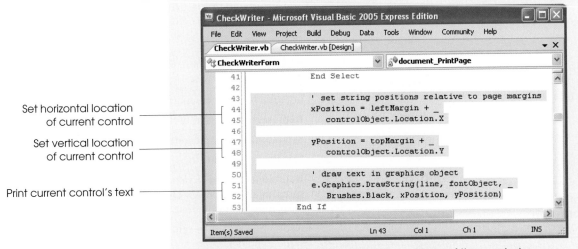

Set horizontal location of current control

Set vertical location of current control

Print current control's text

Figure 26.19 Code to set `String` positions of the controls.

(cont.)

Lines 47–48 perform a similar operation, setting yPosition to the sum of the top margin and *y*-coordinate of the control's location. Lines 51–52 call the DrawString method on the e.Graphics property. The **DrawString** method draws the specified String of text in the Graphics object. The first argument is the String to draw, in this case line. Recall earlier that you set line to the Text property of the current control. The second argument is the font, which is specified by fontObject. The third argument specifies a Brush. You pass the value Brushes.Black, which creates a black brush object to draw the text. The fourth and fifth arguments are the *x*- and *y*-coordinates where the first character of the String prints. Use the xPosition and yPosition variables that you set in lines 44–48 to print the text at the correct location on the page.

4. **Saving the project.** Select **File > Save All** to save your modified code.

SELF-REVIEW

1. The _____ method draws a specified String of text.

    a) String
                b) PrintString

    c) DrawString
                d) Draw

2. Typing Brushes.Black _____.

    a) obtains a black Brush object
          b) retrieves the color of a brush

    c) paints the screen black
          d) creates a Pen object

Answers: 1) c. 2) a.

26.8 Font Class

In the **CheckWriter** application, you used a Font object to specify the style of the text printed on a page. This section introduces the methods and constants contained in the Font class. Note that once a Font has been created, its properties cannot be modified. That means that if you require a different Font, you must create a new Font object with the appropriate settings. That's the reason we created a new Font at line 30 of Figure 26.18 for the DateTimePicker control. There are many versions of the Font constructor for creating custom Fonts to help you do this. Some properties of the Font class are summarized in Fig. 26.20.

Property	Description
Bold	Sets a font to a bold font style if value is set to True.
FontFamily	Represents the FontFamily of the Font (a grouping structure to organize fonts with similar properties).
Height	Represents the height of the font.
Italic	Sets a font to an italic font style if value is set to True.
Name	Sets the font's name to the specified String.
Size	Represents a Single value indicating the current font size measured in design units. (Design units are any specified units of measurement for the font.)
SizeInPoints	Represents a Single value indicating the current font size measured in points.
Strikeout	Sets a font to the strikeout font style if value is set to True (for example, ~~Deitel~~).
Underline	Sets a font to the underline font style if the value is set to True.

Figure 26.20 Font class read-only properties.

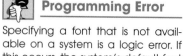

Common Programming Error

Specifying a font that is not available on a system is a logic error. If this occurs, the system's default font will be used instead.

Note that the `Size` property returns the font size as measured in **design units**, whereas `SizeInPoints` returns the font size as measured in points (a more common measurement). The `Size` property can be specified in a variety of ways, such as inches or millimeters. Some versions of the `Font` constructor accept a `Graphics-Unit` argument—an enumeration that allows users to specify the unit of measurement used to describe the font size. Members of the `GraphicsUnit` enumeration include `Point` (1/72 inch), `Display` (1/100 inch), `Document` (1/300 inch), `Millimeter`, `Inch` and `Pixel`. If this argument is provided, the `Size` property contains the size of the font as measured in the specified design unit, and the `SizeInPoints` property contains the size of the font in points. For example, if you create a `Font` having size 1 and specify that `GraphicsUnit.Inch` will be used to measure the font, the `Size` property will be 1, and the `SizeInPoints` property will be 72 because there are 72 points in an inch. If you create a new `Font` object without specifying a `GraphicsUnit`, the default measurement for the font size is `Graphics-Unit.Point` (thus, the `Size` and `SizeInPoints` properties will be equal). [*Note!* There is no way to change the properties of a `Font` object—to use a different font, you must create a new `Font` object.]

The `Font` class has a number of constructors. Most require a font name, which is a `String` representing a font currently supported by the system. Common fonts include *SansSerif* and *Serif*. Constructors also require the font size as an argument. Last, `Font` constructors usually require a font style, specified by an element of the **FontStyle** enumeration: `FontStyle.Bold`, `FontStyle.Italic`, `FontStyle.Regular`, `FontStyle.Strikeout` and `FontStyle.Underline`.

SELF-REVIEW

1. The most common measurement of font size is _____.

   a) points   b) inches

   c) pixels   d) millimeters

2. _____ is an example of a font style.

   a) `Bold`   b) `Italic`

   c) `StrikeOut`   d) All of the above.

   Answers: 1) a. 2) d.

26.9 Previewing and Printing the Check

After defining how objects are printed in the `document_PrintPage` event handler, you must define what occurs when each `Button` is clicked. You begin with the `printButton_Click` event handler to specify the functionality when clicking the **Print** Button. You will write this event handler in the following box.

Defining the **printButton_Click** *Event Handler*

1. ***Creating the printButton_Click event handler.*** In the Windows Form Designer, double click the **Print** Button. The `printButton_Click` event handler appears in the `CheckWriter.vb` file.

2. ***Creating a PrintDocument object.*** Add lines 85–86 of Fig. 26.21 into the event handler. The `PrintDocument` object is used to help print the check. Be sure to add the comments and line-continuation characters as shown in Fig. 26.21 so that the line numbers in your code match those presented in this tutorial.

(cont.)

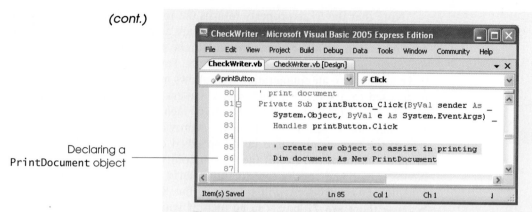

Declaring a
PrintDocument object

Figure 26.21 Code that creates the `PrintDocument` object.

3. *Specifying the PrintPage event handler.* Add lines 88–90 of Fig. 26.22 into the event handler. These lines specify the event handler called when the `PrintPage` event is raised. Lines 89-90 use the **AddHandler** statement to associate the `PrintPage` event of the document object with the event handler specified after the **AddressOf** operator (the document_PrintPage event handler that you created earlier in this tutorial). To execute the code in the event handler, you must provide the name of the event handler you created to handle the event after operator `AddressOf`.

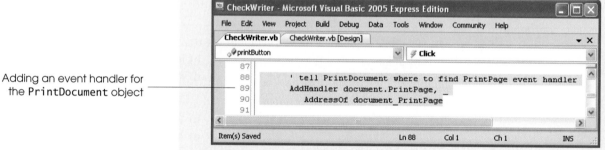

Adding an event handler for
the PrintDocument object

Figure 26.22 Code that adds an event handler to the `PrintDocument` object.

4. *Verifying that the user has a printer.* Add lines 92–96 of Fig. 26.23 to the `printButton_Click` event handler. Line 93 uses the property **PrinterSettings.InstalledPrinters.Count** to determine how many printers are installed on the user's computer. If there are no printers installed (that is, if the `Count` property returns 0), the user cannot print or preview the document. Line 94 in the body of the `If...Then` statement displays an error message by calling procedure `ErrorMessage`, which you will define in the next box. Line 95 exits the event handler using the `Return` keyword.

5. *Printing the document.* Add lines 98–99 of Fig. 26.24 to the printButton_Click event handler. Line 99 calls the `Print` method of the document object. The `Print` method, in turn, raises the `PrintPage` event each time it needs output for printing. Your `PrintPage` event handler then executes and uses a `Graphics` object to draw. The `Graphics` object is obtained from the `Graphics` property of the `PrintPageEventArgs` class. In this case, the `PrintPageEventArgs` object was passed as argument e. The document_PrintPage method uses this `PrintPageEventArgs`' `Graphics` object to call the `DrawRectangle` and `DrawString` methods.

6. *Saving the project.* Select **File > Save All** to save your modified code.

(cont.)

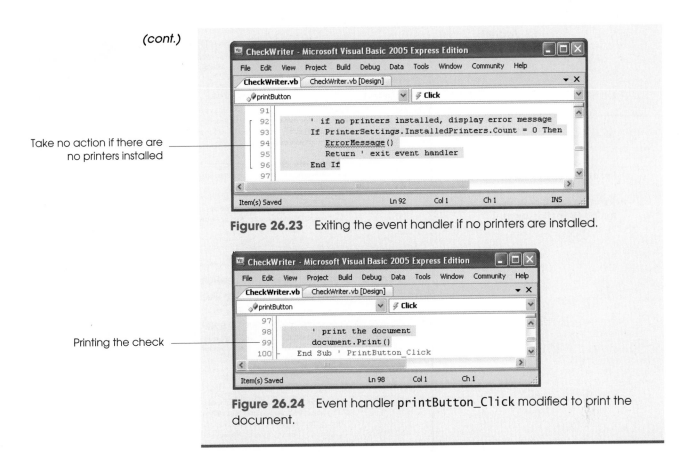

Take no action if there are no printers installed

Figure 26.23 Exiting the event handler if no printers are installed.

Printing the check

Figure 26.24 Event handler `printButton_Click` modified to print the document.

Now that you have defined the `printButton_Click` method, you will complete the application by coding the `Click` event handler for the **Preview** Button. When this Button is clicked, a dialog appears allowing the user to preview the check before printing it. You will create the `previewButton_Click` event handler to enable this feature in the following box.

Defining the `previewButton_Click` *Event Handler*	1. *Creating the `previewButton_Click` event handler.* In the Windows Form Designer, double click the **Preview** Button. The `previewButton_Click` event handler appears in the `CheckWriter.vb` file.
	2. *Creating the `PrintDocument` object and adding the `PrintPage` handler.* Add lines 107–112 of Fig. 26.25 into the event handler. As in the `printButton_Click` event handler, line 108 creates a new `PrintDocument` object named document. Lines 111–112 specify that the `PrintDocument` object's `PrintPage` event handler is method `document_PrintPage`.
	3. *Verifying that the user has a printer.* Add lines 114–118 of Fig. 26.26 to the `printButton_Click` event handler. These lines of code are exactly the same as the code from *Step 4* of the previous box. An error message is displayed if there are no installed printers.
	4. *Specifying the `PrintPreviewDialog` object's `Document` property.* Add line 120 of Fig. 26.27 into the event handler. Recall that when you created the `PrintPreviewDialog` object, you learned that its `Document` property specifies the document to preview. This property requires that its value be of type `PrintDocument`, the same class you use to print the check. This line sets `previewObject`'s `Document` property to document (the `PrintDocument` you created at line 108).

(cont.)

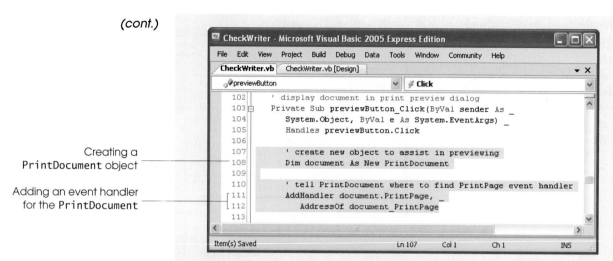

Figure 26.25 Event handler `previewButton_Click` modified to create `PrintDocument` and add `PrintPage` event handler.

Creating a `PrintDocument` object

Adding an event handler for the `PrintDocument`

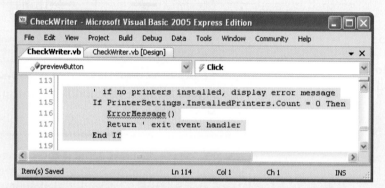

Figure 26.26 Exiting the print preview event handler if no printers are installed.

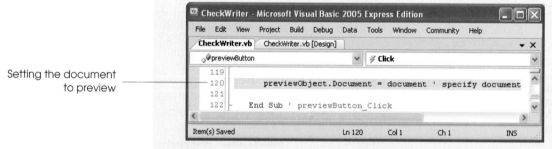

Setting the document to preview

Figure 26.27 Event handler `previewButton_Click` modified to set the `PrintPreviewDialog` object's `Document` property.

5. ***Showing the Print preview dialog.*** Add line 121 into the event handler, as shown in Fig. 26.28. This line invokes the `PrintPreviewDialog` object's `ShowDialog` method to display the **Print preview** dialog that displays how the `PrintDocument` will appear when printed. To display the document, the `PrintPreviewControl` of the `PrintPreviewDialog` raises the `Print-Page` event. Rather than using the `Graphics` object to print a page using your printer, the `PrintPreviewDialog` uses the `Graphics` object to display the page on the screen.

(cont.)

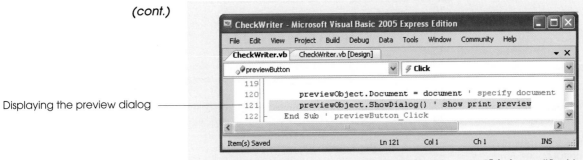

Displaying the preview dialog

Figure 26.28   Event handler `previewButton_Click` modified to show preview dialog.

6. ***Defining the ErrorMessage procedure.*** Add lines 124–131 of Fig. 26.29 into your application. Lines 127–130 display an error message to the user indicating that printing and print previewing the check is not possible if there is no printer installed on the computer.

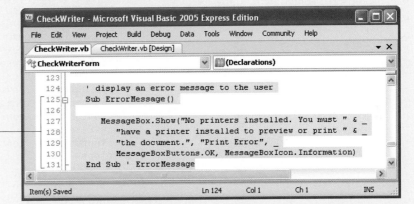

Method to display error message

Figure 26.29   Displaying an error message when no printer is installed.

7. ***Running the application.*** Select **Debug > Start Debugging** to run your application. Enter the information for the check, and click the **Preview Button**. The check will be displayed in the print preview. Use the **Print Button** to print the check. Verify that the check prints out to your default printer (if you have a printer set up).

8. ***Closing the application.*** Close your running application by clicking its close box.

9. ***Closing the IDE.*** Close the Visual Basic IDE by clicking its close box.

Figure 26.30 presents the source code for the **CheckWriter** application. The lines of code that contain new programming concepts that you learned in this tutorial are highlighted.

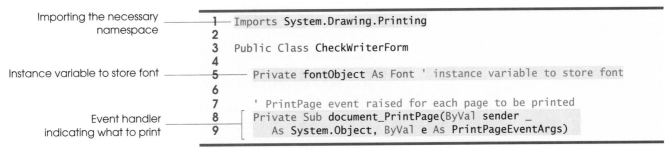

Importing the necessary namespace

Instance variable to store font

Event handler indicating what to print

```
1  Imports System.Drawing.Printing
2
3  Public Class CheckWriterForm
4
5     Private fontObject As Font ' instance variable to store font
6
7     ' PrintPage event raised for each page to be printed
8     Private Sub document_PrintPage(ByVal sender _
9        As System.Object, ByVal e As PrintPageEventArgs)
```

Figure 26.30   **CheckWriter** application code. (Part 1 of 3.)

```
10
11     Dim yPosition As Single
12     Dim xPosition As Single
13
14     ' represent left margin of page
15     Dim leftMargin As Single = e.MarginBounds.Left
16
17     ' represent top margin of page
18     Dim topMargin As Single = e.MarginBounds.Top
19     Dim line As String = Nothing
20     Dim controlObject As Control
21
22     ' iterate over the form, printing each control
23     For Each controlObject In Me.Controls
24        ' we do not want to print Buttons
25        If controlObject.GetType.Name <> "Button" Then
26           line = controlObject.Text
27           Select Case controlObject.Name
28              ' underline the date
29              Case "dateTimePicker"
30                 fontObject = New Font("Tahoma", 8.25, _
31                    FontStyle.Underline)
32              ' draw a box around amount
33              Case "amountTextBox"
34                 e.Graphics.DrawRectangle(Pens.Black, _
35                    amountTextBox.Location.X + leftMargin, _
36                    amountTextBox.Location.Y + topMargin - 4, _
37                    amountTextBox.Width, amountTextBox.Height)
38                 fontObject = controlObject.Font ' default font
39              Case Else
40                 fontObject = controlObject.Font ' default font
41           End Select
42
43           ' set string positions relative to page margins
44           xPosition = leftMargin + _
45              controlObject.Location.X
46
47           yPosition = topMargin + _
48              controlObject.Location.Y
49
50           ' draw text in graphics object
51           e.Graphics.DrawString(line, fontObject, _
52              Brushes.Black, xPosition, yPosition)
53        End If
54     Next ' control
55
56     ' draw necessary formatting lines
57     e.Graphics.DrawLine(Pens.Black, _
58        payeeTextBox.Location.X + leftMargin, _
59        payeeTextBox.Location.Y + topMargin + 15, _
60        550, payeeTextBox.Location.Y + topMargin + 15)
61
62     e.Graphics.DrawLine(Pens.Black, _
63        paymentTextBox.Location.X + leftMargin, _
64        paymentTextBox.Location.Y + topMargin + 15, _
65        490, paymentTextBox.Location.Y + topMargin + 15)
66
67     e.Graphics.DrawLine(Pens.Black, _
68        memoTextBox.Location.X + leftMargin, _
69        memoTextBox.Location.Y + topMargin + 15, _
70        325, memoTextBox.Location.Y + topMargin + 15)
71
```

Labels (left margin annotations):

- Using type **Single** to store coordinates (lines 11–12)
- Variable to store left margin value (line 15)
- Variable to store top margin value (line 18)
- Variable to refer to a control on the **Form** (line 20)
- Iterate through the controls on the **Form** (line 23)
- Obtaining the name of a type of reference (line 25)
- Creating a **Font** object (line 30)
- Drawing a rectangle using the **DrawRectangle** method (lines 34–37)
- Drawing a text using the **DrawString** method (lines 51–52)

Figure 26.30   CheckWriter application code. (Part 2 of 3.)

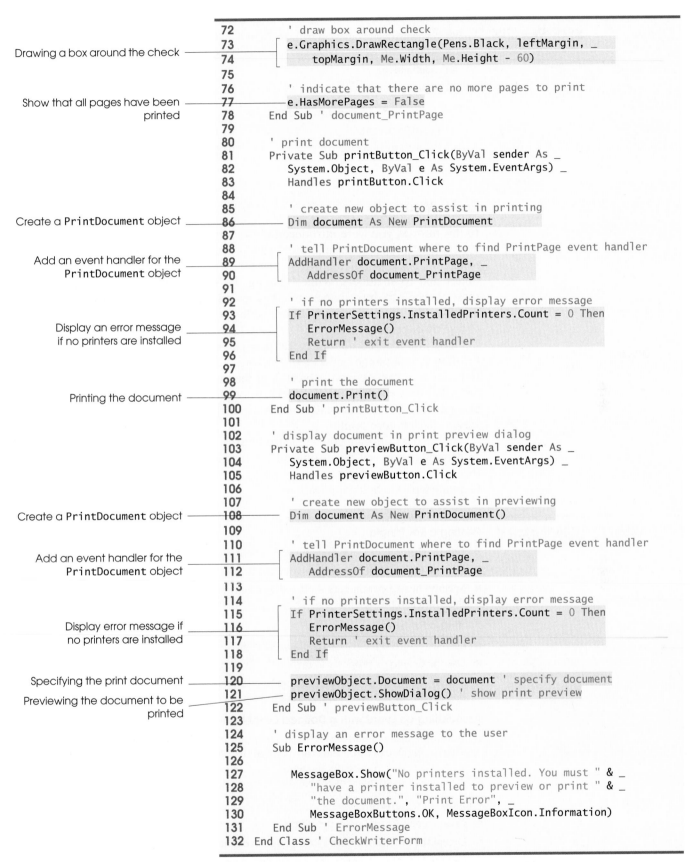

Drawing a box around the check

Show that all pages have been printed

Create a `PrintDocument` object

Add an event handler for the `PrintDocument` object

Display an error message if no printers are installed

Printing the document

Create a `PrintDocument` object

Add an event handler for the `PrintDocument` object

Display error message if no printers are installed

Specifying the print document

Previewing the document to be printed

```
72          ' draw box around check
73          e.Graphics.DrawRectangle(Pens.Black, leftMargin, _
74             topMargin, Me.Width, Me.Height - 60)
75
76          ' indicate that there are no more pages to print
77          e.HasMorePages = False
78       End Sub ' document_PrintPage
79
80       ' print document
81       Private Sub printButton_Click(ByVal sender As _
82          System.Object, ByVal e As System.EventArgs) _
83          Handles printButton.Click
84
85          ' create new object to assist in printing
86          Dim document As New PrintDocument
87
88          ' tell PrintDocument where to find PrintPage event handler
89          AddHandler document.PrintPage, _
90             AddressOf document_PrintPage
91
92          ' if no printers installed, display error message
93          If PrinterSettings.InstalledPrinters.Count = 0 Then
94             ErrorMessage()
95             Return ' exit event handler
96          End If
97
98          ' print the document
99          document.Print()
100      End Sub ' printButton_Click
101
102      ' display document in print preview dialog
103      Private Sub previewButton_Click(ByVal sender As _
104         System.Object, ByVal e As System.EventArgs) _
105         Handles previewButton.Click
106
107         ' create new object to assist in previewing
108         Dim document As New PrintDocument()
109
110         ' tell PrintDocument where to find PrintPage event handler
111         AddHandler document.PrintPage, _
112            AddressOf document_PrintPage
113
114         ' if no printers installed, display error message
115         If PrinterSettings.InstalledPrinters.Count = 0 Then
116            ErrorMessage()
117            Return ' exit event handler
118         End If
119
120         previewObject.Document = document ' specify document
121         previewObject.ShowDialog() ' show print preview
122      End Sub ' previewButton_Click
123
124      ' display an error message to the user
125      Sub ErrorMessage()
126
127         MessageBox.Show("No printers installed. You must " & _
128            "have a printer installed to preview or print " & _
129            "the document.", "Print Error", _
130            MessageBoxButtons.OK, MessageBoxIcon.Information)
131      End Sub ' ErrorMessage
132   End Class ' CheckWriterForm
```

Figure 26.30   CheckWriter application code. (Part 3 of 3.)

SELF-REVIEW

1. When you associate an event with an event handler, keyword _____ is used to specify the location of the event handler.

    a) `AddHandler`   b) `AddressOf`

    c) `HandlerEvent`   d) Both a and b.

2. The _____ object contains the `PrintPage` event.

    a) `PrintDocument`   b) `PrintPreviewDialog`

    c) `PrintPreviewControl`   d) `PrintDialog`

Answers: 1) b. 2) a.

26.10 Wrap-Up

In this tutorial, you were introduced to the topic of graphics and printing. You created a **CheckWriter** application that allows you to enter data in a check and print it using the printer installed on your computer. You learned how to use the `Graphics` object and its members. While building the **CheckWriter** application, you used these concepts to draw shapes and `Strings` using graphics objects such as `Pens` and `Brushes`. You also learned how to use code to create fonts to apply to text you wish to display or print.

You also learned about several new classes, including `PrintPreviewDialog`, `PrintPreviewControl` and `PrintDocument`. You used the `PrintDocument` class to create a `PrintDocument` object. You then used its `PrintPage` event to execute code that draws and prints the check when the user clicks the **Print** Button. You also added a `PrintPreviewDialog` in your application, allowing the user to preview a check before printing it.

In the next tutorial, you will learn how to use multimedia in your applications. In particular, you will be introduced to Microsoft Agent, a technology used to add three-dimensional animated characters to a program. You will use this technology to create a phone book application.

SKILLS SUMMARY

Printing a Rectangle

- Use the `PrintPageEventArgs` object's `Graphics` property.
- Use the `Graphics` property to invoke the `DrawRectangle` method.
- Specify the five parameters—a `Brush` (or `Pen`) object, the *x*-coordinate, the *y*-coordinate, the width and the height.

Printing a `String`

- Use the `PrintPageEventArgs` object's `Graphics` property.
- Use the `Graphics` property to invoke the `DrawString` method.
- Specify the five parameters: the string to print, the font style, the `Brush` object, the *x*-coordinate and the *y*-coordinate of where to begin printing the string.

Associating an Event with a Defined Event Handler

- Follow the format `AddHandler` *objectName*.*eventName*, `AddressOf` *eventHandlerName*, where *objectName* represents the name of the object with which the event will be associated, *eventName* represents the name of a valid event and *eventHandlerName* represents the name of the defined event handler to be associated with the specified event.

Printing a Document

- Create a new `PrintDocument` object.
- Define the `PrintDocument`'s `PrintPage` event handler to specify what to print.
- Use the `PrintDocument` to invoke the `Print` method.

Displaying a Print Preview Dialog

■ Create a `PrintPreviewDialog` object.

■ Specify the `PrintDocument` to preview in the `PrintPreviewDialog`'s Document property.

■ Invoke the `PrintPreviewDialog`'s ShowDialog method.

KEY TERMS

AddHandler statement—Adds an event handler for a specific event.

AddressOf operator—Specifies the location of an event handler associated with an event.

API (application programming interface)—The interface used by a program to access the operating system and various services on the computer.

Brush object—An object used to specify drawing parameters when drawing solid shapes.

Control—A type that can be used to declare variables for referencing controls on the Form.

coordinate system—A scheme for identifying every possible point on the computer screen.

design units—Any specified units of measurement for the font.

dithering—Using small dots of existing colors to form a pattern that simulates a desired color.

Document property—Property of the `PrintPreviewDialog` that allows you to specify the document that will be displayed in the dialog.

DrawLine method of the Graphics class—Draws a line of a specified color between two specified points.

DrawRectangle method—Draws the outline of a rectangle of a specified size and color at a specified location.

DrawString method—`Graphics` method that draws the specified `String`.

Font class—Contains properties that define unique fonts.

FontFamily class—Represents the `FontFamily` of the Font (a grouping structure to organize fonts with similar properties).

FontStyle enumeration—Provides constants for specifying a font's style. These include `FontStyle.Bold`, `FontStyle.Italic`, `FontStyle.Regular`, `FontStyle.Strikeout` and `FontStyle.Underline`.

FromArgb method of the Color class—Creates a new `Color` object from RGB values and from an alpha value.

GDI+ (Graphics Device Interface)—An application programming interface (API) that provides classes for creating two-dimensional vector graphics.

GetName method of the FontFamily class—Returns the name of the `FontFamily` object.

HasMorePages property of the PrintPageEventArgs class—Specifies whether there are more pages to print. When `False`, the `PrintPage` event is no longer raised.

MarginBounds.Left property of the PrintPageEventArgs class—Specifies the left margin of a printed page.

MarginBounds.Top property of the PrintPageEventArgs class—Specifies the top margin of a printed page.

Me keyword—References the current object.

opacity—Amount of transparency of the color.

Pen object—Specifies drawing parameters when drawing shape outlines.

Print method—`PrintDocument` method used to print a document.

PrintDocument class—Allows the user to describe how to print a document.

PrintPage event—Occurs when the data required to print the current page is needed.

PrintPageEventArgs class—Contains data passed to a `PrintPage` event.

PrintPreviewDialog class—Previews a document in a dialog box before it prints.

PrinterSettings.InstalledPrinters.Count property—Determines how many printers are installed on the user's computer.

Single data type—Stores floating-point values. `Single` is similar to `Double`, but is less precise and requires less memory.

System.Drawing.Printing namespace—Allows your applications to access all services related to printing.

UseAntiAlias property—Property of class `PrintPreviewDialog` that makes the text in the `PrintPreviewDialog` appear smoother on the screen.

vector graphics —Graphics created by a set of mathematical properties called vectors, which include the graphics' dimensions, attributes and positions.

x-**axis**—Describes every horizontal coordinate.

x-**coordinate**—Horizontal distance (increasing to the right) from the left of the drawing area.

y-**axis**—Describes every vertical coordinate.

y-**coordinate**—Vertical distance (increasing downward) from the top of the drawing area.

CONTROLS, EVENTS, PROPERTIES & METHODS

Font This class is used to define the font face, size and style of text throughout an application.

■ *Properties*

`Bold`—Sets the weight of the text.

`Italic`—Sets the angle of the text.

`Size`—Sets the size of the text.

`FontFamily`—Contains a `FontFamily` object, which is used to store font face information.

`FontStyle`—Specifies the style applied to a `Font` object.

Graphics The class that contains methods used to draw text, lines and shapes.

■ *Methods*

`DrawLine`—Draws a line of a specified size and color.

`DrawEllipse`—Draws the outline of an ellipse of a specified size and color at a specified location.

`DrawRectangle`—Draws the outline of a rectangle of a specified size and color at a specified location.

`DrawString`—Draws a `String` in a specified font and color at a specified position.

`FillEllipse`—Draws a solid ellipse of a specified size and color at the specified location.

`FillRectangle`—Draws a solid rectangle of a specified size and color at the specified location.

PrintDocument This class allows you to specify how to print a document.

■ *Event*

`PrintPage`—Raised when data required to print a page is needed.

■ *Method*

`Print`—Uses a `Graphics` object to print a page.

PrinterSettings This class stores information about the system's printer settings.

■ *Property*

`InstalledPrinters.Count`—Returns the number of printers installed on the system.

PrintPageEventArgs This class contains data passed to a `PrintPage` event.

■ *Properties*

`HasMorePages`—Specifies if there are more pages to print. When `False`, the `PrintPage` event is no longer raised.

`MarginBounds`—Specifies the margin of the printed page.

  `Left`—Specifies the left margin of the page.

  `Top`—Specifies the top margin of the page.

PrintPreviewDialog [□ PrintPreviewDialog] This control is used to display how a document will look when it is printed.

- *Properties*

  Document—Specifies the document that the control will preview. The document must be of type PrintDocument.

  Name—Specifies the name used to access the PrintPreviewDialog control programmatically.

  UseAntiAlias—Specifies whether the dialog will display a smoothed image.

- *Method*

  ShowDialog—Used to display the PrintPreviewDialog to the user.

MULTIPLE-CHOICE QUESTIONS

26.1 The RGB value (0, 0, 255) represents _____.

- a) Color.Red
- b) Color.Green
- c) Color.Blue
- d) Color.Yellow

26.2 The _____ property of the PrintPreviewDialog object makes text appear smoother.

- a) AntiAlias
- b) UseAntiAlias
- c) Alias
- d) UseAlias

26.3 Use a _____ object to allow the users to preview a document before it is printed.

- a) PrintPreviewDialog
- b) PrintDocument
- c) Print
- d) PrintPreviewControl

26.4 The _____ event handler specifies what will be printed.

- a) OnPaint
- b) Print
- c) Document
- d) PrintPage

26.5 To display the preview dialog of the _____ object, call method ShowDialog.

- a) PrintPreviewDialog
- b) PrintDocument
- c) PrintDialog
- d) Both a and b.

26.6 Set the _____ property to False to indicate that there are no more pages to print.

- a) Document
- b) HasMorePages
- c) TerminatePrint
- d) Both a and b.

26.7 The Print method sends a _____ object to the printer for printing.

- a) Graphics
- b) PrintDocument
- c) PrintPreviewDialog
- d) Brush

26.8 Keyword _____ references the current object.

- a) This
- b) Class
- c) Me
- d) Property

26.9 Opacity is the _____ value of a color.

- a) red
- b) transparency
- c) dithering
- d) blue

26.10 Design units are used to specify the _____ of a Font.

- a) Size
- b) Name
- c) FontFamily
- d) Style

EXERCISES

26.11 (*CheckWriter Modified to Print Background Images*) Modify the **CheckWriter** application to display and print a background for the check. The GUI should look similar to Fig. 26.31. Users can select a background image. The image should appear in the **Print preview** dialog box and also should print as a background to the check.

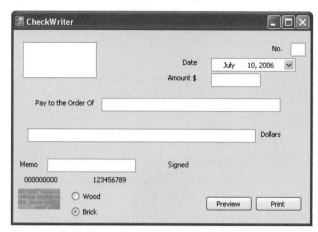

Figure 26.31 Modified **CheckWriter** GUI.

a) *Copying the template to your working directory.* Copy the directory C:\Examples\ Tutorial26\Exercises\ModifiedCheckWriter to your C:\SimplyVB directory.

b) *Opening the application's template file.* Double click CheckWriter.sln in the CheckWriter directory to open the application.

c) *Creating the CheckedChanged event handler.* Double click the **Wood** RadioButton to create its CheckedChanged event handler.

d) *Defining the CheckedChanged event handler.* Define the RadioButton's Checked-Changed event handler to notify the application when users have made a background selection. If the **Wood** RadioButton is selected, then a preview of the wooden back-ground should display in previewPicture. Otherwise, if the **Brick** RadioButton is selected, then a preview of the brick background should display in previewPicture.

e) *Modifying the document_PrintPage event handler.* Modify event handler document_PrintPage to print the background image. [*Hint:* Use the DrawImage method to display the background image to print. DrawImage takes five arguments: The image file, the *x*-coordinate, the *y*-coordinate, the width and the height.] To print the image in the background, the DrawImage method must be the first method called on the Graphics object.

f) *Running the application.* Select **Debug > Start Debugging** to run your application. Enter data into the input fields and select either the **Wood** or **Brick** RadioButton. Verify that the appropriate image is displayed to the left of the RadioButtons. Click the **Preview** Button and verify that the check is displayed with the proper back-ground. Close the preview and repeat this process selecting the background you had not selected before.

g) *Closing the application.* Close your running application by clicking its close box.

h) *Closing the IDE.* Close the Visual Basic IDE by clicking its close box.

26.12 (*Company Logo Designer Application*) Develop a **Company Logo** application that allows users to design a company logo (Fig. 26.32). The application should provide the user with RadioButtons to allow the selection of the next shape to draw. TextBoxes should be provided to allow the user to enter the dimensions of the shapes.

a) *Copying the template to your working directory.* Copy the directory C:\Examples\ Tutorial26\Exercises\CompanyLogo to your C:\SimplyVB directory.

b) *Opening the application's template file.* Double click CompanyLogo.sln in the Com-panyLogo directory to open the application.

c) *Defining the Add Button's Click event handler.* Create the **Add** Button's Click event handler. Define the event handler so that the shape that users specify is drawn on the PictureBox. Use the CreateGraphics method on the PictureBox to retrieve the Graphics object used to draw on the PictureBox. [*Note:* The TextBoxes labeled **X1:, Y1:, X2:** and **Y2:** must contain integers to draw a line. Also, the TextBoxes labeled **X:, Y:, Width:** and **Height:** must contain integers to draw any other shape.]

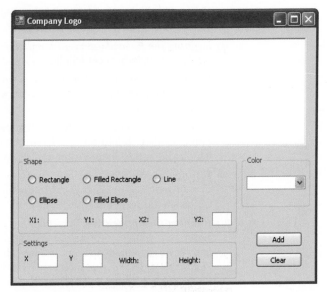

Figure 26.32 Company Logo GUI.

d) *Defining the Clear Button's Click event handler.* Create the **Clear** Button's Click event handler, and define it so that the PictureBox is cleared. [*Hint:* To clear the entire PictureBox, use the PictureBox's Invalidate method. The Invalidate method is often used to refresh (update) graphics of a control. By using the Invalidate method without specifying a graphic to draw, the PictureBox clears.] Also ensure that all TextBoxes are cleared when the **Clear** Button is clicked.

e) *Running the application.* Select **Debug > Start Debugging** to run your application. Use the RadioButtons and TextBoxes to display at least one of each type of shape. Use different colors for the different shapes. Click the **Clear** Button to clear the shapes.

f) *Closing the application.* Close your running application by clicking its close box.

g) *Closing the IDE.* Close the Visual Basic IDE by clicking its close box.

26.13 (*Letter Head Designer Application*) Create a **Letter Head** application that allows users to design stationery for company documents (Fig. 26.33). Allow users to specify the image that will serve as the letterhead.

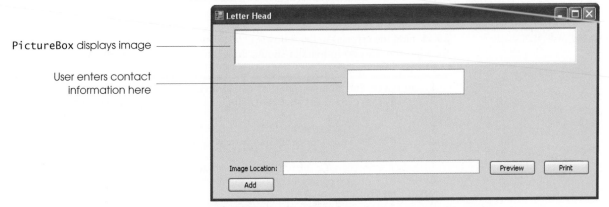

PictureBox displays image ⎯⎯⎯

User enters contact information here ⎯⎯⎯

Figure 26.33 Letter Head GUI.

a) *Copying the template to your working directory.* Copy the directory C:\Examples\Tutorial26\Exercises\LetterHead to your C:\SimplyVB directory.

b) *Opening the application's template file.* Double click LetterHead.sln in the LetterHead directory to open the application.

c) *Creating a `PrintPreviewDialog` control*. Add a `PrintPreviewDialog` control to allow users to preview the letterhead before it is printed.

d) *Defining the `PrintPage` event handler*. Allow users to print the document by defining the `PrintPage` event handler as you did in the **CheckWriter** application.

e) *Defining the `printButton_Click` event handler*. The `printButton_Click` event handler should tell the `PrintDocument` where to find the `PrintPage` event handler, as in the **CheckWriter** application, and print the document.

f) *Defining the `previewButton_Click` event handler*. The `previewButton_Click` event handler should tell the `PrintDocument` where to find the `PrintPage` event handler, as in the **CheckWriter** application, and then show the preview dialog.

g) *Testing the application*. The `Letterhead.png` image file, located in `C:\Examples\Tutorial26\Exercises\Images` has been provided for you to test the application's letter head image capability.

h) *Running the application*. Select **Debug > Start Debugging** to run your application. Enter your contact information and specify the location of an image. [*Note:* An image has been supplied in an `Images` directory, located in your `C:\Examples\Tutorial26\Exercises` directory.] The image should be displayed in the `Picture-Box` at the top of the `Form`. Click the **Preview** Button and verify that the image and contact information is displayed in the preview. Finally, click the **Print** Button to verify that the letterhead prints with the appropriate image and contact information.

i) *Closing the application*. Close your running application by clicking its close box.

j) *Closing the IDE*. Close the Visual Basic IDE by clicking its close box.

What does this code do? ▶ **26.14** What is the result of the following code? Assume that `output_PrintPage` is defined.

```
1   Private Sub printButton_Click(ByVal sender As System.Object, _
2      ByVal e As System.EventArgs) Handles printButton.Click
3
4      Dim output As New PrintDocument()
5
6      AddHandler output.PrintPage, _
7         AddressOf output_PrintPage
8
9      output.Print()
10
11  End Sub ' printButton_Click
```

What's wrong with this code? ▶ **26.15** Find the error(s) in the following code. This is the definition for a `Click` event handler for a `Button`. This event handler should draw a rectangle on a `PictureBox` control.

```
1   Private Sub drawImageButton_Click(ByVal sender As System.Object, _
2      ByVal e As System.EventArgs) Handles drawImageButton.Click
3
4      ' create an orange colored brush
5      Dim brush As SolidBrush = New SolidBrush(Orange)
6
7      ' create a Graphics object to draw on the PictureBox
8      Dim graphicsObject As Graphics = mainPicture.AcquireGraphics
9
10     ' draw a filled rectangle
11     graphicsObject.FillRectangle(brush, 2, 3, 40, 30)
12
13  End Sub ' drawImageButton_Click
```

26.16 (*Screen Saver Simulator Application*) Develop an application that simulates a screen saver. This application should add random-colored, random-sized, solid and hollow shapes at different positions of the screen (Fig. 26.34). Copy the C:\Exercises\ Tutorial26\ScreenSaver directory, and place it in your C:\SimplyVB directory. The design of the Form has been created, which consists of a black Form and a Timer control. In the ScreenSaver.vb code view, the DisplayShape method has been provided and the Timer's tick event handler has already been defined for you.

You must write the rest of the DisplayShape method code. Create the Graphics object from the Form using the Form's CreateGraphics method, and specify random colors, sizes and positions for the filled and hollow shapes that will be displayed on the screen. The width and height of the shapes should be no larger than 100 pixels.

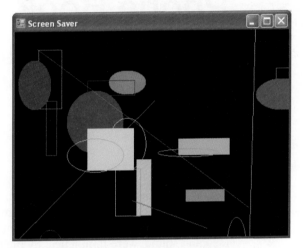

Figure 26.34 Screen Saver running.

26.17 (*Enhanced Screen Saver Simulator Application*) Enhance the **Screen Saver Simulator** application from Exercise 26.16 by modifying the Timer control's Tick event handler. Add code to this event handler so that after a specified amount of time, the screen should clear the displayed shapes. After the screen clears, random shapes should continue to display. Also, use the FromArgb method so that you can specify random opacity (alpha values) for the colors. You should pass four arguments to this method. The first argument is the alpha value, the second is the red value, the third is the green value and the fourth is the blue value.

27

Objectives

In this tutorial, you will learn to:
- Download components necessary to run Microsoft Agent.
- Enhance Windows applications using multimedia.
- Create applications that interact with users.
- Add controls to the **ToolBox**.
- Use Microsoft Agent in a Visual Basic application.
- Obtain the mouse position.
- Use data type **Short**.

Outline

27.1 Microsoft Agent
27.2 Downloading Microsoft Agent Components
27.3 Test-Driving the Phone Book Application
27.4 Constructing the Phone Book Application
27.5 Wrap-Up

Phone Book Application

Introducing Multimedia Using Microsoft Agent

When computers were first introduced, they were large and expensive and were used primarily to perform arithmetic calculations. **Multimedia** applications, which use a variety of media, including graphics, animation, video and sound, were impractical by the high cost and slow speed of computers. However, today's affordable, ultra-fast processors make multimedia-based applications commonplace. As the market for multimedia explodes, users are purchasing computers with faster processors, larger amounts of memory and wider communications bandwidths needed to support multimedia applications.

Exciting new three-dimensional multimedia applications interact with the user by means of animation, audio and video. Multimedia programming is an entertaining and innovative field, but one that presents many challenges. Visual Basic enables you to include multimedia presentations in your applications.

In this tutorial, you will explore the **Microsoft Agent** technology, which uses entertaining, animated three-dimensional cartoon characters to interact with the application user. You will create a phone book application that uses one of the predefined Agent characters.

27.1 Microsoft Agent

In this tutorial, you will create a phone book application that displays people's phone numbers, using Microsoft Agent to interact with users and enhance the application. This application must meet the following requirements:

Application Requirements

A software company's customer-service department is responsible for calling clients. It needs a quick way to access clients' phone numbers and has asked you to develop an application that stores and retrieves the names and numbers of their clients. The customer service employees want an application that employs multimedia (using a Microsoft Agent character, Peedy the Parrot) to allow them to retrieve phone numbers by speaking clients' names and also by selecting clients' names with the mouse.

Microsoft Agent is a technology used to add **interactive animated characters** to Windows applications or Web pages. Microsoft Agent characters can speak (by using voice synthesis) and respond to user input (by using speech recognition). Microsoft employs its Agent technology in such applications as Word, Excel and PowerPoint to help users understand how to use the application.

The Microsoft Agent control provides you with access to four pre-defined characters—*Genie* (a genie), *Merlin* (a wizard), *Peedy* (a parrot) and *Robby* (a robot). Each character contains unique animations that you can use in applications to illustrate different instructions and actions. For instance, the Peedy character-animation set includes several flying animations which you can use to move Peedy across the screen. Microsoft provides basic information on Agent technology at

```
www.microsoft.com/msagent
```

Microsoft Agent technology makes it possible to interact with applications and Web pages by using speech. When the user speaks into a microphone, the control uses a **speech-recognition engine**, an application that translates vocal sound input from a microphone into a language that the computer understands. The Microsoft Agent control also uses a text-to-speech engine, which allows the Microsoft Agent characters to speak lines of text. A **text-to-speech engine** is an application that translates typed words into sound that users hear through headphones or speakers connected to a computer. Microsoft provides speech-recognition and text-to-speech engines for several languages at

```
www.microsoft.com/products/msagent/downloads.htm
```

SELF-REVIEW
1. A _____ translates typed words into sound.
   a) speech-recognition engine   b) text-to-speech engine
   c) character-animation set   d) All of the above.

2. The application that translates vocal sound input from a microphone to a language understood by the computer is called the _____.
   a) speech-recognition engine   b) text-to-speech engine
   c) character-animation set   d) All of the above.

Answers: 1) b. 2) a.

27.2 Downloading Microsoft Agent Components

Microsoft Agent characters can be used as visual aids for applications. The Agents also allow users to speak to, listen to and interact with the characters. This tutorial demonstrates how to use the Microsoft Agent characters to build the **Phone Book** application. To run this tutorial's application, you must download and install the Agent control, speech-recognition engine, text-to-speech engine and Peedy character definition from the Microsoft Agent Web site. Begin by visiting

```
www.microsoft.com/products/msagent/downloads.htm
```

This page (Fig. 27.1) displays a list of Microsoft Agent downloads. The first component you need to download is the Agent character file. Click the **Microsoft Agent character files** link (Fig. 27.1).

Clicking this link directs users to the location where the Microsoft Agent character files can be downloaded (Fig. 27.2). Select the Peedy character from the drop-down list, and click the **Download selected character** link. Save the file Peedy.exe to your computer, and install the Peedy character files by double clicking this file.

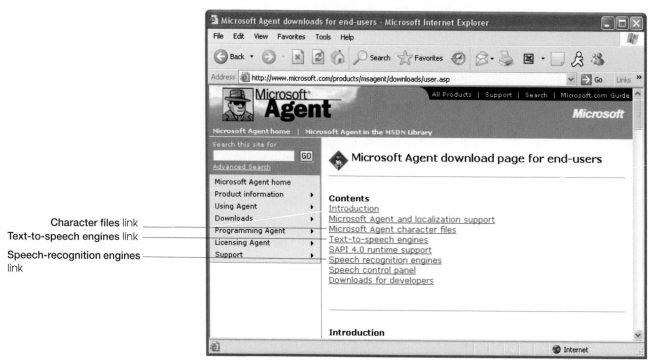

Character files link
Text-to-speech engines link
Speech-recognition engines link

Figure 27.1 Microsoft Web page containing Agent-related downloads.

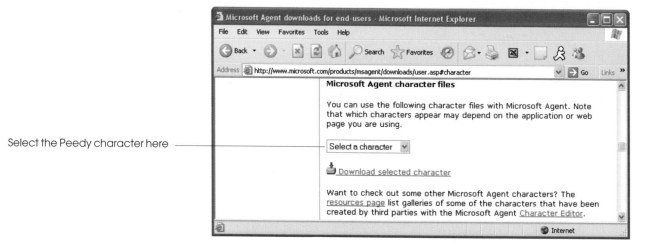

Select the Peedy character here

Figure 27.2 Location for downloading the Microsoft Agent character.

Next, you will download the text-to-speech engine. Return to the **Microsoft Agent Downloads Contents** list by scrolling to the top of the current page, and click the **Text-to-speech engines** link. Click the ComboBox to display the drop-down list, and select the engine that supports American English. Click the **Download selected engine** link to save the file tv_enua.exe. Double click this file once it has been downloaded to install the text-to-speech engine. You may need to restart your machine after this installation.

You must also download the speech-recognition engine. Return to the **Microsoft Agent Downloads Contents** list by scrolling to the top of the current page, and click the **Speech recognition engines** link. Click the **Download Microsoft Speech Recognition Engine** link to save the file actcnc.exe. Double click this file once it has been downloaded to install the speech-recognition engine. The installation process will walk you through the configuration of your micro-phone. Once you have downloaded and installed all the components, you are ready to use Microsoft Agent.

27.3 Test-Driving the Phone Book Application

Recall that you will be creating the **Phone Book** application to allow users to search for a phone number using an interactive Microsoft Agent character. The **Phone Book** application that you build in the next section will contain people's names and phone numbers for the customer-service department. You begin by test-driving the completed application. Then you will learn the additional Visual Basic technologies that you will need to create your own version of this application.

Test-Driving the Phone Book Application

1. ***Opening the completed application.*** Open the directory C:\Examples\ Tutorial27\CompletedApplication\PhoneBook to locate the **Phone Book** application. Double click PhoneBook.sln to open the application in the Visual Basic IDE.

2. ***Running the Phone Book application.*** Select **Debug > Start Debugging** to run the application (Fig. 27.3).

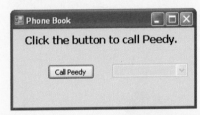

Figure 27.3   **Phone Book** application Form.

3. ***Calling Peedy.*** Click the **Call Peedy** Button to display Peedy. Peedy flies onto the screen into a position beneath the Form, waves and speaks the instructions shown in Fig. 27.4. When he is finished speaking, Peedy goes into a resting position (Fig. 27.5).

ComboBox disabled until Peedy arrives

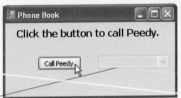

Figure 27.4   Peedy appears after **Call Peedy** button is clicked.

Figure 27.5   Peedy in a resting pose.

4. ***Using the ComboBox to select a name.*** After Peedy appears on the screen, the ComboBox is enabled. Select the name Howard from the list (Fig. 27.6). Note that the **Call Peedy** Button is disabled because Peedy is already on the screen. After Howard is selected, Peedy executes several animations. He first appears to be thinking (Fig. 27.7), tells you Howard's number (Fig. 27.8), then smiles for the user (Fig. 27.9).

(cont.)

Disabled **Call Peedy** Button ————

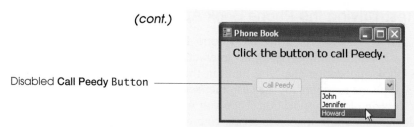

Figure 27.6   Selecting a name from the **ComboBox**.

Figure 27.7   Peedy thinking.

Figure 27.8   Peedy communicates Howard's phone number.

Figure 27.9   Peedy smiles after speaking phone number.

5. ***Providing a voice command.*** Press the *Scroll Lock* key. A box appears beneath Peedy (called a **status box**) that displays information about Peedy's actions. The status box states that Peedy is listening for your command, as in Fig. 27.10. Speak the name John into your microphone.

Figure 27.10   Peedy listening for a voice command.

If Peedy hears and understands your command, the status box displays the command he heard, as in Fig. 27.11. Otherwise, you must repeat the command clearly, so that Peedy can understand. When Peedy successfully hears your command, he gestures as if he is thinking about your request. He then displays John's phone number, as in Fig. 27.12. You will have noticed that Peedy performs several gestures during this application. You will learn how to control these gestures later in the tutorial.

(cont.)

Figure 27.11   Peedy heard voice command.

Figure 27.12   Peedy displays requested phone number.

6. ***Viewing the context menu.*** Right click Peedy and notice that a context menu appears (Fig. 27.13). Selecting one of the names (**John, Jennifer** or **Howard**) will cause the same actions to occur as when a name was chosen from the ComboBox.

Commands in pop-up window ——————

| Open Voice Commands Window |
| Hide |
| John |
| Jennifer |
| Howard |

Figure 27.13   Context menu window.

7. ***Closing the application.*** Close your running application by clicking its close box.

8. ***Closing the IDE.*** Close the Visual Basic IDE by clicking its close box.

SELF-REVIEW

1. The _____ displays information about the Microsoft Agent character's actions.
   a) balloon   b) status box
   c) help window   d) text window

2. You must press the _____ key for Peedy to listen to your voice commands.
   a) *Shift*   b) *Number Lock*
   c) *Scroll Lock*   d) *Insert*

Answers: 1) b. 2) c.

27.4 Constructing the Phone Book Application

Now that you have test-driven the **Phone Book** application, you need to analyze the application, using pseudocode. The Microsoft Agent character, Peedy, helps the user search for a specific telephone number. The user can click the ComboBox to select a name and retrieve the specified telephone number. However, thanks to the enhancement of the Microsoft Agent character, the user also can communicate verbally with Peedy. The user can retrieve a phone number simply by pressing the *Scroll Lock* key and speaking the name of a person into a microphone connected to the computer. Peedy listens for a name, and if he recognizes it, displays and speaks the number to the user. The following pseudocode describes the basic operation of the **Phone Book** application when the **Call Peedy** Button is clicked.

```
When the Form loads
    Display names in the ComboBox
    Load Peedy the Parrot character into the Agent control
    Obtain Peedy the Parrot from the Agent control's Characters property
    Add names as commands for Peedy the Parrot

When the user clicks the Call Peedy Button:
    Display Peedy the Parrot and have the parrot speak the instructions
    Enable ComboBox containing people's names
    Disable the Call Peedy Button

When the user selects a name from the ComboBox:
    Have Peedy the Parrot speak and display (in a conversation bubble) the name
        and phone number of the person selected by the user

When the user speaks a name to Peedy the Parrot:
    Have Peedy the Parrot speak and display (in a conversation bubble) the name
        and phone number of the person selected by the user

When Peedy the Parrot hides:
    Disable ComboBox containing people's names
    Enable the Call Peedy Button
```

Now that you have test-driven the **Phone Book** application and studied its pseudocode representation, you will use an ACE table to help you convert the pseudocode to Visual Basic. Figure 27.14 lists the actions, controls and events that will help you complete your own version of this application.

Action/Control/Event (ACE) Table for the Phone Book Application

Action	Control/Object	Event
Label the application's controls	`instructions-Label`	
	`PhoneBookForm`	Load
Display names in the ComboBox	`nameComboBox, nameList`	
Load Peedy the Parrot character into the Microsoft Agent control	`mainAgent`	
Obtain Peedy the Parrot from the Agent control's Characters property	`mainAgent, mspeaker`	
Add names as commands for Peedy the Parrot	`mspeaker, nameList`	
	`callButton`	Click
Display Peedy the Parrot and have the parrot speak the instructions	`mspeaker`	
Enable ComboBox containing people's names	`nameComboBox`	
Disable the Call Peedy Button	`callButton`	

Figure 27.14   ACE table for the **Phone Book** application. (Part 1 of 2.)

Action	Control/Object	Event
	nameComboBox	Selected-IndexChanged
Have Peedy the Parrot speak the name and phone number of the person selected by the user	nameComboBox, nameList, numberList, mspeaker	
	mainAgent	Command
Have Peedy the Parrot speak the name and phone number of the person selected by the user	nameComboBox, nameList, numberList, mspeaker	
	mainAgent	HideEvent
Enable ComboBox containing people's names	nameComboBox	
Enable the Call Peedy Button	callButton	

Figure 27.14 ACE table for the **Phone Book** application. (Part 2 of 2.)

Now that you understand the purpose of the **Phone Book** application, you will begin to create it. In the next box, you follow the instructions for adding the Microsoft Agent control to your **Toolbox**.

Customizing the Toolbox for the Phone Book Application

1. *Copying the template to your working directory.* Copy the C:\Examples\ Tutorial27\TemplateApplication\PhoneBook directory to your C:\ SimplyVB directory.

2. *Opening the application's template file.* Double click PhoneBook.sln in the PhoneBook directory to open the application in the Visual Basic IDE. If the project does not open in design view, switch to design view at this time.

3. *Adding the Microsoft Agent to the Toolbox.* Before you begin designing the Form, you must make the Microsoft Agent accessible because it is not part of the FCL. To do this, you must add the Microsoft Agent control to the **Toolbox** window. Right click the **All Windows Forms** group in the **Toolbox**, then select **Choose Items…**, as in Fig. 27.15. The **Choose Toolbox Items** dialog appears (Fig. 27.16). Select the **COM Components** tab and search for the **Microsoft Agent Control 2.0** item. Then click its CheckBox to select the control, as in Fig. 27.16. Click the **OK** Button. The Agent control now appears in the **Windows Forms** group in the **Toolbox**, as in Fig. 27.17.

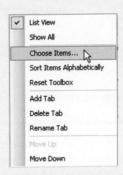

Figure 27.15 **Tools** menu.

4. *Saving the project.* Select **File > Save All** to save your modified code.

(cont.)

Select **CheckBox**

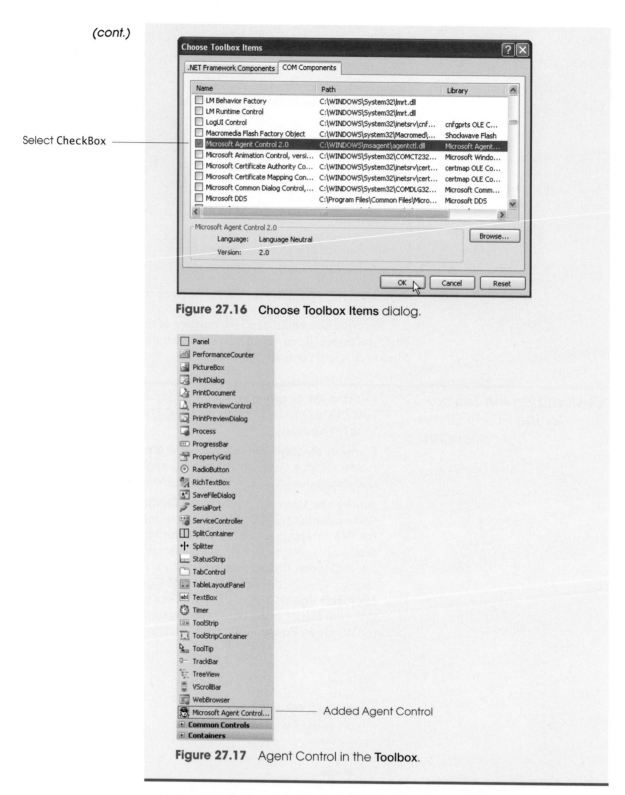

Figure 27.16 **Choose Toolbox Items** dialog.

Added Agent Control

Figure 27.17 Agent Control in the **Toolbox**.

The visual design of the Form (with the exception of the Agent control) is provided in the template application. The next step after adding the Microsoft Agent control to the **Toolbox** is to place a Microsoft Agent control on the Form.

<table>
<tr>
<td style="vertical-align:top; width:33%">

Adding the Microsoft Agent Control to the Application

Good Programming Practice

Controls in a container should not overlap. Place your controls so that they are clearly separated from one another, making the design of your application a clean one.

</td>
<td style="vertical-align:top">

1. *Placing the Microsoft Agent control on the Form.* To meet the application requirements, you must add a Microsoft Agent control to your Form, which will be used to display and manage the actions of the Microsoft Agent characters in your application. Drag and drop the Microsoft Agent control from the **Toolbox** onto the Form. Change the Microsoft Agent control's Name property from the default (AxAgent1) to mainAgent. Change the Microsoft Agent control's Location property to 16, 48 (Fig. 27.18). The control icon is not visible when the application runs, so the location of the control does not affect the application's appearance. However, it is good practice to place the control in a way that does not overlap another control on the Form. Though you set the Agent control's Location property in this step, you will write code later that will determine where the Agent character appears when the application is running. As you saw in the test-drive, the Microsoft Agent character can be displayed outside the application's Form.

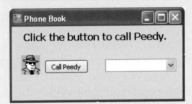

Figure 27.18   Form format of **Phone Book**.

2. *Running the application.* Select **Debug > Start Debugging** to run your application (Fig. 27.19). The **Call Peedy** Button will be used to make the Agent (in this case, Peedy) appear on the screen. However, clicking the Button does not cause any action to take place yet, because the Button's Click event handler has not been defined. Note that the ComboBox next to the **Call Peedy** Button is disabled. You will use code to enable and fill the ComboBox with names shortly.

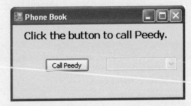

Figure 27.19   **Phone Book** Form with no functionality.

3. *Closing the application.* Close the application by clicking its close box.

</td>
</tr>
</table>

Now that you have placed the Agent control on the application's Form, you'll define the **Phone Book** application's event handlers that will define how the Agent responds to user actions. You begin writing code in the following box.

<table>
<tr>
<td style="vertical-align:top; width:33%">

Using Code to Display the Peedy Agent Character

</td>
<td style="vertical-align:top">

1. *Declaring instance variables.* To view the code file, select **View > Code**. Declare the instance variables you will use in several event handlers by inserting lines 3–11 of Fig. 27.20 within this Form's class definition. In addition to the Microsoft Agent object, mainAgent, that manages all the application's characters, you also need an object to represent the current character (sometimes referred to as the speaker). In this example, the current character will always be Peedy the Parrot. Line 3 creates a variable to represent this Agent character. The mspeaker variable is declared as an **Agent-Objects.IAgentCtlCharacter** object.

</td>
</tr>
</table>

(cont.)

Create an Agent character variable

List of names in phone book

List of phone numbers in phone book

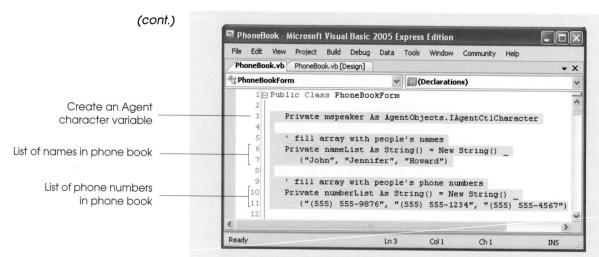

Figure 27.20 Declaring and creating arrays in **Phone Book**.

The arrays `nameList` and `numberList` are then declared and filled. The `nameList` array (lines 6–7) stores the names of people in the phone book (`John`, `Jennifer` and `Howard`), and the `numberList` array (lines 10–11) stores the corresponding phone number for each person (`(555) 555-9876`, `(555) 555-1234` and `(555) 555-4567`).

2. ***Writing code that executes when the application loads.*** The next step in creating the **Phone Book** application is to use the Form's Load event to execute code before the application becomes available to the user. Double click the Form in the Windows Form Designer to generate the Load event handler, and enter code view. Add lines 18–23 of Fig. 27.21 into the Load event handler. The `counter` variable (line 19) is used to iterate through the `nameList` array in the For...Next statement (lines 21–23). This statement fills the ComboBox with the contact names that are stored in the `nameList` array. This allows the user to select names by using the ComboBox instead of speaking the name to Peedy.

Declaring a counter variable

Adding names to the ComboBox

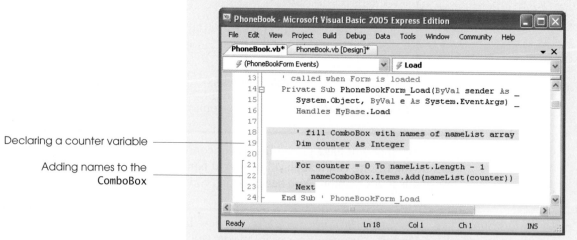

Figure 27.21 Adding items to the ComboBox.

(cont.)

3. ***Initializing the Peedy Agent character.*** Insert lines 25–29 of Fig. 27.22 into the event handler. Lines 26–27 load the Peedy character into `mainAgent`. The first argument of the `Load` method is a `String` used to represent the Agent character being loaded. In this case, use the `String` `"Peedy"`. The second argument is a `String` representing the file where the character is defined (`"Peedy.acs"`).

Several characters can be loaded into a Microsoft Agent control. In this example, however, we will only be using Peedy the Parrot, so no more characters will be loaded. Line 29 assigns the loaded character to `mspeaker`. The character is accessed using the **Characters** property of our Microsoft Agent control. The variable `mspeaker` can now be used to represent the Peedy Agent character. It is not necessary to create a separate object of type `AgentObjects.IAgentCtlCharacter`—the Peedy character can be accessed with the expression `mainAgent.Characters("Peedy")`. We have created `mspeaker` to increase application clarity.

Loading the Peedy character ————

Assigning Peedy to the Agent character variable ————

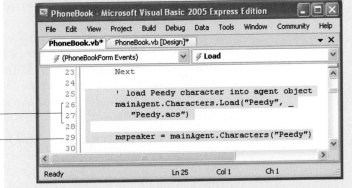

Figure 27.22   Loading the Microsoft Agent character.

4. ***Inserting commands in the Agent Commands context menu.*** Insert lines 31–37 of Fig. 27.23 to your event handler. This code uses the same counter from the previous step in its `For...Next` statement (lines 32–37). The header of the `For...Next` statement resets the counter variable's value to 0. Then the `For...Next` statement adds names from the `nameList` to the Peedy character as voice-enabled commands. The list of valid commands for a character is stored in the **Commands** property of `AgentObjects.IAgentCtlCharacter` objects.

Method **Add** of the `Commands` property adds a new command to the command list. The `Add` method takes five arguments. The first three arguments are `String`s, and the last two are `Boolean` values. The first argument identifies the command name. This value enables access to the command from your application. The second argument is a `String` that appears in a context menu when the user right clicks Peedy. The third `String` represents the word(s) Peedy listens for when users make a verbal request. The fourth argument indicates whether the command is enabled. If so, the Agent character will respond to the spoken command. The final argument specifies whether the command is visible in the `Commands` context menu, which you have already seen in Fig. 27.13.

(cont.)

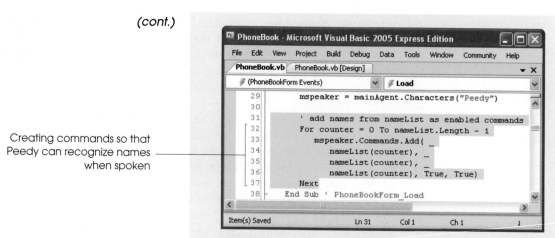

Creating commands so that
Peedy can recognize names
when spoken

Figure 27.23   Adding commands to Peedy's context menu.

In this example, you set the first three arguments to the same value in the `nameList` array and set the last two arguments to `True` for each name. Now Peedy will understand users if they speak any of the names found in the `nameList` array—`John`, `Jennifer` or `Howard`.

A **Command** event is raised when the user selects the command from the Commands pop-up window or speaks the command into a microphone. Command events are handled by the Command event handler of the Microsoft Agent control (`mainAgent`, in this example).

5. ***Defining the `callButton_Click` event handler.*** After defining the Form's Load event, you must create an event handler for the **Call Peedy** Button. When this Button is clicked, Peedy appears and interacts with the user. To create the **Call Peedy** Button's `Click` event handler, double click the **Call Peedy** Button in the Windows Form Designer. Insert lines 44–49 of Fig. 27.24.

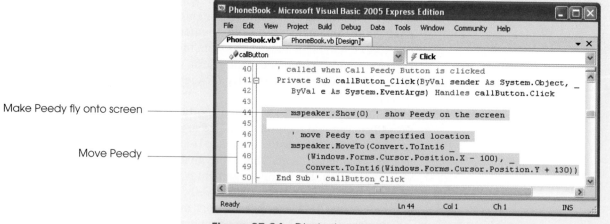

Make Peedy fly onto screen

Move Peedy

Figure 27.24   Displaying the Microsoft Agent character.

Line 44 uses the **Show** method to display Peedy on the screen. Specifying 0 as the argument makes Peedy fly onto the screen and land at his default location. If 1 is passed to the method, Peedy's image pops onto the screen at his default location (without the flying animation).

(cont.)

After the Show method is called, Peedy appears at (or flies to) the default position on the screen. The command in lines 47–49 causes Peedy to move to a new location. These lines use the **MoveTo** method of the mspeaker Agent object. Method MoveTo takes two arguments—an *x*-coordinate and a *y*-coordinate, both of type **Short**. The Short data type stores whole numbers like the Integer data type, but Short variables occupy less space in memory and therefore can store a smaller range of values. **Convert.ToInt16** converts the value of Cursor.Position.X - 100 to a Short value, where **Cursor.Position.X** contains the current position of the mouse pointer. We have subtracted 100 to specify a position that is 100 pixels to the left of the mouse pointer. The same was done for the *y*-coordinate. In this case, the method moves the Agent character 100 pixels to the left and 130 pixels below the mouse pointer at the time the **Call Peedy** Button is clicked. This keeps Peedy near the application Form.

6. ***Coding Peedy's greeting.*** Insert lines 51–61 of Fig. 27.25 into your Click event handler. Line 51 uses the **Play** method to command Peedy to perform an action. This method plays the character animation specified by the String argument that is passed. In this line, Peedy's Wave animation is played—he waves hello to the user. [*Note:* We use only a few of the Peedy character's available animations. To see a listing of the available animations, please visit `msdn.microsoft.com/library/default.asp?url=/library/en-us/msagent/peedy1st_53xw.asp`.]

Lines 54–59 call method **Speak** twice to specify what Peedy says. The argument passed to the Speak method contains the String that Peedy speaks by using the computer's speakers. This String also appears in a conversation balloon above his head. You have already seen an example of this in Fig. 27.4. In this example, you provide the instructions for using the **Phone Book** application. After Peedy displays the instructions, he is positioned in his rest pose (Fig. 27.5) by passing "RestPose" (line 61) to the Play method.

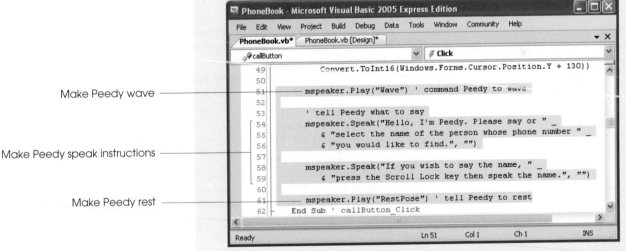

Make Peedy wave

Make Peedy speak instructions

Make Peedy rest

Figure 27.25 Code that defines Microsoft Agent's actions when Peedy first appears on the screen.

(cont.)

7. ***Enabling and disabling controls.*** Now that you have made the Agent character available by clicking the **Call Peedy** Button, you should disable the Button and allow the ComboBox to be used. Insert lines 63–64 of Fig. 27.26 into your `Click` event handler. These lines set `callButton`'s `Enabled` property to `False` and set `nameComboBox`'s `Enabled` property to `True` while the Agent character is on the screen. Recall that the ComboBox is disabled by default. You disable the **Call Peedy** Button because Peedy is on the screen at this point.

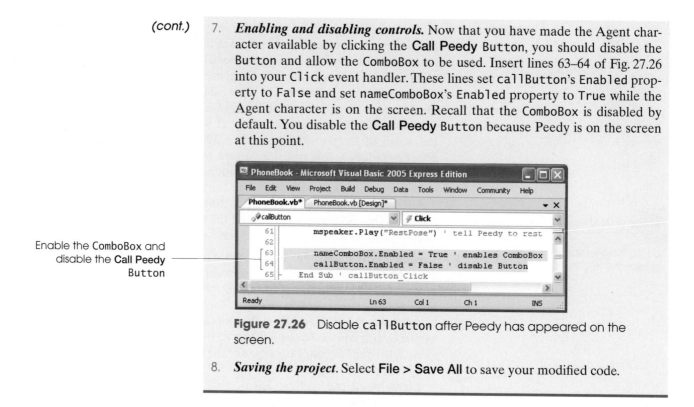

Enable the ComboBox and disable the **Call Peedy** Button

Figure 27.26 Disable `callButton` after Peedy has appeared on the screen.

8. ***Saving the project.*** Select **File > Save All** to save your modified code.

Now that you have written code to display Peedy on the screen and have him speak to the user, you must insert code that allows Peedy to respond to user input. Peedy needs to display and read a phone number when the user selects a valid name, either by speaking, by using the context menu or by using the ComboBox. You will enable these features in the following box.

Completing the Phone Book Application

1. ***Defining the `mainAgent_Command` event handler.*** Event handler `mainAgent_Command` runs when the Command event is raised. Recall that this happens when a user speaks a command to the Agent character by using the microphone (while pressing the *Scroll Lock* key). The event is also raised if the user selects a command from Peedy's context menu. You can generate the event handler by selecting `mainAgent` from the **Class Name** ComboBox and Command from the **Method Name** ComboBox. Insert lines 72–74 of Fig. 27.27 into this event handler.

Lines 73–74 declare the `commandObject` variable, which stores values of type **`AgentObjects.IAgentCtlUserInput`**. This object is used to retrieve the commands that users give Peedy. Note that you use function `CType` to convert the first argument to the type of object specified by the second argument. This line converts the user input to type `AgentObjects.IAgentCtl-UserInput`. You do this to access the name of the command the Agent received.

(cont.)

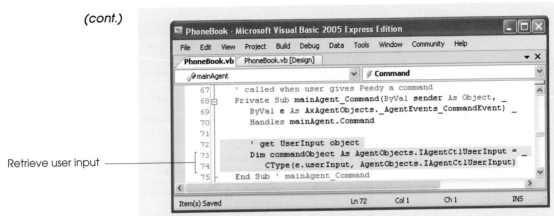

Figure 27.27 Event handler `mainAgent_Command` defined.

2. *Interpreting user input and displaying a phone number.* Insert lines 76–89 of Fig. 27.28 into your code. Line 76 creates a counter variable that is used in a For...Next statement (lines 81–89). The body of this statement contains an If...Then statement (lines 82–88). The code inside the If...Then statement executes if the user's command matches one of the voice-enabled commands you added earlier by using the `nameList` array. Using the counter variable, the For...Next statement iterates through each index of the array, comparing the command name (for example, `John`) to the name in the array. If the names match, the body of the If...Then statement plays Peedy's `Think` animation (line 83) and uses Peedy to speak and display the requested phone number (lines 84–86). After speaking the phone number, Peedy smiles (the `Pleased` animation played at line 87).

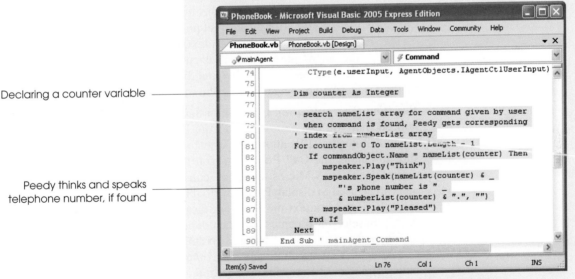

Figure 27.28 Finding the spoken or selected name.

3. *Creating the **nameComboBox_SelectedIndexChanged** event handler.* You must now write code to display a phone number if the user chooses a name from nameComboBox. Double click the ComboBox in the Windows Form Designer to generate the `nameComboBox_SelectedIndexChanged` event handler, and enter code view. Insert lines 97–111 of Fig. 27.29 into the event handler.

(cont.)

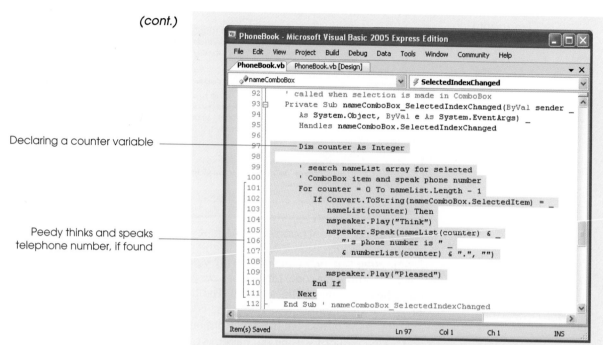

Declaring a counter variable

Peedy thinks and speaks
telephone number, if found

Figure 27.29 Event handler `nameComboBox_SelectedIndexChanged`.

This `ComboBox` allows users who are unable to access the voice-recognition engines to use the application. Much as in the `Command` event handler, lines 101–111 search the array for a `String` that matches the selected item in the `ComboBox`. If a match is found, then Peedy's `Think` animation plays (Fig. 27.7), and the phone number is provided. After Peedy states the number, his `Pleased` animation plays, indicating that he is content with his ability to provide the user with the correct phone number (Fig. 27.9).

The `nameComboBox_SelectedIndexChanged` method executes code similar to the `mainAgent_Command` event handler. The only difference is that the `Command` method is invoked by verbal requests, whereas this method is invoked by selecting items in the `nameComboBox`.

4. **Resetting the application's controls when Peedy is hidden.** You may have noticed that you can choose **Hide** from Peedy's context menu (when you right click Peedy). This allows the user to hide the Peedy character, but be sure to enable the **Call Peedy** Button to allow the user to make Peedy reappear. [*Note:* A Microsoft Agent icon also appears in your system tray and can be used to display Peedy by double clicking it, or by selecting **Show** from the icon's context menu.] Also, disable the `ComboBox` to prevent the user from selecting a name from the `ComboBox` while Peedy is hidden.

When the user selects **Hide**, a **HideEvent** is raised. To generate the `HideEvent` event handler, select `mainAgent` from the Class Name ComboBox and `HideEvent` from the Method Name ComboBox. Then insert lines 119–120 of Fig. 27.30 into the event handler. These lines enable the **Call Peedy** Button and disable the `ComboBox`.

5. **Running the application.** Select **Debug > Start Debugging** to run your application. Click the **Call Peedy** Button to display the Peedy Microsoft Agent character. Use Peedy to determine what phone numbers are stored in the application.

6. **Closing the application.** Close your running application by clicking its close box.

7. **Closing the IDE.** Close the Visual Basic IDE by clicking its close box.

(cont.)

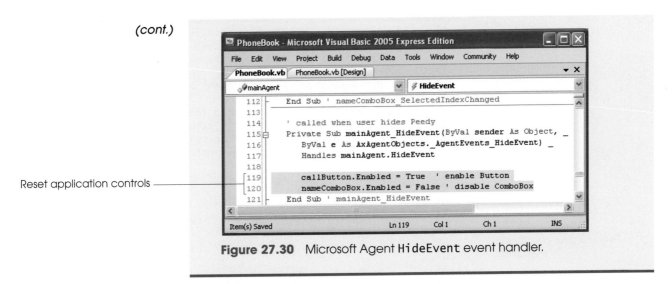

Figure 27.30 Microsoft Agent `HideEvent` event handler.

Figure 27.31 presents the source code for the **Phone Book** application. The lines of code that contain new programming concepts that you learned in this tutorial are highlighted.

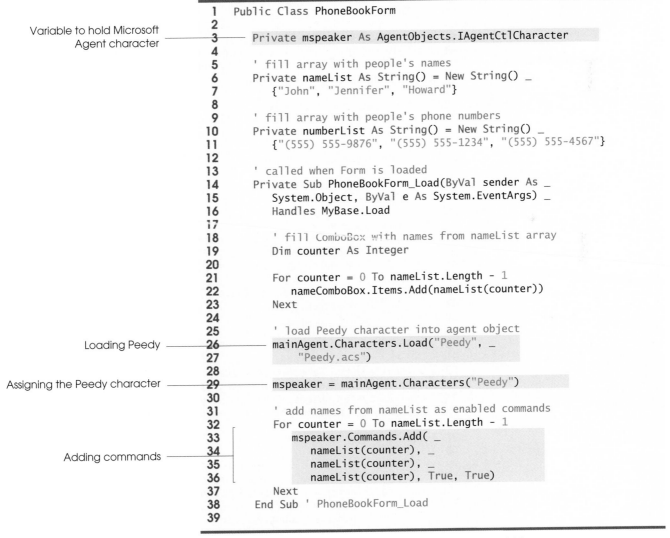

Figure 27.31 **Phone Book** application code. (Part 1 of 3.)

```vbnet
40      ' called when Call Peedy button is clicked
41      Private Sub callButton_Click(ByVal sender As System.Object, _
42         ByVal e As System.EventArgs) Handles callButton.Click
43
44         mspeaker.Show(0) ' show Peedy on the screen
45
46         ' move Peedy to a specified location
47         mspeaker.MoveTo(Convert.ToInt16 _
48            (Windows.Forms.Cursor.Position.X - 100), _
49            Convert.ToInt16(Windows.Forms.Cursor.Position.Y + 130))
50
51         mspeaker.Play("Wave") ' command Peedy to wave
52
53         ' tell Peedy what to say
54         mspeaker.Speak("Hello, I'm Peedy. Please say or " _
55            & "select the name of the person whose phone number " _
56            & "you would like to find.", "")
57
58         mspeaker.Speak("If you wish to say the name, " _
59            & "press the Scroll Lock key then speak the name.", "")
60
61         mspeaker.Play("RestPose") ' tell Peedy to rest
62
63         nameComboBox.Enabled = True ' enables ComboBox
64         callButton.Enabled = False ' disable Button
65      End Sub ' callButton_Click
66
67      ' called when user gives Peedy a command
68      Private Sub mainAgent_Command(ByVal sender As Object, _
69         ByVal e As AxAgentObjects._AgentEvents_CommandEvent) _
70         Handles mainAgent.Command
71
72         ' get UserInput object
73         Dim commandObject As AgentObjects.IAgentCtlUserInput =
74            CType(e.userInput, AgentObjects.IAgentCtlUserInput)
75
76         Dim counter As Integer
77
78         ' search nameList array for command given by user
79         ' when command is found, Peedy gets corresponding
80         ' index from numberList array
81         For counter = 0 To nameList.Length - 1
82            If commandObject.Name = nameList(counter) Then
83               mspeaker.Play("Think")
84               mspeaker.Speak(nameList(counter) & _
85                  "'s phone number is " _
86                  & numberList(counter) & ".", "")
87               mspeaker.Play("Pleased")
88            End If
89         Next
90      End Sub ' mainAgent_Command
91
92      ' called when selection is made in ComboBox
93      Private Sub nameComboBox_SelectedIndexChanged(ByVal sender _
94         As System.Object, ByVal e As System.EventArgs) _
95         Handles nameComboBox.SelectedIndexChanged
96
97         Dim counter As Integer
98
99         ' search nameList array for selected
100        ' ComboBox item and speak phone number
101        For counter = 0 To nameList.Length - 1
102           If Convert.ToString(nameComboBox.SelectedItem) = _
103              nameList(counter) Then
```

Labels (left margin):
- Showing Peedy → line 44
- Moving Peedy → lines 47–49
- Peedy waves and speaks instructions → lines 54–56
- Command event handler → lines 68–70

Figure 27.31 Phone Book application code. (Part 2 of 3.)

```
104              mspeaker.Play("Think")
105              mspeaker.Speak(nameList(counter) & _
106                "'s phone number is " _
107                & numberList(counter) & ".", "")
108
109              mspeaker.Play("Pleased")
110          End If
111        Next
112     End Sub ' nameComboBox_SelectedIndexChanged
113
114      ' called when user hides Peedy
115      Private Sub mainAgent_HideEvent(ByVal sender As Object, _
116        ByVal e As AxAgentObjects._AgentEvents_HideEvent) _
117        Handles mainAgent.HideEvent
118
119        callButton.Enabled = True   ' enable Button
120        nameComboBox.Enabled = False ' disable ComboBox
121      End Sub ' mainAgent_HideEvent
122  End Class ' PhoneBookForm
```

HideEvent event handler ──── (lines 115-117)

Figure 27.31   **Phone Book** application code. (Part 3 of 3.)

SELF-REVIEW

1. When Peedy is hidden, you can show him by _____.

   a) using method Show

   b) selecting **Show** from Peedy's tray icon context menu

   c) double clicking Peedy's tray icon   d) All of the above.

2. Method _____ is used to relocate the Microsoft Agent character on the screen.

   a) Move   b) Relocate

   c) MoveTo   d) Place

Answers: 1) d. 2) c.

27.5 Wrap-Up

In this tutorial, you were introduced to Microsoft Agent and learned how it can be used to enhance software applications. You learned what Microsoft Agent is used for and how to download all the necessary components. You then wrote code to use a Microsoft Agent character, Peedy the Parrot.

Using Peedy, you created an application that interacts with the user by listening to the user's commands and by answering using speech. You used the Show and MoveTo methods to show Peedy and move him on the screen. You also used Peedy's Speak method to speak instructions and phone numbers to the user. You then learned how to control Peedy's gestures, such as Wave and Think, not only to entertain the user but also to signal visually what the application is doing.

Tutorials 28–31 present you with a Web-based bookstore application case study. You will learn how to build an application that can be accessed by using a Web browser. In Tutorial 28, You will be introduced to the concept of a multi-tier application, and you will take your first steps toward building a three-tier application, which you will complete in the subsequent tutorials.

SKILLS SUMMARY

Adding a Control to the Toolbox

- Right click the **All Windows Forms** group in the **Toolbox**, then select **Choose Items....**
- In the **Choose Toolbox Items** dialog locate the control you wish to add then click its CheckBox to select the control.
- Click the **OK** Button. The control now appears in the **All Windows Forms** group in the **Toolbox**.

Displaying The Microsoft Agent to Users

- Load the desired Microsoft Agent, using the `Characters.Load` method.
- Call the Microsoft Agent object's Show method.

Allowing Verbal Communication with the Agent

- Add voice-enabled commands, using the Microsoft Agent's `Commands.Add` method.
- Define the Commands event handler.

Causing the Agent to Speak

- Call the Microsoft Agent's Speak method.
- Specify the `String` that the Microsoft Agent character should speak.

Causing Agent to Perform Actions

- Call the Microsoft Agent character's `Play` method.
- Specify the animation that the Microsoft Agent character should display.

KEY TERMS

Add method of the Commands property—Adds a command to a Microsoft Agent character.

AgentObject.IAgentCtlCharacter object—References a Microsoft Agent character.

AgentObject.IAgentCtlUserInput object—Stores the user input retrieved from a Microsoft Agent character.

Characters property of AxAgent control—Used to access a specific Microsoft Agent character.

Command event—Raised when a user speaks a command to a Microsoft Agent character or selects a command from a character's context menu.

Commands property—Sets which commands the Microsoft Agent character can understand as input from the user.

Convert.ToInt16 method—Converts data to type `Short`.

Cursor.Position property—Contains the *x*- and *y*-coordinates of the mouse cursor on the screen (in pixels).

HideEvent event—Raised when a Microsoft Agent character is hidden.

interactive animated characters—The Microsoft Agent technology adds such characters to Windows applications and Web pages. These characters can interact with the user through mouse clicks and microphone input.

Microsoft Agent—A technology used to add interactive animated characters to Windows applications and Web pages.

MoveTo method—Relocates the Microsoft Agent character on the screen.

multimedia—The use of various media, such as sound, video and animation, to create content in an application.

Play method—Plays a Microsoft Agent character animation.

Short data type—Variables of this type hold small integer values.

Show method—Displays a Microsoft Agent character on the screen.

Speak method—Used to have the Microsoft Agent character speak text to the user.

speech-recognition engine—Application that translates vocal sound input from a microphone into a language that the computer understands.

status box—A box that appears below a Microsoft agent character that displays information about the character's actions.

text-to-speech engine—Application that translates typed words into spoken sound that users hear through headphones or speakers connected to a computer.

GUI DESIGN GUIDELINES

Microsoft Agent Control

- Locate the Microsoft Agent character near the application Form.
- Use Microsoft Agent character gestures to indicate actions the user should take, or a response to an action the user has already taken.

CONTROLS, EVENTS, PROPERTIES & METHODS

Convert The Convert class converts the value of a data type to another data type.

- *Methods*

  ToChar—Converts a value into a character (of data type Char).

  ToDecimal—Converts the value from another data type to type Decimal.

  ToInt16—Converts the value from another data type to type Short.

  ToInteger—Converts the value from another data type to type Integer.

  ToDouble—Converts the value from another data type to type Double.

  ToString—Converts the value from another data type to type String.

IAgentCtlCharacter This class is used to represent the Agent character that is used in the application.

- *Property*

  Commands—Contains the commands the character will recognize.

- *Methods*

  Show—Displays the character on the screen.

  MoveTo—Moves the character to a specified location on the screen.

  Play—Plays character animations.

  Speak—Specifies the text to be spoken by the character.

  Commands.Add—Adds a new command to the command list for the Agent object.

IAgentCtlUserInput This class is used to retrieve commands from users.

- *Property*

  Name—Retrieves the name of the command given by the user.

Microsoft Agent Control　　🦃 Microsoft Agent Control 2.0　　This control is used to create and manipulate the multimedia features of a Microsoft Agent character.

- *In action*

- *Events*

  Command—Raised when a user gives the Microsoft Agent character a verbal command or selects an option from the character's context menu.

  HideEvent—Raised when a user hides the Microsoft Agent character.

- *Property*

  Location—Specifies the location of the Microsoft Agent control on the Form.

- *Method*

  Characters.Load—Loads a character into the Microsoft Agent control.

MULTIPLE-CHOICE QUESTIONS

27.1 The _____ method is used to specify what the Microsoft Agent will say.

  a) Speak　　　　　　　　　　b) Say

  c) Command　　　　　　　　d) Voice

27.2 The _____ method is used to activate a Microsoft Agent character's animation.

  a) Show　　　　　　　　　　b) Play

  c) Speak　　　　　　　　　　d) Appear

27.3 Method MoveTo takes two arguments. What do these arguments represent?

a) The direction in which the Agent is to move (left, right, up, down).

b) The name of the character and its position.

c) The *x*-coordinate and *y*-coordinate of the location to which the Agent is to move.

d) The name of the character and the direction of movement.

27.4 Which method of IAgentCtlCharacter displays the Microsoft Agent character on the screen?

a) Play

b) Show

c) Speak

d) Appear

27.5 Use the _____ event handler to execute code when users click **Hide** the Agent character context menu.

a) Hide

b) HideEvent

c) Command

d) Disappear

27.6 The Add method of the Commands property _____.

a) adds a new command to the command list

b) joins two commands together

c) displays the Commands pop-up window

d) Both a and c.

27.7 The _____ event handler controls what occurs when users speak to the Agent.

a) Command

b) ClickEvent

c) Click

d) SelectedIndexChanged

27.8 _____ specifies the *x*-coordinate of the mouse cursor on the screen.

a) Cursor.Location.X

b) Cursor.Position.X

c) Mouse.Location.X

d) Mouse.Position.X

27.9 Specifying _____ as a parameter to Peedy's Play method causes him to smile.

a) "Think"

b) "Smile"

c) "Pleased"

d) "Happy"

27.10 Specifying _____ as a parameter to Peedy's Play method causes him to rest.

a) "RestPose"

b) "Rest"

c) "Think"

d) "Pose"

EXERCISES

27.11 (*Appointment Book Application Using Microsoft Agent*) Write an application that allows users to add appointments to an appointment book that uses Microsoft Agent. When the user speaks a person's name, Merlin returns the time and date of the appointment the user has with that person. If the user says "Today," Merlin returns a list of the user's appointments for the day.

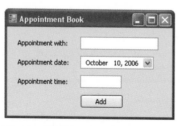

Figure 27.32 Appointment Book GUI.

a) *Downloading the Merlin Microsoft Agent.* Download the Merlin.acs character file from the Microsoft Web site.

b) *Copying the template to your working directory.* Copy the directory C:\Examples\Tutorial27\Exercises\AppointmentBook to your C:\SimplyVB directory.

c) *Opening the application's template file.* Double click AppointmentBook.sln in the AppointmentBook directory to open the application.

d) *Adding the Agent Control to the Form.* Add the Microsoft Agent control to the Form.

e) *Creating module-level variables.* Create three module-level variables of type Array-List to store the date, time and person with whom the user has an appointment. Create a module-level variable of type AgentObjects.IAgentCtlCharacter (as you did in the **Phone Book** application).

f) *Defining the AppointmentsForm_Load event handler.* Load Merlin's character file, display him on the screen and add the "Today" command to the command list.

g) *Defining the addButton_Click event handler.* Define this event handler so that the information provided by the user is added to its corresponding ArrayList. The **Appointment With:** TextBox input should be added to the ArrayList containing the names of people with whom the user has an appointment. The inputs for the appointment date and time should also be added to their respective ArrayLists. Display an error message if the user leaves the **Appointment With:** or the **Appointment Time:** TextBox empty.

h) *Adding voice-enabled commands.* Within the addButton_Click event handler, add a voice-enabled command to the command list that allows the user to speak a name of the person with whom the user has an appointment. This allows the user to check whether there is an appointment with someone by speaking the person's name. The command should also appear in the Commands context menu.

i) *Defining the Agent's Command event handler.* As you did in the **Phone Book** application, define what occurs when a user speaks or selects a command. If the user specifies the Today command, Merlin should tell the user the names of all the people with whom the user has an appointment today. If the user specifies a specific name, Merlin should state the time and date of the user's appointment with this person. If the user did not schedule any appointments, then Merlin should inform the user that no appointments were scheduled.

j) *Running the application.* Select **Debug > Start Debugging** to run your application. Enter various appointments, at least two of which are scheduled for the current day. Input the name of the person you are meeting at one of the appointments by either speaking the name into your microphone or right clicking the agent and selecting that person's name. Verify that the agent repeats back correct information about the appointment. Input the value "Today" by either speaking it into the microphone or right clicking the agent and selecting **Today**. Verify that the agent repeats back all the appointments for the current day.

k) *Closing the application.* Close your running application by clicking its close box.

l) *Closing the IDE.* Close the Visual Basic IDE by clicking its close box.

27.12 (*Modified Craps Game Application Using Microsoft Agent*) Modify the **Craps Game** application from Tutorial 16 to include a Microsoft Agent character.

Figure 27.33 Modified **Craps Game** GUI.

a) *Downloading the Genie Microsoft Agent.* Download the Genie.acs character file from the Microsoft Web site.

b) *Copying the template to your working directory.* Copy the directory C:\Examples\Tutorial27\Exercises\CrapsGameEnhancement to your C:\SimplyVB directory.

c) *Opening the application's template file.* Double click CrapsGame.sln in the Craps-GameEnhancement directory to open the application.

d) *Adding the Agent control to the Form.* Add the Microsoft Agent control to the Form.

e) *Creating a module-level variable.* Create a module-level variable of type AgentObjects.IAgentCtlCharacter (as you did in the **Phone Book** application).

f) *Defining the CrapsGameForm_Load event handler.* Load Genie's character file, and display him on the screen.

g) *Modifying the playButton_Click event handler.* Add code to the playButton_Click event handler to control the Agent. When the user wins the game, Genie should play his Pleased animation and congratulate the user. If the user loses, Genie should play his Confused animation and say that the user has lost. If the user neither wins nor loses, Genie should tell the user to roll again. Make sure to reset him to his RestPose after he plays any animation.

h) *Defining the rollButton_Click event handler.* Add code to the rollButton_Click event handler to control the Agent. If the user "makes the point," Genie should play his Pleased animation and state that the user has won. If the user rolls a 7, Genie should play his Confused animation and say that the user has lost. Otherwise, Genie should tell the user to roll again.

i) *Defining the instructionsButton_Click event handler.* Define event handler instructionsButton_Click to make Genie wave, introduce himself to the user and then explain the rules of the game of craps.

j) *Running the application.* Select **Debug > Start Debugging** to run your application. Click the **Instructions** Button and allow the Agent character to tell you the rules of the game. Use the **Play** and **Roll** Buttons to play a few games of craps. When you need to roll again, verify that the Agent tells you to roll again. Also verify that the Agent informs you whether you have won or lost at the end of each game.

k) *Closing the application.* Close your running application by clicking its close box.

l) *Closing the IDE.* Close the Visual Basic IDE by clicking its close box.

27.13 (*Modified Security Panel Application Using Microsoft Agent*) Modify the **Security Panel** application from Tutorial 12 to include Microsoft Agent.

 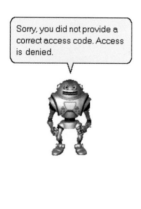

Figure 27.34 Robby from modified **Security Panel** application.

a) *Downloading the Robby Microsoft Agent.* Download the Robby.acs character file from the Microsoft Web site.

b) *Copying the template to your working directory.* Copy the directory C:\Examples\Tutorial27\Exercises\SecurityPanelEnhancement to your C:\SimplyVB directory.

c) *Opening the application's template file.* Double click SecurityPanel.sln in the SecurityPanelEnhancement directory to open the application.

d) *Adding the Agent control to the Form.* Add the Microsoft Agent control to the Form.

e) *Creating a module-level variable.* Create a module-level variable of type AgentObjects.IAgentCtlCharacter (as you did in the **Phone Book** application).

f) *Defining the SecurityPanelForm_Load event handler.* Load Robby's character file, and display him on the screen. Command Robby to tell users to input their access codes.

g) *Modifying the enterButton_Click event handler.* Add code to the enter-Button_Click event handler to use the Microsoft Agent. If the user enters a valid access code, Robby should welcome the user and state the type of employee that the access code represents. If the access code is invalid, then Robby should state that an invalid code was provided and access is denied.

h) *Running the application.* Select **Debug > Start Debugging** to run your application. Enter various access codes. For correct access codes, verify that the Agent tells you what type of employee the access code represents. For incorrect access codes, verify that the Agent tells you that access is denied.

i) *Closing the application.* Close your running application by clicking its close box.

j) *Closing the IDE.* Close the Visual Basic IDE by clicking its close box.

What does this code do? ▶ **27.14** After the user clicks the **Call** Button, what does the following event handler do?

```
1   Private Sub callButton_Click(ByVal sender As System.Object, _
2      ByVal e As System.EventArgs) Handles callButton.Click
3
4      mainAgent.Characters.Load("Genie", "Genie.acs")
5
6      mspeaker = mainAgent.Characters("Genie")
7
8      mspeaker.Show(0)
9
10     mspeaker.Speak("Hello, I'm Genie the special agent!")
11
12  End Sub
```

What's wrong with this code? ▶ **27.15** Find the error(s) in the following code. The event handler should have an Agent object appear and say, "Hello, my name is Merlin." This should happen when the user clicks the **Call** Button.

```
1   Private Sub callButton_Click(ByVal sender As System.Object, _
2      ByVal e As System.EventArgs) Handles callButton.Click
3
4      mainAgent.Characters.Load("Merlin", "Merlin.acs")
5
6      mspeaker = mainAgent.Characters("Merlin")
7
8      Dim number As Integer = 10
9
10     mspeaker.Show(number)
11
12     mspeaker.Play("Hello, my name is Merlin")
13
14  End Sub
```

Programming Challenge ▶ **27.16** (*Enhanced Car Payment Application Using Microsoft Agent*) Enhance the **Car Payment Calculator** application from Tutorial 9 to use the Microsoft Agent, Robby. When the application is executed, Robby should appear on the screen, wave to the user and explain the purpose of the application. After the user enters information into each field of the **Car Payment Calculator** and clicks the **Calculate** Button, Robby should speak the calculated payment amounts and the period (number of months) over which they were calculated. The C:\Examples\Tutorial27\ Exercises\CarPaymentCalculatorEnhancement directory contains the template for this exercise. Copy it to your working directory and open the application to begin the exercise.

28

Bookstore Application: Web Applications

Introducing Visual Web Developer 2005 Express and the ASP.NET Development Server

In previous tutorials, you used Visual Basic to develop Windows applications. These applications contained a GUI with which the user interacted. You can use Visual Basic and Visual Web Developer 2005 Express to create **Web applications**. These applications, also known as Web-based applications, use Visual Basic and Microsoft's **ASP.NET 2.0 technology** to create Web content (data that can be viewed in a Web browser such as Internet Explorer). This Web content includes HTML (HyperText Markup Language) documents and images.

In this tutorial, you will learn important Web-development concepts in the context of the **Bookstore** application. This application consists of two Web pages. The first page displays a list of books. The user selects a book then clicks a Button to direct the browser to a second Web page. In the second page, the server retrieves information about the selected book from a database then that information is displayed for the user in the Web browser. The second Web page also contains a Button that the user can click to return to the first Web page, where the user can then select a different book. After learning the fundamental Web development concepts that are required to understand the **Bookstore** application, you will test-drive the application. In Tutorials 29–31, you will analyze the pseudocode and ACE table and develop the **Bookstore** application.

28.1 Multi-Tier Architecture

Web applications are **multi-tier applications**, sometimes referred to as *n*-tier **applications**. Multi-tier applications divide functionality into separate **tiers** (that is, logical groupings of functionality). The separate tiers of an application can be located on the same computer or on separate computers distributed across any computer network, including the Internet. Figure 28.1 illustrates the basic structure of a multi-tier application.

The **information tier** (also called the **data tier** or the **bottom tier**) maintains data for the application. The information tier for the **Bookstore** application is represented by a SQL Server 2005 Express database that contains book titles, author names, copyright dates, edition numbers, ISBN numbers, book descriptions and file names for each book's cover image.

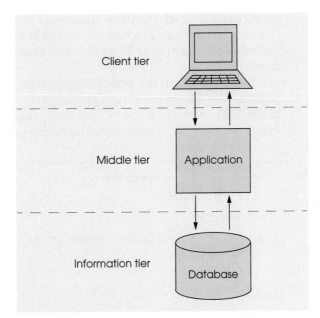

Figure 28.1   Three-tier application model.

The **middle tier**, also called the **business logic** tier, controls interactions between application clients (such as Web browsers) and application data in the information tier. In the **Bookstore** application, the middle-tier code determines which book was selected and which book's information is retrieved from the database. The middle-tier code also determines how the selected book's data will be displayed. The middle tier processes client requests (for example, a request to view a book's information) from the top tier, which we define shortly, and retrieves data from the database (author names, prices, descriptions, etc.) in the information tier. The middle tier then processes data and presents the content to the client. In other words, the middle tier represents the functionality of the Web application.

The **client tier**, or **top tier**, is the application's user interface, which is typically a Web browser. In the **Bookstore** application, the client tier is represented by the pages displayed in the Web browser. The user interacts directly with the **Bookstore** application through the client tier (browser) by selecting from a list and clicking Buttons. The browser reports the user's actions to the middle tier which processes the information. The middle tier can also make requests to and retrieve data from the information tier. The client tier then displays to the user the data retrieved by the middle tier from the information tier.

SELF-REVIEW

1. A database is located in the _____ tier.
   a) top
   b) middle
   c) bottom
   d) client

2. The role of the middle tier is to _____.
   a) display the application's user interface
   b) provide a database for the application
   c) control the interaction between the client and information tiers
   d) control the interaction between the client and the user interface

Answers: 1) c. 2) c.

28.2 Web Servers

A **Web server** is specialized software that responds to client (Web browser) requests by providing requested resources (such as HTML documents). To request documents from Web servers, users must know the locations at which those documents reside. A **URL** (**Uniform Resource Locator**) can be thought of as an address that directs a browser to a resource on the Web. A URL contains a computer name (called a **host name**) or an IP address that identifies the computer on which the Web server resides.

When you access the **Bookstore** application, you provide a URL in a browser to locate the Web pages of the application. In this tutorial, you will use `localhost` in the URL, which is a special host name that identifies the local computer. Normally, you access Web applications through a host name such as `www.deitel.com`.

28.3 Visual Web Developer 2005 Express and the ASP.NET Development Server

In Tutorial 28–Tutorial 31, you will use **Visual Web Developer 2005 Express** (which we'll refer to as Visual Web Developer from this point forward) to test drive and build the **Bookstore** application. Visual Web Developer comes with the **ASP.NET Development Server**—a Web server you can use to test your ASP.NET Web applications. The ASP.NET Development Server is specifically designed for learning and testing purposes to execute Web applications on the local computer and to respond to browser requests from the local computer. Thus, you do not need to be connected to a network to learn Web application development techniques. Unfortunately, the ASP.NET Development Server cannot respond to requests from other computers. After successfully creating an ASP.NET Web application, it is possible to use Visual Web Developer's "Copy Web Site" capability to publish your application to a Microsoft **Internet Information Services (IIS)** Web server so that your application can receive requests from any client on the Web. Since the Web application you will build uses ASP.NET 2.0, the server must have the .NET framework version 2.0 installed.

28.4 Test-Driving the Bookstore Application

In the next three tutorials, you will build an application that displays book information to users upon request. Your **Bookstore** application must meet the following requirements:

> **Application Requirements**
>
> *A bookstore employee receives e-mails from customers asking for information pertaining to the books the store provides online. Responding to the numerous e-mails can be a tedious and time-consuming task. The employee has asked you to create a Web application that allows users to view information about various books online. This information includes the book cover image, author(s), ISBN number, edition number, copyright date and a brief description of the book.*

The **Bookstore** application uses ASP.NET and is designed to allow users to view information about the books offered by the store. You begin by test-driving the completed application. Then, you will learn the additional ASP.NET technologies that you will need to create your own version of this application.

**Test-Driving the
Completed Web-Based
Bookstore Application**

1. ***Opening the Bookstore project.*** In Visual Web Developer, select **File > Open Web Site...** to display the **Open Web Site** dialog. In the dialog that appears, click the **File System** button, browse to `C:\Examples\Tutorial28\CompletedApplication` and select the **Bookstore** folder that contains the Web application. Then click the **Open** button.

2. ***Setting the start page.*** The start page is the first page that loads when you execute the application. To specify the start page, right click the `Books.aspx` file in the **Solution Explorer**, and select **Set As Start Page** (Fig. 28.2). Files with the extension `.aspx` (usually referred to as **Web Forms**, **Web Form Pages** or **ASPX pages**) contain the Web page's GUI. The Web Form file represents the Web page that is sent to the client browser. [*Note:* From this point onward, we refer to Web Form files as ASPX pages.] A Web application can contain several ASPX pages. In this example, `Books.aspx` displays the available books to the user. The page `BookInformation.aspx` displays information about the selected book. You must set `Books.aspx` to appear first so the user can select a book.

Right click the `Books.aspx` page

Select this option to set the start page

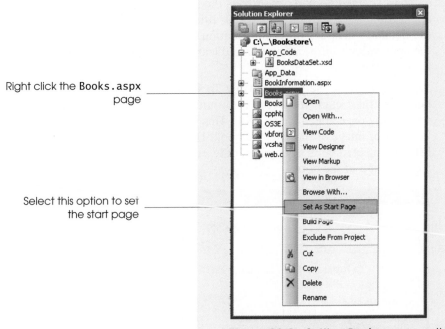

Figure 28.2 Setting `Books.aspx` as the Web application's start page.

3. ***Running the application.*** Select **Debug > Start Debugging** to run the application. The `Books.aspx` page appears in Internet Explorer, as shown in Fig. 28.3. This page displays a `ListBox` containing the available books. Although this `ListBox` looks similar to the `ListBox` control you have used in Windows applications, this `ListBox` is actually a **Web control** (also called an **ASP.NET server control**). Programmers customize ASPX pages by adding Web controls, such as `Labels`, `TextBoxes`, `Buttons` and other GUI components. As you will learn, Web controls look similar to their Windows application counterparts.

Internet Explorer and its HTML content represent the client tier. In Tutorial 29, you will add Web controls, such as `Labels` to display text, a `ListBox` to display the list of available books, `Buttons` to load a different page and a `Table` to display information on a particular book.

(cont.)

Location of `Books.aspx` page

Label controls

ListBox control containing available books

Button control

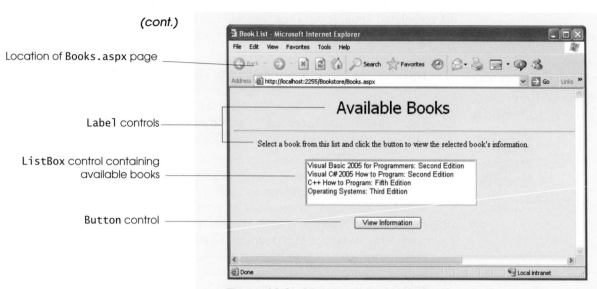

Figure 28.3 Page that displays a list of available books.

The books displayed in the `ListBox` are retrieved from a database. The database, named `Bookstore.mdf`, is the information tier of this three-tier application. Although only the book titles are displayed in the `ListBox`, the database includes other information. In Tutorial 30, you will examine the application's information tier and learn how to connect to the database to access the data.

4. *Selecting a book.* Select **C++ How To Program: Fifth Edition** from the book list then click the **View Information** Button. The `BookInformation.aspx` page appears (Fig. 28.4). This page displays the title, author and book cover image of the selected book. This page also contains a table that lists the selected book's copyright date, edition number, ISBN number and a description of the book.

Location of `BookInformation.aspx` page

When clicked, this Button returns user to `Books.aspx`

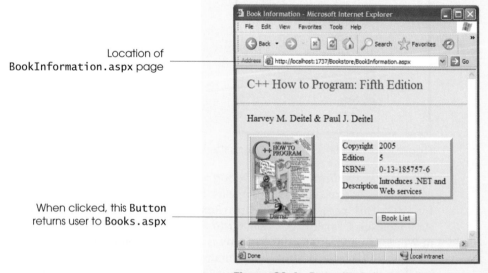

Figure 28.4 Page that displays the selected book's information.

(cont.)

5. ***Returning to Books.aspx.*** After viewing a book's information, users can decide whether they wish to view another book's information. The bottom of this page contains a **Book List** Button that, when clicked, redirects the browser back to the Books.aspx page to redisplay the list of book titles. If you'd like to view information for another book, select a book title then click the **View Information** Button.

6. ***Closing the browser.*** Click the browser's close box to close the browser window. This terminates debugging in Visual Web Developer.

7. ***Closing the IDE.*** Close Visual Basic 2005 by clicking its close box.

This example uses all three tiers of a three-tier application. The information tier is the database from which the application retrieves book information. The middle tier is the code that controls what happens when users interact with the application's Web pages. The client tier is represented by the Web pages in which the user selects books and views their information.

SELF-REVIEW

1. Web controls also are called _____.
   a) ASP.NET server controls
   b) ASP controls
   c) HTML controls
   d) None of the above.

2. In real-world ASP .NET applications, typically clients are _____ that request ASPX pages that reside on Web servers.
   a) Web Form pages
   b) Web controls
   c) Web browsers
   d) None of the above.

Answers: 1) a. 2) c.

28.5 Wrap-Up

In this tutorial, you learned about the components of a three-tier application. You were introduced to the information tier, which maintains the data for the application. You then learned about the client tier, which displays the application's user interface, and the middle tier, which provides the communication between the information and client tiers. Next, you were introduced to Visual Web Developer 2005 Express and its built-in ASP.NET Development Server, which enable you to build and test Web applications on your local computer. You then test-drove the three-tier **Bookstore** application. In doing this, you learned how to run ASP.NET Web-based applications. You were also introduced to ASPX pages, and you learned that Web controls are used to customize these pages.

In the next tutorial, you will create the user interface for this application. You will design the Web pages that display the book list and book information. You will then proceed to Tutorial 30, **Bookstore** Application: Information Tier. This tutorial describes the database used in the application and provides a step-by-step discussion of how the application connects to the database. Our discussion of the **Bookstore** application concludes with Tutorial 31, **Bookstore** Application: Middle Tier where you will build the **Bookstore** application logic.

SKILLS SUMMARY   Opening an Existing Web application in Visual Web Developer 2005 Express

- Launch Visual Web Developer 2005 Express.
- Select **File > Open Web Site...**.

- In the **Open Web Site** dialog, click the **File System** button, then browse to the directory that contains the Web application.
- Select the Web application's directory and click the **Open** button.

Setting the Start Page for a Web Application

- Open the Web application in Visual Web Developer 2005 Express.
- Right click the start page in the **Solution Explorer** window.
- Select **Set As Start Page**.

Testing the Web Application on `localhost`, Using Visual Web Developer 2005

- Open the application in Visual Web Developer 2005.
- Select **Debug > Start Debugging** to run the application.

KEY TERMS

ASP.NET Development Server—A Web server that you can use to test your ASP.NET Web applications. It is specifically designed for learning and testing purposes to execute Web applications on the local computer and to respond to browser requests from the local computer.

ASP.NET 2.0 technology—Can be combined with Visual Basic to create web applications.

ASP.NET server control—Another name for a Web control.

.aspx extension—The filename extension for ASPX pages.

ASPX page—File that specifies the GUI of a Web page using Web controls. Also called Web Forms or Web Form Pages.

bottom tier—The tier (also known as the information tier, or the data tier) containing the application data of a multi-tier application—typically implemented as a database

business logic tier—The tier that controls interaction between the client and information tiers. Also called the middle tier.

client tier—The user interface of a multi-tier application (also called the top tier).

data tier—The tier (also known as the information tier, or the bottom tier) containing the application data of a multi-tier application—typically implemented as a database.

host name—Name of a computer where resources reside.

information tier—Tier containing the application data; typically implemented as a database. Also called the bottom tier or data tier.

Internet Information Services (IIS)—A Microsoft Web server.

IP address—Unique address used to locate a computer on the Internet.

localhost—Host name that identifies the local computer.

middle tier—Tier that controls interaction between the client and information tiers (also called the business logic tier).

multi-tier application—Application (sometimes referred to as an *n*-tier application) whose functionality is divided into separate tiers, which can be on the same machine or can be distributed to separate machines across a network.

n-tier application—Another name for multi-tier applications.

top tier—Tier containing the application's user interface. Also called the client tier.

uniform resource locator (URL)—Address that can be used to direct a browser to a resource on the Web.

Visual Web Developer 2005 Express—A Microsoft tool for building ASP.NET 2.0 Web Applications.

Web applications—Applications that create web content.

Web controls—Controls, such as TextBoxes and Buttons, that are used to customize ASPX pages.

Web Form—Another name for an ASPX page.

Web Form Page—Another name for an ASPX page.

Web server—Specialized software that responds to client requests by providing resources.

MULTIPLE-CHOICE QUESTIONS

28.1 ASPX pages have the _____ extension.
a) `.html`
b) `.wbform`
c) `.vbaspx`
d) `.aspx`

28.2 _____ applications divide functionality into separate tiers.
a) *n*-tier
b) Multi-tier
c) Both a and b.
d) None of the above.

28.3 All tiers of a multi-tier application _____.
a) must be located on the same computer
b) must be located on different computers
c) can be located on the same computer or on different computers
d) must be arranged so that the client and middle tier are on the same computer and the information tier is on a different computer

28.4 The client tier interacts with the _____ tier to access information from the _____ tier.
a) middle; information
b) information; middle
c) information; bottom
d) bottom; information

28.5 A _____ is software that responds to client requests by providing resources.
a) Web server
b) host name
c) Both a and b.
d) None of the above.

28.6 A(n) _____ can be thought of as an address that is used to direct a browser to a resource on the Web.
a) middle tier
b) ASPX page
c) URL
d) query string

28.7 _____ is a Web server.
a) IIS
b) Visual Web Developer 2005 Express
c) Both a and b.
d) None of the above.

28.8 The _____ tier is the application's user interface.
a) middle
b) client
c) bottom
d) information

28.9 The _____ tier contains the application's functionality.
a) middle
b) client
c) top
d) information

28.10 The _____ tier contains the application's data.
a) middle
b) client
c) top
d) information

EXERCISES

28.11 (*Phone Book Application*) Over the next three tutorials, you will create a **Phone-Book** application. This phone book should be a Web-based version of the **PhoneBook** application created in Tutorial 27. [*Note*: This Web application will not use Microsoft Agent.] The **PhoneBook** application should consist of two ASPX pages, which will be named PhoneBook and PhoneNumber. The PhoneBook page displays a DropDownList (a Web control similar to a ComboBox Windows Form control) that contains the names of several people. The names are retrieved from the Phone.mdf database. When a name is selected and the **Get Number** Button is clicked, the client browser is redirected to the PhoneNumber page. The telephone number of the selected name should be retrieved from a database and displayed in a Label on the PhoneNumber page. For this exercise, you need only organize the components (PhoneBook and PhoneNumber ASPX pages, Phone.mdf database and the code that performs the specified functionality) of this Web application into separate tiers. Decide which components belong in which tiers. You will begin building the solution, using Visual Web Developer 2005 Express, in the next tutorial.

28.12 (*US State Facts Application*) Over the next three tutorials, you will create a **US State Facts** application. This application is designed to allow users to review their knowledge about specific U.S. states. This application should consist of two ASPX pages. The first page (named States) should display a ListBox containing 10 different state names. These state names are stored in the StateFacts.mdf database. The user should be allowed to select a state name and click a Button to retrieve information about the selected state from the database. The information should be displayed on a different ASPX page (named StateFacts). The StateFacts page should display an image of the state flag and list the state capital, state flower, state tree and state bird (retrieved from the database) in a Table. You will be provided with images of the state flags. For this exercise, you need only organize the components (States and StateFacts ASPX pages, StateFacts.mdf database and the code that performs the specified functionality) of this Web application into separate tiers. Decide which components belong in which tiers. You will begin building the solution, using Visual Web Developer 2005 Express, in the next tutorial.

Bookstore Application: Client Tier

Introducing Web Controls

In this tutorial, you will create the client tier (user interface) of your three-tier **Bookstore** application, using visual-programming techniques. You will begin by creating the application's project—an ASP.NET Web Site project. You then will learn about Web controls by creating the application's GUI.

29.1 Analyzing the Bookstore Application

Now that you have taken the three-tier **Bookstore** application (in Tutorial 28) for a test-drive, you need to analyze the application components. The following pseudocode describes the basic operation of the **Bookstore** application:

> When the Books page is requested
>> Retrieve the book titles from the database
>> Display book titles in a ListBox
>
> When the user selects a book title from the ListBox and clicks the View Information Button
>> Store the selected book in a variable
>> Redirect the user to the BookInformation page
>
> When the BookInformation page is requested
>> Retrieve the selected book's information from a database
>> Display the book title in a Label
>> Display the authors in a Label
>> Display the cover art in an Image
>> Display the remaining information in a DetailsView table
>
> When the user presses the Book List Button on the BookInformation page
>> Redirect the client browser back to the Books page

The ACE table in Fig. 29.1 lists the actions, controls and events that will help you complete your own version of this application.

679

Action/Control/Event (ACE) Table for the Web-Based Bookstore Application

Action	Control/Object	Event
Label the Books page	`availableLabel`, `instructionsLabel`	
	`Page`	`Load` (for `Books.aspx`)
Display book titles in a ListBox	`bookTitlesListBox`	
	`informationButton`	`Click`
Store the selected book in a variable	`Session`	
Redirect the user to the BookInformation page	`Response`	
	`Page`	`Load` (for `BookInformation.aspx`)
Retrieve the selected book's information from a database	`ProductsTableAdapter`, `ProductsDataTable`, `Session`	
Display the book title in a Label	`bookTitleLabel`	
Display the authors in a Label	`authorsLabel`	
Display the cover art in an image	`bookImage`	
Display the remaining information in a Table	`bookDetailsView`	
	`bookListButton`	`Click`
Redirect the client browser back to the Books page	`Response`	

Figure 29.1 ACE table for the Web-based **Bookstore** application.

29.2 Creating ASPX Pages

Now that you have been introduced to Visual Web Developer, the ASP.NET Development Server and three-tier Web-based application concepts, you will begin creating the **Bookstore** application that you test-drove in the last tutorial.

This Web-based application allows users to view information about books they select. After viewing a book's information, users can return to the page containing the list of books and select another book. You will create the ASP.NET Web application project for the **Bookstore** in the following box.

Creating an ASP.NET Web Application

1. ***Creating the project.*** In Visual Web Developer, select **File > New Web Site...** to display the **New Web Site** dialog (Fig. 29.2). In this dialog, select **ASP.NET Web Site** in the **Templates:** pane. Then select **File System** in the **Location:** drop-down list to create a Web application on your local disk drive. You can specify the location of the project in the **Location:** TextBox. To create a **Bookstore** folder in the **C:\SimplyVB** directory to store your new Web Site, type `C:\SimplyVB\Bookstore` in the **Location:** TextBox. Select **Visual Basic** in the **Language:** TextBox to use Visual Basic to program in the **code-behind files**. The code-behind files provide the ASPX page's functionality and will be discussed further in Tutorial 31. Then click **OK**.

(cont.)

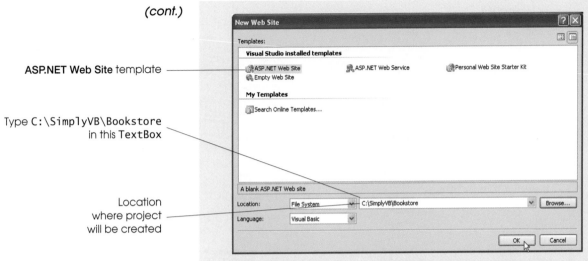

ASP.NET Web Site template ⎯⎯⎯⎯⎯

Type C:\SimplyVB\Bookstore
in this TextBox

Location
where project
will be created

Figure 29.2   Creating an **ASP.NET Web Application** in Visual Studio .NET.

2. *Examining the project files.* The **Solution Explorer** window for the **Bookstore** application is shown in Fig. 29.3. As with Windows applications, Visual Web Developer creates several files for each new **ASP.NET Web Application** project. Default.aspx is the default name for the ASPX page.

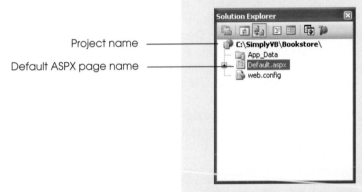

Project name ⎯⎯⎯⎯⎯

Default ASPX page name ⎯⎯⎯⎯⎯

Figure 29.3   **Solution Explorer** window for the Bookstore project.

3. *Viewing the Toolbox.* ASPX pages can be customized by using **Web controls**, which are used in ASPX pages in much the same way as Windows controls are used for Windows Forms. You'll use Web controls to create the user interface of your **Bookstore** application. Figure 29.4 shows the **Standard** controls listed in the **Toolbox**. If the **Toolbox** is not currently displayed, Select **View > Toolbox**.

The left part of the figure displays the beginning of the Web controls list, and the right part of the figure displays the remaining Web control groups. Note that some of the control icons, such as Label, TextBox and Button, are the same as the Windows controls presented earlier in the book. Although some of these control names look the same, the functionality provided by Web controls is different. Web controls can be used only with ASPX pages.

(cont.)

Standard tab ——

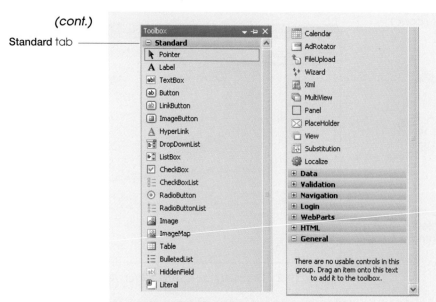

Figure 29.4 **Web Forms** tab in **Toolbox**.

4. *Viewing the ASPX page in Design mode.* When you create a Web application, an ASPX page will be displayed in the **Web Form Designer** (Fig. 29.5). [*Note:* We do not apply a Lucida font to the word "Form" (in "Web Form Designer") because Web Forms are not instances of class Form.] Unlike the Windows Form Designer, the Web Form Designer contains two different viewing modes. The first mode is the **Design mode**. Figure 29.5 shows the ASPX page displayed in **Design** mode for Default.aspx. It consists of a blank white page on which you drag and drop components, such as Buttons and Labels, from the **Toolbox**. If the **Design** mode for the ASPX page is not currently displayed, click the **Design** button, in the lower-left corner of the Web Form Designer. **Design** mode should be used when you want to visually create the ASPX page's GUI by dragging and dropping Web controls onto the ASPX page.

Source Button ——

Design Button (selected) ——

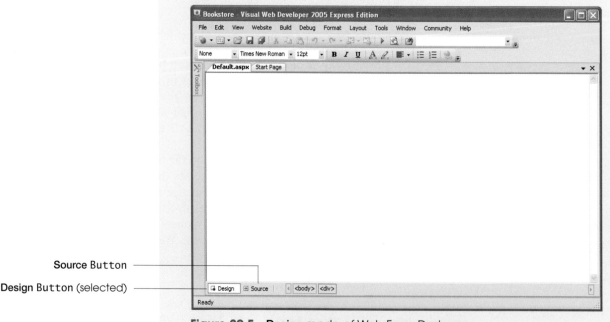

Figure 29.5 **Design** mode of Web Form Designer.

(cont.)   5. ***Switching to Source mode.*** The Web Form Designer also can display the ASPX page in **Source** mode using HTML code (Fig. 29.6). Click the **Source** button. ASPX pages are defined using a combination of HTML and ASP.NET markup. ASP.NET markup is the set of instructions processed on the Web server's machine. ASP.NET markup is often converted into HTML and sent to a browser client as part of a response to a client request. You use **Source** mode when you wish to view your ASPX page's markup. You also can use this mode to edit the markup. When you click the **Design** button, the Web Form Designer switches to **Design** mode.

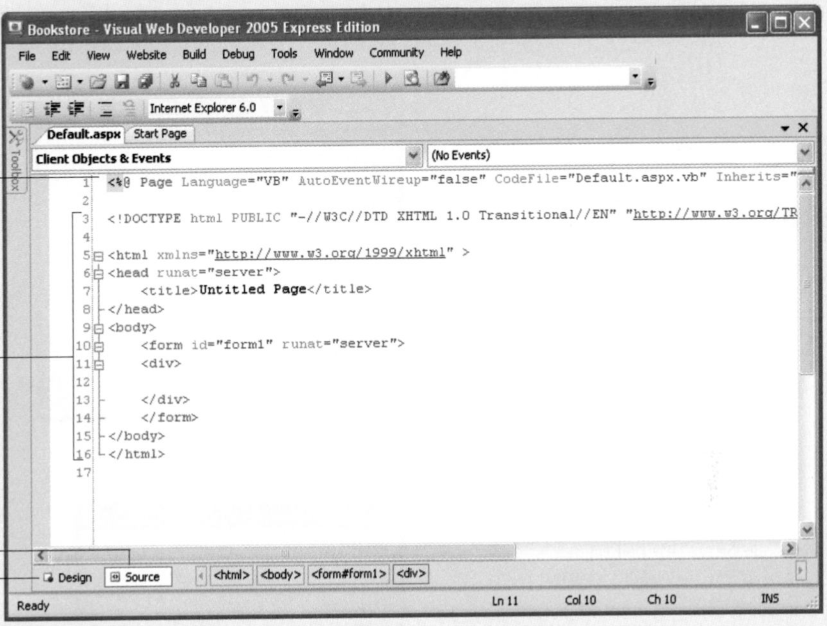

This portion is highlighted by default in Visual Studio .NET (This is an example of ASP markup)

HTML markup

Source Button (selected)
Design Button

Figure 29.6   Source mode of Web Form Designer.

6. ***Saving the project to your Bookstore directory.*** Select **File > Save All** to save all the files in your Web application.

SELF-REVIEW   1. _____ mode allows you to view the ASPX page's markup.
    a) **Source**   b) **Design**
    c) Web control   d) Markup

2. Some Web control names are the same as Windows control names,_____.
    a) because their functionality is the same
    b) but the functionality provided by Web controls is different
    c) because both Web controls and Windows controls can be used in Web applications
    d) None of the above.

Answers: 1) a. 2) b.

29.3 Designing the Books.aspx Page

This **Bookstore** application consists of two ASPX pages, which you create one at a time. The first page of the **Bookstore** application will be named Books.aspx. This page will display the list of available books. You design the first ASPX page in the following box.

**Creating the
Books.aspx Page**

1. *Renaming the ASPX page.* After you have viewed the contents of the default ASPX page (Default.aspx), you will want to give this ASPX page a meaningful name. Select the Default.aspx file in the **Solution Explorer** window. Change the **File Name** property in the **Properties** window from Default.aspx to Books.aspx (Fig. 29.7).

In **Design** mode, click the Web Form Designer. The properties of the ASPX page should display in the **Properties** window. Note that ASPX pages are listed with the identifier **DOCUMENT** in the Component Object Box (Fig. 29.8) because they do not have individual names. Select the **Title** property, and change Untitled Page to Book List. This step sets the text that is displayed in the client browser's title bar.

Change the File Name's
property value to Books.aspx

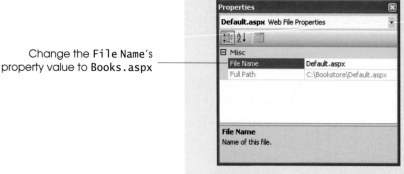

Figure 29.7 Setting the **File Name** property of the ASPX page.

Component Object Box
displays **DOCUMENT** for
ASPX pages

Title property changed to
Book List

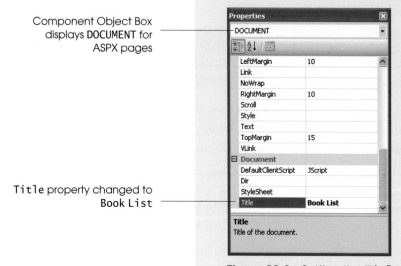

Figure 29.8 Setting the Title property of Books.aspx.

**Good Programming
Practice**

Change the ASPX page's name to a unique and meaningful name for easy identification. The name you choose must end with the .aspx extension for the page to be identified as an ASPX page.

2. *Changing the background color of the ASPX page.* Now you are ready to begin creating the GUI. Make sure you are in **Design** mode of the designer. First change the **BgColor** property of the Books.aspx page so that the background color of Books.aspx is set to light blue. Select BgColor in the **Properties** window, and click the ellipsis (...) to display the **Color Picker** dialog (Fig. 29.9). Click the **Web Palette** tab, and select light blue, as shown in Fig. 29.9. Click **OK**. The background color of the Books.aspx page is now light blue.

(cont.)

Web Palette tab

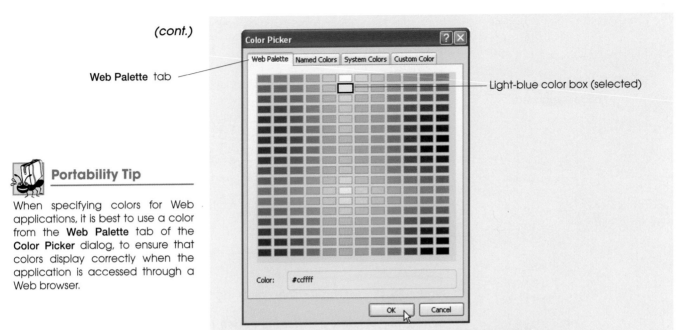

Light-blue color box (selected)

Figure 29.9   Light blue selected in the **Color Picker** dialog.

Portability Tip

When specifying colors for Web applications, it is best to use a color from the **Web Palette** tab of the **Color Picker** dialog, to ensure that colors display correctly when the application is accessed through a Web browser.

Good Programming Practice

Web controls with names and functionality similar to those of Windows controls should be given the same suffixes recommended in earlier tutorials. For example, a Label Web control with the text Available Books can be named available-Label.

3. ***Creating a Label.*** Next, click the Label Web control in the **Standard** group of the **Toolbox**. Drag and drop the control

onto the Books.aspx page. The Label should appear on the ASPX page in the upper-left corner (Fig. 29.10). View its properties in the **Properties** window. Select the ID property, and change Label1 to availableLabel. The **ID property** is used to identify controls, much like the Name property in Windows controls. Now change the Label's Text property from Label to Available Books. Set the Label's font size by setting Size, under the Font property, to XX-Large (Fig. 29.11). Set the Label's font to Tahoma by clicking the down arrow next to property Name (also under the Font property) and selecting **Tahoma** from the list that appears. To display the words correctly in the Label, you will need to set the height and width of the control. Set the **Height** property of the Label to 42px, and set the **Width** to 221px.

Label Web control

Figure 29.10   Label control displayed in the ASPX page.

(cont.)

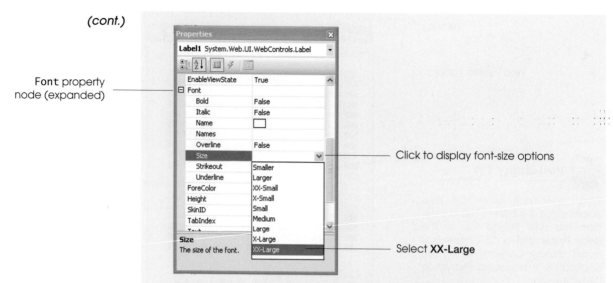

Figure 29.11 Setting the font size of the `Label` control.

4. *Setting the absolute positioning option to allow positioning of Web controls.* Changing the positioning options of the application to **Absolutely positioned** will allow you to modify the position of controls on the Web Form by dragging and dropping the controls. [The default positioning option does not allow you move controls using the drag and drop technique.] To set absolute positioning, select **Tools > Options...** to display the **Options** dialog. In this dialog, ensure that the **Show all settings** checkbox is checked, then expand the **HTML Designer node** and click **CSS Positioning**. In the **Positioning options** GroupBox that appears in the right of the dialog, check the top checkbox and select **Absolutely positioned** in the drop-down list below (Fig. 29.12). Then click **OK**.

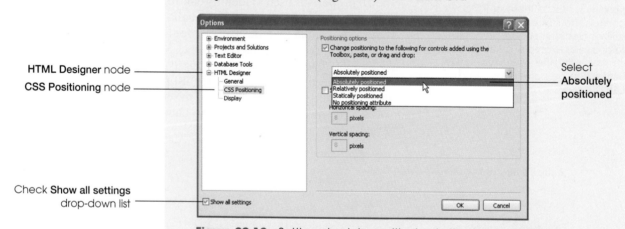

Figure 29.12 Setting absolute positioning in the **Options** dialog.

5. *Setting the exact position of the `Label`.* To set the exact location of the `Label`, select it then select **Format > Style...** to display the **Style Builder dialog** (Fig. 29.13). In the dialog, click **Position** to display the positioning options. **Absolutely positioned** should already be selected in the **Position mode** drop-down list. Specify 16 pixels (**px**) for the **Top** position and 208 pixels for the **Left** position. Click **OK**. The `Label` should now be repositioned on the page (Fig. 29.14).

(cont.)

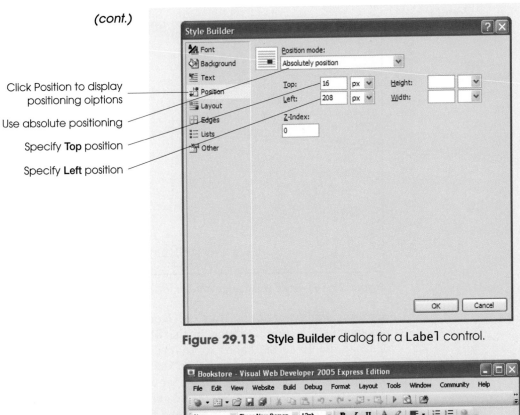

Click Position to display
positioning oiptions

Use absolute positioning

Specify **Top** position

Specify **Left** position

Figure 29.13   **Style Builder** dialog for a **Label** control.

Repositioned **Label**
Web control

Figure 29.14   Complete **Label** displayed in **Design** mode.

6. ***Creating a Horizontal Rule.*** Drag and drop the Horizontal Rule control (found in the **HTML** group in the **Toolbox**),

> ═ Horizontal Rule

and place it beneath `availableLabel`. A **Horizontal Rule** inserts a horizontal line on a Web page. You use it to separate content on your ASPX page. A Horizontal Rule is a type of **HTML control**. As you know, HTML controls correspond to standard HTML elements. In this case study, assume that a control is a Web control unless we explicitly tell you that it is an HTML control. In the **Properties** window, set the `Id` property of the Horizontal Rule to `booksHorizontalRule`. Next, click the `Style` property value in the **Properties** window. Click the ellipsis (**...**) that appears in the `Style` field. The **Style Builder** dialog appears (Fig. 29.15). Click **Position** in the left pane of the dialog. Make sure the **Position mode** is set to **Absolutely positioned**. Set the **Top:** value to 80px, the **Left:** value to 8px, the **Height:** value to 4px and the **Width:** value to 100%. Click **OK**. These settings position the Horizontal Rule 80 pixels from the top edge of the page and 8 pixels from the left edge of the page. The height of the control is now 4 pixels. Setting the width to 100% ensures that the Horizontal Rule extends to the entire width of the page.

Good Programming Practice

When naming a Horizontal Rule control, use the suffix `Horizontal-Rule` following a word that describes the control's use.

(cont.)

Position Tab

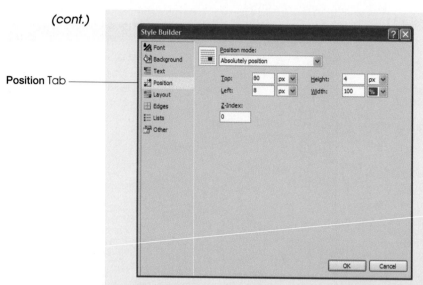

Figure 29.15 **Style Builder** dialog for the `Horizontal Rule` control.

7. *Creating another Label.* After the Horizontal Rule is in place, create another Label control (found in the **Standard** group in the **Toolbox**). Change the ID of the Label to `instructionsLabel`. In the **Properties** window, change the Text property to "`Select a book from this list and click the button to view the selected book's information`". Then set the font size to Medium. Set the height to 18px and the width to 531px. Select **Format > Style...** to display the **Style Builder** dialog. Then absolutely position the Label 95 pixels from the top and 54 pixels from the left and click **OK**.

8. *Creating a ListBox.* The next control you will place on this page is a List-Box. The **ListBox** will contain a list of the available books offered by the bookstore. In the next two tutorials, you will retrieve information from the database to populate the ListBox with book titles. Drag and drop the ListBox control,

> `ListBox`

and place it below `instructionsLabel`. Change the ID property of the ListBox to `bookTitlesListBox`. In the **Properties** window, set the Height to 100 pixels and the Width to 330 pixels. Select **Format > Style...** to display the **Style Builder** dialog. Then absolutely position the ListBox 134 pixels from the top and 147 pixels from the left and click **OK**. [*Note:* Unbound appears in the ListBox because no items have been added to it.]

9. *Adding a Button control.* Below the ListBox add a Button (found in the **Standard** tab in the **Toolbox**). Drag and drop the Button control,

> `ab Button`

onto the ASPX page. Change the Button's ID to `informationButton`, and change its Text property to `View Information`. Set its Width to 130 pixels in the **Properties** window. Select **Format > Style...** to display the **Style Builder** dialog. Then absolutely position the Button 241 pixels from the top and 241 pixels from the left and click **OK**. The `Books.aspx` page should now appear as shown in Fig. 29.16.

(cont.)

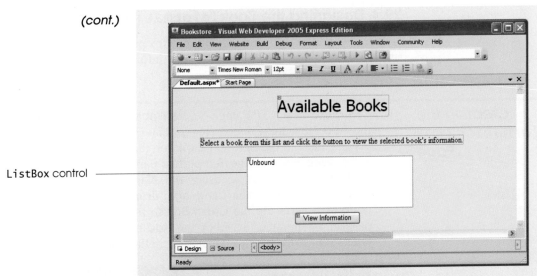

Figure 29.16 **Design** mode of Books.aspx.

10. *Adding a RequireFieldValidator control.* To make sure that a book in the bookTitlesListBox is selected when the informationButton Button is clicked, the application uses a RequiredFieldValidator control. You'll configure the RequiredFieldValidator to display an error message when no title is selected in the bookTitlesListBox. The Required-FieldValidator is located in the **Validation** group in the **Toolbox**. Drag and drop

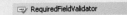

onto the ASPX page. Change the RequiredFieldValidator's ID property to bookRequiredFieldValidator. Select **Format > Style...** to display the **Style Builder** dialog. Then absolutely position the RequiredField-Validator 273 pixels from the top and 243 pixels from the left and click **OK**.

11. *Selecting the control to validate.* In design mode, click the bookRe-quiredFieldValidator control. Select bookTitlesListBox in the **ControlToValidate** ComboBox of the **Properties** window. This causes the bookRequiredFieldValidator to only display an error message when nothing is selected in the bookTitlesListBox specifically.

12. *Setting the RequiredFieldValidator's error message.* In the **Properties** window, set the **Text** property to Please select a book. Now each time the informationButton is clicked while no book is selected in bookTitlesListBox, Please select a book is displayed in the position of the bookRequiredFieldValidator control.

13. *Saving the project.* Select **File > Save All** to save your modified code.

SELF-REVIEW   1. Use the _____ property to change the name of a **Web Forms** control.

    a) Text   b) Name

    c) ID   d) Value

2. The Horizontal Rule is a(n) _____ control.

    a) **Web Forms**   b) **HTML**

    c) **Data**   d) **Windows Forms**

Answers: 1) c. 2) b.

29.4 Designing the `BookInformation.aspx` Page

Now that you have designed the `Books.aspx` page, you will design the `BookInformation.aspx` page, which displays the information about the book that was selected from the `ListBox`.

Creating the
BookInformation.aspx
Page

1. *Creating a new ASPX page.* Select **Website > Add New Item...**, to display the **Add New Item** dialog (Fig. 29.17). [*Note:* You can also right click the project name in the **Solution Explorer**, then select **Add > Add New Item...**] Select **Web Form** in the **Templates:** pane, and rename the ASPX page to `BookInformation.aspx`, using the **Name:** TextBox. Make sure **Visual Basic** is selected in the **Language:** drop-down list, and check the **Place code in a separate file CheckBox** to place the Visual Basic code for the page in a separatae file. Click the **Add** button. A new ASPX page named `BookInformation.aspx` will appear in the **Solution Explorer** window.

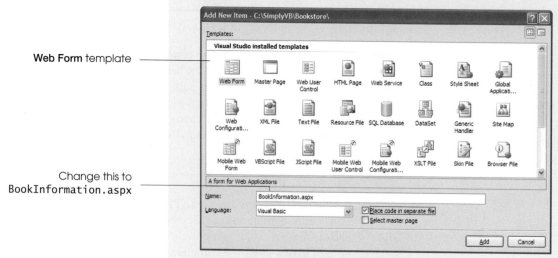

Web Form template

Change this to
BookInformation.aspx

Figure 29.17 **Add New Item - Bookstore** dialog.

2. *Changing the background color.* If the file does not open in **Design** mode, switch to **Design** mode at this time. Change the background color of this page to light blue, as you did in *Step 2* of the box *Creating the Books.aspx Page*.

3. *Creating the bookTitleLabel Label.* Create a new `Label` by double clicking the `Label` control in the **Standard** group of the **Toolbox**. This `Label` will display the title of the book selected by the user. You do not yet know what book title will be selected, so clear the `Text` property of this `Label`. The `Text` property will be set in Tutorial 31. Change the `ID` property of the `Label` to `bookTitleLabel`, set the font size to `X-Large` and set the `Fore-Color` to `Blue`. The **ForeColor** property specifies the color of the text that displays on the `Label`. To set the `ForeColor`, select the `ForeColor` property in the **Properties** window, and click the down arrow that appears in the `ForeColor` field. Click the **Web** tab and select `Blue` to set the forecolor (Fig. 29.18). Set the height to `41px` and the width to `700px`. Select **Format > Style...** to display the **Style Builder** dialog. Then absolutely position the `Label` 15 pixels from the top and 20 pixels from the left and click **OK**.

(cont.)

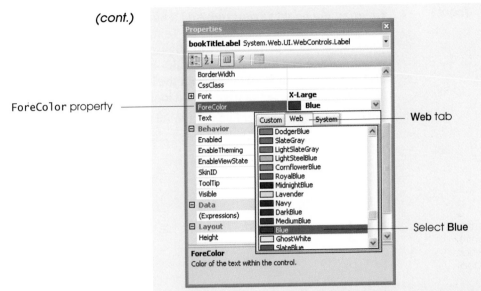

Figure 29.18 Setting a Label's ForeColor property.

4. ***Creating the Horizontal Rule.*** Drag and drop a Horizontal Rule beneath the bookTitleLabel Label. Set the Id property to informationHorizontalRule. Select **Format > Style...** to display the **Style Builder** dialog. Then absolutely position the Horizontal Rule 64 pixels from the top and 0 pixels from the left and set its width to 100%. Then click **OK**.

5. ***Creating the authorsLabel Label.*** After adding the Horizontal Rule, create another Label. Name the Label authorsLabel by setting its ID property, and change its Font property's Size to Large. Set the height of the Label to 34px and the width to 700px. Clear the **Text** property for this Label, because you do not know which book will be selected. You will set this text in Tutorial 31. Select **Format > Style...** to display the **Style Builder** dialog. Then absolutely position the Label 82 pixels from the top and 20 pixels from the left and click **OK**.

6. ***Creating the Image control.*** Now you must add the **Image control** that displays the cover of the selected book. Drag and drop the Image control,

from the **Standard** group in the **Toolbox** window. Change the Image control's ID property to bookImage. Leave the Height and Width properties blank to allow the Image control to be automatically resized each time a new image is loaded. Specify the BorderStyle as Outset, and set the **BorderWidth** to 5 pixels.

The **BorderStyle** property specifies the type of border that displays around the Image. Setting BorderStyle to Outset gives the Image a raised-control appearance. Property BorderWidth specifies the width of the border of the Image control. Setting BorderWidth to 5 causes the border to be 5 pixels thick. Select **Format > Style...** to display the **Style Builder** dialog. Then absolutely position the Image 122 pixels from the top and 20 pixels from the left and click **OK**.

Good Programming Practice

When naming an Image Web control, use the suffix Image following a word that describes what the Image will display.

(cont.)

7. **Creating the bookListButton.** Add a Button to the page. Set the Button's ID to bookListButton, and set its Text to Book List. In the **Properties** window, set the Width property to 80 pixels. Select **Format > Style...** to display the **Style Builder** dialog. Then absolutely position the Button 267 pixels from the top and 270 pixels from the left and click **OK**. The design of the BookInformation.aspx page should look like Fig. 29.19.

8. **Saving the project.** Select **File > Save All** to save your modified code.

Image Web control
(*Note:* The control will be resized when an image is loaded)

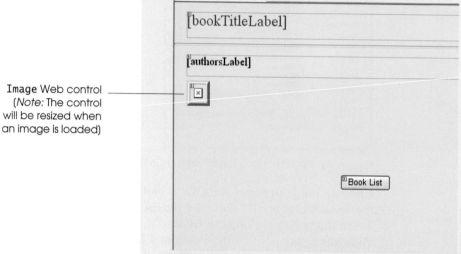

Figure 29.19 Design of the BookInformation.aspx page without the Table.

You are now ready to add the DetailsView control to the page. The DetailsView will display the book information in a structured manner. You will add the DetailsView in the following box.

Adding the DetailsView Control

1. **Creating the DetailsView control.** From the **Data** group of the **Toolbox**, drag and drop the DetailsView control,

onto the page. In the **Properties** window, change the ID of the DetailsView to bookDetailsView, set the BorderStyle to OutSet and change the BorderWidth to 5 pixels. Also, make sure the **Gridlines** property has value Both. The Gridlines property displays separators between the cells (known as **cell borders**) in the DetailsView. Setting Gridlines to Both displays both horizontal and vertical separators between each cell. Set the Width property to 220px. Do not modify the Height property's default value (50px). Select **Format > Style...** to display the **Style Builder** dialog. Then absolutely position the DetailsView 127 pixels from the top and 200 pixels from the left and click **OK**.

2. **Placing text into DetailsView cells.** The information that will be displayed in the DetailsView is currently unknown. You will specify the information that will be displayed in the DetailsView in Tutorial 31. Your BookInformation.aspx page will look like Fig. 29.20.

3. **Saving the project.** Select **File > Save All** to save your modified code.

(cont.)

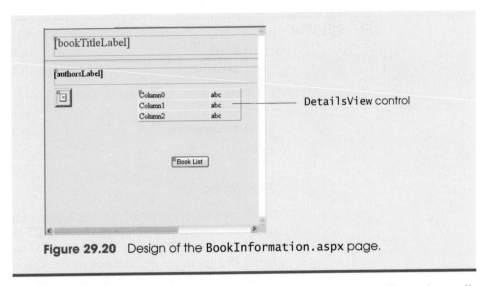

Figure 29.20   Design of the `BookInformation.aspx` page.

Now that you have completed the user interface design, you will run the application. You have specified only the **Bookstore** application's user interface; therefore, it does not have any functionality.

Running the Bookstore
Application

1. ***Testing the application.*** Ensure that the `Books.aspx` page is the start page by right clicking it in the **Solution Explorer** and selecting **Set As Start Page**. Next, select **Debug > Start Debugging** to run your application. [*Note:* A **Debugging not Enabled** dialog may pop up. Make sure the top `RadioBut-ton`, **Modify the Web.config file to enable debugging**, is selected, then click **OK** so the application can be executed in debug mode.] The `Books.aspx` page appears (Fig. 29.20). Note that the `ListBox` does not contain any book titles, because you have not yet set up the database connections to retrieve the information. Click the **View Information** `Button`. The `RequiredFieldValidator` displays a message because you did not select a book, but nothing else happens. Currently, you have specified only the visual aspects of the page. Thus, users are not forwarded to `BookInforma-tion.aspx` when the **View Information** `Button` is clicked.

Empty `ListBox` control —

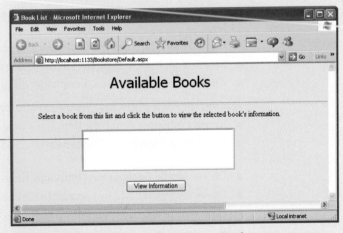

Figure 29.21   Empty `ListBox` of the `Books.aspx` page.

2. ***Closing the application.*** Close your running application by clicking the browser's close box.

3. ***Closing the IDE.*** Close Visual Web Developer by clicking its close box.

SELF-REVIEW

1. The _____ property is used to set the width of an Image control's border.
   - a) `Width`
   - b) `BorderStyle`
   - c) `BorderWidth`
   - d) None of the above.

2. Use the _____ property to display cell borders between `TableCells` in a `Table`.
   - a) `Gridlines`
   - b) `BorderStyle`
   - c) `BorderWidth`
   - d) `Separator`

Answers: 1) c. 2) a.

29.5 Wrap-Up

In this tutorial, you created the ASPX pages for your three-tier **Bookstore** application. You learned how to create an ASP.NET Web application and how to add Web controls to the ASPX pages. In doing so, you were introduced to Visual Web Developer's **Design** mode and **Source** mode. You learned that **Design** mode is used to create the user interface by dragging and dropping Web controls on the ASPX page, while **Source** mode allows you to view and edit the page's markup.

You learned how to use absolute positioning and the **Style Builder** dialog to set the exact position of a control. You used absolute positioning to drag and drop controls and the **Style Builder** dialog to place controls by specifying their top and left positions in pixels. The Web controls you used in this tutorial included `Labels`, `Buttons`, a `ListBox`, an `Image` and a `DetailsView`. You also set the `Image` and `DetailsView` controls' `BorderStyle` property to `Outset` and `BorderWidth` property to 5 pixels, which gave each control a raised appearance.

In the next tutorial, you'll connect to and access the database, or information tier, of the application, which contains information about the books in the bookstore. You'll use Visual Web Developer's **Query Builder** to build statements that can retrieve the data from the database. After you have configured the database access, Tutorial 31 will enable you to create the middle tier of the bookstore, which specifies the functionality of the ASPX pages.

SKILLS SUMMARY

Creating a local ASP.NET Web Application

- Select **File > New Website...**
- Select the **ASP.NET Web Site** icon from the **Templates:** pane in the **New Web Site** dialog.
- Choose **File System** in the **Location:** drop-down list.
- Specify a location to store the file on your system.
- Choose **Visual Basic** in the **Language:** drop-down list and click **OK**.

Adding an ASPX Page to a Web Application

- Select **Website > Add New Item...**, to display the **Add New Item** dialog.
- Select **Web Form** in the **Templates:** box, and rename the ASPX page in the **Name:** TextBox.
- Choose **Visual Basic** in the **Language:** drop-down list.
- Check the **Place code in a separate file** checkbox.
- Click **Add** to add the new ASPX page to the Web Application.

Setting a Web Control's Location

- Select the Web control.
- Select **Format > Style...** to display the **Style Builder** dialog.
- In the dialog. click **Position** to display the positioning options. Select **Absolutely position** from the **Position mode** drop-down list.
- Specify the **Top** and **Left** positions.

Changing to Design Mode
- Click the **Design** mode button beneath the ASPX page in the Web Form Designer.

Changing to Source Mode
- Click the **Source** mode button beneath the ASPX page in the Web Form Designer.

KEY TERMS

`BgColor` **property of an ASPX page**—Specifies the page's background color.

`BorderStyle` **property**—Specifies the type of border that displays around an `Image` or `DetailsView`.

`BorderWidth` **property**—Specifies the border width of an `Image` or `DetailsView`.

Button Web control—Allows users to perform an action.

cell borders—The separators between the cells in a `DetailsView`.

Design mode—Displays the ASPX page's GUI at design time.

`DetailsView` **control**—A control in the **Data** group of the **Toolbox** that allows you to display information in a structured manner

`ForeColor` **property**—Specifies font color for `Label` controls.

`Gridlines` **property of a** `DetailsView`—Specifies whether the `DetailView`'s cell borders display.

`Height` **property**—Allows you to specify the height of a Web control.

Horizontal Rule HTML control—Displays a line to separate controls on an ASPX page.

HTML controls—Correspond to HTML elements.

`ID` **property**—Specifies the name of a Web control.

`Image` **Web control**—Displays an image in an ASPX page.

`Label` **Web control**—Displays text on an ASPX page.

`ListBox` **Web control**—Displays a list of items.

`px`—Specifies that the size is measured in pixels.

Source mode—Displays the ASPX page's markup at design time.

Style Builder dialog—The dialog that enables you to specify styles, such as position, for your Web controls.

`Title` **property of an ASPX page**—Specifies the page's title that displays in the title bar of the browser.

Web Control—Controls that are used to construct web applications.

Web Form Designer—The design area in Visual Web Developer that enables you to visually build your ASPX pages.

`Width` **property**—Allows you to specify the width of a Web control.

CONTROLS, EVENTS, PROPERTIES & METHODS

ASPX page   The page on which controls are dropped to design the GUI.
- *Property*

`BgColor`—Specifies the ASPX page's background color.

Button   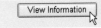   This control allows the user to raise an action or event.

- *In action*

> | View Information |

- *Properties*
    `Height`—Specifies the height of the `Button`.
    `ID`—Specifies the name of the `Button`. The name should be suffixed with `Button`.
    `Text`—Specifies the text displayed on the `Button`.
    `Width`—Specifies the width of the `Button`.

DetailsView 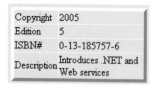 This control is usually used to organize data in a tabular format.

■ *In action*

Copyright	2005
Edition	5
ISBN#	0-13-185757-6
Description	Introduces .NET and Web services

■ *Properties*

BorderStyle—Specifies the appearance of the DetailsView's border.

BorderWidth—Specifies the width of the DetailsView's border.

Gridlines—Specifies the format in which table cell separators are displayed.

ID—Specifies the name used to access the DetailsView control programmatically. The name should be suffixed with DetailsView.

Horizontal Rule ── Horizontal Rule This control displays a line on the ASPX page. It is usually used to separate different areas of the ASPX page.

■ *In action*

─────────────────

■ *Properties*

Id—Specifies the name of the Horizontal Rule. The name should be suffixed with HorizontalRule.

Style—Allows you to specify where to position the Horizontal Rule on the ASPX page.

Image Image This control displays an image on the ASPX page.

■ *In action*

■ *Properties*

BorderStyle—Specifies the appearance of the Image's border.

BorderWidth—Specifies the width of the Image's border.

Height—Specifies the height of the Image control.

ID—Specifies the name used to access the Image control programmatically. The name should be suffixed with Image.

Width—Specifies the width of the Image control.

Label A Label This control displays text on the ASPX page that the user cannot modify.

■ *In action*

Available Books

■ *Properties*

Height—Specifies the height of the Label.

ID—Specifies the name used to access the Label programmatically. The name should be suffixed with Label.

Name (under the expanded Font property in the **Solution Explorer**)—Specifies the name of the font used for the Label's text.

Size (under the expanded Font property in the **Solution Explorer**)—Specifies the size of the Label's text.

Text—Specifies the text displayed on the Label.

Width—Specifies the width of the Label.

ListBox   ListBox   This control allows the user to view and select from multiple items in a list.

■ *In action*

```
Visual Basic 2005 for Programmers: Second Edition
Visual C# 2005 How to Program: Second Edition
C++ How to Program: Fifth Edition
Operating Systems: Third Edition
```

■ *Properties*

Height—Specifies the height of the ListBox.

ID—Specifies the name used to access the ListBox control programmatically. The name should be suffixed with ListBox.

Width—Specifies the width of the ListBox.

RequiredFieldValidator   RequiredFieldValidator   This control enables you to specify that an element in a Web form is required before a form can be submitted.

■ *In action*

Please select a book

■ *Properties*

ControlToValidate—Specifies the Web form element that is required before the form can be submitted.

Height—Specifies the height of the RequiredFieldValidator.

ID—Specifies the name used to access the RequiredFieldValidator control programmatically. The name should be suffixed with RequiredFieldValidator.

Text—Specifies the text that will be displayed if the required Web form element is not supplied when the Web form is submitted.

Width—Specifies the width of the RequiredFieldValidator.

MULTIPLE-CHOICE QUESTIONS

29.1 You change the _____ property of the ASPX page to specify the color that displays in the background of the page.

   a) BackColor   b) BgColor

   c) BackgroundColor   d) Color

29.2 Button, Label and ListBox Web controls can be dragged onto a Web form from the _____.

   a) **Toolbox**   b) **Properties** window

   c) **Solution Explorer**   d) None of the above.

29.3 The _____ dialog can be used to specify the position of a Web control on an ASPX page.

   a) **Toolbox**   b) **Style**

   c) **Builder**   d) **Style Builder**

29.4 Unlike the Windows Form Designer, the Web Form Designer _____.

   a) does not provide two viewing modes   b) provides two viewing modes

   c) allows you to design the graphical user interface   d) does not allow you to design the user interface

29.5 The `BorderStyle` property of the `Image` control _____.
    a) specifies the color of the border
    b) specifies the type of border that displays around the `Image` control
    c) specifies the width of the border   d) Both a and b.

29.6 Setting the `BorderStyle` property to `Outset` makes a control appear _____.
    a) raised   b) with a bold border
    c) with the specified border width   d) with the specified border color

29.7 The _____ mode allows you to create the ASPX page's GUI by dragging and dropping controls on the page.
    a) **Source**   b) **Design**
    c) **Visual**   d) **GUI**

29.8 To specify the exact position of a Web control, use _____ positioning.
    a) relative   b) absolute
    c) fixed   d) None of the above.

29.9 The _____ property specifies the number of pixels used to form a border.
    a) `Border`   b) `Width`
    c) `BorderWidth`   d) None of the above.

29.10 The _____ control enables you to specify that an element in a Web form is required before a form can be submitted.
    a) `RequiredField`   b) `Validator`
    c) `RequiredFieldValidator`   d) None of the above.

EXERCISES

[Note: In these exercises, we may ask you to set an ASPX page as the application's start page, meaning that this page will appear first when the application is run. You can set an ASPX page as the start page by right clicking the file in the **Solution Explorer** *and selecting* **Set As Start Page**.*]*

29.11 (*Phone Book Application: GUI*) Create the user interface for the **Phone Book** application. The design for the two pages for this application is displayed in Fig. 29.22.

    a) *Creating an ASP.NET Web application.* Create an ASP.NET Web application project in the `C:\SimplyVB` directory, and name it PhoneBook. Rename the ASPX page to `PhoneBook.aspx` and set `PhoneBook.aspx` as the start page. Also set the page's **Title** property to Phone Book.

    b) *Changing the background color.* Change the background color of your ASPX page (`PhoneBook.aspx`) to the light-yellow **Web Palette** color (located in the sixth column of the 12th row) by using the `BgColor` property as demonstrated in this tutorial. Change the `Title` of the ASPX page to Phone Book.

    c) *Adding a Label.* Create a `Label`, set the font size to X-Large and change the `Text` property to Phone Book Web Application. Absolutely position the `Label` 40px from the left and 17px from the top. Name the control phoneBookLabel.

    d) *Adding another Label.* Create another `Label`, and set the `Text` property to Select a name from the list and click the Get Number Button:. Absolutely position the `Label` 12px from the left and 53px from the top. Name this Web control instructionsLabel.

    e) *Adding a DropDownList Web control.* Create a `DropDownList` Web control by dragging and dropping it from the **Toolbox** onto the ASPX page. The `DropDownList` Web control looks similar to the ComboBox Windows Form control. Set the width to 190px. Absolutely position the `DropDownList` 82px from the left and 91px from the top. Name the `DropDownList` namesDropDownList.

    f) *Adding a Button.* Create a `Button`, set its width to 90px and change the `Text` property to Get Number. Absolutely position the `Button` 125px from the left and 200px from the top. Name the Web control getNumberButton.

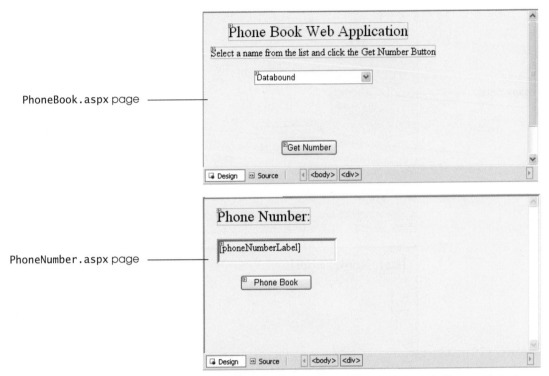

PhoneBook.aspx page

PhoneNumber.aspx page

Figure 29.22   Phone Book application ASPX pages' design.

g) *Adding another ASPX page to the Phone Book application.* Add another ASPX page to the **Phone Book** application, name it PhoneNumber.aspx and change the background to the light-yellow color. Change the Title property to Phone Number.

h) *Adding a Label to the PhoneNumber.aspx.* Create a Label and name it numbersLabel. Set the font size to X-Large and change the Text property to Phone Number:. Absolutely position the Label 20px from the left and 15px from the top.

i) *Adding another Label.* Create another Label, set its BorderStyle to Inset, and set its height and width to 30px and 185px, respectively. Clear the text of the Label. Name the Label phoneNumberLabel. Absolutely position the Label 20px from the left and 63px from the top.

j) *Adding a Button to the PhoneNumber.aspx page.* Create a Button, set its width to 115px and change the Text property to Phone Book. Absolutely position the Button 58px from the left and 120px from the top. Name the Button phoneBookButton.

k) *Saving the project.* Save all the files in your project as you did in *Step 6* of the box, *Creating an ASP.NET Web Application.*

29.12 (*US State Facts Application: GUI*) Create the user interface for the **US State Facts** application. The design for the two pages of this application is displayed in Fig. 29.23.

a) *Creating an ASP.NET Web application.* Create a new ASP.NET Web application project in the C:\SimplyVB directory, and name it USStateFacts. Rename the first ASPX page to States.aspx and set States.aspx as the start page.

b) *Changing the background color.* Change the background color of the States.aspx page to the light-blue **Web Palette** color (located in the sixth column of the second row) by using the BgColor property as demonstrated in this tutorial. Change the Title property of the ASPX page to States.

c) *Adding a Label to States.aspx.* Create a Label Web control, and place it on the page. Set the font size to XX-Large, and change the Text property to States. Absolutely position the Label 200px from the left and 10px from the top. Name the Web control statesLabel.

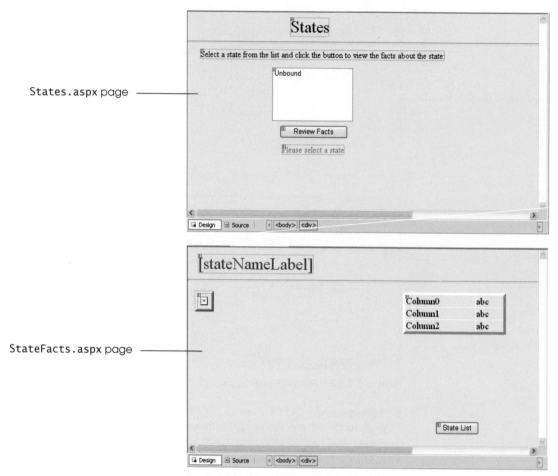

States.aspx page —

StateFacts.aspx page —

Figure 29.23 **US State Facts** application ASPX pages' design.

d) *Adding a Horizontal Rule to States.aspx.* Create a Horizontal Rule, place it on the ASPX page and set its width to 100%. Absolutely position the Horizontal Rule 0px from the left and 55px from the top, and set the Height: to 4px. Name the Horizontal Rule statesHorizontalRule.

e) *Adding another Label to States.aspx.* Create another Label, and place it beneath the Horizontal Rule. Change the font size to Medium, and set the Text property to Select a state from the list and click the button to view facts about that state:. Absolutely position the Label 25px from the left and 70px from the top. Name this Web control instructionsLabel.

f) *Adding a ListBox to States.aspx.* Create a ListBox, and place it on the ASPX page. Set its Height property to 100px and its Width property to 155px. Absolutely position the ListBox 166px from the left and 104px from the top. Name the ListBox statesListBox.

g) *Adding a Button to States.aspx.* Create a Button, and place it on the page. Set its Text property to Review Facts and its Width property to 130px. Absolutely position the Button 181px from the left and 212px from the top. Name the Button factsButton.

h) *Adding a RequireFieldValidator to States.aspx.* Create a RequiredFieldValidator, and place it on the page. Set its ErrorMessage property to Please select a state. and its ControlToValidate to statesListBox. Absolutely position the RequiredFieldValidator 185px from the left and 248px from the top. Name the RequiredFieldValidator statesRequiredFieldValidator.

i) *Adding another ASPX page to the US State Facts application.* Add another ASPX page to the **US State Facts** application and name it StateFacts.aspx. Then change the background color to light blue and the Title property to State Facts.

j) ***Adding a Label to StateFacts.aspx***. Create a Label, name it stateNameLabel, set its font size to XX-Large and change its ForeColor property to Blue. Clear the Label's text. Absolutely position the Label 20px from the left and 13px from the top.

k) ***Adding a Horizontal Rule***. Place the Horizontal Rule beneath the Label. Absolutely position the Horizontal Rule 0px from the left and 60px from the top, and set the Height: to 4px. Change the width to 100%. Name the Horizontal Rule stateFacts-HorizontalRule.

l) ***Adding an Image control to StateFacts.aspx***. Create an Image control and set its BorderStyle to Outset. Change the BorderWidth to 5px. Do not set its height and width to allow the Image control to automatically resize according to the loaded image. Absolutely position the Image 13px from the left and 81px from the top. Name the Web control flagImage.

m) ***Adding a DetailsView to StateFacts.aspx***. Create a DetailsView and name it stateDetailsView. Set the BorderStyle to Outset and the BorderWidth to 5px. Set the Font property's Size to Large. Then set the Width property to 200px. Absolutely position the DetailsView 417px from the left and 82px from the top.

n) ***Adding a Button to StateFacts.aspx***. Create a Button and change its text to State List. Absolutely position the Button 480px from the left and 324px from the top. Name the Button control stateListButton.

o) ***Saving the project***. Save all the files in your project as you did in *Step 6* of the box, *Creating an ASP.NET Web Application*.

Bookstore Application: Information Tier

Examining the Database and Creating Database Components

This tutorial focuses on the Web application's information tier, where the application's data resides. In your **Bookstore** application, the information tier is represented by a Microsoft SQL Server 2005 Express database, Bookstore.mdf, that stores each book's information. Before you begin this tutorial, you should be familiar with the database concepts presented in Tutorial 25.

In this tutorial, you will create the objects that your application will need to connect to and manipulate the database. You also will define the SQL statements that will retrieve data from the database. In fact, the information tier consists solely of the Bookstore.mdf database. The TableAdapter object created in this tutorial is actually part of the middle tier, because it performs the functionality of retrieving data from the database. You create this object here because it interacts with the information tier and does not require any programming. You will complete the **Bookstore** application by creating the middle tier in the next tutorial.

30.1 Reviewing the Bookstore Application

You have taken the three-tier **Bookstore** application for a test-drive (in Tutorial 28) and have designed the GUI by using Web controls and an HTML control (Tutorial 29). Now you are ready to create the database components for the application. Before you begin, you should review the pseudocode and the ACE table (Fig. 30.1) for this application:

When the Books page is requested
    Retrieve the book titles from the database
    Display book titles in a ListBox

When the user selects a book title from the ListBox and clicks the View Information Button
    Store the selected book in a variable
    Redirect the user to the BookInformation page

When the BookInformation page is requested
    Retrieve the selected book's information from a database
    Display the book title in a Label
    Display the authors in a Label
    Display the cover art in an Image
    Display the remaining information in a DetailsView table

When the user presses the Book List Button on the BookInformation page
    Redirect the client browser back to the Books page

Action/Control/Event (ACE) Table for the Web-Based Bookstore Application

Action	Control/Object	Event
Label the Books page	availableLabel, instructionsLabel	
	Page	Load (for Books.aspx)
Display book titles in a ListBox	bookTitlesListBox	
	informationButton	Click
Store the selected book in a variable	Session	
Redirect the user to the BookInformation page	Response	
	Page	Load (for BookInformation.aspx)
Retrieve the selected book's information from a database	ProductsTableAdapter, ProductsDataTable, Session	
Display the book title in a Label	bookTitleLabel	
Display the authors in a Label	authorsLabel	
Display the cover art in an image	bookImage	
Display the remaining information in a Table	bookDetailsView	
	bookListButton	Click
Redirect the client browser back to the Books page	Response	

Figure 30.1   ACE table for the Web-based **Bookstore** application.

30.2 Information Tier: Database

The information tier maintains all the data needed for an application. The database that stores this data may contain product data, such as a description and quantity in stock, and customer data, such as a user name and shipping information.

The **Bookstore** application stores books data in a Microsoft SQL Server 2005 Express database (Bookstore.mdf). This data is retrieved from the database by using Visual Basic code and ADO.NET objects. The database contains one table, named Products, that stores each book's information.

The Products table contains eight fields (columns): ProductID, Title, Authors, Copyright, Edition, ISBN#, Coverart and Description. These fields contain an ID number, the title, authors, copyright date, edition number, ISBN number (a unique number used to reference a book), image name and description of each book, respectively. Figure 30.2 displays the Products table of Bookstore.mdf, using the **Database Explorer** window in **Visual Web Developer 2005**.

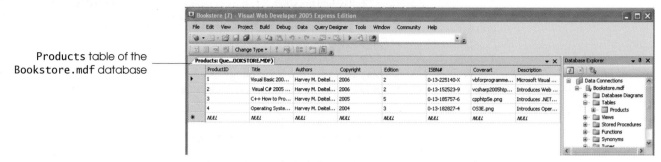

Products table of the
Bookstore.mdf database

Figure 30.2 Products table of the Bookstore.mdf database.

30.3 Using the Server Explorer and Query Builder in ASPX Pages

Before you begin programming this application's middle tier, you must set up the database connections that retrieve data from the database. First, you will add the database to the application in its **App_Data** folder. You will then use the **Query Builder** tool discussed in Tutorial 25 to generate SQL statements to request book information. You will add the database connection in the following box.

Adding the
Bookstore.mdf
Database to the
Bookstore Application

1. ***Opening the Bookstore application in Visual Web Developer.*** Open Visual Web Developer and select **File > Open Web Site...** to display the **Open Web Site** dialog. In this dialog, click **File System**, then locate the **Bookstore** folder in the C:\SimplyVB directory and click the **Bookstore** folder to highlight it. Click the **Open** Button to open the **Bookstore** application.

2. ***Adding a database to the application.*** You must add the **Bookstore** database to the application before accessing its data. This connection will allow you to return information about a specific book from the database to the application. To add a the Bookstore database, right click the **App_Data** folder in the **Solution Explorer** window and select **Add Existing Item...** from the menu (Fig. 30.3) to display the **Add Existing Item** dialog.

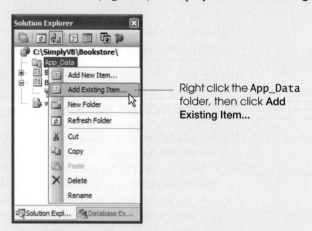

Right click the App_Data
folder, then click **Add**
Existing Item...

Figure 30.3 Adding the Bookstore database to the application in the **Solution Explorer** window.

3. ***Selecting the database.*** You now need to specify the database with which you want to establish a connection. In the **Add Existing Item** dialog, navigate to the **C:\Examples\Tutorial30** directory, select Bookstore.mdf and click **Add** (Fig. 30.4). This establishes the connection to the database. The database file should now appear in your application's **App_Data** folder.

(cont.)

Select **Bookstore.mdf** database (This may display as **Bookstore**, depending on your Windows settings)

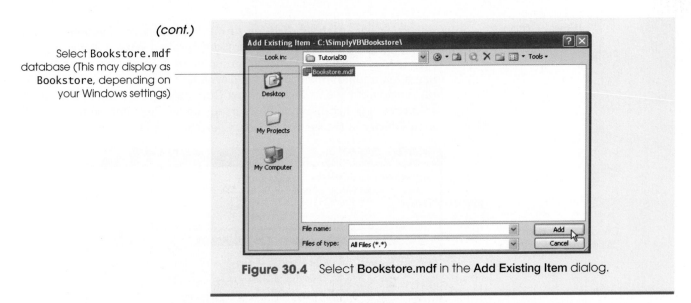

Figure 30.4   Select **Bookstore.mdf** in the **Add Existing Item** dialog.

Now that the database connection has been established, you will add a DataSet that loads the information in **Bookstore.mdf** into the application.

Creating a DataSet from the Bookstore Database

1. ***Adding a DataSet with the Bookstore.mdf data to the ASPX page.*** Select **Website > Add New Item...** to display the **Add New Item** dialog. [*Note:* Make sure the **App_Code** folder is not selected, because the **Add New Item** dialog will not have the same options.] Select **DataSet** in the **Templates:** pane and rename the DataSet to BooksDataSet.xsd in the **Name:** textbox (Fig. 30.5). Click the **Add** button. A dialog appears asking if you would like to put BooksDataSet.xsd in the **App_Code** folder. Click **Yes** (Fig. 30.6). [*Note:* This may take a few seconds.]

Select **DataSet** in **Templates:** pane

Rename DataSet

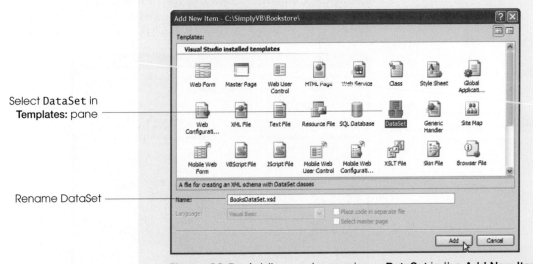

Figure 30.5   Adding and renaming a **DataSet** in the **Add New Item** dialog.

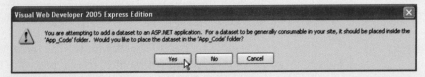

Figure 30.6   Confirming that **BooksDataSet** will be added to the **App_Code** folder.

(cont.)

2. ***Connecting your Web application to the Bookstore.mdf database.*** After the preceding step, the **TableAdapter Configuration Wizard** dialog appears. A `TableAdapter` object extracts information from a database and returns it to an application. In the drop-down list, choose `Bookstore.mdf` (Fig. 30.7). You should not have to click the **New Connection...** Button to browse for `Bookstore.mdf` because you have already added the database to the application, which created the connection. Click **Next >** to continue.

Choose `Bookstore.mdf` from the drop-down list.

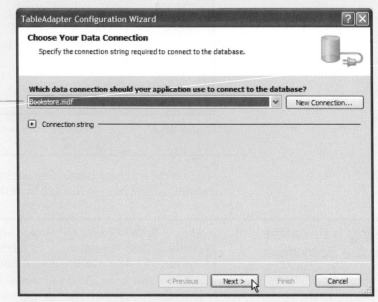

Figure 30.7 Choosing `Bookstore.mdf` as the application's data connection.

3. ***Saving the Connection String.*** In the next screen, ensure that the **Yes, save the connection as:** CheckBox is checked and that `BookstoreConnection-String` is typed in the TextBox below (Fig. 30.8), then click **Next >**.

The name of the connection string is chosen for you based on the `DataSet` name you specified

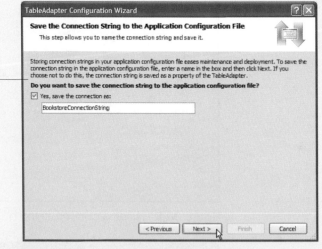

Figure 30.8 Choosing the Connection String.

4. ***Accessing the database.*** The next dialog box allows you to choose the method you want to use to query the `Bookstore.mdf` database. We want the `TableAdapter` to use SQL statements to retrieve information from Bookstore.mdf, so select the **Use SQL statements** radio button (Fig. 30.9), then click **Next >**.

(cont.)

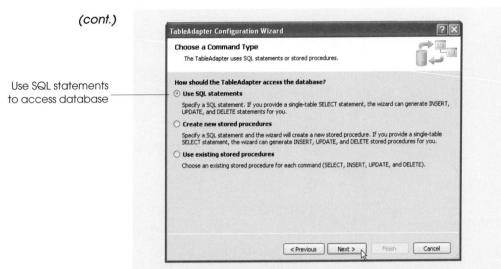

Figure 30.9   Choosing to use SQL statements to access the database.

5. ***Choose the data to be loaded into the table.*** In the **Enter a SQL State-ment** dialog, you can enter a SQL statement that the `TableAdapter` will use to obtain data from `Bookstore.mdf`. Click the **Query Builder...** button (Fig. 30.10) to use the **Query Builder** to generate this SQL statement.

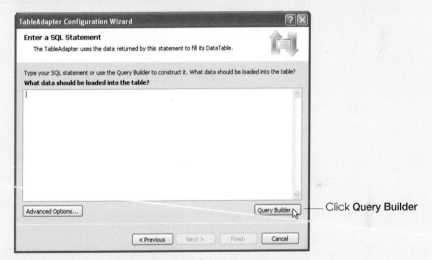

Figure 30.10   Use **Query Builder** to create SQL statement.

6. ***Adding the Products table to the Query Builder dialog***. Before you can use the **Query Builder** dialog, you must select a database table. In the **Add Table** dialog select `Products`, and click the **Add** button (Fig. 30.11). [*Note:* The **Add Table** dialog may take a few seconds to pop up.] Click **Close** to close the **Add Table** dialog.

7. ***Selecting information from the database.*** You are ready to retrieve the val-ues for all eight fields of the `Products` table. In the **Query Builder** dialog, check the ***(All Columns)** checkbox in the `Products` table at the top of the dialog. Your `SELECT` statement should appear as in Fig. 30.12. This state-ment will retrieve the `ProductID`, `Title`, `Authors`, `Copyright`, `Edition`, `ISBN#`, `Coverart` and `Description` field values from the `Products` table of the database. You will later use this information to populate the `List-Box` in the `Books.aspx` page. Click **OK** to close the **Query Builder** dialog. Then click **Finish** to close the **Enter a SQL Statement** dialog.

(cont.)

Select **Products**

Click to add table

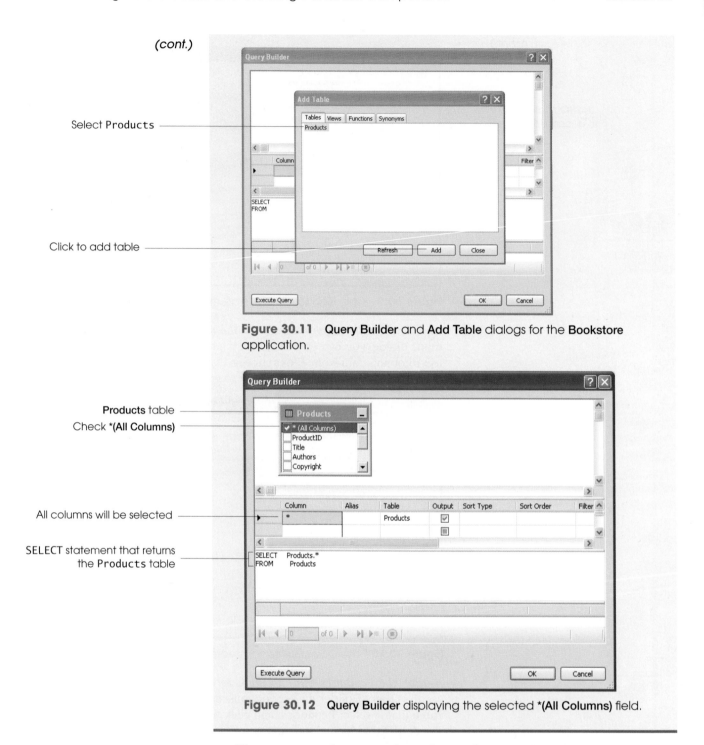

Figure 30.11 **Query Builder** and **Add Table** dialogs for the **Bookstore** application.

Products table
Check ***(All Columns)**

All columns will be selected

SELECT statement that returns the **Products** table

Figure 30.12 **Query Builder** displaying the selected ***(All Columns)** field.

The query you just created can be used to populate the `ListBox` on the `Books.aspx` page. The query returns the entire `Products` table. For the `Details-View` on the `BookInformation.aspx` page, different information is displayed based on the book the user selects in the `ListBox` on the `Books.aspx` page. Therefore, we need a query that selects the information for a specific book. Next, you will add another query with a **WHERE** clause. This query will be used to populate the `DetailsView` on the `BookInformation.aspx` page.

Adding a Query with a
WHERE Clause

1. ***Adding a query with a WHERE clause.*** A WHERE clause in a query enables you to filter the data returned from the database. To add a second query, ensure that the **DataSet Designer** is open by expanding the **App_Code** folder in the **Solution Explorer** and double clicking **BooksDataSet.xsd** to view the **DataSet** designer (Fig. 30.13).

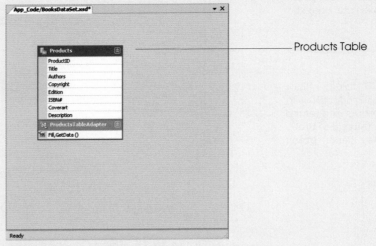

Products Table

Figure 30.13 **DataSet** designer for `BooksDataSet.xsd`.

2. ***Adding a query that selects a specific book.*** Click the `Products` table to select it, then select **Data > Add > Query...** Make sure that the **Use SQL statements** radio button is selected and click **Next >**. In the **Choose a Query Type** dialog, make sure that the **SELECT which returns rows** radio button is selected and click **Next >** (Fig. 30.14). You want to return a row from the database, because each row represents one book.

Select the query type
that returns a row

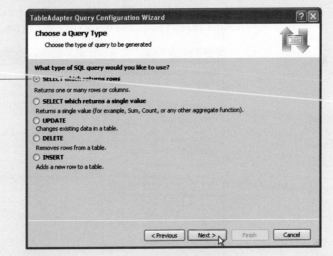

Figure 30.14 Selecting a query type.

3. ***Defining the query.*** In the **Specify SQL SELECT statement** dialog, click the **Query Builder... button**. In the **Products** window, uncheck the `Title`, `Authors`, and `Coverart` checkboxes so only the `ProductID`, `Copyright`, `Edition`, `ISBN#`, and `Description` checkboxes are selected. Then, in the table below, uncheck the **Output** field of `ProductID` and type `@productID` in the `ProductID` **Filter** field. This filter establishes the WHERE clause (Fig. 30.15). Click **OK** to finish the query and return to the **Specify SQL SELECT statement** dialog. Then click **Next >**.

(cont.)

Products window

Only the ProductID, Copyright, Edition, ISBN#, Description CheckBoxes are checked

Selected values appear

SELECT statement that matches ProductID with an input and returns Copyright, Edition, ISBN#, Description

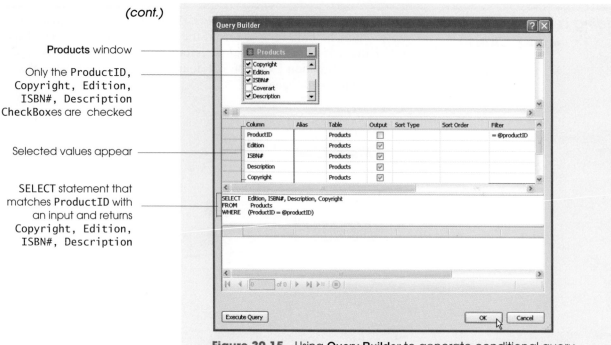

Figure 30.15 Using **Query Builder** to generate conditional query.

4. ***Specifying method names for the queries.*** In the next dialog, change the values in the two textboxes from FillBy and GetDataBy to FillByProductID and GetDataByProductID, respectively (Fig. 30.16). Click **Next >** to confirm that all steps of the **TableAdapter Query Configuration Wizard** have completed successfully, then click **Finish**. A **Microsoft Visual Studio** dialog will appear warning you that the query you just created has a different schema than the main query (Fig. 30.17). Click **OK** to finish in this dialog creating the query. You will later use this information to populate the DetailsView in the BookInformation.aspx page.

Check both query method **CheckBoxes**

Rename query methods

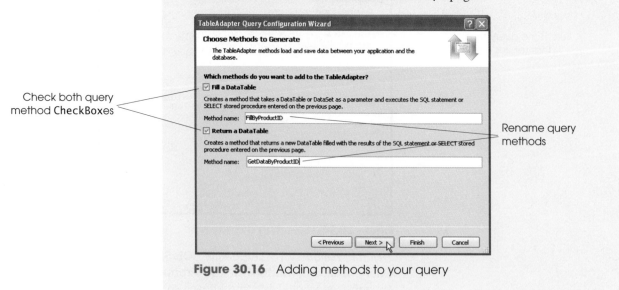

Figure 30.16 Adding methods to your query

(cont.)

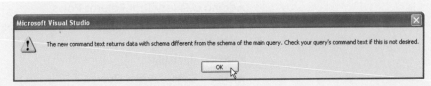

Figure 30.17 Warning dialog displayed because the new query schema is different than the main query

5. *Saving the project.* Select **File > Save All** to save your modified code.

Now that you have added a TableAdapter that uses two SQL queries to retrieve data from Bookstore.mdf, the bookTitlesListBox on the Books.aspx page and the the booksDetailsView on the BookInformation.aspx page can be easily populated, as described in Tutorial 31.

SELF-REVIEW

1. The _____ dialog allows you to select a database table to add to the **Query Builder** dialog.
   a) **Add Table**   b) **Database**
   c) **Database Table**   d) **Data Link Properties**

2. The _____ field in **Query Builder** establishes the **WHERE** clause in the resulting SQL statement.
   a) **Output**   b) **Sort Type**
   c) **Filter**   d) **Sort Order**

Answers: 1) a. 2) c.

30.4 Wrap-Up

In this tutorial, you were introduced to the information tier of the three-tier, Web-based **Bookstore** application. You examined the contents of the Bookstore.mdf database. You configured the information tier of the **Bookstore** application by creating a database connection and a TableAdapter. You used the **Query Builder** to create SQL statements that will retrieve book information from the database.

In the next tutorial, you will create the middle tier of your **Bookstore** application. You will add code to your application to control what data from the database will be displayed on the ASPX page.

SKILLS SUMMARY

Adding a Database Connection Using the Server Explorer Window

■ Right click the **App_Data** folder in the **Solution Explorer** window and select **Add Existing Item...** from the menu.

■ In the **Add Existing Item** dialog, navigate to the directory that contains the desired database. Select the database and click **Add**.

Adding a DataSet to the ASPX Page

■ Select **Website > Add New Item...** to display the **Add New Item** dialog. [*Note:* Remeber to deselect the **App_Code** folder.]

■ Select **DataSet** in the **Templates:** pane and rename the DataSet.

■ In **TableAdapter Configuration Wizard**, choose and save your connection string.

■ Choose a method to access the database (such as using SQL statements).

■ Use **Query Builder** to generate desired SQL statement.

Adding a Query That Returns Rows

■ Open the **DataSet** designer by double clicking the DataSet's name in the **App_Code** folder.

■ Select the table.

■ Select **Data > Add > Query...**

■ Choose the command type.

■ Choose the query type that returns a row.

■ Use **Query Builder** to build the desired SQL statement.

■ Rename the query methods.

KEY TERMS

App_Code folder—The project folder where the DataSet you created is placed.

App_Data folder—The project folder where the database you added is placed.

MULTIPLE-CHOICE QUESTIONS

30.1 _____ is an example of a database product.

a) Sybase
b) Microsoft SQL Server
c) Oracle
d) All of the above.

30.2 The _____ is used when creating SQL statements visually.

a) **Server Explorer** window
b) **Query Builder** tool
c) Both a and b.
d) None of the above.

30.3 DataSets get added to the _____ folder of the application.

a) App_Code
b) App_Data
c) Default
d) None of the above.

30.4 Another name for the database tier is _____.

a) the information tier
b) the bottom tier
c) Both a and b.
d) None of the above.

30.5 A SQL Server 2005 Express database file is placed in the _____ folder.

a) App_Code
b) App_Data
c) Default
d) None of the above.

EXERCISES

30.6 (*Phone Book Application: Database*) Create the database connections and queries for the **Phone Book** application by using the **Server Explorer** window and the **Query Builder** tool.

a) *Opening the application.* Open the **Phone Book** application that you created in Tutorial 29.

b) *Adding the Phone.mdf database to the Phone Book application.* In the **Solution Explorer**, add the database `C:\Examples\Tutorial30\Exercises\Databases\Phone.mdf` to the App_Data folder, as you did in *Steps 2-3* of the box *Adding the Bookstore.mdf Database to the Bookstore Application.*

c) *Adding a DataSet to the Phone Book application.* Add a DataSet to the **Phone Book** application, and name it phoneNumberDataSet. Use the **TableAdapter Configuration Wizard** to connect phoneNumberDataSet to the Phone.mdf database. Proceed through the wizard as demonstrated in the box *Creating a DataSet from the Bookstore Database.* Like *Step 7* of that box, use the **Query Builder** to create a SQL statement that will return all the stored values in the database.

d) *Saving the project.* Select **File > Save All** to save your modified code.

30.7 (*US State Facts Application: Database*) Create the database connections and queries for the **USStateFacts** application by using the **Server Explorer** window and the **Query Builder** tool.

a) *Opening the application.* Open the **US State Facts** application that you created in Tutorial 29.

b) *Adding the `StateFacts.mdf` database to the US State Facts application.* In the **Solution Explorer**, add the database `C:\Examples\Tutorial30\Exercises\Data-bases\StateFacts.mdf` to the App_Data folder, as you did in *Steps 2-3* of the box *Adding the `Bookstore.mdf` Database to the Bookstore Application.*

c) *Adding a DataSet to the US State Facts application.* Add a DataSet to the **US State Facts** application, and name it statesDataSet. Use the **TableAdapter Configuration Wizard** to connect statesDataSet to the StateFacts.mdf database. Proceed through the wizard as demonstrated in the box *Creating a DataSet from the Bookstore Database.* Like *Step 7* of that box, use the **Query Builder** to create a SQL statement that will return all the stored values in the database.

d) *Using Query Builder to add a query with a WHERE clause to the US State Facts application.* As shown in the box, *Adding a Query with a WHERE Clause*, add a query that selects **Capital**, **Flower**, **Tree** and **Bird** from the table using the **StateID** field as the filter for the **WHERE** clause. Like *Step 4* of this box, rename the query methods—in this case to FillByStateID and GetDataByStateID.

e) *Saving the project.* Select **File > Save All** to save your modified code.

Bookstore Application: Middle Tier

Introducing Code-Behind Files and Databound Web controls

In earlier tutorials, you built the client tier and created connections to the information tier of the **Bookstore** application. Using the Visual Web Developer, you were able to design the user interface of this Web-based application. In this tutorial, you will learn about the middle tier and complete the **Bookstore** application by programming the middle tier's functionality. Recall that the middle tier is responsible for interacting with the client and information tiers. The middle tier accepts user requests for data from the client tier, retrieves the data from the information tier (that is, the database) and responds to the client's requests.

31.1 Reviewing the Bookstore Application

You have taken the three-tier **Bookstore** application for a test-drive (in Tutorial 28) and have created the Web controls (Tutorial 29) and database components (Tutorial 30) for the application. Now you will need to write code and create databound Web controls to specify the functionality of the **Bookstore** application. Before you begin to create the middle tier, you should review the pseudocode and the ACE table (Fig. 31.1) for this application:

> When the Books page is requested
> > Retrieve the book titles from the database
> > Display book titles in a ListBox
>
> When the user selects a book title from the ListBox and clicks the View Information Button
> > Store the selected book in a variable
> > Redirect the user to the BookInformation page
>
> When the BookInformation page is requested
> > Retrieve the selected book's information from a database
> > Display the book title in a Label
> > Display the authors in a Label
> > Display the cover art in an Image
> > Display the remaining information in a DetailsView table
>
> When the user presses the Book List Button on the BookInformation page
> > Redirect the client browser back to the Books page

Action	Control/Object	Event
Label the Books page	availableLabel, instructionsLabel	
	Page	Load (for Books.aspx)
Display book titles in a ListBox	bookTitlesListBox	
	informationButton	Click
Store the selected book in a variable	Session	
Redirect the user to the BookInformation page	Response	
	Page	Load (for BookInformation.aspx)
Retrieve the selected book's information from a database	ProductsTableAdapter, ProductsDataTable, Session	
Display the book title in a Label	bookTitleLabel	
Display the authors in a Label	authorsLabel	
Display the cover art in an image	bookImage	
Display the remaining information in a Table	bookDetailsView	
	bookListButton	Click
Redirect the client browser back to the Books page	Response	

Figure 31.1   ACE table for the Web-based **Bookstore** application.

In this tutorial, you will implement the interaction between the user interface and the database of the **Bookstore** application. This means that you will write the code that determines which image will be displayed by the Image control and the code that redirects the client browser to another page when a Button is clicked. You also will use databound controls and queries (created in Tutorial 30) to determine which information will be retrieved from the database and displayed in the DetailsView control.

31.2 Programming the Books Page's Code-Behind File and Creating a Databound ListBox

Although you have designed your **Bookstore** application's GUI and have added database connections, the **Bookstore** currently does not have any other functionality. You will now begin programming your application. You start with the Books.aspx page in the following box.

Changing the Class Name in Books.aspx.vb

1. ***Opening the Bookstore application in Visual Web Developer.*** Open Visual Web Developer, and select **File > Open Web Site...** to display the **Open Web Site** dialog. In this dialog, click **File System**, then locate the **Bookstore** folder in the C:\SimplyVB directory and click the **Bookstore** folder to highlight it. Click the **Open** Button to open the **Bookstore** application.

(cont.)

2. ***Displaying the Books.aspx page's code-behind file in the Solution Explorer.*** Every ASPX page created in Visual Web Developer has a corresponding class written in a .NET language, such as Visual Basic. This class includes event handlers, initialization code, methods and other supporting code and represents the middle tier of your application. The Visual Basic file that contains this class is called the **code-behind file** and provides the ASPX page's functionality. It has the file extension .aspx.vb. If it is not already selected, click the **Nest Related Files** button (Fig. 31.2) in the **Solution Explorer** toolbar. Expand the Books.aspx node to display the code-behind file, Books.aspx.vb (Fig. 31.2).

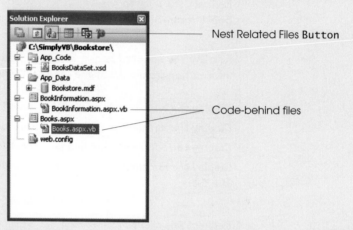

Nest Related Files **Button**

Code-behind files

Figure 31.2 Code-behind files for the Books.aspx and BookInformation.aspx pages in the **Solution Explorer**.

3. ***Viewing the Books.aspx.vb code-behind file.*** Figure 31.3 displays Books.aspx.vb—the code-behind file for Books.aspx. Recall that Visual Studio generates this code-behind file when the project is created. To view this file, double click Books.aspx.vb in the **Solution Explorer** window. [*Note:* You also can right click Books.aspx and select **View Code** to view the code-behind file.] There are no commands in this file because we have not yet started to write event handlers.

Change this class name to Books

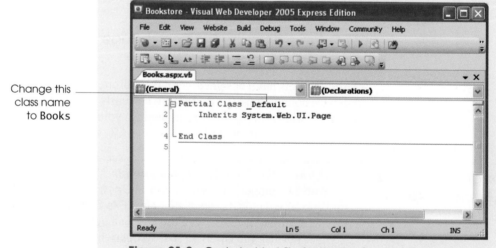

Figure 31.3 Code-behind file for the Books.aspx.

(cont.)

4. ***Changing the class name in Books.aspx.vb.*** Change the class name in line 2 of Books.aspx.vb from _Default to Books (Fig. 31.4). Line 3 of Books.aspx.vb indicates that this class inherits from the Page class. The Page class defines the basic functionality for an ASPX page, much as the Form class defines the basic functionality for a Windows application Form. The Page class is located in the System.Web.UI namespace. The Page class provides properties, methods and events that are useful for creating Web-based applications.

Class name changed to Books

Figure 31.4   Changing the application's class name.

5. ***Modifying the Inherits statement in Books.aspx.*** You also need to go into **Source** mode and change the last part of the Page statement in line 1 of the Books.aspx page from Inherits="_Default" to Inherits="Books" (Fig. 31.5).

```
1    @ Page Language="VB" AutoEventWireup="false" CodeFile="Default.aspx.vb" Inherits="Books" %>
2
3    DOCTYPE html PUBLIC "-//W3C//DTD XHTML 1.0 Transitional//EN" "http://www.w3.org/TR/xhtml1/DTD/x]
4
5    tml xmlns="http://www.w3.org/1999/xhtml" >
6    ead runat="server">
7        <title>Untitled Page</title>
8    head>
9    ody>
10       <form id="form1" runat="server">
11       <div>
12
13       </div>
14       </form>
15   body>
16   html>
```

Figure 31.5   Changing the Books.aspx Inherits statement.

6. ***Saving the project.*** Select **File > Save All** to save your modified code.

Next, you will define the informationButton_Click event handler. This event handler is invoked when the user clicks the **View Information** Button. The event handler determines the selected book and redirects the client browser to the Book-Information page. You create the event handler in the following box.

Defining the Click Event Handler for the Books.aspx Page

1. ***Creating the Click event handler.*** Switch to design mode of the Books.aspx file. Double click the informationButton control. The informationButton_Click event handler should appear in the file Books.aspx.vb.

2. ***Adding code to the Click event handler.*** Add lines 8–12 of Fig. 31.6 to the event handler. Values are not maintained across different ASPX pages. This means that values stored in instance variables cannot be passed from page to page. However, ASP.NET provides **Session** items for sharing values among ASPX pages. Line 9 allows information to be maintained across the **Book-store** application's ASPX pages by adding a **key-value pair** to the Session object. A key-value pair associates a value with a corresponding name (key) which identifies the value.

(cont.)

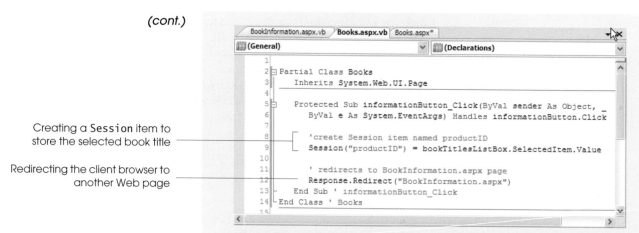

Figure 31.6 `informationButton_Click` event handler definition.

Creating a `Session` item to store the selected book title

Redirecting the client browser to another Web page

In this case, the key is the name `productID`, and the value is the `ProductID` of the selected book, which is determined by `bookTitlesListBox.SelectedItem.Value`. The storage of key-value pairs across Web pages is made possible by **session state**, which is ASP.NET's built-in support for tracking data. Session state enables the current user's information (including the book the user has selected) to be maintained across a browser session.

After the `productID` key has been provided with a value, the page redirects the client browser by calling `Response.Redirect` (line 12). The **Response** object is a predefined ASP.NET object (inherited from class `Page`) that provides methods for responding to clients. **Redirect** is one of the `Response` object's methods, which is used to specify the Web page to which the client browser will be redirected. `Response.Redirect` takes the URL of the page to which the client browser redirects as an argument. When the redirect occurs, the session-state information in the `Session` object is passed to the `BookInformation` page and can be used in that page.

3. *Saving the project.* Select **File > Save All** to save your modified code.

To populate the `bookTitlesListBox` control with the titles of the textbooks, an `ObjectDataSource`, often called a **business object**, is used to connect the application's bottom tier with the user interface. Thus, a business object is part of the middle tier of an application and mediates interactions between the other two tiers. In an ASP.NET Web application, a `TableAdapter` typically serves as the business object that retrieves the data from the bottom-tier database and makes it available to the top-tier user interface through a `DataSet`.

Creating a Databound ListBox using an ObjectDataSource

1. *Binding data to an existing ListBox.* Switch to design mode of the **Books.aspx** file, and select the `bookTitlesListBox` control. Click the black triangle in the upper-right corner of the `bookTitlesListBox` (Fig. 31.7) to open the **ListBox Tasks** menu. [*Note:* You can also right click the `ListBox` and select **Show Smart Tag**.] In this menu, click **Choose Data Source...** to open the **Data Source Configuration Wizard**.

2. *Choosing a data source.* In the **Choose a Data Source** dialog of the **Data Source Configuration Wizard**, select **<New Data Source...>** from the **Select a data source:** ComboBox (Fig. 31.8). This opens the **Choose a Data Source Type** dialog.

(cont.)

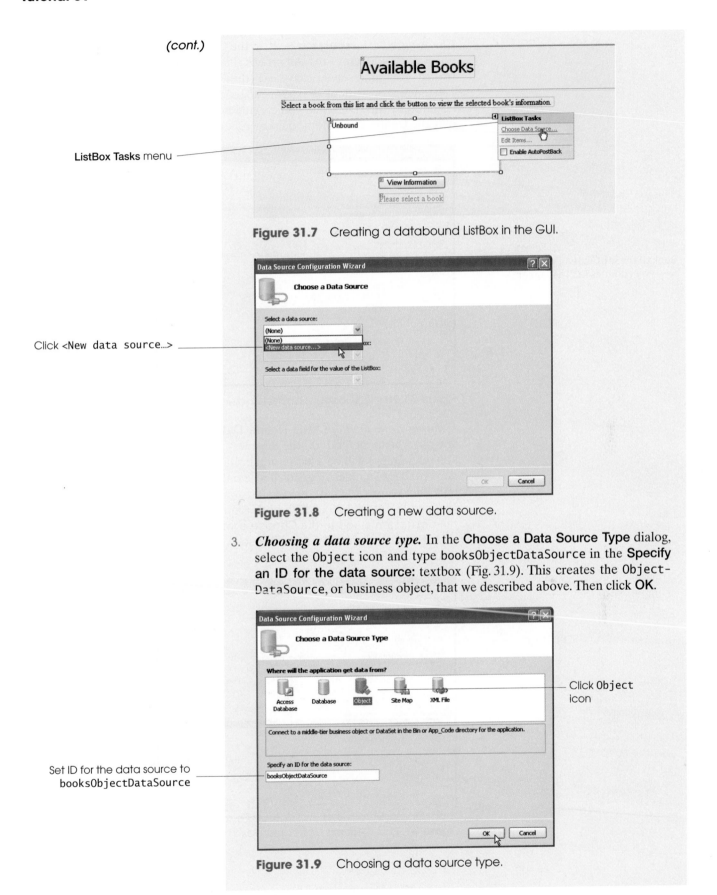

Figure 31.7   Creating a databound ListBox in the GUI.

ListBox Tasks menu —

Click <New data source...> —

Figure 31.8   Creating a new data source.

3. ***Choosing a data source type.*** In the **Choose a Data Source Type** dialog, select the Object icon and type booksObjectDataSource in the **Specify an ID for the data source:** textbox (Fig. 31.9). This creates the Object-DataSource, or business object, that we described above. Then click **OK**.

Click Object icon

Set ID for the data source to booksObjectDataSource

Figure 31.9   Choosing a data source type.

(cont.)

4. ***Choosing a business object.*** Next, in the **Choose a Business Object** dialog, select BooksDataSetTableAdapters.ProductsTableAdapter (Fig. 31.10). [*Note:* You may need to save the project to see the Products-TableAdapters.] BooksDataSetTableAdapters is a namespace that was declared by the IDE when you created BooksDataSet. Click **Next >** to display the **Define Data Methods** screen.

Select
BooksDataSetTableAdapters.
ProductsTableAdapter

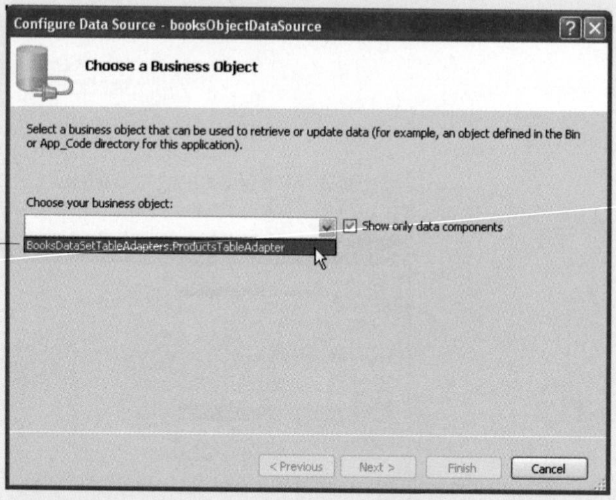

Figure 31.10   Choosing a business object.

5. ***Defining data methods.*** The **Define Data Methods** screen allows you to specify which method of the business object (in this case, Products-TableAdapter) will be used to obtain the data accessed through the booksObjectDataSource. You can choose only methods that return data, so the only choices provided are the GetData and GetDataByProductID methods (defined in Tutorial 30), which both return a ProductsDataTable. Choose the GetData method in the **Choose a method:** ComboBox (Fig. 31.11) and click **Finish** to return to the **Choose a Data Source** dialog of the **Data Source Configuration Wizard**.

SELECT tab

Select
GetData()
method

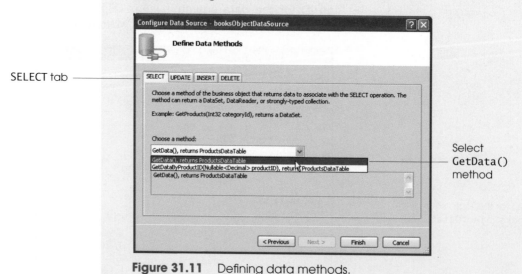

Figure 31.11   Defining data methods.

(cont.)

6. ***Finish choosing a data source.*** After returning to the **Choose a Data Source** dialog, the newly created data source, booksObjectDataSource, should be selected in the top ComboBox. The middle combobox allows you to choose the field in the Products table to display in bookTitlesListBox. Choose Title in this ComboBox. The bottom ComboBox allows you to choose the field that represents a value associated with each item displayed in book-TitlesListBox. Choose ProductID in this ComboBox (Fig. 31.12). Thus, when the bookTitlesListBox is rendered in a Web browser, the list items will display the titles of the textbooks, but the underlying values associated with each item will be the product IDs of the textbooks. Finally, click **OK** to bind the ListBox to the specified data. Note that the text inside the ListBox in design mode now reads Databound instead of Unbound. Also note that an ObjectDataSource control will now be displayed on the page in **Design** mode, but will not be visible in the Web Browser when the program is executed.

Select Title field to be
displayed

Select productID field to be
stored as values associated with
displayed fields

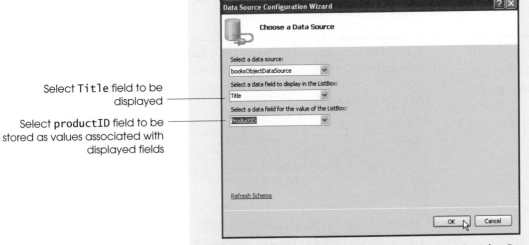

Figure 31.12   Finish defining Data Source for ListBox.

7. ***Saving the project.*** Select **File > Save All** to save your modified code.

Before you begin to program the BookInformation.aspx.vb code-behind file, you need to place images of the book covers in the Bookstore directory so the application can access them. The BookInformation.aspx page will display the cover image of the selected book. You will learn how to place the images in the following box.

Adding Images to the Bookstore Directory

1. ***Locating the images.*** Use Windows Explorer to locate the C:\Examples\Tutorial31\Images directory, which contains images of the book covers.

2. ***Placing the images in the Bookstore directory.*** Copy the four images vcsharp2005htp.png, cpphtp5e.png, vbforprogrammers2.png and OS3E.png, and paste them into the Bookstore directory that is located in the C:\SimplyVB directory on your computer. You can also drag these images directly into the C:\SimplyVB\Bookstore directory a the top of the **Solution Explorer** window in Visual Web Developer. These image files will be used when you program the BookInformation.aspx page.

1. The _____ class defines the basic functionality for an ASPX page.

   a) `Form`   b) `WebForm`

   c) `Page`   d) None of the above.

2. The Page class is located in namespace _____.

   a) `System.Web.UI`   b) `System.Data`

   c) `System.WebForm`   d) `System.Collections`

Answers: 1) c. 2) a.

31.3 Coding the `BookInformation` Page's Code-Behind File and Creating a Databound `DetailsView`

The `BookInformation.aspx` page displays information about the book the user selected. In the following box, you will add the code to the `Page_Load` event handler of the `BookInformation.aspx` page that will retrieve the requested book's information from the database.

Defining the Page_Load Event Handler for the BookInformation.aspx Page

1. **Changing the class name.** Right click `BookInformation.aspx` in the **Solution Explorer** window, and select **View Code** to view the code-behind file `BookInformation.aspx.vb`. Make sure that the class name is `BookInformation` (Fig. 31.13).

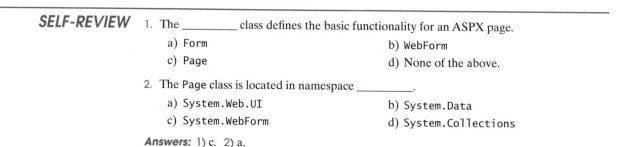

Class name should be `BookInformation`

Figure 31.13 `BookInformation` class.

2. **Inserting the Page_Load event handler.** When the `BookInformation.aspx` page is loaded, we want the book's information to be displayed immediately. An ASPX page's **Page_Load** event handler is invoked automatically when the page is loaded. To insert a `Page_Load` event handler into the `BookInformation` class, select **(Page Events)** from the **Class name** drop-down list, then select **Load** from the **Method name** drop-down list.

Class name drop-down list

Method name drop-down list

Select **Load** from **Method name** drop-down list

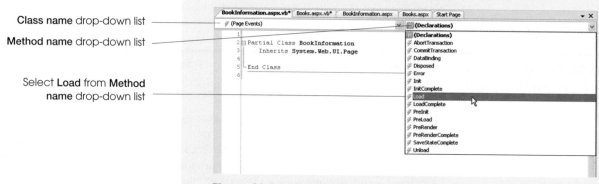

Figure 31.14 `BookInformation` class.

(cont.)   3. ***Creating a `ProductsDataTable` object to hold the Bookstore database information.*** Add lines 8–26 of Fig. 31.15 to the `Page_Load` event handler of the `BookInformation.aspx` page. Lines 9–10 create a `ProductsTable-Adapter` object named `productsAdapter` to connect the application with the Bookstore database. This object reads information from the database and returns it to the application. Lines 13–14 create `productsTable`, an object of class `ProductsDataTable`, to store the information returned by `productsAdapter`. The `productsAdapter.GetData()` method call in line 14 returns a `ProductsDataTable` containing the information from the database's `Products` table.

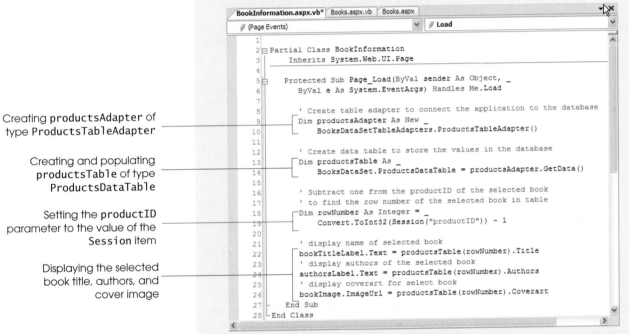

Creating `productsAdapter` of type `ProductsTableAdapter`

Creating and populating `productsTable` of type `ProductsDataTable`

Setting the `productID` parameter to the value of the `Session` item

Displaying the selected book title, authors, and cover image

```
1
2 Partial Class BookInformation
3     Inherits System.Web.UI.Page
4
5     Protected Sub Page_Load(ByVal sender As Object, _
6         ByVal e As System.EventArgs) Handles Me.Load
7
8         ' Create table adapter to connect the application to the database
9         Dim productsAdapter As New _
10            BooksDataSetTableAdapters.ProductsTableAdapter()
11
12         ' Create data table to store the values in the database
13         Dim productsTable As _
14            BooksDataSet.ProductsDataTable = productsAdapter.GetData()
15
16         ' Subtract one from the productID of the selected book
17         ' to find the row number of the selected book in table
18         Dim rowNumber As Integer = _
19            Convert.ToInt32(Session("productID")) - 1
20
21         ' display name of selected book
22         bookTitleLabel.Text = productsTable(rowNumber).Title
23         ' display authors of the selected book
24         authorsLabel.Text = productsTable(rowNumber).Authors
25         ' display coverart for select book
26         bookImage.ImageUrl = productsTable(rowNumber).Coverart
27     End Sub
28 End Class
```

Figure 31.15 `Page_Load` event handler modified to set a parameter value and open a database connection.

4. ***Finding the index of the selected book.*** The index in the `productsTable` of the selected book can be found using the book's `ProductID` field. Recall that in the `Books.aspx` page, you stored the `ProductID` of the selected book in the `Session` item with the key `productID`. Since row indices begin at zero in the `productsTable`, and the `ProductID`s in our database begin at one, we subtract one from the `ProductID` and store this value in variable `rowNumber` (lines 18–19). Line 19 uses the `Session` item to retrieve the `ProductID` of the selected book.

5. ***Accessing the stored data for the selected book.*** In the `productsTable` of type `ProductsDataTable`, information for a specific book can be accessed via the book's index, which is stored in `rowNumber`. The expression `productsTable(rowNumber)` (seen in lines 22, 24 and 26) indicates the book that was selected. Line 22 uses `productsTable(rowNumber).Title` to set `bookTitleLabel`'s **Text** property to the selected book's title. Line 24 uses `productsTable(rowNumber).Authors` to set `authorsLabel`'s **Text** property to the selected book's authors. Line 26 sets the `Image` control's `ImageUrl` property to the name of the selected book's cover image using `ProductsDataTable(rowNumber).Coverart`.

6. ***Saving the project.*** Select **File > Save All** to save your modified code.

The final event handler you define in the BookInformation.aspx page is the bookListButton_Click event handler. This event handler allows the user to return to the list of available books. You create this event handler in the following box.

Defining the bookListButton_Click Event Handler for the BookInformation Page

1. **Creating the bookListButton_Click event handler.** Now you are ready to define the event handler for the bookListButton Button. Select the Book-Information.aspx page and switch to design mode. Double click the **Book List** Button to create the bookListButton_Click event handler. The **Book List** Button is used to redirect the client browser to the Books.aspx page.

2. **Adding code to the event handler.** Add lines 33–34 of Fig. 31.16 to the bookListButton_Click event handler. Line 34 redirects the user to the Books.aspx page by calling Response.Redirect.

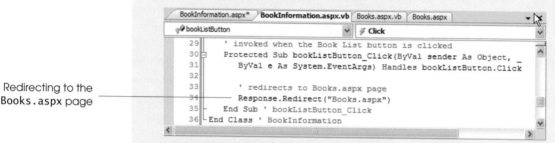

Redirecting to the Books.aspx page

Figure 31.16 Definition of the bookListButton_Click event handler.

3. **Saving the project.** Select **File > Save All** to save your modified code.

No code in BookInformation.aspx.vb's code-behind files is necessary to display the selected book's ISBN#, Edition, Copyright, and Description in the DetailsView control. Below we demonstrate how to populate the DetailsView control in the design mode of BookInformation.aspx using a databound DetailsView control.

Creating a Databound DetailsView Using an ObjectDataSource

1. **Making an existing DetailsView databound.** Switch to design mode of the BookInformation.aspx page and select the bookDetailsView control. Click the black triangle in the upper-right corner of the bookDetailsView (Fig. 31.17) to display the **DetailsView Tasks** menu. Select **<New Data Source...>** in the **Choose Data Source:** ComboBox. This opens the **Choose a Data Source Type** dialog of the **Data Source Configuration Wizard**.

2. **Choosing a data source type.** In the **Choose a Data Source Type** dialog, select the Object icon and type informationObjectDataSource in the **Specify an ID for the data source:** textbox, then click **OK**. This will automatically direct you to the **Choose a Business Object** dialog. Then, in the **Choose a Business Object** dialog, select BooksDataSetTable-Adapters.ProductsTableAdapter and click **Next >**. This will bring you to the **Define Data Methods** screen.

(cont.)

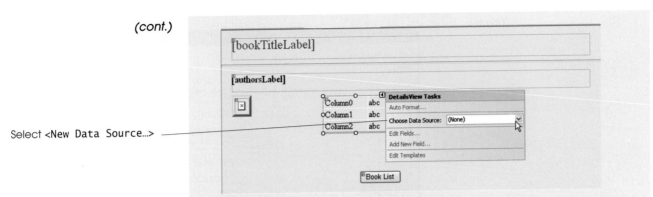

Figure 31.17 Select <New Data Source...> in the **Choose Data Source:** TextBox.

3. *Defining data methods.* The **Define Data Methods** screen allows you to specify which method of the business object (in this case, ProductsTable-Adapter) will be used to obtain the data accessed through the products-ObjectDataSource. In the **Select** tab, choose GetDataByProductID in the **Choose a method:** ComboBox (Fig. 31.18). Recall that this method was defined in Tutorial 30 and that it specifies a parameter indicating which book to select. Click **Next >** to move to the **Define Parameters** dialog.

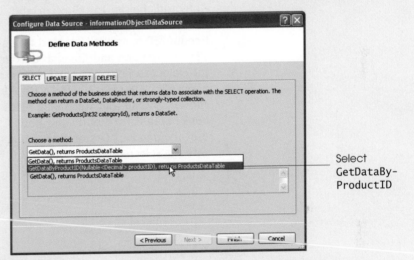

Figure 31.18 Defining the data methods.

4. *Defining data parameters.* The **Define Parameters** dialog allows you to specify the value for @productID that is used by ProductsTableAdapter in the WHERE clause when executing the GetDataByProductID method. Recall that the selected book's ProductID was stored using a Session object in informationButton's Click event in the Books.aspx page. To access this stored value, select Session in the **Parameter Source:** drop-down list. A **Session Field:** textbox will appear. Type productID in this textbox (Fig. 31.19). This will use the Session object's key (productID) to retrieve the corresponding value—the selected book's ProductID, which can be used in the WHERE clause described above. Now click **Finish**. After returning to BookInformation.aspx's designer, note that the books-DetailsView now lists all the fields in your Products table.

(cont.)

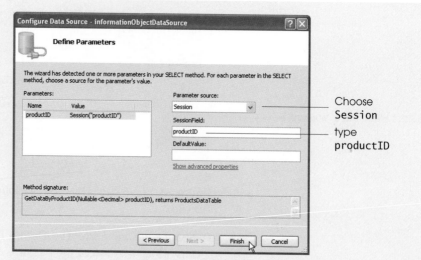

Figure 31.19 Defining the query's parameters.

5. *Specifying the displayed fields.* In the **DetailsView Tasks** menu, click **Edit Fields...** (Fig. 31.20) to display the **Fields** dialog (Fig. 31.21). In the **Selected fields** ListBox in the dialog's lower-left corner, highlight ProductID and click the Button with a red **X** on it. This removes ProductID from the **Selected fields** ListBox. Repeat this step, removing Title, Authors and Coverart from the list. When the only items left in the **Selected fields** list box are Copyright, Edition, ISBN# and Description, click **OK** (Fig. 31.22). In **Design** mode, the booksDetailsView now shows only the four remaining fields. Now when a book is selected in the bookTitlesListBox on the Books.aspx page, ProductsTableAdapter uses the productID stored in the Session object to fill bookDetailsView with the selected book's Copyright, Edition, ISBN# and Description.

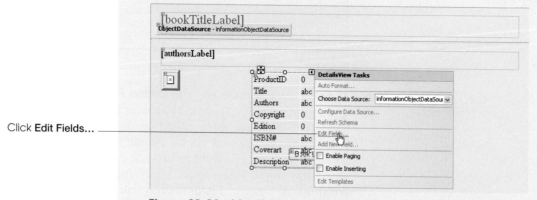

Figure 31.20 Modifying the displayed fields in the DetailsView.

(cont.)

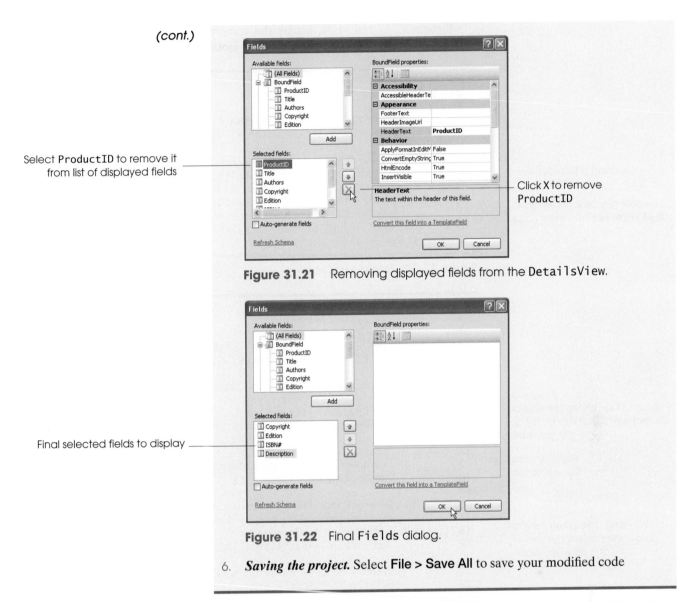

Select **ProductID** to remove it from list of displayed fields

Click **X** to remove **ProductID**

Figure 31.21   Removing displayed fields from the **DetailsView**.

Final selected fields to display

Figure 31.22   Final **Fields** dialog.

6. *Saving the project.* Select **File > Save All** to save your modified code

Now that you have completed the **Bookstore** application, you will test it to ensure that it is functioning properly in the following box.

Testing Your Completed Bookstore Application

1. *Running the application.* Select **Debug > Start Debugging** to run your application. Select a book title from the **ListBox**, and click the **View Information Button**. This application performs the same functions as the completed **Bookstore** application that you test-drove in Tutorial 28. If no book title is selected when the **View Information Button** is clicked, the **RequiredFieldValidator** tells the user to **Please select a book**.

2. *Closing the application.* Close your running application by clicking the browser's close box.

3. *Closing the IDE.* Close Visual Web Developer by clicking its close box.

Figures 31.23 and 31.24 display the complete code listing for the Books.aspx and BookInformation.aspx pages of the **Bookstore** application, respectively.

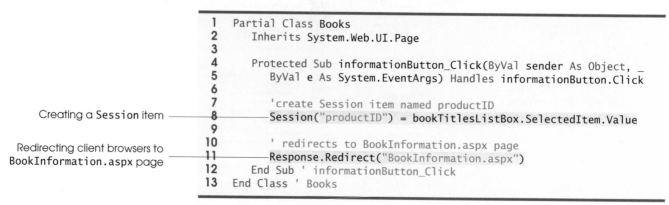

Creating a Session item

Redirecting client browsers to BookInformation.aspx page

```
1  Partial Class Books
2     Inherits System.Web.UI.Page
3
4     Protected Sub informationButton_Click(ByVal sender As Object, _
5        ByVal e As System.EventArgs) Handles informationButton.Click
6
7        'create Session item named productID
8        Session("productID") = bookTitlesListBox.SelectedItem.Value
9
10       ' redirects to BookInformation.aspx page
11       Response.Redirect("BookInformation.aspx")
12    End Sub ' informationButton_Click
13 End Class ' Books
```

Figure 31.23   Books.aspx code.

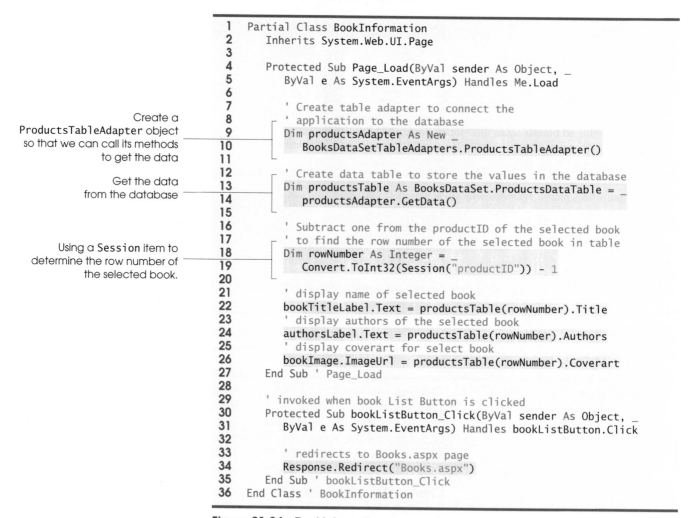

Create a ProductsTableAdapter object so that we can call its methods to get the data

Get the data from the database

Using a Session item to determine the row number of the selected book.

```
1  Partial Class BookInformation
2     Inherits System.Web.UI.Page
3
4     Protected Sub Page_Load(ByVal sender As Object, _
5        ByVal e As System.EventArgs) Handles Me.Load
6
7        ' Create table adapter to connect the
8        ' application to the database
9        Dim productsAdapter As New _
10          BooksDataSetTableAdapters.ProductsTableAdapter()
11
12       ' Create data table to store the values in the database
13       Dim productsTable As BooksDataSet.ProductsDataTable = _
14          productsAdapter.GetData()
15
16       ' Subtract one from the productID of the selected book
17       ' to find the row number of the selected book in table
18       Dim rowNumber As Integer = _
19          Convert.ToInt32(Session("productID")) - 1
20
21       ' display name of selected book
22       bookTitleLabel.Text = productsTable(rowNumber).Title
23       ' display authors of the selected book
24       authorsLabel.Text = productsTable(rowNumber).Authors
25       ' display coverart for select book
26       bookImage.ImageUrl = productsTable(rowNumber).Coverart
27    End Sub ' Page_Load
28
29    ' invoked when book List Button is clicked
30    Protected Sub bookListButton_Click(ByVal sender As Object, _
31       ByVal e As System.EventArgs) Handles bookListButton.Click
32
33       ' redirects to Books.aspx page
34       Response.Redirect("Books.aspx")
35    End Sub ' bookListButton_Click
36 End Class ' BookInformation
```

Figure 31.24   BookInformation.aspx code.

SELF-REVIEW   1. A(n) _____ reads data from a database.

  a) TableAdapter   b) SQL statement

  c) Query Builder   d) DataSet

Answers: 1) a.

31.4 Internet and Web Resources

Please take a moment to visit each of these sites briefly. To save typing time, use the hot links on the enclosed CD or at www.deitel.com.

www.asp.net
This Microsoft site overviews ASP.NET and provides ASP.NET tutorials. The site also includes the IBuySpy e-commerce storefront example that uses ASP.NET and links to Web sites where users can purchase books.

www.asp101.com/aspplus
This site overviews ASP.NET and includes articles, code examples and links to ASP.NET resources.

www.411asp.net
This resource site provides users with ASP.NET tutorials and code samples. The community pages allow users to ask questions, answer questions and post messages.

www.aspfree.com
This site provides free ASP.NET demos and source code. It also provides a list of articles on various topics and a frequently asked questions (FAQs) page.

31.5 Wrap-Up

In this tutorial, you programmed the middle tier of your three-tier **Bookstore** application. By defining methods and event handlers, you specified the actions that execute when the user interacts with ASPX pages. You learned about Session objects and how they are used to maintain session state between ASPX pages. You also learned about the Response.Redirect method to redirect the client browser to other ASPX pages.

After learning about Sessions and Response.Redirect, you used them in the **Bookstore** application. You began with the first ASPX page of the application, Books.aspx. This page retrieved the book titles from the database and displayed the titles in a ListBox control when the ASPX page was loaded. You also retrieved the corresponding product IDs from the database and used them to represent the underlying values associated with each displayed item. You did this by defining a databound ListBox. You then defined the actions that would occur when the user clicks the **View Information** Button. In the Click event handler, you created a Session item to store the product ID of the book selected by the user. You also used the Response.Redirect method in the Click event handler to direct users from the Books.aspx page to the BookInformation.aspx page.

You then defined the BookInformation.aspx page's Page_Load event handler to display the title, authors and cover of the selected book. Recall that you used the value stored in the Session object to determine the book's product ID selected by the user. You also used a databound DetailsView control to display the copyright date, ISBN number, edition, and description of the selected book. Through programming, you were able to control the flow of data from the information tier to the client tier, completing the three-tier **Bookstore** application. You also learned about ASP.NET resources available on the Web.

In the next tutorial, you will learn how to handle exceptions, which are indications of problems that occur during an application's execution. You will use exception handling to verify user input. Throughout the text, you have been using Val to perform this functionality. In the next tutorial, you will learn a more sophisticated technique for handling invalid user input.

SKILLS SUMMARY

Accessing the Code-Behind File
- Click the **Nest Related Files** button in the **Solution Explorer** window.
- Click the plus box next to the desired ASPX page to display the corresponding code-behind file name.

■ Double click the code-behind file name to view the code-behind file.

Creating Databound Controls

■ Click the black triangle in the upper-right corner of the `bookTitlesListBox` to open the **ListBox Tasks** menu. You can also right click the `ListBox` and select `Show Smart Tag`.

■ In this menu, click **Choose Data Source...**.

■ Follow the steps in the **Data Source Configuration Wizard**.

Creating and Using a `Session` Item

■ Type `Session("`*nameOfKey*`")`, where *nameOfKey* represents the key in a key-value pair. Assign this item a value in an assignment statement.

■ Use `Session("`*nameOfKey*`")` to retrieve the item's value.

Redirecting the Client Browser to Another Web Page

■ Type `Redirect.Response("`*URLOfPage*`")`, where *URLOfPage* represents the URL of the page to which the client browser redirects.

KEY TERMS

business object—A middle-tier object that retrieves data from the bottom-tier database and makes it available to the top-tier user interface.

code-behind file—Visual Basic .NET file that contains a class which provides an ASPX page's functionality.

key-value pair—Associates a value with a corresponding key, which is used to identify the value.

ObjectDataSource—Serves as a middle-tier object that retrieves data from the bottom-tier database and makes it available to the top-tier user interface for databound controls.

Page class—Defines the basic functionality for an ASPX page.

Page_Load—An event handler that executes any processing necessary to display a Web page.

Response.Redirect method—Redirects the client browser to another Web page.

SelectedItem.Value property of ListBox—Returns the value of the selected item.

session state—ASP.NET's built-in support for tracking data throughout a browser session.

Session object—Object that is maintained across several Web pages containing a collection of key-value pairs that are specific to a given user.

CONTROLS, EVENTS, PROPERTIES & METHODS

ASPX page Page on which controls are dropped to design the GUI.

■ *Event*

Load—Raised when the ASPX page is created.

■ *Property*

BgColor—Specifies the Web Form's background color.

Image 🖼 Image   This control displays an image on the ASPX page.

■ *In action*

■ *Properties*

BorderStyle—Specifies the appearance of the Image's border.

BorderWidth—Specifies the width of the Image's border.

Height—Specifies the height of the Image control.

ID—Specifies the name used to access the Image control programmatically. The name should be suffixed with Image.

ImageUrl—Specifies the location of the image file.

Width—Specifies the width of the Image control.

Label   A Label   This control displays text on the ASPX page that the user cannot modify.

■ *In action*

Available Books

■ *Properties*

Height—Specifies the height of the Label.

ID—Specifies the name used to access the Label programmatically. The name should be suffixed with Label.

Name (under the expanded Font property in the **Solution Explorer**)—Specifies the name of the font used for the Label's text.

Size (under the expanded Font property in the **Solution Explorer**)—Specifies the size of the Label's text.

Text—Specifies the text displayed on the Label.

Width—Specifies the width of the Label.

ListBox   ☰ ListBox   This control allows the user to view and select from multiple items in a list.

■ *In action*

```
Visual Basic 2005 for Programmers: Second Edition
Visual C# 2005 How to Program: Second Edition
C++ How to Program: Fifth Edition
Operating Systems: Third Edition
```

■ *Properties*

Height—Specifies the height of the ListBox.

ID—Specifies the name used to access the ListBox control programmatically. The name should be suffixed with ListBox.

SelectedIndex—Returns the index of the selected item in the ListBox.

SelectedItem.Value—Returns the value of the selected item in the ListBox.

Width—Specifies the width of the ListBox.

Response This class provides methods for responding to clients.

■ *Method*

Redirect—Redirects the client browser to the specified location.

MULTIPLE-CHOICE QUESTIONS

31.1 The Page_Load event handler _____.

    a) redirects the client browser to different Web pages

    b) defines the functionality when a Button is clicked

    c) executes any processing necessary to display a Web page

    d) defines the functionality when a Web control is selected

31.2 The Response.Redirect method _____.

    a) refreshes the current Web page

    b) sends the client browser to a specified Web page

    c) responds to user input

    d) responds to the click of a Button

31.3 Session items are used in the **Bookstore** application because _____.

a) variables in ASP.NET Web applications must be created as Session items

b) values need to be shared among Web pages

c) Session items are simpler to create than instance variables

d) Both a and b.

31.4 Session state is used for _____ in ASP.NET.

a) tracking user-specific data   b) running an application

c) using a database   d) None of the above.

31.5 The file extension for an ASPX code-behind file is _____.

a) `.asp`   b) `.aspx`

c) `.aspx.vb`   d) `.code`

31.6 The Response object is a predefined ASP.NET object that _____.

a) connects to a database

b) retrieves information from a database

c) creates Web controls

d) provides methods for responding to client requests

31.7 The `Response.Redirect` method takes a(n) _____ as an argument.

a) URL   b) `Integer` value

c) `Boolean` value   d) `OleDbConnection` object

31.8 The _____ property specifies the image that an Image control displays.

a) `ImageGIF`   b) `ImageURL`

c) `Image`   d) `Display`

31.9 The Visual Basic .NET file that contains the ASPX page's corresponding class is called the _____.

a) ASPX file   b) code-behind file

c) class file   d) None of the above.

31.10 Information can be maintained across Web pages by adding a _____ to the Session object.

a) key-value pair   b) number

c) database connection object   d) None of the above.

EXERCISES

31.11 (*Phone Book Application: Functionality*) Define the middle tier for the **Phone Book** application. The running application is shown in Fig. 31.25.

a) *Opening the application.* Open the **Phone Book** application that you created in Tutorial 29 and continued to develop in Tutorial 30.

b) *Populating the namesDropDownList with names in the PhoneBook.aspx page.* In a process similar to the one demonstrated in the box *Creating a Databound ListBox Using an ObjectDataSource*, you need to make namesDropDownList databound. As shown in *Steps 2 and 3* of that box, connect namesDropDownList to a new Object-DataSource called nameObjectDataSource. Then select the automatically generated business object, phoneNumberDataSetTableAdapters.PhoneTableAdapter. Choose the GetData() data method to return data to the DropDownList. Then set the DropDownList's display field to Name and its value field to IDNumber.

c) *Creating the Get Number Button's Click event handler for the PhoneBook.aspx page.* Double click the **Get Number** Button to create the Click event's event handler.

d) *Creating a Session item.* In the Click event handler, create a Session item with the key IDNumber to store the selected IDNumber.

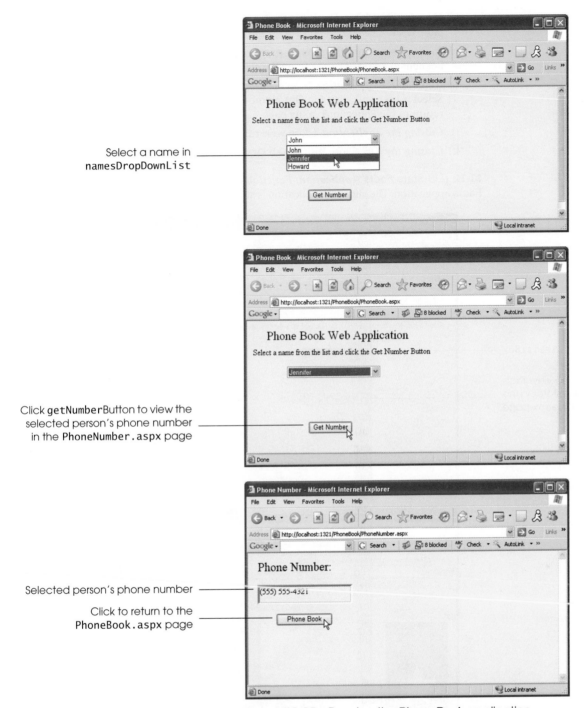

Select a name in
`namesDropDownList`

Click `getNumberButton` to view the
selected person's phone number
in the `PhoneNumber.aspx` page

Selected person's phone number

Click to return to the
`PhoneBook.aspx` page

Figure 31.25   Running the **Phone Book** application.

e) ***Redirecting to the PhoneNumber.aspx page.*** In the Click event handler, use the `Response.Redirect` method to redirect the client browser to the PhoneNumber.aspx page.

f) ***Defining the Page_Load event handler for the PhoneNumber.aspx page.*** As you did in *Step 3* in the box, *Defining the Page_Load Event Handler for the BookInformation.aspx Page*, create a `PhoneTableAdapter` object named `numberAdapter`. Then create a `PhoneDataTable` object named `numberTable` and populate it using the method `numberAdapter.GetData()`. Next, find the row number in the `Phone.mdf` database of the selected person and store it in an `Integer` item named `rowNumber`. Using `rowNumber`, retrieve the appropriate phone number stored in the `phoneNumber` field of `phoneTable` and assign it to `phoneNumberLabel`'s `Text` property.

g) *Creating the Phone Book Button's C1ick event handler for the PhoneNumber.aspx page.* Double click the **Phone Book** Button to create the Click event's event handler.

h) *Redirecting to the PhoneBook.aspx page.* In the Click event handler, use method Response.Redirect to redirect the client browser to the PhoneBook.aspx page.

i) *Running the application.* Select **Debug > Start Debugging** to run your application. Select a user and click the **Get Number** Button. Click the **Phone Book** Button to return to the PhoneBook.aspx page.

j) *Closing the application.* Close your running application by clicking its close box.

k) *Closing the IDE.* Close Visual Web Developer by clicking its close box.

31.12 (*US State Facts Application: Functionality*) Define the middle tier for the **US State Facts** application. The running application is shown in Fig. 31.26.

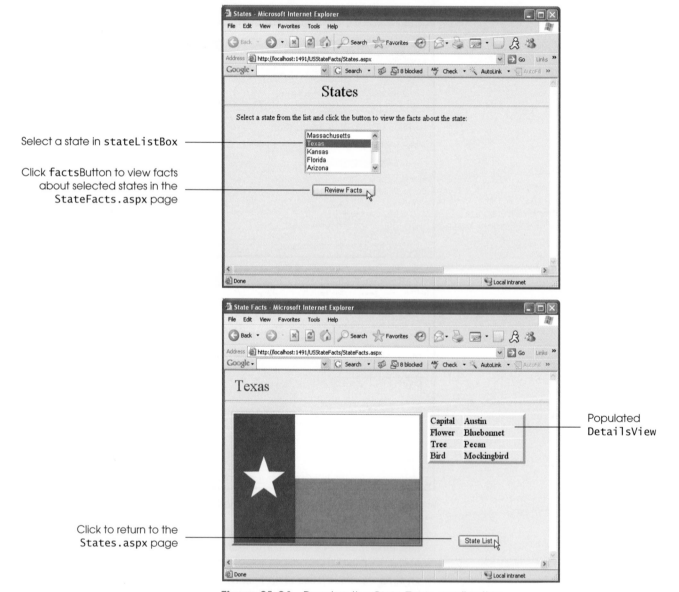

Select a state in stateListBox

Click factsButton to view facts about selected states in the StateFacts.aspx page

Populated DetailsView

Click to return to the States.aspx page

Figure 31.26 Running the **State Facts** application.

a) *Opening the application.* Open the **US State Facts** application that you created in Tutorial 29 and continued to develop in Tutorial 30.

b) *Copying the FlagImages directory to your project directory.* Copy the directory C:\Examples\Tutorial31\Exercises\Images\FlagImages to the USStateFacts directory.

c) ***Populating the ListBox with state names in the States.aspx page.*** Similar to the process demonstrated in the box, *Creating a Databound ListBox Using an Object-DataSource,* you need to make statesListBox databound. As shown in *Steps 2 and 3,* connect statesListBox to a new ObjectDataSource named statesObjectDataSource. Then select the automatically generated business object, statesDataSetTableAdapters.StatesFactsTableAdapter. Choose the GetData() data method to return data to the DropDownList. Then set the ListBox's display field to Name and its value field to StateID.

d) ***Creating the Review Facts Button's Click event handler for the States.aspx page.*** Double click the **Review Facts** Button to create the Click event's event handler.

e) ***Creating a Session item.*** Create a Session item named stateID in the Click event handler and assign it the state name that the user selects from the ListBox.

f) ***Redirecting to the StateFacts.aspx page.*** In the Click event handler, use the Redirect.Response method to redirect the client browser to the StateFacts.aspx page.

g) ***Defining the Page_Load event handler of StateFacts.aspx page.*** Similar to *Step 3* in the box, *Defining the Page_Load Event Handler for the BookInformation.aspx Page,* create a StateFactsTableAdapter object named stateAdapter. Then create a StateFactsDataTable object named stateTable and populate it using the method stateAdapter.GetData(). Next find the row number of the selected state in the StateFacts.mdf database and store it in an Integer item named rowNumber. Using rowNumber, retrieve the appropriate state name stored in the Name field of stateTable and set it equal to stateNameLabel's Text property. Also retrieve the file name for the appropriate flag image stored in the Image field of stateTable and store it in flagImage's ImageURL property. [*Note:* You will need to prefix the file name of the image with FlagImages\.]

h) ***Creating the State List Button's Click event handler for the StateFacts.aspx page.*** Double click the **State List** Button to create the Click event handler.

i) ***Redirecting to the States.aspx page.*** In the Click event handler use the Redirect.Response method to redirect the client browser to the States.aspx page.

j) ***Displaying the state facts in the DetailsView.*** Similar to the process demonstrated in the box, *Creating a Databound DetailsView Using an ObjectDataSource,* you need to make stateDetailsView databound. As shown in *Steps 2 and 3,* connect stateDetailsView to a new ObjectDataSource named factsObjectDataSource and select the automatically generated business object, statesDataSetTableAdapters.StatesFactsTableAdapter. Choose the GetDataByStateID() data method to return data to the DropDownList. Then select Session as the **parameter source** and enter stateID as the **SessionField**. Now, like *Step 5,* edit the displayed fields so that only Capital, Flower, Tree and Bird appear in the DetailsView.

k) ***Running the application.*** Select **Debug > Start Debugging** to run your application. Select a state and click the **Review Facts** Button. Click the **State List** Button to return to the States.aspx page.

l) ***Closing the application.*** Close your running application by clicking its close box.

m) ***Closing the IDE.*** Close Visual Web Developer by clicking its close box.

TUTORIAL

32

Enhanced Car Payment Calculator Application

Introducing Exception Handling

In this tutorial, you will learn about **exception handling**. An **exception** is an indication of a problem that occurs during an application's execution. The name "exception" comes from the fact that problems only occur infrequently—if the "rule" is that a statement normally executes correctly, then the "exception to the rule" is that a problem occurs. Exception handling enables you to create applications that can resolve (or handle) exceptions during application execution. In many cases, handling an exception allows an application to continue executing as if no problem had been encountered.

This tutorial begins with a test-drive of the **Enhanced Car Payment Calculator** application, then overviews exception handling concepts and demonstrates basic exception-handling techniques. You will learn the specifics of exception handling with the **Try**, **Catch** and **Finally** blocks and the architecture of exception classes.

32.1 Test-Driving the Enhanced Car Payment Calculator Application

In this tutorial, you will enhance the **Car Payment Calculator** application from Tutorial 9 by adding exception-handling statements. This application must meet the following requirements:

> **Application Requirements**
>
> *A bank wishes to only accept valid data from users on their car loans. Although the application you developed in Tutorial 9 calculates a result when incorrect data is entered, this result does not correctly represent the user's input. Alter the **Car Payment Calculator** application to allow users to enter only Integers in the **Price:** TextBox and **Down payment:** TextBox. Similarly, only allow users to enter Double values in the **Annual interest rate:** TextBox. If the user enters anything besides an Integer for the price or down payment, or a Double for the interest rate, a message dialog should be displayed instructing the user to input proper data. The interest rate should be entered such that an input of 5 is equal to 5%.*

The original **Car Payment Calculator** application used the Val function to set the value of the variables used in the application. This ensured that the payment calculation was always performed using numeric values. However, as discussed in Tutorial 5, the value returned by Val is not always the value the user intended to input. For example, if the user accidently inputs a character in the middle of the down payment, Val will return the numeric value up until it reaches the character. Any number after the character will be lost, and the calculation will be incorrect. Also, Val does not prevent the user from entering a Double value for the price or down payment, for which Integer values are expected. You will add exception handling to the **Car Payment Calculator** application so that when invalid input is entered, the user will be asked to enter valid input and the application will not calculate monthly payments. If the user provides valid input, the application will calculate the monthly payments for a car when financed for 24, 36, 48 and 60 months. Users input the car price, the down payment and the annual interest rate. You begin by test-driving the completed application. Then you will learn the additional Visual Basic technologies that you will need to create your own version of this application.

Test-Driving the Enhanced Car Payment Calculator Application

1. *Opening the completed application.* Open the directory C:\Examples\ Tutorial32\CompletedApplication\EnhancedCarPaymentCalculator to locate the **Car Payment Calculator** application. Double click Enhanced-CarPaymentCalculator.sln to open the application in the Visual Basic IDE.

2. *Running the Enhanced Car Payment Calculator application.* Select **Debug > Start Debugging** to run the application (Fig. 32.1).

Figure 32.1 Running the completed **Enhanced Car Payment Calculator** application.

3. *Entering an invalid value in the Down payment: TextBox.* Enter 16900 in the **Price:** TextBox, 6000.50 in the **Down payment:** TextBox and 7.5 in the **Annual interest rate:** TextBox (Fig. 32.2).

4. *Attempting to calculate the monthly payment amounts.* Click the **Calculate** Button to attempt to calculate the monthly payment. Note that an error message dialog (Fig. 32.3) appears.

5. *Entering non-numeric data in the Down payment: TextBox.* Change the value 6000.50 in the **Down payment:** TextBox to 600p (Fig. 32.4). Click the **Calculate** Button to attempt to display the monthly payment in the Text-Box. The message dialog shown in Fig. 32.3 appears again (a non-numeric character like p cannot be entered when an Integer is expected).

(cont.)

Figure 32.2 Entering an invalid value in the **Down payment:** TextBox.

Displaying a message when an exception is thrown ———

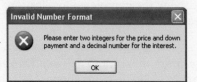

Figure 32.3 Message dialog displayed when incorrect input is entered.

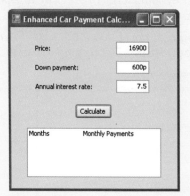

Figure 32.4 Entering non-numeric data in the **Down Payment:** TextBox.

6. ***Entering non-numeric data in the Annual interest rate: TextBox.*** Change the value 600p in the **Down payment:** TextBox to 6000. Enter 7.5% in the **Annual interest rate:** TextBox (Fig. 32.5). Click the **Calculate** Button to attempt to calculate the monthly payment. The message dialog shown in Fig. 32.3 appears again (7.5 is the correct input; entering the % character is incorrect).

Figure 32.5 Entering non-numeric data in the **Annual interest rate:** TextBox.

(cont.)   7. ***Correcting the input.*** Change the value 7.5% in the **Annual interest rate:** TextBox to 7.5, and click the **Calculate** Button to display the monthly payments (Fig. 32.6).

Results displayed only when valid input is entered

Figure 32.6   Displaying monthly payments after input is corrected.

8. ***Closing the application.*** Close your running application by clicking its close box.

9. ***Closing the IDE.*** Close the Visual Basic IDE by clicking its close box.

32.2 Introduction to Exception Handling

Application logic frequently tests conditions that determine how application execution should proceed. Consider the following pseudocode:

Perform a task

If the preceding task did not execute correctly
    Perform error processing

Perform the next task

If the preceding task did not execute correctly
    Perform error processing

...

In this pseudocode, you begin by performing a task. Then you test whether the task executed correctly. If not, you perform error processing. Otherwise, you continue with the next task. Although this form of error checking works, intermixing application logic with error-handling logic can make the application difficult to read, modify, maintain and debug—especially in large applications. In fact, if problems occur infrequently, intermixing application and error-handling logic can degrade an application's performance, because the application must explicitly test for errors after each task to determine whether the next task can be performed.

Exception handling enables you to remove error-handling code from the code that implements your application's logic, thereby improving application clarity and enhancing modifiability. You can decide to handle only the exceptions you choose—all exceptions, all exceptions of a certain type or all exceptions in a group of related types. Such flexibility reduces the likelihood that errors will be overlooked and makes the application more robust.

A method **throws an exception** if a problem occurs during the method execution but the method is unable to correct the problem. There is no guarantee that there will be an **exception handler**—code that executes when the application detects an exception—to process that kind of exception. If there is, the exception handler catches and handles the exception. An **uncaught exception**—an exception that does not have an exception handler—might cause application execution to terminate.

1. An _____ executes when the application detects an exception.

   a) exception code
   b) exception processor
   c) exception handler
   d) None of the above.

2. A method will _____ an exception if a problem occurs during the method execution but the method is unable to correct the problem.

   a) throw
   b) catch
   c) return
   d) None of the above.

Answers: 1) c. 2) a.

32.3 Exception Handling in Visual Basic

Visual Basic provides **Try blocks** to enable exception handling. A Try block consists of the Try keyword followed by a block of code in which exceptions might occur. The purpose of the Try block is to contain statements that might cause exceptions and statements that should not execute if an exception occurs.

At least one Catch block (also called an exception handler) or a Finally block must appear after the Try block, immediately before the **End Try** keywords. A **Catch block** specifies a parameter that identifies the type of exception the exception handler can process. The parameter enables the Catch block to interact with the caught exception object. A Catch block that does not specify a parameter can catch all exception types. A parameterless Catch block should be placed after all other Catch blocks. After the last Catch block, an optional **Finally block** provides code that always executes, whether or not an exception occurs.

If an exception occurs in a Try block, the Try block terminates immediately. As with any other block of code, when a Try block terminates, local variables declared in the block go out of scope. Next, the application searches for the first Catch block (immediately following the Try block) that can process the exception type that occurred. The application locates the matching Catch by comparing the thrown exception's type with each Catch block's exception-parameter type. A match occurs if the exception type matches the Catch block's parameter type. When a match occurs, the code associated with the matching Catch executes. When a Catch block finishes processing, local variables declared in the Catch block (and the Catch's parameter) go out of scope. Any of the Try block's remaining Catch blocks are ignored, and execution resumes at the first line of code after the End Try keywords if there is no Finally block. Otherwise, execution resumes at the Finally block.

If there is no Catch block that matches the exception thrown in the corresponding Try block, the execution resumes at the corresponding Finally block (if it exists). After the Finally block executes, the exception is passed to the method that called the current method, which then attempts to handle the exception. If the calling method does not handle the exception, the exception is again passed to the previous method in the call chain. If the exception goes unhandled, Visual Basic will display a dialog providing the user with information about the exception. The user can then choose to exit or continue running the application, although the application may not execute correctly due to the exception.

If no exceptions occur in a Try block, the application ignores the Catch block(s) for that Try block. Application execution resumes with the next statement after the End Try keywords if there is no Finally block. Otherwise, execution resumes at the Finally block. A Finally block (if one is present) will execute whether or not an exception is thrown in the corresponding Try block or any of its corresponding Catch blocks.

Sometimes a `Catch` block may decide either that it cannot process a certain exception or that it can only partially process the exception. In such cases, the exception handler can defer the handling (or perhaps a portion of it) to another `Catch` block. The handler achieves this by **rethrowing the exception** using the **Throw** statement

> `Throw` *exceptionReference*;

where *exceptionReference* is the parameter for the exception in the `Catch` block. When a rethrow occurs, the next enclosing Try block (if any), which is normally in the calling method, detects the rethrown exception and attempts to catch it.

Another feature in Visual Basic 2005 related to exception handling is the `using` statement, which concisely represents a `Try...Finally` that automatically deallocates a resource after it is used in the Try block. The `using` statement is beyond the scope of this book. For information on `using`, visit `msdn2.microsoft.com/en-us/library/htd05whh.aspx`. Also, you should investigate the `IDisposable` interface (`msdn2.microsoft.com/en-us/library/system.idisposable.aspx`), which is a required part of implementing code with the `using` statement.

SELF-REVIEW

1. The _____ (if any) is/are always executed regardless of whether an exception occurs.
   - a) `Catch` block
   - b) `Finally` block
   - c) both `Catch` and `Finally` blocks
   - d) None of the above.

2. If no exceptions occur in a Try block, the application ignores the _____ for that block.
   - a) `Finally` block
   - b) `Return` statement
   - c) `Catch` block(s)
   - d) None of the above.

Answers: 1) b. 2) c.

32.4 Constructing the Enhanced Car Payment Calculator Application

Now that you've been introduced to exception handling, you will construct your **Enhanced Car Payment Calculator** application. The following pseudocode describes the basic operation of the application:

```
When the user clicks the Calculate Button:
    Clear the ListBox of any previous text

    Try
        Get the car price from the Price: TextBox
        Get the down payment from the Down payment: TextBox
        Get the annual interest rate from the Annual interest rate: TextBox
        Calculate the loan amount (price minus down payment)
        Calculate the monthly interest rate (annual interest rate divided by 1200)
        Calculate and display the monthly payments for 2, 3, 4 and 5 years
    Catch
        Display the error message dialog
```

Now that you have test-driven the **Enhanced Car Payment Calculator** application and studied its pseudocode representation, you will use an ACE table to help you convert the pseudocode to Visual Basic. Figure 32.7 lists the actions, controls and events that will help you complete your own version of this application.

Action	Control/Class/Object	Event
Label all the application's components	`stickerPriceLabel`, `downPaymentLabel`, `interestLabel`	Application is run
	`calculateButton`	`Click`
Try Clear the ListBox of any previous text	`paymentsListBox`	
Get the car price from the **Price:** TextBox	`stickerPrice-TextBox`	
Get the down payment from the **Down payment:** TextBox	`downPayment-TextBox`	
Get the annual interest rate from the **Annual interest rate:** TextBox	`interestTextBox`	
Calculate the loan amount		
Calculate the monthly interest rate		
Calculate and display the monthly payments	`paymentsListBox`	
Catch Display the error message dialog	`MessageBox`	

Figure 32.7 **Enhanced Car Payment Calculator** application ACE table.

Now that you've analyzed the **Enhanced Car Payment Calculator** application's components, you will learn how to place exception handling in your application's code.

Handling a Format Exception

1. ***Copying the template to your working directory.*** Copy the `C:\Examples\Tutorial32\TemplateApplication\EnhancedCarPaymentCalculator` directory to your `C:\SimplyVB` directory.

2. ***Opening the Enhanced Car Payment Calculator application's template file.*** Double click `EnhancedCarPaymentCalculator.sln` in the `EnhancedCarPaymentCalculator` directory to open the application in the IDE.

3. ***Studying the code.*** View lines 25–27 of Fig. 32.8. Lines 25–26 read the `Integer` values from the **Down payment:** and **Price:** TextBoxes, respectively. Line 27 reads a `Double` value from the **Annual interest rate:** TextBox. These lines are different from the ones in the **Car Payment Calculator** application that you developed in Tutorial 9. These three statements now must explicitly convert the data in the TextBoxes to `Integer` and `Double` values, using the methods of the `Convert` class, because **Option Strict** is set to `On`. However, these statements still use the `Val` function, which could cause the application to use incorrect data in its calculation, producing invalid results.

   Method `Convert.ToInt32` throws a `FormatException` if it cannot convert its argument to an `Integer`. The **FormatException** class represents exceptions that occur when a method is passed an argument that is of the wrong type (and cannot be implicitly converted to the correct type). The call to the `Convert.ToInt32` method does not currently throw an exception when the application is run because `Val` converts its argument to a numeric value. This numeric value is the argument passed to `Convert.ToInt32`, so an `Integer` value will always be created. The `Convert.ToDouble` method performs in a similar manner by throwing a `FormatException` if it cannot convert its argument to a `Double`.

(cont.)

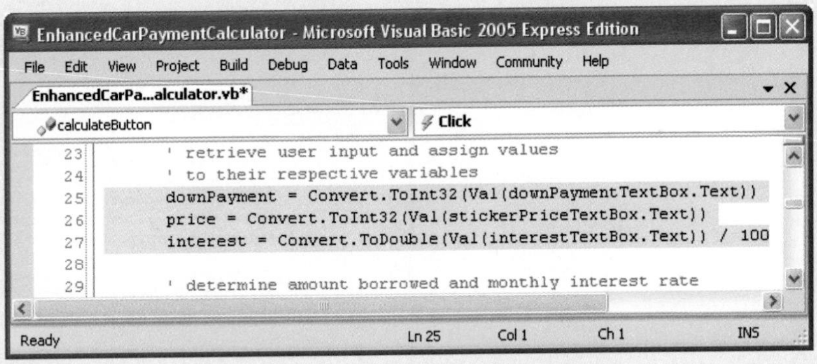

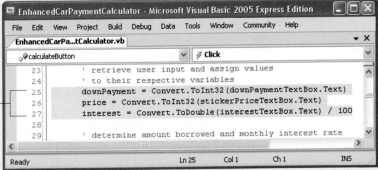

Figure 32.8 Val ensures data is in numeric format.

4. ***Changing the existing code.*** Change lines 25–27 of your template application to match lines 25–27 of Fig. 32.9 by removing the Val function call and the parentheses that designate its argument. Removing the Val function call will cause Convert.ToInt32 and Convert.ToDouble to throw an exception if incorrect input is entered into one of the TextBoxes. This will allow you to add code later in this box to catch the exception and ask the user to enter correct data.

Removing the Val method call allows exceptions to be thrown

Figure 32.9 Removing the Val function call from the application.

5. ***Causing a FormatException.*** Select **Debug > Start Debugging** to run your application. Enter the input of Fig. 32.4 and click the **Calculate** Button. The **Exception Assistant** shown in Fig. 32.10 appears, informing you that an exception has occurred. Note that the exception assistant indicates where the exception occurred and the type of the exception, and provides links to helpful information on handling the exception. Close the **Exception Assistant** by clicking its close box. Then, stop debugging by selecting **Debug > Stop Debugging**.

6. ***Adding a Try block to your application.*** Add lines 23–24 of Fig. 32.11 to your application; however, do not press *Enter* when you are done typing line 24. Instead, when you are done typing this line, add line 51 of Fig. 32.12 to your application. Line 24 begins the Try block, and line 51 ends the Try...Catch statement. The code contained between these two lines is the code that might throw an exception and code that you do not want to execute if an exception occurs. Note that the Try keyword in line 24 is underlined, indicating a syntax error. Adding the Try keyword to your application creates a syntax error until a corresponding Catch or Finally block is added to the application. In the next step, you will add a Catch block to fix the error in line 24.

(cont.)

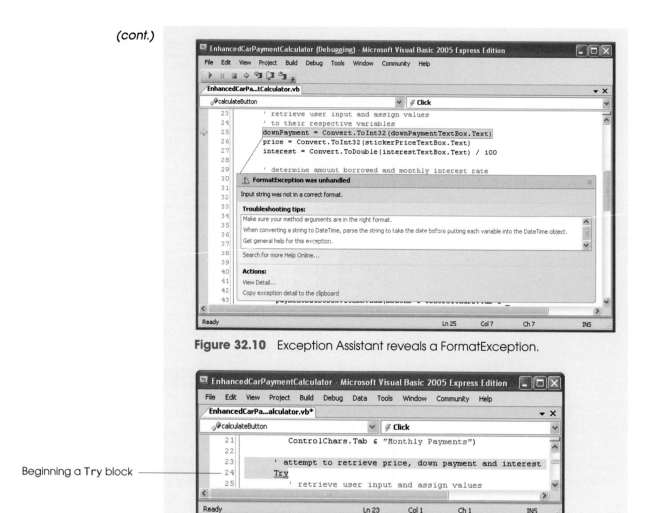

Figure 32.10 Exception Assistant reveals a FormatException.

Beginning a **Try** block ———

Figure 32.11 Enabling exception handling using a **Try** block.

Ending the **Try** statement ———

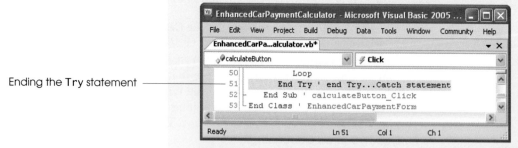

Figure 32.12 Ending the **Try...Catch** block with the **End Try** keywords.

7. ***Adding a Catch block to your application***. Add lines 52–53 of Fig. 32.13 to your application. The **Catch** keyword designates the beginning of a **Catch** block. A **Catch** block ends when either another **Catch** block, a **Finally** block or the **End Try** keywords are reached. Line 53 specifies that this **Catch** block will execute if a **FormatException** is thrown. So this code will execute if the user enters invalid input in one of the **TextBoxes**. Note that the **Try** keyword in line 24 is no longer underlined, because adding a **Catch** block fixed the error in that line.

(cont.)

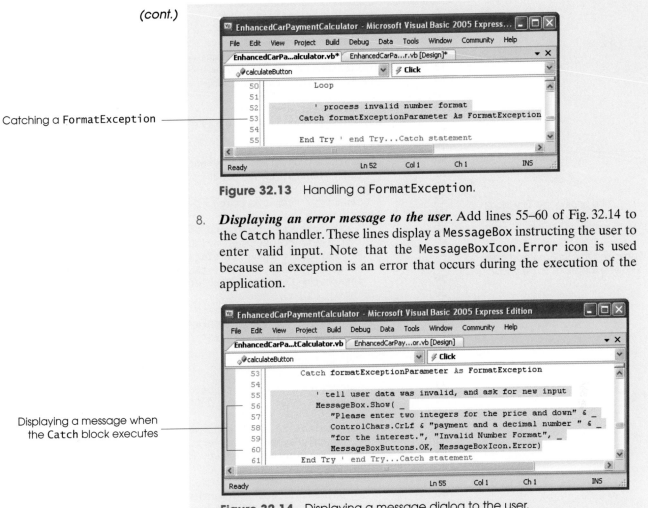

Figure 32.13　Handling a `FormatException`.

8. ***Displaying an error message to the user.*** Add lines 55–60 of Fig. 32.14 to the `Catch` handler. These lines display a `MessageBox` instructing the user to enter valid input. Note that the `MessageBoxIcon.Error` icon is used because an exception is an error that occurs during the execution of the application.

Figure 32.14　Displaying a message dialog to the user.

9. ***Running the application.*** Select **Debug > Start Debugging** to run your application. Enter valid input, and verify that the output contains the correct monthly payment amounts. Enter invalid input to ensure that the `MessageBox` is displayed. Test the application with several invalid values in the different `TextBox`es.

10. ***Closing the application.*** Close your running application by clicking its close box.

11. ***Closing the IDE.*** Close the Visual Basic IDE by clicking its close box.

Figure 32.15 presents the source code for the **Enhanced Car Payment Calculator** application. The lines of code that contain new programming concepts that you learned in this tutorial are highlighted.

```
1   Public Class EnhancedCarPaymentForm
2
3       ' handles Calculate Button's Click event
4       Private Sub calculateButton_Click(ByVal sender As System.Object, _
5           ByVal e As System.EventArgs) Handles calculateButton.Click
6
7           Dim years As Integer = 2        ' repetition counter
8           Dim months As Integer = 0       ' payment period
```

Figure 32.15　**Enhanced Car Payment Calculator** Application. (Part 1 of 2.)

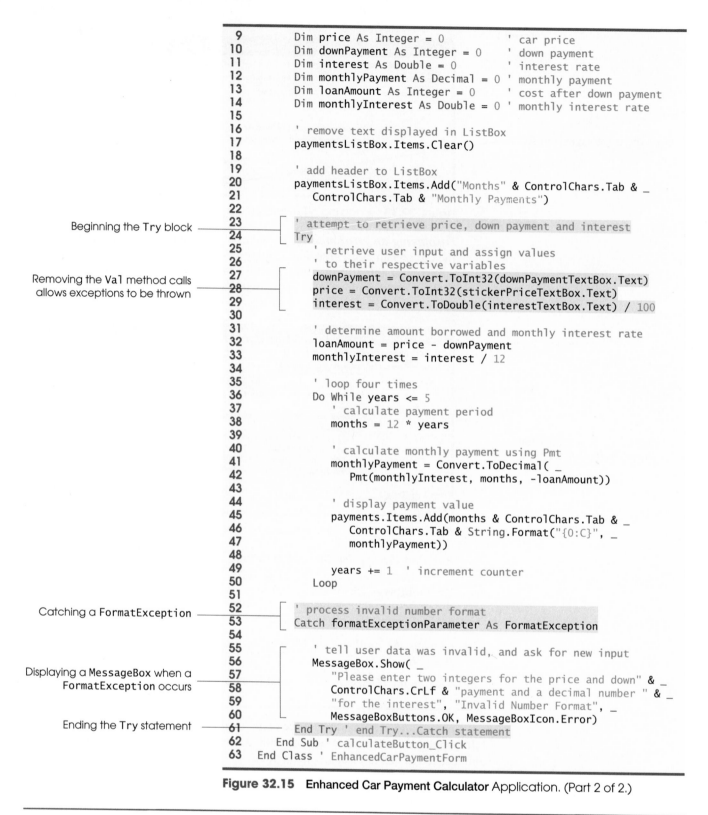

```
 9        Dim price As Integer = 0              ' car price
10        Dim downPayment As Integer = 0       ' down payment
11        Dim interest As Double = 0           ' interest rate
12        Dim monthlyPayment As Decimal = 0    ' monthly payment
13        Dim loanAmount As Integer = 0        ' cost after down payment
14        Dim monthlyInterest As Double = 0    ' monthly interest rate
15
16        ' remove text displayed in ListBox
17        paymentsListBox.Items.Clear()
18
19        ' add header to ListBox
20        paymentsListBox.Items.Add("Months" & ControlChars.Tab & _
21           ControlChars.Tab & "Monthly Payments")
22
23        ' attempt to retrieve price, down payment and interest
24        Try
25           ' retrieve user input and assign values
26           ' to their respective variables
27           downPayment = Convert.ToInt32(downPaymentTextBox.Text)
28           price = Convert.ToInt32(stickerPriceTextBox.Text)
29           interest = Convert.ToDouble(interestTextBox.Text) / 100
30
31           ' determine amount borrowed and monthly interest rate
32           loanAmount = price - downPayment
33           monthlyInterest = interest / 12
34
35           ' loop four times
36           Do While years <= 5
37              ' calculate payment period
38              months = 12 * years
39
40              ' calculate monthly payment using Pmt
41              monthlyPayment = Convert.ToDecimal( _
42                 Pmt(monthlyInterest, months, -loanAmount))
43
44              ' display payment value
45              payments.Items.Add(months & ControlChars.Tab & _
46                 ControlChars.Tab & String.Format("{0:C}", _
47                 monthlyPayment))
48
49              years += 1  ' increment counter
50           Loop
51
52        ' process invalid number format
53        Catch formatExceptionParameter As FormatException
54
55           ' tell user data was invalid, and ask for new input
56           MessageBox.Show( _
57              "Please enter two integers for the price and down" & _
58              ControlChars.CrLf & "payment and a decimal number " & _
59              "for the interest", "Invalid Number Format", _
60              MessageBoxButtons.OK, MessageBoxIcon.Error)
61        End Try ' end Try...Catch statement
62     End Sub ' calculateButton_Click
63  End Class ' EnhancedCarPaymentForm
```

Beginning the Try block — (line 23–24)

Removing the Val method calls allows exceptions to be thrown — (lines 27–29)

Catching a FormatException — (lines 52–53)

Displaying a MessageBox when a FormatException occurs — (lines 55–60)

Ending the Try statement — (line 61)

Figure 32.15 Enhanced Car Payment Calculator Application. (Part 2 of 2.)

SELF-REVIEW   1. If you are attempting to catch multiple errors, you may use several _____ blocks after the _____ block.

a) Try, Catch

b) Catch, Try

c) Finally, Try

d) None of the above.

2. The exception you wish to handle should be declared as a parameter of the _____ block.

    a) `Try`   b) `Catch`

    c) `Finally`   d) None of the above.

Answers: 1) b. 2) b.

32.5 Wrap-Up

In this tutorial, you learned exception-handling concepts and when to use exception handling in Visual Basic. You learned how to use a `Try` block with `Catch` blocks to handle exceptions in your applications. You also learned that the `Throw` statement can be used to rethrow an exception that cannot be handled in the `Catch` block. Next, you applied your knowledge of exception handling in Visual Basic to enhance your **Car Payment Calculator** application to check for input errors. You used a `Try` block to enclose the statements that might throw `FormatExceptions` and a `Catch` block to handle the `FormatExceptions`.

SKILLS SUMMARY

Handling an Exception

- Enclose in a `Try` block any code that might generate an exception and any code that should not execute if an exception occurs.

- Follow the `Try` block with one or more `Catch` blocks. Each `Catch` block is an exception handler that specifies the type of exception it can handle.

- Follow the `Catch` blocks with an optional `Finally` block that contains code that should always execute.

KEY TERMS

Catch block—Also called an exception handler, this block executes when the corresponding `Try` block in the application detects an exceptional situation and throws an exception of the type the `Catch` block declares.

End Try—Indicates the end of a sequence of blocks containing a `Try` block, followed by one or more `Catch` blocks and an optional `Finally` block.

exception—An indication of a problem that occurs during an application's execution.

Exception Assistant—A window that appears indicating where an exception has occurred, the type of exception, and information on handling the exception.

exception handler—A block that executes when the application detects an exceptional situation and throws an exception.

exception handling—Processing problems that occur during application execution.

Finally block—An optional block of code that follows the last `Catch` block in a sequence of `Catch` blocks or the `Try` block if there are no `Catch`es. The `Finally` block provides code that always executes, whether or not an exception occurs.

FormatException class—An exception of this type is thrown when a method cannot convert its argument to a desired numeric type, such as `Integer` or `Double`.

rethrow the exception—The `Catch` block can defer the exception handling (or perhaps a portion of it) to another `Catch` block by using the `Throw` statement.

Throw statement—The statement used to rethrow an exception in a `Catch` block.

throws an exception—A method throws an exception if a problem occurs while the method is executing.

Try block—A block of statements that might cause exceptions and statements that should not execute if an exception occurs.

uncaught exception—An exception that does not have an exception handler. Uncaught exceptions might terminate application execution.

MULTIPLE-CHOICE QUESTIONS

32.1 Dealing with exceptional situations as an application executes is called _____.
a) exception detection
b) exception handling
c) exception resolution
d) exception debugging

32.2 A(n) _____ is always followed by at least one `Catch` block or a `Finally` block.
a) `if` statement
b) event handler
c) `Try` block
d) None of the above.

32.3 The method call `Convert.ToInt32( "123.4a" )` will throw a _____.
a) `FormatException`
b) `ParsingException`
c) `DivideByZeroException`
d) None of the above.

32.4 If no exceptions are thrown in a `Try` block, _____.
a) the `Catch` block(s) are skipped
b) all `Catch` blocks are executed
c) an error occurs
d) the default exception is thrown

32.5 A(n) _____ is an exception that does not have an exception handler, and therefore might cause the application to terminate execution.
a) uncaught block
b) uncaught exception
c) error handler
d) thrower

32.6 A `Try` block can have _____ associated with it.
a) only one `Catch` block
b) several `Finally` blocks
c) one or more `Catch` blocks
d) None of the above.

32.7 The _____ statement is used to rethrow an exception from inside a `Catch` block.
a) `Rethrow`
b) `Throw`
c) `Try`
d) `Catch`

32.8 _____ marks the end of a `Try` block and its corresponding `Catch` and `Finally` blocks.
a) `End Try`
b) `End Finally`
c) `End Catch`
d) `End Exception`

32.9 A `Finally` block is located _____.
a) after the `Try` block, but before each `Catch` block
b) before the `Try` block
c) after the `Try` block and the `Try` block's corresponding `Catch` blocks
d) Either b or c.

32.10 A(n) _____ is executed if an exception is thrown from a `Try` block or if no exception is thrown.
a) `Catch` block
b) `Finally` block
c) exception handler
d) All of the above.

EXERCISES

32.11 (*Enhanced Miles Per Gallon Application*) Modify the **Miles Per Gallon** application (Exercise 13.13) to use exception handling to process the `FormatExceptions` that occur when converting the strings in the TextBoxes to `Doubles` (Fig. 32.16). The original application allowed the user to input the number of miles driven and the number of gallons used for a tank of gas to determine the number of miles the user was able to drive on one gallon of gas.

   a) *Copying the template to your working directory.* Copy the directory `C:\Examples\Tutorial32\Exercises\EnhancedMilesPerGallon` to your `C:\SimplyVB` directory.

   b) *Opening the application's template file.* Double click `EnhancedMilesPerGallon.sln` in the `EnhancedMilesPerGallon` directory to open the application.

   c) *Adding a Try block.* Find the `calculateMPGButton_Click` event handler. Enclose all of the code in this event handler in a `Try` block.

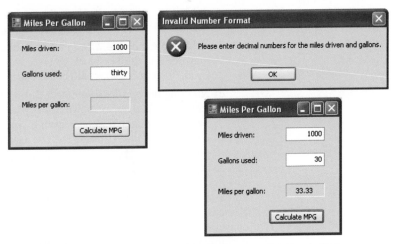

Figure 32.16 Enhanced **Miles Per Gallon** application's GUI.

d) *Adding a Catch block.* After the Try block you added in *Step c*, add a Catch block to handle any FormatExceptions that may occur in the Try block. Inside the Catch block, add code to display an error message dialog.

e) *Running the application.* Select **Debug > Start Debugging** to run your application. Enter invalid data, as shown in Fig. 32.16, and click the **Calculate MPG** Button. A MessageBox will appear asking you to enter valid input. Enter valid input and click the **Calculate MPG** Button again. Verify that the correct output is displayed.

f) *Closing the application.* Close your running application by clicking its close box.

g) *Closing the IDE.* Close the Visual Basic IDE by clicking its close box.

32.12 (*Enhanced Prime Numbers Application*) Modify the **Prime Numbers** application (Exercise 13.17) to use exception handling to process the FormatExceptions that occur when converting the strings in the TextBoxes to Integers (Fig. 32.17). The original application took two numbers (representing a lower bound and an upper bound) and determined all of the prime numbers within the specified bounds, inclusive. An Integer greater than 1 is said to be prime if it is divisible by only 1 and itself. For example, 2, 3, 5 and 7 are prime numbers, but 4, 6, 8 and 9 are not.

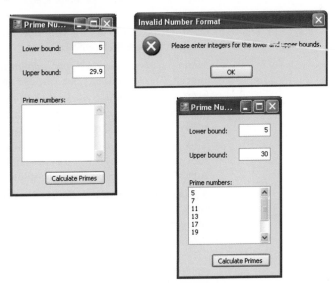

Figure 32.17 Enhanced **Prime Numbers** application's GUI.

a) *Copying the template to your working directory.* Copy the directory C:\Examples\Tutorial32\Exercises\EnhancedPrimeNumbers to your C:\SimplyVB directory.

b) *Opening the application's template file.* Double click EnhancedPrimeNumbers.sln in the EnhancedPrimeNumbers directory to open the application.

c) *Adding a Try block.* Find the calculatePrimesButton_Click event handler. Enclose all the code following the variable declarations in a Try block.

d) *Adding a Catch block.* Add a Catch block that catches any FormatExceptions that may occur in the Try block you added to calculatePrimesButton_Click in *Step c*. Inside the Catch block, add code to display an error message dialog.

e) *Running the application.* Select **Debug > Start Debugging** to run your application. Enter invalid data, as shown in Fig. 32.17, and click the **Calculate Primes** Button. A MessageBox should appear asking you to enter valid input. Enter valid input and click the **Calculate Primes** Button again. Verify that the correct output is displayed.

f) *Closing the application.* Close your running application by clicking its close box.

g) *Closing the IDE.* Close the Visual Basic IDE by clicking its close box.

32.13 (*Enhanced Simple Calculator Application*) Modify the **Simple Calculator** application (Exercise 6.13) to use exception handling to process the FormatExceptions that occur when converting the strings in the TextBoxes to Integers and the DivideByZeroException when performing the division (Fig. 32.18). We will define what a DivideByZeroException is shortly. The application should still perform simple addition, subtraction, multiplication and division.

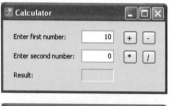

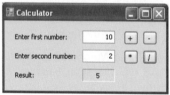

Figure 32.18 Enhanced **Simple Calculator** application.

a) *Copying the template to your working directory.* Copy the directory C:\Examples\ Tutorial32\Exercises\EnhancedSimpleCalculator to your C:\SimplyVB directory.

b) *Opening the application's template file.* Double click EnhancedSimpleCalculator.sln in the EnhancedSimpleCalculator directory to open the application.

c) *Adding a Try block to the addButton_Click event handler.* Find the addButton_Click event handler. Enclose the body of addButton_Click in a Try block.

d) *Adding a Catch block to the addButton_Click event handler.* Add a Catch block that catches any FormatExceptions that may occur in the Try block that you added in *Step c*. Inside the Catch block, add code to display an error message dialog.

e) *Adding a Try block to the subtractButton_Click event handler.* Find the subtractButton_Click event handler, which immediately follows addButton_Click. Enclose the body of the subtractButton_Click in a Try block.

f) *Adding a Catch block to the subtractButton_Click event handler.* Add a Catch block that catches any FormatExceptions that may occur in the Try block that you added in *Step e*. Inside the Catch block, add code to display an error message dialog.

g) *Adding a Try block to the multiplyButton_Click event handler.* Find the mulitplyButton_Click event handler, which immediately follows subtractButton_Click. Enclose the body of the multiplyButton_Click in a Try block.

h) *Adding a Catch block to the multiplyButton_Click event handler.* Add a Catch block that catches any FormatExceptions that may occur in the Try block that you added in *Step g*. Inside the Catch block, add code to display an error message dialog.

i) *Adding a Try block to the divideButton_Click event handler.* Find the divideButton_Click event handler, which immediately follows multiplyButton_Click. Enclose the body of the divideButton_Click in a Try block.

j) *Adding a Catch block to the divideButton_Click event handler.* Add a Catch block that catches any FormatExceptions that may occur in the Try block that you added in *Step i.* Inside the Catch block, add code to display an error message dialog.

k) *Adding a second Catch block to the divideButton_Click event handler.* Immediately following the first Catch block inside the divideButton_Click event handler, add a Catch block to catch any DivideByZeroExceptions. A **DivideByZeroException** is thrown when division by zero in integer arithmetic occurs. Inside the Catch block, add code to display an error message dialog.

l) *Running the application.* Select **Debug > Start Debugging** to run your application. Enter valid input for the first number and 0 for the second number, then click the Button for division. A MessageBox should appear asking you not to divide by 0. Enter invalid input (such as letters) for the first and second numbers, then click any one of the Buttons provided. This time a MessageBox should appear asking you to enter valid input. Enter valid input and click any one of the Buttons provided. Verify that the correct output is displayed.

m) *Closing the application.* Close your running application by clicking its close box.

n) *Closing the IDE.* Close the Visual Basic IDE by clicking its close box.

What does this code do? ▶ **32.14** What does the following code do, assuming that value1 and value2 are both declared as Doubles?

```
1   Try
2
3       value1 = Convert.ToDouble(input1TextBox.Text)
4       value2 = Convert.ToDouble(input2TextBox.Text)
5
6       outputTextBox.Text = (value1 * value2).ToString
7
8   Catch formatExceptionParameter As FormatException
9
10      MessageBox.Show( _
11          "Please enter decimal values.", _
12          "Invalid Number Format", _
13          MessageBoxButtons.OK, MessageBoxIcon.Error)
14
15  End Try
```

What's wrong with this code? ▶ **32.15** The following code should add integers from two TextBoxes and display the result in resultTextBox. Assume that value1 and value2 are declared as Integers. Find the error(s) in the following code:

```
1   Try
2
3       value1 = Convert.ToInt32(input1TextBox.Text)
4       value2 = Convert.ToInt32(input2TextBox.Text)
5
6       outputTextBox.Text = (value1 + value2).ToString
7
8   End Try
9
10  Catch formatExceptionParameter As FormatException
11
12      MessageBox.Show( _
13          "Please enter valid Integers.", _
14          "Invalid Number Format", _
15          MessageBoxButtons.OK, MessageBoxIcon.Error)
16
17  End Catch
```

32.16 (*Enhanced Vending Machine Application*) The **Vending Machine** application from Tutorial 3 has been modified to use exception handling to process the IndexOutOfRangeExceptions that occur when selecting items out of the range 0 through 7 (Fig. 32.19). This type of exception will be defined shortly. To get a snack, the user must type the number of the desired snack in the TextBox, then press the **Dispense Snack:** Button. The name of the snack is displayed in the output Label.

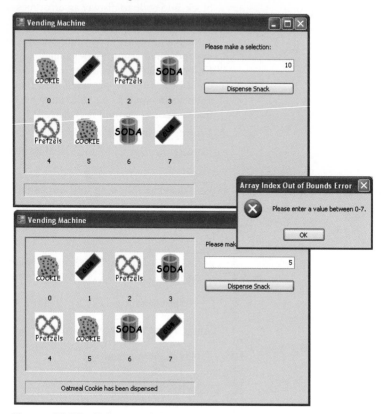

Figure 32.19 Enhanced **Vending Machine** application.

a) *Copying the template to your working directory.* Copy the directory C:\Examples\ Tutorial32\Exercises\EnhancedVendingMachine to your C:\SimplyVB directory.

b) *Opening the application's template file.* Double click EnhancedVendingMachine.sln in the EnhancedVendingMachine directory to open the application.

c) *Adding a Try block.* Find the dispenseButton_Click event handler. Enclose all of the code in the event handler in a Try block.

d) *Adding a Catch block.* Add a Catch block that catches any FormatExceptions that may occur in the Try block that you added to dispenseButton_Click in *Step c*. Inside the Catch block, add code to display an error message dialog.

e) *Adding a second Catch block.* Immediately following the Catch block you added in *Step d*, add a second Catch block to catch any IndexOutOfRangeExceptions that may occur. An **IndexOutOfRangeException** occurs when the application attempts to access an array with an invalid index. Inside the Catch block, add code to display an error message dialog.

f) *Running the application.* Select **Debug > Start Debugging** to run your application. Make an out-of-range selection (for instance, 32) and click the **Dispense Snack** Button. Verify that the proper MessageBox is displayed for the invalid input. Enter letters for a selection and click the **Dispense Snack** Button. Verify that the proper MessageBox is displayed for the invalid input.

g) *Closing the application.* Close your running application by clicking its close box.

h) *Closing the IDE.* Close the Visual Basic IDE by clicking its close box.

Operator Precedence Chart

Operators are shown in decreasing order of precedence from top to bottom with each level of precedence separated by a horizontal line. Visual Basic operators associate from left to right.

Operator	Type
TypeOf	type comparison
^	exponentiation
+	unary plus
–	unary minus
*	multiplication
/	division
\	integer division
Mod	modulus
+	addition
–	subtraction
&	concatenation
<<	bitwise left shift
>>	bitwise right shift
=	relational is equal to
<>	relational is not equal to
<	relational less than
<=	relational less than or equal to
>	relational greater than
>=	relational greater than or equal to
Like	pattern matching
Is	reference comparison
Not	logical negation
And	logical AND without short-circuit evaluation
AndAlso	logical AND with short-circuit evaluation
Or	logical inclusive OR without short-circuit evaluation
OrElse	logical inclusive OR with short-circuit evaluation
Xor	logical exclusive OR

Figure A.1   Operator list (in order of operator precedence).

APPENDIX

ASCII Character Set

The digits in the left column of Fig. B.1 are the left digits of the decimal equivalent (0–127) of the character code, and the digits in the top row of Fig. B.1 are the right digits of the character code. For example, the character code for "F" is 70, and the character code for "&" is 38.

Most users of this book are interested in the ASCII character set used to represent English characters on many computers. The ASCII character set is a subset of the Unicode® character set used by Visual Basic .NET to represent characters from most of the world's languages.

	0	1	2	3	4	5	6	7	8	9
0	nul	soh	stx	etx	eot	enq	ack	bel	bs	ht
1	nl	vt	ff	cr	so	si	dle	dc1	dc2	dc3
2	dc4	nak	syn	etb	can	em	sub	esc	fs	gs
3	rs	us	sp	!	"	#	$	%	&	'
4	(	)	*	+	,	-	.	/	0	1
5	2	3	4	5	6	7	8	9	:	;
6	<	=	>	?	@	A	B	C	D	E
7	F	G	H	I	J	K	L	M	N	O
8	P	Q	R	S	T	U	V	W	X	Y
9	Z	[	\	]	^	_	'	a	b	c
10	d	e	f	g	h	i	j	k	l	m
11	n	o	p	q	r	s	t	u	v	w
12	x	y	z	{			}	~	del		

Figure B.1 ASCII character set.

GUI Design Guidelines

This appendix contains a complete list of the GUI design guidelines presented at the end of each tutorial. The guidelines are organized by tutorial; within each tutorial section, they are organized by control.

Tutorial 3: Welcome Application (Introduction to Visual Programming)

Overall Design

■ Use colors in your applications, but not to the point of distracting the user.

Form

■ Choose short and descriptive Form titles. Capitalize words that are not articles, prepositions or conjunctions. Do not use punctuation.

■ Use Tahoma font to improve readability for controls that display text.

Label

■ Use Labels to display text that users cannot change.

■ Ensure that all Label controls are large enough to display their text.

PictureBox

■ Use PictureBoxes to enhance GUIs with graphics that users cannot change.

■ Images should fit inside their PictureBoxes. This can be achieved by setting PictureBox property SizeMode to StretchImage.

Tutorial 4: Designing the Inventory Application (Introducing TextBoxes and Buttons)

Overall Design

■ Although you can drag a Label control to a location on the Form, the Location property can be used to specify a precise position.

■ Place an application's output below and/or to the right of the Form's input controls.

Button

- Buttons are labelled using their `Text` property. These labels should use book-title capitalization and be as short as possible while still being meaningful to the user.
- Buttons should be stacked downward from the top right of a `Form` or arranged on the same line starting from the bottom right of a `Form`.

Form

- Changing the `Form`'s title allows users to identify the application's purpose.
- Form titles should use book-title capitalization.
- Change the `Form` font to Tahoma to be consistent with Microsoft's recommended font for Windows.

Label

- The `TextAlign` property of a descriptive `Label` should be set to `MiddleLeft`. This ensures that text within groups of `Label`s align.
- A descriptive `Label` should be placed above or to the left of the control that it identifies.
- A descriptive `Label` should have the same height as the `TextBox` it describes if the controls are arranged horizontally.
- A descriptive `Label` and the control it identifies should be aligned on the left if they are arranged vertically.
- Align the left sides of a group of descriptive `Label`s if the `Label`s are arranged vertically.
- A `Label` can be used to display output to the user. Use a descriptive `Label` to identify each output `Label`.
- Output `Label`s should look different from descriptive `Label`s to focus the user's attention. This can be done by setting the `BorderStyle` property to `Fixed3D` and the `TextAlign` property to `MiddleCenter`.
- If several output `Label`s are arranged vertically to display numbers used in a mathematical calculation (such as in an invoice), use the `MiddleRight` `TextAlign` property.
- A descriptive `Label` should use sentence-style capitalization and the control it identifies should be aligned on the top if they are arranged horizontally.

TextBox

- Use `TextBox`es to input data from the keyboard.
- `TextBox`es should have descriptive `Label`s indicating the input expected from the user.
- Make `TextBox`es wide enough for expected input.

Tutorial 7: Wage Calculator Application (Introducing Algorithms, Pseudocode and Program Control)

Overall Design

- Format all monetary amounts using the `C` (currency) format specifier.

TextBox

- When using multiple `TextBox`es vertically, align the `TextBox`es on their right sides, and where possible make the `TextBox`es the same size. Left-align the descriptive `Label`s for such `TextBox`es.

Tutorial 8: Dental Payment Application (Introducing CheckBoxes and Message Dialogs)

CheckBox

- A `CheckBox`'s label should be descriptive and as short as possible. When a `CheckBox` label contains more than one word, use book-title capitalization.
- Align groups of `CheckBox`es either horizontally or vertically.

Message Dialog

■ Text displayed in a dialog should be descriptive and as short as possible.

Tutorial 9: Car Payment Calculator Application (Introducing the Do While...Loop and Do Until...Loop Repetition Statements)

ListBox

■ A ListBox should be large enough to display all of its content or large enough that scrollbars may be used easily.

■ Use headers in a ListBox when you are displaying tabular data. Adding headers improves readability by indicating the information that will be displayed in the ListBox.

Tutorial 10: Class Average Application (Introducing the Do...Loop While and Do...Loop Until Repetition Statements)

Button

■ Disable a Button when its function should not be available to users.

■ Enable a disabled Button when its function once again should be available to users.

Tutorial 11: Interest Calculator Application (Introducing the For...Next Repetition Statement)

NumericUpDown

■ A NumericUpDown control should follow the same GUI Design Guidelines as a single-line TextBox.

■ Use a NumericUpDown control to limit the range of user input.

TextBox

■ If a TextBox will display multiple lines of output, set the Multiline property to True and left-align the output by setting the TextAlign property to Left.

■ If a multiline TextBox will display many lines of output, limit the TextBox height and use a vertical scrollbar to allow users to view additional lines of output.

Tutorial 12: Security Panel Application (Introducing the Select Case Multiple Selection Statement)

Overall Design

■ If your GUI is modeling a real-world object, your GUI design should mimic the physical appearance of the object.

TextBox

■ Mask passwords or other sensitive pieces of information in TextBoxes.

Tutorial 14: Shipping Time Application (Using Dates and Timers)

DateTimePicker

■ Use a DateTimePicker to retrieve date and time information from the user.

■ Each DateTimePicker should have a corresponding descriptive Label.

■ If the user should specify a time of day or a date and time, set the DateTimePicker's ShowUpDown property to True. If the user should specify a date, set the DateTimePicker's ShowUpDown property to False to allow the user to select a day from the month calendar.

GroupBox

■ GroupBox titles should be concise and should use book-title capitalization.

■ Use GroupBoxes to group related controls on the Form visually.

Tutorial 17: Flag Quiz Application (Introducing One-Dimensional Arrays and ComboBoxes)

ComboBox

- Each ComboBox should have a descriptive Label that describes the ComboBox's contents.
- If a ComboBox's content should not be editable, set its DropDownStyle property to Drop-DownList.

Tutorial 18: Sales Data Application (Introducing Two-Dimensional Arrays, RadioButtons and the MSChart Control)

RadioButton

- Use RadioButtons when the user should choose only one option in a group.
- Always place each group of RadioButtons in a separate container (such as a GroupBox).
- Align groups of RadioButtons either horizontally or vertically.

Tutorial 19: Microwave Oven Application (Building Your Own Classes and Objects)

Panel

- Use Panels to organize groups of related controls where the purpose of those controls is obvious. If the purpose of the controls is not obvious, use a GroupBox in place of a Panel, because GroupBoxes can contain captions.
- A Panel can display scrollbars if that Panel is not large enough to display all of its controls at once. To increase readability, we suggest avoiding the use of scrollbars on a Panel. If the Panel is not large enough to display all of its contents, increase the size of the Panel.
- Although it is possible to have a Panel without a border (by setting the BorderStyle property to None), use borders on your Panels whenever possible. This helps to increase readability and organization.

Tutorial 20: Shipping Hub Application (Introducing Collections, the For Each...Next Statement and Access Keys)

Overall Design

- Set a control's TabStop property to True only if the control is used to receive user input.
- Use the TabIndex property to define the logical order in which the user should enter data. Usually the tab order transfers the focus of the application from top to bottom and left to right.
- Use access keys to allow users to "click" a control using the keyboard.

Tutorial 22: Typing Application (Introducing Keyboard Events, Menus and Dialogs)

MenuStrip

- Use book-title capitalization in menu item text.
- Use separator bars in a menu to group related menu items.
- If clicking a menu item opens a dialog, an ellipsis (...) should follow the menu item's text.

Tutorial 27: Phone Book Application (Introducing Multimedia Using Microsoft Agent)

Microsoft Agent Control

- The Microsoft Agent character should be located near the application Form when the character is displayed on the screen.
- Use Microsoft Agent character gestures to indicate actions the user should take, or a response to an action the user has already taken.

APPENDIX

Visual Basic 2005 Express Windows Form Designer Tools

This book presents many controls that are available in Visual Basic 2005 Express. In all, there are 67 items available to you by default in the **Toolbox**. This appendix contains a chart (Fig. D.1) indicating the purpose and usage of most of these. A list of Web resources can be found after the chart.

Icon	Item	Purpose	Usage
▶	Pointer	Allows you to select and modify elements in the IDE. The pointer is not a control.	Allows the user to navigate a GUI.
	Background-Worker	Performs tasks asynchronously to the thread of the main application.	Used to execute time consuming tasks in the background.
	Binding-Navigator	Creates a ToolStrip to access and modify data.	Used to add, delete, update and navigate through data.
	BindingSource	Simplifies the process of binding controls to a data source.	Acts as data source to which components can bind to access data.
ab	Button	Allows users to indicate that an action should be performed.	Most commonly used to execute code when clicked.
☑	CheckBox	Allows the user to select or deselect an option.	Becomes checked when selected and unchecked when deselected.
	Checked-ListBox	Provides the user with a checkable list of items.	Much like a CheckBox, but all options are contained in a format similar to that of a ListBox.

Figure D.1 Visual Basic 2005 Express Windows Form Designer Tools. (Part 1 of 5.)

759

Icon	Item	Purpose	Usage
	ColorDialog	Allows the user to display the Windows **Color** dialog.	Used to retrieve a user's color selection in an application.
	ComboBox	Provides a short list of items in a drop-down menu.	Allow the user to view, enter new text in or search with a search String from multiple items in a list.
	ContextMenu-Strip	Displays a menu of programmer-defined options when the user right-clicks an object.	Provide additional options or features as a shortcut.
	DataGridView	Displays data within a chart.	Represent ADO.NET data in a scrollable chart.
	DataSet	Allows users to create a dataset.	Used to interact with data (typically from a database).
	DateTime-Picker	Allows users to choose the date and time.	Display or allow the selection of a time and date.
	DomainUpDown	Displays string values, using the up and down arrows.	Select strings from an Object collection.
	ErrorProvider	Displays errors regarding a control to the user.	Inform the user if there is an error associated with the control.
	EventLog	Allows interaction with Windows event logs.	Read, write, update and delete event log entries and entire logs.
	FileSystem-Watcher	Listens to the file system change notifications.	Raise events when a directory or a file in a directory changes.
	FlowLayout-Panel	Arranges its contents in a horizontal or vertical flow direction.	Used to specify flow direction, wrapping or clipping.
	Folder-BrowserDialog	Used to browse, select and create new folders.	Used when the application user should not be allowed to select files.
	FontDialog	Displays a font dialog that includes all available fonts installed on the computer.	Used to retrieve a user-specified font format and size in an application.
	GroupBox	Allows controls to be grouped together.	Organize related controls separately from the rest of the Form.
	HelpProvider	Provides additional help features for a specific control.	Create additional help features for a control.
	HScrollBar	A horizontal scrollbar.	Allow users to view text or graphics that may be too large to display horizontally in a control.

Figure D.1   Visual Basic 2005 Express Windows **Form** Designer Tools. (Part 2 of 5.)

Icon	Item	Purpose	Usage
	ImageList	A manageable list of images.	Store a list of images for use in other controls, such as a ListView or menu.
A	Label	Displays text to the user.	Identify specific items on the Form or display general-purpose text.
A	LinkLabel	Similar to a Label control but can include hyperlinks.	Display a hyperlink label that, when clicked, will open a file or Web page.
	ListBox	Provides a list of items.	Allow the user to view and select from multiple items in a list.
	ListView	Displays a group of items with identifiable icons.	Display a list of items (such as files) much like Windows Explorer.
#_	MaskedTextBox	Distinguish between proper and improper user input.	Enable programmers to specify the format of text input.
	MenuStrip	Creates a menu object on a Form.	Allow users to select options from menus, adding functionality to the application.
	MonthCalendar	Allows the user to select the date and time from a calendar that displays one month at a time.	Retrieve a user's date selection from a calendar.
	NotifyIcon	Creates icons that are displayed in a status area, usually while an action is performed in the background.	Remind the user that a certain process is running in the background of the application.
	NumericUpDown	Contains a number that is increased or decreased by clicking the up or down arrows.	Allow the user to specify a number in programmer-defined increments.
	OpenFile-Dialog	Displays a dialog to assist the user in selecting a file.	Retrieve user's file-name selection.
	PageSetup-Dialog	Displays a dialog to allow the user to change a document's page properties.	Allow users to modify the page settings and printer options.
	Panel	Similar to a GroupBox, but can include a scrollbar.	Group controls separately on the Form.
	PictureBox	Displays images.	Allow users to view graphics in an application.
	PrintDialog	Allows the user to select a printer and printing options.	Shown to retrieve user selection for printing options.

Figure D.1   Visual Basic 2005 Express Windows Form Designer Tools. (Part 3 of 5.)

Icon	Item	Purpose	Usage
	PrintDocument	Executes the printing process.	Accessed to print documents.
	PrintPreview-Control	Allows the user to preview a document before printing it.	Display a preview of the document.
	PrintPreview-Dialog	A dialog used to display a PrintPreviewControl.	Display a print-preview dialog.
	Process	Provides access to local and remote processes.	Enable the programmer to start and stop local system processes.
	ProgressBar	Displays a visual representation of the progress of an action or set of actions.	Inform the user of the completeness of an operation.
	PropertyGrid	Provides a user interface for browsing an object's properties.	Display the properties of another GUI control.
	RadioButton	Provides the user with a list of options from which only one or none can be selected.	Allow users to select at most one option from several.
	RichTextBox	Creates a TextBox control with advanced text-editing capabilities.	Allow users to perform more sophisticated editing beyond the features of a TextBox.
	SaveFile-Dialog	Assists the user in selecting a location in which to save a file.	Allow files to be saved.
	SerialPort	Provides access to serial ports.	Interact with a device that is connected to a serial port.
	Split-Container	Two panels, separated by a movable bar.	Group controls separately on the Form in resizable areas.
	Splitter	Allows the user to resize a docked control within an application.	Give the users the ability to change the size of a control.
	StatusStrip	Display useful information regarding the Form or objects in the application.	Notify the user of information not intended for the body of a Form.
	TabControl	Displays available tab pages in which you can place other controls.	Allow multiple tab pages on a Form.
	TableLayout-Panel	A panel that dynamically lays out its controls in a grid.	Allow controls to dynamically resize based on the current set of controls displayed.
	TextBox	Accepts user input from the keyboard. Can also be used to display text.	Used to retrieve user input from the keyboard.

Figure D.1   Visual Basic 2005 Express Windows **Form** Designer Tools. (Part 4 of 5.)

Icon	Item	Purpose	Usage
	Timer	Performs an action at programmer-specified intervals. A `Timer` is not visible to the user.	Allow the action of an event through a specific amount of time.
	ToolStrip	Contains icons representing specific commands.	Provide the user with options in a toolbar.
	ToolStrip-Container	Provides panels for managing other controls.	Used to organize one or more `ToolStrip`, `StatusStrip`, and `MenuStrip` controls.
	ToolTip	Displays text information about an object when the mouse cursor is over it.	Display additional information to the user.
	TrackBar	Allows the user to set a value from a specified range.	Similar to the scrollbar, but includes a range of values.
	TreeView	Displays a tree structure of objects, using nodes.	Display a hierarchical representation of a collection of objects.
	VScrollBar	Allows users to view text or graphics that may be too large to display vertically in a control.	Enable a vertical scrollbar in the control.
	WebBrowser	Provides a managed wrapper for the `WebBrowser` ActiveX control.	Used to embed Web browsing capabilities in an application.

Figure D.1   Visual Basic 2005 Express Windows **Form** Designer Tools. (Part 5 of 5.)

D.1 Internet and Web Resources

A great way to learn about controls not covered in this book is to use them. Several Web sites provide information to help you get started. The following sites should help you as you explore new features of Visual Basic 2005 Express:

msdn2.microsoft.com/en-us/library/xfak08ea.aspx
This site provides documentation for the most commonly used Windows **Form** controls, grouped by function.

www.exforsys.com/content/view/1515/350/
This site provides articles describing features and usage of common controls in Visual Basic 2005. You will also find links to discussions of more advanced topics in other languages.

msdn2.microsoft.com/en-us/library/3xdhey7w.aspx
This Web page provides a more technical description of controls you can use on a Windows **Form**.

E

A P P E N D I X

Keyword Chart

The table of Fig. E.1 contains a complete listing of Visual Basic keywords. Many of these keywords are discussed throughout the text.

Visual Basic Keywords

AddHandler	AddressOf	Alias	And
AndAlso	Ansi	As	Assembly
Auto	Boolean	ByRef	Byte
ByVal	Call	Case	Catch
CBool	CByte	CChar	CDate
CDbl	CDec	Char	CInt
Class	CLng	CObj	Const
Continue	CSByte	CShort	CSng
CStr	CType	CUInt	CULng
CUShort	Date	Decimal	Declare
Default	Delegate	Dim	DirectCast
Do	Double	Each	Else
ElseIf	End	Enum	Erase
Error	Event	Exit	False
Finally	For	Friend	Function
Get	GetType	Global	GoTo
Handles	If	Implements	Imports
In	Inherits	Integer	Interface
Is	IsNot	Lib	Like
Long	Loop	Me	Mod
Module	MustInherit	MustOverride	MyBase
MyClass	Namespace	Narrowing	New

Figure E.1   Visual Basic keywords. (Part 1 of 2.)

Visual Basic Keywords

Next	Not	Nothing	NotInheritable
NotOverridable	Object	Of	On
Operator	Option	Optional	Or
OrElse	Overloads	Overridable	Overrides
ParamArray	Partial	Preserve	Private
Property	Protected	Public	RaiseEvent
ReadOnly	ReDim	REM	RemoveHandler
Resume	Return	SByte	Select
Set	Shadows	Shared	Short
Single	Static	Step	Stop
String	Structure	Sub	SyncLock
Then	Throw	To	True
Try	TryCast	TypeOf	UInteger
Using	When	While	Widening
With	WithEvents	WriteOnly	Xor

The following are keywords, although they are not used in Visual Basic

EndIf	GoSub	Let	Variant	Wend

Figure E.1 Visual Basic keywords. (Part 2 of 2.)

A

access key—Keyboard shortcut that allows the user to perform an action on a control using the keyboard.

accessor—Method-like code units that handle the details of modifying and returning data.

action expression (in the UML)—Used in an action state within a UML activity diagram to specify a particular action to perform.

action state—An action to perform in a UML activity diagram that is represented by an action-state symbol.

action-state symbol—A rectangle with its left and right sides replaced with arcs curving outward that represents an action to perform in a UML activity diagram.

action/decision model of programming—Representing control statements as UML activity diagrams with rounded rectangles indicating *actions* to be performed and diamond symbols indicating *decisions* to be made.

active tab—The tab of the document displayed in the IDE.

active window—The window that is currently being used—sometimes referred to as the window that has the focus.

activity diagram—A UML diagram that models the activity (also called the workflow) of a portion of a software system.

Ada—A programming language, named after Lady Ada Lovelace, that was developed under the sponsorship of the U.S. Department of Defense (DOD) in the 1970s and early 1980s.

Add method of class `ArrayList`—Adds a specified object to the end of an `ArrayList`.

Add method of `Items`—Adds an item to a `ListBox` control.

Add method of the `Commands` property—Adds a command to a Microsoft Agent character.

`AddHandler` statement—Adds an event handler for a specific event.

`AddressOf` operator—Specifies the location of an event handler associated with an event.

ADO.NET—Part of Microsoft.NET that is used to interact with databases.

`AgentObject.IAgentCtlCharacter` object—References a Microsoft Agent character.

`AgentObject.IAgentCtlUserInput` object—Stores the user input retrieved from a Microsoft Agent character.

algorithm—A procedure for solving a problem, specifying the actions to be executed and the order in which they are to be executed.

Alphabetical icon—The icon in the **Properties** window that, when clicked, sorts properties alphabetically.

AndAlso operator—A logical operator used to ensure that two conditions are *both* true before choosing a certain path of execution. Performs short-circuit evaluation.

API (application programming interface)—The interface used by a program to access the operating system and various services on the computer.

App_Code folder—The project folder where the `DataSet` you created is placed.

App_Data folder—The project folder where the database you added is placed.

argument—Inputs to a function that provide information the function needs to perform its task.

arithmetic and logic unit (ALU)—The "manufacturing" section of the computer. The ALU performs calculations and makes decisions.

arithmetic operators—The operators +, -, *, /, \, ^ and Mod.

array—A data structure containing data items of the same type.

array bounds—Integers that determine what indices can be used to access an element in an array. The lower bound is 0; the upper bound is the length of the array minus one.

`Array.Sort` method—Sorts the values of an array into ascending order.

`ArrayList` class—Performs the same functionality as an array, but has resizing capabilities.

As keyword—Used in variable declarations. Indicates that the following word (such as `Integer`) is the variable type.

ASP.NET—.NET software that helps programmers create applications for the Web.

ASP.NET 2.0 technology—Can be combined with Visual Basic to create web applications.

ASP.NET Development Server—A Web server that you can use to test your ASP.NET Web applications. It is specifically designed for learning and testing purposes to execute Web applications on the local computer and to respond to browser requests from the local computer.

ASP.NET server control—Another name for a Web control.

.aspx extension—The filename extension for ASPX pages.

ASPX page—File that specifies the GUI of a Web page using Web controls. Also called Web Forms or Web Form Pages.

assembler—A translator program that converts assembly-language programs to machine language at computer speeds.

assembly language—A type of programming language that uses English-like abbreviations to represent the fundamental operations on the computer.

assignment operator—The "=" symbol used to assign values in an assignment statement.

assignment statement—A statement that copies one value to another. An assignment statement contains an "equals"-sign (=) operator that causes the value of its right operand to be copied to its left operand.

asterisk (*)—Multiplication operator. The operator's left and right operands are multiplied together.

attribute—Another name for a property of an object.

auto-hide—A space-saving IDE feature used for windows such as **Toolbox**, **Properties** and **Dynamic Help** that hides a window until the mouse pointer is placed on the hidden window's tab.

AutoSize property of a Label—Specifies whether a Label is automatically resized to accomodate the text in the Label.

B

BackColor property—Specifies the background color of the Form or a control.

BackColor property of class Form—Returns the Color value used as the background color of the Form.

backslash (\)—Integer division operator. The operator divides its left operand by its right and returns an integer result.

bandwidth—The information-carrying capacity of communications lines.

BASIC (Beginner's All-Purpose Symbolic Instruction Code)—A programming language that was developed in the mid-1960s by Professors John Kemeny and Thomas Kurtz of Dartmouth College as a language for writing simple programs. Its primary purpose was to familiarize novices with programming techniques.

Beep function—Causes your computer to make a beep sound.

BgColor property of an ASPX page—Specifies the page's background color.

binary digit—A digit that can assume one of two values.

binary operator—Requires two operands.

BindingNavigator—A control that allows you to manipulate and navigate data on a databound Form.

bit—Short for "binary digit." A digit that can assume one of two values.

block—A group of code statements.

block scope—Variables declared inside control statements, such as an If...Then statement, have block scope. Block scope begins at the identifier's declaration and ends at the block's final statement (for example, End If).

body of a control statement—The set of statements that are enclosed in a control statement.

book-title capitalization—A style that capitalizes the first letter of the each word in the text (for example, **Calculate Total**).

Boolean data type—A data type that has the value True or False.

BorderStyle property—Specifies the type of border that displays around an Image or DetailsView.

BorderStyle property—Specifies the appearance of a Label's border, which allows you to distinguish one control from another visually. The BorderStyle property can be set to None (no border), FixedSingle (a single dark line as a border), or Fixed3D (giving the Label a "sunken" appearance).

Both value of ScrollBars property—Used to display both horizontal and vertical scrollbars on the bottom and right side of a TextBox.

bottom tier—The tier (also known as the information tier, or the data tier) containing the application data of a multi-tier application—typically implemented as a database

bounding box of an ellipse—Specifies an ellipse's location, width and height.

break mode—The IDE mode when application execution is suspended. This mode is entered through the debugger.

breakpoint—A location where execution is to suspend, indicated by a solid maroon circle.

brush—Used to fill shapes with colors.

Brush object—An object used to specify drawing parameters when drawing solid shapes.

bug—A flaw in a program that prevents it from executing correctly.

built-in data type—A data type already defined in Visual Basic, such as an Integer (also known as a primitive data type).

business logic tier—The tier that controls interaction between the client and information tiers. Also called the middle tier.

business object—A middle-tier object that retrieves data from the bottom-tier database and makes it available to the top-tier user interface.

Button control—Commands the application to perform an action.

Button property of class MouseEventArgs—Specifies which (if any) mouse button is pressed.

Button Web control—Allows users to perform an action.

ByRef keyword—Used to pass an argument by reference.

byte—Eight bits.

ByVal—The keyword specifying that the calling procedure should pass a copy of its argument's value in the procedure call to the called procedure.

C

call-by-reference—See *pass-by-reference.*

call-by-value—See *pass-by-value.*

callee—The procedure being called.

caller—The procedure that calls another procedure. Also known as the calling procedure.

Cancel value of DialogResult enumeration—Used to determine whether the user clicked the **Cancel** Button of a dialog.

caret (^)—Exponentiation operator. This operator raises its left operand to a power specified by the right operand.

Case Else statement—Optional statement whose body executes if the Select Case's test expression does not match an expression of any Case.

case sensitive—The instance where two words that are spelled identically are treated differently if the capitalization of the two words differs.

Case statement—Statement whose body executes if the Select Case's test expression matches an expression of any Case.

Catch block—Also called an exception handler, this block executes when the corresponding Try block in the application detects an exceptional situation and throws an exception of the type the `Catch` block declares.

Categorized icon—The icon in the **Properties** window that, when clicked, sorts properties categorically.

cell borders—The separators between the cells in a `Details-View`.

Central Processing Unit (CPU)—The part of the computer's hardware that is responsible for supervising the operation of the other sections of the computer.

Char structure—Stores characters (such as letters and symbols).

character set—The set of all characters used to write applications and represent data items on a particular computer. Visual Basic uses the Unicode character set.

Characters property of AxAgent control—Used to access a specific Microsoft Agent character.

Chars property of class String—Returns the character located at a specific index in a `String`.

CheckBox control—A small square GUI element that either is blank or contains a check mark.

CheckBox label—The text that appears alongside a `CheckBox`.

Checked property of RadioButton control—When `True`, displays a small dot in the control. When `False`, the control displays an empty white circle.

Checked property of the CheckBox control—Specifies whether the `CheckBox` is checked (`True`) or unchecked (`False`).

CheckedChanged event—Raised when a `RadioButton`'s state changes.

CheckFileExists property of class OpenFileDialog—Enables the user to display a warning if a specified file does not exist.

class—The type of a group of related objects. A class specifies the general format of its objects; the properties and actions available to an object depend on its class. An object is to its class much as a house is to its blueprint.

class definition—The code that belongs to a class, beginning with keywords `Public Class` and ending with keywords `End Class`.

Class Keyword—Reserved word required to begin a class defintion.

class name—The identifier used to identify the name of a class in code.

Clear method of Items—Deletes all the values in a `ListBox`'s control.

Click event—An event raised when a user clicks a control.

client—When an application creates and uses an object of a class, the application is known as a client of the class.

client tier—The user interface of a multi-tier application (also called the top tier).

Close method of class StreamWriter or StreamReader—Used to close the stream.

COBOL (COmmon Business Oriented Language)—A programming language that was developed in the late 1950s by a group of computer manufacturers in conjunction with government and industrial computer users. This language is used primarily for business applications that manipulate large amounts of data.

code editor—A window where a user can create, view or edit an application's code.

code view—A mode of the Visual Basic IDE where the application's code is displayed in an editor window.

code-behind file—Visual Basic .NET file that contains a class which provides an ASPX page's functionality.

collection—A class used to store groups of related objects.

collection type of a For Each...Next statement—Specifies the array or collection through which you wish to iterate.

Collections namespace—Contains collection classes such as `ArrayList`.

Color structure—Contains several predefined colors as properties.

ColorDialog class—Used to display a dialog from which the user can select colors.

column—The second dimension of a two-dimensional array.

ComboBox control—Combines a `TextBox` with a `ListBox`.

Command event—Raised when a user speaks a command to a Microsoft Agent character or selects a command from a character's context menu.

Commands property—Sets which commands the Microsoft Agent character can understand as input from the user.

comment—A line of code that follows a single-quote character (`'`) and is inserted to improve an application's readability.

Community menu—The menu of the IDE that contains commands for sending questions directly to Microsoft, checking question status, sending feedback on Visual Basic and searching the CodeZone developer center and the Microsoft developers community site.

compiler—A translator program that converts high-level-language programs into machine language.

component object box—The `ComboBox` at the top of the **Properties** window that allows you to select the `Form` or control object whose properties you want set.

component tray—The area below the Windows Form Designer that contains controls, such as `Timers`, that are not part of the graphical user interface.

computer—A device capable of performing computations and making logical decisions at speeds millions and even billions of times faster than the speeds at which human beings carry out the same tasks.

omputer program—A set of instructions that guides a computer through an orderly series of actions.

computer programmer—A person who writes computer programs.

condition—An expression with a true or false value that is used to make a decision.

connection—Represents the connection between an application and its data source.

connection string—Specifies the path to a database file on disk, as well as some additional settings that determine how to access the database.

consistent state—A way to maintain the values of an object's instance variables such that the values are always valid.

constant—A variable whose value cannot be changed after its initial declaration.

constructor—A method that initializes a class object or structure value when it is created.

container—An object that contains controls such as a `GroupBox`.

Contents command—The command that displays a categorized table of contents in which help articles are organized by topic.

context-sensitive help—A help option (launched by pressing *F1*) that provides links to articles that apply to the current content (that is, the item selected with the mouse pointer).

control—A reusable GUI component, such as a `GroupBox`, `RadioButton`, `Button` or `Label`.

Control—A type that can be used to declare variables for referencing controls on the `Form`.

control structure (control statement)—An application component that specifies the order in which statements execute (also known as the flow of control).

control structure (statement) nesting—Placing one control statement in the body of another control statement.

control structure (statement) stacking—A set of control statements in sequence. The exit point of one control statement is connected to the entry point of the next control statement in sequence.

ControlChars.Tab constant—Represents a tab character.

controlling expression—Value compared sequentially with each `Case` until either a match occurs or the `End Select` statement is reached. Also known as a test expression.

Convert class—Provides methods for converting data types.

Convert.ToDecimal method—Converts a value to type `Decimal`, which is appropriate for monetary calculations.

Convert.ToInt16 method—Converts data to type `Short`.

coordinate system—A scheme for identifying every possible point on the computer screen.

Count property of ArrayList—Returns the number of objects contained in the `ArrayList`.

Count property of Items—Returns the number of `ListBox` items.

counter—A variable often used to determine the number of times a block of statements in a loop will execute.

counter-controlled repetition—A technique that uses a counter variable to determine the number of times that a block of statements will execute. Also called definite repetition.

CreateGraphics method—Creates a `Graphics` object on a `Form` or control.

criteria of WHERE clause—Indicates the specific records from which data will be retrieved or manipulated.

CType function—Function that converts the type of its first argument to the type specified by the second argument.

currency format—Used to display values as monetary amounts.

CurrentDirectory property of System.Environment—Returns the directory from which the application is executing as a fully qualified path name.

Cursor.Position property—Contains the *x*- and *y*-coordinates of the mouse cursor on the screen (in pixels).

CustomFormat property of a DateTimePicker control—The `DateTimePicker` property that contains the programmer-specified format string with which to display the date and/or time when `DateTimePicker` `Format` property is set to `Custom`.

D

data hierarchy—Collection of data items processed by computers that become larger and more complex in structure as you progress from bits, to characters, to fields and up to larger data structures.

Data menu—The menu of the IDE that contains commands for interacting with databases.

Data Source configuration Wizard—Wizard used to add a data source connection to the application.

Data Sources window—Window used to connect application to a data source (e.g. a database) and create a series of databound controls.

data structure—Groups and organizes related data.

data tier—The tier (also known as the information tier, or the bottom tier) containing the application data of a multi-tier application—typically implemented as a database.

database—Organized collection of data.

Database Explorer window—Window used to view and manipulate database information in the Visual Basic 2005 IDE.

database management system (DBMS)—Collection of programs designed to create and manage databases.

DataSet—A class that is designed specifically to store data from databases that are connected to the application.

DataSource property of class ComboBox—Specifies the source of items listed in a `ComboBox`.

DataTable—Allows you to store related information in memory in rows and columns.

Date structure—A structure whose properties can be used to store and display date and time information.

Date variable—A variable of type `Date`, capable of storing date and time data.

Date.Now—Returns the current system time and date.

DateChanged event of MonthCalendar control—Raised when a new date (or a range of dates) is selected.

DateTimePicker control—Retrieves date and time information from the user.

Debug menu—The menu of the IDE that contains commands for debugging and running an application.

debugger—A tool that allows you to analyze the behavior of your application to determine whether it is executing correctly.

debugging—The process of fixing errors in an application.

Decimal data type—Used to store monetary amounts.

decimal digits—The digits 0, 1, 2, 3, 4, 5, 6, 7, 8 and 9.

decision symbol—The diamond-shaped symbol in a UML activity diagram that indicates that a decision is to be made.

declaration—The reporting of a new variable to the compiler. The variable can then be used in the Visual Basic code.

declare a variable—Report the name and type of a variable to the compiler.

default property—The value of a property that provides the initial characteristics of an object when it is first created.

DefaultBackColor property—Contains the default background color for a `Panel` control.

definite repetition—See *counter-controlled repetition*.

descriptive Label—A `Label` used to describe another control on the `Form`. This helps users understand a control's purpose.

Design mode—Displays the ASPX page's GUI at design time.

design mode—IDE mode that allows you to create applications using Visual Studio .NET's windows, toolbars and menu bar.

design units—Any specified units of measurement for the font.

design view—The IDE view that contains the features necessary to begin creating Windows applications.

Designer.vb file—The file containing the declarations and statements that build an application's GUI.

DetailsView control—A control in the **Data** group of the **Toolbox** that allows you to display information in a structured manner

dialog—A window that displays messages to users or gathers input from users.

DialogResult enumeration—An enumeration that contains values corresponding to standard dialog `Button` names.

diamond symbol—A symbol (also known as the decision symbol) in a UML activity diagram; this symbol indicates that a decision is to be made.

Dim keyword—Indicates the declaration of a variable.

Directory.GetCurrentDirectory—A method of class `Directory` in the `System.IO` namespace that returns a `String` containing the path to the directory that contains the application.

dismiss—Synonym for close.

dithering—Using small dots of existing colors to form a pattern that simulates a desired color.

divide-and-conquer technique—Constructing large applications from small, manageable pieces to make development and maintenance of large applications easier.

Do Until...Loop repetition statement—A control statement that executes a set of body statements until its loop-termination condition becomes `True`.

Do While...Loop repetition statement—A control statement that executes a set of body statements while its loop-continuation condition is `True`.

Document property—Property of the `PrintPreviewDialog` that allows you to specify the document that will be displayed in the dialog.

dot operator—See *member access operator*.

dotted line—A UML activity diagram symbol that connects each UML-style note with the element that the note describes.

Double data type—Stores both whole and fractional numbers. Normally, `Double`s store floating-point numbers.

double-selection statement—A statement, such as `If...Then...Else`, that selects between two different actions or sequences of actions.

double-subscripted array—See *two-dimensional array*.

Do...Loop Until repetition statement—A control statement that executes a set of statements until the loop-termination condition becomes `True` after the loop executes.

Do...Loop While repetition statement—A control statement that executes a set of statements while the loop-continuation condition is `True`; the condition is tested after the loop executes.

DrawLine method of the Graphics class—Draws a line of a specified color between two specified points.

DrawRectangle method—Draws the outline of a rectangle of a specified size and color at a specified location.

DrawString method—`Graphics` method that draws the specified `String`.

DropDownList value of DropDownStyle property—Specifies that a `ComboBox` is not editable.

DropDownStyle property of class ComboBox—`ComboBox` property that specifies the appearance of the `ComboBox`.

dynamic content—A type of content that is animated or interactive.

dynamic resizing—A capability that allows certain objects (such as `ArrayList`s) to increase or decrease in size based on the addition or removal of elements from that object. Enables the `ArrayList` object to increase its size to accommodate new elements and to decrease its size when elements are removed.

E

element—An item in an array.

element of a For Each...Next statement—Used to store a reference to the current value of the collection being iterated.

ElseIf keyword—Keyword used for the nested conditions in nested `If...Then...Else` statements.

embedded parentheses—Another term for nested parentheses.

empty string—A string that does not contain any characters.

Enabled property—Specifies whether a control such as a `Button` appears enabled (`True`) or disabled (`False`).

Enabled property of a TextBox—Determines whether the `TextBox` will respond to user input.

Enabled property of class ComboBox—Specifies whether a user can select an item from a `ComboBox`.

End Class keywords—Reserved words required to end a class defintion.

End Enum keywords—End an enumeration.

End Function keywords—Indicates the end of a `Function` procedure.

End Select keywords—Terminates the `Select Case` statement.

End Sub keywords—Indicates the end of a `Sub` procedure.

End Try—Indicates the end of a sequence of blocks containing a `Try` block, followed by one or more `Catch` blocks and an optional `Finally` block.

EndsWith method of class String—Determines whether a `String` ends with a particular substring.

Enum keyword—Begins an enumeration.

enumeration—A group of related, named constants.

equality operators—Operators = (is equal to) and <> (is not equal to) that compare two values.

event—A user action that can trigger an event handler.

event handler—A section of code that is executed (called) when a certain event is raised (occurs).

event-driven program—A program that responds to user-initiated events, such as mouse clicks and keystrokes.

exception—An indication of a problem that occurs during an application's execution.

Exception Assistant—A window that appears indicating where an exception has occurred, the type of exception, and information on handling the exception.

exception handler—A block that executes when the application detects an exceptional situation and throws an exception.

exception handling—Processing problems that occur during application execution.

executable statement—Actions that are performed when the corresponding Visual Basic application is run.

explicit conversion—An operation that converts a value of one type to another type using code to (explicitly) tell the application to do the conversion. An example of an explicit conversion is to convert a value of one type to another type using a `Convert` method.

expression list—Multiple expressions separated by commas. Used for `Cases` in `Select Case` statements, when certain statements should execute based on more than one condition.

extensible language—A language that can be "extended" with new data types. Visual Basic is an extensible language.

F

field—Column in a table of a database.

field—Group of characters that conveys some meaning. For example, a field consisting of uppercase and lowercase letters can represent a person's name.

FileName property of class `OpenFileDialog`—Specifies the file name displayed in the dialog.

FillEllipse method of class `Graphics`—The method of the `Graphics` class that draws an ellipse. This method takes as arguments a brush, a `Color`, the coordinates of the upper-left corner of the ellipse's bounding box and the width and height of the bounding box. If the width and height are the same, a circle is drawn.

final state—Represented by a solid circle surrounded by a hollow circle in a UML activity diagram; the end of the workflow after an application performs its activities

Finally block—An optional block of code that follows the last `Catch` block in a sequence of `Catch` blocks or the `Try` block if there are no `Catch`es. The `Finally` block provides code that always executes, whether or not an exception occurs.

FixedSingle value of a `Label`'s `BorderStyle` property—Specifies that the `Label` will display a thin, black border.

Flat value of the `FlatStyle` property of a `Button`—Specifies that a `Button` will appear flat.

FlatStyle property of a `Button`—Determines whether the `Button` will appear flat or three-dimensional.

floating-point division—Divides two numbers (whole or fractional) and returns a floating-point number.

focus—Designates the window currently in use.

Focus method—Transfers the focus of the application to the control on which the method is called.

Font class—Contains properties that define unique fonts.

Font property—Specifies the font name, style and size of any displayed text in the `Form` or one of its controls.

FontDialog class—Used to display a dialog from which the user can choose a font and its style.

FontFamily class—Represents the `FontFamily` of the `Font` (a grouping structure to organize fonts with similar properties).

FontStyle enumeration—Provides constants for specifying a font's style. These include `FontStyle.Bold`, `FontStyle.Italic`, `FontStyle.Regular`, `FontStyle.Strikeout` and `FontStyle.Underline`.

For Each...Next repetition statement—Iterates through elements in an array or collection.

For keyword—Begins the `For...Next` statement.

ForeColor property—Specifies font color for `Label` controls.

Form—The object that represents the Windows application's graphical user interface (GUI).

format control string—A string that specifies how data should be formatted.

Format property of a `DateTimePicker` control—The `DateTimePicker` property that allows the programmer to specify a predefined or custom format with which to display the date and/or time.

format specifier—Code that specifies the type of format that should be applied to a string for output.

FormatException class—An exception of this type is thrown when a method cannot convert its argument to a desired numeric type, such as `Integer` or `Double`.

formatting—Modifying the appearance of text for display purposes.

Fortran (Formula Translator)—A programming language developed by IBM Corporation in the mid-1950s to create scientific and engineering applications that require complex mathematical computations.

For...Next header—The first line of a `For...Next` repetition statement. The `For...Next` header specifies all four essential elements for the counter-controlled repetition of a `For...Next` repetition statement.

For...Next repetition statement—Repetition statement that handles the details of counter-controlled repetition. The `For...Next` statement uses all four elements essential to counter-controlled repetition in one line of code (the name of a control variable, the initial value, the increment or decrement value and the final value).

Framework Class Library (FCL)—.NET's collection of "pre-packaged" classes and methods for performing mathematical calculations, string manipulations, character manipulations, input/output operations, error checking and many other useful operations.

FROM SQL keyword—Specifies table from which to get data.

FromArgb method of the `Color` class—Creates a new `Color` object from RGB values and from an alpha value.

FullOpen property of class `ColorDialog`—Property that, when `True`, enables the `ColorDialog` to provide a full range of color options when displayed.

Function keyword—Begins the definition of a Function procedure.

Function procedure—A procedure similar to a Sub procedure, with one important difference: Function procedures return a value to the caller, whereas Sub procedures do not.

functionality—The actions an application can execute.

G

GDI+ (Graphics Device Interface)—An application programming interface (API) that provides classes for creating two-dimensional vector graphics.

Get accessor—Used to retrieve a value of a property.

GetName method of the FontFamily class—Returns the name of the FontFamily object.

GetUpperBound method of class Array—Returns the largest index of an array.

Graphical User Interface (GUI)—The visual part of an application with which users interact.

Graphics class—Provides methods for drawing shapes.

Gridlines property of a DetailsView—Specifies whether the DetailView's cell borders display.

GroupBox control—Groups related controls visually.

guard condition—An expression contained in square brackets above or next to the arrows leading from a decision symbol in a UML activity diagram that determines whether workflow continues along a path.

H

hardware—The various devices that make up a computer, including the keyboard, screen, mouse, hard drive, memory, CD-ROM, DVD and processing units.

HasMorePages property of the PrintPageEventArgs class—Specifies whether there are more pages to print. When False, the PrintPage event is no longer raised.

header—A line of text at the top of a ListBox that clarifies the information being displayed.

Height property of a Web control—Allows you to specify the height of a Web control.

Height property of a Form—This property, a member of property Size, indicates the height of the Form or one of its controls in pixels.

HideEvent event—Raised when a Microsoft Agent character is hidden.

high-level language—A type of programming language in which a single program statement accomplishes a substantial task. High-level languages use instructions that look almost like everyday English and contain common mathematical notations.

Horizontal Rule HTML control—Displays a line to separate controls on an ASPX page.

Horizontal value of ScrollBars property—Used to display a horizontal scrollbar on the bottom of a TextBox.

host name—Name of a computer where resources reside.

HTML (HyperText Markup Language)—A technology for describing Web content.

HTML controls—Correspond to HTML elements.

HyperText Markup Language (HTML)—A language for marking up information to share over the World Wide Web via hyperlinked text documents.

HyperText Transfer Protocol (HTTP)—The protocol that enables HTML files to be transmitted over the World Wide Web.

I

icon—The graphical representation of commands in the Visual Studio .NET IDE.

ID property—Specifies the name of a Web control.

identifier—A series of characters consisting of letters, digits and underscores used to name program units such as classes, controls and variables.

If…Then—Selection statement that performs an action (or sequence of actions) based on a condition. This is also called the single-selection statement.

If…Then…Else—Selection statement that performs an action (or sequence of actions) if a condition is true and performs a different action (or sequence of actions) if the condition is false. This is also called the double-selection statement.

Image property—Indicates the file name of the image displayed in a PictureBox.

Image Web control—Displays an image in an ASPX page.

Image.FromFile—A method of class Image that returns an Image object containing the image located at the path you specify.

immutable—An object that cannot be changed after it is created. In Visual Basic, Strings are immutable.

implicit conversion—An operation that converts a value of one type to another type without writing code to (explicitly) tell the application to do the conversion.

Imports keyword—Used to import namespaces.

Increment property of a NumericUpDown control—Specifies by how much the current number in the NumericUpDown control changes when the user clicks the control's up (for incrementing) or down (for decrementing) arrow.

index—An array element's position number, also called a subscript. An index must be zero, a positive integer or an integer expression. If an application uses an expression as an index, the expression is evaluated first, to determine the index.

index of an ArrayList—The value with which you can refer to a specific element in an ArrayList, based on the element's location in the ArrayList.

indexed array name—The array name followed by an index enclosed in parentheses. The indexed array name can be used on the left side of an assignment statement to place a new value into an array element. The indexed array name can be used in the right side of an assignment to retrieve the value of that array element.

IndexOf method of class String—Returns the index of the first occurrence of a substring in a String. Returns -1 if the substring is not found.

infinite loop—An error in which a repetition statement never terminates.

information tier—Tier containing the application data; typically implemented as a database. Also called the bottom tier or data tier.

initial state—Represented by a solid circle in a UML activity diagram; the beginning of the workflow before the application performs the modeled activities.

initializer list—The required braces ({ and }) surrounding the initial values of the elements in an array. When the initializer list is empty, the elements in the array are initialized to the default value for the array's data type.

input device—Devices such as the keyboard and the mouse that are used to interact with a computer.

input unit—The "receiving" section of the computer that obtains information (data and computer programs) from various input devices, such as the keyboard and the mouse.

Insert method of class ArrayList—Inserts a specified object into the specified location of an ArrayList.

Insert method of class String—String method that inserts its second argument (a String) at the position specified by the first argument.

instance variable—Declared inside a class but outside any procedure of that class. Instance variables have module scope.

instant-access application—Application that immediately locates a particular record of information.

instantiate an object—Create an object of a class.

Int32.MaxValue constant—The largest possible Integer—more specifically, 2,147,483,647.

integer—A whole number, such as 919, –11, 0 and 138624.

Integer data type—Stores integer values.

integer division—Integer division takes two Integer operands and yields an Integer result. The fractional portion of the result is discarded.

Integrated Development Environment (IDE)—A software tool that enables programmers to write, run, test and debug programs quickly and conveniently.

IntelliSense feature—Visual Basic IDE feature that aids the programmer during development by providing windows listing available class members and pop-up descriptions for those members.

interactive animated characters—The Microsoft Agent technology adds such characters to Windows applications and Web pages. These characters can interact with the user through mouse clicks and microphone input.

internal Web browser—The Web browser (Internet Explorer) included in Visual Basic 2005 Express, with which you can browse the Web.

J

Join method of class String—Concatenates the elements in a String array, separated by the first argument. A new String containing the concatenated elements is returned.

K

key-value pair—Associates a value with a corresponding key, which is used to identify the value.

keyboard event—Raised when a key on the keyboard is pressed or released.

KeyChar property of class KeyPressEventArgs—Contains data about the key that raised the KeyPress event.

KeyData property of class KeyEventArgs—Contains data about the key that raised the KeyDown event.

KeyDown event—Generated when a key is initially pressed. Use to handle the event raised when a key that is not a letter key is pressed.

KeyEventArgs class—Stores information about special modifier keys.

KeyPress event—Generated when a key is pressed. Use to handle the event raised when a letter key is pressed.

KeyPressEventArgs class—Stores information about character keys.

Keys enumeration—Contains values representing keyboard keys.

KeyUp event—Generated when a key is released.

keyword—A word in code reserved for a specific purpose. By default, these words appear in blue in the IDE and cannot be used as identifiers.

L

Label—Control that displays text the user cannot modify.

Label Web control—Displays text on an ASPX page.

LastIndexOf method of class String—Returns the index of the last occurrence of a substring in a String. Returns –1 if the substring is not found.

left operand—The expression on the left side of a binary operator.

Left value of MouseButtons enumeration—Used to represent the left mouse button.

length of an array—The number of elements in an array.

Length property of class Array—Contains the length (or number of elements in) an array.

Length property of class String—Returns the number of characters in a String.

line-continuation character—An underscore character (_) preceded by one or more spaces, used to continue a statement to the next line of code.

ListBox control—Allows the user to view items in a list. Items can be added to or removed from the list programmatically.

ListBox Web control—Displays a list of items.

literal String objects—A String constant written as a sequence of characters in double quotation marks (also called a string literal).

Load event of a Form—Raised when an application initially executes.

local variable—Declared inside a procedure or block, such as the body of an If...Then statement. Local variables have either procedure scope or block scope.

localhost—Host name that identifies the local computer.

Locals window—Allows you to view the state of the variables in the current scope during debugging.

location bar—The ComboBox in Visual Basic's internal Web browser where you can enter the name of a Web site to visit.

Location property—Specifies the location of the upper-left corner of a control. This property is used to place a control on the Form precisely.

logic error—An error that does not prevent the application from compiling successfully, but does cause the application to produce erroneous results.

logical exclusive OR (Xor) operator—A logical operator that is True if and only if one of its operands results in True and the other results in False.

logical operators—The operators (for example, AndAlso, OrElse, Xor and Not) that can be used to form complex conditions by combining simple ones.

loop—Another name for a repetition statement.

loop-continuation condition—The condition used in a repetition statement (such as a Do While...Loop) that enables repetition to continue while the condition is True and that causes repetition to terminate when the condition becomes False.

loop-termination condition—The condition used in a repetition statement (such as a Do Until...Loop) that enables repetition to continue while the condition is False and that causes repetition to terminate when the condition becomes True.

M

m-by-n array—A two-dimensional array with m rows and n columns.

machine language—A computer's natural language, generally consisting of streams of numbers that instruct the computer how to perform its most elementary operations.

margin indicator bar—A margin in the IDE where breakpoints are displayed.

MarginBounds.Left property of the PrintPageEventArgs class—Specifies the left margin of a printed page.

MarginBounds.Top property of the PrintPageEventArgs class—Specifies the top margin of a printed page.

masking—Hiding text such as passwords or other sensitive pieces of information that should not be observed by other people as they are typed. Masking is achieved by using the PasswordChar property of the TextBox for which you would like to hide data. The actual data entered is retained in the TextBox's Text property.

masking character—Used to replace each character displayed in a TextBox when the TextBox's data is masked for privacy.

Max method of class Math—A Shared method of class Math which returns the greater of its two arguments.

MaxDate property of a DateTimePicker control—The DateTime-Picker property that specifies the latest value that the DateTimePicker will allow the user to enter.

MaxDropDownItems property of class ComboBox—Property of the ComboBox class that specifies how many items can be displayed in the drop-down list. If the ComboBox has more elements than this, it will provide a scrollbar to access all of them.

Maximum property of a NumericUpDown control—Determines the maximum input value in a particular NumericUpDown control.

MaxLength property of TextBox—Specifies the maximum number of characters that can be input into a TextBox.

.mdf file—A database file of SQL Server 2005 Express.

Me keyword—References the current object.

member access operator—Also known as the dot operator (.). Allows programmers to access a control's properties using code.

member-access modifier—Keywords used to specify what members of a class a client may access. Includes keywords Public and Private.

members of a class—Methods, variables, and properties declared within the body of a class.

memory unit—The rapid-access, relatively low-capacity "warehouse" section of the computer, which stores data temporarily while an application is running.

memory—Another name for the memory unit.

menu—Design element that groups related commands for Windows applications. Although these commands depend on the application, some—such as **Open** and **Save**—are common to many applications. Menus are an integral part of GUIs, because they organize commands without cluttering the GUI.

Menu Designer mode in the Visual Basic IDE—Design mode in the IDE that allows you to create and edit menus and menu items.

menu item—Command located in a menu that, when selected, causes the application to perform an action.

MenuStrip control—Allows you to add menus to your application.

merge symbol (in the UML)—A diamond symbol in the UML that joins two flows of activity into one flow of activity.

MessageBox class—Provides a method for displaying message dialogs.

MessageBox.Show method—Displays a message dialog.

MessageBoxButtons constants—The identifiers that specify Buttons that can be displayed in a MessageBox dialog.

MessageBoxIcon constants—Identifiers that specify icons that can be displayed in a MessageBox dialog.

method—A procedure contained in a class, performs a task and possibly returns information when it completes the task.

method—A procedure contained in a class.

microprocessor—The chip that makes a computer work (that is, the "brain" of the computer).

Microsoft .NET—Microsoft's vision for using the Internet and the Web in the development, engineering and use of software. .NET includes tools such as Visual Studio and programming languages such as Visual Basic.

Microsoft Agent—A technology used to add interactive animated characters to Windows applications and Web pages.

Microsoft Developer Network (MSDN)—An online library that contains articles, downloads and tutorials on technologies of interest to Visual Basic developers.

middle tier—Tier that controls interaction between the client and information tiers (also called the business logic tier).

MinDate property of a DateTimePicker control—The DateTime-Picker property that specifies the earliest value that the DateTimePicker will allow the user to enter.

Minimum property of a NumericUpDown control—Determines the minimum input value in a particular NumericUpDown control.

minus box—The icon that, when clicked, collapses a node.

Mod (modulus operator)—The modulus operator yields the remainder after division.

modifier key—Key such as *Shift*, *Alt* or *Control* that modifies the way that an application responds to a keyboard event.

module scope—Begins at the identifier after keyword Class and terminates at the End Class statement, enables all procedures in the same class to access all instance variables defined in that class.

MonthCalendar control—Displays a calendar from which a user can select a range of dates.

mouse event—Generated when a user interacts with an application using the computer's mouse.

MouseButtons enumeration—Defines constants, such as Left and Right, to specify mouse buttons.

MouseDown event—Generated when a mouse button is pressed.

MouseEventArgs class—Specifies information about a mouse event.

MouseMove event—Generated when a mouse pointer is moved.

MouseUp event—Generated when the mouse button is released.

MoveTo method—Relocates the Microsoft Agent character on the screen.

multi-tier application—Application (sometimes referred to as an *n*-tier application) whose functionality is divided into separate tiers, which can be on the same machine or can be distributed to separate machines across a network.

Multiline property of a TextBox control—Specifies whether the TextBox is capable of displaying multiple lines of text. If the property value is True, the TextBox may contain multiple lines of text; if the value of the property is False, the TextBox can contain only one line of text.

multimedia—The use of various media, such as sound, video and animation, to create content in an application.

multiple-selection statement—Performs one of many actions (or sequences of actions) depending on the value of the controlling expression.

multiplication operator—The asterisk (*) used to multiply two operands, producing their product as a result.

mutually exclusive options—A set of options of which only one can be selected at a time.

N

***n*-tier application**—Another name for multi-tier applications.

name of a variable—The identifier used in an application to access or modify a variable's value.

Name property—Assigns a unique and meaningful name to a control for easy identification.

namespace—A group of related classes in the Framework Class Library.

narrowing conversion—A conversion where the value of a "larger" type is being assigned to a variable of a "smaller" type, where the larger type can store more data than the smaller type. Narrowing conversions can result in loss of data, which can cause subtle logic errors.

nested parentheses—When an expression in parentheses is found within another expression surrounded by parentheses. With nested parentheses, the operators contained in the innermost pair of parentheses are applied first.

nested statement—A statement that is placed inside another control statement.

.NET Framework—Microsoft-provided software that executes applications, provides the Framework Class Library (FCL) and supplies many other programming capabilities.

New keyword—Used to call a constructor when creating an object.

New Project dialog—A dialog that allows you to choose what type of application you wish to create.

Next method of class Random—A method of class Random that, when called with no arguments, generates a positive Integer value between zero and the constant Int32.MaxValue, and, when called with arguments, generates an Integer value in a range constrained by those arguments.

NextDouble method of class Random—A method of class Random that generates a positive Double value that is greater than or equal to 0.0 and less than 1.0.

nondestructive memory operation—A process that does not overwrite a value in memory.

None value of ScrollBars property—Used to display no scrollbars on a TextBox.

Not (logical negation) operator—A logical operator that enables a programmer to reverse the meaning of a condition: A True condition, when logically negated, becomes False, and a False condition, when logically negated, becomes True.

note—An explanatory remark (represented by a rectangle with a folded upper-right corner) describing the purpose of a symbol in a UML activity diagram.

Nothing keyword—Used to clear a reference's value.

Now property—The property of structure Date that retrieves your computer's current time.

NumericUpDown control—Allows you to specify maximum and minimum numeric input values. Also allows you to specify an increment (or decrement) when the user clicks the up (or down) arrow.

O

object technology—A packaging scheme for creating meaningful software units. The units are large and are focused on particular application areas. There are date objects, time objects, paycheck objects, file objects and the like.

ObjectDataSource—Serves as a middle-tier object that retrieves data from the bottom-tier database and makes it available to the top-tier user interface for databound controls.

objects—Reusable software components that model items in the real world.

off-by-one error—The kind of logic error that occurs when a loop executes for one more or one fewer iteration than is intended.

one-dimensional array—An array that uses only one index.

opacity—Amount of transparency of the color.

OpenFileDialog control—Enables an application to use the **Open** dialog, which allows users to specify a file to be opened.

operand—An expression on which an operator performs its task.

Option Strict—When set to **On**, **Option Strict** causes the compiler to check all conversions and requires the programmer to perform an explicit conversion for all narrowing conversions (for example, conversion from **Double** to **Decimal**).

OrElse operator—A logical operator used to ensure that either *or* both of two conditions are **True** in an application before a certain path of execution is chosen.

output device—A device to which information that is processed by the computer can be sent.

output Label—A **Label** used to display calculation results.

output unit—The section of the computer that takes information the computer has processed and places it on various output devices, making the information available for use outside the computer.

P

PadLeft method of class String—Adds characters to the beginning of a string until the length of the string equals the specified length.

Page class—Defines the basic functionality for an ASPX page.

Page_Load—An event handler that executes any processing necessary to display a Web page.

palette—A set of colors.

Panel control—Used to group controls. Unlike **GroupBoxes**, **Panels** do not have captions.

Parameter Info **feature of the Visual Basic IDE**—Provides the programmer with information about procedures and their arguments.

parameter list—A comma-separated list in which the procedure declares each parameter variable's name and type.

parameter variable—A variable declared in a procedure's parameter list that can be used in the body of the procedure.

Pascal—A programming language designed for teaching structured programming, named after the 17th-century mathematician and philosopher Blaise Pascal.

pass-by-reference—When an argument is passed by reference, the called procedure can access and modify the caller's original data directly. Keyword **ByRef** indicates pass-by-reference (also called call-by-reference).

pass-by-value—When an argument is passed by value, the application makes a copy of the argument's value and passes the copy to the called procedure. With pass-by-value, changes to the called procedure's copy do not affect the original variable's value. Keyword **ByVal** indicates pass-by-value (also called call-by-value).

PasswordChar property of a TextBox—Specifies the masking character for a **TextBox**.

Peek method of class StreamReader—Returns the next character to be read or **-1** if there are no more characters to read in the file (that is, the end of the file has been reached).

Pen object—Specifies drawing parameters when drawing shape outlines.

persistent data—Data maintained in files.

PictureBox—Control that displays an image.

pin icon—An icon that enables or disables the auto-hide feature.

pixel—A tiny point on your computer screen that displays a color.

Play method—Plays a Microsoft Agent character animation.

plus box—An icon that, when clicked, expands a node.

Pmt function—A function that, given an interest rate, a time period and a monetary loan amount, returns a **Double** value specifying the payment amount per specified time period.

position number—A value that indicates a specific location within an array. Position numbers begin at 0 (zero).

primary key—Field (or combination of fields) in a database table that contains unique values used to distinguish records from one another.

primary memory—Another name for the memory unit.

primitive data type—A data type already defined in Visual Basic, such as **Integer** (also known as a built-in data type).

Print method—**PrintDocument** method used to print a document.

PrintDocument class—Allows the user to describe how to print a document.

PrinterSettings.InstalledPrinters.Count property —Determines how many printers are installed on the user's computer.

PrintPage event—Occurs when the data required to print the current page is needed.

PrintPageEventArgs class—Contains data passed to a **PrintPage** event.

PrintPreviewDialog class—Previews a document in a dialog box before it prints.

Private keyword—Member-access modifier that makes members accessible only to that class.

procedural programming language—A programming language (such as Fortran, Pascal, BASIC and C) that focuses on actions (verbs) rather than things or objects (nouns).

procedure—A set of instructions for performing a particular task.

procedure body—The declarations and statements that appear after the procedure header but before the keywords End Sub or End Function. The procedure body contains Visual Basic code that performs actions, generally by manipulating or interacting with the parameters from the parameter list.

procedure call—Invokes a procedure, specifies the procedure name and provides arguments that the callee (the procedure being called) requires to perform its task.

procedure definition—The procedure header, body and ending statement.

procedure header—The first line of a procedure (including the keyword Sub or Function, the procedure name, the parameter list and the Function procedure return type).

procedure name—Follows the keyword Sub or Function and distinguishes one procedure from another. A procedure name can be any valid identifier.

procedure scope—Variables declared inside a procedure but outside a control structure have procedure scope. Variables with procedure scope cannot be referenced outside the procedure in which they are declared.

program control—The task of ordering an application's statements in the correct order.

programmer-defined class (programmer-defined type)—A class defined by a programmer, as opposed to classes predefined in the Framework Class Library.

programmer-defined procedure—A procedure created by a programmer to meet the unique needs of a particular application.

project—A group of related files that compose an application.

properties—Object attributes, such as size, color and weight.

Properties window—The window that displays the properties for a Form or control object.

property—Specifies a control or Form object's attributes, such as size, color and position.

Property keyword—Reserved word indicating the definition of a class property.

pseudocode—An informal language that helps programmers develop algorithms.

pseudorandom numbers—A sequence of values produced by a complex mathematical calculation that simulates random-number generation.

Public keyword—Member-access modifier that makes instance variables or methods accessible wherever the application has a reference to that object.

px—Specifies that the size is measured in pixels.

Q

Query Builder—Visual Basic 2005 tool that allows you to specify the statements that retrieve information from and modify information in databases.

R

RadioButton control—Appears as a small circle that is either blank (unchecked) or contains a smaller dot (checked). Usually these controls appear in groups of two or more. Exactly one RadioButton in a group is selected at one time.

random-access memory—An example of primary memory.

Random class—Contains methods to generate pseudorandom numbers.

ReadLine method of class StreamReader—Method of class StreamReader that reads a line from a file and returns it as a String.

ReadOnly property of a NumericUpDown control—Determines whether the input value can be typed by the user.

real-time error checking—Feature of the Visual Basic IDE that provides immediate notification of possible errors in your code. For example, syntax errors are indicated by blue, jagged underlines in code.

record—A collection of related fields. Usually a Class in Visual Basic composed of several fields (called member variables in Visual Basic).

record key—Identifies a record and distinguishes it from all other records.

rectangular array—A type of two-dimensional array that can represent tables of values consisting of information arranged in rows and columns. Each row contains the same number of columns.

redundant parentheses—Unnecessary parentheses in an expression to make the expression easier to read.

reference—A variable to which you assign an object.

relational operators—Operators < (less than), > (greater than), <= (less than or equal to) and >= (greater than or equal to) that compare two values (also known as comparison operators)

Remove method of class String—Deletes characters from a String. The first argument contains the index in the String at which to begin removing characters, and the second argument specifies the number of characters to remove.

RemoveAt method of class ArrayList—Removes the object located at a specified location of an ArrayList.

repetition statement—Allows the programmer to specify that an action or actions should be repeated, depending on the value of a condition.

repetition structure (or repetition statement)—Allows the programmer to specify that an action or actions should be repeated, depending on the value of a condition.

Replace method of class String—Returns a new String object in which every occurrence of a substring is replaced with a different substring.

Response.Redirect method—Redirects the client browser to another Web page.

rethrow the exception—The Catch block can defer the exception handling (or perhaps a portion of it) to another Catch block by using the Throw statement.

Return keyword—Signifies the return statement that sends a value back to the procedure's caller.

Return statement—Used to return a value from a procedure.

return type—Data type of the result returned from a Function procedure.

reusing code—The practice of using existing code to build new code. Reusing code saves time, effort and money.

RGB value—The amount of red, green and blue needed to create a color.

right operand—The expression on the right side of a binary operator.

Right value of MouseButtons enumeration—Used to represent the right mouse button.

row—The first dimension of a two-dimensional array.

rules of operator precedence—Rules that determine the precise order in which operators are applied in an expression.

run mode—IDE mode indicating that the application is executing.

runtime error—An error that has its effect at execution time.

S

scale an image—The process of changing an image's width and height to fit a specified area.

scope—The portion of an application in which an identifier (such as a variable name) can be referenced. Some identifiers can be referenced throughout an application; others can be referenced only from limited portions of an application (such as within a single procedure or block).

screen scraping—The process of extracting desired information from the HTML that composes a Web page.

ScrollBars property of a TextBox control—Specifies whether a TextBox has a scrollbar and, if so, of what type. By default, property ScrollBars is set to None. Setting the value to Vertical places a scrollbar along the right side of the TextBox.

secondary storage media—Devices such as magnetic disks, optical disks and magnetic tapes on which computers store files.

secondary storage unit—The long-term, high-capacity "warehouse" section of the computer.

Select Case statement—The multiple-selection statement used to make a decision by comparing an expression to a series of conditions. The algorithm then takes different actions based on those values.

Select Resource dialog—Used to import files, such as images, to any application.

SELECT SQL keyword—Used to request specified information from a database.

SelectedIndex property of class ComboBox—Specifies the index of the selected item. Returns –1 if no item is selected.

SelectedIndexChanged event of ComboBox—Raised when a new value is selected in a ComboBox.

SelectedItem.Value property of ListBox—Returns the value of the selected item.

SelectedValue property of class ComboBox—Specifies the value of the selected item.

selection structure (or selection statement)—Selects among alternative courses of action.

SelectionStart property of MonthCalendar control—Returns the first (or only) date selected.

sender event argument—Event argument that contains a reference to the GUI component that raised the event (also called the source of the event).

sentence-style capitalization—A style that capitalizes the first letter of the first word in the text. Every other letter in the text is lowercase, unless it is the first letter of a proper noun (for example, Cartons per shipment).

separator bar—Bar placed in a menu to separate related menu items.

sequence structure (or sequence statement)—Built into Visual Basic—unless directed to act otherwise, the computer executes Visual Basic statements sequentially.

sequential execution—Statements in an application are executed one after another in the order in which they are written.

sequential-access file—File which contains data that is read in the order that it was written to the file.

Session object—Object that is maintained across several Web pages containing a collection of key-value pairs that are specific to a given user.

session state—ASP.NET's built-in support for tracking data throughout a browser session.

Set accessor—Provides data-validation capabilities to ensure that the value is set properly.

Short data type—Variables of this type hold small integer values.

short-circuit evaluation—The evaluation of the right operand in AndAlso and OrElse expressions occurs only if the first condition meets the criteria for the condition.

Show method—Displays a Microsoft Agent character on the screen.

ShowDialog method of class FontDialog or ColorDialog—The method that displays the dialog on which it is called.

ShowDialog method of the OpenFileDialog class—Displays the **Open** dialog and returns the result of the user interaction with the dialog.

ShowUpDown property of a DateTimePicker control—The Date-TimePicker property that, when true, allows the user to specify the time using up and down arrows, and, when false, allows the user to specify the date using a calendar.

simple condition—Contains one expression.

Single data type—Stores floating-point values. Single is similar to Double, but is less precise and requires less memory.

single-entry/single-exit control structure (or statement)—A control statement that has one entry point and one exit point. All Visual Basic control statements are single-entry/single-exit control statements.

single-quote character(')—Indicates the beginning of a code comment.

single-selection statement—The If...Then statement, which selects or ignores a single action or sequence of actions.

size of a variable—The number of bytes required to store a value of the variable's type.

Size property—Property that specifies the height and width, in pixels, of the Form or one of its controls.

SizeMode property—Property that specifies how an image is displayed in a PictureBox.

sizing handle—Square that, when enabled, can be used to resize the Form or one of its controls.

small circles (in the UML)—The solid circle in an activity diagram represents the activity's initial state, and the solid circle surrounded by a hollow circle represents the activity's final state.

software—The set of applications that run on computers.

software reuse—The reuse of existing pieces of software, an approach that enables programmers to avoid "reinventing the wheel," helping them develop applications faster.

solid circle (in the UML)—A UML activity diagram symbol that represents the activity's initial state.

SolidBrush class—Defines a brush that draws with a single color.

solution—Contains one or more projects.

Solution Explorer—A window that provides access to all the files in a solution.

Sorted property of class ComboBox—When set to True, sorts the items in a ComboBox alphabetically.

Source mode—Displays the ASPX page's markup at design time.

Speak method—Used to have the Microsoft Agent character speak text to the user.

special characters—Characters that are neither digits nor letters.

special symbols—$, @, %, &, *, (,), -, +, ", :, ?, / and the like.

speech-recognition engine—Application that translates vocal sound input from a microphone into a language that the computer understands.

Split method of class String—Splits the words in a String whenever a space is reached.

SQL Server 2005 Express—A relational databases management system built by Microsoft.

Sqrt method of class Math—A Shared method of class Math which returns the square root of its argument.

Start Page—The initial page displayed when Visual Studio .NET is opened.

StartsWith method of class String—Determines whether a String starts with a particular substring.

state button—A button that can be in the on/off (true/false) state.

statement—A unit of code that, when compiled and executed, performs an action.

status box—A box that appears below a Microsoft agent character that displays information about the character's actions.

Step keyword—Optional component of the For...Next header that specifies the increment (that is, the amount added to the control variable each time the loop is executed).

straight-line form—The manner in which arithmetic expressions must be written left to right to be represented in Visual Basic code.

stream—Object that has access to a sequence of characters.

StreamReader class—Provides methods for reading information from a file.

StreamWriter class—Provides methods for writing information to a file.

StretchImage—Value of PictureBox property SizeMode that scales an image to fill the PictureBox.

string constant—A String constant written as a sequence of characters in double quotation marks (also called a string literal).

string literal—A String constant written as a sequence of characters in double quotation marks (also called a literal String object).

String variable—A variable that stores a series of characters.

string-concatenation operator (&)—This operator combines its two operands into one value

String.Format method—Formats a string.

structured programming—A disciplined approach to creating programs that are clear, correct and easy to modify.

structured programming—A technique for organizing program control to help you develop applications that are easy to understand, debug and modify.

Structured Query Language (SQL)—Language often used by relational databases to perform queries and manipulate data in relational databases.

Style Builder dialog—The dialog that enables you to specify styles, such as position, for your Web controls.

Sub keyword—Begins the definition of a Sub procedure.

Sub procedure—A procedure similar to a Function procedure, with one important difference: Sub procedures do not return a value to the caller, whereas Function procedures do.

submenu—Menu within another menu.

subscript—See *index*.

substring—A sequence of characters in a String.

Substring method of class String—Returns characters from a string, corresponding to the arguments passed by the user, that indicate the start and the end positions within a String.

syntax—Specifies how a statement must be formed to compile without syntax errors.

syntax error—An error that occurs when program statements violate the grammatical rules of a programming language.

System.Drawing.Printing namespace—Allows your applications to access all services related to printing.

System.IO namespace—Contains methods to access files and directories.

T

TabIndex property—A control property that specifies the order in which focus is transferred to controls on the Form when the *Tab* key is pressed.

table—A two-dimensional array used to contain information arranged in rows and columns.

TableAdapter—Object that controls interactions between your application and a connected database.

table—Used to store related information in rows and columns. (Represented by key term DataTable.)

TableAdapter Query Configuration Wizard—Wizard used to create queries that return specific data from a DataSet.

TabStop property—A control property that specifies whether a control can receive the focus when the *Tab* key is pressed.

Tahoma font—The Microsoft-recommended font for use in Windows applications.

temporary variable—Used to store data when swapping values.

text file—A file containing human-readable characters.

Text property—Sets the text displayed on a control.

text-to-speech engine—Application that translates typed words into spoken sound that users hear through headphones or speakers connected to a computer.

TextAlign property—Specifies how text is aligned within a Label.

TextBox control—Retrieves user input from the keyboard.

TextChanged event—Occurs when the text in a TextBox changes.

Throw statement—The statement used to rethrow an exception in a Catch block.

throws an exception—A method throws an exception if a problem occurs while the method is executing.

Tick event of a Timer control—Raised after the number of milliseconds specified in the Timer control's Interval property has elapsed (if Enabled is True).

Timer control—Wakes up at specified intervals to execute code in its Tick event handler.

Title property of an ASPX page—Specifies the page's title that displays in the title bar of the browser.

To keyword—Used to specify a range of values. Commonly used in For…Next headers to specify the initial and final values of the statement's control variable.

ToChar method of class Convert—Converts a single character String to type Char.

ToLongDateString method of type Date—Returns a String containing the date in the format "Wednesday, October 30, 2002."

ToLower method of class String—Creates a new String object that replaces every uppercase letter in a String with its lowercase equivalent.

tool tip—The description of an icon that appears when the mouse pointer is held over that icon for a few seconds.

toolbar—A bar that contains Buttons that, when clicked, execute commands.

toolbar icon—A picture on a toolbar Button.

Toolbox—A window that contains controls used to customize Forms.

Tools menu—A menu of the IDE that contains commands for accessing additional IDE tools and options that enable customization of the IDE.

ToolStripMenuItem class—Class which allows you to add menu items to a MenuStrip control.

top tier—Tier containing the application's user interface. Also called the client tier.

ToShortTimeString method of type Date—Returns a String containing the time in the format "4:00 PM."

ToString method—Returns a String representation of the object or data type on which the method is called.

ToUpper method of class String—Creates a new String object that replaces every lowercase letter in a String with its uppercase equivalent.

ToUpper method of structure Char—Returns the uppercase representation of the character passed as a parameter.

transfer of control—Occurs when an executed statement does not directly follow the previously executed statement in the written application.

transferring the focus—Selecting a control in an application.

transition—A change from one action state to another that is represented by transition arrows in a UML activity diagram.

Transmission Control Protocol/Internet Protocol (TCP/IP)—The combined set of communications protocols for the Internet.

Trim method of class String—Removes all whitespace characters from the beginning and end of a String.

truth table—A table that displays the Boolean result of a logical operator for all possible combinations of True and False values for its operands.

Try block—A block of statements that might cause exceptions and statements that should not execute if an exception occurs.

two-dimensional array—A double-subscripted array that contains multiple rows of values.

type of a variable—Specifies the kind of data that can be stored in a variable and the range of values that can be stored.

U

UML (Unified Modeling Language)—An industry standard for modeling software systems graphically.

unary operators—An operator that takes only one operand.

uncaught exception—An exception that does not have an exception handler. Uncaught exceptions might terminate application execution.

Unicode—A character set containing characters that are composed of two bytes. Characters are represented in Visual Basic using the Unicode character set.

uniform resource locator (URL)—Address that can be used to direct a browser to a resource on the Web.

UseAntiAlias property—Property of class PrintPreviewDialog that makes the text in the PrintPreviewDialog appear smoother on the screen.

V

Val function—Filters a number from its argument if possible. This avoids errors introduced by the entering of nonnumeric data when only numbers are expected. However, the result of the Val function is not always what the programmer intended.

value of a variable—The piece of data that is stored in a variable's location in memory.

Value property of a DateTimePicker control—Stores the value (such as a time) in a DateTimePicker control.

ValueChanged event of a DateTimePicker—Raised when a user selects a new day or time in the DateTimePicker control.

variable—A location in the computer's memory where a value can be stored.

vector graphics—Graphics created by a set of mathematical properties called vectors, which include the graphics' dimensions, attributes and positions.

Vertical value of ScrollBars property—Used to display a vertical scrollbar on the right side of a TextBox.

visual programming—Technique in which Visual Basic processes your programming actions (such as clicking, dragging and dropping controls) and writes code for you.

visual programming with Visual Basic—Instead of writing detailed program statements, the programmer uses Visual Studio's graphical user interface to conveniently drag and drop predefined controls into place, and to label and resize them. Visual Studio writes much of the Visual Basic program, saving the programmer considerable effort.

Visual Studio—Microsoft's integrated development environment (IDE), which allows developers to create applications in a variety of .NET programming languages.

Visual Web Developer 2005 Express—A Microsoft tool for building ASP.NET 2.0 Web Applications.

volatile memory—Memory that is erased when the machine is powered off.

W

Watch window—A Visual Basic IDE window that allows you to view variable values as an application is being debugged.

Web applications—Applications that create web content.

Web controls—Controls, such as `TextBoxes` and `Buttons`, that are used to customize ASPX pages.

Web Form—Another name for an ASPX page.

Web Form Designer—The design area in Visual Web Developer that enables you to visually build your ASPX pages.

Web Form Page—Another name for an ASPX page.

Web server—Specialized software that responds to client requests by providing resources.

Web-safe colors—Colors that display the same on different computers.

WHERE SQL keyword—Specifies criteria that determine which rows to retrieve.

whitespace character—A space, tab or newline character.

widening conversion—A conversion in which the value of a "smaller" type is assigned to a variable of a "larger" type—that is, a type that can store more data than the smaller type.

Width property—Allows you to specify the width of a Web control.

Width property—This setting, a member of property `Size`, indicates the width of the `Form` or one of its controls, in pixels

Windows application—An application that executes on a Windows operating system.

workflow—The activity of a portion of a software system.

World Wide Web (WWW)—A communications system that allows computer users to locate and view multimedia documents (such as documents with text, graphics, animations, audios and videos).

World Wide Web Consortium (W3C)—A forum through which qualified individuals and companies cooperate to develop and standardize technologies for the World Wide Web.

WriteLine method of StreamWriter—Method of class `StreamWriter` that writes a `String` and a line terminator to a file.

X

X property of class MouseEventArgs—The property of class `MouseEventArgs` that specifies the x-coordinate of the mouse event.

x-axis—Describes every horizontal coordinate.

x-coordinate—Horizontal distance (increasing to the right) from the left of the drawing area

Y

Y property of class MouseEventArgs—The property of class `MouseEventArgs` that specifies the y-coordinate of the mouse event.

y-axis—Describes every vertical coordinate.

y-coordinate—Vertical distance (increasing downward) from the top of the drawing area.

Z

zeroth element—The first element in an array.

The DEITEL® Suite of Products...

HOW TO PROGRAM BOOKS

The Deitels' acclaimed *How to Program Series* has achieved its success largely due to the innovative pedagogy used to teach key programming concepts. Their signature *LIVE-CODE Approach*, icon-identified programming tips and comprehensive exercises form the backbone of a series of books that has taught over one million students the craft of programming.

C++ How to Program Fifth Edition

BOOK / CD-ROM

©2005, 1500 pp., paper (0-13-185757-6)

The complete authoritative DEITEL® LIVE-CODE introduction to programming with C++! The Fifth Edition takes a new, easy-to-follow, carefully developed early classes and objects approach to programming in C++. The text includes comprehensive coverage of the fundamentals of object-oriented programming in C++. It includes a new optional automated teller machine (ATM) case study that teaches the fundamentals of software engineering and object-oriented design with the UML 2.0 in Chapters 1-7, 9 and 13. Additional integrated case studies appear throughout the text, including the `Time` class (Chapter 9), the `Employee` class (Chapters 12 and 13) and the `GradeBook` class (Chapters 3-7). The book also includes a new interior design including updated colors, new fonts, new design elements and more.

Small C++ How to Program Fifth Edition

©2005, 900 pp., paper (0-13-185758-4)

Based on chapters 1-13 (except the optional OOD/UML case study) and appendices of *C++ How to Program, Fifth Edition, Small C++* features a new early classes and objects approach and comprehensive coverage of the fundamentals of object-oriented programming in C++. Key topics include applications, variables, memory concepts, data types, control statements, functions, arrays, pointers and strings, inheritance and polymorphism.

Java™ How to Program Sixth Edition

BOOK / CD-ROM

©2005, 1500 pp., paper (0-13-148398-6)

The complete authoritative DEITEL® LIVE-CODE introduction to programming with the new Java™ 2 Platform Standard Edition 5.0! *Java How to Program, Sixth Edition* is up-to-date with J2SE™ 5.0 and includes comprehensive coverage of the fundamentals of object-oriented programming in Java; a new early classes and objects approach; a new interior design including new colors, new fonts, new design elements and more; and a new optional automated teller machine (ATM) case study that teaches the fundamentals of software engineering and object oriented design with the UML 2.0 in Chapters 1-8 and 10. Additional integrated case studies appear throughout the text, including GUI and graphics (Chapters 3-12), the `Time` class (Chapter 8), the `Employee` class (Chapters 9 and 10) and the `GradeBook` class (Chapters 3-8). New J2SE 5.0 topics covered included input/output, enhanced `for` loop, autoboxing, generics, new collections APIs and more.

Small Java™ How to Program Sixth Edition

BOOK / CD-ROM

©2005, 700 pp., paper (0-13-148660-8)

Based on chapters 1-10 of *Java™ How to Program, Sixth Edition, Small Java* is up-to-date with J2SE™ 5.0, features a new early classes and objects approach and comprehensive coverage of the fundamentals of object-oriented programming in Java. Key topics include applications, variables, data types, control statements, methods, arrays, object-based programming, inheritance and polymorphism.

Visual Basic® 2005 How to Program Third Edition

BOOK / CD-ROM

©2006, 1500 pp., paper (0-13-186900-0)

The complete authoritative DEITEL® LIVE-CODE introduction to Visual Basic programming. *Visual Basic® 2005 How to Program, Third Edition* is up-to-date with Microsoft's Visual Basic 2005. The text includes comprehensive coverage of the fundamentals of object-oriented programming in Visual Basic including a new early classes and objects approach and a new optional automated teller machine (ATM) case study that teaches the fundamentals of software engineering and object-oriented design with the UML 2.0 in Chapters 1, 3–9 and 11. Additional integrated case studies appear throughout the text, including the `Time` class (Chapter 9), the `Employee` class (Chapters 10 and 11) and the `Gradebook` class (Chapters 4–9). This book also includes discussions of more advanced topics such as XML, ASP.NET, ADO.NET and Web services. New Visual Basic 2005 topics covered include partial classes, generics, the `My` namespace and Visual Studio's updated debugger features.

Visual C++ .NET® How To Program

BOOK / CD-ROM

©2004, 1400 pp., paper (0-13-437377-4)

Written by the authors of the world's best-selling introductory/intermediate C and C++ textbooks, this comprehensive book thoroughly examines Visual C++® .NET. *Visual C++® .NET How to Program* begins with a strong foundation in the introductory and intermediate programming principles students will need in industry, including fundamental topics such as arrays, functions and control statements. Readers learn the concepts of object-oriented programming, then the text explores such essential topics as networking, databases, XML and multimedia. Graphical user interfaces are also extensively covered, giving students the tools to build compelling and fully interactive programs using the "drag-and-drop" techniques provided by Visual Studio .NET 2003.

C How to Program
Fifth Edition

BOOK / CD-ROM

©2007, 1200 pp., paper
(0-13-240416-8)

C How to Program, Fifth Edition—the world's best-selling C text—is designed for introductory through intermediate courses as well as programming languages survey courses. This comprehensive text is aimed at readers with little or no programming experience through intermediate audiences. Highly practical in approach, it introduces fundamental notions of structured programming and software engineering and gets up to speed quickly. The Fifth Edition includes new chapters on the C99 standard and an introduction to game programming with the Allegro C Library.

Visual C#® 2005
How to Program
Second Edition

BOOK / CD-ROM

©2006, 1589 pp., paper
(0-13-152523-9)

The complete authoritative DEITEL® LIVE-CODE introduction to C# programming. *Visual C#® 2005 How to Program, Second Edition* is up-to-date with Microsoft's Visual C# 2005. The text includes comprehensive coverage of the fundamentals of object-oriented programming in C#, including a new early classes and objects approach and a new optional automated teller machine (ATM) case study that teaches the fundamentals of software engineering and object-oriented design with the UML 2.0 in Chapters 1, 3–9 and 11. Additional integrated case studies appear throughout the text, including the **Time** class (Chapter 9), the **Employee** class (Chapters 10 and 11) and the **Gradebook** class (Chapters 4–9). This book also includes discussions of more advanced topics such as XML, ASP.NET, ADO.NET and Web services. New Visual C# 2005 topics covered include partial classes, generics, the **My** namespace, .NET remoting and Visual Studio's updated debugger features.

Advanced Java™ 2 Platform How to Program

BOOK / CD-ROM

©2002, 1811 pp., paper
(0-13-089560-1)

Expanding on the world's best-selling Java textbook—*Java™ How to Program*— *Advanced Java™ 2 Platform How To Program* presents advanced Java topics for developing sophisticated, user-friendly GUIs; significant, scalable enterprise applications; wireless applications and distributed systems. Primarily based on Java 2 Enterprise Edition (J2EE), this textbook integrates technologies such as XML, JavaBeans, security, JDBC™, JavaServer Pages (JSP™), servlets, Remote Method Invocation (RMI), Enterprise JavaBeans™ (EJB), design patterns, Swing, J2ME™, Java 2D and 3D, XML, design patterns, CORBA, Jini™, JavaSpaces™, Jiro™, Java Management Extensions (JMX) and Peer-to-Peer networking with an introduction to JXTA.

Internet & World Wide Web How to Program
Third Edition

BOOK / CD-ROM

©2004, 1250 pp., paper
(0-13-145091-3)

Teaches the fundamentals needed to program on the Internet. This text provides in-depth coverage of introductory programming principles, various markup languages, and relational databases—all the skills and tools needed to create dynamic Web-based applications.

Python How to Program

BOOK / CD-ROM

©2002, 1376 pp., paper
(0-13-092361-3)

Python How to Program provides a comprehensive introduction to Python— a powerful object-oriented programming language with clear syntax and the ability to bring together various technologies quickly and easily.

XML How to Program

BOOK / CD-ROM

©2001, 934 pp., paper
(0-13-028417-3)

This book is a comprehensive guide to programming in XML. It teaches how to use XML to create customized tags and includes chapters that adress markup languages for science and technology, multimedia, commerce and many other fields.

Perl How to Program

BOOK / CD-ROM

©2001, 1057 pp., paper
(0-13-028418-1)

This comprehensive guide to Perl programming emphasizes the use of the Common Gateway Interface (CGI) with Perl to create powerful, dynamic multi-tier Web-based client/server applications.

e-Business & e-Commerce How to Program

BOOK / CD-ROM

©2001, 1254 pp., paper
(0-13-028419-X)

e-Business & e-Commerce How to Program explores programming technologies for developing Web-based e-business and e-commerce solutions, and covers e-business and e-commerce models and business issues.

THE BUZZ ABOUT THE DEITEL® SUITE OF PRODUCTS!

Deitel & Associates garners worldwide praise for its best-selling *How to Program Series* of books and its signature *LIVE-CODE Approach*. See for yourself what our readers have to say:

"I'm glad to see the early treatment of objects done so well. This is perhaps the most comprehensive Visual Basic.NET text accessible to the beginner."
— Gavin Osborne, Saskatchewan Institute of Applied Science and Technology

"A great book for the novice programmer for learning VB. NET quickly and writing programs with significantly improved performance, and vastly improved readability."
— Sujay Ghuge, Verizon Information Technology

"The book is comprehensive, correct and crystal clear. No other textbook comes close in carefully explaining the intricacies of this powerful language."
— James Huddleston, Independent Contractor

"This book is one of the best of its kind. It is an excellent 'objects first' coverage of C++ that remains accessible to beginners. The example-driven presentation is enriched by the optional OOD/UML ATM cases study that contextualizes the material in an ongoing software engineering project."
— Gavin Osborne, Saskatchewan Institute of Applied Science and Technology

"I am continually impressed with the Deitels' ability to clearly explain concepts and ideas, which allows the student to gain a well-rounded understanding of the language and software development."
— Karen Arlien, Bismarck State College

"Great early introduction to classes and objects. The combination of live-code examples and detailed figures provides a unique visualization of C++ concepts."
— Earl LaBatt, University of New Hampshire

"Probably the most complete coverage of learning through examples in published material today. This material is such high quality —it is unbelievable. The ATM is super."
— Anne Horton, AT&T Bell Laboratories

Java How to Program, 6/e is an excellent book to learn how to program in Java. The book does an excellent job describing the new features included in the JDK 5.0, including generics and formatted output. The book is easy to read with numerous, simple-to-follow code examples."
— Doug Kohlert, Sun Microsystems

"An excellent combination of C#, UML and pseudocode that leads the reader to create good applications and well designed algorithms, using the best practices! Few books mix all of this so well. Great idea and great work!"
— Jose Antonio Seco, Adalucia's Parlament, Spain

"The writing style is comprehensive, systematic and clear. Nothing is either skipped or glossed over. Of particular note is the authors' attention to good software engineering concepts, and the wide selection of code examples provides excellent reinforcement for the practical application of developing Java skills."
— Dean Mellas, Computer and information Sciences, Cerritos College

"Good job! Introduces OOP without burying the reader in complexity. I think the level of conceptual detail is perfect. This will be a great help the next time I teach 101."
— Walt Bunch, Chapman University

"The new edition... is by far the best student-oriented textbook on programming in the C language—the Deitels have set the standard-again! A thorough, careful, student-oriented treatment of not just the langauge, but more importantly, the ideas, concepts, and techniques of programming! The addition of 'live code' is also a big plus—encouraging active participation by the student. A great text!"
— Richard Albright, Goldey-Beacom College

"Once again the Deitel team has produced another academic winner. From start to finish they have the novice programmer in mind... They give enough theory so the students can learn the "why" and not just the "how." The book is an interesting text with practical examples to tie together the theory and the practice. I strongly recommend it as a VB 2005 book for beginning VB students regardless of their academic major."
— Harlan Brewer, Select Engineering Services, Inc.

"Bravo for a wonderful learning experience! I have seen (and bought) lots of programming books (Basic, C, C++) over the years, yours is number one on my list. Wow... it is a joy to work with. Thanks."
— Thomas J. McGrail, Longs, SC

www.deitel.com   www.prenhall.com/deitel
www.InformIT.com/deitel

ORDER INFORMATION

SINGLE COPY SALES:
Visa, Master Card, American Express, Checks, or Money Orders only
Toll-Free: 800-643-5506; Fax: 800-835-5327

GOVERNMENT AGENCIES:
Prentice Hall Customer Service
(#GS-02F-8023A)
Tel: 201-767-5994; Fax: 800-445-6991

COLLEGE PROFESSORS:
For desk or review copies, please visit us on the World Wide Web at www.prenhall.com

CORPORATE ACCOUNTS:
Quantity, Bulk Orders totaling 10 or more books.
Purchase orders only — No credit cards.
Tel: 201-236-7156; Fax: 201-236-7141
Toll-Free: 800-382-3419

CANADA:
Pearson Technology Group Canada
10 Alcorn Avenue, suite #300
Toronto, Ontario, Canada M4V 3B2
Tel: 416-925-2249; Fax: 416-925-0068
E-mail: phcinfo.pubcanada@pearsoned.com

UK/IRELAND:
Pearson Education
Edinburgh Gate
Harlow, Essex CM20 2JE UK
Tel: 01279 623928; Fax: 01279 414130
E-mail: enq.orders@pearsoned-ema.com

EUROPE, MIDDLE EAST & AFRICA:
Pearson Education
P.O. Box 75598
1070 AN Amsterdam, The Netherlands
Tel: 31 20 5755 800; Fax: 31 20 664 5334
E-mail: amsterdam@pearsoned-ema.com

ASIA:
Pearson Education Asia
317 Alexandra Road #04-01
IKEA Building
Singapore 159965
Tel: 65 476 4688; Fax: 65 378 0370

JAPAN:
Pearson Education
Nishi-Shinjuku, KF Building 101
8-14-24 Nishi-Shinjuku, Shinjuku-ku
Tokyo, Japan 160-0023
Tel: 81 3 3365 9001; Fax: 81 3 3365 9009

INDIA:
Pearson Education Indian Liaison Office
90 New Raidhani Enclave, Ground Floor
Delhi 110 092, India
Tel: 91 11 2059850 & 2059851
Fax: 91 11 2059852

AUSTRALIA:
Pearson Education Australia
Unit 4, Level 2
14 Aquatic Drive
Frenchs Forest, NSW 2086, Australia
Tel: 61 2 9454 2200; Fax: 61 2 9453 0089
E-mail: marketing@pearsoned.com.au

NEW ZEALAND/FIJI:
Pearson Education
46 Hillside Road
Auckland 10, New Zealand
Tel: 649 444 4968; Fax: 649 444 4957
E-mail: sales@pearsoned.co.nz

SOUTH AFRICA:
Pearson Education
P.O. Box 12122
Mill Street
Cape Town 8010 South Africa
Tel: 27 21 686 6356; Fax: 27 21 686 4590

LATIN AMERICA:
Pearson Education Latinoamerica
815 NW 57th Street Suite 484
Miami, FL 33158
Tel: 305 264 8344; Fax: 305 264 7933

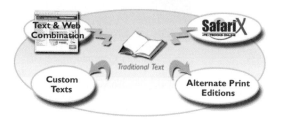

DEITEL® BUZZ ONLINE NEWSLETTER

Each issue of our free, e-mail newsletter, the *DEITEL® BUZZ ONLINE*, is now sent to over 51,000 opt-in subscribers. This weekly newsletter provides updates on our publishing program, our instructor-led professional training courses, timely industry topics and the continuing stream of innovations and new Web 2.0 business ventures emerging from Deitel.

Each issue of our newsletter includes:

- Resource centers on programming languages, Internet and Web technology, and more.
- Updates on all Deitel publications of interest to students, instructors and professionals.
- Free tutorials and guest articles. (part of the Deitel Free Content Initiative)
- Information on our instructor-led professional training courses taught worldwide.

the deitel®
www.deitel.com
Your Information Resource for Building Web 2.0 Businesses
buzz online

June 12, 2006

In this Issue ...

New! Java Enterprise Edition 5 (Java EE 5) Resource Center
Coming in August ! *Simply Visual Basic, 2/e* (College Textbook)
Coming in August ! *C How to Program, 5/e* (College Textbook)
Just Published! *Visual Basic 2005 for Programmers, 2/e* (Deitel Developer Series)
Just Published! *Visual Basic 2005 How to Program, 3/e* (College textbook)
Miss Last Week's Newsletter? Check Out Our OpenGL Resource Center
Check Out Our New C# Books! *Visual C# 2005 How to Program, 2/e* (College textbook)
C# for Programmers, 2/e (Deitel Developer Series)
Check Them Out! All Deitel Resource Centers
Looking for Training? Check out Deitel Dive Into™ Series On-site Corporate Training Delivered to Groups Worldwide
New at Deitel Labs!
Come Work with Us This Fall! Deitel Honors Internship Program

New! Java Enterprise Edition 5 (Java EE 5) Resource Center

The Java Enterprise Edition 5 (Java EE 5) Resource Center is your guide to the latest release of Java Enterprise Edition. It includes the best online resources to help you get started with Java Enterprise Edition 5 (Java EE 5) development. In our Java Enterprise Edition 5 (Java EE 5) Resource Center you'll find:

- Java EE resources from Sun Microsystems, including articles, tutorials, the latest Java Platform Enterprise Edition 5 Specification and more.
- Downloads of Java EE sample applications demonstrating Enterprise JavaBeans 3.0, web services, JAXB, JNDI, JDBC, security and more.
- Enterprise Java Beans 3.0 resources including the specification, an overview of the EJB 3.0 API, sample chapters and books.
- Resources for the Java API for XML-based Web Services (JAX-WS) 2.0, including the JAX-WS 2.0 specification, tutorials and articles.
- The "Introduction to Java EE 5 Technology" tutorial from NetBeans.org.
- Projects for GlassFish (an open source Java EE 5 application server) including frameworks, applications, interoperability techniques and tools.
- The JavaServer Pages specification, plus Java Server Pages articles, white papers and books.
- A slide presentation that walks through the features of the Java EE.
- Links to the Java EE 5 forums at Sun Microsystems.

- Detailed ordering information, additional book resources, code downloads and more.
- Available in both HTML or plain-text format.
- Previous issues are archived at: `www.deitel.com/newsletter/backissues.html`

Recent Deitel Publications

Java How to Program, 6/e

ISBN: 0131483986
Pages: 1576
Order your copy now from
Amazon or InformIT
Demo the free Cyber Classroom
Read the Table of Contents
Read the Preface
Check This Out! Java Resource Center

"Probably the most complete coverage of learning through examples in published material today. This material is such high quality—it's unbelievable. The [optional] ATM OOD/UML case study is super!" —Anne Horton, AT&T Bell Laboratories

Read more testimonials...

C++ How to Program

ISBN: 0131857576
Pages: 1536
Order your copy now from
Amazon or InformIT
Demo the free Cyber Classroom
Read the Table of Contents
Read the Preface
Check This Out! C++ Resource Center

"This book is one of the best of its kind. It is an excellent "objects first" coverage of C++ that remains accessible to beginners. The example-driven presentation is enriched by the optional OOD/UML ATM case study that contextualizes the material in an ongoing software engineering project." —Gavin Osborne, Saskatchewan Institute

Read more testimonials...

Small How to Program Series

Small How to Program Series textbooks bring the solid and proven pedagogy of our *How to Program Series* texts to new, smaller texts that are focused on CS1 courses. The *Small How to Program Series* Java and C++ texts include the FREE online Cyber Classroom.

Small Java How to Program, 6/e

ISBN: 0131486608
Pages: 624
Order your copy now from
Amazon or InformIT
Read the Table of Contents
Read the Preface
Check This Out! Java Resource Center

"This new Chapter 3 introduces OOP without burying the reader in complexity. I think the level of conceptual detail is perfect. This will be a great help the next time I teach 101. ... I was introduced to JHTP by my students who pleaded with me to drop our current assigned text in favor of JHTP. No other text comes close to its quality of organization and presentation. Its Live-Code approach to presenting exemplary code makes a big difference in the learning outcome." —Walt Bunch, Chapman University

Read more testimonials...

Small C++ How to Program, 5/e

ISBN: 0131857584
Pages: 848
Order your copy now from
Amazon or InformIT
Read the Table of Contents
Read the Preface
Check This Out! C++ Resource Center

"I am continually impressed with the Deitels' ability to clearly explain concepts and ideas, which allows the student to gain a well-rounded understanding of the language and software development." —Karen Arlien, Bismarck State College

Read more testimonials...

Computer Science Theory and Practice
Operating Systems, 3/e

ISBN: 0131828274
Pages: 1300
Order your copy now from
Amazon or InformIT
Read the Table of Contents
Read the Preface
Windows Vista Resource Center

Operating Systems, 3/e, Testimonials

"This book is excellent; a superb mix of theory and application; spot-on accuracy, relevancy and application of case studies to the theory of OS design." —Robert Love, MontaVista Software, Inc.

"Deitel understands the Linux kernel very well and is very good at explaining it. Even though I have been a heavy Linux user and SysAdmin for eight years and have hacked both Linux and Unix kernels, I learned a lot." —Bob Toxen, Author of Real World Linux Security, 2/e and Contributor to Berkeley Unix

Simply Series (for the classroom, self-study and distance learning programs)

This Deitel *Simply Series* combines the our signature *live-code approach* (emphasizing complete, working programs, rather than code snippets, and always showing sample outputs) with an *application-driven methodology*, in which readers build real-world applications that incorporate programming fundamentals. Using a *step-by-step tutorial approach*, readers learn programming basics. Each successive tutorial builds on previous concepts and introduces new programming features. Many *Simply Series* books also include higher-end topics such as database programming, multimedia and graphics, and Web applications development. These books are appropriate for the classroom, for self-study and for distance learning programs.

Turn the page to find out more about Deitel & Associates!

To sign up for the *DEITEL® BUZZ ONLINE* newsletter, visit
`www.deitel.com/newsletter/subscribe.html`.

www.deitel.com   www.prenhall.com/deitel
www.InformIT.com/deitel